America

A CONCISE HISTORY

Seattle
★ Olympia
● Portland
★ Salem

WASHINGTON
Columbia R.
● Spokane

OREGON

Boise

IDAHO

Snake R.

Great
Falls

Missouri R.

Helena ★

MONTANA

Yellowstone R.
Billings

**NORTH
DAKOTA**

Bismarck ★

SOUTH DAK
Pierre ★

WYOMING

Cheyenne ★

NEBRASKA
North Platte R.
Pl

● Reno
★ Carson City

NEVADA

● Sacramento

San Francisco ● Oakland
San Jose ●

Sacramento R.

Great
Salt Lake
★ Salt
Lake
City

UTAH

Green R.

**R
O
C
K
Y
M
O
U
N
T
A
I
N
S**

South Platte R.
● Denver
★

COLORADO
● Colorado
Springs

KANS
Arkansas R.

Fresno ●

CALIFORNIA
Mt Whitney
Elev. 14,494 ft.

**S
I
E
R
R
A
N
E
V
A
D
A**

▲ Death Valley
Elev. -282 ft.

● Las Vegas

Colorado R.

Pacific Ocean

● Los Angeles
Salton Sea
Elev. -235 ft.

San Diego ●

ARIZONA

★ Phoenix

● Tucson

Santa Fe ★

Albuquerque ●

NEW MEXICO

El Paso ●

Rio Grande

Pecos R.

● Amarillo

OKLAHO

TEXAS

Colorado R.

San A

Nueces R.

MEXICO

Honolulu ●
Pacific Ocean
HAWAII

0   100
Miles

22°
20°
160°   155°

70°

RUSSIA

BROOKS RA.

ALASKA

Yukon R.
● Fairbanks

ALASKA RA.
▲ Mt. McKinley
20,320 ft.
● Anchorage

CANADA

International Date Line

Bering Sea

50°
180°   175°   165°   155°

60°

Gulf of Alaska

● Juneau

0   400
Miles

145°   135°

120°   115°   110°

Executive editor: Paul Shensa
History editor: Katherine E. Kurzman
Development editor: Jennifer E. Sutherland
Production editors: Elizabeth Geller/Shuli Traub
Production supervisors: Stacey B. Alexander/Scott Lavelle
Art director: Lucy Krikorian
Text design: Design Associates
Graphic arts manager: Demetrios Zangos
Photo research: Photosearch
Cover art: *The Station on the Morris and Essex Railroad* by Edward L. Henry.
   Collection of the Chase Manhattan Bank.
Cartography: Mapping Specialists, Ltd.
Composition: TSI Graphics
Printing and binding: R.R. Donnelley & Sons Company

Library of Congress Catalog Card Number: 97-62265

4 3 2 1 0 9
f e d c b a

For information, write: Bedford/St. Martin's, 75 Arlington Street,
Boston, MA 02116   (617) 426-7440

ISBN: 1-57259-400-4

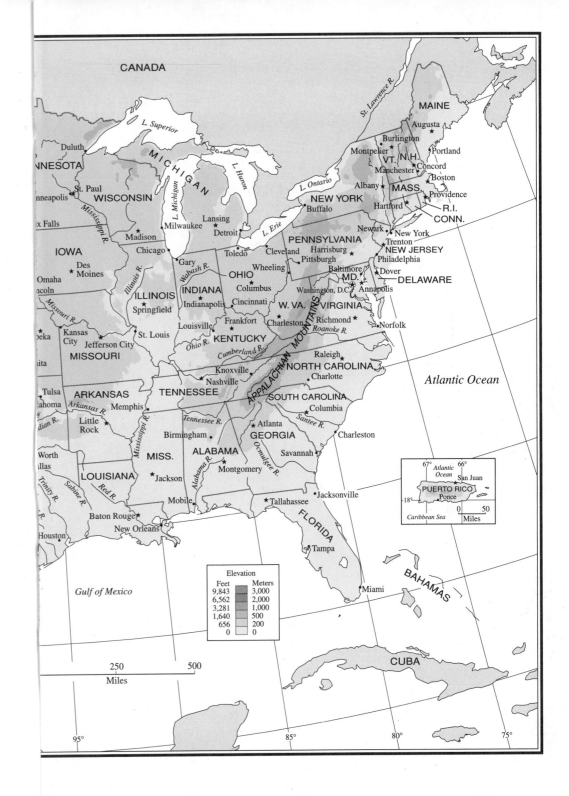

Michael P. Conzen
University of Chicago
Advisory Editor for Cartography

America
A CONCISE HISTOR

James A. Henretta
University of Maryland

David Brody
University of California, Davis

Lynn Dumenil
Occidental College

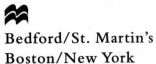

Bedford/St. Martin's
Boston/New York

For Our Teachers and Students

PREFACE

*A*merica: *A Concise History* presents a succinct overview of the American experience in a handy, low-cost format while preserving the structure, balance, and inclusive vision of *America's History*, Third Edition, by James A. Henretta, W. Elliot Brownlee, David Brody, Susan Ware, and Marilynn S. Johnson. Designed as a single-column paperback, the text feels and reads less like a traditional course book and will prove more inviting to the average undergraduate.

Through an intensive development process, we've created an original text in *America: A Concise History*, narrated in a lively style and filled with new insights. Lynn Dumenil, professor of history at Occidental College, has brought her expertise as a cultural historian of twentieth-century America to the author team and has taken prime responsibility for the decades since 1914. James Henretta has rewritten all the chapters through the Civil War (Chapters 1–15), and David Brody revisits Chapters 16–22.

To write a text that would be forty percent shorter than our comprehensive survey while maintaining a strong narrative line, we decided to focus each part of *America: A Concise History* around a few themes and to link our discussions so that students could trace developments over the entire span of U.S. history. We give special emphasis to the evolution of political institutions and policies, the changing character of social groups, the increasing complexity of cultural life, and the interaction between people and their environment. This selective thematic approach provides students with a coherent overview of American history, which instructors can enrich with supplemental readings.

Most important, *America: A Concise History* presents a *balanced* narrative of our nation's past. In our discussions of government and politics, diplomacy and war, we show how they affected—and were affected by—ethnic groups and economic conditions, intellectual beliefs and social change, and religious and moral values of the times. Our text integrates social and political history, probing the lives of the rich diversity of people who have become Americans and analyzing the institutions—political, economic, and religious—that represent a common national identity.

FEATURES

To assist students while they read, *America: A Concise History* has a clear chronology and a strong conceptual framework. Each volume is divided into three parts, with each corresponding to a distinct phase of development. Every part begins at a crucial turning point, such as the Cold War, and emphasizes the dynamic forces at work. Part openers contain **Thematic Timelines** that highlight key developments and brief **Part Essays** that focus on the crucial engines of historical change that created new conditions of life. This part organization will help students understand the major themes in each period of American history, to see that bits and pieces of historical data acquire significance as part of a larger pattern of development.

Throughout the main text we have tried to mix quotations from ordinary Americans into the narrative to create a vivid account. Moving students further back into the context of the historical moment, each chapter includes two **American Voices**, first-person excerpts from letters, diaries, autobiographies, and public testimony that paint a striking picture of the social or political life of the time. These selections, virtually all newly selected and edited for *America: A Concise History*, bring history alive and remind students that the past is much more than a chronicle of the great and powerful.

Each chapter is enhanced by a selection of maps and contemporary illustrations and concludes with a **Timeline** listing important events. Finally, the Documents section reprints the Declaration of Independence and the Constitution of the United States, and the appendix lists statistical information. Also included is a comprehensive list of suggestions for further reading, organized by the headings in each chapter.

SUPPLEMENTS

Users of *America's History* have always cited the ancillary package as a key to the book's success in the classroom. We thus felt it very important to make all the materials for the big book available to adopters of *America: A Concise History*. The *Instructor's Resource Manual* provides an abundance of material to aid instructors in planning the course and enhancing student involvement, including specially commissioned Historiographic Essays and Documents Modules that focus on native Americans, African-Americans, Latino-Americans, women, and constitutional and diplomatic history. One hundred and ten full-color transparencies reproduce maps and figures from the textbook, as well as a selection of fine art and historic photographs. The *Who Built America?* CD-ROM, called "a truly exciting, high-quality electronic book" by *The Wall Street Journal*, covers the period from 1876 to World War I.

In addition, however, several key ancillaries have been specially prepared to support teaching with the concise book; the *Instructor's Resource Manual, Test Bank, Student Guides*, and *Documents Collection* have all been rewritten to take account of the important changes in coverage and approach. Finally, a new ancillary is available for people who use a brief text as a core around which to array a variety of supplements; *Using The Bedford Series in History and Culture with* America: A Concise History provides concrete suggestions for using two dozen volumes from this highly regarded series in conjunction with our text.

American History: A Concise Documents Collection, Volumes 1 and 2

by Douglas Bukowski

For instructors who like to use a variety of brief primary sources in class, a set of readings has been prepared to accompany *America: A Concise History*. For each chapter in the text, a corresponding chapter in this collection includes five to seven excerpts from important sources in political, social, economic, and cultural history. For each reading a helpful headnote gives students context on the author and selection. A series of three to five questions follow the reading to help students think critically about the source. At the end of each chapter, additional questions tie the readings together, inviting students to think about how this diverse set of pieces reflects the complex tenor of the time.

Student Guide, Volumes 1 and 2

Vol. 1 by Stephen J. Kneeshaw (College of the Ozarks); Timothy R. Mahoney (University of Nebraska–Lincoln); Linda Gies (Eastern New Mexico University); and Barbara M. Posadas (Northern Illinois University); Vol. 2 by Thomas R. Frazier (Baruch College, emeritus)

Specially prepared for *America: A Concise History*, the *Student Guide* will help conscientious students improve their performance in the course by developing better learning skills and study habits. The guide begins with an introduction by Gerald J. Goodwin (University of Houston) on how to study history, which is followed by discrete sections for each chapter that reinforce major themes and test on the book's coverage. Each chapter includes a summary of the essential facts and ideas of the text chapter, with fill-in questions; the timeline from the textbook with short explanations of the significance of each event; a glossary; skill-building exercises based on a map, table, or figure; exercises for the American Voices; and a self-test.

Instructor's Resource Manual, Volumes 1 and 2

Vol. 1 by Timothy R. Mahoney (University of Nebraska–Lincoln) and Linda Gies (Eastern New Mexico University); Vol. 2 by Thomas R. Frazier (Baruch College, emeritus), Stephen J. Kneeshaw (College of the Ozarks), and Linda Gies

The *Instructor's Resource Manual* contains materials to aid instructors in teaching *America: A Concise History* and enhance student involvement. For each chapter of the textbook the resources include a list of chapter themes, a brief summary, an annotated timeline from the textbook with additional information, lecture suggestions, class discussion starters, topics for writing assignments, and suggested topics for research. In addition, the *Instructor's Resource Manual* includes nine historiographic essays by outstanding scholars on topics like populism, a guide to writing about history by Gerald J. Goodwin (reprinted in the Student Guide), and a film and video guide by Stephen J. Kneeshaw.

Using The Bedford Series in History and Culture with *America: A Concise History*

by Scott Hovey

Recognizing that many instructors use a brief core text to provide a backbone around which to array supplements, Bedford/St. Martin's has made the Bedford series volumes available at a discount to adopters of *America: A Concise History*. This short guide by Scott Hovey gives practical suggestions for using a dozen volumes from the Bedford series with each volume of this concise text, providing links between text and supplement as well as ideas for starting discussions focused on a single primary-source volume.

Test Bank, Volumes 1 and 2

by Thomas L. Altherr and Adolph Grundman (Metropolitan State College of Denver), and James Miller

The *Test Bank* provides 80 to 110 questions for each chapter of *America: A Concise History*, including multiple-choice questions, fill-ins, and short and long essay questions. Computerized test-generation systems are also available for IBM-compatible and Macintosh platforms.

ACKNOWLEDGMENTS

The scholars and teachers who reviewed our manuscript saved us from many mistakes and made suggestions that enhanced the cogency of our interpretations. All have used concise texts in their courses, and their classroom experience has helped us create a book that will meet the needs of today's diverse students. Special thanks are due to: Thomas Blantz, University of Notre Dame; John Buenker, University of Wisconsin–Parkside; Emmett Essin, East Tennessee State University; David Huehner, University of Wisconsin–Washington County; John Johnson, University of Northern Iowa; Stephen Kneeshaw, College of the Ozarks; Chana Lee, Indiana University; Robert Martin, University of Northern Iowa; Carl Moneyhon, University of Arkansas–Little Rock; John S. Nader, State University of New York at Delhi; Steven Reiss, Northeastern Illinois University; and Kenneth Scherzer, Middle Tennessee State University.

As the authors of *America: A Concise History*, we know better than anyone else how much this book is the work of other hands and minds. We are grateful to Paul Shensa, who helped us to conceive this book, and to Jennifer Sutherland who, as always, held us to the highest scholarly standards as she masterfully edited our text. We also thank our editorial and production team for their dedicated efforts: Stacey B. Alexander, Elizabeth Geller, Lawrence Guerra, Cindy Joyce, Fernando Quinones, Shuli Traub, and Demetrios Zangos. Finally, we want to express our appreciation for the invaluable assistance of Patricia Deveneau, Lawrence Peskin, and Norman Cohen, whose work contributed in many ways to the intellectual vitality of *America: A Concise History*.

James A. Henretta
David Brody
Lynn Dumenil

CONTENTS

LIST OF MAPS

America

A CONCISE HISTORY

ECONOMY From Subsistence to Prosperity	GOVERNMENT From Monarchy to Republic	RELIGION From Hierarchy to Pluralism	SOCIETY The Evolution of Cultures
1450 Native American subsistence economy Europeans fish off North American coast	Rise of monarchical states in Europe	Protestant Reformation (1517)	Spanish confront Pueblo peoples of New Mexico
1600 First staple crops: furs and tobacco	James I rules by "divine right" Virginia House of Burgesses (1619)	English Puritans and Catholics found colonies in America	Calvinism and freehold ideal in New England White servitude and African slavery in Chesapeake colonies
1640 New England trade with sugar islands Mercantilism: First Navigation Act (1651)	Puritan Revolution Stuart restoration (1660) Bacon's rebellion (1675)	Religious liberty in Rhode Island Anglicanism is state church in Virginia	Eastern Woodland Indians retreat inland Aristocratic ideal in Chesapeake
1680 Tobacco trade stagnates Rice cultivation expands	Dominion of New England (1686–89) Glorious Revolution	Quakers create religious liberty in Pennsylvania Rise of toleration	African-American languge and culture
1720 Mature farm economy in North Imports from Britain increase	Rise of the assembly Challenge to "deferential" politics	German and Scots-Irish pietists arrive First Great Awakening	Cultural diversity in Mid-Atlantic colonies Franklin and the American Enlightenment
1760 Trade boycotts encourage manufacturing	Tenant and yeoman uprisings Ideas of popular sovereignty	Evangelical Baptists Quebec Act protects Catholicism (1774)	Sense of American identity

PART 1

THE CREATION OF AMERICAN SOCIETY

1450–1775

For thousands of years the first Americans lived isolated from the rest of the world, developing a rich diversity of societies adapted to the different environments of the continent. The coming of Europeans tore the fabric of these societies to shreds. European settlers transplanted their own societies to the New World—their economic practices, their political systems, their cultures, their religions. But in learning to live in the new land, the men and women who came to England's North American colonies eventually created distinctly new societies.

First, thanks to the abundant resources of eastern North America, the settlers compiled a record of economic achievement. Plenty replaced poverty as the settlers created a bustling economy and, in New England and the Mid-Atlantic colonies, prosperous communities of independent farm families. In the southern colonies the price of prosperity for a few was oppression and captivity for the rest—indentured servitude for many whites and, later, slavery for almost all blacks.

Second, white men of property created an increasingly free and competitive political system. The first English settlers brought authoritarian institutions to America, but arbitrary rule gradually gave way to new kinds of local government that included representative assemblies with real power.

Third, the diversity of religious belief among the settlers eroded support for an established church and promoted the new ideal of religious toleration.

Finally, conditions in the English colonies fostered the creation of new social identities. Many had a unique outlook or language, such as the cultures created by African-Americans and German-Americans. But after 1720 the values and the practices of the European settlers—English, Scots, Scots-Irish, Dutch, German—converged as a result of the religious revivals of the Great Awakening and the dissemination of Enlightenment thought. The result was a new American identity based on the English language, British legal and political institutions, and shared experiences.

CHAPTER 1

WORLDS COLLIDE: EUROPE AND AMERICA

- Native American Worlds
- Traditional European Society in 1450
- Europe and the World, 1450–1550
- The Protestant Reformation and the Rise of England, 1500–1630

In 1492 the peoples of Europe and America lived in separate worlds, unaware of each other's existence. An estimated 70 million native Americans, the descendants of migrants from Asia, populated the vast continents of the Western Hemisphere. Across the Atlantic Ocean another 70 million people inhabited the much less extensive lands of Western Europe. Around 1450 a few Europeans, hungry for the trade and riches of Asia, began to venture far from their native shores. Within a few decades Christopher Columbus, an Italian navigator in the service of Spain, encountered the lands and peoples of the Americas, setting off a collision of cultures that changed the course of world history. The subsequent arrival in the Western Hemisphere of enslaved Africans—first in the West Indies and by 1550 in Brazil—added another dimension to the unfolding story.

How did Europeans become leaders in world trade and extend their influence across the Atlantic? What was the character of the native Americans' life and culture, and what made their societies vulnerable to conquest by European adventurers? How did England, an insignificant nation in 1492, acquire the political will and economic resources to establish colonies in North America? And what led to the transatlantic trade in enslaved Africans? In the answers to these questions lie the origins of the United States.

NATIVE AMERICAN WORLDS

When the Europeans arrived, the great majority of native Americans—probably 40 million—lived in Mesoamerica (present-day Mexico and Guatemala) and another 10 million resided in lands to the north (present-day United States and Canada). Some lived in simple agricultural communities, but the majority resided in societies ruled by warrior-kings and priests. In Mesoamerica and Peru, Indian peoples created civilizations whose art, religion, society, and economy were as complex as those of Europe and the Mediterranean.

The First Americans

The first people who lived in the Western Hemisphere were migrants from Asia. Some might have come by water, but most probably came by land. Strong archaeological evidence suggests that during the last Ice Age, which began about 30,000 years ago, small bands of hunters followed herds of game across a land bridge between Siberia and Alaska. A tale of the Tuscarora Indians, who lived in present-day North Carolina, tells of a famine in the old world and a journey over ice toward where "the sun rises," a trek that brought their ancestors to a lush forest with abundant food and game. Most anthropologists believe that this migratory stream continued for about 20,000 years, until the glaciers melted and the rising ocean waters submerged the land bridge. Then the people of the Western Hemisphere, who by that time had moved as far south as the tip of South America and as far east as the Atlantic coast of North America, were cut off from the rest of the world for 400 generations.

For another 3,000 years the first Americans lived as hunter-gatherers, subsisting on the abundant wildlife and vegetation. But about 3000 B.C. some native American peoples began to develop horticulture, most notably in present-day Mexico. These inventive farmers planted avocado, chili peppers, and cotton and learned how to breed maize, or Indian corn, as well as tomatoes, potatoes, and manioc, crops that would eventually enrich the food supply of the entire world. Over the centuries the Indian peoples bred corn into a much larger, extremely nutritious plant that was hardier, had more varieties, and had a higher yield per acre than wheat, barley, and rye, the staple cereals of Europe. They also learned to cultivate beans and squash and plant them together with corn; this provided a nutritious diet and preserved soil fertility, allowing intensive farming and high yields. The resulting agricultural surplus laid the economic foundation for populous and wealthy societies in Mexico, in Peru, and for a time in the Mississippi Valley.

The Maya and the Aztecs

The flowering of civilization in Mesoamerica began among the Mayan peoples of the Yucatan Peninsula of Mexico and the neighboring rain forests of

Chacmool Statue
Striking statues of a reclining man, called Chacmools, were prominent features of many Mayan temples. Priests placed sacrifices and gifts to the gods on the Chacmools' flat stomachs.

Guatemala. The Maya built large religious centers, urban communities with elaborate systems of water storage and irrigation. By A.D. 300 the Mayan city of Tikal had at least 20,000 inhabitants, mostly farmers who worked the nearby fields and whose labor was used to build huge stone temples. An elite class claiming descent from the gods ruled Mayan society, living in splendor on goods and taxes extracted from peasant families. Drawing on traditions that stretched back to the Olmec people, who had lived along the Gulf of Mexico around 700 B.C., skilled Mayan artisans decorated temples and palaces with art depicting warrior-gods and complex religious rituals. Mayan astronomers created a calendar that recorded historical events and predicted eclipses of the sun and the moon with remarkable accuracy. The Maya also developed hieroglyphic writing to record royal lineages and noteworthy events, including wars.

Beginning around A.D. 800, Mayan civilization declined. Some evidence suggests that a two-century-long dry period caused a decline in population and an economic crisis which prompted overtaxed peasants to desert the temple cities and retreat into the countryside. By A.D. 900 many religious centers had been abandoned, but other Mayan city-states lasted until the Spanish invasion, and emigrants may have carried Mayan technology and culture into the Mississippi Valley.

As the Mayan empire flourished in the Yucatan, a second major Mesoamerican civilization developed in the central Valley of Mexico around the city of Teotihuacán, with its magnificent Pyramid of the Sun. At its zenith about A.D. 500 Teotihuacán had more than 100 temples, about 4,000 apartment buildings, and a population of at least 100,000. By A.D. 800 Teotihuacán had also declined, probably because of a long-term drop in rainfall and recurrent invasions by seminomadic peoples. Eventually the militant Toltecs from the deserts of northern Mexico took control of Teotihuacán and created a great empire, only to be overtaken by another warrior tribe, the Aztecs.

The Aztecs entered the Valley of Mexico from the north and settled on an island in Lake Texcoco. There, in A.D. 1325, they began to build a new city, Tenochtitlán (present-day Mexico City). They learned the settled ways of the resident peoples, mastered their complex irrigation systems, and established an elaborate culture with a hierarchical social order. Priests and warrior nobles ruled over twenty clans of free Aztec commoners who farmed communally owned land, and the nobles used huge numbers of non-Aztec slaves and serfs to labor on their private estates. Artisans worked in stone, pottery, cloth, leather, and especially obsidian (hard volcanic glass used to make sharp-edged weapons and tools).

The Aztecs remained an aggressive tribe and soon subjugated most of central Mexico. Their rulers demanded both economic and human tribute from scores of subject tribes, gruesomely sacrificing untold thousands of men and women to the god of war. Aztec merchants, organized in a hereditary guild, created far-flung trading routes and imported furs, gold, textiles, food, and obsidian. By A.D. 1500 Tenochtitlán had grown into a great metropolis with splendid palaces and temples and over 200,000 inhabitants. The Aztecs' wealth, strong institutions, and military power posed a formidable challenge to any adversary, at home or from afar.

The Indians of the North

The Indians who lived north of the Rio Grande were much fewer in number and less formidable in military strength. In A.D. 1500 and for most of the preceding centuries these Indians lived in hundreds of dispersed communities of a few thousand people (see Map 1.1). Most were organized in self-governing tribes composed of *clans*—groups of related families that had a common identity and a real or legendary common ancestor. They were led by local chiefs who, aided by the clan elders, led ceremonies and regulated personal life. For example, elders encouraged individuals to share food and other scarce goods, promoting an ethic of reciprocity rather than one of accumulation. Elders banned marriage between members of the same clan, a rule that helped prevent inbreeding, and granted families use-rights over certain planting grounds and hunting areas, since the concept of private ownership of land was virtually unknown in Indian culture. Clan leaders also resolved personal feuds, disciplined individuals who violated customs, and decided whether to go to war.

MAP 1.1

Native American Peoples, 1492

Native Americans populated the entire Western Hemisphere at the time of Columbus's arrival, having created diverse cultures that ranged from the centralized agriculture-based empires of the Maya and the Aztecs to seminomadic tribes of hunter-gatherers. The sheer diversity among Indians—of culture, language, tribal identity—inhibited united resistance to the European invaders.

However, their power was far less than that of the Mayan and Aztec nobles, because their kinship-based system of government was locally based and worked by consensus, not by coercion.

Over the centuries some of these tribes exerted influence over neighboring peoples through trade or conquest. The earliest expansive Indian culture appeared in the eastern woodlands of North America as the inhabitants increased the food supply by domesticating plants, settled in large villages, and exchanged goods. By A.D. 100 the vigorous Hopewell people of present-day Ohio had spread their influence through trade from present-day Wisconsin to

Louisiana. They built large burial mounds and surrounded them with extensive circular, rectangular, or octagonal earthworks that in some cases still survive. The Hopewell people buried their dead with art: copper beaten into elaborate designs, crystals of quartz, mica cut into the shapes of serpents and human hands, and stone pipes carved to represent frogs, hawks, bears, and other animals. For unknown reasons, their elaborate trading network gradually collapsed around A.D. 400.

A second complex culture developed in the Southwest. By A.D. 600 farming peoples in present-day Arizona were using irrigation to grow two crops a year, fashioning fine pottery, and worshiping their gods on platform mounds. In New Mexico, the Mogollon peoples developed large multiroom stone structures after A.D. 1000, while the Anasazi built residential-ceremonial villages in steep cliffs as well as devising a road system and various astronomical devices. But these cultures gradually collapsed after A.D. 1250 as long periods of drought and invasions by the Navajos and the Apache disrupted food production. The descendants of these Pueblo peoples—including the Zuni and the Hopi—later built strong but smaller and more dispersed village societies.

Casas Grandes Pot
The artistically and architecturally talented Mogollon and Anasazi peoples of Arizona and New Mexico took utilitarian objects—such as this ordinary pot—and decorated them with black-on-white designs. Their cultures flourished from 1000 to 1250, after which they slowly declined.

The last large-scale culture to emerge north of the Rio Grande was the Mississippian civilization. Beginning about A.D. 800, the advanced farming technology of Mesoamerica spread into the Mississippi River Valley, perhaps carried by emigrants fleeing from warfare among the Maya. New strains of maize and beans, planted on productive river bottomland, provided a protein-rich diet for the resident peoples and created an agricultural surplus. A robust culture based on small fortified temple cities quickly emerged. By A.D. 1150 the largest city, Cahokia (near present-day St. Louis), had a population of 10,000 and more than 100 temple mounds. As in Mesoamerica, the tribute paid by peasant cultivators supported a privileged class of nobles and priests who patronized skilled artisans. However, by A.D. 1350 this Mississippian civilization was in rapid decline, undermined by urban diseases such as tuberculosis and warfare over the fertile bottomlands.

The values and institutions of Mississippian civilization endured for centuries and accounted for the fierce resistance by the Indians of this region to Spanish and French invaders. As late as 1700 French traders and priests who encountered the Natchez people found a society rigidly divided among hereditary chiefs, two intermediate groups of nobles and honored people, and a bottom class of peasants. Undoubtedly influenced by Mesoamerican rituals, the Natchez practiced human sacrifice; the death of a chief called for the sacrifice of his wives and the enlargement of a ceremonial mound to bury their remains. Because of their stratified social order, eighteenth-century British settlers would call the Mississippian peoples (the Choctaw, Creeks, Chickasaw, Cherokee, and Seminole) the Five Civilized Tribes.

The most important legacy of the Mississippian civilization was its agricultural practices. Although farming in Mesoamerica was the province of both sexes, among the eastern Woodland peoples it became the work of women. Over the centuries Indian women became adept horticulturalists, using flint hoes and superior strains of corn, squash, and beans to reduce the dependence of their peoples on gathering and hunting. In the summer many tribes lived in semipermanent villages of domed wigwams where women cultivated fields, passing the right to use them to their daughters. Because of the importance of farming, a matrilineal inheritance system developed among many eastern Indians, including the Five Nations of the Iroquois. The ritual lives of these peoples also focused on religious ceremonies related to the agricultural cycle, such as the Iroquois green corn and strawberry festivals. While Indians ate better as a result of these advances in farming, they enjoyed few material comforts. Their lives were harsh, and their populations grew slowly.

In A.D. 1500 most Indians north of the Rio Grande had resided on the same lands for generations, but there were no great Indian empires and no major cities or religious centers. And because the peoples spoke many different languages (no fewer than sixty-eight east of the Mississippi River), there were few alliances among tribes. Neither their social organization nor their historical experience prepared them to deal collectively with the European invaders.

Women and Agriculture
As a Dutch traveler reported, Indian women planted corn by making "heaps like mole hills, each about two and a half-feet from the others" into which they put "five or six seeds." By planting two acres, a woman typically harvested 60 bushels of shelled corn, half the calories required by five persons for a year. Because of their economic contribution, women had a high status among many eastern Woodland peoples.

TRADITIONAL EUROPEAN SOCIETY IN 1450

In A.D. 1450 few observers would have predicted that the European peoples would become the overlords of the Western Hemisphere. A thousand years after the fall of the Roman empire Europe remained a backward society. Most Europeans, like most native Americans, were exploited peasants or poor farmers who had little knowledge of the wider world. Their lives and those of their descendants who would migrate to the Americas were shaped by the cultural and religious values of the traditional rural world.

The Peasantry

There were only a few large cities in Western Europe before A.D. 1450: Rome, Paris, Amsterdam, London, the city-states of northern Italy. More than 90 percent of the population consisted of peasants living in small rural communities. Usually families owned or leased a small dwelling in the village center and had the right to farm strips of land in the surrounding fields. The fields were not divided by fences or hedges, making cooperative farming a necessity. Each year the male householders decided which crops to plant and how many cows and sheep each family could graze on the commonly used meadows. Because there were few merchants or good roads, most families exchanged surplus grain and meat with their neighbors or bartered their farm products for the services of local millers, weavers, and blacksmiths. Most peasants yearned to be yeomen, under no obligation to a landlord and owning enough land to support a family in comfort, but relatively few achieved that goal. Most men and women lived hard, unvarying lives in the towns or regions of their birth.

Sustenance required unremitting labor. Other than water- or wind-powered mills for grinding grain, raw muscle was the major source of energy. While horses and oxen strained to break the soil with primitive wooden plows, men staggered as they guided them from behind. At harvest time workers cut hay, wheat, rye, and barley with hand sickles, but output was at most one-tenth of a modern yield.

As among the native Americans, nearly all aspects of European peasant life followed a seasonal pattern. The agricultural year began in March or April, when the ground thawed and dried, allowing the villagers to begin the exhausting work of spring plowing and planting. Peasants cut the first crop of hay in June and stored it as winter fodder for their livestock. During these busy spring months men sheared the thick winter wool of their sheep, which the women washed and spun into yarn. In the summer life became more relaxed. Families could mend their fences or repair their barns and houses. August and September often were marked by grief as infants and old people succumbed to epidemics of fly-borne dysentery. Fall brought the strenuous harvest time, but once the crops were in, people celebrated with solemn feasts of thanksgiving and riotous bouts of merrymaking. As winter approached, peasants slaughtered excess livestock and salted or smoked the meat. During the cold months they completed the tasks of threshing grain and weaving textiles and had time to visit friends and relatives in nearby villages. Many rural people died in January and February, victims of the cold and viral diseases. Then, just before the agricultural cycle began again in the spring, rural residents held carnivals to celebrate with drink and dance the end of the long winter night.

For most peasants the margin of existence was thin, and this situation corroded family relations. About half of all peasant children died before the age of twenty-one. Malnourished mothers fed their babies sparingly, calling them "greedy and gluttonous" little beasts, and many newborn girls were "helped to die" so that their older brothers would have enough to eat. To relieve overcrowding at home and instill discipline, English parents commonly sent their children to live as servants in other households, where they often were mistreated. Violence—assault, murder, rape—was much more prevalent than in the modern world, and hunger and disease were constant companions. "I have seen the latest epoch of misery," a French doctor reported as famine and plague struck. "The inhabitants . . . lie down in a meadow to eat grass, and share the food of wild beasts."

Often destitute, usually exploited and dominated by landlords and aristocrats, many peasants simply accepted their condition, but others did not. It would be the deprived rural classes of England and Western Europe, hoping for a better life for themselves and their children, who would supply the majority of white migrants to the Western Hemisphere.

Hierarchy and Authority

In the traditional European social order, as in the Aztec and Mayan empires, authority came from above. Kings and princes owned vast tracts of land and lived in splendor off the labor of the peasantry. Monarchs sought to extend their power by levying royal taxes, creating law courts, and conscripting men for military service. Yet they were far from supreme, given the power of the nobles, each of whom also owned large estates and controlled hundreds of peasant families. Collectively, these noblemen had the power to challenge royal authority. They had their own legislative institutions, such as the French *parlements* and the English House of Lords, and enjoyed special privileges, such as the right to a trial before a jury of their peers. Because nobles had direct control over the peasantry, monarchs had little choice but to appoint them as local judges and militia officers. But after 1450 kings began to undermine the power of the nobility and create more centralized states, laying the basis for overseas expansion.

Just as kings and nobles ruled the polity, the men in peasant families ruled their women and children. The man was the head of the house, his power justified by the teachings of the Christian Church. As one English clergyman put it, "The woman is a weak creature not embued with like strength and constancy of mind"; law and custom consequently "subjected her to the power of man." Upon marriage, an English woman assumed her husband's surname and usually moved to his village. She was required (under the threat of legally sanctioned physical "correction") to submit to her husband's orders. Moreover, she surrendered to her husband the legal right to all her property, including her clothes. Upon his death she received only a dower, usually the use during her lifetime of one-third of the family's land and goods.

A father controlled the lives of his children with equal authority, demanding that they work for him until their middle or late twenties. Then a landowning peasant would provide land to sons and dowries to daughters and choose marriage partners of appropriate wealth and status for them. In many regions fathers bestowed most of the land on the eldest son in the inheritance practice known as *primogeniture* (preference to the firstborn male). Custom called for landless brothers and sisters to work on their brother's farm in return for food and shelter, but the small size of most peasant holdings forced many younger children to join the ranks of the roaming poor.

In this world of scarcity the individual had to submit to the discipline of superiors or to the consensus of the village community. As among the eastern Woodland Indians, local authorities strictly regulated individual behavior for the common good; for example, in Germany they granted marriage licenses only to couples with enough property to support a family. Officials also imposed limits on what could be charged for the staff of life: a loaf of bread, a sack of flour or grain. Fearful of change, they made tradition the measure of existence. "After a thing had been practiced for so long that it becomes a Custom," an English clergyman proclaimed, "that Custom is Law." In such a society few men—and even fewer women—had much personal freedom or individual identity.

Hierarchy and authority prevailed in the traditional European social order both because of the power of established institutions and because, in a violent and unpredictable world, they offered ordinary people a measure of security. These values, which migrants carried with them to America, would shape the character of family life and the social order there well into the eighteenth century.

The Power of Religion

The Roman Catholic Church served as the great unifying force in Western European society. By A.D. 1000 Christianity had converted virtually all of pagan Europe. The pope, as head of the Catholic Church, directed a vast hierarchy of cardinals, bishops, and priests. Latin, the language of scholarship, was preserved by Catholic priests and monks, and Christian dogma provided a common understanding of God, the world, and human history. Equally important, the Church provided another bulwark of authority and

Christ's Crucifixion
This graphic portrayal of Christ's death on the cross by the German painter Grünewald sought to remind believers of the reality of death and the need for repentance. [Mathias Grünewald, Isenheim Altarpiece (central panel), Colmar, Musée Unterlinden, Giraudon/Art Resource]

discipline in society. Every village had a church, and holy shrines dotted the byways of Europe.

Christian doctrine penetrated deeply into the everyday lives of peasants. Over the centuries the Church had adopted a religious calendar that followed the agricultural cycle and transformed pagan festivals into Christian holy days. Thus the winter solstice, which for pagans marked the return of the sun and the victory of light over darkness, became the feast of Christmas. This merging of the sacred and the agricultural cycle endowed all worldly events with meaning. Few Christians believed that events occurred by chance; they were the result of God's will. To avert famine and plague, peasants turned to priests for spiritual guidance and offered prayers to Christ and the saints. God's presence in the world was renewed continually through the sacrament of Holy Communion. According to Catholic doctrine, priests had the power to change sacramental bread and wine into the body and blood of Christ. By consuming the bread of the Host, peasants could partake in the divine.

The Church taught that Satan constantly challenged God by tempting people into evil. If prophets spread unusual doctrines, they were surely the tools of Satan. If a devout Christian fell mysteriously ill, the sickness might be the result of an evil spell cast by a witch in league with Satan. Crushing other religions and suppressing false doctrines (heresies) among Christians was an obligation of rulers and a principal task of the new orders of Christian knights. Between A.D. 1096 and 1291 successive armies of Christians, led by European kings and nobles, embarked on a series of Crusades to expel Muslims from the Holy Land where Jesus had lived.

The Crusaders succeeded in gaining control of much of Palestine, but the impact on Europe was more profound. Religious warfare reinforced and intensified its Christian identity, resulting in renewed persecution of Jews and their expulsion from many European countries. Many Jewish refugees went to Germany, only to be driven farther east, to Poland, over the next few centuries. The Crusades also broadened the intellectual and economic horizons of the privileged classes of Western Europe, bringing them into contact with the advanced Muslim peoples of the Mediterranean region who controlled the trade among Europe, Asia, and Africa and led the world in scholarship.

EUROPE AND THE WORLD, 1450–1550

Around A.D. 1450 Europeans shook off the lethargy of their traditional agricultural society with a major revival of learning, the Renaissance. Inspired by new knowledge and a new optimism, the rulers of Portugal and Spain commissioned Italian navigators to find new trade routes to India and China. These maritime adventurers soon brought Europeans into direct contact with the peoples of Africa, Asia, and the Americas, beginning a new era in world history.

Renaissance Beginnings

Stimulated by the wealth and learning of the Arab world, first Italy and then the countries of northern Europe experienced the rebirth of learning and cultural life now known as the Renaissance. Arab traders had access to the fabulous treasures of the East, such as silks and spices, and Arab societies had acquired magnetic compasses, water-powered mills, and mechanical clocks. In great cultural centers such as Alexandria and Cairo in Egypt, Arab scholars carried on the legacy of Christian Byzantine civilization, which had preserved the great achievements of the Greeks and Romans in religion, medicine, philosophy, mathematics, astronomy, and geography. Through Arab learning, the peoples of Europe reacquainted themselves with their own classical heritage.

The Renaissance had the most profound impact on the upper classes. Merchants from the Italian city-states of Venice, Genoa, and Pisa dispatched ships to Alexandria, Beirut, and other eastern Mediterranean ports, where they purchased goods from China, India, Persia, and Arabia and sold them throughout Europe. The enormous profits from this commerce created a new class of merchants, bankers, and textile manufacturers who conducted trade, lent vast sums of money, and spurred technological innovation in silk and wool production. This moneyed elite ruled the republican city-states of Italy and created the concept of civic humanism, an ideology that celebrated public virtue and service to the state and would profoundly influence European and American conceptions of government.

Drawing inspiration from classical Greek and Roman (rather than Christian) sources, Renaissance intellectuals were optimistic in their view of human nature and celebrated individual potential. Embracing the confident psychology of the Renaissance, they saw themselves not as prisoners of blind fate or victims of the forces of nature but as many-sided individuals with the capacity to change the world.

This energetic view appealed to Renaissance rulers. In *The Prince* (1513), Niccolò Machiavelli, inspired by the state-building activities of the ambitious monarchs of France and Western Europe, provided unsentimental advice on how monarchs could increase their political power. Kings followed his advice, creating royal law courts and bureaucracies to reduce the power of the landed classes and seeking alliances with merchants and manufacturers. Monarchs allowed merchants to trade throughout their realms and granted privileges to artisan guilds, encouraging both domestic manufacturing and foreign trade. In return, these rulers extracted taxes from towns and loans from merchants to support their armies and officials. This alliance of monarchs, merchants, and royal bureaucrats challenged the power of the agrarian nobility, while the increasing wealth of the monarchical nation-state propelled Europe into its first age of expansion.

Portugal Penetrates Africa and Asia

Under the direction of Prince Henry (1394–1460), Portugal led the great surge of expansion. Henry was a many-sided individual, at once a Christian warrior and a Renaissance humanist. As a general of the Crusading Order of Christ, he had fought the Muslims in North Africa, an experience which reinforced his desire to extend the bounds of Christendom—and Portuguese power. As a humanist, Henry patronized Renaissance thinkers and relied on Arab and Italian geographers for the latest knowledge about the shape and size of the continents. Imbued with the spirit of the Renaissance, he tried to fulfill the predictions of his horoscope: "to engage in great and noble conquests and to attempt the discovery of things hidden from other men."

Because Arab and Italian merchants dominated trade in the Mediterranean, Henry sought an ocean route to the wealth of Asia. In the 1420s he established a center for exploration and ocean mapping and sent out ships to sail the African coast. His seamen soon discovered and settled the islands of Madeira and the Azores. By 1435 Portuguese sea captains were roaming the coast of West Africa, seeking ivory and gold in exchange for salt, wine, and fish. By the 1440s they were trading in humans as well, the first Europeans to engage in the African slave trade. For centuries Arab merchants had conducted a brisk overland trade in slaves, buying sub-Saharan Africans captured during local ethnic conflicts and selling them throughout the Mediterranean region. At first the Portuguese transported enslaved West Africans to sugar estates in Madeira and the Azores. Later they would carry hundreds of thousands of slaves to toil and die on the sugar plantations of Brazil and the West Indies.

After Henry's death in 1460 Portuguese adventurers continued to look for a direct ocean route to Asia. In 1488 Bartholomeu Dias rounded the Cape of Good Hope, the southern tip of Africa, and ten years later Vasco da Gama reached India. Although the Arab, Indian, and Jewish merchants who controlled the trade along India's Malabar Coast tried to exclude him, da Gama acquired a highly profitable cargo of cinnamon and pepper (used to flavor and preserve meat). To capture this commerce for Portugal, da Gama returned to India in 1502 with twenty-one fighting vessels, which outmaneuvered and outgunned the Arab fleets. The plunder-hungry Portuguese burned cities and seized the property of rival traders. Soon the Portuguese government set up fortified trading posts for its merchants at key points around the Indian Ocean and opened trade routes from Africa to Indonesia and up the coast of Asia to China and Japan. Portuguese merchants could undersell Arab traders because their ships held more and traveled faster than overland caravans. In a momentous transition, Portuguese replaced Arabs as the leaders in world commerce and the trade in African slaves.

Spain and America

Spain quickly followed Portugal's example. As Renaissance rulers, King Ferdinand of Aragon and Queen Isabella of Castile saw national unity and commerce as the keys to power and prosperity. Married in their teens in an arranged match, the young rulers (1474–1516) combined their kingdoms and completed the centuries-long campaign (the *reconquista*) to oust the Moors (Arabs) from their realm. In 1492 their armies reconquered Granada, the last outpost of Islam in Western Europe. Continuing their effort to use the Catholic religion to build a sense of "Spanishness," Ferdinand and Isabella launched a brutal Inquisition against suspected Christian heretics and expelled or forcibly converted thousands of Jews. Simultaneously they sought new opportunities for trade and empire.

Because Portugal controlled the southern, or African, approach to Asia, Isabella and Ferdinand listened with interest to proposals for a western route to the riches of the East. Its main advocate was Christopher Columbus, a forceful Genoese sea captain who, after many failed ventures, was determined to become rich and famous. Misinterpreting the findings of Italian geographers, Columbus persuaded the Spanish monarchs that the Atlantic Ocean, long feared by Arab sailors as an endless "green sea of darkness," was little more than a narrow channel of water separating Europe from Asia. Dubious at first, Ferdinand and Isabella finally agreed to arrange financial backing from Spanish merchants and charged Columbus not only to discover a new trade route to China but also to carry Christianity to other peoples.

Columbus set sail with three small ships on August 3, 1492. Six weeks later, after a voyage of 3,000 miles, he finally found land, disembarking on one of the islands of the present-day Bahamas on October 12, 1492. Although surprised by the rude living conditions of the natives, Columbus expected them to be quickly "delivered and converted to our holy faith." With ceremony and solemnity, he claimed the islands for Spain and for Christendom.

Believing he had reached Asia—"the Indies," in fifteenth-century parlance—Columbus called the native inhabitants "Indians" and labeled the islands "the West Indies." He then explored the Caribbean islands, demanding gold from the local Tainos and Arawak peoples. Buoyed by the natives' stories of rivers of gold lying "to the west," Columbus left forty men on the island of Hispaniola and returned triumphantly to Spain, taking several Tainos to display to Isabella and Ferdinand.

The Spanish monarchs were sufficiently impressed by his discovery to support three more voyages over the next twelve years. During those expeditions Columbus began the transatlantic slave trade, carrying a few hundred Indians to bondage in Europe and importing black slaves from Africa to work as artisans and farmers in the Spanish settlements. However, he failed to find either golden treasures or great kingdoms, and his death in 1506 went virtually unrecognized. Ignoring Columbus, a German geographer gave the new continents the name of a Florentine merchant, Amerigo Vespucci, who traveled to South America around 1500 and called it a *nuevo mundo*, a New World. For its part, the Spanish Crown was determined to make it a Spanish world.

AMERICAN VOICES

Columbus's First Impressions of Native Americans

As a well-traveled mariner, Columbus knew the world and its peoples. But he was clearly puzzled by the first "Indians" he encountered: their lack of clothes and iron weapons, skin color, and painted bodies. To maintain his belief that he had reached Asia, he visualized a more advanced civilization on the mainland.

Because I knew that they were a people to be delivered and converted to our holy faith rather by love than by force, [I] gave to some among them some red caps and some glass beads, which they hung around their necks, and many other things of little value. At this they were greatly pleased and became so entirely our friends that it was a wonder to see. . . .

They all go naked as their mothers bore them, and the women also, although I saw only one very young girl. . . . Their hair is coarse almost like the hairs of a horse's tail and short; they wear their hair down over their eyebrows, except for a few strands behind, which they wear long and never cut. Some of them are painted black, and they are the colour of the people of the Canaries, neither black nor white, and some of them are painted white and red. . . .

They do not bear arms or know them, for I showed to them swords and they took them by the blade and cut themselves through ignorance. They have no iron. Their spears are certain reeds, without iron, and some of these have a fish hook at the end, while others are pointed in various ways. . . . I saw some who bore marks of wounds on their bodies . . . and they indicated to me that people came from other islands, which are near, and wished to capture them, and they defended themselves. And I believed and still believe that they come here from the mainland to take them for slaves. They should be good servants and of quick intelligence, . . . and I believe that they would easily be made Christians, for it appeared to me that they had no creed.

SOURCE: Bartolomé de Las Casas, *The Journal of Christopher Columbus* (1847/70), trans. by Cecil Jane, rev. and annotated by L. A. Vigneras (London: Hakluyt Society, 1960), pp. 39–41.

The Conquest

Although Columbus had found no gold, rumors of riches to the west encouraged Spanish adventurers to follow in his footsteps. Most of these men were not explorers or merchants but hardened veterans of the Moorish wars who were eager to get rich. The Spanish Crown offered them plunder, estates in the conquered territory, and titles of nobility in return for creating an empire. After subduing the Arawak and Tainos on Hispaniola, these military adventurers explored the mainland in search of booty. Juan Ponce de León searched for gold and slaves along the coast of Florida in 1513 and gave the peninsula its name. Vasco Núñez de Balboa crossed the Isthmus of Darien

(Panama) in 1513, not finding gold but becoming the first European to see the Pacific Ocean.

The first great success of the Spanish *conquistadors* (conquerors) occurred in Mexico (see Map 1.2). In 1519 Hernando Cortés landed on the Mexican coast with 600 men and marched toward the Aztec capital of Tenochtitlán. Fortuitously, Cortés arrived in the very year in which Aztec mythology had predicted the return of the god Quetzalcoatl to his earthly kingdom. Believing that Cortés might be the returning god, Moctezuma, the Aztec ruler, acted indecisively. After the failure of an ambush against the conquistadors, he allowed Cortés to proceed without challenge to Tenochtitlán and received him with great ceremony, only to become his captive. When Moctezuma's forces attempted to expel the invader, they were confronted by superior European military technology. The sight of the Spaniards in full armor, with cannon that shook the heavens, made a deep impression on the Aztecs, who had learned how to purify gold and fashion it into ornate religious objects but did not produce iron tools or weapons. Moreover, the Aztecs had no wheeled carts or cav-

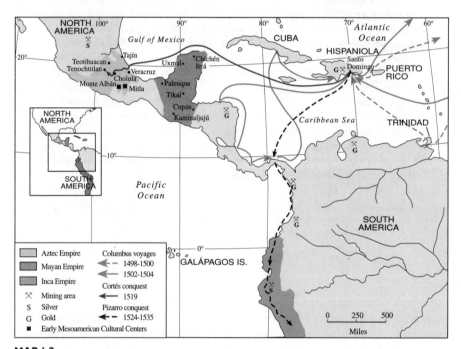

MAP 1.2
The Spanish Conquest
The Spanish first invaded the islands of the Caribbean. Rumors of a magnificent golden civilization led to Cortés's attack on the Aztec empire in 1519. Thanks to the devastating impact of European diseases on Indian peoples, Spanish conquistadors soon conquered the Mayan temple cities and the Inca empire in Peru, completing one of the great conquests in world history.

AMERICAN VOICES

Aztec Elders Describe the Spanish Conquest

uring the 1550s Friar Bernardino de Sahagún published the Florentine Codex: General History of New Spain, *in which the Aztecs described their reaction to the invading Europeans and the devastating impact of smallpox.*

Moctezuma enjoyed no sleep, no food, no one spoke to him. Whatsoever he did, it was as if he were in torment. . . . And when he had so heard what the messengers reported, he was terrified, he was astounded. . . . Especially did it cause him to faint away when he heard how the gun, at [the Spaniards'] command, discharged: how it resounded as if it thundered when it went off. It indeed bereft one of strength; it shut off one's ears. And when it discharged, something like a round pebble came forth from within. Fire went showering forth; sparks went blazing forth. And its smoke smelled very foul. . . .

All iron was their war array. In iron they clothed themselves. With iron they covered their heads. Iron were their swords. Iron were their crossbows. Iron were their shields. Iron were their lances. And those which bore them upon their backs, their deer [horses], were as tall as roof terraces.

And their bodies were everywhere covered; only their faces appeared. They were very white; they had chalky faces; they had yellow hair, though the hair of some was black. . . . And when Moctezuma so heard, he was much terrified. It was as if he fainted away. His heart saddened; his heart failed him. . . .

[Soon] there came to be prevalent a great sickness, a plague. It was in Tepeilhuitl that it originated, that there spread over the people a great destruction of men. Some it indeed covered [with pustules]; they were spread everywhere, on one's face, on one's head, on one's breast. There was indeed perishing; many indeed died of it. No longer could they walk; they only lay in their abodes, in their beds. . . . There was much perishing. Like a covering, covering-like, were the pustules. Indeed, many people died of them, and many just died of hunger. There was death from hunger; there was no one to take care of another; there was no one to attend to another.

SOURCE: Friar Bernardino de Sahagún, *Florentine Codex: General History of New Spain*, trans. by Arthur J. O. Anderson and Charles E. Dibble (Salt Lake City: University of Utah Press, 1975), Book 12, pp. 17–20, 26, 83.

alry, and their warriors, fighting on foot with flint- or obsidian-tipped spears and arrows, were no match for mounted Spanish conquistadors, wielding steel swords and protected by heavy armor.

Still, the vast population of the Aztec empire could easily have crushed the European invaders if the Indian peoples had remain united and healthy. But Cortés exploited the widespread resentment against the Aztecs, forming military alliances and raising thousands of troops from subject peoples who had seen their wealth expropriated by Aztec nobles and their people sacrificed to the Aztec sun god. The Aztec empire collapsed, the victim not of superior Spanish military technology but of a vast internal rebellion of Indian peoples.

As the Spanish sought to impose their dominion over these peoples, they had a silent ally—disease. Separated from Eurasia for thousands of years, the inhabitants of the Western Hemisphere had no immunities to common European diseases. Smallpox, influenza, and measles ravaged the native American peoples, killing tens of thousands of warriors, depriving the people of leaders, and sapping the morale of the survivors. Exploiting this demographic weakness, Cortés quickly extended Spanish rule over the entire Valley of Mexico, and his lieutenants subdued the rest of the highland peoples and then moved against the Maya in the Yucatan Peninsula, eventually conquering them as well.

In the late 1520s Francisco Pizarro led a new military expedition to the mountains of Peru, home of the rich and powerful Inca empire. By the time Pizarro reached Peru, half the population had died from European diseases, which had been spread by Indian traders. Weakened militarily and fighting over succession to the throne, the Inca nobility was easy prey for Pizarro's army. In little more than a decade Spain had become the master of the wealthiest and most populous regions of the Western Hemisphere.

In their ceaseless quest for gold Spanish adventurers were the first Europeans to see large sections of the southern and western United States (see Map 2.1 and the accompanying discussion on page 31). But despite many years and thousands of miles of exploration, they found no gold and few other riches, and so Spanish settlement was limited to Mesoamerica and South America.

Nonetheless, the Spanish invasion and European diseases changed life forever throughout the Western Hemisphere. Virtually the entire Indian population of Hispaniola—some 1 million people—was wiped out by disease and warfare. In Mesoamerica as a whole in 1500 there were probably 40 million Indians; by 1650 that region had only 3 million native Americans. In Peru the population plummeted from 9 million in 1533 to fewer than half a million a century later. The Pueblo peoples of the Southwest and the Mississippian chiefdoms of Florida and the Southeast may have suffered equally catastrophic losses from diseases introduced by the expeditions led by Francisco Vázquez de Coronado and Hernando de Soto.

In Mesoamerica, Spanish overlords ruthlessly exploited the surviving native Americans, forcing them to work on vast plantations to raise crops for local consumption and cattle whose hides were exported to Europe. The Spaniards also altered the natural environment by introducing grains and grasses which supplanted the native flora. Horses, first brought over by Cortés, gradually spread throughout the Western Hemisphere and in the following centuries dramatically changed the way of life of many Indian peoples, especially on the Great Plains of the United States.

The food products of the Western Hemisphere—maize, tomatoes, potatoes, manioc—had an equally great impact on Europe and Africa, increasing agricultural yields and stimulating the growth of populations. Also, the gold and silver that had honored Aztec gods now flowed into the countinghouses of Spain and into the treasury of its monarchs, making that nation the most powerful in Europe for more than a century.

By that time, the once magnificent civilizations of Mexico and Peru lay in ruins and the surviving native Americans had lost much of their cultural identity. Spanish priests suppressed their traditional gods and converted them to Catholicism; as early as 1531 an Indian convert reported a vision of a dark-skinned Virgin Mary, later known as the Virgin of Guadalupe. Soon Spanish bureaucrats imposed taxes and supervised the lives of the Indians, and 500,000 Spanish migrants eventually settled on their lands. Because nearly 90 percent of the Spanish settlers were men and took Indian women as wives or mistresses, the result was a substantial *mestizo* (mixed-race) population. Around 1800, at the end of the colonial era, Spanish America had about 17 million people: 7.5 million Indians, 3.2 million Europeans, 1 million Africans, and 5.5 million people of mixed race and a mixed cultural heritage.

Indians resisted assimilation by retreating into the mountains, but they never had the numbers or the power to oust the Spanish invaders or their descendants. Today only a single Indian tongue, Guarani in Paraguay, is a recognized national language, and no native American state sits in the United Nations. For the original Americans the consequences of the European intrusion in 1492 were tragic and irreversible.

THE PROTESTANT REFORMATION AND THE RISE OF ENGLAND, 1500–1630

Christian fervor had played an important role in the expansionary policies of Portugal and Spain, but now it divided Europe into opposing camps of Catholics and Protestants. A Protestant rebellion in the Spanish Netherlands drained the newfound wealth of the Spanish Crown even as England was undergoing a major economic transformation, giving it the resources to expand into North America and bringing about a new collision of European and Indian peoples.

The Protestant Movement

Over the centuries the Catholic Church had become a large and wealthy institution, controlling vast resources throughout Europe. Renaissance popes and cardinals were among the leading patrons of the arts, but some also misused the Church's wealth. Pope Leo X (1513–1521) was the most notorious, receiving half a million ducats a year from the sale of religious offices. In England, Cardinal Thomas Wolsey set an equally poor example by giving church positions to his relatives. Ordinary priests and monks sometimes used their authority to obtain economic or sexual favors. One English reformer denounced the clergy as a "gang of scoundrels" who should be "rid of their vices or stripped of their authority," but he was ignored. Other reformers, such as Jan Hus of Bohemia, were tried and executed as heretics.

In 1517 Martin Luther, a German monk and professor at the university in Wittenberg, nailed his famous Ninety-five Theses to the door of the castle church. That widely reprinted document condemned the sale of *indulgences*—church certificates that pardoned a sinner from punishments in the afterlife. Luther argued that redemption could come only from God through grace, not from the church for a fee. He was excommunicated by the pope and threatened with punishment by King Charles I of Spain, who in 1519 became head of the Holy Roman Empire, which embraced most of Germany. Northern German princes (with their own grudges against the emperor) embraced Luther's doctrines and protected him from arrest.

Luther broadened his attack, articulating positions that differed from Roman Catholic doctrine in three major respects. First, Luther rejected the doctrine that Christians could win salvation through good deeds, arguing that people could be saved only by grace, which came as a gift from God. Second, he downplayed the role of clergymen as mediators between God and the people, proclaiming, "Our baptism consecrates us all without exception and makes us all priests." As a consequence he also rejected the exclusive authority of the pope to interpret Scripture. Third, Luther said that believers must look to the Bible (not church doctrine) as the ultimate authority in matters of faith. So that everyone could read the Bible, he translated it from Latin into German. Embracing Luther's views, most princes in northern Germany broke from Rome, in part because they wanted the power to appoint bishops and control the Church's property.

Peasants as well as princes heeded Luther's attack on authority and, to his dismay, mounted protests of their own. In 1524 some German peasants rebelled against their manorial lords and were ruthlessly suppressed. Fearing social revolution, Luther urged obedience to established political institutions. Ten years later a group of Anabaptists (so called because they rejected infant baptism) seized control of the city of Münster. They established polygamy, abolished most rights to private property, and placed political power in the hands of "Saints"—those who felt God had saved them through grace. Catholic and Lutheran troops joined together to quell the Anabaptists, who became a symbol to conservatives of the dangers of religious dissent.

For his part, Emperor Charles dispatched armies to Germany to restore his political authority and Catholicism, unleashing a generation of warfare. Eventually the Peace of Augsburg (1555) restored order by allowing princes to decide whether their subjects were to be Catholic or Protestant. Most southern German rulers installed Catholicism as the official religion, while those in the north made Lutheranism the state creed.

The most rigorous Protestant doctrine was established in Geneva, Switzerland, under the leadership of the French theologian John Calvin. Even more than Luther, Calvin stressed the omnipotence of God and the corruption of human nature. His *Institutes of the Christian Religion* (1536) depicted God as an awesome and absolute sovereign who governed the "wills of men so as to move precisely to that end directed by him." Calvin preached the doctrine of *predestination*—the idea that God had chosen certain people for salvation even before they were born, condemning the rest to eternal damnation. In Geneva he set up a model Christian community, eliminating bishops and placing spiritual power in the hands of ministers chosen by the members of each congregation. For Geneva's Calvinists the state had the duty to remake society into a disciplined religious community. Accordingly, ministers and pious laymen ruled the city, prohibiting frivolity and luxury.

Despite widespread persecution, Calvinists won converts all over Europe. Calvinism was adopted by the Huguenots in France, by reformed churches in Belgium and Holland, and by Presbyterians in Scotland.

In England, King Henry VIII (1509–1547) initially opposed the spread of Protestantism in his kingdom. But when the pope denied his request for a divorce from Catherine of Aragon, Henry broke with Rome and made himself the head of a national Church of England (which granted his divorce). Henry made few changes in doctrine, organization, and ritual. But after the reign of his daughter, Queen Mary (1553–1557), who briefly restored Catholicism as the state religion and executed 300 Protestant clergymen, there was growing sentiment against Catholic beliefs and rituals.

Henry's younger daughter, Queen Elizabeth I (1558–1603), sought a middle way. She approved a Protestant confession of faith that incorporated both the Lutheran doctrine of salvation by grace and the Calvinist belief in predestination. To mollify traditionalists Elizabeth retained the Catholic ritual of Holy Communion—now conducted in English rather than in Latin—as well as the hierarchy of bishops and archbishops.

Elizabeth's compromises angered radical Protestants, who condemned the power of bishops as "anti-Christian and devilish and contrary to the Scriptures" and called for major changes in church organization. Many reformers took inspiration from the presbyterian system pioneered in Calvin's Geneva and developed fully by John Knox for the Church of Scotland; there, local congregations elected lay elders (presbyters), who assisted ministers in running the church. By 1600, 500 ministers in the Church of England wanted to eliminate bishops and install a presbyterian form of church government.

By this time many English Protestants were calling themselves "unspotted lambs of the Lord" or (embracing a term initially devised to insult them) "Puritans." To a greater extent than most Protestants they wanted to purify the church of "false" teachings and practices. Following radical Calvinist principles, Puritans condemned many traditional religious rites, such as Holy Communion, as magical or idolatrous; instead, their services were focused on a carefully argued sermon on ethics or dogma. Puritans also placed special emphasis on the idea of a "calling," the duty to serve God in one's work. To ensure that all men and women had access to God's commands, they encouraged everyone to read the Bible, thus promoting widespread literacy. Finally, most Puritans wanted authority over spiritual and financial matters to rest primarily with the local congregation, not with bishops or even presbyterian synods. Eventually a stream of Puritan migrants would carry these radical Protestant doctrines to America.

The Dutch and the English Challenge Spain

Luther's challenge to Catholicism came just two years before Cortés conquered the Aztec empire, and the two events remained linked. Gold and silver from Mexico and Peru made Spain the wealthiest nation in Europe and King Philip II (1556–1598) its most powerful ruler. In addition to Spain, Philip presided over wealthy states in Italy, the commercial and manufacturing provinces of the Spanish Netherlands (Holland and Belgium), and, after 1580, Portugal and all its possessions in America, Africa, and the East Indies.

Philip, an ardent Catholic, tried to root out Protestantism in the Netherlands, which had become wealthy from trade with the vast Portuguese empire and from the weaving of wool and linen. To protect their Calvinist faith and political liberties, the Dutch and Flemish provinces revolted in 1566, and in 1581 the seven northern provinces declared their independence, becoming the Dutch Republic (or Holland). When Elizabeth I of England dispatched 6,000 troops to assist the Dutch cause, Philip found a new enemy. In 1588 he sent the Spanish Armada—130 ships and 30,000 men—against England. Philip planned to reimpose Catholicism in England and then wipe out Calvinism in Holland. But the Armada failed utterly, as English ships and a fierce storm destroyed the Spanish fleet. Nor was this the end of Spanish disasters. Philip had spent much of his American gold on foreign wars, undermining the Spanish economy and prompting the migration of hundreds of thousands of Spaniards to America. By the time of his death in 1598, Spain was in serious decline.

As Spain faltered, Holland prospered. Amsterdam emerged as the financial capital of northern Europe, and the Dutch Republic replaced Portugal as the dominant European power in Asia and coastal Africa. The Dutch also looked across the Atlantic, investing in sugar plantations in Brazil and the Caribbean and establishing fur-trading posts in North America.

England also emerged as an important European state, its economy stimulated by a rise in population from 3 million in 1500 to 5 million in 1630. An equally important factor was the state-supported expansion of the merchant community. English merchants had long supplied high-quality wool to European weavers and, around 1500, created a domestic system of manufacturing. In this *outwork* (or *putting-out*) system merchants bought wool and provided it to landless peasants, who spun and wove the wool into cloth. The merchants then sold the finished product in English and foreign markets.

The government helped merchant capitalists expand production by setting low rates for wages. To increase exports, Elizabeth I awarded bonuses to manufacturers who sold goods in foreign markets and granted special privileges to merchant groups such as the Muscovy Company, providing it with a monopoly

Elizabeth I (1558–1603)
Attired in richly decorated clothes, Queen Elizabeth I celebrates the destruction of the Spanish Armada (pictured in background) and proclaims her nation's imperial ambitions. The
queen's hand rests on a globe, asserting England's claims in the Western Hemisphere.

on the export of English cloth to Russia. Similar charters were granted to the
Levant Company (Turkey) in 1581, the Guinea Company (Africa) in 1588, and
the East India Company in 1600.

This system of state-supported manufacturing and trade became known as
mercantilism. English monarchs, like the rulers of many European states, used
mercantilist policies to increase exports and reduce imports, thus obtaining a
favorable balance of trade. Gold and silver flowed into the country in payment
for English manufactures, stimulating further economic expansion and enriching the merchant community. Increased trade also meant higher revenues
from import duties, which swelled the royal treasury and enhanced the power
of the national government. By 1600 the success of these merchant-oriented

policies made overseas colonization possible. The English (as well as the Dutch) now had the merchant fleets and economic wealth to challenge Spain's monopoly in the Western Hemisphere.

Social Change and the Puritan Exodus

Other economic changes in England (as well as continuing religious conflict) provided a large body of willing settlers. The massive expenditure of American gold and silver by Philip II of Spain had doubled the money supply of Europe and sparked a major economic transition—known today as the Price Revolution—which brought about profound social changes.

In England, the nobility were the first casualties of the price revolution. Aristocrats had customarily rented out their estates on long leases for fixed rents, gaining a secure income and plenty of leisure. As one English nobleman put it, "We eat and drink and rise up to play and this is to live like a gentleman." Then inflation struck. In two generations the price of goods tripled, but the nobility's income barely increased.

As the wealth and status of the aristocracy declined, that of the yeomen and the gentry rose. The *gentry* (substantial landholders who lacked the titles and legal privileges of the aristocracy) had smaller but more efficiently managed estates than the nobility. They kept pace with inflation by renting land on short leases at higher rates. *Yeomen*, described by a European traveler as "middle people of a condition between gentlemen and peasants," owned small amounts of land which they worked with family help. Since their labor costs remained constant, yeomen's sale of wheat—which now sold for two or three times its traditional price—brought increasing profits, which they used to build substantial houses and provide land for their children.

Economics influenced politics. As aristocrats lost wealth, their branch of Parliament, the House of Lords, declined in influence. At the same time, members of the rising gentry entered the House of Commons and, supported by yeomen, demanded new rights and powers for that house, such as control of taxation. Thus the price revolution encouraged the rise of governing institutions in which rich commoners and small property owners had a voice, a development with profound consequences for English—and American—political history.

Peasants and farm laborers made up three-fourths of the population of England, and their lives also were transformed by the price revolution. Many of these rural folk lived in open-field settlements, but the rise of domestic manufacturing increased the demand for wool, prompting profit-minded landlords and wool merchants to persuade Parliament to pass enclosure acts. These acts allowed owners to fence in open fields and put sheep to graze on them. Thus dispossessed, peasant families lived on the brink of poverty by spinning and weaving wool or by working as wage laborers on large estates.

Wealthy men had "taken farms into their hands," an observer noted in 1600, "and rent them to those that will give most, whereby the peasantry of England is decayed and become servants to gentlemen."

These changes set the stage for a substantial migration to America. As land prices continued to rise, thousands of yeomen families looked across the Atlantic for land for their children. The enclosure movement created an even greater number of impoverished peasants, who were prepared to go to America as indentured servants.

And now there were enterprising men ready to establish a permanent English presence in America. The first attempts, all failures, occurred in the 1580s. Sir Humphrey Gilbert's settlement in Newfoundland collapsed for lack of financing, and Sir Ferdinando Gorges's colony along the coast of Maine foundered because of inadequate supplies and the harsh climate. Sir Walter Raleigh's three expeditions to North Carolina ended in disaster when the famous "lost" colony of Roanoke vanished without a trace. After these failures, merchants replaced minor gentry as the leaders of the colonization movement. To provide adequate funding, they formed *joint-stock companies*, which sold shares of stock to many investors. A royally chartered joint-stock venture, the Virginia Company of London, founded the first permanent English settlement in America at Jamestown (Virginia) in 1607. The investors hoped to grow rich by finding gold and exploiting the labor of the natives to mine it. In any event, they prospered by transporting tens of thousands of English indentured servants to the new colony.

While English merchants promoted settlement in Virginia, thousands of English men and women contemplated migration to America to escape a new wave of religious conflict. Elizabeth's successor, King James I (1603–1625), rejected most Puritan and Presbyterian reforms. He remarked bitterly that Presbyterians favoring representative institutions of church government "agreeth as well with a monarchy as God with the Devil." Like other European monarchs, James maintained that kings drew their authority directly from God and thus had a "divine right" to rule. As for the congregationalist-minded Puritans, James threatened to "harry them out of the land, or else do worse."

Radical Protestants took the king at his word and began to flee, first to the Dutch Republic and then to New England and the West Indies. Religious intolerance also drove English Catholics to America. Thousands of other settlers accompanied the Catholics and Puritans, fleeing poverty or hoping for greater prosperity.

These migrations from England would bring about a new collision between the European and native American worlds. Just as the intrusion of the Spanish into Mesoamerica around 1500 had changed forever the history of that region, the coming of the English—and Dutch and French—to eastern North America a century later would produce a similar spectacle of disease and war and cultural conflict.

CHAPTER I TIMELINE

30,000–10,000 B.C.	Settlement of the Americas
3000–2000 B.C.	Cultivation of maize begins
A.D. 100–400	Hopewell culture in Mississippi Valley
300	Rise of Mayan civilization
500	Zenith of Teotihuacán civilization
700–1100	Spread of Arab Muslim civilization
800–1350	Mississippian culture
1096–1291	Crusades bring Europeans into contact with Islamic civilization
1212–1492	Spanish *reconquista*
1325	Aztecs establish capital at Tenochtitlán
1415–1500	Portuguese establish maritime empire
1450–1550	Italian Renaissance
1492	Christopher Columbus's first voyage to America
1513	Juan Ponce de León explores Florida
1517	Martin Luther starts Protestant Reformation
1519	Hernando Cortés leads Spanish conquest of Mexico
1534	Henry VIII establishes Church of England
1536	John Calvin's *Institutes of The Christian Religion*
1550–1630	Price revolution English mercantilism Enclosure movement
1556–1598	Philip II, king of Spain
1558–1603	Elizabeth I, queen of England
1560s	English Puritan movement begins
1603–1625	James I, first Stuart king of England

CHAPTER 2

THE INVASION AND SETTLEMENT OF NORTH AMERICA, 1550–1700

- Imperial Conflicts and Rival Colonial Models
- The Chesapeake Experience
- Puritan New England
- The Indians' New World

Establishing colonies in distant lands was not for the faint of heart. First came a long voyage in small ships over uncharted waters. Then the migrants, weakened by weeks of travel, spoiled food, and shipboard diseases, faced the challenge of life in an alien land inhabited by potentially hostile peoples. The risks were great and the rewards uncertain, yet tens of thousands of Europeans crossed the Atlantic during the seventeenth century, driven by poverty and persecution at home or drawn by the lures of the New World: land, wealth, and—as one group of pious settlers put it—advancing the "gospell of the Kingdome of Christ in those remote parts."

For native Americans, European invasion and settlement were nothing short of catastrophic. Whether they came as missionaries, fur traders, or settlers, the white-skinned people spread havoc. European diseases, sporadic warfare, and religious conversion threatened Indian peoples with the loss of their lives, lands, and age-old cultures. European-style warfare "slays too many men," protested the Narragansett. The first century of cultural contact foretold the course of North American history: the advance of the invaders and the dispossession of the Indian peoples.

IMPERIAL CONFLICTS AND RIVAL COLONIAL MODELS

New Spain represented the first colonial model in America: the Spanish regime forced the Indians to convert to Catholicism and work digging gold and farming large estates for Spanish overlords. This coercive model was much less effective in the less densely populated lands north of the Rio Grande, where other Europeans founded different types of colonies and interacted in different ways with the Indians. New France and New Netherland developed as huge fur-trading empires, while the English built thriving settler colonies in New England and the Chesapeake. Each of these four colonial models had a distinctive character and goal.

Spanish Supremacy Challenged

By the 1560s few Spanish officials still dreamed of finding rich Indian empires north of Mexico. Now their main goal was to prevent other European nations from establishing settlements from which they could attack the Spanish treasure fleet. Roving English "sea dogs" were already plundering Spanish possessions in the Caribbean, and French corsairs were attacking Spanish treasure ships, halving the Spanish Crown's revenue. Equally ominously, French Protestants began to settle in Florida, long claimed by Spain. In response King Philip II ordered that the Frenchmen in Fort Caroline, Florida, be "cast . . . out by the best means," and Spanish troops massacred 300 members of the "evil Lutheran sect."

To safeguard Florida, in 1565 Spain established a fort at St. Augustine, the first permanent European settlement in the future United States. It also founded a dozen other military outposts and religious missions, one as far north as Chesapeake Bay, but these were soon destroyed by Indian attacks.

These military setbacks prompted the Spanish Crown to adopt a new policy toward native Americans. The Comprehensive Orders for New Discoveries, issued in 1573, placed the "pacification" of new lands primarily in the hands of missionaries, not conquistadors. Franciscan friars promptly established missions in the Pueblo world visited by Coronado two generations before, naming the area *Nuevo México* (see Map 2.1). But in 1598 Juan de Oñate led an expedition of 500 soldiers and settlers into New Mexico to establish a fort and a trading villa. Oñate's men seized corn and clothing from the Pueblo peoples and murdered or raped those who resisted. When Indians of the Acoma pueblo killed 11 Spanish soldiers, the remaining troops destroyed the pueblo, killing 500 men and 300 women and children. Faced by now-hostile Indian peoples, most of the settlers withdrew.

Meanwhile, Spain confronted a new threat in the Atlantic. In 1586 the English sea captain Sir Francis Drake sacked the important port city of Cartagena (in present-day Colombia) and nearly wiped out St. Augustine. These attacks, along with the settlement of Virginia in 1607 and that of French Quebec in 1608, alarmed the Spanish authorities. To maintain its claim to the entire continent, the Spanish Crown reinforced the garrison at St. Augustine and revived the Franciscan missions in New Mexico. However, Spanish officials decided that an outpost in California would not be worth the cost, delaying permanent European occupation of that area until 1769.

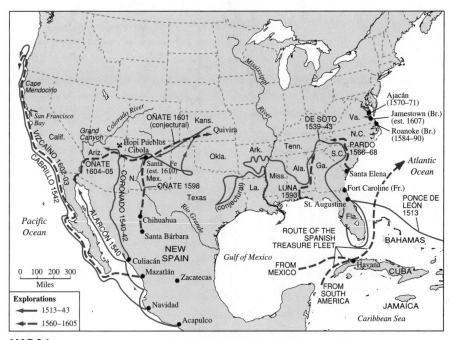

MAP. 2.1

New Spain Looks North, 1513–1610

The quest for gold drew Spanish adventurers deep into North America. Cortés himself dispatched the first expeditions along the Pacific coast, and in the 1540s Hernando de Soto and Francisco Vázquez de Coronado led expeditions that penetrated as far north as Kansas and Tennessee. In 1565 the Spanish founded a permanent settlement at St. Augustine in present-day Florida; in 1610, after the explorations of Juan de Oñate, they settled Santa Fe in New Mexico.

New Spain: Territory and Missions

The Catholic Church was Spain's primary colonizer north of the Rio Grande, although the Crown also granted large tracts of land to a few influential settlers. Franciscan friars established missions in Georgia, northern Florida, and especially New Mexico. The friars built their missions and churches near existing Indian pueblos and villages and often learned Indian languages. Protected by Spanish soldiers, they smashed the religious idols of the native Americans and, to win their allegiance to the Christian god, dazzled them with rich vestments, gold crosses, and silver chalices.

For the Franciscans, religious conversion and cultural assimilation went hand in hand. They introduced the European practice of having men instead of women grow most of the crops and encouraged the Indians to talk, cook, dress, and walk like Spaniards. Sexual sinners and spirit worshipers were punished, usually by whipping. Most native Americans tolerated the Franciscans out of fear of military reprisals or in hopes of learning their spiritual secrets.

Conversion in New Mexico
Franciscan friars introduced Catholicism to the Indian peoples north of the Rio Grande, assisted by nuns of various religious orders. This 1631 engraving shows La V. M. María de Jesús de Agreda preaching to a nomadic people (*los chichimecos*) in New Mexico.

But when Christian prayers failed to prevent European diseases and soldiers from devastating their communities, many Indians returned to their ancestral religions.

Spanish rule was hardly benevolent. Monks and settlers alike systematically exploited Indian labor, ignoring laws intended to protect the native peoples. Franciscan missions depended on Indian workers, who grew the crops and carried them to market, often on their backs. Privileged Spanish landowners collected tribute from the native population, usually in goods but often through forced labor. They also "ransomed" native American women and children who had been captured by nomadic Indian peoples and forced them to work as slaves.

By 1680 years of forced tribute, drought, and raids by Navajos and Apache threatened many pueblos in New Mexico with extinction. Led by Popé, an Indian *shaman* (priest), the peoples of two dozen pueblos mounted a carefully coordinated rebellion, killing over 400 Spaniards and forcing the remaining 2,000 colonists to flee 300 miles down the Rio Grande to El Paso. The Pueblo peoples desecrated churches and tortured and killed twenty-one missionaries. Reconquered a decade later, they rebelled again in 1696, only to be subdued. Exhausted by war but now able to practice their own religion and avoid forced labor, the Pueblo peoples accepted their dependent position, joining with the Spanish to defend their lands against attacks by nomadic Indians.

New France: Furs and Souls

In the 1530s Jacques Cartier had claimed the lands bordered by the Gulf of St. Lawrence for France, but the first permanent settlement came only in 1608, with the founding of Quebec. Even then, few French men and women migrated to America. Many French peasants held strong legal rights to their village lands, and few had been displaced by the enclosure of common fields. Moreover, the French government wanted an ample supply of farm laborers and military recruits and offered few incentives to migrants. Finally, the Catholic monarchs barred Huguenots (French Protestants) from Quebec, fearing that they would undermine state interests. Consequently, New France did not develop as a settler colony. In 1698 its European population was only 15,200, compared with the 100,000 settlers in the English colonies.

Instead, New France became a vast fur-trading enterprise, and French explorers traveled deep into the continent to seek new suppliers and claim new lands (see Map 2.2). In 1673 Jacques Marquette reached the Mississippi River in present-day Wisconsin and traveled as far south as Arkansas. Exploration of the majestic river was completed in 1681 by Robert de La Salle, who sought fortune as well as fame. As a French priest noted with disgust, La Salle's expedition hoped "to buy all the Furs and Skins of the remotest Savages, who, as they thought, did not know their Value; and so enrich themselves in one single voyage." To honor Louis XIV, the Sun King, La Salle named the region Louisiana; soon it included the thriving port of New Orleans on the Gulf of Mexico.

Despite their small numbers, French traders and explorers had a disastrous impact on native Americans living near the Great Lakes. By introducing European diseases, they unwittingly triggered epidemics that killed 25 to 90 percent of the native population, and by providing a market for deerskins and beaver pelts, they set in motion a devastating series of Indian wars. Beginning in the 1640s, the New York Iroquois seized control of the fur trade by launching aggressive wars against the Huron and many Algonquin peoples, forcing them to migrate to the north and west.

While French traders amassed furs, French priests sought converts among both the dispossessed Huron and the belligerent Iroquois. Between 1625 and 1763 hundreds of Jesuit priests lived among the Indians and, to a greater extent than the Spanish Franciscans, came to understand their values. One Jesuit reported a Huron belief that "our souls have desires which are inborn and concealed, yet are made known by means of dreams" and used it to explain the Christian doctrines of immortality and salvation. Indians at first welcomed the "Black Robes" as powerful spiritual beings with magical secrets, such as the ability to forge iron, but skepticism grew when prayers to the Christian

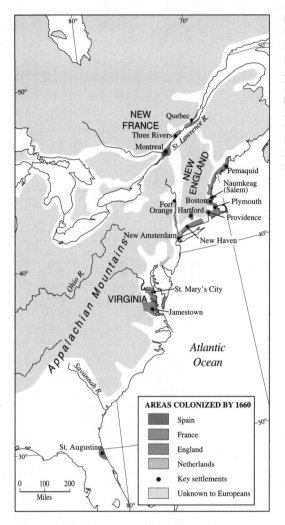

MAP 2.2

Eastern North America in 1660

Four European nations had permanent settlements in eastern North America by 1660, but only England had substantial numbers of settlers—some 25,000 in New England and another 15,000 in the Chesapeake. The English settlements hugged the coastline, leaving most of the land in the hands of native American peoples.

god did not protect them from disease, famine, and enemy attack. A Peoria chief charged that "His fables are good only in his own country; we have our own, which do not make us die as his do."

Unlike the Spanish Franciscans, the French missionaries did not use Indians for forced labor, and they prevented brandy from becoming a bargaining item in the French fur trade as rum had become in the English. Moreover, the French Jesuits won converts by addressing Indian needs. In the 1690s young Illinois women embraced the cult of the Virgin Mary because they could use its emphasis on chastity to assert the Algonquin belief that unmarried women were "masters of their own body." Still, most Indians who had the choice found it more satisfying to hold on to their traditional values than to adopt European religious beliefs.

New Netherland: Commerce

Unlike the French and Spanish, the Dutch in North America had little interest in religious conversion. Their eyes were fastened on commerce, for the Dutch Republic was the trading hub of Europe. Henry Hudson, an Englishman employed by the Dutch East India Company, found and named the Hudson River in 1609, and a few years later the Dutch established fur-trading posts on Manhattan Island and at Fort Nassau (present-day Albany). In 1621 the Dutch government chartered the West India Company, giving it a trade monopoly in West Africa and exclusive authority to establish outposts in America. The company set up new trading stations in Connecticut, New Jersey, Delaware, and Pennsylvania and in 1624 "purchased" Manhattan Island from the Indians, founding the town of New Amsterdam as the capital of New Netherland.

These wilderness outposts attracted few Dutch settlers, and their small size made them vulnerable to invasion from New England or New France. To encourage migration, the West India Company granted huge estates along the Hudson River to wealthy Dutchmen, stipulating that each proprietor settle fifty tenants on his land within four years or lose it; by 1646 only one proprietor, Kiliaen Van Rensselaer, had succeeded. The population in Dutch North America remained small, reaching only 1,500 at the time of the English conquest in 1664.

Although New Netherland failed as a settler colony, it flourished briefly as a fur-trading enterprise. In the 1640s the Dutch seized prime farming land from the Algonquin peoples and took over their trading network, in which corn and wampum from Long Island were exchanged for furs from Maine. The Algonquin responded with force. By the end of a bloody two-year war more than two hundred Dutch residents and a thousand Indians had been killed, many in brutal massacres of women, children, and elderly men. After the war the Dutch West India Company largely ignored its crippled North American settlement, concentrating instead on the profitable importation of African slaves to its sugar plantations in Brazil.

Moreover, Dutch officials in New Amsterdam ruled shortsightedly. Governor Peter Stuyvesant rejected the demands of English settlers on Long Island for a representative system of government, alienating the colony's increasingly diverse population of Dutch, English, and Swedish migrants. Consequently, in 1664, during an Anglo-Dutch war, the population of New Amsterdam offered little resistance to an English invasion and subsequently accepted English rule. For the rest of the century the renamed towns of New York and Albany remained small fur-trading centers, Dutch-English outposts in a region still dominated by native Americans.

The English Model: Land and Settlers

The first English settlement in North America was also an economic venture. In 1606 the ambitious merchant stockholders of the Virginia Company of

London received a charter from James I that granted them the right to exploit North America from present-day North Carolina to southern New York. To honor the memory of Elizabeth I, the "Virgin Queen," the company's directors named the region Virginia. They promised to settle the land and "propagate the *Christian* religion" among the "infidels and Savages."

But trade for gold and other valuable goods was the main goal, and the first expedition in 1607 included no settlers, ministers, or women. The company retained ownership of all the land in Virginia and appointed a governor and a small council to direct the migrants, who were its employees or "servants." They were expected to procure their own food and ship anything of value—gold, exotic crops, and Indian merchandise—back to England.

The traders were unprepared for the challenges they would face. Some were young gentlemen with personal ties to the shareholders of the Virginia Company but no experience in living off the land: a bunch of "unruly Sparks, packed off by their Friends to escape worse Destinies at home." The rest were cynical adventurers bent on conquering the Indians for their gold or turning a quick profit from trade. Like the company's directors, they expected to find established towns with ample supplies of food and labor and Indians with gold to trade for English cloth and tinware.

Arriving in Virginia after a hazardous four-month voyage, the newcomers settled on a swampy peninsula on a river. They named both their new home (Jamestown) and the waterway (James River) after their sovereign. The traders found forty different Indian peoples who willingly exchanged corn for English goods but had little else to offer and no interest in working for them. Unfortunately, the settlers did not want to plant crops and raise food for themselves. All they wanted, one of them noted, was to "dig gold, refine gold, load gold."

But there was no gold and not much food, only illness and disease. Of the 120 Englishmen who embarked on the expedition, only 38 were alive nine months later. Although the Virginia Company had sent 1,200 settlers to Jamestown, by 1611 fewer than half remained. "Our men were destroyed with cruell diseases, as Swellings, Fluxes, Burning Fevers, and by warres," one of the leaders reported, "but for the most part they died of meere famine."

Powhatan, the leading chief of some two dozen tribes near Jamestown, was prepared to trade with the English if they supported him against his Indian rivals. But when desperate traders raided Indian villages for food and the new governor demanded that he acknowledge the sovereignty of James I, Powhatan accused the English of coming "not to trade but to invade my people and possess my country." Nevertheless, the Indian chief, whom Governor John Smith described as a "grave majestical man," sought peace with the English, giving his daughter Pocahontas in marriage to the adventurer John Rolfe in 1614.

Rolfe played a leading role in the colony until his death in 1622. After importing seeds from the West Indies, he began to cultivate tobacco, which was already popular in England as a result of imports from Spanish America. Soon tobacco became the basis of economic life in Virginia, cultivated primarily by hundreds of poor white English laborers. Then, as Rolfe noted in 1619, "a Dutch man of warre . . . sold us twenty Negars." Those black workers were the first Africans in English North America and, in a sense, the first African-Americans.

As hopes for the Indian trade declined and tobacco exports rose, the Virginia Company instituted a new and far-reaching set of policies. In 1617 it allowed individual settlers to own land, granting 100 acres to every freeman in Virginia, and established a *headright* system in which every incoming head of a household had a right to 50 acres of land and 50 additional acres for every adult family member or servant. The company also approved a system of representative government. The House of Burgesses, which first convened in Jamestown in 1619, had the authority to make laws and levy taxes, although its legislative acts could be vetoed by the governor or nullified by the company. By 1622 these incentives of land ownership and local self-government had attracted about 4,500 new English recruits. Virginia was about to become a settler colony.

A second tobacco-growing settler colony developed in neighboring Maryland, but it had very different roots. Maryland was owned by an aristocrat, Cecilius Calvert, who carried the title Lord Baltimore. In 1632 Charles I, the successor to James I, gave Baltimore a charter that made him the proprietor of the territory bordering the vast Chesapeake Bay. Baltimore could sell, lease, or give this land away as he wished. He also had the authority to appoint public officials and to found churches and appoint ministers.

Baltimore wanted Maryland to become a refuge from persecution for his fellow English Catholics. He therefore devised a policy of religious toleration intended to minimize confrontations between Catholics and Protestants, instructing the governor (his brother, Leonard Calvert) to allow "no scandall nor offence to be given to any of the Protestants" and to "cause All Acts of Romane Catholicque Religion to be done as privately as may be." In 1634, 20 gentlemen (mostly Catholics) and 200 artisans and laborers (mostly Protestants) established St. Mary's City overlooking the mouth of the Potomac River. The population grew quickly, for the Calvert family carefully planned and supervised the colony's development, hiring skilled artisans and offering ample grants of land to wealthy migrants.

The booming European market for tobacco ensured Maryland's economic future, but political and religious conflict threatened its stability. When Governor Leonard Calvert tried to govern without the "Advice, Assent, and Approbation" of the freemen of the colony, as the charter specified, a representative assembly elected by the freemen insisted on the right to initiate legislation, which Lord Baltimore grudgingly granted. Uprisings by Protestant settlers also threatened Maryland's religious mission. To protect his Catholic coreligionists, who remained a minority, Lord Baltimore managed to persuade the Assembly to enact a Toleration Act (1649) that granted religious freedom to all Christians. By midcentury England had populated the lands near Chesapeake Bay with thousands of settlers.

THE CHESAPEAKE EXPERIENCE

The English colonies in the Chesapeake Bay region were an economic success for some but a social and moral disaster for many more. Settlers forcefully dispossessed Indians of their lands, and prominent families ruthlessly exploited the labor of white indentured servants and enslaved laborers from Africa, pursuing their dreams of wealth by ruling the society by deceit and force of arms.

Settling the Tobacco Colonies

In Virginia the influx of settlers sparked all-out war with the Indians. The land-hungry farmers coveted land that the native Americans had cleared and were using. The English demands alarmed Opechancanough, Powhatan's brother and successor. After forming an alliance with other Chesapeake tribes, in 1622 the chief launched a surprise attack, killing nearly a third of the white population and vowing to drive the rest into the ocean. The English retaliated by burning the Indians' cornfields to deprive them of food, a strategy that secured the safety of the colony by the late 1620s.

The cost of the war was high. The Indians killed many settlers and burned property, but their own losses were even worse. The time of coexistence was past. As one English militiaman put it, "[we now felt we could] by right of Warre, and law of Nations, invade the Country, and destroy them who sought to destroy us; whereby wee shall enjoy their cultivated places . . . possessing the fruits of others' labour."

Distressed by the Indian uprising, James I dissolved the Virginia Company, accusing its directors of mismanagement, and created a royal colony. Now the king and his ministers appointed the governor and a small advisory council. The House of Burgesses was retained, but any legislation it enacted required ratification by the king's Privy Council. James also legally established the Church of England in Virginia, so that all property owners had to pay taxes to support the clergy. These institutions—a royal governor, an elected assembly, and an established Anglican church—became the model for royal colonies throughout English America.

Tobacco was the primary factor shaping the early history of the Chesapeake colonies. Indians had long used tobacco leaves as a medicine and a stimulant. By the 1620s English men and women began to crave tobacco and the nicotine it contained, smoking, chewing, and snorting it with abandon. Initially James I condemned the use of this "vile Weed" and warned that its "black stinking fumes" were "baleful to the nose, harmful to the brain, and dangerous to the lungs." But his attitude changed as revenues from a tobacco duty, or import tax, filled the royal coffers.

European demand for tobacco set off a forty-year economic boom in the Chesapeake, and thousands of profit-hungry migrants flocked to the region. "All our riches for the present do consist in tobacco," a planter remarked in

The Tobacco Economy
Tobacco provided a bare livelihood for family farmers but brought wealth to those who exploited the labor of indentured servants and slaves. The workers cured the tobacco stalks by hanging them for several months in a well-ventilated shed; then they stripped the leaves and packed them tightly into large barrels, or "hogsheads," for shipment to Europe.

1630. Exports rose from about 3 million pounds in 1640 to 10 million pounds in 1660. Planters moved up the river valleys, establishing large farms (plantations) that were distant from one another but easy to reach by water. The scarcity of towns meant a much weaker sense of community than existed in the open-field villages of rural England.

Unfortunately, mosquitoes flourished in the mild Chesapeake climate, spreading malaria and weakening people's resistance to other diseases. Pregnant women were especially hard hit. Many died after bearing a first or second child, and so settler families were small. Malaria, smallpox, fever, and dysentery took such a toll that while more than 15,000 settlers arrived in Virginia between 1622 and 1640, the population rose only from 2,000 to 8,000.

For most of the seventeenth century life in the Chesapeake colonies remained harsh and short. Most men never married because there were few women. Families often were disrupted by early death; rarely did both parents survive to see their children grow to adulthood. As a result, unmarried young men and orphaned children accounted for a substantial portion of the population, making Chesapeake society very different from that in England.

Servants and Masters

Despite the dangers, by 1700 over 80,000 English settlers had moved to Virginia and another 20,000 had arrived in Maryland. English shipping registers provide insight into their motivation. Three-quarters of the 5,000 migrants from Bristol were men, mostly under twenty-five years old; many had traveled hundreds of miles searching for work. Once in Bristol, these penniless sojourners were persuaded by merchants and sea captains to sign labor contracts called *indentures* and embark for the Chesapeake. The indentures bound them to work in return for room and board for a period of four or five years (or, in the case of younger servants, until age twenty-one).

For merchants, servants represented valuable cargo because their contracts fetched high prices in the labor-starved Chesapeake. For plantation owners, they were an incredible bargain. During the tobacco boom a male indentured servant could produce five times his purchase price in a year. Furthermore, servants were counted as household members, and so planters in Virginia received 50 acres of land for each one they imported.

Most masters ruled their servants with an iron hand, beating them for bad behavior and withholding permission to marry. If a servant ran away or became pregnant, a master went to court to increase the term of service. Female servants were especially vulnerable to abuse. As a Virginia law of 1692 stated, "dissolute masters have gotten their maids with child; and yet claim the benefit of their service." Uncooperative servants had their contracts sold to new masters. As an Englishman remarked in disgust, in Virginia "servants were sold up and down like horses."

For most indentured servants this ordeal did not provide the hoped-for escape from poverty. Half the men died before receiving their freedom, and another quarter remained poor; only a quarter acquired some property and respectability. Surviving female servants generally fared better because men in the Chesapeake had grown "very sensible of the Misfortune of Wanting Wives." Many married their masters or other well-established men. By migrating to the Chesapeake, these few—and very fortunate—men and women escaped a life of landless poverty in England.

The Seeds of Revolt

During the boom years of the 1620s tobacco sold for twenty-four pence a pound; forty years later it was fetching barely one-tenth as much. Overproduction in the Chesapeake caused a collapse of the tobacco market.

Political decisions made in England contributed to the decline. In 1651, in an effort to exclude Dutch ships and merchants from England's overseas possessions, Parliament passed an Act of Trade and Navigation. Revised and

Hard Times in Early Virginia

The lot of an indentured servant in Virginia was always hard, especially before 1630, when food was scarce and Indians were a constant danger. In 1623 Richard Frethorne begged his parents to buy out the remaining years of his labor contract so that he could return to England.

Loving and kind father and mother . . . this is to let you understand that I your child am in a most heavy case by reason of the nature of the country . . . it causes much sickness, as the scurvy and the bloody flux [severe dysentery], and diverse other diseases, which make the body very poor and weak, and when we are sick there is nothing to comfort us. For since I came out of the ship, I never ate anything but peas and loblollie [gruel]. As for deer or venison I never saw any since I came into this land. There is indeed some fowl, but we are not allowed to go and get it, but must work hard both early and late for a mess of water gruel and a mouthful of bread and beef.

People cry out day and night, Oh that they were in England without their limbs and would not care to lose any limb to be in England again . . . we live in fear of the enemy every hour. . . . We are in great danger, for our plantation is very weak, by reason of the dearth, and sickness of our company. . . .

I have nothing to comfort me, nor there is nothing to be gotten here but sickness and death, except that one had money to lay out in some things for profit; but I have nothing at all, no not a shirt to my back, but two rags nor no clothes, but one poor suit, nor but one pair of shoes . . . my cloak is stolen by one of my own fellows, and to his dying hours would not tell me what he did with it, but some of my fellows saw him have butter and beef out of a ship, which my cloak [no] doubt paid for. . . .

SOURCE: Susan M. Kingsbury, ed., *The Records of the Virginia Company of London* (Washington, D.C., Library of Congress, 1935), vol. 4, pp. 58–60.

extended in 1660 and 1663, the Navigation Acts permitted only English or colonial-owned ships to enter American ports. They also required the colonists to ship certain "enumerated articles," including tobacco, only to England. Because the king imposed ever higher import duties, the English market grew slowly. Moreover, Chesapeake planters could no longer legally trade with Dutch merchants, who paid the highest prices. As a result, by the 1670s planters got only one penny a pound for their crop.

Nonetheless, the number of planters in Virginia and Maryland grew and tobacco exports continued to increase, from 20 million pounds annually in the 1670s to 41 million pounds between 1690 and 1720. But profit margins were thin, and the Chesapeake ceased to be a land of upward social mobility.

Yeomen families earned just enough to scrape by or fell into debt and had to sell their land. Even harder hit were newly freed indentured servants, who were entitled to 50 acres of land. Low tobacco prices made it nearly impossible for them to pay the necessary claim fees or buy the tools and seed needed to plant tobacco. Most ex-servants had to sell their labor again, signing new indentures or becoming wage workers or tenant farmers.

Gradually the economic life of the Chesapeake colonies came to be dominated by an elite of planter-landlords and merchants. Established landowners prospered by dividing their ample estates and leasing small plots to the growing army of former servants. They also lent money at high interest rates to hard-pressed yeomen families. Some well-to-do planters became commercial middlemen, setting up small retail stores or charging a commission for storing the tobacco of their poorer neighbors and selling it to English merchants. In Virginia this elite accumulated nearly half the land by soliciting favors from royal governors and filing fictitious headright claims. In Maryland wealthy planters controlled labor with equal success; in one county they owned about 40 percent of the work force through the indenture system.

As these aggressive entrepreneurs confronted a growing number of young landless laborers, social divisions intensified, reaching a breaking point during the corrupt regime of Governor William Berkeley. Berkeley first served as governor of Virginia between 1642 and 1652, when he won fame by putting down a major Indian revolt. As governor again beginning in 1660, he made large land grants to himself and to members of his council, who exempted their own lands from taxation and appointed friends as county judges and local magistrates. Berkeley suppressed dissent in the House of Burgesses by assigning land grants to friendly legislators and appointing their relatives to the posts of sheriff, tax collector, and justice of the peace. Once his favorites were in power, the governor refused to call new elections.

Social and political unrest increased when the corrupt Burgesses changed the voting system to exclude landless freemen, who constituted half the adult white male population. Property-holding yeomen retained the vote but were unhappy about falling tobacco prices, rising taxes, and political corruption. The Virginia elite—unlike the English aristocracy and gentry—was too newly formed and crudely ambitious to command the respect of the lower orders.

Bacon's Rebellion

In 1675 a new Indian conflict sparked a social revolution. By this time the Indians in Virginia were few and weak, their numbers having dwindled from about 30,000 in 1607 to a mere 2,000. Most lived on lands guaranteed by treaty that were coveted by some of the 40,000 whites now in Virginia. Most wealthy planters lived in the coastal districts and opposed armed expansion into Indian territory, as did the planter-merchants who traded with the native Americans for furs. But poor freeholders and aspiring tenants who wanted cheap land insisted that the Indians be expelled or exterminated.

Fighting broke out when Virginia militiamen murdered thirty Indians. Defying orders from Governor Berkeley, a larger force of 1,000 militiamen then surrounded a fortified Susquehannock village and killed four chiefs. The outraged Susquehannock retaliated by killing eighty whites in raids on outlying plantations. Berkeley did not want war, which would disrupt the fur trade, and proposed a defensive military policy, asking the House of Burgesses in March 1676 to raise money to build a series of frontier forts. Western settlers dismissed this strategy as useless, a plot by the "grandees," as one freeman called them, to impose high taxes on the yeomen and to take "all our tobacco into their own hands."

Nathaniel Bacon emerged as the leader of the westerners. A wealthy and bold man, he had recently arrived from England and settled on a frontier estate. Although he was only twenty-eight, Bacon commanded the respect of his neighbors because of his high status—Berkeley had made him a member of the governor's council—and vigor. When Berkeley refused to grant Bacon a military commission, Bacon marched his frontiersmen against the Indians anyway, slaughtering some of the peaceful Doeg people and triggering a political upheaval that overshadowed the Indian question.

Condemning the frontiersmen as "rebels and mutineers," Berkeley expelled Bacon from the council and placed him under arrest. Then, realizing the rebel leader's military power, the governor reinstated him, agreed to legislative elections, and accepted the far-reaching political reforms enacted by the new House. The Burgesses, who now included influential supporters of Bacon, curbed the powers of the governor and the council and cut their patronage powers by converting many local offices into elected posts. The legislature also restored voting rights to landless freemen.

Those much-needed reforms did not end the rebellion. Bacon was bitter at Berkeley, and the poor farmers, indentured servants, and blacks in his army were resentful of exploitation by the "grandees" and eager to flaunt their power. Backed by 400 armed men, Bacon seized control of the colony and issued a "Manifesto and Declaration of the People," demanding the death or removal of all Indians and an end to the rule of wealthy "parasites." "The poverty of the country," Bacon proclaimed, "is such that all the power and sway is got into the hands of the rich." In the bloody civil war that followed Bacon's army burned Jamestown to the ground and plundered the plantations of Berkeley's allies. When Bacon died suddenly from dysentery in October 1676, the governor took his revenge, dispersing the rebel army, seizing the estates of well-to-do rebels, and hanging twenty-three men.

Bacon's rebellion was a pivotal event. Although planter-merchants continued to dominate the colony, they no longer tolerated rule by a corrupt oligarchy. They limited the governor's authority and found public positions for substantial and politically ambitious property owners like Bacon. The planter-merchant elite also appeased the lower social orders by cutting their taxes and supporting an expansionist military policy that promised them access to Indian lands.

The uprising also contributed to the emergence of a new labor system: African slavery. Slavery in the Chesapeake had grown because of a scarcity of English indentured servants, but now its expansion was fueled by the elite's desire to forestall another rebellion by freed white servants. To maintain their privileged class position, the leaders of Virginia and Maryland committed themselves and their descendants to a social system based on the exploitation of enslaved blacks.

PURITAN NEW ENGLAND

The Puritan exodus to America was both a worldly quest for land and a moral effort to preserve the "pure" Christian faith. This blend of realism and idealism gave a distinctive character to the Puritans' experiment. Even as the migrants to New England went about the task of creating a society of independent property-owning farm families, they continued to promote a spiritual vision, giving a moral dimension to American history.

The Puritan Migration

From the beginning New England differed from other European settlements. New Spain and Jamestown were populated initially by unruly male adventurers, and New France and New Netherland by commercial-minded fur traders. By contrast Plymouth, the first permanent community in New England, was settled by women and children as well as men, most of whom were members of pious Protestant families—the Pilgrims.

The Pilgrims were radical Protestants who had separated completely from the Church of England, thus earning the name "Separatists." Seeking freedom to practice their creed, the Pilgrims left England and settled among like-minded Dutch Calvinists in Holland. Subsequently, thirty-five of them decided to migrate to America, where they hoped to maintain their English identity. Led by William Bradford and joined by sixty other migrants from England, they founded the Plymouth colony in 1620.

Before sailing to America aboard the *Mayflower*, the Pilgrims organized themselves into a joint-stock corporation and secured financial backing from sympathetic Puritan merchants. Their stated intention was to settle in the territory granted to the Virginia Company, but by accident or design they landed on the coast of New England. There, outside the jurisdiction of Virginia and lacking a charter from King James I, they created their own covenant of government, the Mayflower Compact, to "combine ourselves together into a civill body politick." This document was the first "constitution" adopted in North America. It translated into political terms the Pilgrims' long-standing belief in the autonomy of the religious congregation and, while recognizing the sovereignty of the king, produced a system of self-government based on the rule of law.

The first winter in America tested the Pilgrims. As in Jamestown, hunger and disease took a heavy toll; of the 100 migrants who arrived in November, only half survived until the spring. Thereafter the Plymouth colony—unlike Virginia— became a healthy and thriving community because the cold climate inhibited the spread of mosquito-borne diseases and the religious discipline established a strong work ethic. Unlike the gold-hungry adventurers in Virginia, the Pilgrims quickly built solid houses and planted ample crops. Their numbers grew rapidly, to 3,000 by 1640, prompting the creation of ten new towns with extensive powers of self-government. A new legal code (1636) provided for a colonywide system of representative government and a rudimentary bill of rights.

The Pilgrims were devout Christians and tried to live according to the laws and ethics of the Bible, which in their view required limiting the power of the state over religion. As "Separatists," they had cut themselves off from the Church of England and believed that each congregation should be self-governing, free from control by either a religious or a political hierarchy. In that sense they anticipated the "separation of church and state."

Meanwhile, England was plunging deeper into religious turmoil. King Charles I (1625–1642) reaffirmed his father's support for the Church of England but personally repudiated some Protestant doctrines, such as justification by faith. The Puritans, who had gained many seats in Parliament, accused the king of "popery." Charles's response was to dissolve Parliament in 1629. For the next decade he ruled by "divine right," raising money through royal edicts, customs duties, and the sale of monopolies. The king's arbitrary rule struck at the dignity of the landed gentry, who expected to exercise authority through the House of Commons. The merchant community, a stronghold of Puritanism, was also displeased as higher tariffs ate away at their profits. Then, in 1633, the king chose William Laud, who loathed Puritans, to head the Church of England. Laud removed hundreds of Puritan ministers, forcing Anglican rituals on their congregations and prompting thousands of Puritans to seek refuge in America.

In 1630, 900 Puritans boarded eleven ships and sailed across the Atlantic under the leadership of John Winthrop, a well-educated and highly regarded country squire. Using a corporate (trading) charter granted by the king for use in England, the Puritans established the Massachusetts Bay colony in the area around Boston. Like the Pilgrims, the Puritans envisioned a reformed Christian society, a genuinely "new" England. However, rather than break with the Church of England, they hoped to reform it (hence, they were "non-Separatists"). Many Puritans saw themselves as central actors in a great drama, a "saving remnant" chosen by God to preserve the true faith in America. The Lord "has sifted a whole nation," a Puritan minister declared, "that he might send choice grain over into this Wilderness."

Winthrop believed that England was morally corrupt and "overburdened with people." He sought land and opportunity for his children and a place in history for his people. "We must consider that we shall be as a City upon a Hill," Winthrop told his fellow passengers aboard the ship *Arbella* in 1630. "The eyes of all people are upon us." Once in America, Winthrop and his associates transformed their joint-stock business corporation, the General Court of shareholders, into a colonial legislature. Over the next decade about 10,000

Puritans migrated to the Massachusetts Bay colony, along with 10,000 others fleeing hard times in England.

The Puritans created representative political institutions that were locally based, with the governor as well as the assembly and council elected by the colony's freemen. However, to ensure rule by the godly, the Puritans limited the right to vote and hold office to men who were Puritan church members. Eschewing the religious toleration of the Pilgrims, they established Puritanism as the state-supported religion and barred members of other faiths from conducting services. Massachusetts Bay became a religious commonwealth with the Bible as the legal as well as spiritual guide. For example, following a biblical rule, Puritans divided inheritances among all children, with a double portion going to the oldest son. "Where there is no Law," the government advised local magistrates, they should rule "as near the law of God as they can."

Puritans and Pequots

Seeing themselves as God's chosen people, the Puritans viewed their intrusions on native American lands from a moral perspective. "By what right or warrant can we enter into the land of the Savages," they asked themselves while still in England, "and take away their rightfull inheritance from them and plant ourselves in their places?" John Winthrop thought that a disastrous smallpox epidemic of 1633 that killed hundreds of Indians provided a clear answer to that question. "If God were not pleased with our inheriting these parts," he pointed out, "Why doth he still make roome for us by diminishing them as we increase?" Citing the Book of Genesis, the magistrates of Massachusetts Bay declared that because the Indians had not "subdued" most of their land by plowing or fencing it, they had no "just right" to it.

Imbued with moral righteousness, the Puritans often treated native Americans with a brutality equal to that of Spanish conquistadors and Nathaniel Bacon's frontiersmen. In 1637 Pequot warriors attacked Puritan farmers who had begun to intrude onto their lands in the Connecticut River Valley. As sporadic violence escalated into war, Puritan militiamen and their Indian allies led a surprise attack on a Pequot village and massacred about 500 men, women, and children. "God laughed at the Enemies of his People," one soldier boasted, "filling the Place with Dead Bodies." The survivors were ruthlessly tracked down and sold into slavery in the Caribbean. In the end the Pequot people were virtually exterminated.

Like most Europeans, English Puritans viewed the Indians as "savages," culturally inferior people who did not deserve civilized treatment. But the Puritans were not racist as the term is understood today. To them, native Americans were neither genetically inferior nor members of a different race—they were white people with sun-darkened skins. "Probably the devil" delivered these "miserable savages" to America, wrote the Puritan minister Cotton Mather, "in hopes that the gospel of the Lord Jesus Christ would never come here to destroy or disturb his absolute empire over them."

This interpretation inspired attempts at conversion. John Eliot, a Puritan minister, translated the Bible into Algonquian and undertook missions to Indians outside Boston and on Cape Cod. Because Puritans demanded that Indians conform to English customs and master Puritan theology, only a few native Americans became full members of Puritan congregations. However, the Puritans created "praying towns" that, like the Spanish Franciscans' missions in New Mexico, attempted to control the Indian population. Within a generation more than a thousand Indians lived under Puritan supervision in fourteen special mission towns. They were forbidden to practice their native religion, required to conform to the laws of Massachusetts, and initially denied the right to own the land on which they lived. Thus, a combination of European diseases, military force, and Christianization pacified most of the Algonquin peoples who lived along the seacoast of New England, guaranteeing, at least temporarily, the safety of the white settlers.

Religion and Society, 1630–1670

By eliminating bishops and elaborate rituals, the Puritans were seeking to re-create the simplicity of the first Christians. They devised a democratic church structure controlled by the *laity*—the ordinary members of the congregation—hence their name, *Congregationalists*. Influenced by John Calvin, Puritans embraced predestination, believing that God had chosen a few "elect" men and women (the Saints) for salvation and had condemned the rest to damnation. Consequently, the Saints set extraordinarily high standards for church membership, rigorously examining those who applied. Even the Saints lived in great anxiety, for they could never be sure that they were really among the elect.

Puritans dealt with the uncertainties of divine election in three ways. Some congregations stressed the conversion experience: when God infused a soul with grace, the person was "born again" and *knew* that salvation was at hand. Other Puritans stressed "preparation," the confidence in redemption that came from years of spiritual guidance and church discipline. Still others believed that God had entered into a *covenant*, or contract, with them, promising to treat them as a divinely "chosen people" as long as they ordered their lives in accordance with His laws.

To maintain God's favor, Puritan magistrates purged their society of religious dissidents. One target was Roger Williams, the minister of Salem. Williams preferred the Pilgrims' separation of church and state and condemned the legal establishment of Congregationalism in Massachusetts Bay. He taught that political magistrates should have authority over only the "bodies, goods, and outward estates of men," not their spiritual lives. Moreover, he questioned the Puritans' right to seize (rather than buy) Indian lands. The Puritan magistrates banished him from Massachusetts Bay.

Williams and his followers resettled in Rhode Island in 1636, founding the town of Providence on land acquired from the Narragansett Indians. Other religious dissidents founded Portsmouth and Newport. In 1644 these towns

Changing Images of Death
Death—sudden and arbitrary—
was a constant presence in the
preindustrial world. Pre-1700 New
England gravestones often depicted
death as a frightening skull, warning people to repent of their sins.
After 1700 a smiling cherub
adorned many gravestones, suggesting a more optimistic view of
the afterlife.

obtained a corporate charter from the English Parliament that granted them
full authority "to rule themselves." In Rhode Island there was no legally established church; every congregation was autonomous, and individual men and
women could worship God as they pleased.

Puritan magistrates also felt threatened by Anne Hutchinson, the wife of a
merchant and a mother of seven who worked as a midwife. Hutchinson held
weekly prayer meetings in her house—often attended by as many as sixty
women—in which she accused certain Boston clergymen of placing undue emphasis on church laws and good behavior. In words that recalled Martin Luther's
rejection of indulgences, Hutchinson argued that salvation was not something
that people could earn; there was no "covenant of works." Instead, salvation was
bestowed by God through the "covenant of grace." Hutchinson accepted the importance of revelation: the direct communication of truth by God to the individual believer. Since this doctrine diminished the role of ministers and, indeed, of all
established authority, Puritan magistrates found it heretical.

The magistrates also resented Hutchinson because of her sex. Like other Christians, Puritans believed in the equality of souls: both men and women could be saved. When it came to the governance of church and state, however, women were seen as being clearly inferior to men. As the Pilgrim minister John Robinson put it, women "are debarred by their sex from ordinary prophesying, and from any other dealing in the church wherein they take authority over the man." Puritan women could never be ministers, lay preachers, or even voting members of the congregation.

In 1637 the Massachusetts Bay magistrates put Hutchinson on trial for heresy, accusing her of believing that inward grace or truth frees an individual from the rules of the church. Hutchinson defended her views with great skill and tenacity, and even Winthrop admitted that she was "a woman of fierce and haughty courage." But the judges found her guilty and berated her for not attending to "her household affairs, and such things as belong to women." Banished, she followed Roger Williams into exile in Rhode Island, settling eventually in New York, where she was killed in an Indian raid in 1643.

The coercive policies of the magistrates, along with the desire for better land, prompted some Puritans to leave Massachusetts Bay. In 1636 Thomas Hooker led a hundred settlers to the Connecticut River Valley, where they established the town of Hartford. Others followed, settling along the river at Wethersfield and Windsor. In 1639 the Connecticut Puritans adopted the Fundamental Orders, a plan of government that included a representative assembly and a popularly elected governor. Connecticut was patterned after Massachusetts Bay, with a firm union of church and state and a congregational system of church government, but voting rights were extended to most property-owning men—not just church members.

As Puritans established themselves in America, England fell into a religious war. When Archbishop Laud imposed a new prayer book on Presbyterian Scotland, a Scottish Presbyterian army invaded England. Thousands of English Puritans—including scores of Puritans who had returned from America— rose up in revolt, demanding greater authority for Parliament and an end to arbitrary royal rule. After four years of civil war the Parliamentary forces led by Oliver Cromwell were victorious. In 1649 Parliament executed Charles I, proclaimed a republican commonwealth, and imposed a presbyterian system of governance on the Church of England.

The Puritan triumph was short-lived. Popular support for the commonwealth quickly ebbed, especially when Cromwell took dictatorial control of the government in 1653. After his death a repentant Parliament summoned Charles I's son, Charles II, to the throne. In 1660 the monarchy was restored, and bishops reclaimed their authority in the Church of England. For many Puritans, Charles II's accession represented the victory of the Antichrist—the false prophet described in the last book of the New Testament.

The outlook in New England seemed hardly less grim, for many younger Puritans had not experienced conversion and become full church members. Their "deadness of soul" threatened the Puritan experiment, since they could not present their own children for baptism. To preserve Puritanism, ministers devised the Halfway Covenant in 1662; it altered traditional Calvinist dogma by allowing unconverted Puritans to baptize their children. Not conversion but birth became the key to church membership. Thus, in the First Church of Milford, Connecticut, in the period 1639–1770, 72 percent of the members belonged to the thirty-six families who had established the original congregation.

The Halfway Covenant began a new phase of the Puritans'"errand into the wilderness." They had come to New England to preserve the "pure" Christian church, expecting to return in triumph to a Europe ready to receive the true Gospel. Since that sacred mission had been dashed by the Restoration in England, Puritan ministers articulated a new vision: they exhorted their congregations to create a new society in America based on their faith and ideals.

Richard Mather (1596–1669)
Mather migrated to New England in 1635 after Archbishop Laud stripped him of his pulpit. His son Increase Mather was a leading Boston clergyman, as was his grandson Cotton Mather, the author of *Magnalia Christi Americana*, an epic of the Puritan adventure in New England.

The Puritan Imagination and Witchcraft

Like the native Americans they encountered in New England, the Puritans believed that the physical world was full of supernatural forces. This faith in "spirits" stemmed in part from Christian teachings, such as the Catholic belief in miracles and the Protestant faith in the powers of "grace." Devout Christians saw signs of God's (or Satan's) power in blazing stars, deformed births, and other unusual events. Noting that "more Ministers' Houses than others proportionably had been smitten with Lightning," Samuel Sewell, a prominent Massachusetts minister, wondered "what the meaning of God should be in it."

The respect for spiritual "forces" reflected certain pagan assumptions that were held by both ordinary people and highly educated individuals. When Sewell moved into a new house, he tried to fend off evil spirits by driving a metal pin into the floor. And thousands of Puritans followed pagan astrological charts printed in farmers' almanacs to determine the best times to plant crops, marry off their children, and make other important decisions.

Zealous ministers attacked many of these beliefs and practices and condemned "cunning" individuals who claimed to have special powers as healers or prophets. Many ordinary Christians looked on folk doctors or conjurers as "wizards" or "witches" who acted at the command of Satan. Between 1647 and 1662 civil authorities in Massachusetts and Connecticut hanged fourteen people for witchcraft, mostly older women who, their accusers claimed, were "double-tongued," "had an unruly spirit," or in some way challenged prevailing customs.

The most dramatic episode of witch-hunting took place in Salem, Massachusetts, in 1692. The causes were complex and involved group rivalries and deception. Poor and resentful farmers in a rural area of Salem apparently sought to retaliate against certain wealthier church members by bringing charges of witchcraft against their families and friends. Things got out of hand when judges allowed the introduction of dubious evidence. Massachusetts authorities arrested 175 people and executed 20, 19 of them women. Fear and suspicion spread into the neighboring village of Andover. Its people "were much addicted to sorcery," claimed one observer, and "there were forty men in it that could raise the Devil as well as any astrologer."

The Salem episode, together with the imposition of royal government in Massachusetts in 1692, marked a turning point for New England. The intense religiosity of the first two generations of Puritans was dealt a blow by popular revulsion against the mass executions at Salem; there would be no more legal prosecutions for witchcraft. The European Enlightenment which began around 1675 also promoted a more rational view of the world. Increasingly, educated people explained accidents and sudden deaths with theories about natural forces, not with religion, satanism, astrology, or witchcraft. Unlike Samuel Sewell (who died in 1730), well-read men of the next generation, such as Benjamin Franklin, would conceive of lightning not as a supernatural sign but as a natural phenomenon.

A Freeholding Society

In creating New England communities, Puritans consciously avoided the worst features of traditional Europe. They did not wish to live in a society dominated by a few wealthy landowners or under a distant government that levied oppressive taxes.

Local rule and freehold property were essential to the Puritans' concept of a God-fearing "just society." To fashion a world of independent communities and landowning families, New England governments relied on land-distribution policies. The General Courts of Massachusetts Bay and Connecticut did not adopt the Chesapeake headright system, which favored wealthy planters, or give thousands of acres of land to favored individuals. Instead, they bestowed the title to a township on a group of settlers, or proprietors, who distributed the land among themselves. The title was given in *fee simple*, which meant that the proprietors' families held the land outright, free from manorial obligations or feudal dues; they could sell, lease, or rent it as they pleased.

Widespread ownership of land did not imply equality of wealth or status. Like most Europeans of that time, Puritans embraced a social and economic hierarchy that provided order and security in an uncertain world. "God had Ordained different degrees and orders of men," proclaimed the wealthy Boston merchant John Saffin, "some to be Masters and Commanders, others to be Subjects, and to be commanded." Consequently, town proprietors normally bestowed the largest plots of land on men of high social status, who often became political leaders. However, all male heads of families received some land and had a voice in the town meeting, the main institution of local government.

Local communities in New England had much more political power than did most peasant villages in Europe. Each year the town meeting chose selectmen to manage town affairs. It also levied taxes; enacted ordinances regarding fencing, lot sizes, and road building; and regulated the use of common fields for grazing livestock and cutting firewood. Beginning in 1634, each town in Massachusetts Bay elected its own representatives to the General Court. As the number of towns increased, the representative assembly gained authority at the expense of the governor and magistrates, further enhancing local control.

The rough economic equality in the farming communities of New England gradually declined. The larger proprietors owned enough land to divide among all their sons, usually three or four. Smallholders could provide land for only some of their sons, the rest of whom became landless. Newcomers who lacked the rights of proprietors were the least well off, for they had to buy land or work as tenants or laborers. By 1702, in Windsor, Connecticut, landless sons and newcomers accounted for no less than 30 percent of the male taxpayers. It would take years of saving or migration to a new town for these men and their families to become freeholders.

Despite these inequalities, nearly all New Englanders had an opportunity to acquire property, and even those at the bottom of the social scale enjoyed some economic security. When he died in the 1690s, Nathaniel Fish was one of the poorest men in Barnstable, Massachusetts, yet he owned a two-room cottage, 8 acres of land, an ox, and a cow. For him and thousands of other settlers New England had proved to be the promised land, a new world of opportunity.

THE INDIANS' NEW WORLD

Native Americans on the eastern seaboard were also living in a new world, but for them it was a bleak, dangerous, and conflict-ridden place. They responded to European invasion and settlement in a variety of ways: banding together in new tribes, retreating to the Appalachian Mountains, and on occasion doing battle with the Europeans.

Metacom's War

By the 1670s the white population of New England had reached 55,000 while the Indian population continued to decline from an estimated 120,000 in 1570, to 70,000 in 1620, to barely 16,000 in 1670. Like Opechancanough in Virginia and Popé in New Mexico, Metacom, leader of the Wampanoag

Metacom (King Philip), Chief of the Wampanoag
The Indian uprising of 1675 left an indelible mark on the historical memory of New England. This painting of 1850 was used by traveling performers to tell the story of King Philip's War and was done on semitransparent cloth so that it could be lit from behind for dramatic effect. (Shelburne Museum)

AMERICAN VOICES

The Unredeemed Captive

A decade and a half after Metacom's War, Indians mounted new attacks against Massachusetts frontier settlements. In 1704 Mohawk Indians attacked the town of Deerfield and took back to French Canada 112 prisoners, including seven-year-old Eunice Williams. Most of the captives were returned or ransomed, and in 1713 Peter Schulyer, an Albany fur trader, sought the return of Eunice Williams, who was now sixteen.

I arrived from Albany at Mont Reall [Montreal] on ye 15th of April. . . . Monsr. De Vaudruille [Vaudrieuil], Governor and Chief of Canada . . . gave me all the Encouragement I could immagine for her to go home. . . . Accordingly I went to the ffort of Caghenewaga [Kahnawake] being accompanied by one of the Kings officers and a ffrench Interpreter [and] likewise another of the Indian language. . . .

I thought fitt first to apply mySelf to the priests . . . And [as I] was informed before that this infant (As I may say) was married to a young Indian, I therefore proposed to know the Reason why this poor captive should be Married to an Indian being a Christian born . . . said he they came to me to Marry them. . . . And if he would not marry them they matter'd not, for they were resolved never to leave on the other. . . . He sent for her, who presently came with the Indian She was married to both together. She looking very poor in body, bashfull in the face, but proved harder than Steel in her breast. . . .

I first Spoak to her in English, Upon wch she did not Answr me; And I believe She did not understand me, she being very Young when she was taken. . . . I Imployed my Indian Languister to talk to her . . . but could not get one word from her. . . . And I could not prevail wth her to go home . . . that she might only go to see her father, And directly return hither again. . . .

And these two words ["Jaghte oghte, a plaine denyall"] were all we could gett from her; in allmost two hours time that we talked with her . . . and the time growing late and I being very Sorrowfull, that I could not prevail upon nor get one word more from her I took her by the hand and left her in the priest's house.

[Eunice Williams remained among the Mohawk, bore two daughters, twice visited her English brothers and sisters, and died in Canada in 1785, aged eighty-nine.]

SOURCE: John Demos, *The Unredeemed Captive: A Family Story from Early America* (New York, Knopf, 1994), pp. 101–108.

tribe, concluded that only united resistance could stop the advance of the Puritans. Forging a military alliance with the Narragansett and Nipmuck peoples in 1675, Metacom attacked white settlements throughout New England. Bitter fighting continued into 1676, ending only when Metacom was killed.

The war was a deadly affair. The Indians burned 20 percent of the English towns in Massachusetts and Rhode Island and killed 5 percent of the adult white population. But their own losses—from famine and disease as well as battles—were much larger, perhaps 25 percent of the population. Many survivors were sold into slavery in the Caribbean, including Metacom's wife and nine-year-old son.

Subsequently, most New England Indians accepted their dependent status, surviving as a separate group on the margins of white society. They had suffered a double tragedy, losing both their land and the integrity of their traditional cultures.

The Fur Trade and the Inland Peoples

The Indian peoples in the interior of North America remained independent, but few were able to maintain their customary way of life. Epidemics and drunkenness sapped the vitality of many peoples. As tribes exchanged furs for iron utensils and cloth blankets, they lost their traditional artisan skills—making fewer flint hoes, clay pots, and skin garments. After two or three generations some eastern Indians had to rely on European manufacturers for many basic goods. To the west of the Appalachians traditional subsistence activities remained strong because canoes could carry only small quantities of imported goods.

The greatest threat to the cultures of the inland peoples was the fur trade. Eager for European trade goods, Indian families and villages began to claim exclusive hunting and trapping rights over an area, undermining clan unity. More important, conflict between tribes increased as rival bands of hunter-warriors competed to control the trade in furs. The Iroquois peoples of New York were the most successful. Organized in large towns of 500 to 2,000 persons and united in a great "longhouse" confederation (the Five Nations), the Iroquois virtually destroyed the neighboring Eries and the Neutrals and forced the Huron to move north of the Great Lakes. Then they pushed a dozen Algonquian-speaking peoples—Ottawa, Fox, Sauk, Kickapoo, Miami, Illinois—out of their traditional lands north of the Ohio River. The Algonquin crowded into a newly formed multitribal region west of Lake Michigan (present-day Wisconsin). Commitment to battle increased the influence of those who made war, and so the balance of power shifted from elders to headstrong young warriors.

The fur trade also transformed the Indians' relationship with the natural world. Native Americans were animists in religion, believing that everything—animals, trees, rocks—had a living spirit that demanded respect. Each clan in a tribe venerated an animal as its *totem*, or symbol, often considering themselves descendants of that animal. Tribesmen could hunt those totem animals only if they followed certain customs. As they skinned beavers or butchered deer for food and clothing, they thanked their spirits by offering prayers or burning tobacco and respectfully burying the carcasses and entrails. As they killed more and more animals for their fur, the Indians sensed the displeasure of the natural world. The epidemics that swept their communities confirmed their fears: the spirits of the animals were taking their revenge. The warriors of the Micmac of Nova Scotia confessed that they no longer knew "whether the beavers are among our friends or our enemies."

America had become a new world for its Indian peoples. All the invaders—Dutch and French fur traders no less than Spanish conquistadors and English settlers—had undermined traditional native American societies, forcing their members to fashion new ways of life.

CHAPTER 2 TIMELINE	
1565	Spain establishes St. Augustine, Florida
1573	Spanish Comprehensive Orders for New Discoveries
1598	Acoma War in New Mexico
1607	English adventurers settle Jamestown, Virginia
1608	Samuel de Champlain founds Quebec
1619	First Africans arrive in Chesapeake Virginia House of Burgesses convened
1620	Pilgrims found Plymouth colony
1620–1660	Tobacco boom in Chesapeake colonies
1621	Dutch West India Company chartered
1622	Opechancanough's uprising; Virginia becomes a royal colony (1624)
1625	Jesuits begin missionary work in Canada
1630	Puritans found Massachusetts Bay colony
1634	Maryland settled
1636	Roger Williams settles Rhode Island
1637	Pequot War Anne Hutchinson banished
1640s	Five Iroquois Nations go to war over fur trade
1649–1660	Puritan Commonwealth in England
1660–1678	William Berkeley, governor of Virginia
1660–1720	Poor tobacco market Indentured servitude declines
1664	English conquer New Netherland
1675–1676	Bacon's rebellion Metacom's uprising
1680	Popé's Rebellion in New Mexico
1692	Salem witchcraft trials

CHAPTER 3

THE BRITISH EMPIRE IN AMERICA, 1660–1750

- The Politics of Empire, 1660–1713
- The Imperial Slave Economy
- The New Politics of Empire, 1713–1750

By 1660 English traders and settlers had pushed aside the native Americans and founded two clusters of colonies along the eastern coast of North America. The pace of settlement quickened as British officials encouraged the migration of tens of thousands of English men and women to the mainland and the importation of even greater numbers of enslaved Africans to grow sugar on the islands of the West Indies. As the American colonies grew in size, numbers, and wealth, they changed in character, becoming crucial parts of a transatlantic system of trade and forming the first British Empire.

The British Empire was the product of calculated policy, not chance. To protect their increasingly valuable colonies from European rivals—the Dutch in New Netherland, the French in Quebec and the West Indies, and the Spanish in Florida—English officials expanded the navy and repeatedly went to war. As a result, imperial warfare was a major factor in the century between 1660 and 1750.

A long struggle over imperial administrative control emerged as a second significant theme. To profit from the products and commerce of the American settlements, the home government attempted to control their trade through strict mercantilist economic regulations and to subordinate local political institutions to imperial direction. While never completely successful, these policies worked well enough to create a prosperous empire and make England a dominant power in Europe.

THE POLITICS OF EMPIRE, 1660–1713

In the first decades of settlement the Chesapeake and New England colonies were governed in a haphazard fashion. Taking advantage of the upheaval produced by civil war in England, local oligarchies of Puritan magistrates and tobacco-growing planters governed as they wished. With the restoration of the monarchy in 1660, royal bureaucrats tried to impose order on the unruly settlements.

The Restoration Colonies

In 1660 Charles II ascended to the English throne. A generous but extravagant man who was always in debt, Charles rewarded his aristocratic supporters and paid his creditors with millions of acres of American land. In 1663 he gave the Carolinas, an area long claimed by Spain and populated by thousands of Indians, to eight friends. The next year all the territory between the Delaware and Connecticut rivers went to his brother James, the duke of York. James took possession of the conquered province of New Netherland, renaming it New York after himself, and passed on the ownership of New Jersey to two of the Carolina proprietors.

In one of the great land grabs in history, a few English aristocrats had won title to vast provinces. Like Maryland, their new colonies were proprietorships; they owned all the land and could rule as they wished as long as the laws conformed broadly to those of England. Most proprietors sought to create a traditional social order presided over by a gentry class and a legally established Church of England. Thus, the Fundamental Constitutions of Carolina (1669) prescribed a manorial system with a powerful nobility and a mass of serfs.

This aristocratic scheme was pure fantasy. The first settlers in North Carolina, poor families from Virginia, refused to work on large manors and chose to live on modest farms, raising grain and tobacco. Indeed, farmers in Albemarle County, angered by taxes on tobacco exports and by the annual *quitrents* (small payments that acknowledged the lordship of the proprietors), rebelled in 1677. After deposing the governor, they forced the proprietors to abandon most of their financial claims.

The colonists of South Carolina, many of whom had come from Barbados (by then an overcrowded sugar island), refused both the Fundamental Constitutions and the payment of quitrents. The settlers from Barbados brought their African slaves and used them to raise cattle and food crops for export to the West Indies. They also opened a lucrative trade with native Americans, exchanging English manufactured goods for furs and Indian slaves. The market in Indian slaves encouraged slave-raiding attacks on Franciscan missions in Florida, threatening war with Spain and in 1715 prompting a violent war with the resident Yamasee people. South Carolina remained an ill-governed, violence-ridden frontier settlement until the 1720s.

In stark contrast to the Carolinas, the proprietary colony of Pennsylvania (which included present-day Delaware) pursued a pacifistic policy toward native Americans and became prosperous. In 1681 Charles II bestowed the colony on William Penn in payment of a large debt owed to Penn's father. Born to wealth and destined for courtly pursuits, the younger Penn converted to the Society of Friends (Quakers), a radical Protestant sect, and used his prestige to spread its influence. Pennsylvania, his greatest achievement, was designed as a refuge for Quakers, who were persecuted in England because they refused to serve in the army and pay taxes to support the Church of England.

Like the Puritans, the Quakers wanted to restore the simplicity and spirituality of early Christianity. But Quakers were not Calvinists, who restricted salvation to a small elect. Quakers followed the teachings of their founders George Fox and Margaret Fell, who argued that all men and women could be saved because God had imbued each person with an inner "light" of grace or understanding. In Quaker meetings for worship there was no minister or sermon; members sat in silence until moved to speak by the inner light.

Penn's Frame of Government (1681) was a radical document for its time because it guaranteed political liberty and religious freedom and allowed Christians of all denominations to vote and hold office. Thousands of Quakers, primarily from the middling classes of northwestern England, settled along the Delaware River in or near the city of Philadelphia, which Penn himself planned. The proprietor sold land at low prices—and in fee simple—and, to attract other Protestant settlers, advertised in Dutch and German. In 1683 migrants from the German province of Saxony founded Germantown (just outside Philadelphia) and were soon joined by thousands of other Germans attracted by fertile land and the prospect of freedom from religious warfare. Ethnic diversity, pacifism, and freedom of conscience made Pennsylvania the most open and democratic Restoration colony.

From Mercantilism to Dominion

Beginning in the 1650s, the English government extended to America the mercantilist policies used to control its foreign trade. To oust Dutch merchants from the English colonies, the Navigation Act of 1651 required that goods imported into England or its American settlements be carried on English-owned ships. New acts in 1660 and 1663 strengthened the ban on foreign merchants and stipulated that colonial sugar, tobacco, and indigo could be shipped only to England. To provide more business for English merchants, the acts also required that European exports to America pass through England. To enforce these laws and raise money, the Revenue Act of 1673 imposed a "plantation duty" on sugar and tobacco exports and created a staff of customs officials to collect it.

The English government backed its mercantilist policy with force. "What we want," declared the duke of Albemarle, "is more of the trade the Dutch now have." In three commercial wars between 1652 and 1674 the English navy drove the Dutch from New Netherland and ended Dutch supremacy in the West African slave trade. Meanwhile, English merchants expanded their fleets and dominated Atlantic commerce.

Many Americans resisted the mercantilism of Charles II as burdensome and intrusive. Edmund Randolph, a customs official in Massachusetts, reported that the Puritan-dominated government took "no notice of the laws of trade," welcoming Dutch merchants, importing goods from the French sugar islands, and claiming that its royal charter exempted it from most of the new regulations. Outraged, Randolph called for English troops to "reduce Massachusetts to obedience." The Lords of Trade and Plantations (the committee that managed colonial affairs) pursued a punitive legal strategy instead. In 1679 they denied the claim of Massachusetts Bay to the adjoining province of New Hampshire, creating a separate colony with a royal governor. To bring the Puritan colony directly under English control, in 1684 the Lords persuaded the English Court of Chancery to annul the charter of Massachusetts Bay on the grounds that its government had virtually outlawed the Church of England and violated the Navigation Acts.

The accession to the throne of James II (1685–1688), an admirer of France's despotic Louis XIV and of "divine right" monarchy, prompted the Lords of Trade to create a centralized imperial system in America. Backed by the king, in 1686 the Lords revoked the corporate charters of Connecticut and Rhode Island and merged them with the Massachusetts Bay and Plymouth colonies to form a new royal province, the Dominion of New England. Two years later they added New York and New Jersey to the Dominion, creating a single colony from the Delaware River to Maine.

These actions went far beyond mercantilism, which had respected the political autonomy of the various colonies while regulating their trade, and extended to America the authoritarian model of colonial administration practiced in Ireland. James II appointed Sir Edmund Andros, a former military officer, as governor of the Dominion, empowering him to abolish the existing legislative assemblies and rule by decree. In Massachusetts Andros advocated public worship in the Church of England, offending Puritan Congregationalists, and banned town meetings, angering villagers who prized local self-rule. Even worse, he challenged all land titles granted under the original Massachusetts charter. He offered to provide new deeds, but not in fee simple; title holders would be required to pay an annual quitrent. The Puritans protested to the king, but James refused to restore the old charter.

The Glorious Revolution of 1688

James II angered English political leaders as much as Andros alienated the Americans. The king revoked the charters of many English towns, rejected the advice of Parliament, and aroused popular opposition by openly practicing Roman Catholicism. In 1688, when James's Spanish Catholic wife gave birth to a son, the prospect of a Catholic heir to the throne ignited a quick and

The Target of the Glorious Revolution
The stance and facial expression of James II (1685–1688) suggest his arrogant personality. The king's arbitrary actions and Catholic sympathies prompted rebellions in England and America and cost him the throne.

bloodless coup known as the Glorious Revolution. Backed by popular protests and the army, Protestant parliamentary leaders forced James into exile and enthroned Mary, his Protestant daughter by his first wife, and her Dutch husband, William of Orange. Queen Mary II and King William III agreed to rule as constitutional monarchs, accepting a Declaration of Rights that limited royal prerogatives and increased personal liberties and parliamentary powers.

The coup leaders felt a need to justify their substitution of one monarch for another. John Locke provided that justification in his *Two Treatises on Government* (1690), which rejected divine right theories of monarchial rule and argued that the legitimacy of government rests on the consent of the governed and that individuals have inalienable natural rights to life, liberty, and property. Locke's celebration of individual rights and representative government had a lasting influence in America, where many political leaders wanted to increase the powers of the colonial assemblies.

More immediately, the Glorious Revolution sparked popular rebellions in Massachusetts, Maryland, and New York. When the news of the coup reached

Boston in April 1689, Puritan leaders seized Governor Andros and shipped him back to England. William and Mary agreed to break up the Dominion of New England, creating the new royal colony of Massachusetts (which included Plymouth and Maine), but refused to restore all the Puritans' powers. According to the new charter of 1692, the king would appoint the governor (and naval officers to enforce customs regulations), all male property owners (not just Puritan church members) would have the vote, and members of the Church of England would enjoy religious freedom.

The uprising in Maryland had both religious and economic causes. Since 1660 tobacco prices has been falling, threatening the livelihoods of smallholders, tenant farmers, and former indentured servants, most of whom were Protestant. They resented the rising taxes and the high fees imposed by wealthy proprietary officials, who were primarily Catholics. When Parliament ousted James II in England, a Protestant Association quickly removed the officials appointed by the Catholic Lord Baltimore. The Lords of Trade suspended Baltimore's proprietorship, imposed royal government, and established the Church of England as the colony's official church. This settlement lasted until 1715, when Benedict Calvert, the fourth Lord Baltimore, converted to the Anglican faith and the Crown restored the proprietorship to the Calvert family.

In New York the rebellion against the Dominion of New England was supported by both English settlers angered by James's prohibition of representative institutions and Dutch Protestants who welcomed Queen Mary and her Dutch husband to the English throne. Dutch artisans in New York City helped oust Lieutenant Governor Nicholson, an Andros appointee and an alleged Catholic sympathizer, and rallied behind a new government led by Jacob Leisler, a migrant German soldier who had married into a prominent Dutch merchant family. At first Leisler found supporters among all classes and ethnic groups, but when he freed debtors from prison and championed a more democratic town-meeting form of government, most wealthy merchants (who had traditionally controlled the city government) turned against him. In 1691 a new royal governor took control of New York, restored the representative assembly, and supported the wealthy classes against the Dutch artisans. Leisler was indicted for treason, convicted by an English jury, hanged, and then decapitated. A new merchant-dominated Board of Aldermen passed ordinances that lowered artisans' wages. Conflict between the Leislerian and anti-Leislerian factions continued until the 1710s.

In both America and England the Glorious Revolution of 1688–1689 began a new phase in imperial history. The uprisings in Boston and New York toppled the authoritarian Dominion and restored internal self-government, while in England the new constitutional monarchy enhanced the political power of financiers and merchants, who reestablished a mercantile empire based on trade, rejecting James II's plan for an imperial dominion based on bureaucratic rule. This policy gave free rein to enterprising merchants and to the emerging American representative assemblies. Although Parliament created a new Board of Trade (1696) to supervise the American settlements, it had little success. Settlers and proprietors resisted the Board's attempt to install royal governors in all the colonies, as did many English political leaders, who feared an increase in royal power. Consequently, the empire remained diverse, an odd mixture of corporate governments (Connecticut and Rhode Island) and proprietary institutions (Pennsylvania, Maryland, the Carolinas) in colonies that were of minor economic importance and royal governments in the great staple-producing settlements (the West Indies, Virginia) and elsewhere (Massachusetts, New York, New Jersey).

Imperial Warfare

Beginning in 1689, Britain and France fought a century-long series of wars to determine which nation would be dominant in Western Europe. The first of these conflicts to have a major impact in the Western Hemisphere was the War of the Spanish Succession (1702–1713), which pitted Britain against France and Spain. In North America the British tried to protect their growing settlements in the Carolinas by launching an attack against Spanish Florida. An expedition from South Carolina burned St. Augustine but failed to capture the fort. Then the Carolinians armed Creek and Chickasaw warriors and Indians who had fled from forced labor at Spanish missions. This Indian army destroyed the remaining Franciscan missions in northern Florida, attacked the Spanish settlement at Pensacola, and massacred the Apalachee who remained loyal to the Spaniards. To preserve control of Florida and protect Havana in nearby Cuba, the Spanish reinforced St. Augustine and launched unsuccessful attacks against Charleston, South Carolina.

Native Americans also took part in the fighting in the Northeast between the French in Quebec and the Puritan colonies in New England. To halt the expansion of English settlement, French officials provided supplies and arms to pro-French Abenaki and Mohawk warriors, who destroyed English settlements along the coast of Maine and in 1704 attacked the western Massachusetts town of Deerfield, where they killed 48 residents and carried 112 into captivity (see American Voices, p. 54). New England responded to these raids by launching attacks against French settlements, joining with British troops to seize Port Royal. However, in 1710 a major British-American expedition against the French stronghold at Quebec failed miserably.

The New York frontier remained quiet because France and England did not want to disrupt the lucrative fur trade and because most of the Iroquois nations had adopted a new policy of "aggressive neutrality." The Five Iroquois peoples—the Mohawk, Oneida, Onondaga, Cayuga, and Seneca—had long lived in a strong political confederation and during the 1670s had entered into a "covenant chain" of alliances with the English governors of New York and the Algonquin tribes of New England. However, during the 1690s pro-British and pro-French factions among the Iroquois fought one another in a devastating "beaver war." Subsequently the Five Nations adopted a neutralist stance, exploiting their central location by trading with the English and the French but refusing to fight for either side. The Delaware leader Teedyuscung explained this strategy by showing his people a pictorial message from the Iroquois: "You see a Square in the Middle, meaning the Lands of the Indians; and at one End, the Figure of a Man, indicating the English; and at the other End, another, meaning the French. Let us join together to defend our land against both."

Stymied militarily in America, Britain used victories in Europe to win major territorial and commercial concessions in the Treaty of Utrecht (1713). From France, Britain obtained Newfoundland, Acadia (Nova Scotia), the Hudson Bay region of northern Canada, and access to the western Indian trade (see Map 3.1). From Spain, Britain acquired the strategic fortress of Gibraltar at the entrance to the Mediterranean and commercial privileges in Spanish America. These gains solidified Britain's commercial supremacy and brought peace to eastern North America for a generation.

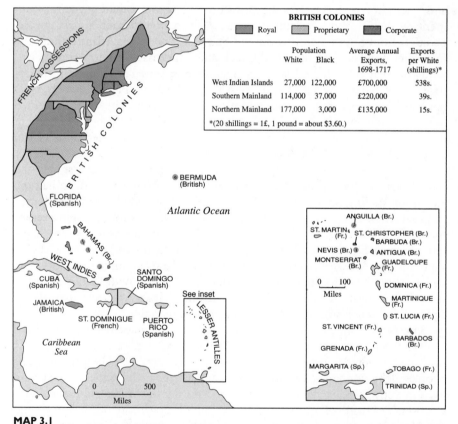

MAP 3.1

Britain's American Empire, 1713

Britain's West Indian colonies were small in size—mere dots on the Caribbean Sea—but large in economic importance. Their sugar plantations brought wealth to England and provided markets for the farm products of northern mainland colonies.

In the Southwest the Spanish established permanent settlements in Texas, beginning at San Antonio in 1718, to protect the silver mines in northern New Spain from attacks from French Louisiana. This expansion of Spanish influence was opposed by the prosperous town-dwelling Caddo peoples, one of whose confederacies, the "Kingdom of Tejas," would give Texas its name. The Caddo had expelled the Spanish Franciscans in 1693, blaming them for a fatal smallpox epidemic. A generation later the Tejas refused baptism (believing "that the [holy] water kills them") and successfully resisted Spanish control by turning to the French for firearms and trade goods. Like the Iroquois, the Caddo peoples had learned how to turn European rivalries and warfare to their own advantage.

THE IMPERIAL SLAVE ECONOMY

Britain's interest in American affairs reflected the increasing importance to its trade of the staple crops of sugar, tobacco, and rice. Using land seized from native Americans, European merchants and planters had created a new agricultural and commercial order which historians call the South Atlantic system. At the core of the new system of production stood enslaved labor from Africa.

The African Background

Vast and diverse, West Africa stretches from present-day Senegal to Cameroon and then extends southward to Congo and Angola. In 1500 tropical rain forest covered much of the coast, but a series of great rivers—the Senegal, Gambia, Volta, Niger, and Congo—provided relatively easy access to the woodlands, plains, and savanna of the interior.

Most residents farmed small plots and lived in extended families in small villages. Normally, men cleared the land and women planted and harvested the crops. On the plains of the savanna, millet, cotton, and livestock were the primary products, while the forest peoples grew yams and harvested oil-rich palm nuts. Forest dwellers exchanged kola nuts, a mild stimulant, for the textiles and leather goods produced by savanna dwellers. Similarly, salt produced along the seacoast was traded for iron or gold mined in the hills of the interior.

Most West Africans spoke related languages but were divided into hundreds of distinct cultural and political groups. A majority of the people lived in hierarchical, socially stratified societies ruled by princes. Others resided in stateless societies organized by family and lineage (much like those of the Woodland Indians of eastern North America). Both women and men had secret societies that cut across lineage and clan loyalties in stateless cultures and checked the powers of rulers in princely states. These societies provided sexual education for the young, conducted adult initiation ceremonies, and, by shaming individuals and officials, enforced a code of public conduct and private morality.

Spiritual beliefs varied greatly. Although some West Africans had been converted to the Muslim faith and believed in a single god, most recognized a variety of deities ranging from a remote creator-god who seldom interfered in human affairs to numerous spirits that lived in the earth, animals, and plants. Male blacksmiths (who had mastered the secrets of iron making) and female potters (who had transformed the basic elements of earth, water, and fire) captured these spiritual powers in amulets, "power generators" that protected those who wore them. Africans also paid homage to their ancestors, who were believed to inhabit a spiritual world from which they could intercede in behalf of their descendants. Royal families paid elaborate homage to their ancestors in an attempt to give themselves an aura of divinity.

At first European traders had a positive impact on life in West Africa by introducing new plants and animals. Portuguese merchants carried coconuts from East Africa, oranges and lemons from the Mediterranean, and pigs from Western Europe. From the Americas traders brought sweet potatoes, peanuts, papaya, pineapples, and tobacco. American maize and cassava (manioc) gradually displaced millet and yams as staples in the West African diet; in many areas their higher yields promoted population growth.

Portuguese merchants expanded existing trade networks, stimulating the African economy. European iron bars and metal products joined kola nuts and salt moving inland; grain, gold, ivory, and cotton textiles flowed to the coast to provision European ships. This inland trade remained in the hands of Africans because of disease; Europeans were quickly stricken by yellow fever, malaria, and dysentery, and their death rate was more than 50 percent a year.

Europeans soon joined in the trade in humans. Unfree status had existed for many centuries in West Africa. Some people were held in bondage as security for debts; others were sold into servitude by their kin, often in return for food in times of famine; still others were war captives. Although treated as property and exploited as agricultural laborers, slaves usually were considered members of the society that had enslaved them and sometimes were treated as kin. Most retained the right to marry, and their children were often free. A small proportion of unfree West Africans were "trade slaves," sold from one kingdom to another or carried overland to the Mediterranean region, mostly by Arab traders. Thus, the first Portuguese in Senegambia found that the Wolof king

> supports himself by raids which result in many slaves from his own as well as neighboring countries. He employs these slaves in cultivating the land allotted to him; but he also sells many to the Azanaghi [Arab] merchants in return for horses and other goods, and also to the Christians, since they have begun to trade with these blacks.

The demand for labor in the Western Hemisphere gradually transformed the scale and nature of African slavery (see Map 3.2). Between 1440 and 1550 Portuguese traders carried a few thousand Africans each year to sugar plantations

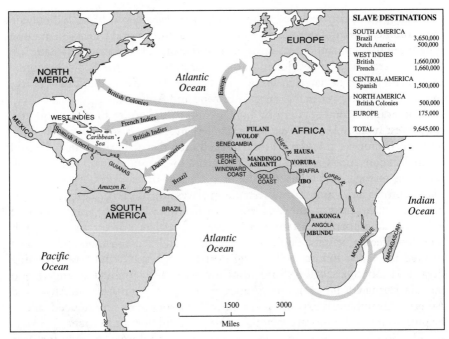

SLAVE DESTINATIONS	
SOUTH AMERICA	
Brazil	3,650,000
Dutch America	500,000
WEST INDIES	
British	1,660,000
French	1,660,000
CENTRAL AMERICA	
Spanish	1,500,000
NORTH AMERICA	
British Colonies	500,000
EUROPE	175,000
TOTAL	9,645,000

MAP. 3.2

The Atlantic Slave Trade

West Africa was home to scores of peoples and dozens of kingdoms. Some states, such as Dahomey, became aggressive slavers, taking tens of thousands of war captives and selling them to European traders. About 15 percent of these enslaved Africans died on the transatlantic voyage, the brutal "middle passage"; most of the survivors labored on sugar plantations in Brazil and the British and French West Indies.

in Madeira and the Azore Islands. Between 1550 and 1700, Portuguese and Dutch merchants annually transported about 10,000 Africans across the Atlantic to Brazil and the Caribbean. Then English and French merchants took over this trade in humans, developing African-run slave-catching systems that extended far into the interior. Between 1700 and 1810 they carried about 7 million Africans—800,000 in the 1780s alone—to toil and die in the Americas, primarily on sugar estates in the West Indies.

The South Atlantic System

Sugar was the cornerstone of the South Atlantic system, its cultivation fueled by a new European craving for sweetness, which previously had been available only from honey and fruit juices. Imitating Dutch and Portuguese planters in Brazil, English and French merchants developed sugar plantations in the West Indies, beginning with Barbados around 1650. By 1700 they were investing heavily in the Leeward Islands and Jamaica; by 1750 Jamaica had 700 large sugar plantations worked by more than 105,000 enslaved Africans.

Sugar production required fertile land, many laborers to plant and cut the cane, and heavy equipment to process it into raw sugar and molasses. Because only wealthy merchants or landowners had the capital to outfit a plantation, a planter-merchant elite developed in the sugar industry. As the Scottish econo-mist Adam Smith declared in his famous treatise *The Wealth of Nations* (1776), sugar was the most profitable crop in Europe and America.

The South Atlantic system brought wealth to the entire English economy. Most West Indian planters lived as "absentees" in England, spending their prof-its there. Moreover, the Navigation Acts required that American sugar be sold to English consumers or sent through England to continental markets; by 1750 reexports of sugar and tobacco accounted for half of all British exports. Sub-stantial profits also came from the trade in slaves, for the Royal African Com-pany sold male slaves in the West Indies for five times what it paid for them in Africa. To transport slaves (and machinery and settlers) to America, shipyards built hundreds of vessels. Thousands of English and Scottish men and women worked in related industries: building port facilities and warehouses, refining sugar and tobacco, distilling rum from molasses (a by-product of sugar), and manufacturing textiles and iron products for the growing markets in Africa and America. Commercial expansion also provided a supply of experienced sailors, helping to make the Royal Navy the most powerful fleet in Europe.

The South Atlantic system was an economic and human tragedy for West Africa and the parts of East Africa, such as Madagascar, where slavers also preyed. Between 1550 and 1870 the Atlantic slave trade uprooted about 15 million Africans, diminishing the wealth and population of the continent. Overall, the iron, tinware, rum, and cloth that entered the African economy in exchange for slaves was worth from one-tenth (in the 1680s) to one-third (by the 1780s) as much as the goods those slaves produced.

In addition, the slave trade changed the nature of West African society by encouraging centralized states and military conquest. In 1739 an observer noted that "whenever the King of Barsally wants Goods or Brandy . . . the King goes and ransacks some of his enemies' towns, seizing the people and selling them." War and slaving became a way of life in Dahomey, where the royal house made the sale of slaves' a state monopoly and used the resulting ac-cess to European guns to create a military despotism. Dahomey's army, which included a contingent of 5,000 women, systematically raided the interior for captives, exporting thousands of slaves each year. The Asante kings also used the firearms and wealth acquired through the Atlantic trade to create a bu-reaucratic empire of 3 million to 5 million people. Yet slaving remained a choice, not a necessity. The old and still powerful Kingdom of Benin, famous for its cast bronzes and carved ivory, resolutely opposed the slave trade, pro-hibiting the export of male slaves for over a century (see American Voices, p. 70).

The trade in humans changed many aspects of African life. Class divi-sions hardened as people of noble birth sold those of lesser status. Gender relations shifted as well. Men constituted two-thirds of the slaves sent across

An African King
This striking bronze plaque from Benin, an important kingdom in West Central Africa, depicts a mounted king, his attendants, and (probably) his children.

the Atlantic both because European planters paid more for men and because African traders directed women captives into local slave markets. The resulting imbalance between the sexes allowed some African men to take several wives, changing the nature of marriage. Most important, the Atlantic trade prompted harsher forms of slavery in Africa, eroding the dignity of human life there as well as on the plantations of the Western Hemisphere.

The Slave Trade in Africa

The demand for black laborers in the Americas disrupted African society, encouraging wars among peoples and forever changing millions of lives. The narrative of Venture Smith describes how this affected many Africans.

I was born at Dukandarra, in Guinea, about the year 1729. My father's name was Saungm Furro, Prince of the tribe of Dukandara. My father had three wives. Polygamy was not uncommon in that country, especially among the rich, as every man was allowed to keep as many wives as he could maintain. By his first wife he had three children. The eldest of them was myself, named by my father, Broteer. . . .

The first thing worthy of notice which I remember was, a contention between my father and mother, on account of my father marrying his third wife without the consent of his first and eldest, which was contrary to the custom generally observed among my countrymen. In consequence of this rupture, my mother left her husband and country, and travelled away with her three children to the eastward. I was then five years old . . .; [a year later] the difference between my parents had been made up . . . and I was once more restored to my paternal dwelling in peace and happiness. . . .

[Shortly afterwards] my father learned that the place had been invaded by a numerous army, from a nation not far distant, . . . instigated by some white nation who equipped them [with guns] and sent them to subdue and possess the country. . . . The army of the enemy was large, I should suppose consisting of about six thousand men. Their leader was called Baukurre. After destroying the old prince [my father], they decamped and immediately marched towards the sea, lying to the west, taking with them myself and the women prisoners. . . .

All of us were then put into the castle, and kept for market. On a certain time I and other prisoners were . . . rowed to a vessel belonging to Rhode Island. . . . I was brought on board by one Robertson Mumford, steward of said vessel, for four gallons of rum, and a piece of calico, and called VENTURE, on account of his having purchased me with his own private venture. Thus I came by my name. All the slaves that were bought for that vessel's cargo, were two hundred and sixty.

SOURCE: John Bayles, ed., *Black Slave Narratives* (New York: Macmillan, 1970), pp. 36–44.

Slavery and Society in the Chesapeake

The first Africans arrived in Virginia in 1619, but for the next forty years their numbers remained small and they were not legally enslaved. English common law acknowledged indentured servitude but not *chattel slavery*—the ownership of one human being by another. If planters wanted legalized slavery, they would have to create it. In the West Indies and South Carolina they did exactly that, enacting statutes permitting chattel slavery in the first decade of settlement.

The law of slavery developed more slowly in the tobacco colonies of Maryland and Virginia. About 400 Africans were living in the Chesapeake colonies in 1649, making up 2 percent of the population; by 1670 the proportion of blacks had reached only 5 percent. Africans were forced to work hard and were ill fed and ill clothed, but so were most English indentured servants. A significant number of black workers received their freedom by completing a term of service or converting to Christianity. Some African Christian freemen even purchased slaves or bought the labor contracts of English servants, suggesting that religion and personal initiative were as important as race in determining social status at this time. By becoming a Christian and a planter, an enterprising African could aspire to near equality with the English settlers.

Beginning in the 1660s, for unclear reasons, legislatures in the Chesapeake colonies enacted laws that lowered the status of Africans. Perhaps the English-born elite grew more conscious of race as the number of Africans increased. By 1671 the Virginia House of Burgesses had forbidden Africans to own guns or join the militia. It had also barred them—"tho baptized and enjoying their own Freedom"—from buying the labor contracts of white servants and specified that conversion to Christianity did not qualify Africans for eventual freedom. Being black was becoming a mark of inferior legal status, and being a slave was becoming a permanent and hereditary condition.

Subsequently African slavery expanded not because it was "necessary"—white families and English indentured servants could have continued to grow tobacco and could have cultivated rice and sugar as well—but because it was profitable. After Bacon's rebellion of 1675–1676, planters imported thousands of Africans, primarily because the growing slave trade made them less expensive than white indentured servants (who were in short supply and thus more costly) but also because slaves had few legal rights and could be disciplined more strictly. A law of 1692 prohibiting sexual intercourse between English and Africans was intended to separate white and black workers and create a racially divided society. Finally, in 1705, a Virginia statute explicitly defined virtually all resident Africans as slaves: "All servants imported or brought into this country by sea or land who were not Christians in their native country shall be accounted and be slaves." The Chesapeake elite had chosen to create a society based on enslaved black laborers, who numbered 10 percent of the Chesapeake population by 1700 and 20 percent by 1720.

These years witnessed significant changes among whites as well. As settlement moved inland after 1675, away from the disease-ridden lowlands, English migrants lived long enough to form stable families and communities. When death rates had been high, many husbands had named their wives as executors of their estates and legal guardians of their children. Now they bestowed those powers on their male kin. Reaffirming the primacy of male heirs, they also limited widows' portions to the traditional one-third share during their lifetimes. Men reassumed their customary control of family property.

The reappearance of strict patriarchy within the family mirrored larger social developments. The planter elite now stood at the top of a rural social hierarchy, exercising authority over a small yeoman class, a large group of white tenant farmers, and a growing host of enslaved black laborers. Wealthy planters used Africans to grow food as well as export tobacco; build houses, wagons, and tobacco casks; and make shoes and clothes. By increasing their self-sufficiency, the planter elite survived the depressed tobacco market between 1680 and 1720. Small-scale planters who used family labor to grow tobacco fared less well, falling deeper into debt.

However, the Virginia gentry paid attention to the concerns of middling and poor whites, reducing their taxes and allowing them to vote. The strategy of the leading families—the Carters, Lees, Randolphs, Robinsons—was to curry favor with the voters at election time, bribing them with rum, money, and the promise of favorable legislation. In return, yeomen planters were expected to elect their wealthy neighbors to political office and defer to their authority. This political horse trading enhanced the power of the planter elite at the expense of the royal governor. It also created solidarity among whites, as did the spread of African slavery; by 1770 there were 500,000 slaves in the southern mainland colonies, roughly one-third of the population, and 60 percent of the English families in the Chesapeake owned at least one slave.

As time passed, affluent Chesapeake planters modeled themselves after the English aristocracy. Between 1720 and 1750 they replaced their modest wooden houses with brick mansions. They and their wives read English journals, imported English clothes, and dined in the English fashion. Planters hired English tutors to teach etiquette to their daughters and sent their sons to London to be educated as gentlemen. Most of these young men returned to America, married, and followed in their fathers' footsteps, managing plantations and participating in politics. Gentry women deferred to their husbands' authority, reared pious children, and maintained elaborate social networks. Using the profits of the South Atlantic system, the planter-merchants of the Chesapeake formed an increasingly well-educated, refined, and stable ruling class.

The Expansion of Slavery

For the enslaved Africans at the bottom of the social scale, the South Atlantic system was an unrelieved tragedy. Torn from their village homes, captives were marched in chains to coastal ports. From there they made the perilous "middle passage" to the New World in hideously overcrowded ships. Some Africans jumped overboard, choosing to drown rather than endure more suffering. Nearly a million (15 percent of the 8 million who crossed the Atlantic between 1700 and 1810) died on the journey, mostly from dysentery, smallpox, or scurvy.

Africans who toiled in the sugar islands faced the harshest conditions. Planting and harvesting sugarcane required intense labor under a tropical sun, with a pace set by the overseer's whip. With sugar prices high and the cost of slaves low, many planters worked slaves to death and then imported more. Between 1708 and 1735 about 85,000 Africans were brought into Barbados, but the black population increased only from 42,000 to 46,000.

Conditions were less severe in Maryland and Virginia, where many slaves lived relatively long lives. Tobacco was a less physically demanding crop than sugar, and epidemic diseases did not spread as easily because the plantations were small and dispersed. Also, because tobacco profits were low, planters could not constantly buy new slaves and therefore treated those they had less harshly. Tobacco planters attempted to increase their work force through reproduction, purchasing higher numbers of female slaves and encouraging large families. In 1720 women made up about a third of the African population of Maryland, and the black population had begun to increase naturally. One absentee owner instructed his plantation agent "to be kind and indulgent to the breeding wenches, and not to force them when with child upon any service or hardship that will be injurious to them." By midcentury American-born slaves constituted a majority among Chesapeake blacks.

The most oppressive conditions for slaves existed in South Carolina. The colony had grown slowly until Africans from rice-growing cultures turned rice into a profitable export crop around 1700. To expand production, white planters imported tens of thousands of Africans, who by the 1710s made up a majority of the colony's population and 80 percent of those living in the rice-growing lowlands. Mosquito-borne epidemic diseases took thousands of African lives, while overwork killed many more slaves, for moving tons of dirt to build irrigation works was brutally hard. As in the West Indies, there were many deaths and few births.

Community and Resistance

Slaves regarded each other not as Africans but as members of a specific people: Mende, Hausa, Ibo, Yoruba. To prevent slave revolts, white planters consciously enhanced this sense of cultural diversity. "The safety of the Plantations," declared a widely read English pamphlet, "depends upon having Negroes from all parts of Guiny, who do not understand each other's languages and Customs and cannot agree to Rebel."

Africans found it in their interest to transcend this cultural diversity. The largely African-born population of the South Carolina lowlands created a new and widely understood language, the Gullah dialect, using English and African words in an African grammatical structure. In the Chesapeake, where there were more American-born blacks and a less concentrated slave population, a European visitor in the mid-eighteenth century reported that "all the blacks spoke very good English." A common language was one prerequisite

Hulling Rice in Georgia
In this early twentieth-century photograph, the descendants of enslaved women use traditional
African mortar-and-pestle technology to separate the hard outer shell from grains of rice.

for the creation of African-American communities. The growth of stable
family and kin networks was another. A high death rate inhibited the creation of multigenerational families in South Carolina, but after 1725 blacks in
the Chesapeake were able to establish enduring families and extended kin
networks.

African-Americans gradually developed a culture of their own, passing on family names, traditions, and knowledge to the next generation. Aspects of the slaves' African heritage could be seen in wood carvings, the giant wooden mortars and pestles used to hull rice, and the design of shacks. Many African-Americans retained traditional Muslim religious beliefs or relied on the spiritual powers of conjurers. Others adopted Protestant Christianity, reshaping its doctrines, ethics, and rituals to fit their needs and creating a spiritually rich and long-lasting religious culture.

However, slaves had few opportunities for education and accumulated few material goods. A well-traveled European who visited a slave hut in Virginia in the late eighteenth century found it to be

> more miserable than the most miserable of the cottages of our peasants. The husband and wife sleep on a mean pallet, the children on the ground; a very bad fireplace, some utensils for cooking. . . . They work all week, not having a single day for themselves except for holidays.

African Culture in South Carolina
The dance and the musical instruments are of Yoruba origin, the contribution of Africans from the Niger River–Slave Coast region (the homeland of the Yoruba), an area that accounted for one-sixth of the slaves imported into South Carolina before 1770.

Sadism under Slavery

Planters relied on various incentives to extract work from their African slaves. A few used rewards, providing cooperative laborers with food, leisure, and better treatment. Many more relied on force, extracting work by whipping recalcitrant laborers. Some went further, as described by Philip Fithian, a Princeton graduate employed as tutor by a Virginia planter.

When I am on the Subject, I will relate further, what I heard Mr George Lees Overseer, one Morgan, say the other day that he himself had often done to Negroes, and found it useful; He said that whipping of any kind does them no good, for they will laugh at your greatest Severity; But he told us he had invented two things, and by several experiments had proved their success.—For Sulleness, Obstinacy, or Idleness, says he, Take a Negro, strip him, tie him fast to a post; take then a sharp Curry-Comb, + curry him severely til he is well scrap'd; + call a Boy with some dry Hay, and make the Boy rub him down for several Minutes, then salt him, & unlose him. He will attend to his Business (said the inhuman Infidel) afterwards!—But savage Cruelty does not exceed His next diabolical Invention—To get a Secret from a Negro, says he, take the following Method—Lay upon your Floor a large thick plank, having a peg about eighteen Inches long, of hard wood, & very Sharp, on the upper end, fixed fast in the plank—then strip the Negro, tie the Cord to a staple in the Ceiling, so as that his foot may just rest on the sharpened Peg, then turn him briskly round, and you would laugh (said our informer) at the Dexterity of the Negro, while he was releiving his Feet on the sharpen'd Peg!

SOURCE: Philip Vickers Fithian, *Journals and Letters, 1767–1774* (Williamsburg, Va.: Colonial Williamsburg Press, 1934), pp. 50–51.

Slaves resisted the rigorous work routine at their peril. To punish slaves who disobeyed, refused to work, or ran away, planters resorted to the lash and the amputation of fingers, toes, and ears. Declaring the chronic runaway Ballazore an "incorrigeble rogue," Robert "King" Carter of Virginia ordered all his toes cut off: "nothing less than dismembering will reclaim him." Thomas Jefferson, who witnessed such cruelty on his father's plantation in mid-eighteenth-century Virginia, noted that each generation of whites was "nursed, educated, and daily exercised in tyranny," for the relationship "between master and slave is a perpetual exercise of the most unremitting despotism on the one part, and degrading submission on the other."

White violence was related to the size and density of the slave population. English planters in the predominantly African West Indies routinely branded troublesome slaves with hot irons. In South Carolina the outnumbered whites maintained authority by imposing strict regulations. Black workers were forbidden to leave the plantation without special passes, and rural patrols enforced those regulations.

Slaves dealt with their plight in a variety of ways. Some bargained with their owners, agreeing to do extra work in return for better food and clothes. Others resisted by working slowly or stealing. Still others attacked their owners or overseers even though this was punishable by mutilation or death. A successful rebellion was nearly impossible because whites were armed and, outside of coastal South Carolina, more numerous than Africans. Some newly arrived slaves without ties to African-American culture escaped to the frontier, where they tried to establish African villages or, more often, married into Indian tribes. Others, especially those fluent in English, fled to towns, where they tried to pass as free blacks.

The largest slave uprising of the eighteenth century, the Stono rebellion, occurred in the late 1730s, when the governor of Spanish Florida promised freedom and land to slaves who ran away from South Carolina. At least sixty-nine slaves reportedly escaped to St. Augustine, and rumors circulated "that a Conspiracy was formed by Negroes in Carolina to rise and make their way out of the province." When war between England and Spain broke out in 1739, seventy-five Africans killed a number of whites near the Stono River, stole guns and ammunition, and marched south toward Florida. Unrest swept the countryside, but the white militia killed many of the Stono rebels and dispersed the rest, preventing a general uprising. Frightened whites tightened plantation discipline and imported fewer new slaves. For Africans the price of active resistance was high.

The Northern Maritime Economy

The South Atlantic system encompassed nonslaveholding farmers in the northern mainland colonies because the sugar islands provided a ready market for bread, lumber, fish, and meat. As a West Indian explained in 1647, planters in the islands "had rather buy food at very dear rates than produce it by labour, so infinite is the profit of sugar works." By 1700 the economies of the West Indies and New England were tightly interwoven. After 1720 farmers and merchants in New York, New Jersey, and Pennsylvania entered this trade, shipping wheat, corn, and bread to the sugar islands.

The South Atlantic system tied the whole British Empire together. In return for sugar exports to England, West Indian planters received *bills of exchange* (credit slips) from London merchant houses. The planters used those bills to buy slaves and reimburse American merchants for the crops produced by northern farmers. Farmers and merchants then exchanged the bills for British manufactures, completing the cycle.

American merchants in Boston, Philadelphia, and New York invested some of their profits in new ships and factories. In Boston, Newport, and Providence they refined raw sugar into finished loaves (previously imported from England) and distilled West Indian molasses into rum. By the 1740s Boston distillers were exporting more than half a million gallons of rum annually. In addition, merchants in smaller ports, such as Salem and Marblehead, built a major fishing industry, providing mackerel and cod to feed the slaves of the sugar islands and to export to southern Europe. Southern merchants transformed Baltimore into a major port by developing a bustling trade in wheat, while Charleston traders exported deerskins, indigo, and rice to European markets.

The expansion of commerce in the eighteenth century fueled rapid growth in American port cities and coastal towns. By 1750 Newport, Rhode Island, and Charleston, South Carolina, had nearly 10,000 residents apiece, Boston 15,000, and New York almost 18,000. The largest port was Philadelphia, whose population reached 30,000 by 1776, the size of a large European provincial city. Smaller coastal towns were centers of the shipbuilding and lumber industries. By the 1740s seventy sawmills dotted the Piscataqua River in New Hampshire, providing low-cost wood for homes, warehouses, and especially shipbuilding. Taking advantage of the Navigation Acts, which allowed colonists to build and own trading vessels, scores of shipwrights turned out oceangoing ships, while hundreds of other artisans made ropes, sails, and metal fittings for the new fleet. Shipyards in Boston and Philadelphia launched about 15,000 tons of oceangoing vessels annually; eventually colonial-built ships made up about a third of the British merchant fleet.

The impact of the South Atlantic system extended into the interior of North America. A small fleet of trading vessels sailed back and forth between Philadelphia and the villages along the Delaware Bay, exchanging cargoes of European goods for barrels of flour and wheat. In the 1750s hundreds of professional teamsters in Maryland moved to market 370,000 bushels of wheat and corn and 16,000 barrels of flour annually—over 10,000 wagon trips. To service this traffic entrepreneurs and artisans set up taverns, livery stables, and barrel-making shops in small towns along the wagon roads, providing additional jobs. The prosperous interior town of Lancaster, Pennsylvania, boasted more than 200 artisans, both German and English. The South Atlantic system thus provided not only markets for farmers (by far the largest group of northern residents), but also opportunities for merchants, artisans, and workers in country towns and seaport cities.

At the top of seaport society stood a small group of wealthy landowners, who lived off their rents, and prosperous merchants. By 1750 about forty merchants controlled over 50 percent of Philadelphia's trade and had taxable assets averaging £10,000, a huge sum at the time. Like the Chesapeake gentry, these prosperous northern merchants imitated the British upper classes, importing design books from England and building Georgian-style mansions to showcase their wealth. Their wives created a genteel culture, decorating their houses with fine furniture and entertaining guests at elegant dinners.

Artisan and shopkeeper families formed the middle ranks of seaport society and numbered nearly half the population. Innkeepers, butchers, seamstresses, shoemakers, weavers, bakers, carpenters, masons, and dozens of other specialists socialized among themselves, formed mutual-help societies, and worked to gain a *competency*—an income sufficient to maintain their families in modest comfort and dignity. Wives and husbands often worked as a team, teaching the "mysteries of the craft" to their children. The most prosperous owned their own houses and shops (sometimes run by widows continuing a family business). Some artisans aspired to wealth and status, an entrepreneurial ethic that prompted them to hire apprentices and expand production. Most craft workers were not well-to-do, however; these middling people had taxable assets averaging about £300. Many of them were quite poor; a tailor was lucky to accumulate £30 worth of property in his lifetime.

Laboring men and women formed the lower ranks of urban society. Boston, Philadelphia, and New York needed hundreds of dockworkers to unload manufactured goods and molasses from inbound ships and reload the ships with barrels of wheat, fish, and rice for export; these demanding jobs often were filled by black slaves and white indentured servants. Hundreds of merchant seamen lived in the poor wards of port cities, along with unskilled men who worked for wages. Poor women—whether single, married, or widowed—could eke out a living by washing clothes, spinning wool, or working as servants or prostitutes. To make ends meet, most laboring families sent their children out to work at an early age. Indispensable to the economy yet without homes of their own, these bound laborers, wage earners, and merchant seamen lived in crowded tenements in back alleys. In good times hard work brought family security or enough money to drink cheap New England rum in waterfront taverns.

Periods of stagnant commerce affected everyone, threatening merchants with bankruptcy and artisans with irregular work. For laborers and seamen, whose household budgets left no margin for sickness or unemployment, depressed trade meant hunger, dependence on charity handed out by town-appointed overseers of the poor, and—for the most desperate—a life of petty thievery. Involvement in the South Atlantic system between 1660 and 1750 brought uncertainty as well as opportunity to northern workers and farmers.

THE NEW POLITICS OF EMPIRE, 1713–1750

The triumph of trade changed the politics of empire. British ministers, pleased with the prosperous commerce in staple crops, were content to rule the colonies with a gentle hand. The colonists enjoyed a significant degree of self-government and economic autonomy, allowing them to challenge the rules of the mercantilist system.

The Rise of the Assembly

Before 1689 political affairs in most colonies were dominated by proprietors, royal governors, and authoritarian elites, reflecting the view that "Authority should Descend from *Kings* and *Fathers* to *Sons* and *Servants*," as a royalist political philosopher put it. In the Glorious Revolution of 1688 the English political faction known as the Whigs challenged that outlook, winning the fight for a constitutional monarchy that limited the authority of the Crown. Their ideal government would divide power among the monarchy, the aristocracy, and the commons. Whigs did not advocate democracy but did believe that nonnoble property owners should have some political power, especially over the levying of taxes. When Whig politicians forced William and Mary to accept a Declaration of Rights in 1689, they strengthened the powers of the House of Commons at the expense of the Crown.

American representative assemblies copied the English Whigs and insisted on maintaining their authority over taxes, refusing to fund military projects and other programs advocated by royal governors. Gradually the legislatures won partial control of patronage and the budget, angering imperial bureaucrats and absentee proprietors. "The people in power in America," complained the proprietor William Penn during a struggle with the Pennsylvania Assembly, "think nothing taller than themselves but the Trees." In Massachusetts during the 1720s the assembly refused repeatedly to obey the king's instructions to provide a permanent salary for the royal governor; subsequently legislatures in North Carolina, New Jersey, and Pennsylvania declined to pay their governors any salary for several years.

The Rise of an American Gentry
George Wyllys (1710–1796) came from a family of political leaders in Connecticut and served as secretary of the colony from 1730 to 1796. The emergence of capable and well-educated men such as Wyllys (note the books in his library) bolstered the growing power of the American representative assemblies.

The rise of the assembly created an elitist rather than a democratic political system. Although most property-owning white men had the right to vote after 1700, only men of considerable wealth and status stood for election. In Virginia in the 1750s seven members of the influential Lee family sat in the House of Burgesses and, along with other powerful Virginia families, dominated its major committees. In New England descendants of the original Puritans had intermarried and formed a core of political leaders. "Go into every village in New England," John Adams said in 1765, "and you will find that the office of justice of the peace, and even the place of representative, have generally descended from generation to generation, in three or four families at most."

Neither elitist assemblies nor wealthy property owners could impose unpopular edicts on the people. The crowd actions that had overthrown the Dominion of New England in 1689 were a regular part of political life in England and America and were used to achieve social and economic aims. Mobs upheld community values: in New York they closed houses of prostitution, while in Salem, Massachusetts, they ran people with infectious diseases out of town. Other mobs had economic motives, rioting to prevent merchants from exporting grain from Boston during a wartime shortage in 1710 and proprietors from forcing their tenants from disputed lands in New Jersey in the 1730s and 1740s. When officials in Boston tried to restrict the sale of farm produce to a designated public marketplace, a crowd destroyed the building and defied the authorities to arrest them. "If you touch One you shall touch All," an anonymous letter warned the sheriff, "and we will show you a Hundred Men where you can show one."

Such expressions of popular power, combined with the growing power of the assemblies, undermined the old authoritarian system. By the 1750s most colonies had representative political institutions that were broadly responsive to popular pressure and increasingly immune from British control.

Salutary Neglect

British colonial policy during the reigns of George I (1714–1727) and George II (1727–1760) contributed significantly to the rise of American self-government. Royal bureaucrats relaxed their supervision of internal colonial affairs, focusing instead on defense and trade. Two generations later the British political philosopher Edmund Burke would praise this strategy as "salutary [healthy] neglect."

Salutary neglect was a by-product of the political system developed by Sir Robert Walpole, leader of the Whigs in the House of Commons between 1720 and 1742. Using appointments, pensions, and gifts, Walpole transformed the formerly antagonistic relationship between king and Parliament into one of cooperation. But his tactics offended the self-described Real (or Radical) Whigs, who argued that by using patronage and bribery to create a strong Court (or Crown) party, Walpole had betrayed the constitutional monarchy established by the Glorious Revolution. A Country party of landed gentle-men warned that high taxes, a bloated royal bureaucracy, and a standing army threatened the liberties of the people.

The arguments of the Radical Whigs and the Country party appealed to Americans who wanted to enhance the power of the provincial assemblies. In their eyes the royal governors in America still had too much arbitrary power; they pointed to Governor William Cosby of New York, whose salary demands and selling of offices threw the province into political chaos for a decade. American Whigs warned that colonial governors, emulating Walpole, would use land grants and political appointments to control the assemblies.

Walpole's patronage policies weakened the imperial system in a more di-rect fashion by filling the Board of Trade with men of little talent. These "placemen" did little, weakening the morale of more capable imperial offi-cials. When Governor Gabriel Johnson went to North Carolina in the 1730s, determined to "make a mighty change in the face of affairs" by curbing the assembly, he was soon discouraged by the lack of support from other British officials. Forsaking reform, he decided "to do nothing which can be reason-ably blamed, and leave the rest to time, and a new set of inhabitants."

Salutary neglect did not "cause" Americans to seek independence; in fact, in the short run mild rule under Walpole strengthened the colonists' alle-giance to Britain (as did the increasing popularity of British goods and cul-ture). But the legislative autonomy allowed by salutary neglect did encourage Americans to expect a position of political equality within the empire.

Consolidating the Mercantile System

Walpole's main preoccupation during the years of salutary neglect was to pro-tect British commercial interests from foreign threats. One of his major initia-tives was the new colony of Georgia. In the early 1730s General James Oglethorpe and a group of social reformers successfully petitioned King George II for land south of the Carolinas. They named the new colony in honor of the king and planned it to be a refuge for Britain's poor. Envisioning a society of small farms worked by independent landowners and white inden-tured servants, the trustees of Georgia limited most land grants to 500 acres and, unlike other British colonies, initially outlawed slavery.

Walpole arranged for Parliament to subsidize Georgia because he wanted to protect the valuable rice colony of South Carolina from Spanish Florida. Spain had long resented the British presence in Carolina and was outraged by the expansion into Georgia, where Spanish Franciscans had Indian missions. In addition, English merchants had steadily increased their trade in slaves and manufactured goods to Spain's colonies in Mesoamerica, eventually control-ling two-thirds of that trade, and Spanish officials wanted to resist this often il-legal commercial imperialism. In 1739 Spanish naval forces sparked the so-called War of Jenkins' Ear by mutilating Robert Jenkins, an English sea cap-tain who was trading illegally with the Spanish West Indies.

Walpole jumped on this provocation to begin the first significant military conflict in America in a generation. In 1740 British regulars commanded by Governor Oglethorpe, together with provincial troops from South Carolina and Georgia and some Indian allies, launched an unsuccessful expedition against St. Augustine, which was defended by Spanish soldiers and escaped African slaves. Later that year the governors of the other mainland colonies raised 2,500 volunteers, who joined a British naval force in an assault on the Spanish seaport of Cartagena (in present-day Colombia). The attack failed, and instead of enriching themselves with Spanish booty, hundreds of colonial troops died of tropical diseases.

The War of Jenkins' Ear became part of a general European conflict, the War of the Austrian Succession. The British and French navies clashed in the West Indies, but initially there was little fighting along the long frontier between the Anglo-American colonies and French Canada. Then, in 1745, more than 3,000 New England militiamen, supported by a British naval squadron, captured the powerful French naval fortress of Louisbourg, which protected the entrance into the St. Lawrence River. The Treaty of Aix-la-Chapelle (1748) returned Louisbourg to France, but the war secured the territorial integrity of Georgia by reaffirming British military superiority in that region.

An unexpected threat to British economic ascendancy in North America was American competition, which British officials were determined to eliminate. According to the mercantilist Navigation Acts, colonies could produce only agricultural goods and raw materials; the more profitable manufacturing of goods and the provision of commercial services were reserved for the home country. In 1699 Parliament had prohibited Americans from marketing colonial-made textiles; in 1732 the ban was extended to the sale of hats, and in 1750 to iron products such as plows, axes, and skillets.

However, the Navigation Acts had a major loophole because they allowed Americans to own ships and transport goods. Colonial merchants exploited those provisions, securing 95 percent of the commerce between the mainland and the West Indies and 75 percent of the trade in manufactures shipped from London and Bristol. Quite unexpectedly, British mercantilism had created a dynamic and wealthy community of colonial merchants.

The flour, fish, and meat produced by the rapidly growing mainland colonies raised another set of problems for the British authorities. By the 1720s the British sugar islands could not absorb these goods, and so colonial merchants sold them in the French West Indies. These supplies helped French planters produce low-cost sugar, undercutting British sales in Europe. When American rum distillers began to prefer cheap French molasses to the British product, planters petitioned Parliament for help. The resulting Molasses Act of 1733 permitted the mainland colonies to export fish and farm products to the French islands but, to enhance the competitiveness of British molasses, placed a high tariff on French molasses. American merchants and public officials protested that the act would cut farm exports and cripple their distilling industry, making it more difficult for colonists to purchase British goods. When

Parliament ignored their petitions, American merchants continued importing French molasses and bribed customs officials to ignore the new tax. Luckily, sugar prices rose in the mid-1730s, and the act was not enforced.

The lack of adequate currency in the colonies led to another confrontation. American merchants sent most of the specie and bills of exchange they earned in the West Indian trade to Britain to pay for manufactured goods, draining the domestic money supply. To remedy this problem, the assemblies of ten colonies established land banks which lent paper money to farmers, taking their land as collateral. Farmers used the paper money to buy tools or livestock or to pay their creditors, thereby stimulating trade. But some assemblies, such as that of Rhode Island, issued large amounts of currency, causing it to fall in value, and required merchants to accept it. Creditors, especially English merchants, rightly complained that they were being forced to accept worthless currency. In 1751 Parliament passed a Currency Act that prevented all the New England colonies from establishing new land banks and prohibited the use of public currency to pay private debts.

These economic conflicts angered a new generation of British political leaders, who believed that the colonies already had too much autonomy. In 1749 Charles Townshend of the Board of Trade charged that American assemblies had assumed many of the "ancient and established prerogatives wisely preserved in the Crown." Townshend and other officials were determined to replace salutary neglect with a more rigorous system of imperial control.

CHAPTER 3 TIMELINE

1651	First Navigation Act
1660	Restoration of Charles II
1660s	Barbados becomes sugar island
	Virginia moves toward slave system
	New Navigation Acts
1664	New Netherland captured; becomes New York
1669	Fundamental Constitutions of Carolina
1681	William Penn founds Pennsylvania
1686–1689	Dominion of New England
1688–1689	Glorious Revolution in England and rebellions in Massachusetts, Maryland, and New York
1696	Board of Trade created
1705	Virginia statute defines slavery
1714–1750	British policy of "salutary neglect"
	Rise of American assemblies
1718	Spanish missions and garrison in Texas
1720–1742	Sir Robert Walpole chief minister
1720–1750	Dahomey becomes "slaving" state
	Black natural increase in Chesapeake
	Rice exports from Carolina soar
	Africans in Carolina create Gullah language
	Planter aristocracy in southern colonies
	Expansion of seaport cities on mainland
1732–1733	Georgia colony chartered
	Molasses Act
1739	Stono rebellion
	War of Jenkins' Ear
1750	Iron Act
1751	Currency Act

GROWTH AND CRISIS IN AMERICAN SOCIETY, 1720–1765

- Freehold Society in New England
- The Mid-Atlantic: Toward a New Society, 1720–1765
- The Enlightenment and the Great Awakening, 1740–1765
- The Midcentury Challenge: War, Trade, and Land, 1750–1765

By 1720 Britain's North American settlements were well established. The early dangers were past. The Indians in coastal areas had been expelled or pacified and the colonists produced enough food to feed themselves and send a surplus to markets in Europe and the West Indies. Steady immigration, the slave trade, and natural increase had brought the population to 400,000.

During the next 45 years, natural increase more than doubled the population of New England, while the mid-Atlantic colonies, with their promise of freehold land, political liberties, and religious tolerance, drew hundreds of thousands of new migrants from Europe. In addition, tens of thousands of enslaved Africans were imported into the southern settlements. By 1765 the mainland population had grown fivefold, to almost 2 million people.

As the new arrivals and the landless younger children of long-settled families moved west in search of opportunities, they fought with each other and reignited conflict with native peoples and with the other European powers contesting for dominance of North America, France and Spain.

FREEHOLD SOCIETY IN NEW ENGLAND

In the 1630s the Puritans had migrated from a country where a handful of nobles and gentry owned 75 percent of the arable land and farmed it by using servants, leaseholding tenants, and wage laborers. In their new home they had created a long-lived yeoman society in which farm families owned 70 percent of the land as *freeholders*—without feudal dues or leases.

Farm Families: Women's Place

The Puritans' egalitarianism did not extend to the family, which by law and custom remained a patriarchy. Men claimed power in the state and authority in the family. The Reverend Benjamin Wadsworth of Boston advised women in his pamphlet *The Well-Ordered Family* (1712) that being richer, more intelligent, or of higher social status than their husbands mattered little: "Since he is thy Husband, God has made him the head and set him above thee." Their duty, Wadsworth concluded, was "to love and reverence him."

Throughout their lives women saw at firsthand that their role was a subordinate one. Small girls watched their mothers defer to their fathers. As young adults they learned that their marriage portions were inferior in kind and size to those of their brothers; daughters received not land but money, livestock, or household goods. Ebenezer Chittendon of Guilford, Connecticut, for example, left all his land to his sons, decreeing that "Each Daughter have half so much as Each Son, one half in money and the other half in Cattle."

Throughout New England women were raised to be dutiful helpmeets (helpmates) to their husbands. Farmwives spun thread and yarn from flax or wool and wove it into shirts and gowns. They knitted sweaters and stockings, made candles and soap, churned milk into butter and pressed curds into cheese, brewed malt into beer, preserved meats, and mastered dozens of other household tasks. The most exemplary or "notable" practitioners of these domestic arts won praise from the community, for their labor was crucial to the rural household economy.

Reproduction—being a mother—was no less central a task. Most women married in their early twenties; by their early forties they had given birth to six or seven children, usually delivered with the aid of midwives. A large family sapped a woman's emotional strength, focusing her energies on domestic activities for about twenty of her most active years. A Massachusetts mother explained that she had no time for religious activities because "the care of my Babes takes up so large a portion of my time and attention."

In long-settled communities a gradual reduction in farm size prompted many couples to have fewer children. After 1750 women in Andover, Massachusetts, bore an average of only four children and thus gained the time and energy to pursue other tasks. Farm women made extra yarn, cloth, or cheese to exchange with neighbors or sell to shopkeepers, enhancing their families' standard of living. Or, like Susan Huntington of Boston (who had the good fortune to be rich), they spent more time in "the care & culture of children, and the perusal of necessary books, including the scriptures."

Yet women's lives remained tightly bound by a web of legal and cultural restrictions. While ministers often praised the piety of the women in their

Tavern Culture
By the eighteenth century many taverns were run by women, such as this "Charming Patroness," who needed all her charm to deal with the raucous clientele. It was in taverns, declared the puritanical John Adams, that "diseases, vicious habits, bastards, and legislators are frequently begotten."

congregations, they excluded them from church governance. Thus, after Hannah Heaton questioned the authority of her Congregationalist minister, thinking him unconverted and a "blind guide," she quit her husband's church and sought out one of the few sects (mostly Quaker or Baptist) that welcomed questioning women and allowed them to become spiritual leaders. But Heaton was an exception. Most women in New England remained constrained by the conventional view that, as Timothy Dwight put it, women should be "employed only in and about the house and in the proper business of the sex."

Farm Property: Inheritance

As the base of early American economic life, land was much prized. "The hope of having land of their own & becoming independent of Landlords is what chiefly induces people into America," an official reported in the 1730s. But acquiring a farmstead was only the first step toward independence, because most migrating Europeans also wanted to provide for the next generation. Parents who were propertyless or poor indentured their sons and daughters to more prosperous households, where they would have enough to eat and could learn the ways of the world. When the indentures ended at age eighteen or twenty-one, the more ambitious young men would begin the slow ten- to twenty-year climb up the agricultural ladder, from servant to laborer to tenant and finally to freeholder. Luckier sons and daughters in successful farm families received a marriage portion when they reached marriageable age—usually twenty-three to twenty-five.

The *marriage portion*—land, livestock, or farm equipment—served several purposes, both repaying children for their labor and ensuring their loyalty during their parents' old age. It also allowed parents to choose their children's partners, which they did not hesitate to do because everyone's future prosperity depended on a wise choice. Normally, children had the right to refuse an unacceptable match, but they did not have the luxury of "falling in love" with whomever they pleased.

Marriage under English common law was hardly a contract between equals. A bride relinquished to her husband the legal ownership of her land and personal property. After her husband's death, she received the right to use (but not to sell) a third of the family's estate. Death or remarriage canceled this use-right, and her portion was divided among the children. In this way the widow's property rights were subordinated to those of the family "line," which stretched, through the children, across the generations.

To preserve the ideal of a freehold society based on family property, some fathers willed the farm to a male child, specifying that it remain undivided and in the family forever. These fathers provided their other children with money, apprenticeship contracts, or frontier tracts with which to become freeholders in other communities. Other parents required the oldest son to pay money or goods to the younger children in return for the family farm. Finally, some yeomen moved to frontier regions, where life was hard but land for the children was cheap and abundant. "The Squire's House stands on the Bank of the Susquehannah," the traveler Philip Fithian reported from the Pennsylvania backcountry. "He tells me that he will be able to settle all his sons and his fair Daughter Betsy on the Fat of the Earth."

The historic accomplishment of these farmers was the creation of whole communities composed of independent property owners. A French visitor remarked on the sense of personal worth and dignity in this rural world, which contrasted sharply with European peasant life. Throughout the northern colonies, he wrote, he had found "men and women whose features are not marked by poverty, by lifelong deprivation of the necessities of life, or by a feeling that they are insignificant subjects and subservient members of society."

The Crisis of Freehold Society

With each generation the population of New England doubled, mostly as a result of natural increase. The Puritan colonies had about 100,000 people in 1700, 200,000 in 1725, and almost 400,000 in 1750. In long-settled areas farms had been divided and subdivided, leaving parents in a quandary. In the 1740s the Reverend Samuel Chandler of Andover, Massachusetts, was "much distressed for land for his children," seven of whom were boys. By the 1750s in the neighboring town of Concord, about 60 percent of farmers owned less land than their fathers had.

Because parents had less to give their children, they had less control over their lives. The system of arranged marriages broke down as young people engaged in premarital sex and then used pregnancy to win their fathers' permission to marry. Throughout New England the number of firstborn children conceived before marriage rose spectacularly, from about 10 percent in the 1710s to 30 percent or more in the 1740s. Given another chance, young people "would do the same again," an Anglican minister observed, "because otherwise they could not obtain their parents' consent to marry."

New England families met the threat to the freeholder ideal through a variety of strategies. Many parents chose to have smaller families by using primitive methods of birth control. Others joined with neighbors to petition the provincial government for new land grants. As they moved inland—eventually into New Hampshire and the future Vermont—they hacked new communities out of the forest. Still others used their small plots in established communities more productively, replacing the traditional English crops of wheat and barley with high-yielding potatoes and Indian corn. Corn offered a hearty food for humans, and its leaves furnished feed for cattle and pigs, which in turn provided milk and meat. In time New England developed a livestock economy, becoming the major supplier of salted and pickled meat to the West Indies. By 1770 preserved meat accounted for about 5 percent of the value of all exports from the mainland colonies.

Finally, New England farmers compensated for their smaller plots by exchanging goods and labor, developing the full potential of what one historian has called the "household mode of production." Men lent each other tools, draft animals, and grazing land. Women and children joined other families in spinning yarn, sewing quilts, and shucking corn. Farmers plowed fields owned by artisans and shopkeepers, who repaid them with shoes, furniture, or store credit. Typically, no money changed hands; instead, farmers, artisans, and shopkeepers recorded their debts and credits in personal account books and every few years "balanced" the books by transferring small amounts of cash. The system allowed households—and the entire economy—to achieve maximum output, preserving the freehold ideal.

THE MID-ATLANTIC: TOWARD A NEW SOCIETY, 1720–1765

Unlike New England, which was settled mostly by English Puritans, the mid-Atlantic colonies of New York, New Jersey, and Pennsylvania became home to peoples of differing origins, languages, and religions. Strong ethnic and linguistic ties bound German settlers to one another, as did deep sectarian loyalties among Scots-Irish Presbyterians, English and Welsh Quakers, German Lutherans, and Dutch Reformed Protestants.

Opportunity and Equality

Ample fertile land and a long growing season attracted migrants to the mid-Atlantic, and profits from wheat financed its settlement. Between 1720 and 1770 wheat prices doubled because of a population explosion in Western Europe. By 1770 the value of the wheat, corn, flour, and bread shipped from the middle colonies to Europe and the West Indies amounted to over 15 percent of all mainland exports. This prosperity helped the combined population of New York, New Jersey, and Pennsylvania surge from 50,000 in 1700 to 120,000 in 1720 and 350,000 in 1765.

As the population rose, so did the demand for land. Nonetheless, many migrants refused to settle in New York's Hudson River Valley, which, unlike the predominantly freehold colonies of Pennsylvania, New Jersey, and New England, was inhabited primarily by tenant farmers. There, long-established Dutch families presided over manors created by the Dutch West India Company and wealthy English families, such as the Morris and Heathcote clans, dominated vast tracts granted by early English governors (see Map. 4.1). These propertied families sought to live like European gentry, but few migrants were interested in becoming their tenants. In 1714 only 82 tenants lived on the vast manor of Rensselaerswyck. But as freehold land became scarce in eastern New York, more families were forced to accept tenancy leases. Manorial lords attracted tenants by granting them long leases and the right to sell any improvements they made to the next tenant. Thus, Rensselaerswyck had 345 tenants in 1752 and nearly 700 by 1765.

Most tenant families hoped that with hard work and luck they could acquire freehold farmsteads. But though these grain-growing farmers prospered, they rarely became rich because preindustrial technology limited their output. One worker with a hand sickle could reap only half an acre a day; any ripe uncut grain promptly sprouted and became useless. The cradle scythe, an agricultural tool introduced during the 1750s, doubled or tripled the amount of grain a worker could cut. Even so, a family with two adult workers could not harvest more than about 15 acres of wheat in a growing season, a yield of perhaps 150 to 180 bushels of grain. After family needs were met, the remaining surplus might be worth £15—enough to buy salt and sugar, tools, cloth, and perhaps a few acres of land.

Unlike New York, rural Pennsylvania was initially a land of equality. In Chester County the original migrants arrived with approximately equal resources. They lived simply in small houses with one or two rooms, a sleeping loft, a few benches or stools, some wooden trenchers (platters), and a few wooden noggins (cups). Only the wealthiest families ate off pewter or ceramic plates imported from England or Holland. The rise of the wheat trade and an influx of poor settlers introduced marked social divisions. By the 1760s some Chester County farmers had grown wealthy by hiring propertyless laborers to raise large quantities of wheat for market sale. Others had become successful entrepreneurs, providing newly arrived settlers with land, equipment, goods, and services. Gradually a new class of wealthy agricultural capitalists—large-scale

MAP 4.1

The Hudson River Manors
Dutch and English manorial lords dominated the fertile eastern shores of the Hudson River Valley, leasing small farms to German tenant families and refusing to sell land to migrants from overcrowded New England. This powerful elite produced leading American families, such as the Roosevelts.

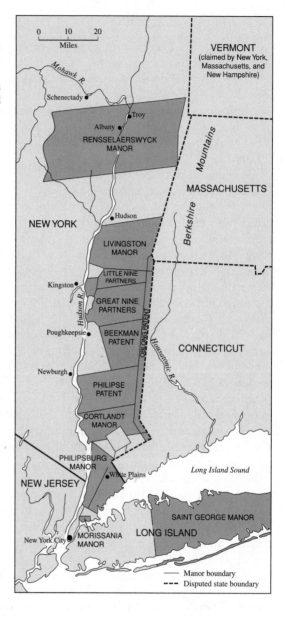

farmers, rural landlords, speculators, storekeepers, and gristmill operators—accumulated estates that included mahogany tables, four-poster beds, couches, table linen, and imported Dutch dinnerware.

At the bottom of the social order nearly half of all white men were propertyless. Some landless men, the sons of property owners, would eventually inherit at least part of the family estate, but just as many were Scots-Irish *inmates*—single men or families "such as live in small cottages and have no taxable property, except a cow." In the predominantly German settlement of Lancaster, Pennsylvania, a merchant noted an "abundance of Poor people" who "maintain their Families with great difficulty by day Labour." Although Scots-Irish and German migrants hoped to become tenants and eventually landowners, a sharp rise in land prices prevented many from realizing their dreams.

Merchants and artisans took advantage of the ample supply of labor by organizing a putting-out system. They bought wool or flax from large-scale producers and paid propertyless workers and subsistence farmers to spin it into yarn or weave it into cloth. An English traveler reported in the 1760s that hundreds of Pennsylvanians had turned "to manufacture, and live upon a small farm, as in many parts of England." Indeed, in many places the colonies had become as crowded and socially divided as rural England (see American Voices, p. 94), and many farm families feared—with good reason—a return to the lowly status of the European peasant.

Ethnic Diversity

The middle colonies were not a melting pot in which European cultures blended into a homogeneous "American" outlook; they were a patchwork of ethnically and religiously diverse communities. A traveler in Philadelphia in 1748 found no fewer than twelve religious denominations, including Anglicans, Quakers, Swedish and German Lutherans, Scots-Irish Presbyterians, and even Roman Catholics. Large communities of German sectarians, such as the Moravians in Bethlehem and Nazareth, Pennsylvania, added to this diversity.

Migrants usually kept their ethnic identities, often by marrying within their own groups or maintaining the customs of their native lands. The major exception were the Huguenots, Calvinists expelled from France who settled in New York and various seacoast cities; they gradually lost their French ethnic identity by intermarrying with other Protestants. More typical were the Welsh Quakers. Seventy percent of the children of the original Welsh migrants to Chester County, Pennsylvania, married other Welsh Quakers, as did 60 percent of the third generation.

Members of the Society of Friends (Quakers) became the dominant social group in Pennsylvania, at first because of their numbers and later, despite a huge influx of new migrants after 1720, because of their wealth and influence. Quakers controlled Pennsylvania's representative assembly until the 1750s and exercised considerable power in New Jersey. Pacifists, they avoided war with native Americans. In 1682 William Penn negotiated a treaty with the Delaware Indians; later the Pennsylvania government purchased land from the Indians rather than seizing it by force. These conciliatory policies enabled Pennsylvania to avoid a major Indian war until the 1750s, unlike the other British colonies. Some Quakers extended their egalitarian values to their relations with blacks. After 1750 most Quaker meetings condemned the institution of slavery, and some expelled members who continued to keep slaves.

The Distress of an Indentured Servant

B*etween 1720 and 1775 thousands of poor Europeans came to the mainland colonies as indentured servants and were sold to the highest bidder. "They sell the servants here as they do their horses, and advertise them as they do their beef and oatmeal," wrote an astonished British officer. James Revel, a servant sold to a planter in the Virginia backcountry, described his ordeal in verse.*

Some view'd our limbs, and other's turn'd us round,
Examining like Horses, if we're sound,
What trade are you, my Lad, says one to me,
A Tin-man, Sir, that will not do, says he.
   Some felt our hands and view'd our legs and feet,
And made us walk, to see we were compleat; . . .
   If any like our look, our limbs, our trade,
The Captain then a good advantage made. . . .

Down to the harbour I was took again,
   On board of a sloop, and loaded with a chain;
Which I was forc'd to wear both night and day,
For fear I from the sloop should get away. . . .
   And when the sloop with loading home was sent
An hundred mile we up the river went
The weather cold and very hard my fare,
My lodging on the deck both hard and bare,
   At last to my new master's house I came,
At the town of Wicoccomoco call'd by name,
Where my Europian clothes were took from me,
Which never after I again could see.
   A canvas shirt and trowsers then they gave,
With a hop-sack frock in which I was to slave:
No shoes nor stocking had I for to wear,
Nor hat, nor cap, both head and feet were bare.
   Thus dress'd into the Field I must next go,
Amongst tobacco plants all day to hoe,
At day break in the morn our work begun,
And so held to the setting of the Sun.

SOURCE: Bernard Bailyn, *Voyagers to the West* (New York: Knopf, 1986), pp. 327, 348.

The Quaker vision of a "peaceable kingdom" attracted many Europeans seeking freedom and opportunity, including Germans who fled from war, religious persecution, and poverty in their homeland. First to arrive, in 1683, was a group of Mennonites attracted by a pamphlet promising religious freedom. In the 1720s religious upheaval and population growth in southwestern Germany and Switzerland stimulated a wave of migrants. "Wages were far better," Heinrich Schneebeli reported to his friends in Zurich after an exploratory trip to Pennsylvania, and "one also enjoyed there a free unhindered exercise of religion." Beginning in 1749, thousands of Germans and Swiss fled their overcrowded and war-torn societies; by 1756, 37,000 of these migrants had landed in Philadelphia.

German settlements soon dominated certain areas of Pennsylvania, while other groups moved down the Shenandoah Valley into the western parts of Maryland, Virginia, and the Carolinas. Some Germans and Swiss came to America as *redemptioners*—a type of indentured servant—but many more came with some resources, determined to improve the lives of their children.

Most German migrants were content to live in a British-defined political community, for few came from the governing classes and many rejected political activism on religious grounds. They slid easily into the status of loyal subjects of the German-born (and German-speaking) king of England, engaging in politics only to protect their religious liberty and property

A Quaker Meeting for Worship
Quakers met for worship in plain, unadorned buildings and sat in silence, waiting for inspiration by the "inner light." In this British work, entitled *Quaker Meeting*, an elder (his hat hung on a peg above his head) speaks to the congregation. Women spoke frequently, an experience that prepared Quaker women to play a leading role in the nineteenth-century women's rights movement. (Museum of Fine Arts, Boston)

rights—insisting, for example, that as in Germany, married women should have property rights. Moreover, they guarded their language and cultural heritage carefully, encouraging their American-born children to take marriage partners of their own ancestry. A minister in North Carolina admonished his congregation "not to contract any marriages with the English or Irish," explaining that "we owe it to our native country to do our part that German blood and the German language be preserved in America." Thus, these migrants and their descendants spoke to each other and read newspapers in German, conducted church services in German, and preserved German agricultural practices. English visitors to the middle colonies remarked that German women were "always in the fields, meadows, stables, etc. and do not dislike any work whatsoever."

The Scots-Irish formed the largest group of eighteenth-century migrants from Europe, some 150,000 in number. They were the descendants of Presbyterian Scots who around 1650 had been sent to Ireland to bolster English control of its Catholic population. Once in Ireland, however, the Scots had faced discrimination and economic regulation by the English. The Test Act of 1704 excluded Scottish Presbyterians as well as Irish Catholics from holding public office in Ireland. English mercantilist regulations placed heavy import duties on the woolen goods Scots-Irish weavers produced, and Scots-Irish farmers were heavily taxed. "Read this letter, Rev. Baptist Boyd," a New York settler wrote back to his minister, "and tell all the poor folk of ye place that God has opened a door for their deliverance . . . all that a man works for is his own; there are no revenue hounds [tax collectors] to take it from us here." Lured by such reports, after 1720 thousands of Scots-Irish sailed for Philadelphia and then migrated to central Pennsylvania and southward down the Shenandoah Valley into Maryland and Virginia. Like the Germans, the Scots-Irish were determined to keep their culture. They held to their Presbyterian faith and promoted marriage within the church.

A Pluralistic Society

In Western Europe religious pluralism was condemned, and even in America most ministers remained committed to an established church and government enforcement of religious rules. Throughout Pennsylvania "the preachers do not have the power to punish anyone, or to force anyone to go to church," complained the minister Gottlieb Mittelberger. As a result, "Sunday is very badly kept. Many people plough, reap, thresh, hew or split wood and the like." Thus, Mittelberger concluded, "Liberty in Pennsylvania does more harm than good to many people, both in soul and body."

However, religious sects in Pennsylvania enforced moral behavior among their members through communal self-discipline. For example, each Quaker family attended a weekly worship meeting and a monthly discipline meeting. Four times a year a committee met with each family to make certain the children were receiving proper religious instruction. The committee also reported on the moral behavior of adults; a Chester County meeting disciplined one of its members "to reclaim him from drinking to excess and keeping vain company." Permission to marry was granted only to couples with sufficient land, livestock, and equipment to support themselves and their future children. The children of well-to-do Friends received ample marriage portions and usually married within the sect, while those who lacked resources remained unmarried or married non-Quakers. In Chester County about two-thirds of the young men and women who married outside the faith were barred from Quaker meetings. Thus, communal sanctions effectively sustained a self-contained and prosperous Quaker community.

In the 1750s Quaker dominance in Pennsylvania finally came under attack. Scots-Irish Presbyterians on the frontier challenged the pacifism of the Quaker-dominated assembly, demanding a more aggressive Indian policy. Many of the newer German migrants also opposed the Quakers; they wanted laws that respected their inheritance customs and representation in proportion to their numbers in the provincial assembly. As an observer noted, Scots-Irish Presbyterians, German Baptists, and German Lutherans had begun to form "a general confederacy" against the Quakers; but they found it difficult to unite because of "a mutual jealousy, for religious zeal is secretly burning."

During the 1760s and again during the War for Independence, latent religious and ethnic passions would break out, yet the mid-Atlantic experiment in freedom and diversity would survive. In the centuries to come cultural pluralism, an open political order, and passionate ethnic and social conflicts would characterize much of American society.

THE ENLIGHTENMENT AND THE GREAT AWAKENING, 1740–1765

Two great European cultural movements reached America between the 1730s and the 1760s: the Enlightenment and Pietism. The *Enlightenment*, which emphasized the power of human reason to shape the world, appealed especially to better-educated men and women from merchant or planter families and to urban artisans. *Pietism*, an emotional, evangelical religious movement that stressed a Christian's relation to God, attracted many social groups, especially farmers and urban laborers. The two movements promoted independent thinking in different ways; together they transformed American intellectual and cultural life.

The Enlightenment in America

Most early Americans relied on religious precepts or folk wisdom to explain the workings of the natural world. Thus, Swedish settlers in Pennsylvania attributed magical powers to the great white mullein, a common wildflower.

When they had a fever, a traveler reported, they would "tie the leaves around their feet and arms." Even educated people believed that events occurred for reasons that today would be considered magical. When a measles epidemic struck Boston in the 1710s, the Puritan minister Cotton Mather tried to contain it by "getting the Blood of the Great Passover sprinkled on our Houses." Like most Christians, Mather believed that the earth stood at the center of the universe and that God intervened directly in human affairs.

Early Americans held to these beliefs despite the Scientific Revolution, which had challenged both traditional Christian and folk world views. As early as the 1530s the astronomer Copernicus had observed that the earth traveled around the sun, rather than vice versa, implying a more modest place for humans in the universe. Other scholars had conducted experiments using empirical methods—actual observed experience—to learn about natural phenomena. Eventually the English scientist Isaac Newton, in his *Principia Mathematica* (1687), used mathematics to explain the movement of the planets around the sun. Newton's laws of motion and concept of gravity described how the universe could operate without God's constant intervention, undermining traditional Christian explanations of the cosmos.

In the century between the publication of Newton's book and the outbreak of the French Revolution in 1789, the philosophers of the European Enlightenment applied scientific reasoning to all aspects of life, including social institutions and human behavior. Enlightenment thinkers believed that human beings could observe, analyze, understand, and improve their world. They advanced four fundamental principles: the lawlike order of the natural world, the power of human reason, the natural rights of individuals (including the right to self-government), and the progressive improvement of society.

In his *Essay Concerning Human Understanding* (1690), John Locke emphasized the impact of environment, experience, and reason on human behavior, proposing that the character of individuals and societies was not fixed by God's will but could be changed through education and purposeful action. His *Two Treatises on Government* (1690) advanced a revolutionary theory: political authority was not divinely ordained but sprang from "*social compacts*" people made to preserve their "natural rights" to life, liberty, and property. In Locke's view, not princes but people conferred political legitimacy, so that governments might change through the decision of a majority.

The Enlightenment ideas of Locke and others came to America with books and travelers and quickly affected educated colonists' conceptions of religion, science, and politics. As early as the 1710s the Reverend John Wise of Ipswich, Massachusetts, combined Locke's political principles with Calvinist theology to defend the decision of Congregational churches to vest power in lay members. Wise argued that just as the "social compact" formed the basis of political society, the religious covenant made the congregation—not bishops or monarchs, as in the Church of England—the interpreter of spiritual authority. When a smallpox epidemic threatened Boston in the 1720s, Cotton Mather sought a scientific rather than a religious remedy, joining with a prominent Boston physician to support the new technique of inoculation.

Enlightenment Philanthropy: The Philadelphia Hospital
This imposing structure, built in 1753, embodied two Enlightenment principles: purposeful action could improve society, and the world should express reason and order, exhibited here in the symmetrical facade. Etchings such as this one, *A Southeast Prospect of the Pennsylvania Hospital*, c. 1761, by John Streeper and Henry Dawkins, bolstered Philadelphia's reputation as the center of the American Enlightenment.

The epitome of the Enlightenment in America was Benjamin Franklin. Born in Boston in 1706 to a devout Calvinist family and apprenticed to a printer as a youth, Franklin became a self-made, self-taught man. As a tradesman, printer, and journalist in Philadelphia, he formed "a club of mutual improvement" which met weekly to discuss "Morals, Politics, or Natural Philosophy." Franklin's imagination was shaped by Enlightenment literature, not by the Bible. In fact, as he explained in his *Autobiography*, "from the different books I read, I began to doubt of Revelation itself."

Like many urban artisans, wealthy Virginia planters, and affluent seaport merchants, Franklin became a *deist*. Influenced by Enlightenment science, deists believed that God had created the world but allowed it to operate in accordance with the laws of nature. The deists' God was a rational being, a divine "watchmaker" who did not intervene directly in history or in people's lives. Rejecting the authority of the Bible, deists relied on people's "natural reason" to define a moral code. Adherence to the code, they believed, would be rewarded by God after death.

Franklin popularized the practical outlook of the Enlightenment—in *Poor Richard's Almanac*, which was read by thousands—and contributed to it himself. In 1743 he helped found the American Philosophical Society, an institution devoted to "the promotion of useful knowledge"; he invented bifocal lenses for eyeglasses, an improved stove (the Franklin stove), and the lightning rod. Franklin's book on electricity, first published in England in 1751, was praised by the English scientist Joseph Priestley as the greatest contribution to science since Newton.

Franklin's city, Philadelphia, became the showplace of the American Enlightenment, boasting a circulating library filled with the latest scientific treatises from Europe and the first American medical school (1765). Quaker and Anglican merchants built a Hospital for the Sick Poor in 1751 and in 1767 added a Bettering House to shelter the aged and disabled and offer employment to the poor. In Philadelphia and other American cities ambitious printers published newspapers and gentleman's magazines, the first significant nonreligious publications to appear in the colonies. Thus, the European Enlightenment added a secular dimension to colonial intellectual life, preparing the way for American contributions to republican political theory during the Revolutionary Era.

Pietism in America

As a few Americans—mostly urban artisans and merchants and wealthy Virginia planters—turned to deism, many other Americans embraced the European devotional movement known as Pietism. Forsaking theological arguments, Pietists emphasized devout, or "pious," behavior, emotional church services, and striving for a mystical union with God. Their teachings came to America with German migrants in the 1720s and sparked a religious revival among many farmers, artisans, and laborers. In Pennsylvania and New Jersey the Dutch minister Theodore Jacob Frelinghuysen moved from church to church, preaching rousing, emotional sermons to German settlers. In private prayer meetings he harnessed their enthusiasm and encouraged lay members to preach a message of spiritual urgency to growing congregations. A decade later William Tennent and his son Gilbert, Presbyterian clergymen who copied Frelinghuysen's approach, led revivals among Scots-Irish migrants in the same area.

Simultaneously, an American pietistic movement was born in Puritan New England. Puritanism had begun in England during the 1580s as part of an earlier pietistic upsurge, but over the decades many Puritan congregations had lost their religious zeal. In the 1730s the minister Jonathan Edwards sought to restore spiritual commitment to the Congregational churches in the Connecticut River Valley. A philosopher as well as an effective preacher, Edwards urged his hearers—especially young men and women—to commit themselves to a life of piety and prayer.

George Whitefield, a young English evangelist, transformed the local revivals into a "Great Awakening" that spanned the mainland settlements. Whitefield had experienced conversion after reading German pietistic tracts and was influenced by John Wesley, the founder of English Methodism, who combined enthusiastic preaching with disciplined "methods" of worship. Whitefield carried Wesley's style to America and enjoyed equally great success, preaching throughout the mainland colonies from 1739 to 1741.

From Georgia to Massachusetts huge crowds of "enthusiasts" greeted the young preacher. "Religion is become the Subject of most Conversations," the *Pennsylvania Gazette* reported. "No books are in Request but those of Piety and Devotion." The usually skeptical and restrained Benjamin Franklin was so impressed by Whitefield's oratory that when the preacher asked for contributions, Franklin emptied his pockets "wholly into the collector's dish, gold and all." By the time the evangelist reached Boston, the Reverend Benjamin Colman reported, the people were "ready to receive him as an angel of God."

Whitefield owed his appeal partly to his compelling personal presence. "He looked almost Angelical; a young, slim, slender Youth . . . Cloathed with Authority from the Great God," wrote a Connecticut farmer (see American Voices, page 102). Like most evangelical preachers, Whitefield did not read his sermons but spoke from memory, as if inspired, raising his voice for dramatic effect, gesturing eloquently, and making striking use of biblical metaphors. The young preacher evoked a deep emotional response when he impressed on his listeners that they had all sinned and must seek salvation. Hundreds of men and women suddenly felt the "new light" of God's grace within them. Afterward, strengthened and self-confident, these New Lights were prepared to follow in Whitefield's footsteps.

Religious Upheaval in the North

Like all cultural explosions, the pietistic revival was controversial. Conservative ministers such as Charles Chauncy of Boston condemned (and feared) the "cryings out, faintings and convulsions" produced by emotional preaching. These "Old Lights" persuaded the Connecticut legislative assembly to prohibit traveling preachers from speaking to established congregations without the ministers' permission. When Whitefield returned to Connecticut in 1744, he found many pulpits closed to him. But the New Lights won repeal of the law in 1750, resisting attempts by civil authorities to silence them. "I shall bring glory to God in my bonds," a dissident preacher wrote from jail. Dozens of farmers, women, and artisans roamed the countryside, condemning the Old Lights as "unconverted" sinners.

During the Great Awakening both New Lights and Baptists questioned government involvement in religion. In New England many New Lights left the established Congregational Church; by 1754 they had founded 125 "separatist" churches. Other dissidents joined Baptist congregations, which favored a greater separation of church and state. According to the Baptist preacher Isaac Backus, "God never allowed any civil state upon earth to impose religious taxes." In New York and New Jersey the Dutch Reformed Church split in two, as New Lights resisted conservative church authorities in the Netherlands.

The Awakening also challenged the authority of ministers, whose education and biblical knowledge had once commanded respect. Gilbert Tennent questioned those qualifications in an influential pamphlet, *The Dangers of an Unconverted Ministry*, maintaining that not theological training but conversion

AMERICAN VOICES

The Power of a Preacher

George Whitefield's reputation as an inspired preacher drew thousands to his sermons, including Nathan Cole and his wife, a Connecticut farm couple.

Now it please God to Send Mr. Whitefield into this land; and my hearing of his preaching at Philadelphia, like one of the old apostles . . . I felt the Spirit of God drawing me by conviction; I longed to see and hear him and wished he would come this way. . . . Then of a sudden, in the morning about 8 or 9 of the clock there came a messenger and said Mr. Whitefield . . . is to preach at Middletown this morning at ten of the clock.

And when we came within about half a mile of the road that comes down . . . to Middletown, on high land I saw before me a cloud or fog rising . . . [and] a noise something like a low rumbling thunder and presently found it was the noise of horses' feet coming down the road, and this cloud was a cloud of dust made by the horses' feet . . . and as I drew nearer it seemed like a steady stream of horses and their riders. . . . And when we got to Middletown old meeting house there was a great multitude, it was said to be 3 or 4000 of people, assembled together. . . .

When I saw Mr. Whitefield come upon the scaffold, he looked almost Angelical; a young, slim, slender Youth before some thousands of people with a bold undaunted countenance. And my hearing how God was with him everywhere as he came, it solemnized my mind and put me into a trembling fear before he began to preach; for he looked as if he was cloathed with Authority from the Great God, and a sweet solemnity sat upon his brow, and my hearing him preach gave me a heart wound. By God's blessing my old foundation was broken up, and I saw that my righteousness would not save me.

SOURCE: Merrill Jensen, ed., *American Colonial Documents to 1776 (English Historical Documents*, vol. 9) (New York: Oxford University Press, 1955), pp. 544–545.

qualified ministers to hold office. Reasserting Luther's commitment to the priesthood of all believers, Tennent suggested that anyone who had experienced the saving grace of God could speak with ministerial authority. Not long afterward, the Baptist Isaac Backus celebrated this spiritual democracy, noting that "the common people now claim as good a right to judge and act in matters of religion as civil rulers or the learned clergy."

By joining in religious revivals, farm families reaffirmed a cooperative work ethic and questioned economic competition and the pursuit of wealth. "In any truly Christian society," Tennent explained, "mutual *Love* is the *Band and Cement*"—not the mercenary values of the marketplace. Suspicious of merchants and land speculators and dismayed by the erosion of traditional morality, Jonathan Edwards spoke for many rural Americans when he charged that a "private niggardly spirit" was more suitable "for wolves and other beasts of prey, than for human beings."

As religious enthusiasm spread, churches founded new colleges to educate their youth and train ministers. New Light Presbyterians established the College of New Jersey (Princeton) in 1746, and New York Anglicans founded King's College (Columbia) in 1754. Baptists set up the College of Rhode Island (Brown); the Dutch Reformed Church subsidized Queen's College (Rutgers) in New Jersey. The true intellectual legacy of the Awakening, however, was not education for the few but a new sense of religious authority among the many.

Social and Religious Conflict in the South

In the southern colonies religious conflict took an intensely social form, especially in Virginia. Although the established Church of England was supported by public taxes, it had never ministered to most Virginians. African-Americans (about 40 percent of the population) were generally ignored by the church, and landless whites (another 20 percent) attended irregularly. Middling white freeholders, who accounted for about 35 percent of the population, formed the core of most Anglican congregations. But prominent planters and their families (5 percent of the population) held real power in the church and used their control of parish finances to discipline Anglican ministers. One clergyman complained that dismissal awaited any minister who "had the courage to preach against any Vices taken into favor by the leading Men of his Parish."

The Great Awakening challenged both Anglicanism and the power of elite planters. In 1743 the bricklayer Samuel Morris, inspired by his reading of George Whitefield's sermons, led a group of Virginia Anglicans out of the established church. Seeking a more vital religious experience, Morris and his followers invited New Light Presbyterian ministers from Scots-Irish settlements along the Virginia frontier to lead their prayer meetings. Soon these local revivals spread across the backcountry and into the so-called Tidewater region along the Atlantic coast, threatening the social authority of the Virginia gentry. Planters and their well-dressed families were used to arriving at Church of England services in elaborate carriages drawn by well-bred horses. Some routinely flaunted their power by marching in a body to their seats in the front pews. These potent reminders of the gentry's social superiority would vanish if freeholders attended New Light Presbyterian rather than Church of England services. Moreover, religious pluralism would threaten the gentry's ability to tax the masses to support the established church.

To prevent the spread of New Light doctrines, Virginia's governor denounced the "false teachings," and Anglican justices of the peace closed down Presbyterian meetinghouses. Their harassment kept most white yeomen families and poor tenants within the Church of England, as did the fact that most Presbyterian ministers were highly educated and sought converts mainly among skilled workers and propertied farmers.

By contrast, the evangelical Baptist preachers who came to Virginia in the 1760s drew their congregations primarily from the poor, offering solace and hope in a troubled world. Their central ritual was adult baptism, often by complete immersion in water. Once men and women had experienced the infusion of grace—had been "born again"—they were baptized in an emotional public ceremony that celebrated the Baptists' shared fellowship. During the 1760s thousands of yeomen and tenant farm families in Virginia were drawn to revivalist meetings by the enthusiasm and democratic ways of Baptist preachers.

Even slaves were welcome at Baptist revivals. As early as 1740 George Whitefield had openly condemned the brutality of slaveholders and urged that Africans be brought into the Christian fold. In South Carolina and Georgia a handful of New Light planters took up this challenge, but the hostility of the white population and the commitment of many Africans to their ancestral religions kept the number of converts low. The first sizeable conversion of slaves took place in the 1760s among second- and third-generation African-Americans in Virginia. Hundreds of those slaves, who knew English and English ways, joined Baptist churches run by ministers who taught that all people were equal in God's eyes.

The ruling gentry reacted violently to the Baptists, who posed a threat to their dominance. The Baptists courted blacks and poor whites and emphasized equality by calling one another "brother" and "sister." Baptist preachers urged their followers to work hard and lead virtuous lives and condemned customary pleasures of Chesapeake men such as gambling, drinking, whoring, and cockfighting. In response, Anglican sheriffs and justices of the peace broke up Baptist services by force. In Caroline County, Virginia, an Anglican posse attacked one Brother Waller, who was attempting to pray when, a fellow Baptist reported, "he was violently jerked off the stage; they caught him by the back part of his neck, beat his head against the ground, and a gentleman gave him twenty lashes with his horsewhip." Despite such attacks, about 20 percent of Virginia's whites and hundreds of enslaved blacks had joined Baptist churches by 1775. In the South as in the North, Protestant revivalism was on the way to becoming a dominant American religious tradition.

Although Anglican slaveholders retained their economic and political power in Virginia, the revival gave meaning to the lives of poor families. Through membership in more democratic churches, white yeomen and tenant farmers asserted their economic interests. Moreover, as Baptist ministers spread Christianity among slaves, the cultural gulf between blacks and whites shrank, undermining one justification for slavery and giving blacks a new sense of spiritual identity. Within a generation African-Americans would develop their own versions of Protestant Christianity.

THE MIDCENTURY CHALLENGE: WAR, TRADE, AND LAND, 1750–1765

In 1745 Governor Shirley of Massachusetts predicted that within a century the population of Britain's mainland colonies would equal that of France and "lay a foundation for a Superiority of British power upon the continent of Europe." In fact, this shift in the balance of diplomatic power began within two decades when the colonists joined in a Great War for Empire that undermined French influence not only in Europe but in Asia and America as well.

The French and Indian War

In 1750 the interior of North America was still inhabited by Indians, who intended to remain in control. Most French settlers lived along the St. Lawrence River, near the fur-trading centers of Montreal and Quebec (see Map 4.2). The more numerous British inhabitants had not ventured across the Appalachian Mountains, both because the lands to the west offered few natural transportation routes and because of Indian resistance. For a generation native Americans had bargained for guns and subsidies from British and French officials and firmly resisted the intrusion of white settlers. However, their strategy of playing off the French against the British was breaking down as European governments refused to pay the rising cost of the "gifts" the Indians demanded as part of the "play-off" system. Along the Ohio River the Delaware and Shawnee declared their independence from the Iroquois, creating more instability. To shore up England's alliance with the Six Nations, the Board of Trade called for a great intercolonial meeting with the Iroquois at Albany, New York, in June 1754.

A central issue was the Anglo-American demand for Indian lands, the result of population growth in New England and the South, and the huge migration of Europeans to the middle colonies. In an unsuccessful bid to settle Scottish migrants west of Albany, British agents bestowed manufactured goods on the Mohawk. To the south, Governor Dinwiddie of Virginia and a group of prominent planters organized the Ohio Company in 1749. Supported by influential London merchants, they obtained a royal grant of 200,000 acres along the upper Ohio River, with the promise of 300,000 more. These intrusions infuriated the Iroquois, who complained, "We don't know what you Christians, English and French intend; we are so hemmed in by both, that we have hardly a hunting place left."

Britain's movement into the Ohio Valley alarmed the French, who countered by constructing Fort Duquesne at the point where the Monongahela and Allegheny rivers join to form the Ohio (present-day Pittsburgh). The confrontation escalated in 1754 when Dinwiddie dispatched an expedition led by Colonel George Washington, a young planter eager to speculate in western lands, to support the claims of the Ohio Company. In July 1754 French troops seized Washington and his men, prompting expansionists in Virginia and Britain to demand war. But the British prime minister, Henry Pelham, urged calm: "There is such a load of debt, and such heavy taxes already laid upon the people, that nothing but an absolute necessity can justifie our engaging in a new War."

William Pitt, a rising British statesman, and Lord Halifax, the new head of the Board of Trade, strongly advocated a policy of expansionism in the

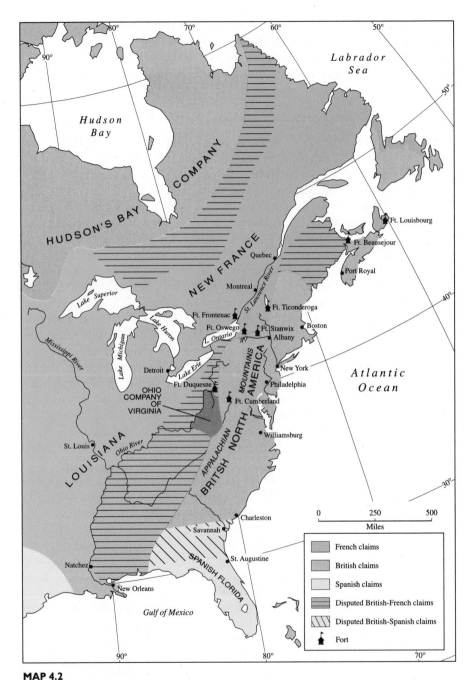

MAP 4.2

European Spheres of Influence, 1754

France laid claim to vast areas of North America and tried to counter the numerical superiority of British settlers through alliances with Indian peoples. For their part, native Americans played off one European power against another. By expelling the French from North America, the Great War for Empire disrupted this system, leaving Indian peoples on their own in resisting Anglo-American settlers.

colonies. Even before news of the fighting reached London, the Board of Trade had considered a proposal for a "union between ye Royal, Proprietary, & Charter Governments," but decided instead to dispatch a military governor-general and ask the colonial assemblies to finance a series of defensive forts. For their part, the Anglo-American delegates to the intercolonial meeting in Albany, New York, responded to the French threat by devising a Plan of Union. Primarily the work of Benjamin Franklin, the Albany Plan proposed that the colonies send delegates to a continental assembly that would assume responsibility for all western affairs: trade, Indian policy, and defense. But the proposed union, which was to be presided over by a royal governor-general, never materialized because the provincial assemblies wanted to preserve their authority and the imperial government feared the consequences of convening the great assembly.

Instead, Halifax and Pitt persuaded the ministry to dispatch naval and military forces to America, where they joined with colonial militia in attacking French forts. In June 1755 British and New England troops captured Fort Beauséjour in Nova Scotia (Acadia) and deported 6,000 Acadians, some of whom eventually settled in Louisiana. In July, as 1,400 British regulars and 450 Virginia militiamen advanced on Fort Duquesne, they were surprised by a small force of French and a larger group of Delaware and Shawnee, who had decided to side with the French. In the ensuing battle the British commander, General Edward Braddock, lost his life and half his troops. "We have been beaten, most shamefully beaten, by a handfull of Men," Washington complained bitterly as he led the survivors back to Virginia.

The Great War for Empire

In 1756 the fighting in America had spread to Europe, where the conflict later became known as the Seven Years' War. Britain and Prussia aligned themselves against France and Austria. When Britain decided to mount major offensives in India and West Africa as well as in North America and the West Indies, the conflict quickly became a Great War for Empire. Britain had reaped unprecedented profits from its overseas trading empire and was determined to crush France, the main obstacle to further expansion.

William Pitt, who was appointed Secretary of State in 1756, was the grandson of the East Indies merchant "Diamond" Pitt and a committed expansionist. Pitt was a haughty man constantly at odds with his colleagues. "I know that I can save this country," he declared, "and that I alone can." Indeed, Pitt was a master of strategy, both commercial and military, and his goal was to cripple France by attacking its colonies. In planning the critical campaign against New France, Pitt exploited a demographic advantage: on the North American mainland, Britain's 2 million subjects outnumbered the French 14 to 1. To mobilize the colonists, Pitt agreed to pay half the cost of their troops and supply them with arms and equipment. He then committed a major British fleet and thousands of British regulars to the American conflict, appointing three young officers— James Wolfe, Jeffrey Amherst, and William Howe—as the top commanders.

In 1758 the British forced the French to abandon Fort Duquesne, which they renamed Fort Pitt, and then captured Louisbourg. The following year Wolfe attacked Quebec; after several failed attacks, 4,000 British troops scaled the high cliffs protecting the city and overwhelmed the French. Quebec's fall was the turning point of the war. The Royal Navy prevented French reinforcements from crossing the Atlantic; when British forces captured Montreal in 1760, the conquest of Canada was complete.

Indian peoples from New York to Michigan grew increasingly concerned as British armies and traders occupied French forts, curtailed their "gifts" and supplies of gunpowder, and used rum to cheat them out of furs. Fearing an influx of Anglo-American settlers, the Ottawa chief Pontiac sought to restore the old French alliance, declaring, "I am French, and I want to die French." Neolin, a Delaware prophet, went further, urging a repudiation of all Europeans and a return to native American traditions. In 1763 Pontiac led a group of loosely confederated tribes in a major uprising, capturing nearly every British garrison west of Fort Niagara and besieging the fort at Detroit. But the Indian alliance gradually weakened, and British military expeditions defeated the Delaware near Fort Pitt and broke the siege of Detroit. In the peace settlement that followed, Pontiac and his allies accepted the British as their new political "fathers." In return, the British addressed the Indians' concerns by temporarily barring Anglo-Americans from settling west of the Appalachians by establishing the Proclamation Line of 1763.

Elsewhere the British went from success to success. Fulfilling Pitt's dream, the East India Company captured French commercial outposts and took control of trade in large sections of India. British forces seized French Senegal in West Africa, the French sugar islands of Martinique and Guadeloupe, and the Spanish colonies of Cuba and the Philippine Islands. When the war ended, Pitt was no longer in office, but his maritime strategy had extended British power around the world.

The Treaty of Paris of 1763 confirmed the triumph, granting Britain sovereignty over half the continent of North America, including French Canada, all French territory east of the Mississippi River, and Spanish Florida. Spain received Louisiana west of the Mississippi, along with the restoration of Cuba and the Philippines. The French empire in North America was reduced to a handful of sugar islands in the West Indies and two rocky islands off the coast of Newfoundland. The transatlantic British empire was at the height of its power.

British Economic Growth

Britain owed its triumph in large part to its unprecedented economic resources. Since 1700, when it had wrested control of many oceanic trade routes from the Dutch, Britain had been the dominant commercial power. By 1750 it was becoming the first country to undergo the Industrial Revolution. New

Pontiac
This portrait depicts Pontiac as both an Indian, symbolized by the necklace of bear claws, and as a European-style ruler with a regal demeanor and a flowing robe. Pontiac did indeed partake of two worlds, absorbing French culture as he asserted his Indian identity.

technology and work discipline made Britain the first—and for over a century the most powerful—nation in the world.

New machines and new business practices were enabling Britain to produce more wool and linens, more iron tools, paper, chinaware, and glass than ever before—and to sell those goods at lower prices. British artisans had designed and built water- and steam-driven machines that powered lathes for shaping wood, jennies and looms for spinning and weaving textiles, and hammers for forging iron. The new machines produced goods far faster than human hands could. Furthermore, the entrepreneurs who ran the new factories drove their employees hard, forcing them to keep pace with the machines and work long hours. To market these products, English and Scottish merchants launched aggressive campaigns in the rapidly growing mainland colonies, extending a full year's credit instead of the traditional six months to American traders. Soon Americans were purchasing 20 percent of all British exports.

This first "consumer revolution" raised the living standard of many Americans. Colonial merchants and storekeepers stocked larger inventories (on credit) and offered credit to their customers, allowing settlers to buy equipment and household goods for their farms. Americans paid for those goods by increasing their agricultural exports. Scottish merchants helped Virginia planters and Scots-Irish migrants settle the Piedmont, a region of plains and rolling hills just inland from the Tidewater counties. They granted the settlers ample credit to purchase land, slaves, and equipment and took their tobacco crop in payment, exporting it to expanding markets in France and central Europe. By the 1760s South Carolina planters were sending indigo valued at £117,000 a year to English textile factories and exporting about 65 million pounds of rice a year to Holland and southern Europe. New York, Pennsylvania, Maryland, and Virginia became the breadbasket of the Atlantic world, supplying Europe's exploding population with wheat at ever increasing profits. In Philadelphia wheat prices jumped almost 50 percent between 1740 and 1765.

This first American spending binge, like most subsequent splurges, landed many consumers in debt. Even during the boom times of the 1750s and 1760s exports paid for only 80 percent of imported British goods. The remaining 20 percent—millions of pounds—was financed by the British merchants who extended credit. Moreover, the boom ended when the war in America wound down and Britain slashed its troop levels and military expenditures. The loss of military markets, contracts, and cash subsidies made it more difficult for Americans to purchase British goods. Merchants looked anxiously at their overstocked warehouses and feared bankruptcy. "I think we have a gloomy prospect before us," a Philadelphian noted in 1765, "as there are of late some Persons failed, who were in no way suspected." The increase in transatlantic trade had raised living standards but also had made Americans more dependent on overseas creditors and international economic conditions.

Land Conflicts and Western Uprisings

In good times or bad the colonial population continued to grow, and that (combined with the shortage of arable land in long-settled areas) caused political conflict over land rights. With each new generation the problem got worse. In 1738 families who traced their American ancestry back four generations had founded the town of Kent, Connecticut, at the generally accepted western boundary of the colony. The next generation had to find somewhere else to go. In 1749 Connecticut farmers formed the Susquehannah Company, and a few years later petitioned the legislature to assert jurisdiction over the

Wyoming Valley in northeastern Pennsylvania, where some of them had settled. But the Penn family reaffirmed its proprietary rights over the valley and issued its own land patents. Soon rival land claimants were burning down one another's houses. To avert further violence the governments of Pennsylvania and Connecticut referred the dispute to the authorities in London, where it remained undecided at the time of independence.

Land disputes also broke out along the imprecise border between New York and Massachusetts, when hundreds of yeomen families from New England moved into the disputed territory and refused to accept tenancy leaseholds from manorial landlords. Instead, the migrants purchased freehold titles from land speculators in Massachusetts and encouraged long-settled Dutch and German tenants to rebel against the landlords. In 1766 New England migrants and tenant farmers in Westchester, Dutchess, and Albany counties refused to pay rent and used mob violence to close the courts. At the behest of the royal governor, General Thomas Gage and two British regiments joined local sheriffs and manorial bailiffs to suppress the tenant uprising and evict the squatters.

Simultaneously, in New Jersey and the southern colonies, resident landowners and English aristocrats revived long-dormant seventeenth-century land charters. Judges supported most of their legal claims. For example, court decisions upheld the right of Lord Granville, an heir of one of the original Carolina proprietors, to collect quitrents in North Carolina and awarded ownership of the entire northern neck of Virginia (along the Potomac) to Lord Fairfax.

This revival of proprietary power underscored the growing strength of the landed gentry and the increasing resemblance between rural societies in Europe and America. High-quality land east of the Appalachians was getting more expensive, and much of it was controlled by English aristocrats, manorial landlords, and wealthy speculators. Tenants and even yeomen farmers feared they soon might be reduced to the status of European peasants.

As farmers moved west in search of cheap freehold land, they found themselves in the middle of disputes over Indian policy, political representation, and debts. In Pennsylvania, Scots-Irish migrants who lived along the frontier wanted to push the Indians out of the colony, but pacifistic Quakers prevented such military action. In 1763 a band of Scots-Irish farmers, the Paxton Boys, took matters into their own hands and massacred twenty native Americans. When Governor John Penn tried to bring the murderers to justice, about 250 armed Scots-Irish advanced on Philadelphia. Benjamin Franklin intercepted the angry mob at Lancaster and arranged a compromise, narrowly averting a battle. Prosecution of the accused men failed for lack of witnesses. Although the Scots-Irish dropped their demand for the expulsion of the Indians, the episode left a legacy of racial hatred and political resentment. A decade later the Scots-Irish would take their revenge against the Indians in the west and the Quaker and Anglican elite in the east.

Violence broke out in the backcountry of South Carolina as well, where land-hungry whites and Cherokee had clashed repeatedly during the war

A Backcountry Road
The first settlers in interior valleys lived in small, crude log cabins that were strung out along the road. Loneliness and desolation, suggested here by a solitary rider, were overcome by concerted efforts to build social communities, often through church-centered activities.

with France. After the war ended in 1763 a group of vigilantes, the Regulators, tried to impose order on outlaw bands of whites roaming the countryside. The Regulators whipped people suspected of poaching or stealing property. They also demanded that the eastern-controlled government provide more local courts, fairer taxes, and greater local representation in the provincial assembly. The eastern-dominated assembly, wanting to suppress the Regulators but fearing slave revolts on lowland rice plantations, refused to send troops to the backcountry. The assembly therefore compromised, creating locally controlled courts in the west and reducing fees for legal documents but refusing to reapportion the legislature or lower western taxes. Eventually a rival group, the Moderators, raised an armed force of its own and forced the Regulators to accept the authority of the colonial government. Like the Paxton Boys in Pennsylvania, the South Carolina Regulators attracted attention to western needs but ultimately failed to wrest power from the eastern elite.

Another political controversy arose in the newly settled backcountry of North Carolina. After the Great War for Empire tobacco prices plummeted, carrying many farmers into debt and into court. Eastern judges directed sheriffs to seize the property of bankrupt farmers and auction it off to pay creditors and court costs. Backcountry farmers resented merchants' lawsuits, not just because they generated high fees for lawyers and court officials but also because they violated local custom. As in rural New England, farmers were used to making loans among neighbors on the basis of mutual trust and often allowed the loans to remain unpaid for years.

To save their farms, North Carolina debtors created their own Regulator movement. They intimidated judges, closed down courts, and broke into jails to free their comrades. But the Regulators also proposed a coherent program of democratic reforms. Their leader, Herman Husband, told his followers not to vote for "any Clerk, Lawyer, or Scotch merchant. We must make these men subject to the laws or they will enslave the whole community." The Regulators demanded passage of a law allowing them to pay their taxes in the "produce of the country" rather than in cash. They also wanted legal fees reduced and (like the South Carolina Regulators) greater legislative representation and fairer taxes so that each person would be taxed "in proportion to the profits arising from his estate." In 1771 the royal governor mobilized the eastern militia and defeated a large Regulator force at the Alamance River; seven insurgent leaders were summarily executed. Not since Leisler's revolt in New York in 1689 had political conflict caused so much bloodshed in America.

In 1771 as in 1689, colonial conflicts became intertwined with imperial politics. In far-off Connecticut the Reverend Ezra Stiles defended the Regulators. "What shall an injured & oppressed people do," he asked, when faced with "Oppression and tyranny (under the name of Government)?" Stiles's remarks reflected growing resistance to British imperial control, a result of the changes that had occurred in the mainland colonies between 1720 and 1765. America was still a dependent society closely tied to Britain by trade, culture, and politics, but it was also an increasingly complex society with the potential for an independent existence. British policies would determine the direction the maturing colonies would take.

CHAPTER 4 TIMELINE

1700s	Freehold ideal in rural communities Arranged marriages common Woman's "place" as subordinate helpmate
1700–1714	New Hudson River manors created
1720s	Germans and Scots-Irish settle in middle colonies
1730s	Enlightenment ideas spread to America Tennents lead Presbyterian revivals Jonathan Edwards preaches in New England
1739	George Whitefield and the Great Awakening
1740–1760s	Population pressure in New England Ethnic pluralism in middle colonies Rising grain and tobacco prices Increasing rural inequality
1740s	Old Lights versus New Lights New colleges founded
1743	Franklin founds American Philosophical Society
1749	Ohio Company; Susquehannah Company
1750s	Industrial Revolution begins in England "Consumer revolution" raises American debt Indian "play-off" system breaks down
1754	French and Indian War begins Albany Congress
1755	French Acadians deported
1759	Fall of Quebec
1760s	New York and New England border conflicts Regulator movements in the Carolinas Evangelical Baptists in Virginia
1763	Treaty of Paris ends Great War for Empire Pontiac leads Indian uprising Paxton Boys in Pennsylvania

TOWARD INDEPENDENCE: YEARS OF DECISION, 1763–1775

- The Reform Movement, 1763–1765
- The Dynamics of Rebellion, 1765–1766
- The Growing Confrontation, 1767–1770
- The Road to War, 1771–1775

As the Great War for Empire ended, the American colonists rejoiced over the triumph of British arms. But twelve years later many of them were angry and had themselves taken up arms to resist British authority. How had it happened, asked the president of King's College in New York, that such a "happily situated" people had decided to "hazard their Fortunes, their Lives, and their Souls, in such a Rebellion"?

Unlike other colonial peoples of the time, Americans lived in a prosperous, stable society with a strong tradition of representative government. This unique historical circumstance created experienced leaders and a self-confident populace capable of supporting an independence movement. When the home government made a determined attempt to reform the imperial system, Americans rebelled. The long overdue but disastrous reforms prompted a violent response which began a downward spiral of political conflict and ideological debate that ended in civil war.

This course of events was hardly predictable in 1765, when the Americans were indeed a "happily situated" people. And it was far from inevitable, for Britain and its colonies had lived for decades in a peaceful and prosperous union. Purposeful British statecraft could have saved the empire. Instead, passionate Patriot agitation brought about its demise.

THE REFORM MOVEMENT, 1763–1765

The Great War for Empire had a mixed legacy. By driving the French out of Canada, Britain had achieved dominance over eastern North America (see Map 5.1). But the cost of the triumph was high: a mountain of debt that prompted the British ministry to impose new taxes on its American possessions and, more fundamentally, to redefine the empire as one not of mercantilist regulation but of imperial dominion.

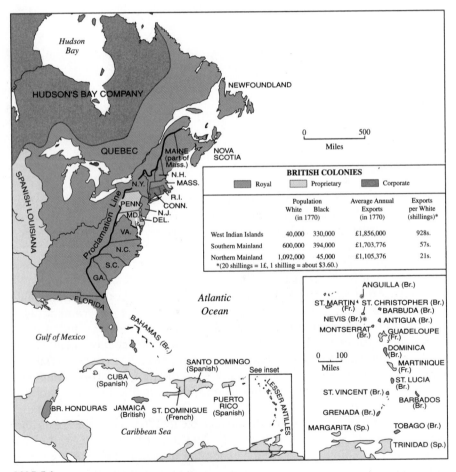

MAP 5.1

Britain's American Empire in 1763

In 1763 Britain was dominant in the West Indies and controlled all of eastern North America. British troops occupied the conquered colonies of Florida and Quebec and sought to prevent Anglo-American settlement west of the Proclamation Line.

The Legacy of War

The war made visible the differences between British and colonial society, for the fighting brought thousands of British troops to the mainland colonies. Many Americans were shocked by the arrogance of upper-crust British officers. British soldiers, a Massachusetts militiaman wrote in his diary, "are but little better than slaves to their officers." The hostility was mutual. General James Wolfe complained that colonial troops were drawn from the dregs of society and that "there was no depending on them in action."

The war also exposed the weakness of British administrative control, especially that of the royal governors. In theory governors had extensive political powers, including command of the provincial militia, but in reality they had to share power with the colonial assemblies. Britain's Board of Trade complained that in Massachusetts "almost every act of executive and legislative power is ordered and directed by votes and resolves of the General Court." This situation, British officials agreed, had to change.

Imperial authorities began by enforcing the Navigation Acts strictly. Before the war American merchants had routinely bribed customs officials to circumvent the Molasses Act of 1733. To curb such corruption, in 1762 Parliament passed a Revenue Act that prohibited English customs appointees from leasing their positions to deputies, who often accepted bribes. In addition, the ministry instructed the Royal Navy to stop the flourishing wartime trade between the mainland colonies and the French islands. The fact that French armies attempting "to Destroy one English province, are actually supported by Bread raised in another" was absurd, declared an outraged British politician.

This more restrictive policy culminated in 1763 with the deployment of a large peacetime army of about 10,000 men in North America. The decision stemmed from a variety of motives. First, the ministry wanted to discourage rebellion by the 60,000 French residents of the newly captured province of Quebec and to protect Florida, which Spain wanted back. Second, Pontiac's rebellion had underscored the need for a substantial military garrison along the frontier both to awe the Indians and to deter land-hungry whites from settling west of the Proclamation Line of 1763. Finally, some British politicians feared that with the French gone from Canada, Americans would seek greater freedom from imperial control. As Henry Knox, a Treasury official who once had served the Crown in Georgia, put it: "The main purpose of Stationing a large Body of Troops in America is to secure the Dependence of the Colonys on Great Britain." By stationing an army in America, the British ministry was indicating its willingness to use force to preserve its authority.

A more immediate problem was Britain's national debt, which had nearly doubled as a result of the war, from £75 million in 1754 to £133 million in 1763. To pay the rising interest charges, Lord Bute, the new prime minister, would have to raise taxes. Treasury officials advised against increasing the land tax, at an all-time high and paid by the propertied classes, whose support the government needed. Bute therefore imposed higher import duties on tobacco and sugar, which manufacturers passed on to British consumers in the form of higher prices. The ministry also increased *excise levies*—essentially sales taxes—on goods such as salt, beer, and distilled spirits, passing along the costs of the war to the king's ordinary subjects.

To collect these taxes and duties, the British government doubled the size and increased the powers of its bureaucracy. Customs agents and informers patrolled the coasts of southern Britain, arresting smugglers and seizing tons of goods, such as French wines and Flemish textiles, on which import duties had not been paid. Convicted smugglers faced heavy penalties, including death or "transportation" to America as indentured servants.

Thus, the price of empire abroad had turned out to be debt and a more powerful government at home—developments that confirmed the worst fears of the opposition, the Radical Whigs and Country Party landlords, who had long emphasized the dangers of a big and expensive government. The Treasury, they charged, was now at the mercy of the "monied interest," the banks and financiers who were reaping millions of pounds in interest from government bonds. The bureaucracy, they protested, was bloated, filled with thousands of "worthless *pensioners* and *placemen*." Worried by this corruption, reformers demanded that Parliament be made more representative. The Radical Whig John Wilkes demanded an end to "rotten boroughs"—tiny districts whose voters were controlled by wealthy aristocrats and merchants. In domestic affairs as in colonial policy, the war had transformed political life, creating a more active and arguably a more oppressive government.

British Reform Strategy

This political transformation was particularly apparent in colonial affairs. A new generation of British officials was determined to reform the imperial system. The first to take action was George Grenville, who became prime minister in 1763. The following year Grenville won enactment of a Currency Act, which protected the financial interests of British merchants by banning the use of paper money as legal tender throughout the colonies. Then he introduced a new Navigation Act, the Sugar Act of 1764, to replace the widely evaded Molasses Act of 1733. Treasury officials had looked closely at the pattern of colonial trade and had convinced Grenville that the mainland settlers had to sell some of their wheat, fish, and lumber in the French islands. Without the molasses, sugar, and bills of exchange those sales brought, the colonists would lack the funds to buy British manufactured goods. Therefore, Treasury officials resisted demands from British sugar planters to cut off trade between the mainland and the French islands by reviving the duty of 6 pence per gallon on French molasses. Instead, they recommended a smaller duty of 3 pence per gallon, arguing that it would allow British molasses to compete with the cheaper French product without destroying the mainland's export trade or distilling industry.

This carefully crafted policy garnered little support among American merchants and manufacturers, however. Many New England traders, such as John

Hancock of Boston, had made their fortunes by smuggling French molasses and thus had never paid the duty. Their profits would be cut severely by the new regulations. These merchants, joined by New England distillers, who feared a rise in the price of molasses, orchestrated a political campaign against the Sugar Act. Publicly, they protested that the new tax would wipe out trade with the French islands. Privately, they vowed to evade the duty by smuggling or by bribing officials. Merchants and their allies also raised constitutional objections to the new legislation. The speaker of the Massachusetts House of Representatives argued that the duties constituted a tax, so that the Sugar Act was "contrary to a fundamental Principall of our Constitution: That all Taxes ought to originate with the people."

The Sugar Act of 1764 raised other constitutional issues as well. To enforce the duties, the act extended the jurisdiction of *vice-admiralty courts*—maritime tribunals composed only of a judge—denying the accused a hearing before a common-law jury. For half a century colonial legislatures had vigorously opposed vice-admiralty courts; to limit their power, lawmakers had extended the jurisdiction of colonial courts to cover customs offenses occurring in the seaports or coastal waters. As a result, merchants charged with violating the Navigation Acts often were tried in common-law courts and acquitted by local juries. By extending the jurisdiction of vice-admiralty courts to all customs offenses wherever they occurred, the Sugar Act closed this loophole.

The powers given to the vice-admiralty courts revived old American fears and raised new constitutional objections. An influential Virginia planter charged that the courts illegally discriminated against British subjects living in America: the colonists "were not sent out to be the Slaves but to be the Equals of those that remained behind," he asserted. John Adams, a young Massachusetts lawyer who was defending John Hancock on a charge of smuggling, took a similar position. "Is there not in this Clause a Brand of Infamy, or Degradation, and Disgrace, fixed upon every American?" Adams demanded to know. "Is he not degraded below the rank of an Englishman?"

Although the logic of these arguments was compelling, some of the facts were wrong. The new vice-admiralty legislation did not discriminate against Americans but simply extended British legal practices to America. Vice-admiralty courts had long played a major role in Britain, where they were unpopular among both smugglers and political leaders who feared unbridled royal power. The real issue was the growing authority of the British state. Having lived for decades under a policy of salutary neglect, Americans knew that the new British policy challenged the existing constitutional structure of the empire. As a committee of the Massachusetts House put it, the Sugar Act and other British edicts "have a tendency to deprive the colonies of some of their most essential Rights as British subjects."

For their part, British officials insisted on Parliament's supremacy and denied that the colonists could claim the privileges inscribed in their royal charters or the traditional rights of Englishmen. When Royal Governor Francis Bernard of Massachusetts heard that the Massachusetts assembly had objected to the Sugar Act, claiming no taxation without representation, he asserted that Americans did not have that constitutional right. "The rule that a *British* subject shall not be bound by laws or liable to taxes, but what he has consented to by his representatives," Bernard argued, "must be confined to the inhabitants of Great Britain only." In the eyes of most British officials and politicians, Americans were second-class subjects of the king, their rights limited by the Navigation Acts and the national interests of the British state, as determined by Parliament.

The Stamp Act

The issue of taxation brought about the first great imperial crisis. When Grenville introduced the Sugar Act, he also announced his intention to seek a stamp tax to cover part of the cost of keeping 10,000 British troops in America—some £200,000 per year (about $15 million today). The new tax would raise revenue by requiring stamps (similar to modern postage stamps) on court documents, land titles, contracts, playing cards, newspapers, and other printed items. A similar English tax that had been levied since 1694

George Grenville, Architect of the Stamp Act
As prime minister from 1764 to 1766, Grenville assumed leadership of the movement for imperial reform and taxation. But most British politicians believed that the colonies should be better regulated and share the cost of the empire.

was yielding an annual revenue of £290,000; Grenville hoped the American levy would raise at least £60,000 a year. The prime minister knew that some Americans would object to the tax on constitutional grounds, and so he asked explicitly whether any member of the House of Commons doubted "the power and sovereignty of Parliament over every part of the British dominions, for the purpose of raising or collecting any tax." No one rose to object.

Confident of Parliament's support, Grenville vowed to impose a stamp tax in 1765. This challenge threw the London agents of the colonial legislatures into confusion. They all agreed that the assemblies could not apportion their defense budget among themselves; the colonies had met together only once, at the Albany Congress of 1754, and not a single assembly had accepted that body's proposals.

Benjamin Franklin, representing the Pennsylvania assembly, countered Grenville's initiative with an innovative proposal for American representation in Parliament. "If you chuse to tax us," he suggested to a British friend, "give us Members in your Legislature, and let us be one People." But with the exception of William Pitt, British politicians rejected Franklin's radical idea. They argued that the colonists were "virtually" represented in the home legislature by the merchants who sat in Parliament and by other members with interests in America. Colonial leaders were equally skeptical of Franklin's plan; Americans were "situate at a great Distance from their Mother Country," the Connecticut assembly declared in a printed pamphlet that was quickly sent to London, and therefore "cannot participate in the general Legislature of the Nation." Influential merchants in Philadelphia, worried that a handful of colonial delegates would be powerless in Parliament, warned Franklin "to beware of any measure that might extend to us seats in the Commons."

The way was clear for Grenville to introduce the Stamp Act both to raise revenue and to assert a constitutional principle, "the Right of Parliament to lay an internal Tax upon the Colonies," as his chief assistant observed. The ministry's plan worked smoothly. The House of Commons refused to accept American petitions opposing the act and passed the new legislation by an overwhelming vote of 205 to 49. At the request of General Thomas Gage, commander of British military forces in America, Parliament also passed a Quartering Act that directed colonial governments to provide barracks and food for the British troops stationed in the colonies. Finally, Parliament approved Grenville's proposal that violations of the Stamp Act be tried in vice-admiralty courts.

The design was complete. Using the doctrine of Parliamentary supremacy, Grenville had begun to fashion a genuinely imperial administrative system, run by British officials without regard for the American assemblies. He thus provoked a constitutional confrontation not only on the specific issues of taxation, jury trials, and quartering of the military but on the fundamental question of representative self-government.

THE DYNAMICS OF REBELLION, 1765–1766

Grenville had thrown down the gauntlet to the Americans. Although the colonists had often opposed unpopular laws and arbitrary governors, they had never before faced a reform-minded ministry and Parliament. But Patriots— as the defenders of American rights came to be called—took up Grenville's challenge, organizing to protest the acts, rioting in the streets, and delivering speeches that bordered on treason.

The Crowd Rebels

In May 1765 the eloquent young Virginian Patrick Henry addressed the House of Burgesses and blamed the legislation on the new king, George III (1760–1820). Comparing George to the tyrannical Charles I, Henry seemed to call for a new republican revolution. Dismayed by Henry's nearly treasonous remarks, the Burgesses nonetheless endorsed his attack on the Stamp Act, declaring that any attempt to tax the colonists without their consent "has a manifest Tendency to Destroy American freedom." In Massachusetts, James Otis, another republican-minded firebrand, persuaded the House of Representatives to call for a general meeting of all the colonies in New York in October to consider a "loyal and humble representation" to the king and Parliament "to implore Relief" from the act.

Nine colonial assemblies sent delegates to the Stamp Act Congress, which devised a set of Resolves protesting strongly against the loss of American "rights and liberties," especially trial by jury. The delegates contested the constitutionality of the Stamp and Sugar acts, declaring that only the colonists' elected representatives could impose taxes on them. They also rejected, because of their distance from Britain and their local interests, direct representation in the House of Commons. Then, assuring Parliament that Americans "glory in being subjects of the best of Kings having been born under the most perfect form of government," the delegates humbly petitioned for repeal of the Stamp Act. Other influential Americans advocated nonviolent resistance through a boycott of British goods.

Popular resentment was not so easily contained. When the act went into effect on November 1, disciplined mobs led by men who called themselves the Sons of Liberty demanded the resignation of newly appointed stamp-tax collectors, most of whom were native-born colonists. In Boston the Sons of Liberty made an effigy of the collector Andrew Oliver, which they beheaded and burned; then they destroyed a new brick building that Oliver owned. Two weeks later Bostonians attacked the house of Lieutenant Governor Thomas Hutchinson, a defender of social privilege and imperial authority, breaking the furniture, looting the wine cellar, and burning the library (see American Voices, p. 124).

In nearly every colony similar crowds of angry people—the "rabble," as their detractors called them—intimidated royal officials. Near Wethersfield, Connecticut, 500 farmers and artisans confronted the locally prominent tax

A British View of American Mobs
The cartoonist depicts the Sons of Liberty as sadists, subjecting a British
excise officer to physical abuse, and as wanton destroyers of property,
dumping tea into the harbor. The Liberty Tree in the background raises
the question: Does Liberty mean Anarchy?

collector, Jared Ingersoll, and forced his resignation. One rioter "lookt upon
this as the Cause of the People," he shouted, and would not "take Directions
about it from any Body." In New York nearly 3,000 shopkeepers, artisans, laborers, and seamen marched through the streets, breaking street lamps and
windows and crying "Liberty!"

AMERICAN VOICES

The Threat of Mob Rule

To Josiah Quincy, Jr., a Boston gentleman, the destruction of the house of Chief Justice Thomas Hutchinson in August 1765 raised the prospect of popular tyranny and "lawless despotism."

There cannot, perhaps, be found in the records of time a more flagrant instance to what a pitch of infatuation an incensed populace may arise than the last night afforded. . . . The populace of Boston . . . assembled in King's Street; where, after having kindled a fire, they proceeded, in two separate bodies, to attack the houses of two gentlemen of distinction . . . and did great damage in destroying their houses, furniture, &c., and irreparable damage in destroying their papers. Both parties . . . then unitedly proceeded to the Chief-Justice's house, who, not expecting them, was unattended by his friends who might have assisted, or proved his innocence. . . .

This rage-intoxicated rabble . . . beset the house on all sides, and soon destroyed every thing of value. . . . The destruction was really amazing. . . .

The distress a man must feel on such an occasion can only be conceived by those who the next day saw his Honor the Chief-Justice come into court . . . with tears starting from his eyes, and a countenance which strongly told the inward anguish of his soul.

> GENTLEMEN [he said]: There not being a quorum of the court without me, I am obliged to appear. Some apology is necessary for my dress: indeed, I had no other. Destitute of every thing. . . .

> I call my Maker to witness, that I never, in New England or Old, in Great Britain or America, neither directly nor indirectly, was aiding, assisting, or supporting—in the least promoting or encouraging—what is commonly called the Stamp Act; but, on the contrary, did all in my power, and strove as much as in me lay, to prevent it. . . .

Who, that marks the riotous tumult, confusion, and uproar of a democratic . . . state [would not fly] . . . to that best asylum, that glorious medium, the British Constitution? . . . May ye never lose it through a licentious abuse of your invaluable rights. . . .

SOURCE: Reprinted from *Proceedings of the Massachusetts Historical Society*, 1st ser., 1791–1883 (20 vols., 1879–1884), Vol. 4 (1858–1860), pp. 47–51.

Although the strength of the Liberty mobs was surprising, crowd actions were a fact of life in both Britain and America. Every November 5 Protestant mobs on both sides of the Atlantic celebrated Guy Fawkes Day by burning the pope in effigy to mark the failure of a Catholic uprising in 1605. Colonial mobs regularly destroyed houses used as brothels and rioted to protest the impressment of merchant seamen by the Royal Navy. The Stamp Act crowds were simply acting according to tradition.

The leaders of the Sons of Liberty were mostly minor merchants or skilled artisans who knew each other from their jobs, churches, or neighborhoods. The mobs they led were composed of a diverse mixture of established artisans, struggling journeymen, and poor laborers and seamen. Many were drawn into the streets by economic issues. Imports of low-priced British shoes and other manufactured goods threatened the livelihood of some artisans, and so they opposed a stamp tax that would lower their declining standard of living. Unlike "the Common people of England," a well-traveled colonist observed, "the people of America . . . never would submitt to be taxed that a few may be loaded with palaces and Pensions and riot in Luxury and Excess, while they themselves cannot support themselves and their needy offspring with Bread."

Other crowd members were moved by the religious passions aroused by the Great Awakening. These evangelical Protestants led disciplined, hardworking lives and resented the arrogance and immorality of British military officers and the corruption of royal bureaucrats. Still other crowd members had imbibed from their parents and grandparents the antimonarchical sentiments of the seventeenth-century Puritan revolution. A letter sent to a Boston newspaper promising to save "all the Freeborn Sons of America" from "tyrannical ministers" was signed "Oliver Cromwell." Finally, a substantial portion of many mobs included apprentices, journeymen, day laborers, and unemployed sailors—young men seeking adventure and excitement who, when fortified by drink, were ready to resort to violence.

Throughout the colonies popular resistance nullified the Stamp Act, lending a democratic cast to the emerging American Patriot movement. "Nothing is wanting but your own Resolution," a New York Son of Liberty declared during the upheaval, "for great is the Authority and Power of the People." On Guy Fawkes Day (November 5, 1765), New York Lieutenant Governor Cadwallader Colden, fearing an assault on Fort George, where the stamps were stored, called on General Gage to use his small military force against the crowd. Gage refused. "Fire from the Fort might disperse the Mob, but it would not quell them," he told Colden, "and the consequence would in all appearances be an Insurrection, the Commencement of Civil War." Frightened collectors distributed few stamps, and angry Americans coerced officials into accepting legal documents without them.

Slow communication across the Atlantic meant that the ministry's response to this resistance would not be known until the following spring. But royal officials clearly could no longer count on the deferential political behavior that had ensured stability in the colonies for three generations. "What can a Governor do without the assistance of the Governed?" the Philadelphia customs collector lamented.

Ideological Roots of Resistance

The American resistance movement began in the seaport cities because urban residents were directly affected by British policies. The Stamp Act taxed goods used by merchants and lawyers, such as newspapers and legal documents; the Sugar Act raised the cost of molasses to urban merchants and distillers; and the Currency Act complicated everyone's trade and financial transactions. Moreover, British firms had begun selling low-cost manufactured goods directly to colonial shopkeepers, threatening the livelihood of American artisans and merchants. All in all, an official in Rhode Island reported, the interests of Britain and the colonies were increasingly "deemed by the People almost altogether incompatible in a Commercial View."

At first the colonists framed their protests narrowly in terms of economic and political self-interest. One pamphleteer complained that colonists were being compelled to give the British "our money, as oft and in what quantity they please to demand it." Other writers alleged that the British had violated particular "liberties and privileges" embodied in colonial charters. But American Patriots gradually broadened the terms of debate by defining "liberty" as an abstract ideal—as a "natural right" of all people—rather than a set of historical privileges. Pamphlets of remarkable political sophistication circulated throughout the colonies, providing the resistance movement with both an intellectual rationale and a political agenda.

As Patriot merchants and lawyers formulated their arguments, they drew on three intellectual traditions. The first was English *common law*—the centuries-old body of legal rules and procedures that protected the king's subjects against arbitrary acts by the government. In 1761 the Boston lawyer James Otis had cited English legal precedent in the famous Writs of Assistance case, in which he disputed the constitutionality of a general search warrant permitting customs officials to inspect the property and possessions of any and all persons. Similarly, in demanding a jury trial for John Hancock, John Adams invoked common-law tradition. "This 29th Chap. of Magna Charta," Adams argued, referring to an ancient English document that had established the right to trial by jury, "has for many Centuries been esteemed by Englishmen, as one of the noblest Monuments, one of the firmest Bulwarks of their Liberties." Adams and other lawyers protested again when the terms of appointment for colonial judges were altered from "during good behavior" to "at the pleasure" of the royal governor, arguing that the change in wording compromised the independence of the judiciary. Customary legal practices and common-law rights, they maintained, could not be abridged by bureaucratic edict or even parliamentary statute.

A second major intellectual resource for educated Americans was the rationalist thought of the Enlightenment. Unlike common-law attorneys, who valued precedent and venerated the ways of the past, Enlightenment philosophers such as David Hume and Frances Hutcheson questioned the past and relied on reason to discover and correct social ills. The urban elite also was influenced by the political philosopher John Locke, who argued that all individuals possessed certain "natural rights," such as life, liberty, and property, which government was responsible for protecting. And they celebrated French theorists such as Montesquieu, who devised institutional curbs to prevent the arbitrary exercise of political power.

The republican and Whig strands of the English political tradition provided the third ideological basis for the American Patriot movement. In some places, particularly Puritan New England, Americans had long venerated the Commonwealth era—the brief period between 1649 and 1660 when England was a republic. After the Glorious Revolution of 1688 many colonists had welcomed the constitutional restrictions placed on the monarchy by English Whigs, such as the ban on royally imposed taxes. Later, many educated Americans absorbed the arguments of Radical Whig spokesmen who denounced political corruption. "Bribery is so common," John Dickinson of Pennsylvania had complained during a visit to London in the 1750s, "that there is not a borough in England where it is not practiced." These republican and Radical Whig sentiments predisposed many Americans to distrust imperial reform. Joseph Warren, a Boston physician and Patriot, reported that many townspeople thought the Stamp Act was intended "to force the colonies into rebellion," after which the ministry would use "military power to reduce them to servitude."

Thus, the ideology of Enlightenment thinkers, common-law attorneys, and Radical Whig critics of ministerial policy endowed colonial opposition to British control with high moral significance, turning a series of tax protests into a broad resistance movement.

The Informal Compromise of 1766

In Britain, Parliament was in turmoil, with different political factions advocating radically different responses to the American challenge. George III had replaced Grenville with a new prime minister, Lord Rockingham, who led a group of tradition-minded politicians (labeled Old Whigs by one historian) that opposed Grenville's policies toward the colonies. But hard-liners in Parliament, outraged by the popular rebellion in America, demanded that imperial reform continue. They wanted to dispatch British soldiers to the seaport cities to suppress the riots and force the Americans to submit to the constitutional supremacy of Parliament. "The British legislature," declared Chief Justice Sir James Mansfield, "has authority to bind every part and every subject, whether such subjects have a right to vote or not."

Rockingham tried to reconcile the various factions to a common policy. Three groups were willing to repeal the Stamp Act, but for very different reasons. The Old Whigs advocated repeal because they believed that America was important not as a source of tax revenue but as a source of "flourishing and increasing trade" that added to the national wealth. Some Old Whigs even agreed with the colonists that the new tax was unconstitutional. British merchants also favored repeal, because an American boycott of British goods had caused a drastic fall in their sales. In January 1766 the leading commercial centers of London, Liverpool, Bristol, and Glasgow deluged Parliament with petitions, pointing out the threat to British prosperity. "The Avenues of Trade are all shut up," a Bristol merchant with large inventories on hand complained. "We have no Remittances and are at our Witts End for want of Money to fulfill our Engagements with our Tradesmen." Finally, former Prime Minister William Pitt demanded that "the Stamp Act be repealed absolutely, totally, and immediately" because it was a failed policy. Pitt's view of the constitutional issues was ambiguous; he argued both that Parliament could not tax the colonies and that British authority over America was "sovereign and supreme, in every circumstance of government and legislation whatsoever."

Rockingham gave each side just enough to claim victory. To assist British merchants and mollify colonial opinion, he repealed the Stamp Act and ruled out the use of troops against colonial crowds. He also modified the Sugar Act, reducing the duty on French molasses from 3 pence to 1 penny a gallon but extending it to British molasses as well. Thus, the revised Sugar Act not only regulated foreign trade, which most American politicians accepted, but taxed a British product, which some colonists saw as unconstitutional. Finally, Rockingham pacified imperial reformers and hard-liners with the Declaratory Act of 1766, which explicitly reaffirmed the British Parliament's "full power and authority to make laws and statutes . . . to bind the colonies and people of America . . . in all cases whatsoever."

Because the Stamp Act crisis ended quickly, it might have been forgotten quickly. In 1766 the constitutional status of the American provinces remained uncertain, but political positions had not yet hardened. Leaders of goodwill could still hope to work out an imperial relationship that was acceptable to both sides.

Mixing Business and Politics, 1766
Hurt by the colonists' trade boycott, British manufacturers campaigned for repeal of the Stamp Act. To celebrate repeal—and expand the market for its teapots in America—the Cockpit Hill factory in Derby quickly produced a commemorative design.

THE GROWING CONFRONTATION, 1767–1770

The compromise of 1766 was short-lived. Within a year political rivalries in Britain sparked a new and more prolonged struggle with the American provinces. On both sides of the Atlantic economic self-interest and ideological rigidity aggravated the conflict, resurrecting the passions and violence of 1765 and dashing prospects for a quick resolution of the crisis.

The Townshend Initiatives

Often the course of history is changed by a small event—a leader's illness, a personal grudge, a chance remark. So it was in 1767, when Rockingham's Old Whig ministry collapsed and George III named William Pitt to head the new ministry. Pitt, the master strategist of the Great War for Empire, was chronically ill with gout and frequently missed cabinet meetings and Parliamentary debates, leaving Chancellor of the Exchequer Charles Townshend in command. Pitt was sympathetic toward America; Townshend was not. Since his service on the Board of Trade in the 1750s, Townshend had favored imperial reform; at last he had the power to push it through. When Townshend presented the military budget to Parliament in 1767, his longtime rival Lord Grenville rose to demand again that the colonists pay for the British troops in America. On the defensive, Townshend made an unplanned, fateful policy decision. Convinced of the necessity of imperial reform and eager to reduce the English land tax, he promised that he would find a new source of revenue in America.

The new tax legislation, known as the Townshend Act of 1767, was intended to free royal officials from financial dependence on the American legislatures, enabling them to enforce Parliamentary laws and royal directives. The tax imposed duties on paper, paint, glass, and tea imported into the colonies and was expected to raise about £40,000 a year. To pacify Grenville, part of the revenue would defray military expenses, but the major part would be used to pay the salaries of governors, judges, and other imperial officials. To enhance further the power of the royal bureaucracy, Townshend devised the Revenue Act of 1767. The new act created a Board of American Customs Commissioners in Boston and vice-admiralty courts in Halifax, Boston, Philadelphia, and Charleston. These administrative innovations were far-reaching, and posed a greater threat to American autonomy than did the small sums raised by the import duties.

New York gave Townshend another chance to challenge the colonial assemblies when it refused to comply with the Quartering Act of 1765. Fearing an unlimited drain on its treasury, the New York legislature first denied General Gage's requests for barracks and supplies and then limited its assistance. Unsatisfied, the British ministry instructed New York to assume complete financial responsibility for its defense against Indian attacks. If the assembly refused, some members of Parliament threatened that an extra port duty would be imposed on New York imports and exports to raise the needed funds. The earl of Shelburne, the new secretary of state, went even further, suggesting the appointment of a military governor with authority to seize funds from New York's treasury to pay for quartering the troops and "to act with Force or Gentleness as circumstances might make necessary." Townshend decided on a less provocative measure, the so-called Restraining Act of 1767, which suspended the New York assembly until it submitted to the Quartering Act. Faced with the loss of self-government, New Yorkers appropriated the required funds.

The Restraining Act was of great significance because it threatened Americans with the loss of their representative governments. The British Privy Council had always supervised the assemblies, invalidating about 5 percent of all colonial laws (such as those establishing land banks or vesting new powers in the assemblies). Townshend's Restraining Act went much further by declaring American governmental institutions to be completely dependent on Parliamentary favor.

America Again Resists

The Townshend Duties revived the constitutional debate over taxation. During the Stamp Act crisis some Americans had suggested that "external" duties on trade (which Britain had always regulated) were acceptable but that direct or "internal" taxes (which had never before been levied) were not. Townshend thought this distinction between internal and external taxes "perfect nonsense," but told Parliament that "since Americans were pleased to make that distinction, he was willing to indulge them [and] . . . to confine himself to regulations of Trade." Most colonial leaders refused to accept the legitimacy of Townshend's measures, however. They agreed with John Dickinson, author of *Letters from a Farmer in Pennsylvania* (1768), that the real issue was not whether the tax was internal or external but the intention of the legislation. Because the Townshend duties were not designed to regulate trade but to bring revenue to the imperial government, they amounted to taxes imposed without consent.

Americans debated the wisdom of a new boycott of British goods. In February 1768 the Massachusetts House of Representatives sent a letter to the other assemblies condemning the Townshend Act for taxing the colonists and thereby infringing on their "natural & constitutional Rights." In April Boston merchants began a new boycott of British imports, and New York traders followed in August. Philadelphia merchants, sailors, and dockworkers, who were more heavily involved in direct trade with Britain, refused to join the movement, believing they had too much to lose. Nonetheless, public support for nonimportation gradually spread to smaller port cities, such as Salem, Newport, and Baltimore, and into the countryside. In Puritan New England, ministers and public officials supported the boycott by condemning "luxury and dissipation" and the use of "foreign superfluities" and promoted the domestic manufacture of necessities such as paper and cloth.

American women, ordinarily excluded from playing a prominent role in public affairs, became crucial to the nonimportation movement through their production of "homespun" textiles. During the Stamp Act crisis, groups of young women with ties to Patriot leaders had underscored their support for the cause by increasing their output of yarn and cloth. The contest over the Townshend duties elicited support from a much broader group of women, including many pious farmwives who assembled to spin yarn at the homes of their ministers. Some gatherings were openly patriotic, such as one in Berwick, Maine, where the spinners, "as true Daughters of Liberty," celebrated American goods, "drinking rye coffee and dining on bear venison." Many more women's groups combined their support for nonimportation with charitable work by spinning flax and wool to donate to the needy.

Newspapers celebrated these women, prompting thousands of others to redouble their efforts at the spinning wheel and loom. One Massachusetts town proudly claimed an annual output of 30,000 yards of cloth; East Hartford, Connecticut, reported 17,000 yards. Although this surge in domestic production did not compensate for the loss of British imports, which had averaged about 10 million yards a year, it inspired support for nonimportation in hundreds of communities.

Indeed, the boycott as well as new crowd actions united thousands of Americans in a common political movement. The Sons of Liberty published the names of merchants who imported British goods, broke their store windows, and harassed their employees. Many merchants deeply resented the crowds' attacks on their reputations and property. Fearing mob rule, they condemned nonimportation and stood by the royal governors. Still, in March 1769 most Philadelphia merchants finally responded to public pressure and joined the nonimportation movement. Two months later the members of the Virginia House of Burgesses agreed not to buy duted articles, British luxuries, or slaves. "The whole continent from New England to Georgia seems firmly fixed," the *Massachusetts Gazette* proudly announced; "like a strong, well-constructed arch, the more weight there is laid upon it, the firmer it stands; and thus with America, the more we are loaded, the more we are united." Reflecting colonial self-confidence, Benjamin Franklin called for a return to the pre-1763 mercantilist system. "It is easy to propose a plan of conciliation," Franklin declared: "*repeal* the laws, *renounce* the right, *recall* the troops, *refund* the money, and *return* to the old method of requisition."

British patience was exhausted. When a copy of the Massachusetts House's letter opposing the Townshend duties reached London in the late spring of 1768, Lord Hillsborough, the secretary of state for American affairs, branded it as "unjustifiable opposition to the constitutional authority of Parliament." He instructed Governor Francis Bernard to dissolve the House if it refused to rescind its action. To strengthen the "Hand of Government" in Massachusetts and assist the Commissioners of the Customs, who had been forced by a mob to take refuge on a British naval vessel, Hillsborough dispatched four regiments of troops to Boston.

Hillsborough's goal was to prepare for an armed showdown with the radical Boston Patriots. By the end of 1768 a thousand British regulars were encamped in Boston, and military coercion was a very real prospect. General Gage accused public leaders in Massachusetts of "Treasonable and desperate Resolves" and advised the ministry to "Quash this Spirit at a Blow." Parliament responded by threatening to appoint a special commission to hear evidence of treason, and King George supported Hillsborough's plan to repeal the Townshend duties in all the colonies except Massachusetts. Once the rebellious New Englanders were isolated, the British army would bring them to their knees.

The stakes had risen. In 1765 American resistance to taxation had provoked a Parliamentary debate. In 1768 it produced a plan for military coercion.

The Second Compromise

At this critical moment the British ministry's resolve faltered. A food shortage in Britain caused riots across the countryside; in the highly publicized "Massacre of Saint George Fields," troops killed seven demonstrators. The Radical Whig John Wilkes, supported by associations composed of merchants, tradesmen, and artisans, stepped up his attacks on government corruption and won election to Parliament. Overjoyed, American Patriots drank toasts in Wilkes's honor and purchased thousands of teapots and drinking mugs emblazoned with his picture. Riots in Ireland over the growing military budget there added to the ministry's difficulties.

The American trade boycott also began to hurt. Normally the mainland colonies had an annual trade deficit of £500,000, but in 1768 they imported less from Great Britain, cutting the deficit to £230,000. In 1769 the boycott had a major impact. By continuing to export tobacco, rice, fish, and other goods to Britain while refusing to buy its manufactured goods, Americans accumulated a trade surplus of £816,000. To revive their flagging fortunes, British merchants and manufacturers petitioned Parliament for repeal of the Townshend duties. Government revenues, nearly 70 percent of which came from excise taxes and duties on imported goods, had also suffered. By late 1769 merchants' petitions had persuaded some ministers that the Townshend duties were a mistake, and the king had withdrawn his support for Hillsborough's plan.

Early in 1770 Lord North became prime minister and arranged a new compromise. Arguing that it was foolish to tax British exports to America (raising their price and decreasing consumption), North persuaded Parliament to repeal the duties on glass, paper, paint, and other manufactured items. But he retained the tax on tea as a symbol of Parliament's supremacy. Gratified, merchants in New York and Philadelphia rejected pleas from Patriots in Boston to continue the boycott. Indeed, most Americans did not insist on strict adherence to their constitutional principles and did not contest the symbolic levy on tea. Instead, they simply avoided paying the tax by drinking smuggled tea.

Even violence in New York City and Boston did not rupture the compromise. During the boycott New York artisans and workers had taunted British troops, mostly with words but occasionally with stones and fists. In retaliation the soldiers tore down a Liberty Pole (a Patriot flagpole), setting off a week of street fighting. In Boston friction between the townsmen and British soldiers over constitutional principles, in particular the legitimacy of the occupation of the town by a Standing Army, and everyday issues, such as competition for part-time jobs, sparked the "Boston Massacre." In March 1770, menaced by a mob of laborers and seamen, a group of soldiers fired into the crowd, killing five men, including one of the leaders, Crispus Attucks, an escaped slave who was working as a seaman. A Radical Whig pamphlet accused the British of deliberately planning the massacre.

Although most Americans remained loyal to the empire, five years of conflict over taxes and constitutional principles had significantly altered their sentiments. In 1765 American public leaders had accepted Parliament's authority; the Stamp Act Resolves had opposed only certain "unconstitutional" legislation. By 1770 the most outspoken Patriots—Benjamin Franklin in Pennsylvania, Patrick Henry in Virginia, and Samuel Adams in Massachu-

Patrick Henry, a Great Orator
Henry drew on evangelical Protestantism to create a new mode of political oratory. "His figures of speech . . . were often borrowed from the Scriptures," a contemporary noted, while his style and speech conveyed "the earnestness depicted in his own features." (Shelburne Museum, Shelburne, Vt. Photograph by Ken Burris)

setts—had repudiated Parliamentary supremacy, claiming equality for their assemblies. Franklin wanted to redefine the empire to make Britain and the colonies "distinct and separate states" united under "the same Head, or Sovereign, the King." His proposal horrified Thomas Hutchinson, the American-born royal governor of Massachusetts, who rejected the idea of "two independent legislatures in one and the same state." For Hutchinson, the British Empire was a whole, its sovereignty indivisible. "I know of no line," he told the Massachusetts House of Representatives, "that can be drawn between the supreme authority of Parliament and the total independence of the colonies."

There the matter rested. The British had twice tried to impose taxes on the colonies, and American Patriots had twice forced them to retreat. If Parliament insisted on exercising its claim to sovereignty, at least some Americans would have to be subdued by force. Fearful of civil war, the ministry hesitated to take the final fateful step.

THE ROAD TO WAR, 1771–1775

The repeal of the Townshend duties in 1770 restored harmony to the British Empire. For the next three years most disputes were resolved peacefully. Yet below the surface lay strong fears and passions and mutual distrust. Suddenly, in 1773, those undercurrents erupted, overwhelming any hope for compromise. In less than two years the Americans and the British stood on the brink of war.

The Tea Act

Radical Boston Patriots who wanted greater rights for the colonies continued to warn Americans of the dangers of imperial domination. In November 1772 Samuel Adams persuaded the Boston town meeting to establish a Committee of Correspondence "to state the Rights of the Colonists of this Province." Within a few months eighty Massachusetts towns had similar committees. Other colonies copied the practice when the British government set up a royal commission to investigate the burning of the *Gaspée*, a British customs vessel, in Rhode Island. The commission's powers, particularly its authority to send Americans to Britain for trial, first aroused the Virginia House of Burgesses, which created a Committee of Correspondence "to communicate with the other colonies" about the situation in Rhode Island. By July 1773 committees had sprung up in Connecticut, New Hampshire, and South Carolina.

Parliament's passage of a Tea Act in May 1773 initiated the chain of events that led directly to civil war. Lord North had designed the act to provide financial relief for the British East India Company, which was deeply in debt because of military expeditions undertaken to extend British trade in India. The Tea Act provided the company with a government loan and, more important, eliminated the customs duties on the company's tea as it passed through Britain.

Lord North failed to understand how unpopular the Tea Act would be in America. Since 1768, when the Townshend Act had placed a duty of 3 pence a pound on tea, American traders had been importing Dutch tea illegally. By the 1770s about 90 percent of the tea consumed in the colonies was contraband. However, the Tea Act was designed to make the East India Company's tea cheaper than Dutch tea. Radical Patriots accused the ministry of bribing Americans to give up their principles; as an anonymous woman wrote in the *Massachusetts Spy*, "the use of tea is considered not as a *private* but as a *public* evil . . . a handle to introduce a variety of . . . oppressions amongst us." One such oppression was the East India Company's decision to distribute the tea directly to shopkeepers, a tactic that would eliminate most colonial merchants from the trade. "The fear of an Introduction of a Monopoly in this Country," General Haldimand reported from New York, "has induced the mercantile part of the Inhabitants to be very industrious in opposing this Step and added Strength to a Spirit of Independence already too prevalent."

The Committees of Correspondence took the lead in organizing resistance to the Tea Act. They held public bonfires at which they persuaded their fellow citizens (sometimes gently, sometimes not) to consign British tea to the flames. The Sons of Liberty also prevented East India Company ships from landing new supplies. By forcing the Company's captains to return the tea to Britain or store it in public warehouses, the Patriots effectively nullified the legislation.

Governor Thomas Hutchinson of Massachusetts, determined to uphold the Tea Act, hatched a scheme to land the tea and collect the tax. When a shipment of tea arrived on the *Dartmouth*, he had the ship passed through customs immediately, after which it could not depart without paying the tax. If the tea duty were not paid within twenty days, by law customs officials could seize the cargo, land it with the help of the British army, and sell the tea at auction. But Patriots foiled the governor's plan by raiding the *Dartmouth*: a group of artisans and laborers disguised as Indians boarded the ship, broke open the 342 chests of tea (valued at about £10,000, or roughly $800,000 today), and threw them into the harbor (see American Voices, p. 136). "This destruction of the Tea is so bold and it must have so important Consequences," John Adams wrote in his diary, "that I cannot but consider it as an Epoch in History."

The British Privy Council was outraged, as was the king. "Concessions have made matters worse," George III declared. "The time has come for compulsion." Early in 1774 Parliament decisively rejected a proposal to repeal the duty on American tea and instead enacted four Coercive Acts to force Massachusetts into submission. A Port Bill closed Boston Harbor until the East India Company received payment for the destroyed tea. A Government Act annulled the Massachusetts charter and prohibited most local town meetings. A new Quartering Act required the colony to build barracks or accommodate

AMERICAN VOICES

Mob Discipline at the Boston Tea Party

George Robert Twelves Hewes, a poor Boston shoemaker, became a Patriot in part because a British soldier had refused to pay him for a pair of shoes. His account of the Tea Party describes the discipline imposed by the Sons of Liberty both on their followers and on other citizens.

It was now evening, and I immediately dressed myself in the costume of an Indian, equipped with a small hatchet. . . . After having painted my face and hands with coal dust in the shop of a blacksmith, I repaired to Griffin's wharf, where the ships lay that contained the tea. When I first appeared in the street . . . I fell in with many who were dressed, equipped and painted as I was . . . and marched in order to the place of our destination. . . . The name of him who commanded the division to which I was assigned, was Leonard Pitt. . . .

As soon as we were on board the ship, [Pitt] appointed me boatswain, and ordered me to go to the captain and demand of him the keys to the hatches. . . . We then were ordered by our commander to open the hatches, and take out all the chests of tea and throw them overboard . . . first cutting and splitting the chests with our tomahawks. . . .

Several attempts were made by some of the citizens of Boston and its vicinity, to carry off small quantities of [the tea] for their family use. . . . One Captain O'Conner, whom I knew well, came on board for that purpose . . . filled his pockets, and also the lining of his coat. . . . We were ordered to arrest him. . . . I seized him by the skirt of his coat, and . . . tore it off. . . .

The next day we nailed the skirt of his coat . . . to the whipping post in Charlestown, the place of his residence, with a label on it, commemorative of the occasion which had thus subjected the proprietor to the popular indignation.

SOURCE: James Hawkes, *A Retrospect of the Boston Tea-Party.* . . . (Boston: 1834), pp. 37–41.

soldiers in private houses. To protect royal officials from Massachusetts juries, a Justice Act allowed the transfer of trials for capital crimes to other colonies or to Britain.

In response, Patriot leaders throughout the mainland condemned these "Intolerable Acts" and rallied support for Massachusetts. In far-off Georgia, a Patriot warned the "Freemen of the Province" that "every privilege you at present claim as a birthright, may be wrested from you by the same authority that blockades the town of Boston." "The cause of Boston," George Washington declared from Virginia, "now is and ever will be considered as the cause of America." The activities of the Committees of Correspondence had created a firm sense of unity.

In 1774 Parliament passed the Quebec Act, which heightened the Americans' sense of common danger. The law extended the boundaries of Quebec into the Ohio River Valley, threatening to restrict the western boundaries of Virginia and other seaboard colonies. It also gave legal recognition to Roman Catholicism—a humane concession to French Canadians but one that aroused old religious hatreds, especially in New England, where Puritans associated Catholicism with arbitrary royal government. Although the ministry had not intended the Quebec Act as a coercive measure, many colonial leaders saw it as another demonstration of Parliament's power to intervene in American domestic affairs.

The Continental Congress Responds

American leaders called for a new all-colony assembly, the Continental Congress. The newer colonies—Florida, Quebec, Nova Scotia, and Newfoundland—did not attend, but delegates chosen by all the other mainland assemblies (except Georgia, whose legislature was effectively controlled by a royal governor) met in Philadelphia in September 1774. New England delegates to the First Continental Congress advocated political union and defensive military preparations. Southern leaders, fearing a British plot "to overturn the constitution and introduce a system of arbitrary government," favored a new economic boycott. But many delegates from the middle colonies held out for a political compromise.

Led by Joseph Galloway of Pennsylvania, these men of "loyal principles" outlined a scheme for a new imperial system that resembled the Albany Plan of Union of 1754. Under Galloway's proposal, America would have a legislative

Religion and Rebellion
Many American Protestants hated bishops and the ecclesiastical power they represented. This cartoon warned that the Quebec Act of 1774, which allowed the practice of Catholicism in Canada, was part of a plot by the Church of England to impose bishops on the American colonies.

council selected by the colonial assemblies and a president-general appointed by the king. The new council would have veto power over Parliamentary legislation that affected America. Despite this feature, however, the delegates refused to endorse Galloway's plan. With British troops occupying Boston, it was thought to be too conciliatory.

Instead, the First Continental Congress passed a Declaration of Rights and Grievances that condemned the Coercive Acts and demanded their repeal. It also repudiated the Declaratory Act of 1766, which had proclaimed Parliament's supremacy over the colonies, and demanded that Britain restrict its supervision of American affairs to matters of external trade. Finally, the Congress began a program of economic retaliation, beginning with nonimportation and nonconsumption agreements that would take effect in December 1774. If Parliament did not repeal the Intolerable Acts by September 1775, all colonial exports to Britain, Ireland, and the West Indies would be cut off. Thus, ten years of constitutional conflict had culminated in all-out commercial warfare.

Even at this late date a few British leaders continued to hope for compromise. In January 1775 the earl of Chatham (William Pitt) asked Parliament to give up its claim to tax the colonies and recognize the Continental Congress as a lawful body. In return for these and other concessions, he suggested, the Congress should acknowledge Parliamentary supremacy and grant a continuing revenue to help defray the British national debt.

But the British ministry had backed down twice; a third retreat was impossible. The honor of the nation was at stake. The ministry rejected Chatham's plan, branding the Continental Congress an illegal assembly. It also dismissed a proposal by Lord Dartmouth, the colonial secretary, to send commissioners to America to negotiate a settlement. Instead, Lord North set stringent terms: Americans must pay for their own defense and administration and acknowledge Parliament's authority to tax them. To put teeth in these demands, North imposed a naval blockade on American trade with foreign nations and ordered General Gage to suppress dissent in Massachusetts. "Now the case seemed desperate," the prime minister told former Governor Thomas Hutchinson, who was living in exile in London. "Parliament would not— could not—concede. For aught he could see it must come to violence."

The Rising of the Countryside

Ultimately, the success of the urban-led Patriot movement would depend on support from the large rural population. At first most farmers had little interest in imperial issues. Their lives were deeply rooted in the soil, and their prime allegiance was to family and community. But the French and Indian War had taken their sons away and raised their taxes. In Newtown, Long Island, for example, farmers had paid an average of 10 shillings a year in taxes until 1754; by 1756 their taxes had jumped to 30 shillings a year to cover military expenses. Peace brought them only slight relief; the Quartering Act cost each Newtown resident 20 shillings in taxes in 1771. Rural Americans found these increases onerous, though in fact they paid much lower taxes than did most Britons.

The urban-led nonimportation movements of 1765 and 1769 also raised the political consciousness of many rural Americans. When the Continental Congress declared a new economic boycott of British goods in 1774, it easily established a network of local Committees of Safety and Inspection to support it. Appealing to rural thriftiness, the Congress condemned those who wore expensive imported clothes to funerals, approving only "a black crape or ribbon on the arm or hat for gentlemen, and a black ribbon and necklace for ladies." In Concord, Massachusetts, eighty percent of male heads of families and a number of single women signed a Solemn League and Covenant vowing support for nonimportation.

Patriots also appealed to the yeoman tradition of agricultural independence, which was everywhere under attack. Arable land had become scarce and expensive in long-settled regions; in many new communities merchants were seizing farmsteads for delinquent debts. The new demands of the British government would further drain "this People of the Fruits of their Toil," complained the town meeting of Petersham, Massachusetts. "The duty on tea," added a Patriot pamphlet, "was only a prelude to a window-tax, hearth-tax, land-tax, and poll-tax, and these were only paving the way for reducing the country to lordships." By the 1770s many northern yeomen felt personally threatened by British imperial policy.

Despite their higher standard of living, southern slaveowners had similar fears. Many Chesapeake planters had fallen deeply into debt to British merchants. Accustomed to being masters on their plantations, they resented their financial dependence and feared the prospect of political dependence raised by the Coercive Acts. Influential planters worried that once Parliament had subdued Massachusetts, it might seize control of Virginia's county courts and House of Burgesses, depriving the gentry of the political power it had enjoyed so long. This threat moved Patriot planters to action. "The spark of liberty is not yet extinct among our people," one planter declared, "and if properly fanned by the Gentlemen of influence will, I make no doubt, burst out again into a flame."

While many wealthy planters and affluent merchants supported the Patriot cause, other prominent Americans worried that resistance to Britain would destroy respect for all political institutions, ending in mob rule. When the Sons of Liberty turned to violence to enforce nonimportation, their fears increased. One well-to-do New Yorker complained, "No man can be in a more abject state of bondage than he whose Reputation, Property and Life are exposed to the discretionary violence . . . of the community."

Other social groups also refused to support the resistance movement. In regions where many wealthy landlords became Patriots, such as the Hudson Valley of New York, tenant farmers often favored the maintenance of imperial authority. Similar social divisions prompted some backcountry Regulators in North Carolina and farmers on the eastern shore of Chesapeake Bay in Maryland to oppose the policies advocated by the local Patriot gentry. Ethnic and religious conflicts in the middle colonies prompted thousands of ordinary colonists to remain loyal to the king. Many Quakers and Germans in

Pennsylvania and New Jersey tried to remain neutral because of pacifist religious principles or from fear of political change.

Beginning in 1774, prominent Americans of "loyal principles"—mostly royal officials, merchants with military contracts, clergy of the Church of England, and well-established lawyers—denounced the Patriot movement, accusing it of seeking independence. They coalesced in a small but articulate pro-British party. But in most areas they failed to organize potential supporters and were therefore unable to affect the course of events. A Tory Association started by Governor Wentworth of New Hampshire drew only fifty-nine members, fourteen of whom were the governor's relatives. At this crucial juncture Americans who favored resistance to British rule commanded the allegiance—or at least the acquiescence—of the majority of white Americans.

The Failure of Compromise

When the Continental Congress met in September 1774, New England was already openly defying British authority. In August 150 delegates from neighboring towns had gathered in Concord, Massachusetts, for a Middlesex County Congress. The illegal convention had advised Patriots to close the royal courts of justice and transfer their political allegiance to the popularly elected House of Representatives. Armed crowds had prevented judges appointed by the royal governor from holding court and had harassed supporters of the imperial regime.

General Thomas Gage, by then the military governor of Massachusetts, tried desperately to maintain imperial power. In September 1774 he ordered British troops in Boston to seize Patriot armories and storehouses at Charlestown and Cambridge. In response, 20,000 colonial militiamen mobilized to safeguard military supply depots in Concord and Worcester. The Concord town meeting voted to raise a defensive force, the famous Minutemen, to "Stand at a minutes warning in Case of alarm." Increasingly, Gage's authority was limited to Boston, where it rested primarily on the bayonets of his 3,500 troops. Meanwhile, the Massachusetts House met on its own authority, issued regulations for the collection of taxes, strengthened the militia, and assumed the responsibilities of government.

Even before the news of Massachusetts's defiance reached London, the colonial secretary, Lord Dartmouth, had proclaimed Massachusetts to be in a state of "open rebellion." Declaring that "force should be repelled by force," he ordered Gage to march quickly against the "rude rabble." On the night of April 18, 1775, Gage dispatched 700 soldiers to capture colonial leaders and supplies at Concord. But Paul Revere and two other Bostonians warned the Patriots, and at dawn on April 19 local militiamen met the British first at Lexington and then at Concord. The skirmishes took a dozen lives. As the British retreated along the narrow roads to Boston, they were repeatedly ambushed by militiamen from neighboring towns. By the end of the day, 73 British soldiers were dead, 174 wounded, and 26 missing. British fire had killed 49 American militiamen and wounded 39. Thus, twelve years of conflict over taxes and constitutional principles had ended in civil war.

CHAPTER 5 TIMELINE

1754–1763	Salutary neglect ends British national debt doubles
1760	George III becomes king
1762	Revenue Act reforms customs service
1763	Proclamation Line restricts western settlement Peacetime army in America Grenville becomes prime minister
1764	Currency Act Sugar Act Colonists oppose vice-admiralty courts Franklin proposes American representation in Parliament
1765	Stamp Act Quartering Act Stamp Act Congress and riots
1765–1766	First nonimportation movement
1766	First Compromise: Rockingham repeals Stamp Act and enacts Declaratory Act
1767	Townshend duties "Restraining Act" in New York
1768	Second nonimportation movement begins Daughters of Liberty make homespun cloth British army occupies Boston
1770	Second Compromise: North repeals most Townshend duties Boston Massacre
1772	*Gaspée* burned in Rhode Island Colonial Committees of Correspondence
1773	Tea Act Boston Tea Party
1774	Coercive Acts punish Massachusetts Quebec Act First Continental Congress Third nonimportation movement Loyalists organize
1775	British ministry orders Gage to suppress rebellion Battles of Lexington and Concord

THEMATIC TIMELINE

	GOVERNMENT Creating Republican Institutions	ECONOMY Expanding Commerce and Manufacturing	SOCIETY Defining Liberty and Equality	CULTURE Pluralism and National Identity
1775	State constitutions written Independence declared (1776)	Wartime expansion of manufacturing	Gradual emancipation in North Murray, "On the Equality of the Sexes" (1779)	Paine's *Common Sense* (1776) calls for an American republic
1780	Articles of Confederation (1781) U.S. Constitution (1787)	Bank of North America (1781) Commercial recession (1783–89)	Virginia Statute of Religious Freedom (1786) Idea of republican motherhood	Land ordinances create national domain Webster defines American English
1790	Bill of Rights (1791) First national parties: Federalists and Republicans	First Bank of the United States (1791–1811) States charter business corporations Outwork system expands	Sedition Act limits press freedom (1798)	Indians form Western Confederation Regional differences—New England, South, Mid- Atlantic—persist
1800	Revolution of 1800 Activist state legislatures Chief Justice Marshall asserts judicial power	Cotton economy expands into Old Southwest Farm productivity improves Embargo encourages domestic manufacturing	New Jersey ends woman suffrage (1807) U.S. ends legal importation of African slaves (1808)	African-Americans absorb Protestant Christianity Tecumseh develops Indian identity
1810	Triumph of Republican party State constitutions democratized	Second Bank of the United States (1816–1836) Supreme Court protects contracts and corporations	Expansion of suffrage for white men End of established churches in New England (1820s)	War of 1812 tests national unity Second Great Awakening shapes American identity

PART 2

THE NEW REPUBLIC
1775–1820

The American war is over, Benjamin Rush declared in 1787, "but this is far from being the case with the *American revolution.*... It remains yet to establish and perfect our new forms of government." The job was even greater than Rush imagined, for the republican revolution of 1776 challenged traditional values and institutions in many spheres of life.

The first and most fundamental challenge was to create a republican system of government. In 1775 no one in America knew what powers the central and state governments should have or how they should be organized. It took time and experience to find out; the state constitutions and the U.S. Constitution of 1787 were great experiments in self-rule. One unexpected result was the appearance of political parties, new institutions that initially threatened to divide the nation.

Second, Americans had to achieve economic independence, a task that involved the creation of new systems of banking, manufacturing, and transportation and the extension of the national economy into the vast lands of the trans-Appalachian West.

Third, the new nation needed to define the meaning of liberty and equality. Resisting demands from some women and African-Americans that the new republic guarantee equal rights for all, American leaders restricted full citizenship and social equality to white men. A few prominent Americans did suggest a political role for women as "republican mothers" who would train their sons as patriots, while others advocated marriages based on the principle of equality. The impact of republican ideas was more dramatic in religion, as most states abolished established churches and many citizens flocked to democratically organized denominations.

The final challenge was to create a national identity from a diversity of peoples and regions. Gradually political institutions began to unite Americans, as did their increasing participation in the market economy and evangelical Protestant churches.

WAR AND REVOLUTION, 1775–1783

- Toward Independence, 1775–1776
- The Perils of War and Finance, 1776–1778
- The Path to Victory, 1778–1783
- Republicanism Defined and Challenged

The battles at Lexington and Concord transformed American Patriots into rebels willing to use military force to achieve their political ends. Although only a minority of Patriots demanded independence, the outbreak of fighting gave the advantage to the most intrepid. By the end of 1775 radicals dominated local meetings, provincial assembles, and the Continental Congress and demanded a complete break from Britain. "To know whether it be the interest of the continent to be independent," declared Thomas Paine, "we need only ask this easy, simple question: Is it the interest of a man to be a boy all his life?" Responding to such sentiments, on July 4, 1776, Patriot leaders formally severed American ties to Great Britain by agreeing to a Declaration of Independence.

More momentously, the rebels became revolutionaries, as they created new republican state governments. "From subjects to citizens the difference is immense," remarked the South Carolina physician and Patriot David Ramsey. "Each citizen of a free state contains, within himself, by nature and the constitution, as much of the common sovereignty as another." Repudiating aristocratic and monarchical rule, the Patriots placed sovereignty in the people, launching the age of democratic revolutions.

TOWARD INDEPENDENCE, 1775–1776

The Battle of Concord was fought on April 19, 1775, but fourteen months would elapse before the rebels formally broke with Britain. In the meantime, Patriot legislators in most colonies threw out their royal governors and created the two essentials for independence: a government and an army.

Civil War

Armed struggle in Massachusetts lent urgency to the Second Continental Congress, which met in Philadelphia in May 1775. Soon after the Congress opened, more than 3,000 British troops attacked new American fortifications on Breed's Hill and Bunker Hill, overlooking Boston. Three assaults, at the cost of 1,000 British casualties, finally dislodged the Patriot militia. Inspired by his countrymen's valor, John Adams exhorted the Congress to rise to the "defense of American liberty" by calling for volunteers and creating a Continental army headed by George Washington of Virginia. More cautious delegates and those with Loyalist sympathies opposed these measures, warning that they would lead to more violence and commit the colonists irretrievably to rebellion. After bitter debate, Congress approved the proposals—but as Adams lamented, only "by bare majorities."

Despite the blood that had been shed, a majority in Congress still hoped for reconciliation with Britain. Led by John Dickinson of Pennsylvania, these moderates passed an Olive Branch petition, expressing loyalty to George III and asking him to seek the repeal of oppressive Parliamentary legislation. But zealous Patriots such as Samuel Adams of Massachusetts and Patrick Henry of Virginia tried to mobilize anti-imperial sentiment by winning passage of a Declaration of the Causes and Necessities of Taking Up Arms. Americans dreaded the "calamities of civil war," it asserted, but were "resolved to die Freemen rather than to live [as] slaves." The king decided the issue by refusing to receive the petition.

Instead, in August 1775 George III issued a Proclamation for Suppressing Rebellion and Sedition. The following month the Congress launched an invasion of Canada, hoping to unleash a popular uprising and add a fourteenth colony to the rebellion. Patriot forces easily took Montreal, but in December they failed to capture Quebec. To aid the Patriot cause American merchants waged financial warfare, implementing the Congress's resolution to cut off all exports to Britain and its West Indian possessions. By cutting the trade in tobacco and disrupting the production of sugar, they hoped to undermine the British economy. Parliament retaliated at the end of 1775 with a Prohibitory Act that outlawed all trade with the rebellious colonies.

Meanwhile, the fighting in Massachusetts sparked skirmishes between Patriots and Loyalists in Virginia. In June 1775 the Patriot-dominated

House of Burgesses forced the royal governor, Lord Dunmore, to take refuge on a British warship in Chesapeake Bay. Branding the Patriots "traitors," the governor organized two military forces—one white, the Queen's Own Loyal Virginians, and one black, the Ethiopian Regiment. Then, in November, Dunmore issued a controversial proclamation of his own, offering freedom to slaves and indentured servants who joined the Loyalist cause. Faced with the possibility of black uprisings as well as military attack, Patriot planters threatened runaway slaves with death and called for a final break with Britain.

In North Carolina, demands for independence grew more insistent in response to British military threats. Early in 1776 North Carolina's royal governor, Josiah Martin, tried to reestablish imperial authority with a force of 1,500 Scottish Highlanders from the Carolina backcountry. But the Patriot militia in the low country quickly mobilized and in February defeated Martin's army at the Battle of Moore's Creek Bridge, capturing more than 800 troops. As the violence escalated, radical Patriots transformed the assembly into an independent Provincial Congress; in April that body instructed its representatives in Philadelphia "to concur with the Delegates of other Colonies in declaring Independency, and forming foreign alliances." Virginia followed suit. In May, led by George Mason, James Madison, Edmund Pendleton, and Patrick Henry, Patriots called a special convention at which they resolved unanimously to support independence.

Common Sense

The break with Britain did not come easily, for most Americans retained a deep loyalty to the Crown. Joyous crowds had toasted the health of George III after the repeal of the Stamp Act; even as the imperial crisis worsened, Benjamin Franklin had proposed that the king rule over autonomous American assemblies. Americans had condemned tax legislation enacted by Parliament, not the king or the institution of monarchy.

The very structure of American society supported their loyalty. Americans used the same metaphors of age and family to describe imperial rule and social authority. They often pictured the colonies as the dependent offspring—the children—of Britain, the "mother country." Just as the settlers respected male elders in town meetings, churches, and families, so they obeyed the king as the father of his people. Denial of the king's legitimacy might threaten all paternal authority and weaken the hierarchical social order. Nonetheless, by 1775 many Americans were accusing George III of actively supporting oppressive legislation and ordering military retaliation against them.

Surprisingly, agitation against the king became especially intense in Philadelphia, the largest but hardly the most tumultuous seaport city. Because Philadelphia merchants harbored Loyalist sympathies, the city had been slow to join the boycott against the Townshend duties. But artisans, who accounted for about half the city's population, were destined to become a powerful force in the Patriot movement. Worried that British imports threatened their small-scale manufacturing enterprises and that Parliament was attempting to abolish their "just Rights and Privileges," they organized a Mechanics Association. By February 1776 forty artisans sat with forty-seven merchants on the Philadelphia Committee of Resistance, the extralegal body that enforced the latest trade boycott.

The artisans acted out of both economic self-interest and religious ideology. Some artisans, and even more of the city's laborers, were Scots-Irish Presbyterians who had left northern Ireland to escape the hard times created by British mercantilist policies. Many Scots-Irish were also followers of Gilbert Tennent and other New Light ministers. As pastor of Philadelphia's Second Presbyterian Church, Tennent had told his congregation that all men and women were equal before God. Translating that assertion into political terms, New Light Presbyterians shouted in street demonstrations that they had "no king but King Jesus." Republican ideas derived from the European Enlightenment also circulated freely in Pennsylvania. Well-educated scientists and statesmen such as Benjamin Franklin and Benjamin Rush questioned not only the wisdom of George III but the idea of monarchy itself.

At this pivotal moment, with popular sentiment in flux, a single pamphlet tipped the balance. In January 1776 Thomas Paine published *Common Sense*, a call for independence and republicanism phrased in language the general public could understand and respond to. Paine, a minor bureaucrat in England, had been fired from the Customs Service for wage agitation. In 1774, with a letter of introduction from Benjamin Franklin, he had migrated to Philadelphia, where he met Benjamin Rush and others who shared his republican sentiments. In *Common Sense* Paine called George III "the hard hearted sullen Pharaoh of England" and blasted the British system of "mixed government," which yielded only "monarchical tyranny in the person of the King and aristocratical tyranny in the persons of the peers." *Common Sense* went through twenty-five editions and reached hundreds of thousands of homes. Its message was clear: reject the arbitrary powers of king and Parliament and create independent republican states. "A government of our own is our natural right," Paine concluded. "'TIS TIME TO PART."

Independence Declared

Throughout the colonies, Patriot conventions, inspired by Paine's arguments and escalating military conflict with Loyalists, called urgently for a break from Britain. In June 1776 Richard Henry Lee presented the Virginia Convention's resolution to the Continental Congress: "That these United Colonies are, and of right ought to be, free and independent states . . . absolved from all allegiance to the British Crown." Faced with certain defeat, staunch Loyalists and anti-independence moderates withdrew from the Congress, leaving committed Patriots to take the fateful step. On July 4, 1776, the Congress approved a Declaration of Independence.

Affirming the Declaration of Independence
The mood in the room is solemn as Congress formally declares independence from Great Britain. The delegates were now traitors to their country and king, their fortunes and even lives hinging on the success of Patriot arms.

The main author of the Declaration was Thomas Jefferson, a young Virginia planter and legislative leader who had mobilized resistance to the Coercive Acts with the pamphlet *A Summary View of the Rights of British America*. Now Jefferson sought to legitimize the colonies' independence by blaming the rupture on the king. To persuade domestic critics and foreign observers, he condemned the imperial acts that had oppressed Americans, heaping most of the blame on George III: "He has plundered our seas, ravaged our coasts, burned our towns, and destroyed the lives of our people. . . . A prince, whose character is thus marked by every act which may define a tyrant, is unfit to be the ruler of a free people."

Jefferson, who was steeped in the ideas and rhetoric of the European Enlightenment, preceded these accusations with a proclamation of "self-evident" truths: "that all men are created equal"; that they possess the "unalienable rights" of "Life, Liberty, and the pursuit of Happiness"; that government derives its "just powers from the consent of the governed" and can rightly be overthrown if it "becomes destructive of these ends." In linking these doctrines of individual liberty and popular sovereignty with independence, Jefferson established revolutionary republicanism as a defining value of the new nation.

For Jefferson as for Paine, the pen would prove mightier than the sword. Almost overnight many halfhearted Americans became republican revolutionaries. In rural hamlets and seaport cities, crowds celebrated the Declaration by burning George III in effigy; in New York City, they toppled a huge statue of the king. These acts of destruction broke the Patriots' psychological ties to the mother country and the father monarch. Americans were ready to create *republics*, state governments that would derive their authority from the people.

THE PERILS OF WAR AND FINANCE, 1776–1778

The Declaration of Independence prompted Britain to launch a full-scale military assault against the Patriots. For the next two years British forces outfought the Continental army commanded by George Washington, winning nearly every battle. A few inspiring American victories kept the rebellion alive, but in late 1776 and during the winter of 1777–1778 at Valley Forge, the Patriot cause hung in the balance.

War in the North

When the British decided to use military force to crush the American revolt, few observers gave the rebels a chance. Great Britain had 11 million people, compared with the colonies' population of 2.5 million, nearly 20 percent of whom were slaves. The British also had a profound economic advantage because of the immense profits from the South Atlantic system and the emerging Industrial Revolution. These financial resources paid for the most powerful navy in the world, a standing army of 48,000 men, and thousands of German mercenaries. Moreover, British military officers had been tested in combat, and their soldiers were well armed. The imperial government also had the support of tens of thousands of Loyalists in America as well as many Indian tribes hostile to white expansion.

By contrast, the rebellious Americans were militarily weak. They had no navy, and General Washington's poorly trained army consisted of about 18,000 troops, mostly short-term militiamen hastily recruited by state governments in Virginia and New England. The Patriots could field thousands more militiamen, but only for short periods and only near their own farms and towns. Although many American officers were capable veterans of the French and Indian War, even the most experienced had never commanded a large force or faced a disciplined army capable of the intricate maneuvers of European warfare.

To exploit this advantage Britain's prime minister, Lord North, acted swiftly after the unexpected American invasion of Canada in 1775. He ordered an ambitious military mobilization and replaced the ineffective General Gage with a new commander, General William Howe. Howe had served in the colonies during the French and Indian War and had distinguished himself in the siege of Quebec. North ordered him to capture New

York City and seize control of the Hudson River, actions that would isolate the radical Patriots in New England from the other colonies. In July 1776, as the Continental Congress was declaring independence in Philadelphia, Howe was landing 10,000 troops—British regulars and German mercenaries—outside New York City. By August the British army in New York had swollen to 32,000 soldiers, supported by a fleet of thirty warships and 10,000 sailors.

British superiority was immediately apparent. On August 27, 1776, Howe attacked the Americans in the Battle of Long Island and forced their retreat to Manhattan Island. There Howe outflanked Washington's troops, nearly trapping them on several occasions. Outgunned and outmaneuvered, the Continental army again retreated, first to Harlem Heights, then to White Plains, and finally across the Hudson River to New Jersey. By December the British army had pushed the rebels out of New Jersey and across the Delaware River into Pennsylvania, forcing Congress to flee from Philadelphia to Baltimore.

From the Patriots' perspective, winter came just in time, for in the eighteenth century military campaigns were customarily halted during the cold months. The overconfident British let down their guard, allowing the Americans to score a few triumphs. On Christmas night in 1776, Washington crossed the Delaware River and staged a surprise attack on Trenton, New Jersey, forcing the surrender of a thousand German mercenaries (Hessians). Then, in early January 1777, the Continental army won a small engagement at nearby Princeton. The two victories raised sagging Patriot morale and allowed the Continental Congress to return to Philadelphia. Bright stars in a dark night, these momentary triumphs could not mask British military superiority. These are the times, wrote Tom Paine, that "try men's souls."

Armies and Strategies

Instead of following up his victories with a ruthless pursuit of the retreating Americans, Howe was content to demonstrate his superior power, hoping to convince the Continental Congress that resistance was futile. He had opposed the Coercive Acts of 1774 and hoped to negotiate a compromise with the rebels. Howe's caution also reflected the conventions of eighteenth-century warfare, which prescribed outmaneuvering the opposing forces and winning their surrender rather than destroying them. The British general was well aware that his troops were 3,000 miles from supplies and reinforcements. In case of a major defeat, replenishing his force would take six months. Although Howe's tactics were understandable, they cost the British the opportunity to nip the rebellion in the bud.

Howe's failure to win a decisive victory was paralleled by Washington's success in avoiding a major defeat. He too was cautious, challenging Howe on occasion but retreating in the face of superior strength. As Washington advised Congress, "On our Side the War should be defensive." His strategy was to draw the British away from the seacoast, extend their lines of supply, and sap their morale while keeping the Continental army intact as a symbol and instrument of American resistance.

Congress had promised Washington a regular force of 75,000 men, but the Continental army never reached half that number. Yeomen militiamen preferred to serve in local units rather than join the Continental forces. Consequently, the army drew recruits from the lower ranks of society. General William Smallwood of Maryland commanded soldiers who were either poor American-born youths or older foreign-born men—British ex-convicts and former indentured servants. Such men enlisted not for reasons of patriotism but for a bonus of $20 in cash (about $200 today) and the promise of 100 acres of land. Molding these recruits into a fighting force took time. In the face of a British artillery bombardment or flank attack, many men panicked; hundreds of others deserted, unwilling to submit to the discipline and danger of military life. The soldiers who stayed resented the contemptuous way Washington and other American officers treated the camp followers—the women who came along with the recruits and took care of their material and emotional needs.

Such support was crucial, for the Continental army was poorly supplied and faintly praised. Radical Whig Patriots had long viewed a peacetime standing army as a threat to liberty; even in wartime they preferred the militia to a professional force. Consequently, the Continental army lacked adequate supplies and pay. General Philip Schuyler of New York complained that his troops were "weak in numbers, dispirited, naked, destitute of provisions, without camp equipage, with little ammunition, and not a single piece of cannon." Given these handicaps, Washington was fortunate not to have suffered an overwhelming defeat in the first year of the war.

Victory at Saratoga

Howe's failure to achieve a decisive victory surprised and dismayed Lord North and his colonial secretary, Lord George Germain, who now realized that restoration of the empire would require a long-term military commitment. Accepting the challenge, the government increased the British land tax to finance the war and prepared to mount a major campaign in 1777.

The isolation of New England remained the primary British goal and was to be achieved by a three-pronged attack on Albany, New York. General John Burgoyne was to lead a large contingent of British regulars from Quebec to Albany. A second, smaller force of Iroquois warriors (who had allied themselves with the British to protect their land from American settlers) would attack from the west under Colonel Barry St. Leger. To reinforce Burgoyne from the south, Germain ordered Howe to dispatch a force northward from New York City (see Map 6.1).

Howe wanted to attack Philadelphia, the home of the Continental Congress and the Continental army, and end the rebellion with a single victory. With Germain's apparent approval, Howe set his forces in motion. Rather than

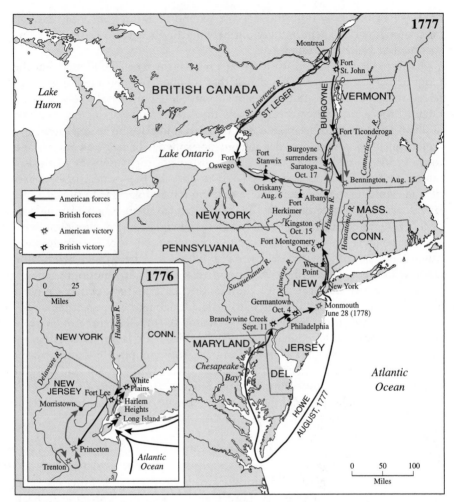

MAP 6.1
The War in the North
In 1776 the British drove Washington's army across New Jersey into Pennsylvania. The Americans counterattacked at Trenton and Princeton and camped for the winter at Morristown. In 1777 General Howe captured Philadelphia from the south; Colonel St. Leger and General Burgoyne launched invasions from Canada but were defeated at Oriskany, Bennington, and then Saratoga, the turning point of the war.

march overland through New Jersey, the troops sailed south from New York and then up Chesapeake Bay to approach Philadelphia from the southwest. Howe's troops easily outflanked the American positions along Brandywine Creek, forcing Washington to withdraw. On September 26 the British marched triumphantly into Philadelphia, half assuming that the capture of the rebels' capital would end the uprising. But the Continental Congress fled into the interior, determined to continue the struggle.

The British paid a high price for Howe's decision to attack Philadelphia, for it contributed directly to Burgoyne's defeat. Initially Burgoyne's troops had sped across Lake Champlain, overwhelming the American defenses at Fort Ticonderoga and driving toward the upper reaches of the Hudson River. Then they stalled, for Burgoyne—"Gentleman Johnny," as he was called—fought with style, not speed, weighed down by comfortable tents and ample stocks of food and wine. Burgoyne's progress was further impeded by General Horatio Gates, whose troops felled trees across the crude wagon trail Burgoyne was following and raided his long supply lines to Canada.

By the end of the summer Burgoyne's army—6,000 regulars (half of them German mercenaries) and 600 Loyalists and Indians—was in trouble, bogged down in the wilderness near Saratoga, New York. In August, 2,000 American militiamen left their farms to fight a bitter battle at nearby Bennington, Vermont, depriving British raiders of much-needed supplies of food, horses, and oxen. Meanwhile, Patriot militiamen in the Mohawk Valley forced St. Leger and the Iroquois to retreat. Because Howe needed additional troops to occupy Philadelphia, the British commander in New York City recalled the troops he had sent toward Albany. While Burgoyne waited for help, thousands of Patriot militiamen from Massachusetts, New Hampshire, and New York joined Gates's forces. They "swarmed around the army like birds of prey," an alarmed English sergeant wrote in his journal, and on October 17, 1777, forced Burgoyne to surrender.

The battle at Saratoga proved to be the turning point of the war. The Americans captured 5,000 British troops and their equipment. More important, their victory virtually assured the success of American diplomats in Paris, who were seeking a military alliance with France. Patriots on the home front were delighted, though their joy was muted by wartime difficulties.

Wartime Trials

The war exposed tens of thousands of civilians to deprivation, displacement, and death. "An army, even a friendly one, are a dreadful scourge to any people," a Connecticut soldier wrote from Pennsylvania. "You cannot imagine what devastation and distress mark their steps." New Jersey was particularly hard hit by the fighting, as British and American armies marched back and forth across the state. Those with reputations as Patriots or Loyalists fled their homes to escape arrest—or worse—as soldiers and partisans looted farms, seeking food or political revenge. Wherever the armies went, drunk and disorderly troops harassed or raped women and girls. Families lived in fear of their approach.

Indeed, the War of Independence became a civil war. In New England mobs of Patriot farmers beat suspected Tories or destroyed their property. "Every Body submitted to our Sovereign Lord the Mob," a Loyalist preacher lamented. Patriots organized Committees of Safety to collect taxes, send food and clothing to the Continental army, and impose fines or jail sentences on those who failed to support the cause. "There is no such thing as remaining neutral," declared the Committee of Farmington, Connecticut.

The new state governments were not politically secure, and many teetered on the brink of bankruptcy. To finance the war they borrowed gold, silver, or British currency from wealthy individuals. When those funds ran out, they had to find a new means of feeding, clothing, and paying the troops. Since opposition to taxation had fueled the independence movement, Patriot officials were reluctant to increase taxes. Instead, the states created a new monetary system based on the dollar (not the English pound) and issued $260 million in currency and transferable bonds. Theoretically, the new notes could be redeemed at a stated time in gold or silver, but since they were printed in huge quantities and were not backed by tax revenues or mortgages on land, many Americans refused to accept them at face value. North Carolina's paper money came to be worth so little, even the state government refused it.

The monetary system created by the Continental Congress collapsed too, despite the efforts of the Philadelphia merchant Robert Morris, the "financier of the Revolution." The Congress was completely dependent on funds requisitioned from the states, which frequently paid late or not at all. To raise money Congress depended on loans, but with no revenue of its own, it could not assure creditors they would be repaid. Congress therefore borrowed $6 million from France, which it used as security to encourage wealthy Americans to purchase $27 million in Continental loan certificates. When those funds and other French and Dutch loans were exhausted, Congress followed the lead of the states and financed the war by printing bills of credit. Between 1775 and 1779 it issued $191 million in bills, which were used as currency. By 1780 tax revenues from the states had retired only $3 million, and the value of the bills fell dramatically.

The excess of currency created the worst inflation in American history. The amount of goods available for purchase—both domestic foodstuffs and foreign manufactures—had shrunk significantly because of the fighting and the British naval blockade, while the amount of money in circulation had multiplied. Because more currency was chasing fewer goods, prices rose rapidly. In Maryland, for example, a bag of salt that had cost $1 in 1776 sold for $3,900 a few years later. Unwilling to accept worthless currency, hardpressed farmers refused to sell their crops, even to the Continental army. To supply their own needs, farmers used barter—trading wheat for tools or clothes—or sold goods only to those who could pay in gold or silver. Women, distressed by the high prices for sugar, tea, and bread, formed mobs and seized the goods they needed from storekeepers. Civilian morale and social cohesion crumbled, causing some Patriot leaders to doubt that the rebellion could succeed.

A Flood of Paper Currency
The Continental Congress issued this bill in 1776, declaring it to be worth "SIX Spanish Milled DOLLARS" or the equivalent in gold or silver, but by 1780 most Americans no longer had confidence in the currency and its value collapsed to virtually nothing, giving rise to the phrase "not worth a continental."

Fears reached their peak during the winter of 1777–1778. Howe camped in Philadelphia and with his officers partook of the finest wines, foods, and entertainment the city could offer. Washington's army retreated to Valley Forge, some 20 miles to the west, where about 12,000 soldiers and hundreds of camp followers suffered horribly. "The army . . . now begins to grow sickly," a surgeon confided to his diary. "Poor food—hard lodging—cold weather—fatigue—nasty clothes—nasty cookery. . . . Why are we sent here to starve and freeze?" Nearby farmers refused to help. Some were pacifists—Quakers and German sectarians—unwilling to support either side. Others were self-interested, hoarding their grain in hopes of higher prices in the spring or willing to accept only the gold and silver offered by British quartermasters. "Such a dearth of public spirit, and want of public virtue," Washington complained—but to no effect. By spring, a thousand of his hungry soldiers had vanished into the countryside and another 3,000 had died from malnutrition and disease, along with scores of camp followers. One winter at Valley Forge took as many American lives as had two years of fighting against General Howe.

AMERICAN VOICES

The Ordeal at Valley Forge

The Patriots nearly lost their army—and their struggle for independence—during the winter of 1777–1778. Of the 12,000 soldiers camped at Valley Forge, 3,000 died. The memoir of James Sullivan Martin, a private from Connecticut, describes the beginning of their ordeal.

While we lay here [en route to Valley Forge] there was a Continental thanksgiving ordered by Congress, and the army had all the cause in the world to be particularly thankful, if not for being well off, at least that it was no worse, and we were ordered to participate in it. We had nothing to eat for two or three days previous, except what the trees of the fields and forests afforded us. But we must now have what Congress said—a sumptuous thanksgiving. . . . And what do you think it was, reader? Guess. You cannot guess. . . . I will tell you: it gave each and every man *half a gill* [about one-fourth cup] of rice and a *tablespoon full* of vinegar! . . .

We arrived at Valley Forge in the evening: it was dark. There was no water to be found, and I was perishing with thirst. I searched for water till I was weary and came to my tent without finding any. Fatigue and thirst, joined with hunger, almost made me desperate. I felt at that instant as if I would have taken victuals or drink from the best friend I had on earth by force. . . . Two soldiers, whom I did not know, passed by; they had some water in their canteens. . . . I tried to beg a draught of water from them, but . . . at length I persuaded them to sell me a drip for three pence, Pennsylvania currency, which was every cent of property I could then call my own, so great was the necessity I was then reduced to.

SOURCE: Linda R. Monk, ed., *Ordinary Americans: U.S. History through the Eyes of Everyday People* (Alexandria, VA: Close Up Publications, 1994), pp. 32–33.

THE PATH TO VICTORY, 1778–1783

The Patriots' prospects improved dramatically in 1778, when the United States formed a military alliance with France, the most powerful nation on the European continent. The alliance brought the Americans money, troops, and supplies and changed the conflict from a colonial rebellion to an international war.

The French Alliance

France and America were unlikely partners. France was Catholic and a monarchy; the United States, largely Protestant and a federation of republics. The two peoples had been on opposite sides in wars from 1689 to 1763. But

France was intent on avenging its defeat in the French and Indian War and its loss of Canada. In 1776 the comte de Vergennes, the French foreign minister and an early supporter of American independence, persuaded King Louis XVI to extend a secret loan to the rebellious colonies and supply them with gunpowder. Early in 1777 Vergennes opened commercial and military negotiations with Benjamin Franklin and two other American diplomats, Arthur Lee and Silas Deane. When news of the American victory at Saratoga reached Paris in December 1777, Vergennes urged the king to approve a formal alliance with the Continental Congress.

Franklin and his associates craftily exploited the rivalry between France and Britain, using the threat of a negotiated settlement with Britain to win an explicit French commitment to American independence. The Treaty of Alliance of February 6, 1778, specified that once France had entered the war against Great Britain, neither partner would sign a separate peace before the "liberty, sovereignty, and independence" of the United States were assured. The American diplomats pledged that their government would recognize any French conquests in the West Indies.

The alliance with France gave new life to the Patriots' cause. With access to military supplies and European loans, the American army soon strengthened and hopes soared. "There has been a great change in this state since the news from France," a Patriot soldier reported from Pennsylvania; farmers— "mercenary wretches," he called them—"were as eager for Continental Money now as they were a few weeks ago for British gold."

With renewed energy and purpose, the Congress addressed the demands of the officer corps for pensions. Most officers came from the upper ranks of society and used their own funds to equip themselves and sometimes their men as well. In return they demanded pensions for life at half pay. John Adams condemned the petitioners as "Mastiffs, scrambling for rank and pay like apes for nuts," but General Washington urged Congress to grant the pensions, warning the lawmakers that "the salvation of the cause depends upon it." Congress agreed to grant the officers half pay after the war, but only for seven years.

Meanwhile, the war was becoming increasingly unpopular in Britain. Radical agitators and republican-minded artisans supported American demands for greater rights and campaigned for political reform at home, including broadened voting rights and more equitable representation for cities in Parliament. The landed gentry and urban merchants protested against continuing increases in the land tax and the stamp duty as well as new levies on carriages, wine, and imported goods. "It seemed we were to be taxed and stamped ourselves instead of inflicting taxes and stamps on others," a British politician complained.

But George III remained determined to crush the rebellion. If America won independence, he warned Lord North, "the West Indies must follow them. Ireland would soon follow the same plan and be a separate state, then this island would be reduced to itself, and soon would be a poor island indeed."

Worried about a possible Franco-American alliance, however, the king allowed North to seek a negotiated settlement. In February 1778 Parliament repealed the Tea and Prohibitory acts and, in an amazing concession, renounced its right to tax the colonies. North appointed a commission headed by Lord Carlisle to negotiate with the Continental Congress and offer a return to the constitutional "condition of 1763," before the Sugar and Stamp acts. But the gesture was too little too late. The Patriots, now allied with France, rejected the overture.

War in the South

The French alliance expanded the war but did not rapidly conclude it. When France entered the conflict in June 1778, it was hoping to capture a rich sugar island and therefore concentrated its naval forces in the West Indies. Spain, which joined the war in 1779, also had its own agenda: in return for naval assistance to France, it wanted to regain Florida and Gibraltar.

The British ministry, beset by war on many fronts, settled on a modest strategy. It would use its army to recapture the rich tobacco- and rice-growing colonies of Virginia, the Carolinas, and Georgia and then rely on local Loyalists to hold and administer them. The British knew that Scottish Highlanders in North Carolina retained an especially strong allegiance to the Crown and hoped to recruit other Loyalists from the ranks of the Regulators, the enemies of the low-country Patriot planters. The ministry also hoped to take advantage of southern racial divisions. In 1776 over 1,000 slaves had fought for Lord Dunmore under the banner "Liberty to Slaves!"; thousands more might support a new British offensive. At the least, racial divisions would undermine the Patriots' military efforts. Because African-Americans formed 30 to 50 percent of the population, whites were afraid to arm them. For the same reason many planters refused to allow their sons or white overseers to join the Continental forces, fearing that their absence would encourage slave revolts.

Implementing this southern strategy became the responsibility of Sir Henry Clinton, who replaced the discredited Howe. In June 1778 Clinton ordered the main British army to evacuate Philadelphia and move to more secure quarters in New York. In December he launched his southern campaign, capturing Savannah, Georgia, and mobilizing hundreds of blacks to build barricades and unload supplies. Then Clinton moved inland, capturing Augusta early in 1779. By the end of the year, with the help of local Loyalists, the British had reconquered Georgia, and 10,000 troops were poised for an assault on South Carolina. To counter this threat, the Continental Congress suggested that South Carolina raise 3,000 black troops, but the state assembly overwhelmingly rejected the proposal.

During most of 1780 British forces marched from victory to victory (see Map 6.2). In May Clinton forced General Benjamin Lincoln and his 5,000 troops to surrender at Charleston, South Carolina. Shortly afterward Lord Cornwallis assumed control of the British forces and sent out expeditions to

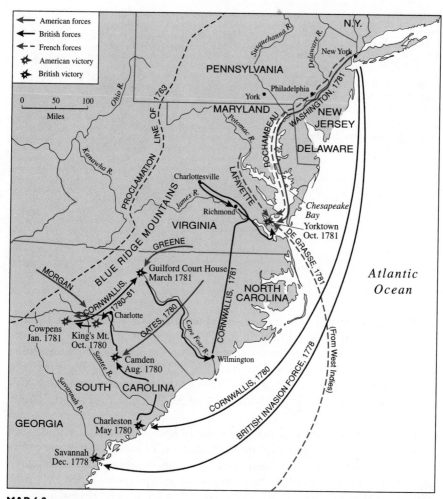

MAP 6.2

The Campaign in the South

The British ministry's southern strategy started well. British forces captured Savannah in December 1778 and Charleston in May 1779. Brutal guerrilla warfare raged in the interior over the next eighteen months. When Cornwallis carried the battle into Virginia in late 1781, a French and American army surrounded his forces at Yorktown, aided by the French fleet under Admiral de Grasse.

secure the countryside. In August Cornwallis routed an American force commanded by General Horatio Gates, the hero of Saratoga, at Camden. Only about 1,200 Patriot militiamen joined Gates at the battle in Camden—a fifth of the number at Saratoga. Many of them panicked and fled without firing a shot, handing the British control of South Carolina. Hundreds of enslaved African-Americans fled to freedom in Florida, while hundreds more sought protection behind British lines, providing labor for the invading army.

James Lafayette
Born into slavery in Virginia, in 1781 James Lafayette served as a spy for the American army commanded by the marquis de Lafayette, receiving his freedom as a reward and adopting Lafayette's surname. The two Lafayettes met again in 1824, when the Frenchman visited the United States.

Then the tide of battle turned. The Dutch declared war against Britain, completing its diplomatic isolation, and France dispatched troops to America. The French decision was partly the work of the marquis de Lafayette, a republican-minded aristocrat who had offered his services to the American cause long before the alliance of 1778. In 1780 Lafayette persuaded Louis XVI to send General comte de Rochambeau and 5,500 men to Newport, Rhode Island.

General Washington replaced Gates with Nathanael Greene, who devised a new military strategy to recapture the Carolinas. To make the best use of Patriot militiamen, many of whom were "without discipline and addicted to plundering," Greene divided them into small groups commanded by strong leaders and directed them to harass the larger but less mobile British forces. In October 1780 a militia force of Patriot farmers defeated a regiment of Loyalists at King's Mountain, North Carolina, taking about a thousand prisoners. Led by the "Swamp Fox," General Francis Marion, American guerrillas won a series of small but fierce battles in South Carolina, while General Daniel Morgan led another band to a bloody victory at Cowpens, North Carolina, in January 1781. But Loyalist garrisons and militia remained powerful, assisted by the well-organized Cherokee, who hoped to protect their lands by attacking American settlers and troops. "We fight, get beaten, and fight again," General Greene declared doggedly. In March 1781 Greene's soldiers fought Cornwallis's seasoned army to a draw at North Carolina's Guilford Court House.

Weakened by this war of attrition, Cornwallis decided to concede the southernmost states to Greene and seek a decisive victory in Virginia. Aided by reinforcements from New York, the British general invaded Virginia's Tidewater region. There Benedict Arnold, the infamous traitor to the Patriot cause, led Cornwallis's troops up and down the James River, where they met only slight resistance from a small American force commanded by Lafayette. Then, in May 1781, as the two armies sparred near the York Peninsula in Virginia, France ordered its large fleet from the West Indies to North America.

Emboldened by the ample forces at his disposal, Washington launched a well-coordinated attack. Feinting an assault on New York City, he secretly marched General Rochambeau's army from Rhode Island to Virginia, where it joined his own troops. Simultaneously, the French fleet massed off the coast of Virginia, establishing control of Chesapeake Bay. By the time the British discovered Washington's audacious plan, Cornwallis was surrounded, his 9,500-man army outnumbered two to one on land and cut off from reinforcement or retreat by sea. Abandoned by the British navy, Cornwallis surrendered at Yorktown on October 19, 1781.

The Franco-American victory at Yorktown broke the resolve of the British government, which lacked the will or resources to fight a long war of attrition. "Oh God! It is all over!" Lord North exclaimed when he heard the news. The combined French and Spanish fleet menaced the British sugar islands, Dutch merchants were capturing European markets from British traders, and a newly formed group of European states—the League of Armed Neutrality—was demanding an end to Britain's commercial blockade of France. Isolated diplomatically in Europe, stymied militarily in America, and lacking public support at home, the British ministry gave up active prosecution of the war.

The Patriot Advantage

Angry members of Parliament demanded an explanation. How could mighty Britain, victorious in the Great War for Empire, be defeated by a motley group of colonists? The ministry blamed the military leadership, pointing with some justification to a series of blunders. Why had Howe not been more ruthless in pursuing Washington's army in 1776? How could Howe and Burgoyne have failed to coordinate the movement of their armies in 1777? Why had Cornwallis marched deep into the powerful state of Virginia in 1781?

While historians have been critical of the military command, they also have noted the high odds against British success, given broad-based American support for the rebel cause. Although only a third of the white population zealously supported the Patriots, another third was supportive enough to pay the taxes imposed by state governments. Moreover, unlike most revolutionaries, the Patriots were led by experienced politicians who commanded public support. And even though the Continental army had to be built from scratch and was never very large, it was fighting on its own territory with the assistance of thousands of militiamen. The more than 55,000 Tories and thousands of native Americans who fought for the British could not offset these advantages. Once the rebels had the financial and military support of France, they could reasonably hope for victory. A charismatic leader such as William Pitt

Patriot Soldiers at Yorktown, 1781
A French observer captured the diversity of the American forces: a black infantryman from
Rhode Island, a French soldier, a buckskin-clad rifleman from Virginia, and (holding the gun-
nery torch) an artilleryman from the Continental army.

might have suppressed the rebellion, but ordinary politicians and mediocre
generals were destined to fail.

Americans, by contrast, had the inspired leadership of George Washington
as commander of the Continental army. Washington deferred to the civil authorities, winning respect and support from the Congress and the state governments alike. Confident of his own abilities, he recruited outstanding military
officers such as the Prussian Baron von Steuben to instill discipline in the ranks
of the fledgling Continental army and turn it into a respectable fighting force.

Washington had a greater margin for error than the British generals, because Patriots controlled local governments and could mobilize the militia to
intervene at crucial moments. Thousands of militiamen had besieged General
Gage in Boston in 1775, surrounded Burgoyne at Saratoga in 1777, and forced
Cornwallis from the Carolinas in 1781. In the end the American people decided the outcome of the conflict. Preferring Patriot rule, they refused to support Loyalist forces or accept imperial control in British-occupied areas.
Consequently, while the British won many military victories, they achieved
little, and their defeats at Saratoga and Yorktown proved catastrophic.

Diplomatic Triumph

After Yorktown diplomats took two years to conclude the war. Peace talks began
in Paris in April 1782, but the French and Spanish stalled for time, hoping for a

major naval victory or territorial conquest. Their delaying tactics infuriated the American diplomats—Benjamin Franklin, John Adams, and John Jay—who feared that drawn-out negotiations would tempt France to sacrifice American interests. For this reason the Americans negotiated secretly with the British; if necessary they were prepared to cut their ties to France and sign a separate peace. The British ministry also was eager to obtain a quick settlement. Many members of Parliament no longer supported the war, and ministers feared the loss of a rich West Indian sugar island. Once again Franklin and his colleagues exploited the rivalry between Britain and France.

In the bipartite Treaty of Paris, signed on September 3, 1783, Great Britain formally recognized American independence. Britain retained Canada, which now had a southern boundary at the Great Lakes. All the land south of the lakes between the Appalachian Mountains and the Mississippi River, which Britain had wrested from France just twenty years before, was ceded to the new American republic. Although this territory was still the domain of unde-feated native Americans, Britain did not secure its allies' rights to the land by insisting on a separate Indian territory. Leaving the Indians to their fate, nego-tiators promised to withdraw British garrisons from the region "with all con-venient speed." As an Indian of the Wea people complained, "In endeavouring to assist you it seems we have wrought our own ruin." Other treaty provisions granted Americans fishing rights off Newfoundland and Nova Scotia, forbade the British from "carrying away any negroes or other property," and guaran-teed freedom of navigation on the Mississippi to British subjects and Ameri-can citizens "forever." In its only concessions, the American government promised not to hinder British merchants from recovering prewar debts and to recommend to the state legislatures that they return property that had been confiscated from Loyalists and treat them as equal citizens.

In the Treaty of Versailles, signed at the same time as the Treaty of Paris, Britain made peace with France and Spain. Neither American ally gained very much. Spain reclaimed Florida from Britain but failed in its main objective of retaking Gibraltar. France had the pleasure of reducing British power, but its only territorial gain was the Caribbean island of Tobago. Moreover, the war had quadrupled France's national debt; only six years later cries for tax relief and political liberty at home would spark the French Revolution. Only the Americans profited handsomely from the treaties, which gave them indepen-dence and opened up the interior of the North American continent for settlement.

REPUBLICANISM DEFINED AND CHALLENGED

From the moment they became revolutionary republicans, Americans began to define the character of their new social order. In the Declaration of Inde-pendence Thomas Jefferson had turned to John Locke, the philosopher of *pri-vate* liberty, when he declared a universal human right to "Life, Liberty, and the pursuit of Happiness." But Jefferson and many other Americans also lauded "republican virtue," an enlightened quest for the *public* interest. As the New Hampshire constitution phrased it, "Government [was] instituted for the common benefits, protection, and security of the whole community." The tension between self-interest and public interest would shape the new nation's future.

Republican Ideals and Wartime Pressures

Simply put, a republic is a state without a monarch. Yet for many Americans republicanism was not just a political system but a social philosophy. "The word *republic*" in Latin, wrote Thomas Paine, "means the *public good*," which citizens have a duty to secure. "Every man in a republic is public property," asserted the Philadelphia Patriot Benjamin Rush (who eventually extended the notion to include women as well). "His time and talents—his youth—his manhood—his old age—nay more, life, all belong to his country."

Reflecting this concern with public virtue, the Continental Congress praised the self-sacrifice of the militiamen who fought and fell at Lexington and Concord, Saratoga and Camden. It condemned as a "total loss of virtue," as Henry Laurens of South Carolina put it, the wartime demand by Continental officers for lifetime pensions. Raised as gentlemen, officers were supposed to be exemplars of virtue who gave freely to the republic.

But as the war continued, military self-sacrifice diminished. During the winters of 1779 and 1780 Continental troops stationed at Morristown, New Jersey, mutinied, unwilling to endure low pay and sparse rations. To restore authority, Washington ordered the execution of several leaders of the revolt but urged Congress to use monetary incentives—back pay and new clothing—to pacify the recruits. Later in the war, unrest among officers erupted at Newburgh, New York, where Washington had to use his personal authority to thwart a potentially dangerous challenge to the Congress's policies.

Economic distress also tested the republican virtue of ordinary citizens. The British naval blockade had nearly destroyed the New England fishing industry and had cut off the supply of European manufactured goods. British occupation of Boston, New York, and Philadelphia had also cut domestic trade and manufacturing. As unemployed shipwrights, dock laborers, masons, coopers, and bakers left the cities and drifted into the countryside, New York City's population declined from 21,000 residents in 1774 to less than half that by the war's end. In the Chesapeake the British blockade deprived tobacco planters of European markets, forcing them to turn to the cultivation of grain, which could be sold at home.

Everywhere the scarcity of goods brought a sharp rise in prices and widespread appeals for government regulation. Hard-pressed consumers decried merchants and traders as "enemies, extortioners, and monopolizers." But when, in 1777, a convention of New England states limited price increases to 75 percent above the prewar level, many farmers and artisans refused to sell their goods at the set prices. In the end, a government official admitted, consumers had to pay the market price "or submit to starving."

The struggle over regulation came to a head in Philadelphia. After the British withdrawal in 1778, severe food shortages and soaring prices prompted a sharp conflict over regulated versus free trade. Artisans and laborers persuaded a town meeting to establish a Committee on Prices, which set wholesale and retail prices for thirty-two commodities, and justified this regulation by invoking the traditional concept of the "just price." But merchants, led by the financier Robert Morris, condemned the price controls and espoused the "classical liberal" ideas of free trade and enlightened self-interest. Regulation, Morris noted, would only encourage farmers to store their crops, whereas allowing prices to rise would bring goods to market and relieve scarcity. Most farmers agreed with Morris, as did members of the Continental Congress, including Benjamin Franklin, who condemned price controls as "contrary to the nature of commerce."

Nonetheless, most Philadelphians favored "fair" trade rather than "free" trade. At a second town meeting in August 1779, 2,115 Philadelphians voted for regulation, and only 281 against it. In practice, however, many artisan-republicans—shoemakers, tanners, and bakers—found that they could not support their families on fixed prices and did not abide by them. In civilian life as in the military, self-interest tended to triumph over republican virtue.

In those difficult times Patriot women contributed to both the war effort and the well-being of their families by increasing their production of homespun cloth. One Massachusetts town produced 30,000 yards of homespun, while women in Elizabeth, New Jersey, promised "upwards of 100,000 yards of linnen and woolen cloth." Other women assumed the burdens of farm production while their men were away at war. Some went into the fields, plowing, harvesting, and loading grain, while others supervised hired laborers or slaves, in the process acquiring a taste for decision making. "We have sow'd our oats as you desired," Sarah Cobb Paine wrote to her absent husband; "had I been master I should have planted it to Corn." Taught from childhood to act selflessly—to value the welfare of their fathers, brothers, and husbands above their own—most Patriot women did not experience a conflict between republican virtue and self-interest. Their contribution to the war effort boosted their self-esteem and prompted some to claim greater rights in the new republican society. It also sparked an increase in farm household productivity that would soon create a dynamic rural economy.

Spiraling inflation posed the most severe challenge to American families and the notion of public virtue. By 1778 so much currency had been printed that a family needed \$7 in Continental bills to buy goods worth \$1 in gold or silver. The ratio increased to 42 to 1 in 1779 and 100 to 1 in 1780. When the rate of exchange between Continental currency and specie reached 146 to 1 in 1781, not even the most virtuous Patriots would accept paper money. To restore its value, the Continental Congress asked the states to assess taxes that could be paid at the rate of 40 paper dollars to every silver dollar. This plan redeemed \$120 million in Continental bills but enriched speculators who had bought Continental bills at a rate of 100 to 1.

War Mobilization
A few American women actually fought in the war, and thousands more trav-
eled with the Continental army, providing the troops with food and support.
This 1779 woodcut, which illustrated a poem by a "Daughter of Liberty," was
meant to symbolize the wartime contributions of the women of Marblehead,
Massachusetts. (Collection of The New-York Historical Society)

At the end of the war speculators still held $71 million in Continental
notes, hoping they could eventually redeem the currency at an even greater
profit. "Private Interest seemed to predominate over the public weal," a
leading Patriot complained.

Ultimately, the sacrifices made by hundreds of thousands of ordinary
Americans financed the struggle for independence. Farmers and artisans who
had received Continental bills for supplies and soldiers who had taken them
as pay sacrificed the most. The currency literally depreciated in their pockets.

Individually the losses were small, amounting to a tiny "currency tax" every time an ordinary citizen received a paper dollar, kept it a week, and then spent it. Collectively they paid the huge cost of the war.

The Loyalist Exodus

As the war turned in favor of the Patriots, more than 100,000 Loyalists, fearing for their lives, emigrated to the West Indies, Britain, and Canada. The exodus disrupted the established social order, for some of the Loyalists were wealthy and politically powerful merchants, lawyers, and landowners. Although some Patriots wanted to seize the property the "traitors" left behind, most public officials thought that confiscation would be contrary to Patriot principles. For example, the Massachusetts Constitution of 1780 declared that every citizen should be protected "in the enjoyment of his life, liberty, and property, according to the standing laws"; Massachusetts officials extended those rights to most Loyalists.

Thus, there was no government-led social revolution. Most states seized only a limited amount of Loyalist property and sold it to the highest bidder, usually a wealthy Patriot rather than a yeoman or foot soldier. In a few cases confiscations did produce a democratic result. In North Carolina, about half the new owners of Loyalist lands were small-scale farmers. And on the former Philipse manor in New York, Patriot tenants successfully converted their leases into fee-simple ownership. But in general the revolutionary upheaval did not drastically alter the structure of rural society.

Social turmoil was greater in the cities, as Patriot merchants replaced Tories at the top of the economic ladder. In Massachusetts the Lowell, Higginson, Jackson, and Cabot families moved their trading enterprises to Boston to fill the vacuum created by the departure of the Hutchinsons and Apthorps. In Philadelphia, small-scale traders stepped into the vacancies created by the collapse of Anglican and Quaker mercantile firms. In the countinghouses as on the battlefield, Patriots emerged triumphant. The War of Independence replaced a tradition-oriented economic elite—one that invested its profits from trade in real estate, becoming *rentier* landlords—with a group of entrepreneurial-minded republican merchants who promoted new trading ventures and domestic manufacturing.

The Problem of Slavery

During the war thousands of southern slaves had sought freedom by fleeing behind British lines. Two neighbors of Richard Henry Lee, the Virginia Patriot, lost "every slave they had in the world." When the British army evacuated Charleston, more than 6,000 former slaves went with them; another 4,000 left from Savannah. Hundreds of black Loyalists settled permanently in Canada. Over 1,000 others, poorly treated and settled on inferior land in Nova Scotia, sought a better life in the abolitionist settlement in Sierra Leone, West Africa.

Thousands of African-Americans also served the Patriot cause. Free blacks from New England enrolled in Patriot units such as the First Rhode Island

Company and the Massachusetts "Bucks." In Maryland, Patriots recruited a large number of slaves for military service and later freed them, a policy rejected by other southern states. But many slaves struck informal bargains with their Patriot masters, trading loyalty in wartime for a promise of eventual liberty. In 1782 the Virginia assembly passed an act allowing *manumission* (liberation); within a decade planters had freed 10,000 slaves.

Slavery revealed a contradiction in the Patriots' republican ideology. "How is it that we hear the loudest *yelps* for liberty among the drivers of Negroes?" the British author Samuel Johnson chided. Some white Patriots took his point to heart. "I wish most sincerely there was not a Slave in the province," Abigail Adams wrote to her husband, John, as Massachusetts went to war. "It always appeared a most iniquitous Scheme to me—to fight ourselves for what we are daily robbing and plundering from those who have as good a right to freedom as we have."

The Quakers, whose belief in religious equality had made them sharp critics of many social inequities, took the lead in condemning slavery. Beginning in the 1750s, the Quaker evangelist John Woolman had urged Friends to free their slaves; during the war many North Carolina Quakers did so. Other rapidly growing pietistic groups, notably the Methodists and the Baptists, also advocated emancipation and admitted both enslaved and free blacks to their congregations. In 1784 a conference of Virginia Methodists declared that slavery was "contrary to the Golden Law of God on which hang all the Law and Prophets."

Enlightenment philosophy also played a role in the debate. John Locke had argued that ideas were not innate but stemmed from a person's impressions and experiences in the world. Accordingly, Enlightenment thinkers suggested that the oppressive conditions of slavery, not inherent inferiority, accounted for the debased situation of Africans in the Western Hemisphere. As one American put it, "A state of slavery has a mighty tendency to shrink and contract the minds of men." Anthony Benezet, a Quaker philanthropist who funded a school for blacks in Philadelphia, defied popular opinion in declaring that African-Americans were "as capable of improvement as White People."

By 1784, Massachusetts had abolished slavery outright and three other states—Pennsylvania, Connecticut, and Rhode Island—had provided for its gradual termination. Within another twenty years every state north of Delaware had implemented a policy of gradual emancipation. The laws gave priority to white property rights, for they required blacks to endure a few more years of unpaid labor. Thus, the New York Emancipation Edict of 1799 granted freedom only to enslaved children—not their parents—and only at age twenty-five. As late as 1810, 30,000 blacks in the northern states—nearly a fourth of their African-American population—were still enslaved. Whites moved slowly toward emancipation because they feared that freed blacks would compete with them for jobs and housing. More menacing was the possibility of race melding. In 1786 Massachusetts reenacted a colonial-era law that prohibited whites from marrying blacks, Indians, or mulattoes.

AMERICAN VOICES

Benjamin Banneker Tests Jefferson's Commitment to Natural Rights

In Notes on Virginia *(1785) Jefferson suggested the inherent inferiority of the black race. In this letter of 1791 Benjamin Banneker, a free African-American farmer and mathematician who authored an almanac and helped survey the District of Columbia, asks Jefferson to reconsider.*

I suppose it is a truth too well attested to you, to need a proof here, that we are a race of Beings who have long laboured under the abuse and censure of the world . . . considered rather as brutish than human, and Scarcely capable of mental endowments. . . .

I hope . . . you will readily embrace every opportunity to eradicate that train of absurd and false ideas and opinions which so prevail with respect to us, and that your Sentiments are concurrent with mine, which are that the one universal Father has given to us all . . . the Same Sensations, and endued us all with the same faculties. . . . Sir I freely and Chearfully acknowledge, that I am of the African race, and, in that colour which is natural to them of the deepest dye. . . .

Sir, Suffer me to recall to your mind that time in which the Arms and tyranny of the British Crown were exerted with very powerful effort in order to reduce you to a State of Servitude. . . . This, Sir, was a time in which you clearly saw into the injustice of a State of Slavery [and] . . . that you publickly held forth this true and invaluable doctrine . . . : "We hold these truths to be Self evident, that all men are created equal . . ."; but Sir how pitiable it is to reflect, that . . . in detaining by fraud and violence so numerous a part of my brethren under groaning captivity and cruel oppression . . . you would at the Same time be found guilty of that most criminal act, which you professedly detested in others, with respect to yourselves.

SOURCE: John J. Patrick, ed., *Founding the Republic: A Documentary History* (Westport, CT: Greenwood Press, 1995), pp. 102–105.

The tension between the republican values of liberty and property was greatest in the South, where slaves, who made up 30 to 60 percent of the population, represented a huge financial investment. Some planters, moved by religious principles or oversupplied with workers on declining tobacco plantations, allowed blacks to buy their freedom through paid work as artisans or laborers. By 1810 manumission and self-purchase had raised the number of freed blacks in Maryland to about a third of the African-American population. But emancipation was never seriously considered in the rice-growing areas of South Carolina and Georgia. The North Carolina legislature condemned Quaker manumissions as "highly criminal and reprehensible" and ordered that free blacks be reenslaved or expelled from the state. In 1792 the Virginia legislature made manumission more difficult. Following the lead of Thomas Jefferson, who owned more than a hundred slaves, the Chesapeake gentry argued that slavery was a "necessary evil" required to maintain white supremacy and the luxurious planter life style.

The southern debate over emancipation ended in 1800 when Virginia authorities thwarted a slave uprising planned by the free black Gabriel Prosser, who was hanged with about thirty of his followers. "Liberty and equality have brought the evil upon us," a letter to the *Virginia Herald* proclaimed in the aftermath, for such doctrines are "dangerous and extremely wicked in this country, where every white man is a master, and every black man is a slave."

A Republican Religious Order

Political revolution broadened the appeal of religious liberty, forcing Patriot lawmakers to devise a new relationship between church and state. Before 1776 only the Quaker- and Baptist-controlled colonies of Pennsylvania and Rhode Island had repudiated the idea of an established church. The most dramatic change came in Virginia, where the Church of England had been the established church. There most Anglicans renounced allegiance to the king, the titular head of the Church of England, and in 1778 reorganized themselves as the Protestant Episcopal Church of America. To win support for the war, the Episcopalians accepted the legitimacy of Presbyterian and Baptist churches, undermining the idea of an established church. Leading Virginia Patriots who embraced the Enlightenment also questioned the wisdom of state-supported churches. In 1776 James Madison and George Mason persuaded the Virginia convention to issue a Declaration of Rights that would guarantee the "free exercise of religion" to all Christians.

After the Revolution an established church and compulsory religious taxes were no longer the norm. Baptists in particular opposed the use of taxes to support religion. In Virginia their political influence prompted lawmakers to reject a bill supported by George Washington and Patrick Henry, which would have imposed a general tax to fund all Christian churches. Instead, in 1786 the Virginia legislature enacted Thomas Jefferson's Bill for Establishing Religious Freedom, which made all churches equal before the law and granted direct financial support to none. In New York and New Jersey the sheer number of churches—Episcopalian, Presbyterian, Dutch Reformed, Lutheran, and Quaker, among others—prevented legislative agreement on an established church or compulsory religious taxes.

Still, many Americans argued that a firm union of church and state would promote morality and respect for authority. "Pure religion and civil liberty are inseparable companions," a group of North Carolinians advised their minister. "It is your particular duty to enlighten mankind with the unerring principles of truth and justice, the main props of all civil government." Accepting this premise, most state governments provided churches with indirect aid by exempting their property and ministers from taxation. Thus the separation of church and state came slowly, especially in New England, where Congregationalist ministers who had strongly supported the independence movement were able to preserve a legally established church until the 1830s. But even there religious taxes could now be used to support Baptist and Methodist churches as well as the established Congregationalists.

Freedom of conscience proved equally controversial. In Virginia, Jefferson's Bill for Establishing Religious Freedom instituted the principle of liberty of conscience by outlawing religious requirements for political and civil posts. However, other states enforced religious criteria for voting and office holding, penalizing individuals who dissented from the doctrines of Protestant Christianity. The North Carolina constitution of 1776 disqualified from public office any citizen "who shall deny the being of God, or the Truth of the Protestant Religion, or the Divine Authority of the Old or New Testament." New Hampshire's constitution contained a similar provision until 1868.

Americans who were influenced by Enlightenment values condemned such restrictions on freedom of conscience. Leading American Patriots, including Thomas Jefferson and Benjamin Franklin, argued that God had given human beings the power of reason so that they could determine moral truths for themselves. To protect society from "ecclesiastical tyranny," they demanded complete freedom of expression.

Many evangelical Protestants also favored freedom of conscience, but their main goal was to protect their churches from state control. The New England minister Isaac Backus warned Baptists not to incorporate their churches or accept state funding because that might lead to state control. In Connecticut a devout Congregationalist welcomed "voluntarism" (the voluntary funding of churches by their members) because it allowed the laity to control the clergy, furthering "the principles of republicanism." In religion as in politics, Americans had begun to create a new republican order.

CHAPTER 6 TIMELINE

1775	Second Continental Congress meets in Philadelphia Battle of Bunker Hill Olive Branch petition Lord Dunmore's proclamation to slaves American invasion of Canada
1776	Patriots skirmish with Loyalists in South Thomas Paine's *Common Sense* Declaration of Independence (July 4) General Howe defeats Washington in New York
1777	Patriot women assist war economy Howe occupies Philadelphia Gates defeats Burgoyne at Saratoga Continental army suffers at Valley Forge Paper currency creates inflation
1778	Franco-American alliance (February 6) Lord North seeks negotiated settlement British begin "southern" strategy by capturing Savannah
1780	General Clinton captures Charleston French army lands in Rhode Island
1781	Cornwallis invades Virginia; surrenders at Yorktown Large-scale Loyalist emigration
1782	Slave manumission act in Virginia (reversed in 1792)
1783	Treaty of Paris (September 3)
1786	Virginia Bill for Establishing Religious Freedom
1800	Gabriel Prosser's rebellion in Virginia

CHAPTER 7

THE NEW POLITICAL ORDER, 1776–1800

- Creating New Institutions, 1776–1787
- The Constitution of 1787
- The Political Crisis of the 1790s

Many revolutions end in political chaos or military rule, but the new American republic escaped those unhappy fates. The Loyalist exodus ended support for the monarchy, and most Continental army officers supported civilian rule. Still, General George Washington stunned the world in 1783 when he voluntarily left public life to return to his plantation. "Tis a Conduct so novel," the painter Jonathan Trumbull reported from London, "so inconceivable to People [here], who, far from giving up powers they possess, are willing to convulse the empire to acquire more." Washington's retirement left power in the hands of the Patriot leaders, who were committed to representative government.

Fashioning republican institutions absorbed the energy and intellect of an entire generation. Between 1776 and 1800 Americans not only wrote new state and federal constitutions but also devised a system of politics that was responsive to the popular will. When a bill was introduced into a state legislature, grumbled Ezra Stiles, the conservative president of Yale College, every elected official "instantly thinks how it will affect his constituents," not the public good. What Stiles disparaged as an excess of democracy, most ordinary Americans welcomed. For the first time their interests were represented in the halls of government.

CREATING NEW INSTITUTIONS, 1776–1787

The Revolution of 1776 was both a struggle for home rule (independence) and, in the words of the historian Carl Becker, a conflict over "who should rule at home." Who would control the new republican institutions, traditional elites or ordinary citizens? Where would power reside, in the national government or the states?

The State Constitutions: How Much Democracy?

In May 1776 the Continental Congress had urged Americans to suppress royal authority and establish new governing institutions. Most states quickly complied. Within six months Virginia, Maryland, North Carolina, New Jersey, Delaware, and Pennsylvania had written new constitutions and Connecticut and Rhode Island had transformed their colonial charters into republican constitutions by deleting references to the king.

The Declaration of Independence had stated the principle of popular sovereignty: governments derive "their just powers from the consent of the governed." In the heat of revolution, many Patriots gave this clause a democratic twist. In North Carolina the backcountry farmers of Mecklenburg County instructed their delegates to the state's constitutional convention to "oppose everything that leans to aristocracy or power in the hands of the rich and chief men exercised to the oppression of the poor." Voters in Virginia elected a new assembly that "was composed of men not quite so well dressed, nor so politely educated, nor so highly born," an observer remarked. Delaware's constitution declared that "the Right of the People to participate in the Legislature, is the Foundation of Liberty and of all free government."

This outlook received its fullest expression in Pennsylvania, where a coalition of Scots-Irish farmers, Philadelphia artisans, and Enlightenment-influenced intellectuals created the most democratic government in America or Europe. Pennsylvania's constitution abolished property owning as a test of citizenship, granting all men who paid taxes the right to vote and hold office. It also created a *unicameral* (one-house) assembly with complete legislative power. No council or upper house was reserved for the wealthy, and no governor exercised veto power. Other constitutional provisions mandated an extensive system of elementary education, protected citizens from imprisonment for debt, and called for a society of economically independent freemen.

Pennsylvania's democratic constitution alarmed many leading Patriots, who believed that voting and officeholding should be restricted to "men of learning, leisure and easy circumstances." Jeremy Belknap of New Hampshire insisted that "the people be taught . . . that they are not able to govern themselves." He and other conservative Patriots feared that popular rule would lead to the tyranny of legislative majorities, allowing ordinary citizens to use their numerical advantage to tax the rich.

From Boston, John Adams denounced Pennsylvania's unicameral legislature as "so democratical that it must produce confusion and every evil work." To counter its appeal, Adams composed his *Thoughts on Government* and sent the treatise to friends at constitutional conventions in other states. Adams adapted the British Whig theory of mixed government (in which power was shared by the king, lords, and commons) to a republican society. To preserve liberty, he recommended dispersing authority by assigning the different functions of government—lawmaking, administering, and judging—to separate branches. Thus, legislatures would make the laws, which would be enforced by the executive and the judiciary. Adams also called for a *bicameral* (two-house) legislature in which men of property in the upper house would check the excesses of popular majorities in the lower house. As a further curb on democracy, he proposed an elected governor with the power to veto laws and an appointed—not elected—judiciary to review them. Adams argued that this plan was republican because the people would elect both the chief executive and the legislature.

Leading Patriots endorsed Adams's scheme both because they feared democracy and because it resembled the governments of the colonial period. Most states adopted constitutions that provided for bicameral legislatures in which membership in both houses was elective. Recalling the arbitrary conduct of royal governors, most also reduced the powers of the executive; only three gave veto power to the governor. Many states retained property qualifications for voting, however. Thus, in New York, while 90 percent of white men could vote in assembly elections, only 40 percent could vote for the governor and the upper house. The most flagrant use of property to maintain the power of the elite occurred in South Carolina, where the 1778 constitution required candidates for governor to have a debt-free estate of £10,000 (about $600,000 today), senators to be worth £2,000, and assemblymen to own property valued at £1,000. These provisions ruled out officeholding for about 90 percent of white men.

Nonetheless, post-Revolutionary politics had a democratic tinge. State constitutions apportioned seats in the lower houses of the legislatures on the basis of population, giving farmers in western areas the representation they had long demanded. Indeed, backcountry residents were able to transfer state capitals from merchant-dominated seaports such as New York City and Philadelphia to inland cities such as Albany and Harrisburg. Even conservative South Carolina moved its seat of government inland, from Charleston to Columbia.

Most of the state legislatures were filled by new sorts of political leaders. After the war, noted one observer, ordinary voters were less likely to elect their social "betters" to office and chose men of "middling circumstances" who knew "the wants of the poor." By the mid-1780s, middling farmers and urban artisans controlled the lower houses in most northern states and formed a sizable minority in southern assemblies. These "middling men" took the lead in opposing the collection of back taxes and other measures that tended "toward the oppression of the people."

The political legacy of the Revolution was complex. Only in Pennsylvania and Vermont were radical Patriots able to take power and create democratic

AMERICAN VOICES

An Attack on Patrick Henry's Social Policies

Even before the war ended, democratic-minded state legislators advanced policies designed to assist ordinary voters. In Virginia, Patrick Henry spoke for yeomen farmers and debtors in seeking to reduce the burden of military service, cut taxes, and allow debts to be paid in depreciated paper currency. Such measures were condemned by privileged representatives, as in this letter from J. P. (Jack) Custis to his stepfather, George Washington.

Patrick Henry, who possesses the most unbounded influence over the House, is, in my opinion, the most absurd politician in the world. He moved, the other day, that the [military] draft, which has taken place in many counties . . . should be reduced from eighteen months to twelve months. Absurd as this motion must appear to every reasonable man, it did not want espousers, though, fortunately, the number was too small, and the motion was lost. . . .

He [Patrick Henry] is also desirous that half of the tax which was laid, to furnish bounties for the recruits should be remitted; although half of the State, or two thirds, have paid it, or are prepared to do so. This matter is not yet determined, and I am afraid he will succeed. . . . By this means, all authority will be lost, and the State thrown into the greatest confusion.

A law was passed yesterday, making all the money that hath been emitted, by Congress or this State, a legal tender, in discharge of all debts and Contracts whatsoever; except specific contracts, expressing the contrary. It is also proposed to emit ten million more. This tender act, iniquitous as it is, was carried by a majority of two to one, and will forever cast a reflection on the justice of the State.

SOURCE: J. P. Custis to George Washington, March 16, 1781, reprinted in the *William and Mary Quarterly*, 3rd ser., 43 (April 1986), 288–289.

governmental institutions. Yet everywhere, the day-to-day politics of electioneering and interest-group bargaining became much more responsive to the demands of ordinary citizens.

Equally important, the extraordinary excitement of the Revolutionary Era tested the dictum that only men could engage in politics. While men continued to control all public institutions—legislatures, juries, government offices—upper-class women entered into political debate, filling their letters and diaries (and undoubtedly their conversations) with opinions on public issues. "The men say we have no business [with politics]," Eliza Wilkinson of South Carolina complained in 1783, "but I won't have it thought that because we are the weaker sex as to bodily strength we are capable of nothing more than domestic concerns. They won't even allow us liberty of thought, and that is all I want."

American women did not demand complete equality with men, but they did want to end discriminatory customs and legal rules. Abigail Adams demanded equal legal rights for married women, pointing out that under existing common law they could not own most forms of property and could not enter into a contract or initiate a lawsuit without their husbands' action. "Men would be tyrants" if they continued to hold such power over women, Adams declared to her husband, criticizing him and other Patriots for "emancipating all nations" from monarchical despotism while "retaining absolute power over Wives."

Although men paid some attention to women's requests, they were generally unwilling to question their own dominant position. Most husbands remained patriarchs; even young men who embraced the republican ideal of "companionate" marriage did not support a public role for their wives and daughters. With the partial exception of New Jersey, which granted the vote to unmarried and widowed women of property until 1807, women remained second-class citizens, unable to participate directly in American political life.

The republican belief in the need for an educated citizenry provided an avenue for the most important advances made by American women. In her 1779 essay "On the Equality of the Sexes" (published in 1790), Judith Sargent Murray compared the intellectual faculties of men and women, arguing that women had an equal capacity for memory and superior imagination. Murray conceded that most women were inferior to men in judgment and reasoning,

Judith Sargent (Murray), Age 19
The well-educated daughter of a Massachusetts merchant, Judith Sargent endured a difficult seventeen-year marriage to John Stevens, during which she wrote "On The Equality of the Sexes." After Stevens's death, she wed the Reverend John Murray, who became a leading Universalist. Her portrait, painted around 1771 by John Singleton Copley, captures Murray's skeptical view of the world, which enabled her to question customary gender roles.

but only because of a lack of training: "We can only reason from what we know," and most women had been denied "the opportunity of acquiring knowledge." In the 1790s the attorney general in Massachusetts persuaded a jury that girls had an equal right to schooling under the state constitution. With greater access to public elementary schools and new female academies, many young women became literate, knowledgeable, and intellectually prepared for a role in public life. By 1850 as many women as men in the northeastern states would be able to read and write, and literate women would challenge their subordinate legal and political status.

The Articles of Confederation

As the Patriots moved toward independence in 1776, they envisioned a central government with limited powers. Carter Braxton of Virginia thought the Continental Congress should have the power to "regulate the affairs of trade, war, peace, alliances, &c." but "should by no means have authority to interfere with the internal police [governance] or domestic concerns of any Colony."

This outlook informed the Articles of Confederation, passed by Congress in November 1777. The first national constitution provided for a loose confederation in which "each state retains its sovereignty, freedom, and independence" as well as all powers and rights not "expressly delegated" to the United States. The Articles gave the confederation the authority to declare war and peace, make treaties with foreign nations, adjudicate disputes between the states, borrow and print money, and requisition funds from the states "for the common defense or general welfare." These powers were to be exercised by a central legislature, the Congress, in which each state had one vote regardless of its wealth or population. There was no separate executive branch or judiciary. Important laws needed approval by at least nine of the thirteen states, and changes in the Articles required unanimous consent.

Because of disputes over western lands, the Articles were not ratified by all the states until 1781. States with no claims to land in the West, such as Maryland and Pennsylvania, refused to ratify the Articles until Virginia and other states that did have such claims (based on royal charters in which boundaries stretched to the Pacific Ocean) agreed to relinquish them to Congress to create a common national domain in the West. Threatened by Cornwallis's army in 1781, Virginia finally agreed to give up its land claims (see Map 7.1 for the dates of the actual cessions), and Maryland, the last holdout, then ratified the Articles.

Formal ratification of the Articles was anticlimactic, because the Congress had been exercising de facto constitutional authority for four years, raising the Continental army and negotiating with foreign nations. The Confederation's weakness stemmed primarily from its limited fiscal powers. Lacking the authority to impose taxes, the Congress had to requisition funds from the state legislatures and hope they would pay, which they usually failed to do. Faced with the prospect of the Confederation's bankruptcy in 1780, General

MAP 7.1

Western Land Claims

The Confederation Congress resolved conflicting claims by the states by creating a "national domain." Between 1781 and 1802 all the seaboard states with western land claims ceded them to the national government. The Confederation Congress divided the domain into territories, opening them to citizens from all states and providing them with self-governing institutions and the prospect of statehood.

Washington called urgently for a national system of taxation, warning Patriot leaders that otherwise "our cause is lost."

In response, nationalist-minded members of Congress sought to expand the Confederation's authority. Robert Morris, who became superintendent of finance in 1781, persuaded Congress to charter the Bank of North America, a private institution in Philadelphia, hoping to use its notes to stabilize the inflated Continental currency. Morris also developed a comprehensive financial plan that apportioned some war expenses among the states in proportion to their landed wealth while centralizing control of army expenditures and foreign debt. He hoped that the existence of a national debt would draw attention to the Confederation's need for the power to impose an import duty.

But the nationalists were largely stymied by resistance to an increase in the Confederation's powers, which required the unanimous consent of the states. In 1781 Rhode Island rejected Morris's proposal for an import duty of 5 percent. Two years later New York refused to accept a similar plan, pointing out that it had opposed British import duties and would not accept them from Congress. Rather than send funds to Congress (which might use them to repay debt-holding citizens of other states), some states paid interest directly to their own citizens. By 1786 Pennsylvania, Maryland, New York, and New Jersey had assumed nearly one-third of the domestic debt, showing that the Confederation was essentially a league of states rather than an effective central government.

Despite its limited powers, the Congress successfully planned the settlement of the trans-Appalachian West. The Congress needed to assert the Confederation's title to this great treasure in order to sell it and raise revenue for the government. Thus, in 1783 Congress began to negotiate with Indian tribes, hoping to persuade them that the Treaty of Paris had extinguished their land rights. The Congress also bargained with white squatters, allowing them to stay only if they paid for their lands. Congress wanted to secure an orderly settlement of western lands and their eventual admission to the Union. Given the natural barrier of the Appalachian Mountains, many members of Congress feared that westerners might establish separate republics or even link up with Spanish Louisiana. The danger was real: in 1784 thousands of settlers—"white savages," John Jay called them—set up a new state, Franklin, in what is now eastern Tennessee. To preserve its authority over the West, Congress refused to recognize Franklin or consider its application to join the Confederation. Instead, the delegates directed the states of Virginia, North Carolina, and Georgia to administer the process of creating new states south of the Ohio River.

To the north of the Ohio, Congress established a national domain, issuing three ordinances for the settlement and administration of the Northwest Territory. The Ordinance of 1784, written by Thomas Jefferson, called for the admission of states carved out of the territory as soon as their populations equaled that of the smallest existing state. To deter squatters, the Land Ordinance of 1785 established a grid surveying system and specified that the lands be surveyed before settlement (see Map 7.2). Land was to be sold in fee simple and mostly in large blocs, a provision that favored large-scale investors and speculators.

Finally, the Northwest Ordinance of 1787 provided for the creation of three to five territories, which would eventually become the states of Ohio, Indiana, Illinois, Michigan, and Wisconsin. Reflecting the Enlightenment social philosophy of Jefferson and other Patriots, the ordinance prohibited slavery in those territories and earmarked funds from the sale of some land for the support of schools. Each new territory would be ruled by a governor and

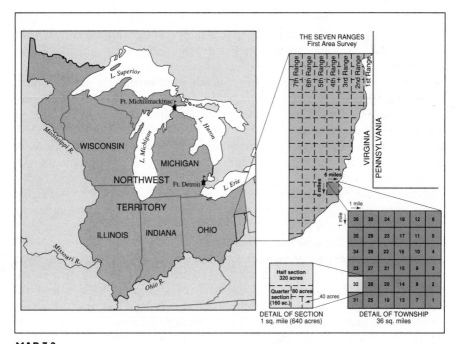

MAP 7.2

Land Divisions in the Northwest Territory
The ordinances of 1785 and 1787 divided the Northwest Territory into uniform sections or townships. The townships were about the same size as New England communities, 36 square miles, and were divided into thirty-six sections of 1 square mile, or 640 acres, surveyed in a grid pattern. The ordinances favored speculators over yeomen by requiring that half the townships be sold in single blocks of 23,040 acres.

judges appointed by Congress. Once the number of free adult men reached 5,000, settlers could elect their own legislature. When the population grew to 60,000, residents could write a republican constitution and apply to join the Confederation. Once admitted, a new state would enjoy all the rights and privileges of the existing states.

The land ordinances of the 1780s were a great and enduring achievement. They provided for the orderly settlement of the West while reducing the prospect of secessionist movements and preventing the emergence of dependent "colonies." The ordinances also added a new "western" dimension to the national identity. The United States was no longer confined to thirteen governments on the eastern seaboard; it had space to expand.

The Postwar Crisis

Whatever the future of the West, postwar conditions in the East were grim. Peace had brought a recession rather than a return to prosperity. The war had destroyed many American merchant ships and cut the export of tobacco and other farm goods. The British Navigation Acts, which once had nurtured colonial commerce, now barred Americans from trading with the British West Indies. And low-priced British manufactures flooded American markets, driving many artisans and wartime textile firms out of business.

State governments emerged from the war with large debts and worthless currencies. Speculators—wealthy merchants and landowners—who had purchased state debt certificates for far less than face value advocated high taxes so that the bonds could be redeemed quickly at full value. But yeomen farmers and artisans, hard hit by the postwar recession, demanded tax relief. To assist debtors, many states enacted laws allowing them to pay creditors in installments. Other states printed more paper currency in an effort to extend credit. Although wealthy men deplored these actions as destructive of "the just rights of creditors," the stopgap measures probably prevented a major social upheaval.

In Massachusetts, the lack of debtor-relief legislation provoked the first armed uprising in the new nation. Merchants and creditors had persuaded the legislature to impose taxes to repay the state's war debt rather than to issue more paper currency. When cash-strapped farmers could not pay their debts, creditors hauled them into court, saddling them with high legal fees. In 1786 residents of central and western counties called extralegal meetings to protest the taxes and property seizures, and bands of angry farmers closed the courts by force. The resistance gradually grew into a full-scale revolt led by the former Continental army captain Daniel Shays.

A struggle against taxes imposed by a nonlocal government, Shays's Rebellion resembled colonial resistance to the Stamp Act. "The people have turned against their teachers the doctrines which were inculcated to effect the late revolution," complained the conservative Massachusetts political leader Fisher Ames. But even the Radical Patriots of 1776 condemned the crowd actions as antirepublican. "Those Men, who . . . would lessen the Weight of Government lawfully exercised must be Enemies to our happy Revolution and Common Liberty," charged Samuel Adams. To preserve its authority, the Massachusetts legislature passed a Riot Act outlawing illegal assemblies. Governor James Bowdoin, supported by eastern merchants, equipped a strong fighting force to put down the rebellion and called for additional troops from the Continental Congress. Shays's army dwindled during the winter of 1786–1787, falling victim to freezing weather and inadequate supplies, and Bowdoin's military force easily dispersed the rebels.

The collapsed rebellion provided graphic proof that the costs of war and the fruits of independence were not being shared evenly. Many of those who had suffered while fighting for independence felt they had exchanged one tyranny for another. Massachusetts voters turned Governor Bowdoin out of office, and farmers in New York, northern Pennsylvania, Connecticut, New Hampshire, and Vermont (admitted as a state in 1791) closed courthouses, demanding economic relief. As British officials in Canada predicted the imminent demise of the United States, many Americans feared for the fate of their republican experiment. In these dire times nationalists redoubled their efforts to create a central government equal to the challenges facing the new republic.

An Anti-Shaysite Interviews the Rebels

After Shays's Rebellion, both sides sought to justify their cause. This clever piece, purportedly written by a neutral observer, suggests the rebels' grievances but subtly emphasizes their selfish motives, portraying the "mobility" as anarchists intent on destroying all authority.

What influenced them to thus rise and oppose government? What did they aim at thereby. . . . As therefore I was present with them at the late rising . . . I inquired of an old plough jogger the confessed aim of the people of that assembly. He said, "To get redress of grievances." I asked, "What grievances?" He said, "We have grievances enough; I can tell you mine. I have labored hard all my days, and fared hard. I have been greatly abused, been obliged to do more than my part in the war, been loaded down with [many taxes:] class-rates, town-rates, province-rates, continental-rates, and all rates, lawsuits, and have been pulled and hauled by sheriffs, constables, and collectors, and had my cattle sold for less than they were worth. I have been obliged to pay, and no-body will pay me . . . and the great men are going to get all we have, and I think it is time for us to rise and put a stop to it, and have no more courts, nor sheriffs, nor collectors, nor lawyers. I design to pay no more. . . ."

I next asked a pert lad . . . [who] made a long harangue upon governors, and jobbers, and lawyers and judges . . . and salaries, and fees, and pensions, and such has ten times too much, and such has five times too much, and . . . the great men pocket up all the money and live easy, and we work hard, and we can't pay it, and we won't pay it. . . .

Thus I went from rank to rank, through all the mobility. . . . I got the secrets of their hearts.

SOURCE: Linda R. Monk, ed., *Ordinary Americans: U.S. History through the Eyes of Everyday People* (Alexandria, VA: Close Up Publications, 1994), pp. 42–43.

THE CONSTITUTION OF 1787

From the moment of its creation, the Constitution was a controversial document. This principled and innovative statement of republican political theory, written in a time of crisis, also embodied the values and interests of men with a personal stake in its outcome.

The Rise of a Nationalist Faction

Men who had served the Confederation during the war—as military officers, diplomats, and officials—had acquired a "national" outlook. General Washington, the financier Robert Morris, and the diplomats Benjamin Franklin, John

Jay, and John Adams became advocates of a stronger central government with the power to control foreign commerce and impose tariffs. They knew that without tariff revenue, Congress would be unable to pay the interest on the foreign debt and the nation's credit would collapse. But southern planters opposed tariffs on cheap British textiles and ironware, and key commercial states in the North—New York, Massachusetts, Pennsylvania—had devised their own trade policies, involving subsidies to local merchants as well as tariffs on imported goods.

By 1786 the nationalists were also worried about the creditworthiness of the state governments. Legislatures in Virginia and other southern states had granted tax relief to various groups of citizens, diminishing public revenue and delaying the redemption of state debts. Taxpayers were being led to believe they would "never be compelled to pay," lamented Charles Lee of Virginia, a wealthy bondholder. Moreover, state governments had jeopardized the integrity of private debts by providing legislative relief to debtors. "While men are madly accumulating enormous debts, their legislators are making provisions for their nonpayment," a South Carolina creditor complained.

Nationalists took the initiative in 1786, when James Madison persuaded the Virginia legislature to call a special convention to discuss tariff and taxation policies. Twelve men representing only five states met in Annapolis, Maryland; after their discussion, they called for another meeting in Philadelphia to undertake a broad review of the Confederation. Nationalists in Congress, frightened by Shays's Rebellion, secured a resolution supporting the Philadelphia convention, calling for a revision of the Articles of Confederation "adequate to the exigencies of government and the preservation of the Union." "Nothing but the adoption of some efficient plan from the Convention," a fellow nationalist wrote to James Madison, "can prevent anarchy first & civil convulsions afterwards."

The Philadelphia Convention

In May 1787, fifty-five delegates arrived in Philadelphia, representing every state except Rhode Island, whose legislature opposed any increase in central authority. Some delegates, such as Benjamin Franklin of Pennsylvania, had been leaders of the independence movement. Others, including George Washington and Robert Morris, had become prominent during the war. Several famous Patriots missed the convention. John Adams and Thomas Jefferson were in Europe, serving as the American ministers to Britain and France. The radical Samuel Adams had not been chosen as a delegate by the Massachusetts legislature, while the firebrand Patrick Henry refused to attend because he favored a limited national government. Their places were taken by capable younger men such as James Madison and Alexander Hamilton.

Most delegates to the Philadelphia convention were merchants, slaveholding planters, or "monied men." There were no artisans, backcountry settlers, or tenants and only a single yeoman farmer. Consequently, most delegates supported creditors' property rights and favored a central government that would protect the republic from "the imprudence of democracy," as Hamilton put it.

The delegates began by electing Washington as the presiding officer. To forestall popular opposition, they decided to deliberate behind closed doors. They agreed that each state would have one vote, as in the Confederation, and that a majority of states would decide an issue. Then the delegates exceeded their mandate to revise the Articles of Confederation by agreeing to consider the Virginia Plan, a scheme for a truly national government devised by James Madison. Madison had arrived in Philadelphia determined to fashion a new political order that would ensure government by men of high character. A graduate of Princeton, he had read classical and modern political theory and served in both the Confederation Congress and the Virginia assembly. His experience in Virginia had convinced him of the "narrow ambition" and lack of public virtue of many state political leaders.

Madison's Virginia Plan differed from the Articles of Confederation in three crucial respects. First, it rejected state sovereignty in favor of the "supremacy of national authority." The central government would have the power to overturn state laws and "legislate in all cases to which the separate States are incompetent." Second, the plan called for a *national* republic that drew its authority directly from all the people and had direct power over them. As Madison explained, the new central government would bypass the states, operating directly "on the individuals composing them." Third, the plan created a three-tier national government with a lower house elected by voters, an upper house elected by the lower house, and an executive and judiciary chosen by the entire legislature.

From a political perspective, Madison's plan contained a fatal flaw. By assigning great power to the lower house, whose composition was based on population, it would have increased the influence of the larger states dramatically. Consequently, delegates from the less populous states rejected the plan, fearing, as a Delaware delegate put it, that the states with many inhabitants would "crush the small ones whenever they stand in the way of their ambitious or interested views."

Delegates from the small states rallied behind the New Jersey Plan devised by William Paterson. This plan strengthened the Confederation by giving the central government the power to raise revenue, control commerce, and make binding requisitions on the states. But it preserved the equality of the states by limiting each state to one vote in a unicameral legislature, as in the Confederation. Delegates from the larger states would not accept this provision. However, after a month of debate a bare majority of the states voted to accept the Virginia Plan as the basis for further discussion.

This decision raised the prospect of a dramatically new constitutional system. During the hot, humid summer of 1787 the delegates met six days a week, debating high principles and considering a multitude of technical details.

Experienced and realistic politicians, they knew that their plan had to be acceptable to existing political factions and powerful social groups. Pierce Butler of South Carolina invoked a classical Greek precedent: "We must follow the example of Solon, who gave the Athenians not the best government he could devise but the best they would receive."

Representation remained the central problem. To satisfy both large and small states, the Connecticut delegates suggested amending the Virginia Plan so that the upper house, the Senate, would always seat two members from each state, while seats in the lower chamber, the House of Representatives, would be apportioned on the basis of population. The size of the states' delegations would be determined every ten years on the basis of a national census. This "Great Compromise" was accepted, but only after bitter debate; to some it seemed less a compromise than a victory for the smaller states.

Other state-related matters were quickly settled. One delegate objected to establishing national courts within the states, warning that "the states will revolt at such encroachments." The convention therefore defined the judicial power of the United States in broad terms, vesting it "in one supreme Court" and leaving the new national legislature to decide whether to establish lower courts within the states. The convention also decided against a uniform freehold property qualification for voting. "Eight or nine states have extended the right of suffrage beyond the freeholders," George Mason of Virginia pointed out. "What will people there say if they should be disfranchised?" In another attempt to appease the states, delegates placed the selection of the president in the hands of an *electoral college* that would be chosen on a state-by-state basis. And they specified that state legislatures, not the voters at large, would elect members of the Senate. By giving state governments an important role in the new constitutional system, the delegates hoped to encourage them to accept a reduction in their sovereignty.

Although slavery was not a prominent issue in the debates, discussion of the subject revealed important regional divisions. While no one proposed the abolition of slavery, Gouverneur Morris of New York spoke for many northern delegates in condemning slavery as "a nefarious institution." George Mason, reflecting the outlook of many Chesapeake planters, who already had ample numbers of slaves, argued for prohibition of the Atlantic slave trade. But delegates from the rice-growing states of South Carolina and Georgia insisted that slave imports continue, warning that otherwise their states "shall not be parties to the Union."

For the sake of national unity, the delegates decided to treat slavery as a political rather than a moral issue. To protect the property of slaveowners, they agreed to a "fugitive" clause that would enable masters to reclaim enslaved blacks (or white indentured servants) who had taken refuge in other states. At the insistence of Georgia and South Carolina, they denied Congress the power to regulate slave imports for twenty years. To mollify the northern states, the delegates agreed not to mention slavery explicitly in the Constitution (referring instead to citizens and "all other Persons"), thus denying the institution national legal status. They also refused southern demands to count slaves and citizens equally in determining states' representation in Congress, accepting a compromise proposal in which a slave would be counted as three-fifths of a free person for purposes of representation and taxation.

Having allayed the concerns of small states and slave states, the delegates proceeded to create a powerful, procreditor national government. The finished document declared that the Constitution and all national legislation and treaties made under its authority would be the "supreme" law of the land. It gave the national government broad powers over taxation, military defense, and external commerce as well as the authority to make all laws "necessary and proper" to implement those and other provisions. To establish the fiscal reputation of the central government and protect creditors, the Constitution mandated that the United States honor the existing national debt. Finally, it restricted the ability of state governments to assist debtors by forbidding them to issue money or enact any "Law impairing the Obligation of Contracts."

The proposed Constitution was not a "perfect production," Benjamin Franklin admitted on September 17, 1787, as he urged the forty-one delegates still present to sign it. Yet the great diplomat confessed his astonishment at finding "this system approaching so near to perfection as it does." His colleagues apparently agreed; all but three signed the document.

The Debate over Ratification

The delegates hesitated to submit the Constitution to the state legislatures for their unanimous consent, as required by the Articles of Confederation, because they knew that Rhode Island (and perhaps a few other states) would reject it. Instead, they specified that the Constitution would go into effect upon ratification by special conventions in at least nine of the thirteen states. The Confederation Congress, because of its nationalist sympathies, winked at this extralegal procedure.

A great national debate immediately began, in which the nationalists seized the initiative with two bold moves. First, they called themselves "Federalists," a term that suggested a loose, decentralized system of government and partially obscured their quest for a strong central authority. Second, they launched a coordinated political campaign, publishing dozens of pamphlets and newspaper articles in support of the proposed Constitution.

The opponents of the Constitution, who became known as Antifederalists, came from diverse backgrounds and were less organized than the Federalists. Some, like Governor George Clinton of New York, enjoyed power in a state and feared losing it. Others were rural democrats who pointed out that the Constitution, unlike most state constitutions, lacked a bill of rights; they feared the power of a central government controlled by merchants and creditors. "These lawyers and men of learning and monied men expect to be managers of this Constitution," worried a Massachusetts farmer, "and get all the power and all the money into their own hands and then they will swallow up all of us little folks . . . just as the whale swallowed up Jonah."

Well-educated Americans with a traditional republican outlook also opposed the new system. To keep government "close to the people," they wanted the nation to remain a collection of small sovereign republics tied together only for trade and defense—not the "United States" but the "States United." Citing the French political philosopher Montesquieu, Antifederalists argued that republican institutions were best suited to cities or small states. Melancton Smith of New York warned that the large electoral districts prescribed by the Constitution would give power to a few wealthy upper-class men, whereas "a representative body, composed principally of respectable yeomanry, is the best possible security to liberty." Patrick Henry foresaw a return to the worst features of British rule: high taxes, an oppressive bureaucracy, a standing army, and a "great and mighty President . . . supported in extravagant munificence."

In New York, where ratification was hotly contested, James Madison, John Jay, and Alexander Hamilton countered these arguments in a series of newspaper articles collectively called *The Federalist*. They stressed the need for a strong government to conduct foreign affairs and insisted that central authority would not foster domestic tyranny. Citing Montesquieu's praise for "mixed government" (and drawing on John Adams's *Thoughts on Government*), the authors of *The Federalist* pointed out that national authority would be divided among a president, a bicameral legislature, and a judiciary. Each branch of government would "check and balance" the others, thus preserving liberty.

Indeed, in *The Federalist*, No. 10, Madison maintained that the size of the national republic would be its greatest protection against tyranny. It was "sown in the nature of man," Madison wrote, that individuals would seek power and form factions to advance their interests. Indeed, "a landed interest, a manufacturing interest, a mercantile interest, a moneyed interest, with many lesser interests, grow up of necessity in civilized nations." He argued that the government of a free society should not suppress those groups but instead prevent any one of them from becoming dominant—an end best achieved in a large republic. "Extend the sphere," Madison concluded, "and you take in a greater variety of parties and interests; you make it less probable that a majority of the whole will have a common motive to invade the rights of other citizens."

Unlike the men at the Philadelphia convention, the delegates who met at the state ratifying conventions between December 1787 and June 1788 represented a wide spectrum of Americans, from untutored farmers and middling artisans to well-educated gentlemen. Generally, delegates from the backcountry were Antifederalists, whereas those from the seacoast were Federalists. A coalition of merchants, artisans, and commercial farmers from Philadelphia and its vicinity spearheaded an easy Federalist victory in Pennsylvania. Other early Federalist successes came in the less populous states of Delaware, New Jersey, Georgia, and Connecticut, where delegates counted on a strong national government to offset the power of their larger neighbors.

The Constitution's first real test came in January 1788 in Massachusetts, one of the most populous states and a hotbed of Antifederalist sentiment (see Map 7.3). Influential Patriots, including Samuel Adams and Governor John Hancock, opposed the new constitution, as did Shaysite sympathizers in the west. But Boston artisans, who wanted tariff protection from British imports, supported ratification. Astute Federalist politicians finally won over wavering delegates by warning of political chaos and promising a national bill of rights. By a close vote of 187 to 168, the Federalists carried the day.

Spring brought new Federalist victories in Maryland and South Carolina. When New Hampshire ratified in June, the required nine states had

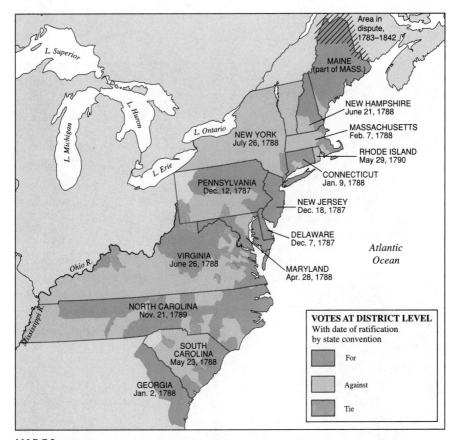

MAP 7.3

Ratifying the Constitution

In 1907 the geographer Owen Libby discovered that most delegates from seaboard or commercial farming districts favored the Constitution while those from backcountry areas opposed it. Subsequent research has confirmed Libby's socioeconomic interpretation in North and South Carolina and Massachusetts; however, other factors influenced delegates in some states with frontier districts, such as Georgia, where the Constitution was ratified unanimously.

approved the Constitution. Nonetheless, the essential states of Virginia and New York had not yet acted. Madison, Jay, and Hamilton, writing in *The Federalist*, used their superb rhetorical skills to win support in those states. Leading Federalists reiterated their promise to amend the Constitution with a bill of rights, addressing a powerful Antifederalist argument. In the end the Federalists won narrowly in Virginia, 89 to 79, and that success carried them to victory in New York by the even smaller margin of 30 to 27. North Carolina and Rhode Island ratified only in 1789 and 1790, respectively.

The Federalists, working against great odds, had created a national republic that reestablished the political authority of the traditional elite. The Revolutionary Era, which had enhanced the power of yeomen and other ordinary Americans, had come to an end.

Federalist Gentry
A prominent New England Federalist, Oliver Ellsworth served as Chief Justice of the United States (1796–1800), while Abigail Wolcott Ellsworth was the daughter of a governor of Connecticut. In 1792 the artist Ralph Earl captured the aspirations of the Ellsworths by giving them an aristocratic demeanor and prominently displaying their mansion (in the window). (Wadsworth Atheneum)

The Constitution Implemented

The Constitution expanded the dimensions of American political life, allowing voters to fill national as well as local and state offices. The Federalists swept the election of 1788, placing forty-four supporters in the first Congress; only eight Antifederalists were elected. The Constitution had specified that electors chosen in the states would select the president and vice-president, and as expected, the electors chose George Washington as president. John Adams received the second highest number of electoral votes and became vice-president. The two men took up their posts in New York City, the temporary home of the national government.

Washington, the military savior of his country, became its political father as well. At fifty-seven, he was a man of great personal dignity and influence. Instinctively cautious, he generally followed the administrative practices of the Confederation, asking Congress to reestablish the existing executive departments: Foreign Affairs (State), Finance (Treasury), and War. The president had the power to appoint major officials with the consent of the Senate; Washington insisted on his authority to remove them as well, an approach that ensured the chief executive's control over the bureaucracy. To head the Department of State, Washington chose Thomas Jefferson, a fellow Virginian and an experienced diplomat. For secretary of the Treasury he turned to Alexander Hamilton, a lawyer and wartime military aide. The new president designated Jefferson, Hamilton, and Secretary of War Henry Knox as his *cabinet*, or advisory body.

The new national charter had created a Supreme Court but left the establishment of the court system to Congress. Because the Federalists wanted national institutions to act directly on individual citizens, the Judiciary Act, passed by Congress in 1789, created a hierarchical federal court system with thirteen *district courts*, one for each state, and three *circuit courts* to hear appeals. As the Constitution specified, the Supreme Court had the final say. Moreover, the Judiciary Act permitted appeals to the Supreme Court of constitutional matters that arose in the state courts, ensuring that national judges would decide contested issues.

The Federalists kept their promise to add amendments to the Constitution. Drawing on lists of rights submitted by the states' ratifying conventions, James Madison, who had been elected to the House of Representatives, submitted nineteen amendments to the first Congress. Twelve received legislative approval, of which ten were ratified by the states by December 1791. The amendments, which became known as the Bill of Rights, both mandated certain legal procedures, such as trial by jury, and safeguarded certain fundamental individual rights, such as freedom of speech and religion. Citizens were guaranteed the right to bear arms so that they might serve in the militia and defend their liberties. The Tenth Amendment limited the authority of the national government by reserving nondelegated powers to the states or the people. In addressing Antifederalists' concerns through the Bill of Rights,

Congress secured the legitimacy of the new government and ensured broad political support for the Constitution.

THE POLITICAL CRISIS OF THE 1790s

The final decade of the century brought fresh political challenges. The Federalists split into two irreconcilable factions over financial policy, and the French Revolution widened rifts over political ideology. In the course of these struggles, Alexander Hamilton and Thomas Jefferson defined contrasting views of the American future.

Hamilton's Program

One of George Washington's most important decisions was his choice of Alexander Hamilton as secretary of the Treasury. An ambitious self-made man, Hamilton had come to the mainland from the West Indies in 1772 and enrolled at King's College in New York. During the war Hamilton's military abilities and personal charm had impressed Washington, who had chosen him as his personal aide. In the 1780s, Hamilton had married the daughter of a wealthy Hudson River landowner and become a leading lawyer in New York City. At the Philadelphia convention Hamilton had condemned the "amazing violence and turbulence of the democratic spirit," calling for an authoritarian government headed by a president with nearly monarchical powers.

As Treasury secretary, Hamilton devised bold policies that enhanced the authority of the national government and favored his immediate acquaintances, many of them financiers and seaport merchants. He outlined his plan in three pathbreaking and interrelated reports to Congress: on public credit (January 1790), a national bank (December 1790), and manufactures (December 1791).

The financial and social implications of Hamilton's "Report on the Public Credit" made it instantly controversial. Congress was to redeem at face value the millions of dollars in securities issued by the Confederation, a *redemption* and *funding* plan that would bolster the government's credit but also provide windfall profits to speculators. For example, the merchant firm of Burrell & Burrell had paid about $600 for Confederation notes with a face value of $2,500; their redemption at face value would bring an enormous profit of $1,900. Hamilton proposed to pay off the Burrells and other noteholders with new government securities, which would pay interest at about 6 percent. He hoped that investors, attracted by the relatively high interest rate, would hold (and not speculate with) the new securities, keeping their value high and enhancing the government's credit.

Hamilton's plan for a *permanent* national debt funded by monied men reawakened Radical Whig and republican fears of scheming British financiers and governmental favoritism. Speaking for the Virginia House of Burgesses, Patrick Henry declared that "to erect, and concentrate, and perpetuate a large monied interest, must prove fatal to the existence of American liberty." Challenging the morality of Hamilton's proposal, James Madison sought to assist the thousands of shopkeepers, farmers, and soldiers who had accepted government securities during the dark days of the war and then sold them to speculators. Madison proposed giving the present bondholders only "the highest price which has prevailed in the market" and distributing the remaining funds to the original owners. But identifying the original owners would have been difficult, and nearly half the members of the House of Representatives owned Confederation securities and stood to profit from Hamilton's plan. Melding practicality with self-interest, the House rejected Madison's proposal by a solid margin and approved Hamilton's plan.

Hamilton then advanced a second proposal that favored wealthy creditors, a plan by which the national government would take over the war debts of the states. This *assumption* plan unleashed the flurry of speculation and governmental corruption that critics of redemption had feared. Before Hamilton announced it, Assistant Secretary of the Treasury William Duer used insider knowledge to buy up the depreciated war bonds of southern states. By the end of 1790 Duer and other northern speculators owned more than half the war bonds of Virginia and the Carolinas, which they sold after the announcement of Hamilton's assumption plan caused bond values to rise.

Concerned members of Congress noted that some states, such as Virginia and Maryland, had already levied high taxes to pay off their war debts; under Hamilton's plan they would be taxed to pay the debts of other states as well. To win congressional support for assumption, Hamilton agreed to repay those states and back their bid to locate the national capital along the banks of the Potomac. In return, Maryland and Virginia gave Hamilton the votes he needed in the House of Representatives.

In December 1790, Hamilton, bolstered by the passage of his redemption and assumption bills, asked Congress to charter a national financial institution, the Bank of the United States. The bank, to be jointly owned by private stockholders and the national government, would make loans to merchants, handle government funds, and issue financial notes. Thus, it would provide a respected medium of exchange for the specie-starved American economy and make the new national debt easier to fund. These considerable benefits persuaded a majority of both houses to enact Hamilton's bill and send it to the president for approval.

At this critical juncture, Secretary of State Thomas Jefferson joined ranks with Madison against Hamilton. Jefferson had condemned the shady dealings in southern war bonds and the "corrupt squadron of paper dealers" who had arranged them. Now he charged that Hamilton's scheme for a national bank was unconstitutional. "The incorporation of a Bank," Jefferson told President Washington, was not "delegated to the United States by the Constitution." In a *strict interpretation* of the national charter, Jefferson maintained that the central government had only the limited powers explicitly assigned to it in the Constitution. In response, Hamilton articulated a *loose interpretation*, noting that Article 1, Section 8, empowered Congress to make "all Laws which shall be necessary and proper" to carry out the Constitution's provisions. In Hamilton's view, "if the *end* be clearly comprehended within any of the specified powers, and if the measure is not forbidden by any particular provision of the Constitution, it may safely be deemed to come within the compass of national authority." Washington agreed and signed the legislation creating the bank.

Hamilton turned now to the final element of his financial system: a national revenue that would be used to pay the interest on the national debt. At Hamilton's insistence, in 1792 Congress imposed a variety of domestic excise taxes, including a duty on whiskey distilled in the United States. But the revenue from those taxes was too small. Although his "Report on Manufactures" (1791) had envisioned an economically powerful nation that was self-sufficient in manufactured goods, the Treasury secretary could not ask for high "protective" tariffs that would help American industries by excluding foreign products. Such tariffs would cut trade, depriving the government of needed revenue. Therefore, Hamilton asked Congress for only a modest increase in customs duties, a tariff for "revenue."

Hamilton's carefully designed plan worked brilliantly. As American trade increased, customs revenue rose steadily (providing about 90 percent of the national government's income from 1790 to 1820), allowing him to fund his redemption and assumption programs. In less than two years he had devised a strikingly modern fiscal system that provided the new national government with financial stability.

Jefferson's Vision

Hamilton paid a high price for this success. By the time Washington began his second four-year term in 1793, Hamilton's financial measures had split the Federalists into irreconcilable factions. Most northern Federalists, in both Congress and the states, adhered to the political alliance led by Hamilton, and most southerners to a rival group headed by Madison and Jefferson. By the elections of 1794 the two factions had acquired names. Hamilton's supporters retained their original name: Federalists; Madison's and Jefferson's supporters were called Democratic-Republicans or simply Republicans.

The southern planters and western farmers who became Republicans rejected Hamilton's economic and social philosophy. Thomas Jefferson, a man of great learning, spoke for them. Well read in architecture, natural history, scientific farming, and political theory, Jefferson embraced the optimistic spirit of the Enlightenment, declaring his belief in the "improvability of the human race." But he knew that progress was not inevitable and deplored both the traditional speculative practices of merchants and financiers and the emerging social divisions of an urban industrial economy. Having visited the manufacturing regions in Britain and seen the masses of propertyless laborers there, Jefferson had concluded that workers who depended on wages lacked the economic independence required to sustain a republic.

Jefferson's vision of the American future was agrarian and democratic. Although he had grown up a privileged slaveowner, he understood the needs of yeomen farmers and other ordinary white Americans. His vision took form in his *Notes on the State of Virginia* (1785): "Those who labor in the earth are the chosen people of God," he declared. When Jefferson drafted the Ordinance of 1784, he had pictured a West settled by productive yeomen farm families. Their grain and meat would feed European nations, which "would manufacture and send us in exchange our clothes and other comforts."

During the 1790s, Jefferson's vision moved closer to reality as turmoil in Europe created new opportunities for American farmers. The French Revolution began in 1789; four years later the French republican government went to war against a British-led coalition of monarchical states. As warfare disrupted European farming, wheat prices leapt from 5 to 8 shillings a bushel and remained high for twenty years. Chesapeake and Middle Atlantic farmers increased their grain exports, reaping substantial profits. A boom in cotton exports, fueled by the mechanization of cloth production in Britain and the invention of the cotton gin at home, boosted the economy of the Lower South. As Jefferson had hoped, European markets brought prosperity to American farmers and planters.

Two Visions of America
Thomas Jefferson and Alexander Hamilton confront each other in these portraits, as they did during the 1790s. Jefferson was pro-French; Hamilton, pro-British. Jefferson favored farmers and artisans; Hamilton supported merchants and financiers. Jefferson believed in democracy and rule by legislative majorities; Hamilton argued for a strong executive and for judicial review.

War and Politics

American merchants profited even more handsomely from the European war. President Washington issued a Proclamation of Neutrality that enabled U.S. citizens to trade with both sides. As neutral carriers, American ships could pass through the British naval blockade along the French coastline; they soon took over the lucrative trade between France and its West Indian sugar islands. The American merchant fleet became one of the largest in the world, increasing from 355,000 tons in 1790 to more than 1.1 million tons in 1808. Commercial earnings rose spectacularly, averaging $20 million annually in the 1790s—twice the value of cotton and tobacco exports. To keep up with demand, shipowners invested in new vessels, providing work for thousands of shipwrights, sail makers, laborers, and seamen. Hundreds of carpenters, masons, and cabinetmakers found work building warehouses and elegant Federal-style town houses for newly affluent merchants. In the 1790s the assessed value of property in New York City soared from $5.8 million to $20.7 million.

At the same time, the passions of the European struggle convulsed the new republic. Many Americans had welcomed the French Revolution of 1789 because it abolished feudalism and established a constitutional monarchy. But the creation of the more democratic French republic in 1792 and the execution of King Louis XVI the following year divided public opinion. On one side artisans praised the egalitarianism of the French republicans: in Boston, Royal Alley became Equality Lane. Like the radical French Jacobins, artisans addressed each other as "citizen" and founded political clubs, most of which were strongholds of Jefferson's Republican party. On the other side the wealthy and those with strong Christian beliefs denounced the Terror (the executions of Louis XVI and his aristocratic supporters) and condemned the new French regime for abandoning Christianity in favor of atheism.

These ideological conflicts sharpened the debate over Hamilton's economic policies and even helped foment a domestic insurrection. In 1794 farmers in western Pennsylvania mounted the Whiskey Rebellion to protest Hamilton's excise tax on spirits, which had raised the price—and thus cut the demand—for the corn whiskey they sold locally and bartered for eastern manufactures. Like the Sons of Liberty of 1765 and the Shaysites of 1786, the Whiskey rebels attacked both local tax collectors and the authority of a distant government. But these protesters also waved banners proclaiming the French revolutionary slogan "Liberty, Equality, and Fraternity!" To uphold national authority (and deter secessionist movements along the frontier), President Washington raised an army of 12,000 troops that soon suppressed the rebels.

Britain's maritime strategy also widened the growing political divisions in the United States. In November 1793 the Royal Navy began to prey on American ships bound for France from the West Indies, seizing more than 250 vessels and confiscating their sugar cargoes. To avoid war, President Washington sent John Jay to Britain to negotiate a broad series of issues. Jay returned with a treaty that required the U.S. government to make "full and complete compensation" to British merchants for all pre–Revolutionary War debts owed by American citizens. The treaty also acknowledged Britain's right to remove French property from neutral ships, overturning the American merchants' claim that "free ships make free goods." In return, the agreement allowed American merchants to submit claims of illegal seizure to arbitration and required the British to end their aid to the western Indians and remove six military garrisons from the Old Northwest. Although Jefferson and his Republican followers denounced Jay's Treaty as too conciliatory, the Senate ratified it by the bare two-thirds majority required by the Constitution. As long as Hamilton and his Federalist allies were in power, the United States would have a pro-British foreign policy.

The Rise of Parties

The appearance of rival political parties marked a new stage in American politics. Although colonial legislatures had often divided into temporary factions based on family alliances, ethnicity, or regional concerns, they lacked well-organized parties. The new state and national constitutions made no provision for organized political bodies. The framers of the various constitutions considered parties unnecessary and dangerous; following classical republican principles, they wanted voters and legislators to act independently and in the public interest.

But the revolutionary ideology of popular sovereignty had drawn ordinary citizens into politics, and the appearance of economic and ideological interest groups sparked the appearance of a competitive party system. Merchants and creditors favored Federalist policies, as did wheat-exporting slaveholders in the Tidewater districts of the Chesapeake. The emerging Republican coalition was more diverse and drew supporters from across the social spectrum. By the mid-1790s it included not only southern planters and western farmers but also artisans in the seaport cities, German and Scots-Irish settlers, and smallholding eastern farmers.

Party identity crystallized during the election of 1796. To prepare for the election, Federalist and Republican leaders called legislative caucuses in Congress and conventions in the states to discuss policies, nominate candidates, and mobilize supporters. On election day voters selected candidates for local, state, and national office not only on their individual merits but as representatives of parties that stood for distinct principles.

Federalist candidates triumphed in the 1796 election, winning a majority in Congress and the electoral college. The new president, John Adams, continued Hamilton's pro-British foreign policy. When the French navy began to seize American merchant ships and agents of Prince Talleyrand, the French foreign minister, solicited a loan and a bribe from American diplomats, Adams urged Congress to prepare for war. To overcome Republican objections, he charged that Talleyrand's agents, whom he dubbed X, Y, and Z, had insulted the honor of the United States. The Federalist-controlled Congress responded by cutting off trade with France and authorizing American privateers to seize French ships. Party conflict, which had begun over Hamilton's domestic policies, now extended to foreign affairs.

The Crisis of 1798–1800

For the first but not the last time in American history a controversial foreign policy prompted domestic protest and governmental repression. With the United States fighting an undeclared war against France, pro-Republican immigrants from Ireland viciously attacked Adams's foreign policy. Some Federalists responded in kind: "Were I president, I would hang them for otherwise they would murder me," declared a Philadelphia pamphleteer. To silence its critics, the administration pushed a series of coercive measures through Congress in 1798. The Naturalization Act increased the residency requirement for citizenship from five to fourteen years; the Alien Act authorized the deportation of foreigners; and the Sedition Act prohibited the publication of ungrounded or malicious attacks on the president or Congress. "He that is not for us is against us," thundered the Federalist *Gazette of the United States*. Prosecutors arrested more than twenty Republican newspaper editors and politicians, accused them of sedition, and imprisoned some of them.

Republicans assailed this legislation and charged that the Sedition Act contradicted the First Amendment's prohibition against "abridging the freedom of speech, or of the press." Although the Sedition Act was probably unconstitutional, Republicans did not appeal to the Supreme Court partly because the Court's power to review congressional legislation had not been established and partly because the Court was packed with Federalists.

Madison and Jefferson took the fight to the state legislatures instead. At their urging, in 1798 the Kentucky legislature declared the Alien and Sedition acts to be "unauthoritative, void, and of no force." State legislators justified their rejection of a congressional law by arguing that the national government owed its existence to a compact among the states, which meant that "each party has an equal right to judge by itself." The Virginia legislature passed a similar resolution, establishing the legal theory for a "states' rights" interpretation of the Constitution.

The debate over the Sedition Act set the stage for the election of 1800. Jefferson, once opposed in principle to political parties, now saw them as a valuable way "to watch and relate to the people" the activities of the government. Republicans strongly supported Jefferson's bid for the presidency, pointing to the wrongful imprisonment of newspaper editors and championing states' rights. President Adams responded to their attacks by reevaluating his foreign policy. Rejecting the advice of Hamilton and others who wanted to intensify the undeclared war with France (so that Federalists would benefit from an upsurge in patriotism), Adams put country ahead of party and entered into diplomatic negotiations which brought an end to the war.

Federalists branded Jefferson an irresponsible pro-French radical, "the archapostle of irreligion and free thought," but their strategy failed. Voters protested against the undeclared foreign war—and the special national tax on land and houses that Congress had imposed to pay for it—by giving Republicans a majority in both houses of Congress and a narrow edge in the electoral college. But the electors gave Jefferson the same number of votes as Aaron Burr of New York (Jefferson's choice for vice-president), throwing the presidential election into the House of Representatives. (The Twelfth Amendment, ratified in 1804, would remedy the constitutional defect that caused the deadlock by requiring electors to vote separately for president and vice-president.)

Ironically, as the era of Federalism and its aristocratic outlook came to an end, Alexander Hamilton ushered in a more democratic era. For thirty-five ballots Federalists in the House of Representatives blocked Jefferson's election. Then the former Treasury secretary intervened. Calling Burr an "embryo Caesar" and the "most unfit man in the United States for the office of president," Hamilton persuaded key Federalists to permit his longtime rival's selection. The Federalists' concern for political stability also played a role. As Senator James Bayard of Delaware explained, "it was admitted on all hands that we must risk the Constitution and a Civil War or take Mr. Jefferson."

Jefferson called the election the "Revolution of 1800," and so it was. The bloodless transfer of power demonstrated that governments elected by the people could be changed in an orderly way, even in times of bitter partisan conflict. In his inaugural address in 1801, Jefferson praised this achievement, declaring: "We are all Republicans, we are all Federalists." The new republican constitutional order of 1776 had survived a quarter-century of domestic conflict and foreign crisis.

CHAPTER 7 TIMELINE

1776	Pennsylvania's democratic constitution John Adams, *Thoughts on Government* Propertied women vote in New Jersey (changed in 1807)
1777	Articles of Confederation (ratified 1781)
1779	Judith Sargent Murray, "On the Equality of the Sexes"
1780s	Postwar commercial recession Creditor-debtor conflicts in states
1781	Bank of North America chartered by Congress
1784	Ordinance outlines policy for new states
1785	Jefferson's *Notes on the State of Virginia*
1786	Annapolis commercial convention Shays's Rebellion
1787	Northwest Ordinance Philadelphia constitutional convention
1787–1788	Ratification conventions *The Federalist* (Jay, Madison, Hamilton)
1789	Judiciary Act establishes federal court system
1790	Hamilton's program: redemption and assumption
1791	Bill of Rights ratified
1793	Democratic-Republican party founded
1794	Whiskey Rebellion
1795	Jay's Treaty
1798	Alien, Sedition, and Naturalization acts Kentucky and Virginia resolutions
1800	Jefferson elected in "Revolution of 1800"

TOWARD A CONTINENTAL NATION, 1790–1820

- Westward Expansion
- Republican Policy and Diplomacy
- Regional Diversity and National Identity

When the thirteen colonies declared independence in 1776, the new nation was confined to a narrow strip of land along the Atlantic seaboard. But the peace treaty of 1783 extended the domain of the United States as far west as the Mississippi River, more than doubling the size of the new republic and adding millions of acres of fertile, well-watered land. Taking advantage of this bonanza, land-hungry eastern farmers and ambitious entrepreneurs streamed across the Appalachian Mountains.

Just as this vast migration began, President Thomas Jefferson doubled the nation's size again with the Louisiana Purchase of 1803. "[No] territory can be too large," declared David Ramsey of South Carolina, "for a people, who multiply with such unequaled rapidity." With extraordinary self-confidence, tens of thousands of ordinary Americans accepted the challenge of settling the interior of the continent, trekking hundreds of miles by foot and wagon, confronting angry Indian peoples, and turning dense forests into productive farmland. By 1820 two million white and black Americans—a number almost equal to the nation's total population in 1776—were living in nine new states and three territories west of the Appalachians. The United States was on its way to becoming a truly "continental" republic.

Settlers Move West through Pennsylvania
Thomas Birch captured the optimistic spirit of migrating families in his 1816 painting *Conestoga Wagon on the Pennsylvania Turnpike*. The woman's arm points to the West, suggesting both her family's destination and the course of national development.

WESTWARD EXPANSION

Westward movement transformed the lives of all Americans. In the East the departure of large numbers of young men and women disrupted long-established communities, while in the West hundreds of thousands of Indians faced forced removal from their ancestral lands.

Native American Resistance

In the Treaty of Paris, Great Britain had relinquished its claims to the trans-Appalachian region and its peoples to the United States. Although native Americans rejected American control, pointing out that they had not signed the treaty and had never been conquered, the Confederation Congress used military threats to force the Iroquois from most of their lands in New York and Pennsylvania. Soon the once-powerful Iroquois were confined to relatively small reservations. In 1785 American negotiators used similar tactics to force the Chipewyan, Delaware, Ottawa, and Wyandot to sign away most of the future state of Ohio. This time the tactic did not work, as these tribes repudiated the agreement and joined the Miami, Shawnee, and Potawatomi in a confederacy to defend their lands. Led by Little Turtle, the Western Confederacy defeated American expeditionary forces in 1790 and 1791.

Fearing an alliance between the Western Confederacy and the British in Canada, President Washington doubled the size of the army to 5,000 men and ordered General "Mad Anthony" Wayne to lead a new expedition. In August 1794 Wayne defeated the Indian allies in the Battle of Fallen Timbers and negotiated a settlement. In the Treaty of Greenville (Ohio) in 1795, the United States acknowledged Indian ownership of the lands in the trans-Appalachian West but successfully asserted the nation's sovereignty over the region. The Indians agreed to place themselves "under the protection of the United States, and no other Power whatever" (see Map 8.1). The agreement was also significant because it increased the likelihood that Britain would comply with its obligation (reaffirmed in Jay's Treaty of 1795) to withdraw its garrisons from the region. Indian resistance had slowed but not stopped the advance of American settlement.

Settlers and Speculators

As the fighting subsided, migrants from the North and the South poured across the Appalachians. Tenant farmers and struggling yeomen families in the Chesapeake region headed for Kentucky and Tennessee, fleeing the depleted soils and planter elite of the Tidewater region. As more than 225,000 migrants moved west, a worried landlord complained in the *Maryland Gazette* that "boundless settlements open a door for our citizens to run off and leave us, depreciating all our landed property and disabling us from paying taxes."

The new settlers flocked through the Cumberland Gap into Kentucky and along the Knoxville Road into what would become Tennessee, confident that they would prosper by growing cotton and hemp, which were in great demand. But first they had to gain title to their land. The migrants based their claims on "the ancient cultivation law" governing frontier tracts, invoking the argument of the North Carolina Regulators (see Chapter 4) that the poor had a customary right "from time out of Mind" to occupy "back waste vacant

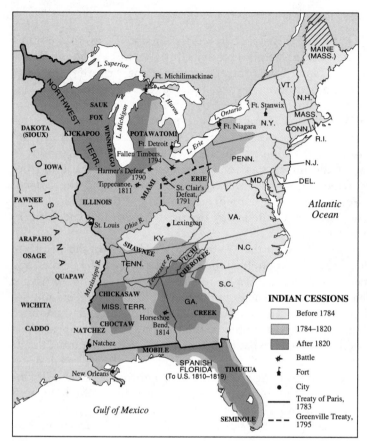

MAP 8.1

Expansion: Military and Diplomatic

On the basis of the peace treaty of 1783, the United States claimed sovereignty over the trans-Appalachian West. When the Indians of the Western Confederacy contested that claim, the American government upheld it by force. Armed diplomacy forced native American peoples to cede by treaty most of their lands east of the Mississippi River.

Lands" sufficient "to provide a subsistence for themselves and their posterity." The Virginia government (which administered the Kentucky territory) allowed "actual settlers" to purchase up to 1,400 acres but allowed twenty-one wealthy individuals and partnerships to acquire handsome tracts averaging 100,000 acres. When Kentucky became a state in 1792, a handful of speculators held title to one-fourth of the land, while half the adult white men owned none and lived as squatters or tenants.

Another wave of migrants flowed out of New England into New York State and beyond, planting new yeoman farm communities in the Great Lakes region. Even though some New England farmers had moved north into New

Hampshire and Vermont and east along the coast of Maine in search of land, many New England communities remained overcrowded. Seeking to provide farmsteads for their children, thousands of New England parents hitched their oxen and horses to wagons and carried tools, plows, and household goods to the fertile plains and rolling hills of upstate New York. By 1820, 800,000 migrants were living in a string of settlements stretching from Albany to Buffalo. Thousands more had pressed on to Ohio.

This vast migration was organized not by governments or joint-stock companies but by the people themselves. To lighten the economic and emotional burdens of migration, many settlers moved in large family groups. As a traveler reported from central New York: "The town of Herkimer is entirely populated by families come from Connecticut. We stayed at Mr. Snow's who came from New London with about ten male and female cousins." Members of Congregational churches often migrated together, transplanting the strong religious and cultural traditions of New England to western communities.

As in Kentucky, much land in New York was snapped up by politically well-connected speculators. In the 1780s the financier Robert Morris acquired 1.3 million acres in the Genesee region of central New York for $75,000—about 6 cents an acre. Speculation drove up the price of farms, making it difficult for yeomen families to realize their dream of landed independence. Thousands of settlers signed lease-purchase agreements with the Dutch-owned Holland Land Company only to become mired in debt because of high interest rates and the difficulty of transporting goods to market. Soon the number of tenants far surpassed the number of freeholders in the counties west of the Genesee River. Having fled declining prospects in the East, these farmers found themselves at the bottom of the economic ladder in the West.

The massive exodus drained eastern towns of money and workers, forcing established farmers to plant different crops and improve their equipment. In New England farmers turned to potatoes, a nutritious, high-yielding crop. In the wheat-growing Middle Atlantic states enterprising farmers replaced metal-tipped wooden plows with cast-iron models that dug a deeper furrow and required a single yoke of oxen instead of two or three. Cast-iron plows reduced the cost of livestock and labor, enabling farmers to maintain production levels even if their sons and daughters had gone west.

Eastern farmers also took advantage of the progressive farming methods advocated by British agricultural reformers. Wealthy "improvers" rotated their crops to maintain the soil's fertility, ordering workers or tenants to plant nitrogen-rich clover and follow it with wheat, corn, wheat, and then clover. In Pennsylvania crop rotation increased the average wheat yield from 12 to 25 bushels per acre. Yeomen diversified their output by raising sheep and selling the wool to textile manufacturers. And they adopted a year-round planting cycle, sowing wheat in the winter and planting corn in the spring to provide fodder for their milk cows. Farm women and girls milked the cows and made butter and cheese to sell in the growing towns and cities.

The "Onion Maidens" of Wethersfield, Connecticut
Founded in 1634 and densely settled by 1750, Wethersfield remained prosperous through agricultural innovation, turning after 1790 to market gardening. Women played a dominant role in this intensive horticulture,
which made Wethersfield the "onion capital" of the United States.

Rural families were now laboring twelve months a year. But whether they
were hacking fields out of western forests or carting manure to replenish eastern
soils, their labor was rewarded by higher output and income. Westward migration
boosted the entire American economy as it improved the quality of rural life.

The Transportation Bottleneck

The geography of the American continent remained an obstacle to economic
advancement. In America as in Europe, the patterns of settlement and trade

had long been determined by water routes. Farmers without access to rivers had to haul their crops by oxcart over narrow dirt trails that turned to mud-holes during the wet season. Even in dry weather, ox-drawn carts moved slowly and carried only small loads. They were expensive, too, costing 30 cents a ton-mile, or roughly five times as much as water transport. Incredibly, Pennsylvania farmers paid as much to send wheat and corn 30 miles overland to Philadelphia as merchants did to ship it from Philadelphia to London. Consequently, settlers paid premium prices for land along navigable streams and speculators bought up likely sites for towns along the Ohio, Tennessee, and Mississippi rivers, on which farmers floated their produce to New Orleans. Without access to waterways or good roads, western settlers could not afford to send goods to distant markets.

The enhancement of inland trade became a high priority for the new state governments, which actively encouraged transportation ventures. Between 1793 and 1812, the Pennsylvania legislature granted corporate charters to fifty-five private turnpike companies and Massachusetts chartered over a hundred. The turnpike companies charged tolls for the use of the level gravel roads they built, but the roads cut travel time significantly. State governments and private entrepreneurs also dredged rivers to make them navigable and constructed short canals, mostly to bypass waterfalls or rapids. By 1816 the United States had about 100 miles of canals, but only three were more than 2 miles long and none breached the great Appalachian barrier.

Despite these transportation bottlenecks, white Americans continued to migrate westward. They knew it would take a generation to clear land; build houses, barns, and roads; and plant orchards. But they were confident that their sacrifices would yield future security—a farmstead and an independent livelihood for themselves and their children. Slowly, thousands of yeomen and tenant families turned forests into farms, transforming the landscape of the trans-Appalachian West.

REPUBLICAN POLICY AND DIPLOMACY

Between 1801 and 1825 three Republicans from Virginia—Thomas Jefferson, James Madison, and James Monroe—each served two terms as president. Supported by voters in the new western states and by strong majorities in Congress, the Virginia Dynasty reversed many Federalist policies, completing what Jefferson called the Revolution of 1800.

The Jeffersonian Presidency

Thomas Jefferson was perhaps the most accomplished and versatile statesman in American history. A seasoned diplomat and an insightful political philosopher, he was also a superb politician. On becoming president in 1801, Jefferson won over some of his Federalist opponents by appointing them to major government posts; he used other patronage positions to bolster the Republican party in New England. But the new president still faced a government filled with his opponents, especially in the judiciary. The most important Federalist judge was the formidable John Marshall of Virginia, who had been appointed chief justice of the United States by John Adams in January 1801 (he would serve until 1835). Moreover, the outgoing Federalist-controlled Congress had passed a Judiciary Act in 1801, creating sixteen new judgeships, six additional circuit courts, and a variety of patronage posts, which Adams had filled in a series of "midnight appointments" just before leaving office. The Federalists "have retired into the judiciary as a stronghold," Jefferson complained, "and from that battery all the works of Republicanism are to be beaten down and erased."

Republicans in Congress fought back by repealing the Judiciary Act and impeaching two Federalist judges for their partisan political activities, winning the removal of one. For his part, James Madison, the new secretary of state, refused to deliver the commission of one of Adams's midnight appointees, prompting the famous case of *Marbury v. Madison* (see Chapter 9). Subsequently, Jefferson pursued a conciliatory policy, judging each Federalist bureaucrat on the basis of his ability. During eight years as chief executive, he removed only 109 of 433 Federalist officeholders.

Nonetheless, Jefferson and his party were determined to reverse Federalist policies and shrink the national government to what they considered its proper constitutional size and shape. When the Alien and Sedition acts expired, the Republican Congress did not reenact them, seeing them as politically motivated and unconstitutional. Jefferson also abolished all internal taxes, including the excise tax that had sparked the Whiskey Rebellion of 1794, and reduced the size of the army and navy. He reluctantly accepted the Bank of the United States, which he had condemned as unconstitutional in 1791, because of its importance to the nation's economy. But Jefferson was still opposed to a large public debt, and so he appointed Albert Gallatin, a brilliant Swiss-born fiscal conservative, as Treasury secretary. By cutting expenditures and using customs revenues to redeem government bonds, Gallatin reduced the debt from $83 million in 1801 to $45 million in 1808. With Jefferson and Gallatin at the helm, the nation was no longer run in the interest of northeastern creditors and merchants.

Jefferson and the West

Long before he became president Jefferson had championed the settlement of the West. He had celebrated the yeoman farmer in *Notes on the State of Virginia* (1785), helped compose the Confederation's land ordinances, and strongly supported Pinckney's Treaty of 1795, which allowed westerners to ship crops down the Mississippi for export through Spanish-held New Orleans.

As president, Jefferson had a new opportunity to encourage western settlement. The ordinance of 1785, which had set land policy for the national domain, had favored speculators over yeomen. It specified that half the land be sold in blocs of 23,040 acres at a minimum price of $1 per acre, making direct purchase impossible for all but the wealthy (see Map 7.2, page 181). The other half was to be divided into parcels of 640 acres, but even those were prohibitively expensive for many migrants, who lacked the cash to buy high-quality or well-located land. Poorer settlers demanded better terms, but the Federalist-dominated Congresses of the 1790s instead doubled the minimum price to $2 per acre. Many Federalist politicians were eastern landlords who were determined not to lose their tenants to cheap land in the West.

Because Jefferson wanted to see the West populated with yeomen farm families, the Republicans in Congress won the passage of new laws in 1800 and 1804 reducing the minimum allotment to 320 and then 160 acres and allowing payment in installments over four years. Eventually the Land Act of 1820 reduced the minimum purchase to 80 acres and the price to $1.25 per acre, enabling a farmer with only $100 in cash to buy a western farm.

But international events challenged Jefferson's vision for the West. In 1799 the daring general Napoleon Bonaparte seized power in revolution-torn France and began an ambitious campaign to establish a French empire in both Europe and America. In 1800 Napoleon coerced Spain into signing a secret treaty returning Louisiana to France; two years later Spanish officials began restricting American access to New Orleans. Meanwhile, Napoleon had mobilized an expeditionary force to restore French rule in Haiti (or Saint-Domingue), a rich sugar island that had been seized by rebellious black slaves led by Toussaint L'Ouverture.

Napoleon's actions prompted Jefferson to question his party's traditionally pro-French foreign policy. Trade down the Mississippi River, guaranteed by Pinckney's Treaty of 1795 with Spain, was crucial to the West; any nation that denied Americans access to New Orleans, Jefferson declared, must be "our natural and habitual enemy." To avoid crossing swords with Napoleon, Jefferson instructed Robert R. Livingston, the American minister in Paris, to purchase New Orleans.

Jefferson's diplomacy yielded a magnificent prize: the entire territory of Louisiana. In 1802 the French invasion of Haiti was faltering, the victim of yellow fever and spirited black resistance, and a new war was threatening to break out in Europe. Acting with characteristic decisiveness, Napoleon gave up his dream of an empire in America and in April 1803 offered to sell Louisiana. For about $15 million ($180 million today), Livingston and James Monroe, the American ambassador to Britain, concluded what became known as the Louisiana Purchase (see Map 8.3, page 227). "We have lived long," Livingston remarked to Monroe, "but this is the noblest work of our lives."

The magnitude of the Louisiana Purchase forced the president to reconsider his interpretation of the Constitution. Jefferson had always been a strict constructionist, arguing that the national government possessed only the powers "expressly" delegated to it in the Constitution. But there was no provision in the Constitution for adding new territory. Given his dreams for the West, Jefferson was pragmatic: adopting a loose interpretation, he used the treaty-making powers granted by the Constitution to complete the deal with France.

A scientist as well as a statesman, Jefferson wanted detailed information about the physical features of the new territory and its plant and animal life. In 1804 he sent his personal secretary, Meriwether Lewis, to explore the region along with William Clark, an army officer. Aided by Indian guides, Lewis and Clark traveled up the Missouri River, across the Rocky Mountains, and (venturing beyond the Purchase) down the Columbia River to the Pacific Ocean. After two years they returned with the first maps of the immense wilderness and vivid accounts of its natural resources and native American inhabitants.

The Louisiana Purchase was a stunning accomplishment, doubling the size of the nation at a single stroke, but it brought a new threat. New England Federalists had long feared that western expansion would diminish their region's power, and some of them now talked openly of leaving the Union. When Alexander Hamilton refused to support their plan for a separate confederation, the northeastern secessionists turned to Aaron Burr, the ambitious vice-president, who was seeking election as governor of New York. After Hamilton accused Burr of plotting to dismember the nation, Burr killed him in a duel—the preferred aristocratic method for settling personal disputes—and was indicted for murder.

This tragic event propelled Burr into yet another secessionist scheme. After completing his term as vice-president early in 1805, he moved west to avoid prosecution. There he conspired with General James Wilkinson, the military governor of the Louisiana Territory. Their plan remains a mystery, but it is thought to have involved either the capture of Spanish territory in Mexico or a rebellion to establish Louisiana as a separate nation headed by Burr. Whatever their intentions, Wilkinson betrayed his ally, arresting Burr on a charge of treason as the former vice-president led an armed force down the Ohio River.

In a highly publicized and politicized trial presided over by Chief Justice John Marshall, Burr was acquitted. But the verdict in Burr's trial was less important than the dangers to national unity that the trial revealed. The Republicans' expansionist policies had increased sectional tension and party conflict, giving new life to states' rights sentiments and secessionist schemes.

The Road to War

Meanwhile, the outbreak of the Napoleonic Wars in Europe (1802–1815) had begun to draw the new nation into European conflicts. Great Britain and France, the major belligerents, refused to respect American neutrality, claiming the right to board merchant ships and confiscate cargoes destined for each other's ports. While on board, the British often removed sailors they suspected of deserting the Royal Navy and *impressed* them back into military service. Between 1802 and 1811 British officers seized nearly 8,000 sailors, many of whom were American citizens.

Long-simmering American resentment erupted in 1807, when a British warship attacked the U.S. Navy vessel *Chesapeake*, killing or wounding twenty-one men and seizing four alleged deserters. "Never since the battle of

Lexington have I seen this country in such a state of exasperation as at present," Jefferson declared. The president demanded monetary reparations and an end to impressment. To demonstrate his resolve, he barred British warships from American ports, preventing their resupply. The British government apologized and promised compensation but continued to seize French goods from American ships and impress suspected deserters.

To protect American interests while avoiding war, Jefferson pursued a policy of peaceful coercion. Working closely with Secretary of State James Madison, the president devised the Embargo Act of 1807. This legislation prohibited American ships from leaving their home ports until Britain and France repealed their restrictions on U.S. trade. Though the embargo was imaginative—an economic weapon similar to the nonimportation movements between 1765 and 1775—it was also naive. Jefferson and Madison overestimated the belligerents' dependence on American shipping and underestimated resistance from New England merchants, who feared the embargo would ruin them. The embargo crippled American exports, which plunged from $108 million in 1806 to $22 million in 1808, hurting farmers as well as merchants and prompting Federalists to demand its repeal. "Would to God," exclaimed one Federalist, "that the Embargo had done as little evil to ourselves as it has done to foreign nations."

Despite public discontent with the embargo, voters elected James Madison to the presidency in 1808. Madison promptly acknowledged the embargo's failure. He replaced it with the Nonintercourse Act, which permitted trade with all nations except France and Britain, and offered the promise of normal commerce if the belligerents respected America's neutral rights. When Britain and France ignored this overture, Madison bowed to pressure from Congress and accepted an act that reopened legal trade but threatened to cut off trade with any nation interfering with American commerce. But the British ministry refused to alter its policies, and the astute Napoleon exploited the ill-conceived legislation. Publicly exempting American commerce from seizure, the French emperor instructed his customs officials privately to ignore the exemption. "The Devil himself could not tell which government, England or France, is the most wicked," an exasperated congressman declared.

Republicans were pretty sure it was Britain; congressmen from the West accused Governor-General James Craig of Canada of providing military assistance to native Americans in the Ohio River Valley. Bolstered by British goods and guns, the Shawnee chief Tecumseh, assisted by his brother, the Prophet Tenskwatawa, had revived the Western Confederation. The two leaders had constructed a new ideology that blended ancestral religious values with Christian teachings. Like other Indian leaders before them, they called for a ban on liquor, less dependence on European goods, and an end to the cohabitation of Indian women and white men. To symbolize the religious roots of Indian resistance, Tecumseh centered his confederacy in a sacred town at the junction of the Tippecanoe and Wabash rivers. He traveled widely among southern tribes in hopes of winning their support.

**Tenskwatawa, "The Prophet,"
1836**
Although his brother Tecumseh
was the greater leader, Tenskwatawa added a spiritual dimension to native American resistance,
urging a holy war against white
settlers. His religious message tran-
scended differences among Indian
peoples, helping to create a formidable political and military alliance.

To prevent further land cessions, Tecumseh revived the doctrine of common tribal ownership of the territory north of the Ohio River and vowed to
exclude white settlers. But thousands of white settlers already lived in the
West, and their concerns had a decisive impact on American policy. Expansionists in Congress condemned British support of Tecumseh and threatened
to retaliate by invading Canada and seizing Florida from Spain, Britain's ally.
Urged on by such talk, some Americans living near and in the western (pan-
handle) region of Florida took up arms and tried to annex it to the United
States. Meanwhile, southern planters campaigned for the conquest of eastern
Florida to prevent slaves from taking refuge among the Seminole Indians. In
1811, responding to Indian raids in the Indiana Territory, Governor William
Henry Harrison marched on Prophetstown, Tenskwatawa's sacred village,
fended off the confederation's warriors at the Battle of Tippecanoe, and
burned the town to the ground.

Prompted by these events, Henry Clay of Kentucky, the new Speaker of
the House of Representatives, and John C. Calhoun, a rising young congressman from South Carolina, pushed Madison toward war with Great Britain.
With national elections approaching, Madison bowed to pressure from western and southern War Hawks and abandoned the strategy of economic coercion. He demanded that the British respect American sovereignty in the West
and neutral rights on the Atlantic. When the British failed to respond quickly

enough, Madison asked Congress for a declaration of war. In June 1812 a sharply divided Senate voted 19 to 13 for war; the House of Representatives concurred, 79 to 49.

The causes of the War of 1812 have been much debated. Officially, the United States went to war because of violations of its neutral rights: the seizure of its ships and the impressment of its sailors. But the patterns of voting in Congress and in the election of 1812 suggest that the war was fought as much for land as for maritime rights. The war was opposed by Federalist congressmen and by a majority of voters in New England and the Middle Atlantic states, who gave 89 electoral votes to the Federalist candidate for president, De Witt Clinton of New York.

Madison amassed 128 electoral votes, mostly in the South and West—regions whose congressmen had heeded the demands of their constituents and voted for war. Western farmers were angry because the British blockade had cut the price of their crops. Settlers in frontier districts demanded war against the Indians and their British allies. War Hawks in Congress eyed new territory in Florida and Canada and hoped war would discredit the Federalists and underscore America's independence from Britain. Many Americans had been enraged by British arrogance; Republicans exploited this anger to mobilize support for the war. As President Madison put it, "National honor is national property of the highest value."

The War of 1812

The War of 1812 was a near disaster for the United States both militarily and politically. Republican congressmen had predicted an easy victory in Canada, but when General William Hull invaded western Canada in the summer of 1812, he was immediately forced to retreat. Nonetheless, American forces stayed on the offensive. Commodore Oliver Hazard Perry defeated a small British flotilla on Lake Erie, and in October 1813 General William Henry Harrison defeated a combined British and Indian force at the Battle of the Thames, killing Tecumseh, who had become a general in the British army. Another American force captured and burned the Upper Canada capital of York (now Toronto) but, lacking men and supplies, quickly withdrew.

Political divisions in the United States prevented a major invasion of Canada. Federalist governors in the New England states opposed the war and prohibited their militias from fighting outside their states. Boston merchants and banks declined to lend money to the federal government—some actually invested in British bonds instead—making the war difficult to finance. In Congress, Daniel Webster, a dynamic young representative from New Hampshire, led Federalist opposition to higher taxes and tariffs. To force a negotiated peace, Webster discouraged enlistment and successfully opposed the conscription of state militiamen into the national army. Having led a divided nation into war, Madison and the Republicans were unable to strike the British in Canada, their weakest point.

In the Atlantic, the small American navy proved no match for the Royal Navy. Although the British lost scores of merchant vessels to American privateers in the first months of the war, thereafter the Royal Navy redeployed its fleet and British commerce moved in relative safety. By 1813 Britain had taken the initiative at sea: a flotilla of warships moved up and down the American coastline, interfering with shipping and threatening seaport cities. In 1814, the fleet sailed up Chesapeake Bay and British army units stormed ashore to attack the District of Columbia. There they set fire to government buildings in retaliation for the destruction of York. The troops advanced on Baltimore where they were finally repulsed by courageous American resistance at Fort McHenry. After two years of sporadic warfare, the United States was stalemated in Canada and on the defensive along the Atlantic, its new capital city in ruins.

Sectional opposition to the war strengthened in 1814. The Massachusetts legislature called for a convention "to lay the foundation for a radical reform in the National Compact." In December New England Federalists gathered in Hartford, Connecticut. Some delegates to the Hartford Convention proposed outright secession by their states, but the majority favored a revision of the Constitution. Their object was to reverse the declining role of the Federalist party—and New England—in the expanding nation. To end the Virginia Dynasty, the delegates proposed a constitutional amendment limiting the presidency to a single four-year term, rotating the office among citizens from different states. Other Federalists suggested amendments restricting commercial embargoes to sixty days and requiring a two-thirds majority in Congress to declare war, prohibit trade, or admit a new state.

A minority in the nation and divided among themselves, the Federalists could hope to prevail only if the war continued to go badly—a very real prospect. In the late summer of 1814 a planned British invasion of the Hudson River Valley had been narrowly averted by an American naval victory at the Battle of Lake Champlain. Then, in December, British transports landed thousands of seasoned veterans at New Orleans, threatening to cut off the West's access to the sea. The United States was under pressure from both north and south. The only hopeful sign was that Britain had finally defeated Napoleon in Europe and wanted peace with the United States.

In August 1814 the British entered into negotiations with an American delegation at Ghent, Belgium. The American commissioners—John Quincy Adams, Albert Gallatin, and Henry Clay—at first demanded territory in Canada and Florida, but British diplomats insisted on a buffer state between the United States and Canada to serve as a refuge for their native American allies. In the end both sides realized that the small concessions they might win at the bargaining table were not worth the cost of prolonging the war. The Treaty of Ghent, signed on Christmas Eve, 1814, restored the prewar borders of the United States and left unresolved disputes to future negotiations.

These results hardly justified three years of fighting and a sharply divided nation. But a final victory in combat lifted Americans' morale. Before news of the Treaty of Ghent reached the United States, newspaper headlines proclaimed

AMERICAN VOICES

A Kentucky Soldier Describes the Battle of New Orleans

For Americans, the Battle of New Orleans was a glorious victory that brought an upbeat end to an inglorious war. For the British, the clash was a bloody disaster, as this account by a Kentucky soldier makes clear.

The official report said the action lasted two hours and five minutes, but it did not seem half that length of time to me. It was so dark that little could be seen, until just about the time the battle ceased. The morning had dawned to be sure, but the smoke was so thick that everything seemed to be covered up in it. Our men did not seem to apprehend any danger, but would load and fire just as fast as they could, talking, swearing, joking all the time. . . .

When the smoke cleared away and we could obtain a fair view of the field, it looked at first glance like a sea of blood. It was not blood itself which gave it this appearance, but the red coats in which the British soldiers were dressed. Straight out before our position, for about the width of space which we supposed had been occupied by the British column, the field was entirely covered with prostrate bodies. In some places they were lying in piles of several, one on top of the other. . . .

Individuals could be seen in every possible attitude. Some lying quite dead, others mortally wounded, pitching and tumbling about in the agonies of death. Some had their heads shot off, some their legs, some their arms. Some were laughing, some crying, some groaning, and some screaming. . . .

SOURCE: Linda R. Monk, ed., *Ordinary Americans: U.S. History through the Eyes of Everyday People* (Alexandria, VA: Close Up Publications, 1994), pp. 47–48.

"ALMOST INCREDIBLE VICTORY!! GLORIOUS NEWS." On January 8, 1815, General Andrew Jackson's troops had crushed the British forces attacking New Orleans. Jackson's victory made the rugged, slaveowning Tennessee planter a national hero and a symbol of the emerging West. Yet Jackson dominated the battlefield not through the marksmanship of his Kentucky sharpshooters in coonskin caps but through a traditional deployment of regular troops, including a contingent of French-speaking black Americans, the Corps d'Afrique. The Americans fought from carefully constructed breastworks and were amply supplied with cannon, which rained "grapeshot and cannister bombs" on the massed British formations. With 700 Redcoats dead and 2,000 wounded or taken prisoner, the British lost thousands of their finest troops. American casualties totaled only 13 dead and 58 wounded. The victory redeemed the nation's battered pride and, with the coming of peace, undercut the Hartford Convention's demands for a revised Constitution. The young nation's political institutions had survived a divisive war.

The tumultuous era of the early republic thus came to an end. Peace in Europe ended two decades of political conflict over foreign policy and hastened the demise of the Federalists, whose elitist policies garnered little support in an expanding, increasingly democratic nation. "No Federal character can run with success," Gouverneur Morris of New York lamented, and the election results of 1818 bore out his pessimism. Republicans now outnumbered Federalists 37 to 7 in the Senate and 156 to 27 in the House of Representatives.

The decline of the Federalists prompted contemporary observers to dub James Monroe's two terms as president (1817–1825) the Era of Good Feeling. Actually, national political harmony was more apparent than real, for the Republican party—by then home to many former Federalists—soon split into factions that struggled over power, patronage, and, after 1820, economic policy.

REGIONAL DIVERSITY AND NATIONAL IDENTITY

During the colonial period four separate American cultures had emerged: New England, the Middle Atlantic, the Chesapeake, and the Lower South. The political divisions of the War of 1812 showed that regional differences remained strong. As the migrants transplanted their seaboard cultures to the interior, American life became even more diverse.

Atlantic Seaboard Societies

Observers had long noticed the contrast between the race- and class-divided societies of the Chesapeake and the freehold farming regions of the North. A British traveler detected both religious "fanaticism" and "a great strain of industry among all ranks of people" in New England. Visitors to the Chesapeake commented on the rude manners and heavy drinking of white tenant farmers and small freeholders, who had a "passion for gaming at the billiard table, a cock-fight or cards."

These popular stereotypes reflected genuine cultural differences. Because of its Puritan heritage, New England had a strong tradition of primary schooling and Bible reading. As a result, in 1790 most of the men and more than half the women in New England could read and write. By contrast, the slaveholding elite that ruled southern society refused to provide schooling for ordinary whites. Most white women and a third of white men in the Chesapeake could not even write their names and had to sign wills and marriage licenses with a mark such as an "X."

Holidays were another sign of regional differences. In Virginia, South Carolina, and other states with an Anglican religious heritage, Christmas was an occasion for feasting and celebration. Not so in New England, where ministers condemned such celebrations as profane; most churches in that region did not celebrate Christmas until the 1850s. New England's holiday was Thanksgiving, which commemorated the trials and triumphs of the first Pilgrim and Puritan settlers. Indeed, the region's history contributed to its strong sense of identity. By the 1820s most men and women had ties to large clans that could trace their American roots back six or seven generations. No fewer than 281 members of the Newhall clan were living in Lynn, Massachusetts, in the 1820s, along with 259 Breeds, 195 Alleys, and 162 Johnsons. In a very real sense, New England was a society of interrelated families.

The culture of the Middle Atlantic region was more diverse, for the settlers there had consciously maintained their distinct ethnic identities. In Pennsylvania, New Jersey, and western Maryland, Quakers and Scots-Irish had married largely within their own ethnic groups, while Germans had held on to their language and customs, especially in farming towns. As a visitor to Hanover, Maryland, noted around 1820, "The inhabitants are all German. Habits, speech, newspapers, cooking—all German." This diversity within and between regions delayed the emergence of an American national identity.

Political events occasionally reminded isolated farmers and ethnic communities that they were members of a larger nation. During the War of 1812 Americans began to refer to the federal government as "Uncle Sam": "The letters U.S. on government waggons &c are supposed to have given rise to it," reported a newspaper in Troy, New York. War patriotism gave instant popularity to "The Star Spangled Banner," written by Francis Scott Key during the battle at Fort McHenry.

Newspapers brought national news and advertisements to small towns and rural areas. Political parties subsidized some papers in an effort to create a national debate on various legislative issues. The influential *Niles Weekly Register*, established in Baltimore in 1811, and the *North American Review*, founded in Boston in 1815, carried news from Europe and the port cities to every region. But only members of certain elites—merchants, politicians, lawyers—participated fully in the emerging national culture. Most Americans lived out their lives in the local cultures into which they had been born.

The Old Northwest

When Jedidiah Morse published *American Geography* in 1793, he listed three "grand divisions of the United States": northern, middle, and southern. In the 1819 edition he added a new section: "Western States and Territories." Initially this region lacked a culture of its own. When 176 residents of Granville, Massachusetts, moved to Ohio, they transplanted their Congregational church whole, complete with ministers and elders, along with their system of freehold agriculture. Throughout the trans-Appalachian West, most "new" communities were not new; they were old communities that had moved inland.

Cut off from most trade with outside markets, settlers made their own clothes, repaired old tools, and bartered goods and labor with their neighbors.

"A noble field of Indian corn stretched away into the forest on one side," an English visitor to an Ohio farm in the 1820s noted, waxing romantic,

and immediately before the house was a small potato garden, with a few peach and apple trees. The woman told me that they spun and wove all the cotton and woollen garments of the family, and knit all the stockings; her husband, though not a shoemaker by trade, made all the shoes. She manufactured all the soap and candles they use. All she wanted with money, she said, was to buy coffee, tea, and whiskey, and she could "get enough any day by sending a batch of butter and chickens to market."

Self-sufficiency meant a low standard of living. As late as 1840, per capita income in the Old Northwest was only 70 percent of the national average.

Apart from its relative poverty, the Northwest's distinctiveness lay in the conflict among competing cultural traditions. As New Englander Lucy Maynard wrote home from central Illinois, "Our neighbors are principally from . . . Kentucky, some from Virginia, all friendly but very different from our people in their manner and language and every other way." In Indiana these differences sparked a twenty-year struggle between education-conscious migrants from New England and tax-shy yeomen from the southern states. Because of such diverse cultural traditions, the states of the Old Northwest resembled the mixed societies of the Middle Atlantic region.

Slavery Moves into the Old Southwest

While poor whites fled from the Chesapeake, migrating first to Kentucky and then to the Old Northwest, wealthy planters carried slavery into the Old Southwest—the future states of Alabama, Mississippi, and Louisiana. At the Philadelphia convention in 1787 slaveowners from Georgia and South Carolina had preserved the Atlantic slave trade for twenty more years. By 1808, the year Congress ended the trade, Georgia and South Carolina rice growers had imported 250,000 new African workers—as many as had been imported in the entire colonial period. The black population throughout the South also grew through reproduction, increasing from half a million in 1775 to 1.8 million in 1820.

Many Africans and African-Americans still toiled on tobacco and rice plantations. When soil exhaustion lowered tobacco production in the Tidewater region of the Chesapeake, planters took the crop to the Virginia Piedmont, North Carolina, Kentucky, and Tennessee. Simultaneously, white planters in Louisiana—some of them refugees from black-controlled Haiti—established a booming sugar economy. Slaves in Louisiana, like those on the sugar plantations of the West Indies, were brutally exploited and died quickly from disease and overwork.

However, it was a new crop—cotton—that provided the main impetus for the expansion of slavery. For centuries most Europeans had worn clothing made from wool or flax. Although English manufacturers had taken up cotton

A Migrant Recalls the Frontier Experience

B*orn around 1810, Reuben Davis grew up on the Alabama frontier, where his slaveowning father had migrated to find land and opportunities for his many children.*

Both my parents were born in Virginia, and remained there after marriage until ten children were added to their family. They then removed to Tennessee, and settled near Winchester. . . .

When I was about five years of age, my father removed from Tennessee to North Alabama. The land had been recently purchased from the Indians, and many of them yet roamed the dense forests of that section. I well remember how I hunted with these wild companions, and was taught by them to use the bow and arrow. Even now I can recall something of the emotion excited in my youthful breast by the wild yells of a party of drunken savages passing near my father's house. . . .

At that time the country was as wild and unsettled as possible; there were no laws, no schools, and no libraries. Every man did what was right in his own eyes, but in spite of general recklessness and lawlessness, there was a rough code of honor and honesty which was rarely broken. The settlers lived a life of great toil and many privations, but they were eminently social, kindly, and friendly. . . . My brothers and myself, assisted by six colored hands, cultivated the land, and attended school only about three months in the year. . . .

There was this great advantage that, while none were very wealthy, few were poor enough to suffer actual want. . . . The simple habits of the laboring man were not shamed by the ostentation of his more prosperous neighbor; and there was none of that silent, perpetual contrast of luxury and penury, which now adds bitterness to class hatreds.

SOURCE: Reuben Davis, *Recollections of Mississippi and Mississippians* (Boston: Houghton, Mifflin & Company, 1890), pp. 2–4.

spinning and weaving, cotton textiles had remained a minor industry until 1750. Then a European population explosion increased the demand for cloth just as the technological breakthroughs of the Industrial Revolution began to boost production and lower prices. Rising consumer demand generated a huge demand for cotton goods, which manufacturers met with the use of the newly invented water-powered spinning jenny and weaving mule.

Since independence American planters had grown a smooth-seed, long-fiber variety of cotton on the sea islands of the southern Atlantic coast. In the 1790s, Eli Whitney and other inventors developed machines to separate the rough seeds from the fiber of short-staple cotton, which could be grown in most areas of the South. The combination of British demand and American innovation created a new agricultural industry and a massive demand for land and labor. In South Carolina and Georgia, thousands of white planters moved into the interior to grow cotton. After the War of 1812, production spread to Alabama and Mississippi, which entered the Union in 1817 and 1819, respectively. In a single year a government land office in Huntsville, Alabama, sold $7 million of uncleared land. The expression "doing a land-office business"—a metaphor for rapid commercial expansion—dates from this time.

For enslaved blacks, the coming of cotton meant social upheaval. Entire black communities were uprooted from the Chesapeake and Lower South and forced to move west with their masters. Thousands more young women and men were sold by their owners to domestic slave traders, who resold them to planters in the new tobacco regions and booming cotton states. By 1820 whites had relocated more than 250,000 African-Americans. Torn from their loved ones, African-Americans had to rebuild their lives, laboring "from day clean to first dark" on frontier plantations in Alabama and Mississippi. "I am Sold to a man by the name of Peterson a trader," lamented a Georgia slave. "My Dear wife for you and my Children my pen cannot Express the griffe I feel to be parted from you all."

Early antislavery reformers had hoped that the decline of the tobacco economy and the end of the Atlantic slave trade would allow slavery to "die a natural death." Their dream was shattered when Louisiana, Mississippi, and Alabama joined the Union with state constitutions that permitted slavery. When Missouri applied for admission on a similar basis in 1819, antislavery forces rallied. Congressman James Tallmadge of New York proposed a ban on the importation of slaves into Missouri and the gradual emancipation of its black inhabitants, setting off a bitter debate in Congress. When whites in Missouri refused to end slavery, the northern majority in the House of Representatives blocked the territory's admission to the Union. In response, southerners used their power in the Senate, which was equally divided between eleven free and eleven slave states, to withhold statehood from Maine, which was seeking to separate from Massachusetts. Tempers flared in the heat of debate. Senator Thomas W. Cobb of Georgia accused Tallmadge of kindling "a fire which all the waters of the ocean cannot put out and which seas of blood can only extinguish."

The controversy raged for two years before Representative Henry Clay of Kentucky persuaded the House to accept a series of agreements known collectively as the Missouri Compromise. Maine would enter the Union as a free state in 1820 and Missouri as a slave state the following year, a bargain that preserved the sectional balance in the Senate and set a precedent for the admission of states in pairs, one free and one slave. To mollify antislavery sentiment in the House of Representatives, southern congressmen accepted a ban on slavery in the rest of the Louisiana Territory north of latitude 36° 30′, Missouri's southern boundary (see Map 8.2).

In 1821 as in 1787, white leaders in the North and the South gave priority to the Union, finding complex ways to reconcile their regions' interests.

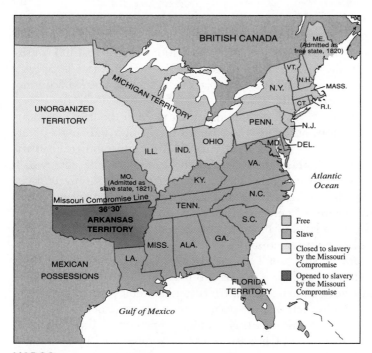

MAP 8.2
The Missouri Compromise, 1820
The Missouri Compromise resolved for a generation the issue of slavery in
the lands of the Louisiana Purchase. Slavery was forbidden north of the
compromise line, 36° 30′ north latitude, with the exception of Missouri,
which entered the Union as a slave state. The compromise provided for the
nearly simultaneous admission of Maine, maintaining an equal number of
free and slave states in the Senate.

But the task had become more difficult. The delegates at the Constitutional
Convention had resolved their sectional differences in two months; Congress
took two years to craft the Missouri Compromise, and there was no guarantee that it would work. The fates of the West, the Union, and the black race
had become inextricably intertwined. As Thomas Jefferson exclaimed at the
time, the Missouri controversy "like a fire-bell in the night, awakened and
filled me with terror."

African-American Society and Culture

After 1800 a more unified African-American culture developed in the United
States for three reasons. First, the end of the transatlantic slave trade in 1808
made it unnecessary to assimilate newly arrived Africans. Even in South Carolina only about 20 percent of the slaves in 1820 had been born in Africa.

Second, the movement of slavery into the Old Southwest had reduced differences among slaves. For example, the Gullah dialect spoken by slaves from the Carolinas gradually died out on the cotton plantations of Alabama and Mississippi, replaced by the black English spoken by slaves from the Chesapeake. Third, especially in northern cities, free blacks consciously created a distinct African-American community.

African cultural elements found an important place in the lives of American blacks. Descriptions of blacks who "danced the Congo and sang a purely African song" appeared as late as 1890. African-Americans also retained the incest taboos of their homeland. Unlike South Carolina's white elite, which allowed marriage between cousins to keep property in the family, enslaved blacks shunned such marriages. For example, on the Good Hope plantation in South Carolina, where 40 percent of the 175 slave children born between 1800 and 1857 were related by blood to just three slaves from Africa, only one marriage took place between cousins.

Because slaveowners forbade legal marriage between blacks (so that slaves could be sold without breaking a marriage bond), African-Americans devised their own rituals. Young men and women first asked their parents' consent to marry and then sought their owner's permission to live together in their own cabin. Following African custom, many couples jumped over a broomstick together in a public ceremony. Christian blacks were often wed by a white or black preacher, but the rites never ended with the customary phrase "until death do you part."

Although forced separations split many black families, the majority of unions were stable. Among the slaves on the Good Hope plantation, about 70 percent of the women conceived all their children by the same man. Black family life was much more fragile in Louisiana, where labor in the sugar fields killed many men.

To maintain their identity, many recently imported slaves in the Lower South bestowed African names on their children. Males born on Friday were often called Cuffee—the name of that day in several West African languages. Most Chesapeake slaves chose names of British origin and bound one generation to another by naming sons after fathers, uncles, or grandfathers. Daughters often were named after grandmothers. Like incest rules and marriage rituals, African-American naming patterns created order in a harsh and arbitrary world.

After the family, the religious community played the most important role in the lives of enslaved African-Americans. Some blacks maintained African practices, invoking traditional spirits in time of need, but many became Christians, absorbing the religious views of white Baptists and Methodists and adapting them to their needs. Black Christians generally ignored the doctrines of original sin and predestination as well as biblical passages that portrayed the church as a lawgiver and symbol of authority. They preferred to envision God as a warrior who had liberated the Jews, his chosen people. "Their cause was similar to the Israelites'," explained a slave conspirator during a thwarted rebellion in Virginia. Slaves also identified with the persecuted Christ, who had suffered and died so that his followers might gain salvation. Amid the manifest injustice of their lives, African-Americans used Christian principles to affirm their equality with whites in the eyes of God.

As local African-American cultural communities developed, the quality of slave life gradually improved. During the eighteenth century the diverse origins of African-born slaves had enabled white men to take easy advantage of blacks—to rape women and punish defiant men by branding them or cutting off their fingers or ears. Although these abuses did not stop after 1800, they were questioned more often. White politicians condemned rape as an aristocratic vice ill suited to a republican society, while the spread of evangelical Christianity prompted many masters to treat slaves more humanely. Meanwhile, by forming stable families and strong communities, African-Americans were better able to resist the worst forms of oppression. They insisted that work gangs be sold "in families" and defied their masters when they were not. One Maryland slave, faced with transport to Mississippi and separation from his wife, "neither yields consent to accompany my people, or to be exchanged or sold," his owner reported. Masters ignored such resistance at their peril, because a slave's relatives might retaliate with arson, poison, or destruction of crops or equipment.

Blacks in the rice-growing lowlands of South Carolina were particularly successful in gaining the right to labor by the *task* rather than work under constant supervision. Each day a worker would have to complete a precisely defined task—turn over a quarter acre of land, hoe half an acre, or pound seven mortars of rice. By working hard, many lowland slaves finished their tasks "by one or two o'clock in the afternoon," a Methodist preacher reported, and had "the rest of the day for themselves, which they spend in working their own private fields . . . planting rice, corn, potatoes, tobacco &c. for their own use and profit." "Should any owner increase the work beyond what is customary," a rice planter in South Carolina warned around 1800, "he subjects himself . . . to such discontent amongst his slaves as to make them of little use to him."

Still, white masters had virtually unlimited power, both legal and physical, over their slaves. In the upland cotton-growing regions of South Carolina and Georgia and in Alabama and Mississippi, owners forced workers to labor in "gangs" that were supervised by black "drivers" or white overseers. Planters sold slaves who were recalcitrant and punished those they viewed as lazy. Particularly on newly settled plantations, profit-conscious masters used the lash to extract labor from exhausted field workers. A few blacks, such as Gabriel Prosser in Virginia (1799) and Denmark Vesey in South Carolina (1822), plotted mass uprisings and murders. But most blacks realized that a revolt was unlikely to be successful. Flight was also perilous. The northern and western states were hotbeds of racial prejudice, and the Fugitive Slave Law (1793) allowed masters to carry escaped slaves back to bondage. In these circumstances, slaves had no option but to build the best possible lives for themselves where they were. Like the oppressed peasantry of Europe, they worked as dependent agricultural laborers and built close-knit communities based on family, kinship, and religion.

Meanwhile, free African-Americans—about 5 percent of all blacks in the United States by 1820—explored the limits of their liberty. Most free blacks earned low wages as farm workers or city laborers and laundresses. Their lives were circumscribed by prejudice: they were usually forbidden to vote, attend public schools, or sit next to whites in churches. But a few African-Americans who were able to make full use of their talents achieved great distinction. The mathematician and surveyor Benjamin Banneker published an almanac and helped lay out the new national capital. Joshua Johnston won praise for his portraiture, and Robert Sheridan acquired a small fortune from his mercantile enterprises. But more impressive and enduring were the institutions this first generation of free African-Americans created. Hundreds of free blacks pooled their resources and talents to found schools, mutual-benefit and fellowship societies, antislavery organizations, and religious denominations such as the AME (African Methodist Episcopal) Church. Over the years these institutions gave free African-Americans a sense of cultural autonomy.

Mount Bethel African Methodist Episcopal Church
After they were segregated in the gallery of Philadelphia's St. George's Methodist Church, a group of African-American Methodists decided to worship "separate from our white brethren." In 1794 they formed the Methodist Bethel Church. Led by Richard Allen, the congregation won legal recognition as an independent "African" church in 1816. Allen became the first bishop of the African Methodist Episcopal Church.

The Fate of Native Americans

"Next to the case of the black race within our bosom," James Madison remarked as he left the presidency in 1817, "that of the red race on our borders is the problem most baffling to the policy of our country." Political opinion was sharply divided. A few influential Americans advocated extermination: "Cut up every Indian Cornfield and burn every Indian town," proclaimed William Henry Drayton of South Carolina, so that their "nation be extirpated and the lands become the property of the public." Many others, including Henry Knox, Washington's first secretary of war, favored assimilation. As a first step, Knox advocated breaking up commonly owned tribal land and redistributing it to individual Indian families. But that idea was rejected by the Indians, who did not normally possess wealth as individuals and wanted to maintain their clans and tribes.

Nonetheless, until the 1820s the U.S. government generally encouraged assimilation. It instructed territorial governors to purchase huge tracts of native American land, opening them to white pioneers and encouraging Indians to settle in farming communities on their remaining territory. And it welcomed the efforts of missionaries to change the Indians' culture. The object, as one Kentucky minister put it, was to make the Indian "a farmer, a citizen of the United States, and a Christian."

Most native Americans resisted attempts to redefine their identity. "Born free and independent," an observer noted, Indians were "struck with horror at whatever has the shadow of despotic power." Many tribes drove out white missionaries and forced converts to Christianity to participate in traditional native American rites. To justify their ancestral values, native American leaders devised dualistic cultural and religious theories. As a Munsee prophet put it, "there are two ways to God, one for the whites and one for the Indians."

Nevertheless, many tribes broke into hostile religious factions. Among the Seneca of New York, for example, the prophet Handsome Lake promoted traditional agricultural ceremonies—such as the green corn dance and the strawberry festival—in which the celebrants gave thanks to the earth, plants, animals, water, and sun. But Handsome Lake also adopted some Christian precepts, such as a belief in heaven and hell, and used them to discourage his followers from drinking alcohol, gambling, and practicing witchcraft. The more conservative among the Seneca, led by Red Jacket, opposed the innovations suggested by white missionaries, such as expecting men to work in the fields. Traditionally, Indian women had been responsible for growing staple foods and had often controlled the inheritance of cultivation rights. Their economic importance gave Indian women some political power; for example, the Shawnee chose female "war" and "civil" chiefs, who could prevent the dispatch of war parties and save captives from being tortured. Consequently, most Indian women insisted on retaining their role as cultivators. Even Christian Indians would not give up their social identities. To view themselves as individuals, as the Europeans demanded, would have been to repudiate the clan, the essence of Indian life.

Only under special circumstances did native Americans accept European ways. When whites attempted to oust the Cherokee from their ancestral lands in Georgia and the Carolinas in 1806 and again in 1817, a small faction of Cherokee mixed-bloods, the Christian offspring of white fur traders and Indian women, attempted to resist removal by adopting some elements of Anglo-American culture. They organized a national council, developed a written language, and in 1827 promulgated a charter of government modeled on the U.S. Constitution. But most full-blooded Cherokee rejected Anglo-American values; seizing control of the national council, they denounced both cultural assimilation and forced removal. As a chief of the neighboring Creeks declared, "We would not receive money for land in which our fathers and friends are buried. We love our land; it is our mother."

Continental Empire: Spain and the United States

Native Americans were not the only obstacles to America's westward expansion. During the reign of Carlos III (1759–1788) Spanish officials had sought to unite the long-settled territories on New Spain's northern border (present-day Florida, Texas, New Mexico, and Arizona) with new Spanish settlements in California. Under the direction of José de Gálvez, Spanish troops had established military presidios at San Diego, Santa Barbara, Monterey, and San Francisco. There and elsewhere along the California coast between 1769 and 1782, the Franciscan friar Junípero Serra had set up religious missions. Spanish ranchers followed, grazing huge herds of cattle.

To pacify the vast region that stretched from California to Florida, the Spanish attempted to contain or exterminate the war-prone Apache and to make more cooperative peoples dependent on Spanish trade through treaties and gifts, especially arms and alcohol. This policy brought peace to New Spain's northern frontier, allowing more Spanish ranchers and farmers to settle in Texas, New Mexico, and Arizona.

New Spain's borderlands empire quickly came under pressure from the newly independent American republic. To deter American settlement west of the Appalachians, Spanish authorities restricted American trade on the Mississippi River in 1784 and entered into an alliance with the Creek peoples. But American threats and military setbacks in Europe forced Spain to accept Pinckney's Treaty of 1795, which gave Americans access to the Mississippi and voided Spanish land claims in the Ohio River Valley. To prevent further American expansion (and curry favor with Napoleon), Spain ceded Louisiana to France in 1800. When the French emperor sold Louisiana to the United States in 1803, Spanish diplomats reacted strongly. They disputed President Jefferson's claim that Louisiana extended to the Rio Grande and the Rocky Mountains, which would have placed all of

Texas and half of New Mexico under American control. Instead, they argued that Louisiana was limited to the land along the Mississippi River (the present-day states of Louisiana, Arkansas, and Missouri). The issue remained unresolved at the end of the War of 1812, along with the status of West Florida, which had been occupied by American troops during the war (see Map 8.3).

The disputes between Spain and the United States were resolved by John Quincy Adams, son of the Federalist president John Adams. John Quincy had joined the Republican party before the War of 1812. As secretary of state under President Monroe, the younger Adams pursued an expansionist western policy. Exploiting a diplomatic crisis created by an unauthorized military expedition into Florida led by General Andrew Jackson, the secretary negotiated the Adams-Onís Treaty of 1819. Spain gave up its claim to the Oregon country and allowed the United States to annex East Florida; in return, the American government renounced its dubious claim to Spanish Texas and accepted a compromise boundary between New Spain and the Louisiana Territory. Adams also negotiated two

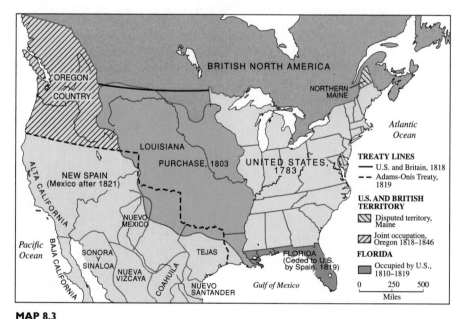

MAP 8.3
Defining the National Boundaries
After the War of 1812, John Quincy Adams negotiated treaties with Great Britain and Spain that made Florida and northern Maine part of the United States and defined the American boundaries with Canada and New Spain (which in 1821 became the independent nation of Mexico). These treaties eliminated the threat of war until the 1840s, providing the young nation with a much needed period of peace.

important agreements with Great Britain. The Rush-Bagot Treaty of 1817 limited naval forces on the Great Lakes, and an agreement in 1818 established the border between the Louisiana Territory and British Canada at the 49th parallel. Adams's diplomacy gave the United States undisputed possession of a vast inland empire.

Secretary Adams and President Monroe had this continental empire in mind when they outlined a new foreign policy that thirty years later became known as the Monroe Doctrine. In an address to Congress in 1823, Monroe warned European powers to stay out of the Western Hemisphere. Monroe's warning was meant for Spain in particular: patriots in Mexico and other Spanish colonies had revolted against Spanish rule and established independent republics, and Monroe was warning Spain not to try to subdue them. Adams and Monroe also hoped to prevent the Russians from extending their fur-trading posts south of Alaska. Thus, Monroe declared that the Americas were not "subject for further colonization" by European nations. In return, he pledged "not to interfere in the internal concerns" of European states. Monroe and Adams had turned their backs on the Old World and were looking westward, envisioning an American empire that would stretch from the Atlantic to the Pacific.

CHAPTER 8 TIMELINE

1790s	White settlers move west; cotton production expands Turnpikes and short canals built
1790–1791	Little Turtle defeats American armies
1792	Kentucky joins Union; Tennessee follows (1796)
1794	Battle of Fallen Timbers; Treaty of Greenville (1795)
1800s	Handsome Lake revival among Seneca
1800	Spain restores Louisiana to France
1801–1807	Gallatin reduces national debt Price of federal land reduced Seizures of American ships and sailors
1803	Louisiana Purchase; Lewis and Clark expedition follows Aaron Burr and western secession
1808	Tecumseh and Tenskwatawa mobilize Indians Congress bans importation of slaves
1810s	Expansion of slavery into Old Southwest Cherokee resist white advance Decline of Federalist party
1811	Battle of Tippecanoe
1812	War of 1812
1815	Battle of New Orleans; Treaty of Ghent
1817	Rush-Bagot Treaty (U.S.–Canadian boundary)
1817–1825	Era of Good Feeling
1819	Adams-Onís Treaty: Florida annexed, Texas boundary defined
1820	Missouri Compromise
1823	Monroe Doctrine

CHAPTER 9

TOWARD A CAPITALIST PROTESTANT REPUBLIC, 1790–1820

- Political Economy: The Capitalist Commonwealth
- Visions of a Republican Social Order
- Protestant Christianity and Women's Lives

For most white Americans July 4, 1826, was a day of celebration. For fifty years they had lived in a self-governing society, free of an arbitrary government that imposed high taxes and an established church that enforced rigid dogma. Not even the deaths of John Adams and Thomas Jefferson on that Independence Day could diminish Americans' optimism. Indeed, for many citizens the timing of the deaths of two former presidents was a sign that God looked with favor on their experiment in self-government. Two of the greatest Founders had died, but the republic lived on.

During that first half-century the nation had matured into a full-fledged "republican" society. It now boasted not only a self-governing polity but also an economic system and a cultural order that reflected many of the values of ordinary citizens. State governments and social reformers had applied republican ideals to traditional institutions such as families, schools, and churches, unleashing a process of change that provided women as well as men with a new social identity. Reflecting the self-confident spirit of the new republic, leading citizens hailed their society as a model for all peoples. "The temperate zone of North America," a Kentucky judge declared in a Fourth of July speech, "already exhibits many signs that it is the promised land of civil liberty, and of institutions designed to liberate and exalt the human race."

POLITICAL ECONOMY: THE CAPITALIST COMMONWEALTH

The American quest for economic independence was longer and more arduous than the struggle for political autonomy. To enhance the prosperity of their citizens, states played a leading role in economic development, creating new legal institutions and providing financial incentives for ambitious entrepreneurs.

A Capitalist Society

Merchants had dominated the economic life of port cities in colonial times; with the departure of the British, they began to set the social and cultural tone as well. America was "a Nation of Merchants," a British visitor reported from Philadelphia in 1798, "always alive to their interests; and keen in the pursuit of wealth in all the various modes of acquiring it." And acquire it they did, especially during the European wars that dragged on from 1792 to 1815. Daring entrepreneurs, such as the fur trader John Jacob Astor and the merchant Robert Oliver, became the nation's first millionaires. Astor migrated from Germany to New York in 1784 and became wealthy by carrying furs from the Pacific Northwest to markets in China. Investing his profits in real estate, he became the largest landowner in New York City. Oliver made his fortune in Baltimore, beginning as an agent for Irish linen merchants and then starting his own mercantile firm. Exploiting the wartime shipping boom, he reaped enormous profits in the West Indian coffee and sugar trade.

To finance the expansion of mercantile enterprises, Americans had to devise an entirely new banking system. Before 1776 economically ambitious colonists were unable to secure loans. Farmers had relied on government-sponsored land banks, pledging their land as security, while merchants such as Oliver had arranged partnerships, borrowed funds from other merchants, or obtained credit from British suppliers. Then, in 1781, several Philadelphia merchants, Robert Morris among them, persuaded the Confederation Congress to charter the Bank of North America to provide short-term commercial loans. Traders in Boston and New York founded similar banks in 1784. Those institutions provided merchants with the credit they needed to finance their transactions, freeing them from dependence on overseas sources of financing.

In 1791, as part of Alexander Hamilton's plan to centralize the expanding American financial system, Congress chartered the Bank of the United States. The bank had the power to issue notes and make commercial loans; although the bank's managers used their lending powers cautiously, profits still averaged a handsome 8 percent annually. By 1805, in response to the continuing demand for commercial credit, the bank had set up branches in eight major cities.

Nonetheless, for political reasons, the First Bank of the United States did not survive. Jeffersonians had long condemned the idea of a national bank, warning that it would produce "a consolidated, energetic government supported by public creditors, speculators, and other insidious men lacking in public spirit of any kind." When the bank's twenty-year charter expired in 1811,

President Madison did not seek its renewal, a decision that forced merchants, artisans, and farmers to turn to their state legislatures. New York chartered the Mechanics' and Farmers' Bank of Albany in 1811, and other states followed suit. By the time Madison chartered the Second Bank of the United States in 1816, there were no fewer than 246 state-chartered banks. Unfortunately, many state banks issued notes without adequate reserves of specie, a shortsighted policy that inhibited commercial growth by undermining the notes' value.

Poorly managed state banks were one cause of the Panic of 1819, a credit crisis sparked by a sharp drop in world agricultural prices. With farm income suddenly cut by a third, many American farmers were unable to pay their creditors, setting in motion successive bankruptcies among local storekeepers, wholesale merchants, and overextended state banks. The economic recession continued for two years, giving many Americans their first taste of the *business cycle*—the periodic expansion and contraction of profits and employment that is an inherent part of a market economy.

The Panic revealed that more and more Americans—artisans and yeomen as well as merchants and southern planters—were dependent on regional or national markets. Before 1790, thousands of artisans in New England and the Middle Atlantic states had handcrafted furniture, tools, wagons, shoes, saddles, clothing, and dozens of other items, but most of those goods had remained within the local community. But some artisans—especially those who worked in large, specialized groups—had an eye on more distant markets. Even before independence, shipbuilders in seacoast towns, iron smelters in Pennsylvania and Maryland, and shoemakers in Lynn, Massachusetts, had sold their products in far-flung markets. During the Revolutionary War, merchants had encouraged rural men and women to make cheese, textiles, paper, and gunpowder. Later, national pride prompted calls for the expansion of *all* domestic handicrafts. "Until we manufacture more," a writer in the *Boston Gazette* declared in 1788, "it is absurd to celebrate the Fourth of July as the birthday of our independence."

Once the war was over, many merchants stopped investing in domestic manufacturing because it was more profitable to sell low-priced British goods. Still, some entrepreneurs continued to develop wider markets for American rural manufactures. For instance, merchants sold goods made on Massachusetts farms not only in Boston but also in other New England seaports. As a Polish traveler in central Massachusetts reported in 1798, "Along the whole road from Boston, we saw women engaged in making cheese."

As rural manufacturing increased, the northeastern regions of the United States took a major step toward a *capitalist* manufacturing economy. At the center of this productive system stood a dynamic group of merchant-entrepreneurs who recruited rural households to manufacture goods in a manner similar to the European *outwork*, or *putting-out*, system (see Chapter 1). At the periphery were hundreds of thousands of farm families that supplied the labor. When a French traveler visited central Massachusetts in 1795, he found "almost all these houses . . . inhabited by men who are both cultivators and artisans; one is a tanner, another a shoemaker, another sells goods, but all are farmers."

This system achieved its greatest success in the shoe and boot trade. In the 1780s merchants and master craftsmen in Lynn, Massachusetts, began buying large quantities of leather, thread, and awls and put thousands of farm families to work. Women and children stitched together the thin leather and canvas uppers; then the half-finished shoes were taken by wagon to Lynn for assembly by journeymen shoemakers. When the Embargo of 1807 cut off competition from British-made shoes, merchants in Lynn and over thirty other Massachusetts towns expanded their output, making millions of shoes.

By the 1820s entrepreneurs had mobilized an enormous work force in the New England countryside. Farm families produced shoes, brooms, palm-leaf hats, and tinware—baking pans, cups, utensils, lanterns. Merchants and peddlers sold those products throughout the United States, creating a *national* market.

These successes stemmed primarily from innovations in organization and marketing rather than in technology. Even as their markets expanded, tinworkers, shoemakers, and other artisans continued to use traditional *preindustrial* manufacturing methods. Power-driven machines—the product of the Industrial Revolution in Britain—were adopted slowly in America, beginning in the

The Household as Factory
The outwork system used the labor of all the members of a rural household. Here the wife spins wool into yarn, which her husband weaves into cloth. One of her children fashions strips of palm leaves into a seat (or perhaps a hat), and the other works at another task. Wage labor increased the incomes of many families and tied them to the emerging market economy.

textile industry. In the 1780s merchants built scores of small mills along the creeks and rivers of New England and the Middle Atlantic states. They installed water-powered machines and hired workers to card and comb wool— and later cotton—into long strands. For several decades, the next steps in the manufacturing process were accomplished under the outwork system rather than in factories. Farm women and children spun the strands into yarn, receiving wages for their work, while men in other households wove the yarn into cloth. In 1810 there were about 2,500 outwork weavers in New England. A decade later more than 12,000 household workers in that region were weaving woolen cloth, which was then taken to water-powered fulling mills to be pounded flat and finished smooth.

The rise of rural manufacturing transformed the agricultural economy. To supply merchants and artisans with raw materials, ambitious farm families switched from mixed-crop agriculture to livestock raising. The shoe business consumed thousands of beef hides each year, the new cheese industry required large herds of dairy cows, and textile mills processed the wool from tens of thousands of sheep. High prices for these raw materials brought prosperity and new businesses to many farming towns. In 1792 Concord, Massachusetts, had one slaughterhouse and five small tanneries; a decade later it had eleven slaughterhouses and six large tanneries. Foul odors from the stockyards and tanning pits drifted over the town, but its residents were able to acquire more goods.

At first, barter transactions were a central feature of the emergent market system, as the records of the book-manufacturing firm of Ebenezer and Daniel Merriam of Brookfield, Massachusetts, demonstrate. When the Merriams began selling books to publishing houses in New York City, Philadelphia, and Boston in the 1810s, they received neither cash nor credit in return but other *books*, which they had to exchange with local storekeepers to get supplies for their business. The Merriams paid their employees on a barter basis; a journeyman printer received the use of a small house, credits at local stores, and a third of his "wages" in books, which he had to peddle for himself to gain more than a literary profit from his labors.

Gradually, a cash economy replaced this complex barter system. Instead of exchanging their surplus crops for household necessities, farm families supplied merchants with specialized goods in return for cash or store credit.

The new capitalist-run market economy had some drawbacks. Rural parents—and their children—now worked longer and harder, making shoes, hats, and cloth during the winter and planting, weeding, and harvesting crops during the warmer seasons. Perhaps more important, they lost some of their economic independence. Instead of working solely for themselves as yeomen farm families, they toiled as part-time wage earners for merchants and manufacturers. The new market system decreased the self-sufficiency of families and communities even as it made them more productive.

But the tide of change was unstoppable and, on the whole, beneficial. Beginning around 1800, per capita income in the United States increased more than 1 percent per year—over 30 percent in each generation. By the 1820s

American Country Furniture
Country artisans, such as the un-known maker of this high chest of drawers from Norwich, Vermont (circa 1780), simplified high-style English designs. Using common woods such as birch and pine rather than expensive mahogany, these rural manufacturers built fur-niture that was both affordable and elegant. (Shelburne Museum)

the extraordinary increase in output, artisan skills, and merchant capital had laid the foundation for the American Industrial Revolution (see Chapter 10). After half a century of political independence, the nation was beginning to achieve economic independence.

State Governments and Mercantilism: The "Commonwealth" System

Throughout the nineteenth century, the most important political institutions in the United States were the state governments. State legislatures took the lead in regulating social life, abolishing slavery in the North but retaining it in the South. They enacted laws governing criminal and civil affairs, set voting re-quirements, established taxation systems, and created and oversaw subordinate county, city, and town governments. Beginning in the late 1810s, many states rewrote their constitutions to make them more democratic, decreasing the property requirements for voting, reapportioning legislatures, and increasing the number of elected (rather than appointed) officials. Consequently, state governments had a much greater impact on the day-to-day lives of Americans than did the national government.

As early as the 1790s, many state legislatures attempted to enhance their states' prosperity by devising an American plan of mercantilism known as the "commonwealth" system. Just as the British Parliament had promoted the imperial economy by passing Acts of Trade, state legislatures enacted measures to stimulate commerce and economic development. In particular, they granted hundreds of *corporate charters* to private businesses that were intended, as the act establishing the Massachusetts Bank put it, to be "of great public utility." Chartered companies were not new, of course; English investors had used them to establish the first American colonies. Under English law, however, colonial governments had been discouraged from creating corporations. As a result, American merchants had financed their mills, shipyards, and trading ventures through private partnerships, which lacked some of the economic advantages of government-chartered corporations, such as tax exemptions and monopoly privileges.

Private partnerships also lacked the funds required to build the large-scale transportation projects—the economic infrastructure—that had become a high priority. State legislatures therefore issued numerous charters of incorporation to promote investment in roads, bridges, and canals. In 1794 the Lancaster Turnpike Company received a monopoly charter from the Pennsylvania assembly to lay a graded gravel road between Lancaster and Philadelphia. The success of the venture set off a boom in turnpike construction. Improved roads soon connected dozens of inland market centers to seaport cities.

By 1800 state governments had granted more than 300 corporate charters. Incorporation enhanced the status of private companies in two ways. First, some charters protected investors by granting them *limited liability*; in the event of a business failure, shareholders' personal assets could not be seized to pay the corporation's debts. Second, most transportation charters included the power of *eminent domain*, which enabled turnpike, bridge, and canal corporations to use the judicial system to force the sale of land along their routes. This power—previously available only to the government—permitted private corporations to take land from property owners for a reasonable price, even if the owners did not want to sell. In granting corporations the power of eminent domain, state legislatures promoted the good of the commonwealth at the expense of the property rights of private citizens.

Such uses of state power by private companies were controversial and, in the eyes of some critics, contrary to republicanism, "which does not admit of granting peculiar privileges to any body of men." Charters not only violated the "equal rights" of all citizens, opponents argued, but limited the sovereignty of the people. As a Pennsylvanian put it, "whatever power is given to a corporation, is just so much power taken from the State, in derogation of the original power of the mass of the community."

Nonetheless, state courts consistently upheld the validity of corporate charters. Judges routinely approved grants of eminent domain to private corporations. "The opening of good and easy internal communications is one of the highest duties of government," a New Jersey court declared.

State mercantilism soon encompassed much more than transportation. In the years immediately following the Embargo of 1807, which cut off goods and credit from Europe, New England state governments awarded charters to 200 iron-mining, textile-manufacturing, and banking firms. Over the next few decades the Pennsylvania legislature was even more active, chartering more than 1,100 corporations and authorizing them to hold over $150 million in capital. Corporations, whether in the form of incorporated towns and cities, incorporated churches and charitable institutions, or chartered private businesses, were becoming a central institution in American society. As one contemporary put it, "the whole political system" was "made up of concatenations of various corporations, political, civil, religious, social and economical."

By 1820 the innovative policies of state governments had created a new political economy: the commonwealth system. This system enhanced the public good as well as the economic and political power of capitalist entrepreneurs. The use of state legislation to encourage business enterprise and improve the general welfare would continue for another generation. In 1820 Missouri lawmakers incorporated the concept of the commonwealth system into that state's first constitution, specifying that "internal improvements shall forever be encouraged by the government of this state."

Law and the "Commonwealth": Republicans versus Federalists

Both Federalists and Republicans endorsed the idea of the commonwealth, but in different ways. Federalists looked to the national government for economic leadership and supported Hamilton's program of *national* mercantilism: a funded debt, tariffs, and a central bank. Jeffersonian Republicans generally relied instead on *state* legislatures to promote economic development. After the War of 1812, some Republicans, led by Henry Clay of Kentucky, began to support national economic initiatives, but many more, including President James Monroe, still opposed them. This fundamental disagreement about the role of the national government would shape political debate for the next thirty years (see Chapter 11).

Differing conceptions of law also separated Federalists and Republicans. From the earliest colonial times, American jurisprudence had followed English common law. In deciding cases, judges relied on *precedents*—previous decisions in similar cases—and assumed, as a Maryland lawyer put it, that "the Common Law takes in the Law of Nature, the Law of Reason and the Revealed Law of God." In this view, which was held by many Federalists, law was venerable and unchanging.

The revolutionary republican doctrine of popular sovereignty undermined the intellectual foundations of the old legal order. In the debate over constitutional principles, many Americans recognized that law was a human invention, the product of politics rather than a sacred body of timeless truths. During the 1790s Thomas Jefferson and other Republican party leaders attacked the common-law system, maintaining that law made by judges following common-law precedent was inferior to the statute ("positive") law enacted by representatives of the people. As a Republican jurist put it, a magistrate "should be governed himself by *positive* law" while executing and enforcing "the will of the supreme power, which is the will of THE PEOPLE."

In response, Federalist judges and politicians warned that popular sovereignty had to be curbed. Without safeguards, representative government would result in the "tyranny of the majority"—the passage of statutes that would infringe on the property rights of individual citizens. To prevent state legislatures from overriding property rights, Federalist lawyers asserted that judges had the power to void laws that violated traditional common-law principles or were contrary to "natural law" or "natural rights" (see Chapter 4).

Because common-law precedents had evolved in a relatively static agricultural economy, they often discouraged new modes of enterprise. For example, capitalist entrepreneurs who erected dams to power flour or textile mills often flooded adjacent farmlands; outraged farmers sued, charging that the dams infringed on their property rights, constituted a public "nuisance," and should be pulled down. At first the farmers won most of these cases, as judges used common-law precedents to rule that interfering with the natural flow of a river for nonfarming purposes was illegal.

But when it became clear that such decisions would stifle economic development, republican-minded state legislatures enacted statutes that overrode common law. In Massachusetts, the Mill Dam Act of 1795 allowed mill proprietors to flood adjacent farmland and required farmers to accept "fair compensation" for their lost acreage. Prodevelopment legislators justified the taking of private property by asserting the superior rights of those who made dynamic, rather than static, use of their property.

State judges with Republican leanings accepted the doctrines of popular sovereignty and legislative power and tended to uphold mill acts. To these judges, *social utility*—the greatest good for the greatest number—justified the government's intrusion into individual citizens' property rights. Such rulings shocked the Federalist lawyer and politician Daniel Webster, who considered them no less than a "revolution against the foundations on which property rests." Although both political parties favored economic development, Federalists gave a higher priority to national mercantilism, common law, and a static theory of property rights; Republicans emphasized state activism, statute law, and a dynamic concept of property.

Federalist Law: John Marshall

When he became president in 1801, Thomas Jefferson warned that his Federalist opponents were retreating into the judiciary, from which fortress "all the works of Republicanism are to be beaten down and erased." The legal career of John Marshall confirmed Jefferson's prediction. Appointed chief justice of the Supreme Court by John Adams in 1801, Marshall upheld Federalist principles until his death in 1835. His success stemmed not from a mastery of legal

Chief Justice John Marshall
A Virginia Federalist, Marshall had a commanding personal presence and made over the United States Supreme Court in his image, transforming it from a minor department to a major institution in American legal and political life.

principles and doctrines—indeed, his opinions usually cited very few precedents—but from the power of his logic and the force of his personality. Until 1821 Marshall dominated his colleagues on the Supreme Court, who largely accepted his definition of the meaning of the Constitution.

Three principles shaped Marshall's jurisprudence: a commitment to judicial authority, the supremacy of national over state legislation, and a traditional, static view of property rights. The celebrated case of *Marbury v. Madison* (1803) demonstrated Marshall's commitment to the first principle: the preeminent power of the judiciary. The case arose from President Adams's controversial "midnight" appointments of Federalist judges just as he was leaving office. As secretary of state in Jefferson's incoming Republican administration, James Madison had refused to commission one of those appointees, William Marbury, as a justice of the peace in the District of Columbia. When Marbury asked the Supreme Court to issue a legal writ on his behalf, Marshall ruled that while Marbury had a right to his commission, that right was not enforceable by the Court. This was so, Marshall declared, because the Judiciary Act of 1789 violated the Constitution by expanding the powers given to the Supreme Court in that document. Marshall's decision was politically astute, condemning Madison's action while avoiding a direct confrontation with the Republican administration.

More important, Marshall's decision marked the first time the Supreme Court had overturned a national law. Five years earlier, during the dispute over the Alien and Sedition acts, the Republican-dominated legislatures in Kentucky and Virginia had asserted their authority to determine the constitutionality of national laws. But the Constitution implied that the Supreme Court held the power of *judicial review*, and Marshall claimed it explicitly: "It is emphatically the province and duty of the judicial department to say what the law is." Thereafter, the doctrine of judicial review evolved slowly. During the first half of the nineteenth century, the Supreme Court and the state courts used it only to overturn *state* laws that conflicted with constitutional principles. Not until the *Dred Scott* decision of 1857 would the Supreme Court void another national law.

Marshall's second principle—nationalism—was most eloquently expressed in the controversial case *McCulloch v. Maryland* (1819). When Congress created the Second Bank of the United States in 1816, it gave that bank the authority to handle the notes of state-chartered banks and thus to monitor their financial reserves. To preserve the independence and competitive position of its state banks, the Maryland legislature passed a statute imposing an annual tax of $15,000 on notes issued by the Second Bank's Baltimore branch. The Second Bank contested the constitutionality of that action, claiming that it infringed on the powers of the national government. In response, lawyers for the state of Maryland adopted Jefferson's argument against the First Bank of the United States, maintaining that Congress lacked the constitutional authority to charter a national bank. Even if such a bank could be created, the lawyers argued, Maryland had a right to tax its activities within the state.

Marshall firmly rejected both arguments. The Second Bank was constitutional, he declared, because its existence was "necessary and proper," given the national government's responsibility to control currency and credit. Like Alexander Hamilton and other Federalists, Marshall preferred a loose construction of the Constitution. "Let the end be legitimate, let it be within the scope of the Constitution and all means which are appropriate, which [are consistent] . . . with the letter and the spirit of the constitution, are constitutional," he wrote. As for Maryland's right to tax all institutions within its borders, the chief justice embraced the nationalist position advanced by Daniel Webster, a fellow Federalist and the legal counsel to the Second Bank. "The power to tax involves the power to destroy," Marshall observed, suggesting that Maryland's bank tax would render the national government "dependent on the states"—a situation that "was not intended by the American people" when the Constitution was ratified.

Marshall asserted the dominance of national statutes over state legislation again in *Gibbons v. Ogden* (1824), which struck down a monopoly the New York legislature had granted to Aaron Ogden for steamboat passenger service across the Hudson River. Asserting that the Constitution gave the federal government the authority to regulate interstate commerce, the chief justice upheld the claim of Thomas Gibbons, who held a federal coasting license.

Marshall also turned to the Constitution to uphold his third principle: property rights. To protect individuals against government interference with their property, Marshall seized on the *contract clause* of the Constitution

(Article I, Section 10), which prohibits the states from passing any law "impairing the obligation of contracts." Delegates at the Philadelphia convention had included this clause primarily to void state laws that protected debtors from merchants and other creditors. But Marshall expanded the scope of the contract clause by using it to defend other property rights against legislative challenge.

For example, the case of *Fletcher v. Peck* (1810) involved a large grant of land made by the Georgia legislature to the Yazoo Land Company. When a newly elected state legislature canceled the grant, alleging that it had been obtained through fraud and bribery, speculators who had already purchased Yazoo lands appealed to the Supreme Court to uphold their titles. Speaking for the Court, Marshall ruled that the purchasers held valid contracts whose provisions could not be impaired by the state of Georgia. This decision was far-reaching. It not only gave constitutional protection against subsequent legislation to those who purchased state-owned lands but, by upholding the rights of out-of-state speculators, also encouraged the development of a national capitalist economy.

The court extended its defense of property rights even further in *Dartmouth College v. Woodward* (1819), in which the trustees of the college contested the state legislature's attempt to turn it into a public institution. The Court ruled that the school's charter, which dated back to colonial times, constituted a contract that could not be tampered with by the New Hampshire legislature. In Marshall's view, Dartmouth College was private property.

Marshall had difficulty persuading his colleagues to accept this position. Although he was still the dominant member, by 1819 five of the seven Supreme Court justices had been appointed by the Republican presidents Jefferson and Madison. Some of those justices embraced the commonwealth ideal, arguing that a public university would better serve the common good. Other Republican judges hesitated to restrict the powers of state legislatures or expand the broad protection for property rights set forth in *Fletcher v. Peck*. Only after months of deliberation—and the preparation of a precedent-filled decision by Associate Justice Joseph Story, a New England jurist with strong Federalist leanings—did the other justices on the Court follow Marshall and rule in favor of the college. In Story's view, *Dartmouth College v. Woodward* not only upheld a static, or "vested," conception of property rights but extended constitutionally protected property rights from individuals to business corporations. Thereafter, corporations would claim that their state-granted charters were "contracts" that protected them forever from regulation or control by the governments that had created them.

Marshall's triumph seemed complete; he had incorporated Federalist principles into the law of the land. Indeed, many of Marshall's legal principles, such as judicial review and corporate rights, would become central fixtures of American law. But even before the chief justice's death in 1835, jurists who valued the rights of states had begun to qualify his nationalist vision, and state legislators evaded the restrictions of the Dartmouth College decision by granting charters that included clauses allowing the state to alter their terms.

As this tactic indicates, the legal conflict between Marshall and his Republican opponents was primarily over the means, not the ends, of economic development. Both sides strongly supported private ownership of property and the expansion of a market economy. Together they laid the legal and political foundations for the American Economic Revolution (see Chapter 10).

VISIONS OF A REPUBLICAN SOCIAL ORDER

After independence, Americans tried to become "republicans" not just in their laws but also in their political outlook, social behavior, and cultural values. Their pursuit of republican ideals was complex and conflict-ridden. It pitted propertyless men against their social betters, increased the tension between men and women, and generated new theories of child rearing and education.

Social Mobility and Democracy for Men

Between 1780 and 1820 hundreds of well-educated Europeans visited the United States to observe life in a republican society. They came from countries with monarchical governments, established churches, male-dominated families, and profound divisions between social classes. And they wondered— as have successive generations of historians—whether America represented a different and more just social order. The French-born essayist Crèvecoeur had no doubts. In his famous *Letters from an American Farmer* (1782), Crèvecoeur wrote that European society was composed "of great lords who possess everything, and of a herd of people who have nothing." America, by contrast, had "no aristocratical families, no courts, no kings, no bishops." Because they lived in a society without hereditary rulers, another writer argued, Americans should value people not for their "wealth, titles, or connections" but for their "talents, integrity, and virtue."

Republican ideology undermined hierarchical authority by proclaiming that all free men were equal before the law. "The law is the same for everyone both as it protects and as it punishes," noted a European traveler. Legal equality was not the same as social uniformity, however. Foreign visitors were well aware that class divisions existed in the United States, but they saw them as differing from those in Europe. The American colonies had never had—and the republican state and national constitutions prohibited—a legally privileged nobility. The absence of a hereditary aristocracy encouraged enterprising Americans to seek upward social mobility and to justify class divisions on the basis of achievements. "In Europe to say of someone that he rose from nothing is a disgrace and a reproach," remarked an aristocratic Polish visitor. "It is the opposite here. To be the architect of your own fortune is honorable. It is the highest recommendation."

Some Americans from long-distinguished families questioned the moral legitimacy of a social order based primarily on financial success. "The aristocracy of Kingston [New York] is more one of money than any village I have ever seen," complained Nathaniel Booth in 1825. Booth's ancestors had once ruled Kingston, but his family had lost its prominence in the rapidly growing Hudson River town. "Man is estimated by dollars," he lamented; "what he is worth determines his character and his position at once." But Booth spoke for only a minority of Americans. For most white men, republicanism meant the opportunity to advance their interests and those of their families. For them, America was the "best poor man's country."

By the 1820s republicanism had also come to mean voting rights for free white men. With the revision of state constitutions and the advent of political democracy, property ownership and high social status no longer constituted the foundation of citizenship. Increasingly, Americans repudiated the hierarchical ideal of Federalists such as Samuel Stone, who had called for "a *speaking* aristocracy in the face of a *silent* democracy." Rejecting the deferential politics of the eighteenth century, they refused to vote for Federalist politicians who flaunted their high social status, with their "top boots, breeches, and shoe buckles," their hair in "powder and queues." Instead, they elected Republican politicians who dressed simply and advocated extending the franchise.

Republican-dominated state legislatures did enact laws to expand political democracy. Maryland extended the vote to all adult men in 1810, and the new states of Indiana (1816), Illinois (1818), and Alabama (1819) provided for a broad male franchise in their constitutions. By the end of the 1820s, only a few states—North Carolina, Virginia, and Rhode Island—required that voters own freehold property. Others, such as Ohio and Louisiana, limited suffrage to men who paid taxes or served in the militia. But a majority of the states had instituted universal white manhood suffrage (see Map 9.1, following page).

Popular pressure brought other constitutional changes as well. Between 1818 and 1821, reform-minded politicians in Connecticut, Massachusetts, and New York revised their state constitutions, reapportioning their legislatures on the basis of population and instituting more democratic forms of local government, such as the election rather than the appointment of judges and justices of the peace. If such "democratic doctrines" had been advanced ten years earlier, the Federalist Chancellor James Kent of New York protested, they "should have struck the public mind with astonishment and terror."

As the status of ordinary white men rose, that of white women and free blacks actually declined. Increasingly, political rights in the new republic depended on gender and race. Among the new states admitted to the Union between 1790 and 1860, only Vermont and Maine gave the vote to free blacks. Existing states, such as Pennsylvania and New York, took the franchise away from free African-Americans or subjected them to substantial property qualifications. Women, who had been excluded from public life by custom, now were explicitly banned from voting by constitutional provisions that limited full citizenship to men. To justify such discrimination, republican legislators in New Jersey (who excluded property-owning women from the vote in 1807) invoked traditional biological and social arguments. As a letter to the editor of a newspaper put it, "Women, generally, are neither by nature, nor habit, nor education, nor by their necessary condition in society fitted to perform this duty with credit to themselves or advantage to the public."

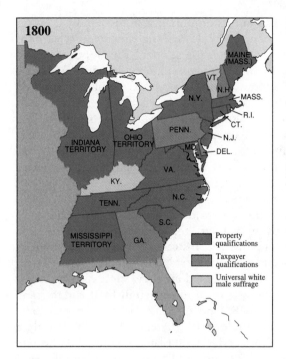

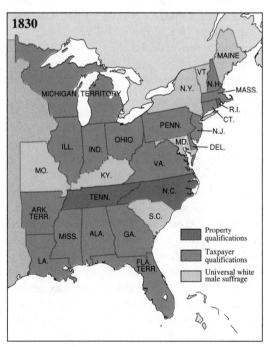

MAP 9.1

The Expansion of Voting Rights for White Men

Between 1800 and 1830 the United States moved steadily toward political democracy. Many states revised their constitutions, replacing property ownership with taxpaying or militia service as a qualification for voting. Some states—both in the East and the West—extended the franchise to all white men. A broader electorate changed the tone of politics, as parties tried to appeal to the interests and values of ordinary people.

Republican Marriage

Despite its limitations republicanism was a revolutionary ideology, which as John Adams lamented, "spread where it was not intended," threatening the husband's control of the family. Both in Europe and in America, husbands had long dominated wives and controlled family property. But in the eyes of some women, subordination to men seemed arbitrary, at odds with their belief in equal natural rights. Patriarchy was not "natural" and could be justified only on pragmatic grounds, "for the sake of order in families," as Mercy Otis Warren put it.

Economic and cultural changes also eroded customary family relations. Landowning parents had long arranged their children's marriages to ensure their own economic well-being during old age. But as land holdings shrank in long-settled rural communities, parents could no longer bequeath substantial farms—the economic incentives they had used to control their children's lives. Young men and women began to choose their own partners, influenced by the new cultural attitude of sentimentalism.

The New Conjugal Family
Grace and Philip Schuyler pose informally with their daughters and encourage their musical and literary talents. The affectionate mood of this early nineteenth-century scene stands in sharp contrast to family portraits painted in earlier eras, which emphasized the authority of the father and the subordinate status of his wife and children. (Collection of the New-York Historical Society)

Originating in Europe during the Romantic movement of the late eighteenth century, *sentimentalism* celebrated the importance of "feeling"—that is, a physical, sensuous appreciation of God, nature, and other human beings. By 1820 sentimentalism had touched all classes of American society. It dripped from the pages of the German and English literary works that were read in educated circles. It fell from the lips of actors in tear-jerking melodramas, which soon became the most popular theatrical entertainments in the United States. And it infused the rhetoric of revivalist preachers, who appealed to the passions of the heart rather than the logic of the mind.

Sentimentalism, in short, encouraged couples to marry for love. Parents had always taken physical attraction and emotional compatibility into account in arranging marriages for their children, but romance in and of itself did not have a high cultural value. Most parents were more concerned with the personal habits and financial resources of a prospective son- or daughter-in-law. A skeptical mother in Virginia remarked that young women should remain single "till they were old enough to form a proper *judgement* of mankind." Wealthy fathers who worried that their resources would be squandered by a free-spending son-in-law often placed funds in legal trusts so that their daughters would not be completely dependent on their husbands. As a Virginia planter wrote to his lawyer, "I rely on you to see the property settlement properly drawn *before the marriage,* for I by no means consent that Polly shall be left to the Vicissitudes of Life." By such means fathers gave up the hope of patriarchal dominance and became paternalists, protecting the interests of children who married for love.

Republicanism made marriage rather than parenthood the fundamental family relationship, and the new youth-run marriage system gave young adults greater freedom. Magazines promoted marriages "contracted from motives of affection, rather than of interest"; this outlook encouraged a young person to seek a spouse who was, as Eliza Southgate of Maine put it, "calculated to promote my happiness." Such freedom had its costs, because young adults often lacked the maturity and experience to choose wisely. Many were disappointed when their spouses failed as providers or faithful companions; a few sought divorces. Before 1800 most petitioners for divorce had charged their spouses with neglect, abandonment, or adultery—serious offenses against the moral order of society—but after that date emotional grounds dominated petitions. One woman complained that her husband had "ceased to cherish her," while a man lamented that his wife had "almost broke his heart." Reflecting these changed cultural values, some states expanded the legal grounds for divorce to include personal cruelty and drunkenness and made divorce available through judicial decree rather than only, as in the past, through a special act of the legislature.

Still, most unions, happy or not, lasted until death and, especially among urban Americans of middling status, were influenced by the republican ideal of a "companionate" marriage. But this noble ideal, in which wives enjoyed "true equality, both of rank and fortune," with their husbands, often foundered in the face of deeply ingrained cultural habits that favored men and laws that placed all

AMERICAN VOICES

A Companionate Marrige: Mary and Henry Lee

After a financial reverse, Henry Lee went to India as a merchant while Mary Lee raised their daughter, Molly, in Boston. Their letters reveal the personal intimacy, social equality, and shared financial responsibility of the ideal republican marriage.

[India] January 12, 1813
My respected and belov'd wife. . . .
You perhaps do not know that I have a partner in my business upon whose judgment I rely in all difficult cases. . . . Are you at a loss to know who this sage adviser is? No other than yourself, my dear wife, from whom I have rec'd many wise counsels which I ought to have benefited by more than I have, as indeed I should if I had followed all of them. . . .

The letters you have written would do honour to any one. They gratify me now almost as much as when first rec'd—the affectionate concern you take in my welfare touches me most sensibly. . . . I cannot help loving you the better for it.

[Boston] 28th Feb'y, Sunday Evening. . . . Oh, my dear, dear husband, when we do meet I believe I shall hold you fast—for it appears to me that almost any labour, if together, would not be too hard for us. . . . I know not why the wife should not work a *little* as well as the husband *labour so hard*, and did I feel a certainty that you would agree with me upon the subject, I should most certainly act upon the principle.

[Boston] 28th October, 1813. . . . The Indigo consigned to Patrick has sold at a very handsome advance; he . . . said that one speculation had afforded you more than all he had done for ever so long. . . . As for the property consigned *to me*, I cannot give a very good account of my stewardship. . . . I have sold all my goods but the handkerchiefs, and I fear they will sell so badly as to make my sales average very badly. They are in Tuckerman's shop.

SOURCE: Frances Rollins Morse, ed., *Henry and Mary Lee, Letters and Journals . . . 1802–1860* (Boston, privately printed, 1926), pp. 78–81.

property in men's hands. Moreover, because the new marriage system discouraged parents from playing an active role in their children's lives, young wives could no longer rely on their parents for emotional or financial support; they became even more dependent on their husbands than their mothers had been. The marriage contract "is so much more important in its consequences to females than to males," a young man at the Litchfield Law School noted astutely in 1820, "for besides leaving everything else to unite themselves to one man, they subject themselves to his authority. He is their all—their only relative—their only hope."

Republican Mothers

Traditionally, most American women had focused their lives on domestic duties: bearing and raising children and work in the home or on the farm. As the changing political order challenged long-standing customs, a few upper-class women sought a public voice. But most women—and certainly most men—did not assume that the egalitarian logic of republican ideology would affect gender roles. Few demanded or even supported a substantial public role for American women. Instead, many clergymen and political leaders promoted the traditional notion of a *separate sphere* for women, but expanded it. Women had special domestic skills and responsibilities, they argued, and should play a leading role in home and family life.

This enhanced domestic role for women stemmed in part from changes in Christian thought. Traditionally, most religious writers had viewed women as morally inferior to men—as sexual temptresses or witches. By 1800 the clergy had begun to hold men responsible for sexual misconduct instead. Moralists now claimed that modesty and purity were inherent in woman's nature, making women uniquely qualified to educate the spirit. Thus, the cultivation of virtue became part of women's sphere.

Political leaders also called on women to ensure the future of the new American republic. In *Thoughts on Female Education* (1787), Benjamin Rush argued that a young woman should receive intellectual training so that she would be "an agreeable companion for a sensible man"; her responsibility, as another moralist put it, was to ensure "his perseverance in the paths of rectitude." Rush and other men of affairs welcomed the emergence of loyal "republican mothers" who would instruct "their sons in the principles of liberty and government." As the author of a list of "Maxims for Republics" put it, "Some of the first patriots of ancient times were formed by their mothers."

Ministers embraced the idea of republican motherhood, devising new roles for women in moral and religious education. "Preserving virtue and instructing the young are not the fancied, but the real 'Rights of Women,'" the Reverend Thomas Bernard told the Female Charitable Society of Salem, Massachusetts, in 1803. He urged his audience to dismiss the public roles advocated by Mary Wollstonecraft, a British republican who had published the pathbreaking feminist manifesto *A Vindication of the Rights of Women* in 1792. Instead, women should be content to care for their children, a responsibility that gave them "an extensive power over the fortunes of man in every generation." While Bernard wanted women to remain in their traditional domestic sphere, he campaigned to enhance its value.

Many American women from the middling classes accepted this limited revision of their role. As a young New England woman wrote in 1803, "She is still *woman,* with duties prescribed her by the God of Nature essentially different from those of *man.*" Some educated women of the upper classes, however, insisted on the equality of the separate male and female worlds. "I will never consent to have our sex considered in an inferior point of light," proclaimed Abigail Adams, the wife of President John Adams, in 1799. And some ministers envisioned a public role for women that was based on their domestic virtues. As Thomas Grimké, a South Carolina minister, asserted, "Give me a host of educated pious mothers and sisters and I will revolutionize a country, in moral and religious taste."

PROTESTANT CHRISTIANITY AND WOMEN'S LIVES

Religion had always been a significant part of American life. But in the decades between 1790 and 1820, a series of revivals planted the values of Protestant Christianity deep in the American national character. In the process, religious revivalism created new public roles for women.

The Second Great Awakening

The revivals that began around 1790 were much more complex than those of the First Great Awakening. In the 1740s most revivals had occurred in existing congregations; fifty years later they took place in frontier camp meetings as well and often involved the creation of new churches and denominations. Even more strikingly, the Second Great Awakening spawned a wide variety of organizations dedicated to social and political reform.

The churches that prospered in the new nation were typically republican in their outlook or organization. Because it was dominated by bishops and priests, the Roman Catholic Church attracted few converts either among Protestants, who embraced Luther's doctrine of the priesthood of all believers, or among the unchurched, who feared clerical power. Few ordinary Americans joined the Episcopal Church, which had a similar hierarchical structure and was dominated by its wealthiest members. The Presbyterian Church was more popular, in part because it was more "republican": ordinary members elected laymen to the synods (congresses) where doctrine and practice were formulated.

Methodism attracted even more adherents. Although bishops took the lead on theological issues and enforced order in the church, the evangelical fervor of early Methodism fostered lay preaching, emotional worship services, and communal singing, which created an egalitarian religious culture. The most democratic forms of church government belonged to Quakers, Baptists, and Congregationalists. No bishops or governing bodies stood above the local congregations, and most decisions—on matters of theology as well as administration—rested with church members. Partly because of their democratic features, Methodist and Baptist churches grew spectacularly; by the early nineteenth century they were the largest religious denominations in the United States.

A continuous wave of revivalism fueled the expansion of Protestant Christianity. Beginning in the 1780s, Baptists and Methodists evangelized the older cities and backcountry of New England. A new sect of Universalists, who repudiated the Calvinist doctrine of predestination and preached universal salvation, attracted thousands of converts, especially in northern New England. After 1800 enthusiastic camp meeting revivals swept the frontier regions of

South Carolina, Kentucky, Tennessee, and Ohio. James McGready, a Scots-Irish Presbyterian preacher, "could so array hell before the wicked," an eyewitness reported, "that they would tremble and Quake, imagining a lake of fire and brimstone yawning to overwhelm them." When frontier preachers got together at a revival meeting, they were electrifying. One young man, James Finley, was so moved by the Cane Ridge, Kentucky, revival of 1802 that he became a Methodist minister:

> The noise was like the roar of Niagara. The vast sea of human beings seemed to be agitated as if by a storm. I counted seven ministers, all preaching at one time, some on stumps, others on wagons. . . . Some of the people were singing, others praying, some crying for mercy. A peculiarly strange sensation came over me. My heart beat tumultuously, my knees trembled, my lips quivered, and I felt as though I must fall to the ground.

Through such revivals, Baptist and Methodist preachers reshaped the spiritual landscape of the South and the Old Southwest. They won over most of the white population and, with the assistance of black ministers, began to implant evangelical Protestant Christianity among African-Americans as well.

Unlike the First Great Awakening, which had split many churches into hostile factions, the Second Awakening brought about friendly competition among Protestant churches to spread the faith to the unconverted. In New England and the Middle Atlantic states, pious women supplemented the work of preachers and lay elders, doubling the amount of organized spiritual energy. In the South and West, Baptist and Methodist preachers traveled constantly. Instead of settling in a congregation, a Methodist cleric followed a circuit, "riding a hardy pony or horse . . . with his Bible, hymn-book, and Discipline." Wherever they went, these "circuit riders" established new churches by searching out devout families, bringing them together for worship, then appointing lay elders to lead the congregation and enforce moral discipline until the circuit rider returned.

Evangelical ministers copied the techniques of George Whitefield and other eighteenth-century revivalists, codifying their intuitive genius in manuals of "practical preaching." To attract converts, preachers were cautioned to emphasize piety over theology; extemporaneous speech was deemed more powerful than a written sermon. "Preach without papers," advised one minister, "seem earnest & serious; & you will be listened to with Patience, & Wonder; both of your hands will be seized, & almost shook off as soon as you are out of the Church."

These missionary innovations attracted converts and shifted the denominational base of American religion toward the Baptists, Methodists, and other evangelical churches. The leading churches of the Revolutionary Era—the Congregationalists, Episcopalians, and Quakers—declined in relative membership. Their leaders and members were content for the most part to maintain their existing congregations or grow slowly through natural increase.

The Second Great Awakening changed the character of American thought—and social action—in dramatic ways. Before the Awakening, the Calvinist preoccupation with human depravity and weakness had shaped the

Peter Cartwright Finds God

A s the son of a pious mother, Peter Cartwright was well prepared to respond to the evangelical message. After becoming a minister in the rapidly growing Methodist Church, he spread the Gospel throughout the Mississippi Valley.

In 1801, when I was in my sixteenth year, my father, my eldest half brother, and myself, attended a wedding about five miles from home, where there was a great deal of drinking and dancing, which was very common at marriages in those days. I drank little or nothing; my delight was in dancing. . . .

[That night] I began to reflect on the manner in which I had spent the day and evening. I felt guilty and condemned. I arose and walked the floor. My mother was in bed. It seemed to me, all of a sudden, my blood rushed to my head, my heart palpitated, in a few minutes I turned blind; an awful impression rested on my mind that death had come and I was unprepared to die. I fell on my knees and asked God to have mercy on me.

My mother sprang from her bed, and was soon on her knees by my side, praying for me, and exhorting me to look to Christ for mercy. . . . Three months rolled away, and still I did not find the blessing of the pardon of my sins. . . .

As there was a great waking up among the Churches, from the revival that had broken out at Cane Ridge [Kentucky], many flocked to sacramental meetings. . . . I went, with weeping multitudes, and bowed before the stand, and earnestly prayed for mercy. In the midst of a solemn struggle of soul, an impression was made on my mind, as though a voice said to me, "Thy sins are all forgiven thee." Divine light flashed all round me, unspeakable joy sprung up in my soul. . . . I have never, for one moment, doubted that the Lord did, then and there, forgive my sins and give me religion.

SOURCE: W. P. Strickland, ed., *Autobiography of Peter Cartwright, The Backwoods Preacher* (New York: Hunt & Eaton, 1856), pp. 34–38.

thinking of many writers, teachers, and statesmen. But by the early nineteenth century, ministers—whether or not they were revivalists—had begun to place greater stress on human ability and individual free will. Their view imparted a new optimism to the intellectual culture of the United States.

In New England, the primary source of the new theology, many educated and economically well-off Congregationalists became Unitarians. Rejecting the concept of the Trinity—God the Father, Son, and Holy Spirit—Unitarians worshiped an indivisible and "united" God (hence the name Unitarian). Reacting against the emotionalism of Methodist and Baptist services, they stressed the power of human reason. "The ultimate reliance of a human being is, and must be, on his own mind," argued the famous Unitarian minister William

Ellery Channing, "for the idea of God is the idea of our own spiritual nature, purified and enlarged to infinity." This emphasis on a believer's reason, a legacy of the Enlightenment, gave Unitarianism a humanistic and individualistic cast. Optimistic ideas affected mainstream Congregational churches as well. Lyman Beecher, the preeminent New England clergyman, accepted the evangelical doctrine of universal salvation. Although he believed humans have a natural tendency to sin, he retreated from the Calvinist doctrine of predestination, declaring that all men and women have the capacity to choose God. In emphasizing choice—the free will of the believer—Beecher testified to the growing confidence in the power of human action.

Reflecting this optimistic outlook, the minister Samuel Hopkins linked individual salvation with social reform through the concept of religious *benevolence*. Benevolence was the practice of disinterested virtue, to be undertaken by those who had received God's sanctifying grace. According to the New York Presbyterian minister John Rodgers, such fortunate individuals had a duty "to dole out charity to their poorer brothers and sisters." Inspired by such arguments, pious merchants founded the New York Humane Society and other charitable organizations. By the 1820s some conservative church leaders were complaining that through their benevolence, lay men and women were devoting themselves to secular reforms—such as the prevention of pauperism—and neglecting spiritual goals. Their criticism was on the mark. It was her belief, the social reformer Lydia Maria Child later recalled, that "the *only* true church organization [is] when heads and hearts unite in working for the welfare of the human-race."

Ideas of benevolence and religious activism spread quickly through the founding of new theological seminaries such as Andover in Massachusetts and Lane in Ohio, two Congregationalist institutions that fostered cooperation among the denominations. As individual clergymen worked together, American Protestant churches became less dogmatic. Many congregations abandoned orthodox books and pamphlets such as the *Watts Hymnal*, which took controversial stances on old theological debates over predestination, and replaced them, a layman explained, with publications that would not give "offense to the serious Christians of any denomination."

Emulating a British innovation, American Protestants founded five interdenominational societies between 1815 and 1826: the American Education Society (1815), the American Bible Society (1816), the American Sunday School Union (1824), the American Tract Society (1824), and the American Home Missionary Society (1826). The new organizations were based in New York, Boston, and Philadelphia, but they ministered to a national congregation. Each year the societies dispatched hundreds of missionaries and distributed tens of thousands of religious pamphlets.

Organization on this scale united the individual energies of thousands of church members in a great collective undertaking, providing the Second Great Awakening with momentum and power. "I want to see our state evangelized," declared one pious New York layman. "Suppose the great State of New York in all its physical, political, moral, commercial, and pecuniary resources should come over to the Lord's side. Why it would turn the scale and could convert the world. I shall have no rest until it is done." For the first time in America, men and women in small villages scattered across the nation saw themselves as part of a large religious movement that could change the course of history.

As a result of the Second Awakening, religion became a central force in American life. On July 4, 1827, the Reverend Ezra Stiles Ely called on the members of the Seventh Presbyterian Church in Philadelphia to begin a "Christian party in politics." In his sermon "The Duty of Christian Freemen to Elect Christian Rulers," Ely set out for the American republic a new religious goal—one Thomas Jefferson and John Adams would have found strange, if not troubling. The two recently deceased presidents had believed that America's mission was to spread political republicanism. In contrast, Ely urged the United States to become an evangelical Christian nation dedicated to religious conversion at home and abroad. As Ely put it, "All our rulers ought in their official capacity to serve the Lord Jesus Christ." The Second Great Awakening had added an intense religious dimension to American politics and the emerging national identity.

Women and Religion

Revivalism created new opportunities for women in the public sphere. In Rhode Island, the preacher Jemima Wilkinson founded a new sect, the Universal Friends. In many Protestant churches, women took advantage of their enhanced moral status by expanding their role in religious and charitable activities. To give but a few examples, in New Hampshire women managed more than fifty local "cent" societies which raised funds for the Society for Promoting Christian Knowledge; evangelical women in New York City founded a charitable institution, the Society for the Relief of Poor Widows; and young Quaker women in Philadelphia ran the Society for the Free Instruction of African Females.

Jemima Wilkinson, the "Universal Friend"
A tall, graceful woman with dark eyes, Jemima Wilkinson had a magnetic personality and a powerful preaching style. Her message blended the Calvinist warning of "a lost and guilty, gossiping, dying World" with a Quaker-inspired social gospel. Like the Shakers, Wilkinson preached celibacy and never married. More controversial, she dressed like a man, wearing a black robe similar to a clergyman's gown.

Women became active in religion and charitable work partly because they were excluded from other spheres of public life and partly because they formed a substantial majority in many denominations. After 1800 no less than 70 percent of the members of New England Congregational churches were women. Some ministers acknowledged their numbers by changing long-standing practices. In many Protestant faiths, men and women had tradition-ally sat on opposite sides of the church during regular Sunday services and ministers had conducted separate prayer meetings for each sex. Now evangel-ical Methodist and Baptist preachers began to encourage mixed praying. Al-though critics condemned the practice as "promiscuous," Presbyterian and Congregational churches in frontier areas achieved impressive results. "Our prayer meetings have been one of the greatest means of the conversion of souls," a minister in central New York reported in the 1820s, "especially those in which brothers and sisters have prayed together."

As women began to transcend traditional gender roles, their religious ac-tivities and organizations became controversial. Many laymen resented the clergy's emphasis on women's moral superiority and the religious and social activism that sprang from it. "Women have a different *calling*," one man argued. "They are neither required nor permitted to be exhorters or leaders in public assemblies. . . . That they *be chaste, keepers at home* is the Apostle's [St. Paul's] di-rection." But many ministers continued to encourage the creation of women's organizations, and women became increasingly conscious of their new social power and public role. By the 1820s, mothers throughout the United States had founded local maternal associations to encourage Christian child raising. Newsletters such as *Mother's Magazine* were widely read in hundreds of small towns and villages, giving women a sense of shared purpose and identity.

In their capacity as moral paragons, women had an immediate and direct impact on social behavior. Imbibing the principle of female virtue, many young women, and the men who courted them, postponed sexual intercourse until after marriage—a form of self-restraint that had not been common in the eighteenth century. In Hingham, Massachusetts, and many other New England towns, about 30 percent of the women who married between 1750 and 1800 had borne a child within eight months of the wedding day. By the 1820s the proportion had dropped to 15 percent.

Religious activism also advanced the education of women. Churches es-tablished scores of seminaries and academies where girls—mostly from the middling classes—received sound intellectual training as well as moral instruc-tion. Emma Willard, the first American to advocate higher education for women, opened the Middlebury Female Seminary in Vermont in 1814 and later founded girls' schools in Waterford and Troy, New York.

Women educated in female academies gradually displaced men from their customary roles as schoolteachers. By the 1820s women were teaching the summer session in many public schools; in the following decade they would work the more demanding winter term as well. Women took over teaching in primary schools because they had few other opportunities and because they would accept lower pay than men would. Women earned $12 to $14 per month with room and board as schoolteachers—less than a farm laborer did. But they benefited from the higher moral status accorded to women and from the imperatives of republican motherhood: they would instruct the young not only at home but also in school. As schoolteachers, women had an acknowledged place in public life that had been beyond their reach in colonial and Revolutionary times. Thus, the Second Great Awakening transformed both the character of American culture and the scope of women's lives.

CHAPTER 9 TIMELINE

1780s	Rural outwork system, especially shoes and textiles
1781	Philadelphia merchants found Bank of North America
1782	St. Jean de Crèvecoeur, *Letters from an American Farmer*
1787	Benjamin Rush, *Thoughts on Female Education*
1790s	State mercantilism encourages economic development Second Great Awakening Republican motherhood defined
1791	First Bank of the United States founded; dissolved in 1811
1794	Lancaster Turnpike Company
1795	Massachusetts Mill Dam Act
1800s	State-chartered banks proliferate Rise of sentimentalism and republican marriage system Women's religious activism and female academies Spread of evangelical Baptists and Methodists Beginnings of benevolent reform
1801	John Marshall becomes chief justice of the United States
1803	*Marbury v. Madison* states theory of judicial review
1807	New Jersey excludes propertied women from suffrage
1810	*Fletcher v. Peck* expands contract clause
1816	Second Bank of the United States chartered
1819	*McCulloch v. Maryland* enhances power of national government *Dartmouth College v. Woodward* protects corporate property rights
1818–1821	Democratic revision of state constitutions
1820s	Women become schoolteachers Growth of cash-based market economy
1824	*Gibbons v. Ogden* establishes federal authority over interstate commerce

	ECONOMY Economic Revolution Creates New Social Classes	GOVERNMENT Creating a Democratic Polity	SOCIETY Reforming People and Institutions	SECTIONALISM From Compromise to Civil War and Reconstruction
1820	Waltham textile factory employs women operatives (1814) Erie Canal completed (1825)	Universal white male suffrage Rise of Jackson and Democratic party	American Colonization Society (1817) "Benevolent" Reform Revivalist Charles Finney	Missouri Compromise (1820) Walker's *Appeal to the Colored Race* (1829)
1830	Protective tariffs aid owners and workers Panic of 1837 cripples union movement	Anti-Masonic movement Whig party formed (1834); Second Party System emerges	Joseph Smith founds Mormonism Female Moral Reform Society (1834)	Nullification crisis (1832) Garrison forms American Anti-Slavery Society (1833)
1840	Irish join labor force *Commonwealth v. Hunt* (1842) legalizes unions	Log Cabin campaign mobilizes voters Antislavery parties: Liberty and Free Soil	Fourierist and other communal settlements founded Seneca Falls Convention (1848)	War with Mexico and Wilmot Proviso (1846) increase sectional conflict
1850	Free labor ideology justifies inequality Panic of 1857	Whig party disintegrates Republican party founded (1854): Third Party System	Stowe's *Uncle Tom's Cabin* (1852)	Compromise of 1850 Kansas-Nebraska Act (1854) and "Bleeding Kansas" *Dred Scott* decision (1857)
1860	Republicans enact agenda: Homestead Act, aid to railroads, high tariffs	Thirteenth Amendment (1865) ends slavery; Fourteenth Amendment (1868) extends legal and political rights	U.S. Sanitary Commission and American Red Cross founded	South Carolina secedes (1860) Confederate States of America (1861–65)
1870	Panic of 1873	Fifteenth Amendment extends vote to black men (1870)	Freed African-Americans create schools and institutions	Compromise of 1877 ends Reconstruction

PART 3

ECONOMIC REVOLUTION AND SECTIONAL STRIFE

1820–1877

Between 1820 and 1877 the United States was transformed from a predominantly agricultural society into one of the world's most powerful industrial economies, a change that affected every aspect of American life.

First, the expansion of markets and the growth of industry revolutionized the economy. High-speed machines and a new organization of labor boosted factory output while a new network of canals and railroads helped create a vast national market. A wealthy elite of business owners emerged at the top of the social order, while the urban middle class grew in size and importance. At the bottom of the scale propertyless workers labored for wages in the new factories and businesses.

Second, these changes spurred the development of political parties and a more open, democratic polity. Farmers, workers, and entrepreneurs turned to politics to improve their economic welfare, while Irish and German immigrants entered the political arena to protect their religion and culture from nativists and reformers. The result was a two-party system that engaged the energies of the vast majority of the electorate.

Third, many Americans troubled by the changes sweeping the country joined reform movements, many with religious roots. Dedicated men and women preached the gospel of temperance, Sunday observance, and prison reform. Others sought more radical change—equal rights for women and the abolition of slavery—and a few pursued their vision in utopian communities.

All these changes sharpened sectional divisions: the North became an urbanizing and industrializing society based on free labor while the South remained a rural, slaveholding one. Conflicts over the expansion of slavery in the West led finally to the secession of the South and a bloody civil war to restore the Union and liberate the slaves. But in the Reconstruction Era that followed, the victorious North failed to extend the full benefits of democracy and opportunity to African-Americans.

CHAPTER 10

THE ECONOMIC REVOLUTION, 1820–1840

- The Coming of Industry: Northeastern Manufacturing
- The Expansion of Markets
- A Changing Social Structure

The United States was founded as an agrarian republic and over the next half-century matured into a commercially advanced agricultural society. Then enterprising Americans initiated a century-long process of change that transformed the nation into the world's most powerful industrial economy. The 1820s and 1830s were crucial decades in this transition, for they saw a dramatic acceleration in the growth of its two central components: the system of manufacturing and the market economy. Together, the "industrial revolution" and the "market revolution" created a new economic structure. A major change in manufacturing methods enabled Americans to increase their economic *productivity* (making far more goods per worker), while the building of new transportation networks—turnpikes, canals, and railroads—allowed those products to be sold throughout the land.

The French aristocrat Alexis de Tocqueville captured a key feature of this economic revolution in his treatise *Democracy in America* (1835). "What most astonishes me," he remarked after a two-year stay in the United States, "is not so much the marvelous grandeur of some undertakings, as the innumerable magnitude of small ones." It was the individual efforts of tens of thousands of artisan-inventors, entrepreneurial storekeepers and manufacturers, and commercially minded farmers that propelled the country into a new economic era. As the editor of *Niles Weekly Register* put it, there was an "almost *universal ambition to get forward.*"

Not all Americans embraced the new ethic of enterprise, and many who did failed to share in the new prosperity. Industrial and commercial expansion created a class-divided society that challenged the founders' vision of an agricultural republic with few distinctions of wealth or power. "The invasion of Nature by Trade with its Money, its Credit, its Steam, its Railroad," the philosopher Ralph Waldo Emerson wrote in 1839, "threatens to . . . establish a new, universal Monarchy."

THE COMING OF INDUSTRY: NORTHEASTERN MANUFACTURING

The Industrial Revolution came to the United States after 1790 as American merchants increased productivity by reorganizing work and building factories. These innovations in manufacturing boosted output and living standards to an unprecedented extent; the average per capita wealth of Americans increased by nearly 1 percent per year—30 percent over the course of a generation. Goods that once had been luxury items became part of everyday life.

New Organization and New Technology

This impressive gain in output stemmed primarily from changes in the organization of production. Since the 1790s American merchants had used their profits from commerce to expand the outwork system, which made domestic manufacturing more efficient even without technological improvements (see Chapter 9). For example, during the 1820s and 1830s outwork transformed the shoe industry as merchants and manufacturers introduced the "division of labor" into the system of production. The employers hired journeymen and set them to work in central shops cutting leather into soles and "uppers." Then they sent out the uppers to shoe binders, usually women who worked at home binding the uppers and sewing in fabric linings. Finally, the manufacturers had other journeymen assemble the shoes in small shops and return them to the central shop for inspection and packing. The new system of production made the master a powerful employer, the "shoe boss," and eroded workers' control over the pace and conditions of labor. This division of labor also dramatically increased the output of shoes while cutting their price.

For tasks that were not suited to the outwork system, entrepreneurs created an even more important new organization, the modern *factory*. They concentrated as many of the elements of production as possible under one roof and divided the work into specialized tasks. For example, in the 1830s Cincinnati merchants built slaughterhouses that included "disassembly" lines for butchering hogs. A simple system of overhead rails moved the carcasses past workers who had specific tasks: splitting the animals, removing various organs, and trimming the carcasses before packers stuffed them in barrels and pickled them. The system was efficient and quick; every hour more than sixty hogs were butchered and packed. In the 1840s Cincinnati was disassembling so many hogs that the city became known as "Porkopolis."

Upper Falls of the Genesee River, 1835
Like many early industries, the prosperous flour mills at Rochester, New York, were located to take advantage of natural resources. The Genesee River provided water to transport grain to the mills, and its falls powered the mill machinery. (Collection of the New-York Historical Society)

The new factories boasted impressive new technology. As early as 1782 the prolific Delaware inventor Oliver Evans had built a highly automated labor-saving flour mill driven by water power. His machinery lifted the grain to the top of the mill, cleaned the grain as it fell into hoppers, ground it into flour, conveyed the flour back to the top of the mill, and then cooled the flour during its descent into barrels. Evans's factory, remarked one observer, "was as full of machinery as the case of a watch." It needed only six men to mill 100,000 bushels of grain a year.

The Textile Industry

The most dramatic gains in productivity occurred when manufacturers in the textile industry *combined* these organizational and technological innovations. In the 1760s textile manufacturers in northern England had begun to use water-driven machines to produce huge quantities of inexpensive cloth, and in the 1790s American entrepreneurs tried to duplicate their success. This task was difficult because British law prohibited the export of textile machinery and the emigration of mechanics who knew how to build it. Lured by high wages or offers of partnerships, thousands of British mechanics disguised themselves as ordinary laborers and set sail for the United States. By 1812 there were more than 300 British mechanics at work in the Philadelphia area alone.

The most important was Samuel Slater, who came to America in 1789. He had worked for Richard Arkwright, the inventor and operator of the most advanced machinery for spinning cotton. Having memorized the design of Arkwright's machinery, the young Slater contacted Moses Brown, a wealthy merchant who had been trying to duplicate British spinning technology. Slater took over the management of Brown's cotton mill in Providence, Rhode Island, and replicated Arkwright's machines. The opening of Slater's mill in 1790 marks the advent of the American Industrial Revolution.

In competing with British mills, American manufacturers had one major advantage: an abundance of natural resources. America's rich agriculture produced a wealth of cotton and wool, and from Maine to Delaware its rivers provided a cheap source of energy. As rivers cascaded downhill from the Appalachian foothills to the Atlantic coastal plain, they were easily harnessed to run power machinery. All along this *fall line* industrial villages and towns sprang up.

However, the British producers easily undersold their American competitors. Thanks to cheap shipping and low interest rates in Britain, it was profitable to import raw cotton from the United States, manufacture it into cloth, and then ship the textiles back across the Atlantic. Moreover, because British companies were better established, they could engage in cutthroat competition, cutting prices briefly but sharply to drive the newer American firms out of business. The most important British advantage was cheap labor. Britain had a larger population—about 12.6 million in 1810 compared with 7.3 million Americans—and thousands of landless laborers who were willing to take low-paying factory jobs. Since unskilled American workers could obtain good pay for farm or construction work, American manufacturers had to pay them higher wages.

To offset these British advantages, American entrepreneurs sought assistance from the federal government. In 1816 Congress passed a tariff that gave cotton cloth manufacturers some protection from low-cost imports. New protective legislation in 1824 levied a tax of 35 percent on imported iron products, woolen and cotton textiles, and various agricultural products, and the rate rose to 50 percent in 1828. But in 1833, under pressure from southern planters, western farmers, and urban consumers—all of whom wanted to keep down the price of manufactured goods—Congress began to reduce tariffs (see Chapter 11). Unable to compete with lower-cost British producers, American textile manufacturers often failed.

American producers adopted two strategies to compete with their British rivals. First, they tried to improve on British technology. In 1811 Francis Cabot Lowell, a wealthy Boston merchant, spent a holiday touring British textile mills. A well-educated and charming young man, he flattered his hosts by asking a great many questions, but his easy manner hid a serious purpose. Lowell listened closely and secretly made detailed drawings of power machinery. Paul Moody, an experienced American mechanic, then copied the machines and made improvements. In 1814 Lowell joined two other merchants,

A New England Mill Worker: Sarah Rice

Between 1815 and 1850 tens of thousands of New England farm girls took jobs in new textile factories. Sarah Rice, who tended looms in a Masonville, Connecticut, mill, explains both the financial advantages of factory labor over work as a domestic servant and the toll on her health taken by fourteen-hour workdays.

Masonville Feb 23d 1845
Dear Father
    I now take my pen in hand to let you know where I am. I have been waiting perhaps longer than I ought to without leting you know where I am yet I had a reason for so doing . . . knowing that you was dolefully prejudiced against a Cotton Factory, and being no less prejudiced myself I thought it best to wait and see how I prospered. . . .
    To be sure it is a noisy place and we are confined more than I like to be but I do not wear out my clothes and shoes as I do when I do house work. If I can make 2 dollars per week beside my board and save my clothes and shoes I think it will be better than to do housework for nine shillings [$1.12] I mean for a year or two. I should not like to spend my days in a mill . . . because I like a Farm to well for that.

Millbury [Massachusetts] Sept 14th 1845
You surely cannot blame me for leaving the factory so long as I realised that it was killing me to work in it. Could you have seen me att the time or a week before I came away you would [have] advised me as many others did to leave immediately. I realise that if I lose my health which is all I possess on earth . . . that I shall be in a sad condition.

SOURCE: Gary Kulik, Roger Parks, Theodore Z. Penn, eds., *The New England Mill Village, 1790–1860* (Cambridge, Mass.: MIT Press, 1982), pp. 389–390.

Nathan Appleton and Patrick Tracy Jackson, to form the Boston Manufacturing Company. Raising the staggering sum of $400,000, they built a textile plant in Waltham, Massachusetts, on the Charles River. The Waltham factory was the first in America to perform all the operations of cloth making under one roof. More important, thanks to Moody's improvements, Waltham's power looms operated at higher speeds than British looms and needed fewer workers.

    The second American strategy was to find less expensive workers. The Boston Manufacturing Company took the lead, pioneering a manufacturing system that became known as the Waltham plan. The company recruited thousands of farm girls and women, who would work at low wages, as textile operatives. To attract these workers, the company provided boardinghouses and cultural activities such as evening lectures. The mill owners reassured anxious parents by enforcing strict curfews, prohibiting alcoholic beverages, and requiring regular church attendance. At Lowell (1822), Chicopee (1823), and other sites in Massachusetts and New Hampshire, the Boston Manufacturing Company built new cotton factories on the Waltham plan; other Boston-owned firms quickly followed suit.

By the early 1830s more than 40,000 young women were working in textile mills in New England. Eleven-year-old Lucy Larcom of Lowell, Massachusetts, went to work in a textile mill, she later recalled, so that she could support herself and not be "a trouble or burden or expense" to her widowed mother. Many operatives sent their savings home to help their fathers pay off farm mortgages, defray the cost of schooling for their brothers, or accumulate a dowry for themselves. Women textile operatives often found their work oppressive and took periodic breaks before moving to another mill, but many gained a new sense of freedom and autonomy. "Don't I feel independent!" a mill worker wrote to her sister in the 1840s. "The thought that I am living on no one is a happy one indeed to me."

The owners of the Boston Manufacturing Company were even happier. By using improved technology and cheap female labor, they finally achieved competitive superiority over their British rivals in American markets. They also had an advantage over textile manufacturers in New York and Pennsylvania, where agricultural employment was better paid than in New England and textile wages consequently were higher. Producers in those states pursued a different strategy, modifying traditional technology to produce higher-quality cloth, also with good results. In 1825 Thomas Jefferson, once a critic of industrialization, expressed his pride in the American achievement: "Our manufacturers are now very nearly on a footing with those of England."

American Mechanics and Technological Innovation

By the 1820s American craftsmen had replaced British immigrants at the cutting edge of technological innovation. Although few had a formal education and once had been viewed as "mean" or even "servile" workers, they now claimed respect as "men professing an ingenious art." One such inventor, Richard Garsed, started working in a textile mill when he was eight years old. Ten years later, in 1837, Garsed experimented with improvements on power looms in his father's factory and in three years nearly doubled their speed. By 1846 he had patented a cam and harness device that allowed elaborately figured fabrics such as damask to be woven by machine.

In the Philadelphia region, the most important inventors came from the remarkable Sellars family. Samuel Sellars, Jr., invented a machine for twisting worsted woolen yarn. His son John devised more efficient ways of using water power to run the family's sawmills and gristmills and built a machine to weave wire sieves. John's sons and grandsons built machine shops that turned out a

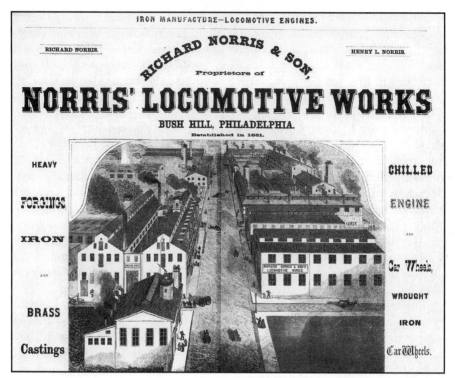

The Norris Locomotive Works
Founded in 1831, the Norris Works became a prime supplier of locomotives to railroads in the
United States and Europe. Its large workshops boasted sophisticated machine tools and could
produce three locomotives every six days. (National Museum of American History, Smithsonian)

variety of new products: riveted leather fire hoses, papermaking equipment,
and eventually locomotives. In 1824 members of the Sellars family and other
mechanics founded the Franklin Institute in Philadelphia. Named after Benjamin Franklin, whom the mechanics admired for his scientific accomplishments and idealization of hard work, the institute fostered a sense of
professional identity. The Franklin Institute published a journal; provided high
school–level instruction in mechanics, chemistry, mathematics, and mechanical drawing; and organized annual fairs to exhibit the most advanced products.
Craftsmen in Ohio and other states soon established their own mechanics institutes, which played a crucial role in diffusing technical knowledge and encouraging innovation. Around 1820 the United States Patent Office issued
about 200 patents on new inventions each year; by 1850 it was awarding 1,000
annually, and ten years later over 4,000.

During these years American mechanics pioneered the development of
machine tools—machines for making other machines. This technical advance
was crucial because it facilitated the rapid spread of the Industrial Revolution.

For example, mechanics serving the textile industry invented lathes, planers, and boring machines that made standardized parts. These machine-tooled parts, which required a minimum of filing and fitting, made it possible to manufacture new spinning jennys and weaving looms at a low cost and to repair broken machines. Moreover, this machinery was precise enough in design and construction to operate at higher speeds than British equipment.

Technological innovation swept through the rest of American manufacturing. For example, in 1832 the mechanics employed by Samuel W. Collins in his Connecticut ax-making company built a vastly improved die-forging machine—a device that pressed and hammered hot metal into dies, or cutting forms. Using the improved machine, a skilled worker could increase his production of ax heads from 12 to 300 a day. A few years later mechanics in Massachusetts perfected a power-driven shoe-stitching machine, boosting the output of well-made boots while cutting the cost.

The most important advances in machine building came in the firearms industry. To fill large-scale contracts from the federal government, Eli Whitney and his coworkers in Connecticut developed machine tools that produced parts that were not only interchangeable but also precision-crafted. After Whitney's death this innovative work in machine design was continued by his partner, John H. Hall, an engineer at the federal armory at Harpers Ferry, Virginia. By the 1840s Hall had developed an array of basic machine tools to work metal: turret lathes, milling machines, and precision grinders. Thereafter, manufacturers could use those machine tools to produce complicated machinery with great speed, at low cost, and in large quantities. With this expansion in the availability of machines, the American Industrial Revolution came of age.

Wage Workers and the Labor Movement

As the Industrial Revolution gathered momentum, it changed the economic system and the character of the American social order. Each decade, more and more white Americans lost their economic independence and took work as wage-earning employees, hired by the day, week, or season (or for a specific job). They had no security of employment and little control over their working conditions.

Some wage workers worked in traditional crafts, such as the building trades. These journeymen artisans—carpenters, housepainters, stonecutters, masons, nailers, and cabinetmakers—had valuable skills and a strong sense of craft identity. Consequently, they were able to form unions and bargain with the master artisans who employed them. The journeymen's main concern was the increasing length of the workday, which deprived them of time to spend with their families or use to improve their education. The traditional workday for artisans had averaged out, over the winter and summer seasons, at about twelve hours; they began at first light, took breaks for lunch and dinner, and stopped at dusk. By the 1820s masters were abusing the old work rules—

scheduling more jobs for summer when the workday was longer and charging customers more while paying journeymen the old daily rate. In response, 600 carpenters in Boston went on strike in 1825, demanding a ten-hour day, 6 A.M. to 6 P.M., with an hour each for breakfast and dinner. Although the Boston protest failed, two years later several hundred journeymen carpenters in Philadelphia won a similar strike for a ten-hour day and then helped found the Mechanics' Union of Trade Associations. This citywide organization of fifty unions and 10,000 Philadelphia wage earners articulated a broad reform program, demanding "a just balance of power . . . between all the various classes."

By the mid-1830s skilled workers in the building trades had forced many urban employers to accept ten hours as the standard workday. In 1835 the Philadelphia city council set a ten-hour day for local public works, and the following year President Andrew Jackson established a ten-hour day at the Philadelphia navy yard. These victories were significant; they gave skilled American workers the same hours that British building-trade workers had enjoyed since the 1750s.

Artisans whose occupations were threatened by industrialization were less successful. As machines changed the nature of their work, shoemakers, hatters, printers, furniture makers, and weavers faced declining incomes, unemployment, and loss of status. To avoid the regimentation of factory work, some artisans moved to small towns or set up small, specialized shops that catered to a limited market. For example, in New York City 800 highly skilled cabinetmakers produced fashionable or custom-made products. In status and income they outranked a much larger group of 3,200 semitrained workers—derogatively called "botches"—who turned out cheap, mass-produced furniture.

In many industries less skilled factory workers banded together to form craft unions to seek higher pay and better working conditions. In 1830 in Lynn, Massachusetts, journeymen shoemakers founded a Mutual Benefit Society that quickly grew into a national union and formed local federations with other craft unions. In 1834 federations from Boston to Philadelphia joined to form the National Trades' Union, the first national union of different trades.

Union leaders mounted a critique of the new industrial order. Afraid that workers were becoming "slaves to a monied aristocracy" (their term for commercial middlemen and capitalist employers), they condemned the new organization of production in which "capital and labor stand opposed." To restore a just society, they devised a *labor theory of value,* arguing that the price of a product should reflect the labor required to make it and should be paid primarily to the producer, to "enable him to live as comfortably as others." Appealing to the spirit of the American Revolution, which had destroyed the aristocracy of birth, they called for a new revolution to destroy the aristocracy of capital. Armed with this artisan-republican ideology and pressed by rapidly increasing prices, in 1836 union men organized nearly fifty strikes for higher wages, many of which were temporarily successful.

This agitation for workers' rights inspired women operatives in cotton and woolen textile mills. As competition among cloth producers cut profit margins and threatened bankruptcy, employers reduced the pay of their workers and imposed more stringent work rules. In 1828 women mill workers in Dover, New Hampshire, struck against new rules, winning some relief; six years later more than 800 Dover women walked out to protest wage cuts. That same year 2,000 women in Lowell, Massachusetts, backed up a strike by withdrawing their savings from an employer-owned bank. The *Boston Transcript* reported that "one of the leaders mounted a pump, and made a flaming . . . speech on the rights of women and the iniquities of the 'monied aristocracy.'"

However powerful the rhetoric, most strikes by factory operatives failed. Employers often fired the leaders, and the rest of the workers either returned to work or moved to another factory. Even the more successful strikes by building-trade workers and shoemakers did not alter the inferior position of wage laborers in the new industrial order. They lacked access to financial capital, business know-how, and a broad education, three key ingredients of success in the new society. In these circumstances, a group of Philadelphia workers declared, "liberty is but an unmeaning word, and equality an equal shadow."

THE EXPANSION OF MARKETS

As American factories turned out more manufactures, merchants and legislators sought faster and cheaper ways to get those products to consumers. Beginning in the 1820s, they promoted the construction of a massive system of canals and roads to link eastern manufacturers and markets to the trans-Appalachian West, where hundreds of thousands of farm families had settled.

The West: Farming New Land

In the generation after independence vast numbers of men and women left the seaboard states, taking with them their savings, personal property, and skills. Some families wanted to acquire enough land to settle their children on nearby farms, re-creating traditional rural communities. Others were more entrepreneurial and hoped for greater profits from the fertile soil of the West. By the 1820s the Carolinas, Vermont, and New Hampshire were losing as many people through migration as they gained through natural increase. Abandoned farms and homes dotted the countryside, their owners gone in search of better lands. "It is useless to seek to excite patriotic emotions" and loyalty to one's state of birth, complained an easterner, "when self-interest speaks so loudly." By 1840 about 5 million people—more than a third of the nation's population—lived west of the Appalachians (see Map 10.1).

These pioneers migrated in three great streams. In the South, plantation owners encouraged by the voracious demand of British factories for raw cotton moved their slaves into the Old Southwest. Deserting depleted fields in

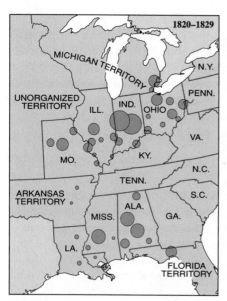
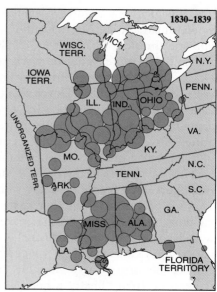

MAP 10.1

Western Land Sales, 1820–1839

In the 1830s hundreds of thousands of migrants settled in the farmlands of the Ohio Valley and the cotton belt of the Old Southwest. Each circle centers on a government land office, and the area of each circle represents the relative amount of land sold at that office.

Georgia and the Carolinas, they established the Cotton Kingdom in the new states of Louisiana (admitted to the Union in 1812), Mississippi (1817), Alabama (1819), Missouri (1821), and Arkansas (1836). "*The Alabama Fever* rages here with great violence," a North Carolina planter complained, "and has *carried off* vast numbers of our Citizens."

Small-scale farmers from the Upper South, especially Virginia and Kentucky, created a second stream as they crossed the Ohio River into the Old Northwest. Some of these migrants were fleeing planter-dominated slave states. In a free community, thought Peter Cartwright, a Methodist lay preacher from southwestern Kentucky, "I would be entirely clear of the evil of slavery . . . [and] could raise my children to work where work was not thought a degradation." These southerners introduced corn and hog farming to Ohio (admitted in 1803), Indiana (1816), and Illinois (1818).

The third stream of migrants came from the overcrowded farms of New England. Thousands had poured into upstate New York during the 1790s, and now thousands more abandoned the rocky soils of Vermont and New Hampshire for the rich lands of the Old Northwest. They wanted to maintain their traditional life as yeomen farmers and keep their children on the land, sparing them from industrial work. These settlers established wheat farms throughout the Great Lakes Basin: northern Ohio, northern Illinois, Michigan (admitted in 1837), Iowa (1846), and Wisconsin (1848).

To meet the demand for cheap land, in 1820 Congress reduced the price of federal land from $2.00 an acre to $1.25—just enough to cover the cost of surveying and sale. For $100 a farmer could buy 80 acres, the minimum required under federal law. With huge quantities of public land available at that price, the market price for all undeveloped land remained low. Many American families saved enough in a few years to make the minimum purchase and used money from the sale of an old farm to finance the move. By 1840 the population center of American society had shifted significantly to the west.

The Transportation Revolution

Extending the market economy into the interior required a revolution in transportation. Previously, most overland trade had been local, consisting of an exchange of goods between towns and nearby rural areas. For example, Philadelphia merchants and artisans traded their textiles and ironware for farm products grown nearby: flour and corn, dairy products, fruits and vegetables, and wood for heating and cooking. More distant trade was virtually impossible because of the lack of a system of well-maintained roads.

To enhance the "common-wealth" of their citizens, the federal and state governments tried to create a larger market. Beginning in the 1790s, they chartered private companies to build toll-charging turnpikes in well-populated areas and subsidized road construction in the West (see Map 10.2). The most significant feat was the National Road, which started in Cumberland, Maryland, passed Wheeling (then in Virginia) in 1818, crossed the Ohio River in 1833, and reached Vandalia, Illinois, in 1850. At first these interregional highways mostly carried migrants and their heavily loaded wagons to the West and herds of livestock to the East, but gradually they became conduits for manufactured goods and farm products. Merchants in the Northeast exchanged textiles, clothing, boots and shoes, muskets, and farm equipment for wheat, corn, whiskey, and hogs from farms in the Great Lakes Basin and the Ohio Valley.

By facilitating regional specialization, improved transportation greatly increased the overall productivity of the American economy. For example, it allowed western farmers to reap the advantages of cheap land and inexpensive factory-made tools. Farmers throughout the North and the West bought the new cast-iron plow invented in 1819 by Jethro Wood, a farmer in upstate New York. Wood's plow cut cultivating time in half, allowing farmers to till much larger fields, and could easily be repaired with replaceable cast-iron parts. Northeastern factories supplied other low-cost, high-quality products to western farmers: shovels and spades fabricated from rolled iron at the Delaware Iron Works, axes forged in a Connecticut factory, steel horseshoes manufactured in Troy, New York. Indeed, the production of farm implements consumed fully half the nation's output of pig iron. For their part, western farmers contributed to the rapid progress of the American Industrial Revolution by providing low-cost cotton, wool, leather, and other raw materials to

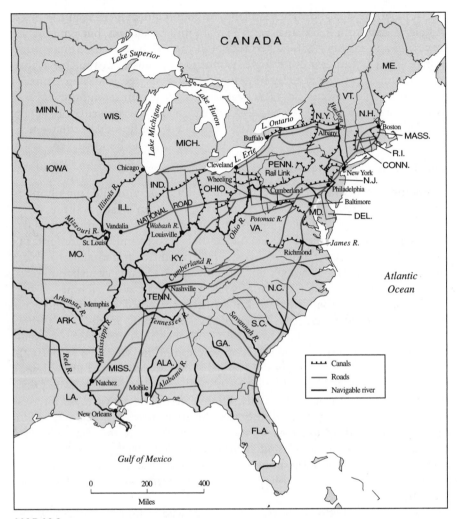

MAP 10.2
The Transportation Revolution: Roads and Canals, 1820–1850
By 1850 the United States had an efficient transportation system based on roads, natural waterways, and canals. Short canals and navigable rivers carried cotton, tobacco, and other products from the upcountry of the seaboard states into the Atlantic commercial system. Major canals—the Erie, Chesapeake and Ohio, and Pennsylvania Mainline—linked major seaport cities to the vast trans-Appalachian region, and a set of regional canals connected most of the Great Lakes region to the Ohio and Mississippi rivers and New Orleans.

eastern manufacturers. In addition, they supplied the abundant and inexpensive grain, meat, vegetables, and fruit that helped maintain the health and vigor of factory workers and urban populations in the Northeast.

To get these goods to market, Americans replaced slow and expensive overland trade with a water-borne transportation system of unprecedented size, complexity, and cost. As early as 1790 entrepreneurs had begun to build canals to connect inland areas with coastal cities and towns, but progress was slow. When the New York legislature began the Erie Canal in 1817, no canal in the United States was longer than 28 miles—a reflection of the huge capital investment canals required and the lack of American engineering expertise. But the New York project had three things in its favor: the vigorous support of New York City merchants, who wanted access to western markets; the backing of New York's governor, DeWitt Clinton, who persuaded the legislature to finance the waterway from tax revenues, tolls, and bond sales to foreign investors; and the relative gentleness of the terrain west of Albany. Even so, the task was enormous. Millions of cubic yards of dirt had to be dug out by hand and hauled away, thousands of tons of rock quarried to build huge locks to raise and lower boats, and vast reservoirs constructed to ensure a steady supply of water. The first great engineering project in American history, the Erie Canal altered the ecology as well as the economy of an entire region.

The Erie Canal was an instant success. The first section, a stretch of 75 miles opened in 1819, immediately generated enough revenue to repay its cost. When the canal was completed in 1825, the 40-foot-wide ribbon of water stretched 364 miles from Albany to Buffalo. The canal carried lightweight

Construction of the Erie Canal
Tens of thousands of workers, primarily poor immigrants from Ireland, built the American canal system. The vast scale of the project and the impressive economic benefits concealed a huge cost in lives. In the marshes near Syracuse a thousand workers fell ill with fever, and many died.

packet boats from New York City to Buffalo in only six days, and 100-ton freight barges pulled by two horses moved along at a steady 24 miles a day, greatly accelerating the flow of goods and cutting transportation costs. (On upstate New York roads, it took four horses to pull a small 1-ton wagon 12 miles in a day.)

The Erie Canal brought prosperity to central and western New York, carrying wheat and meat from farming communities in the interior to eastern cities and foreign markets. In 1818 the mills in Rochester, New York, had processed only 26,000 barrels of flour from the wheat of nearby farmers; ten years later the number soared to 200,000 barrels, and in 1840 to 500,000 barrels. After a trip on the canal, the novelist Nathaniel Hawthorne suggested that its water "must be the most fertilizing of all fluids, for it causes towns with their masses of brick and stone, their churches and theaters, their business and hubbub, their luxury and refinement, their gay dames and polished citizens, to spring up."

The spectacular benefits of the Erie Canal prompted a national canal boom. Civic and business leaders in Philadelphia and Baltimore proposed their own waterways to compete for the trade of the West. Copying New York's fiscal innovations, they persuaded their state governments to allocate tax money to canal projects, making it easier to raise the needed capital. Some state governments invested directly in canal companies or forced state-chartered banks to do so; others offered to guarantee their loans, and this encouraged British and Dutch investors to provide almost three-quarters of the $200 million invested in canals by 1840. Canals quickly became the most important part of the inland American transportation system, connecting the Great Lakes region with the great port cities of New York (via the Erie and Pennsylvania canals) and New Orleans (via the Ohio and Mississippi rivers).

The steamboat, another product of the industrial age, ensured the success of this vast water transportation system. The engineer-inventor Robert Fulton built the first American steamboat, the *Clermont*, which he navigated up the Hudson in 1807. However, the first steamboats were expensive to run because their engines consumed large amounts of wood or coal, and they could not navigate shallow western rivers. During the 1820s engineers broadened the hulls of these boats, and this increased their cargo capacity, speeded loading and unloading, and gave them a shallower draft. This improved design cut the cost of upstream river transport in half, dramatically increasing the flow of goods into the interior. Steam-powered shipping also speeded the transit of people and news. In 1830 a traveler or a letter from New York could go by water to Boston in a day and a half, to Charleston in five days, and to New Orleans or Detroit in two weeks. Thirty years earlier the same journeys, by road or sail, had taken twice as long.

The rapid emergence of this national system of transportation was encouraged by the Supreme Court headed by John Marshall, which struck down state controls over interstate commerce. In the crucial case of *Gibbons v. Ogden* (1824) the Court declared that the federal government had paramount authority over interstate commerce. This decision meant that no local monopolies—or tariffs—would impede the flow of goods and services across the nation.

The Growth of Cities and Towns

Industrialization and the expansion of interregional trade greatly expanded the urban population of the United States. In 1820 there were only 58 towns in the nation with 2,500 to 50,000 people; by 1840 there were 126. During those two decades the number of urban residents grew fourfold, from 443,000 to 1,844,000.

The most rapid growth occurred in the new industrial towns that sprang up along the fall line. In 1822, for example, the Boston Manufacturing Company decided to build a new complex of mills in East Chelmsford, Massachusetts, on the Merrimack River. Within a few years the sleepy river village was transformed into a bustling town, now named Lowell in honor of the company's founder. Hartford, Connecticut, Trenton, New Jersey, and Wilmington, Delaware, also became urban centers as mill owners exploited their water power and recruited workers from the surrounding countryside.

Western commercial cities such as New Orleans, Pittsburgh, Cincinnati, and Louisville grew almost as rapidly. The initial expansion of these cities resulted from their location at points where goods had to be transferred from one mode of transport, such as canal boats or farmers' wagons, to another, such as steamboats or sailing vessels. As the western population grew during the 1830s, St. Louis, Rochester, Buffalo, Cleveland, Detroit, and Chicago emerged as dynamic centers of commerce. Merchants and bankers settled there, developing the marketing, provisioning, and financial services that were essential to farmers and small-town merchants in the hinterland.

The old Atlantic seaports—Boston, New York, Philadelphia, and Baltimore—remained the largest American cities. Traditionally places of commerce, the port cities now became centers of finance and manufacturing. In 1817 New York merchants founded the New York Stock Exchange, which soon became the nation's chief market for securities. The New York metropolis grew at a phenomenal rate, diversifying into small-scale manufacturing and becoming the center of the ready-made clothing industry, which relied on the labor of thousands of low-paid seamstresses. "The wholesale clothing establishments are . . . absorbing the business of the country," a "Country Tailor" complained to the *New York Tribune*, "casting many an honest and hardworking man out of employment [and allowing] . . . the large cities to swallow up the small towns."

New York's growth stemmed primarily from its control of foreign trade. It had the best harbor in the United States, and oceangoing vessels could sail or steam 150 miles up the Hudson River to Albany. The city's merchants exploited these natural advantages. In 1818 four Quaker merchants founded the Black Ball Line as the first transatlantic packet service. Black Ball ships operated on a regular schedule, carrying cargo, people, and mail between New York and European ports such as Liverpool, London, and Le Havre. New York merchants also gained an unassailable lead in commerce with the newly independent Latin American nations of Brazil, Peru, and Venezuela. Finally, they moved into the cotton trade. Their agents in southern ports offered finance, insurance, and shipping to cotton exporters and won for New York a dominant share of the cotton that passed through northern harbors. In their most aggressive stroke New York merchants persuaded the state government to build the Erie Canal, which solidified New York's position as the nation's premier port. By 1840 New York's merchants controlled almost two-thirds of foreign imports and almost half of all foreign trade.

A CHANGING SOCIAL STRUCTURE

The industrial and market revolutions transformed the material lives of many Americans, allowing them to live in larger houses, cook on iron stoves, and wear better-made clothes. But the new economic order also widened social distinctions between a wealthy industrial and commercial elite, a substantial urban middle class, and a mass of propertyless wage earners. By creating a class-divided society, industrialization posed a momentous challenge to American republican ideals.

The Business Elite

Before industrialization, white American society had been divided into various *ranks*, with a group of notables at the top ruling over the "lower orders." But in rural society the different ranks shared a common culture: gentlemen farmers talked easily with yeomen about crop yields and livestock breeds, while their wives conversed with humble farm women about the arts of quilting and preserving food. In the South humble tenants and aristocratic slaveowners shared the same amusements: gambling, cockfighting, and horse racing. Rich and poor attended the same Quaker meetinghouse or sat together in the same Presbyterian or Congregational church. "Almost everyone eats, drinks, and dresses in the same way," a European visitor to Hartford, Connecticut, reported in 1798, "and one can see the most obvious inequality only in the dwellings."

The Industrial Revolution shattered this traditional order and created a society of *classes*, each with its own culture. The new economic system pulled many Americans into cities and made a few of them—merchants, manufacturers, bankers, and landlords—very rich. In 1800 the top 10 percent of the nation's families owned about 40 percent of the wealth; by 1860 the wealthiest 10 percent owned nearly 70 percent. Inequality was greatest in the cities, where the richest 1 percent of the population held more than 40 percent of all tangible property—such as land and buildings—and an even higher share of intangible property—such as stocks and bonds.

Government policies encouraged this accumulation of wealth by placing heavier taxes on the middling and poorer classes than on the rich. The U.S. Treasury raised most of its revenue from tariffs—taxes on imported goods such as textiles that were purchased mostly by ordinary citizens. State and local governments also favored the wealthier classes. They usually taxed real estate and tangible personal property (such as furniture, tools, and machinery) but almost never taxed the stocks and bonds owned by the rich or the inheritances they passed on to their children.

Over time the wealthiest families consciously set themselves apart. Instead of laboring side by side with journeymen and apprentices in small shops, merchants and manufacturers became managers, issuing orders to hundreds of outworkers or factory operatives. Similarly, they chose to live in separate residential areas. Previously many wage earners had lived in the same home or neighborhood as their employers. By the 1830s most employers had stopped providing their workers with housing and moved their families to distinct upper-class enclaves, often at the edge of the city. The desire for greater privacy by privileged families divided many American cities into class-segregated communities for the first time.

The Middle Class

Standing between wealthy owners and entrepreneurs at one end of the social spectrum and nonpropertied wage earners at the other was a growing middle class. In the words of a Boston printer and publisher, the "middling class" was made up of "the farmers, the mechanics, the manufacturers, the traders, who carry on professionally the ordinary operations of buying, selling, and exchanging merchandize." As industry expanded, skilled mechanics were in demand, building contractors and shopkeepers profited as cities grew, commercial-minded farmers benefited from rising prices, and lawyers and surveyors were swamped with clients seeking assistance on legal matters and property boundaries. Middle-class business owners, employees, and professionals were most numerous in the Northeast, where they numbered about 30 percent of the population in 1840, but they could be found in every American town and village, even in the agrarian South.

Increasingly these middling people shared a common style of living that gave them a distinct cultural identity. Husbands had sufficient earnings so that their wives did not have to seek paid work. Typically, middle-class men saved about 15 percent of their income, depositing it in banks and using it to buy a well-built house in a "respectable part of town." They purchased handsome clothes for themselves and their families and drove about town in smart carriages. Their wives and daughters were literate and accomplished; they bought books and pianos as well as commodious furniture for their front parlors. The more affluent among them hired a servant or two to work in the kitchen and the stables. Material comfort became a distinguishing mark of the middle class.

Moral and mental discipline was an equally prominent feature of the middle class. Successful parents wanted to pass their status on to their children. Therefore, they usually provided their offspring with a full high school education (in an era when most white children received only four or five years of elementary education). Ambitious parents were equally concerned with their children's character and stressed discipline, morality, and hard work.

Many middle-class men and women shared the economic and moral values of the business elite, especially a belief in hard work and personal achievement. Puritans and other American Protestants had long believed that work in an earthly "calling" was a duty people owed to God. In the 1820s and 1830s the business elite and the middle class gave this idea a secular twist: they celebrated work as socially beneficial, the key to a higher standard of living for the nation and social mobility for the individual.

Benjamin Franklin gave classical expression to the secular work ethic in his *Autobiography*, which was published in full in 1818 and immediately found a huge audience. Heeding Franklin's suggestion that an industrious man would become a rich one, tens of thousands of young American men worked hard, saved their money, adopted temperate habits, and practiced honesty in their business dealings. Countless magazines, children's books, self-help manuals, and novels taught the same lessons. The ideal of the "self-made man" became a central theme of American popular culture. Just as a rural-producer ethic had united the social ranks in pre-1800 America, this new goal of personal achievement and social mobility tied together the upper and middle classes of the new industrializing society.

The New Urban Poor

As thoughtful members of the business elite and the middle class surveyed the emerging social landscape, they worried that many Americans might never improve their status. A yeomanlike society made up of independent families no longer seemed possible or even advisable. "Entire independence ought not to be wished for," Ithamar A. Beard, the paymaster of the Hamilton Manufacturing Company, told a mechanics' association in 1827. "In large manufacturing towns, many more must fill subordinate stations and must be under the immediate direction and control of a master or superintendent, than in the farming towns."

Beard had a point. By 1840 as many as half the nation's free workers were laboring for others rather than for themselves. The bottom 10 percent of this wage-earning labor force consisted of casual workers—those hired on a short-term basis, often by the day, for the most arduous jobs. Poor women washed clothes, while their husbands and sons carried lumber and bricks for construction projects, loaded ships and wagons, and dug out dirt and stones to build canals. Most casual laborers owned no property except the clothes they wore. During business depressions they bore the brunt of unemployment, and even in the best of times their jobs were unpredictable, seasonal, and dangerous.

Other laborers had greater security of employment, but few were prospering. In Massachusetts in 1825 the daily wage of an unskilled worker was about two-thirds that of a mechanic; two decades later it was less than half as much. The 18,000 needlewomen in New York City in the 1850s were no better off, averaging less than $80 a year. These meager wages did not buy much. While middle-class families spent about one-third of their income on food, poorer urban workers had to spend nearly $2 of every $3 they earned just for sustenance. After paying rent for housing, they were broke—unable to take advantage of the rapidly falling prices of manufactured goods. Only the most fortunate working families could afford to educate their children, pay the fees required for apprenticeship in a trade, or accumulate small dowries so that their daughters could marry men with better prospects. Most had to send their children out to work to help support the family. An economic recession or the death of one of the spouses often threw them into dire poverty. As a charity worker noted, "What can a bereaved widow do, with 5 or 6 little children, destitute of every means of support but what her own hands can furnish (which in a general way does not amount to more than 25 cents a day)."

By the 1830s most urban factory workers, journeymen, and unskilled casual laborers resided in well-defined neighborhoods. Certain blocks were dominated by large, crowded boardinghouses where single men and women lived in unhealthy conditions. Elsewhere landlords converted houses, including the basements and attics, into tiny apartments and used the profits from rentals to build more workers' housing. Often the developers squeezed a number of buildings, interspersed with outhouses and connected by foul-smelling courtyards and dark alleys, onto a single lot.

Living in such distressing conditions, many wage earners turned to the dubious solace of alcohol. Liquor had long been an integral part of American life; beer, wine, and rum had lubricated ceremonies, celebrations, work breaks, barn raisings, and games. But during the 1820s urban wage earners led Americans to new heights of alcohol consumption. Aiding them were western farmers, who distilled corn and rye into gin and whiskey as a low-cost way to get their grain to market. By 1830 the per capita consumption of liquor had risen to more than 5 gallons a year, three times present-day levels.

Drinking patterns changed as well. Workers in many craft unions "swore off" liquor, convinced that it would undermine their skilled work as well as their health and finances. But other workers began to drink on the job—and not just during the traditional 11 A.M. and 4 P.M. "refreshers." Journeymen used apprentices to smuggle whiskey into shops, and then, as one baker recalled, "One man was stationed at the window to watch, while the rest drank." Grogshops and tippling houses appeared on almost every block in working-class districts. The saloons became focal points for urban disorder and crime, including assault, burglary, and vandalism. Fueled by unrestrained drinking, a fistfight among young men one night could turn into a brawl the second night and a full-scale riot the third. The urban police forces, consisting of low-paid watchmen and untrained constables, were unable to contain the lawlessness.

The Benevolent Empire

The disorder and lawlessness among urban wage earners sparked concern among well-to-do Americans. Inspired by the religious ideal of "benevolence," they created a number of reform organizations that historians refer to collectively as the "Benevolent Empire."

During the 1820s Congregational and Presbyterian ministers united with like-minded merchants and their wives to launch a program of social regulation. Their purpose, announced Presbyterian minister Lyman Beecher of Boston, was to restore "the moral government of God." The reformers introduced new forms of moral discipline both into their own lives and into the lives of ordinary working people. They would regulate behavior—by persuasion if possible, by law if necessary.

Although the Benevolent Empire targeted age-old evils such as drunkenness, prostitution, and crime, its methods were new. Instead of relying on church sermons and moral suasion by community leaders, the reformers set out to institutionalize charity and combat evil systematically. They established large-scale organizations—the Prison Discipline Society and the American Society for the Promotion of Temperance, among many others. Each had a managing staff, a network of volunteers and chapters, and a newspaper.

Together, these groups set out to "improve" society. First, they encouraged people to lead well-disciplined and moral lives, campaigning for temperance in drinking habits and the end of prostitution. Beyond that, they persuaded local governments to ban carnivals of drink and dancing, such as the Negro Election Day festivities in New England, which had been enjoyed by whites as well as blacks. Second, they created new institutions for people who were threats to society or were unable to handle their own affairs. Reformers provided homes of refuge for the abandoned children of the poor, removed the insane from isolation in attics and cellars and placed them in newly built asylums, and campaigned for an end of corporal punishment for criminals and their rehabilitation through moral training in penitentiaries.

Women played an increasingly active role in the Benevolent Empire. Since the 1790s upper-class women had sponsored a number of charitable organizations, such as the Society for the Relief of Poor Widows with Small Children, founded in New York in 1797 by Isabella Graham, a devout Presbyterian widow. By the 1820s Graham's society was assisting hundreds of widows and their children in New York City. Her daughter, Joanna Bethune, set up other charitable institutions, including the Orphan Asylum Society and the Society for the Promotion of Industry, which gave subsidized employment as spinners and seamstresses to hundreds of poor women.

Some reformers came to believe that one of the greatest threats to the "moral government of God" was the decline of the traditional Sabbath. As the pace of commercial activity accelerated during the 1820s, merchants and shippers began to conduct business on Sunday, since they did not want their goods and equipment to lie idle one day in every seven. To restore traditional values, in 1828 Lyman Beecher and other ministers formed the General Union for Promoting the Observance of the Christian Sabbath. Union chapters sprang up—usually with women's auxiliaries—from Maine to the Ohio Valley. Seeking a symbolic issue to rally Christians to their cause, the Union focused on a law Congress had enacted in 1810 allowing mail to be transported—though not delivered—on Sunday. To secure its repeal the Union adopted the tactics of a political party, organizing rallies and circulating petitions. Its members also boycotted shipping companies that did business on the Sabbath and campaigned for municipal laws forbidding games and festivals on the Lord's Day.

Not everyone agreed with the program of the Benevolent Empire. Men who labored twelve or fourteen hours six days a week refused to spend their one day of leisure in meditation and prayer. Shipping company managers demanded that the Erie Canal provide lockkeepers on Sundays and joined anti-temperance advocates in arguing that boycotts and laws enforcing morality were "contrary to the free spirit of our institutions." And when the Benevolent Empire proposed to teach Christianity to slaves, white southerners were outraged. Such popular resistance or indifference limited the success of the Benevolent Empire. A different kind of message was required if religious reformers were to do more than preach to the already converted and discipline the already disciplined.

Revivalism and Reform

It was the Presbyterian minister Charles Grandison Finney who brought just such a message to Americans. Finney was not part of the traditional religious elite. Born to poor farmers in Connecticut in 1792, he was determined to join the new middle class as a lawyer. But in 1823 he underwent an intense

Charles Finney, Evangelist
Finney (1792–1875) had a long and influential career after his New York revivals, training a generation of ministers at Oberlin College. This daguerreotype, taken in 1850 while Finney and his second wife, Elizabeth Atkinson, were on a evangelistic tour of Britain, suggests his moral intensity.

conversion experience and decided to become a minister. Beginning in towns along the Erie Canal, Finney conducted emotional revival meetings that ignored deep instruction in church doctrine; what counted for Finney was the will to be saved. God would welcome *any* sinner who submitted to the Holy Spirit, and only an infusion of God's grace, poured into the heart of the believer, made a moral life possible. Finney's ministry drew upon—and greatly accelerated—the Second Great Awakening, the wave of Protestant revivalism that had begun after the Revolution (see Chapter 9).

Finney's message that "God has made man a moral free agent" was particularly attractive to members of the new middle class, who had already chosen to improve their material lives. But he became famous for converting those at the ends of the social spectrum: the haughty rich, who had placed themselves above God, and the abject poor, who seemed lost to drink, sloth, and misbehavior. His goal was to humble the pride of the rich and relieve the shame of the poor by celebrating their common fellowship in Christ. Conversion changed not only people's eternal fate but also their moral standing, identifying them spiritually with earnest, pious middle-class respectability.

Finney's most spectacular triumph came in 1830, when he moved his revivals from small towns to Rochester, New York, a major Erie Canal city. For six months he preached every day and added a new tactic—group prayer meetings in family homes—in which women played an active role. Finney's wife, Lydia, and other pious middle-class wives carried the message to the homes of the unconverted, often while their disapproving husbands were at work. Soon, one convert reported, "You could not go upon the street and hear any conversation, except upon religion."

Finney soon won over the influential merchants and manufacturers of Rochester, who pledged to reform their lives and those of their workers. They would attend church, join the "Cold Water" movement by giving up alcohol, and work steady hours. To encourage their employees to follow suit, wealthy businessmen founded a new Free Presbyterian Church—"free" because members did not have to pay for pew space. This church was specifically designed to serve poor workers: canal laborers, transients, and the settled poor. Other evangelical Protestants soon founded two similar churches. To reinforce the work of those churches, Rochester's business elite established a savings bank to encourage thrift, Sunday schools for poor children, and the Female Charitable Society to provide relief for the families of the unemployed.

The success of the Protestant crusade in Rochester was duplicated by revivalists in cities and towns from New England to the Ohio Valley. Dozens of younger ministers—Baptist and Methodist as well as Congregationalist and Presbyterian—adopted Finney's evangelical message and techniques. In New York City, where Finney established himself after leaving Rochester, the wealthy silk merchants Arthur and Lewis Tappan founded a magazine, *The Christian Evangelist*, to promote his ideas. The success of the revival "has been so general and thorough," concluded a General Assembly of Presbyterians, "that the whole customs of society have changed."

The Vice of Intemperance

John Gough's impoverished English parents shipped him off at age twelve to America, where he found work as a bookbinder in New York City—and turned to drink. In 1842 he converted to temperance and used his eloquence as a lecturer to command high fees and persuade thousands to join the movement.

Will it be believed that I again sought refuge in rum? Yet so it was. Scarcely had I recovered from the fright, than I sent out, procured a pint of rum, and drank it all in less than an hour. And now came upon me many terrible sensations. Cramps attacked me in my limbs, which racked me with agony; and my temples throbbed as if they would burst. . . . Then came on the drunkard's remorseless torturer—delirium tremens, in all its terrors, attacked me. . . . I was at one time surrounded by millions of monstrous spiders, that crawled slowly over every limb, whilst the beaded drops of perspiration would start to my brow, and my limbs would shiver until the bed rattled. . . . I was falling— falling swiftly as an arrow—far down into some terrible abyss. . . .

By the mercy of God, I survived this awful seizure; and when I rose, a weak, broken-down man, and surveyed my ghastly features in the glass, I thought of my mother, and asked myself how I had obeyed the instructions received from her lips. . . . Oh! how keen were my rebukes; and, in the excitement of the moment, I resolved to lead a better life, and abstain from the accursed cup.

For about a month, terrified by what I had suffered, I adhered to my resolution; then my wife came home, and, in my joy at her return, I flung my good resolutions to the wind, and . . . I took a glass of brandy. That glass aroused the slumbering demon. . . . The night of my wife's return, I went to bed intoxicated.

SOURCE: David Brion Davis, ed., *Antebellum American Culture: An Interpretive Anthology* (Lexington, Mass.: Heath, 1979), pp. 402–403.

The temperance movement proved to be the most effective arena for evangelical reform on a national scale. In 1832 evangelicals gained control of the American Temperance Society; within a few years it had grown to 2,000 chapters with more than 200,000 members. The society adapted the methods that had worked so well in the revivals—group confession and prayer, a focus on the family and the spiritual role of women, and sudden, emotional conversion—and took them into virtually every town and city in the North. On one day in New York City in 1841, 4,000 people took the temperance "pledge." The average annual consumption of spirits fell from about 5 gallons per person in 1830 to about 2 gallons in 1845.

Evangelical reformers also reinforced the traditional moral foundations of the American work ethic. Laziness, drinking, and other wasteful habits could not be cured by Benjamin Franklin's patient methods of self-discipline, they argued. Instead, people had to experience the profound change of heart achieved only in religious conversion. With God's grace would come the determination to turn from drink, sloth, and sin. Then even the poorest family could look forward to a prosperous new life. Through such means, evangelical Protestantism reinforced the sense of common identity between the business elite and the middle class and implanted a commitment to individual enterprise and moral discipline among many wage earners. Religion and the ideology of social mobility served as a powerful cement, holding society together in the face of the massive changes brought by the spread of industrial enterprise and the market economy.

CHAPTER 10 TIMELINE

1765	James Hargreaves invents spinning jenny
1782	Oliver Evans develops automated flour mill
1790	Samuel Slater opens a cotton mill in Providence, Rhode Island
1807	Robert Fulton launches the *Clermont*
1810s	Beginning of Cotton Kingdom in Old Southwest
1814	Boston Manufacturing Company opens Waltham cotton mill
1817	Erie Canal begun
1819	Cast-iron plow invented
1820	Minimum price of federal land reduced to $1.25 per acre
1820s	Women become textile operatives Building workers seek ten-hour day Rise of Benevolent Empire
1824	Congress passes major protective tariff *Gibbons v. Ogden* promotes interstate trade
1828	Protective tariff raised
1830s	Expansion of western commercial cities Class-segregated urban neighborhoods Growth of temperance movement Charles Grandison Finney begins Rochester revival
1833	National Road crosses Ohio River

CHAPTER 11

A DEMOCRATIC REVOLUTION, 1820–1844

- Democratizing Politics, 1820–1829
- The Jacksonian Presidency, 1829–1837
- Class, Culture, and the Second Party System

The Economic Revolution transformed the lives of millions of Americans. In the old traditional society most white people had lived and worked together in close-knit communities, and their institutions—the family, the village or urban neighborhood, the artisan's shop, the religious congregation, and the town meeting—had functioned well. But geographic expansion and economic change pushed many people out of those intimate settings and divided society along class lines. The new world was less predictable, less personal, and far more complicated.

To address the problems of the new society, Americans turned not only to evangelical religion but also to democratic politics. In the early years of the nation the slogan had been *republicanism*, rule by property-owning "men of TALENTS and VIRTUE." By the 1820s the watchword had become *democracy*, power exercised by party politicians elected by the people as a whole. "That the majority should govern was a fundamental maxim in all free governments," declared Martin Van Buren, the most talented of the new breed of middle-class professional politicians. By uniting Americans from different classes and regions, the new democratic political parties held together an increasingly fragmented social order.

DEMOCRATIZING POLITICS, 1820–1829

Expansion of the franchise was the most dramatic expression of the democratic revolution. Beginning in the late 1810s, one state after another revised its constitution to remove property qualifications, giving ordinary farmers and wage earners the franchise and laying the foundation for the rise of mass politics. Whatever its flaws, the emerging American political system was the most democratic in the world; nowhere else did ordinary men have so much political power.

The Rise of Popular Politics

In the old agricultural society, wealthy notables—northern landlords, slave-owning planters, and seaport merchants—dominated the political system. As former Supreme Court Justice John Jay put it in 1810, "Those who own the country are the most fit persons to participate in the government of it." The notables managed local elections by building up an "interest": lending money to small farmers, buying supplies from storekeepers and artisans, and treating their workers or tenants to rum at election time. An outlay of £5 for refreshments, an experienced poll watcher told an office seeker, "may produce about 100 votes." As Martin Van Buren, whose father was a tavern keeper, knew from personal experience, this gentry-dominated system excluded men of modest means who lacked land, wealth, and "the aid of powerful family connections."

The first assaults on the old deferential order came in the West. As small-holding farmers and ambitious laborers settled the trans-Appalachian region, they broke free of control by the gentry; "no white man or woman will bear being called a servant," reported a traveler in Ohio. The constitutions of the new states of Indiana (1816), Illinois (1818), and Alabama (1819) prescribed a broad male franchise. Armed with the vote, ordinary citizens usually elected middling men to local and state offices. A well-to-do migrant in Illinois was surprised to find that his plowman "was a colonel of militia, and a member of the legislature." Once in public office, men from modest backgrounds responded to the demands of their constituents, making it easier for farmers to claim "squatters' rights" to unoccupied land, restricting imprisonment for debt, and keeping taxes low.

To deter migration to the West and unrest at home, the elites in most eastern states grudgingly accepted a broader franchise. Responding to reformers who condemned property qualifications as a "tyranny" that endowed "one class of men with privileges which are denied to another," Maryland extended the vote to all adult men in 1810. By the mid-1820s only a few states—North Carolina, Virginia, Rhode Island—required the ownership of freehold property for voting. Others, such as Ohio and Louisiana, limited suffrage to men who paid taxes or served in the militia, but a majority of the states had instituted universal white manhood suffrage.

Popular pressure brought major revisions in the state constitutions of Connecticut, Massachusetts, and New York. Between 1818 and 1821 popularly elected conventions wrote new charters that reapportioned legislatures on the basis of population and instituted more democratic forms of local government, such as the election rather than the appointment of judges and justices of the peace.

The politics of democracy was more complex and contentious than the politics of deference. Newly powerful entrepreneurs and speculators demanded government assistance and protection for their business enterprises and used their wealth to elect friendly candidates and lobby for legislation. Bankers sought charters and opposed limits on interest rates; land speculators petitioned for roads and canals to enhance the value of their holdings and demanded the eviction of squatters. Other Americans entered the political arena for religious and cultural reasons. In 1828 evangelical Presbyterians in Utica, New York, campaigned for town ordinances to restrict secular activities on Sunday; in response, a local Universalist attacked this effort at coercive reform, calling for "Religious Liberty."

The rise of the political party allowed the voices of such ordinary voters to be heard. Political "factions" and "parties" had been condemned as antirepublican by the Founders and had no place in state constitutions or the federal constitution. But as the power of notables declined, the political party emerged as the central element in the American system of government. The new parties were disciplined organizations run by professional politicians from middle-class backgrounds, especially lawyers and journalists. To some observers, they resembled the mechanical innovations of the Industrial Revolution, political "machines" that, like a well-designed textile loom, wove the diverse threads of social groups and economic interests into an elaborate tapestry—a coherent legislative program.

Martin Van Buren of New York was the chief architect—and advocate— of the emerging system of party government. Between 1817 and 1821 Van Buren created the first statewide political machine, the Albany Regency; a few years later the "Little Magician" organized the first nationwide political party, the Jacksonian Democrats. In each case Van Buren repudiated republican principles that disparaged political parties as dangerous to the commonwealth. Indeed, the opposite was true. "All men of sense know that political parties are inseparable from free government," Van Buren argued, because they checked the government's "disposition to abuse power . . . [and] the passions, the ambition, and the usurpations of individuals."

One key to Van Buren's success as a politician was his systematic use of the *Albany Argus* and other party newspapers to promote a *platform* and drum up the vote. *Patronage* was even more important, for the awarding of state jobs gave Van Buren a greater "interest" than any landed aristocrat—some 6,000 appointments to the legal bureaucracy of New York (judges, justices of the peace, sheriffs, deed commissioners, and coroners) carrying salaries and fees worth $1 million. Finally, Van Buren insisted on party *discipline*, requiring state legislators to follow the majority decisions of a party meeting, or *caucus*. On one crucial occasion, Van Buren pleaded with seventeen Republicans to "magnanimously sacrifice individual preferences for the general good" and rewarded their loyalty with patronage and a formal banquet where, an observer wrote, they were treated with "something approaching divine honors."

The Election of 1824

The advance of political democracy disrupted the old system of national politics managed by leading notables. The aristocratic Federalist party virtually disappeared, and the Republican party broke up into competing factions. As the election of 1824 approached, no fewer than five candidates, all calling themselves Republicans, campaigned for the presidency. Three were veterans of President James Monroe's cabinet: Secretary of State John Quincy Adams, the son of John Adams; Secretary of War John C. Calhoun; and Secretary of the Treasury William H. Crawford. The fourth candidate was Speaker of the House Henry Clay from Kentucky, and the fifth was General Andrew Jackson, now a senator from Tennessee. Although Crawford had been selected as the "official" nominee by a poorly attended caucus of the Republicans in Congress, the other candidates refused to accept that result.

Instead, they introduced democracy to national politics by seeking support among ordinary voters. Thanks to democratic reforms, eighteen of the twenty-four states used popular elections (rather than a vote of the state legislature) to choose members of the electoral college. Thus, in three-quarters of the states the struggle for the presidency became literally a "popularity" contest won by the candidate who commanded the most support among the voters and thus among the electors.

The battle was closely fought. Thanks to his diplomatic success as secretary of state, John Quincy Adams enjoyed national recognition. Henry Clay framed his candidacy around the *American System*, a national program of tariffs and internal improvements to promote economic growth. Rejecting Clay's plan for an activist central government, William Crawford of Georgia promised strong support for the rights of the states, a position that enhanced his popularity in the South. Recognizing Crawford's strength in his home region, John C. Calhoun of South Carolina switched to the vice-presidential race and endorsed Andrew Jackson for the presidency.

As the hero of the Battle of New Orleans, Jackson embodied the nationalistic pride that had swelled in the wake of the War of 1812. Born in the Carolina backcountry, Jackson had settled in Nashville, Tennessee, where he had formed ties to influential families through his marriage and his career as an attorney, cotton planter, and slaveowner. His reputation as a man of civic virtue and "plain solid *republican utility*" attracted many voters, and his rise from common origins fit the tenor of the new democratic age. Nominated for the presidency by the Tennessee legislature, Jackson soon commanded nationwide support.

Still, Jackson's strong showing in electoral college surprised most political leaders. He received 99 electoral votes; Adams, 84 votes; Crawford (struck down by a stroke during the campaign), 41; and Clay, 37. Since no candidate had received an absolute majority, the Constitution specified that the House of Representatives would choose the president from among the three leading contenders. This requirement hurt Jackson because many congressmen were horrified at the thought of a rough-hewn westerner and blunt general in the White House; following Henry Clay, they feared Jackson as a "military chieftain." Personally out of the race, Clay resolved to use his powers as Speaker to thwart Jackson's election. By the time the House met in February 1825, Clay had put together a coalition of representatives from New England and the Ohio Valley that voted Adams into the presidency. Adams showed his gratitude by appointing Clay secretary of state, the traditional steppingstone to the highest office.

Clay's appointment was a fatal mistake for both men. John C. Calhoun accused Adams of thwarting the will of the people by using "the power and patronage of the Executive" to select his successor. It was, he wrote, "the most dangerous stab, which the liberty of this country has yet received." Jacksonians in Congress, their numbers increased by the election results, condemned Clay for arranging this "corrupt bargain" and vowed he would never become president.

The Presidency of John Quincy Adams, 1825–1829

As president, Adams called for bold leadership. "The moral purpose of the Creator," he told Congress, was to use the president and every other public official to "improve the conditions of himself and his fellow men." To that end, Adams embraced the American System of national economic development proposed by Henry Clay: (1) a protective tariff to stimulate manufacturing, (2) federally subsidized internal improvements (roads and canals) to aid commerce, and (3) a national bank to provide a uniform currency and control credit.

Adams's policies favored his most loyal supporters, the business elite of the Northeast, and assisted entrepreneurs and commercial farmers in the West. They won little support in the South, which opposed tariffs, and among small-holding farmers, who feared powerful banks. From his deathbed, Thomas Jefferson condemned Adams for promoting "a single and splendid government of [a monied] aristocracy ... riding and ruling over the plundered ploughman and beggared yeomanry." Other politicians objected on constitutional grounds. In 1817 President Madison had vetoed Calhoun and Clay's Bonus Bill (which would have used federal funds to build projects in various states), arguing that it exceeded the national government's constitutional powers, and Adams's program was even more ambitious. There was little public support for an active national government; most politically aware Americans believed that the state governments should assume the primary responsibility for economic development. A hostile Congress defeated most of Adams's proposals, approving only a

John Quincy Adams (1767–1848)
This famous photograph of Adams, taken about 1843, suggests his tenacity and moral commitment, attributes that hindered his effectiveness as president. Ignoring congressional opposition, Adams tried to implement Clay's American System of national mercantilism, a policy that led to the creation of the Democratic party and his defeat in the election of 1828.

few navigation improvements and a short extension of the National Road from Wheeling, Virginia, into Ohio.

The most far-reaching battle of the Adams administration came over tariffs. In 1824, a new tariff had imposed a protective tax of 35 percent primarily on imported manufactures—iron goods and woolen and cotton cloth—and Adams and Clay wanted even higher duties to protect eastern manufacturers. When Van Buren and his Jacksonian allies took control of Congress in 1827, they supported higher tariffs, but for different reasons. By raising tariffs on raw materials and agricultural imports, they hoped to help smallholding farmers. But Van Buren's main objective was to bolster Jackson's prospects in the Middle Atlantic states, which he needed to carry in the 1828 election. "I fear this tariff thing," warned Thomas Cooper of South Carolina; "by some strange mechanical contrivance . . . it will be changed into a machine for manufacturing Presidents, instead of broadcloths, and bed blankets."

Disregarding southern opposition, northern Jacksonians enacted the Tariff of 1828, which raised duties on raw materials *and* manufactures. To win support for Jackson in New York, Pennsylvania, Ohio, and Kentucky, Van Buren and his allies proposed tariffs on flax, hemp, iron, lead, molasses, and raw wool. But to push those rates through Congress, they had to meet the demand of northeastern representatives for a duty of about 50 percent on imported cloth.

The new tariff enraged the South, which gained nothing from the new legislation. As the world's cheapest producer of raw cotton, the South did not need a protective tariff, and by raising the price of British manufactures, the tariff cost southern planters about $100 million a year. They had to buy either high-cost American manufactures, thus enriching northeastern businesses and workers, or highly taxed British goods, thus paying the cost of the national government. This was "little less than legalized pillage" declared an Alabama legislator; with equal fervor other southern politicians denounced the new legislation as the "Tariff of Abominations."

However, most southerners did not blame their tariff woes on Jackson and refused to vote for Adams, who supported not only high tariffs but also the land rights of native Americans in the South. In 1825 U.S. commissioners and a faction of the Creek people had concluded a treaty that ceded the remaining Creek lands in Georgia. When the Creek National Council repudiated the treaty as fraudulent, Governor George M. Troup vowed to take the lands by force. Defying Adams's efforts to help the Indians, Troup attacked the president as a "public enemy . . . the unblushing ally of the savages," and Congress extinguished Creek land titles in Georgia, forcing most of the Creeks to leave the state.

Elsewhere, Adams's primary weakness was political. He was a patrician, the last notable to serve in the White House, and he acted the part: aloof, haughty, paternalistic. Ignoring his waning popularity, Adams failed to use patronage to reward his supporters; indeed, he allowed hostile politicians to keep their appointed positions as long as they were competent. In 1828 Adams "stood" for reelection, telling supporters, "If my country wants my services, she must ask for them."

Martin Van Buren and the professional politicians handling Jackson's campaign had no reservations about "running" for office. Now a senator from New York, Van Buren created the first national campaign organization. His goal was to re-create the old Jeffersonian coalition, uniting farmers and artisans (the "plain Republicans of the North") with the southern slaveowners who had voted Jefferson, Madison, and Monroe into the presidency. John C. Calhoun, Jackson's semiofficial running mate, brought his South Carolina allies into Van Buren's party, and Jackson's close friends in Tennessee rallied voters in the Old Southwest to the cause. With strong direction from above, state leaders orchestrated a newspaper campaign (in New York, fifty Van Burenite papers declared for Jackson on the same day) and mobilized local groups to run mass meetings, torchlight parades, and barbecues to excite public interest. They celebrated Jackson's frontier origins and rise to wealth and fame without the advantages of birth, education, or political intrigue. Old Hickory—the nickname came from the toughest American hardwood tree—was a "natural" aristocrat, a self-made man.

Initially the Jacksonians called themselves Democratic-Republicans, but as the campaign wore on, they became Democrats. The name conveyed their message. The republic, Jacksonians charged, had been corrupted by "special privilege," which they would root out and replace by the rule of the majority—the democracy. "Equality among the people in the rights conferred by government," Jackson would declare, was the "great radical principle of freedom."

Jackson's message appealed to a variety of social groups. His hostility to special privileges for business corporations and to Clay's American System won support among urban workers and artisans in the Northeast who felt threatened by industrialization. In the Southeast and the West, Old Hickory's well-known animus toward native Americans reassured white farmers who favored Indian removal. On the controversial Tariff of Abominations, Jackson benefited from the financial boost it gave to Pennsylvania ironworkers and western farmers; at the same time, he declared his support for a "judicious" tariff, appealing for southern votes by suggesting that the existing rates were too high.

The Democrats' strategy of seeking votes from a wide variety of social and economic groups worked like a charm. In 1824, only about a fourth of the eligible electorate had voted; in 1828, more than half went to the polls, and they voted overwhelmingly for Jackson. The senator from Tennessee received 178 of 261 electoral votes and became the first president from the West, indeed from any state other than Virginia and Massachusetts. The massive outpouring of popular support for Jackson frightened the northern business elite. When the new president came to Washington, warned ex-Federalist Daniel Webster, he would "bring a breeze with him. Which way it will blow, I cannot tell. . . . My *fear* is stronger than my *hope.*" Watching an unruly crowd clamber over the elegant furniture in the White House to shake the hand of the newly inaugurated president, Supreme Court Justice Joseph Story lamented that "the reign of King 'Mob' seemed triumphant."

THE JACKSONIAN PRESIDENCY, 1829–1837

Political democracy—a broad franchise, a disciplined political party, and policies tailored to specific social groups—had carried Andrew Jackson to the presidency. Jackson used that popular mandate to enhance his authority; invoking the sovereignty of the people, he attacked Clay's American System and proposed a different—and more limited—vision of the role of the national government.

Jackson's Political Agenda

To decide policy, Jackson relied primarily on an informal group of advisers, his so-called Kitchen Cabinet. Its most influential members were Francis Preston Blair of Kentucky, who edited the *Washington Globe*; Amos Kendall, also from Kentucky, a Treasury Department official who helped Jackson write many of his state papers; Roger B. Taney of Maryland, who became attorney general and then chief justice of the United States; and, most influential, Secretary of State Martin Van Buren.

AMERICAN VOICES

Republican Majesty . . . and Mobs

When Andrew Jackson came to Washington in 1829, he threatened the author-ity of traditional leaders. Writing to her son, the Washington socialite Margaret Bayard Smith revealed her anxiety about popular democracy.

The inauguration . . . was . . . an imposing and majestic spectacle. . . . Thousands and thousands of people, without distinction of rank, collected in an immense mass around the Capitol, silent, orderly, and tranquil. . . . The door from the Rotunda opens, preceded by the marshall surrounded by the judges of the Supreme Court, the old man [President Jackson] with his grey hair, that crown of glory, advances, bows to the people, who greet him with a shout that rends the air. . . . After reading his speech, the oath was administered to him by the chief justice. The marshall presented the Bible. The president took it from his hand, pressed his lips to it, laid it reverently down, then bowed again to the people. Yes, to the people in all their majesty—and had the spectacle closed here, even Europeans must have acknowledged that a free people, collected in their might, silent and tranquil, restrained solely by a moral power, without a shadow around of military force, was majesty, rising to sublimity, and far surpassing the majesty of kings and princes, surrounded with armies and glittering in gold. . . .

[But at the White House reception] . . . what a scene did we witness!! The *majesty of the people* had disappeared, and [instead] a rabble, a mob . . . scrambling, fighting, romping. . . . The president, after having literally been nearly pressed to death . . . escaped to his lodgings at Gadsby's. Cut glass and bone china to the amount of several thousand dollars had been broken in the struggle to get refreshments. . . . Ladies and gentlemen only had been expected at this [reception], not the people *en masse.* . . . [The] rabble in the president's house brought to my mind descriptions I had read of the mobs in the Tuileries and at Versailles [during the French Revolution].

SOURCE: M. B. Smith to J. B. H. Smith, March, 1829, Smith Family Correspondence, Library of Congress.

Following Van Buren's practice in New York, Jackson used patronage to create a loyal and disciplined party. He insisted on rotation in office: when a new administration came to power, bureaucrats would have to leave government service and return "to making a living as other people do." Dismissing the argument that forced rotation would eliminate expertise, Jackson suggested that most public duties were "so plain and simple that men of intelligence may readily qualify themselves for their performance." William L. Marcy, a New York Jacksonian, put it more bluntly, telling a Senate committee that government jobs were like the spoils of war and that there was "nothing wrong in the rule that to the victor belong the spoils of the enemy." Using the policy of rotation as a *spoils system*, Jackson dispensed government jobs to win support for his legislative program.

Jackson's main priority was to block Clay's American System and overthrow laws that had expanded the powers of the national government. Responding to western supporters who argued that the "voice of the people" called for "economy in the expenditures of the Government," Jackson rejected federal support for most internal improvements. In 1830 he vetoed a bill that would have extended the National Road from Maysville, Ohio, to Lexington, Kentucky, arguing that it was "an infringement of the reserved powers of states." Then Jackson turned his attention to two other parts of the American System: protective tariffs and the national bank. Those issues were so complex and politically charged that it took years of effort—and great political skill—for Jackson to emerge triumphant, but by the end of his two terms in office the American System lay in disarray.

The Tariff and Nullification

The Tariff of 1828 had helped Jackson win the presidency, but it saddled him with a major political crisis. The fiercest opposition to the tariff was in South Carolina, whose slaveowners suffered from chronic insecurity. South Carolina was the only state with an African-American majority—56 percent of the population in 1830—which made it more like Jamaica or Barbados than the rest of the South. Like their West Indian counterparts, South Carolina planters lived in fear of slave rebellions and, by the late 1820s, the forced abolition of slavery. The British Parliament was about to end slavery in the West Indies (and did so in August 1833), and South Carolina planters worried that the U.S. government might do the same. To prevent that outcome, that state's leaders tried to limit the power of the federal government, choosing the tariff as their target.

The crisis began in 1832, when Congress ignored southern demands to repeal the Tariff of Abominations and placed high duties on cloth and iron. In November, leading planters and politicians in South Carolina called a state convention, which boldly adopted an Ordinance of Nullification. The Ordinance declared the tariffs of 1828 and 1832 null and void, forbade the collection of those duties in the state after February 1, 1833, and threatened secession if the federal government tried to collect them.

South Carolina's act of nullification rested on the constitutional arguments developed in a tract published in 1828, *The South Carolina Exposition and Protest*. Written anonymously by Vice-President John C. Calhoun, the *Exposition* challenged the proposition that majority rule lay at the heart of republican government. "Constitutional government and the government of a majority are utterly incompatible," Calhoun wrote. "An unchecked majority is a despotism." To devise a mechanism to check congressional majorities, Calhoun turned to the arguments advanced by the Antifederalists of the 1780s and by Jefferson and Madison in the Kentucky and Virginia resolutions of 1798. Developing a constitutional theory that states' rights advocates would use well

John C. Calhoun (1782–1850)
Calhoun was a brilliant thinker and
a determined politician. Entering
Congress as a nationalist, he
emerged during the 1820s as a
strong opponent of an activist national government, serving as Jackson's vice-president during his first
administration. Beginning with the
nullification controversy, Calhoun
developed a states' rights ideology
that he championed until his
death.

into the twentieth century, Calhoun maintained that sovereignty resided not
in the American people as a whole but in citizens acting through their state
governments. Consequently, a state convention could determine that a congressional law was unconstitutional and declare it null and void within the
state's borders. The law would remain nullified unless three-fourths of the
other states ratified an amendment assigning Congress the power in question;
even then the dissident state could secede from the republic.

Despite his reservations about the national government, Jackson would have
none of this. In January 1830 Senator Daniel Webster had attacked the doctrine
of nullification and states' rights in a famous debate with Senator Robert Hayne
of South Carolina, ending with the resounding appeal: "liberty *and* Union, now
and forever, one and inseparable." Siding with Webster, Jackson confronted Calhoun at a banquet and publicly repudiated his vice-president's ideas by proposing a formal toast: "Our Federal Union—*it must be preserved.*"

The president's response to South Carolina's Nullification Ordinance in
1832 was equally forthright. "Disunion by armed force is *treason,*" he declared in
December. Appealing to patriotism, Jackson asserted that nullification violated
the Constitution and was "*unauthorized by its spirit, inconsistent with every principle
on which it is founded, and destructive of the great object for which it was formed.*" At
Jackson's request, Congress passed a Force Bill authorizing him to use the army
and navy to compel obedience. Simultaneously, Jackson met South Carolina's

objections by winning new legislation that provided for a gradual reduction in duties; by 1842 import taxes would revert to the modest levels set in 1816, and another part of Clay's American System would be eliminated.

The compromise worked. Having saved face on the tariff issue, the South Carolina convention rescinded its nullification of the tariff (while defiantly nullifying the now-meaningless Force Act). Jackson was satisfied. He had established the principle that no state could nullify a law of the United States, providing the basis for Abraham Lincoln's defense of the Union during the secession crisis of 1861.

The Bank War

In the middle of the tariff crisis Jackson faced a major challenge from the supporters of the Second Bank of the United States. The Second Bank stood at the center of the American financial system. A privately managed entity, the Bank had operated since 1816 under a twenty-year charter from the federal government, which owned 20 percent of its stock. Its most important role was to stabilize the nation's money supply. Most American money consisted of notes—in effect, paper money—issued by state-chartered commercial banks. The banks promised to redeem the notes with "hard" money—gold or silver coins, also known as *specie*—on demand. By collecting those notes and regularly demanding specie, the Second Bank kept the state banks from issuing too many notes (which would produce monetary inflation and higher prices).

During the prosperous 1820s, the Second Bank maintained monetary stability and restrained expansion-minded banks in the West, forcing some to close. This policy was welcomed by bankers and entrepreneurs in Boston, New York, and Philadelphia, whose capital was underwriting economic development, but aroused popular hostility. Most Americans did not understand the regulatory role of the Second Bank and feared its ability to force bank closures, which left ordinary citizens holding worthless paper notes. More powerful Americans also opposed the Second Bank and resented the financial power wielded by its president, Nicholas Biddle. Wealthy New York bankers, including supporters of Martin Van Buren, wanted federal monies deposited in their institutions, and some expansion-minded bankers in western cities, including friends of Jackson in Nashville, wanted to escape supervision by a central bank.

But it was a political miscalculation by the supporters of the Second Bank that brought about its downfall. In 1832 Jackson's opponents in Congress, led by Henry Clay and Daniel Webster, persuaded Biddle to request an early recharter of the Bank. They had the votes to get a rechartering bill through Congress and hoped to lure Jackson into an unpopular veto just before the 1832 elections.

Jackson turned the tables on Clay and Webster. He not only vetoed the bank bill but, by justifying his action in a masterful public statement that blended constitutional arguments with class rhetoric and patriotic fervor, became a public hero. Taking Jefferson's position, the president declared that Congress had no constitutional authority to charter a national bank, which was "subversive of the rights of the States." Using the vocabulary of the American Revolution, he attacked the Second Bank as "dangerous to the liberties of the people," a nest of special privilege and monopoly power that promoted "the advancement of the few at the expense of the many . . . the farmers, mechanics, and laborers." Finally, the president evoked popular support by stressing the heavy investment in the Bank's stock by British aristocrats; such a powerful institution should be "*purely American,*" he declared.

Jackson's attack on the Bank carried him to victory in the presidential election of 1832. Rejecting Calhoun as a nullifier and a snob (because of his refusal to welcome Mrs. Peggy Eaton, a cabinet wife, into Washington society), Jackson took a new vice-presidential running mate, Martin Van Buren. Together, Old Hickory and the Little Magician overwhelmed Henry Clay, who headed the National Republican ticket, by 219 to 49 electoral votes. Jackson's most fervent supporters were farmers and workers whose lives had been disrupted by price fluctuations or falling wages. But many promoters of economic growth were also Jacksonians. State bankers welcomed the demise of the Second Bank, and thousands of middle-class Americans—lawyers, clerks, shopkeepers, artisans—cheered his attacks on privileged corporations. They wanted equal opportunity to rise in the world.

Immediately after his reelection Jackson launched a new attack on the Second Bank, which still had four years left on its charter. He appointed Roger B. Taney, a strong opponent of corporate privilege, secretary of the Treasury and had him withdraw the government's gold and silver from the Bank and deposit it in state institutions, which critics called his "pet banks." To justify this abrupt (and probably illegal) act, Jackson claimed that the recent election had given him a mandate to destroy the Second Bank. It was the first time a president had claimed that victory at the polls allowed him to act independently of Congress.

The "Bank War" continued to escalate. In March 1834, Jackson's opponents in the Senate passed a resolution written by Henry Clay censuring the president and warning of despotism: "We are in the midst of a revolution, hitherto bloodless, but rapidly descending towards a total change of the pure republican character of the Government, and the concentration of all power in the hands of one man." Nicholas Biddle sharply reduced loans by the Second Bank, creating a brief recession. But Jackson and Taney refused to recharter the Second Bank, and in 1836 it became a state bank in Pennsylvania, still a wealthy institution but one without public responsibilities.

Jackson had destroyed both national banking—the creation of Alexander Hamilton—and the American System of protective tariffs and internal improvements favored by John Quincy Adams and Henry Clay. The result was a profound change in the policies and powers of the national government. "All is gone," observed a Washington newspaper correspondent. "All is gone, which the General Government was instituted to create and preserve."

Not quite all, for in certain respects Jackson enhanced the powers of the national government and the president. He stood firmly for the Union during the nullification crisis, threatening the use of military force, and he greatly expanded the authority of the nation's chief executive, using the rhetoric of popular sovereignty to declare that "the President is the direct representative of the American people." Jackson's legacy as chief executive, like those of other great presidents, was complex and rich.

Indian Removal

The status of the native American peoples was as difficult an issue as the tariff and the Bank, and it also raised issues of federal versus state power. In the late 1820s, white voices throughout the West called for the removal of Indians and their resettlement west of the Mississippi River. Removal was also favored by many eastern whites, including those who were sympathetic to the native American peoples; in their view it was a humane way to protect them from direct competition with a superior race.

Jackson endorsed Indian removal in his first inaugural address in 1829 and soon began to implement it. The Old Southwest was the home of the so-called Five Civilized Tribes: the Cherokee and Creeks in Georgia, Tennessee, and Alabama; the Chickasaw and Choctaw in Mississippi and Alabama; and the Seminole in Florida. During the War of 1812, Jackson's expeditions against the Creeks had forced them to relinquish millions of acres. But Indian peoples still controlled vast tracts of land, and some of them, especially mixed-blood Christian Cherokee, had adopted European institutions and values. By the 1820s the mixed-blood Cherokee had created a centralized political system, a thriving agricultural economy, and a wealthy slaveowning class (see Chapter 8). Neither the mixed-blood Cherokee cotton planters nor the full-blood traditionalists wanted to leave their lands.

Cherokee preferences carried no weight with Jackson, a committed Indian fighter (and alleged Indian hater). In 1827 the Cherokee adopted a constitution and proclaimed themselves a separate nation within the United States. In response, the Georgia legislature declared that the Cherokee were merely a collection of individuals who were tenants on state-owned land. Upon becoming president, Jackson threw his support to Georgia, withdrawing the federal troops that had protected Indian enclaves there and in Alabama and Mississippi; the states, he argued, were sovereign within their borders.

Jackson then pushed through the Indian Removal Act of 1830, which offered native Americans land west of the Mississippi in exchange for their ancestral holdings. To encourage native Americans to accept these terms, Jackson instructed his agents to promise that in the West "their white brothers . . . will have no claim to the land" so that they "can live upon it, they and all their children, as long as grass grows and water runs." Unwilling to fight against well-armed federal troops and land-hungry American settlers, some seventy Indian peoples negotiated treaties; taken together, those agreements exchanged 100 million acres of land in the East for $68 million and 32 million acres in the West.

As Jackson pursued Indian removal, the Cherokee carried their case to the Supreme Court. They had claimed status as a "foreign nation" under the U.S.

Constitution, but in *Cherokee Nation v. Georgia* (1831), Chief Justice John Marshall denied the claim of national independence. Speaking for a majority of the justices, Marshall declared that Indian peoples enjoyed only partial autonomy and defined them as "domestic dependent nations." However, in *Worcester v. Georgia* (1832), Marshall sided with the Cherokee, voiding Georgia's extension of state law over them and holding that Indian nations were "distinct political communities, having territorial boundaries, within which their authority is exclusive ... [and this is] guaranteed by the United States." But Jackson had no interest in protecting the Cherokee and reputedly responded, "John Marshall has made his decision; now let him enforce it."

Jackson was determined to force removal. In 1832 he dispatched troops to dislodge Chief Black Hawk and his Sauk and Fox followers from rich farmland along the Mississippi River in western Illinois. Rejecting Black Hawk's offer to surrender, the American army pursued him into the Wisconsin Territory. There, on August 3, the pursuit ended in the brutal eight-hour-long Bad Axe Massacre,

Black Hawk (1767–1838)
"It was here that I was born—and here lie the bones of many friends and relatives," Black Hawk declared in 1830. "I ... could never consent to leave it." To protect his ancestral village in Illinois, Black Hawk mobilized Sauk and Fox warriors and forcibly resisted the Indian Removal Act. (Courtesy of the Gilcrease Institute)

which took the lives of 850 of Black Hawk's 1,000 warriors. During the next five years a combination of diplomatic pressure and military power forced virtually all the remaining Indian peoples to move west of the Mississippi.

The Cherokee and the Seminole mounted the greatest resistance. The Cherokee repudiated a treaty that had been signed by a minority faction and refused to leave their lands. By the treaty deadline in May 1838, only 2,000 of the 17,000 Cherokee had departed. During the summer Martin Van Buren, who had succeeded Jackson as president, ordered General Winfield Scott to enforce the treaty. Scott's army rounded up about 14,000 Cherokee and forcibly marched them 1,200 miles to the new Indian Territory (present-day Oklahoma), an arduous journey they remembered as the Trail of Tears (see Map 11.1). Along the way 3,000 Indians died of starvation and exposure. Only the Seminole remained in the Old Southwest. Aided by runaway slaves, many of whom had married into the tribe, the Seminole in Florida fought a guerrilla war into the 1840s against federal

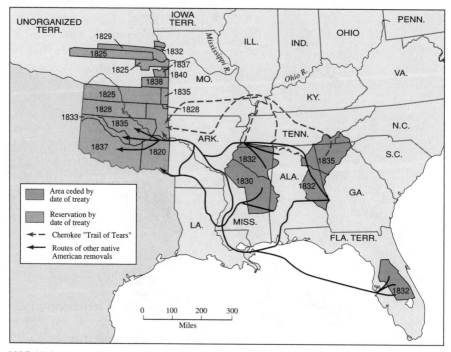

MAP 11.1
The Removal of Native Americans
Between 1820 and 1840 the U.S. government concluded treaties with native Americans in the East, assigning them lands west of the Mississippi River. During the 1830s the Five Civilized Tribes of the Old Southwest (the Cherokee, Chickasaw, Choctaw, Creeks, and Seminole) were forced to move to reservations in the Indian Territory, the present-day state of Oklahoma; other eastern tribes were settled in Kansas.

troops and the state militia. Using military power, the national government had asserted its control over the Indian peoples and forced their removal to the West.

The Jacksonian Legacy

The Jacksonian Democrats used their newfound political power to infuse American institutions with their principles. The process began in 1835, when, after the death of John Marshall, Jackson appointed his close associate Roger B. Taney as chief justice of the Supreme Court. During his long tenure (1835–1864), Taney persuaded the Court to give constitutional legitimacy to Jackson's policies of antimonopoly and states' rights.

Thus, in the landmark case of *Charles River Bridge Co. v. Warren Bridge Co.* (1837), Taney undermined the legal position of chartered monopolies by ruling that the legislative charter held by the Charles River Bridge Company did not convey an exclusive, monopolistic right, since none was explicitly stated. Instead, the legislature retained the power to charter a competing bridge company. As Taney put it: "While the rights of private property are sacredly guarded, we must not forget that the community also has rights, and the happiness and well-being of every citizen depends on their faithful preservation." This decision qualified John Marshall's interpretation of the contract clause in cases such as *Dartmouth College v. Woodward* (1819), which had emphasized the binding nature of public charters and had limited the power of states to alter or repeal them (see Chapter 9). It also encouraged competitive enterprise, opening the way for legislatures to charter railroads that would compete with existing canal and turnpike companies.

Other decisions by the Taney Court retreated from Marshall's nationalist interpretation of the commerce clause and enhanced the regulatory role of state governments. For example, in *Mayor of New York v. Miln* (1837) the Taney Court ruled that New York State could use its "police power" to inspect the health of arriving immigrants. The Taney Court also restored to the states some of the economic powers they had exercised before 1787. In *Briscoe v. Bank of Kentucky* (1837) the Court approved the issuance of currency by a bank owned and controlled by the state of Kentucky, ruling that it did not violate the provision (in Article I, Section 10, of the U.S. Constitution) that forbade states from issuing "bills of credit."

Jacksonian Democrats mounted their own constitutional revolution in the states. Between 1830 and 1860 twenty states called conventions to revise their basic charters, greatly enhancing their democratic aspects. Most states extended the vote to all white men and reapportioned their legislatures on the basis of population. They brought government "near to the people" by cutting the number of appointed posts and mandating the election of most officials, including sheriffs, justices of the peace, and judges. Most constitutions also implemented Jacksonian ideals by prohibiting states from granting special charters to corporations or extending loans or credit guarantees to private businesses. "If there is any danger to be feared in a republican government," declared a New Jersey Democrat, "it is the danger of associated wealth, with special privileges." Finally, the Jacksonian constitutions protected taxpayers by setting strict limits on state indebtedness and encouraging judges to enforce them. As a New York reformer put it, "We will not trust the legislature with the power of creating indefinite mortgages on the people's property." Just as Jackson had undermined the American System of government subsidies on the national level, his disciples in the states subverted the "commonwealth" philosophy of economic development that depended on chartered monopolies and legislative assistance. Declaring that "the world is governed too much," Jacksonians embraced a small-government, laissez-faire outlook that allowed more decisions to be made by ordinary people acting in the marketplace and the voting booth.

CLASS, CULTURE, AND THE SECOND PARTY SYSTEM

The rise of the Democrats and Jackson's tumultuous presidency sparked the creation in the mid-1830s of a second national party—the Whigs. For the next two decades Whigs and Democrats dominated American politics, forming what historians call the Second Party System. Many evangelical Protestants became Whigs, while most Catholics and nonevangelical Protestants joined the Democrats. The two parties competed fiercely for votes, debating issues of economic policy, class power, and moral reform and offering Americans a clear choice between political programs.

The Whig Persuasion

The Whig party began in Congress in 1834, when opponents of Andrew Jackson banded together to protest his policies and high-handed actions. They took the name *Whigs* to identify themselves with the pre-Revolutionary American and British parties—also called Whigs—that had opposed the arbitrary actions of King George III and previous monarchs. The Congressional Whigs charged that "King Andrew I" had violated the Constitution through "executive usurpation." Led by Senators Webster of Massachusetts, Clay of Kentucky, and Calhoun of South Carolina, the Whigs gradually elaborated their plan for the nation's future. During the election of 1836 they formulated a party platform and sought votes among evangelical Protestants and upwardly mobile middle- and working-class citizens in the North.

The Whigs did not preach a message of economic equality. They believed that it was natural for individuals to have different abilities and acquire different amounts of wealth. They reconciled an economic hierarchy with republican ideals by exalting *equality of opportunity*; pointing to the relative absence of permanent distinctions of class and status among white citizens of the United States, they argued that "this is a country of *self-made men*." Like the Federalists, the Whigs envisioned a political world dominated by men of ability and wealth. Unlike the Federalists, they wanted an elite chosen by talent, not birth.

A Whig Cartoon
"Attacking the president as "KING ANDREW THE FIRST," this political cartoon accuses Andrew Jackson of acting like an arbitrary monarch and trampling on the principles of the Constitution. Seeking to turn democratic fervor to the advantage of the Whig party, the caption asked: "Shall he reign over us, or shall the PEOPLE RULE?" (Collection of the New-York Historical Society)

Inspired by a republican Constitution and Christian principles, this select group would govern in the best interests of all the people.

The Whigs also justified elite rule by celebrating the role played by enterprising entrepreneurs and activist governments in increasing the nation's wealth. Suggesting that industrialization had increased social harmony, they welcomed the investments of "moneyed capitalists" as increasing the "chances of improvement to those who had little" and providing "bread, clothing and homes to the poor." As the Whig Congressman Edward Everett told a Fourth of July crowd in Lowell, Massachusetts, there was a "holy alliance" among laborers, owners, and governments. Many workers agreed, especially those holding jobs in the New England textile factories and Pennsylvania iron mills that benefited from state subsidies and protective tariffs. To continue economic progress, Everett and northern Whigs called for a return to the American System of Henry Clay and John Quincy Adams.

Southern Whigs had a different perspective. They condemned Jackson's "executive usurpation" and advocated rapid economic development but opposed the nationalism of the northern Whigs and their belief in high tariffs and social fluidity. Indeed, Calhoun argued that the northern Whig ideal of equal opportunity was contradicted by the reality of slavery and industrial capitalism. "A conflict between labor and capital" was inevitable, he argued, urging southern slaveowners and northern factory owners to unite in a defensive alliance against their common foe: the working class composed of enslaved blacks and propertyless whites.

Most Whig leaders rejected Calhoun's class-conscious vision. "A clear and well-defined line between capital and labor" might fit the slave South or class-ridden Europe, Daniel Webster admitted, but in the North "this distinction grows less and less definite as commerce advances." Webster emphasized the growing importance of the northern middle class, which, attracted by the promise of upward mobility, was becoming the backbone of the Whig party. In the election of 1834 the Whigs won a majority in the House of Representatives by appealing to prosperous farmers, small-town merchants, and skilled industrial workers in New England, New York, and the new communities along the Great Lakes. Those voters were attracted to the Whigs' ideology of individual mobility and commitment to moral reform. Many of them had previously been Anti-Masons, members of a powerful but short-lived political movement directed against the secret Order of Freemasonry. Picking up on Anti-Masonic themes—temperance, equality of opportunity, evangelical religious values—Whigs favored legal curbs on the sale of alcohol and local bylaws that preserved Sunday as a day of worship.

Henry Clay carried the Whig message into the Ohio and Mississippi valleys, where it appealed to farmers, bankers, and shopkeepers who favored public investment in roads, canals, and bridges. But support for the Whigs in the South was fragmentary, resting more on the appeal of specific policies than on agreement with the Whigs' social vision. For example, many nonslaveholding whites in the backcountry voted Whig to break the grip over state politics held by rich planters, most of whom were Democrats. Yet a significant minority of wealthy planters became Whigs, especially those who had invested heavily in railroads, banks, and factories and had close ties to northern markets and New York capitalists. Finally, some states' rights Democrats in Virginia and South Carolina shared former Vice-President Calhoun's anger at Andrew

Jackson's threat to use force to suppress nullification and, like him, joined the Whigs in protest.

In the election of 1836, the Whigs faced Martin Van Buren, the architect of the Democratic party and Jackson's handpicked successor. Van Buren emphasized his and Jackson's opposition to the American System and support for "equal rights." But the Little Magician also promised to preserve American liberty from the coercion implicit in the Whig program of moral reform. He declared himself an "inflexible and uncompromising opponent" of the use of government power to restrict slavery, as many antislavery activists and some Whigs were demanding, and opposed similar plans to enforce temperance or change social mores. The Whigs ran three regional candidates, hoping to garner enough electoral votes to throw the election into the House of Representatives, which they controlled. The plan failed. The Whig tally—73 electoral votes collected by William Henry Harrison of Ohio, 26 by Hugh L. White of Tennessee, and 14 by Daniel Webster—fell far short of Van Buren's 170 votes. Still, the size of the popular vote for Whig candidates—49 percent of the total—showed that the party's message of economic improvement and moral uplift had appealed not only to middle-class Americans but also to farmers and workers with little or no property.

Labor Politics and the Depression of 1837–1843

In seeking the votes of workers, Whigs had to compete with the workingmen's parties that had sprung up in fifteen states between 1827 and 1833. Rising prices and stagnant wages had lowered the standard of living of many urban artisans and wage earners, who feared what they called "the glaring inequality of society." Thus, the Working Men's party in New York City demanded the abolition of private banks, chartered monopolies, and imprisonment for debt. Philadelphia workers demanded higher taxes on the wealthy and a system of universal publicly financed education so that their children could advance into the ranks of the propertied. In 1834 the Working Men's party persuaded the Pennsylvania legislature to authorize free, tax-supported schools.

The ideology underlying the workingmen's parties was artisan republicanism, which called for a society in which (as the radical Democrat Orestes Brownson put it) "instead of one man's working for another and receiving wages thereof, all men will be independent proprietors, working on their own capitals, on their own farms, or in their own shops." This vision led workers to demand "equal rights" and attack legislation that created chartered corporations and monopolistic banks "for the benefit of the rich and the oppression of the poor." "The only safeguard against oppression," argued William Leggett, a leading member of the New York Loco-Foco (Equal Rights) party, "is a system of legislation which leaves to all the free exercise of their talents and industry."

At first the workingmen's parties did well in urban areas, but divisions over policy and voter apathy soon took a toll. By the mid-1830s most politically active

New York Seamstresses Organize

W*orking long hours to earn $1.25 a week, most New York City seamstresses lived in poverty. When clothing contractors cut piecework rates in 1831, the seamstresses organized the United Tailoresses Society, adopted a "bill" of wages, and, as this speech by the society's treasurer, Lavinia Waight, indicates, found a common identity as workers and women.*

That females are imposed upon, and oppressed in almost every stage of action to which the circumstances of their existence render them liable, is a fact, that . . . requires only the reiteration of cases. . . .

Are not females in the first place excluded from equal liberality in the circumstances of their education, incapacitated for the duties of legislation and other matters of like importance, in which, you will all allow, they are equally interested? . . . Why should not women be engaged in the duties of trade and legislation? to whom shall I put the question? to those helpless and oppressed beings who are, and have been, blindfolded by a cunning and designing policy, from a fair view of their own interests?

Shall I then question the lords and tyrants of the world, and the monopolizers of all interest? It is unnecessary. Look to the baneful effects that a degraded and major portion of mankind exhibit to your view. Shall I ask *Nature* if the physical inequalities which she has made, furnish a cause for these evils? or shall I argue from her decrees, a total reversion of the present degraded order of things?

These remarks may be thought by some . . . irrelevant to the immediate purposes of this meeting. I have thought them important links in the chain of oppressions against the truly dominated *weaker sex.* . . .

SOURCE: *New York Daily Sentinel*, February 17, 1831, reprinted in Gerda Lerner, *The Female Experience: An American Documentary* (Bloomington: Indiana University Press, 1977). pp. 278–279.

workers had joined the Democratic party, and they continued to agitate against monopolies, banks, and imprisonment for debt. They also condemned protective tariffs, which gave "bounties to particular interests," and supported legislation placing taxes on the personal property of the wealthy: stocks, bonds, machinery, and furniture. At the same time they shifted their attention to the workplace, taking advantage of the shortage of skilled labor to create new unions in small cities and General Trade Union federations in New York City and Philadelphia.

Employers responded to worker agitation by attacking the union movement. In 1836 clothing manufacturers in New York City agreed not to hire workers belonging to the Union Trade Society of Journeymen Tailors and circulated a list—a so-called blacklist—of its members. The employers also brought lawsuits to overturn *closed shop* agreements that required them to hire only union members. They argued that such contracts violated the common law and, in New York State, legislative statutes that prohibited "conspiracies" in restraint of trade.

Judges usually agreed. In 1835, the New York Supreme Court found that a shoemaker's union in Geneva had illegally caused "an industrious man" to be "driven out of employment." "It is important to the best interests of society," the court declared, "that the price of labor be left to regulate itself." When another court upheld a conspiracy verdict against a New York City tailor's union, a crowd of 27,000 people demonstrated outside city hall and tailors circulated handbills proclaiming that the "Freemen of the North are now on a level with the slaves of the South." In 1836 popular demonstrations encouraged local juries to acquit shoemakers in Hudson, New York, carpet makers in Thompsonville, Connecticut, and plasterers in Philadelphia of similar conspiracy charges. The resistance of workers and their supporters had preserved the unions from legal attack.

At this juncture, the Panic of 1837 threw the American economy into disarray. The Panic began early in 1837, when the Bank of England, needing to increase the domestic supply of specie to bolster the British economy, sharply curtailed the flow of money and credit to America. For the previous decade and a half, British manufacturers and investors had stimulated the American economy, providing southern planters with credit to expand cotton production and purchasing millions of dollars of canal bonds in northern

The Panic of 1837
With their once prosperous economy mired in a deep recession, these New Yorkers had little to celebrate on Independence Day in 1837. This cartoon assails Democratic economic policies by illustrating their results (from right to left): sheriffs auctioning off a debtor's property, mechanics clamoring for work, a mother begging, and disheartened laborers turning to the bottle.

states. As the British economy faltered and textile mills cut their purchases, American cotton prices declined sharply, setting off a financial panic. Unable to collect the debts owned by planters, southern banks closed their doors or refused new requests for credit. By late March a number of New York and Philadelphia mercantile firms had declared bankruptcy, undermining faith in paper bank notes. When more and more customers demanded gold and silver, banks suspended specie payments. Deprived of credit, businesses had to cut production, and so trade, manufacturing, and farming slid into decline. "This sudden overthrow of the commercial credit and honor of the nation" had a "stunning effect," observed Henry Fox, the British minister in Washington. "The conquest of the land by a foreign power could hardly have produced a more general sense of humiliation and grief." Soon the crisis engulfed state governments as tax revenues and canal tolls fell. Nine states defaulted on bonds issued to finance canal building; others declared a moratorium on debt payments, undermining British confidence in the American economy and cutting the flow of new investment. Bumper crops during the late 1830s drove down cotton prices even further, bringing more bankruptcies.

The American economy fell into a deep depression. By 1843 canal construction had dropped 90 percent and prices nearly 50 percent; unemployment rose, reaching almost 20 percent of the work force in seaports and industrial centers. From his pulpit, Henry Ward Beecher described a land "filled with lamentation . . . its inhabitants wandering like bereaved citizens among the ruins of an earthquake, mourning for children, for houses crushed, and property buried forever."

By creating a surplus of skilled workers, the depression devastated the labor movement. In 1837, 6,000 masons, carpenters, and other building-trade workers lost their jobs in New York City, depleting the membership of unions and destroying their bargaining power. By 1843 most local unions and all the national labor organizations had disappeared, along with their newspapers and other publications.

However, two events during the depression years improved the long-term prospects of the labor movement. One was a major legal victory. In *Commonwealth v. Hunt* (1842), Chief Justice Lemuel Shaw of Massachusetts upheld the rights of workers to form unions and enforce a closed shop. Shaw, one of the great jurists of the nineteenth century, overturned common-law precedents by making two critical rulings: (1) a union was not an inherently illegal organization, and (2) union members could legally attempt to enforce a closed shop, even by striking. Shaw's opinion was generally accepted by courts in other states, so that unions were free to organize. However, judges (who were mostly Whigs) found other methods, such as court injunctions, to restrict strikes and boycotts. Labor's second success was political. Continuing Jackson's effort to attract workers to the Democratic party, in 1840 President Van Buren signed an executive order establishing a ten-hour day for federal employees. Significantly, this achievement came after the unions had lost their power in the marketplace, underlining the fact that the struggle between labor and capital—like conflicts over tariffs, banks, and internal improvements—had moved into the political arena.

"Tippecanoe and Tyler Too!"

The depression had a major impact on American politics. Because few people understood the workings of the international economy, many Americans blamed the Democrats for the depression. In particular, they derided Jackson for destroying the Second Bank and issuing the Specie Circular of 1836, which required western settlers to use bullion to pay for land purchases and appeared to trigger the financial panic. Van Buren refused to revoke the Specie Circular or take other actions to reverse the downturn. Holding to his philosophy of limited government, he advised Congress that "the less government interferes with private pursuits the better for the general prosperity." As the depression continued, this laissez-faire outlook commanded less and less political support.

Worse, Van Buren's major piece of economic legislation, the Independent Treasury Act of 1840, actually delayed recovery. In 1833 Van Buren had opposed Jackson's decision to place the government's gold and silver in various state banks. Now he condemned the "pet bank" system as corrupt favoritism and, with great difficulty, won approval for a government-run Independent Treasury to handle public funds. However commendable as a political reform, the Independent Treasury cut economic expansion by pulling federal specie out of state banks (which had used it to back loans) and putting it in government vaults (where it did no good at all).

Determined to exploit Van Buren's weakness, the Whigs organized their first national convention and nominated William Henry Harrison of Ohio for the presidency. A military hero of the Battle of Tippecanoe and the War of 1812, Harrison was well advanced in age (he was sixty-eight) and had little political experience. But the Whig leaders in Congress, Clay and Webster, did not want a strong president; they planned to have Harrison rubber-stamp their program for protective tariffs and a national bank. Party strategists such as Thurlow Weed of New York had chosen Harrison primarily because of his military record and western background, promoting him as the Whig version of Andrew Jackson. An unpretentious, amiable man, Harrison warmed to that task, telling voters that Whig policies were "the only means, under Heaven, by which a poor industrious man may become a rich man without bowing to colossal wealth."

The election of 1840 turned more on style than on substance. Whig pamphleteering, songfests, parades, and well-orchestrated mass meetings dominated the campaign, establishing a new political style. Recognizing the importance of women in evangelical churches and reform organizations, Whigs hailed Harrison as "a good Sunday school . . . church going man," invited "the ladies" to political meetings, and called on women to infuse government and society with "pure morality." Whig speakers assailed "Martin Van Ruin" as a manipulative politician with aristocratic tastes—a devotee of fancy wines and elegant clothes, as indeed he was—and praised Harrison (actually the son of a wealthy planter who had signed the Declaration of Independence) as a self-made soldier and statesman who lived in a simple log cabin and enjoyed hard cider, a drink of the common man.

The 1840 election became the great "log-cabin" campaign, the first election in American history in which two national parties competed for the loyalties of a mass electorate. Articles in the Democrat *Washington Globe* and the Whig *National Intelligencer* carried the parties' messages in the nation's capital and the articles were then reprinted in local Jacksonian and Whig newspapers in thousands of crossroads towns. The Democrats relied on party discipline to bring out the vote, while the Whigs drew on the wealth of the business elite to orchestrate their carnival-like campaign. More than 80 percent of the eligible electorate went to the polls in 1840 (up from less than 60 percent in 1832 and 1836). Heeding the Whig slogan "Tippecanoe and Tyler Too," they voted Harrison into the White House and gave the Whigs a majority in Congress.

The Whig triumph was short-lived. One month after his inauguration, Harrison died of pneumonia and the nation got "Tyler Too." Vice-President John Tyler of Virginia, who became president, was not a typical Whig. Tyler had joined the Whig party primarily because he opposed Jackson's stance against nullification; on economic issues he was an Old Republican, sharing Jackson's hostility to the Second Bank and the American System. Acting

The Log-Cabin Campaign, 1840
During the Second Party System, politics became more democratic as ordinary people voted for candidates who shared their values and life styles. The stars in the corner of this homemade campaign flag evoke patriotism, while the central image falsely portrays William Henry Harrison as a poor frontier farmer.

more like a Democrat than a Whig, Tyler vetoed bills that would have raised tariffs and created a new national bank. Also like Jackson, Tyler favored the West and the common man, and he approved the Preemption Act of 1841, which allowed American citizens and immigrants to stake a free claim to 160 acres of federal land. If they built a house on the property and improved the land, they could purchase it later at the standard price of $1.25 an acre. The act helped cash-poor settlers and accelerated the pace of westward expansion.

The split between Tyler and the Whigs gave the Democrats time to regroup. The party vigorously recruited supporters among subsistence farmers in the North and smallholding planters in the South. It cultivated the votes of the urban working class and was particularly successful among Irish and German Catholic immigrants, whose numbers had increased rapidly during the 1830s. Thanks to these recruits, the Democrats remained the majority party: in most parts of the nation, their program of equal rights, states' rights, and cultural liberty was more attractive than the Whig platform of economic nationalism, moral reform, and individual mobility.

The continuing struggle between Whigs and Democrats, each claiming to speak for "the people," completed the democratic revolution. The United States now boasted universal suffrage for white men as well as a highly organized system of representative government that was responsive to ordinary citizens. In their scope and significance for American life, these political innovations matched the economic advances of the industrial and market revolutions.

CHAPTER 11 TIMELINE

1810s	Revision of state constitutions
	Van Buren creates disciplined party in New York
1825	John Quincy Adams elected president by House; advocates Henry Clay's American System
1827	Philadelphia Working Men's Party organized
1828	Tariff of Abominations
	Andrew Jackson elected president
	The South Carolina Exposition and Protest
1830	Jackson vetoes extension of the National Road
	Indian Removal Act
1831	*Cherokee Nation v. Georgia*
1832	Bad Axe Massacre of Sauk and Fox
	Jackson vetoes rechartering of Second Bank
	South Carolina nullifies Tariff of 1832
1833	Force Bill and Compromise Tariff
1834	Whig Party formed by Clay, Calhoun, and Webster
1835	Roger Taney named chief justice
1837	*Charles River Bridge Co. v. Warren Bridge Co.*
	Panic of 1837 begins depression of 1837–1843
1838	Trail of Tears
1840	Log-cabin campaign
1841	Tyler succeeds Harrison as president
	Preemption Act
1842	*Commonwealth v. Hunt* allows trade unions

CHAPTER 12

THE FERMENT OF REFORM, 1820–1860

- Individualism
- Communalism
- The Women's Movement
- Abolitionism

The whirlwind pace of economic and political change in the 1820s and 1830s transformed the way Americans thought about themselves as individuals and as a society. Increasing opportunities encouraged many men and women in the North to believe that they could improve not just their personal lives but society as a whole. Some dedicated themselves to the cause of reform. Such individuals, the Unitarian minister Henry W. Bellows warned, had committed themselves to the pursuit of "an object, which in its very nature is unattainable—the perpetual improvement of the outward condition."

Many obstacles stood in their way. America's social order was still rigidly divided by race and gender as well as wealth and religious belief. As much as it liberated some individuals, the new industrial and market economy meant new forms of social control for others, such as the strict work discipline imposed on factory operatives. Even the rise of democratic politics brought new forms of social discipline. Party members were "safe if they face the enemy," remarked one of Martin Van Buren's political lieutenants, "but the first man we see *step to the rear*, we *cut down*."

In fact, the first wave of American "improvers," the benevolent reformers of the 1820s, had seized on social discipline as the answer to the nation's ills, championing regular church attendance, temperance, and the strict moral codes of the evangelical churches. Then, in the 1830s and 1840s, a more powerful reform wave spilled out of these conservative channels and washed over

American society, threatening to submerge traditional institutions and values. Mostly middle-class in origin, the new reformers propounded a variety of radical ideals—extreme individualism, communitarianism, sexual equality, the immediate emancipation of slaves—and demanded action to satisfy their visions. The result was a far-reaching intellectual and culture debate that challenged the premises of the American social order.

INDIVIDUALISM

Individualism was a term coined by Alexis de Tocqueville in 1835 following his visit to the United States. He used it to describe people who were "no longer attached to each other by any tie of caste, class, association, or family." Unlike the French political philosopher, who feared the disintegration of society, the New England transcendentalist Ralph Waldo Emerson celebrated this liberation of the individual from the constraints of traditional social ties and institutions. Emerson's vision of individual freedom influenced thousands of ordinary Americans and a generation of important artists and writers.

Emerson and Transcendentalism

Emerson was the leading spokesman for transcendentalism, an intellectual movement rooted in the religious soil of New England. Its first advocates were spiritually inclined young men, often Unitarian ministers from well-to-do New England families, who questioned the constraints imposed by their Puritan heritage. For inspiration they turned to Europe, drawing on a new conception of self and society known as Romanticism. Romantic thinkers, such as the English poet Samuel Taylor Coleridge, rejected the ordered, rational world of the eighteenth-century Enlightenment. Instead they tried to capture the passionate character of the human spirit and sought deeper insights into the mysteries of existence. Drawing on ideas borrowed from the German philosopher Immanuel Kant, English romantics and Unitarian radicals believed that behind the concrete world of the senses was an *ideal* world. To reach this deeper reality, people had to "transcend," or go beyond, the ways in which they normally comprehended the world. By tapping mysterious intuitive powers, people could soar beyond the limits of ordinary experience and gain mystical knowledge of ultimate and eternal things.

Emerson, like his father a Unitarian minister, emerged as the intellectual leader of the transcendentalist movement in 1832 at the age of twenty-nine. After a crisis of conscience he resigned his Boston pulpit, rejecting organized religion in favor of individual moral insight. Emerson moved to Concord, Massachusetts, and turned to writing essays and lecturing, supported in part by a legacy from his first wife. His subject was what he called "the infinitude of the private man," the idea of the radically free individual.

The young philosopher saw people as being trapped in inherited customs and institutions. They wore the ideas of people from earlier times—the tenets of New England Calvinism, for example—as a kind of "faded masquerade" and needed to shed those values and practices. "What is a man born for but to be a Reformer, a Remaker of what man has made?" he asked. For Emerson, an individual's remaking depended on the discovery of his or her own "original relation with Nature," an insight that would lead to a mystical private union with the "currents of Universal Being." The ideal setting for such a discovery was solitude under an open sky, among nature's rocks and trees.

Emerson's genius lay in his capacity to translate vague ideas into examples that made sense to ordinary middle-class Americans. His essays and lectures conveyed the message that all nature was saturated with the presence of God— a pantheistic spiritual outlook that departed from traditional Christian doctrine and underlay his attack on organized religion. Emerson also criticized the new industrial society, predicting that a preoccupation with work, profits, and the consumption of factory-made goods would drain the nation's spiritual energy. "Things are in the saddle," Emerson wrote, "and ride mankind."

The transcendentalist message of inner change and self-realization reached hundreds of thousands of people, primarily through Emerson's writings and lectures. Public lectures had become a spectacularly successful new way of spreading information and fostering discussion among the middle classes. Beginning in 1826, the American Lyceum attempted to "promote the general diffusion of knowledge" by organizing lecture tours by all sorts of speakers— poets, preachers, scientists, reformers—and soon took firm hold, especially in the North. In 1839, 137 local Lyceum groups in Massachusetts invited lecturers to their towns during the fall and winter "season" to speak to more than 33,000 subscribers. Among the hundreds of lecturers on the Lyceum circuit, Emerson was the most popular. Between 1833 and 1860 he gave 1,500 lectures in more than 300 towns in twenty states.

Emerson's celebration of the liberated individual tapped currents that already ran deep in his middle-class audiences. The publication of Benjamin Franklin's *Autobiography* in 1818 had given Americans a down-to-earth model of an individual seeking "moral perfection" through self-discipline. Charles Grandison Finney's account of his conversion experience in 1823 also pointed in Emersonian directions. Finney, the foremost business-class evangelist, pictured his conversion as a mystical union of an individual, alone in the woods, with God. And the great revivalist's message, like that of Emerson, affirmed the importance of individual action. As Finney put it, "God has made man a moral free agent," endowing individuals with the ability to determine their spiritual as well as their worldly fate.

Emerson's Literary Influence

Emerson took as one of his tasks the remaking of American literature. In an address entitled "The American Scholar" (1837) the philosopher issued a literary declaration of independence from the "courtly muse" of old Europe. He urged American writers to celebrate democracy and individual freedom and find inspiration not in the doings and sayings of aristocratic courts but in the "familiar, the low . . . the milk in the pan; the ballad in the street; the news of the boat; the glance of the eye; the form and gait of the body."

A young New England intellectual, Henry David Thoreau (1817–1862), heeded Emerson's call by turning to the American environment for inspiration. Shortly after his graduation from college, Thoreau turned away from society and embraced self-reliance and the natural world, building a cabin at the edge of Walden Pond near Concord, Massachusetts, and living alone there for two years. In 1854 he published *Walden, Or Life in the Woods*, an account of his spiritual search for meaning that went beyond the artificiality of life in a "civilized" society:

> I went to the woods because I wished to live deliberately, confront only the essential facts of life, and see if I could not learn what it had to teach, and not, when I came to die, discover that I had not lived.

Although Thoreau's book had little impact outside transcendentalist circles during his lifetime, *Walden* has become an essential text of American literature and an inspiration to those who reject the dictates of society. Its most famous metaphor provides an enduring justification for independent thinking: "If a man does not keep pace with his companions, perhaps it is because he hears a different drummer." Beginning from this premise, Thoreau became an advocate for social nonconformity and a philosopher of civil disobedience.

As Thoreau sought independence and self-realization for men, Margaret Fuller (1810–1850) explored the possibilities of freedom for women. Born into a wealthy Boston family, Fuller learned to read the classic works of literature in six languages and educated her four siblings. After teaching in a girls' school, she became interested in Emerson's ideas and in 1839 began a transcendental "conversation," or discussion group, for elite Boston women. Soon Fuller was editing the leading transcendentalist journal, the *Dial*, and in 1844 she published *Woman in the Nineteenth Century*, which proclaimed that a "new era" was coming for men and women.

Fuller's philosophy began with the transcendental belief that women, like men, had a mystical relationship with God that gave them identity and dignity. It followed that every woman deserved psychological and social independence—the ability "to grow, as an intellect to discern, as a soul to live freely and unimpeded." Thus, she declared, "We would have every arbitrary barrier thrown down" and "every path laid open to Woman as freely as to Man." Embracing that vision, Fuller became the literary critic of the *New York Tribune* and went to Italy to report on the Revolution of 1848. Her adventurous life brought an early death; returning to the United States at the age of forty, she drowned in a shipwreck. But Fuller's example and writings inspired the rising generation of women reformers.

Another writer who responded to Emerson's call was the poet Walt Whitman (1819–1892). Whitman said that when he first encountered Emerson, he had been "simmering, simmering." Then Emerson "brought me to a boil." Whitman

Margaret Fuller (1810–1850)
This daguerreotype shows Fuller
reading a book and captures her
intense intellectuality and love of
learning. A leading female advocate
of transcendentalism, Fuller used its
doctrines to declare the moral and
intellectual equality of women.

had been a journalist, an editor of the *Brooklyn Eagle* and other newspapers, and an active publicist for the Democratic party. But it was poetry that was the "direction of his dreams." In *Leaves of Grass*, first published in 1855 and constantly revised and expanded for almost four decades afterward, he recorded his attempt to pass a number of "invisible boundaries": between solitude and community, between prose and poetry, and even between the living and the dead.

At the center of *Leaves of Grass* is the individual—the figure of the poet, "I, Walt." He begins alone: "I celebrate myself, and sing myself." But because he has what Emerson called an "original relation" with nature, Whitman claims not solitude but perfect communion with others: "For every atom belonging to me as good belongs to you." Whitman was celebrating democracy as well as himself, arguing that a poet could claim a profoundly intimate, mystical relationship with a mass audience. For Emerson, Thoreau, and Fuller the individual had a divine spark. For Whitman the individual had expanded to *become* divine.

The transcendentalists were not naive optimists. Whitman wrote about human suffering with as much passion as he wrote about everything else. Emerson's accounts of the exhilaration that could come in nature were tinged with anxiety. "I am glad," he said, "to the brink of fear." Thoreau's gloomy judgment of everyday life is well known: "The mass of men lead lives of quiet desperation." Still, such dark murmurings were muted in their work, woven into triumphant and expansive assertions that nothing was impossible for an individual who could break free from tradition, law, and other social restraints.

Emerson's influence also reached two great novelists, Nathaniel Hawthorne and Herman Melville, who had more pessimistic visions. They addressed the opposition between individual transcendence and the legitimate requirements of social order, discipline, and responsibility. Both sounded powerful warnings that unfettered egoism could destroy individuals and those around them. Hawthorne's most brilliant exploration of the theme of excessive individualism appeared in his novel *The Scarlet Letter* (1850). The two main characters, Hester Prynne and Arthur Dimmesdale, challenge their seventeenth-century New England community in the most blatant way—by committing adultery and producing a child. The result of their assertion of individual freedom from social discipline is not liberation but degradation—condemnation by the community.

Melville explored the limits of individualism in even more extreme and tragic terms and emerged as a scathing critic of transcendentalism. He made his most powerful statement in *Moby Dick* (1851), the story of Captain Ahab's obsessive hunt for a mysterious white whale that brings death not only to Ahab but to all but one of his crew. Here the quest for spiritual meaning in nature brings death, not transcendence, to the liberated individual who lacks inner discipline and self-restraint.

Moby Dick was a commercial failure. The middle-class audience that was the primary target of American publishers was unwilling to follow Melville into the dark, dangerous realms of individualism gone mad. Readers also were unenthusiastic about Thoreau's advocacy of civil disobedience and Whitman's boundless claims for a mystical union between the man of genius and the democratic mass. What American readers emphatically preferred were the more modest examples of individualism offered by Emerson.

Brook Farm

To escape the constraints of life in industrializing America, transcendentalists and other radical reformers created ideal communities, or *utopias*. They hoped that these planned societies, which organized life in new ways, would allow members to realize their spiritual and moral potential. The most important communal experiment of the transcendentalists was Brook Farm, founded in 1841. Free from the tension and demands of an urban competitive society, its members hoped to develop their minds and souls and uplift society through inspiration. The Brook Farmers supported themselves by selling milk, vegetables, and hay for cash but organized their farming so that they could remain relatively independent of the market.

The intellectual life at Brook Farm was electric. Hawthorne lived there for a time and later used the setting for *The Blithedale Romance* (1852). All the major transcendentalists, including Emerson, Thoreau, and Fuller, were residents or frequent visitors. A former member recalled that they "inspired the young with a passion for study, and the middle-aged with deference and admiration, while we all breathed the intellectual grace that pervaded the atmosphere." Music, dancing, games, plays, parties, picnics, and dramatic readings filled the leisure hours.

If Brook Farm represented intellectual fulfillment, it faltered in achieving economic self-sufficiency. At first most of its members were ministers, teachers, writers, and students who had few productive skills; to succeed it needed practical men and women. A reorganization in 1844 attracted more farmers and artisans but yielded only marginal economic gains. And these changes resulted in a more disciplined routine that, as one resident put it, suppressed "the joyous spirit of youth." After a devastating fire in 1846, the organizers disbanded and sold the farm.

After the failure of Brook Farm the transcendentalists abandoned their attempts to fashion a new system of social organization. Most accepted the brute reality of industrial society and tried to reform it, especially through the education of workers. However, the passion of the transcendentalists for individual freedom lived on in the movement to abolish slavery, which many of them joined.

COMMUNALISM

Even as Brook Farm faded, thousands of Americans joined other communal settlements during the 1840s, primarily in the Northeast and Midwest (see Map 12.1). Most were ordinary people seeking refuge and security from the seven-year economic depression that had begun with the Panic of 1837. But these rural utopias were also symbols of social protest, explicitly challenging the values of the larger society by organizing themselves along socialist lines with common ownership of property or experimenting with unconventional forms of marriage and family life. In questioning acquisitive capitalist values and traditional gender roles, the communalists pointed to major cultural strains in American society.

The Shakers

The Shakers were the first successful American communal movement and dated back to the era of the Revolution. In 1770 Ann Lee Stanley (Mother Ann), a young cook in Manchester, England, had a vision that she was the second incarnation of Christ; four years later she led a band of eight followers to America, where they established a church near Albany, New York. Because of the ecstatic dances that became part of their worship, the sect became known as "Shaking Quakers" or, more simply, "Shakers." After Mother Ann's death the Shakers decided to withdraw from the evils of the world into strictly run communities of believers. They embraced the common ownership of property, accepted government by the church, and pledged to abstain from alcohol, tobacco, politics, and war. Shakers also eliminated marriage and made a commitment to celibacy, in accordance with Mother Ann's testimony against "the lustful gratifications of the flesh as the source and foundation of human corruption."

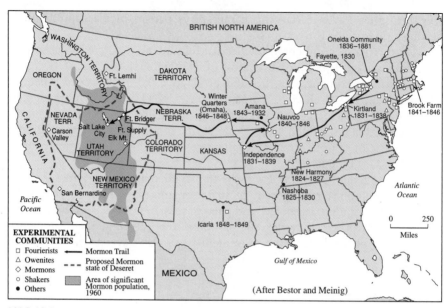

MAP 12.1
Major Communal Experiments before 1860
Some experimental communities sought out frontier locations, but the vast majority simply looked for secluded areas in well-settled regions. The avoidance of the South by these groups is striking. The most successful experimenters by far were the Mormons, who ultimately sought extreme isolation and built an agrarian society in Utah.

The Shakers believed that God was "a dual person, male and female" and that Mother Ann represented God's female element. These doctrines provided the underpinning for their attempt to banish distinctions between the sexes. In practice, Shakers maintained a traditional division of labor between men and women, but they vested the authority for governing each community— in both its religious and its economic spheres—in women and men alike, the Eldresses and Elders.

Beginning in 1787, Shakers founded twenty communities, mostly in New England, New York, and Ohio. Their agriculture and crafts, especially furniture making, acquired a reputation for quality that enabled most of these communities to become self-sustaining and even comfortable. Thanks to this economic success and their ideology of sexual equality, Shaker communities attracted more than 3,000 converts during the 1830s, with women outnumbering men more than two to one. Because Shakers had no children of their own, they had to rely on converts and the adoption of young orphans to replenish their numbers. As these sources dried up in the 1840s and 1850s, the communities stopped growing and eventually began to decline. By the end of the nineteenth century most Shaker communities had disappeared, leaving as their material legacy a distinctive and much-imitated furniture style.

The Fourierist Phalanxes

The rise of the American Fourierist movement in the 1840s was one cause of the Shakers' decline. Charles Fourier (1777–1837) was a French utopian reformer who devised an eight-stage theory of social evolution, predicting the imminent decline of individualism and capitalism. As interpreted by his idealistic American disciple Arthur Brisbane, Fourierism meant "completion of our great political movement of 1776" through new social institutions that would end the "menial and slavish system of Hired Labor or Labor for Wages." In the place of capitalist labor there would be cooperative work and living in groups called *phalanxes*. The members of a phalanx would be its shareholders; they would own all its property in common, including stores and a bank as well as a school and a library. Fourier and Brisbane saw the phalanx as a practical, more humane alternative to the emerging capitalist society and one that would liberate women as well as men. "In society as it is now constituted," Brisbane wrote, "Woman is subjected to unremitting and slavish domestic duties"; in the "new Social Order . . . based upon Associated households," most domestic labor would be eliminated or shared with men.

Brisbane skillfully promoted Fourier's ideas in his influential book *The Social Destiny of Man* (1840), a regular column in Horace Greeley's *New York Tribune*, and hundreds of lectures, many of them in towns along the Erie Canal. These ideas found a receptive audience among educated farmers and craftsmen, who yearned for economic stability and communal solidarity in the wake of the Panic of 1837. In the 1840s Brisbane and his followers started nearly 100 cooperative communities from Massachusetts to Michigan, but almost all were unable to support themselves and quickly collapsed. Despite its failure to establish viable communities, the Fourierist movement was important as an index of both the social dislocation caused by the economic depression and the difficulty of establishing a utopian community in the absence of a charismatic leader or a compelling religious vision.

Noyes and the Oneida Community

The radical minister John Humphrey Noyes was both charismatic and deeply religious. He believed that the Fourierists had failed because their communities lacked the strong religious ethic required for sustained altruism and cooperation and pointed to the success of the Shakers, praising them as the true "pioneers of modern Socialism." Noyes was also attracted by the Shakers' marriageless society and set about creating a community that defined sexuality and gender roles in dramatically new and radical ways.

Noyes was a well-to-do graduate of Dartmouth College who was inspired to join the ministry by the preaching of Charles Finney. When Noyes developed radical doctrines and was expelled from his Congregational Church, he became a leader of "perfectionism." Perfectionism was an evangelical movement that gathered thousands of followers during the 1830s, primarily among religiously minded New Englanders who had settled in New

York. Perfectionists believed that the Second Coming of Christ had already occurred and that people could therefore aspire to perfection in their earthly lives, attaining complete freedom from sin. Unlike most perfectionists (who lived conventional personal lives), Noyes believed that the major barrier to achieving this ideal state was marriage, which did not exist in heaven and should not exist on earth. "Exclusiveness, jealousy, quarreling have no place at the marriage supper of the Lamb," Noyes wrote. He wanted to reform marriage to liberate individuals from sin, as had the Shakers, but his solution was dramatically different: instead of Shaker celibacy, Noyes and his followers embraced *complex marriage*—all the members of his community were married to one another.

Complex marriage was a complex doctrine designed to attain various social goals. Noyes rejected monogamy partly because he wished to free women from being regarded as the property of their husbands. To give women even more freedom, he sought to regulate childbirth (urging men to have intercourse without orgasm) and established community nurseries. By freeing women from endless child bearing and child raising, Noyes hoped to help them become full and equal members of the community.

In the 1830s Noyes gathered his followers in his hometown of Putney, Vermont, but local opposition to the practice of complex marriage prompted him to move the community to Oneida, New York, in 1848. By the mid-1850s more than 200 people were living at Oneida, and it became financially self-sufficient when the inventor of a highly successful steel animal trap joined the community. With the profits from the production of traps, Oneida diversified into making silverware with the brand name Community Plate. After Noyes fled to Canada in 1879 to avoid prosecution for adultery, the community abandoned complex marriage and founded a joint-stock silver manufacturing company, the Oneida Community, Ltd., which survived well into the twentieth century.

As with the Shakers and Fourierists, the historical significance of Noyes and his followers lies neither in their numbers nor in their fine crafts but rather in their effort to create alternative communities that avoided some of the social and sexual divisions of the emergent capitalist industrial society of the United States.

The Mormon Experience

Despite their challenge to marriage and family life—two of the most deeply rooted institutions in American society—neither the Shakers nor the Oneidians aroused fierce hostility to their social experiments. The case was far different with the Mormons, or the Church of Jesus Christ of Latter-Day Saints, the most successful by far of all the communal experiments and yet another alternative to the emerging social order.

The Mormons emerged from the religious ferment that arose among families of Puritan descent who settled along the Erie Canal. The founder of the Mormon Church was Joseph Smith, a vigorous, powerful individual. Born in Vermont in 1805, he moved at the age of ten with his very religious but rather poor farming and shopkeeping family to Palmyra in central New York. In a series of religious experiences that began in 1820, Smith came to believe that God had singled him out to receive a special revelation of divine truth. In 1830 he published *The Book of Mormon*, claiming he had translated it from ancient hieroglyphics on gold plates shown to him by an angel named Moroni. Seeing himself as a prophet to a sinful, excessively individualistic society, Smith organized a church that asserted control over many aspects of life and reaffirmed the primacy of the husband within the family. Like many Protestant ministers, he encouraged his followers to adopt practices central to success in the age of capitalist markets and factories: hard work, saving, and risk taking. Unlike them, Smith placed equal emphasis on a communal framework that would protect the Mormon "New Jerusalem" from outside threats and create a structure for the achievement of human perfection.

Smith struggled for years to establish a sanctuary for his new religion. In the face of persecution in various neighboring settlements, Smith and his growing congregation trekked west, eventually settling in Nauvoo, Illinois, a town they founded on the Mississippi River. By the early 1840s Nauvoo had become the largest utopian community in the United States, with 30,000 inhabitants. But the rigid discipline and secrecy of the Mormons, along with their prosperity, hostility to other sects, and bloc voting in Illinois elections, fueled resentment among their neighbors. Smith turned this resentment into overt hostility when he refused to abide by any Illinois law that he did not approve of personally, asked Congress to turn Nauvoo into a federal territory, and (in 1844) declared himself a candidate for president of the United States.

Moreover, Smith had a new revelation that justified *polygamy*—having more than one wife at the same time. A few Mormon leaders began to practice polygamy, dividing the community from within, while economic and political issues encouraged assaults from without. In 1844 Smith was arrested and charged with treason for allegedly conspiring with foreign powers to create a Mormon colony in Mexico. An anti-Mormon mob stormed the jail where Smith and his brother were being held in Carthage, Illinois, and murdered them.

Now led by Brigham Young, the Mormon elders sought religious independence by leaving the United States to create a new settlement in the western wilderness. In 1846 Young began a phased migration of more than 10,000 people across the Great Plains. (Many of the migrants accepted the practice of polygamy; those who remained in the United States did not. Led by Smith's son, Joseph Smith III, they formed the Reorganized Church of Jesus Christ of Latter-Day Saints, headquartered in Independence, Missouri.) Young's party eventually reached the Great Salt Lake in what was still Mexican territory. Using communal labor and an elaborate irrigation system based on communal water rights, the Mormon pioneers transformed the desert. They quickly spread planned agricultural communities along the base of the Wasatch Range in present-day Utah.

When the United States acquired Utah from Mexico in 1848 (see Chapter 14), Congress rejected a Mormon petition to create a new state, Deseret,

An Illinois "Jeffersonian" Attacks the Mormons

The solidarity of the Mormon community enraged many Illinois residents, who feared the power of the nearly independent city-state at Nauvoo and the 2,000-strong armed "Legion" commanded by Joseph Smith. This letter, probably written by a leading anti-Mormon editor who then published it in his own newspaper, proposes their forcible expulsion from the state.

Mr. Editor,

. . . It is a low pitiable contemptable kind of electioneering, that old Tom Jefferson would have been ashamed of—when a body of men acting under the garb of religion (as the Mormons themselves say they are) shall decide our elections and act together as a body politically, we might as well bid a final farewell to our liberties and the common rights of man.

Now Sir, under all these circumstances, it is high time that every individual should come out and clearly define the position that he occupies. I too am an Anti-Mormon both in principle and in practice. . . . Mr. Editor when I speak harshly of the Mormons . . . I do not mean every individual that advocates the Mormon cause. By no means; that there are some good, law-abiding peaceable citizens belonging to the Mormon profession I verily believe . . . but I am opposed to them because of the unprincipled manner in which the leaders of that fanatical sect, set at defiance the laws of the land . . . (as was the case in Missouri) claiming to be the chosen people of God; not subject to the laws of the state in any respect whatever, and receiving revelations direct from Heaven almost daily commanding them to take the property of the older citizens of the county and confiscate it to the use of the Mormon church. . . .

It was for the commission of such deeds . . . that finally led to their expulsion from that state, and one of the brightest pages in the history of Missouri is that, on which is written "Governor Boggs's exterminating order" directing that the lawless rabble should be driven beyond the limits of the state, or exterminated at their own option. They chose the former, [which was] a most unfortunate thing for the state of Illinois.

SOURCE: David Brion Davis, *Antebellum America: An Interpretive Anthology* (Lexington, Mass.: Heath, 1979), pp. 226–227.

stretching all the way to Los Angeles and San Diego. Instead, it set up the much smaller Utah Territory in 1850, with Young as territorial governor. In 1858 President James Buchanan removed Young from the governorship and, responding to pressure from Christian churches to eliminate polygamy, sent a small army to Salt Lake City. However, the "Mormon War" proved bloodless. Fearing that the forced abolition of polygamy would serve as a precedent for the ending of slavery, Buchanan withdrew the troops. The national govern-

A Mormon Man and His Wives
Only a minority of Mormon men in Utah had more than one wife, and only a few had as many as this homesteader, who stood to profit from their labor. The cabin, although cramped for such a large family, is well built with a brick chimney and—a luxury for any pioneer home—a glass window.

ment did not succeed in pressuring the Utah Mormons to abolish polygamy until 1890, six years before Utah became a state.

Mormons in both Utah and Missouri had succeeded where other social experiments and utopian communities had failed. They endorsed the private ownership of property and encouraged individualistic economic enterprise, accepting the entrepreneurial spirit of market society. But Mormon leaders resolutely used strict religious controls to create disciplined communities and patriarchal families, reaffirming values inherited from the eighteenth century. This blend of economic innovation, social conservatism, and hierarchical leadership continued into the twentieth century, creating a prosperous church with a strong missionary impulse and millions of members.

THE WOMEN'S MOVEMENT

The prominence of gender issues—sexual behavior, marriage, family authority—among Mormons, Shakers, and Noyesites was the product of a broad shift in American culture, particularly in the North. After the American Revolution northern women played a more prominent role in public life, joining religious revivals and reform movements. Slavery was among the targets of women reformers, and their abolitionist activities created great controversy and made some of them into feminists. Feminists argued that women had social and political rights as individuals—rights that equaled those of men.

Origins of the Women's Movement

During the American Revolution, upper-class women had demanded greater legal rights for married women and more educational opportunities for their daughters but had been given only a slightly enhanced status as "republican mothers." Subsequently the Economic Revolution presented young farm women with new opportunities for factory labor but imposed new constraints on many middle-class married women, reinforcing their confinement to a "separate sphere" (see Chapter 9). Rather than working as household producers (the traditional roles of the wives of farmers and artisans), middle-class women became full-time providers of household services, such as child care. At the same time, many of these middle-class women achieved greater authority within their families by joining religious revivals and becoming guardians of morality. Such activities bolstered their self-esteem and encouraged them to enlarge their influence over decisions in all areas of family life, including the timing of pregnancies. Publications such as *Godey's Lady's Book* and Catharine Beecher's *Treatise on Domestic Economy* (1841) taught women how to make their homes more efficient and moral and justified a life of middle-class domesticity.

For most middle-class women a greater influence over family life was enough, but some women used their newfound religious authority to increase their involvement outside the home. Moral reform was among the first of their efforts in the public arena. In 1834 a group of middle-class women founded the New York Female Moral Reform Society and elected Lydia Finney, the wife of the evangelical minister Charles Finney, as its president. Its goals were to end prostitution, redeem fallen women, and protect single women from moral corruption. By 1837 the Society had 250 chapters in towns and villages throughout New York State and 15,000 members. Three years later it had grown into a national association, the American Female Moral Reform Society, with 555 chapters throughout the North. Employing only women as its agents, bookkeepers, and staff, the society attempted to provide moral "government" for factory girls, seamstresses, clerks, and servants who lived away from their families. Women reformers even visited brothels, where they sang hymns, offered prayers, searched for runaway girls, and noted the names of clients. They also founded homes of refuge for prostitutes and homeless women and won the passage of laws regulating sexual behavior—including making seduction a crime—in Massachusetts in 1846 and New York in 1848.

Women also turned their energies to the reform of social institutions, working to improve conditions in almshouses, asylums, hospitals, and jails, which grew in number in the 1830s and 1840s. The Massachusetts reformer Dorothea Dix was a leader in these efforts. Outraged that insane women were jailed alongside criminals, Dix persuaded the Massachusetts legislature to expand the state hospital to accommodate the poor and mentally ill. Dix carried her message to other states, persuading legislatures to expand their public hospitals, and nearly secured Congressional legislation that would have set aside 12.5 million acres of public land to support asylums for the insane.

Both as reformers and as teachers, northern women played a major role in education. From Maine to Wisconsin women vigorously supported the movement led by Horace Mann to expand public elementary schools. As secretary of the newly created Massachusetts Board of Education from 1837 to 1848, Mann lengthened the school year; established teaching standards in reading, writing, and arithmetic; and improved instruction by recruiting well-educated women as teachers. The intellectual leader of the new corps of women educators was Catharine Beecher, who founded academies for young women in Hartford and Cincinnati. In a series of publications Beecher argued that "energetic and benevolent women" were the best qualified to impart moral and intellectual instruction to the young. By the 1850s, most teachers were women both because school boards heeded Beecher's arguments and because women could be paid less than men.

Abolitionism and Women

The public accomplishments of moral reformers such as Dix and Beecher inspired other women to assume public roles, and many of them found a cause in the movement to end slavery. During the Revolutionary Era, Quaker women in Philadelphia had established schools for freed slaves, and subsequently many Baptist and Methodist women endorsed religious arguments

The Grimké Sisters
Sarah Moore Grimké (1792–1873) and Angelina Emily Grimké (1805–1879) joined the Philadelphia Female Anti-Slavery Society and began abolitionist lecturing in 1836. They drew crowds of thousands—and scathing criticism for having lost, as some Massachusetts clergymen put it, "that modesty and delicacy . . . which constitutes the true influence of women in society." The Grimké sisters responded with powerful statements protesting male domination of women.

AMERICAN VOICES

A Feminist Finds Her Voice

In this letter to her friend Lucy Stone, the future feminist leader Antoinette Brown (1825–1921) recounts her confrontation with the president of Oberlin College, the eminent revivalist Charles Grandison Finney, and explores the psychological strain of forging new roles for women.

[June 1848]

Lucy dearest:

The cause of woman is moving on finely here. You know the theological students are required to tell their religious experiences before Prof. Finney. Once or twice when he called for those who had not done so, [James] Tefft mentioned Lettice [Holmes] and me. He looked as though he did not know what to say, and the next time said, "Oh, we don't call upon the ladies." They had all told me we should have to speak, and I felt so badly at what he said that I just began to cry and was obliged to leave the room. . . .

I went over to see him and he certainly seemed to forget that he was talking with a woman. We conversed more than an hour sometimes upon the gravest subjects of philosophy and theology and he expressed himself freely upon the true position of woman . . . that though he did not think she was generally called upon to preach or speak in public because the circumstances did not demand it, still that there was nothing right or wrong in the thing itself and that sometimes she was specially called to speak. . . . A week or two later Professor Finney called upon me to speak in the prayer meeting, and I did so. Told them the exercises of my mind . . . and my determination to preach and speak in public when I was prepared for this. They all seemed surprised and pleased too that I was really expecting to speak.

So, L____, you are going to lecturing, are you? . . . Success to the Truth and to you dearest Lucy so far as you preach it and in the right spirit. I am glad you are going to lecture. . . . Be good, Lucy, be good, and don't be afraid of anybody but speak as though you had a right to.

SOURCE: Nancy Woloch, ed., *Early American Women* (New York: McGraw-Hill, 1997), pp. 273–274. Reproduced with permission of the McGraw-Hill Companies.

against slavery. When William Lloyd Garrison began his radical campaign for *abolition*—the immediate, uncompensated end to slavery—in 1831, a few women rallied to his cause. One of the first Garrisonian abolitionists was Maria W. Stewart, an African-American who spoke to mixed audiences of men and women in Boston in the early 1830s. As the abolitionist movement mushroomed, scores of white women delivered lectures condemning slavery and thousands more conducted home "visitations" to win converts among women and their husbands.

Influenced by abolitionist ideas and their own experience of discrimination, a few women challenged the subordinate status of their sex. The most famous were the abolitionist sisters Angelina and Sarah Grimké. The Grimkés had left their father's South Carolina slave plantation, converted to Quakerism and abolitionism in Philadelphia, and become antislavery lecturers. When some Congregationalist clergymen demanded that they cease speaking to mixed male and female audiences, Sarah Grimké turned to the Christian Bible for justification: "The Lord Jesus defines the duties of his followers in his Sermon on the Mount . . . without any reference to sex or condition," she wrote. "Men and women are CREATED EQUAL! They are both moral and accountable beings and whatever is right for man to do is right for woman." In a debate with Catharine Beecher (who wanted women to exercise power through their domestic activities) Angelina Grimké pushed the argument beyond religion, using Enlightenment principles to claim equal civic rights for women:

It is a woman's right to have a voice in all the laws and regulations by which she is governed, whether in Church or State. . . . The present arrangements of society, on these points are a *violation of human rights, a rank usurpation of power*, a violent seizure and confiscation of what is sacredly and inalienably hers.

By 1840 the Grimkés were asserting that traditional gender roles amounted to the "domestic slavery" of women. Not all abolitionist women shared that view, but many demanded equality with men within the antislavery movement.

Soon women were using the abolitionist movement as a vehicle to improve the condition of their sex. The most prominent example was the novelist Harriet Beecher Stowe, who in the novel *Uncle Tom's Cabin* (1852) charged that among the greatest moral failings of slavery was its destruction of the slave family and the degradation of slave women. Sojourner Truth, a former slave who lectured to both antislavery and women's rights conventions, hammered home the point that women slaves were denied both basic human rights and the protected separate "sphere" enjoyed by free women. "I have ploughed and planted and gathered into barns, and no man could head me—and ain't I a woman?" she asked. Drawn into public life by abolitionism, thousands of northern women had become firm advocates of greater rights not only for African-Americans but for white women.

The Program of Seneca Falls

The commitment to full civil equality for women emerged during the 1840s as activists devised a pragmatic program of reform. While championing the rights of women, they did not challenge the institution of marriage or even the conventional division of labor within the family. Instead, harking back to the efforts of Abigail Adams and other Revolutionary Era women, they tried to strengthen the legal rights of married women, especially with respect to

The Beecher Family, circa 1859
The Beechers were an impressive family. Lyman (center, seated) was one of the leading Protestant ministers of the nineteenth century, as was his son, Henry Ward (far right). Catharine (second from left) was an influential educator and well-known author who emphasized women's authority within the home. Harriet Beecher (Stowe), pictured at the far left, was an antislavery activist and the author of *Uncle Tom's Cabin*.

property. In 1848 New York adopted legislation giving married women greater control over their own property, and similar laws were enacted in fourteen other states. Affluent men provided crucial support for this legislation. They wanted to protect their spouses' assets in case their businesses went into bankruptcy and to guard against dissolute sons-in-law who might waste their daughters' inheritances.

To push forward the nascent women's movement, Elizabeth Cady Stanton and Lucretia Mott, who had become friends at the World's Anti-Slavery Convention in London in 1840, called a convention in Seneca Falls in upstate New York in 1848. The convention outlined for the first time a coherent program for women's equality. Taking the republican ideology of the Declaration of Independence as a starting point, the delegates declared that "all men and women are created equal" but that "the history of mankind is a history of repeated injuries and usurpations on the part of man toward woman, having in direct object the establishment of an absolute tyranny over her." To persuade

Americans to right this long-standing wrong, they resolved to "use every in-strumentality within our power. . . . We shall employ agents, circulate tracts, petition the State and national legislatures, and endeavor to enlist the pulpit and the press on our behalf." By staking out claims for equality for women in public life, the Seneca Falls convention repudiated the idea that the assign-ment of separate spheres for men and women was the natural order of society.

Although most men dismissed the Seneca Falls Declaration as nonsense, it drew women—and a few radical men—into the movement. During the 1850s conventions of women—at the local, regional, and national levels—hammered out a diverse reform program. They called on churches to revise concepts of female inferiority in their theology and worked for legal changes that would give married women control over their property and earnings, guarantee a mother's custody of her children in the event of divorce or the fa-ther's death, and ensure women's right to sue and testify in court. Finally, and above all else, they began a concerted campaign to win the vote for women. In 1851 a national convention of women declared that suffrage was "the corner-stone of this enterprise, since we do not seek to protect woman, but rather to place her in a position to protect herself."

The struggle for legislation required new tactics and new leaders who had talents as organizers rather than lecturers. The most prominent was Susan B. An-thony. Anthony came from a Quaker family and as a young woman had been an active temperance and antislavery reformer. Her experience in the temperance movement, Anthony explained, had taught her "the great evil of woman's utter dependence on man for the necessary means to aid reform movements." In 1851 she joined the movement for women's rights and forged an enduring friendship with Elizabeth Cady Stanton. Anthony created a network of political "captains," all women, who lobbied the state legislature relentlessly. In 1860 her efforts culminated in a New York law granting women the right to collect and spend their own wages (which fathers or husbands previously could insist on controlling), bring suit in court, and, if widowed, acquire full control of the property they had brought to the marriage. Such successes would provide the basis for more aggressive reform attempts after the Civil War.

ABOLITIONISM

For women as well as men, blacks as well as whites, the dominant American reform movement became the drive to end slavery. In part this focus stemmed from the success of other initiatives: the Second Great Awakening had drawn millions of Americans into churches, temperance was on the rise, hospitals for the sick and mentally ill had been created, and prisons had been reformed. But more important was the new attitude of many northern whites toward the South's "peculiar institution." Early nineteenth-century reformers had criti-cized human bondage as contrary to the tenets of republicanism and liberty. Now abolitionists condemned slavery as a *sin* and saw it as their moral duty to end this violation of God's law.

African Colonization

By 1820 republican-minded reformers had persuaded the northern states to abolish slavery and provide for gradual emancipation. They had also induced Congress to outlaw the importation of enslaved Africans and, in the Missouri Compromise, prohibit slavery in most of the Louisiana Purchase. But the most difficult problem remained untouched: ending slavery in the old South and the border states of Kentucky, Tennessee, and Missouri.

The founders of the American Colonization Society, which included President James Monroe, thought they had the answer. Slaveowners would gradually emancipate their slaves—some 1.5 million people in 1820—and the Society would arrange for their resettlement in Africa. The Society's leaders believed, as Henry Clay put it, that racial bondage had placed Kentucky and the other slaveholding states "in the rear of our neighbors . . . in the state of agriculture, the progress of manufactures, the advance of improvement, and the general prosperity of society."

Slavery had to go, as did the freed slaves. Emancipation without colonization, the influential Kentucky Congressman predicted, "would be followed by instantaneous collisions between the two races, which would break out into a civil war that would end in the extermination or subjugation of the one race or the other." Northerners who joined the Colonization Society had much the same outlook. They regarded the 250,000 free blacks in the northern states as "notoriously ignorant, degraded and miserable, mentally diseased, brokenspirited," as one Society report put it, and hoped they would leave.

However, the American Colonization Society was a dismal failure. Despite appeals to wealthy individuals, churches, and state governments, it raised enough money to purchase freedom for only a few hundred slaves. Most free blacks rejected colonization, agreeing with Bishop Richard Allen of the African Methodist Episcopal Church that "this land which we have watered with our *tears* and our *blood* is now our *mother country*." Three thousand African-Americans met in Philadelphia's Bethel Church to condemn colonization, declaring that their goal was to advance in American society using "those opportunities . . . which the Constitution and the laws allow to all." In the end, the Society transported only 6,000 African-Americans to Liberia, a colony it established on the west coast of Africa.

Slave Rebellion

Having rejected colonization, free blacks demanded an end to slavery. To build support for emancipation, in 1827 John Russwurm and Samuel D. Cornish began the first African-American newspaper, *Freedom's Journal*, in New York. The Boston agent for the newspaper was David Walker, a free black from North Carolina who made a living selling secondhand clothes. In 1829 Walker published a stirring pamphlet entitled *Appeal . . . to the Colored Citizens* that ridiculed the religious pretensions of slaveholders, justified slave rebellion, and warned white Americans that the slaves would revolt if justice was delayed.

"We must and shall be free. . . . And woe, woe, will be it to you if we have to obtain our freedom by fighting. . . . I do declare that one good black man can put to death six white men." Within a year Walker's *Appeal* had gone through three printings and had begun to reach free blacks in the South.

In 1830 Walker and other African-American activists called a national convention in Philadelphia. The delegates did not adopt Walker's radical position but urged free blacks to use every legal means to improve the condition of their race and asked for divine assistance in breaking "the shackles of slavery."

As Walker was calling for violent black rebellion from Boston, Nat Turner, a slave in Southampton County, Virginia, staged a bloody revolt—a coincidence that had far-reaching consequences. As a child Turner had taught himself to read and had hoped to be emancipated, but a new master forced him into field work and another master separated him from his wife. Turner became deeply spiritual, seeing visions and concluding that he might have been chosen to carry Christ's burden of suffering in a race war. Taking an eclipse of the sun as an omen, Turner plotted with a handful of relatives and close friends to meet the masters' terror with violence of their own. In August 1831, his men killed almost sixty whites, in many cases dismembering and decapitating them. Turner hoped that a vast army of slaves would rally to his cause, but he had mustered only sixty men by the time a white militia dispersed his poorly armed and exhausted followers. Vengeful whites now took slaves' lives at random. One company of cavalry killed forty in two days, putting the heads of fifteen on poles to warn "all those who should undertake a similar plot." Fifty slaves were prosecuted, and twenty were hanged. After hiding for nearly two months, Turner was captured and hanged, still identifying his mission with Christ's.

Deeply shaken by Turner's rebellion, the Virginia legislature debated a bill providing for gradual emancipation and colonization. When the bill was rejected in 1832 by a vote of 73 to 58, the possibility that southern planters would legislate an end to slavery faded forever. Instead, the southern states marched down another path, toughening their slave codes, limiting the movement of slaves, and prohibiting anyone from teaching them to read. They would meet Walker's radical *Appeal* with radical measures of their own.

Evangelical Abolitionism

Frightened by the prospect of a bloody racial revolution and inspired by the antislavery efforts of free blacks, evangelical northern whites launched a moral crusade to abolish slavery. Previously Quakers, along with some Methodists and Baptists, had freed their own slaves and campaigned for gradual emancipation in the North. Now radical Christian abolitionists demanded that southerners free their slaves immediately. The issue was absolute: slaveowners and their supporters were sinning by depriving slaves of their God-given status as free moral agents. If the slaveowners did not repent, the evangelical abolitionists believed, they faced the prospect of revolution in this world and damnation in the next.

The most uncompromising leader of the abolitionist movement during the 1830s was William Lloyd Garrison. A Massachusetts-born printer, Garrison had collaborated in Baltimore during the 1820s with a Quaker, Benjamin Lundy, who published the *Genius of Universal Emancipation*, the leading antislavery newspaper of the decade. In 1830 Garrison went to jail for seven weeks for libeling a New England merchant engaged in the domestic slave trade. Garrison went on to found his own antislavery weekly, *The Liberator*, in Boston in 1831. The next year he spearheaded the formation of the New England Anti-Slavery Society.

From the outset *The Liberator* took a radical stance. Garrison condemned the American Colonization Society, charging that its real aim was to strengthen slavery by removing troublesome African-Americans who were already free. He attacked the U.S. Constitution for its implicit acceptance of racial bondage, labeling it "a covenant with death, an agreement with Hell." And he demanded the immediate abolition of slavery without reimbursement for slaveholders. As time went on, Garrison concluded that slavery was a sign of deep corruption infesting *all* American institutions and called for comprehensive reform of society.

Theodore Dwight Weld, who joined Garrison as a leading abolitionist, came to the movement from the religious revivals of the 1830s. The son of a

William Lloyd Garrison
As this picture suggests, Garrison was an intense and righteous man. In 1854 he publicly burned the Constitution and declared:"So perish all compromises with tyranny." His attack on slavery began a passionate quest to destroy all institutions that prevented individuals—whites as well as blacks, women as well as men—from discovering their full potential.

Congregationalist minister and inspired by Charles Finney, Weld became an advocate of temperance and educational reform. Turning to abolitionism, he worked in northern Presbyterian and Congregational churches, preaching the moral responsibility of all Americans for the denial of liberty to slaves. In 1834 Weld inspired a group of students at Lane Theological Seminary in Cincinnati to form an antislavery society. Weld's crusade gathered force, buttressed by the theological arguments he advanced in *The Bible against Slavery* (1837). Collaborating closely with Weld were Angelina Grimké, whom he married in 1838, and her sister, Sarah.

Weld and the Grimkés provided the abolitionist movement with a mass of evidence in *American Slavery as It Is: Testimony of a Thousand Witnesses* (1839). The book set out to answer a simple question—"What is the actual condition of the slaves in the United States?"—with evidence from southern newspapers and firsthand testimonies. In one account, Angelina Grimké told of a treadmill that slaveowners used for punishment: "One poor girl, [who was] sent there to be flogged, and who was accordingly stripped naked and whipped, showed me the deep gashes on her back—I might have laid my whole finger in them—*large pieces of flesh had actually been cut out by the torturing lash*." The book sold over 100,000 copies in its first year alone.

In 1833 Weld, Garrison, Arthur and Lewis Tappan, and sixty other delegates, black and white, met in Philadelphia to establish the American Anti-Slavery Society. The Society received financial support from the Tappans, wealthy merchants in New York City. Women abolitionists quickly established their own organizations, such as the Philadelphia Female Anti-Slavery Society, founded by Lucretia Mott in 1833, and the Anti-Slavery Conventions of American Women, formed by a network of local societies in the late 1830s. The women's societies raised money for *The Liberator* and were a major force in the movement, distributing abolitionist literature, collecting tens of thousands of signatures on antislavery petitions, and running schools for free blacks.

Abolitionist leaders developed a two-pronged plan of attack, one part aimed at the general public and the other at politicians. To foster intense public condemnation of slavery, they adopted the tactics of the religious revivalists: large rallies led by stirring speakers, constant agitation by local antislavery chapters, and home visits by agents of the movement. The abolitionists also used the latest techniques of mass communication. Assisted by new steam-powered printing presses, the American Anti-Slavery Society distributed more than 100,000 pieces of literature in 1834. In 1835 the Society launched its "great postal campaign," which flooded the nation, including the South, with a million abolitionist pamphlets. In July 1835 alone abolitionists mailed more than 175,000 items at the New York City post office.

The abolitionists' second strategy was to win support from state and national legislators. In 1835 the American Anti-Slavery Society encouraged local chapters and members to bombard Congress with petitions demanding the abolition of slavery in the District of Columbia, an end to the domestic slave trade, and denial of the admission of new slave states to the Union. By 1838, petitions with nearly 500,000 signatures had arrived in Washington.

This agitation drew thousands of middle-class men and women to abolitionism. During the 1830s the number of local abolitionist societies grew swiftly, from about 200 in 1835 to more than 500 in 1836 and nearly 2,000 by 1840—when they had nearly 200,000 members, including many leading transcendentalists. Emerson condemned the moral failure of a free society that tolerated slavery; Thoreau was even more assertive. In 1846 he protested the Mexican War and slavery by refusing to pay his taxes and submitting to arrest. Two years later he published an anonymous essay entitled "Civil Disobedience" that outlined how individuals, by resisting governments that sanctioned slavery and through loyalty to a higher moral law, could redeem themselves and the state. "A minority is powerless while it conforms to the majority," Thoreau declared, but it becomes "irresistible when it clogs by its whole weight."

Abolitionism Attacked

As Thoreau discerned, the abolitionist crusade had won the wholehearted allegiance of only a small minority—perhaps 10 percent—of white Americans in the North and the sympathy of perhaps twice as many. But men of wealth feared that the abolitionist attack on slave property could turn into a general assault on all property rights. Tradition-minded clergymen warned that the abolitionists threatened the stability of the family by encouraging public roles for women. New York merchants and New England textile producers rallied to the support of their southern customers and suppliers. And many northern wage earners feared that freed slaves willing to work for subsistence wages would pour into northern communities and take their jobs. Moreover, few white northerners believed in civic equality for free blacks. Only five New England states extended suffrage to African-American men, while Connecticut, New Jersey, and Pennsylvania denied them the franchise, as did Ohio, Indiana, and Illinois. Even fewer whites welcomed the prospect of racial mixing and intermarriage.

Moved by such sentiments, northern opponents of abolitionism sometimes turned to violence. Mobs, often led by "gentlemen of property and standing," intimidated free blacks and abolitionists. In 1833 an antiabolitionist mob of fifteen hundred New Yorkers stormed a church in search of Garrison and Arthur Tappan. The next year prominent New Yorkers cheered as a mob of laborers vandalized and set fire to Lewis Tappan's house. Another white mob swept through Philadelphia's African-American neighborhoods, clubbing and stoning residents, destroying homes and churches, and forcing crowds of black women and children to flee the city. In 1835 in Utica, New York, a group of lawyers, local politicians, merchants, and bankers broke up an abolitionist convention and beat several delegates. In the same year a Boston mob dragged Garrison through the streets, threatening to hang him. And two years later in Alton, Illinois, a mob shot and killed an abolitionist editor, Elijah P. Lovejoy.

White southerners reacted to abolitionism with even greater fury. Southern legislatures banned the movement and passed resolutions demanding that northern states follow suit. The Georgia legislature offered a $5,000 reward to anyone who would kidnap Garrison and bring him to the South to be tried for inciting rebellion. In Nashville vigilantes whipped a northern college student for distributing abolitionist pamphlets, and a mob in Charleston attacked the post office and destroyed sacks of abolitionist mail. After 1835, southern postmasters simply refused to deliver mail of suspected abolitionist origin.

Politicians joined the fray. President Andrew Jackson, though a radical on many issues, was a slaveowner and a firm supporter of the southern social order. Jackson privately approved of South Carolina's removal of abolitionist pamphlets from the U.S. mail, and in 1835 he asked Congress to restrict the use of the mails by abolitionist groups. Congress did not comply, but in 1836 the House of Representatives adopted the so-called *gag rule*. Under this rule, which remained in force until 1844, antislavery petitions were automatically tabled when they were received so that they could not become the subject of debate in the House.

Assailed from outside, abolitionists were also divided among themselves. Many antislavery clergymen denounced the public lecturing to mixed audiences by the Grimké sisters and other women as "promiscuous" and immoral. Some male abolitionists left the Anti-Slavery Society because they disagreed with Garrison's broad attack on American institutions.

Garrison grew more radical, supporting pacifism and the abolition of prisons and asylums. Arguing that "our object is *universal* emancipation, to redeem women as well as men from a servile to an equal condition," he demanded that the American Anti-Slavery Society retain a broad platform that supported women's rights. At the convention of the American Anti-Slavery Society in 1840 Garrison precipitated a split with more conservative abolitionists by insisting on equal participation by women and helping to elect Abby Kelley to the organization's business committee. When the movement split, Kelley, Lucretia Mott, and Elizabeth Cady Stanton remained with Garrison in the American Anti-Slavery Society. They recruited new women agents, including Lucy Stone, to proclaim the common interests of enslaved blacks and free women.

Garrison's opponents founded a new organization, the American and Foreign Anti-Slavery Society, which received financial backing from Lewis Tappan. It members worked through their churches to win public support for practical measures against slavery. Other abolitionists turned to electoral politics, establishing the Liberty party and nominating James G. Birney for president in 1840. Birney was a former Alabama slaveowner who had been converted to abolitionism by Theodore Weld and had founded an antislavery newspaper in Cincinnati. Birney and the Liberty party argued that the Constitution did not recognize slavery; that the Fifth Amendment, by barring any

Congressional deprivation of "life, liberty, or property," prevented the federal government from supporting slavery; and that slaves became automatically free when they entered areas of federal authority, such as the District of Columbia and national territories. But Birney won few votes in the election of 1840, and the future of the party and political abolitionism appeared dim.

Coming hard on the heels of popular violence and political suppression, these schisms and electoral failures stunned the abolitionist movement. It had attracted the energies and ideas of thousands of evangelical Protestants, moral reformers, and transcendentalists. But it had aroused the hostility of a substantial majority of the white population, which feared that abolitionism—and the feminist movement that accompanied it—might not reform American society but destroy it. The movement for reform, begun with such confidence in the North in the 1820s, now divided the people of that region and threatened the unity of the nation.

CHAPTER 12 TIMELINE

Year	Event
1817	American Colonization Society founded
1829	David Walker's *Appeal*
1830	Joseph Smith publishes *The Book of Mormon*
1831	William Lloyd Garrison begins publishing *The Liberator* Nat Turner's rebellion
1832	Ralph Waldo Emerson resigns his pulpit New England Anti-Slavery Society founded
1834	New York Female Moral Reform Society established
1836	House of Representatives adopts "gag rule"
1840	Liberty party runs James G. Birney for president
1841	Transcendentalists found Brook Farm Dorothea Dix begins her investigations
1844	Margaret Fuller's *Woman in the Nineteenth Century*
1845	Thoreau withdraws to Walden Pond
1846	Mormons begin trek to Salt Lake
1848	John Humphrey Noyes founds Oneida Community Seneca Falls convention
1851	Herman Melville's *Moby Dick* Susan B. Anthony joins movement for women's rights
1852	Harriet Beecher Stowe's *Uncle Tom's Cabin*
1855	Walt Whitman's *Leaves of Grass*
1858	The "Mormon War"

CHAPTER 13

SECTIONS AND SECTIONALISM, 1840–1860

- The Slave South: A Distinctive Society
- The Northeast: Industry and Culture
- The West: Manifest Destiny

The Economic Revolution increased the wealth of both the North and the South but accentuated long-standing differences between those regions. The North was increasingly industrial and urban, a busy land of movement and markets and individual mobility, while the South remained overwhelmingly agricultural and rural, a vast expanse of white cotton and black slaves. More important, sectional differences were increasingly *felt*, especially in the South. As John C. Calhoun warned in 1850, southerners had come to fear "the long-continued agitation of the slavery question on the part of the North" and the North's growing wealth and political power.

The consciousness of *sectionalism* was more intense and widespread than it had been in the 1790s, when Thomas Jefferson had contested Alexander Hamilton's pronorthern economic program, or the 1830s, when the sections had quarreled over tariffs and the Second Bank. Those were battles over issues. Now the conflict was between different ways of life. By the middle of the nineteenth century northerners and southerners were living in different social systems, with different ways of thinking about the individual and society. Middle-class northerners hailed the new principles of "free labor," individualism, and social mobility; southern slaveowners celebrated the old traditions of slavery, hierarchy, and authority.

Simultaneously, the massive westward migration of Americans shifted the balance of political power to the heartland of the continent, the states of the

Mississippi Valley. The emergence of the West as a distinct section created new opportunities—and dangers. Many Americans came to believe that the nation's future lay in the West, that its "Manifest Destiny" was to extend republican institutions to the Pacific Ocean. But whose institutions: those of the North or those of the South? The issue of westward expansion became inextricably entangled with that of slavery and sectional identity.

THE SLAVE SOUTH: A DISTINCTIVE SOCIETY

The South was a complex society based on race and class. White planters grew rich by exploiting the labor of enslaved African-Americans, who numbered one-third of the South's population. Adopting the outlook of a landed gentry, wealthy planters described themselves as natural aristocrats. While yeomen and tenant families contested the dominance of the planter elite, they ultimately stood with it to support "white supremacy."

The Southern Slave Economy

The South's economy grew rapidly between 1830 and 1860. Planters sold more and more tobacco, rice, sugar, and—above all—cotton in Europe. In the 1840s, after the Cotton Kingdom had swept across the Mississippi River into Texas, the South was producing more than two-thirds of the world's cotton and accounted for almost two-thirds of the total value of American exports.

Unlike northern farmers, who profited primarily by selling to domestic consumers and improving farm technology, southern planters grew wealthy by relying on British markets and capital, fresh land, and slavery. The British connection was crucial. The buoyant demand of British textile mills drove up the price of cotton, while British mercantile houses furnished capital for new plantations. The availability of fresh land was equally significant because cotton ruined the soil more quickly than did most other crops. In the early 1850s an observer described Georgia's eastern plantation belt as "red old hills stripped of their native growth and virgin soil, and washed with deep gullies." By 1860 nearly three-fourths of the South's cotton production came from the region's newer plantations—lands stretching from western Georgia to eastern Texas.

Slavery marched west as millions of acres of new land came into production (see Map 13.1). To clear and plant the land quickly and raise the output of their African-American workers, slaveowners devised a new form of work discipline: a gang labor system that resembled factory work. Planters and overseers on plantations with twenty or more slaves organized the hands into disciplined teams, or *gangs*, and assigned them specific tasks. Using the threat of the whip, white overseers and enslaved black drivers worked their gangs at a feverish pace, clearing and plowing the land or hoeing and picking cotton. In 1854 a traveler glimpsed two gangs returning from work on a well-established Mississippi plantation:

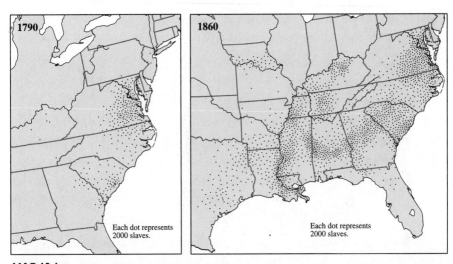

MAP 13.1
Distribution of the Slave Population, 1790–1860
The cotton boom shifted enslaved African-Americans to the Old Southwest. In 1790 most slaves lived and worked on the tobacco plantations of the Chesapeake and in the rice and indigo areas of South Carolina. By 1860 hundreds of thousands were laboring on the cotton and sugar lands of the lower Mississippi Valley and along an arc of fertile cotton land—the "black belt"—sweeping from Mississippi through Georgia.

First came, led by an old driver carrying a whip, forty of the largest and strongest women I ever saw together; they were all in a simple uniform dress of a bluish check stuff, the skirts reaching little below the knee; their legs and feet were bare; they carried themselves loftily, each having a hoe over the shoulder, and walking with a free, powerful swing.

Next marched the plow hands with their mules, "the cavalry, thirty strong, mostly men, but a few of them women."

Thanks to gang labor, fertile western land, and the enormous demand for cotton, slaveowners earned profits on their investments that averaged about 10 percent a year. Even the most successful New England textile mills rarely produced a higher rate of return. But high profits from agriculture created two long-term problems. First, southern investors concentrated their resources in cotton and slaves, so that the percentage of southerners who lived in towns and worked in manufacturing was only half that in the North. The only major cities in the South were the old seaports of Baltimore, Charleston, and New Orleans, which remained predominantly commercial centers.

A second, and more tragic, problem was the low level of education in the South. The wealthy planters who controlled southern society wanted a compliant labor force content with the drudgery of agricultural work. Consequently, they trained most of their slaves as field hands (allowing only a few to learn the arts of the blacksmith, carpenter, and bricklayer) and made little

Harvesting Sugarcane
Growing sugar was arduous work and took the lives of thousands of slaves. In both the West Indies and Louisiana, sugar planters used gang labor to ditch and drain marshlands and plant cane seedlings in long ditches. Harvesting the mature cane and carrying it to the plantation's mill were equally strenuous and, as this watercolor by Franz Holzlhuber shows, were the work of women as well as men.

or no effort to provide blacks, and ordinary whites, with elementary instruction in reading and arithmetic. Some southern states made teaching slaves to read a crime, and no state had a comprehensive system of public schools for whites. As a result, in 1850 most African-Americans and about 20 percent of white southerners were illiterate (compared with less than 1 percent in New England). Lacking cities, factories, and educated workers, the South could not provide a majority of its people with a rising standard of living. In 1860 the per capita income was $141 in the North but only $103 in the South. Enslaved African-Americans and white tenant farmers had little or no property, and landholding yeomen in the back country lacked access to profitable markets. Prosperity was limited primarily to the families—25 percent of the white population—that owned plantations and slaves.

Slaveowning Planters and Yeomen Farmers

Southern society was dominated by planters who owned twenty or more slaves. Making up only 10 percent of all slaveholders (and about 2 percent of whites in the South), they owned about half the slaves. These 10,000 families dominated southern society more completely than the business elite controlled the North. For example, in Alabama in 1850 slaveowners represented only 30 percent of the electorate but 75 percent of the legislators; a fourth of the legislators were large planters who owned fifty or more slaves. Except in the back-country, most county governments in the South were run by substantial planters, who served as justices of the peace and church vestrymen. The members of this elite married their children to one another, and their sons and daughters became commercial and cultural leaders, working as merchants, lawyers, newspaper editors, and ministers and hosting plantation balls and church fetes.

Wealthy planters marked their success by building splendid mansions and indulging in displays of conspicuous consumption. The Greek Revival mansion on the rural estate of John Henry Hammond, a leading South Carolina planter and politician, boasted a center hall that was 53 by 20 feet, its floor embellished with stylish Belgian tiles and expensive Brussels carpets. "Once a year, like a great feudal landlord," a guest recounted, Hammond "gave a fete or grand dinner to all the country people." To retain the allegiance of ambitious men, Hammond and other planters encouraged them to buy slaves and grow rich.

Like all ruling classes, the planters tried to justify their power by endowing it with moral purpose. Responding to abolitionist attacks in the 1830s, they encouraged politicians, newspaper editors, and clergymen to defend slavery as a "positive good" that raised Africans from their savage condition rather than, as in the past, a "necessary evil" to maintain white living standards and prevent racial warfare. Seeking a religious justification, planters noted that the Hebrews, God's chosen people, had owned slaves and that Christ had never condemned slavery. Many defenders of slavery invoked St. Paul's injunction: "Servants, obey your masters."

Southern apologists also trumpeted the virtues of slavery in comparison to "free labor" in the North. They pointed out that few northern factory owners took any interest in the welfare of their workers, who labored long hours for meager pay and lived in unhealthy slums. In contrast, they praised planters as models of "disinterested benevolence" who ensured that enslaved African-Americans were adequately fed and housed and provided for the sick and elderly who could no longer work.

In fact, because of the prosperity of the mid-nineteenth-century plantation system, most slaves were somewhat better clothed and housed than were the poorest whites in both the South and the North. The slaves' food—particularly when supplemented by greens from their own garden plots and by game and fish—was probably better than that of unskilled workers in the North. And on some large plantations, children, the sick, and the elderly received better care than poor northerners did. But few enslaved African-Americans enjoyed a comfortable standard of living, and, unlike northern workers, slaves did not have the freedom to quit their jobs. And they clearly understood that planters gave them material favors not from benevolence but to protect their investment.

As part of the social defense of slavery, writers praised planters' wives as the managers of large households and lauded their work as nurses, caring for sick African-American children. Many writers especially exalted the sexual purity of white plantation women, contrasting them with stereotypical descriptions of passionately sexual black men and women and defending the brutal punishment of male slaves accused of rape or sexual intimacy with white women. Planters' wives became symbols of the moral superiority of whites over blacks.

The reality of plantation life was far more complex. A few planters' wives did enter into consensual sexual relations with African-Americans, and many planters had sex with their female slaves and fathered children by them. "I cannot tell how much I suffered in the presence of these wrongs," Harriet Jacobs confessed in anguish in her autobiography, *Incidents in the Life of a Slave Girl*. For many enslaved women, sexual assault by their masters was compounded by cruel treatment at the hands of mistresses enraged by their husbands' promiscuity.

In contrast to Brazil and the West Indies, interracial sex in the American South did not lead to the acceptance of a multicolored, mixed-race society. To maintain the loyalty of non-slaveowning whites (and ward off abolitionist attacks), planters increasingly relied on an ideology that asserted the equality of all whites and the inferiority of all blacks, including those of mixed ancestry and light skin color. As William Yancey of Alabama explained to a northern audience, "Your fathers and my fathers built this government on two ideas; the first is that the white race is the citizen and the master race, and the white man is the equal of every other white man. The second is that the Negro is the inferior race."

This rigid racial ideology helped unify a white population divided by property and regional outlook. Three-quarters of white families in the South did not own slaves. Some were tenant farmers, but many more were yeomen who owned farms of 50 to 100 acres in hilly regions or the Appalachian backcountry. Yeomen families grew some cotton but primarily raised corn and livestock, especially hogs. Their goals were modest: to preserve their holdings and secure enough new land or goods to set up all their children as farmers.

Wealthy slaveowners often stood in their way, buying up the best land and forcing yeomen into less fertile regions. Planters used their power in the state legislatures to keep taxes low on slaves and other personal property and tax land by acreage rather than by value so that backcountry farmers paid relatively high taxes on their marginal lands. In addition, planters enacted laws that forced yeomen to "fence in" their livestock (sparing themselves the cost of building fences around their large properties) and prohibited them from hunting on unused private lands. Finally, legislatures forced all white men— whether they owned slaves or not—to serve in patrols and militias that deterred slaves from running away or rebelling.

Few white yeomen or tenants welcomed gentry rule, and some actively opposed it. In 1857 Hinton Helper of North Carolina sought to rouse the

"Non-slaveowners of the South! farmers, mechanics and workingmen," warning that "the slaveholders, the arrogant demogogues whom you have elected to offices of honor and profit, have hoodwinked you . . . used you as mere tools for the consummation of their wicked designs." But Helper was forced into exile in the North by the planter elite, which maintained its rule by cutting some taxes, appointing a few yeomen to patronage positions, and making deals with backcountry leaders. Slaveowners also relied on racial prejudice, warning tenants and yeomen that they had to support slavery or face economic competition and race warfare with freed African-Americans. As John Henry Hammond told his poor white neighbors: "In a slave country every *freeman* is an aristocrat."

Enslaved African-Americans

Custom and law relegated slaves to a thoroughly subordinate social position. By law enslaved individuals were *chattel*—personal property. They could be disciplined at the will of their owners and bought and sold as if they were horses. As Thomas Ruffin, a justice of North Carolina Supreme Court, declared in a court decision in 1829, "The power of the master must be absolute to render the submission of the slave perfect."

The domestic slave trade reflected the brutal reality of the slave system. Few slaves arrived from Africa after 1808, when Congress banned American participation in the Atlantic slave trade. But because their birth rate equaled the high level among rural whites, the African-American population grew rapidly, from 1.1 million in 1810 to 3.9 million in 1860. Although many blacks continued to work on the plantations where they had been born, hundreds of thousands were moved by their owners to the expanding Cotton Kingdom in the Old Southwest. Some migrating slaves—perhaps as many as half—moved with relatives and friends as their owners deserted the Carolinas for the fertile plains of the Mississippi Valley. The rest were "sold South" through a new domestic slave trade that provided tobacco and cotton planters in Maryland, Virginia, and other long-settled regions with a major source of income. By the 1850s slaveowners were shipping 25,000 men and women a year westward, breaking up families and communities. "Dey sole my sister Kate," Anna Harris remembered decades later. "Sole her in 1860, and I ain't seed or heard of her since."

In the face of this internal slave trade, African-Americans nurtured family relationships for protection and support. Because slaves were not allowed to make contracts, their marriages were not legally binding. Nonetheless, many unions were durable. If not broken up by sale, couples usually maintained close nuclear families; in their cabins they loved and quarreled, laughed and suffered, much as free people did. Slaves also developed elaborate kinship networks that included distant relations and even individuals who had no blood or marital ties but shared in the life of the family. Elderly slaves played the role of patriarch, conducting religious services and disciplining

---

A Child Learns the Meaning of Slavery

Jacob Stroyer, born into slavery in South Carolina, was emancipated and became a minister in Salem, Massachusetts. In My Life in the South *(1855), Stroyer relates a dramatic incident that revealed his parents' subordinate and powerless status.*

Father . . . used to take care of horses and mules. I was around with him in the barnyard when but a small boy; of course that gave me an early relish for the occupation of hostler, and soon I made known my preference to Colonel Singleton, who was a sportsman and had fine horses. . . . Hence I was allowed to be numbered among those who took care of the fine horses, and learned to ride. . . .

It was not long after I had entered my new work before they put me upon the back of a horse which threw me to the ground almost as soon as I reached his back. . . . When I got up there was a man standing near with a switch in hand, and he immediately began to beat me. . . . This was the first time I had been whipped by anyone except Mother and Father, so I cried out in a tone of voice as if I would say, this is the first and last whipping you will give me when Father gets hold of you.

When I got away from him I ran to Father with all my might, but soon my expectation was blasted, as Father very coolly said to me, "Go back to your work and be a good boy, for I cannot do anything for you." But that did not satisfy me, so I went on to Mother with my complaint and she came out to the man who whipped me. He was a groom, a white man whom master hired to train his horses . . . [and] he took a whip and started for her, and she ran from him, talking all the time. . . .

Then the idea first came to me that I, with my dear father and mother and the rest of my fellow Negroes, was doomed to cruel treatment through life and was defenseless. . . .

SOURCE: Linda R. Monk, ed., *Ordinary Americans: U.S. History through the Eyes of Everyday People* (Alexandria, VA: Close Up Publications, 1994), pp. 71–72.

---

difficult children. Young slaves learned to address their elders by kin titles such as "Aunt" and "Uncle," preparing them for the day when they might be separated from their parents. When parted by sale, members of nuclear and extended families tried to keep track of one another. But the distances were often too great, and many slaves started new families in their new locations. When the Union army registered African-American marriages in Mississippi at the end of the Civil War, officials found that the slave trade had separated about a fourth of the men over forty years old from their first wives.

As migration and the domestic slave trade moved thousands of African-Americans to the Deep South, their working lives became more difficult. The weather was the hottest and conditions the most oppressive in that newly settled region, and the planters were the most brutal because many of them were poor men on the make rather than well-established members of the gentry. Work routines were more demanding as well. Sugar—grown in Louisiana—was the most labor-intensive plantation crop. Work was nearly as strenuous on newly founded cotton plantations in Alabama, Mississippi, Louisiana, Arkansas, and Texas. And the number of enslaved blacks in those states increased from about 500,000 in 1840 to more than 1.5 million in 1860, when they amounted to more than a third of all slaves (see Map 13.1).

To resist gang labor and forced separations, African-Americans used the tactics employed by previous generations of slaves: they feigned illness to slow the pace of work, were deliberately careless with the master's property, losing or breaking tools, and occasionally set fire to houses and barns.

Increasingly, young men resisted by running away. In the 1840s and 1850s tens of thousands of slaves fled from their masters, defying white patrols with bloodhounds, and about 1,000 reached freedom in the North each year. Blacks who lived near a free state had the greatest chance of success. In those areas enslaved women, whose concern for their children often deterred flight, joined the exodus along with their families. The fugitives counted on receiving aid from the "underground railroad," an informal network of white and African-American abolitionists that included free African-Americans in Baltimore, Richmond, Charleston, New Orleans, and other southern cities. In Baltimore, a free African-American sailor lent his identification papers to the future abolitionist Frederick Douglass, who used them to escape to New York and then returned them by mail. Many escaped slaves, such as Harriet Tubman, returned repeatedly to the South, risking reenslavement or death by working with the "railroad."

A few slaves followed the path marked out by David Walker's *Appeal* and Nat Turner's uprising by turning on their masters. But most African-Americans realized that rebellion was more likely to bring death than freedom, and they lacked the strong institutions—such as the communes formed by free peasants or serfs—needed to organize them. Moreover, blacks formed less than half the population in most areas; their southern white adversaries were well armed, unified, and militant; and there were no impenetrable jungles, mountains, and swamps into which they could flee.

In these circumstances, many slaves turned to spiritual resistance derived, especially after 1830, from Protestant Christianity. The Christianity of the slaves repudiated the virtue of obedience: when a white minister urged slaves in Liberty County, Georgia, to obey their masters, he noted that "one half of my audience deliberately rose up and walked off." Black Christianity also downplayed the doctrine of human depravity and developed as a religion of emotional fervor, celebration, and stoic endurance. Religion offered the hope of eventual liberation from life's sorrows and helped many slaves endure their

Harriet Tubman
Harriet Tubman (far left) was born in 1823 and escaped from slavery on a Maryland plantation in 1849. During the next ten years she became a popular abolitionist speaker and led hundred of slaves, including those pictured here, to freedom on the underground railroad. Tubman served as a spy for the Union army during the Civil War and then set up schools for ex-slaves in North Carolina.

bondage. African-American Protestants took heart from stories of the ancient Israelites' escape from Egypt and Christ's compassion for the oppressed. Confident of their special relationship with God, slaves prepared themselves spiritually for emancipation, which they saw as deliverance to the Promised Land.

Free Blacks

While nearly 4 million African-Americans were enslaved in 1860, 500,000 were free. About half the free blacks resided in the North, where they lived as second-class citizens. They were permitted to vote in only four New England states and New York and could testify against whites in court only in Massachusetts. Virtually all public facilities in the North were segregated, and most states denied blacks access to public schools. The federal government did not allow free African-Americans to work for the postal service, claim public lands, or hold a U.S. passport.

Most free African-Americans in the slave states lived in the Upper South, where they faced even greater legal restrictions on their liberty, especially after 1840. Free blacks accused of crimes were often denied a jury trial, and those who lacked work were threatened by vagrancy and apprenticeship laws intended to force them back into slavery. To prove their free status, they had to carry manumission documents; in some states they needed official permission just to travel across county lines. Even if they had good papers, free African-Americans had to be careful; kidnapping followed by sale into slavery was a constant threat.

In both the North and the South, free blacks were consigned by custom or law to the most menial and low-paying work. In rural areas they worked as agricultural laborers or tenant farmers; in towns and cities, as domestic servants, laundresses, or day laborers. However, the shortage of skilled workers in southern cities did create opportunities for a few blacks to become carpenters, blacksmiths, barbers, butchers, and shopkeepers. Skilled African-American workers in Baltimore, Richmond, Charleston, and New Orleans formed their own benevolent societies and churches, which became the core of their urban communities, providing education, recreation, and social welfare programs.

As a privileged group among African-Americans, free blacks felt pulled in two directions: loyalty to the welfare of their families, which often meant assimilating white culture, and loyalty to their race, which meant identifying with the great mass of enslaved African-Americans. In some places wealthier free blacks, particularly the mulatto children of white masters and black women, drew apart from common laborers and field hands and adopted the outlook of the planter class. In New Orleans free African-Americans sponsored an opera company and established literary journals. A few owned land and slaves.

Generally, however, free blacks and enslaved African-Americans saw themselves as one people. "We's different [from whites] in color, in talk and in 'ligion and beliefs," as one put it. Knowing that their freedom was not secure as long as slavery existed, free blacks sought to win freedom for their "brothers" and "sisters." A few free blacks in the South—such as Denmark Vesey, a Charleston, South Carolina, carpenter married to an enslaved woman—plotted rebellion, and many more aided fugitive slaves. In the North free African-Americans supported the abolitionist movement, and some—such as David Walker, Frederick Douglass, and Sojourner Truth—rose to positions of leadership. In the rigid caste system of American race relations, free blacks stood as symbols of hope to enslaved African-Americans and omens of danger to the majority of whites.

THE NORTHEAST: INDUSTRY AND CULTURE

As the planter elite carried slavery into the Old Southwest, the business leaders of the Northeast drove mechanization forward at an increasing pace and, in the 1840s and 1850s, began to incorporate the predominantly rural trans-Appalachian West into the expanding industrial economy. The economic results were phenomenal. By 1860 the United States was third in the world in manufacturing, behind only Great Britain and France.

Factories Triumphant

The American population grew from 17 million in 1840 to over 31 million in 1860, nearly doubling the market for industrial goods. This startling increase stemmed in part from a high birth rate (45 births per thousand people per year, compared with 30 per thousand in Europe) and in part from a massive surge in immigration from Western Europe. As the destination of most immigrants, the northeastern and Great Lakes states dominated this demographic surge, accounting for nearly two-thirds of the population increase.

Northern manufacturers easily met the growing demand for goods. They expanded production not only in the industrial towns, where falling water powered mills, but also in the older seaports and, with stunning swiftness, the towns of the interior, where the coal-powered stationary steam engine was used to run other machines. By 1838 there were about 2,000 steam engines in the United States and 133 in Pittsburgh alone, where they were used in the glass industry, sawmills, machine shops, and iron-rolling mills. The use of steam engines enabled manufacturers to build factories in the largest cities, taking advantage of their cheap labor, capital markets, sophisticated trading services, and eager consumers.

Factory production lay at the heart of industrial expansion. Northern manufacturers built hundreds of new factories that used power-driven machines and assembly-line techniques to turn out vast quantities of well-made goods. Cyrus McCormick of Chicago developed power-driven conveyor belts to assemble reapers, and Samuel Colt built an assembly-line factory in Hartford, Connecticut, to produce his invention—the "six-shooter," as it became known. By the late 1850s Colt's factory was turning out 60,000 weapons annually, and five Connecticut clockmakers were using machine tools to make intricate works for half a million clocks a year. As a team of British observers noted with admiration, those products were made "in large factories, with machinery applied to almost every process, the extreme subdivision of labor, and all reduced to an almost perfect system of manufacture."

The sheer volume of output made some products—Remington rifles, Singer sewing machines, Waltham watches, and Yale locks as well as Colt handguns and McCormick reapers—into household words in the United States and abroad. After showing their machine-tooled goods at the Crystal Palace Exhibition in London in 1851, McCormick and Colt built factories in Great Britain that used American machinery and production techniques. Soon their products dominated many European markets.

Steam power and assembly lines had other, less positive effects, such as sharpening conflict between owners and workers. To pay for their new machinery, manufacturers cut wages, and to use it most efficiently, they increased the pace of work, which employees resisted. For example, in 1845 the weaver Sarah G. Bagley and other operatives formed the Female Labor Reform Association to protest wage cuts and a speedup in a Lowell, Massachusetts, textile mill, but the Association was unable to halt the decline in wages and working conditions. As a result, there was an important change in the labor force throughout the textile industry. Few young Yankee women chose to enter the mills, and most older female employees left to marry and raise families; Irish

McCORMICK'S FIRST REAPER

The McCormick Reaper, 1851
The McCormick reaper was a complex piece of machinery, but it was designed to be assembled and repaired by average farmers. Company advertisements informed potential buyers that the reaper's parts were "numbered and marked with paint, showing the connection of the parts with one another so that they can readily be put together by the farmer." By using reapers to harvest ripe grain before it sprouted, farmers could plant many more acres.

and French-Canadian immigrants—more men than women—took their place, working for low wages and foreshadowing the emergence of an all-male system of factory labor (see Chapter 18).

By the 1850s the supply of machine-made goods often exceeded the demand, prompting the laying off or dismissal of workers. One episode of overproduction preceded the Panic of 1857—a financial crisis sparked by excess railroad investments—and resulted in a full-scale depression. Unemployment remained at about 10 percent until the outbreak of the Civil War in 1861, reminding Americans of the social costs of the new—and otherwise very successful—system of industrial production.

The Culture of the Middle Class

Between 1830 and the Panic of 1857, the per capita income of Americans increased by about 2.5 percent a year, a remarkable rate that the United States has never since matched. This prosperity, along with the availability of inexpensive mass-produced goods, allowed the creation of a new material and intellectual culture. A new urban middle class grew in size and self-awareness, and its outlook lent a distinctive character to northern society.

Improvements in housing were one mark of prosperity and middle-class identity. In the 1830s American carpenters devised a faster method to build wooden houses: the balloon frame. Traditional wood construction depended on the careful fitting together of heavy timbers; in the East experienced housewrights fashioned a strong frame with mortise-and-tenon joints, while in the West farmers fitted trimmed logs together. The *balloon frame*, much lighter in weight (as its name implied) but almost as strong, formed a house with a vertical grid of thin wooden studs joined by nails to cross-pieces at the top and bottom. Once the carpenter had thrown up the frame, he simply nailed wood sheathing to the studs to make the walls and then added a layer of clapboard siding. The new technology reduced the cost of housing by 40 percent, and the four-room balloon-frame house quickly became the standard residence, replacing the typical two-room-with-a-loft house of preindustrial society.

The new house design helped change the character of family life. Urban middle-class parents had already begun to have fewer children by using various means of birth control: abstinence, coitus interruptus, animal skin condoms, and abortions induced by herbs. Larger houses allowed family members to avoid close physical contact with one another. To enhance individual privacy, architects published manuals featuring house plans with many bedrooms. Andrew Jackson Downing, the leading architectural philosopher of the era, lauded the new houses in his famous book *The Architecture of Country Houses* (1850). Downing argued they would promote a "refinement of manners" and strengthen the life of the family, which was "the best social form."

Prosperous urban families lived not only in more space but also in greater luxury. Beds with springs of woven rope or iron wire replaced beds with wooden slats, and as mass-produced ticking and sheeting became available in stores, homemade featherbeds, mattresses, and down pillows became standard items. Middle-class residences now boasted furnaces that heated water for bathing and for radiators that warmed entire rooms, eliciting complaints from visiting Europeans that it was impossible to escape hot air: "It meets you the moment the street-door is opened to let you in, rushes after you when you emerge again, half-stewed and parboiled into the wholesome air."

Most affluent urban house owners acquired goods that eased the burden of traditional domestic chores. Stoves with ovens, including broilers and movable grates, replaced inefficient open hearths. Women now had access to a variety of pots, pans, and kettles; mechanical equipment such as grinders and presses; and washboards. Many middle-class households boasted treadle-operated sewing machines and iceboxes, which ice-company wagons filled daily. After the introduction of the Mason jar in 1858, households vastly increased their ability to preserve perishable foods.

No less important, the technology of the Industrial Revolution allowed the realization of Emerson's dream of a democratic audience for American literature. The Napier steam-driven press (1825) and the Hoe rotary press (1847) led to the mass production of cheap books. The northern middle class provided a virtually insatiable market, buying books or borrowing the nearly 13 million volumes available in over 50,000 public libraries. Publishing houses in New York, Philadelphia, and Boston competed with each other, offering discounts to booksellers, sending sales agents into the field, and recruiting popular authors. Between 1820 and 1850 American book publishers such as Harper Brothers and G. P. Putnam's Sons increased their annual sales from about $2.5 million to $12.5 million. The religious press also contributed to the explosion in print. The American Bible Society and dozens of other organizations published more than 1 million Bibles and 6 million books, pamphlets, and magazines each year.

The new book culture was a distinguishing feature of the northern middle class. Fiction constituted a large proportion of literary consumption. One of the first successful American writers of fiction was James Fenimore Cooper. Beginning with *The Pioneers* (1823) and *The Last of the Mohicans* (1826) and ending with *The Deerslayer* (1841), Cooper built an enormous readership for the adventures of his hero, the frontier scout Leatherstocking. Corresponding in popularity was the poetry of Henry Wadsworth Longfellow, who romanticized the American past in *Hiawatha* (1855) and *The Courtship of Miles Standish* (1858).

Women writers were even more popular among middle-class readers, the majority of whom were female. Catharine Maria Sedgwick won wide popularity in the 1820s, as did Caroline Howard Gilman and Caroline Lee Hentz in the next decade. Writers whose names are virtually unknown today—Sara Parton, Augusta Evans Wilson, and Susan Warner—reached even larger audiences in the 1850s. The sentimental melodramas of these women authors, often punctuated by tearful domestic scenes, helped develop the emerging middle-class identity by suggesting that women occupied a "separate sphere" and could achieve their potential only within the context of marriage and the family. In her last novel, *Married or Single* (1857), Sedgwick concluded that marriage was "the great circumstance" of a woman's life where she could form the character of her husband and children.

The most successful woman novelist of the period was Harriet Beecher Stowe. *Uncle Tom's Cabin* (1852), which sold 350,000 copies in its first year, was first and foremost an antislavery novel, but it was also an argument for the superior morality of women and the importance of family life. Stowe gave the home a deep religious meaning, writing in *The Minister's Wooing* (1859) that it was the "appointed sphere for woman, more holy than cloister, more saintly and pure than church and altar."

The commercial success of women novelists gave an ironic twist to their celebration of the private sphere of home, marriage, and family. These writers were actually engaged in a very public—and commercial—enterprise. Bargaining with their publishers, often making their own living, and supporting their families, they were among the first successful professional women in the United States. These talented and energetic women were erasing the contradiction between "domestic" and "public" life and justifying the independent woman. But they did so in a subtle and unthreatening fashion by promoting morality and thus assuming one of the roles of the minister. Indeed, Caroline Lee Hentz described her writing career as "vocation . . . for which God has endowed me."

Indeed, the thousands of middle-class northern women active in religious and reform organizations were living exemplars of the novelists' heroines, as were the multitude of women teachers who were inspired by the writings of Catharine Beecher (see Chapter 12). To Beecher, "moral and religious education must be the foundation of national instruction" and education must be carried out by "energetic and benevolent women." Thus, the cultural world of the new middle class enhanced not only the material lives of American women but also their intellectual and moral authority.

Immigration and Cultural Conflict

Immigrants from Ireland and the German states formed other new cultural worlds in the northeastern states. There was no federal legislation regulating immigration, and state laws, which attempted to set minimum health standards and exclude paupers, were generally ineffective. Consequently, there were no legal barriers to immigrants fleeing poverty and famine or seeking a better life. Between 1820 and 1860 about 2 million Irish men and women poured into the United States, along with 1.5 million Germans and 750,000 Britons. Most avoided the South because they opposed slavery, shunned blacks, or feared competition from enslaved workers and instead settled in the northern states, where they accounted for nearly a third of white adults by 1860.

The economic situation of immigrants varied greatly. The wealthiest were the British, many of whom were professionals, landowning farmers, and skilled workers. The majority of German immigrants came from farming and artisan families and could afford to buy land in America; many of them settled in the West, especially Missouri and Wisconsin. The poorest migrants were peasants and laborers from Ireland, who fled from a famine in the 1840s caused by a devastating blight on the potato crop and English economic policies that encouraged the exportation of scarce grain. The Irish found new homes in the cities of New England and New York, taking low-skilled jobs in factories, construction projects, docks, warehouses, and private homes. Arriving in dire poverty, they were willing to work for long hours, at low wages, and with great intensity. Irish workers gave a competitive edge to industrialists in New York City and Boston, where they numbered nearly one-third of the population by 1850. For example, each of the largest clothing factories in Boston employed about a hundred young Irishwomen.

Many Irish immigrants, like many unskilled native-born day laborers, lived in poverty, unable to afford the food they needed to keep up with the intense pace of factory work. Crowded living conditions threatened their health, for sanitation systems in large cities were primitive. Poorly sealed privies drained into drinking wells, and open sewers ran through the streets. Epidemics of cholera, yellow fever, typhoid, smallpox, diphtheria, and tuberculosis struck with increasing frequency. In the summer of 1849 cholera epidemics hit New York, St. Louis, and Cincinnati. More than 5,000 people, mostly poor immigrants, died in New York alone.

In times of hardship and sorrow, immigrants turned to their churches. French-Canadians, many Germans, and virtually all the Irish were committed Catholics, and they fueled the growth of the Catholic Church. In the 1840s there were 16 Catholic dioceses and 700 churches in the United States, and the number increased to 45 dioceses and 3,000 churches by 1860. With the guidance of their priests and bishops, the Irish built a network of ethnic institutions: charitable societies, orphanages, militia companies, parochial schools, newspapers, social clubs, and political organizations. These community organizations had few equivalents in Ireland, for they had sprung up to help immigrants in their search for housing, jobs, and education. They also reflected the desire of Irish immigrants to maintain their native culture, to which existing American institutions were indifferent or hostile.

The arrival of the first wave of Irish immigrants in the 1830s produced a rash of anti-Catholic publications. One of the most militant critics of Catholicism was Samuel F. B. Morse, who would later make the first commercial adaptation of the telegraph. In 1834 Morse published *Foreign Conspiracy against the Liberties of the United States*, which warned of a Catholic threat to American republican institutions. The "past history" of Roman Catholics, Morse suggested, and "the fact that they everywhere act together, as if guided by one mind, admonish us to be jealous of their influence . . . in relation to our free institutions." He was especially wary of Irish Catholics, who "kept alive their foreign feelings, associations, habits and manners." Morse advocated the formation of an "Anti-Popery Union" to resist the perceived threat.

Morse believed that Irish Catholics would obey the dictates of Pope Pius IX, who strongly opposed republican reformers in Italy and condemned republicanism as a false political ideology based on the sovereignty of the people rather than the sovereignty of God. Republican-minded Protestant ministers of many denominations shared Morse's fears, and *Foreign Conspiracy* became their textbook. Millions of young Americans read it in Protestant Sunday schools.

The social tensions stemming from industrialization intensified anti-Catholic sentiment. Unemployed Protestant mechanics and poorly paid factory workers attacked Catholics, blaming cheap immigrant labor for their economic woes. They organized Native American Clubs, which called for increasing the waiting period for citizenship from five to twenty-one years, restricting public office to native-born Americans, and using only the Protestant version of the Bible in public schools.

Other native-born citizens supported the anti-Catholic movement for reasons of public policy. They wanted a strong system of public schools and therefore opposed proposals from Catholic clergymen and Democratic legislators in many northeastern states that the local taxes paid by Catholics be reserved for parochial (religious) schools. Evangelical ministers and temperance advocates were alarmed by the abuse of alcohol by some Irish men and called for an end to immigration. This cultural warfare among ethnic and religious groups inhibited the development of a strong labor movement. Many Protestant laborers felt they had more in common with their employers than with their Catholic coworkers.

In almost every city with a large immigrant population, religious and cultural conflicts resulted in violence. In 1834, in Charlestown, Massachusetts, a quarrel between Catholic laborers repairing an Ursuline convent and Protestant workers in a neighboring brickyard turned into a full-scale riot. An anti-Catholic mob drove the residents out of the convent and burned it to the ground. Rioting escalated in the 1840s as the Irish began to acquire political influence in northeastern cities. In Philadelphia the violence peaked in 1844 when the Catholic bishop persuaded public school officials to use both Protestant and Catholic versions of the Bible. Anti-Irish rioting incited by the city's Native American Clubs lasted for two months and escalated into open warfare between Protestants and the Penn-

Anti-Catholic Riot in Philadelphia
When riots against Irish Catholics broke out in Philadelphia in 1844, the governor of Pennsylvania called out the militia to protect Catholic churches, including one (pictured in the background) in which young Irish-Americans had stored muskets for self-defense. The Protestant rioters, depicted by the artist as well-dressed gentlemen, exchanged musket fire with the militia, which eventually restored order but not amity to the religiously divided city.

sylvania militia. Ethnicity and religion now split the North in much the same way (although not to the same extent) that race and class had long divided the South.

THE WEST: MANIFEST DESTINY

During the 1840s and 1850s, American settlers and European immigrants filled up the large geographic area that became known as the Midwest and tied it culturally and economically to the Northeast. Captivated by this westward movement, expansionists declared that it was the nation's "Manifest Destiny" to dominate the entire North American continent. A few political leaders realized that this mission would inevitably create conflicts with Mexico and Great Britain and revive the long-simmering conflict between the North and the South over the expansion of slavery, but their reservations were swept aside by the expansionist fervor. The fate of the nation would soon depend on the fate of the West.

The Midwest

By 1860 nearly one-third of the nation's people lived in the Midwest states— Ohio, Indiana, Illinois, Michigan, and Wisconsin, along with Missouri, Iowa, and Minnesota—where they created a complex society and economy that resembled that of the Northeast. Many settlers had come from New England or New York and had carried their culture, churches, and fraternal lodges with them. Tens of thousands more had migrated from Germany and Ireland, and so the ethnic composition of the Midwest was similar to that of the Northeast.

Strong economic bonds tied the two regions. Most midwesterners were wheat farmers who shipped their crops to northeastern markets on the Great Lakes and the Erie Canal. Midwestern inventors and entrepreneurs drew on the industrial technology and mass-production techniques of northeastern manufacturers to produce low-cost labor-saving goods—especially farm machinery. The story of John Deere was typical. As a blacksmith in Grand Detour, Illinois, Deere made his first steel plow out of old saws in 1837; ten years later he opened a factory in Moline that used mass-production techniques. His steel plows, superior in strength to cast-iron models, quickly dominated the midwestern market. Other companies—McCormick, Hussey, Atkins, and Manny—mass-produced reapers that revolutionized the harvesting of grain. Previously, one worker with a cradle scythe had cut 2 to 3 acres a day. With a self-raking reaper, a farmer could cut 12 acres daily. Because their farms were large and laborers were in short supply, midwesterners led the way in using modern agricultural technology, increasing their productivity more than 20 percent during the 1850s.

Another product of industrial technology—the railroad—cemented the union between the Northeast and the Midwest. As late as 1852 canals were

AMERICAN VOICES

A German Immigrant on Life in Ohio

In 1836 twenty-four-year-old Ernst Stille left his family's overcrowded farm in Prussia and, nearly destitute, settled in Cincinnati. After ten years of hard work, Stille had not achieved his dream of landed independence.

May 20th [1847]
Dearest friends and relatives,
. . . The only people who are really happy here are those who were used to hard work in Germany and with toil and great pains could hardly even earn their daily bread. When people like that come here, even if they don't have any money, they can manage, they rent a room and the husband goes to work, earns his dollar a day and so he can live well and happily with a wife and children. But a lot of people come over here who were well off in Germany but were enticed to leave their fatherland by boastful and imprudent letters from their friends or children and thought they could become rich in America. This deceives a lot of people, since . . . if they want to live in the country and don't have enough money to buy a piece of land that is cleared and has a house then they have to settle in the wild bush and have to work very hard to clear the trees out of the way so they can sow and plant. . . . Here in Cincinnati I know a lot of people who have made it by working hard like Ernst Lots for example he does very well he also owns a brickyard and earns good money. . . . A good worker can do his day's work in 10 hours, earn one dollar and live well on that with a wife and children, and have such good food and drink like the best burgher in Lengerich [Stille's hometown in Germany]. . . .
    My plan is if I stay in good health for the next couple of years to buy a piece of land and live there, since from my childhood I've been used to farming, I'd rather do that than stay in the city all of my life, [but] you can't start very well unless you have 300 dollars.

SOURCE: Wolfgang Helbich, Walter Kamphoefner, and Ulrike Sommer, eds., *News from the Land of Freedom: German Immigrants Write Home* (Ithaca, N.Y.: Cornell University Press, 1991), pp. 85–87. © C.H. Beck'she Verlagsbuchhandlung (Oscar Beck), Munich.

carrying twice the tonnage of railroads, but in the next six years track mileage increased dramatically. The new railroads included trunk lines that stretched across New York and Pennsylvania to provide through traffic from New York City and Philadelphia to Cleveland and Chicago (see Map 13.2). More convenient and faster than canals, railroads became the main carriers of freight by 1859. They hastened the settlement of areas that canal and river transport could not serve and made western farming more profitable by lowering the cost of transporting farm goods to market. This *national* market in wheat forced some eastern farmers out of business and prompted others to turn to market gardening.

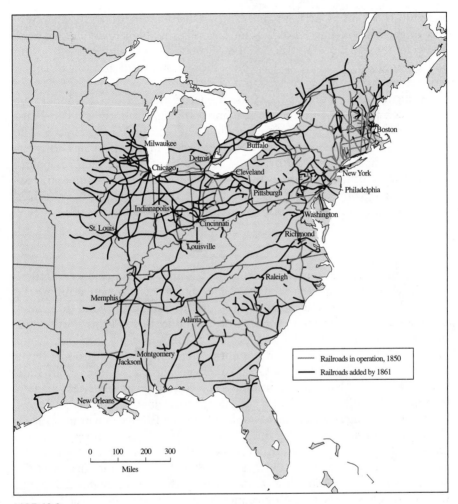

MAP 13.2
Railroads of the North and South, 1850–1860
In the decade before the Civil War the rapid construction of railroads provided the Northeast and the Midwest with extensive and dense transportation systems that stimulated economic development. The South built a much simpler system. In all regions, railroad lines used different track gauges, hindering the efficient flow of traffic. During the war such problems hampered military operations, especially in the South.

Railroads also promoted the development of commercial and manufacturing cities. Entrepreneurs congregated wherever railroad lines converged or met water transport, establishing grain storehouses, flour mills, packing plants, and docks and providing work for hundreds of artisans and laborers. Shopkeepers and insurance brokers quickly followed, as did manufacturers. In 1846 Cyrus McCormick moved his reaper factory from western Virginia to Chicago to be closer to his midwestern customers. As key railroad junctions and industrial centers, St. Louis and Chicago became boom towns. Thanks in part to the balloon-frame house, which was first developed in Chicago, they grew rapidly into cities. By 1860 St. Louis and Chicago had surpassed Boston and Baltimore in size and had become the nation's third and fourth largest cities, respectively, after New York and Philadelphia.

Railroad construction speeded the modernization of the iron industry, a critical component of northeastern manufacturing. Railroads needed high-quality iron, and so Philadelphia rail mills raised their technical standards. The engineering requirements for train engines had a similar effect on steam engine production in the Northeast and the Midwest, where railroads built a large network of machine shops to service their locomotives. Although separated by geography, the Midwest and the Northeast increasingly resembled each other in ethnic composition, cultural values, and technical skills.

Texas

At the same time that northern farmers and European migrants were settling the Midwest, migrants from the Ohio Valley and the South were claiming the best lands in Arkansas and southern Missouri, pushing just beyond their western boundaries to the 95th meridian of longitude. Beyond this north-south line stretched the semiarid Great Plains. In 1820 an army explorer, Major Stephen H. Long, had described the entire area between the Missouri River and the Rocky Mountains as a Great American Desert, "almost wholly unfit for cultivation." Sharing this assumption, land-hungry American planters looked southward toward Mexican territory, especially the province of Texas.

Texas had long been a zone of conflict between European nations. During the eighteenth century the Spanish had employed Tejas or Texas (so called after the local native American word for "friends") as a buffer against the French. After the Louisiana Purchase in 1803, Texas became Spain's buffer against Americans. Although adventurers from the United States did arrive, the Adams-Onís treaty of 1819 guaranteed Spanish sovereignty over Texas.

After winning independence from Spain in 1821, the Mexican government encouraged its own citizens and colonists from the United States to settle in Texas. To win the allegiance of the Americans, the Mexican government granted them some of the best land in Texas (see Map 13.3). One early grantee was Moses Austin, whose son Stephen F. Austin established a thriving American settlement by offering large land grants at a low cost. By 1830 about 7,000 Americans were living in eastern and central Texas, far outnumbering the 3,000 Mexicans in the southwestern towns of Goliad and San Antonio. The Americans did not assimilate Mexican culture and defied various Mexican laws, including an edict of 1829 ending slavery. By 1835, 27,000 Americans and their 3,000 slaves were living in Texas, raising cotton and cattle.

When the Mexican government tried to assert control over Texas, the resident Americans split into two groups. The "peace party," under the leadership of Stephen Austin, worked to win more self-government for the province within

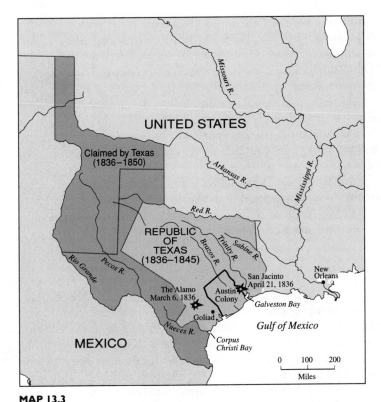

MAP 13.3
American Settlement in Texas
In 1821 Stephen F. Austin established the first organized Anglo-American settlement in Texas on land granted to his father by the Mexican authorities. By 1834 he had issued land titles to more than 1,000 settlers, who grew cotton and exported it from Corpus Christi Bay and Galveston Bay.

Mexico, while the "war party" demanded independence. Austin won significant reforms, but before he could achieve statehood for Texas within Mexico, General Antonio López de Santa Anna became president, appointed a military commandant for Texas, and centralized power in Mexico City. Santa Anna's actions prompted the American war party to provoke a rebellion that most of the American settlers ultimately supported. On March 2, 1836, the rebels proclaimed the independence of Texas and adopted a constitution legalizing slavery.

Santa Anna vowed to put down the rebellion. Four days after the declaration of independence, his army wiped out the garrison defending the Alamo in San Antonio. After capturing the settlement of Goliad, the Mexican chief ordered the execution of 371 rebel prisoners, whom he regarded as mercenaries rather than Texans because they had just arrived from the United States. Santa Anna thought he had crushed the rebellion, but the battle of the Alamo had captured the attention of New Orleans and New York newspapers. Their correspondents romanticized the heroism of the Texans at the Alamo and the deaths of the folk heroes Davy Crockett and Jim Bowie. Using some of the strongest anti-Catholic rhetoric of the day, the newspapers described the Mexicans as tyrannical butchers in the service of the pope. Thousands of American adventurers, lured by Texan offers of land bounties, set sail from New York, the Gulf states, and the Mississippi Valley. Reinforced by the new arrivals and led by General Sam Houston, the rebels routed the Mexicans in the Battle of San Jacinto on April 21, 1836, establishing de facto independence. The Mexican government refused to recognize the new republic but abandoned efforts to reconquer it.

The Texans immediately voted by plebiscite for annexation by the United States, but Presidents Andrew Jackson and Martin Van Buren refused to act. They knew that adding Texas as a slave state would divide the Democratic party and the nation and almost certainly lead to war with Mexico.

Oregon and California

The annexation of Texas became a more pressing issue in the 1840s as American expansionists developed continental ambitions. Those ambitions were captured by the term Manifest Destiny, coined in 1845 by John L. O'Sullivan, the editor of the *Democratic Review*. As O'Sullivan put it, "Our manifest destiny is to overspread the continent allotted by Providence for the free development of our yearly multiplying millions." Behind the rhetoric of Manifest Destiny was a sense of cultural and even racial superiority; "inferior" peoples—such as native Americans—were to be brought under American dominion, taught about republican forms of government, and converted to Protestantism. O'Sullivan left the geographic scope of Manifest Destiny vague but clearly implied that the United States had a divinely inspired mission to bring the entire West, including parts of Mexico and Canada, into the American republic.

In fact, many residents of the Ohio River Valley were casting their eyes westward to the fertile valleys of the Oregon Country, which was claimed by Great Britain as well as the United States. In 1818 a British-American convention had established the 49th parallel as the Canadian-American boundary up to the Rocky Mountains but no farther, allowing both Britons and Americans to settle anywhere in the disputed region. At that time Oregon stretched from the 42nd parallel in the south (the border with the Mexican province of California) to 54° 40′ in the north (the border with Russian Alaska). Subsequently, the British-run Hudson's Bay Company carried on a lucrative fur trade north of the Columbia River, while several hundred Americans settled to the south, mostly in the Willamette Valley. On the basis of this settlement, the United States established a claim to the zone between the 42nd parallel and the Columbia River.

In 1842 American interest in Oregon increased dramatically. Navy lieutenant Charles Wilkes published glowing reports of the potential harbors he had found in the Strait of Juan de Fuca, Admiralty Inlet, and Puget Sound, which were of great interest to New England merchants plying the China trade. Also in 1842 the first large party, over a hundred people, crossed the Oregon Trail that fur traders and explorers had blazed through the Great Plains and the Rocky Mountains (see Map 13.4). Their reports told of a mild climate and fertile soil. "Oregon fever" raged. In May 1843 over a thousand men, women, and children gathered in Independence, Missouri, for the trek to Oregon. The migrants were mostly farming and trading families from Missouri and the Ohio Valley: Kentucky, Tennessee, and the southern parts of Indiana and Ohio. They had more than 100 wagons and 5,000 oxen and cattle. With military-style organization and formations, the pioneers overcame flooding streams, dust storms, dying livestock, and encounters with Indians. After a journey of six months, they reached the Willamette Valley, more than 2,000 miles across the continent. During the next two seasons another 5,000 people reached Oregon.

By the Civil War 350,000 Americans, including many from the Midwest, had braved the Oregon Trail. Over 34,000 people died in the effort, mostly from disease and exposure; only 400 deaths came from Indian attacks. The walking migrants wore 3-foot-deep paths, and their wagons carved 5-foot-deep ruts,

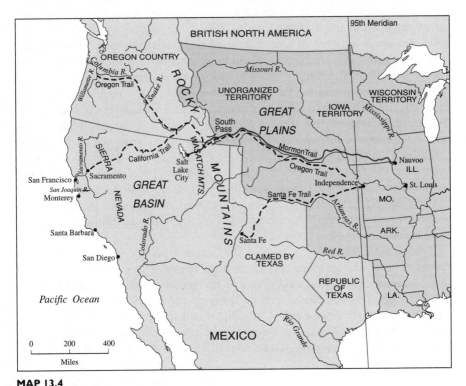

MAP 13.4
Settlement of the Trans-Missouri West
In the 1840s tens of thousands of Americans crossed the Great Plains in huge wagon trains. The Mormons settled in the Salt Lake basin; other pioneers pressed on to Mexican California and the Oregon Country. There was remarkably little crime on these treks because most migrants were deeply religious or were committed to the rule of Anglo-American law, which they enforced through political compacts and self-created institutions.

across sandstone formations in southern Wyoming—tracks that are visible today. Women found the trail especially difficult, for it pulled them away from friends, exaggerated the authority of their husbands, and added to their traditional chores the strenuous work of driving wagons and animals. Some pioneers ended up in the Mexican province of California. They left the Oregon Trail just past Fort Hall on the Snake River and struggled southward down the California Trail, settling in the interior valley of the Sacramento River.

California had been the remotest corner of Spain's American empire, and Spain had established a significant foothold there only in the 1770s, when it built a chain of coastal missions and presidios along the coast (see Chapter 8). New England merchants soon struck up trade with the new California settlements, largely for sea otter pelts that they carried to China. Commerce increased after Mexico won independence from Spain in 1821. To promote the economic development of California, the new Mexican government secularized the California missions, liberating more than 20,000 Indians who had been forced to work for the friars, and promoted large-scale cattle ranching on former mission lands.

The rise of cattle ranching created a new society and economy. While some mission Indians joined native American peoples in the interior of California, many remained in the coastal region. They intermarried with the local *mestizos* (Mexicans of mixed Spanish and Indian ancestry) and worked as laborers and cowboys. New England merchants carried the leather and tallow produced on the large California *ranchos* to customers in the booming Massachusetts boot and shoe industry. To handle the increased business, New England firms dispatched dozens of resident agents to California. Unlike the Americans in Texas, many of those New Englanders assimilated Mexican culture. They married into the families of the elite Mexicans—the *Californios*—and adopted their dress, manners, outlook, and Catholic religion. A crucial exception was Thomas Oliver Larkin, the most successful merchant in Monterey. Larkin established a close working relationship with Mexican authorities and often lent them money, but he remained an American citizen and plotted for the peaceful annexation of California to the United States. In 1843 he became the U.S. consul in California.

Like Larkin, American settlers in the Sacramento Valley had no desire to assimilate into Mexican society. Their legal standing was uncertain because they had received dubious land grants or had squatted without any title. They hoped to emulate the Americans in Texas by colonizing the country, overwhelming what they regarded as an inferior culture, and then seeking annexation by the United States. However, these settlers numbered only about 700 in the early 1840s, compared to the coastal population of 7,000 Mexicans and 300 American traders.

The Election of 1844

The future course of American policy toward California, Oregon, and Texas would be determined by the election of 1844. Since 1836, when Texas first requested annexation to the United States, some southern leaders had favored territorial expansion to protect and extend the slave system. They had been opposed not only by cautious party politicians and northern abolitionists but also (southerners came to think) by British diplomacy. In 1839 Britain and France had intervened in Mexico to force it to pay its foreign debts, and there were rumors that Britain wanted California as payment. Southern leaders also saw evidence that Britain was encouraging Texas to remain independent and had designs on Spanish Cuba, which some southerners wanted to annex as a slave state. It all seemed to add up to a grand scheme concocted by British abolitionists to block American expansion—and the spread of slavery—to the south and west. To thwart this design southern expansionists demanded the annexation of Texas.

Simultaneously, "Oregon fever" and Manifest Destiny altered the political and diplomatic landscape in the North. In 1843 Americans throughout the Ohio Valley and the Great Lakes states called on the federal government to renounce the joint occupation of Oregon and oust the British. Democrats and Whigs jointly organized "Oregon conventions," and in July a bipartisan national convention demanded that the United States seize Oregon all the way to 54° 40′ north latitude, the southern limit of Russian Alaska.

Now that northerners too were demanding expansion, southern Democrats could champion the annexation of Texas without threatening party unity. President John Tyler, disowned by the Whigs because of his opposition to Henry Clay's nationalist economic program, hoped to win reelection in 1844 as a Democrat or as the head of a new political party. To curry favor among expansionists, Tyler proposed both the annexation of Texas and the seizure of Oregon to the 54° 40′ line. In April 1844 Tyler and John C. Calhoun, his new secretary of state, submitted to the Senate a treaty for the annexation of Texas. The treaty was opposed by two other leaders with presidential ambitions: the Democrat Martin Van Buren and the Whig Henry Clay. Each feared alienating northern voters by supporting the annexation of Texas. At their urging, Whigs and northern Democrats united to defeat the treaty.

The annexation of Texas became the central issue in the election. The Democrats passed over Tyler, whom they did not trust, and Van Buren, whom southern Democrats despised for his stance on Texas. Instead, they selected former Governor James K. Polk of Tennessee, a slaveowner who was Andrew Jackson's personal favorite and carried the nickname "Young Hickory." Unimpressive in appearance, Polk was a man of iron will and boundless ambition for the nation. He called for the annexation of Texas and taking all of Oregon. "Fifty-four forty or fight!" became the patriotic cry of his campaign.

The Whigs nominated Henry Clay, who once again championed his American System of internal improvements, high tariffs, and national banking. Throughout the campaign Clay dodged the issue of Texas, finally suggesting that under certain circumstances he might support annexation. His position disappointed thousands of northern Whigs and Democrats who opposed any expansion of slavery. Rather than vote for Clay, some antislavery advocates supported the Liberty party's candidate, James G. Birney of Kentucky. Birney won less than 3 percent of the popular vote but probably took enough votes from Clay in New York to cause him to lose that state by 5,000 votes. By winning New York's 36 electoral votes, Polk won by a margin of 170 to 105 in the electoral college. (Without New York, he would have lost by 141 to 134.)

After Polk's victory, congressional Democrats closed ranks and moved immediately to bring Texas into the Union. Unable to secure a two-thirds majority in the Senate for a treaty with the Texas Republic, they approved annexation by a joint resolution of Congress, which required only a majority vote in each house. Mexico challenged the legality of Congress's action—it had never recognized the independence of the Republic of Texas—and broke off diplomatic relations with the United States. But Polk's strategy of linking Texas and Oregon had been successful. And the continuing dispute with Mexico over Texas would soon give him the opportunity to assert American control over even more territory in the West, fulfilling the dreams of the most ardent advocates of Manifest Destiny.

CHAPTER 13 TIMELINE

1830s	Slavery defended as a "positive good"
	Expansion of Cotton Kingdom and domestic slave trade
	Growth of cattle ranching in Mexican California
1836	Texas proclaims independence from Mexico
1840s	Spread of factory system to many industries
	Large-scale Irish migration caused by potato famine
1842	Overland migration to Oregon begins
1844	Anti-Catholic rioting in Philadelphia
	Texas and Oregon questions dominate election
1845	Lowell Female Labor Reform Association formed
	John L. O'Sullivan coins term *Manifest Destiny*
	Texas admitted to the Union as a slave state
1849	Cholera epidemics in cities
1850	A. J. Downing's *The Architecture of Country Houses*
1850s	Growth in number of fugitive slaves and underground railroad
	Immigrants replace native-born women as textile operatives
	Rise of middle-class consumer culture
	Chicago and St. Louis become major cities
1857	Hinton Helper attacks slaveowning aristocracy
	Financial panic begins economic depression

CHAPTER 14

THE CRISIS OF THE UNION, 1845-1860

- War, Expansion, and Slavery, 1845–1850
- The End of the Second Party System, 1850–1858
- Abraham Lincoln and the End of Union, 1858–1860

For nearly a generation after the Missouri Compromise of 1820 the two major political parties prevented a confrontation between evangelical abolitionism and the proslavery movement by devising programs that were *national* in appeal. But the compromise worked only so long as the territory of the United States remained unchanged. The annexation of Texas in 1846 and the subsequent war with Mexico prompted a fateful political struggle over the extension of slavery into the West.

As politicians searched desperately for a formula to resolve the status of slavery in the new lands, the nation experienced a decade-long series of crises—first over California and fugitive slaves, then over the settlement of Kansas, and finally over the constitutional status of slavery. "That Union should so long have been preserved in a confederacy which contains an element of discord of such magnitude and of so disturbing a nature as that of Slavery is a wonder," Martin Van Buren reflected in 1856. But even as he spoke, the trust and goodwill that had preserved the Union for nearly three generations were being shattered.

WAR, EXPANSION, AND SLAVERY, 1845-1850

James K. Polk and the Democrats had swept to victory in 1844 by promising the immediate annexation of Texas and laying claim to all of Oregon. But

Polk had even greater territorial ambitions: he wanted all of Mexico west of Texas to the Pacific Ocean and was prepared to go to war to get it. What he was not prepared for, though he should have been, was the major crisis over slavery unleashed by the success of his expansionist dreams.

The War with Mexico, 1846–1848

Mexico had not prospered in the twenty-five years since it won independence from Spain in 1821. Its population remained small at seven million people, and its stagnant economy yielded only modest tax revenue, much of which was eaten up by interest payments on foreign debt and a bloated and often corrupt government bureaucracy. Consequently, the Mexican republic lacked the money and people to settle its distant northern provinces. The Spanish-speaking population of California and New Mexico remained small—about 75,000 in 1840—and contributed little to the national economy. Still, the fledgling Mexican government was determined to retain all its historical territories, and when the breakaway Texas Republic accepted American statehood on July 4, 1845, Mexico broke off diplomatic relations with the United States.

President James Polk viewed that action as a great opportunity. Since taking office in March 1845, Polk had moved quickly to implement Congress's resolution annexing Texas and had devised a secret plan to acquire all Mexico's far northern provinces. To intimidate the Mexican government, he ordered General Zachary Taylor and an American army of 2,000 soldiers to occupy the disputed lands between the Nueces River (the historical boundary of the Mexican province of Texas) and the Rio Grande, which the expansionist-minded Texas Republic claimed as its southern and western border (see Map 14.1). Then Polk launched a diplomatic initiative, dispatching John Slidell on a secret mission to Mexico City. Slidell was instructed to secure Mexico's acceptance of the Rio Grande boundary and buy the Mexican provinces of New Mexico and California, paying as much as $30 million. When Slidell arrived in December 1845, Mexican officials refused to see him, declaring that the American annexation of Texas was illegal.

Anticipating the failure of Slidell's mission, Polk had already embarked on an alternative plan to take California. The president's strategy was to foment a revolution that, as in Texas, would lead to the creation of an independent republic and a request for annexation. In October 1845 he had Secretary of State James Buchanan advise Thomas O. Larkin, the U.S. consul in the major port of Monterey, that the United States would protect Californians if they sought independence from Mexico. Larkin immediately encouraged leading Mexican residents to support a peaceful shift of sovereignty. To add military muscle to any uprising, Polk sent orders to John Sloat, the commander of the U.S. naval squadron in the Pacific, to seize San Francisco Bay and California's coastal towns in the event of war. The president also had the War department dispatch Captain John C. Frémont and an "exploring" party of heavily armed soldiers deep into Mexican territory. By December 1845 Frémont had reached California's Sacramento Valley.

MAP 14.1
The War with Mexico, 1846–1848
American forces easily seized Monterey and San Fransisco but encountered strong Mexican resistance in southern California at San Pascual and San Gabriel. In the heart of Mexico, Santa Anna took advantage of the division of American forces to attack the army of Zachary Taylor at Buena Vista (February 1847). Repulsed by Taylor's smaller force, Santa Anna retreated south to Mexico City, where he was decisively defeated by another American army led by Winfield Scott.

Events now moved quickly toward war. When Polk learned of the failure of Slidell's mission, he ordered General Taylor to build a fort near the Rio Grande, hoping to incite an armed response by Mexico. As Ulysses S. Grant, a young officer serving with Taylor, said much later, "We were sent to provoke a fight, but it was essential that Mexico should commence it." When Mexican and American forces clashed near the Rio Grande in May 1846, Polk delivered the war message he had drafted long before, saying that Mexico "has passed the boundary of the United States, has invaded our territory, and shed American blood upon the American soil." Ignoring Whig pleas for a peaceful resolution of the dispute, the Democratic majority in Congress voted for war with Mexico, unleashing large and almost hysterical demonstrations of popular support. To avoid a simultaneous war with Britain over Oregon, the president retreated from his campaign pledge of "fifty-four forty or fight" and accepted a British proposal to divide the Oregon region at the 49th parallel.

As the Senate ratified the Oregon Treaty with Great Britain in June 1846, fighting broke out in California between American naval forces and Mexican authorities. Commander John Sloat landed 250 marines and seamen in Monterey and declared that California "henceforward will be a portion of the United States." American settlers in the interior staged a revolt and, supported by Frémont's forces, captured the town of Sonoma. To ensure American control of California, Polk ordered army units under General Stephen Kearney to capture Santa Fe in New Mexico (which they did in August) and march to the Pacific Ocean. Despite stiff resistance from the Mexicans, American forces secured control of all of California early in 1847 (see Map 14.1).

Zachary Taylor's army in Texas had been equally successful. In May 1846 the American forces had crossed the Rio Grande, occupied Matamoros, and moved south, using their advantage in artillery to win a series of victories against a larger Mexican army. After a fierce six-day battle in September, Taylor took the interior town of Monterrey. Two months later, a U.S. naval squadron in the Gulf of Mexico seized Tampico, Mexico's second most important port. By the end of 1846 the United States controlled much of northeastern Mexico.

Polk expected that these American victories would prompt the Mexicans to sue for peace, but he had underrated their national pride and strength. Under the newly elected president General Antonio Lopez de Santa Anna, Mexico refused to end the fighting. Instead Santa Anna went on the offensive, attacking the depleted units of Zachary Taylor at Buena Vista in February 1847. Only superiority in artillery enabled Taylor to eke out a victory and hold the American line in northeastern Mexico.

To bring Santa Anna to terms, Polk accepted the plan devised by General Winfield Scott, a veteran army officer, to strike deep into the heart of Mexico. In March 1847 Scott captured the port of Veracruz and began the 260-mile march to Mexico City that the Spanish conquistador Hernando Cortés had taken three centuries earlier. Leading Scott's 14,000 troops was a cadre of talented West Point officers who would become famous in the Civil War: Robert E. Lee, George Meade, and P. G. T. Beauregard. Scott's troops crushed Santa Anna's attempt to block their march at Cerro Gordo, and after inflicting heavy losses on the Mexican army at the Battle of Churubusco, his much-depleted troops seized Mexico City in September 1847. Santa Anna was overthrown, and the new Mexican government agreed to make peace. The war was finally over.

The Wilmot Proviso, Free Soil, and the Election of 1848

Initially many Americans viewed the war with Mexico as a noble struggle to extend American republican institutions across the continent. But the conflict quickly became politically divisive. A few Whigs, such as Charles Francis Adams of Massachusetts and Joshua Giddings of Ohio, had opposed the war from the beginning on moral grounds (becoming known as "conscience Whigs"), viewing it as a conspiracy to add new slave states in the West. They argued that the expansion of slavery would jeopardize the Jeffersonian ideal of a yeoman freeholder society and assure control of the federal government by slaveholding Democrats. These antislavery Whigs grew bolder after the elections of 1846, which gave their party control of Congress. After Taylor's victory at Buena Vista in February 1847, Whigs in the House passed a resolution that congratulated the army but condemned the war, declaring that it had been "unconstitutionally and unnecessarily begun by the President." Whigs grew more vocal as American casualties mounted, particularly during the bloody march to Mexico City.

Whig leaders moved toward an antislavery stance partly because their economic program—especially their support for high tariffs—had lost its appeal. In 1846 Polk and the Congressional Democrats had passed the Walker Tariff, which dramatically reduced duties on imported goods. The Walker Tariff came hard on the heels of Britain's repeal of the Corn Laws (which had placed high duties on imported wheat and corn) and seemed to herald the adoption of free trade throughout the Anglo-American world. American consumers welcomed cheaper prices on imported goods, and their increased purchases pushed up tariff revenues, allowing Polk to finance the war without raising taxes. Given the popularity of free trade, the Whigs could no longer count on winning elections by championing higher tariffs.

As a result of Polk's expansionist policy, the Democrats had even worse problems. In August 1846, David Wilmot, a Democratic representative from Pennsylvania, proposed a simple amendment to a military appropriations bill: slavery would be prohibited in any new territories acquired from Mexico. This provision, known as the Wilmot Proviso, quickly became a rallying point for northerners who feared the expansion of slavery. In the House the Democratic party split as supporters of Martin Van Buren joined forces with antislavery Whigs to pass the Proviso. The Senate, dominated by southerners and proslavery northern Democrats, killed it.

In this heated atmosphere, the most fervent Democrat expansionists became even more aggressive. Polk, Secretary of State Buchanan, and Senators Stephen A. Douglas of Illinois and Jefferson Davis of Mississippi wanted the United States to take at least part of Mexico south of the Rio Grande. But some southerners worried that the United States could not absorb the Mexicans, whom they regarded as an "inferior" people, and feared that a longer war would augment the power of the federal government. John C. Calhoun supported taking only California and New Mexico, the most sparsely populated areas of Mexico. Midwestern Democrats also opposed expansion to the south, in part because of their anger at Polk's compromise with Britain over Oregon.

To reunify the Democratic party before the next election, Polk and Buchanan abandoned their expansionist dreams in Mexico and accepted Calhoun's policy. In February 1848 Polk signed the Treaty of Guadalupe Hidalgo, in which the United States agreed to pay Mexico $15 million in return for more than one-third of its territory: Texas north of the Rio Grande, New Mexico, and California (see Map 14.2). The United States also agreed to assume all the claims of its citizens, totaling $3.2 million, against the Mexican government. The Senate ratified the treaty in March 1848.

The passions aroused by the war dominated the election of 1848. The Wilmot Proviso had energized abolitionists who had been seeking a legislative solution to the problem of slavery, and the Senate's refusal to pass it alarmed them. Antislavery advocates now claimed that southern planters and their northern business allies had entered into a massive "Slave Power" conspiracy to expand the bounds of slavery. To defeat this alleged plan, a significant number of northerners joined a new "free-soil" movement. The free-soilers abandoned the Liberty party's focus on the sinfulness of slavery and the natural rights of African-Americans. Instead, they depicted slavery as a threat to republican institutions and yeoman farming and vowed to prevent its geographic expansion. This shift in emphasis—toward keeping the West open for settlement by white

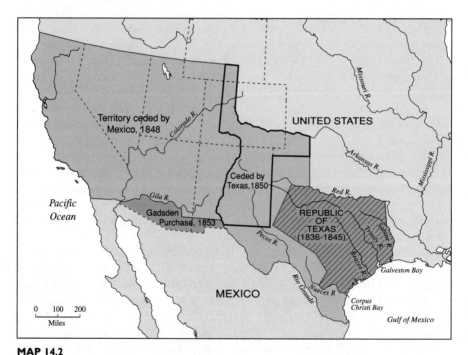

MAP 14.2
The Mexican Cession, 1848
The War with Mexico added a vast territory to the United States: the present states of California, Nevada, Utah, most of Arizona and New Mexico, more than half of Texas, and parts of Wyoming, Colorado, Kansas, and Oklahoma. After Mexico ratified the Treaty of Guadalupe Hidalgo, Polk told Congress that the new territories "constitute of themselves a country large enough for a great empire, and their acquisition is second in importance only to that of Louisiana in 1803."

families and away from freeing slaves—led the radical abolitionist William Lloyd Garrison to denounce free-soil doctrine as racist "whitemanism."

Despite Garrison's hostility, the new political approach worked. The Wilmot Proviso's call for free soil was the first antislavery proposal to attract broad popular support. Hundreds of women in the Great Lakes states joined new female free-soil organizations formed by the American and Foreign Anti-Slavery Society. Frederick Douglass, the foremost black abolitionist, also endorsed free soil, seeing it as the best way to provoke a political struggle between the North and the South that would overthrow slavery. At the same time Douglass urged free-soilers to pay less attention to white demands for land and more attention to the needs of African-Americans, seeking their emancipation in the South and civil rights in the North.

The conflict over slavery took a toll on Polk and the Democratic party. Opposed by free-soilers and exhausted by his rigorous dawn-to-midnight work regime, Polk declined to run for a second term and died three months after leaving office. To maintain unity, the Democrats nominated Senator Lewis Cass of Michigan, an avid expansionist who had advocated buying Cuba, annexing Mexico's Yucatan Peninsula, and taking all of Oregon. Cass campaigned on a platform that was deliberately vague on the question of slavery in the West. He promoted a new idea—*squatter sovereignty*—that would give settlers in each territory the power to determine its status as free or slave.

Cass's political ingenuity failed to hold the party together. Demanding unambiguous opposition to the expansion of slavery, some northern Democrats joined the newly formed Free Soil party, which nominated Martin Van Buren for president. Van Buren's conversion to free soil was genuine, but he also wanted to punish southern Democrats for having denied him the presidential nomination in 1844. To attract Whig votes, the Free Soil party chose a conscience Whig, Charles Francis Adams, as its candidate for vice-president.

To avoid such divisions in their party, the Whigs nominated General Zachary Taylor. Taylor was a southerner and a Louisiana slaveowner, but he had not taken a position on the politically charged issue of slavery in the territories. Equally important, the general's exploits during the War with Mexico had made him a popular hero. Known as "Old Rough and Ready," Taylor possessed a common touch that had won him the affection of his troops. "Our Commander on the Rio Grande," wrote Walt Whitman, "emulates the Great Commander of our revolution"—George Washington.

In 1848, as in 1840, running a military hero worked for the Whigs, but only barely. Taylor took 47 percent of the popular vote against 42 percent for Cass, but the margin in the electoral college was thin: 163 to 127 electoral votes. The Free Soil ticket of Van Buren and Adams made the difference in the election, winning 10 percent of the popular vote and depriving the Democrats of enough votes in New York to cost Cass that state and the presidency. The popularity of the Wilmot Proviso and the rapid growth of the Free Soil party had changed the dynamics of American politics.

1850: Crisis and Compromise

Even before President Taylor took office, events in California had sparked a major political crisis that threatened the Union. In January 1848 (a few months before California formally became part of the United States), workmen building a mill for John A. Sutter discovered flakes of gold in the Sierra Nevada foothills in northern California. Sutter was a Swiss immigrant who arrived in California in 1839, became a Mexican citizen, and established an almost feudal estate in the Sacramento Valley. He tried to keep the discovery a secret, but by May Americans were pouring into the foothills from San Francisco. When President Polk confirmed the discovery in December, the gold rush was on. By January 1849 sixty-one crowded ships had departed from northeastern ports to sail around Cape Horn for San Francisco, and by May 12,000 wagons had crossed the Missouri River, also bound for the goldfields. In 1849 alone more than 80,000 migrants—the "forty-niners"—arrived in California.

The rapid influx of settlers revived the national debate over free soil. The forty-niners, who lived in crowded, chaotic towns and mining camps, demanded the formation of a territorial government to protect their lives and property. To avoid an extended debate over slavery, President Taylor advised the Californians to apply for statehood immediately, and in November 1849 they ratified a state constitution that prohibited slavery. Few of the many southerners who flocked to the goldfields or to San Francisco owed slaves or wanted to; only ranchers in sparsely populated southern California had strongly promoted slavery. For his part, Taylor wanted to attract Free Soilers

California Prospectors
Beginning in 1849, thousands of fortune seekers from all parts of the world converged on the California goldfields. By 1852 the state had 200,000 residents, including 25,000 Chinese, many of whom worked as wage laborers in the goldfields. These prospectors are using a primitive technique—panning—to separate gold from sand and gravel.

The Allure—and Reality—of the Gold Rush

The discovery of gold in California prompted tens of thousands of easterners to head west. Among them were Catherine Haun and her lawyer husband, who, like many others, found adventure but not riches.

Early in January of 1849 we first thought of emigration to California. It was a period of national hard times, and we being financially involved in our business interests near Clinton, Iowa . . . longed to go to the new El Dorado and "pick up" gold enough with which to return and pay off our debts. . . .

Full of the energy and enthusiasm of youth, the prospects of so hazardous an undertaking had no terror for us. Indeed, as we had been married but a few months, it appealed to us as a romantic wedding tour. . . . Some half dozen families of our neighborhood joined us and probably about twenty-five persons constituted our little band. . . .

Eight strong oxen and four of the best horses on the farm were selected to draw our four wagons. . . . Two wagons were filled with merchandise which we hoped to sell at fabulous prices when we should arrive in the "land of gold." The theory of this was good but the practice—well, we never got the goods across the first mountain. . . .

Our caravan had a good many women and children, and although we were probably longer on the journey owing to their presence, they exerted a good influence, as the men did not take such risks with Indians and thereby avoided conflict; . . . more attention was paid to cleanliness and sanitation; and . . . the meals were more regular and better cooked, thus preventing much sickness. . . .

[W]e reached Sacramento on November 4, 1849, just six months and ten days after leaving . . . [but] it was past the middle of January before we reached Marysville—there were only a half dozen houses, all occupied at exorbitant prices. Someone was calling for the services of a lawyer to draw up a will, and my husband offered to do it, for which he charged $150. This seemed a happy omen for success and he hung out his shingle, abandoning all thought of going to the mines.

SOURCE: Diary of Catherine Haun, Huntington Library, San Marino, California (MSS HM 538). Reprinted by permission of The Huntington Library.

and northern Democrats into the Whig party and urged Congress to admit California as a free state.

Southern politicians were alarmed by the swift victory of the antislavery forces in California. Not only had a valuable area been lost to free soil, but the admission of California would threaten the carefully maintained balance in the Senate. In 1845 the entry of Texas and Florida had raised the total of slave states to fifteen, against thirteen free states. However, the entry of Iowa in 1846 and Wisconsin in 1848 had reestablished the balance. Now southern leaders feared that the admission of California would give the North a majority in the Senate as well as the House, placing their section at a political disadvantage from which it would never recover. They were prepared to block the entry of California as a free state unless the federal government guaranteed the future of slavery.

The resulting impasse produced long and passionate debates in Congress. As usual, John C. Calhoun took the most extreme southern position, warning of possible secession by the slave states and civil war. To avoid that outcome, he proposed that slavery be guaranteed in all the territories and that a constitutional amendment be adopted to create a permanent balance of power between the sections. The presidency would become a dual office, with authority divided between executives from the South and the North, each with full veto power.

In making those proposals, Calhoun advanced a radically new constitutional doctrine: Congress had no constitutional authority to regulate slavery in the territories and thus could not exclude slavery from a territory before its admission as a state. This argument ran counter to a half century of practice. Congress had prohibited slavery in the Northwest Territory and, by the Missouri Compromise of 1821, in most of the Louisiana Purchase.

While Calhoun's new doctrine won support in the Deep South, many southerners were prepared to accept a more moderate position with respect to the status of slavery in the West: an extension of the Missouri Compromise line to the Pacific Ocean. This would guarantee slaveowners access to some western territory (in a separate state in southern California, for example) and add more slave states to the Union. Some northern Democrats, including former Secretary of State James Buchanan, also favored this plan as a way to resolve the crisis.

A third alternative was squatter sovereignty, Lewis Cass's platform in the election of 1848, now being championed by Democratic Senator Stephen Douglas of Illinois. Douglas called his plan *popular sovereignty* to emphasize its roots in republican ideology, and it had considerable appeal. Popular sovereignty would place decisions about slavery in the hands of local settlers and their territorial governments rather than in Congress, removing the explosive issue from national politics. However, popular sovereignty was a vague and slippery concept, because it was not clear at what point the people of a territory could legalize or ban slavery—when the territory was first organized or later when it framed a constitution and applied for statehood.

Antislavery advocates were unwilling to accept *any* expansion of slavery, lending credence to Calhoun's warning of the possible breakup of the Union. In 1850 Senator Salmon P. Chase of Ohio, elected by a Democratic–Free Soil coalition, and Senator William H. Seward, a New York Whig, urged federal authorities to contain slavery and then extinguish it completely. Condemning slavery as "morally unjust, politically unwise, and socially pernicious" and invoking "a higher law than the Constitution," Seward demanded bold action to protect freedom, "the common heritage of mankind."

Standing on the brink of disaster, senior Whigs and Democrats desperately sought a compromise. Through a long, complex legislative process, the Whig leaders Henry Clay and Daniel Webster and the Democrat Stephen A. Douglas organized a complex package of six laws known collectively as the Compromise of 1850. To mollify the South, the Compromise included a new Fugitive Slave Act that strengthened a law of 1793 by allowing slaveowners to use federal magistrates to return runaway slaves. To satisfy the North, the Compromise admitted California as a free state, resolved a boundary dispute between New Mexico and Texas in favor of New Mexico through federal assumption of $10 million in unpaid debts of the Republic of Texas, and abolished the slave trade, but not slavery, in the District of Columbia. Finally, the Compromise organized the rest of the lands acquired from Mexico into the territories of New Mexico and Utah on the basis of popular sovereignty.

The Compromise averted a secession crisis in 1850—but only barely. In the midst of the struggle the governor of South Carolina declared that there was not "the slightest doubt" that his state would secede. He and the leaders of Georgia, Mississippi, and Alabama organized special conventions to protect "Southern Rights" and demand secession. Although moderate southern politicians persuaded the convention delegates to support the Compromise, in return they had to agree to support secession in the future if Congress abolished slavery anywhere, failed to recognize slavery in a new territory, or refused to admit a territory with a proslavery constitution into the Union. Lacking the support of other slave states, the "fire-eaters" in South Carolina drew back from secession, averting a constitutional crisis. The fact that the Compromise of 1850 elicited such a passionately negative response throughout the Deep South—and among many northern Whigs and Free Soilers as well—did not augur well for its success.

THE END OF THE SECOND PARTY SYSTEM, 1850–1858

The architects of the Compromise of 1850 hoped that their agreement, like the Missouri Compromise of 1820, would resolve the issue of slavery for another generation. But their hopes were quickly dashed as one conflict after another divided Americans along sectional lines. Demanding freedom for fugitive slaves and free soil in the West, some northerners blocked implementation of the Compromise, while some southerners insisted on the expansion of slavery not just in the West but in the Caribbean. These disputes led to violence and destroyed the Second Party System, deepening the crisis of the Union.

The Fugitive Slave Act

The most controversial element of the Compromise proved to be the Fugitive Slave Act. Under its terms, federal judges or special commissioners in the northern states determined the status of blacks who were accused of being runaway slaves. A commissioner would receive a $10 fee if an alleged fugitive was found to be a runaway but only $5 if he or she was declared a free person—clear encouragement for a slavery verdict. The accused blacks were denied jury trials and even the right to testify; their supporters faced stiff penalties if they defied the law. Because federal marshals were legally required to support slave catchers, the new legislation was effective and many fugitives (as well as some free blacks) were sent to the South and enslaved.

The plight of runaways and the appearance of slave catchers in northern communities aroused popular hostility, and free blacks and abolitionists organized vigilante groups to block enforcement of the act. In October 1850 Theodore Parker and other Boston abolitionists defied the law by helping two slaves escape to freedom and driving a Georgia slave catcher out of town. A year later rioters broke into a courthouse in Syracuse, New York, and freed a fugitive slave. Abandoning pacifism, Frederick Douglass declared that "the only way to make a Fugitive Slave Law a dead letter is to make half a dozen or more dead kidnappers." As if in response, in September 1851 a deadly confrontation took place in the Quaker village of Christiana, Pennsylvania. About twenty African-Americans, including several escaped slaves, exchanged gunfire with a group of slave catchers from Maryland; the slaveowner was killed, and his son was severely wounded. Millard Fillmore, who had become president after the death of Zachary Taylor in 1850, sent troops and federal marshals to arrest thirty-six blacks and four whites and had them indicted for treason. But a jury acquitted one defendant, and northern public opinion forced the government to drop its charges against the rest.

Harriet Beecher Stowe's abolitionist novel, *Uncle Tom's Cabin* (1852), increased northern opposition to the Fugitive Slave Act. The novel tells of a compassionate but weak slaveholder in Kentucky who sells two slaves, Tom and a five-year-old boy, to a slave trader to pay off debts. The beautiful Eliza Harris, the boy's mother, refuses to be separated from her son. With the child in her arms, she crosses the Ohio River on cakes of ice just ahead of the vicious slave trader. Eliza reaches the house of an Ohio politician who, to preserve the Union, had set aside his "private feeling" and voted for a fugitive slave law. His wife persuades him to follow his heart and help Eliza and her child escape to Canada. Meanwhile, Tom has fallen under the control of Simon Legree, a brutal overseer on a southern plantation, who beats Tom to death but never conquers his Christian soul. By translating the moral principles of abolitionism into heartrending personal situations, Beecher's novel evoked a mixture of empathy and outrage throughout the North. More than 300,000 Americans bought copies of *Uncle Tom's Cabin,* and countless families flocked to an emotionally charged stage version produced by local theater companies.

Responding to the growing popular opposition to slave catching, some northern legislatures challenged federal authority by enacting *personal liberty* laws that extended legal rights to accused fugitives. In 1857 the Wisconsin Supreme Court went even further. In *Ableman v. Booth* the Wisconsin judges

Uncle Tom's Cabin
In these illustrations from the original 1852 edition of *Uncle Tom's Cabin*, the engraver portrays Eliza Harris (top panel) as a caring mother and Tom (bottom) as a well-dressed and noble servant. Like the book's text, these images offered whites a sympathetic view of African-Americans, challenging generations of negative stereotypes.

claimed the authority to void federal statutes, ruling that the Fugitive Slave law could not be enforced in their state because it violated the Constitution. Then they contested the power of the federal courts to review their decision, directly challenging a jurisdictional doctrine that had been accepted for more than a generation. When the case was finally considered by the U.S. Supreme Court in 1859, Chief Justice Taney led a unanimous court in affirming the supremacy of federal over state courts—a position that has stood the test of time—and upheld the constitutionality of the Fugitive Slave law. But by that time popular sentiment in many northern states had made it impossible to catch fugitive blacks or secure their conviction. As Douglass had hoped, the act had become a "dead letter."

The Whigs' Decline and the Democrats' Diplomacy

The conflict over fugitive slaves split the Whig party, which went into the election of 1852 weakened by the deaths of Zachary Taylor and Henry Clay, one of its greatest leaders. Passing over Fillmore because of his reputation as an aristocratic snob and vigorous enforcement of the Fugitive Slave Act, the Whigs nominated General Winfield Scott, another hero of the War with Mexico. But about a third of southern Whigs refused to support Scott and, angry over the party's pronorthern economic stance and growing opposition to slavery, threw their support to the Democrats.

The Democrats too were divided. Southerners wanted a candidate who would support Calhoun's position that all territories should be open to slavery, but northern delegates rejected that idea outright. They were committed to the principle of popular sovereignty but were sharply divided among the three candidates—Lewis Cass, Stephen Douglas, and James Buchanan—who supported it. For forty-eight ballots no one could secure the necessary two-thirds majority. Exhausted, the convention settled on a compromise candidate, Franklin Pierce of New Hampshire, a handsome and congenial man reputed to be sympathetic to the South.

The Democrats' cautious strategy paid off, and they swept the election. Pleased by the admission of California as a free state, Martin Van Buren and many other Free Soilers voted for Pierce, reuniting the Democratic party. Conversely, the election fragmented the Whig party. The massive exodus of southerners undermined its status as a national party, and it soon split into sectional wings. The Whigs would never again wage a national campaign.

As president, Pierce pursued an expansionist foreign policy. To assist northern merchants, he supported an ongoing effort to expand trade with Asia by dispatching a mission to Japan that successfully negotiated a commercial treaty. But Pierce was even more solicitous of southern interests. To resolve a dispute over the southern boundary of New Mexico, the president revived Polk's plan to annex Mexican territory south of the Rio Grande. Pierce and his secretary of war, Jefferson Davis, sent James Gadsden to buy a major portion of northern Mexico and Baja (Lower) California. Mexican officials refused to part with those large territories but agreed to the sale of 30,000 square miles of land south of the Gila River. Gadsden, a South Carolina politician and railroad promoter, wanted this territory to expedite the construction of a southern transcontinental railroad to the Pacific. Completed in 1854, the Gadsden Purchase, as it became known, rubbed salt into Mexico's war wounds, reminding it of the power of its northern neighbor.

Pierce's most dramatic foreign policy initiative came in the Caribbean. Southern expansionists had funded three clandestine military expeditions to Spanish Cuba, where they hoped to prod the slaveowning elite into declaring independence. Once Cuba was independent, it would be invited to join the Union as a slave state. In 1853 Pierce covertly supported a new Cuban expedition led by John A. Quitman, a former governor of Mississippi. While Quitman was building up his forces, the Pierce administration threatened war with Spain over the seizure of an American ship, demanding an apology and a large indemnity. But when northern Democrats in Congress refused to support aggressive diplomacy designed to add a new slave state, Pierce and Secretary of State William L. Marcy had to back down.

Still determined to seize Cuba, Marcy instructed the American minister in Madrid "to detach that island from the Spanish dominion" by purchase. When that initiative also failed, Marcy encouraged the minister and the

American diplomats in France and Great Britain to pressure Pierce to seize the island. The result was an inflammatory message to Pierce that became known as the Ostend Manifesto (1854). Invoking the rhetoric of Manifest Destiny, the three American ministers declared that the United States would be justified in seizing Cuba "by every law, human and Divine." Quickly leaked to the press by antiexpansionists, the Ostend Manifesto triggered a new wave of northern resentment against the South and forced Pierce to halt his efforts to acquire Cuba. But the Democrats' policy of expansionism in the Caribbean had already revived northern fears of a "Slave Power" conspiracy.

Kansas-Nebraska and the Rise of New Parties

Almost immediately a new struggle over westward expansion deepened sectional divisions. Because the Missouri Compromise prohibited slavery in the Louisiana Purchase north of 36° 30′, southern senators had delayed the political organization of that area, allowing only the admission of Iowa to the Union in 1846 and the formation of the Minnesota Territory. Even though much of the remaining area was in the "Great American Desert," westward-looking residents of the Ohio River Valley and the Upper South demanded that it be organized for settlement. Senator Stephen A. Douglas of Illinois became their foremost spokesman, championing western development and the building of a northern transcontinental railroad from Chicago to California. In 1854 Douglas introduced a bill to extinguish native American rights on the central Plains and organize a large territory to be called Nebraska. Because Nebraska was north of 36° 30′, it would be a free territory.

Douglas's bill conflicted with the plans of southern senators, who were determined to extend slavery throughout the Louisiana Purchase and, like James Gadsden, hoped that a city in a slaveholding state—New Orleans, Memphis, or St. Louis—would become the eastern terminus of a transcontinental railroad. To win southern support for the organization of Nebraska, Douglas made two major concessions. First, he amended his bill so that it explicitly repealed the Missouri Compromise, which had prohibited slavery in the northern part of the Louisiana Purchase. The region would be organized on the basis of popular sovereignty. Second, Douglas agreed to the formation of two new territories, Nebraska and Kansas, rather than one, giving slaveholders a chance to dominate the settlement of Kansas, the more southern territory (see Map 14.3). To win northern support for this scheme, Douglas argued that Kansas would be settled primarily by non-slaveholders because its climate and terrain were not suited to plantation agriculture. Supported primarily by southern representatives (along with some northern Democrats), the Kansas-Nebraska Act passed in May 1854.

The Kansas-Nebraska Act proved to be the last nail in the coffin of the Second Party System of Whigs and Democrats. Abolitionists and free-soilers

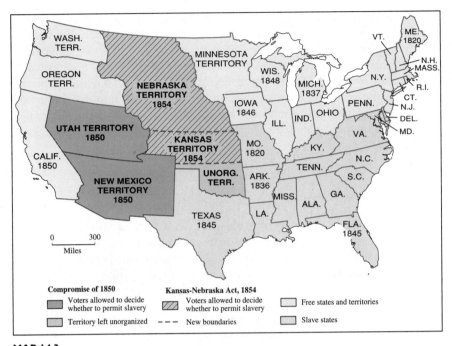

MAP 14.3
The Compromise of 1850 and the Kansas-Nebraska Act, 1854
Vast territories were at stake in the contest over the extension of slavery. The Compromise of 1850 resolved the status of lands in the Far West: California would be a free state, and the settlers of the Utah and New Mexico territories would decide their own fate. The implementation of popular sovereignty in Kansas and Nebraska sparked a local civil war, revealing a fatal flaw in the concept.

denounced the act for opening new territories to slavery, calling it "part of a great scheme for extending and perpetuating supremacy of the slave power." Antislavery northern Whigs and "Anti-Nebraska" Democrats abandoned their respective parties to create a new party, taking the Jeffersonian name *Republican*. Emphasizing uncompromising opposition to the expansion of slavery, the Republicans ran a slate of candidates, primarily in the Midwest, in the congressional election of 1854.

Like most American parties, the Republican party was a coalition of diverse groups—Free Soilers, antislavery Democrats, conscience Whigs—but its founders shared a distinct vision. In the Republican view, slavery produced only two classes of people: masters and slaves. The masters were corrupted by wielding unlimited power, a system of rule that produced habits of subservience, ignorance, and sloth among slaves and poor whites. In contrast, Republicans such as Senator Thaddeus Stevens of Pennsylvania celebrated the virtues of a society based on "the middling classes who own the soil and work it with their own hands." They envisioned communities in which no person would have unlimited power over another and social mobility would prevent the division of society into fixed classes. Abraham Lincoln, an Illinois Whig who became a Republican, articulated the party's vision. "There is no permanent class of hired laborers among us," he argued, and every man had a chance to become an owner. "The man who labored for another last year, this year labors for himself, and next year he will hire others to labor for him." In the face of increasing class divisions in the industrializing North and Midwest, Lincoln and his fellow Republicans asserted the values of republican freedom, individual enterprise, and social mobility.

Competing for Whig and Democratic votes was another new party, the "Know-Nothing," or American, party. The Know-Nothing party had its origins in the anti-immigrant, anti–Catholic passions of the 1840s (see Chapter 13). In 1850 various secret anti–Catholic societies banded together in the Order of the Star-Spangled Banner; a year later they formed the American party. The secrecy-conscious members of the party sometimes answered outsiders' questions by saying "I know nothing," which gave the party its nickname, but its program was far from secret. Know-Nothings attempted to unite northern and southern voters behind a program of nativist opposition to the "alien menace": Irish and German Catholics. Many supported a ban on immigration and advocated literacy tests for voters, which they thought would disfranchise most recent immigrants. In 1854 the Know-Nothings gained control of the state governments of Massachusetts and Pennsylvania and, allied with the Whigs, commanded a majority in the U.S. House of Representatives. The emergence of a new major party led by nativists suddenly became a real possibility.

At that moment the implementation of the Kansas-Nebraska Act created a new political crisis. In 1854 thousands of settlers began to rush into Kansas, putting Douglas's theory of popular sovereignty to the test. On the side of slavery, Senator David R. Atchison of Missouri organized residents of his state to cross into Kansas and vote in crucial elections. Opposing him were agents of the New England Emigrant Aid Society, organized by abolitionists to colonize Kansas with free-soilers. The preference of the Pierce administration was clear. In March 1855 the administration recognized the territorial legislature in Lecompton, Kansas, which had been elected largely by proslavery Missourians who had crossed the border to cast ballots. The territorial legislature declared that questioning the legitimacy of slavery was a felony and aiding a fugitive slave was a capital offense. Pierce assisted the legislature with federal troops and proslavery judicial appointees, but free-soilers rejected the legitimacy of the territorial government.

In May 1856 both sides turned to violence. A proslavery gang, 700 strong, sacked the free-soil town of Lawrence, destroying two newspaper offices, looting stores, and burning down buildings. The attack on Lawrence enraged John Brown, an abolitionist from New York and Ohio, whose free-state militia force arrived too late to save the town. Brown was a complex man with a checkered past. Born in 1800, he had started more than twenty businesses in six states, had fallen into bankruptcy, and had often been sued by his creditors.

Free State Battery, 1856
In Kansas the Civil War began in 1856 as free-soilers from the upper Midwest fought with
proslavery forces from Missouri. "[I am using] my utmost endeavors to change the attitude of
the Free State settlers from a defensive to an offensive warfare," a young man wrote to his
brother in Indiana, but "I found that arms were really scarce." This cannon had seen service in
the War with Mexico.

Nonetheless, he had an intelligence and a moral intensity that won the trust of
influential people, including leading abolitionists. According to a free-soil
minister who knew him, Brown believed "that God had raised him up on
purpose to break the jaws of the wicked." Taking vengeance for the sack of
Lawrence three days later, he and a few followers murdered and mutilated five
proslavery settlers. We must "fight fire with fire" and "strike terror in the
hearts of the proslavery people," Brown declared. The "Pottawatomie massacre," as the killings became known, initiated a guerrilla war in Kansas that
cost about 200 lives.

The violence that began in Kansas spread within a week to the halls of
Congress. In an inflammatory speech, "The Crime against Kansas," Senator
Charles Sumner of Massachusetts denounced the Pierce administration, the
South, and Senator Andrew P. Butler of South Carolina, who Sumner said had
taken "the harlot slavery" as his mistress. Butler's nephew and protégé, Congressman Preston Brooks, took offense at Sumner's attack. Brooks accosted
Sumner at his desk and beat him on the head with a walking cane. Severely
injured, Sumner did not return to the Senate for two and a half years; Massachusetts venerated him as a martyr, keeping his seat open for him. Southern

"Bleeding Kansas": A Southern View

Early in 1856 Axalla John Hoole and his bride left South Carolina to build a new life in Kansas. These letters show that things did not go well from the start and only got worse; after eighteen months the Hooles returned to South Carolina. A Confederate militia captain, Axalla Hoole died in the Battle of Chickamauga in September 1863.

Kansas City, Missouri, Apl. 3d., 1856

My Dear Brother . . .
The Missourians . . . are very sanguine about Kansas being a slave state & I have heard some of them say it *shall* be . . . but generally speaking, I have not met with the reception which I expected. Everyone seems bent on the Almighty Dollar, and as a general thing that seems to be their only thought. . . .

Lecompton, K.T., Sept. 12, 1856

My dear Mother . . .
I have been unwell ever since the 9th of July. . . . I thought of going to work in a few days, when the Abolitionists broke out and I have had to stand guard of nights when I ought to have been in bed, took cold which . . . caused diarrhea. . . . Betsie is well—
    You perceive from the heading of this that I am now in Lecompton, almost all of the Proslavery party between this place and Lawrence are here. We brought our families here, as we thought that we would be better able to defend ourselves. . . .

Lane [and a Free State army] came against us last Friday (a week ago to-day). As it happened we had about 400 men with two cannon . . . but we were acting on the defensive, and did not think it prudent to commence the engagement.

Douglas, K.T., July the 5th., 1857

Dear Sister . . .
I fear, Sister, that [our] coming here will do no good at last, as I begin to think that this will be made a Free State at last. 'Tis true we have elected Proslavery men to draft a state constitution, but I feel pretty certain, if it is put to a vote of the people, it will be rejected, as I feel pretty confident that they have a majority here at this time. The South has ceased all efforts, while the North is redoubling her exertions. . . .

SOURCE: William Stanley Hoole, ed., "A Southerner's Viewpoint of the Kansas Situation, 1856–1857," *Kansas Historical Quarterly* (1934), vol. 3: 43–68, 145–171, passim.

representatives prevented the House from censuring Brooks, and when he resigned, South Carolina voters not only returned him to Congress but also sent
him a batch of new canes to replace the one he had broken in the attack. Passion had replaced compromise as the hallmark of American politics.

Buchanan's Failed Presidency

The violence in Kansas dominated the presidential election of 1856. The Democrats reaffirmed their support for popular sovereignty and the Kansas-
Nebraska Act, but, to counter the impact of "Bleeding Kansas" on northern
voters, turned away from Pierce and nominated James Buchanan of Pennsylvania. A tall, dignified, white-haired figure of sixty-four years, Buchanan was
an experienced but unimaginative and timid politician.

The two-year-old Republican party counted on anger over "Bleeding
Kansas" to boost its fortunes. The party's platform denounced the Kansas-
Nebraska Act and, alleging a "Slave Power" conspiracy to expand slavery, insisted that the federal government prohibit slavery in all the territories. As one
Republican put it, "If we do not exclude slavery from the Territories, it will
exclude us." The platform also called for federal subsidies to transcontinental
railroads, reviving the element of the Whig economic program that was most
popular among midwestern Democrats. For president, the Republicans nominated John C. Frémont, a free-soiler famous for his role in the conquest of
California.

The American party entered the election with high hopes, but it quickly
split into warring factions—North and South—over the struggle in Kansas.
The Republicans cleverly maneuvered the northern faction into endorsing
Frémont and won the support of many Know-Nothing workingmen by
adding anti-Catholic nativism to its program of high tariffs on imported manufactures. As a Pennsylvania congressman declared, "Let our motto be, protection to *everything American, against everything foreign.*" The southern faction of
the American party nominated Millard Fillmore, who ran an effective campaign and won 21 percent of the national vote but only 8 electoral votes.

James Buchanan, the Democrat, won the three-way race. Some southern
Democrats openly threatened secession if Frémont won, and, fearful of such a
cataclysm, enough northern Democrats remained loyal to the party to give
the election to Buchanan, who drew 1.8 million votes (45 percent) to 1.3 million (33 percent) for Frémont. Frémont demonstrated the appeal of the new
Republican party in the North by carrying eleven free states with 114 electoral votes. Buchanan took only five free states, and a small shift of the popular
vote to Frémont in Illinois and Pennsylvania would have won him the
presidency.

The dramatic restructuring of parties was now apparent. The Know-
Nothings had lost their bid to become a major party, and the Republicans had
replaced the Whigs in the contest with the Democrats for national supremacy.
Because the Republicans had no support in the South, the implications for

the sectional crisis were ominous; a victory for the new party might mean the end of the Union. The fate of the Republic hinged on the ability of President Buchanan to achieve a new compromise that would protect free soil in the West and slavery in the South.

Events—and his own values and weaknesses—conspired against Buchanan. Although Congress had long regulated slavery in the territories, its authority to do so had never been subjected to a clear test of constitutionality. In 1856 the case of Dred Scott reached the Supreme Court. Scott was an enslaved African-American who had lived for a time with his master, an army surgeon, in the free state of Illinois and at Fort Snelling in the Wisconsin Territory (later incorporated into the Minnesota Territory), where the Northwest Ordinance (1787) and the Missouri Compromise (1820) prohibited slavery. In his suit, which he filed in Missouri in 1846, Scott claimed that his residence in a free state and a free territory had made him free. In March 1857, only two days after Buchanan's inauguration, the Court announced its decision in *Dred Scott v. Sandford.*

Seven members of the Court concurred on one critical point: Scott remained a slave. But the judges in the majority could not agree on the legal issues raised by the case, and each justice wrote a separate opinion. In the most influential opinion, Chief Justice Roger B. Taney of Maryland declared that blacks, slave *or* free, could not be citizens of the United States and that Scott therefore had no right to sue in federal court. That argument was controversial enough, since free African-Americans could be citizens of a state (which would give them the right to enter federal courts). But Taney went on to make two even more controversial points. First, he repeated John C. Calhoun's argument that because the Fifth Amendment prohibited the taking of property without due process of law, Congress could not prevent southern citizens from taking their slave "property" into the territories or owning it there. Therefore, the chief justice concluded, the Northwest Ordinance and the Missouri Compromise—which prohibited slavery in the territories—had *never* been constitutional, and so Scott's residence at Fort Snelling could not have freed him. Second, Taney declared that Congress could not give to territorial governments any powers that Congress itself did not possess. Since Congress had no authority to prohibit slavery in a territory, neither did a territorial government. Thus Taney also endorsed Calhoun's interpretation of popular sovereignty: only when settlers wrote a constitution and requested statehood could they prohibit slavery.

Five of the seven justices in the majority, including the chief justice, were Democrats from slave states. They and President Buchanan—who privately twisted the arm of his fellow Pennsylvanian, Justice Robert C. Grier, to join the five—intended to make political policy as well as constitutional law. They hoped their decision would be accepted out of respect for the Court and ease the sectional crisis. The result was just the opposite. In a single stroke a Democrat-dominated Supreme Court had declared the Republicans' antislavery platform unconstitutional, a decision the Republicans could never accept.

Led by Senator William H. Seward of New York, they accused the Supreme Court and President Buchanan of participating in the "Slave Power" conspiracy.

Buchanan then made things worse. In early 1858 he recommended the admission of Kansas as a slave state under the constitution written by proslavery forces, the so-called Lecompton constitution. Most observers—including the Democrat Stephen Douglas—believed that constitution had been enacted by fraudulent means. Angered that Buchanan would not permit a referendum in Kansas on the constitution, Douglas broke with the president and his southern allies and mobilized western Democrats and Republicans in the House of Representatives to prevent the admission of Kansas as a slave state. (Kansas would enter the Union as a free state in 1861, after many southern representatives had left Congress.) By pursuing a proslavery agenda—first in the *Dred Scott* decision and then in Kansas—Buchanan had split his party and the nation.

ABRAHAM LINCOLN AND THE END OF UNION, 1858–1860

The crisis of the Union intensified as the national Democratic party fragmented into sectional factions and the Republicans gained the support of a majority of northern voters. During this transition Abraham Lincoln emerged as the pivotal figure in American politics, the only Republican leader whose policies and temperament might have saved the Union. But few southerners trusted Lincoln, and his election threatened to unleash the secessionist movement that had menaced the nation since 1850.

Lincoln's Early Career

The rise of the middle class in the small towns of the Ohio River Valley shaped Lincoln's early career. He came from a farming family of modest means that, searching for prosperity, had moved from Kentucky, where Lincoln was born in 1809, to Indiana and then Illinois. In 1831 Lincoln rejected the life of a farmer and began working as a store clerk in New Salem, Illinois. There he won the admiration of the young men who hung out in local saloons, who elected him captain of a company of militia. A socially ambitious young man, Lincoln also sought entry into the cultured world of the middle class, becoming a member of the New Salem Debating Society. With the help of the local schoolmaster he mastered English grammar and elementary mathematics, and another villager introduced him to Shakespeare.

Lincoln's ambition was "a little engine that knew no rest," as a close associate later remarked. Admitted to the bar in 1837, Lincoln moved to Springfield, the small country town that had become the new state capital. There he met Mary Todd, the daughter of a successful Kentucky businessman and politician; they married in 1842. The couple were a picture in contrasts. Her tastes were aristocratic; his were humble. She was volatile; he was easygoing and deliberate.

Bouts of depression, which plagued Lincoln throughout his life, tried her patience and tested his character. Entering political life, Lincoln served four terms as a Whig in the lower house of the Illinois legislature, where he promoted education, state banking, and internal improvements such as turnpikes, canals, and railroads. An effective speaker, he campaigned actively for William Henry Harrison in 1840 and for his political hero, Henry Clay, in 1844. In 1846 Lincoln won election to Congress.

Abraham Lincoln
Abraham Lincoln was the most photographed man of his time, yet none of the photographs convey his wit, charm, and intelligence. The photography of that day required subjects to stand absolutely still for long periods, causing Lincoln to appear as a formal, rather distant man or, as here, giving him a sad and abstracted air.

As a member of Congress during the War with Mexico, Lincoln had been forced to take a stand on the contentious issue of slavery. He had long felt that slavery was unjust and in 1838 had condemned mob violence against abolitionists. But Lincoln had little sympathy for abolitionism and did not believe that the federal government had the constitutional authority to tamper with slavery in the southern states. Still, he knew that the Whig party had to hold the allegiance of the growing number of people opposed to the expansion of slavery.

Lincoln sought a middle ground. He supported the appropriations bill that sustained Polk's war in Mexico but, to express opposition to the spread of slavery, voted for the Wilmot Proviso. He also proposed the gradual abolition of bondage in the District of Columbia, advancing a plan that would provide compensation to slaveowners and require approval in a referendum of the "free white citizens" of the District. Lincoln argued that such measures—firm opposition to the expansion of slavery, gradual emancipation, and the colonization of freed slaves in Africa and elsewhere—represented the only practical way to address the issue. But his ideas were derided by both sides. Abolitionists assailed him as "the slave hound of Illinois," and proslavery voters in southern Illinois condemned his support for the Wilmot Proviso. Dismayed, Lincoln withdrew from politics and devoted his energies to an increasingly lucrative legal practice representing railroads and manufacturers in Illinois.

Lincoln returned to the political fray after the passage of Stephen Douglas's Kansas-Nebraska Act. Attacking Douglas's position on popular sovereignty in what became known as his Peoria address, Lincoln articulated a clear position on slavery. He would not threaten the institution in areas where it existed, but would use the authority of the national government to exclude it from the territories. Beyond that, Lincoln expressed his conviction that the nation must eventually cut out slavery like a "cancer."

Abandoning the Whig party in favor of the Republicans, Lincoln soon emerged as their leader in Illinois. Campaigning for the U.S. Senate against Stephen Douglas in 1858, Lincoln alerted his audiences to the dangers of the "Slave Power" conspiracy. He warned that the proslavery Supreme Court might soon declare that the Constitution "does not permit a *state* to exclude slavery from its limits," just as it had decided (in *Dred Scott*) that "neither Congress nor the territorial legislature can do it." In that event, he continued, "we shall *awake* to the *reality* . . . that the *Supreme Court* has made *Illinois* a *slave* state."

The fear that slavery would be extended throughout the nation was widely felt in the North in the wake of the *Dred Scott* decision and informed Lincoln's famous "House Divided" speech. Quoting from the Bible, "A house divided against itself cannot stand," he predicted a constitutional crisis that would bring either the triumph or the demise of slavery:

> I believe this government cannot endure permanently half *slave* and half *free*. I do not expect the Union to be dissolved—I do not expect the house to *fall*—but I do expect it will cease to be divided. It will become *all* one thing, or *all* the other.

Lincoln's Victory and the Nation's Fate

Lincoln's 1858 duel with Stephen Douglas for the U.S. Senate attracted national interest because of Douglas's prominence and Lincoln's reputation as a formidable speaker. To increase his national reputation, Lincoln challenged Douglas to a series of seven debates. During those debates Lincoln attacked slavery as an institution that subverted equality of opportunity. While expressing doubts about the innate abilities of those of African descent and rejecting proposals that would give them social and political equality, he declared that blacks were entitled to "all the natural rights enumerated in the Declaration of Independence." This meant, Lincoln explained, that "in the right to eat the bread, without leave of anybody else, which his own hand earns," the black was "the equal of every living man." Taking the offensive, Lincoln pressed Douglas to explain how he could accept the *Dred Scott* decision (which allowed slaveowners to bring their property into the territories) and at the same time advocate popular sovereignty.

In a debate in Freeport, Illinois, Douglas responded by reformulating popular sovereignty. In what became known as the Freeport doctrine, he asserted that settlers could exclude slavery from a territory simply by not adopting local legislation to protect it. Even if territorial governments lacked the power to prohibit slavery, as Taney had argued in his *Dred Scott* opinion, municipalities could still do so by refusing to support the "peculiar institution." Douglas's Freeport statement upset both proslavery advocates, who feared they would be denied the victory won in the *Dred Scott* decision, and abolitionists, who were not convinced that local regulations would halt the expansion of slavery. Nonetheless the Illinois state legislature reelected the "Little Giant," as Douglas was called, to the Senate. Yet Lincoln had established himself as a national leader, and the Republican party, by winning control of the House of Representatives in the election of 1858, had moved a step closer to national power.

In the wake of Republican gains, southern Democrats divided into two groups. Moderates such as Senator Jefferson Davis of Mississippi, who were known as Southern Rights Democrats, pursued the traditional policy of seeking ironclad commitments to protect slavery in the territories. Radicals such as Robert Barnwell Rhett of South Carolina and William Lowndes Yancey of Alabama abandoned cooperation and actively promoted secession. They proposed extreme measures, such as the reopening of the Atlantic slave trade, in the hope of driving a wedge between the North and the South.

Radical northerners played into their hands. In 1858 William Seward declared that freedom and slavery were locked in "an irrepressible conflict." In October 1859, the militant abolitionist John Brown led eighteen heavily armed black and white men in a raid that seized the federal arsenal at Harpers Ferry, Virginia. Brown's explicit purpose was to provide arms for a slave rebellion that would establish an African-American state in the South. The local militia and U.S. Marines under the command of Colonel Robert E. Lee quickly reclaimed the arsenal, capturing Brown and killing ten of his party. Republican leaders disavowed Brown's raid, but Democrats called his plot, in

the words of Stephen Douglas, "a natural, logical, inevitable result of the doctrines and teachings of the Republican party." Fueling the Democratic charges
were letters that linked six leading abolitionists to the financing of Brown's
raid. The group included two Unitarian ministers, Theodore Parker, who was
active in the underground railroad, and Thomas Wentworth Higginson, a free-
soiler who would command a regiment of African-American soldiers during
the Civil War. Higginson admitted his involvement and declared that Brown's
"acquittal or rescue would do half as much good as [his] being executed; so
strong is the personal sympathy with him."

Virginia gave the abolitionists the Christian martyr they wanted. Brown
was charged with treason, sentenced to death, and hanged. At a church meeting in Concord, Massachusetts, Henry David Thoreau described Brown as "an
angel of light," "the bravest and humanest man in all the country." Slaveholders
were horrified by northern admiration of Brown and looked toward the future with fear. "The aim of the present black republican organization is the
destruction of the social system of the Southern States, without regard to consequences," warned one newspaper.

Nor could the South count on the Democratic party to protect its interests. At the April 1860 party convention, northern Democrats rejected Jefferson Davis's program to protect slavery in the territories, prompting the
delegates from eight southern states to leave the hall. When neither Douglas
nor anyone else could win the required two-thirds majority for the presidential nomination, the convention adjourned. At a second Democratic
convention in Baltimore, northern and western delegates nominated Douglas; southern Democrats met separately and nominated Buchanan's vice-
president, John C. Breckinridge of Kentucky. The Democratic party had
broken into two sectional pieces.

The Republicans sensed victory. They courted white voters by opposing
both slavery and racial equality: "Missouri for white men and white men for
Missouri," declared that state's Republican platform. On the national level, the
Republican convention chose Lincoln as its presidential candidate. Lincoln's
position on slavery was more moderate than that of the best-known Republicans, Senator William H. Seward of New York and Salmon P. Chase of Ohio,
who demanded measures that would lead to abolition. Lincoln also conveyed
a compelling egalitarian image that appealed to smallholding farmers and
wage earners. And Lincoln's home territory—the rapidly growing Midwest—
was crucial in the competition between Democrats and Republicans. The
Republican platform followed Lincoln's views and struck a moderate tone,
upholding free soil in the West and denying the right of states to secede but
ruling out direct interference with slavery in the South. In addition, the platform endorsed the old Whig program of economic development, which had
gained increasing support in the Midwest, especially after the Panic of 1857.

The Republican strategy was successful. Lincoln received only 40 percent
of the popular vote but won every northern and western state except New

Jersey and garnered a majority in the electoral college. Douglas drew support from all regions except the South (taking 30 percent of the total vote) but won electoral votes only in Missouri and New Jersey. Breckinridge captured every state in the Deep South as well as Delaware, Maryland, and North Carolina, while John Bell, a former Tennessee Whig who became the nominee of the Constitutional Union party, carried the Upper South states where the Whigs had been strongest: Kentucky, Tennessee, and Virginia. As the vote indicated, the nation had divided into two antagonistic sections.

The Republicans had united the Northeast, the Midwest, and the Far West behind free soil and had seized national power. To many southerners, it now seemed time to think carefully about the meaning of Lincoln's words of 1858, that the Union must "become all one thing, or all the other."

CHAPTER 14 TIMELINE

Year	Event
1845	Polk inaugurated
	Texas accepts admission to the Union
	Slidell's mission
1846	United States declares war on Mexico
	Oregon treaty ratified
	Walker Tariff lowers tariffs
	Wilmot Proviso introduced in Congress
1847	Winfield Scott captures Mexico City
1848	Gold discovered in California
	Treaty of Guadalupe Hidalgo
	Free Soil party organized
1850	Compromise of 1850
1851	American party formed
1854	Kansas-Nebraska Act
	Republican party formed
	Ostend Manifesto
	Know-Nothing movement peaks
1856	"Pottawatomie massacre"
	James Buchanan elected president
1857	*Dred Scott v. Sandford*
1858	Buchanan backs Lecompton constitution
	Lincoln-Douglas debates
1859	John Brown's raid on Harpers Ferry
1860	Abraham Lincoln elected president

CHAPTER 15

TWO SOCIETIES AT WAR, 1861–1865

- Secession and Military Stalemate, 1861–1862
- Toward Total War
- The Turning Point: 1863
- The Union Victorious, 1864–1865

For political leaders in the South, the victory of Abraham Lincoln and the Republicans in 1860 presented a clear and immediate danger. They knew that Lincoln regarded slavery as morally wrong and that the Republicans would unite northern society against the "Slave Power." There would be no extension of slavery into the territories. Moreover, unlike any preceding president, Lincoln owed the South not a single electoral vote. Soon, a southern senator warned, "cohorts of Federal office-holders, Abolitionists, may be sent into [our] midst." The result would be waves of bloody slave revolts.

To save slavery, radical southern leaders embarked on the dangerous journey of secession, leading their states out of the Union and establishing their own nation. If Lincoln and the Republicans would not allow them to leave peacefully, they would fight.

And so came the Civil War. Called the "War between the States" by southerners and the "War of the Rebellion" by northerners, the struggle resolved once and for all the great issue of slavery and redefined the character of the Union. The cost was high: more lives lost than in all the nation's subsequent wars put together and a century-long legacy of bitterness between the triumphant North and the vanquished South.

SECESSION AND MILITARY STALEMATE, 1861–1862

After Lincoln's election in November 1860, secessionist fervor swept through the Deep South. In the four months before Lincoln's inauguration in March 1861, political leaders in Washington struggled to forge a new compromise that (like those of 1787, 1820, and 1850) would preserve the Union.

Choosing Sides

The movement toward secession was most rapid in South Carolina—the home of Calhoun, nullification, and the Southern Radical movement. Robert Barnwell Rhett and other South Carolina fire-eaters had been planning for secession since 1850 and called a convention to achieve their goal. On December 20, the convention voted unanimously to dissolve "the union now subsisting between South Carolina and other States."

Moving quickly, fire-eaters in the six cotton states of the Deep South called similar conventions and organized vigilante groups and militia. In early January, in an atmosphere of public celebration, Mississippi enacted a secession ordinance. Within a month Florida, Alabama, Georgia, Louisiana, and Texas had also left the Union (see Map 15.1). In early February the jubilant secessionists met in Montgomery, Alabama, to proclaim a new nation—the Confederate

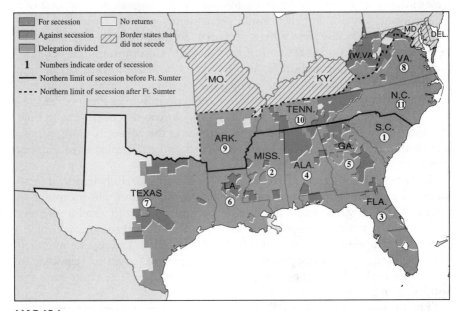

MAP 15.1
The Process of Secession
The states with the highest concentration of slaves (see Map 13.1) led the secessionist movement and, after the attack on Fort Sumter, were joined by the states of the Upper South. Yeoman farmers in Tennessee and the backcountry of Alabama, Georgia, and Virginia opposed secession but, except in the future state of West Virginia, generally supported the Confederate war effort.

States of America. They adopted a provisional constitution and named Jefferson Davis, a former U.S. senator and secretary of war, as provisional president.

Secessionist fervor was less intense in the eight Upper South states (Virginia, Delaware, Maryland, North Carolina, Kentucky, Tennessee, Missouri, and Arkansas). In January 1861 the legislatures of Virginia and Tennessee voted to resist any federal invasion of the seceded states but went no further. Seeking a compromise that would restore the Union, Upper South leaders proposed federal guarantees for slavery in the states where it existed.

Meanwhile, the Union government floundered. In his last message to Congress in December 1860, President Buchanan declared secession illegal but said that the federal government lacked the authority to restore the Union by force. South Carolina immediately claimed that Buchanan's message implied recognition of its independence and demanded the surrender of Fort Sumter, a federal garrison in Charleston harbor. Reluctant to turn over federal property, Buchanan decided to test the secessionists' resolve by ordering an unarmed merchant ship to resupply the fort. When the South Carolinians fired on the ship, Buchanan backed down, refusing to order the navy to escort it into the harbor.

As the crisis continued, Buchanan urged Congress to find a compromise. The proposal that received the most support was submitted by Senator John J. Crittenden of Kentucky, an aging follower of Henry Clay, one of the architects of the Compromise of 1850. Crittenden won congressional approval of a constitutional amendment that would permanently protect slavery from federal interference in any state where it existed. To deal with the territories, he called for the westward extension of the Missouri Compromise line (36° 30′ North) to the California border. Slavery would be barred north of the line and protected to the south, including any territories "hereafter acquired." After consulting with President-elect Lincoln, congressional Republicans rejected Crittenden's plan for the territories. Lincoln was determined to uphold the doctrine of free soil and feared that extending the Missouri Compromise line would encourage the South to embark on an imperialist expansion of slavery into Mexico, the Caribbean, and Latin America.

In his inaugural address on March 4, 1861, Lincoln carefully balanced a call for reconciliation with a firm commitment to the Union. He promised to permit slavery in states where it existed but stood firm for free soil in the territories. Most important, he stated that secession was illegal and that acts of violence in its support constituted insurrection. He announced that he intended to enforce federal law throughout the Union and—of particular relevance to Fort Sumter—hold federal property in the seceded states. The choice was the South's: return to the Union or face war.

The decision came quickly. Within a month of Lincoln's inauguration the garrison at Fort Sumter urgently needed supplies. To maintain his credibility, the new president dispatched a relief expedition, informing South Carolina that it would not land troops or arms unless the delivery of food and medicine was disrupted. Jefferson Davis and his government welcomed Lincoln's decision, believing that a confrontation would turn the wavering Upper South against the North and win foreign support for the Confederate cause. Resolving to take the fort before the arrival of the Union ships, Davis authorized General P. G. T. Beauregard to demand its surrender. When Major Robert Anderson refused to comply, the Confederate forces opened fire, forcing him to surrender on April 14. The next day Lincoln called 75,000 state militiamen into federal service for ninety days to put down an insurrection "too powerful to be suppressed by the ordinary course of judicial proceedings." All talk of compromise was past.

Northern states responded to Lincoln's call to arms with enthusiasm. Asked to provide thirteen regiments of volunteers, Republican Governor William Dennison of Ohio sent twenty. "The lion in us is thoroughly roused," he explained. Many northern Democrats were equally committed to the Union cause. As Stephen Douglas declared six weeks before his death: "Every man must be for the United States or against it. There can be no neutrals in this war, *only patriots—or traitors.*"

The white residents of the Upper South now had to choose between the Union and the Confederacy, and their decision was crucial. Those eight states accounted for two-thirds of the South's white population, more than three-fourths of its industrial production, and well over half its food and fuel. They were home to many of the nation's best military leaders, including Colonel Robert E. Lee of Virginia, a career officer whom General-in-Chief Winfield Scott recommended to Lincoln as field commander of the new Union army. And they were geographically strategic. Kentucky, with its 500-mile border on the Ohio River, was essential to the movement of troops and supplies. Maryland was vital to the Union's security because it surrounded the nation's capital on the north.

The weight of history decided the outcome in Virginia, the original home of American slavery. Three days after the fall of Fort Sumter, a Virginia convention passed an ordinance of secession by a vote of 88 to 55. The dissenting votes came mainly from the yeoman-dominated northwestern counties (see Map 15.1); elsewhere in Virginia whites rallied to the Confederate cause. Refusing Scott's offer to command the Union troops, Robert E. Lee resigned from the army. "Save in defense of my native state," Lee told Scott, "I never desire again to draw my sword." North Carolina, Tennessee, and Arkansas joined Virginia in the Confederacy.

Lincoln moved aggressively to hold the rest of the Upper South. In May he ordered General George B. McClellan to take control of northwestern Virginia, thus securing the railway line between Washington and the Ohio Valley. In October voters there overwhelmingly approved the creation of a new state, West Virginia, which was admitted to the Union in 1863. The Union cause was much less popular in Maryland, where support for slavery was strong. A pro-Confederate mob attacked Massachusetts troops marching between railroad stations in Baltimore, causing the war's first combat deaths: four soldiers and twelve civilians. When other Maryland secessionists destroyed railroad bridges and telegraph lines, Lincoln ordered military occupation of the state and imprisoned suspected secessionists, including members of the state legislature. He released them only in November 1861, after Unionists had gained control of the Maryland legislature.

In Missouri, the key to communications and trade on the Missouri and upper Mississippi rivers, Lincoln mobilized support among the large German-American community. In July a force of German-American militia defeated Confederate sympathizers commanded by the governor. Despite continuing raids by Confederate guerrilla bands led by William Quantrill and Jesse and Frank James, the Union retained control of Missouri.

In Kentucky secessionist and Unionist sentiment was evenly balanced, so Lincoln moved cautiously. Not until August, after Unionists had taken control of the state government, did he order federal troops to cut Kentucky's thriving export trade in horses, mules, whiskey, and foodstuffs to the Lower South. When the Confederacy responded by moving troops into Kentucky, the Unionist legislature asked for federal protection. In September, Illinois volunteers under the command of the relatively unknown brigadier general Ulysses S. Grant crossed the Ohio River and drove the Confederates out. Of the eight states of the Upper South, Lincoln had kept four (Delaware, Maryland, Kentucky, and Missouri) and a portion of a fifth (western Virginia) in the Union.

War Aims and Military Initiatives

After secession, Confederate leaders called on their people to defend the independence of the new nation. At his inauguration in February 1861, Jefferson Davis identified the Confederate cause with that of the American Revolution; like their grandfathers, white southerners were fighting against tyranny and for the "sacred right of self-government." As Davis put it, the Confederacy sought "no conquest, no aggrandizement, no concession of any kind from the states with which we were lately confederated; all we ask is to be let alone." The decision to focus on the defense of the Confederacy (and not to conquer western territories) gave southern leaders a strong advantage: they needed only a military stalemate to guarantee Confederate independence.

Lincoln made his first major statement on Union goals and strategy in a speech to Congress on July 4, 1861. Rejecting General Winfield Scott's plan to use economic sanctions and a naval blockade to persuade the Confederates to return to the Union, Lincoln called for an aggressive miliary strategy to put down the rebellion. He saw secession as an attack on republican government and the rule of law, America's great contribution to world history. The issue was simple: "whether a constitutional republic, or a democracy—a government of the people, by the same people—can or cannot maintain its territorial integrity against its domestic foes." Only by crushing the rebellion could the nation preserve its principles.

The president knew that the northern public wanted a strike toward Richmond, the Confederate capital, and he hoped an early victory would end the rebellion. He therefore dispatched General Irwin McDowell and an army of 30,000 men to attack P. G. T. Beauregard's force of 20,000 troops at Manassas, a major rail junction in Virginia 30 miles southwest of Washington. McDowell attacked strongly on July 21 near Manassas Creek (also called Bull Run), but panic swept through his troops during a Confederate counterattack. For the first time Union soldiers heard the hair-raising rebel yell. "The peculiar corkscrew sensation that it sends down your backbone under these circumstances can never be told," one Union veteran wrote. "You have to feel it." McDowell's troops retreated in disarray to Washington, along with the many civilians who had come to observe the battle. The victorious Confederate troops also dispersed, confused and without the wagons and supplies they needed to pursue McDowell's army.

It was now clear that the rebellion would not be easily crushed. To bolster northern morale, which had been shattered by the rout at Bull Run, Lincoln replaced McDowell with General George B. McClellan and signed bills for the enlistment of a million additional men, who would serve for three years in the newly created Army of the Potomac. A cautious military engineer, McClellan spent the winter of 1861–1862 training raw recruits, and in 1862 he launched the first major offensive of the war, a thrust toward Richmond. In a maneuver that required skillful logistics, the Union general transported about 100,000 troops by boat down the Potomac River and Chesapeake Bay and then up the peninsula between the York and James rivers toward the South's capital. But McClellan failed to anticipate a Confederate counterstroke. In May a Confederate army under Thomas J. ("Stonewall") Jackson marched rapidly north up the Shenandoah Valley, threatening Washington. To head off the danger, Lincoln diverted 30,000 troops from McClellan's army, but Jackson, a brilliant general, defeated three Union armies in the valley. Then Jackson joined the Confederates' formidable commanding general, Robert E. Lee, who had confronted McClellan outside Richmond. Lee launched a ferocious attack that lasted for seven days (June 25–July 1), suffering heavy casualties (20,000 to the Union's 10,000). But McClellan failed to exploit his advantage, refusing to renew the offensive unless he received fresh troops. Lincoln ordered the withdrawal of the Army of the Potomac, and Richmond remained secure.

Lee promptly went on the offensive, hoping for victories that would humiliate Lincoln's government. Joining with Jackson in northern Virginia, Lee routed a Union army in the Second Battle of Bull Run (August 1862) and then struck north through western Maryland, where he met with near disaster. When Lee divided his force—sending Jackson to capture Harpers Ferry in West Virginia—a copy of his orders fell into McClellan's hands. But the Union general again failed to pursue his advantage, delaying his attack until Lee's depleted army had occupied a strong defensive position behind Antietam Creek, near Sharpsburg, Maryland. Outnumbered 87,000 to 50,000, Lee desperately fought off McClellan's attacks. Just as Union regiments were about to overwhelm his right flank, Jackson's troops arrived, saving the Confederates from a major defeat. Appalled by his casualties, McClellan let Lee retreat to Virginia.

The fighting at Antietam was savage. A Wisconsin officer described his men as "loading and firing with demoniacal fury and shouting and laughing hysterically." At a critical point in the battle a sunken road, nicknamed Bloody Lane, was filled with Confederate bodies two and three deep, and the attacking Union troops knelt on "this ghastly flooring" to shoot at the retreating Confederates. The battle at Antietam on September 17, 1862, remains the bloodiest single day in U.S. military history. Together, the Confederate and Union dead numbered 4,800 and the wounded 18,500, of whom 3,000 soon died. (In comparison, 6,000 Americans were wounded or killed on D-Day in World War II.)

In public Lincoln declared Antietam a victory, but privately he believed that McClellan should have fought Lee to the finish. A masterful organizer of men and supplies, McClellan lacked the stomach for a major commitment of his forces. Dismissing McClellan, Lincoln began a long search for an effective replacement. His first choice was Ambrose E. Burnside, who proved to be more daring but less competent. In December, after heavy losses in futile attacks against well-entrenched Confederate forces at Fredericksburg, Virginia, Burnside resigned his command and Lincoln replaced him with Joseph ("Fighting Joe") Hooker. As 1862 ended, the Confederates had some reason to be content: the war in the East was a stalemate.

In the West, Union forces had been more successful. Their goal was to control the Ohio, Mississippi, and Missouri rivers, dividing the Confederacy into isolated pieces and reducing the mobility of its armies. The decision of Kentucky not to join the rebellion had already given the Union dominance in the Ohio River Valley. In 1862 the Union army launched a series of highly innovative land and water operations to gain control of the Tennessee and Mississippi rivers as well. As the northern part of the Union strategy, General Ulysses S. Grant used riverboats clad with iron plates to take Fort Henry on the Tennessee River and Fort Donelson on the Cumberland. Grant then moved south along the Tennessee to seize critical railroad lines. A Confederate army under Albert Sidney Johnston and P. G. T. Beauregard caught Grant by surprise early in April near a small log church named Shiloh. Grant relentlessly threw troops into the battle, forcing a Confederate withdrawal but taking huge casualties. Grant described a large field "so covered with dead that it would have been possible to walk over the clearing in any direction, stepping on dead bodies, without a foot touching the ground." At the cost of many lives Grant had maintained the Union's military momentum in the West.

Three weeks later, Union naval forces commanded by David G. Farragut struck from the south, moving through the Mississippi Delta from the Gulf of Mexico to capture New Orleans. The Union now held the South's financial center and largest city as well as a major base for future naval operations. Union victories in the West had thus significantly undermined Confederate strength in the Mississippi Valley.

TOWARD TOTAL WAR

The carnage at Antietam and Shiloh had made it clear that the war would be long and costly. After Shiloh, Grant later noted, he "gave up all idea of saving the Union except by complete conquest." The conflict now became a *total war*—a struggle that arrayed the entire resources of the two societies against each other and eventually would result in warfare against enemy civilians. Aided by a strong party and a talented cabinet, Lincoln skillfully mobilized the North for all-out war, organizing an effective central government. Jefferson Davis was far less successful in harnessing the resources of the South, because the eleven states of the Confederacy remained deeply suspicious of centralized rule.

Mobilizing Armies and Civilians

Initially, patriotic fervor filled both armies with eager volunteers. The call for soldiers was especially successful in the South, which had a strong military tradition and an ample supply of trained officers. But the initial surge of enlistments fell off as the people saw the realities of war: heavy losses to disease and dreadful battlefield carnage. Soon both governments faced the necessity of forced enlistment.

The Confederacy was the first to act. In April 1862, after the defeat at Shiloh, the Confederate Congress imposed the first legally binding draft in American history. One law extended all existing enlistments for the duration of the war; another required three years of military service from all able-bodied men between the ages of eighteen and thirty-five. In September, after the heavy casualties at Antietam, the age limit was raised to forty-five. The Confederate draft had two loopholes. First, it exempted one white man— either the planter or an overseer—for each twenty slaves, allowing men on large plantations to avoid military service. Second, drafted men could hire substitutes. Before this provision was repealed in 1864, the price for a substitute had risen to $300 in gold, about three times the annual wages of a skilled worker. Laborers and yeomen farmers angrily complained that it was "a rich man's war and a poor man's fight."

Consequently, some southerners refused to serve, and the Confederate government lacked the power to compel them. Because the Confederate constitution vested sovereignty in the individual states, strong governors such as Joseph Brown of Georgia and Zebulon Vance of North Carolina simply ignored Davis's first draft call in early 1862. Elsewhere, state judges issued writs of *habeas corpus* (a legal process designed to protect people from arbitrary arrest and detention) and ordered the Confederate army to release protesting draftees. The Confederate Congress was reluctant to override the judges' authority to free conscripted men, but military need prompted it to suspend habeas corpus for two periods totaling sixteen months. These measures, along with popular enthusiasm and long enlistments, enabled the Confederate government to keep substantial armies in the field well into 1864.

The Union government was able to take a more authoritarian stance toward potential foes and ordinary citizens. To prevent opposition to the war, Lincoln suspended habeas corpus and imprisoned thousands of Confederate sympathizers without trial. The president also extended martial law to civilians who discouraged enlistment or resisted the draft, making them subject to military courts rather than local juries. This firm policy had the desired effect. The Militia Act of 1862 set a quota of volunteers for each state, and enough recruits came forward to satisfy Union needs for a year. As the scale of hostilities increased, Congress passed the Enrollment Act of 1863, which instituted higher quotas but allowed them to be met with volunteers or conscripts. To avoid conscription, northern officials enticed volunteers with cash bounties, prompting the enlistment or reenlistment of almost a million men. As in the South, wealthy men could avoid the draft by providing a substitute or paying a $300 commutation, or exemption, fee.

The Enrollment Act sparked the first significant opposition to the northern war effort, as thousands of recent immigrants refused to serve. Northern Democrats exploited this resentment by charging that Lincoln was drafting

Draft Riots in New York City
The Enrollment Act of 1863 enraged many workers and recent Irish and German immigrants who opposed the war. In July in New York City they took out their anger on free blacks. As the club-waving mob hangs an African-American, three others escape by climbing over a fence. The violence against blacks received wide publicity (this engraving appeared in the *Illustrated London News* on August 8, 1863) and generally strengthened support for the Union war effort.

poor whites in order to free the slaves and flood the cities with black laborers. Some Democrats opposed the war, believing that the South should be allowed to secede; others simply wanted to protect the interests of immigrants, most of whom were Democrats. In July 1863 hostility to the draft and to African-Americans spilled onto the streets of New York City. For five days immigrant Irish and German workers ran rampant, burning the draft office, sacking the homes of important Republicans, and attacking the police. The rioters lynched and mutilated at least a dozen African-Americans, drove hundreds of black families from their homes, and burned down the Colored Orphan Asylum. Lincoln rushed in Union troops, who killed more than a hundred rioters and suppressed the insurrection, but many immigrants continued to oppose conscription.

The Union government's determination to wage total war won greater support among native-born citizens. In 1861 prominent New Yorkers established the United States Sanitary Commission. Its task was to provide medical services and prevent a repeat of the debacle of the recently concluded Crimean War between Britain and Russia, in which disease had accounted for over three-fourths of British casualties. Through its network of 7,000 local auxiliaries, the Sanitary Commission gathered supplies; distributed clothing, food, and medicine to the army; improved the sanitary standards of camp life; and recruited battlefield nurses and doctors for the Union Army Medical Bureau. These efforts were not consistently successful. Diseases—dysentery, typhoid, and malaria as well as childhood viruses such as mumps and measles, to which many rural men had not developed an immunity—killed twice as many Union soldiers (about 250,000) as died in combat. Surgeons inadvertently took more lives by spreading infection than they saved by performing operations. Still, because of better sanitation and high-quality food, the mortality rate among Union troops from disease and wounds was substantially lower than that in other major nineteenth-century wars. Confederate soldiers were less fortunate. Although thousands of white women volunteered as nurses, the Confederate health system was poorly organized. Thousands of southern soldiers contracted scurvy because of the lack of vitamin C in their diets, and they died from camp diseases at higher rates than did Union soldiers.

Women took a leading role in the Sanitary Commission and other wartime agencies. As superintendent of female nurses, Dorothea Dix became the first woman to receive a major federal appointment. Dix used her influence to combat the prejudice against women treating men, opening a new occupation to women. Thousands of educated Union women joined the war effort as clerks in the expanding governmental bureaucracy. In the South women staffed the efficient Confederate postal service. Indeed, in both sections millions of women assumed new economic responsibilities and worked with far greater intensity. They took over many farm tasks previously done by men and went to work in schools and textile, clothing, and shoe factories. A number of women even took on military duties as spies, scouts, and (disguised as men)

The Common Lemon: The Difference between Life and Death

In the Civil War disease took more lives than bullets did, and the northern toll would have been even higher without the work of the doctors and nurses of the United States Sanitary Commission. As this narrative by the volunteer nurse and reformer Jane Swisshelm indicates, public support was also crucial—in this case by providing lemons, which were rich in vitamin C and inhibited a common hospital disease.

About nine o'clock I returned to the man I had come to help. I had sat by him but a few moments when I noticed a green shade on his face. It darkened, and his breathing grew labored—then ceased. I think it was not more than twenty minutes from the time I observed the green tinge until he was gone. I called the nurse, who brought . . . a surgeon [and I knew], by the sudden shadow on his face when he saw the corpse, that he was alarmed; and when he had given minute directions for the removal of the bed and its contents, the washing of the floor and sprinkling with chloride of lime, I went close to his side, and said in a low voice:

"Doctor, is not this hospital gangrene?"

"I am very sorry to say, madam, that it is."

"Then you want lemons!"

"We would be glad to have them!"

"Glad to have them?" I repeated, in profound astonishment, "why, you *must* have them!"

He seemed surprised at my earnestness, and set about explaining: "We sent to the Sanitary Commission last week, and got half a box."

"Seven hundred and fifty wounded men! Hospital gangrene, and half a box of lemons!" . . .

I went to the head nurse . . . who . . . gave me writing materials, and I wrote a short note to the *New York Tribune*:

"Hospital gangrene has broken out in Washington, and we want lemons! *lemons!* LEMONS! LEMONS! No man or woman in health, has a right to a glass of lemonade until these men have all they need; send us lemons!"

I signed my name and mailed it immediately, and it appeared next morning. . . . That day lemons began to pour into Washington, and soon, I think, into every hospital in the land. . . . If there was any more hospital gangrene that season I neither saw nor heard of it.

SOURCE: Jane Swisshelm, *Half a Century* (Chicago: Jansen, McClurg, 1880), pp. 251–253.

soldiers. As the nurse Clara Barton, who later founded the American Red Cross, recalled, "At the war's end, woman was at least fifty years in advance of the normal position which continued peace would have assigned her."

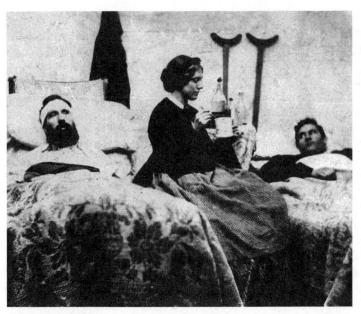

Hospital Nursing
Working as nurses in battlefront hospitals, thousands of Union and Confederate women gained firsthand experience of the horrors of war. Most nurses were unpaid volunteers, cooking and cleaning for their patients as well as tending their wounds. A sense of calm prevails in this behind-the-lines Union hospital in Nashville, where those who survived their wounds were sent to recover.

Mobilizing Resources and Money

Wars usually are won by the side with superior resources and economic organization, and in this regard the Union entered the war with a distinct advantage. With nearly two-thirds of the American people, about two-thirds of the nation's railroad mileage, and nearly 90 percent of American industrial output, the North's economy was far superior to the South's. The North had an especially great advantage in the manufacture of cannon and rifles because many of its arms factories were equipped for mass production.

But the Confederate position was far from weak. Virginia, North Carolina, and Tennessee had substantial industrial capacity. Richmond, with its Tredegar Iron Works, was an important industrial center, and in 1861 the Confederacy transported to Richmond the gun-making machinery captured at the U.S. armory at Harpers Ferry. The production of the Richmond armory, the purchase of Enfield rifles from Britain, and the capture of 100,000 Union rifles enabled the Confederacy to provide every infantryman with a modern weapon by 1863.

Moreover, with 9 million people, the Confederacy could mobilize enormous armies. While one-third of that number were slaves, their masters kept them in the fields, producing food for the armies and cotton for export. The Confederacy counted on "King Cotton" to provide revenue to purchase clothes, boots, blankets, and weapons from abroad. They also counted on cotton as a diplomatic weapon, hoping that the British, who depended on southern cotton to supply their textile factories, would grant diplomatic recognition and provide military and economic aid. Although the British government never recognized the Confederate States of America as an independent nation, it did regard the conflict as a war, and that gave the rebels the status of a belligerent power with the right under international law to borrow money and purchase weapons. Thus the odds did not necessarily favor the Union, despite its superior resources.

The outcome would depend on the success of the two governments in mobilizing the resources of their societies. Lincoln and the Republicans had a clear economic agenda. To build political support for their party and boost industrial output, they enacted virtually the entire program of national mercantilism previously advocated by Henry Clay and the Whig party. First, the Republicans raised tariffs, winning praise from northeastern manufacturers and laborers and farmers who feared competition from cheap foreign labor. Second, Secretary of the Treasury Salmon P. Chase created a national banking system—an important element of every modern centralized government—by linking thousands of local banks. This integrated system was far more effective in raising capital and controlling inflation than earlier efforts by the First and Second banks of the United States had been. Finally, the Lincoln administration devised a far-reaching system of internal improvements. In 1862 Congress fulfilled the Republican promise to build transcontinental railroads, chartering the Union Pacific and Central Pacific railways and subsidizing them lavishly. It gave those railroads 20 square miles of federal land for every mile of track they put down and in 1864 provided a similar subsidy to the Northern Pacific. In addition, the Republicans moved aggressively to provide northern farmers with "free land" in the West. The Homestead Act of 1862 gave heads of families or individuals age twenty-one or older the right to 160 acres of public land after five years of residence and improvement. This economic program sustained the allegiance of a majority of northerners to the Republican party while bolstering the Union's ability to fight the war.

In contrast, the Confederate government had a much less coherent economic policy. True to its states' rights philosophy, the Confederacy left most economic matters in the hands of the state governments. But as the realities of total war became clear, the Davis administration took some extraordinary measures: it built and operated shipyards, armories, foundries, and textile mills; commandeered food and scarce raw materials such as coal, iron, copper, and lead; requisitioned slaves to work on fortifications; and exercised direct control over foreign trade. These coercive measures were resented as the war wore on, because the Confederate leaders failed to explain their wartime needs or cope with misery on the home front. To sustain the war effort they increasingly counted on racial solidarity: Jefferson Davis warned whites that a Union victory would destroy slavery "and reduce the whites to the degraded position of the African race."

For both the North and the South, the cost of fighting a total war was enormous. In the Union, government spending shot up from less than 2 percent of gross national product to about 15 percent. To pay for those expenditures, the Republicans established a powerful modern state that raised money in three ways. First, the government increased taxes by raising tariffs, placing excise duties on consumer goods, and for the first time imposing direct taxes on business corporations, large inheritances, and incomes. These levies paid for about 20 percent of the cost of the war.

The sale of Treasury bonds financed 65 percent of the northern war effort. Following the advice of Jay Cooke, a Philadelphia banker, the Treasury paid interest on the bonds in gold and marketed them widely. Using newspaper advertisements and 2,500 subagents, Cooke persuaded nearly a million northern families to buy war bonds. In addition, the National Banking acts of 1863 and 1864 induced many state banks to purchase Treasury bonds by offering them a national charter, which freed them from certain taxes and offered other economic advantages. By the end of 1865, the number of national banks had tripled and their purchases of U.S. bonds had increased nearly fourfold.

The Union financed most of the remaining cost of the war by printing paper money. As with the "Continentals" issued during the War for Independence, these Treasury notes—known as *greenbacks*—were backed by faith in the government rather than by specie. The Legal Tender Act of 1862 authorized the issue of $150 million in greenbacks and required the public to accept them as legal tender. Unlike the Continentals, this paper money did not depreciate significantly in value because it was issued in limited amounts, funding about 15 percent of wartime expenses. By imposing broad-based taxes, borrowing from the middle class as well as the wealthy, and creating a national monetary system, the Union government created the financial foundations of a modern nation-state, raising huge sums and directly involving millions of citizens in the war effort.

The financial demands on the South were just as great, but it lacked a powerful central government that could tax and borrow. The Confederate Congress fiercely opposed taxes on cotton exports and slaves, the most valuable property of wealthy planters. Taxes fell primarily on urban middle-class and non-slaveholding yeomen farm families, who refused to pay. Consequently, the Confederacy covered less than 5 percent of its expenditures through taxation. The government paid for another 35 percent by borrowing, although many wealthy planters refused to buy large quantities of Confederate bonds and foreign bankers were equally wary.

Thus the Confederacy was forced to finance about 60 percent of its expenses with unbacked paper money. The flood of currency created soaring inflation, which was compounded by counterfeit copies of the poorly printed Confederate notes. As the huge supply of money (and shortages of goods) brought rising food prices, riots broke out in more than a dozen southern cities and towns. In Richmond several hundred women broke into bakeries, crying, "Our children are starving while the rich roll in wealth." Things got worse as the paper money depreciated. By the spring of 1865 prices had risen to ninety-two times their 1861 levels. Inflation not only undermined civilian morale but also caused farmers to refuse to accept Confederate money for their produce. Supply officers had to seize what they needed, offering payment in worthless IOUs. Fearful of a strong government and taxation, the Confederacy was forced to violate the property rights of its citizens to sustain the war.

THE TURNING POINT: 1863

By 1863 the Lincoln administration had mobilized northern society, creating a complex war machine and a coherent economic and financial system. "Little by little," the young diplomat Henry Adams noted at his post in London, "one began to feel that, behind the chaos in Washington power was taking shape; that it was massed and guided as it had not been before." Slowly but surely the tide of battle shifted toward the Union.

Emancipation

From the beginning of the conflict, antislavery Republicans had tried to persuade their party to make abolition a Union war aim. They based their argument not just on morality but on "military necessity," pointing out that slave-grown crops sustained the Confederate war effort. As Frederick Douglass put it, "the very stomach of this rebellion is the Negro in the form of a slave. Arrest that hoe in the hands of the Negro, and you smite the rebellion in the very seat of its life." As war casualties mounted in 1862, Lincoln and some Republican leaders accepted Douglass's argument and began to redefine the war as a struggle against slavery—the cornerstone of southern society.

But it was enslaved African-Americans who forced the issue by seizing freedom for themselves. Exploiting the disorder of wartime, tens of thousands of slaves escaped and sought refuge behind Union lines. The first Union official to confront this issue was General Benjamin Butler. When three slaves reached his camp on the Virginia coast in May 1861, he labeled them "contraband of war" and refused to return them to their owner. His term stuck, and for the rest of the war slaves behind Union lines were known as *contrabands*. Within a few months a thousand contrabands were camping with Butler's army. To define their status and undermine the Confederate war effort, in August 1861 Congress passed the First Confiscation Act, which authorized the seizure of all property—including slaves—used to support the rebellion.

Radical Republicans, who had long condemned slavery, now saw a way to use the war to end it. By the spring of 1862 leading Radicals—Treasury secretary Chase; Charles Sumner, chair of the Senate Committee on Foreign Relations; and Thaddeus Stevens, chair of the House Ways and Means Committee— had pushed moderate Republicans toward abolition. In April Congress enacted legislation ending slavery in the District of Columbia, with compensation for owners. In June it outlawed slavery in the federal territories, finally enacting the Wilmot Proviso and the Republicans' free-soil policy. And in July Congress passed the radical Second Confiscation Act, which, overriding the property rights of Confederate slaveowners, declared "forever free" all fugitive slaves and all slaves captured by the Union army.

Lincoln now seized the initiative from the radicals. In July 1862 he prepared a general proclamation of emancipation and, viewing the battle of Antietam as "an indication of the Divine Will," issued it on September 22, 1862. Based on the president's war powers, the proclamation declared Lincoln's intention to free the slaves in all states still in rebellion on January 1, 1863. The seceding states had a hundred days to preserve slavery by returning to the Union. None chose to do so.

The proclamation was politically astute. Since Lincoln needed to keep the loyalty of the border states still in the Union, he left slavery intact there. He also wanted to win the allegiance of the areas occupied by Union armies—western and central Tennessee, western Virginia, and southern Louisiana, including New Orleans—so he left slavery untouched there. Consequently, because Lincoln's order had no practical effect within the Confederacy, the Emancipation Proclamation did not free a single slave. Yet it dramatically changed the nature of the conflict. The struggle to preserve the Union had become, as Lincoln put it, a war of "subjugation" in which "the old South is to be destroyed and replaced by new propositions and ideas."

As a war aim, emancipation was extremely controversial. During the congressional election of 1862 the Democrats denounced emancipation as unconstitutional, warned of slave uprisings and massive bloodshed in the South, and claimed that a "black flood" would wash away the jobs of northern workers. Democrat Horatio Seymour won the governorship of New York by declaring that if abolition was the purpose of the war, the South should not be conquered. Other Democrats swept to victory in New York, Pennsylvania, Ohio, and Illinois, and the party gained 34 seats in Congress. However, the Republicans still held a 25-seat majority in the House and had gained 5 seats in the Senate. Lincoln refused to retreat. On New Year's Day, 1863, he signed the Emancipation Proclamation. As a gesture to northerners who sympathized with the South and feared race warfare, Lincoln urged slaves to "abstain from all violence." But he now justified emancipation as an "act of justice." "If my name ever goes into history," he said, "it was for this act."

Vicksburg and Gettysburg

The fate of the proclamation would depend on the success of Union armies and the Republicans' ability to win support for their program. The outlook was not encouraging. Not only had Democrats registered gains in the election of 1862, there was increased popular support for Democrats who favored a negotiated peace. Two brilliant victories by Lee, whose army defeated Hooker's forces at Fredericksburg (December 1862) and Chancellorsville, Virginia (May 1863), caused a further erosion of northern support, as did rumors of a new draft.

At this crucial juncture, General Grant mounted a major offensive in the West designed to split the Confederacy in two. Grant drove south along the west

AMERICAN VOICES

Triumph and Tragedy at Vicksburg

As James K. Newton of the 14th Wisconsin Volunteers celebrated the capture of the Confederate stronghold of Vicksburg on July 4, 1863, he was forced to confront the high cost of victory.

My Dear Parents,

. . . In my opinion I had about as glorious a 4th of July as I could wish to spend. Early in the morning our Reg't was ordered to be in readiness to march at a minutes notice; we fell in, and stacked arms; all of us expecting to spend the day in Vicksburg, and—we were not disappointed. . . .

It looked strange to see Uncle Sam's troops marching through the city, and the Secesh [secessionists] standing in groups at every street corner . . . [those Confederate soldiers] are only too glad to be paroled, and allowed to go home for a while. . . . I presume there are a great many conflicting reports up north, as to what was gained on our side by the surrender of Vicksburg. I should not wonder if the Copperheads [southern supporters] up there made it out to be not much of a victory after all, but notwithstanding what *they say*, and the stories that they circulate, the truth will come out in the end. . . . We have now undisputed possession of the Miss: River. We have taken 31,000 prisoners; 45,000 stand of small arms; over 100 cannon; and nearly 100 stands of Colors. All this we have gained. . . .

I have sad news to write again, and I might as well tell it now as at any other time. Henry Cady is dead: he died on the 1st day of July . . . that makes three of our Comp'y who have died in that hospital, and all for the want of proper care.

"Little Cady"—as we all called him, was universally acknowledged to be the best boy in the Comp'y; . . . The boys all moarn for him, but myself especially, for he was like a brother to me . . . I can but hope that he has gone to that better world where sin, pain, and sorrow can not enter.

SOURCE: Stephen E. Ambrose, ed., *A Wisconsin Boy in Dixie: Civil War Letters of James K. Newton* (Madison: University of Wisconsin Press, 1961), pp. 80–83. Reprinted by permission of The University of Wisconsin Press.

bank of the Mississippi and then moved his troops across the river near Vicksburg, where he defeated two Confederate armies and laid siege to the city. After repelling Union assaults for six weeks, the exhausted and starving Vicksburg garrison surrendered on July 4, 1863. Five days later Union forces took Port Hudson, Louisiana, establishing Union control of the Mississippi. Grant had cut Louisiana, Arkansas, and Texas off from the rest of the Confederacy.

Grant's initial advance down the Mississippi had caused a division over strategy within the Confederate leadership. Davis and other civilian leaders wanted to throw in reinforcements to defend Vicksburg and send troops to

Tennessee to draw Grant out of Mississippi. But Lee, buoyed by his recent victories over Hooker, favored a new invasion of the North. He argued that a military thrust into the free states would relieve the pressure on Vicksburg by drawing the Union armies east. Beyond that, Lee hoped for a major victory that would undermine northern support for the war.

Lee won out. In June 1863 he maneuvered his army north through Maryland into Pennsylvania. The Army of the Potomac moved along with him, positioning itself between Lee and Washington. The two great armies met in an accidental but decisive confrontation at Gettysburg, Pennsylvania (see Map 15.2). On the first day of battle, July 1, Lee drove the Union's advance guard to the south of town. There General George G. Meade, who had just taken over command of the Union forces from Hooker, placed his troops in well-defended hilltop positions and called up reinforcements. By the morning of the second day Meade had 90,000 troops to 75,000 for Lee. Aware that he was outnumbered but bent on victory, Lee attacked both of Meade's flanks but failed to turn them. General Richard B. Ewell, assigned to attack the Union right, was unwilling to risk his men in an all-out assault, and General Longstreet, on the Union left, was unable to dislodge Meade's forces from Little Round Top.

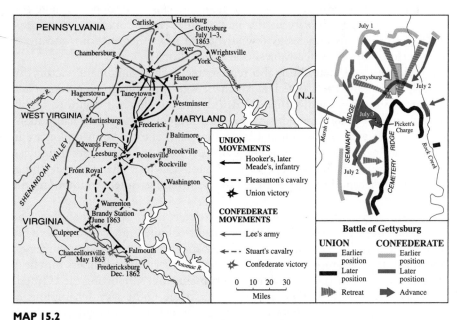

MAP 15.2
The Battle of Gettysburg, 1863
After Lee's victory at Chancellorsville in May, the two armies jockeyed for position as the Confederate forces moved northward. At Gettysburg, the victory of the Union army commanded by General George Meade was primarily the result of superior numbers and its well-fortified position along Cemetery Ridge, which gave its units a major tactical advantage.

On July 3 Lee decided to attempt a frontal assault on the center of the Union lines. He had enormous confidence in his troops and realized that this might be his last chance to inflict a crushing psychological defeat on the North. After the heaviest artillery barrage of the war, Lee ordered 14,000 men under General George E. Pickett to take Cemetery Ridge. But Meade had reinforced the center of his line with artillery and his best troops. When Pickett's men charged across a mile of open terrain, they were met by massive fire and thousands were killed, wounded, or captured. By the end of the battle, Lee had suffered 28,000 casualties, one-third of the Army of Northern Virginia, and Meade had lost 23,000 killed or wounded, making Gettysburg the most lethal battle of the Civil War.

Gettysburg was a great Union victory; never again would a southern army invade the North. But shocked by the bloodletting, Meade allowed the remaining Confederate soldiers to escape, thus losing an opportunity to end the war. "As it is," Lincoln brooded, "the war will be prolonged indefinitely."

Nonetheless, the outcome at Gettysburg and the simultaneous Union victory at Vicksburg amounted to a major turning point in the conflict. In the fall of 1863, Republicans reaped the political gains of those victories by sweeping state and local elections in Pennsylvania, Ohio, and New York. In the South, the military setbacks accentuated war weariness. The Confederate elections of 1863 went sharply against the politicians who supported Jefferson Davis, and a large minority in the new Confederate Congress was outspokenly hostile to his policies. A few advocated peace negotiations, and many more criticized the ineffectiveness of the war effort.

Vicksburg and Gettysburg also represented a great diplomatic victory for the North, ending the Confederacy's chances to gain foreign recognition and acquire advanced weapons. In 1862 British shipbuilders had begun to supply armed cruisers to the Confederacy, and one of them, the *Alabama*, had sunk or captured more than a hundred Union merchant ships. Union diplomats in London despaired of preventing the scheduled delivery of two other ironclad cruisers in mid-1863. But news of the Union victories changed everything, and the American minister persuaded the British government to impound the ships.

Cotton was not "King" and had not determined British policy, as the South had hoped. British manufacturers had stockpiled raw cotton before the war, and when those stocks were depleted, they found new sources in Egypt and India. Equally important, the dependence of British consumers on cheap wheat from the North deterred the government from supporting the Confederacy. Finally, British workers and reformers were enthusiastic champions of abolition, which the Emancipation Proclamation had established as a Union war aim. The results at Vicksburg and Gettysburg confirmed British neutrality by demonstrating the military might of the Union. The British did not want to risk Canada or their merchant marine by provoking a strong, well-armed United States.

THE UNION VICTORIOUS, 1864–1865

The Union victories of 1863 made it clear that the South could not win the war on the battlefield, but the Confederacy still hoped for a stalemate and a negotiated peace. Lincoln and his generals faced the daunting task of winning a quick and decisive military victory; otherwise a majority of northern voters might well desert the Republican party and its policies.

Soldiers and Strategy

Free 'African-Americans and fugitive slaves had tried to enlist in the Union army as early as 1861, and the black abolitionist Frederick Douglass had embraced their cause: "Once let the black man get upon his person the brass letters, 'U.S.,'. . . a musket on his shoulder and bullets in his pockets, and there is no power on earth which can deny that he has earned the right to citizenship in the United States." Such an outcome frightened many northern whites, who were determined to keep blacks subjugated. Moreover, most Union generals doubted that former slaves would make good soldiers, and so the Lincoln administration initially refused to encourage black aspirations for military service.

The Emancipation Proclamation changed popular thinking and military policy. If blacks were to benefit from a Union victory, some northern whites argued, they should share in the fighting and dying. The valor exhibited by the first African-American regiments also influenced northern opinion. In January 1863 Thomas Wentworth Higginson, the white abolitionist commander of the First South Carolina (Black) Volunteers, wrote a glowing newspaper account of their military prowess: "No officer in this regiment now doubts that the key to the successful prosecution of the war lies in the unlimited employment of black troops." The War department authorized the enlistment of free blacks and contraband slaves, and as white resistance to conscription increased, the Lincoln administration recruited as many African-Americans as it could. Without black soldiers, the president suggested in the autumn of 1864, "we would be compelled to abandon the war in three weeks." By the following spring there were nearly 200,000 African-American soldiers and sailors.

Military service did not end racial discrimination. Black soldiers served under white officers in segregated regiments and were used primarily to build fortifications, garrison forts, and guard supply lines. At first they were paid less than white soldiers ($7 versus $13 per month), and only a few were promoted to higher ranks. Despite such treatment, African-Americans volunteered for military service in disproportionate numbers and diligently served the Union cause. They knew they were fighting for freedom and the possibility of a new social order. "Hello, Massa," said one black soldier to his former master, who had been taken prisoner. "Bottom rail on top dis time." The worst fears of the secessionists had come true: through the agency of the Union army, slaves had risen in a great rebellion.

Black Soldiers in the Union Army
Tens of thousands of African-Americans volunteered for military service and a chance to fight for the freedom of their people. These soldiers were members of the 107th Colored Infantry. In January 1865 their regiment participated in the daring capture of Fort Fisher, which protected Wilmington, North Carolina, the last Confederate port open to blockade runners.

As African-Americans enlisted in the ranks, Lincoln finally found a commanding general in whom he had confidence. In March 1864 he put General Ulysses S. Grant in charge of all the Union armies and approved Grant's plan to advance simultaneously against all the major Confederate forces. Both the general and the president wanted a decisive victory before the election of 1864.

As the successful western campaigns of 1863 showed, Grant understood how to fight a modern war—a war relying on industrial technology and directed at an entire society. At Vicksburg he had besieged an entire city and forced its surrender. A few months later, in November 1863, he had used the North's edge in technology to advantage, utilizing railroad transport to charge to the rescue of a Union army near Chattanooga, Tennessee, and drive an invading army back into Georgia. Moreover, Grant was willing to accept heavy casualties in assaults on strongly defended positions, abandoning the caution of earlier Union commanders. "To conserve life, in war," Grant wrote, "is to fight unceasingly." Grant's aggressive tactics earned him a reputation as a butcher both of his own men and of enemy armies, which he pursued relentlessly when they were in retreat. Finally, to crush the South's will to resist, the new Union commander was willing to terrorize the civilian population.

In May 1864 Grant ordered major new offensives on two fronts. Personally taking charge of the 115,000-strong Army of the Potomac, he set out to destroy Lee's force of 75,000 troops in Virginia. Simultaneously he instructed

General William Tecumseh Sherman, who shared his views on modern warfare, to invade Georgia and take Atlanta. As Sherman prepared for battle, he wrote that "all that has gone before is mere skirmish. The war now begins."

Grant advanced toward Richmond, hoping to force Lee to fight in open fields, where the Union's superior manpower and artillery could prevail. Lee, remembering Gettysburg, maintained strong defensive positions, attacking only when he held a tactical advantage. He seized such opportunities twice, winning narrow victories in the battles of the Wilderness on May 5–7 and Spotsylvania Court House on May 8–12. Nevertheless Grant drove on toward Richmond. In early June he attacked Lee at Cold Harbor but withdrew after losing 7,000 men in a frontal assault. Grant had severely eroded Lee's forces, which had suffered 31,000 casualties, but Union losses were even higher at 55,000 men.

The fighting took a heavy psychological toll. "Many a man has gone crazy since this campaign began from the terrible pressure on mind and body," complained a Union officer. Previous battles had lasted only a few days and had been separated by long intervals. But in this campaign Grant's relentless advance toward Richmond and Lee's defensive tactics produced sustained fighting and grueling attrition. In June, Grant pulled some of his troops away from Richmond to lay siege to Petersburg, an important railroad center. Protracted trench warfare, which foreshadowed that of World War I, made the spade as important as the sword. Soldiers built complex networks of trenches, tunnels, and artillery emplacements for almost 50 miles around Richmond and Petersburg. An officer described the continuous artillery firing and sniping as "living night and day within the 'valley of the shadow of death.'" The stress was especially great for the outnumbered Confederate troops, who spent months in the muddy, sickening trenches without rotation to the rear. As time passed, Lincoln and Grant felt pressures of their own; the enormous casualties and continued military stalemate threatened Lincoln with defeat in the November election.

The outlook for the Republicans worsened when raids by Jubal Early's cavalry near Washington in early July forced Grant to divert his best troops from the Petersburg campaign. To punish and control the Shenandoah Valley, which provided a base for Early and food for Lee's army, Grant ordered General Philip H. Sheridan to turn the region into "a barren waste." During the fall Sheridan's troops conducted a scorched-earth campaign, destroying grain supplies, barns, farming implements, and gristmills. This terrorism went beyond the military norms of the day, for most officers regarded civilians as noncombatants and feared that a punitive policy against the population would erode military discipline. But Grant's decision to carry the war to Confederate civilians had changed the definition of conventional warfare.

The Election of 1864 and the "March to the Sea"

As the siege at Petersburg dragged on, Lincoln's reelection hopes came to rest on General William Sherman in Georgia. Sherman had gradually penetrated to within about 30 miles of Atlanta, a great railway hub that controlled the heart of the Confederacy. Although his army outnumbered that of General Joseph E. Johnston 90,000 to 60,000, he avoided a direct attack and slowly pried the Confederates out of one defensive position after another. Finally, on June 27, at Kennesaw Mountain, Sherman engaged Johnston in a set battle, in which he suffered 3,000 casualties while inflicting only about 600. By late July the Union general had laid siege to Atlanta, but the next month brought little gain. Like Grant, Sherman seemed bogged down in a hopeless campaign.

Meanwhile, the presidential campaign of 1864 was well under way. In June the Republican convention endorsed Lincoln's war measures, demanded the unconditional surrender of the Confederacy, and called for a constitutional amendment to abolish slavery. To attract Democratic support, the party temporarily renamed itself the National Union party and nominated Andrew Johnson, a Unionist Tennessee Democrat, for vice-president. The Democratic convention met in late August and nominated General George B. McClellan. The delegates declared their opposition to emancipation but were divided over continuing the war. By threatening to bolt the convention, the "Peace Democrats" forced through a platform calling for "a cessation of hostilities" and a convention to restore peace "on the basis of the Federal Union." Although personally a "War Democrat," McClellan promised if elected to recommend an immediate armistice and a peace convention. Rejoicing in "the first ray of real light I have seen since the war began," Confederate Vice-President Alexander Stephens declared that if Atlanta and Richmond held out, Lincoln might be defeated, and northern Democrats then be persuaded to accept the independence of the South.

But on September 2, Atlanta fell. In a stunning move, Sherman pulled his troops from the trenches and swept around the city to destroy its roads and rail links to the rest of the Confederacy, forcing its surrender. In her diary Mary Chestnut, a slaveowning plantation mistress, despaired of victory: "We are going to be wiped off the earth." Amid the 100-gun salutes in northern cities that greeted the news of Sherman's victory, McClellan repudiated the Democratic peace platform. But Republicans charged that he was still a peace candidate and that *Copperheads* (a poisonous snake and the name bestowed on Peace Democrats by Republican newspapers) were hatching treasonous plots in the border states.

Sherman's success in Georgia gave Lincoln a clear-cut victory in November. He took 212 of 233 electoral votes, winning 55 percent of the popular vote in the free and border states and carrying every state except Delaware, Kentucky, and New Jersey. Republicans won 145 of the 185 seats in the House of Representatives and increased their Senate majority to 42 of 52 seats. Many of those victories hinged on the votes of Union troops, most of whom wanted the war to continue until the Confederacy met every Union demand, including emancipation.

Already the pace of legal emancipation had accelerated. In 1864 Maryland and Missouri amended their constitutions to free their slaves, and the three occupied states of Tennessee, Arkansas, and Louisiana followed suit. Abolitionists still worried that the Emancipation Proclamation, based on the president's wartime powers, would lose its force at the end of the war and that southern states would reestablish slavery. Urged on by Lincoln, the new Republican-dominated Congress took the final step toward full legal emancipation. On January 31, 1865, it approved the Thirteenth Amendment, which prohibited slavery throughout the United States. Slavery was nearly dead.

And so was the Confederacy. After the capture of Atlanta, Sherman declined to follow the retreating Confederate army into Tennessee and decided on a bold strategy. Rather than spread his troops dangerously thin by protecting supply lines to the rear, he would "cut a swath through to the sea," living off the land. To persuade Lincoln and Grant to approve this unconventional plan, Sherman pointed out that such a march would devastate Georgia and score a major psychological victory. It would be "a demonstration to the world, foreign and domestic, that we have a power [Jefferson] Davis cannot resist."

Sherman carried out the concept of total war he and Sheridan had pioneered: destruction of the enemy's economic resources and will to resist. "We are not only fighting hostile armies," Sherman wrote, "but a hostile people, and must make old and young, rich and poor, feel the hard hand of war." He

Atlanta in Ruins
As the Confederate army retreated from Atlanta, it blew up factories to keep them out of Union hands. Sherman's forces destroyed the remaining industries, including the roundhouse (on the right) and car repair sheds of the Georgia Central Railroad. The devastation of Atlanta and Georgia during Sherman's "march to the sea" was a severe blow to Confederate morale.

left Atlanta in flames and during his 300-mile march to the sea destroyed rail-roads, property, and supplies (see Map 15.3). A Union veteran wrote that "[we] destroyed all we could not eat, stole their niggers, burned their cotton & gins, spilled their sorghum, burned & twisted their R.Roads and raised Hell generally." The havoc so demoralized Confederate soldiers that many deserted and fled home to their loved ones. When Sherman reached Savan-nah, Georgia, in mid-December, the 10,000 Confederate defenders left with-out a fight.

In February 1865 Sherman invaded South Carolina. He planned to link up with Grant at Petersburg and along the way punish the state where secession had begun. "The truth is," Sherman wrote, "the whole army is burning with an insatiable desire to wreak vengeance upon South Carolina." His troops cut a comparatively narrow swath across the state but ravaged the countryside even more thoroughly than they had in Georgia. By March Sherman had reached North Carolina and was on the verge of linking up with Grant and crushing Lee's army.

Sherman's march exposed an internal Confederate weakness: rising class resentment on the part of poor whites. Long angered by the "twenty-Negro" exemption from military service given to slaveowners and their overseers and fearing that the Confederacy was doomed, ordinary southern farmers increas-

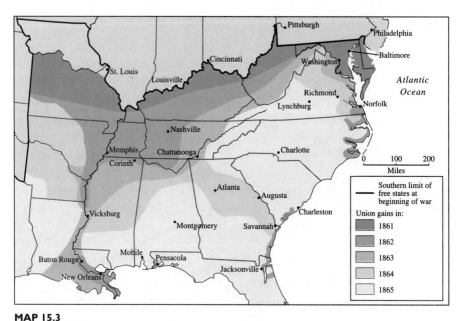

MAP 15.3
The Conquest of the South, 1861–1865
It took four years for the Union army to occupy the territory of the Confederacy, much of which remained under southern control until the last year of the war. Most of the Union's victories came on the western front, where its control of strategic lines of communication allowed it to mount large-scale attacks against Confederate armies.

Lee's Surrender
Lee surrendered to Grant in the parlor of a modest farmer, Wilmer McLean, who could not escape the war. McLean had fled to Appomattox for peace and quiet after leaving a Manassas home, which Confederate soldiers had used as a headquarters and Union forces had shelled during the first major battle of the war.

ingly resisted conscription and desertion became widespread. By early 1865 the Confederacy was experiencing such a severe manpower crisis that its leaders decided to take an extreme measure: arming the slaves. Urged on by Lee, the Confederate Congress voted to enlist black soldiers; Davis issued an executive order granting freedom to all blacks who served in the Confederate army. But the war ended too soon to reveal whether any slaves would have fought for the Confederacy.

The final act of the war took place in Virginia. In April 1865 Grant finally forced Lee into a showdown by gaining control of the crucial railroad junction at Petersburg and cutting off his supplies. Lee abandoned the defense of Richmond and turned west, hoping to join up with Confederate forces in North Carolina. While Lincoln visited the ruins of the Confederate capital, mobbed by joyful former slaves, Grant cut off Lee's escape route. On April 9, almost precisely four years after the attack on Fort Sumter, Lee surrendered to Grant at Appomattox Court House, Virginia. In accepting the surrender of the impeccably dressed Confederate general, Grant set a tone of egalitarianism and generosity, wearing an unpressed jacket and muddy trousers and allowing Lee's men to take their horses home for spring planting. By May 26 all the Confederate generals had laid down their arms, and the Confederate army and government simply dissolved.

The armies of the Union had destroyed the Confederacy and much of the South's economy. Its factories, warehouses, and railroads were in ruins, as were many of its farms and some of its most important cities. Almost 260,000 Confederate soldiers had paid for secession with their lives. Most significant, the Union had been preserved and slavery destroyed. But the cost of victory was enormous in money, wasted resources, and lives. Over 360,000 Union soldiers were dead, and hundreds of thousands were maimed and crippled. The hard and bitter war was over, and a reunited nation turned to the tasks of peace, which were to be equally hard and bitter.

CHAPTER 15 TIMELINE

1861	Confederate States of America formed (February 4)
	Abraham Lincoln inaugurated (March 4)
	Confederates fire on Fort Sumter (April 12)
	Virginia convention votes to secede (April 17)
	First Battle of Bull Run (July 21)
	General Benjamin Butler declares runaway slaves "contraband of war"
1862	Congress passes Legal Tender Act
	Homestead Act and federal aid to transcontinental railroads
	Battle of Shiloh (April 6–7)
	Confederacy introduces first draft
	Battle of Antietam (September 17)
	Preliminary Emancipation Proclamation (September 22)
1863	Lincoln issues Emancipation Proclamation (January 1)
	Enrollment Act begins draft in North; riots in New York City (July)
	Battles of Gettysburg (July 1–3) and Vicksburg
1864	Tariffs raised
	Ulysses S. Grant advances on Richmond; siege of Petersburg
	Atlanta falls to William T. Sherman (September 2)
	Lincoln reelected, and Sherman marches through Georgia
1865	Robert E. Lee surrenders (April 9)
	Ratification of Thirteenth Amendment

CHAPTER 16

RECONSTRUCTION, 1865–1877

- Presidential Reconstruction
- Radical Reconstruction
- Redemption

In his second inaugural address, President Abraham Lincoln spoke of the need to "bind up the nation's wounds." No one knew better than Lincoln how daunting a task that would be. Foremost, of course, were the terms for restoring the states in rebellion to the Union. But the war had opened more fundamental questions. Slavery was finished. That much was certain. But what system of labor should replace plantation slavery? What rights should the freedmen be accorded beyond emancipation itself? How far should the federal government go to settle these questions? And who should decide? the president? or the Congress?

While the war was still on, the North began to grope for answers. Relying on his wartime powers, Abraham Lincoln in December 1863 offered a general amnesty to all but high-ranking Confederates willing to pledge loyalty to the Union and accept the abolition of slavery. When 10 percent of a state's 1860 voters had taken this oath, they could organize a new government and apply for restoration to the Union. Only states under military occupation—Louisiana, Arkansas, and Tennessee—took advantage of Lincoln's generous offer, but he hoped Confederates elsewhere might also be induced to abandon the rebellion.

Although it reflected his conciliatory bent, Lincoln's Ten Percent Plan was really aimed at subverting the southern war effort. What it also did was to reveal the rocky road that lay ahead for Reconstruction. Thus, in Louisiana, sugar planters showed little remorse for the crime of slavery. On the contrary, with the aid of the occupying federal forces, they tried to regain control over the freed slaves, buttressed by oppressive curfew and vagrancy regulations. But the Louisiana freedmen fought right back. Led by the free black community of New Orleans, they began to agitate for political rights. No less than their former masters, ex-slaves intended to be actors in the savage drama of Reconstruction.

With Louisiana very much in mind, Republicans in Congress put forth a stricter substitute for Lincoln's Ten Percent Plan. The initiative came from the Radical wing of the party—those bent on a stern peace and full rights for the freedmen—but with broad support among more moderate Republicans. The Wade-Davis bill, passed on July 2, 1864, laid down, as conditions for the restoration of the rebellious states to the Union, an oath of allegiance by a majority of each state's adult white men, new state governments formed and operated only by those who had never carried arms against the Union, and permanent disfranchisement of Confederate civil and military leaders. The Wade-Davis bill served notice that the congressional Republicans were not about to hand reconstruction policy over to the president.

Lincoln was not perturbed. Rather than openly challenging Congress, he executed a "pocket" veto of the Wade-Davis bill by not signing it before Congress adjourned. At the same time he initiated informal talks with congressional leaders aimed at finding a common ground. The last speech he ever delivered, on April 11, 1865, demonstrated Lincoln's cautious realism. Reconstruction, he pleaded, had to be regarded as a practical, not a theoretical, problem. It could be solved only if Republicans remained united, even if that meant compromising, and only if the defeated South gave its consent, even if that meant forgiveness. What the speech showed, above all, was Lincoln's sense of the fluidity of events, of policy toward the South as an evolving, not a fixed, position.

What course Reconstruction might have taken had Lincoln lived is one of the great unanswered questions of American history. On April 14, 1865—five days after Lee's surrender at Appomattox—Lincoln was shot in the head at Ford's Theater in Washington by an unstable actor named John Wilkes Booth. Ironically, Lincoln might have been spared if the war had dragged on longer, for Booth and his Confederate associates had originally plotted to kidnap the president to force a negotiated settlement. Without regaining consciousness, Lincoln died on April 15.

At one stroke John Wilkes Booth had sent Lincoln to martyrdom, hardened many northerners against the South, and handed the presidency to a man utterly lacking in Lincoln's moral sense and political judgment, Vice-President Andrew Johnson.

PRESIDENTIAL RECONSTRUCTION

At the end of the Civil War, a very big constitutional question remained in dispute—whether, on seceding, the Confederate states had legally left the

Union. If so, then these states became conquered territories, and the terms of their readmission demanded the gravest consideration by the Congress. If not, if even in defeat they retained their constitutional status, the initiative for restoring them to the Union might appropriately be taken by the president. This was Andrew Johnson's view, and by an accident of timing, he was free to act on it. For, under leisurely rules that went back to the early republic, the 39th Congress elected in November 1864 was not scheduled to convene until December 1865.

Johnson's Initiative

Andrew Johnson was a self-made man and a former slaveholder from the hills of eastern Tennessee. A Jacksonian Democrat, he saw himself as the champion of the common man. He hated what he called the "bloated, corrupt aristocracy" of the Northeast, and he was just as disdainful of the southern planters, whom he blamed for the poverty of his own yeoman farmers. Johnson's political career had taken him to the U.S. Senate, where he remained when the war broke out, loyal to the Union. After federal forces captured Nashville, Johnson became Tennessee's military governor. The Republicans nominated him for vice-president in 1864 in an effort to promote wartime political unity and to court the support of southern Unionists.

In May 1865, just a month after Lincoln's death, Johnson launched his own plan for restoration. He offered amnesty to all southerners, irrespective of their part in the rebellion, who took an oath of allegiance to the Union, but excluding high-ranking Confederate officials and the wealthier planters, whom

Andrew Johnson
The president was not an easy man. This photograph of Andrew Johnson (1808–1875) conveys some of the personal qualities that contributed so centrally to his failure to reach an agreement with Republicans on a program of moderate reconstruction.

Johnson held responsible for secession. Such persons could be pardoned only by presidential order. He appointed provisional governors for the southern states, and laid down as conditions for their restoration only that they revoke their ordinances of secession, repudiate their Confederate debts, and ratify the Thirteenth Amendment, which abolished slavery. Within months all the former Confederate states had met Johnson's requirements and had functioning, elected governments.

At first Republicans responded favorably. The moderates among them were sympathetic to Johnson's states' rights argument that it was up to the states, not the federal government, to settle questions of the ballot and civil equality for the freedmen. Even the Radicals were optimistic. They liked the stern treatment of Confederate leaders, and they hoped that the new southern state governments would respond positively to Johnson's conciliatory approach and offer the vote at least to African-Americans who were literate and owned property.

Nothing of the sort happened. Instead, the newly seated southern legislatures moved to restore slavery in all but name. They enacted laws—known as Black Codes—designed to drive the freedmen back to the plantations, to restrict their freedom of movement, and to deny them equality before the law. Localities set curfews; insisted that blacks who wanted to live in town obtain white sponsors; and, in an effort to prevent political mobilization, sharply restricted rights of assembly. The new governments had mostly been formed by ex-Whigs and southern Unionists, but when it came to racist attitudes, not a lot distinguished them from the Confederates. The latter, moreover, swiftly filtered back into the corridors of power. It turned out that Johnson, despite his hard words against them, forgave ex-Confederate leaders easily, so long as he got the satisfaction of making them submit to his personal authority. His perceived indulgence of their efforts to restore white supremacy emboldened the ex-Confederates. They packed the delegations to the new Congress with old comrades—nine members of the Confederate Congress; seven former officials of Confederate state governments; four generals and four colonels; and even the vice-president of the Confederacy, Alexander Stephens.

When Congress convened in early December 1865, the Republicans refused to admit the southern delegations, effectively blocking Johnson's reconstruction program. Although relations with the president had already cooled, the Republicans assumed he would work cooperatively with them in formulating the new terms on which the South would be readmitted to Congress. To that end, a House-Senate committee—the Joint Committee on Reconstruction—was formed and began public hearings on conditions in the South. By now, the worst of the Black Codes had been rescinded, but in place of laws aimed specifically at blacks the states brought forth nonracial ordinances that accomplished the same repressive ends. On top of that, a wave of violence erupted across the South, intended to terrorize the freedmen into submission. In Tennessee, a Nashville paper reported in early 1867 that white gangs "are riding about whipping, maiming and killing all negroes who do not obey the orders of their former masters, just as if slavery existed." Listening to the vivid testimony of officials, observers, and victims, Republicans concluded the South had embarked on a concerted effort to circumvent the Thirteenth Amendment. The only possible response was for the federal government to intervene.

Back in March 1865, the previous Congress had established the Freed-man's Bureau to provide emergency aid to ex-slaves and refugees during the chaotic transition from war to peace. Now, under the leadership of the moderate Republican Senator Lyman Trumbull, Congress voted to extend the Bureau's life, gave it direct funding for the first time, and authorized its agents to step into cases where blacks were being denied the "civil rights belonging to white persons."

More extraordinary was Trumbull's proposal for a civil rights bill, declaring all persons born in the United States to be citizens and granting them, without regard to race, equal rights of contract, access to the courts, and protection of person and property. Trumbull's bill nullified all state laws depriving citizens of these rights, authorized U.S. attorneys to bring enforcement suits in the federal courts, and provided for fines and imprisonment for anyone, including public officials, guilty of depriving a citizen of civil rights. In response to an unrepentant South, Republicans of the most moderate persuasion concluded that the federal government had to assume responsibility for securing the basic civil rights of the freedmen.

Acting on Freedom

While Congress debated, African-Americans as best they could acted on their own idea of freedom. News of emancipation left them exultant and hopeful. Freedom meant many things. It meant reuniting separated families, the end of punishment by the lash, the ability to move around, the opportunity to establish schools, churches, and social clubs, and, not least, the chance to engage in politics. Across the South, blacks held mass meetings, paraded, and formed organizations. In the cities, where free blacks took the lead, Union Leagues and Equal Rights Leagues worked to give the freedmen a political voice. With the encouragement of Freedmen's Bureau agents, state conventions also began to meet, invariably passing resolutions demanding equality before the law and the right to vote—"an essential and inseparable element of self-government."

First of all, however, came economic independence, which emancipated blacks believed was the basis for true freedom. During the Civil War they had acted on this assumption whenever Union armies drew near. During the final months of the war, when the Union directed its military operations against civilians, freedmen found greater opportunities to win control of land. Most visibly, General William T. Sherman reserved vast tracts of coastal lands in Georgia and South Carolina—the Sea Islands and abandoned plantations within 30 miles of the coast—for liberated slaves, and settled them on 40-acre tracts. Sherman only wanted to relieve the pressure the refugees were placing

AMERICAN VOICES

A Plea for Land

*F*ollowing is a painfully written letter by the ex-slaves of Edisto Island to President Andrew Johnson, pleading for a reversal of his order that the lands they now worked be returned to the plantation owners.

Edisto Island S.C. Oct 28th, 1865.
To the President of these United States. We the freedmen Of Edisto Island South Carolina have learned . . . with deep sorrow and Painful hearts of the possibility of government restoring These lands to the former owners. . . . Here is where secession was born and Nurtured Here is where we have toiled nearly all Our lives as slaves and were treated like dumb Driven cattle. This is our home, we have made These lands what they are. . . . Shall not we who Are freedmen and have always been true to this Union have the same rights as are enjoyed by Others? Have we broken any Law of these United States? have we forfeited our rights of property In Land?—If not then! are not our rights as A free people and good citizens of these United States To be considered before the rights of those who were Found in rebellion against this good and just Government. . . . And we who have been abused and oppressed For many long years But be subject To the will of these large Land owners? God forbid.
    . . . We the freedmen of this Island and the State of South Carolina—Do hereby petition to you as the President of these United States, that some provisions be made by which Every colored man can purchase land. and Hold as his own. We wish to have A home if It be but A few acres. . . . May God bless you in the Administration of your duties as the President Of these United States is the humble prayer Of us all.—

In behalf of the Freedmen
Henry Bram
Committee   Ishmael. Moultrie
yates. Sampson

SOURCE: Eileen Boris and Nelson Lichtenstein, eds., *Major Problems in the History of American Workers: Documents and Essays* (Lexington, MA: Heath, 1990), 137–139.

---

on his army as it marched across the lower South. But the freedmen assumed that Sherman's order meant that the land would be theirs.

As the war ended, resettlement became the responsibility of the Freedmen's Bureau, which was charged with distributing confiscated land to "loyal refugees and freedmen" and with regulating labor contracts between freedmen and planters. The Freedmen's Bureau also worked with the large number of northern voluntary associations that sent missionaries and teachers to the South to establish schools for former slaves.

With the encouragement of the Freedmen's Bureau, blacks across the South occupied confiscated or abandoned land, including half a million acres of "Sherman" land in Georgia and South Carolina. Many families stayed on their old plantations in the hope that they could claim some of the land after the war. When the South Carolina planter Thomas Pinckney returned home, his freed slaves told him, "We ain't going nowhere. We are going to work right here on the land where we were born and what belongs to us."

Johnson's amnesty plan, entitling pardoned Confederates to recover property seized during the war, brought these hopes to an abrupt halt. In October 1865, Johnson ordered General Oliver O. Howard, head of the Freedmen's Bureau, to tell Sea Island blacks that the land they occupied would have to be restored to the white owners. When Howard reluctantly obeyed, the dispossessed farmers protested: "Why do you take away our lands? You take them from us who have always been true, always true to the Government! You give them to our all-time enemies! That is not right!" In the Sea Islands and elsewhere, former slaves resisted efforts to remove them. Often led by black veterans of the Union army, they fought pitched battles with plantation owners and bands of ex-Confederate soldiers. In this warfare federal troops often backed the local whites, who generally prevailed in recapturing their former holdings.

As returning planters prepared for a new growing season, a great battle began to take shape over the labor system that would replace slavery. Convinced that blacks could not work without supervision, planters insisted on retaining the gang system of plantation labor, only now paying low wages instead of the food, clothing, and shelter their slaves had once received. Many freedmen voted with their feet. Thousands of families abandoned their old plantations, seeking better lives and more freedom in the towns and cities of the South. Those who remained in the countryside refused to work the cotton fields under the hated gang labor or negotiated tenaciously over the terms of their labor contracts. What was freedom all about if not to have a bit more leisure time, to work less intensely than they had as slaves, and to work for themselves and their families? Whatever system of labor finally might emerge, it was clear that the freedmen and their families would never settle for anything resembling the old plantation system.

The efforts of former slaves to control their own lives ran counter to deeply entrenched white attitudes. "The destiny of the black race," asserted one Texan, could be summarized "in one sentence—subordination to the white race." Southern whites, a Freedmen's Bureau official observed, could not "conceive of the negro having any rights at all." When freedmen resisted, white retribution was swift and often terrible. In Pine Bluff, Arkansas, "after some kind of dispute with some freedmen," whites set fire to their cabins and lynched twenty-four of the inhabitants—men, women, and children. The toll of murdered and beaten blacks mounted into untold thousands. The governments established under Johnson's plan only put the stamp of legality on the pervasive efforts to enforce white supremacy. Blacks "would be *just as well* off

Wage Labor of Ex-Slaves
This photograph, taken in South Carolina shortly after the Civil War, shows former slaves being led from the cotton fields. Although they now worked for wages, they were probably organized into a gang not far removed from the earlier slave gangs. Their plug-hatted crew leader is dressed much as his slave-driving predecessor would have been.

with no law at all or no Government," concluded a Freedmen's Bureau agent, as with the justice they got under the restored white rule.

In this unequal struggle, blacks turned to Washington. "We stood by the government when it wanted help," a black Mississippian wrote President Johnson. "Now . . . will it stand by us?"

Congress versus President

Andrew Johnson was, alas, not the man to ask. In February 1866, he vetoed the Freedmen's Bureau bill, declaring it unconstitutional because Congress lacked authority to provide a "system for the support of indigent people" and because the states most directly affected by its provisions were not yet represented in Congress. The Bureau, said Johnson, was an "immense patronage," showering benefits on blacks never granted to "our own people." A month later, rebuffing the outraged critics of his Freedman's Bureau veto, Johnson vetoed Trumbull's Civil Rights bill, again arguing that federal protection of black civil rights constituted "a stride toward centralization." His racism, hitherto muted, now blazed forth. In his view, granting blacks the privileges of citizenship was discriminatory, operating "in favor of the colored and against the white race," and threatening all manner of evil consequences, including miscegenation.

Taken by surprise, the Republicans were galvanized into action. They failed, just barely, to override Johnson's veto of the Freedmen's Bureau bill, but in early April, they got the necessary two-thirds majorities in both houses and enacted the Civil Rights bill into law. This was a truly historic event, the first time Congress had prevailed over a presidential veto on a major piece of legislation. In July the Freedmen's Bureau was renewed over a second Johnson veto.

Anxious to consolidate their victory, Republicans moved to enshrine black civil rights in an amendment to the Constitution. They were already upset by the dividend the South had gained from emancipation: a jump in federal representation because, under the Constitution, the slave population had counted as only three-fifths, whereas as free persons blacks counted fully (even if they could not vote). Now this question was bundled with civil rights into what became the Fourteenth Amendment. Section 2 reduced a state's representation in the House of Representatives by the percentage of adult male citizens who were denied the vote. Intended to prod the South toward enfranchising the freedmen, Section 2 was quickly overtaken by events and had no lasting significance, save for the insertion of the word *male* into the Constitution, which, to the outrage of woman suffragists, cast women out from the gathering movement toward universal suffrage. The heart of the Fourteenth Amendment was Section 1, which declared that "all persons born or naturalized in the United States" were citizens. No state could abridge "the privileges or immunities of citizens of the United States," deprive "any person of life, liberty, or property, without due process of law," or deny anyone "the equal protection of the laws." These phrases were vague, intentionally so, but they established the constitutionality of the Civil Rights Act and, more important, the basis on which the courts and Congress could establish an enforceable standard of equality before the law in the states.

For the moment, however, the Fourteenth Amendment was most important for its impact on national politics. With the 1866 congressional elections approaching, Johnson somehow figured he had a winning issue in the Fourteenth Amendment. He denounced it, and urged the states not to ratify it. Months earlier, Johnson had begun to maneuver politically against the Republicans, aiming to build a coalition of white southerners, northern Democrats, and conservative Republicans under the banner of "National Union." For discredited Democrats, Johnson's scheme offered the cloak of respectability, and they eagerly seized it. Any hope of creating a new national party, however, was shattered by Johnson's intemperate behavior and by escalating violence in the South. Sympathetic Republicans and ex-Whigs backed off, a dissension-ridden National Union convention in July ended inconclusively, and Johnson's campaign against the Fourteenth Amendment became, effectively, a campaign for the Democratic party. In late August Johnson embarked on a disastrous "swing around the circle"—a railroad tour from Washington to Chicago and St. Louis and back. It was unprecedented for a president to campaign personally, and Johnson made matters worse by engaging in shouting matches with hecklers and by insulting members of the hostile crowds.

The 1866 congressional elections inflicted a humiliating defeat on Johnson. The Republicans, having won a three-to-one majority in Congress, considered themselves "masters of the situation," free to proceed "entirely regardless of [Johnson's] opinions or wishes." As a referendum on the Fourteenth Amendment, moreover, the election registered strong popular support for the civil rights of the freedmen. The Republican Party emerged with a new sense of unity—a unity coalescing not at the center, but on the left, around the root-and-branch program of the Radical minority.

The Radicals represented the abolitionist strain within the Republican party. Most of them hailed from New England, or from the area of the upper Midwest settled by New Englanders. In the Senate, they were led by Charles Sumner of Massachusetts; in the House, by the redoubtable Thaddeus Stevens from Pennslyvania. For them, Reconstruction was never primarily about restoring the Union; rather, it was about remaking southern society. "The foundations of their institutions . . . must be broken up and relaid," declared Stevens, "or all our blood and treasure will have been spent in vain." Only a handful went as far as Stevens in demanding that the plantations be broken up into small farms for the former slaves. But the Radicals had no qualms about expanding the powers of the national government to protect the civil rights of the freedmen and, more than that, grant them the suffrage. Radicals were aggressively partisan. They regarded the Republican party as the instrument of the Lord, and black votes as the means by which the party could dominate the South and bring about its regeneration.

At first, in the months after the surrender at Appomattox, few but the Radicals themselves imagined they had any chance of putting across so extreme a program. Black suffrage especially seemed beyond reach, since the northern states themselves (excepting in New England) denied blacks the vote at this time. And yet, as fury mounted against the intransigent South, Republicans became ever more radicalized until, in the wake of the smashing victory of 1866, they embraced the Radicals' vision of a reconstructed South.

RADICAL RECONSTRUCTION

Afterward, thoughtful southerners admitted that the South had brought radical Reconstruction on itself. "We had, in 1865, a white man's government in Alabama," remarked the man who had been Johnson's provisional governor, "but we lost it." The state's "great blunder" was not to "have at once taken the negro right under the protection of the laws." Remarkably, the South remained defiant even after the 1866 congressional elections. Every state legislature (except, back in July, Tennessee) rejected the Fourteenth Amendment, mostly by virtual acclamation. It was as if they could not imagine that governments installed under the presidential imprimatur and fully functioning might be swept away. But that, in fact, is just what the Republicans intended to do.

Congress Takes Command

The Reconstruction Act of 1867, enacted in March by the Republican Congress, organized the South as a conquered land, dividing it (with the exception of Tennessee) into five military districts, each under the command of a Union general. The price for reentering the Union was granting the vote to the freedmen and disfranchising the South's prewar leadership class—anyone who had taken an oath of loyalty to the Constitution as an officeholder or a commissioned officer and then had participated in the rebellion. Each military commander was ordered to register all eligible adult males, black as well as white, to supervise the election of state conventions, and to make certain that the new state constitutions contained guarantees of black suffrage. Congress would readmit a state to the Union if its voters ratified the constitution, if that document proved acceptable to Congress, and if the new state legislature approved the Fourteenth Amendment (thus ensuring the needed ratification by three-fourths of the states). Johnson vetoed the act, but Congress overrode the veto. By 1870, all ten of the ex-Confederate states had met the requirements and were readmitted to the Union.

Republicans also checkmated President Johnson. The Tenure of Office Act, a companion to the Reconstruction Act, required Senate consent for the removal of any official whose appointment had required Senate confirmation. Congress chiefly wanted to protect Secretary of War Edwin M. Stanton, a Lincoln holdover and the only member of Johnson's cabinet who favored radical Reconstruction. In his position Stanton could do much to prevent Johnson from frustrating the goals of Reconstruction. Congress also required the president to issue all orders to the army through its commanding general, Ulysses S. Grant.

Seemingly defeated, Johnson appointed generals recommended by Stanton and Grant to command the five military districts in the South. But he was just biding his time. In August 1867, after Congress had adjourned, he "suspended" Stanton and replaced him with Grant, believing that the general would act like a good soldier and follow orders. Next Johnson replaced four of the commanding generals, including Philip H. Sheridan, Grant's favorite cavalry general. Johnson, however, had misjudged Grant, who publicly registered his opposition to the president's machinations. When the Senate reconvened in the fall, it overruled Stanton's suspension. Grant, now an open enemy of Johnson's, resigned so that Stanton could resume his office.

In February 1868 Johnson dismissed Stanton. House Republicans lashed back by using the power granted them by the Constitution to impeach—to charge federal officials with "Treason, Bribery, or other high Crimes and Misdemeanors." The House overwhelmingly (128 to 47) brought eleven counts of criminal misconduct, nine of which dealt with violations of the Tenure of Office Act, against the president.

The case went to the Senate, which the Constitution empowers to act as a court in impeachment cases, presided over by Chief Justice Salmon P. Chase. After an eleven-week trial, thirty-five senators on May 15 voted for conviction, one vote short of the two-thirds majority required. Seven moderate Republicans had broken ranks, voting for acquittal along with twelve Democrats. The reluctant Republicans were overwhelmed by the drastic nature of the attack on Johnson; Congress had removed federal judges from office, but never a president. Even if Johnson had broken the law, they felt, the real issue was a political disagreement between Congress and the president. They feared that a conviction based on a policy dispute would establish a dangerous precedent and undermine the presidency, which seemed too high a price just to punish Johnson.

In any case, even without being convicted, Johnson had been defanged, and he was helpless for the remainder of his term to alter the course of Reconstruction.

The impeachment controversy made Grant, already the North's most popular war hero, a Republican hero as well, and he easily won the party's presidential nomination in 1868. In the fall campaign he supported radical Reconstruction, but he also urged reconciliation between the sections. His Democratic opponent was Horatio Seymour, a former governor of New York and a Peace Democrat who almost declined the nomination, certain that the Democrats could not overcome their identification with the disloyal South. As Seymour feared, the Republicans "waved the bloody shirt," stirring up old wartime emotions against the Democrats to great effect. Grant won about the same share of the northern vote (55 percent) that Lincoln had in 1864, and received 214 of 294 electoral votes. The Republicans also retained two-thirds majorities in both houses of Congress.

In the wake of their smashing victory, the Republicans quickly produced the last major piece of Reconstruction legislation—the Fifteenth Amendment, which forbade either the federal government or the states to deny citizens the right to vote on the basis of race, color, or "previous condition of servitude." Proponents of the amendment were aware that it left open the use of poll taxes and property or literacy tests to discourage blacks from voting. But northern states also valued such qualifications, employing them against immigrants and the "unworthy" poor. A California senator warned that in his state, with its rabidly anti-Chinese sentiment, any restriction on that power would "kill our party as dead as a stone." Despite grumbling by Radical Republicans, the amendment passed without modification in February 1869. Congress required the unreconstructed states of Virginia, Mississippi, Texas, and Georgia to ratify it before they were readmitted to the Union. A year later the Fifteenth Amendment became part of the Constitution.

If the Fifteenth Amendment troubled some proponents of black suffrage, this was nothing as compared to the outrage felt by women's rights advocates. They had fought the good fight for so many years for the abolition of slavery, only to be abandoned by their male allies when the chance finally came to get the vote for women. How could the suffrage be granted to ex-slaves, Elizabeth Cady Stanton demanded to know, but not to them? The Fifteenth Amendment opened up a schism in the ranks of the women's movement. In 1868 a group led by Lucy Stone broke with the American Equal Rights Association, which had declared against the Fifteenth Amendment, and formed the New England Woman Suffrage Association. Its goal was to maintain an alliance with the Republicans in the forlorn hope that, once Reconstruction had been settled, it would be time for woman suffrage.

The South during Radical Reconstruction

Between 1868 and 1871 all the southern states met the congressional stipulations and rejoined the Union. Protected by federal troops and encouraged by northern party leaders, state Republican organizations took hold across the South and won control of the newly established Reconstruction governments. These Republican administrations remained in power for periods ranging from a few months in Virginia to nine years in South Carolina, Louisiana, and Florida (see Map 16.1). African-Americans participated prominently in the Reconstruction governments. In Alabama, Florida, South Carolina, Mississippi,

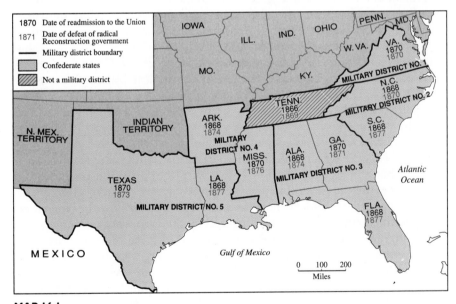

MAP 16.1
Reconstruction
The federal government organized the Confederate states into five military districts during radical Reconstruction. For each state the first date indicates when that state was readmitted to the Union; the second date shows when radical Republicans lost control of the state government. All the ex-Confederate states rejoined the Union from 1868 to 1870, but the periods of radical rule varied widely. Radicals lasted only a few months in Virginia; they held on until the end of Reconstruction in Louisiana, Florida, and South Carolina.

and Louisiana they constituted an outright majority of registered voters. They provided the votes for Republican victories in those states and in Georgia, Virginia, and North Carolina as well, where they accounted for nearly half the registered voters.

Democratic ex-Confederates mocked and scorned black Republican officeholders as ignorant field hands who could only play at politics, and they referred to whites who became Republicans as *scalawags*—an ancient Scots-Irish term for runty, worthless animals. Whites who had come from the North they denounced as *carpetbaggers*—self-seeking interlopers who carried all their belongings in cheap suitcases called carpetbags.

Actually, few southern Republicans conformed to the hostile stereotypes. Some carpetbaggers did come south for personal profit, but they also brought capital and skills. Union army veterans taken with the South—its climate, people, and economic opportunities—also figured heavily among the carpetbaggers. And interspersed with the self-seekers were many idealists anxious to advance the cause of emancipation. The scalawags were even more diverse. Some were former slaveowners, ex-Whigs and even ex-Democrats, drawn to Republicanism as the best way to attract northern capital to southern railroads, mines, and factories. In southwest Texas, the large population of Germans was strongly Republican. They sent to Congress Edward Degener, an immigrant and a San Antonio grocer whom Confederate authorities had imprisoned and whose sons had been executed for treason. Most numerous among the scalawags were yeomen farmers from the back-country districts who wanted to rid the South of its slaveholding aristocracy. Scalawags had generally fought against, or at least refused to support, the Confederacy; they believed that slavery had victimized whites as well as blacks. "Now is the time," a Georgia scalawag wrote, "for every man to come out and speak his principles publickly [*sic*] and vote for liberty as we have been in bondage long enough."

The Democrats' stereotypes of black political leaders were just as false. Until 1867 most African-American leaders in the South came from the elite that had been free before the Civil War. With the formation of the reconstructed Republican governments in 1867, this diverse group of ministers, artisans, shopkeepers, and former soldiers reached out to the freedmen. African-American speakers, some financed by the Republican Congressional Committee, fanned out into the old plantation districts and drew ex-slaves into political leadership. Still, few of the new leaders were field hands; most had been preachers or artisans. The literacy of one ex-slave, Thomas Allen, who was a Baptist minister and shoemaker, helped him win election to the Georgia legislature. "In my county," he recalled, "the colored people came to me for instructions, and I gave them the best instructions I could. I took the *New York Tribune* and other papers, and in that way I found out a great deal, and I told them whatever I thought was right."

Many of the African-American leaders who emerged in 1867 had been born in the North or had spent many years there. They moved south when radical Reconstruction opened up the prospect of meaningful freedom. Like

Hiram R. Revels
In 1870 Hiram R. Revels (1822–1901) was elected to the U.S. Senate from Mississippi to fill Jefferson Davis's former seat. Revels was a free black from North Carolina who had migrated to the North and attended Knox College in Illinois. He recruited blacks for the Union army and as an ordained Methodist minister served as chaplain of a black regiment in Mississippi, where he settled after the war.

white migrants, many were veterans of the Union army. Some had fought in the antislavery crusade, some were employed by the Freedmen's Bureau or northern missionary societies, and a few came from free families and had gone north for an education. Others had escaped from slavery and were returning home, like Blanche K. Bruce, who first taught school in Missouri and then in 1874 became Missisippi's second black U.S. senator.

Although never proportionate to the size of the black population, African-American officeholders held positions of importance throughout the South. In 1868 they constituted a majority in the lower house of the South Carolina legislature. They were heavily represented in the state's executive offices, elected three members of Congress, and won a seat on the state supreme court. Across the South generally, twenty African-Americans served as governor, lieutenant governor, secretary of state, treasurer, or superintendent of education, more than six hundred served as state legislators, and sixteen served in the U.S. House of Representatives. Almost all who became state executives had been free before the Civil War, but in the legislatures most black members had been slaves.

The Republicans who took office had ambitious plans for a reconstructed South. They modernized state constitutions and made more offices elective. They established hospitals, penitentiaries, and asylums for orphans and the insane. Republican governments built roads in areas where roads had never existed. They poured money into rebuilding the region's railroad network. And they did all this without federal financing. Southern Republicans fell far short of making their vision a reality, but they accomplished more than their critics gave them credit for.

To pay for their ambitious programs the Republican governments copied the taxes that northern states had relied on since the Jacksonian period. These were general property taxes applying not only to real estate but to personal wealth as well. The goal was to make planters pay their fair share of taxes and to broaden the tax base by forcing them to sell off uncultivated land. In many plantation counties, especially in South Carolina, Louisiana, and Mississippi, former slaves served as tax assessors and collectors, administering the taxation of their one-time owners.

Increasing tax revenues never managed to overtake the burgeoning obligations assumed by the Reconstruction governments. State debts mounted rapidly, and, as interest payments on bonds fell into arrears, public credit collapsed. On top of that, much of the spending was wasted, especially the aid to railroads, or ended in the pockets of state officials. Corruption was endemic to American politics, of course, present in the southern states before the Republicans came on the scene, and rampant everywhere in this era, not least in the Grant administration itself. But there was no question that, in the free-spending atmosphere of the early Republican regimes, corruption was especially luxuriant or that it was damaging to the cause of radical Reconstruction.

A Freedmen's School
An 1866 sketch from *Harper's Weekly* of a Vicksburg, Mississippi, school run by the Freedmen's Bureau illustrates the desire for education by ex-slaves of all ages. Because most southern blacks were farmers, schools often offered night classes that left students free for field work during the day.

Nothing, however, could dim the achievement in public education. Here the South had lagged woefully; only Tennessee had a system of public schooling. Republican state governments vowed to make up for lost time, viewing education as the foundation for a democratic order. African-Americans of all ages rushed to attend the newly established schools, even when they had to pay tuition. An elderly man in Mississippi explained his desire to go to school: "Ole missus used to read the good book [the Bible] to us . . . on Sunday evenin's, but she mostly read dem places where it says, 'Servants obey your masters.' . . . Now we is free, there's heaps of tings in that old book we is just suffering to learn." By 1875 about half of all the children in Florida, Mississippi, and South Carolina were enrolled in school.

Except in New Orleans, the new schools were segregated. Most African-Americans did not complain. They seemed to agree that integration was an issue for a later day; they shared Frederick Douglass's judgment that separate schools were "infinitely superior" to no schools at all.

The building of schools was part of a larger effort by African-Americans to fortify the institutions that had sustained their spirit during the days of slavery. Most important, they strengthened family life as the cornerstone of new communities. Families moved away from the slave quarters, usually building homes scattered around their old plantations (see Map 16.2, following page). Husbands, wives, and children who had been separated were reunited, sometimes after journeys of hundreds of miles. Couples stepped forward to record marriages that had not been recognized under slavery. Many women refused to work in the fields. Instead, they insisted on tending gardens, managing households, and bringing education and religion to their children. Wives asserted their independence, opening individual bank accounts, refusing responsibility for their husbands' debts at country stores, and bringing complaints of abuse and lack of child support to the Freedmen's Bureau.

Religious belief had deep roots in nineteenth-century slave society. Now, in freedom, the African-Americans buttressed their new communities by founding their own churches. They left their old white-dominated congregations, where they had been relegated to segregated balconies and denied any voice in church governance, and built churches of their own. These churches joined together to form African-American versions of the Southern Methodist and Southern Baptist denominations, including, most prominently, the National Baptist Convention and the African Methodist Episcopal Church. Everywhere the robust black churches served not only as places of worship but as schools, social centers, and political meeting halls.

Black ministers were community leaders and often held political office during Reconstruction. Charles H. Pearce, a Methodist minister in Florida, declared, "A man in this State cannot do his whole duty as a minister except he looks out for the political interests of his people." Calling for the brotherhood of man and the special destiny of the ex-slaves as the new "Children of Israel," black ministers provided a powerful religious underpinning for the Republican politics of their congregations.

MAP 16.2

The Barrow Plantation

Comparing the 1860 map of this central Georgia plantation with the 1881 map reveals the changing patterns of black residence and farming. In 1860 the slave quarters were clustered near the planter's house, which sat on a small hilltop. The free sharecroppers of 1881 built cabins along the spurs or ridges of land between the streams, scattering their community over the plantation. A black church and school were built by this date. A typical sharecropper on the plantation earned most of his income from growing cotton.

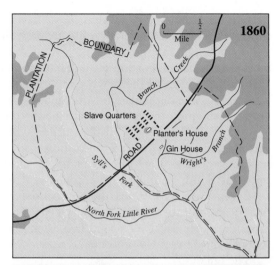

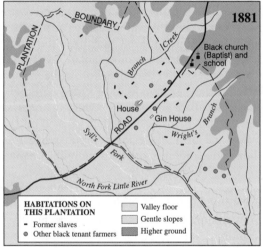

REDEMPTION

Ex-Confederates were blind to the benefits of radical Reconstruction. Indeed, no amount of achievement could have persuaded them that it was anything but an abomination, undertaken without their consent, and intended to deny them their rightful place in southern society. Led by the planters, ex-Confederates calling themselves the Redeemers staged a massive counterrevolution—one designed to "redeem" the South and restore them to political power under the banner of the Democratic party.

Counterrevolution

Insofar as they could win at the ballot box, the Democrats took that route. They worked hard to get ex-Confederates restored to the rolls of registered voters, they appealed to racial solidarity and southern patriotism, and they attacked black suffrage as a threat to white supremacy. By 1869, the Democrats had enough votes to regain office in Tennessee, and a year later, Virginia. But force was equally acceptable. Throughout the Deep South, especially where black voters were heavily concentrated, ex-Confederate planters and their supporters organized secret societies and waged campaigns of terrorism against blacks and their white allies.

The most widespread of these groups, the Ku Klux Klan, first appeared in 1866 as a Tennessee social club but quickly became a paramilitary force under the ferocious leadership of Nathan Bedford Forrest, the Confederacy's most decorated cavalry general. Forrest was notorious for a wartime incident at Fort Pillow, Tennessee, when his troops massacred African-American soldiers after they had surrendered.

By 1870 the Klan was operating almost everywhere in the South in concert with the Democratic party. The Klan murdered and whipped Republican politicians, burned black schools and churches, and attacked party gatherings. In October 1870 a group of Klansmen assaulted a Republican rally in Eutaw, Alabama, killing four African-Americans and wounding fifty-four. Such terrorist tactics enabled the Democrats to seize power in Georgia and North Carolina in 1870 and to make substantial gains elsewhere. An African-American politician in North Carolina wrote, "Our former masters are fast taking the reins of government."

Congress responded by passing a series of Enforcement Acts in 1870 and 1871, including the Ku Klux Klan Act. These laws authorized President Grant to use federal prosecutions, military force, and martial law to suppress conspiracies to deprive citizens of the rights to vote, to hold office, to serve on juries, and to enjoy equal protection of the law. Federal agents penetrated the Klan and gathered evidence that provided the basis for widespread arrests; federal grand juries indicted more than 3,000 Klansmen. In South Carolina, where the Klan was most deeply entrenched, federal troops occupied nine counties and drove as many as 2,000 Klansmen from the state.

The Grant administration's assault on the Klan raised the spirits of southern Republicans, but it also emphasized how dependent they were on the federal government. If they were to prevail over ex-Confederate terrorism, they needed what one southern Republican described as "steady, unswerving power from without."

Northern Republicans, however, had no stomach for an endless guerrilla war in the South. They grew weary of the financial costs of Reconstruction and the continuing bloodshed it seemed to produce. Although re-elected handily in 1872, Grant did not take his victory as a mandate for holding to his interventionist course. Prosecuting Klansmen under the Enforcement Acts was

AMERICAN VOICES

White Terror

*A*lthough Mississippi remained Republican until 1876, this letter from a party
organizer attests to the stubborn white resistance to radical Reconstruction.
Without federal bayonets, a town like Brandon would never be secure for the
Republicans.

Brandon, Mississippi, June 21, 1868
Dear Sir:
    I came here at the most exciting time probably that this place has known
since the war. The democrats had a great meeting. . . . After this I learned a
paper was circulated for [the colored men] to sign, in which they promised to
vote the democratic ticket, and about a 100 names were received. The colored
men were induced to do this by threats of being discharged. . . . Supplies have
already been stopped from those who would not promise to vote the democratic ticket. One man informs me his horse and wagon, valued at $150, is to
be sold to satisfy an attachment for $9, on Saturday next, if not paid before; he
has owing him $100 and over from white men; none will pay, nor will the sale
be stopped unless he votes democratic; but he is true steel and no signs of
backing down. Several colored men have had their lives threatened, and from
the best information I can get there will be a row here unless a squad of
troops are sent here to keep order. There is not a white republican in town. . . .
    Since writing the above, and while out about ten minutes from my room, a
K.K.K. warning was put under my door. Below is a copy:

    The bloody dagger is drawn; the trying hour is at hand; beware! Your
    steps are marked; the eye of dark chief is upon you. First he warns; then
    the avenging dagger flashes in the moonlight.
        By order of the Grand Cyclops. . . .

    Make a request of the post commander for the troops to be here on elec-
tion day, or have them sent over on Wednesday, if possible.
    Excuse haste, and my scribbling, mistakes, &c.
                                                Respectfully yours,
                                                D. S. Harrison

SOURCE: Stanley I. Kutler, ed., *Looking for America*, 2d ed. (New York: Norton, 1979), 36–37.

an uphill battle. U.S. attorneys usually faced all-white juries, and the Justice
department lacked the resources to prosecute effectively. After 1872, prosecutions began to drop off, and many Klansmen received hasty pardons; few served
significant prison terms. Moreover, the Supreme Court undercut the Enforcement Acts by ruling that the Fourteenth Amendment protected citizens from

Klan Portrait, 1868
Two armed Klansmen from
Alabama pose proudly in their
disguises. Northern audiences saw
a lithograph based on this photograph in *Harper's Weekly* in
December 1868.

actions by the *states*, not by other citizens, so that federal prosecution of private
groups like the Klan became legally questionable.

The faltering zeal for Reconstruction in the North, however, had much
broader sources. The worst depression in the nation's history struck in 1873,
and the North became preoccupied with its own economic problems. Northern business interests complained that the turmoil of Reconstruction retarded
the South's economic recovery and harmed their investment opportunities.
Sympathy for the freedmen also began to wane. The North was flooded with
one-sided, often racist reports, such as James S. Pike's *The Prostrate State* (1873),
of extravagant, corrupt Republican rule and a South in the grip of "a mass of
black barbarism." In the 1874 elections, the Republicans suffered a crushing
defeat, losing control of the House of Representatives for the first time since
secession, and also losing seven normally Republican northern states to the
Democrats. For Republican party strategists, the political costs in a disillusioned
North began to outweigh their hopes for a Republican-dominated South.

In a kind of self-fulfilling prophecy, the unwillingness of the Grant administration to shore up Reconstruction guaranteed that it would fail. Republican

governments that were denied federal help found themselves overwhelmed by ex-Confederate politicians during the day and by terrorists at night. Democrats overthrew Republican governments in Texas in 1873, in Alabama and Arkansas in 1874, and in Mississippi in 1875.

The Mississippi campaign showed all too clearly what the Republicans were up against. As elections neared in 1875, paramilitary groups such as the Rifle Clubs and the Red Shirts operated openly. Often local Democrats paraded armed, as if they were militia companies. They identified black leaders in assassination lists called "dead-books"; broke up Republican meetings; provoked rioting that left hundreds of African-Americans dead; and threatened voters, who still lacked the protection of the secret ballot. Mississippi's Republican governor, Adelbert Ames, a Congressional Medal of Honor winner from Maine, appealed to President Grant for federal troops, but Grant refused. Ames then contemplated organizing a state militia but ultimately decided against it, believing that only blacks would join. Rather than escalate the fighting and turn it into a racial war, he conceded victory to the terrorists.

By 1877 Republican governments, backed by token U.S. military units, remained in only three states: Louisiana, South Carolina, and Florida. Elsewhere, the ex-Confederates were back in the saddle.

Sharecropping

In the meantime, the freedmen were locked in a great economic struggle with their former owners. In 1869, the Republican government of South Carolina had established a land commission empowered to buy property and resell it on easy terms to the landless. In this way about 14,000 black families acquired farms. South Carolina's land distribution plan showed what was possible, but it was the exception, not the rule. Despite a lot of rhetoric, Republican regimes elsewhere did little to help the freedmen fulfill their dreams of becoming independent farmers. Federal efforts proved equally feeble. The Southern Homestead Act of 1866 offered 80-acre grants to settlers, limited for the first year to freedmen and southern Unionists. The advantage was strictly symbolic, however, since the public land made available to homesteaders was off the beaten track in swampy, infertile parts of the lower South, and since, in any case, they lacked the resources to get started. Only about a thousand families finally succeeded. There was no reversing President Johnson's order restoring confiscated lands to ex-Confederates, even after the Radical Republicans had the power to do so. Property rights, it seemed, trumped everything else. The Freedman's Bureau, which had earlier championed the land claims of the ex-slaves, now devoted itself to teaching them how to be good agricultural laborers.

So, while they yearned for farms of their own, most freedmen started out landless, and with no option but to work for their former owners. But not, they vowed, under the conditions of slavery—no gang work, no overseers, no fines or punishments, no regulation of their private lives or personal freedom. They were willing to work for wages, provided the pay was high enough, as it

Sharecropping
This sharecropping family seems proud of its new cabin and crop of cotton, which it planted in every available bit of ground. But the presence of the white landlord in the background suggests that sharecropping was only a limited kind of economic freedom.

was, for example, on the great sugar plantations of Louisiana taken over after the war by northern investors. The problem was that cotton planters lacked the money to pay wages, at least until the crop came in, and sometimes, in lieu of a straight wage, they offered a share of the crop. As a *wage*, sharecropping was a bad deal for the freedmen, but it opened up interesting possibilities. They quickly realized that, if they could be paid in shares for their work, they could pay in those same shares to rent the land they worked. This form of land tenantry, already familiar in parts of the South among white farmers, the freedmen now seized on for the independence it offered them. Planters resisted, believing, as one wrote, that "wages are the only successful system of controlling hands." But, in a battle of wills that broke out all across the cotton South, the planters yielded to "the inveterate prejudices of the freedmen, who desire to be masters of their own time."

Thus there sprang up, quite spontaneously, a distinctively southern system of agricultural labor—*sharecropping*, in which the freedmen worked as renters, exchanging their labor for the use of land, house, implements, and sometimes seed and fertilizer. Typically they turned over between half and two-thirds of their crops to the landlord. The sharecropping system joined laborers and the owners of land and capital in a common sharing of risks and returns. But it was a very unequal relationship, given the force of southern law and custom on the white landowner's side, and given the dire economic circumstances of the sharecroppers. Starting out in poverty, they had no way of making it through the first growing season without borrowing for food and supplies.

Country storekeepers stepped in. Bankrolled by their northern suppliers, they "furnished" the sharecroppers and took as collateral *liens* on their crops. Under laws passed by the new Democratic regimes, crop liens effectively transferred the crops to the storekeeper, leaving sharecroppers only the proceeds that remained after their debts had been paid. Once indebted at one store, the sharecropper was no longer free to shop around, and became an easy target for exhorbitant prices, usurious interest rates, and crooked bookkeeping. As cotton prices declined during the 1870s, more and more sharecroppers failed to settle accounts and fell into permanent debt. And if the merchant was also the landowner, or conspired with the landowner, the debt became a pretext for forced labor, or *peonage*, although evidence now suggests that sharecroppers generally managed to pull up stakes and move on once things became hopeless. Sharecroppers always thought twice about moving, however, because part of their "capital" was being known and well-reputed in their home communities. Freedmen who lacked that local standing generally found sharecropping hard going and likely ended up in the ranks of agricultural laborers.

In the face of so much adversity, black families struggled to better themselves. By the end of Reconstruction, about one-quarter of them had managed to save enough to rent with cash payments. Land ownership was harder to achieve. In many places whites would not sell to blacks or jacked up prices exhorbitantly. For the sake of independence, however, black farmers persevered. Eventually they owned about a third of the land they cultivated, but rarely the best land and usually at a cost greater than its fertility warranted.

For the freedmen, sharecropping was not the worst choice; it certainly beat laboring for their former owners. But for southern agriculture, the costs were devastating. Sharecropping committed the South inflexibly to cotton, the one cash crop capable of satisfying the financial demands of landowners and furnishing merchants. Crop diversification declined, costing the South its self-sufficiency in grains and livestock. And with farms leased year-to-year, neither tenant nor owner had any incentive to improve the property. The crop-lien system lined merchants' pockets with unearned profits—economists estimate the excessive rate of profit at 13.5 percent—that might otherwise have gone into agricultural improvement. The result was a stagnant farm economy, blighting the South's future and condemning it to economic backwardness—a kind of retribution, in fact, for the fresh injustices visited on the people it had once enslaved.

The Political Crisis of 1877

Northerners were scarcely aware of the South's agrarian revolution. National politics had moved on, and other concerns absorbed the voter. Foremost was the stench of scandal that hung over the White House. In 1875 Grant's secretary of the treasury, Benjamin Bristow, exposed the so-called Whiskey Ring, a network of distillers and government agents who had defrauded the Treasury of millions of dollars of excise taxes on liquor. The ringleader was a Grant appointee, and Grant's own private secretary, Orville Babcock, had a hand in the scandal. The others went to prison, but Grant stood by Babcock, possibly perjuring himself to save his secretary from jail. On top of this, the economy had fallen into a severe depression after 1873. Grant's administration responded ineffectually, rebuffing the pleas of debtors for relief by increasing the money supply (see Chapter 19). Among the casualties of the depression was the Freedman's Savings and Trust Company, which had been sponsored by the Freedman's Bureau and held the small deposits of thousands of ex-slaves. When the bank failed in 1874, Congress refused to compensate the depositors, and many lost their life savings. In denying their pathetic pleas, Congress was signaling also that Reconstruction had lost its moral claim on the country.

Abandoning Grant, the Republicans in 1876 nominated Rutherford B. Hayes, governor of Ohio, a colorless figure but untainted by corruption or by strong convictions—in a word, a safe man. His Democratic opponent was Samuel J. Tilden, governor of New York, a wealthy lawyer with ties to Wall Street and a reform reputation for helping to break the grip of the thieving Tweed Ring on New York City politics. The Democrat Tilden, of course, favored "home rule" for the South but so, more discretely, did the Republican Hayes. Reconstruction actually did not figure prominently in the campaign and was mostly subsumed under broader Democratic charges of "corrupt centralism" and "incapacity, waste, and fraud." By now, Republicans had essentially written off the South, and scarcely campaigned there. Not a lot was said about the states still ruled by Reconstruction governments—Florida, South Carolina, and Louisiana.

Once the returns started coming in on election night, however, those three states began to loom very large indeed. Tilden led in the popular vote and, victorious in key northern states, seemed headed for the White House. But sleepless politicians at Republican headquarters realized that if they kept Florida, South Carolina, and Louisiana, Hayes would win by a single electoral vote. The campaigns in those states had been bitterly fought, replicating the Democratic assaults on blacks that had overturned Republican regimes everywhere else in the South. But Republicans still controlled the election machinery in those states, and, citing Democratic fraud and intimidation, they could certify Republican victories. The audacious announcement came forth from Republican headquarters: Hayes had carried the three southern states and won the election. But, of course, newly elected Democratic officials in the three states also sent in electoral votes for Tilden, and, when Congress met in early 1877, it faced two sets of electoral votes from those states.

The Constitution does not provide for this contingency. All it says is that the president of the Senate (in 1877, a Republican) opens the electoral certificates before the House (Democratic) and the Senate (Republican) and that "The votes shall then be counted." For weeks, ever since the November election, an air of crisis had gripped the country. There was wild talk of inside deals, of a new election, even of a violent coup and civil war. Just in case, the commander of the army, General William T. Sherman, deployed four artillery companies in Washington. Finally, Congress decided to appoint an electoral commission to settle the question. The commission included seven Republicans; seven Democrats; and, as the deciding member, David Davis, a Supreme Court justice not known to have fixed party loyalties. But Davis disqualified himself by accepting an Illinois seat in the Senate. He was replaced by Republican Justice Joseph P. Bradley, and by 8 to 7, the commission awarded the disputed votes to Hayes.

Outraged Democrats had one more trick up their sleeves. They controlled the House, and they set about stalling a final count of the electoral votes so as to prevent Hayes's inauguration on March 4. But a week before, secret Washington talks had begun between southern Democrats and Ohio Republicans representing Hayes. Other issues may have been on the table, but the main thing was the situation in South Carolina and Louisiana, where Republican governors physically occupied the statehouses, protected by Union troops. But for the disputed federal election, ironically, the military would not have intervened, and the ex–Confederate Redeemers would already have seized power. Exactly what deal was struck, or how involved Hayes himself was, will probably never be known, but on March 1 the House Democrats suddenly ended their filibuster, the ceremonial counting of votes went forward, and Hayes was inaugurated on schedule. He soon ordered the Union troops back to their barracks, and the Republican regimes in South Carolina and Louisiana fell. Reconstruction had ended.

In 1877 political leaders on all sides seemed ready to say that what Lincoln had called "the work" was complete. But for the freedmen, the work had only begun. Reconstruction turned out to have been a magnificent aberration, a magnum leap beyond what most white Americans actually felt was due their black fellow citizens. Redemption represented a sad falling back to the norm. Still, something real had been achieved—three rights-defining amendments to the Constitution; some elbow room to advance economically; and, not least, a stubborn confidence among blacks that, by their own efforts, they could lift themselves up. Things would, in fact, get worse before they got better, but the work of the Reconstruction was imperishable and could never be effaced.

CHAPTER 16 TIMELINE

1863	Lincoln announces his Ten Percent Plan
1864	Wade-Davis bill passed by Congress Lincoln gives Wade-Davis bill a "pocket" veto
1865	Freedmen's Bureau established Lincoln assassinated; Andrew Johnson succeeds as president Johnson implements his restoration plan
1866	Republicans fail to override Johnson's veto of Freedmen's Bureau bill Civil Rights Act passes over Johnson's veto of Freedmen's Bureau bill Johnson makes disastrous "swing around the circle" Johnson defeated in congressional elections
1867	Reconstruction Acts Tenure of Office Act
1868	Impeachment crisis Fourteenth Amendment ratified Ulysses S. Grant elected president
1870	Ku Klux Klan at peak of power Enforcement Acts passed by Congress Fifteenth Amendment ratified
1871	Ku Klux Klan Act passed by Congress
1872	Grant's re-election as president
1873	Panic of 1873 ushers in depression of 1873–1877
1874	Democrats win majority in House of Representatives
1875	Whiskey Ring scandal undermines Grant administration
1877	Congressional compromise makes Rutherford B. Hayes president after disputed election Reconstruction ends

THEMATIC TIMELINE

	ECONOMY The Triumph of Industrialism	GOVERNMENT From Inaction to Progressive Reform	SOCIETY Rise of Urban Culture	DIPLOMACY An Emerging World Power
1877	Carnegie launches modern steel industry Knights of Labor becomes national movement (1878)	Election of Rutherford B. Hayes ends Reconstruction	National League founded (1876) Dwight L. Moody pioneers urban revivalism	U.S. becomes a net exporter
1880	Swift pioneers vertically integrated firm American Federation of Labor founded (1886)	Chinese Exclusion Act (1882) Civil service reform (1883)	Electrification transforms city life First *Social Register* defines high society (1888)	Diplomacy of inaction Naval buildup begins
1890	U.S. surpasses Britain in iron and steel output Economic depression (1893–97) F.W. Taylor introduces scientific management	Populist party founded (1892) McKinley defeats Bryan's free silver crusade (1896) Black disfranchisement and racial segregation in the South	Immigration from southeastern Europe rises sharply Settlement houses spread progressive ideas to cities Hearst's *New York Journal* pioneers yellow journalism	Social Darwinism and Anglo-Saxonism promote expansionism Spanish-American War (1898–99); conquest of the Philippines
1900	Great merger movement Industrial Workers of the World founded (1905)	Theodore Roosevelt attacks the trusts Hepburn Act enforces government's regulation of railroads (1906) Women take leading roles in social reform	Muckraking journalism Movies begin to overtake vaudeville	Panama cedes Canal Zone to United States (1903) Roosevelt Corollary to Monroe Doctrine (1904) Root-Takahira agreement (1908)
1910	Ford builds first automobile assembly line	Revival of the struggle for civil rights; NAACP founded (1910) New Freedom legislation creates Federal Reserve, FTC	Urban liberalism	Taft's Dollar Diplomacy promotes American business Wilson proclaims U.S. neutrality in World War I

PART 4

A MATURING INDUSTRIAL SOCIETY

1877-1914

The decade after Reconstruction marked a watershed in American life. For the first time, farmers no longer constituted a majority of the nation's work force. America's future was now linked to its industrial development. As heavy industry emerged and the railroad system was completed, nationwide firms began to dominate American enterprise. The modern labor movement emerged, and, as immigration surged, the foreign-born and their children became America's workers.

The demands of industrialism for western resources largely drove the final surge of settlement across the Great Plains and to the Pacific, in the process overwhelming the native American inhabitants, disrupting the long-established Hispanic communities of the Southwest, and attracting a multiethnic population from Europe, Asia, and Mexico. The phenomenal growth of the cities was likewise the product of industrialism. An urban way of life emerged unlike anything seen before in America.

In this era of economic expansion, there seemed little need for government intervention. The major parties were robust, but their vitality stemmed from a political culture of popular participation and the informal functions they performed as organized machines. The political status quo was upset by the rise of the Populist party during the depressed 1890s. The Republicans turned back that challenge in 1896, but they then had to contend with another economic concern—the concentration of corporate industry—that dominated the Progressive Era. In those years, the nation addressed a host of reform issues, including political corruption, urban problems, and the demands of African-Americans for equality.

Finally, the United States began to assert itself globally, warring with Spain in 1898, acquiring an overseas empire, and pressing for open markets in Latin America and Asia. As World War I approached, there would be no evading the entanglements that came with America's status as a Great Power.

CHAPTER 17

THE AMERICAN WEST

- The Great Plains
- The Far West

During the last decades of the nineteenth century, American society seemed at odds with itself. From one angle the nation looked like an advanced industrial society, with great factories and mills and enormous, crowded cities. But from another angle America still seemed to be a frontier country, with pioneers streaming onto the Great Plains, repeating the old dramas of "settlement" they had been performing ever since Europeans first set foot on the continent. Not until the census of 1890 did the federal government declare that a "frontier of settlement" no longer existed: the country's "unsettled area has been so broken into . . . that there can hardly be said to be a frontier line."

That same year, 1890, the country surpassed Great Britain in the production of iron and steel. Newspapers reported Indian wars and labor strikes in the same edition. The last tragic episode in the suppression of the Sioux, the massacre at Wounded Knee, South Dakota, occurred only eighteen months before the great Homestead steel strike of 1892. This alignment of events from the distant worlds of factory and frontier was not accidental. The final surge of settlement across the Great Plains and the Far West was powered primarily by the dynamism of American industrialism.

THE GREAT PLAINS

During the 1860s agricultural settlement reached the western margins of the high-grass prairie country. Beyond, roughly at the 98th meridian, stretched vast semiarid lands uninviting to farmers accustomed to woodlands and ample rainfall (see Map 17.1). The geologic event that created the Great Plains had occurred 60 million years before, when the Rocky Mountains had been thrust up out of the ocean covering western North America. With no outlet, the shallow inland sea to the east dried up, forming a hard pan on which sediment washing down from the mountains built up a loose, featureless surface layer. The mountain barrier also made for a dry climate, because the moisture-laden winds from the Pacific spent themselves on the western slopes. Only vegetation capable of withstanding the periodic droughts and bitter winters could take hold on the plains. The short gramma grass, the linchpin of this fragile ecosystem, matted the easily blown soil into place and sustained a rich wildlife dominated by the grazing pronghorn antelope and buffalo. What the dry short-grass country had not sustained, until Indians began migrating there in quite recent times, was human settlement.

Indians of the Great Plains

Probably a hundred thousand native Americans lived on the Great Plains at mid-nineteenth century. They were a diverse people, divided into six linguistic families and at least thirty tribal groupings. On the eastern margins and along the Missouri River, the Mandan, Arikara, and Pawnee planted maize and beans and lived in permanent villages. The ravaging smallpox and measles brought by Europeans decimated these concentrated, sedentary tribes. Less vulnerable to epidemics were the hunting tribes that had migrated to the Great Plains since the seventeenth century: Kiowa and Comanche in the southwest; Arapaho and Cheyenne on the central plains; and, to the north, Blackfeet, Crow, Cheyenne, and the great Sioux nation.

Originally the Sioux had been eastern prairie people, occupying semiper-manent settlements in the lake country of northern Minnesota. With fish and game dwindling, some Sioux tribes drifted westward and around 1760 began to cross the Missouri River. These Sioux became a nomadic people, living in portable skin tepees and following the buffalo. Splendid hunters and formidable fighters, the Sioux claimed the entire Great Plains north of the Arkansas River as their hunting grounds.

The westernmost Sioux—they called themselves the Teton people, or Lakota (meaning "allies")—made up a loose confederation of seven tribes. In the winter months the tribes broke up into small bands, but each spring they assembled and prepared for the summer hunt, and for battle. Mostly, raiding parties rode forth intent on capturing ponies and taking scalps, but occasionally, long columns of warriors mounted serious territorial campaigns against rival tribes. The Sioux, it must be remembered, were an invading people who dominated the northern Great Plains by driving out or subjugating longer-settled tribes.

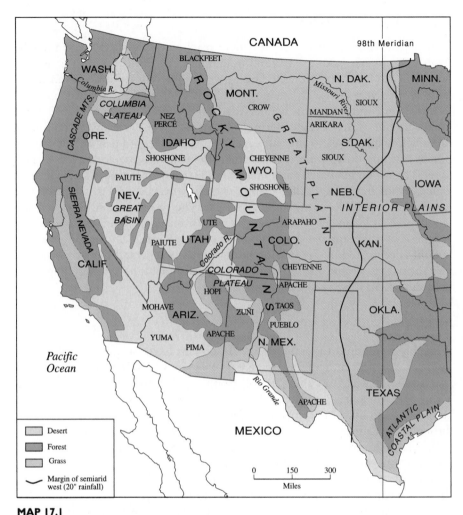

MAP 17.1
The Natural Environment of the West
As settlers pushed into the Great Plains beyond the line of semiaridity, they sensed the over-whelming power of the natural environment. In a landscape without trees for fences and barns and without adequate rainfall, ranchers and farmers had to relearn their business. The native Americans peopling the plains and mountains had learned to live in this environment, but this knowledge counted for little against the ruthless pressure of the settlers to domesticate the West.

A society that celebrates the warrior virtues is likely to define gender roles sharply. But before the Sioux acquired horses, chasing down the buffalo had in-volved the entire community. Women and men worked collectively to construct a "pound" and channel the herds in the right direction. With the arrival of horses, however, the hunt changed, and gender roles became more fixed. On horseback, the men became highly efficient hunters. The women stayed behind to prepare the mounting piles of buffalo skins. This was laborious, painstaking work, heavily burdening the Sioux women, but also enriching the tribe.

Living so close to nature, depending on its bounty for survival, the Sioux saw sacred meaning in every manifestation of the natural world. Unlike Europeans, they conceived of God not as a supreme being but as, in the words of the ethnologist Clark Wissler, "a controlling power or series of powers pervading the universe"—Wi, the sun; Skan, the sky; Maka, the earth; Inyan, the rock. Below these came the moon, wind, buffalo, and so on, down through a hierarchy embodying the entire natural order.

By prayer and fasting in some isolated place, Sioux prepared themselves to experience those mysterious powers. The vision, when a supplicant achieved it, attached itself to some object—a feather, the skin of an animal, or a shell— which was tied into a sacred bundle that became the person's lifelong talisman. For the tribe as a whole, Sacred Pipe bundles served as the symbolic and ceremonial core of Sioux religion. In the Sun Dance, the entire tribe engaged in the rites of coming of age, fertility, the hunt, and combat, followed by four days of fasting and dancing in supplication to Wi, the sun.

The world of the Teton Sioux was not self-contained. All along they had traded pelts and buffalo robes for the produce of the agriculturalist Indians. These exchanges expanded to the white traders who appeared on the upper Missouri River during the eighteenth century. Although the buffalo provided most of the essentials of life, the Sioux came to rely as well on the traders' pots, kettles, blankets, knives, and firearms. The trade system they entered was linked to the Euro-American market economy, yet it was also integrated into the Sioux way of life. Everything depended on the survival of the Great Plains as the Sioux had found it—wild grassland on which the antelope and buffalo ranged free.

Intruders

On first encounter, white Americans saw no better use for the Great Plains. After exploring a drought-stricken stretch in 1820, Major Stephen H. Long declared it "almost wholly unfit for cultivation, and of course uninhabitable by a people depending upon agriculture for their subsistence."

For years thereafter, maps marked the plains region as the Great American Desert. With that notion in mind, Congress formally designated the Great Plains in 1834 as permanent Indian country. Trade with the Indians would continue, but now it would be closely supervised and licensed by the federal government, with the Indian country otherwise off limits to white intrusion.

Events swiftly overtook the nation's solemn commitment to the native Americans. During the 1840s settlers began moving westward to Oregon and California. Instead of serving as a buffer against the British and Mexicans, the Indian country became a bridge to the Pacific. The first wagon train headed west for Oregon from Missouri in 1842. Soon thousands of emigrants traveled the Oregon Trail to the Willamette Valley or, cutting south beyond Fort Hall, down into California. Approaching that juncture in 1859, it seemed to Horace

Greeley as if "the white coverings of the many emigrant and transport wagons dotting the landscape" gave "the trail the appearance of a river running through great meadows, with many ships sailing on its bosom." Only these "ships" left behind not a trailing wake of foam, but a rutted landscape devoid of grass and game and littered with abandoned wagons and rotting garbage.

Talk about the need for a railroad to the Pacific soon began to be heard in Washington. How else could the distant territories formally acquired from Mexico and Britain in 1848 be firmly linked to the Union? The project languished while North and South argued over the terminus for the route to the Pacific. Meanwhile, the Indian country was crisscrossed by overland freight lines and Pony Express riders. In 1861, telegraph lines brought San Francisco into instant communication with the East. The next year, with the South in rebellion, the federal government finally moved forward with the transcontinental project.

No private company could be expected to foot the bill by itself. The construction costs were staggering, and, in the short run, not much traffic could be expected beyond the well-populated states. So the federal government awarded generous land grants along the right-of-way, plus millions of dollars in loans, to the two companies that undertook the transcontinental project.

The Union Pacific, building westward from Omaha, made little headway until the Civil War ended, but then advanced rapidly across Indian country, reaching Cheyenne, Wyoming, in November 1867. It took the Central Pacific nearly that long, moving eastward from Sacramento, to cross the crest of the Sierra Nevada. Both then worked furiously—since the government subsidy was based on miles of track laid—until, to great fanfare, the tracks met at Promontory Point, Utah, in 1869. None of the other land-grant railroads made it as far as the Rockies before the Panic of 1873 hit, throwing them into bankruptcy and bringing work to an abrupt halt.

By then, however, railroad tycoons had changed their minds about the Great Plains. No longer did they see it through the eyes of the Oregon-bound settlers, as a place to be gotten through en route to the Pacific. Rail transportation, they realized, was laying the basis for the economic exploitation of the Great Plains. This calculation spurred the railroad boom that followed the economic recovery of 1878. Construction soared. Forty thousand miles of track were laid west of the Mississippi during the 1880s, linking southern California via the Southern Pacific Railroad to New Orleans and via the Santa Fe to Kansas City, and also linking the Northwest via the Northern Pacific Railroad to St. Paul, Minnesota.

Of all the beckoning opportunities, most obvious was cattle raising. The grazing buffalo made it easy to imagine the Great Plains as cow country. But first, the buffalo had to go. A small market for buffalo robes had existed for years. Then, in the early 1870s, eastern tanneries discovered how to cure the hides, and a huge market suddenly developed. The systematic slaughter of the buffalo began. Already diminished by disease and shrinking pasturage, the great herds almost vanished within ten years. Many people spoke out against this mass killing, but no way existed to stop people bent on making a quick dollar. Besides, as General Philip H. Sheridan pointed out, exterminating the buffalo would starve the Indians into submission and open up the feeding grounds for cattle.

About 5 million head of longhorn cattle roamed south Texas in 1865, hardly worth bothering about because they could not be profitably marketed. That year, however, the Missouri Pacific Railroad reached Sedalia, Missouri. At that terminal, which connected to hungry eastern markets, a $3 longhorn might command $40. With this incentive, Texas ranchers inaugurated the famous Long Drive. Cowboys began to herd cattle hundreds of miles north to the railroads that were pushing west across Kansas.

At Abilene, Texas, and at Ellsworth and Dodge City, in Kansas, ranchers sold their cattle and trail-weary cowboys went on a binge. These wide-open cattle towns captured the nation's imagination as symbols of the Wild West. The reality was much more ordinary. The cowboys, many of them blacks and Hispanics, were in fact farmhands on horseback, working long hours under harsh conditions for small pay. Colorful though it seemed, the Long Drive was actually a makeshift means of bridging a gap in the developing transportation system. As soon as railroads reached the Texas range country during the 1870s, ranchers abandoned the hazardous and wasteful Long Drive.

The Texas ranchers owned or leased the land they used, sometimes in huge tracts. North of Texas, where the land was in the public domain, cattlemen simply helped themselves, treating the land as a free commodity for anyone who seized it and put it to use. Hopeful ranchers would spot a likely area

The Cowboy at Work
Open-range ranching, in which cattle from different ranches grazed together, gave rise to distinctive traditions. At the roundup, cowboys separated the cattle by owner and branded the calves. The cowboy, traditionally a colorful figure, was really a farmhand on horseback, with the skills to work on the range. He earned twenty-five dollars a month, plus meals and a bed in the bunkhouse, in return for long hours of grueling, lonesome work.

along a creek and claim as much land as they could qualify for as settlers under federal homesteading laws, plus what might be added by fraudulent claims taken out by one or two ranch hands. By a common usage that quickly became established, ranchers had a "range right" to all the adjacent land rising up to the divide—the point where the land sloped down to the next creek.

News of easy money traveled fast. Calves were selling at $5 a head, steers at maybe $60 on the Chicago market. Rail connections were in place or coming in. And the grass was free. Profits of 40 percent per annum were almost ensured. The rush was on, drawing from as far away as Europe both the smart money and the romantics (like the recent Harvard graduate Teddy Roosevelt) eager for a taste of the Wild West. By the early 1880s the plains overflowed with cattle, decimating the grass and trampling the water holes.

A cycle of good weather only postponed the inevitable disaster. When it came—a hard winter in 1885, a severe drought the following summer, then record blizzards and bitter cold—cattle died by the hundreds of thousands. An awful scene of rotting carcasses greeted the cowhands riding out onto the range the following spring. On top of that, beef prices plunged when hard-pressed ranchers dumped the surviving cattle on the market. The boom collapsed and investors fled, leaving behind a more enduring ecological disaster: the native grasses never recovered from the relentless overgrazing in the drought cycle.

Open-range ranching came to an end. Ranchers fenced their land and planted hay for the winter. No longer would cattle be left to fend for themselves on the open range. Elsewhere, Hispanic grazers from New Mexico brought sheep in to feed on the forbs and woody plants that had replaced the native grasses. Sheep raising, previously scorned by ranchers as unmanly and resisted as a threat to cattle, became a major enterprise in the sparser high country. Some ranchers even sold out to the despised "nesters"—those who wanted to try farming the Great Plains.

Homesteaders

The movement of farmers onto the plains was not exactly spontaneous. Powerful interests devoted themselves to overcoming the notion of a Great American Desert. Foremost were the railroads, eager to sell off the public land they had been granted—180 million acres of it—and develop traffic for their routes. They advertised aggressively, offered cut-rate tickets, and sold off their land holdings at bargain prices. Land speculators, steamship lines, and the western states and territories did all they could to encourage settlement of the Great Plains. So did the federal government, with its offer under the Homestead Act (1862) of 160 acres of public land to settlers.

"Why emigrate to Kansas?" asked a testimonial in *Western Trail*, the Rock Island Railroad's gazette. "Because it is the garden spot of the world. Because it will grow anything that any other country will grow, and with less work. Because it rains here more than any other place, and at just the right time." As if

Preaching the Word of God

P*astor Carl Johan Nyvall of the Swedish Mission Friends describes his itinerant ministry on the Great Plains, 1876.*

I heard to my surprise that some sixty or seventy Swedish immigrants, planning to settle in this vicinity [Kearney, Nebraska], were to arrive by train from the East. My friend and I met the group at the station. . . . I preached the Word of God twice for these pilgrims and it seemed that their hearts at this time were more receptive than usual. . . .

When one gets to know through firsthand contacts what pioneer life in America is like, one wonders how people can endure it. . . . Even though the settlers may have . . . sixty to eighty acres of cultivated fields, they themselves live . . . in wretched wooden sheds, in sod houses, or in dugouts. . . . A visitor is happy if he is given a place in the same bed as the family. . . . Preachers who would serve the Lord in America by seeking out the scattered immigrants must be prepared for severe privations.

B*ut preachers got in return the warmest of welcomes, as one of Pastor Nyvall's Swedish colleagues found after the long journey to one homestead:*

Some hours' sleep. I looked out the window. . . . Round about were arranged wagon seats and planks, where a large group of people had gathered. . . . When I had preached for some forty minutes, I jumped down from the box, but then a thickset man said, "You ought to know, Pastor, that we have come a long way and that we don't have meetings so often, so please, go and get up on the box again." There was nothing else to do. An equally long sermon again. Baskets and boxes were now opened. There was plenty of food. F. said, "We will go on with the meeting as soon as we have eaten." So, up on the box again. The Lord was with us. Oh, what an advantage to be able to preach for these people!

SOURCE: H. Arnold Barton, ed., *Letters from the Promised Land* (Minneapolis: University of Minnesota Press, 1975), 170–172.

to confirm the optimists, an exceptionally wet cycle occurred between 1878 and 1886. "As the plains are settled up we hear less and less of drouth, hot winds, alkali and other bugbears that used to hold back the adventurous," remarked one Nebraska man. Some settlers attributed the increased rainfall to soil cultivation and tree planting. Others credited God. As a settler on the southern plains remarked, "The Lord just knowed we needed more land an' He's gone and changed the climate."

Buffalo Chips
With no trees around for firewood, settlers on the plains had to make do with dried cow and buffalo droppings. Gathering the "buffalo chips" must have been a regular chore for Ada McColl on her homestead near Lakin, Kansas (1893).

No amount of optimism, however, could dispel the pain of migration. "That last separating word *Farewell!* sinks deeply into the heart," one pioneer woman recorded in her diary, thinking of family and friends left behind. Emigrants had always taken parting as a kind of death, with reunion unlikely "on this side of the dark river." But then came the treeless plains. "Such an air of desolation," wrote a Nebraska-bound woman; and from another woman in Texas, "such a lonely country."

For some women, this hard experience had a liberating side. Prescribed gender roles broke down as women shouldered men's work and became self-reliant in the face of danger and hardship. When husbands died or broke down, wives took up the reins and operated farms on their own. Under the Homestead Act, which accorded widows and single women the same rights as men, women filed 10 percent of the claims. "People afraid of coyotes and work and loneliness had better leave ranching alone," advised one woman homesteader. "At the same time, any woman who can stand her own company . . . will certainly succeed; will have independence, plenty to eat all the time, and a home of her own in the end."

Even with a man around, however, a woman contributed crucially to the farm enterprise. Farming might be thought of as a dual economy, in which men's labor brought in the big wage at season's end, while women's labor provisioned the family day by day and produced a steady bit of money for groceries. And if the crop failed, it was women's labor that carried the family through. No wonder farming communities placed a high premium on marriage: a mere 2.4 percent of Nebraska women in 1900 had never married.

Male or female, the vision of new land to be farmed drove people onto the plains. By the 1870s, the midwestern states had filled up, and farmers looked hungrily westward. The same excitement took hold in northern Europe. Not only Germans came, but also, for the first time, Russians, Norwegians, and Swedes. At the peak of the "American fever" in 1882, over 105,000 Scandinavians emigrated to the United States. Swedish and Norwegian became the primary languages in parts of Minnesota and the Dakotas. Roughly a third of the farmers on the northern plains were foreign-born.

The motivation for most settlers, American or European, was to better themselves economically. But for some southern blacks, Kansas briefly represented something more precious—the modern land of Canaan. In the spring of 1879, with Reconstruction over and federal protection withdrawn, black communities fearful of white vengeance were swept by religious enthusiasm for Kansas. Within a month or so, some 6,000 blacks from Mississippi and Louisiana joined the exodus, most of them with nothing more than the clothes on their backs and faith in the Lord. How many of these "Exodusters" remained is hard to say, but the 1880 census reported 40,000 blacks in Kansas—by far the largest African-American concentration in the West aside from Texas, whose expanding cotton frontier attracted hundreds of thousands of black migrants during the 1870s and 1880s.

No matter where they came from, homesteaders found the plains an alien land. A cloud of grasshoppers might descend and destroy a crop in a day; a brushfire or hailstorm could do the job in an hour. What forested land had always provided—springs for water, lumber for cabins and fencing, ample firewood—was absent. For shelter, settlers often cut dugouts into hillsides and, after a season or two, erected sod houses made of turf from the ground. The absence of trees, on other other hand, meant far less labor clearing the land. New technology and better seed overcame obstacles once thought insurmountable. Steel plows enabled homesteaders to break the tightly matted ground, and barbed wire provided cheap fencing against roaming cattle. Strains of hard-kernel wheat tolerant of the extreme temperatures of the plains came in from Europe. A homesteader would harvest good crops while the wet cycle held, and begin to anticipate the wood-frame house, deep well, and full coal bin that might make life tolerable on the plains.

Then, in the late 1880s, the dry years came and silenced such hopeful calculations. "From day to day," reported the budding novelist Stephen Crane from Nebraska, "a wind hot as an oven's fury . . . raged like a pestilence," destroying the crops and leaving farmers "helpless, with no weapon against this terrible and inscrutable wrath of nature." Land only recently settled emptied out as homesteaders fled in defeat. The Dakotas lost 50,000 settlers between 1885 and 1890, and comparable departures occurred up and down the drought-stricken plains.

Other settlers held on grimly. Stripped of the illusion that rain followed the plow, the survivors came to terms with the semiarid climate prevailing west of the 98th meridian. Mormons in the area near the Great Salt Lake (see

Chapter 13) had demonstrated how irrigation could turn a wasteland into a garden. But the Great Plains mostly lacked the surface water needed for irrigation. The answer lay in dry-farming methods, which involved deep planting to bring subsoil moisture to the roots and quick harrowing after rainfalls to turn over a dry mulch that slowed evaporation. Dry farming developed most fully on the corporate farms that covered up to 100,000 acres in the Red River Valley in North Dakota. Even family farms could not survive with less than 300 acres of cereal crops and machinery for plowing, planting, and harvesting. Dry farming was not for the unequipped homesteader.

By the turn of the century the Great Plains had fully submitted to agricultural development. About half the nation's cattle and sheep, a third of its cereal crops, and nearly three-fifths of its wheat came from the newly settled lands. In this process there was little of the "pioneering" that Americans associated with the westward movement. The railroads came before the settlers; eastern capital financed the ranching bonanza; and agriculture depended on sophisticated dry-farming techniques and modern machinery.

And where was the economic capital of the Great Plains? Far off in Chicago. There, at the hub of the nation's rail system, the wheat pit traded western grain and consigned it to world markets, and the great packing houses slaughtered western cattle and supplied the nation with sausage, bacon, and sides of beef. In return, western ranchers got lumber, barbed wire, McCormick reapers, and Sears Roebuck catalogs. Chicago was truly "nature's metropolis."

The Impact on the Indians

What of the native Americans who had inhabited the Great Plains? Basically, their fate has been told in the foregoing account of western settlement. "The white children have surrounded me and have left me nothing but an island," lamented the great Sioux chief Red Cloud in 1870, the year after the completion of the transcontinental railroad. "When we first had all this land we were strong; now we are all melting like snow on a hillside, while you are grown like spring grass."

No matter that provision for a permanent Indian country had been written into federal law and ratified by treaties with various tribes. As incursions into their lands increased from the late 1850s onward, the Indians struck back all along the frontier: the Apache in the Southwest, the Cheyenne and Arapaho in Colorado, the Sioux in the Wyoming and Dakota territories. The Indians hoped that if they resisted stubbornly enough and exacted a high enough price, the whites would tire of the struggle and leave them in peace. This reasoning seemed not altogether fanciful, given the country's exhaustion after the Civil War. But the federal government did not give up; instead, it formulated a new reservation policy for dealing with the western Indians.

Few whites questioned the necessity of moving the native Americans out of the path of settlement and into reservations. That, indeed, had been the fate of the eastern and southern tribes. Now, however, Indian removal was linked to something new: a planned approach to weaning the Indians from their tribal way of life. Under the guidance of the Office of Indian Affairs, they would be wards of the government until they learned "to walk on the white man's road."

The government set aside two extensive areas for the Indians. It allocated the southwestern quarter of the Dakota Territory—present-day South Dakota west of the Missouri River—to the Teton Sioux tribes. It assigned what is now Oklahoma to the southern Plains Indians as well as to the Five Civilized Tribes—the Choctaw, Cherokee, Chickasaw, Creek, and Seminole—who had been forceably removed there thirty years before (see Chapter 11). Scattered reservations went to the Apache, Navajo, and Ute in the Southwest and to the mountain Indians in the Rockies and beyond.

That the Indians would resist was inevitable. "You might as well expect the rivers to run backward as that any man who was born a free man should be contented when penned up and denied liberty to go where he pleases," said Chief Joseph of the Nez Percé tribe. Under the leadership of Chief Joseph, the Nez Percé undertook in 1877 a remarkable 1,500-mile march from eastern Oregon almost to Canada trying to escape confinement in a small reservation.

The U.S. Army was thinly spread, having been cut back after the Civil War to a total force of 27,000. But these were seasoned troops, including 2,000 black cavalrymen of the Ninth and Tenth regiments, whom Indians called, with grim respect, "buffalo soldiers." Technology also favored the army. Telegraph communications and railroads enabled the troopers to be quickly concentrated; repeating rifles and Gatling guns increased their firepower. As fighting intensified in the mid-1870s, a reluctant Congress appropriated funds for more western troopers. Tribal rivalries meant that the army always had Indian allies. Worst of all for the Indians, however, beyond the formidable U.S. Army or their own disunity, was the overwhelming impact of white settlement.

Resisting the reservation solution, the Indians fought on for years—in Kansas in 1868–1869; in the Red River Valley of Texas in 1874; and sporadically in New Mexico among the Apache, until the capture of Geronimo in 1886. On the northern plains the crisis came in 1875, when the Indian Office, despite a treaty guarantee, ordered the Sioux to vacate their Powder River hunting grounds and withdraw to the reservation.

Led by Sitting Bull, Sioux and Cheyenne warriors gathered on the Little Big Horn River to the west of the Powder River country. In a typical concentrating maneuver, army columns from widely separated forts converged on the Little Big Horn from three sides. The Seventh Cavalry, commanded by George A. Custer, came upon the main Sioux encampment on June 25, 1876. Disregarding orders, the reckless Custer sought out battle on his own. He attacked from three sides, hoping to capitalize on the element of surprise. But his forces were stretched too thin. The other two groups fell back with heavy losses to defensive positions, but Custer's force of 256 men was surrounded and annihilated by Crazy Horse's warriors. It was a great victory, but not a decisive one. The day of reckoning was merely postponed.

Weakened by unrelenting military pressure and increasing physical privation, the Sioux bands one by one gave up and moved onto the reservation. Last to come in were Sitting Bull's followers. They had retreated to Canada, but in 1881, after five hard years, they recrossed the border and surrendered at Fort Buford, Montana.

It was not Indian resistance but relentless white pressure that wrecked the reservation solution. In the mid–1870s prospectors began to dig gold in the Black Hills—sacred land to the Sioux and entirely inside their reservation. Unable to hold back the prospectors or buy out the Sioux, the government opened the Black Hills to gold seekers at their own risk. In 1877, after Sioux resistance had crumbled, federal agents forced the tribes to cede the western third of their Dakota reservation.

The Indian Territory of Oklahoma met the same fate. Two million acres in the heart of the territory had not been assigned to any tribe, and white homesteaders coveted that fertile land. The "Boomer" movement, stirred up initially by railroads running across the Indian Territory during the 1880s, agitated tirelessly to open this so-called Oklahoma District to settlers. In 1889 the government gave in and placed the Oklahoma District under the Homestead Act. On April 22, 1889, a horde of claimants rushed in and staked out the entire district within a few hours. Two tent cities—Guthrie with 15,000 people and Oklahoma City with 10,000—were in full swing by nightfall.

The completion of the land-grabbing process was hastened, ironically, by the avowed friends of the native Americans. The Indians had never lacked sympathizers, especially in the East. After the Civil War, reformers created the Indian Rights Association. The movement got a boost from Helen Hunt Jackson's powerful book *A Century of Dishonor* (1881), which told the story of the unjust treatment of the Indians. The reformers, however, had little sympathy for the tribal way of life. They could imagine no other future for the Indian than assimilation into white society. And they felt that defense of Indian lands against white encroachment was hopeless without granting them the property protections that Americans enjoyed as private owners.

The resulting policy was called *severalty*—the division of reservation lands into individually owned parcels. With the blessing of reformers, the Dawes Severalty Act of 1887 authorized the division of tribal lands, with 160 acres for each family head and smaller parcels for individuals. The land would be held in trust by the government for twenty-five years, and the Indians would become U.S. citizens. Remaining reservation lands would be sold off, with the proceeds placed in an Indian education fund.

The Sioux were among the first to bear the brunt of the Dawes Act. The federal government, announcing that it had gained the Sioux' approval, opened their "surplus" land to white settlement on February 10, 1887. But no surveys had been made, nor any provision for the Sioux living in the ceded

Becoming White

Z itkala-Sa, afterward the author Gertrude Simmons Bonnin, recalled in 1900 her painful transformation from Sioux child to pupil at a mission school.

The first day . . . a paleface woman, with white hair, came up after us. We were placed in a line of girls who were marching into the dining room. These were Indian girls, in stiff shoes and closely clinging dresses. The small girls wore sleeved aprons and shingled hair. As I walked noiselessly in my soft moccasins, I felt like sinking into the floor, for my blanket had been stripped from my shoulders. . . . Late in the morning, my friend Judewin gave me a terrible warning. Judewin knew a few words of English; and she had overheard the paleface woman talk about cutting our long, heavy hair. Our mothers had taught us that only unskilled warriors who were captured had their hair shingled by the enemy. Among our people, short hair was worn by mourners, and shingled hair by cowards! . . . In spite of myself, I was carried downstairs and tied fast in a chair. I cried aloud, shaking my head all the while until I felt the cold blades of the scissors against my neck, and heard them gnaw off one of my thick black braids. Then I lost my spirit. . . .

Now, as I look back upon the recent past, I see it from a distance, as a whole. I remember how, from morning till evening, many specimens of civilized peoples visited the Indian school. The city folks with canes and eyeglass, the countrymen with sunburned cheeks and clumsy feet . . . alike astounded at seeing the children of savage warriors so docile and industrious. . . .

In this fashion many have passed through the Indian schools during the last decade, afterward to boast of their charity to the North American Indian. But few there are who have paused to question whether real life or long lasting death lies beneath this semblance of civilization.

SOURCE: Linda K. Kerber and Jane De-Hart Mathews, eds., *Women's America: Refocusing the Past*, 2d ed. (New York: Oxford University Press, 1987), 254-257.

areas. On top of these signs of bad faith, drought wiped out the Indians' crops. It seemed beyond endurance. The Sioux had lost their ancestral lands. They faced a future as farmers that was alien to all their traditions. And immediately confronting them was a hard winter of starvation.

But news of salvation had also come. An Indian messiah, a holy man who called himself Wovoka, was preaching a new religion on a Paiute reservation in Nevada. In a vision, Wovoka had gone to heaven and received God's word that the world would be regenerated. The whites would disappear, all the Indians of past generations would return to earth, and life on the Great Plains would go back to the time of the roaming buffalo. All this would come to pass in the spring of 1891. Awaiting that great day, the Indians should follow Wo-

The Dead at Wounded Knee
In December 1890 U.S. soldiers massacred about 146 Sioux men, women, and children in the
Battle of Wounded Knee in South Dakota, in the last big fight on the northern plains between
Indians and whites. Black Elk, a Sioux holy man, related that "after the soldiers marched away
from their dirty work, a heavy snow began to fall . . . and it grew very cold." The body of
Yellow Bird lay frozen where it had fallen.

voka's commandments and practice the Ghost Dance. This daylong ritual of
dancing and praying sent participants into trancelike states during which their
spirits rose to heaven. As the frenzy of the Ghost Dance swept through some
Sioux encampments in the fall of 1890, resident whites became alarmed and
called for army intervention.

Among the Minneconjou, the medicine man Yellow Bird had stirred up a
fervent Ghost Dance following. But the Minneconjou chief Big Foot had
fallen desperately ill with pneumonia, and the Minneconjou had agreed to
come in under military escort to Wounded Knee Creek on December 28.
The next morning, when the soldiers attempted to disarm the Indians, a battle
exploded in the encampment. Among the U.S. troopers, 25 died; among the
Indians, 146 men, women, and children perished, many of them shot down as
they fled.

Wounded Knee was the final episode in the long war of suppression of
the Plains Indians. The process of severalty now proceeded without hindrance. On the Dakota lands the Teton Sioux fared relatively well, and many
of the younger generation settled down as small farmers and stock grazers.
Ironically, the more fortunate tribes were probably those occupying reservation lands that did not attract white settlement, and thus were bypassed by
the severalty process. The flood of whites into South Dakota and Oklahoma,
on the other hand, left the Indians as small minorities in lands once wholly
theirs—20,000 Sioux in a South Dakotan population of 400,000 in 1900,
70,000 of various tribes in a population of a million when Oklahoma became a state in 1907.

THE FAR WEST

On the western edge of the Great Plains, the Rocky Mountains rise up to form a great barrier between the flat eastern two-thirds of the country and the rugged Far West. Beyond the Rockies lie two vast plateaus: on the north side the Columbia plateau, extending into eastern Oregon and Washington; and flanking the southern Rockies, the Colorado plateau. Where they break off, the plateaus carve out the desertlike Great Basin that covers eastern Utah and all of Nevada. Separating this arid interior from the Pacific are two great mountain ranges—the Sierra Nevada and, to the north, the Cascades—beyond which lies a coastal region that is cool and rainy to the north but increasingly dry as one proceeds southward until in southern California rainfall becomes almost as sparse as in the interior.

What most impressed Americans about this far western country was its sheer inhospitability. The Far West could not be occupied in standard American fashion—that is, by a multitude of settlers moving westward along a broad front; blanketing the land; and, homestead by homestead, bringing it under cultivation. The wagon trains moving to Oregon's Willamette Valley adopted an entirely different strategy of occupation—the planting of widely scattered settlements in a vast, mostly barren landscape. This had been New Spain's strategy ever since it had sent the first contingents of settlers 700 miles northward from Mexico into the upper Rio Grande Valley in 1598. When the Southwest was taken by the United States 250 years later, major Hispanic settlements existed in New Mexico and California, and lesser settlements were scattered along the borderlands into south Texas. At that time, aside from Oregon, the only significant Anglo settlement was around the Salt Lake in Utah, where Mormons had moved to escape persecution and plant a New Zion. Fewer than 100,000 Euro-Americans—roughly 25,000 of them Anglo, the rest Hispanic—lived in the entire Far West in 1848.

The Mining Frontier

More emigrants would be coming in, certainly, but the nation's newly acquired western territory seemed unlikely to be much of a magnet. California was "hilly and mountainous," noted a U.S. naval officer in 1849, too dry for farming and surely not "susceptible of supporting a very large population." He had not taken account of the recent discovery of gold in the Sierra foothills, however. California would indeed support a very large population, drawn not by the lure of arable land but by dreams of gold.

Extraction of mineral wealth became the basis for the Far West's development (see Map 17.2, following page). This meant, first of all, explosive growth. By 1860, when the Great Plains was still Indian country, California was a booming state with 300,000 residents. There was also a burst of city building. San Francisco quickly became a bustling metropolis—it had 57,000 residents by 1860—the hub of a mining empire that stretched to the Rockies. Finally, the distinctive pattern of geographically dispersed settlement persisted, driven

MAP 17.2

The Mining Frontier

The Far West was America's gold country because of its geological history. Veins of gold and silver form when molten material from the earth's core is forced up into fissures caused by the tectonic movements that create mountain ranges, such as the ones that dominate the far western landscape. It was these veins, the product of mountain-forming activity many thousands of years earlier, that prospectors began to discover after 1848 and furiously exploit.

now, however, by a proliferation of mining sites and by people moving not from east to west, but from west to east, coming mainly from California.

By the mid-1850s, as easy pickings in the California gold country diminished, disappointed prospectors began to pull out and spread across the West in hopes of striking it rich elsewhere. Gold was discovered on the Nevada side of the Sierras, in the Colorado Rockies, and along the Fraser River in British Columbia. New strikes occurred in Montana and Wyoming during the 1860s, a decade later in the Black Hills of South Dakota, and in the Coeur d'Alene region of Idaho during the 1880s.

As the news of each gold strike spread, a wild, remote area turned almost overnight into a mob scene of prospectors, traders, gamblers, prostitutes, and saloon keepers. At least 100,000 fortune seekers flocked to the Pike's Peak area of Colorado in the spring of 1859. Trespassers on government or Indian land, the prospectors made their own law. The mining codes devised at community meetings limited the size of a mining claim to what a person could reasonably work. This kind of informal lawmaking also became an instrument for excluding or discriminating against Mexicans, Chinese, and African-Americans in the gold fields. And it turned into hangman's justice for the many outlaws who infested the mining camps.

The heyday of the prospectors was always brief. They were equipped only to skim gold from the surface of the earth and from streambeds. Extracting the metal locked in underground lodes required mine shafts and crushing mills, which took capital, technology, and business organization. The original claim holders quickly sold out after exhausting the surface gold or when a generous bidder came along. At every gold-rush site the prospector soon gave way to entrepreneurial development and large-scale mining. Rough mining camps turned into big towns.

Nevada's Virginia City started out as a bawdy, ramshackle mining camp, but after the opening of the Comstock lode in 1859, it boasted a stock exchange, ostentatious mansions for the mining kings, fancy hotels, and even Shakespearean theater. Virginia City remained a boom town nevertheless. It was a magnet for job seekers of both sexes: men labored as miners for $4 a day, and many working-class women became dance-hall entertainers and prostitutes because that was the best chance offered them by the city's bonanza economy. In 1870 men outnumbered women two to one. There were a hundred saloons, and brothels lined D Street.

In its final stage the mining frontier passed into the industrial world. At some sites gold and silver proved less important than the commoner metals—copper, lead, zinc—for which there was a huge demand in eastern manufacturing. Copper mining thrived in the Butte district of Montana. In the 1890s, Idaho's Coeur d'Alene silver district became the nation's main source of lead and zinc. Entrepreneurs raised capital, built rail connections, devised technology for treating the lower-grade copper deposits, constructed smelting facilities, and recruited a labor force.

Miners were industrial workers and, like other workers, they organized trade unions. But relations with management, once they soured during the depressed 1890s, became unusually violent. In 1892 at Coeur d'Alene, striking miners fought gun battles with company guards, sent a car of explosive powder careening into the Frisco mine, and threatened to blow up processing plants. Martial law was declared, strikers were crowded into "bullpens" (enclosed stockades), and the strike was broken. Similarly violent strikes took place at Cripple Creek, Colorado, in 1894; at Leadville, Colorado, in 1896; and again at Coeur d'Alene in 1899.

If the Far West had lacked mineral wealth, its history would certainly have been very different. Before the discovery of gold at Sutter's Mill, Oregon's Willamette Valley, not dry California, attracted most westward-bound settlers. And, were it not for the gold rush, California would likely have remained like the Willamette Valley—an economic backwater lacking markets for its products and slow to build population. In 1860, already a state, Oregon had scarcely 25,000 inhabitants, and its principal city, Portland, was little more than a village. Booming California pulled Oregon out of the doldrums by creating a market for the state's produce and timber. During the 1880s Oregon and Washington (which became a state in 1889) grew prodigiously. Where scarcely a hundred thousand settlers had lived twenty years earlier, there were nearly three-quarters of a million by 1890. Portland and, even more dramatically, Seattle had blossomed into important commercial centers, both prospering from a robust mixed economy of farming, ranching, logging, and fishing.

At a certain point, especially as railroads opened up eastern markets, this diversified growth became self-sustaining. But what had triggered it, what had provided the first markets and underwritten the service infrastructure, was the bonanza mining economy, at the hub of which, metropolis for the entire Far West, stood San Francisco.

Hispanics, Chinese, Anglos

California was the anchor of two distinct far western regions. First, it joined with Oregon and Washington to form the Pacific slope. Second, by climate and Spanish heritage, California was linked to the Southwest, which today includes Arizona, New Mexico, and Texas. There, along a 1,500-mile borderland, settlements had been planted over many years by the rulers of New Spain. Most populous and best established were the settlements along the upper Rio Grande Valley in New Mexico; the main town, Santa Fe, over 200 years old, contained 4,635 residents in 1860. At the other end, in California, a Hispanic population was spread thinly in the old presidio towns along the coast and on a patchwork of great ranchos.

The economy of this Hispanic crescent consisted primarily of cattle and sheep ranching. In south Texas there were modest-sized, family-run rancheros. Everywhere else the social order was highly stratified. At the top stood an elite—beneficiaries of royal land grants, proudly Spanish, and devoted to the traditional life of a landed aristocracy. Below them, with little in between, was a laboring population of servants, artisans, *vaqueros* (cowboys), and farm workers. New Mexico also contained a large *mestizo* population, a peasantry of mixed Hispanic and Indian blood, who were Spanish-speaking and Catholic, but who, in their village life and farming methods, were faithful to their Pueblo Indian heritage.

Pueblo Indians, although long past the golden age of their civilization, still occupied much of the Rio Grande Valley, making the New Mexico countryside a patchwork of Hispanic and Pueblo settlements. To the north a vibrant new people, the Navajo, had appeared, warriors like the Apache from whom they had sprung but also skilled craft workers and sheep raisers.

New Mexico was one place where European and native American cultures managed a successful, if uneasy, coexistence, and where the Indian inhabitants were equipped to hold their own against the Anglo challenge. In California, by contrast, the Hispanic occupation had been harder on the native hunter-gatherer peoples, undermining their tribal structure, reducing them to forced labor, and making them easy prey for the aggressive Anglo miners and settlers, who, in short order, nearly wiped out California's once numerous Indian population.

The fate of the Hispanic Southwest after its incorporation into the United States depended on the rate of Anglo immigration. In New Mexico, which remained off the beaten track even after the arrival of railroads in the 1880s, the Santa Fe elite more than held its own, incorporating the Anglo newcomers into Hispanic society through intermarriage and business partnerships. In California, on the other hand, the seizure of the great ranchos by the Anglos was relentless, even though the 1848 peace treaty with Mexico had recognized the property rights of the resident *californios* and had made them U.S. citizens. Around San Francisco the rancho system disappeared almost in a puff of smoke. Farther south, where Anglos were slow to arrive, the dons held on longer, but by the 1880s just a handful of the original families still retained their Mexican land grants.

The New Mexico peasants found themselves similarly embattled. Crucial to their livelihood was the right to graze on common lands. But this was a customary right that could not withstand legal challenge when Anglo ranchers established title and began putting up fences. The peasants responded as best they could. Traditionally, women had always raised much of the family food in small gardens, participated in the village bartering system, made the clothes, and plastered the adobe houses. With the loss of the common lands, the men began to leave the villages seasonally to work on the railroads or in the Colorado mines and sugar-beet fields, earning crucial dollars while leaving the village economy in their wives' hands.

Elsewhere, hard-pressed Hispanic peasants struck back for what they considered rightfully theirs. When Anglo ranchers began to fence in common lands in San Miguel County, the New Mexicans long settled there, *los pobres* (the poor ones), organized themselves as masked raiders and in 1889 and 1890 mounted an effective campaign of harassment against the interlopers. When Anglo farmers swarmed into south Texas after 1900, bent on exploiting new irrigation methods, the displaced *Tejanos* responded with sporadic but persistent night-riding attacks. Much of the raiding by Mexican "bandits" from across the border in the years before World War I was really a civil war waged by embittered *Tejanos* who had lived north of the Rio Grande for generations.

These *Tejanos*, however, like the New Mexico villagers who became seasonal wage laborers, could not avoid being driven into the ranks of a Mexican-American working class as the Anglo economy developed. This same development also began to attract increasing numbers of immigrants from Old Mexico.

All along the Southwest borderlands, economic activity was picking up in the late nineteenth century. Railroads were being built, copper mines were opening in Arizona, cotton and vegetable agriculture was developing in south Texas, and fruit growing was being introduced in southern California. In Texas the Hispanic population increased from about 20,000 in 1850 to 165,000 in 1900. Some Mexicans came as contract workers for railway track gangs and harvest crews; virtually all were relegated to the lowest-paying and most backbreaking work; and everywhere they were discriminated against and reviled by higher-status Anglo workers.

What stimulated the Mexican migration was the enormous demand for workers by a region undergoing explosive economic development. Hence the exceptionally high numbers of immigrants in the California population of this era: between 1860 and 1890 roughly one-third were foreign-born—more than twice the level for the country as a whole. Many came from Europe; most numerous were the Irish, followed by the Germans and British. But there was also another group that was unique to the West—the Chinese.

Attracted first by the California gold rush of 1849, 200,000 Chinese came to the United States over the next three decades. In those years they consti- tuted a considerable minority of California's population, around 9 percent. Because virtually all Chinese were actively employed, they represented a much larger proportion of the state's labor force, probably a quarter. Elsewhere in the West, at the crest of mining activity, their presence could surge remark- ably—for example, to over 25 percent of Idaho's population in 1870.

The coming of the Chinese to North America was part of a worldwide Asian migration that began in the mid-nineteenth century. Driven by poverty, Chinese went to Australia, Hawaii, and Latin America; Indians to Fiji and South Africa; and Javanese to Dutch colonies in the Caribbean. Most of these Asians migrated as indentured servants, which in effect made them the prop- erty of others. In America indentured servitude was no longer lawful, so the Chinese came as free workers. Their passage was financed by a *credit-ticket sys- tem*, by which they were able to borrow passage money from a broker while retaining their personal freedom and their right to choose their employers.

Once in America, Chinese immigrants normally entered the orbit of the Six Companies, a powerful confederation of Chinese merchants in San Fran- cisco's Chinatown. Most of the arrivals were unattached men eager to earn a stake and return to their native Cantonese villages. The Six Companies not only acted as an employment agency but also provided new arrivals with the social and commercial services they needed to survive in an alien world. The few Chinese women—the male-female ratio was thirteen to one—worked mostly as servants or prostitutes, sad victims of the desperate poverty that drove the Chinese to America.

Until the early 1860s, when surface mining played out, Chinese men la- bored mainly in the California gold fields—as prospectors where the white miners permitted it, as laborers and cooks where they did not. When con- struction began on the transcontinental railroad, the Central Pacific hired Chinese workers. Eventually Chinese constituted four-fifths of the railroad's labor force, doing most of the pick-and-shovel labor of laying the railroad track across the Sierras. Many were recruited directly from around Canton by labor agents to work in gangs under the control of "China bosses," who not only supervised but fed, housed, paid, and often cheated them.

When the transcontinental railroad was completed in 1869, the Chinese scattered. Some continued to work in construction gangs for the railroads, while others labored on swamp-drainage projects in the Central Valley and then became agricultural workers, and if they were lucky, small farmers and

Building the Central Pacific
Chinese laborers work on the great trestle spanning the canyon at Secret-
town in the Sierra Nevada.

orchardists. The mining districts of Idaho, Montana, and Colorado also attracted large numbers of Chinese, but according to the 1880 census, nearly
three-quarters remained in California. "Wherever we put them, we found
them good," remarked Charles Crocker, one of the promoters of the Central
Pacific. "Their orderly and industrious habits make them a very desirable class
of immigrants."

White workers, however, did not share the employers' enthusiasm for Chinese labor. In other parts of the country, racism was directed against African-
Americans; in California, where there were few blacks, it found a target in the
Chinese. "They practice all the unnameable vices of the East," wrote the young
journalist Henry George. "They are utter heathens, treacherous, sensual, cowardly and cruel." Sadly, this vicious racism was intertwined with labor's republican ideals. The Chinese, argued George, would drive out free labor, "make
nabobs and princes of our capitalists, and crush our working classes into the
dust . . . substitut[ing] . . . a population of serfs and their masters for that population of intelligent freemen who are our glory and our strength." The anti-
Chinese agitation climaxed in San Francisco in the late 1870s, when mobs
ruled the streets. The fiercest agitator, an Irish teamster named Denis Kearney,
quickly became a dominant figure in the California labor movement. Under
the slogan "The Chinese Must Go!" Kearney led the Workingmen's party
against the state's major parties. Democrats and Republicans, however, jumped
on the bandwagon, joining together in 1879 to write a new state constitution
replete with anti-Chinese provisions and pressuring Washington to take up the

issue. In 1882 Congress finally passed the Chinese Exclusion Act, which barred the further entry of Chinese laborers into the country.

Chinese immigration effectively came to an end, but not the job opportunities that had attracted the Chinese in the first place. The West's agricultural development intensified the demand for cheap labor, especially in California, which was shifting from wheat, the state's first great cash crop, to fruits and vegetables. This intensive agriculture required a lot of workers—so-called "stoop labor," meagerly paid, and mostly seasonal. This was not, as one San Francisco journalist put it, "white men's work." That ugly phrase serves as a touchstone for California agricultural labor as it would thereafter develop—a kind of caste labor system, which always drew some downtrodden, footloose whites, yet was basically defined along color lines. But if not the Chinese, then who? First, Japanese immigrants, who came in increasing numbers and by the early twentieth century constituted half the state's agricultural labor force. Then, when anti-Japanese agitation closed off that population flow in 1908, Mexico became the next, essentially permanent, provider of migratory workers for California's booming commercial agriculture.

The irony of the state's social evolution is painful to behold. Here was California, a land of limitless opportunity, boastful of its democratic egalitarianism. Yet, simultaneously and from its very birth, it was a racially torn society, at once exploiting and despising the Mexican and Asian minorities whose hard labor helped make California the enviable land it was.

Golden California

Life in California contained all that the modern world of 1890 had to offer—cosmopolitan San Francisco, comfortable travel, a high living standard, colleges and universities, even resident painters and writers. Yet California was remote from the rest of America, a long journey away and, of course, differently and spectacularly endowed by nature. Location, environment, and history conspired to set California somewhat apart from the American nation. And so, in certain ways, did the Californians.

What Californians yearned for was a cultural tradition of their own. Closest to hand was the bonanza era of the Forty-Niners. California had the good fortune of attracting to its parts one Samuel Clemens. Clemens did a bit of prospecting, became a reporter in San Francisco, and adopted the pen name Mark Twain.

Listening to the old miners of Angel's Camp in 1865, Twain jotted one tale down in his notebook, as follows:

> Coleman with his jumping frog—bet stranger $50—stranger had no frog, and C. got him one:—in the meantime stranger filled C's frog full of shot and he couldn't jump. The stranger's frog won.

In Twain's hands, this fragment was transformed into a tall tale that caught the imagination of the country and made his reputation as a humorist. "The

Celebrated Jumping Frog of Calaveras County" had somehow encapsulated the entire world of make-or-break optimism in the mining camps.

In short stories such as "The Luck of Roaring Camp" and "The Outcasts of Poker Flat," Twain's fellow San Franciscan Bret Harte developed this theme in a more literary fashion and firmly implanted it in California's memory. But this bonanza past was too raw, too suggestive of the tattered beginnings of so many of the state's leading citizens—in short, too disreputable—for an up-and-coming society.

Then, in 1884, Helen Hunt Jackson published her novel *Ramona*. In this story of a half-caste girl caught between two cultures, Jackson intended to advance the cause of the Indians, but she placed her tale in the evocative context of Old California, and that rang a bell. By then, the Spanish missions—disestablished by the Mexican government back in 1833, long before the influx of Yankees—had fallen into total disrepair and the missionaries were wholly forgotten, their Indian converts scattered and in dire poverty. Now that lost world of "sun, silence and adobe" became all the rage. Sentimental novels and histories appeared in abundance. There was a movement to restore the missions. Many communities began to stage Spanish fiestas, and the mission style of architecture enjoyed a great vogue among developers.

In its Spanish past California found the cultural traditions it needed. The same kind of discovery was taking place elsewhere in the Southwest, although in the case of Santa Fe and Taos there really were live Hispanic roots to celebrate.

All this enthusiasm was, of course, strongly tinged with commercialism. And so was a second distinctive feature of California's development—the exploitation of its climate. The southern part of the state was neglected, thinly populated, and too dry for anything but grazing and some chancy wheat growing. What it did have was an abundance of sunshine. At the beginning of the 1880s there burst upon the country amazing news of the charms of southern California. "There is not any malaria, hay fever, loss of appetite, or languor in the air; nor any thunder, lightning, mad dogs . . . or cold snaps." This publicity was mostly the work of the Southern Pacific Railroad, which had reached Los Angeles in 1876 and was eager for business. When the Santa Fe Railroad arrived in 1885, a furious rate war broke out and fares from Chicago or St. Louis to Los Angeles fell to $25 or less. Thousands of people, mostly midwesterners, poured in. Los Angeles County, which had less than 3 percent of the state's population in 1870, had 12 percent by 1900. By then southern California had firmly established itself as the land of sunshine and orange groves. It had found a way to translate climate into riches.

That California was specially favored by nature some Californians knew even as the great stands of redwoods and sugar pine were being hacked down, the soil depleted by the relentless cycle of wheat crops, the streams polluted, and the hills torn apart by reckless mining techniques. Back in 1864 influential Americans who had seen the Sierras prevailed on Congress to grant to the state of California "the Cleft, or Gorge in the granite peak of the Sierra Nevada Mountain, known as Yosemite Valley," which would be reserved "for public

Kitty Tatch and Friend on Glacier Point, Yosemite
From the time the Yosemite Valley was set aside in 1864 as a place for "public pleasuring, resort, and recreation," it attracted a stream of tourists eager to experience the grandeur of the American West. As is suggested by this photograph taken sometime in the 1890s, the magic of Yosemite was enough to set even staid young ladies dancing.

pleasuring, resort, and recreation." When the young naturalist John Muir arrived in California four years later, he headed straight for Yosemite Valley. Its "grandeur . . . comes as an endless revelation," he wrote. Muir, and others like him, became devoted to studying the High Sierras and protecting them from "despoiling gain-seekers . . . eagerly trying to make everything immediately and selfishly commercial." One result was the creation of California's national parks in 1890—Yosemite, Sequoia, King's Canyon. Another was the formation in 1892 of the Sierra Club, which became a powerful voice for the defenders of California's wilderness.

Champions of California's wild lands won some battles and lost some. Advocates of water-resource development insisted that California's irrigated agriculture and thirsty cities could not grow without tapping the abundant snowpack of the Sierras. By the turn of the century, Los Angeles faced a water crisis that threatened its growth. The answer was a 238-mile aqueduct to the Owens River in the southern Sierras. A bitter controversy blew up over this

immense project, driven by the objections of local residents and preservation-
ists to the flooding of the beautiful Owens Valley. More painful was the defeat
suffered by John Muir and his allies in their battle to save the Hetch Hetchy
gorge, north of Yosemite National Park. In 1913, after years of controversy, the
federal government approved the damming of Hetch Hetchy to serve the
water needs of San Francisco.

When the stakes became high enough, nature lovers like John Muir generally came out on the short end. Even so, something original and distinctive
had been added to California's heritage—the linking of a society's well-being
with the preservation of its natural environment.

CHAPTER 17 TIMELINE

1849	California Gold Rush
	Chinese migration begins
1862	Homestead Act
1864	Yosemite Valley reserved as public park
1865	Long Drive of Texas longhorns begins
1867	U.S. government adopts reservation policy for Plains Indians
1868	Indian treaty confirms Sioux rights to Powder River hunting grounds
1869	Union Pacific–Central Pacific transcontinental railroad completed
1874	Barbed wire invented
1875	Sioux ordered to vacate Powder River hunting grounds; war breaks out
1876	Battle of Little Big Horn
1877	San Francisco anti-Chinese riots
1879	Exoduster migration to Kansas
1882	Chinese Exclusion Act
1884	Helen Hunt Jackson's novel *Ramona*
1886	Dry cycle begins on the Great Plains
1887	Dawes Severalty Act
1889	Oklahoma opened to white settlement
1890	Indian massacre at Wounded Knee, South Dakota

CHAPTER 18

CAPITAL AND LABOR IN THE
AGE OF ENTERPRISE, 1877–1900

- Industrial Capitalism Triumphant
- The World of Work
- The Labor Movement

The year that Reconstruction ended, 1877, also marked the end of the first great crisis of America's industrializing economy. In 1873, four years earlier, a severe depression had set in, bankrupting 47,000 firms and driving down wholesale prices by about 30 percent. Hundreds of thousands of workers lost their jobs, and suffering was widespread. Before long the foundations of the social order began to shake.

On July 16, 1877, railroad workers went on strike against the Baltimore and Ohio (B&O) system to protest wage cuts. In railway towns along the B&O tracks crowds cheered as the strikers attacked company property and prevented trains from running. The strike spread across the country. In Pittsburgh the Pennsylvania roundhouse went up in flames on July 21. At many rail centers rioters and looters roamed freely. Only the arrival of federal troops restored order. On August 15 President Rutherford B. Hayes wrote in his diary: "The strikers have been put down *by force.*" Never had the nation edged so close to social revolution.

And then recovery came. Within months the economy was booming again. In the next fifteen years, the output of manufactured goods increased over 150 percent. America's confidence in its industrial future rebounded. "Upon [material progress] is founded all other progress," asserted a railroad president in 1888. "Can there be any doubt that cheapening the cost of necessaries and conveniences of life is the most powerful agent of civilization and progress?"

INDUSTRIAL CAPITALISM TRIUMPHANT

Economic historians speak of the late nineteenth century as the age of the Great Deflation. Prices fell worldwide, not only in the United States (see Figure 18.1). Normally, falling prices signal economic stagnation: there is not enough demand for the available goods and services. For England, a mature industrial power, the Great Deflation did indeed indicate economic decline. But not for the United States; its industrial expansion went into high gear during the Great Deflation. Because of increasing manufacturing efficiencies, American firms could cut prices *and* yet earn profits that could finance still better equipment.

Basic Industry

By the 1870s, industry was long established in America. But the early factories had really been appendages of the agricultural economy. The goods they produced—textiles, shoes, paper, and furniture—were consumer goods that used familar raw materials and mostly replaced homemade or artisan-made goods (articles made by skilled workers). Gradually, however, a different kind of demand developed. This was the result of the surging economic growth of the country. Railroads needed locomotives; new factories needed machinery; and the expanding cities needed trolley lines, sanitation systems, and commercial buildings. Railroad equipment, machinery, and construction materials were *capital* goods—that is, goods that themselves added to the productive capacity of the economy.

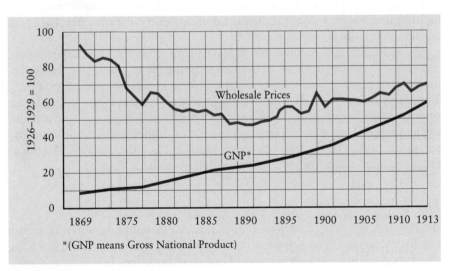

*(GNP means Gross National Product)

FIGURE 18.1
Business Activity and Wholesale Prices, 1869–1913
This graph shows the key feature concerning the performance of the late nineteenth-century economy: namely, that while output was booming, the price for goods was falling.

Central to the development of the capital-goods sector was a new technology for manufacturing steel. The country already produced large quantities of wrought iron, whose malleability made it easily worked by country blacksmiths and farmers. But wrought iron was expensive—it was produced in small batches by skilled puddlers and rollers—and did not stand up under heavy use as railway track. In 1856 the British inventor Henry Bessemer perfected a method for refining raw pig iron into an essentially new product—steel—that was harder and more durable than wrought iron. Others adopted Bessemer's process, but it was Andrew Carnegie who demonstrated its revolutionary importance.

An iron maker and former railroad man, Carnegie in 1872 erected a massive steel mill outside Pittsburgh, designed to take maximum advantage of Bessemer's method. Named the Edgar Thompson Works after Carnegie's admired boss at the Pennsylvania Railroad, his mill combined all the stages of production—smelting, refining, and rolling—into a single integrated operation. Iron ore entered the blast furnaces at one end and, with no break in operations, came out the other end as finished steel rails. The Edgar Thompson Works was hugely profitable, and became a model for the modern steel industry. Large, integrated steel plants swiftly replaced the small iron mills that had once dotted western Pennsylvania.

The technological breakthrough in steel spurred the intensive exploitation of the country's rich mineral resources. Once iron ore began to be shipped down the Great Lakes from the Mesabi range in northern Minnesota, the industry was assured of an ample supply of its primary raw material. The other key ingredient, coal, came in equal abundance from the great Appalachian field that stretched from Pennsylvaina down to Alabama. A minor enterprise before the Civil War, coal production doubled every decade after 1870, exceeding 400 million tons a year by 1910.

As steam engines became the nation's primary energy source, prodigious amounts of coal began to be consumed by railroads and factories. Earlier reliant on water power, industries rapidly converted to steam-driven machinery. The steam turbine, a further innovation introduced in the 1880s, utilized continuous rotation rather than the back-and-forth motion of the conventional steam engine. With the coupling of the steam turbine to the electric generator, the nation's energy revolution was completed, and after 1900 America's factories began a massive conversion to electric power.

The Railroads

Before the Civil War, most goods moved quite efficiently by water. But from the first appearance of primitive locomotives on iron tracks in the 1830s, Americans fell in love with railroads. They were impatient for the year-round, on-time service that canal barges and riverboats could never provide. By 1860, with a network of tracks already covering the states east of the Mississippi, the railroad clearly was on the way to being industrial America's mode of transportation (see Map 18.1).

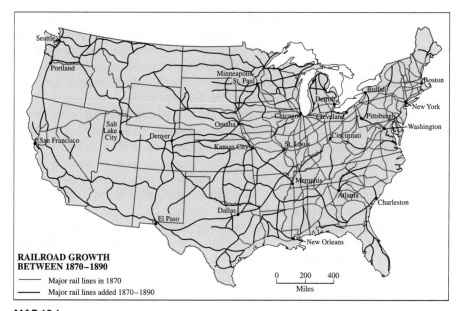

MAP 18.1
The Expansion of the Railroad System, 1870–1890
In 1870, the nation had 53,000 miles of rail track; in 1890, 167,000 miles. That burst of construction essentially completed the nation's rail network, although there would be additional expansion for the next two decades. The main areas of growth were in the South and west of the Mississippi. The Great Plains and the Far West accounted for over 40 percent of all railroad construction in this period.

The question was, who would pay for it? Railroads could be state enterprises, like the canals. Or, alternatively, they could be financed by investors trying to make money. Unlike most European countries, the United States chose to leave railroads to private enterprise. Even so, government played a big role. Many states offered financial aid, mostly by buying railroad bonds, but also, as in Maine and Texas, by offering land grants from the public domain. Land grants were the principal means by which the federal government encouraged interregional railroads; huge tracts went to the transcontinental railroads, because of the national interest in tying the Far West to the rest of the country.

The most important boost that government gave the railroads, however, was not money or land but a legal form of organization—the *corporation*—that enabled them to raise private capital in prodigious amounts. Investors who bought stock in the railroads—and thus became their legal owners—enjoyed *limited liability*: they risked only the money they had invested. A corporation also could borrow money by issuing interest-bearing bonds, which was how the railroads mostly raised the funds they needed.

The actual responsibility for railroad building generally was handed over to a construction company, which, despite the name, was really another part of the elaborate financing system. Hiring contractors and suppliers often involved persuading them to accept the railroad's bonds as payment and, when that failed, wheeling and dealing to raise cash by selling or borrowing on the bonds. Since the promoters of the railroad and the owners of the construction company were one and the same, the opportunities for plunder were enormous. The most notorious construction company, the Union Pacific's Credit Mobilier, siphoned probably half the money it paid out into the pockets of the promoters.

Railroad promotion was not for the faint of heart. Most successful were promoters with the best access to capital—their own or others'. Cornelius Vanderbilt started with the fortune he had made in the steamboat business. He consolidated previously independent lines up the Hudson River and across New York State, and ultimately developed the New York Central into a trunk line to Chicago that was rivaled only by the Pennsylvania Railroad. James J. Hill, who without federal subsidy made the Great Northern into the best of the transcontinental railroads, was certainly the nation's champion railroad builder. In contrast, Jay Gould, who at one time or another controlled the Erie, Wabash, Union Pacific, and Missouri Pacific systems, always remained a stock-market speculator at heart.

Railroad development in the United States was often sordid, fiercely competitive, and subject to boom and bust. Yet vast sums of capital were raised and a network was built exceeding that of the rest of the world combined. By 1900 virtually no corner of the country lacked rail service.

The railroads also became increasingly efficient. The early system, built by competing local companies, had been a jumble of discontinuous segments. Gauges of track—the width between the rails—varied widely, and at many points railroads were not connected. As late as 1880 goods shipped from Massachusetts to South Carolina had to be unloaded eight times and physically moved to new freight cars across a river or at the other side of a city.

Beginning with the Civil War years, however, pressure increased for a better-organized rail system. In 1883 the railroads rebelled against the jumble of local times that made scheduling a nightmare, and acting on their own, divided the country into the four standard time zones that we still use. By the end of the 1880s a standard track gauge (4 feet, 8½ inches) had been adopted across the country. Fast-freight firms and standard accounting procedures enabled shippers to use the railroad network as if it were a single unit, moving their goods without breaks in transit, transfers between cars, or the other delays that had once bedeviled them.

At the same time, railroad technology was advancing. Durable steel rails permitted heavier traffic. Locomotives became more powerful and capable of pulling more freight cars. To control the greater mass being hauled, the inventor George Westinghouse perfected the automatic coupler, the air brake, and the friction gear for starting and stopping a long line of cars. Costs per ton-mile fell by 50 percent between 1870 and 1890, resulting in a steady drop in freight rates for shippers.

The railroads brilliantly met the transportation needs of the maturing industrial economy. However, this achievement did not stem from any orderly plan; it sprang from the competitive energy of a freewheeling market economy. For the railroads, the costs of unrestrained growth were painfully high. On many routes there were too many railroads, and competitors fought for the available traffic by cutting rates to the bone. Many were saddled with huge bonded debt from the extravagant construction years; about a fifth of these bonds failed to pay interest, even in a pretty good year like 1889. When the economy turned bad, as it did in 1893, the weaker roads inevitably went under; a third of the industry (by track mileage) declared bankruptcy.

Out of the rubble came a major railroad reorganization. This was primarily the handiwork of Wall Street. Investment banks such as J. P. Morgan & Co. had sprung up to market the stocks and bonds issued by railroads. And when railroads fell into bankruptcy the investment bankers stepped in to pick up the pieces. They persuaded investors to help out by accepting lower interest rates or by putting up more money. And they eased the competitive pressures on the railroads by consolidating rivals. By the early twentieth century, half a dozen great regional systems had emerged and the nerve center of American railroading had shifted to Wall Street.

Mass Markets and Large-Scale Enterprise

The railroads sparked a revolution in how goods were marketed. Until well into the industrial age, all but a few manufacturers operated on a small scale, producing mainly for nearby markets. And they left distribution to wholesale merchants and commission agents. Then, after the Civil War, the scale of economic activity began to grow dramatically. "Combinations of capital on a scale hitherto wholly unprecedented constitute one of the remarkable features of modern business methods," the economist David A. Wells wrote in 1889. He could see "no other way in which the work of production and distribution can be prosecuted." What was there about the nation's economic activity that led to Wells's sense of inevitability?

The key to large-scale enterprise lay in the American market. Immigration and a very high birthrate swelled the population from 40 million in 1870 to over 60 million in 1890. People flocked to the cities. The railroads brought these dense consuming markets within the reach of distant producers. The telegraph, fully operational by the Civil War, speeded communications. Unlike Europe, America was not carved up into many national markets; no political frontiers impeded the flow of goods across the continent. Nowhere else did manufacturers have so vast and accessible an internal market for their products.

How they took advantage of that opportunity is perhaps best seen in the case of the meat-packing industry. With the opening of the Union Stock Yards in 1865, Chicago became the cattle market for the country. Cattle came in by rail from the Great Plains; were auctioned off at the Chicago stockyards; and then were shipped to eastern cities, where, as before, they were slaughtered in local "butchertowns." Such an arrangement—with distribution nationalized but processing still local—adequately met the demand of an exploding urban population and could have done so indefinitely. In Europe no further development ever did occur.

But Gustavus F. Swift, a shrewd Chicago cattle dealer from Massachusetts, saw the future differently. He objected that livestock deteriorated en route to the East, and that local slaughterhouses were too small to use waste by-products and cut labor costs. If dressed beef could be kept fresh in transit, Swift realized, he could concentrate the processing in Chicago. Once his engineers developed an effective cooling system, Swift invested in a fleet of refrigerator cars and constructed an immense beef-processing plant at the Chicago stockyards.

This was only the beginning of Swift's innovations. Since no refrigerated warehouses existed in the cities to which he shipped his chilled beef, Swift built his own network of branch houses. Next, he established a fleet of wagons to distribute his products to retail butcher shops. Swift constructed additional facilities to process the fertilizer, chemicals, and other usable by-products from his slaughtering operations. He also began to handle other perishable goods, so that he could fully utilize his refrigerator cars and branch houses. As demand grew, Swift built more packing houses in other stockyard centers, including Kansas City, Kansas; Fort Worth, Texas; and Omaha, Nebraska.

Step by step, Swift created a new kind of enterprise, the *vertically integrated* firm—a national company capable of handling within its own structure all the functions of an industry. In effect, Swift & Co. replaced a large number of small, specialized firms with one multifunctional national firm. Swift's lead was followed by several big Chicago packers who had already built big processsing plants that produced preserved pork products. By 1900 five firms, all of them nationally organized and vertically integrated, produced nearly 90 percent of the meat shipped in interstate commerce.

In most other fields, no single innovation was so decisive as Swift's refrigerator car. But others did share Swift's insight that the essential step was to identify a mass market and then develop a national enterprise capable of serving it. In the petroleum industry, John D. Rockefeller built the Standard Oil Company partly by taking over rival firms, but he also developed a national distribution system to reach the enormous market for kerosene as a fuel for lighting and heating homes. The Singer Sewing Machine Company formed its own sales organization, using both retail stores and door-to-door salesmen. Through such distribution systems, manufacturers provided technical information, credit, and repair facilities for their products.

American society prepared its citizens to be consumers of the standardized goods produced by national manufacturers and sold by mass marketers. The high rate of geographic mobility broke down the local loyalties that were so strong in Europe. Social class in America, though by no means absent, was blurred at the edges and did not, for example, call for class-specific ways of dressing. Foreign visitors often noted that ready-made clothing made it difficult to tell salesgirls from debutantes on city streets.

The American consumer's receptivity to standardized goods should not be exaggerated. Gustavus Swift, for example, encountered great resistance to his Chicago beef. How could it be wholesome weeks later in Boston or Philadelphia? Cheap prices helped, but advertising mattered more. Modern advertising was born in the late nineteenth century, bringing brand names and a billboard-cluttered urban landscape. By 1900 companies spent over $90 million a year for space in newspapers and magazines. Advertisements urged readers to bathe with Pears' soap, eat Uneeda biscuits, sew on a Singer machine, and snap pictures with a Kodak camera. The active molding of demand for brand names became a major function of American business.

The New South

For the South, catching up with the industrial North was no easy task. The antebellum (prewar) plantation economy had strongly impeded industrial development. The slave states had few cities, a primitive distribution system, and not much manufacturing. This modest infrastructure was quickly restored after the Civil War. And then, in 1877, with both Reconstruction and economic depression ended, a railroad boom developed. Track mileage doubled in the next decade and, at least by that measure, the South became nearly competitive with the rest of the country.

But the South remained overwhelmingly agricultural. The sharecropping system, which required a cash crop (see Chapter 16), committed the South to cotton despite soil depletion, low productivity, and unprofitable prices. Wages for southern farm labor fell steadily, dropping to scarcely half the national average by the 1890s—roughly 75 cents a day without board, for a farm laborer.

From this low agricultural wage, surprisingly, sprang the South's hopes for industrialization. Consider, for example, how southern textile mills got started in the Piedmont upcountry of North Carolina, South Carolina, and Georgia in the mid-1870s. The mills recruited workers from the surrounding hill farms, where people struggled to make ends meet. To attract them, mill wages had to be higher than farm earnings, but not much higher. Paying rock-bottom wages, the new mills had a big competitive advantage over the long-established New England industry.

The labor system that evolved likewise reflected southern rural society. To begin with, it was a family system. "Papa decided he would come because he didn't have nothing much but girls and they had to get out and work like men," recalled one woman. It was not Papa, in fact, but his girls whom the mills wanted, for work as spinners and loom tenders. Only they could not be recruited individually: no right-thinking parent would have permitted that. There was, on the other hand, no objection to hiring by families; after all, everyone had been expected to work on the farm. And so the family system of mill labor developed, in which half or more of the operatives were women and the work force was very young. In the 1880s, a quarter of all southern textile workers were under fifteen years of age.

The hours were long—twelve hours a day was the norm—but life in the mill villages was, in the words of one historian, "like a family." Employers tended to be highly paternalistic, providing company housing and a variety of services. The mill workers themselves built close-knit, supportive communities, but for whites only. Although blacks sometimes worked as day laborers and janitors, they hardly ever got production jobs in the cotton mills.

Cheap, abundant labor might have been termed the South's most valuable natural resource. But the region was blessed with other natural resources as well (see Map 18.2). From its rich soil came tobacco, the South's second cash crop. When cigarettes became fashionable in the 1880s, the young North Carolina entrepreneur James B. Duke seized the new market by taking advantage of a southern invention—James A. Bonsack's machine for producing cigarettes automatically. Blacks stemmed and stripped the leaf as they always had, but Duke followed the textile example and restricted machine-tending to white women.

Lumbering, by contrast, was largely integrated, with a labor force evenly divided between black and white men. The extensive pine forests of the South were rapidly—heedlessly is perhaps the better word—exploited in these years.

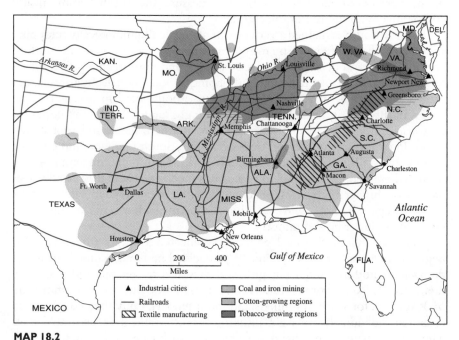

MAP 18.2
The New South, 1900
The economy of the Old South focused on raising staple crops, especially cotton and tobacco. In the New South staple agriculture continued to dominate but there was marked industrial development as well. Industrial regions developed, producing textiles, coal and iron, and wood products. By 1900 the South's industrial pattern was well defined.

Alabama's coal and iron ore deposits also attracted investors; by 1890 the Birmingham district was producing nearly a million tons of iron and steel a year.

Despite the South's high hopes, this burst of industrial development did not lift the region out of poverty. In 1900 two-thirds of all southerners made their living from the soil, just as they had in 1870. Moreover, the industries that did develop were either extractive, as with forestry and mining, or engaged in low-end processing of coarse products. Industry by industry, the key statistic—the value added by manufacturing—showed the South consistently lagging behind the North.

Southerners tended to blame the North: the South was a "colonial" economy controlled by New York and Chicago. There was some truth to this charge. Much of the capital—by no means all—did come from the North. And the integrating processes of the economy did subordinate regional to national interests. When the railway network moved to a uniform gauge in 1886, the southern railroads converted to the northern standard. Nor did northern interests hesitate to use their muscle to maintain the interregional status quo. Railroads, for example, varied freight rates so that it was cheap for southern cotton and timber to flow out and for northern manufactured goods to flow in.

Yet in the end the South's economic backwardness was mostly of its own making. The crowning irony was that the great advantage of the South—its cheap labor—also kept it from becoming a more technologically advanced economy. First, low wages discouraged employers from replacing workers with machinery. Second, low wages attracted labor-intensive industry, such as textiles. Third, a cheap labor market discouraged investment in education because of the likelihood that better-educated workers would flee to higher-wage markets.

What distinguished the southern labor market was that racially rooted barriers *insulated* it from the rest of the country: the normal flow of workers back and forth did not occur and wage differences did not narrow. So long as this condition persisted, the South would remain a tributary economy, a supplier on unequal terms to the advanced industrial heartland of the North.

THE WORLD OF WORK

In a free-enterprise system, profit drives business. But the industrial order is not populated only by profit makers. It includes—in vastly larger numbers—wage earners. What is done for profit always affects those who work for wages, but never so drastically as in the late nineteenth century.

Labor Recruits

Wherever it took hold, industrialism set people in motion. Artisans moved into factories. Farm folk migrated to the cities. An industrial labor force emerged. This happened in the United States just as it did in European countries, but with a difference: the United States could not rely primarily on its native-born population for a supply of workers.

Except in the South, native-born white Americans no longer wanted factory work. Rural Americans were highly mobile in the late nineteenth century, and of those who moved, about half ended up in cities. But the jobs they took were as white-collar workers in offices and retail stores. Rural blacks would certainly have opted for factory jobs had they been given the chance. Modest numbers—280,000—did migrate to northern cities between 1870 and 1910, but they were restricted to casual labor, janitorial work, and, for the women, domestic service. Employers turned black applicants away from the factory gates because immigrant workers already supplied them with as much cheap labor as they needed.

The great migration from the Old World had started in the 1840s, when over a million Irish peasants fled the potato famine. In the following years, as European agriculture became increasingly commercialized, peasant populations grew and outstripped the available land. The peasant economy failed first in Germany and Scandinavia and then, later in the nineteenth century, across Austria-Hungary, Russia, Italy, and the Balkans. Although the majority of migrants to America had always been drawn from Europe's peasant villages, large

Immigrant Workers
Many native-born Americans resented the influx of peasant immigrants from eastern and southern Europe that began in the 1880s. In fact, the newcomers, more than any other group, operated the machines, laid the railroad tracks, and performed the heavy construction labor that built the nation's cities. They were Europe's gift—its most vigorous and hardworking people.

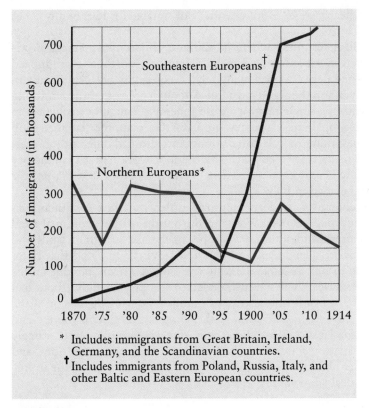

* Includes immigrants from Great Britain, Ireland, Germany, and the Scandinavian countries.
† Includes immigrants from Poland, Russia, Italy, and other Baltic and Eastern European countries.

FIGURE 18.2
American Immigration, 1870–1914
This graph shows the surge of European immigration in the late nineteenth century. While northern Europe continued to send substantial numbers, it was overshadowed after 1895 by southern Europeans pouring into America to work in mines and factories.

numbers of seasoned workers also came, attracted by the higher wages or cut loose by economic disruptions in Europe.

Ethnic origin largely determined the kind of work that the immigrants found in America. Skilled workers generally sought the same types of jobs they had held in the Old World. The Welsh worked as tin-plate workers, the English as miners, the Germans as machinists and traditional artisans, the Belgians as glassworkers, and the Scandinavians as seamen on Great Lakes boats. For common labor, employers had long counted on the brawn of Irish rural immigrants. As industrialization advanced, the demand for unskilled workers increased, helping to stimulate the heavy migration from southern and eastern Europe that began in the 1880s (see Figure 18.2). Italian and Slavic immigrants without industrial skills flooded into American factories. Heavy, low-paid labor became the domain of the recent immigrants. Blast-furnace jobs, one investigator heard, were "Hunky work," not suitable for him or any other American.

Not only skill determined where immigrants ended up in American industry. The newcomers, although generally traveling on their own, moved within well-defined networks, following relatives or fellow villagers already in America and relying on them to land a job. A high degree of ethnic clustering resulted, even within a single factory. At the Jones and Laughlin steelworks in Pittsburgh, for example, the carpentry shop was German, the hammer shop Polish, and the blooming mill Serbian. Immigrants also had different job preferences. Men from Italy, for example, liked outdoor work better than factory labor. And, already accustomed to it, they worked in gangs under a *padrone* (boss), much as they had in Italy.

Immigrants entered a modern industrial order, but they saw their surroundings through peasant eyes. With the disruption of the traditional rural economies of eastern and southern Europe, many had lost their lands and fallen into the class of dependent, propertyless servants. To avoid that bitter fate—to find the means to remain among the landed—many peasant immigrants came to America. They never intended to stay permanently. About half did return, departing from America in great numbers during depression years. No one knows how many left because they had saved enough money and how many left for lack of work. For their American employers, it scarcely mattered. What mattered was that they willingly took the worst jobs, and melted away when the jobs dried up. For the new industrial order, the immigrants made an ideal labor supply.

Working Women

Between 1870 and 1900 the number of wage-earning women jumped by almost two-thirds. Women made up a quarter of the labor force in 1900, and had become essential to America's industrial economy. The opportunities they found were shaped by gender—by the fact that they were women. Contemporary beliefs about womanhood largely determined which women took jobs and how they were treated once they became wage earners.

Wives were not supposed to work outside the home, and in fact fewer than 5 percent did so in 1890. The typical working woman at that time was under twenty-four and unmarried. Only among African-Americans did married women work for wages, in numbers that ranged over 30 percent. When older white women worked, remarked one observer, it "was usually a sign that something had gone wrong"—that they were widows or alone for other reasons.

Since women were held to be inherently different from men, it followed that they should not be permitted to do "men's work." Nor, regardless of the value of their labor, could they be paid a man's wage. A woman did not require a "living wage" because, as one investigator reported, "it is expected that she has men to support her." At the turn of the century the weekly wage of women factory workers came to roughly $7, or $3 less than that of unskilled men and $5 below the average for all industrial workers.

Women's work fell into three categories. One of every three women worked as a maid or in some other type of domestic service. Another third held "female" white-collar jobs in teaching, nursing, sales, and office work. The remaining third worked in industry, heavily concentrated in the garment trades and textile mills, but present also in many other industries as inspectors, packers, and assemblers and in other "light" occupations. Few worked as supervisors, fewer in the crafts, and nearly none as day laborers.

Just how jobs came to be defined as male or female—in sociological lingo, the "sex-typing" of occupations—is not easy to explain. The jobs of telephone operator and store clerk, originally held by men, had by the 1890s been taken over by women. Wherever an occupation became female-dominated, it was redefined as having feminine qualities, even though very similar or even identical work elsewhere was done by men. Once a job was identified as women's work, it became unsuitable for men. There were no male telephone operators by 1900.

Switchboard Operators
When the first telephone exchange was set up in Boston in 1878, it was operated by teenage boys, which followed the practice set in the telegraph industry. During the 1880s, however, young women increasingly replaced the boys, and by 1900 switchboard operation was defined strictly as women's work. In this photograph of a telephone exchange in Columbus, Ohio, in 1907, the older woman at left has risen to the position of supervisor, but it is the two men in the picture who are clearly in charge.

Getting Organized

Rose Schneiderman (1882–1972) typified the young Jewish garment workers who became the firebrands of their industry. Schneiderman went on to an illustrious career as a unionist and reformer.

We had no idea that there was a union in our industry and that women could join it. Nor did we have a full realization of the hardships we were needlessly undergoing. There was the necessity of owning a sewing machine before you could work. Then you had to buy your own thread. But the worst of it was the incredibly inefficient way in which work was distributed. Because we were all pieceworkers, any time lost during the season was a real hardship. . . .

We formed a committee composed of my friend Bessie Mannis, who worked with me, myself, and a third girl. Bravely we ventured into the office of the United Cloth Hat and Cap Makers Union. . . . We were told that we would have to have at least twenty-five women. . . . We waited at the doors of factories and, as the girls were leaving for the day, we would approach them and speak our piece. . . . Within days we had the necessary number, and in January 1903 we were chartered as Local 23, and I was elected secretary. . . .

The only cloud in the picture was mother's attitude toward my becoming a trade unionist. She kept saying I'd never get married because I was so busy—a prophecy which came true. . . .

That June we decided to put our strength to the test. . . . On Saturdays . . . we women had to hang around until three or four o'clock before getting our pay. I headed a committee which informed Mr. Fox that we wanted to be paid at the same time as the men. . . . He didn't say outright that he agreed; he wouldn't give us that much satisfaction. But on the first Saturday in July, when we went for our pay at twelve noon, there it was ready for us.

SOURCE: Rose Schneiderman, *All for One* (1967), reprinted in Irving Howe and Kenneth Libo, eds., *How We Lived* (New York: New American Library, 1979), 139–41.

As with men's work, ethnicity played a big part in the distribution of women's jobs among particular groups. White-collar jobs were reserved for the native-born, increasingly including, however, the second-generation daughters of immigrants. And as with men, ethnicity created clustering patterns in women's jobs; in the case of Italian families, for instance, it restricted women to subcontracted tasks, such as sewing, that could be done at home.

But if ethnicity mattered at the workplace, gender mattered at least as much. Women's identity gave their work distinctive meaning. Department store clerks, for example, developed a work culture and language just as robust as that of any male craft group. The most important fact about wage-earning women was their youth. For many, their first job freed them from family discipline. It was an opportunity to be independent; to form friendships with other young women; and to experience, however briefly, a fun-loving time of nice clothes, dancing, and other "cheap amusements."

To some degree, their youthful preoccupations made it easier for working women to accept the miserable terms under which they labored. But this did not mean that they lacked a sense of group solidarity and self-respect. Nice clothes might appear frivolous to the casual observer, but they also conveyed the message that the working girl considered herself as good as anyone. Rebellious youth culture sometimes united with job grievances to produce astonishing strike movements, as, for example, by the Jewish garment workers of New York and the Irish-American telephone operators of Boston.

Disapproval of job-holding wives, although expressed in sentimental and moral terms, was based on solid necessity. From the standpoint of the labor market, the basic economic unit was the individual employee. For workers, however, the family was the economic unit, to which the wife contributed crucially. Cooking, cleaning, and tending the children were not income-producing activities and were not reckoned in terms of money. But everyone knew that the family economy depended on the wife's household contribution. Therefore, her place was in the home.

Except among the high-paid crafts, however, working-class families found the going hard on a single income. The rockiest period came during a family's child-bearing years, when there were many mouths to feed and only the earnings of the father to provide the food. Thereafter, as the children grew up, the family income began to increase. Not only unmarried sons and daughters but the younger children as well contributed their share. In 1900 one of every five children under sixteen worked. "When the people own houses," remarked a printer from Fall River, "you will generally find that it is a large family all working together."

By the 1890s all the northern industrial states had passed laws prohibiting child labor and limiting work-hours for teenagers. Most of these states also required school attendance for a certain number of weeks each year. Working-class families continued to rely on second incomes, but this money came more and more from the wives. After 1890 the proportion of working married women crept steadily upward. About a fifth of the wives of unskilled and semiskilled men in Chicago held jobs in 1920. Wage-earning wives and mothers were on their way to becoming a primary part of America's labor force.

Autonomous Labor

No one supervised the nineteenth-century coal miner. He was a tonnage worker, paid for the amount of coal he produced. He provided his own tools, worked at his own pace, and knocked off early when he chose. Such autonomous craft workers—almost all of them men—flourished in many branches of nineteenth-century industry. They were mule spinners in cotton

AMERICAN VOICES

A Miner's Son

John Brophy (1883–1963), an important mine union official in the twentieth century, recalls what mining was like in his boyhood.

I got a thrill at the thought of having an opportunity to go and work in the mine, to go and work along side my father. . . . It was a great satisfaction to me that my father was a skilled, clean workman with everything kept in shape, and the timbering done well. . . . It's plain that the individual miner in those early days had considerable freedom of judgment. I think that was one of the great satisfactions that a miner had—that he was his own boss within his workplace. . . .

The miner is always aware of danger, that he lived under dangerous conditions in the workplace. . . . Then there is the further fact that the miner by and large lived in purely mining communities which were often isolated. They developed a group loyalty under all these circumstances. They were both individualists and they were group conscious. . . . You find time and again miners, in an effort to rescue their fellow workers, taking chances which quite often meant death for thmeselves. . . .

Along with that is a sense of justice. There was the very fact the miner was a tonnage worker and that he could be short weighed and cheated in various ways, and that the only safeguard against it was organization. . . . The miner in my day in the United States was aware that all knowledge didn't start with his generation. . . . At least on one side of my family there are at least four generations of [British] miners, and I say this with a sense of pride; very much so. I'm very proud of the fact that there is this long tradition of miners who have struggled with the elements.

SOURCE: Jerold S. Auerbach, ed., *American Labor: The Twentieth Century* (Indianapolis: Bobbs-Merrill, 1969), 44–48.

mills; puddlers and rollers in iron works; molders in stove making; and machinists, glassblowers, and skilled workers of many other types.

In the shop they abided by the *stint*, a limit they themselves placed on the amount they would produce each day. This informal system of limiting output infuriated efficiency-minded engineers. But to the worker it signified personal dignity and "unselfish brotherhood" with fellow employees. The male craft worker took pride in maintaining a "manly" bearing, toward both his fellows and the boss. One day a shop in Lowell, Massachusetts, posted regulations requiring all employees to be at their posts in work clothes at the opening bell and to remain, with the shop door locked, until the dismissal bell. A machinist promptly packed his tools and quit, declaring that he had not "been brought up under such a system of slavery."

Underlying this ethical code was a keen sense of the craft group, each with its own history and customs. Hatters, masters of the art of applying fur felting to top hats and bowlers, had a language of their own. When a hatter was hired, he was "shopped"; if fired, he was "bagged"; when he quit work, he "cried off"; and when he took an apprentice, the boy was "under teach." The hatters, most of whom worked in Danbury, Connecticut, or Orange, New Jersey, formed a distinctive, self-contained community.

The craft worker's skills were crucial to nineteenth-century production. He was valued also for the responsibilities he assumed. He hired his own helpers, supervised their work, and paid them from his earnings. In an era when the scale of production was expanding, autonomous craft workers relieved their employers of the burden of shop-floor management. Many factory managers deliberately shifted this responsibility to employees. A system of inside contracting developed in metal-fabricating firms that did precise machining and complex assembling. Contractor-employees hired and paid their own men and supervised them.

Dispersal of authority was thus characteristic of nineteenth-century industry. The aristocracy of the workers—the craftsmen, inside contractors, and foremen—enjoyed a high degree of autonomy. However, their subordinates often paid dearly for that independence. The opportunities for abuse were endless. Any worker who paid his helpers from his own pocket might be tempted to exploit them. In the Pittsburgh area, foremen were known as "pushers," notorious for driving their gangs mercilessly. On the other hand, industrial labor in the nineteenth century remained on a human scale. People dealt with each other face to face, and often developed cohesive ties within the shop. Striking craft workers commonly received the support of helpers and laborers, and labor gangs sometimes walked out on behalf of a popular foreman.

Systems of Control

As technology advanced and modern management emerged, workers increasingly lost the proud independence that had characterized nineteenth-century craft work.

One source of this de-skilling process was a new system of production—Henry Ford called it "mass production"—that lent itself to mechanization. Agricultural implements, typewriters, bicycles, and, after 1900, automobiles were assembled from standardized parts. The machine tools that cut, drilled, and ground these metal parts had originally been manned by skilled machinists. But because they produced long runs of a single item, these machine tools became more specialized; they became *dedicated* machines—machines set up to do the same job over and over—and the need for skilled operatives disappeared. In the manufacture of sewing machines, one machinist complained in 1883, "the trade is so subdivided that a man is not considered a machinist at all. One man may make just a particular part of a machine and may not know anything whatever about another part of the same machine." Such a worker, noted an observer, "cannot be master of a craft, but only master of a fragment."

Employers were attracted to dedicated machinery because it increased output; the impact on workers was not uppermost in their minds. They recognized that mechanization made it easier to discipline their workers, but that was only an incidental benefit. Gradually, however, the idea took hold that managing workers might itself be a way to reduce the cost of production.

The pioneer in this field was Frederick W. Taylor. An expert on metal-cutting methods, Taylor believed that the same engineer's approach might be applied to managing workers, hence the name for his method: *scientific management*. In order to get the maximum work from the individual worker, Taylor suggested two basic reforms. The first would eliminate the brain work from manual labor. Managers would assume "the burden of gathering together all of the traditional knowledge which in the past has been possessed by the workmen and then of classifying, tabulating, and reducing this knowledge to rules, laws, and formulae." The second reform, a logical consequence of the first, would deprive workers of the authority they had exercised on the shop floor. Workers would "do what they are told promptly and without asking questions or making suggestions. . . . The duty of enforcing . . . rests with the management alone."

Once they had the knowledge and the power, managers would put labor on a "scientific" basis. This meant subjecting each task to a *time-and-motion study*, in which an engineer analyzed and timed each job with a stopwatch. Workers would be paid at a *differential rate*—that is, a certain amount if they met the stopwatch standard, and a higher rate for additional output. Taylor claimed that his techniques would guarantee optimum worker efficiency. His assumption was that only money mattered to workers and that they would automatically respond to the lure of higher earnings.

Scientific management was not, in practice, a roaring success. Implementing it proved very expensive, and workers stubbornly resisted the job-analysis method. "It looks to me like slavery to have a man stand over you with a stopwatch," complained one iron molder. A union leader insisted that "this system is wrong, because we want our heads left on us." Far from solving the labor problem, as Taylor claimed it would, scientific management embittered relations on the shop floor.

Yet Taylor achieved something of fundamental importance. He was a brilliant publicist, and his teachings spread throughout American industry. Taylor's disciples moved beyond his simplistic economic psychology, creating the new professions of personnel administration and industrial psychology, which claimed to know how to get more and better labor from workers. A threshold had been crossed into the modern era of labor management.

So the circle closed on American workers. With each advance, the quest for efficiency cut deeper into their cherished autonomy. The process occurred unevenly. For textile workers the loss had come early. Miners and iron workers felt it much more slowly. Others, such as construction workers, escaped the process almost entirely. But increasing numbers of workers found themselves in an environment that crushed any sense of mastery or even understanding.

THE LABOR MOVEMENT

Wherever industrialization has taken hold, workers have organized and formed labor unions. However, the movements they built have varied from one industrial society to another. In the United States, workers were especially uncertain about the path they wanted to take. Only in the 1880s did the American labor movement settle into a fixed course.

Reformers and Unionists

Thomas B. McGuire, a New York wagon driver, was ambitious. He had saved $300 from his wages "so that I might become something of a capitalist eventually." But his venture as a cab driver in the early 1880s soon failed:

> Corporations usually take that business themselves. They can manage to get men, at starvation wages, and put them on a hack, and put a livery on them with a gold band and brass buttons, to show that they are slaves—I beg pardon; I did not intend to use the word slaves; there are no slaves in this country now—to show that they are merely servants.

Slave or liveried servant, the symbolic meaning was the same to McGuire. He was speaking of the crushed aspirations of the independent American worker.

What would satisfy the Thomas McGuires of the nineteenth century? Only the establishment of an *egalitarian society*, one in which every citizen might hope to become independent. This republican goal did not mean returning to the agrarian past, but rather moving beyond the existing industrial order to a juster system that did not distinguish between capitalists and workers. All would be "producers" laboring together in what was commonly called the "cooperative commonwealth." This was the ideal that inspired the Noble and Holy Order of the Knights of Labor.

Founded in 1869 as a secret society in Philadelphia, the Knights of Labor spread to other cities, and by 1878 had become a national movement. The Order's elaborate ritual and ceremony gave nineteenth-century workers a sense of belonging very much like that offered by the fraternalism of the Masons or Odd Fellows. For the Knights, however, fraternalism was harnessed to labor-reform advocacy. The goal was to "give voice to that grand undercurrent of mighty thought, which is today [1880] crystallizing in the hearts of men, and urging them on to perfect organization through which to gain the power to make labor emancipation possible."

But how was "emancipation" to be achieved? Through cooperation, the Knights argued. Funds would be raised to set up cooperative factories and shops owned and run by the employees. As these cooperatives flourished and spread, American society would be transformed into a cooperative commonwealth. But little was actually done. Instead, the Knights devoted themselves to "education." The Knights's leader, Grand Master Workman Terence V. Powderly, regarded the organization as a vast educational society that ought to be open to almost anyone (excluding lawyers and saloonkeepers). The cooperative commonwealth would arrive in some mysterious way as more and more "producers" became members and learned the group's message from lectures, discussions, and publications. Social evil would not end in a day, but "must await the gradual development of educational enlightenment."

The labor reformers expressed the higher aspirations of American workers. Another kind of organization—the trade union—tended to their day-to-day needs. Unions had long been central in the lives of craft workers. Apprenticeship rules regulated entry into a trade, and the *closed shop*—by reserving all jobs for union members—kept out lower-wage and incompetent workers. Union rules specified the terms of work, sometimes in minute detail. The trade union also expressed the social identity of the craft. A Birmingham iron worker claimed that his union's "main object was to educate mechanics up to a standard of morality and temperance, and good workmanship." Some unions emphasized mutual aid. Because operating trains was a high-risk occupation, the railroad brotherhoods provided accident and death benefits and encouraged members to assist one another. On the job and off, the unions played a big part in the lives of craft workers.

The earliest unions organized locally workers in the same craft, sometimes limited, especially among German workers, to a single ethnic group. As expanding markets broke down their insularity, these unions began to form national organizations, starting with the International Typographical Union in 1852. By the 1870s molders, ironworkers, bricklayers, and about thirty other trades had formed national unions.

The practical job interests they espoused might have seemed a far cry from the reform ideals of the Knights of Labor. But both kinds of motives arose from a single workers' culture. Seeing no conflict, many workers carried membership cards in both the Knights of Labor and a trade union. The careers of many labor leaders, including Powderly, likewise embraced both kinds of activity. For many years even the functional lines were indistinct. At the local level, little separated a trade assembly of the Knights from a local trade union; both engaged in fraternal and job-oriented activities.

Trade unions generally barred women, and so did the Knights until, in 1881, women shoe workers in Philadelphia struck in support of their male co-workers, and won the right to form their own local assembly. By 1886 probably 50,000 women belonged to the Knights of Labor. Their courage on the picket line prompted Powderly's rueful remark that women "are the best men in the Order." For a handful of women, such as the hosiery worker Leonora M. Barry, the Knights provided a rare chance to take up leadership roles as organizers and officials. Similarly, the Knights of Labor grudgingly expanded the opportunity for black workers to join out of the need for solidarity and, just as important, in deference to the Order's egalitarian principles. The Knights could rightly boast that their "great work has been to organize labor which was previously unorganized."

Samuel Gompers
This is a photograph of the labor leader in his forties taken when he was visiting striking miners in West Virginia, an area where mine operators resisted unions with special fierceness. The photograph was taken by a company detective.

The Triumph of "Pure and Simple" Unionism

In the early 1880s the Knights began to rival the trade unions. Boycott campaigns against the products of "unfair" employers achieved impressive results. With the economy booming and workers in short supply, the Knights began to win strikes, including a major victory against Jay Gould's Southwestern railway system in 1885. Workers flocked into the organization, and its membership jumped from 100,000 to perhaps 700,000 in less than a year. For a brief time the Knights stood poised as a potential industrial-union movement capable of bringing all workers into its fold.

Frightened by this success, the national trade unions began to insist on a clear separation of roles, with the Knights confined to the field of labor reform. This was partly a battle over turf, but it also reflected deepening divergence of labor philosophies.

The ideological assault on the Knights was led by Samuel Gompers, a union cigar maker from New York City. Gompers hammered out the philosophical position that would become known as "pure and simple" unionism. His starting point was that grand theories and schemes such as those that excited the labor reformers should be avoided like the plague. Unions, Gompers thought, should focus instead strictly on concrete, achievable gains, and they should organize workers not as an undifferentiated mass of "producers," but by craft and occupation. The battleground should be where workers could mobilize their power, which was where they worked, not in the quicksands of politics. While the Knights dreamt of a cooperative commonwealth, pure-and-simple unionists concerned themselves strictly with the here-and-now. "No matter how just," Gompers pronounced, "unless the cause is backed up with power to enforce it, it is going to be crushed and annihilated."

The struggle for the eight-hour day that began in 1886 crystallized the tensions between the rival movements. Both, of course, favored a shorter workday, but for different reasons. For the Knights, it was desirable because workers had duties "to perform as American citizens and members of society." Trade unionists took a more hard-boiled view of the eight-hour day: it would spread the available jobs among more workers, protect them against overwork, and (like higher wages) make life easier for them. When the trade unions set May 1, 1886, as the deadline for achieving the eight-hour day, the leadership of Knights objected. But workers everywhere responded enthusiastically, and as the deadline approached, a wave of strikes and demonstrations broke out.

In Chicago four strikers died on May 3 in a battle at the McCormick agricultural-implement works. German-American anarchists, revolutionary advocates of a stateless society, called a protest meeting the next evening at Haymarket Square. When police moved in to break it up, someone threw a bomb that killed and wounded several of the police. With no proof of their involvement, the anarchists were tried and found guilty of criminal conspiracy. Four were executed, one committed suicide, and the others received long prison sentences. They were victims of one of the great miscarriages of American justice.

The antiunion hysteria set off by the Haymarket affair enabled employers to take the offensive against the campaign for an eight-hour day. They broke strikes violently, compiled blacklists of strikers, and forced others to sign so-called *yellow-dog contracts* guaranteeing that as a condition of employment, they would not join a labor organization. If trade unionists needed any further confirmation of the tough world in which they lived, they found it in Haymarket and its aftermath.

In December 1886, having failed to persuade the Knights of Labor to desist from union activity, the national trade unions formed the American Federation of Labor (AFL), with Samuel Gompers as president. The AFL in effect locked into place the trade-union structure as it had evolved by the 1880s. Underlying this structure was the conviction that workers had to take the world as it was, not as they dreamed it might be.

The Knights of Labor never recovered from the employer counteroffensive after the Haymarket affair. Powderly retreated to the rhetoric of labor reform, but wage earners had lost interest, and he was unable to formulate a workable new strategy. By the mid-1890s, the Knights of Labor had faded away.

Industrial War

The trade unions were conservative, in that they accepted the economic order; all they wanted was a larger share for working people. But it was precisely that claim against their profits that made American employers so opposed to collective bargaining. In the 1890s they unleashed a fierce counterattack on the trade-union movement.

In Homestead, Pennsylvania, site of one of Carnegie's great steel mills, the skilled workers thought themselves safe from that threat. Mostly homeowners, they elected fellow workers to public office and considered the town very much their community. And they had faith in Andrew Carnegie, who had advocated in a famous magazine article the right of workers to combine, and also of a property right in their jobs that forbade the use of strikebreakers by employers.

Espousing high-toned principles made Carnegie feel good; but, alas, the bottom line made him feel even better. Carnegie decided that collective bargaining had become too expensive. With the new machinery he was installing, Carnegie was confident that his skilled workers could be replaced, and the union broken. Lacking the stomach for the hard battle ahead, Carnegie hid himself in his remote castle in Scotland. But he left behind a second-in-command eminently qualified for the job. This was Henry Clay Frick, a former coal baron and a veteran of labor wars in the coal fields.

After some perfunctory bargaining Frick announced that, effective July 1, 1892, the company would no longer deal with the Amalgamated Association of Iron and Steel Workers. The plant had already been fortified so that strikebreakers could be brought in to resume operations. At stake for Carnegie's employees now were not just wage cuts but the defense of a way of life. Town authorities turned away the county sheriff when he tried to take possession of the plant. The entire community—women no less than men—mobilized in defense of the union.

Behind hastily erected barricades, the strikers opened fire on barge loads of Pinkertons trying to approach the plant at dawn on July 6. When the Pinkertons surrendered after a bloody battle, they were mercilessly pummeled by the enraged women of Homestead as they were herded to the railway station. Frick appealed to the governor of Pennsylvania, who called out the state militia and placed Homestead under martial law. The great steelworks was taken over and opened to strikebreakers, while union leaders and town officials were arrested on charges of riot, murder, and treason.

The Homestead strike ushered in a decade of strife in which working people faced not only the great power of corporate industry, but the even greater power of their own government. The fullest demonstration of that hard reality came at a place that seemed an even less likely site for class warfare than Homestead. Pullman, Illinois, was a model factory town built by George M. Pullman, inventor of the sleeping car, which brought comfort and luxury to railway travel. When the Panic of 1893 struck, business fell off and Pullman cut wages, but not the rents for company housing. When a workers' committee finally complained to him in May 1894, Pullman responded that he saw no connection between his roles as employer and landlord. As for the committee members, they were fired.

The strike that ensued would have been only a footnote in American labor history, but for the fact that the Pullman workers belonged to the American Railway Union (ARU), a rapidly growing industrial union of railroad workers. Its leader, Eugene V. Debs, directed ARU members not to handle Pullman sleeping cars, which, although operated by the railroads, were owned and serviced by the Pullman Company. This was a *labor boycott*, in which force was applied at a secondary point (the railroads) to bring pressure on the primary target (Pullman). Since the railroads insisted on running the Pullman cars, a far-flung strike soon spread across the country, threatening the entire economy.

Quite deliberately, the railroads maneuvered to bring the federal government into the dispute. Their hook was the U.S. mail cars, which they attached to every train hauling Pullman cars. When strikers stopped these trains, the railroads appealed to President Grover Cleveland to protect the U.S. mail. It so happened that the attorney-general, Richard Olney, was a former railroad lawyer who unabashedly sided with his former employers. When federal troops failed to get the trains running again, Olney obtained court orders forbidding the ARU leaders to conduct the strike. Debs refused to obey; he was held in contempt of court and jailed. Now leaderless and uncoordinated, the strike quickly fell apart. No one could doubt why the great Pullman boycott had failed: it had been crushed by the naked use of government power on behalf of the railroad companies.

American Radicalism in the Making

No one who had known him as a young man would have thought that one day Eugene Debs would become the nation's leading socialist. A native of Terre Haute, Indiana, a prosperous railroad town, Debs grew up believing in the essential goodness of American society. A popular young man-about-town, Debs considered a career in politics or business, but instead got involved in the local labor movement. In 1880, at the age of twenty-five, he was elected national secretary-treasurer of the Brotherhood of Locomotive Firemen, one of the craft unions representing the skilled operating trades on the railroads. Increasingly bothered by his union's indifference to the welfare of low-paid track and yard laborers, Debs unexpectedly resigned from his comfortable post to devote himself to a new organization, the

The Pullman Strike
Chicago was the hub of the railwork network and the strategic center of the battle between the Pullman boycotters and the trunk line railroads. For the strikers, the crucial thing was to prevent those trains with Pullman cars attached from running; for the railroads, it was to get the trains through at any cost. The arrival of federal troops meant that the trains would move and that the strikers would be defeated.

American Railway Union, that would organize all railroad workers irrespective of skill—that is, an *industrial union.*

The Pullman strike visibly changed Debs. Sentenced to six months in the federal penitentiary, Debs came out of jail an avowed radical, committed to a lifelong struggle against a system that enabled employers to enlist the powers of government to beat down working people. Initially Debs identified himself as a Populist, but he quickly gravitated toward the socialist camp.

German refugees had brought the ideas of Karl Marx, the radical German philosopher, to America after the failed 1848 revolutions in Europe. Little noticed by most Americans, Marxist socialism struck deep roots in the growing German-American communities of Chicago and New York. In 1877 the Socialist Labor party was formed, and from that time onward Marxist socialism maintained a continuing, if narrowly based, presence in American politics.

When Eugene Debs appeared in their midst in 1897, the socialists were in a state of crisis. Despite the economic upheaval just ending, they had failed to make much headway. Many blamed the party head, Daniel De Leon, an ideological purist not greatly interested in attracting voters. Debs joined in the revolt against the dogmatic De Leon. When the rival Socialist Party of America was formed in 1901, it was with the aim of building a broad-based political movement.

A spellbinding campaigner, Debs talked socialism in an American idiom, making Marxism understandable and persuasive to many ordinary Americans. Under him the new party began to break down ethnic barriers and attract American-born voters. In Texas, Oklahoma, and Minnesota, socialism exerted a powerful appeal among cotton and wheat farmers. The party was also highly successful at attracting women activists. Inside of a decade, with a national network of branches and state organizations, the Socialist party had become a force to be reckoned with in American politics.

For some radical unionists, especially veterans of the fierce labor wars in the West (see Chapter 17), electoral politics seemed too tame. Led by Ed Boyce and "Big Bill" Haywood, the Western Federation of Miners joined with left-wing socialists in 1905 to create a new movement, the Industrial Workers of the World (IWW). The *Wobblies*, as IWW members were called, fervently supported the Marxist class struggle—but strictly in the industrial field. By action at the point of production and by an unending struggle against employers—ultimately by means of a general strike—they believed that the workers themselves would bring about a revolution. A workers' society would emerge, run directly by the workers through their industrial unions. The term *syndicalism* describes this brand of workers' radicalism.

In both its major forms—the politically oriented Socialist party and the syndicalist IWW—American radicalism flourished after the crisis of the 1890s, but only on a limited basis. Socialists and Wobblies lived, in a sense, on the tolerance of society. They would later be crushed without ceremony. Nevertheless, they served a larger purpose. American radicalism, by its sheer vitality, bore witness to what was exploitative and unjust in the new industrial order.

CHAPTER 18 TIMELINE

1869	Knights of Labor founded in Philadelphia First transcontinental railroad completed
1872	Montgomery Ward, first mail-order house, founded Andrew Carnegie starts construction of Edgar Thompson steelworks near Pittsburgh
1873	Panic of 1873 ushers in economic depression
1875	John Wanamaker establishes first department store in Philadelphia
1877	Baltimore and Ohio workers initiate nationwide railroad strike
1878	Gustavus Swift introduces refrigerator car
1883	Railroads establish national time zones
1886	Haymarket Square bombing in Chicago American Federation of Labor (AFL) founded
1890	U.S. surpasses Britain in producing iron and steel
1892	Homestead steel strike crushed
1893	Panic of 1893 starts depression of the 1890s Wave of railroad bankruptcies; reorganization by investment bankers begins
1894	President Cleveland sends troops to break Pullman boycott
1895	Frederick W. Taylor expounds scientific management Southeastern European immigration exceeds northern European immigration for the first time
1901	Eugene V. Debs helps found Socialist party
1905	Industrial Workers of the World (IWW) launched

CHAPTER 19

THE POLITICS OF LATE NINETEENTH-CENTURY AMERICA

- The Politics of the Status Quo, 1877–1893
- The Crisis of American Politics: The 1890s
- Race and Politics in the South

Ever since the founding of the Republic, foreign visitors had been coming to America to study its political system. Most famous of the early observers was Alexis de Tocqueville, the author of *Democracy in America* (1832). When an equally brilliant visitor, the Englishman James Bryce, sat down to write his own account fifty years later, he decided that Tocqueville's great book could not serve as his model. For Tocqueville, Bryce noted, "America was primarily a democracy, the ideal democracy, fraught with lessons for Europe." In his own book, *The American Commonwealth* (1888), Bryce was much less rhapsodic. Tocqueville's robust democracy had devolved over the next half-century into the dreary machine politics of post–Civil War America.

Bryce was anxious that his European readers not misunderstand him. Europeans needed to be aware of "the existence in the American people of a reserve of force and patriotism more than sufficient to sweep away all the evils now tolerated, and to make a politics of the country worthy of its material grandeur and of the private virtues of its inhabitants." Bryce was ultimately an optimist: "A hundred times in writing this book have I been disheartened by the facts I was stating: a hundred times has the recollection of the abounding strength and vitality of the nation chased away these tremours."

Just what it was that Bryce found so disheartening in the practice of American politics is this chapter's first subject; the second is the underlying vitality that Bryce sensed, and how it re-emerged and began to reinvigorate the nation's politics by the century's end.

THE POLITICS OF THE STATUS QUO, 1877–1893

In times of national ferment, as a rule, public life becomes magnified. Leaders emerge. Electoral campaigns debate great issues. The powers of government expand. In the Civil War era, the nation's public institutions had been severely tested, not least by the contested presidential election of 1876. In 1877, with the Republican Rutherford B. Hayes safely settled in the White House, the era of sectional strife finally ended.

Political life went on, but drained of its earlier drama. In the 1880s there were no Lincolns, no great national debates. There remained an irreducible core of public functions and even, as on the question of railroad regulation, grudging acceptance of new governmental involvement. But the dominant rhetoric celebrated that government which governed least, and as compared to the Civil War era, American government did govern less.

The National Scene

There were five presidents from 1877 to 1893: Rutherford B. Hayes (Republican, 1877–1881), James A. Garfield (Republican, 1881), Chester A. Arthur (Republican, 1881–1885), Grover Cleveland (Democrat, 1885–1889), and Benjamin Harrison (Republican, 1889–1893). All were estimable men. Hayes,

Grover Cleveland
In the years after Reconstruction, Americans did not look for charismatic personalities or dramatic leadership in their presidents. They preferred men who accepted the limits of executive power, men of "sound conservatism." Grover Cleveland fitted the bill to perfection. For political reformers, Cleveland had the additional virtues of independence and personal integrity. He best represented the late nineteenth-century ideal of the American president.

Garfield, and Harrison boasted distinguished war records. Hayes had served effectively as governor of Ohio for three terms, and Garfield had done well as a congressional leader. Arthur, despite his reputation as a machine politician, had demonstrated fine administrative skills as head of the New York customs house. Cleveland had made his mark as reform mayor of Buffalo and governor of New York. None was a charismatic leader, but circumstances, more than personal qualities, explain why none of these presidents made a larger mark on history.

The president's most demanding job was to dispense political patronage. Under the spoils system, government jobs were treated as rewards for those who had served the winning party. Reform of this system became urgent after President Garfield was shot in 1881. His assassin, Charles Guiteau, was a deranged religious fanatic, but advocates of civil-service reform blamed his death on the poisonous atmosphere of the spoils system. The resulting Pendleton Act of 1883 created a list of jobs to be filled on the basis of examinations administered by the new Civil Service Commission. The list originally covered only a small percentage of federal appointments, however, and patronage remained a preoccupation in the White House. Though standards of public administration did rise, there was no American counterpart to the elite professional civil services taking shape in Britain and Germany in these years.

The functions of the executive branch were, in any event, very modest. Of the 100,000 federal employees in 1880, fully 56 percent worked for the U.S. Post Office. During the 1880s the important government departments— Treasury, State, War, Navy, Interior—were sleepy places carrying on largely routine duties. Virtually all federal funding came from customs duties and excise taxes on liquor and tobacco. These sources produced more money than the government spent. The question of how to reduce the federal *surplus* ranked as one of the most troublesome issues of the 1880s.

On matters of national policy the presidents took a back seat to Congress. But Congress functioned badly. Party discipline was weak, and procedural rules frequently blocked legislative business. The Democrats favored states' rights, while the Republicans were heirs to the Whig enthusiasm for federally assisted economic development. After Reconstruction, however, the Republicans backed away from that activist position and, in truth, party differences became muddy. On most leading issues of the day—civil-service reform, the currency, and regulation of the railroads—the divisions occurred within the parties, not between them.

Only the tariff remained a potent partisan issue. From Lincoln's administration onward, high duties had protected American industry from imported goods. The Democrats, free traders by tradition, regularly attacked Republican protectionism. In practice, however, the tariff was a negotiable issue like any other. Congressmen voted their constituents' interests, regardless of party rhetoric. As a result, every tariff bill was a patchwork of bargains among special interests.

Issues were treated gingerly partly because the parties were so equally balanced. The Democrats, in retreat immediately after the Civil War, quickly regrouped, and by the end of Reconstruction stood on virtually equal terms with the Republicans. Every presidential election from 1876 to 1892 was decided by a thin margin, and neither party gained permanent command of Congress. Political caution seemed wise; any false move on national issues might tip the scales to the other side.

The weakening of principled politics was evident in the Republicans' retreat from their Civil War legacy. The major unfinished business after 1877 involved the plight of the former slaves. The Republican agenda called for federal funding to combat illiteracy and, even more threatening to the South, federal protection for black voters in southern congressional elections. Neither measure managed to make it through Congress, however. The Republicans back-pedaled on the race issue and gradually abandoned the blacks to their fate.

That did not stop Republican orators from "waving the bloody shirt" against the Democrats. Service in the Union army gave candidates a strong claim to public office, and veterans' benefits always stood high on the Republican agenda. The Democrats played the same game in the South as the defenders of the Lost Cause.

Alternatively, campaigns could descend into comedy. In the hard-fought election of 1884, for example, the Democrat Grover Cleveland burst on the scene as a reformer, fresh from his victories over corrupt machine politics as Buffalo mayor and New York governor. But years earlier Cleveland, a bachelor, had fathered an illegitimate child, and throughout the campaign he was dogged by the ditty, "Maw, Maw, where's Paw? He's in the White House, haw-haw-haw." His opponent, James G. Blaine, got tangled up in the scandalous charge by a too ardent Republican supporter that the Democrats were the party of "Rum, Romanism and Rebellion." In the midst of all the mudslinging, the issues got lost.

The Ideology of Individualism

The characteristics of public life in the 1880s—the inactivity of the federal government, the evasiveness of the political parties, and the absorption in politics for its own sake—derived ultimately from the conviction that little was at stake in public affairs. In 1887 Cleveland vetoed a small appropriation for drought-stricken Texas farmers with the remark that "though the people support the Government, the Government should not support the people." Governmental activity was itself considered a bad thing. All that the state could do, said Republican Senator Roscoe Conkling, was "to clear the way of impediments and dangers, and leave every class and every individual free and safe in the exertions and pursuits of life." Conkling was expressing the political corollary to the doctrine of *laissez faire*—the belief that that government was best which governed least.

A flood of popular writings trumpeted the individualist creed, from the rags-to-riches tales of Horatio Alger to the stream of success manuals with

Facing the World
The cover of this Horatio Alger
novel (1893) captures the myth of
opportunity. Our hero "Harry
Vane" is a poor but earnest lad,
valise packed, ready to make his
way in the world and, despite the
many obstacles thrown in his path,
sure to succeed. In some 135 books
Horatio Alger repeated this story,
with minor variations, for an eager
reading public that numbered in
the millions.

such titles as *Thoughts for the Young Men of America, or a Few Practical Words of Advice to those Born in Poverty and Destined to be Reared in Orphanages* (1871). It was a lesson celebrated in the lives of such self-made men as Andrew Carnegie, whose book *Triumphant Democracy* (1886) paid homage to a nation that had enabled a penniless Scottish child to rise from bobbin boy to steel magnate.

From the pulpit came the assurances of the Episcopal bishop William Lawrence of Massachusetts that "Godliness is in league with riches." Bishop Lawrence was voicing a tradition in American Protestantism that went back to the Puritans: success in one's earthly calling signified the promise of eternal salvation. It was all too easy for a conservative ministry to make morally reassuring the furious acquisitiveness of industrial America. "To secure wealth is an honorable ambition," intoned the Baptist minister Russell H. Conwell in his lecture "Acres of Diamonds," a text for what became known as the Gospel of Wealth.

American individualism drew strong intellectual support from science. In *The Origin of Species* (1859) the British naturalist Charles Darwin had developed a bold hypothesis to explain the evolution of plants and animals. In nature, Darwin wrote, all living things struggle and compete. Individual members of a species are born with characteristics that better enable them to survive in their particular environment: camouflage coloring for a bird, for example, or resistance to thirst in a desert animal. These survival characteristics, since they are heritable, become dominant in future generations, and the species evolves. This process of evolution, which Darwin called *natural selection*, created a revolution in biological science.

Drawing on Darwin, the British philosopher Herbert Spencer developed an elaborate analysis of how human society had evolved through competition and "survival of the fittest." Social Darwinism, as Spencer's ideas became known, was championed in America by William Graham Sumner, a sociology professor at Yale. Competition, said Sumner, is a law of nature that "can no more be done away with than gravitation." And who are the fittest? "The millionaires. . . . They may fairly be regarded as the naturally selected agents of society. They get high wages and live in luxury, but the bargain is a good one for society."

Social Darwinists argued against any interference with social processes. "The great stream of time and earthly things will sweep on just the same in spite of us," Sumner wrote in a famous essay, "The Absurd Attempt to Make the World Over" (1894). As for the government, it had "at bottom . . . two chief things . . . with which to deal. They are the property of men and the honor of women. These it has to defend against crime."

The Courts

Suspicion of government not only paralyzed political initiative; it also shifted power away from the executive and legislative branches. "The task of constitutional government," declared Sumner, "is to devise institutions which shall come into play at critical periods to prevent the abusive control of the powers of a state by the controlling classes in it." Sumner meant the judiciary. From the 1870s onward the courts increasingly accepted the role that he assigned to them, becoming the guardians of the rights of private property.

Under the federal system as it was understood in the late nineteenth century, the states retained primary responsibility for social welfare and economic regulation. The basis for this authority was the *police powers* of the states to ensure the health, safety, and morals of their citizens. How to strike a balance between the general welfare and the liberty of individuals to pursue their private interests was the dominant legal issue of the era. Most states, caught up in the conservative ethos of the day, were themselves cutting back on expenditures and public services. Even so, there were more than enough state initiatives to alarm vigilant judges. Thus, in the landmark case *In Re Jacobs* (1885) the New York Supreme Court struck down a state law prohibiting cigar manufacturing in tenements on the grounds that such regulation exceeded the police powers of the state.

For the U.S. Supreme Court, the crucial weapon was the Fourteenth Amendment (1868), which prohibited the states from depriving "any person of life, liberty, or property, without due process of law." The due-process clause had been adopted during Reconstruction to protect the civil rights of the former slaves. But due process protected the property rights and contractual liberty of any "person," and corporations counted as persons. So interpreted, the Fourteenth Amendment became by the turn of the century a powerful means of restraining the states in the use of their police powers to regulate private business.

The Supreme Court erected similar barriers against the federal government through a narrow reading of the Constitution. In 1895 the Court ruled that the federal power to regulate interstate commerce did not cover manufacturing, and struck down a federal income tax law. And over matters where federal power was undeniable—such as the regulation of railroads—the Supreme Court watched like a hawk for undue interferences with the rights of property.

Power conferred status. The law, not politics, attracted the ablest people and held the public's esteem. A Wisconsin judge boasted: "The bench symbolizes on earth the throne of divine justice. . . . Law in its highest sense is the will of God." Judicial supremacy reflected how dominant the ideology of individualism had become in industrial America, and also how low American politicians had fallen in the esteem of their countrymen.

Cultural Politics

Yet for all the criticism leveled against it, politics figured centrally in the nation's life. Proportionately more voters turned out in presidential elections from 1876 to 1892 than at any other time in American history. People voted Democratic or Republican for a lifetime. National conventions attracted huge crowds. "The excitement, the mental and physical strains," remarked an Indiana Republican after the 1888 convention, "are surpassed only by prolonged battle in actual warfare, as I have been told by officers of the Civil War who latter engaged in convention struggles." The convention he described had nominated the colorless Benjamin Harrison on a routine platform. What was all the excitement about?

For one thing, politics was a lively part of the nation's culture. During the election season the party faithful marched in impressive torchlight parades. Party paraphernalia flooded the country—handkerchiefs, mugs, posters, and buttons imprinted with the Democratic donkey or the Republican elephant, symbols that had been adopted in the 1870s. In 1888 the presidential hopefuls were pictured on cards, like baseball players, packed into Honest Long Cut tobacco. Campaigns had the suspense of baseball pennant races, plus the excitement of the circus coming to town. In an age before movies and radio, politics ranked as one of the great American forms of mass entertainment.

Party loyalty was a deadly serious matter, however. Long after the Civil War, emotions remained high. Among family friends in Cleveland, recalled the urban reformer Brand Whitlock, the Republican party was "a synonym for patriotism, another name for the nation. It was inconceivable that any self-respecting person should be a Democrat." Or, in the South, that any self-respecting person could be a Republican.

Beyond these sectional differences, the most important determinants of party loyalty were religion and ethnicity. Statistically, northern Democrats tended to be foreign-born and Catholic, while Republicans tended to be native-born and Protestant. Among Protestants, the more *pietistic* a person's faith—that is, the more personal and direct the believer's relationship to God—the more likely he or she was to be a Republican, and to favor using the powers of the state to regulate individual behavior.

During the 1880s ethnic tensions began to build up in many cities. One issue was the place of foreign languages in the schools. Immigrant groups, especially the Germans, wanted their children taught in their own languages. In

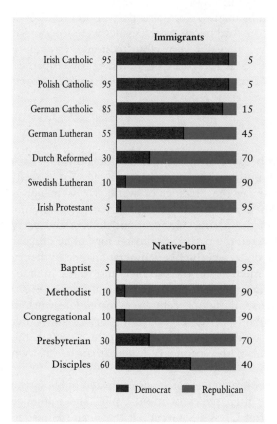

FIGURE 19.1

Ethnocultural Voting Patterns in the Midwest, 1870–1892 These figures demonstrate how voting patterns among midwesterners reflected ethnicity and religion in the late nineteenth century. Especially striking is the overwhelming preference by immigrant Catholics for the Democratic party. Among Protestants there was an equally strong preference for the Republican party by certain groups of immigrants (Swedish Lutherans and Irish Protestants) and native-born (Free Will Baptists, Methodists, and Congregationalist), but other Protestant groups were more evenly divided in their party preferences.

response, native-born Americans passed laws making English the language of instruction. Religion was an even more explosive educational issue. Catholics fought a losing battle over public aid for parochial schools. By 1900 such aid had been prohibited by twenty-three states. In Boston a furious controversy broke out in 1888 over the use of an anti-Catholic history textbook. When the school board withdrew the offending book, angry Protestants mounted a campaign to throw the moderates off the board and return the text to the curriculum.

Then there was the question of public morals. In many states so-called blue laws restricted activity on Sundays. When Nebraska banned Sunday baseball, the state supreme court approved the law as a blow struck in "the contest between Christianity and wrong." But German and Irish Catholics, who saw nothing evil in a bit of fun on Sunday, considered blue laws a violation of their personal freedom. Ethnocultural conflict also flared over the liquor question. Many states adopted strict licensing and local-option laws governing the sale and consumption of alcoholic beverages. Indiana permitted drinking, but only joylessly in rooms containing "no devices for amusement or music . . . of any kind."

Because the hottest ethnocultural issues of the day—education, the liquor question, and observance of the Sabbath—were also party issues, they lent deep significance to party affiliation. And because these issues were fought out mostly at the state and local level, they hit very close to home. Crusading Methodists thought of Republicans as the party of morality. For embattled Irish and German Catholics the Democratic party was the defender of their freedoms.

Organizational Politics

Political life was also important because of the remarkable organizational activity it generated. By the 1870s both major parties had evolved formal, well-organized structures. At the base lay the precinct or ward, whose meetings could be attended by all party members. County, state, and national committees ran the ongoing business of the parties. Conventions determined party rules, adopted platforms, and selected the party's candidates for public office.

Party administration seemed, on its face, highly democratic, since in theory all power derived from the party members in the precincts and wards. In practice, however, the parties were run by unofficial internal organizations—*machines*—which consisted of insiders willing to accept discipline and do work in exchange for getting on the public payroll, or pocketing bribes and other forms of "graft." The machines tended toward one-man rule, although the "boss" ruled more by the consent of the secondary leaders than by his own absolute power.

Absorbed in the tasks of power brokerage, party bosses treated public issues as somewhat irrelevant. And the high stakes of money, jobs, and influence made for intense factionalism. After Ulysses S. Grant left the White House in

The Levi P. Morton Association
The top-hatted gentlemen in this photograph constituted the local Republican party organization of Newport, Rhode Island, named in honor of Levi P. Morton, Benjamin Harrison's
vice president. The maleness of party politics leaps from the photograph and asserts more
clearly than a thousand words why the suffragist demand for the right to vote was met with
ridicule and disbelief.

1877, the Republican party divided into two warring factions—the Stalwarts,
who followed Senator Roscoe Conkling of New York, and the Halfbreeds, led
by James G. Blaine of Maine. The split was sparked by a personal feud between
Conkling and Blaine, but it persisted because of a furious struggle over patronage. The Halfbreeds represented a newer Republican generation that was
more inclined to pay lip service to political reform, and less committed to the
shopworn Civil War issues. But issues were secondary in the war between
Stalwarts and Halfbreeds. These factions were really fighting over the spoils of
party politics.

　　And yet the record was not wholly negative. Machine politics raised the
standards of governance in certain ways. Disciplined professionals, veterans
of machine politics, improved the performance of state legislatures and the
Congress. More important, party machines filled a void in the nation's public
life. They did informally much of what the governmental system left undone,
especially in the cities (see Chapter 20).

　　But machine politics never managed to win public legitimacy. Many of
the nation's social elite—intellectuals, well-to-do businessmen, and old-line
families—resented a politics that excluded people like themselves, the "best
men." There was, too, a genuine clash of values. Political reformers called for

"disinterestedness" and "independence"—the opposite of the self-serving ca-
reerism and party regularity fostered by the machine system. Many of them
had earned their spurs as Liberal Republicans who had broken from the party
and fought President Grant's reelection in 1872.

In 1884 Carl Schurz, Edwin L. Godkin, and Charles Francis Adams, Jr.,
again left the Republican party because they associated its presidential candidate, James G. Blaine, with corrupt politics. Mainly from New York and Massachusetts, these Republicans became known as Mugwumps—a derisive bit of
contemporary slang, supposedly of Indian origin, referring to pompous or
self-important persons. The Mugwumps threw their support to the Democrat
Grover Cleveland, and may have ensured his victory by providing the margin
for him in New York State.

After the 1884 election, the enthusiasm for reform spilled over into local
politics, spawning good-government campaigns across the country. Although
they won some municipal victories, the Mugwumps were more effective at
molding public opinion. Controlling the respectable newspapers and journals
and strategically placed in the urban world, the Mugwumps defined the terms
of political debate and denied the machine system public legitimacy.

The Mugwumps were reformers, but not on behalf of social justice. The
problems of working people did not evoke their sympathy, nor did they favor
using the powers of the state to ease the suffering of the poor. As far as the
Mugwumps were concerned, that government was best that governed least.
Theirs was the brand of "reform" perfectly in keeping with a politics of the
status quo.

Women's Political Culture

The young Theodore Roosevelt, an up-and-coming Republican state politician in 1884, referred to the Mugwumps contemptuously as "man-milliners"
(makers of ladies' hats). The sexual slur was not accidental. In attacking organizational politics, the Mugwumps were challenging one of the bastions of male
society. At party meetings and conventions, men carried on not only the business of politics, but also the satisfying rituals of male sociability amid cigar
smoke and whiskey. Politics was identified with manliness. It was competitive.
It dealt in the commerce of power. It was frankly self-aggrandizing. Party politics, in short, was no place for a woman.

So, naturally, the woman suffrage movement met fierce opposition in
these years. Blocked in their efforts to get a constitutional amendment, suffragists concentrated on state campaigns. But except in Wyoming, Idaho,
Colorado, and Utah, the most they could win was women's right to vote for
school boards or on tax issues. "Men are ordained to govern in all forceful
and material things, *because they are men*," asserted an antisuffrage resolution,
"while women, by the same decree of God and nature, are equally fitted to
bear rule in a higher and more spiritual realm"—that is to say, not in
politics.

Yet this invocation of the doctrine of "separate spheres" did open a channel for women to enter public life. "Women's place is Home," acknowledged the journalist Retha Childe Dorr. "But Home is not contained within the four walls of an individual house. Home is the community. The city full of people is the Family. . . . And badly do the Home and Family need their mother." So believing, women had since the early nineteenth century engaged in charitable and reform activities. Women's organizations fought prostitution, assisted the poor, agitated for the reform of women's prisons, and tried to expand educational and job opportunities for women. Since many of these goals required state intervention, women's organizations of necessity became politically active, but not, they stressed, out of any desire to participate in partisan politics or to gain the ballot. Quite the contrary: women were bent on creating their own political sphere.

No issue joined home and politics more poignantly than did the liquor question. Just before Christmas in 1873 the women of Hillsboro, Ohio, began to hold vigils in front of the town's saloons, pleading with the owners to close down and end the suffering of families of hard-drinking fathers. Thus began a spontaneous uprising of women that spread across the country and closed an estimated 3,000 saloons. From this agitation came the Woman's Christian Temperance Union (WCTU), which after its formation in 1874 rapidly blossomed into the largest organization of women in the country.

Because it excluded men, the WCTU was the spawning ground for a new generation of women leaders. Under the guidance of Frances Willard, who became president in 1879, the WCTU moved beyond temperance and adopted a "Do-Everything" policy. Alcoholism, women recognized, was not simply a personal failing; it stemmed from larger social problems in American society. Willard also wanted to attract women who had no particular interest in the liquor question. By 1889 the WCTU had thirty-nine departments concerned with labor, social purity, health, and international peace as well as temperance.

Most important, the WCTU was drawn to woman suffrage. This was necessary, Willard argued, "because the liquor traffic is entrenched in law, and law grows out of the will of majorities, and majorities of women are against the liquor traffic." Women needed the vote, said Willard, to fulfill their social responsibilities *as women*. This was very different from the claim made by the suffragists—that the ballot was an inherent right of all citizens *as individuals*—and was less threatening to masculine pride.

Not much changed in the short run. But by linking women's social concerns to women's political participation, the WCTU helped lay the groundwork for a fresh attack on male electoral politics in the early twentieth century. And in the meantime, even without the vote, the WCTU demonstrated how potent a voice women could find in the public arena, and how energetic a political culture they could build.

THE CRISIS OF AMERICAN POLITICS: THE 1890s

Ever since the end of Reconstruction in 1877 national politics had been stalemated by two evenly balanced parties. This equilibrium finally began to break down late in the 1880s. Benjamin Harrison's election to the presidency in 1888 was the last of the cliff-hanger victories: the Democratic candidate, Grover Cleveland, actually got a larger popular vote. Thereafter, the tide went heavily against the Republicans. In 1890 Democrats took the House of Representatives decisively, capturing 235 seats to the Republicans' 88, and won a number of governorships in normally Republican states. In 1892 Cleveland regained the presidency by the largest margin in twenty years.

Had everything else remained equal, the events of 1890 and 1892 might have opened a long period of Democratic supremacy. But everything else did not remain equal. By the time of Cleveland's inauguration, rising farm foreclosures and railroad bankruptcies signaled economic trouble. On May 3, 1893, the stock market crashed. In Chicago 100,000 jobless workers walked the streets; nationwide, the unemployment rate soared to over 20 percent. As always in hard times, suffering and unrest mounted alarmingly.

As the economic crisis of the 1890s set in, which party would prevail, and on what platform, became an open question. The first challenge arrived from the West and the South, where the grievances of farmers had begun to crystallize into the radical program of the Populist party.

The Populist Revolt

Farmers were of necessity joiners. They needed organization to overcome their social isolation and to obtain crucial economic services—hence the enormous appeal of the Granger movement, which had spread across the Midwest after 1867, and, after its decline, of the farmers' alliances that began to spring up among southern and western farmers. From scattered organizational beginnings, two dominant organizations emerged. One was the Farmers' Alliance of the Northwest, which was confined mainly to the midwestern states. More dynamic was the National (or Southern) Farmers' Alliance, which in the mid-1880s spread rapidly from Texas onto the Great Plains and eastward into the cotton South, as "travelling lecturers" extolled the virtues of cooperative activity and reminded farmers of "their obligation to stand as a great conservative body against the encroachments of monopolies and . . . the growing corruption of wealth and power." While thus recapitulating Granger resentment against railroads and merchants that had fueled earlier third-party movements, the alliances conceived of themselves as agents of social and economic reform, rather than as new political parties.

The Texas Alliance established a massive cooperative, the Texas Exchange, that marketed the crops of cotton farmers and provided them with cheap

En Route to a Populist Rally, Dickinson County, Kansas
Farm people traveled miles to rallies and meetings for the chance to voice their grievances and socialize with like-minded folks. This tradition infused Populism with a special fervor. Gatherings such as the one these Kansans were heading for were a visible sign of what Populism meant—a movement of the "people."

credit. When cotton prices fell sharply in 1891, the Texas Exchange failed. The Texas Alliance then proposed a new scheme: a *subtreasury system* that would enable farmers to store their crops in public warehouses. Farmers would be able to borrow against those crops from a federally supplied fund at low interest rates until prices rose enough so their cotton could be profitably marketed. The subtreasury plan would provide the same credit and marketing functions as had the defunct Texas Exchange, but with a crucial difference: the federal government would play the key role. When the subtreasury plan was rejected by the Democratic party as too radical, the Texas Alliance decided to strike out in politics independently.

These events in Texas revealed, with special clarity, a process of politicization that went on throughout the Alliance movement. Across the South and the West, as state alliances grew stronger and more impatient, they began to field independent slates. In 1890 third parties won control of the Nebraska and Kansas legislatures and in the South captured several governorships and eight state legislatures. These successes led to the formation of the national People's (Populist) party in 1892. In the elections that year, with the veteran third-party campaigner James B. Weaver as their presidential candidate, the Populists captured a million votes and carried four western states

Angry Farmers

*In his testimony Datus E. Meyer, a Minnesota farmer, details the farmers' griev-
ances against the railroads. But underlying is his sense of the farmers as victims
of powers beyond their control—hence the demand for government intervention that
was one of the hallmarks of Populism.*

St. Paul, Minnesota, June 25 1885

Mr. Meyer. There is very great discontent among the smaller farmers of
the State in regard to [the railroads]. . . . I can produce for you freight
receipts that will show where car-loads of stuff have been brought from
Springfield, Ohio, to Saint Paul at a charge of $65, a distance of about
800 miles, and carried to Saint Vincent, a distance of about 400 miles,
and charged $155. . . . Then there were discriminations proved [that]
they absolutely refused to allow a small farmer to have a car at all, in
which to load his corn and ship it away, unless he put it through that elevator system . . . on account of having given the exclusive privilege to
those elevator lines. . . .

You know how hard farmers are to organize; and yet there are over
three hundred secret organizations in this State, organized for the purpose of obtaining redress. . . .

The Chairman. They have a right now to go into court and sue if they
are charged an unreasonable rate?

Mr. Meyer. That is true. But suppose a farmer sues under the common
law. The railroads have their attorneys hired and paid for all the time,
and they can carry that suit on until an ordinary farmer is ruined. He
cannot contend with the railroads.

The Chairman. What would you have done?

Mr. Meyer. I would put a commission between the farmer and the
railroads that would see that he obtains justice. That is what I would
have done, and what the farmers desire shall be done. You can depend
on that.

SOURCE: U.S. Senate, Select Committee on Interestate Commerce, *Report*, 49 Cong., 1 Sess. (1886), Part 2, 1335–1337,
reprinted in Stanley I. Kutler, ed., *Looking for America* (2d ed., New York: W.W. Norton, 1975), II, 171–174.

(see Map 19.1). For the first time agrarian protest truly challenged the national two-party system.

The challenge was driven as much by ideology as by the quest for political
power. Populism contained a strong radical bent. The problems afflicting farmers, Populists felt, could stem only from some basic evil. They identified this evil
as the "money power" that controlled the levers of the economic system. "There

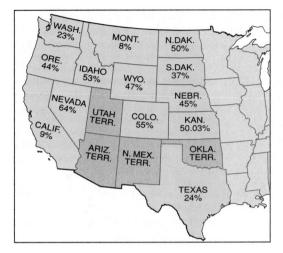

MAP 19.1

The Heyday of Western Populism, 1892

This map shows the percentage of the popular vote won by James B. Weaver, the People's party candidate, in the presidential election of 1892. Except for California and Montana, the Populists won broad support across the West and genuinely threatened the established parties in that region.

are but two sides," proclaimed a Populist manifesto. "On the one side are the allied hosts of monopolies, the money power, great trusts and railroad corporations. . . . On the other are the farmers, laborers, merchants and all the people who produce wealth. . . . Between these two there is no middle ground."

By this reasoning, farmers and workers formed a single producer class. Thus the Texas-based alliance renamed itself in 1889 the National Farmers' Alliance and Industrial Union. The title was not merely empty rhetoric. Organized in Knights of Labor assemblies, Texas railroad workers and Colorado miners cooperated with the farmers' alliances, got their support in strikes, and actively participated in forming state Populist parties. In its explicit class appeal—in recognizing that "the irrepressible conflict between capital and labor is upon us"—Populism parted company from the two mainstream parties.

Populism was distinguished also by the many women in the movement. In the established parties, the grass-roots organizations—the local political clubs—were for men only. Populism, on the other hand, arose from a network of suballiances that had formed for largely social purposes and that welcomed women. Although women were active as speakers and lecturers, few of them achieved high office in the alliances, and their role diminished with the formation of the Populist party. In deference to the southern wing, the party platform was silent on woman suffrage. Still, neither Democrats nor Republicans would have countenanced a spokeswoman such as the fiery Mary Elizabeth Lease, who became famous for calling on farmers "to raise less corn and more hell." Lease insisted just as strenuously on Populism's "grand and holy mission . . . to place the mothers of this nation on an equality with the fathers."

In an age dominated by laissez-faire doctrine, what most distinguished Populism from the major parties was its positive attitude toward the state. The Populist program declared: "We believe that the powers of government—in other words, of the people—should be expanded as rapidly and as far as the good sense of an intelligent people and the teachings of experience shall justify, to the end that oppression, injustice and poverty should eventually cease in the land."

The Omaha platform, adopted at the founding convention in 1892, called for nationalization of the railroads and communications; protection of the land, including natural resources, from monopoly and foreign ownership; a graduated income tax; the Texas Alliance's subtreasury plan; and the free and unlimited coinage of silver. From this array of issues, free silver emerged as the overriding demand of the Populist party.

In the early 1890s rock-bottom prices wreaked havoc among cotton, wheat, and corn growers. Under this pressure, farmers turned to free silver, which they hoped would, by increasing the money supply, raise farm prices and give them some relief. In addition, free silver would bring in hefty contributions from silver-mining interests. These mine operators, scornful though they might be of Populist radicalism, yearned for the day when the government would buy at a premium price all the silver they could produce, and to that end they were prepared to support the Populists.

Free silver was opposed by urban social democrats such as Henry Demarest Lloyd of Chicago and by agrarian radicals such as Georgia's Tom Watson. They pleaded that free silver not be made the leading party issue because it would undercut the broader Populist program and drive away wage earners, who had no enthusiasm for inflationary measures. Any chance of a farmer-labor alliance that might transform Populism into an American version of a social-democratic party would be doomed. As Lloyd complained, free silver was "the cowbird of reform," stealing in and taking over the nest that others had built.

Although fiercely debated within the party, the outcome was never in doubt: the political appeal of free silver was simply too great. But once Populists made that choice, they had fatally compromised their party's capacity to maintain an independent existence. For free silver was not an issue over which the Populists held a monopoly. Free silver was, on the contrary, a question at the very center of mainstream politics in the 1890s.

Money and Politics

In a rapidly developing economy, such as nineteenth-century America's, the money supply is bound to be a big political issue. Money has to increase rapidly enough to meet the economy's needs, or growth will be stifled. How fast the money supply should grow, however, is a question that creates sharp divisions. Debtors and producers of goods want a larger money supply: more money in circulation inflates prices and reduces the real cost of borrowing. The "sound-money" people—creditors, individuals on fixed incomes, people in the slower-growing sectors of the economy—have an opposite interest.

Civil War policies had very much magnified the money question. Before the war, the main source of the nation's money supply had been the banknotes issued by several thousand state banks. The Banking Act of 1863, however, sharply curtailed the freedom of these banks to create money. The economic impact of this nationalizing action was not immediately felt because the Lincoln administration itself was printing large amounts of paper money—greenbacks, so-called—to finance the Civil War. Afterward, however, the sound money interests lobbied powerfully for a return to the bimetallic policy prevailing ever since the founding of the Republic, which was to base the federal currency on the amount of *specie*—gold and silver—held by the U.S. Treasury. The issue was hotly contested for a decade, but in 1875 the inflationists were defeated, and the circulation of greenbacks as legal tender—that is, backed by nothing more than the good faith of the federal government—came to an end. With the state banknotes also in short supply, the country entered an era of chronic deflation and tight credit.

This was the context out of which the silver question emerged. The country had always operated on a bimetallic standard, but the supply of silver had gradually tightened and, as it became more valuable as metal than as money, silver disappeared from circulation. In 1873 silver was officially dropped as a medium of exchange. Soon afterward, great silver discoveries occurred in the West; silver prices fell. Inflationists began to agitate for a resumption of the traditional bimetallic policy: at the ratio of sixteen to one, silver would flow into the Treasury and greatly expand the volume of currency.

With so much at stake for so many people, the currency question became one of the staples of post-Reconstruction politics. Twice the prosilver coalition in Congress won modest victories. First, under the Bland-Allison Act of 1878, the U.S. Treasury was required to purchase and coin between $2 million and $4 million worth of silver each month. Then, in the more sweeping Sherman Silver Purchase Act of 1890, an additional 4.5 million ounces of silver bullion was to be purchased monthly, to serve as the basis for new issues of U.S. Treasury notes.

These legislative battles, although hard-fought, cut across party lines in the characteristic fashion of post-Reconstruction politics. In the early 1890s, silver suddenly became a defining issue between the parties; in particular, it had a radicalizing effect on the Democratic party.

When the crash of 1893 hit, the Democrats held power in Washington. The party in office usually gets blamed if the economy falters, but President Cleveland made things worse for the Democrats. When jobless marchers arrived in Washington in 1894 to appeal for federal relief, Cleveland's response was to disperse them forcibly and arrest their leader, Jacob S. Coxey. Cleveland's brutal handling of the Pullman strike further alienated the labor vote. Nor was he able to deliver on his campaign promise for tariff reform. He lost control of the battle when the unpopular McKinley Tariff of 1890 came up for revision in Congress. The resulting Wilson-Gorman Tariff of 1894, which he allowed to pass into law without his signature, caved in to special interests and left the most important rates largely unchanged.

Most disastrous, however, was Cleveland's rigidity on the silver question. Cleveland was a committed sound-money man. Nothing that happened after the depression set in—not collapsing prices, not the suffering of farmers, not the groundswell of support for free silver within his own party—budged Cleveland.

The Election of 1896

At their national convention in Chicago in 1896, the Democrats repudiated Cleveland and turned left. The leader of the triumphant silver Democrats was William Jennings Bryan of Nebraska. Bryan was a political phenomenon. Only thirty-six years old, he had already served two terms in Congress and become a passionate advocate of free silver. He was a skilled politician, and no less important, an inspiring public speaker. Bryan, remarked the journalist Frederic Howe, was "pre-eminently an evangelist . . . the vox ex cathedra of the Western self-righteous missionary mind." With biblical fervor, Bryan swept up his audiences when he joined the debate on free silver at the Democratic convention. He locked up the presidential nomination with a stirring attack on the gold standard: "You shall not press down upon the brow of labor this crown of thorns, you shall not crucify mankind on a cross of gold."

Bryan's nomination meant that the Democrats had become the party of free silver; his "cross of gold" speech meant that the money question would turn into a national crusade. No one could be neutral on this defining issue. Silver Republicans bolted their party; gold Democrats went for a splinter Democratic ticket or supported the Republican party. Even the Prohibition party split into gold and silver wings. The Populists, meeting after the Democratic convention, accepted Bryan as their candidate. The free-silver issue had become so vital that they could not do otherwise. Although they nominated their own vice-presidential candidate, the Georgian Tom Watson, the Populists found themselves for all practical purposes absorbed into the Democratic silver crusade.

The Republicans took up the challenge. Their key party leader was Mark Hanna, a wealthy Cleveland ironmaker, a brilliant political manager, and an exponent of the new industrial capitalism. Hanna orchestrated an unprecedented money-raising campaign among America's corporate interests. His candidate, William McKinley of Ohio, personified the virtues of Republicanism, standing solidly for high tariffs, honest money, and prosperity. While Bryan broke with tradition and crisscrossed the country in a furious whistlestop campaign, the dignified McKinley received delegations at his home in Canton, Ohio. Bryan orated with moral fervor; McKinley talked of industrial progress and a full dinner pail.

Not since 1860 had the United States witnessed such a hard-fought election over such high stakes. For the middle class, sound money stood symbolically for the soundness of the social order. With jobless workers tramping the streets and bankrupt farmers up in arms, Bryan's fervent assault on the gold standard struck fear in many hearts. Republicans denounced the Democratic platform as "revolutionary and anarchistic," and Bryan's supporters as "social misfits who have almost nothing in common but opposition to the existing order and institutions."

McKinley won handily, with 271 electoral votes to Bryan's 176. He kept the ground Republicans had regained in the 1894 midterm elections and pushed into Democratic strongholds, especially in the cities. Boston, New York, Chicago, and Minneapolis, all taken by Cleveland in 1892, went for

McKinley in 1896. Bryan ran strongly only in the South, in silver-mining states, and in the Populist West. But the gains his evangelical style brought him in some Republican rural areas did not compensate for his losses in traditionally Democratic urban districts.

The paralyzing equilibrium of American politics ended in 1896. The Republicans had skillfuly handled both the economic and the cultural challenges. They persuaded the nation that they were the party of prosperity and shifted some of the burdens of morality politics onto the Democrats. The Republicans had become the nation's majority party. In 1896, too, electoral politics regained its place as an arena for national debate, setting the stage for the reform politics of the Progressive Era.

RACE AND POLITICS IN THE SOUTH

When Reconstruction ended in 1877, so did the hopes of African-Americans that they would enjoy the equal rights of citizenship promised them by the Fourteenth and Fifteenth amendments. Schools were strictly segregated. Access to jobs, to justice, and to social welfare was racially determined and unequal. But segregation in public accommodations was not yet legally required, and practices varied a good deal across the South. Only on railroads, as travel became more common, did whites begin to demand that blacks be excluded from first-class cars, with the result that southern railroads became after 1887 the first public accommodation subject to segregation laws.

In politics, the situation was even more fluid. Blacks had not been driven from politics. On the contrary, their turnout at elections was not far from that of whites. But blacks did not participate on equal terms with whites. In the Black Belt areas, where African-Americans sometimes outnumbered whites, voting districts were gerrymandered (redivided) to ensure that while blacks got some offices, political control remained in white hands. Blacks, moreover, were routinely intimidated during political campaigns. Even so, an impressive majority remained staunchly Republican, refusing, as the last black Congressman from Mississippi told his House colleagues in 1882, "to surrender their honest convictions, even upon the altar of their personal necessities."

Whatever hope blacks entertained for better days, however, faded during the 1880s and then, in the next decade, expired in a terrible burst of racist terrorism.

Biracial Politics

No democratic society can survive if it does not enable competing economic and social interests to be heard. In the United States the two-party system performs that role. The Civil War crisis severely tested the two-party system, because, in both the North and the South, political opposition came to be seen as treasonous. In the victorious North, despite the best efforts of the Republicans, the Democrats shed their disgrace and reclaimed their status as a major party. In the defeated South, however, the scars of war cut deep, and

Reconstruction cut even deeper. The struggle for "home rule" empowered southern Democrats. They had "redeemed" the South from Republican domination, hence the name they adopted: Redeemers. Cloaked in the mantle of the Lost Cause, the Redeemers claimed a monopoly on political legitimacy.

The Republican party did not fold up, however. On the contrary, it soldiered on, sustained by strong black loyalty, by a hard core of white support, by patronage from Republican national administrations, and by a key Democrat weakness. This was the gap between the universality the Democrats claimed as the party of Redemption and the reality that the party was controlled by an economic elite indifferent to the plight of poor whites.

Class antagonism, although often muted by sectional patriotism, was never absent from southern society. The Civil War had brought out long-smoldering differences between hill-country farmers and planters. Fresh sources of conflict now arose from the sharecropping system—which increasingly included whites as well as blacks—and from an emerging industrial working class. In the late 1880s, agrarian discontent boiled over, welling out of the farmers' alliances that sprang up across the South and spawning a formidable Populist challenge to Redeemer rule.

What distinguished the South was not that it experienced intense agrarian protest—so did the West—but that this agrarian challenge provoked a crisis in the South's one-party system. Refusing to accept any opposition as legitimate, the ruling Democrats stuffed ballot boxes, intimidated black voters, murdered opponents, and stirred up racial hatred by shouting "Negro domination!"

But Populists were themselves uneasy about black participation. Racism cut through southern white society and, so some thought, most infected the lowest rungs. "The white laboring classes here," wrote an Alabaman in 1886, "are separated from the Negroes, working all day side by side with them, by an innate consciousness of race superiority," which "excites a sentiment of sympathy and equality with the classes above them, and in this way becomes a healthy social leaven." Yet when times got bad enough, hard-pressed whites could also see blacks as fellow victims. "They are in the ditch just like we are," asserted one white Texan. Southern Populists never fully reconciled these contradictory impulses. They never questioned the conventions of social inequality. But once agrarian protest turned political, the logic of racial solidarity became hard to deny.

Kept out of the Southern Alliance, black farmers had organized separately into the Colored Farmers' Alliance, gaining thereby a certain amount of leverage with the emerging Populist movement. The realities of partisan politics, once the alliances turned against the conservative Democrats, clinched the argument for interracial unity. Where the Populists fused with the Republican party, as in North Carolina and Tennessee, they automatically became allies of black leaders and gained a black constituency. Where fusion did not happen and the Populists fielded independent tickets, they needed to appeal to black voters. "The accident of color can make no difference in the interest of farmers, croppers, and laborers," argued the Georgian Tom Watson. "You are kept

apart that you may be separately fleeced of your earnings." By making this interracial appeal, even if not always wholeheartedly, the Populists put at risk the
foundations of conservative southern politics.

White Reaction

The conservative Democrats played the race card to the hilt, parading as the
"white man's party" while denouncing the Populists for courting "Negro
rule." Yet they shamelessly competed for the black vote. In this, they had many
advantages: money; control of the local power structures; a paternalistic relationship to the black community. When all else failed, mischief at the polls enabled the Democrats to beat back the Populists. Thus the Mississippian Frank
Burkitt's bitter attack on the conservatives: they were "a class of corrupt
office-seekers" who had "hypocritically raised the howl of white supremacy
while they debauched the ballot boxes . . . disregarded the rights of the blacks
. . . and actually dominated the will of the white people through the instru-
mentality of the stolen negro vote."

In the midst of these deadly struggles the Democrats decided to settle matters once and for all. An effort to disfranchise the blacks, hitherto hesitant,
now turned into a potent section-wide movement (see Map 19.2). In 1890

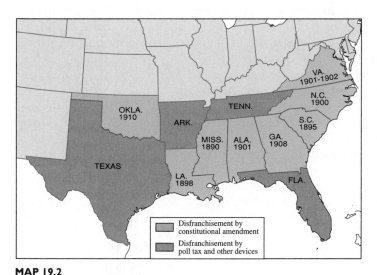

MAP 19.2
Disfranchisement in the South
In the midst of the Populist challenge to Democratic rule in the South, a
movement to deprive blacks of the right to vote spread across the South.
By 1910 every southern state except Tennessee, Arkansas, Texas, and
Florida had made constitutional changes designed to prevent blacks from
voting, and these four states accomplished much the same result through
other methods. For the next half century the political process in the South
would be for whites only.

Mississippi adopted a literacy test that effectively drove blacks out of politics. The motives behind it were cynical, but the literacy test could be dressed up as a reform for Mississippians tired of electoral fraud and violence. Their children and grandchildren, argued one influential figure, should not be left "with shotguns in their hands, a lie in their mouths and perjury on their lips in order to defeat the negroes." This logic even persuaded some weary Populists: Frank Burkitt, for example, was arguing *for* the Mississippi literacy test in the words quoted in the previous paragraph.

The race issue had helped to bring down the Populists; now it helped reconcile them to defeat. Embittered poor whites, deeply ambivalent all along about interracial cooperation, turned their fury on the blacks. Insofar as disfranchising measures asserted militant white supremacy, poor whites approved. It was important, of course, that they themselves be partially protected by lenient enforcement and by exemptions. But poor whites were not protected from property and poll-tax requirements, and many stopped voting.

Poor whites might have objected more had their spokesmen not been given a voice within the Democratic party. A new brand of southern politician came forward to speak for them. Tom Watson, the fiery Georgia Populist, rebuilt his political career as a brilliant practitioner of race baiting. Starting in the early 1900s, he and other racial demagogues thrived throughout the South.

The color line, hitherto incomplete, became rigid and comprehensive. Segregated seating in trains, widely adopted in the late 1880s, provided a precedent for the legal separation of the races. The enforcing legislation, known as Jim Crow laws, soon applied to every type of public facility—restaurants, hotels, streetcars, even cemeteries. In the 1890s the South became for the first time a society fully segregated by law.

The U.S. Supreme Court soon ratified the South's decision. In the case of *Plessy v. Ferguson* (1896) the Court ruled that segregation was not *discriminatory*—that is, it did not violate black civil rights under the Fourteenth Amendment—provided that blacks received accommodations equal to those of whites. The "separate but equal" doctrine of course had little regard for the realities of southern life: segregated facilities were rarely if ever "equal" in any material sense, and segregation was itself intended to underscore the inferiority of blacks. With a similar disregard for reality, the Supreme Court in *Williams v. Mississippi* (1898) validated the disfranchising devices of the southern states: so long as race was not a specified criterion for disfranchisement, the Fifteenth Amendment was not being violated even though the practical effect was the virtual exclusion of blacks from politics in the South.

Race hatred became an accepted part of southern life, manifested in a wave of lynchings and race riots and in the public abuse of blacks. For example, Benjamin R. Tillman, governor of South Carolina and after 1895 a U.S. senator, denounced blacks as "an ignorant and debased and debauched race." This ugly racism came from several sources, including job competition between whites

A Black Man on Segregation

W*hen C. H. Johnson, a porter at an auction house, spoke up before a visiting Senate committtee in 1883, the movement for a segregated South was just gathering steam. But even then, Johnson makes clear, southern blacks were not deceived about the fraudulence of "separate but equal."*

Columbus, Ga., November 20, 1883

Question. Do you feel as though your people have had a fair chance to be heard by the committee?

Answer. I do. . . .

Q. And you think they have said all they want to say?

A. Well, I won't say that they did that. . . . It is just like as it was in the time of slavery . . . and they have got the same feelings now, a great many of them, and they want to say things, but they are afraid of the white people. . . .

Q. What do you mean by social equality?

A. . . . If I get on the cars to ride from here to Montgomery, or to Atlanta, although I pay the same fare that you pay—they make me do that—I do not have the same accommodations.

Q. Suppose you have a car just as good as the one white folks have, but are not allowed to go into their car, will that be satisfactory?

A. But that is not going to be done. They are not going to make a law of that kind. . . .

Q. That would be a different case. I am supposing a case where the accommodations provided for the two races are just the same.

A. . . . I would be satisfied. But don't allow a man to come in over my wife, or any other lady that respects herself as a lady, swearing and spitting and cursing around. . . . I do not want to kick up a fuss with any one, or with white people about getting in amongst them . . . but if a colored man comes along and pays the same fare that the white man pays, he has the same rights as the white man. . . .

SOURCE: U.S. Senate, Committee on the Relations between Capital and Labor, *Report* (1885), IV, 635–638, reprinted in Stanley I. Kutler, ed., *Looking for America* (2d ed., New York: W.W. Norton, 1979), II, 234–238.

and blacks during the depressed 1890s, and white anger against a less submissive black generation born after slavery.

But what had triggered the antiblack offensive was the political crisis in the South over Populism. From then on, white supremacy propped up the one-party system that the Redeemers had been fighting for ever since Reconstruction. If the southern elite had to share political power with demagogic poor white leaders such as Tom Watson, it would be on terms agreeable to them— the exclusion from the political arena of any serious challenge to the economic status quo.

The Black Response

Southern blacks in many places resisted white oppression as best they could. When Georgia adopted the first Jim Crow law applying to streetcars in 1891, Atlanta blacks declared a boycott, and over the next fifteen years blacks boycotted segregated streetcars in at least twenty-five cities. "Do not trample on our pride by being 'jim crowed,'" the Savannah *Tribune* urged its readers: "Walk!" Ida Wells-Barnett emerged as the most outspoken black crusader against lynching, so enraging the Memphis white community by the editorials in her newspaper *Free Speech* that she was forced to leave the city in 1892. Some blacks were drawn to the Back-to-Africa movement, despairing of ever finding justice in America. But emigration was not a real choice, and African-Americans everywhere had to bend to the raging forces of racism, and find a way to survive.

Booker T. Washington, the foremost black leader of his day, marked out the path in a famous speech in Atlanta in 1895. Washington retreated from the defiant stand of an older generation of black abolitionists exemplified by Frederick Douglass, who died the same year that the Atlanta speech launched Washington into national prominence. Washington was conciliatory toward the South; it was a society that blacks understood and loved. He considered "the agitation of the question of social equality the extremest folly." Washington accepted segregation, provided that blacks had equal facilities. He accepted literacy tests and property qualifications for the vote, provided that they applied equally to blacks and whites.

Washington's doctrine came to be known as the Atlanta Compromise. His approach was "accommodationist," in the sense that it avoided a direct assault on white supremacy. Despite the humble face he put on before white audiences, however, Washington did not concede the struggle. Behind the scenes he did his best to resist Jim Crow laws and disfranchisement. More important, his Atlanta Compromise, while abandoning the field of political protest, opened up a second front of economic struggle.

Booker T. Washington sought to capitalize on a southern dilemma about the economic role of the black population. Racist dogma dictated that blacks be kept down, effectively reinforcing their image as lazy, shiftless workers. But for the South to prosper, it needed an efficient labor force. Washington made this need the target of his efforts. As founder of the Tuskegee Institute in Alabama in 1881, Washington advocated *industrial education*—manual and agricultural training. He preached the virtues of thrift, hard work, and property ownership. Washington's industrial education program won generous support from northern philanthropists and businessmen.

Washington assumed that black economic progress would be the key to winning political and civil rights. He regarded members of the white southern

Booker T. Washington
In an age of severe racial oppression, Washington emerged as the acknowledged leader of blacks in the United States. He was remarkable both as spokesman to white Americans and for his deep understanding of the aspirations of black Americans. Born a slave, Washington suffered the indignities experienced by all blacks. But he also understood what it took to gain white support—and to maneuver around white hostility—in the black struggle for equality.

elite as crucial allies, because ultimately only they had the power to change the South. More important, they could see "the close connection between labor, industry, education, and political institutions." When it was in their economic interest, when they had grown dependent on black labor and black enterprise, white men of business and property would recognize the justice of black rights. As Washington put it, "There is little race prejudice in the American dollar."

For twenty years after his Atlanta address Booker T. Washington dominated the organized African-American community. In an age of severe racial oppression, no black dealt more skillfully with the elite of white America or wielded greater political influence. Black leaders knew Washington as a hard taskmaster. Intensely jealous of his authority, he did not regard opposition kindly. Black politicians, educators, and editors stood up to him at their peril.

Even so, opposition surfaced after 1900, especially among younger, educated blacks. They thought Washington was conceding too much. He instilled black pride, but of a narrowly middle-class and utilitarian kind. What about the special genius of blacks that W. E. B. Du Bois celebrated in his collection of essays, *The Souls of Black Folk* (1903)? And what of the "talented tenth" of the black population, whose promise could only be stifled by manual education? Blacks also became increasingly impatient with Washington's silence on segregation and lynching. By the time of his death in 1915, Washington's approach had been superseded by a strategy that relied on the courts and political leverage, not on black self-help and accommodation.

CHAPTER 19 TIMELINE	
1874	Woman's Christian Temperance Union founded
1877	Rutherford B. Hayes inaugurated; end of Reconstruction
1881	President James A. Garfield assassinated
1883	Pendleton Civil Service Act
1884	Mugwump reformers bolt the Republican party to support Grover Cleveland, first Democrat elected president since 1856
1887	Interstate Commerce Act creates the Interstate Commerce Commission to regulate railroads Florida adopts first law segregating railroad travel
1888	James Bryce's *The American Commonwealth*
1890	The McKinley Tariff Democrats sweep Congressional elections, inaugurating brief era of Democratic party dominance Mississippi becomes first state to adopt literacy test to disfranchise blacks
1892	People's (Populist) Party founded
1893	Panic of 1893 leads to national depression Repeal of Sherman Silver Purchase Act (1890)
1894	Coxey's Army
1895	Booker T. Washington sets out Atlanta Compromise
1896	Election of William McKinley; free-silver campaign crushed *Plessy v. Ferguson* upholds constitutionality of "separate-but-equal" facilities
1897	Economic depression ends

CHAPTER 20

THE RISE OF THE CITY

- Urbanization
- City People
- Upper Class/Middle Class

In 1820 America was a land of farmers. Barely 5 percent of the people lived in towns or cities. But after that, decade by decade, the urban population swelled until, by 1900, one of every five Americans lived in cities of over 100,000 residents. Nearly a tenth of the nation—6.5 million persons—lived in just three great cities: New York, Chicago, and Philadelphia.

The city was the arena of the nation's vibrant economic life. Here the factories went up, and here the new immigrants settled, constituting in 1900 about a third of the residents of major American cities. Here, too, lived the millionaires and a growing white-collar middle class. For all these people, the city was more than a place to make a living. It provided the setting for an urban culture unlike anything seen before in the United States. City people, although differing vastly among themselves, became distinctively and recognizably urban.

URBANIZATION

The march to the cities seemed inevitable to nineteenth-century Americans. "The greater part of our population must live in cities," declared the Congregational minister Josiah Strong. "In due time we shall be a nation of cities." Urbanization became inevitable because of its link to another inevitability of American life—industrialism.

The Economic Sources of City Growth

Until the Civil War, cities had been centers of commerce, not industry. They were the places where merchants bought and sold goods for distribution into the interior or shipment out to the world market. Early industry, on the other hand, was largely rural because factories needed water power from streams, access to fuel and raw materials, and workers recruited from the countryside.

After midcentury, industry began to move into the city. Once steam engines came along, mill operators no longer needed to locate along streams. In the iron industry coal replaced charcoal as the primary fuel, so iron makers did not have to be near forests. Improved transportation, especially the railroads, enabled businesses to select the best sites in relation to supplies and markets. The result was a geographic concentration of industry. Iron makers gravitated to Pittsburgh because of its access not only to coal and iron ore, but also to markets for iron and steel products. Chicago, ideally located between livestock suppliers and consuming markets, became a great meat-packing center in the 1870s.

As factories became bigger, their size contributed to urban growth. A plant that employed thousands of workers instantly created a small city in its vicinity, sometimes a company town like Aliquippa, Pennsylvania, which became body and soul the property of the Jones and Laughlin Steel Company. Many firms set up their plants near a large city so they could draw on its labor supply and transportation facilities, as George Pullman did when he

TABLE 20.1

Ten Largest Cities by Population, 1870 and 1910

1870		1910	
City	Population	City	Population
1. New York	942,292	New York	4,766,883
2. Philadelphia	674,022	Chicago	2,185,283
3. Brooklyn*	419,921	Philadelphia	1,549,008
4. St. Louis	310,864	St. Louis	687,029
5. Chicago	298,977	Boston	670,585
6. Baltimore	267,354	Cleveland	560,663
7. Boston	250,526	Baltimore	558,485
8. Cincinnati	216,239	Pittsburgh	533,905
9. New Orleans	191,418	Detroit	465,766
10. San Francisco	149,473	Buffalo	423,715

*Brooklyn was consolidated with New York in 1898.
SOURCE: U.S. Census data.

located his sleeping-car works southwest of Chicago. Sometimes these outlying industrial towns were absorbed into the nearby metropolis, as happened
to Pullman.

The established commercial cities also became more industrial. Warehouse
districts could readily be converted to small-scale manufacturing; a distribution network and transportation facilities were right at hand. In addition, as
gateways for immigrants, port cities offered abundant cheap labor. Boston,
Philadelphia, Baltimore, and San Francisco became hives of small-scale, labor-
intensive industrial activity. New York's enormous pool of immigrant workers
made that city a magnet for the garment trades, cigar making, and light industry. New York was, in fact, the nation's largest producer of manufactured
goods.

City Building

The commercial cities of the early nineteenth century had been compact
places, densely settled around a harbor or along a river. As late as 1850, when it
had 565,000 people, greater Philadelphia covered only 10 square miles. From
the foot of Chestnut Street on the Delaware River a person could walk to almost anywhere in the city within forty-five minutes. Thereafter, as it developed, Philadelphia spilled out and, like American cities everywhere, engulfed
the surrounding countryside.

A downtown area emerged, usually in what had been the original commercial city. Downtown in turn broke up into shopping, financial, warehous-
ing, manufacturing, hotel and entertainment, and red-light districts. Although
somewhat fluid at their edges, all these districts were well-defined areas of specialized activity. Moving out from the center, industrial development tended
to follow the arteries of transportation—railroads, canals, and rivers—and, at
the city's outskirts, to create concentrations of heavy industry.

While highly congested at the center, American cities actually had lower
densities than European cities: 22 persons per acre for fifteen American cities
in 1890, for example, versus 157.6 per acre for a comparable group of German
cities. Given this difference, the development of efficient urban transportation
had a much higher priority in the United States than in Europe.

The first innovation, dating back to the 1820s, was the omnibus, an elon-
gated version of the horse-drawn carriage. Much more efficient was the
horsecar. The key thing was that it ran on iron tracks, so that the car could
carry more passengers, move them at a faster clip through congested city
streets, and reach out into the suburbs. From the 1840s onward, horsecars were
the mainstay of urban transit across America.

Then came the electric trolley car. Its development was the work primarily of Frank J. Sprague, an engineer once employed by Thomas A. Edison. In
1887 Sprague designed an electricity-driven system for Richmond, Virginia: a
"trolley" carriage running along an overhead power line was attached by cable
to streetcars equipped with an electric motor—hence the name trolley car.

Traffic Jam in Downtown Chicago, 1905
The purpose of urban transit systems was to move masses of people rapidly
and efficiently through the city. However, better transportation brought
more congestion as well, as this scene of gridlock at Randolf and Dearborn
streets in Chicago shows.

After Sprague's success, the trolley swiftly displaced the horsecar and became
the primary means of public transportation for most American cities.

In the great metropolitan centers, however, mounting congestion called
for the removal of public transit from the streets. In 1879 the first elevated
lines went into operation on Sixth and Ninth avenues in New York City.
Powered at first by steam engines, the "els" converted to electricity following
Sprague's success with the trolley. Chicago developed elevated transit most
fully. New York, on the other hand, turned to the subway. Although Boston
opened a short underground line in 1897, it was the completion in 1904 of a
subway running the length of Manhattan that demonstrated the full potential
of the high-speed underground train. Mass transit had become *rapid* transit.

Equally remarkable was the architectural revolution sweeping metropolitan business districts. With steel girders, durable plate glass, and the passenger
elevator available by the 1880s, a wholly new way of construction opened up.
A steel skeleton would support the building, and the walls, previously weight-
bearing, would serve as curtains enclosing the structure; the sky, so to speak,
became the limit.

The first "skyscraper" to be built on this principle was the ten-story Home
Insurance Building (1885) in Chicago. Although this pioneering effort was itself conventional in appearance—it looked just like the other commercial
buildings in the downtown district—its steel-girdered technology liberated

the aesthetic perceptions of American architects. A Chicago school sprang up, dedicated to the design of buildings whose form expressed, rather than masked, their structure and function. The masterpiece of the Chicago school was Louis Sullivan's Carson, Pirie, Scott and Company department store (1904). Chicago pioneered skyscraper construction, but New York, with its unrelenting need for prime downtown space, took the lead after the mid-1890s. Completed in 1913, the fifty-five-story Woolworth Building marked the beginning of the modern Manhattan skyline.

For ordinary citizens, the electric lights that dispelled the gloom of the city at night probably offered the most dramatic evidence that times had changed. The mainstay of city lighting since the early nineteenth century had been gaslight—illuminating gas produced from coal—but, at 12 candlepower, gaslight was too dim to brighten the downtown streets and the city's public spaces. The first use of electricity, when generating technology made it commercially feasible in the 1870s, was for arc lights that illuminated the city streets and public buildings. Electric lighting then entered the American home thanks to Thomas Edison's invention of a serviceable light bulb in 1879. Edison's motto—"Let there be light!"—truly described the experience of the modern city.

Manhattan's First Skyscraper
The Tower Building at 50 Broadway was completed in 1889. To the modern eye, this first New York skyscraper seems modest and old-fashioned. Compared with its squat neighbors, however, it was a revolutionary building based on new principles of slender, soaring architecture.

Before it had any significant effect on industry, electricity gave the city its modern tempo, lifting and lowering elevators, powering streetcars and subway trains, turning night into day. Meanwhile, Alexander Graham Bell's telephone (1876) speeded up communication beyond anything imagined previously. By 1900, 1.5 million telephones were in use, linking urban people into a network of instant communication.

The Private City

City building was very much an exercise in private enterprise. The lure of profit spurred the great innovations—the trolley car, electric lighting, the sky-scraper, the elevator, the telephone—and drove urban real-estate develop-ment. The investment opportunities looked so tempting that new cities sprang up almost overnight from the ruins of the Chicago fire of 1871 and the San Francisco earthquake of 1906. Real-estate interests, eager to develop subdivi-sions, often were instrumental in pushing streetcar lines outward from the central districts of cities.

America produced what the urban historian Sam Bass Warner has called the "private city"—a city shaped primarily by the actions of many private in-dividuals, all pursuing their own goals and bent on making money. The pre-vailing belief was that the sum of such private activity would far exceed what the community could accomplish through public effort. This meant that the city itself handled only functions that could not be undertaken efficiently or profitably by private enterprise.

Despite that limitation, American cities actually compiled an impressive record in the late nineteenth century. Though by no means free of the corrup-tion and wastefulness of earlier days, city governments became more centralized, better administered, and above all, more expansive in the functions they under-took. Nowhere in the world were there more massive public projects: water aqueducts, sewage systems, street paving, bridge building, extensive park systems.

Yet streets, mainly a matter of convenience for the people, were often filthy. "Three or four days of warm spring weather," remarked a New York journalist, would turn Manhattan's garbage-strewn, snow-clogged streets into "veritable mud rivers." The environment likewise suffered. A visitor to Pitts-burgh noted "the heavy pall of smoke which constantly overhangs her . . . until the very sun looks coppery through the sooty haze." As for the lovely hills ris-ing from the rivers, "they have been leveled down, cut into, sliced off, and ruthlessly marred and mutilated." Pittsburgh presented "all that is unsightly and forbidding in appearance, the original beauties of nature having been ruthlessly sacrificed to utility."

It was not that America lacked an urban vision. On the contrary, an abid-ing rural ideal had exerted a powerful influence on American cities for many years. Frederick Law Olmsted, who designed New York's Central Park before the Civil War and many other city parks in later years, wanted cities that exposed people to the beauties of nature. One of Olmsted's projects, the

Chicago World's Fair of 1893, gave rise to the influential "City Beautiful" movement. The results included larger park systems; broad boulevards and parkways; and, after the turn of the century, zoning laws and planned suburbs. But cities usually heeded urban planners too little and far too late. "Fifteen or twenty years ago a plan might have been adopted that would have made this one of the most beautiful cities in the world," Kansas City's park commissioners reported in 1893. At that time, "such a policy could not be fully appreciated." Nor, even if Kansas City had foreseen its future, would it have shouldered the "heavy burden" of trying to shape its development. The American city had placed its faith in the dynamics of the marketplace, not the restraints of a planned future.

Hardest hit by urban growth were the poor. In earlier times low-income city residents had lived in makeshift wooden structures in the alleys and back streets and, increasingly, in the subdivided homes of more prosperous families that had fled to better neighborhoods. When rising land values after the Civil War made this practice unprofitable, speculators began to build housing specifically designed for the urban masses. In New York City, the dreadful result was five- or six-story tenements housing twenty or more families in cramped, airless apartments. In New York's Eleventh Ward an average of 986 persons occupied each acre, a density matched only in Bombay, India.

Reformers recognized the problem but seemed unable to solve it. Some favored model tenements financed by public-spirited citizens willing to accept a limited return on their investment. When private philanthropy failed to make much of a dent in the problem, cities turned to housing codes. The most advanced of these was New York's Tenement House Law of 1901, which required interior courts, indoor toilets, and fire safeguards for new structures, but did little for existing housing stock. Commercial development had pushed up land values in downtown areas. Only high-density, cheaply built housing could earn a sufficient profit for the landlords of the poor. This economic fact defied nineteenth-century solutions.

A Balance Sheet: Chicago and Berlin

Chicago and Berlin had virtually equal populations in 1900. Their histories were, however, profoundly different. Seventy years earlier, when Chicago was just a muddy frontier outpost, Berlin was a city of 250,000, and the royal seat of the Hohenzollerns of Prussia.

With German unification in 1871, the imperial authorities rebuilt Berlin on a grander scale. "A capital city is essential for the state, to act as a pivot for its culture," proclaimed the Prussian historian Heinrich von Treitschke. Berlin served that national purpose—as "a center where Germany's political, intellectual, and material life is concentrated, and its people can feel united." Chicago had no such pretensions. It was strictly a place of business, made great by virtue of its strategic grip on the commerce of America's industrial heartland. Nothing in Chicago evoked the grandeur of Berlin's boulevards or its monumental palaces and public buildings, nor were Chicagoans ever witness to anything like the pomp and ceremony of Berlin's imperial parades up broad, tree-lined Unter den Linden to the national cathedral.

Yet as a functioning city Chicago was in many ways superior to Berlin. Chicago's waterworks pumped 500 million gallons of water a day, or 139 gallons of water per person, while Berliners had to make do with 18 gallons. Flush toilets, a rarity in Berlin in 1900, could be found in 60 percent of Chicago's homes. Chicago's streets were lit by electricity, while Berlin still relied mostly on gaslight. Chicago had a much bigger streetcar system, twice as much acreage devoted to parks, and a public library containing many more volumes. And Chicago had just completed an amazing sanitation project, reversing the course of the Chicago River so that its waters—and the city's sewage—would flow away from the lake, and southward down into the Illinois and Mississippi rivers.

Giant sanitation projects were one thing; an inspiring urban environment was something else. For well-traveled Americans admiring of things European, the sense of inferiority was palpable. "We are enormously rich," admitted the journalist Edwin L. Godkin, "but . . . what have we got to show? Almost nothing. Ugliness from an artistic point of view is the mark of all our cities." Thus the balance sheet: an urban infrastructure that was superb by nineteenth-century standards, but "no municipal splendors of any description, nothing but population and hotels."

CITY PEOPLE

When the budding writer Hamlin Garland and his brother arrived in Chicago from rural Iowa in 1881, they knew immediately that they had entered a new world: "Everything interested us. . . . Nothing was commonplace, nothing was ugly to us." In one way or another every city-bound migrant, whether from the American countryside or from a foreign land, experienced something of this exhilaration and wonder.

But with the opportunity and boundless variety came disorder and uncertainty. The urban world was utterly unlike the rural communities the newcomers had left. In the countryside every person had been known to his or her neighbors. Mark Twain found New York "a splendid desert, where a stranger is lonely in the midst of a million of his race. . . . Every man rushes, rushes, rushes, and never has time to be companionable [or] to fool away on matters which do not involve dollars and duty and business." If rural roles and obligations had been well understood, in the city the only predictable relationships were those dictated by the marketplace.

The newcomers could never re-create in the city the worlds they had left behind. But they found ways to gain a sense of belonging, they built a multitude of new institutions, and they learned how to function in an impersonal, heterogeneous environment. An urban culture emerged, and through it there developed a new breed of American who was entirely at home in the modern city.

Newcomers

At the turn of the century, upward of 30 percent of the residents of New York, Chicago, Boston, Cleveland, Minneapolis, and San Francisco were foreign-born. The biggest ethnic group in Boston was Irish; in Minneapolis, Swedish; in most other northern cities, German. But by 1910 the influx from southern and Eastern Europe had changed the ethnic complexion of many of these cities. In Chicago, Poles took the lead; in New York, Eastern European Jews; in San Francisco, Italians.

All these immigrants—old and new—brought with them experiences and customs from the homeland that shaped their lives in the New World. But as the older "walking cities" disappeared, so did the opportunities for intermingling with the older populations. The later arrivals from southern and Eastern Europe had little choice about where they lived; they needed to be near their jobs and to find cheap housing. Some gravitated to the outlying factory districts; others settled in the congested downtown ghettos. The immigrants did not settle randomly in these districts, however. In New York, Italians crowded into the Irish neighborhoods west of Broadway, and Russian and Polish Jews pushed the Germans out of the Lower East Side. A colony of Hungarians lived around Houston Street, and Bohemians occupied the Upper East Side between Fiftieth and Seventy-sixth streets.

Capitalizing on the fellow feeling that drew ethnic groups together, a variety of institutions sprang up to meet the immigrants' needs. Wherever substantial numbers lived, newspapers appeared. In 1911 the 20,000 Poles in Buffalo, New York, supported two Polish-language daily papers. Immigrants throughout the country avidly read *Il Progresso Italo-Americano* and the Yiddish-language *Jewish Daily Forward*, both published in New York City. Companionship could always be found on street corners, in barbershops and club rooms, and in saloons. Italians marched in saint's day parades, Bohemians gathered in singing societies, and New York Jews patronized a lively Yiddish theater. To provide help in times of sickness and death, the immigrants organized mutual-aid societies. The Italians of Chicago had sixty-six of these organizations in 1903, composed mainly of people from particular provinces and towns. Immigrants built a rich and functional institutional life in urban America, to an extent unimagined in their native villages.

The great African-American migration to northern cities was just beginning at the turn of the century. The black population of New York increased by 30,000 between 1900 and 1910, making New York second only to Washington, D.C., as a black urban center, but the 91,000 blacks in New York in 1910 represented fewer than 2 percent of the population, and that was true of Chicago and Cleveland as well.

Despite their relatively small numbers, urban blacks could not escape discrimination. They retreated from the scattered black neighborhoods of older times into concentrated ghettos—Chicago's Black Belt on the south side, for example, or the early outlines of New York's Harlem. In employment, race prejudice cut down job opportunities. While 26 percent of Cleveland's blacks had been skilled workers in 1870, only 12 percent were by 1890, and entire occupations such as barbering (except for a black clientele) disappeared. Two-thirds of Cleveland's blacks in 1910 worked as domestics and day laborers, with little hope of moving up the job ladder.

In the face of pervasive discrimination, urban blacks built their own communities. They created a flourishing press; fraternal orders; a vast array of women's organizations; and a middle class of doctors, lawyers, and small business owners. Above all, there were the black churches—twenty-five in Chicago in 1905, mainly Methodist and Baptist. More than any other institution, remarked one scholar in 1913, it was the church "which the Negro may call his own. . . . A new church may be built . . . and . . . all the machinery set in motion without ever consulting any white person. . . . [It] more than anything else represents the real life of the race." As in the southern countryside, the church was the central institution for city blacks, and the preacher the most important local citizen. Manhattan's Union Baptist Church, housed like many others in a storefront, attracted the "very recent residents of this new, disturbing city" and, ringing with spirituals and fervent prayer, made Christianity come "alive Sunday mornings."

Ward Politics

Race and ethnicity tended to divide the newcomers and turn them in on themselves. Politics, on the contrary, acted as a powerful instrument for integrating them into the larger urban society. Every migrant to an American city automatically became a ward resident, and by living on a particular street, immediately acquired a spokesman at city hall in the form of an alderman. Immigrants learned very quickly that if they needed anything from city hall, the alderman was the person to see. That was how streets got paved, or water mains extended, or variances granted—so that, for example, in 1888 Vito Fortounescere could "place and keep a stand for the sale of fruit, inside the stoop-line, in front of the northeast corner of Twenty-eighth Street and Fourth Avenue" in Manhattan, or the parishioners of Saint Maria of Mount Carmel could set off fireworks at their Fourth of July picnic.

Machine control of political parties, although present at every level, flourished most luxuriantly in the big cities. Urban machines depended on a loyal grass-roots constituency. So each ward was divided into election districts of a few blocks, with a district captain who reported to the ward boss (who might also be the alderman). The main jobs of these functionaries were to be accessible and, as best they could, to serve the needs of the party faithful.

The machine similarly served the business community. Contractors sought city business; gas companies and streetcar lines wanted licenses and privileges; manufacturers needed services and not-too-nosy inspectors; and the liquor trade and numbers racket relied on a tolerant police force. All of them turned to the machine boss and his lieutenants. In addition to these everyday functions, the machine continuously mediated among conflicting interests and oiled the wheels of city government.

Of course, the machine exacted a price for these services. The tenement dweller gave his vote. The businessman wrote a check. Corruption permeated this informal system. Some of the money that changed hands inevitably ended in the pockets of machine politicans. This "boodle" could take the form of outright corruption—kickbacks by contractors; protection money from gamblers, saloonkeepers, and prostitutes; payoffs from gas and trolley companies. The Tammany ward boss George Washington Plunkitt, however, insisted that he had no need for kickbacks and bribes. He favored what he called "honest graft," the easy profits that came to savvy insiders. Plunkitt made most of his money building wharves on Manhattan's waterfront. One way or another, legally or otherwise, machine politics rewarded its supporters.

For the young and ambitious, this was reason enough to favor the machine system. In the mid-1870s, over half Chicago's forty aldermen were foreign-born, sixteen of them Irish immigrants. The first Italian was elected to the board in 1885, the first Pole in 1888. Blacks did not manage to get on Chicago's board of aldermen until after 1900, but Baltimore's Eleventh Ward elected an African-American in 1890 and Philadelphia had three black aldermen by 1899. As a ladder for social mobility, machine politics (like professional sports, entertainment, and organized crime) was the most democratic of American institutions.

For the ordinary tenement dweller, however, the machine had a more modest value. It acted as a rough-and-ready social service agency, providing jobs for the jobless, a helping hand for a bereaved family, and an ally against an unfeeling city bureaucracy. The Tammany ward boss Plunkitt had a "regular system" when fires broke out in his district. He arranged for housing for burned-out families, to "fix them up till they get things runnin' again. It's philanthropy, but it's politics, too—mighty good politics."

Plunkitt was an Irishman, and so were most of the ward politicians controlling Tammany Hall. But by the 1890s Plunkitt's Fifteenth District was filling up with Italians and Eastern European Jews. In general the New York Irish had no love for these newer immigrants, but Plunkitt played no favorites. On any given day (as recorded in a diary) he might attend an Italian funeral in the afternoon and a Jewish wedding in the evening, and at each he probably paid his respects with a few Italian words or a bit of Yiddish.

In an era when so many forces acted to isolate ghetto communities, politics served an *integrating* function, cutting across ethnic lines and giving immigrants and blacks a stake in the larger urban order.

Religion and Ethnicity

For most immigrants, religion was an abiding concern and was so intertwined with their ethnic identity as to be inseparable from the story of how they adapted to American life.

AMERICAN VOICES

Bintel Brief

The Yiddish phrase bintel brief *means "bundle of letters." That was the name of the famous column of the* Jewish Daily Forward *devoted to letters from immigrant readers about their trials and tribulations in America.*

I was born in a small town in Russia, and until I was sixteen I studied in *Talmud Torahs* and *yeshivas*, but when I came to America I developed spiritually and became a freethinker. Yet every year when the time of *Rosh Hashana* and *Yom Kippur* comes around I become very gloomy. . . . So strong are my feelings that I enter the synagogue, not in order to pray to God but to heal and refresh my aching soul by sitting among *landsleit* [countrymen] and listening to the cantor's sweet melodies. The members of my Progressive Society don't understand. They say I am a hypocrite. . . . What do you think? *Answer:* No one can tell another what to do with himself on *Yom Kippur.*

I am a Russian revolutionist and a freethinker. Here in America I became acquainted with a girl who is also a freethinker. We decided to marry, but the problem is that she has Orthodox parents, and if we refuse a religious ceremony we will be cut off from them forever. I don't know what to do. Therefore, I ask you to advise me how to act. *Answer:* There are times when it is better to be kind in order not to grieve old parents.

I am a young man of twenty-five, and I recently met a fine girl. She has a flaw, however—a dimple in her chin. It is said that people who have this lose their first husband or wife. I love her very much. But I'm afraid to marry her lest I die because of the dimple. *Answer:* The tragedy is not that the girl has a dimple in her chin but that some people have a screw loose in their heads.

SOURCE: Irving Howe and Kenneth Libo, eds., *How We Lived* (New York: New American Library, 1979), 88–90.

About 250,000 Jews, mostly of German origin, were living in America when the Eastern European Jews began to arrive in the 1880s. The German Jews, well established and prosperous, had embraced Reform Judaism, abandoning religious practices "not adapted to the views and habits of modern civilization." Anxious to preserve their traditional piety, the Yiddish-speaking immigrants from Eastern Europe founded their own Orthodox synagogues, often in vacant stores and ramshackle buildings, and practiced Judaism in the old way.

In the villages of Eastern Europe, however, Judaism had stood not only for worship and belief, but for an entire way of life. Insular though it might be, ghetto life in the American city could not re-create the communal environment on which strict religious observance depended. "The very clothes I wore and the very food I ate had a fatal effect on my religious habits," confessed the hero of Abraham Cahan's novel *The Rise of David Levinsky* (1917). "If you . . . attempt to bend your religion to the spirit of your surroundings, it breaks. It falls to pieces." Levinsky shaved off his beard and plunged into the Manhattan clothing business. Orthodox Judaism survived this shattering of faith, but only by sharply reducing its claims on the lives of the faithful.

Catholics faced much the same problem. The issue, explicitly defined within the Roman Catholic Church as "Americanism," turned on how far Catholicism should respond to American society. Should Catholic children attend parochial or public schools? Should they intermarry with non-Catholics? Should the traditional education for the clergy be changed? Bishop John Ireland of St. Paul, Minnesota, felt that "the principles of the Church are in harmony with the interests of the Republic." But traditionalists, led by Archbishop Michael A. Corrigan of New York, denied the possibility of such harmony and argued in effect for insulating the Church from the pluralistic American environment.

Immigrant Catholics generally supported the Church's conservative wing, because they wanted to preserve their religion as they had known it in Europe. But their concerns were not purely religious; church life also had to

Immaculate Heart of Mary Church, 1908
In crowded immigrant neighborhoods the church rose from undistinguished surroundings to assert the centrality of religious belief in the life of the community. This photograph is a view of Immaculate Heart of Mary Church taken from Polish Hill in Pittsburgh in 1908.

express their ethnic identities. Newly arrived Catholics wanted their own parishes where they could celebrate their own customs, speak their own languages, and establish their own parochial schools. When they became numerous enough, they also demanded their own bishops.

The severity of the challenge depended partly on the religious convictions of each ethnic group. Italian men, for example, were known for religious apathy. Many Italians, moreover, harbored strong anticlerical feelings, much strengthened by the papacy's opposition to the unification of Italy. On the other hand, the church played so important a part in the lives of Polish immigrants that they resented any interference by the Catholic hierarchy. In 1907 fifty parishes formed the Polish National Catholic Church of America, which adhered to Catholic ritual without recognizing the pope's authority.

On the whole, however, the Church managed to satisfy the immigrant faithful. It met the demand for representation in the hierarchy by appointing immigrant priests as auxiliary bishops within existing dioceses. And ethnic parishes also flourished. Before World War I, American Catholics worshiped in more than 2,000 foreign-language churches, and many others were bilingual. Not without strain, the Catholic Church made itself a central institution for the expression of ethnic identity in urban America.

For the Protestant churches, the city posed different but not easier challenges. With each wave of immigration, the Protestant population in the cities lost ground. Seventeen Protestant churches moved out of lower Manhattan during the twenty years after 1868, as the area below Fourteenth Street filled up with immigrants.

Every major city retained great downtown churches where wealthy Protestants worshiped. Some of these churches, richly endowed, took pride in nationally prominent pastors, including Henry Ward Beecher of Plymouth Congregational Church in Brooklyn and Phillips Brooks of Trinity Episcopal Church in Boston. But the eminence of these churches, with their fashionable congregations and imposing edifices, could not disguise the growing remoteness of Protestantism from much of its urban constituency. "Where is the city in which the Sabbath day is not losing ground?" lamented a minister in 1887. The families of businessmen, lawyers, and doctors could be seen in any church on Sunday morning, he noted, "but the workingmen and their families are not there."

To counter this decline, the Protestant churches responded in two ways. They evangelized among the unchurched and the indifferent, for example, through the Sunday-school movement. Protestants also made their churches instruments of social uplift. Starting in the 1880s, many city churches provided such facilities as reading rooms, day nurseries, clubhouses, and vocational classes. Sometimes the churches linked evangelism and social uplift. The Salvation Army, which arrived from Great Britain in 1879, spread the gospel of repentance among the urban poor and built an assistance program that ranged from soup kitchens to homes for former prostitutes. When all else failed, the down-and-outers of American cities knew they could count on the Salvation Army.

The social meaning that people sought in religion explained the enormous popularity of a book called *In His Steps* (1896). The author, the Congregational minister Charles M. Sheldon, told the story of a congregation that resolved to live by Christ's precepts for one year. "If the church members were all doing as Jesus would do," Sheldon asked, "could it remain true that armies of men would walk the streets for jobs, and hundreds of them curse the church, and thousands of them find in the saloon their best friend?"

The most potent form of urban evangelism—revivalism—said little about social uplift. From their origins in the eighteenth century, revival movements had steadfastly focused on individual redemption. The defeat of earthly problems, revivalists believed, would follow the conversion of the people to Christ. Beginning in the mid-1870s, revival meetings swept through the cities.

The pioneering figure was Dwight L. Moody, a former Chicago shoe salesman and YMCA official. After preaching in Britain for two years, Moody returned to America in 1875. With his talented choir leader and hymn writer, Ira D. Sankey, Moody staged revival meetings that drew thousands. He preached an optimistic, uncomplicated, nondenominational message. Eternal life could be had for the asking, Moody shouted as he held up his Bible. His listeners needed only "to come forward and take, TAKE!"

Many other preachers followed in Moody's path. The most notable was Billy (William Ashley) Sunday, a hard-drinking former outfielder for the Chicago White Stockings who had mended his ways and found religion. Like Moody and other city revivalists, Sunday was a farm boy. His rip-snorting cries against "Charlotte-russe Christians" and the "booze traffic" carried the ring of rustic America. By realizing that many people remained villagers at heart, revivalists found a key for bringing city dwellers back into the church.

Leisure in the City

City people compartmentalized life's activities, setting workplace apart from home and working time apart from free time. "Going out" became a necessity, demanded not only as relief from a day of hard work but as proof that life was better in the new world than in the old. "He who can enjoy and does not enjoy commits a sin," a Yiddish-language paper told its readers. And enjoyment now meant buying a ticket and being entertained.

Amusement parks went up at the end of trolley lines in cities across the country. Most glittering was Luna Park at New York's Coney Island—"an enchanted, storybook land of trellises, columns, domes, minarets, lagoons, and lofty aerial flights. . . . It was a world removed—shut away from the sordid clatter and turmoil of the streets." In fact, that escape from everyday urban life explains the appeal of amusement parks. The creators of Luna Park intended it to be "a different world—a dream world . . . where all is bizarre and fantastic . . . gayer and more different from the every-day world."

The theater likewise attracted huge audiences. Chicago had six vaudeville houses in 1896 and twenty-two in 1910. Originating in cheap variety and minstrel shows, vaudeville cleaned up its routines, making them suitable for the entire family, and turned itself into thoroughly professional entertainment handled by national booking agencies. With its standard program of nine singing, dancing, and comedy acts, vaudeville attained enormous popularity just as the movies arrived. The first primitive films, a minute or so of humor or glimpses of famous people, appeared in 1896 in penny arcades and as filler in vaudeville shows. Within a decade, millions of city people were watching narrative films of increasing length and artistry at nickelodeons (named after the 5-cent admission charge) across the country.

For young unmarried workers, the cheap amusements of the city created a new social space. "I want a good time," a New York clothing operator told an investigator. "And there is no . . . way a girl can get it on $8 a week. I guess if anyone wants to take me to a dance he won't have to ask me twice." Hence the widespread ritual among the urban working class of "treating." The girls spent what money they had on dressing up; their beaus were expected to pay for the fun. Parental control over courtship broke down, and amid the bright lights and lively music of the dance hall and the amusement park, working-class youth forged a more easygoing culture of sexual interaction and pleasure seeking.

The geography of the big city reserved ample space for commercialized sex. Prostitution was not new to urban life, but in the late nineteenth century it became less hidden and ghettoized. New York's Tenderloin, running northward from Twenty-third Street between Fifth and Eighth avenues and eventually up to Times Square and beyond, was also the locale of the city's fanciest restaurants, the best hotels, and the theater district. On the side streets many of the brownstones, abandoned by their well-to-do owners for more fashionable parts of town, were taken over by brothels. The nearby concert saloons—the forerunners of the nightclub—featured not only stage shows and bars but also well-dressed prostitutes working the premises.

The Tenderloin and the Bowery were also the sites of a robust gay subculture. The long-held notion that homosexual life was covert—"in the closet"—in Victorian America appears not to be true, at least not in the country's premier city. Homosexuality was illegal, but as with prostitution, the law was mostly a dead letter. In certain corners of the city a gay world flourished, with a full array of saloons, meeting places, and drag balls, which were widely known and often patronized by uptown "slummers."

Of all forms of male diversion, none was more specific to the city, nor so spectacularly successful, than professional baseball. The game's promoters decreed that baseball had been created in 1839 by Abner Doubleday in the village of Cooperstown, New York. Actually, baseball was neither of American origin—it developed from the British game of rounders—nor a product of rural life.

Organized play began in the early 1840s in New York City, where a group of gentlemen enthusiasts competed on an empty lot. During the next twenty years the aristocratic tone of baseball disappeared. Clubs sprang up across the country, and intercity competition developed on a scheduled basis. In 1868 baseball became openly professional, as other teams followed the lead of the Cincinnati Red Stockings in signing players to contracts at a negotiated salary for the season.

Big-time commercial baseball came into its own with the launching of the National League in 1876. The team owners were profit-minded businessmen who carefully shaped the sport to please the fans. Wooden grandstands gave way to the concrete and steel stadiums of the early twentieth century, such as Fenway Park in Boston, Forbes Field in Pittsburgh, and Shibe Park in Philadelphia.

For the urban multitudes baseball grew into something more than an occasional afternoon at the ballpark. By rooting for the home team, fans found a way of identifying with the city they lived in. Amid the diversity and anonymity of urban life, baseball acted as a bridge among strangers.

Most efficient at this task, however, was the newspaper. James Gordon Bennett, founder of the *New York Herald* in 1835, wanted "to record the facts . . . for the great masses of the community." The news was whatever interested city readers, starting with crime, scandal, and sensational events. After the Civil War Charles A. Dana of the *New York Sun* added the human-interest story, which made news of ordinary, insignificant happenings. Newspapers also targeted specific audiences. A women's page offered recipes and fashion news, separate sections covered sports and high society, and the Sunday supplement helped fill the weekend hours.

Joseph Pulitzer, Publisher
Pulitzer (1847–1911) left Hungary at seventeen because he wanted to be a soldier, and his best chance was with the Union army in America. He was the greatest newspaper publisher of the century, extraordinary for his insight into what an urban reading public wanted from a newspaper and because he came to this task as a foreigner, without English as his mother tongue and without roots in American society.

When Joseph Pulitzer, the owner of the *St. Louis Post-Dispatch*, invaded New York in 1883 by buying the *World*, a furious circulation war broke out. In 1895 William Randolph Hearst, who owned the *San Francisco Examiner*, bought the *New York Journal* and challenged the *World*. Hearst developed a sensational style of newspaper reporting that became known as *yellow journalism*. The term, linked to the first comic strip to appear in color, "The Yellow Kid" (1895), referred to a type of reporting that treated accuracy as secondary to a good story.

"He who is without a newspaper," said the great showman P. T. Barnum, "is cut off from his species." Barnum was speaking of city people and their hunger for information. By meeting this need, newspapers revealed their sensitivity to the public they served.

The Higher Culture

In the midst of this popular ferment, new institutions of higher culture were taking shape in America's cities. A hunger for the cultivated life was not, of course, specifically urban. Before the Civil War the lyceum movement had sent lecturers to the remotest towns, bearing messages of culture and learning. The Chautauqua movement, founded in upstate New York in 1874, carried on this work of cultural dissemination. However, large cultural institutions such as museums, public libraries, opera companies, and symphony orchestras could flourish only in metropolitan centers.

The first major art museum, the Corcoran Gallery of Art, opened in Washington, D.C., in 1869. New York's Metropolitan Museum of Art, started in rented quarters two years later, moved in 1880 to its permanent site in Central Park and launched an ambitious program of art acquisition. When J. P. Morgan became chairman of the board in 1905, the Metropolitan's preeminence was assured. The Boston Museum of Fine Arts was founded in 1876, and Chicago's Art Institute in 1879.

Top-flight orchestras also appeared, first in New York under the conductors Theodore Thomas and Leopold Damrosch in the 1870s and then in Boston and Chicago during the next decade. National tours by these leading orchestras planted the seeds for orchestral societies in many other cities. Public libraries grew from modest collections (in 1870 only seven had as many as 50,000 books) into major urban institutions. The greatest library benefactor was Andrew Carnegie, who announced in 1881 that he would build a library in any city that was prepared to maintain it. By 1907 Carnegie had spent more than $32.7 million to establish about a thousand libraries throughout the country.

The late nineteenth century was the great age not only of money making but also of money *giving*. The new millionaires patronized the arts partly as a civic duty, and partly to help establish themselves in society. But museums and opera houses also received generous support out of a sense of national pride.

"In America there is no culture," pronounced the English critic G. Lowes Dickinson in 1909. Science and the practical arts, yes, "every possible application of life to purposes and ends," but "no life for life's sake." Such conde-scending remarks received a respectful hearing because of a deep sense of cul-tural inferiority to the Old World. In 1873 Mark Twain and Charles Dudley Warner published a novel, *The Gilded Age*, satirizing America as a land of money-grubbers and speculators. This enormously popular book touched a nerve in the American psyche. Its title has in fact been appropriated by histo-rians to characterize the late nineteenth century—America's "Gilded Age"—as an age of materialism and cultural shallowness.

Some members of the upper class, like the novelist Henry James, despaired of the country and moved to Europe. But the more common response was to try to raise the nation's cultural level. The newly rich had a hard time of it. They did not have much opportunity to cultivate a taste for art, and a great deal of what they collected was mediocre and garish. On the other hand, George W. Vanderbilt, grandson of the rough-hewn Cornelius Vanderbilt, was an early champion of French Impressionism, and the coal and steel baron Henry Clay Frick built a brilliant art collection that is still housed, as a public museum, in his mansion in New York City. The enthusiasm of moneyed Americans—not always well directed—largely fueled the great cultural insti-tutions that sprang up during the Gilded Age.

A deeply conservative idea of culture sustained this generous patronage. The aim was to embellish life, not to probe or reveal its meaning. "Art," says the hero of the Reverend Henry Ward Beecher's sentimental novel *Norwood* (1867), "attempts to work out its end solely by the use of the beautiful, and the artist is to select out only such things as are beautiful." The idea of culture also took on an elitist cast: Shakespeare, once a staple of popular stage entertain-ment (in various bowdlerized versions), was appropriated into the domain of "serious" theater. And simultaneously, the world of culture became feminized. "Husbands or sons rarely share those interests," noted one observer. In Ameri-can life, remarked the clergyman Horace Bushnell, men represented the "force principle," women the "beauty principle."

UPPER CLASS/MIDDLE CLASS

In the compact city of the early nineteenth century, class distinctions had been expressed by the way men and women dressed, how they behaved, and the deference they demanded from or granted to others. As the industrial city grew, these interpersonal marks of class began to lose their force. In the anonymity of a large city, recognition and deference no longer served as mechanisms for conferring status. Instead, people began to rely on external signs: conspicuous display of wealth; membership in exclusive clubs and orga-nizations; and above all, choice of neighborhood.

For the poor, place of residence depended, as it always had, on the location of their work. But for higher-income urbanites, where to live became a matter of personal means and social preference.

The Urban Elite

As early as the 1840s Boston merchants had taken advantage of the new railway service to escape the congested central city for the rural life of Milton, Newton, and other outlying towns. By 1848 roughly 20 percent of Boston's businessmen were making the long trip by train from the countryside to their downtown offices. Ferries that plied the harbor between Manhattan and Brooklyn or New Jersey served the same purpose for New Yorkers. As commercial development engulfed downtown residential areas, the exodus from cities by the well-to-do spread across America. In Cincinnati wealthy families settled on the scenic hills rimming the crowded, humid tableland that ran down to the Ohio River. On those hillsides, a traveler noted in 1883, "the homes of Cincinnati's merchant princes and millionaires are found . . . elegant cottages, tasteful villas, and substantial mansions, surrounded by a paradise of grass, gardens, lawns, and tree-shaded roads."

Despite the temptations of country life, many of the very richest people preferred the heart of the city. Chicago boasted its Gold Coast; San Francisco, Nob Hill; Denver, Quality Hill; and Manhattan, Fifth Avenue. The New York novelist Edith Wharton recalled how the comfortable midcentury brownstones gave way to the "'new' millionaire houses," which spread northward beyond Fifty-ninth Street and up Fifth Avenue along Central Park. By carving out fashionable areas in the heart of a city, the rich visibly demonstrated their capacity to assert their will over the larger society.

But great fortunes did not automatically confer high social standing. An established elite stood astride the social heights, even in such relatively raw cities as San Francisco and Denver. It had taken only a generation—and sometimes less—for money made in commerce or real estate to shed its tarnish and become "old" and genteel. In older cities such as Boston, wealth passed intact through several generations, creating a closely knit tribe of Brahmin families that kept moneyed newcomers at bay. Elsewhere urban elites tended to be more open, but only to the socially ambitious who were prepared to make visible and energetic use of their money.

The richest and most successful people gravitated to New York. The tycoon Frank Cowperwood, in Theodore Dreiser's novel *The Titan* (1914), reassured his unhappy wife that if Chicago society would not accept them, "there are other cities. Money will arrange matters in New York—that I know. We can build a real place there, and go in on equal terms, if we have money enough." New York thus came to be a magnet for millionaires. The city attracted them not only because of its importance as a financial center, but for the opportunities it offered for display and social recognition.

This infusion of wealth shattered the older elite society of New York. Seeking to be assimilated into the upper class, the flood of moneyed newcomers simply overwhelmed it. There followed a curious process of reconstruction, a deliberate effort to define the rules of conduct and identify those who properly "belonged" in New York society.

The key figure in this process was Ward McAllister, a southern-born lawyer who made a quick fortune in gold-rush San Francisco before devoting himself to a second career as the arbiter of New York society. In 1888 McAllister compiled the first *Social Register*, which would serve as a "record of society, comprising an accurate and careful list" of all those deemed eligible for New York society. McAllister instructed the socially ambitious on how to select guests, set a proper table, arrange a ball, and launch a young lady into society. To top things off, McAllister got the idea of "the Four Hundred"—the true cream of New York society. His list corresponded to those invited to Mrs. William Astor's great ball of February 1, 1892.

Americans were adept at making money, remarked the journalist Edwin L. Godkin in 1896, but they lacked the European traditions for spending it. "Great wealth has not yet entered our manners," Godkin remarked. "No rules have yet been drawn to guide wealthy Americans in their manner of life." In their struggle to find the rules and establish the manners, the moneyed elite made an indelible mark on urban life. If there was magnificence in the American city, that was mainly their handiwork. And if there was conspicuous waste and display, that too was their doing.

The Suburban World

The middle class left a smaller imprint on the public and cultural faces of urban society. Its members, unlike the rich, preferred privacy and retreated into the domesticity of suburban comfort and family life.

The emerging corporate economy spawned a new middle class. Bureaucratic organizations required managers, accountants, and clerks. Industry called for engineers, chemists, and designers, while the distribution system needed salesmen, advertising executives, and buyers. These salaried ranks increased sevenfold between 1870 and 1910, at a much faster rate than any other occupational group. Nearly 9 million people held white-collar jobs in 1910, more than a fourth of all employed Americans.

The salaried middle class was overwhelmingly urban. Some of its members lived within the city, in the row houses of Baltimore and Boston or the comfortable apartment buildings of New York City. But far more preferred to escape from the clamor and congestion of the city. They were attracted by a persisting "rural ideal." They agreed with the landscape architect Andrew Jackson Downing, who thought that "nature and domestic life are better than the society and manners of town." With the extension of trolley service from the city center, middle-class Americans followed the wealthy into the countryside. All sought what a Chicago developer promised for his North Shore subdivision in 1875—"qualities of which the city is in a large degree bereft, namely, its pure air, peacefulness, quietude, and natural scenery."

No major American city escaped rapid suburbanization during the last third of the nineteenth century. City limits everywhere expanded rapidly. By

1900 more than half Boston's people lived in "streetcar suburbs" outside the original city. The U.S. Census of 1910 reported that nationwide about 25 percent of the urban population lived in suburbs beyond the city limits.

The geography of the suburbs was truly a map of class structure in America, because where a family lived told where it ranked. The farther the distance from the center of the city, the finer the houses and the larger the lots. The affluent had the leisure and flexible schedules to travel the long distance into town. People closer in wanted direct transit lines convenient to home and office. Working-class suburbanites were more likely to have more than one wage earner in the family, less secure employment, and jobs requiring movement around the city. They needed easy access to crosstown transit lines, which ran closer in to the city center.

Divisions within suburbs, although always a precise measure of economic ranking, never became rigid. People in the city center who wanted to better their lives moved to the cheapest suburbs. Those already settled there fled from these newcomers, in turn pushing the next higher group farther out in search of space and greenery. Suburbanization was the sum of countless individual decisions. Each move represented an advance in living standards—not only more light, air, and quiet, but better housing than the city afforded. Suburban houses typically had more space and better design, as well as indoor toilets; hot water; central heating; and, by the turn of the century, electricity.

The suburbs also restored a basic opportunity that had seemed sacrificed by rural Americans when they moved to the city. In the suburbs, home ownership again became the norm. "A man is not really a true man until he owns his home," propounded the Reverend Russell H. Conwell in "Acres of Diamonds," his famous sermon on the virtues of making money.

The small town of the rural past had fostered community life. Not so the suburbs. The grid street pattern, while efficient for laying out lots and providing utilities, offered no natural focus for group life. Nor did the stores and services that lay scattered along the trolley-car lines. Suburban development conformed to the economics of real estate and transportation, and so did the thinking of middle-class home seekers entering the suburbs. They wanted a house that gave them good value and convenience to the trolley line.

The need for community had lost some of its force for middle-class Americans. Two other attachments assumed greater importance: work and family.

Middle-Class Families

In the preindustrial economy farmers, merchants, and artisans had carried on their work within family units, which counted as members not only blood relatives, but all others living and working in the household. As industrialism progressed, economic activity moved out of the household, especially for the middle class. The father left the home to earn a living, and children spent more years in school. Clothing was bought ready-made, food came increasingly in cans and packages. Middle-class families became smaller, excluding all

Middle-Class Domesticity
For middle-class Americans the home was a place of nurture, a refuge from the world of competitive commerce. Perhaps that explains why their residences were so heavily draped and cluttered with bric-a-brac, every space filled with overstuffed furniture. All of it emphasized privacy and pride of possession. The young woman shown playing the piano symbolizes another theme of American domesticity—wives and daughters as ornaments and as bearers of culture and refinement.

but nuclear members, typically consisting by 1900 of husband, wife, and three children.

Within this family circle, relationships became intense and affectionate. "Home was the most expressive experience in life," recalled the literary critic Henry Seidel Canby of his growing up in the 1890s. "Though the family might quarrel and nag, the home held them all, protecting them against the outside world." In a sense, the family served as a refuge from the competitive, impersonal business world. The quiet, tree-lined streets created a domestic place insulated from the hurly-burly of commerce and enterprise.

The burdens of this domesticity fell heavily on the wife. It was nearly unheard of for her to seek an outside career. Her job was to manage the household. "The woman who could not make a home, like the man who could not support one, was condemned," Canby remembered. But with fewer children, the wife's workload declined. Moreover, servants still played an important part in middle-class households. In 1910 there were about 2 million domestic servants, the largest job category for women.

"We Did Not Know Whether . . . Women's Health Could Stand the Strain of Higher Education"

M Carey Thomas (1857–1935), president of Bryn Mawr College for many years, recalls her dreams of college as a girl growing up in Baltimore in the 1870s.

The passionate desire of women of my generation for higher education was accompanied thruout its course by the awful doubt, felt by women themselves as well as by men, as to whether women as a sex were physically and mentally fit for it. . . . I often remember praying about it, and begging God that if it were true that because I was a girl I could not successfully master Greek and go to college and understand things to kill me at once, as I could not bear to live in such an unjust world. . . .

We did not know when we began whether women's health could stand the strain of college education. We were haunted in those early days by the clanging chains of that gloomy little specter, Dr. Edward H. Clarke's *Sex in Education*. With trepidation of spirit I made my mother read it, and was much cheered by her remark that, as neither she, nor any of the women she knew, had ever seen girls or women of the kind described in Dr. Clarke's book, we might as well act as if they did not exist. . . .

When . . . I went to Leipzig to study after graduating from Cornell, my mother used to write me that my name was never mentioned to her by the women of her acquaintance. I was thought by them to be as much a disgrace to my family as if I had eloped with the coachman. . . .

We are now [1908] living in the midst of great and, I believe on the whole beneficent, social changes which are preparing the way for the coming economic independence of women. . . . The passionate desire of the women of my generation for a college education seems, as we study it now in the light of coming events, to have been part of this greater movement.

SOURCE: Linda K. Kerber and Jane De Hart-Mathews, eds., *Women's America: Refocusing the Past* (2d ed., New York: Oxford University Press, 1987), 263–265.

As household work eased, higher-quality homemaking became the new ideal. This was the message of Catharine Beecher's best-selling book *The American Woman's Home* (1869) and of such magazines as the *Ladies' Home Journal* and *Good Housekeeping*, which first appeared during the 1880s. In addition to her domestic duties, the wife had the higher calling of bringing sensibility, beauty, and love to the household. "We owe to women the charm and beauty of life," wrote one educator. "For the love that rests, strengthens and inspires, we look to women." In this idealized view, the wife made the home a refuge for her husband and a place of nurture for their children.

Womanly virtue, even if a happy marriage depended on it, by no means put wives on equal terms with their husbands. Although the legal status of married women—the right to own property, control separate earnings, make contracts, and get a divorce—improved markedly during the nineteenth century, sufficient legal discrimination remained to establish their subordinate role within the family. More important, custom dictated a wife's submission to her husband. She relied on his ability as the family breadwinner, and despite her superior virtues and graces, she ranked as his inferior in vigor and intellect. Her mind could be employed "but little and in trivial matters," wrote one prominent physician, and her proper place was as "the companion or ornamental appendage to man."

No wonder bright, independent-minded women rebelled against marriage. The marriage rate in the United States fell to its lowest point during the last forty years of the nineteenth century. More than 10 percent of women of marriageable age remained single, and the rate was much higher among college graduates and professionals. Married life, remarked the writer Vida Scudder, "looks to me often as I watch it terribly impoverished, for women."

Around 1890 a change set in. Although the birth rate continued to decline, more young people married, and at an earlier age. These developments reflected the beginnings of a sexual revolution in the American middle-class family. Experts began to abandon the notion, put forth by one popular medical text, that "the majority of women (happily for society) are not very much troubled by sexual feeling of any kind." In succeeding editions of his book *Plain Home Talk on Love, Marriage, and Parentage*, the physician Edward Bliss Foote began to favor a healthy sexuality that gave pleasure to both women and men.

During the 1890s the artist Charles Dana Gibson created the image of the "new woman" in his drawings for *Life* magazine. The Gibson girl was tall, spirited, athletic, and chastely sexual. She eshewed bustles, hoop skirts, and hourglass corsets, preferring shirtwaists and other natural styles that did not hide or disguise her female form. In the city, women's sphere began to take on a more public character. Among the new urban institutions catering to women, the most important was the department store, which became a temple for women's emerging role as consumers.

The children of the middle class went through their own revolution. In the past, American children had been regarded as an economic asset—added hands for the family farm, shop, or countinghouse. That no longer held true for the urban middle class. Parents stopped treating their children as working members of the family. There was such a thing as "the juvenile mind," lectured Jacob Abbott in his book *Gentle Measures in the Management and Training of the Young* (1871). The family was responsible for providing a nurturing environment in which the young personality could grow and mature.

Preparation for adulthood became increasingly linked to formal education. School enrollment went up 150 percent between 1870 and 1900. High school attendance, while still encompassing only a small percentage of teenagers, increased at the fastest rate. As the years between childhood and adulthood began to stretch out, a new stage of life—adolescence—emerged. While rooted in a lengthening period of family dependency, adolescence shifted much of the socializing role from parents to peer group. A youth culture—one of the hallmarks of American life in the twentieth century—was starting to take shape.

CHAPTER 20 TIMELINE

Year	Event
1869	Corcoran Art Gallery opens in Washington, D.C.
1871	Chicago fire
1873	Mark Twain and Charles Dudley Warner publish *The Gilded Age*
1875	Dwight L. Moody launches urban revivalist movement
1876	Alexander Graham Bell patents the telephone National Baseball League founded
1878	Electric arc-light system installed in Philadelphia
1879	Thomas Edison's incandescent light bulb Salvation Army arrives from Britain
1881	Carnegie offers to build libraries for every American city
1883	Brooklyn Bridge opens Joseph Pulitzer purchases the *New York World*
1885	William Jenney builds first steel-frame structure, Chicago's Home Insurance Building
1888	First electric trolley line constructed in Richmond, Virginia
1893	Chicago World's Fair "City Beautiful" movement
1895	William Randolph Hearst enters New York journalism The comic strip "The Yellow Kid" appears
1897	Boston builds first American subway
1901	New York Tenement House Reform Law
1904	New York subway system opens
1906	San Francisco earthquake
1913	Woolworth Building, New York City

THE PROGRESSIVE ERA

- The Course of Reform
- Progressivism and National Politics

On the face of it, the political ferment of the 1890s ended with the election of 1896. After the bitter struggle over free silver, the victorious Republicans had no stomach for political crusades. William McKinley's administration devoted itself to maintaining business confidence: sound money and high tariffs were the order of the day. The main thing, as party chief Mark Hanna said, was to "stand pat and continue Republican prosperity."

Yet beneath the surface a deep uneasiness was taking hold of the country. For more than half a century Americans had been absorbed in developing their nation. At the beginning of the twentieth century they paused, looked around, and began to add up the costs—a frightening concentration of corporate power, a restless working class, misery in the cities, corrupt machine politics. The heritage of an earlier America seemed to be giving way to the demands of the new industrial order.

Now, with the crisis of the 1890s over, reform became an absorbing concern for many Americans. It was as if social awareness had reached a critical mass around 1900, and set reform activity going as a major, self-sustaining phenomenon. For this reason the years from 1900 to World War I have come to be known as the Progressive Era.

THE COURSE OF REFORM

Historians have sometimes spoken of a progressive "movement." But progressivism was not a movement in any meaningful sense. There was no single

AMERICAN VOICES

Muckraking

In this autobiographical account Charles Edward Russell, a newpaperman, describes how he got into muckraking journalism and what he thought it was all about. He never did, by the way, get back to writing music.

All America had been accustomed to laud and bepraise the makers of great fortunes. . . . Now, of a sudden, men began to discover that these great and adored fortunes had been gathered in ways that not only grazed the prison gate but imposed burdens and disadvantages upon the rest of the community. . . . In the shock of this discovery, a literature of exposition arose. . . .

Pure accident cast me, without the least desire, into the pursuit of this fashion. I had finally withdrawn from the newspaper business, and having enough money to live modestly I was bent upon carrying out a purpose long cherished [to compose music]. Upon this task I was intent when the whole business was upset with a single telegram.

One day, Mr. J. W. Midgley, who was a famous expert on railroad rates and conditions . . . let loose a flood of startling facts about the impositions practised by the owners and operators of refrigerator cars. My friend, Mr. Erman J. Ridgway . . . of *Everybody's Magazine* wired asking me to see Mr. Midgley [who] positively refused all offers to become an exposé writer. [So] Ridgway wire[d] asking me to furnish the article *Everybody's* wanted. I had not the least disposition to do so, except only that Ridgway was my friend. . . . The next thing I knew a muckrake was put into my hand and I was plunged into the midst of the game. . . .

I wrote two or three articles on the refrigerator car scandal and then went on to write a series on the methods of the Beef Trust. . . . We were all up and away, full of the pleasures of the chase . . . and all that business about poetry and music sheets forgotten. It was exhilarating sport, hunting the money octopus.

SOURCE: Charles Edward Russell, *Bare Hands and Stone Walls* (New York, Charles Scribner's Sons, 1933), 135–139.

progressive constituency, no agreed-upon agenda, no unifying organization or leadership. At different times and places, different social groups became active. People who were reformers on one issue might be conservative on another. The term *progressivism* embraces a widespread, many-sided effort after 1900 to build a better society.

A new style of popular journalism triggered much of this reform activity. During the 1890s magazines such as *Collier's* and *McClure's* had found a wide audience of urban readers. Unlike the highbrow *Atlantic Monthly* and *Harper's*, these bright new magazines, which sold for only a dime, specialized in lively and informative reporting. Almost by accident—Lincoln Steffens's article "Tweed Days in St. Louis" in the October 1902 issue of *McClure's* is credited with getting things started—editors discovered that what most interested readers was the exposure of corruption in American life.

In a series of powerful articles, Lincoln Steffens wrote about "the shame of the cities"—the corrupt ties between business and political machines. Ida M. Tarbell attacked Standard Oil, and David Graham Phillips told how money controlled the Senate. William Hard exposed industrial accidents in "Making Steel and Killing Men" (1907) and child labor in "De Kid Wot Works at Night" (1908). Hardly a sordid corner of American life escaped the scrutiny of these tireless reporters. They were moralists as well, infusing their factual accounts with personal indignation. "The sights I saw," wrote the pioneering slum investigator Jacob Riis, "gripped my heart until I felt I must tell of them, or burst, or turn anarchist."

Theodore Roosevelt, among many others, thought these journalists went too far. In a 1906 speech he compared them to the man with a muckrake in *Pilgrim's Progress* (by the seventeenth-century English preacher John Bunyan), too absorbed with raking the filth on the floor to look up and accept a celestial crown. Thus the term *muckraker* became attached to journalists who exposed the underside of American life. Their efforts were in fact health-giving. More than any other group, the muckrakers called the people to arms.

Political Reformers

Progressives framed their intentions in terms of high ideals. Their cause, pronounced Theodore Roosevelt, "is based in the eternal principles of righteousness." But in pursuit of reform, they were not all drawn to the same targets. Nor, in making their choices, were progressives indifferent to their own self-interest. In politics especially, the battles for reform reflected mixed motives of power politics and civic betterment.

In many cities the demand for good government came from local businessmen. Taxes went up, they complained, but needed services always lagged. There had to be an end, as one manufacturer said, to "the inefficiency, the sloth, the carelessness, the injustice and the graft of city administrations." The solution, argued John Patterson of the National Cash Register Company, was to get rid of old-fashioned party rule and put "municipal affairs on a strict business basis."

In 1900 a hurricane devastated Galveston, Texas, drowning 5,000 people and destroying the municipal port. Local businessmen took over and, in the process of rebuilding the city, replaced the mayor and board of aldermen with a five-member commission. The Galveston plan, although widely copied, had a serious flaw: it gave too much power to the individual commissioners. Dayton, Ohio, solved this problem by assigning policy matters to a nonpartisan commission and administrative functions to an appointed city manager. The commission-manager reform was chiefly the work of the business community and overtly a matter of the bottom line.

It was also a way of grabbing power. By making elections citywide and professionalizing city administration, municipal reformers attacked the ward politics that had favored ethnic and working-class groups. In fact, municipal reform contained a decidedly antidemocratic bias. "Ignorance should be excluded from control," said former Mayor Abram Hewitt of New York in 1901. "City business should be carried on by trained experts selected upon some other principle than popular suffrage."

Other urban progressives, however, opposed such elitism. Mayor Brand Whitlock of Toledo, Ohio, believed "that the cure for the ills of democracy was not less democracy, as so many people were always preaching, but more democracy." Whitlock's administration not only attacked municipal corruption and inefficiency, but also concerned itself with the needs of Toledo's working people. An increasing number of cities came under the leadership of such progressive mayors, including Samuel M. "Golden Rule" Jones in Toledo, Tom Johnson in Cleveland, and Mark Fagan in Jersey City. By combining popular programs and campaign magic, they won over the urban masses and challenged the rule of the machines.

The major battleground for democratic reform, however, was not the cities, but the states. Robert M. La Follette of Wisconsin led the way. Born in 1855, La Follette had followed a conventional party career as a lawyer, as district attorney, and then as congressman for three terms before breaking with the Wisconsin Republican machine in 1891, allegedly because the top party boss had tried to bribe him. La Follette became a tireless advocate of political reform, battling the Republican old guard for a decade before finally winning the governorship in 1900 on a platform of higher taxes for corporations, stricter utility and railroad regulation, and political reform.

La Follette's key proposal was a direct primary law requiring political parties to choose candidates by means of popular elections rather than in machine-run conventions. Enacted in 1903, the direct primary both expressed La Follette's political ideals and suited his particular political talents. The party regulars opposing him were insiders, more comfortable in the caucus room than out campaigning. But that was where La Follette, a superb campaigner, excelled. The direct primary gave La Follette an iron grip on the Republican party that he did not relinquish until his death twenty-five years later.

What was true of La Follette was more or less true of all successful progressive politicians. Albert B. Cummins of Iowa, Harold U'Ren of Oregon, and Hiram Johnson of California all supported democratic ideals, and all skillfully used the direct primary as the steppingstone to political power. If they were newcomers—as Woodrow Wilson was when he left academic life to enter New Jersey politics in 1910—they showed a quick aptitude for politics and gained a solid mastery of the trade. They practiced a new kind of popular politics, which in a reform age could be a more effective route to power than the backroom techniques of the old-fashioned machine politicians.

Robert M. La Follette
La Follette was transformed into a political reformer when a Wisconsin Republican boss attempted to bribe him in 1891. As he described it in his *Autobiography,* "Out of this awful ordeal came understanding; and out of understanding came resolution. I determined that the power of this corrupt influence . . . should be broken." This photograph captures La Follette at the top of his form, taking his case in 1897 to the people of Cumberland, Wisconsin.

The Woman Progressive

Reform movements arise through a process of *recruitment.* Why do people enlist in a great cause? Each mobilized group—the progressive politicians just described, for example—is linked in some personal way to the evil crying out for correction. For middle-class women of the Progressive Era, the link was between being wives and mothers and being responsible for the social well-being of their communities.

Middle-class women had long borne the burden of humanitarian work in American cities. As voluntary investigators, they visited needy families, assessed their problems, and referred them to relief agencies.

After many years of such dedicated charity work, Josephine Shaw Lowell of New York City concluded that giving assistance to the poor was not enough. "If the working people had all they ought to have, we should not have the paupers and criminals," she declared. "It is better to save them before they go under, than to spend your life fishing them out afterward." Lowell founded the New York Consumers' League in 1890. Her goal was to improve the wages and working conditions of female clerks in the city's stores.

From these modest beginnings the league spread to other cities, and blossomed into the National Consumers' League in 1899. By then the women at its head had lost faith in voluntary action; only the state had the power to rescue poor urban families. Under the crusading Florence Kelley, formerly a chief factory inspector in Illinois, the Consumers' League became a powerful lobby for protective legislation for women and children.

Among its achievements, none was more important than the *Muller v. Oregon* decision (1908), which upheld Oregon's ten-hour workday for women workers. The Consumers' League recruited the brilliant Boston lawyer Louis D. Brandeis to defend the Oregon law before the Supreme Court. In his brief, Brandeis devoted a scant two pages to the narrow constitutional issue—whether, under its police powers, Oregon had the right to regulate women's working hours. Instead, Brandeis rested his case on data gathered by the Consumers' League showing how long hours damaged women's health and family roles. The *Muller* decision, which accepted Brandeis's reasoning, cleared the way for a wave of protective laws across the country.

Women's organizations became a mighty lobbying voice on behalf of women and children. Their victories included the first law providing public assistance for mothers with dependent children, in Illinois in 1911; the first minimum wage law for women, in Massachusetts in 1912; in many states, more effective child labor laws; and at the federal level, the Children's and Women's bureaus in the Labor Department, in 1912 and 1920, respectively. The welfare state, insofar as it arrived in America in these years, was what women progressives had made of it; they had erected a "maternalist" welfare system.

Meanwhile, other women were launching the settlement-house movement. In 1889, inspired by Toynbee Hall in the London slums, two young American women, Jane Addams and Ellen Gates Starr, established Hull House on Chicago's West Side. During the next fifteen years, scores of settlement houses sprang up in the slum neighborhoods of the nation's cities. Hull House had meeting rooms, an art gallery, clubs for children and adults, and a kindergarten. Addams herself led battles for garbage removal, playgrounds, better street lighting, and police protection. At the Henry Street Settlement in New York City, Lillian D. Wald made visiting nursing a major service.

Besides the modest good they did in the slum neighborhoods, the settlement houses also satisfied the needs of middle-class residents for meaningful lives. In a famous essay Jane Addams spoke of the "subjective necessity" of the settlement house. She meant that it was as much a response to the desire of educated young men and women to serve as it was a response to the needs of slum dwellers. Addams, for example, had grown up in a comfortable Illinois family. After college she faced an empty future, as an ornamental wife if she married, as a sheltered spinster if she did not. Hull House became her salvation, enabling her to "begin with however small a group to accomplish and to live."

Almost imperceptibly, women activists like Jane Addams and Florence Kelley breathed new life into the suffrage movement. Why should a woman who was capable of running a settlement house or lobbying a bill be denied the right to vote? If women had the right to vote, moreover, they would demand more enlightened legislation and better government. And finally, by encouraging working-class women to help themselves, women progressives got a whole new class interested in fighting for suffrage.

In 1903 social reformers founded the National Women's Trade Union League. Financed and led by wealthy supporters, the league organized women workers, played a considerable role in their strikes, and perhaps most important, helped to develop working-class leaders, such as Rose Schneiderman (see American Voices, Chapter 18, page 488) for New York garment workers and Agnes Nestor among Illinois glove workers. Athough they often resented the patronizing ways of their well-to-do patrons, trade-union women identified their cause with the broader struggle for women's rights.

In Britain, suffragists had begun to picket Parliament, assault politicians, and go on hunger strikes while in jail. Following their lead, Alice Paul, a young Quaker who had lived in Britain, applied confrontational tactics to the

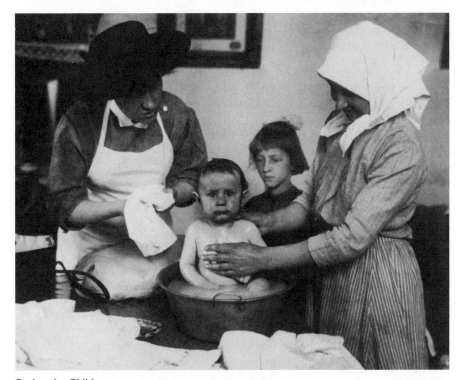

Saving the Children
In the early years at Hull House, Jane Addams recalled, toddlers sometimes arrived for kindergarten tipsy from a breakfast of bread soaked in wine. To settlement-house workers, the answer to such ignorance was in child care education, and so began the program to send visiting nurses into immigrant homes. They taught mothers the proper method of caring for children—including, as this photograph shows, the daily infant bath, in a dishpan if necessary.

AMERICAN VOICES

Tracking Down Lead Poisoning

Alice Hamilton (1869–1970) studied medicine over the objections of her socially prominent family in Fort Wayne, Indiana. When she landed a job teaching pathology in Chicago in 1897, Hamilton at last had her chance to fulfill her dream of living at Jane Addams's Hull House. That experience launched her on an illustrious career as a pioneer in industrial medicine—one of the many paths to social reform opened up by settlement-house work.

Living in a working-class quarter, coming in contact with laborers and their wives, I could not fail to hear tales of the dangers that working men faced, of cases of carbon-monoxide poisoning in the great steel mills, of painters disabled by lead palsy, of pneumonia and rheumatism among the men in the stockyards. . . . At the time I am speaking of [1910] Professor Charles Henderson . . . persuaded [the governor] to appoint an Occupational Disease Commission, the first time a state had ever undertaken such a survey. . . .

One case, of colic and double wristdrop, which was discovered in the Alexian Brothers' Hospital, took me on a pretty chase. The man, a Pole, said he had worked in a sanitary-ware factory, putting enamel on bathtubs. I had not come across this work in the English or German authorities on lead poisoning, and had no idea it was a lead trade. . . . The management assured me that no lead was used in the coatings and invited me to inspect the workrooms. . . . Completely puzzled, I made a journey to the Polish quarter to see the palsied man and heard from him I had not even been in the enameling works, only the one for final touching up. The real one was far out on the Northwest Side. I found it and discovered that enameling means sprinkling a finely ground enamel over a red hot tub where it melts and flows over the surface. I learned that the air is thick with enamel dust . . . rich in red oxide of lead. A specimen . . . proved to contain as much as 20 per cent soluble lead—that is, lead that dissolves into solution in the stomach. Thus I nailed down the fact that sanitary-ware enameling is a dangerous lead trade in the United States, whatever was true of England or Germany.

SOURCE: W. Elliot Brownlee and Mary M. Brownlee, eds., *Women in the American Economy: A Documentary History* (New Haven: Yale University Press, 1976), 285–287.

American battle for woman suffrage. Rejecting the slower route of enfranchisement by the states (see Map 21.1), Paul advocated a constitutional amendment that in one stroke would give women across the country the right to vote. In 1916 Paul organized the militant National Woman's party.

The National American Woman Suffrage Association (NAWSA), from which Paul had split off, was also rejuvenated. Carrie Chapman Catt, a skilled political organizer from the New York movement, took over as national leader in 1915. Under her guidance, NAWSA brought a broad-based organization to the campaign for a federal amendment.

In the midst of this suffrage struggle something new and more fundamental began to happen. A younger generation of college-educated women, out in the world and self-supporting, refused to be hemmed in by the social constraints of women's "separate sphere." "Breaking into the Human Race" was the intention they proclaimed at a mass meeting in New York in 1914. "We intend simply to be ourselves," declared the chair Marie Jenny Howe, "not just our little female selves, but our whole big human selves."

The women at this meeting called themselves *feminists*, a term that was just coming into use. In this, its first incarnation, *feminism* meant freedom for full personal development. Thus did Charlotte Perkins Gilman, famous for her advocacy of communal kitchens as a means of liberating women from homemaking, imagine the new woman: "Here she comes, running, out of prison and off pedestal; chains off, crown off, halo off, just a live woman."

Feminists were militantly prosuffrage, but unlike their more traditional suffragist sisters, they did not stake their claim on any presumed uplifting effect of the women's vote on American politics. Rather, they demanded the right to vote

Suffragists on Parade, 1912
After 1910 the suffrage movement went into high gear. Suffragist leaders decided to demand a constitutional amendment rather than rely on gaining the vote state by state. In 1912 they served notice on both parties that they meant business and, as shown in this suffragist parade in New York, made their demands a visible part of the presidential campaign.

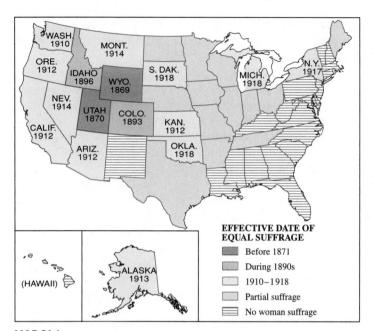

MAP 21.1
Woman Suffrage, 1869–1918
By 1909, after more than sixty years of agitation, only four lightly populated western states had granted women full voting rights. A number of
other states offered partial suffrage, limited mostly to voting for school
boards and such issues as taxes. Between 1910 and 1918, as the effort
shifted to the struggle for a constitutional amendment, eleven states (and
Alaska) joined the list granting full suffrage. The most stubborn resistance
was in the South.

because they considered themselves fully equal to men. At the point that the suffrage movement was about to triumph, it was overtaken by a larger revolution
that redefined the struggle for women's rights as a battle against all the constraints
that prevented women from achieving their potential as human beings.

Feminism brought forth a new and more radical type of woman social
progressive: Margaret Sanger. As a public health nurse in New York City,
Sanger had been repeatedly asked by immigrant women the "secret" of how
to avoid having more babies. When one of her patients died of a botched
abortion, Sanger decided to devote herself to teaching poor immigrant
women about birth control. This activity was illegal under nineteenth-century
laws that treated birth-control literature and contraceptive devices as obscene
materials. While it was easy enough for the educated middle class to evade
these laws, birth control could reach the poor only through an open campaign
of education. Undeterred by police raids or public disapproval, Sanger gave
speeches, published pamphlets, and in 1916 opened the first birth-control
clinic in the United States. If her ends were not different from Jane Ad-

dams's—both wanted to uplift the downtrodden—the means Sanger used posed a more provocative challenge to the status quo.

Urban Liberalism

Thirty minutes before quitting time on Saturday afternoon, March 25, 1911, fire broke out at the Triangle Shirtwaist Company in downtown New York City. The flames trapped the workers, mostly young immigrant women. Forty-seven leapt to their deaths; another ninety-nine never reached the windows. The tragedy caused a national furor, and led two months later to the creation of the New York State Factory Commission.

In the next four years the commission developed a remarkable program of labor reform: fifty-six laws dealing with fire hazards, unsafe machines, industrial homework, and wages and hours for women and children. The chairman of the commission was Robert F. Wagner; the vice-chairman, Alfred E. Smith. Both were Tammany Hall politicians, Democratic party leaders in the state legislature. They established the commission, participated fully in its work, and marshaled the party regulars to pass the proposals into law. All this Wagner and Smith did with the approval of the Tammany machine.

Tammany's reform role reflected something new in urban politics. Party machines increasingly recognized their limitations as social agencies in the modern industrial age. Only the state could prevent future Triangle fires, or cope with the evils of factory work and city poverty. A new generation had entered machine politics. Al Smith and Robert Wagner, men of social vision, absorbed the lessons of the Triangle investigation. They formed durable ties with such middle-class progressives as the social worker Frances Perkins, who sat on the commission as the representative of the New York Consumers' League. Historians have labeled this development *urban liberalism*.

City machines, always pragmatic, adopted urban liberalism without much of an ideological struggle. The same could not be said of trade unions, the other institution that represented American working people. The American Federation of Labor (AFL) had strongly opposed state interference in labor's affairs. Samuel Gompers preached that workers should not seek from government what they could accomplish by their own economic power and self-help. *Voluntarism*, as trade unionists called this doctrine, did not die out, but it weakened substantially during the progressive years.

In the early twentieth century the labor movement came under severe attack by the courts. In the *Loewe v. Lawlor* case (1908), the Supreme Court found a labor boycott—a call by the Hatters' Union for people not to patronize the antiunion D. E. Loewe & Company—to be a conspiracy in restraint of trade under the Sherman Act and awarded triple damages to the company. Hundreds of union members stood to lose their homes and life savings until the labor movement raised the money to pay the fines. Even worse was the employers' ability to get *injunctions*—court orders—prohibiting a union from carrying on a strike or boycott.

Only a political response could blunt these assaults on labor's economic weapons. In its "Bill of Grievances" of 1906, the AFL demanded that Congress grant unions immunity from court attack. Rebuffed, the unions decided to become more politically active, entering campaigns and giving nonpartisan support to candidates who favored their program.

Once into politics, the labor movement had difficulty denying the case for social legislation. The AFL, after all, claimed to speak for the entire working class. When muckrakers exposed exploitation of workers and middle-class progressives came forward with solutions, how could the labor movement fail to respond? Gompers served on the Triangle factory commission, and if— according to Frances Perkins—he was a less eager student than the Tammanyite members, learn he did. In state after state, organized labor joined the battle for progressive legislation and increasingly became its strongest advocate.

Conservative labor leaders offered the excuse that protective laws were for women and children, who could not defend themselves. In practice, however, trade unions became more flexible about legislative protection for men as well, especially regarding workers' compensation for industrial accidents. Between 1910 and 1917 all the industrial states enacted insurance laws covering factory injuries.

Compared to Europe, however, the United States was slow to protect workers against the hazards of modern industrial life. Health insurance and unemployment compensation, although popular in Europe, scarcely made it onto the American political agenda. Old-age pensions, which Britain adopted in 1908, got a serious hearing, only to come up against an odd barrier. The United States already had a pension system of a kind, for Civil War veterans: as many as half of all native-born men over sixty-four or their surviviors were drawing benefits in the early twentieth century. It did not help, moreover, that the Republican party had shamelessly exploited veterans' pensions for partisan purposes; or that administration of the program was notoriously corrupt and laced with patronage; or finally, that easy access to veterans' benefits often reinforced fears of state-induced dependency.

Not until another generation had experienced the Great Depression would the country be ready for social insurance. A secure old age, unemployment compensation, health insurance—these human needs of a modern industrial order were beyond the reach of urban liberals in the Progressive Era.

Cultural Pluralism Embattled

Urban liberalism was driven not only by the plight of the downtrodden but by a sharpening attack on immigrants. Old-stock evangelical Protestants had long agitated for laws that would impose their moral and cultural norms on American society. After 1900 this impulse again beat strongly, expressing, in fact, one strand of progressive reform. The Anti-Saloon League, which called itself "the Protestant church in action," became a formidable force for prohibition in many states. The outlawing of liquor was related to other reform targets, for the saloon bred dirty politics and poverty. Like progressives on other fronts, prohibitionists pronounced their movement the "Revolt of Decent Citizens."

The moral-reform agenda expanded to include a new goal: restricting the immigration of southern and Eastern Europeans into the United States. La Follette's close adviser, Edward A. Ross of the University of Wisconsin, denounced the "pigsty mode of life" of immigrants. The danger, respected social scientists argued, was that the nation's Anglo-Saxon population would be "mongrelized" and its civilization swamped by "inferior" Mediterranean and Slavic cultures. Feeding on this fear, the Immigration Restriction League spearheaded a movement to end America's historic open-door policy. Like prohibition, immigration restriction was considered by its proponents to be a progressive reform.

Urban liberals thought otherwise. They bitterly resented the attacks on the worthiness of urban immigrants. Prohibition, protested one Catholic academic, was "despotic and hypocritical domination." The Tammany politician Martin McCue accused the Protestant ministry of "seeking to substitute the policeman's nightstick for the Bible."

In many ways, certainly until the Great Depression, ethnocultural issues provided a stronger basis for urban liberal politics than did economics. And because the Democrats cultivated the immigrant vote, they became destined to be the majority party once a second generation came of age. The shift from Republican domination, although not completed until the 1930s, began during the Progressive Era.

Racism and Reform

The direct primary was the flagship of progressive politics—the crucial reform, as La Follette said, for returning politics to "the people." The primary originated not in Wisconsin, however, but in the South, and by the time La Follette got his primary law in 1903, primaries were already operating in seven southern states.

In the South, however, the primary was a *white* primary. Since the Democratic nomination was tantamount to election, to be excluded from the primary meant in effect to be disfranchised. The direct primary was a reform *intended* to drive blacks out of politics.

How could democratic reform and white supremacy be thus wedded together? Because of the racism of the age. In a 1902 book on Reconstruction, Professor John W. Burgess of Columbia University denounced the Fifteenth Amendment, granting blacks the vote, as a "monstrous thing." Burgess was southern-born, but he was confident that his northern audience saw the "vast differences in political capacity" between blacks and whites, and approved of black disfranchisement. Even the Republican party offered no rebuttal. Indeed, as president-elect in 1908, William Howard Taft applauded the southern laws as necessary to "prevent entirely the possibility of domination by . . . an ignorant electorate." Taft reassured southerners that "the federal government has nothing to do with social equality."

In the North, racial tensions were on the rise. Over 200,000 blacks migrated from the South between 1900 and 1910. Their arrival in northern cities invariably sparked white resentment. Attacks on blacks became widespread. In 1908 a bloody race riot broke out in Springfield, Illinois. Equally reflective of racist sentiment was the huge success of D. W. Griffith's epic film *Birth of a Nation* (1915), which depicted Reconstruction as a moral struggle between rampaging blacks and a chivalrous Ku Klux Klan. Woodrow Wilson found the film's history "all so terribly true." His Democratic administration marked a low point for the federal government as the ultimate guarantor of equal rights: during Wilson's tenure, segregation of the U.S. civil service would have gone into effect but for an outcry among black leaders and influential white allies.

In these bleak years a core of young black professionals, mostly northern-born, began to fight back. The key figure was William Monroe Trotter, the pugnacious editor of the *Boston Guardian* and an outspoken critic of Booker T. Washington. "The policy of compromise has failed," Trotter argued. "The policy of resistance and aggression deserves a trial." In this endeavor, Trotter was joined by W. E. B. Du Bois, a Harvard-trained sociologist and author of *Souls of Black Folk*. In 1906 the two of them, having broken with Washington, called a meeting of twenty-nine supporters at Niagara Falls—but in Canada, because no hotel on the U.S. side would admit blacks. The Niagara movement, which resulted from that meeting, had an impact far beyond the scattering of members and local bodies it organized. The principles it affirmed would define the struggle for the rights of African-Americans: first, encouragement of black pride by all possible means; second, an uncompromising demand for full political and civil equality; and above all, the resolute denial "that the Negro-American assents to inferiority, is submissive under oppression and apologetic before insults."

Going against the grain, a handful of white reformers rallied to the African-American cause. Among the most devoted was Mary White Ovington, who grew up in an abolitionist family. Like Jane Addams, Ovington became a settlement-house worker, but among urban blacks in New York rather than in an immigrant Chicago neighborhood. News of the Springfield race riot of 1908 changed her life. Convinced that her duty was to fight racism, Ovington called a meeting of sympathetic white progressives, which led to the formation of the National Association for the Advancement of Colored People (NAACP) in 1909.

The Niagara movement, torn by internal disagreements, was breaking up, and most of the black activists joined the NAACP. The organization's national leadership was dominated by whites, but with one crucial exception. Du Bois became the editor of the NAACP's journal, *The Crisis*. With a passion that only a black voice could provide, Du Bois used that platform to proclaim the demand for equal rights.

In social welfare, the National Urban League became the lead organization, uniting in 1911 the many groups serving black migrants arriving in northern cities. Like the NAACP, the Urban League was interracial, including both white reformers such as Ovington and black welfare activists such as William Lewis Bulkley, a New York school principal who was the main architect of the Urban League. In the South, social welfare was very much the province of black women, whose civic activities to some degree filled the vacuum left by the disfranchisement of black men. Black women's progressivism sprang organizationally from the churches and schools, but also from the southern affiliates of the National Association of Colored Women's Clubs, which had started in 1896. And because their activities seemed unthreatening to white supremacy, black women reached across the color line and found allies and supporters among white women in the South.

Progressivism was a house of many chambers. Most were infected by the respectable racism of the age, but not all. A saving remnant of white progressives rallied to the cause of African-Americans. In the interracial NAACP and Urban League, and in such black organizations as the National Association of Colored Women's Clubs, the national institutions were formed that would lead the black struggle for a better life over the next half-century.

PROGRESSIVISM AND NATIONAL POLITICS

The gathering forces of progressivism were slow to reach the national scene. Reformers had been spurred by immediate and visible problems. Washington seemed remote from the battles they were waging in their cities and states. But in 1906 Robert La Follette moved from the governor's office in Wisconsin to the U.S. Senate. Other seasoned progressives, also ambitious for a wider stage, made the same move. By 1910 a highly vocal progressive bloc was making itself heard in both houses of Congress.

Progressivism came to national politics not via Congress, however, but via the presidency. This was partly because the White House provided a "bully pulpit"—to use Theodore Roosevelt's phrase—for mobilizing national opinion. But just as important was the twist of fate that brought Roosevelt to the White House on September 14, 1901.

The Making of a Progressive President

Except for his upper-class background, Theodore Roosevelt was cut from much the same cloth as other progressive politicians. Born in 1858, he came from a wealthy old-line New York family, attended Harvard, and might have chosen the life of a leisured man of letters. Instead, scarcely out of college, he plunged into Republican politics, and in 1882 he entered the New York State legislature. His reasons matched the high-minded motives of other budding progressives. Roosevelt always identified himself—loudly—with the cause of righteousness. But he did not scorn power and its uses. He showed contempt for the amateurism of the Mugwumps—"those political and literary hermaphrodites," he called them—and much preferred the professionalism of party politics.

Returning from the Spanish-American War the hero of San Juan Hill (see Chapter 22), Roosevelt captured the New York governorship in 1898. During his single term he clearly signaled his reformist inclinations by pushing through civil-service reform and a tax on corporate franchises. He discharged the corrupt superintendent of insurance over the Republican party's objections, and asserted his confidence in the government's capacity to improve the life of the people.

Hoping to neutralize Roosevelt, the party bosses promoted him in 1900 to a dead-end job, as William McKinley's vice-president. Roosevelt accepted reluctantly. But on September 6, 1901, an anarchist named Leon F. Czolgosz shot the president. When McKinley died eight days later, Roosevelt became president. It was a sure bet, groaned Republican boss Mark Hanna, that "that damn cowboy" would make trouble in the White House.

Roosevelt in fact moved cautiously, attending first of all to politics. He skillfully used the patronage powers of the presidency to gain control of the Republican party. But Roosevelt was also restrained by uncertainty about what reform role the federal government ought to play. At first the new president might have been described as a progressive without a cause.

Even so, Roosevelt displayed his activist bent. An ardent outdoorsman, he devoted part of his first annual message to Congress to conservation. Unlike John Muir (see Chapter 17, page 472), Roosevelt was not a preservationist devoted to defending the nation's wilderness. Rather, he wanted to *conserve* the country's resources. He was not against commercial development as long as it was regulated and mindful of the public interest. In 1902 he backed the Newlands Reclamation Act, which designated the proceeds from public land sales for irrigation in arid regions. His administration expanded the national forest reserve; upgraded the management of public lands; and to the chagrin of some Republicans, energetically prosecuted violators of federal land laws. In the cause of conservation, Roosevelt demonstrated his enthusiasm for exercising executive authority and his disdain for those who sought profit "by betraying the public."

Roosevelt showed the same determination in the face of the anthracite coal strike of 1902. Anthracite, or hard coal, was the main fuel for home heating in those days. As cold weather approached, it became urgent to settle the strike. The United Mine Workers (UMW), led by John Mitchell, were willing to submit to arbitration, but the mine operators adamantly refused to recognize the union. Advised that he had no legal grounds for intervening, the president nevertheless called both sides to a White House conference on October 1, 1902. When the operators balked, Roosevelt threatened a government takeover of the mines. He also persuaded the financier J. P. Morgan to use his considerable influence with them. At that point, the mine operators caved in. Roosevelt appointed an arbitration commission to rule on the issues, another unprecedented step. Although not especially sympathetic to organized labor, TR became infuriated by the "arrogant stupidity" of the mine owners. "Of all the forms of tyranny the least attractive and the most vulgar is the tyranny of mere wealth," Roosevelt wrote in his autobiography. He was prepared to deploy all his presidential authority against the "tyranny" of irresponsible business.

Regulating the Marketplace

The economic issue that most troubled Roosevelt was the assault on the competitive market by big business. The drift toward large-scale enterprise had been under way for many years, as entrepreneurs sought the efficiencies of nationwide, vertically integrated firms (see Chapter 18). But, additionally, creating bigger businesses meant gaining power to control markets. Controlling markets was the motive behind the scramble to merge rival firms in the aftermath of the depression of the 1890s. These mergers—*trusts*, as they were called—greatly increased the degree of business concentration in the economy. Of the 73 largest industrial companies in 1900, 53 had not existed three years earlier. By 1910, 1 percent of the nation's manufacturers accounted for 44 percent of the nation's industrial output.

Roosevelt's uneasiness became evident as early as his first annual message to Congress, in which he referred to the "real and grave evils" of economic concentration. But what weapons could the president use in response?

The basic legal principles upholding free competition were already firmly established. Under *common law*—the body of judge-made legal precedents America had inherited from Britain—it was illegal for anyone to restrain or monopolize trade. Persons who were economically injured by such actions could sue for damages. These common-law rights had been enacted into statutory law in many states during the 1880s and then, because the problem spilled over state jurisdictions, had been incorporated into the Sherman Antitrust Act of 1890 and become part of federal law.

Neither Cleveland nor McKinley had been much inclined to enforce the Sherman Act. But the law was there to be used. Its potential rested above all on the fact that it incorporated common-law principles of unimpeachable validity. In the right hands, the Sherman Act could be a strong weapon against the abuse of economic power.

Roosevelt made his opening move in 1903 by establishing the Bureau of Corporations, empowered to investigate business practices. On the basis of evidence gathered by the bureau, the Justice Department was able to mount antitrust suits. The department had already filed such a suit in 1902 against the Northern Securities Company, a combination of the railroad systems of the Northwest. In a landmark decision, the Supreme Court ordered Northern Securities dissolved in 1904.

In the presidential election that year, Roosevelt handily defeated a weak conservative Democratic candidate, Judge Alton B. Parker. Now president in

J. Pierpont Morgan
J. P. Morgan was a giant among American financiers. He had served an apprenticeship in investment banking under his father, a leading Anglo-American banker in London. A gruff man of few words, Morgan had a genius for instilling trust and the strength of will to persuade others to follow his lead and do his bidding—qualities the great photographer Edward Steichen captured in this portrait.

his own right, Roosevelt stepped up the attack on the trusts. He took on forty-five of the nation's giant firms, including Standard Oil, American Tobacco, and Du Pont. His rhetoric rising, Roosevelt became the nation's trustbuster, a crusader against "predatory wealth."

But Roosevelt was not antibusiness. He regarded large-scale enterprise as a natural result of modern industrialism. Only firms that abused their power deserved punishment. But how would those companies be identified? Under the Sherman Act, following common-law practice, the courts decided whether an act in restraint of trade was "unreasonable," that is, actually harmed the public interest. The courts thus had the discretion to evaluate the actions of corporations on a case-by-case basis. In 1897, however, the Supreme Court repudiated this "rule of reason" in the *Trans-Missouri* case. Now, even if the impact on the market was harmless, actions that restrained or monopolized trade would automatically violate the Sherman Act.

Little noticed when it was first decided, *Trans-Missouri* placed Roosevelt in an awkward position. He had no desire to hamstring legitimate business activity, but he could not rely on the courts to distinguish between "good" and "bad" trusts. The only solution was for Roosevelt to assume that responsibility. This the president could do because it was up to him—or his attorney general—to decide whether or not to initiate antitrust prosecutions in the first place.

In November 1904, with an antitrust suit looming, the United States Steel Corporation approached Roosevelt and proposed a deal: cooperation in exchange for preferential treatment. The company would open its books to the Bureau of Corporations; if the bureau found evidence of wrongdoing, the company would be warned privately and given a chance to set matters right. Roosevelt accepted this "gentlemen's agreement" because it solved a serious dilemma for him. He could accommodate the realities of the modern industrial order while maintaining his public image as the champion against the trusts.

The railroads posed a different kind of problem for Roosevelt. As quasi-public enterprises, they had always been subject to regulation, beginning at the federal level in 1887 with the establishment of the Interstate Commerce Commission (ICC), the nation's first federal regulatory agency. Like the Sherman Act, however, railroad regulation remained pretty much a dead letter in its early years. Convinced that the railroads needed firm regulation, Roosevelt pushed through the Elkins Act of 1903, which prohibited discriminatory rebates, that is, reductions on published rates for preferred or powerful customers. Then, with the 1904 election behind him, Roosevelt launched his drive for real railroad regulation.

The central issue was government rate-setting, which the conservative Republican bloc in Congress firmly opposed. In 1906, after nearly two years of wrangling, Congress passed the Hepburn Railway Act, which empowered the ICC to set maximum rates upon complaint of a shipper, and to prescribe uniform methods of bookkeeping. But as a concession to conservatives, the courts retained broad powers to review the ICC's rate decisions.

The Hepburn Act was a triumph of Roosevelt's skills as a political operator. He had maneuvered brilliantly against determined opposition and come away with the essentials of what he wanted. Despite grumbling by Senate progressives critical of any compromise, Roosevelt was satisfied. He had achieved a landmark expansion of the government's regulatory powers over business.

The regulation of consumer products, another hallmark of progressive reform, was very much the handiwork of muckraking journalists—in particular, Samuel Hopkins Adams's riveting series of articles on the patent-medicine business in *Collier's* in 1905. For a time, industry lobbies stymied pure food and drug legislation. Then, in 1906, Upton Sinclair's novel *The Jungle* appeared. Sinclair had meant to expose labor exploitation in Chicago meat-packing plants, but his graphic descriptions of rotten meat and filthy conditions excited—and sickened—the nation. President Roosevelt weighed into the legislative battle, initiating a federal investigation of the stockyards. Within months, the Pure Food and Drug Act and the Meat Inspection Act were passed, and another administrative agency was added to the federal bureaucratic structure Roosevelt was building: the Food and Drug Administration.

During the 1904 presidential campaign Roosevelt had taken to calling his program the Square Deal. This kind of labeling was new to American politics, introducing a political style that dramatized issues, mobilized public opinion, and asserted leadership. But the Square Deal meant something of substance as well. After many years of passivity and weakness, the federal government was

Campaigning for the Square Deal
When William McKinley ran for president in 1896, he sat on his front porch in Canton, Ohio, and received delegations of voters. But Theodore Roosevelt considered the presidency a "bully pulpit" and used the office brilliantly to mobilize public opinion and assert his leadership. The preeminence of the presidency in American public life began with Roosevelt's administration. Here, at the height of his crusading powers, he stumps for the Square Deal in the 1904 election.

reclaiming the role it had abandoned after the Civil War. Now, however, the target was the new economic order. When companies misused corporate power, the government had to step in and assure ordinary Americans a "square deal."

The Fracturing of Republican Progressivism

Roosevelt was well aware that his Square Deal was built on nineteenth-century foundations. Antitrust doctrine, in particular, seemed to him inadequate in the face of a large-scale industrial order. Better, Roosevelt felt, to empower the federal government to oversee big business than to try to enforce an archaic competitive market. Roosevelt's final presidential speeches dwelt on the need for a reform agenda for the twentieth century. This was the task he bequeathed to his chosen successor, William Howard Taft.

Taft was an admirable man in many ways. An able jurist and a superb administrator, he had served Roosevelt loyally as governor-general of the Philippines and as secretary of war. He was an avowed Square Dealer. But he was not by nature a progressive politician. He disliked the give-and-take of politics, he distrusted power, and he generally deferred to Congress. In fundamental ways, moreover, Taft was conservative. He revered the processes of the law and, unlike Roosevelt, found it hard to trim his means to fit his ends.

Taft's Democratic opponent in the 1908 campaign was William Jennings Bryan. This was Bryan's last hurrah, and he made the most of it. Eloquent as ever, Bryan attacked the Republicans as the party of the "plutocrats," and outdid them in urging tougher antitrust legislation, lower tariffs, stricter railway regulation, and advanced labor legislation. Bryan's campaign moved the Democratic party into the mainstream of national progressive politics, but that was not enough to offset Taft's advantages as Roosevelt's candidate.

Taft won comfortably, and he entered the White House with a mandate to pick up where Roosevelt had left off. That, alas, was not to be.

By 1909 the ferment of reform had unsettled the Republican party. On the right, the conservatives were bracing themselves against further losses. Led by the formidable Senator Nelson W. Aldrich of Rhode Island, they were still a force to be reckoned with. On the left, progressive Republicans were rebellious. They had broad popular support—especially in the Midwest—and in Robert La Follette they had a fiery leader. The progressives felt that Roosevelt had been too easy on business, and with him gone from the White House, they intended to make up for lost time. Reconciling these conflicting forces within the Republican party would have been a daunting task for the most accomplished politician. For Taft, it spelled disaster.

First there was the tariff. Progressives considered protective tariffs a major reason why the trusts had sprung up. Although Taft had campaigned for tariff reform, he was won over by the conservative Republican bloc and ended up approving the Payne-Aldrich Tariff Act of 1909, which sheltered eastern industry from foreign competition.

Next came the Pinchot-Ballinger affair. U.S. Chief Forester Gifford Pinchot, an ardent conservationist and a chum of Roosevelt's, accused Secretary of the Interior Richard A. Ballinger of conspiring to transfer Alaskan public lands rich in natural resources to a private syndicate. When Pinchot aired the charges in January 1910, Taft fired him for insubordination. Despite Taft's strong conservationist credentials, in the eyes of the progressives he was marked for life by the Pinchot-Ballinger affair as a friend of the "interests" plundering the nation's resources.

Solemnly pledged to carry on Roosevelt's tradition, Taft found himself propelled into the conservative Republican camp, an ally of "Uncle Joe" Cannon, the dictatorial speaker of the House of Representatives. When a House revolt finally broke Cannon's power in 1910, it was regarded as a defeat for the president as well. Largely in reaction to Taft, the reformers in the Republican party turned into a distinct, organized faction. By 1910 they were calling themselves "Progressives," or in more belligerent moments, "Insurgents." Taft answered by trying to purge them in the Republican primaries that year.

The Progressives emerged from the 1910 elections stronger and angrier. In January 1911 they formed the National Progressive Republican League and began a drive to take over the Republican party. Though La Follette was their leader, the Progressives knew that their best chance to capture the presidency lay with Theodore Roosevelt.

Roosevelt, home from a year-long safari in Africa, yearned to reenter the political fray. He would have been troublesome for Taft under any circumstances. As it was, the president's handling of the Progressives fed Roosevelt's mounting sense of outrage. But Roosevelt was too loyal a party man to defy the Republican establishment, and too astute a politician not to recognize that a Republican party split would benefit the Democrats. He could be spurred into rebellion only by a true clash of principles. On the question of the trusts, just such a clash materialized.

Roosevelt had managed to reconcile public policy and economic reality during his administration by distinguishing between good and bad trusts. But this was a makeshift solution that depended on a president who was willing to stretch his powers to the limit. Taft had no such inclination. His legalistic mind rebelled at the notion that he as president should decide which trusts should be prosecuted. The Sherman Act was on the books. "We are going to enforce that law or die in the attempt," Taft promised grimly.

In its *Standard Oil* decision (1911), the Supreme Court eased Taft's problem by reasserting the common-law principle of the "rule of reason," which meant that, once again, the courts themselves would distinguish between good and bad trusts. With that burden lifted from the executive branch, Attorney General George W. Wickersham stepped up the pace of antitrust actions.

United States Steel became an immediate target. Among the charges against the Steel Trust was that it had violated the antimonopoly provision of the Sherman Act by acquiring the Tennessee Coal and Iron Company (TCI) in 1907. Roosevelt had personally approved the acquisition as a necessary step—so U.S. Steel representatives had explained it to him—to prevent a financial collapse on Wall Street. Taft's suit against U.S. Steel thus amounted to an attack on Roosevelt: he had as president arranged for U.S. Steel to circumvent the Sherman Act. Nothing was better calculated to propel Roosevelt into action than an issue that was both an affair of personal honor and a question of broad principle.

The country did not have to choose between breaking up big business and submitting to corporate rule, Roosevelt argued. There was a third way. The federal government could be empowered to oversee the nation's industrial corporations to make sure they acted in the public interest. They would be regulated by a federal trade commission as if they were natural monopolies or public utilities.

In a speech in Osawatomie, Kansas, in August 1910, Roosevelt made his case for what he called the New Nationalism. The central issue, he argued, was human welfare versus property rights. In modern society, property had to be controlled "to whatever degree the public welfare may require it." The government would become "the steward of the public welfare."

This formulation removed the restraints from Roosevelt's thinking. He took up the cause of social justice, adding to his program a federal child labor law, regulation of labor relations, and a national minimum wage for women. Most radical, perhaps, was Roosevelt's attack on the legal system. Insisting that the courts should not be making social policy, Roosevelt proposed sharp curbs on their powers, even raising the possibility of popular recall of court decisions. Beyond these specifics, the New Nationalism advanced a new political philosophy. Roosevelt was proposing a *statist* solution—an enormous expansion of the role of the federal government—to the problem of corporate power.

Early in 1912, Roosevelt announced his candidacy for the presidency and immediately swept the progressive Republicans into his camp. A bitter party battle ensued. Roosevelt won the states that held primary elections, but Taft controlled the party organizations elsewhere. Dominated by the party regulars, the Republican convention chose Taft.

Roosevelt, considering himself cheated out of the nomination, bolted from the Republicans and created a new Progressive party, soon nicknamed the "Bull Moose" party. In a crusading campaign, Roosevelt offered the New Nationalism to the people.

Woodrow Wilson and the New Freedom

While the Republicans battled among themselves, the Democrats were on the move. The scars caused by the free silver campaign of 1896 had faded, and in the 1908 campaign William Jennings Bryan had established the rejuvenated party's progressive credentials. The Democrats made dramatic gains in 1910, taking over the House of Representatives for the first time since 1892 and capturing a number of traditionally Republican governorships. After fourteen years as the party's standard-bearer, Bryan reluctantly made way for a new generation of leaders.

The ablest was Woodrow Wilson of New Jersey. Wilson was an academic, a noted political scientist, and president of Princeton University. In 1910, with no political experience, he accepted the Democratic nomination for governor of New Jersey. As governor, Wilson compiled a brilliant record: he cleaned up the boss system and passed a direct primary law, workers' compensation, and stronger regulation of railroads and utilities. Wilson went on, in a bruising battle, to win the Democratic presidential nomination in 1912.

Wilson possessed, to a fault, the moral certainty that characterized the progressive politician. A brilliant speaker, he almost instinctively assumed the mantle of righteous reform. Only gradually, however, did he hammer out, in reaction to Roosevelt's New Nationalism, a coherent reform program, which he called the New Freedom.

Wilson actually had much in common with Roosevelt. "The old time of individual competition is probably gone by," Wilson stressed. Like Roosevelt, he opposed not bigness but the abuse of economic power. Nor did Wilson think that the abuse of power could be prevented without a strong federal government. He parted company from Roosevelt over *how* government should restrain private power.

As he warmed to the debate, Wilson cast the issue in fundamental terms. "This is a struggle for emancipation," he proclaimed in October 1912. "If America is not to have free enterprise, then she can have freedom of no sort whatever." Wilson also scorned Roosevelt's social program. Welfare might be benevolent, he declared, but it also would be paternalistic and contrary to the traditions of a free people.

How, then, did Wilson propose to deal with the problem of corporate power? Court enforcement of the Sherman Act was Wilson's basic answer. His task was to figure out how to make that long-established antitrust approach work better. In this effort Wilson relied heavily on a new adviser, Louis D. Brandeis, famous as the "people's lawyer" for his public service in many progressive causes (including the landmark *Muller* case).

An expert on regulatory matters, Brandeis understood that an all-powerful trade commission was likely to end up not as defender of the public interest, but in a cozy relationship with the industries it was supposed to regulate. Nor did Brandeis believe that bigness meant efficiency. On the contrary, he argued, trusts were wasteful compared with firms that vigorously competed in a free market. The main thing was to prevent the trusts from unfairly using their power to curb free competition.

The 1912 election fell short of being a referendum on the New Nationalism versus the New Freedom. The outcome turned on a more humdrum reality: Wilson was elected because he kept the traditional Democratic vote, while the Republicans split between Roosevelt and Taft. Although he won by a landslide in the electoral college, Wilson received only 42 percent of the popular vote—115,000 fewer votes than Bryan had amassed against Taft in 1908. At best it could be said that the 1912 election signified that the American public was in the mood for reform. Only 23 percent, after all, had voted for the one candidate who stood for the status quo, President Taft. Woodrow Wilson's own reform program, however, had not received a mandate from the people.

Yet the 1912 election proved decisive in the history of national reform. The debate between Roosevelt and Wilson had brought forth, in the New Freedom, a program capable of finally resolving the crisis over corporate power that had gripped the nation for a decade. Just as important, the election created a rare legislative opportunity in Washington. Wilson became president with the Democrats in firm control of both houses of Congress, united in their eagerness to get on with the New Freedom.

Wilson chose a flanking attack on the problem of economic power. Long out of power, the Democrats were hungry for tariff reform. From the prevailing average of 40 percent, the Underwood Tariff Act of 1913 pared rates down to an average of 25 percent. Targeting especially the trust-dominated industries, Democrats confidently expected the Underwood Tariff to spur competition and reduce prices for consumers by opening protected American markets to foreign products.

Wilson's administration then turned to the nation's banking system, whose key weakness was the absence of a central reserve bank. The main function of central banks at that time was to regulate commercial banks and back them up in case they could not meet their obligations to depositors. In practice, this role had been assumed by the great New York banks, which handled the accounts of outlying banks and assisted them when they came under pressure. However, if the New York banks weakened, the entire system could collapse. This had nearly happened in 1907, when the Knickerbocker Trust Company failed and panic swept through the nation's financial markets.

The need for a reserve system became widely accepted, but the form it should take was hotly debated. Wall Street wanted a centralized system controlled by the bankers. Rural Democrats and their spokesman, Senator Carter Glass of Virginia, preferred a decentralized network of reserve banks. Progressives in both parties agreed that the essential feature should be public control over the reserve system. The bankers, whose practices were already under scrutiny by Congress, were on the defensive in this contest.

President Wilson, no expert to begin with, learned quickly and reconciled the reformers and bankers. The monumental Federal Reserve Act of 1913 gave the nation a banking system that was resistant to financial panic. The act delegated reserve functions to twelve district reserve banks, which would be controlled by their member banks. The Federal Reserve Board imposed public regulation on this regional structure. In one stroke the act strengthened the banking system and placed a measure of restraint on the "money trust."

Having dealt with tariff and banking reform, Wilson turned to the problem of corporate power. He wanted to rely on the Sherman Act, but was not sure how to make its antitrust principles more effective. Was it feasible to write strict definitions of illegal practices? Wilson finally decided that it was not. In the Clayton Antitrust Act of 1914, amending the Sherman Act, the definition of illegal practices was left flexible, subject to the test of whether the effect "substantially lessen[ed] competition or tend[ed] to create a monopoly."

As for Brandeis's advocacy of a trade commission, the problem was how much power and what functions it should have. Wilson was understandably hesitant, given his principled opposition to Roosevelt's conception of a powerful trade commission overseeing American business. Ultimately, under the 1914 law establishing it, the Federal Trade Commission (FTC) received broad powers to investigate companies and issue "cease and desist" orders against unfair trade practices that violated antitrust law. FTC decisions, however, were subject to court review, so that Wilson's entire program was situated within the original conception of antitrust enforcement. As before, it would ultimately be up to the courts to decide which business practices were illegal. Despite a good deal of commotion, this arduous legislative process was actually an exercise in consensus building. Wilson himself had opened the debate in a conciliatory way. "The antagonism between business and government is over," he said, and the time was ripe for a program representing the "best business judgment in America." Afterward, Wilson felt he had brought the long controversy over corporate power to a successful conclusion, and in fact he had. Steering a course between Taft's conservatism and Roosevelt's radicalism, Wilson had carved out a middle way that brought to bear the powers of government without threatening the constitutional order, and that curbed abuse of corporate power without threatening the capitalist system.

On social policy, too, Wilson charted a middle way. During the 1912 campaign he had denounced Roosevelt's social program as paternalistic. The most Wilson was willing to accept was cosmetic language in the Clayton Act stating that labor and farm organizations were not illegal combinations. He rejected exempting them from antitrust prosecution.

The labor vote had grown increasingly important to the Democratic party, however. As his second presidential campaign drew nearer, Wilson lost some of his scruples about prolabor legislation. In 1915 and 1916 he championed a host of bills beneficial to American workers: a federal child labor law, the Adamson eight-hour law for railroad workers, and the landmark Seamen's Act, which eliminated age-old abuses of sailors aboard ship. Likewise, after earlier resistance, in 1916 Wilson approved the Federal Farm Loan Act, which provided the low-interest rural credit system long demanded by farmers.

Wilson encountered the same dilemma that confronted all successful progressives: the claims of moral principle versus the unyielding realities of political and economic life. Progressives were high-minded but not radical. They saw evils in the system, but they did not consider the system itself to be evil. They also prided themselves on being realists as well as moralists. So it stood to reason that Wilson, like other progressives who achieved power, would find his place at the center.

CHAPTER 21 TIMELINE

1887	Interstate Commerce Commission established
1889	Jane Addams and Ellen Gates Starr found Hull House
1890	Sherman Antitrust Act
1893	Economic depression (until 1897)
1899	National Consumers' League founded
1900	Robert M. La Follette elected Wisconsin governor First commission form of city government in Galveston, Texas
1901	President McKinley assassinated; Theodore Roosevelt succeeds United States Steel Corporation formed
1902	President Roosevelt settles national anthracite strike
1903	National Women's Trade Union League
1904	Supreme Court dissolves the Northern Securities Company
1906	Hepburn Railway Act AFL adopts Bill of Grievances Upton Sinclair's *The Jungle*
1908	*Muller v. Oregon* upholds regulation of working hours for women Federal Council of Churches founded William Howard Taft elected president
1909	NAACP formed
1910	Roosevelt announces the New Nationalism Woman suffrage movement revives; suffrage victory in Washington State
1911	*Standard Oil* decision restores "rule of reason" Triangle Shirtwaist fire
1912	Progressive party formed Woodrow Wilson elected president
1913	Federal Reserve Act Underwood Tariff
1914	Clayton Antitrust Act

CHAPTER 22

AN EMERGING WORLD POWER, 1877–1914

- The Roots of Expansion
- An American Empire
- Onto the World Stage

I n 1881 Great Britain sent a new envoy to Washington. He was Sir Lionel Sackville-West, son of an earl, brother-in-law of the Tory leader Lord Denby, but otherwise distinguished only as the lover of a celebrated Spanish dancer. His well-connected friends wanted to park Sir Lionel somewhere comfortable, but out of harm's way. So they made him minister to the United States.

Twenty years later such an appointment would have been unthinkable. All the European powers had by then elevated their missions in Washington to embassies, and staffed them with top-of-the-line ambassadors. And they treated the United States, without question, as a fellow Great Power.

In Sir Lionel's day, the United States had scarcely cast a shadow on world affairs. America's army in 1881 was smaller than Bulgaria's; its navy ranked thirteenth in the world. Two decades later, however, the United States was flexing its muscles. It had just made short work of Spain in a brief but decisive war and acquired for itself an empire that stretched from Puerto Rico to the Philippines. America's standing as a rising naval power was manifest, and so was its aggressive assertion of national interest in the Caribbean and the Pacific.

The European powers could not be sure what America's role would be, since the United States retained its traditional policy of nonalignment in European affairs. But in chanceries across the Continent, the importance of the

United States was universally acknowledged, and its likely response to every event carefully assessed.

How the United States emerged onto the world stage in the years before World War I is the subject of this chapter.

THE ROOTS OF EXPANSION

In 1880 the United States had a population of 50 million, and by that measure it ranked with the great European powers. In industrial production the nation was second only to Britain and was rapidly closing the gap. Anyone who doubted the military prowess of the Americans needed only to recall the ferocity with which they had fought one another in the Civil War. The great campaigns of Lee, Sherman, and Grant had entered the military textbooks and were closely studied by army strategists everywhere.

Nor, when its vital interests were at stake, had the United States shown itself to be lacking in diplomatic vigor. The Civil War had put the United States at odds with both France and Britain. In the case of France, the issue involved the establishment in Mexico of a puppet regime under Archduke Maximilian, regarded by the United States as a threat to its security in the Southwest. When American troops under General Philip Sheridan began to mass on the Mexican border in 1867, the French military withdrew, abandoning Maximilian to a Mexican firing squad. With Britain, the thorny issue involved damages to Union shipping by the *Alabama* and other Confederate sea raiders operating from English ports. American hopes of achieving the annexation of Canada out of this dispute were dashed by Britain's grant of dominion status to Canada in 1867. But four years later, after lengthy negotiations, Britain expressed regret for its unneutral acts against the Union and agreed to the arbitration of the *Alabama* claims, settling to America's satisfaction the last outstanding diplomatic issue of the Civil War.

Diplomacy in the Gilded Age

In the years that followed, the United States lapsed into diplomatic inactivity, not out of weakness but for lack of any clear national purpose in world affairs. The business of building the nation's industrial economy absorbed Americans and turned their attention inward. And while the new international telegraphic cables provided the country with swift overseas communication after the 1860s, wide oceans still kept the world at a distance and gave Americans a sense of isolation and security.

In these circumstances, with no external threat to be seen, what was the point of maintaining a big navy? After the Civil War, the fleet gradually deteriorated. Of the 125 ships on the navy's active list, only about 25 were seaworthy at any one time. During the administration of Chester A. Arthur (1881–1885) a modest upgrading program began, commissioning new ships, raising the standards for the officer corps, and founding Naval War College. But the fleet remained small, without a unified naval command and with little more to do than maintain coastal defenses.

The conduct of diplomacy was likewise of little account. Appointment to the foreign service was mostly through the spoils system. American ministers and consular officers were a mixed lot, with many idlers and drunkards among the hard-working and competent. Domestic politics, moreover, made it difficult to develop a coherent foreign policy. Although diplomacy was an executive responsibility, the U.S. Senate jealously guarded its constitutional right to give "advice and consent" on treaties and diplomatic appointments. For its part the State Department tended to be inactive, exerting little control over either policy or its missions abroad. In remote parts of the world the American presence was often primarily religious: the intrepid missionaries bent on Christianizing the native populations of Asia, Africa, and the Pacific islands.

In the Caribbean the United States remained the dominant power, but the expansionist enthusiasms of the Civil War era subsided. Nothing came of the grandiose plans of William H. Seward, Andrew Johnson's secretary of state, nor of President Grant's efforts to purchase Santo Domingo in 1870, and the Senate regularly blocked later moves to acquire bases in Haiti, Cuba, and Venezuela. The long-cherished interest in an interoceanic canal across Central America also faded. Despite its claims of exclusive building rights, the United States stood by when a French company headed by the builder of the Suez Canal, Ferdinand de Lesseps, started to dig across the Panama isthmus in 1880. That project failed after a decade, but the reason was bankruptcy, not American opposition.

Diplomatic activity in Latin America quickened when James G. Blaine became secretary of state in 1881. He got involved in a border dispute between Mexico and Guatemala, tried to settle a war Chile was waging against Peru and Bolivia, and called the first Pan-American conference. Blaine's interventions in Latin American disputes went badly, however, and his successor canceled the Pan-American conference after Blaine left office in late 1881. This was a characteristic instance of Gilded Age diplomacy, driven partly by partisan politics and carried out without any clear sense of national purpose.

Pan-Americanism—the notion of a community of American states—took root, however, and Blaine, returning in 1889 for a second stint at the State Department, took up the plans by the outgoing Cleveland administration for a new Pan-American conference. But little came of it, except for an agency in Washington that was later named the Pan-American Union. Any Latin American goodwill won by Blaine's efforts was soon blasted by the humiliation the United States visited upon Chile because of a riot against American sailors in the port of Valparaiso in 1891. Threatened with war, Chile was forced to apologize to the United States and to pay an indemnity of $75,000.

In the Pacific, American interest centered on Hawaii. With a climate ideal for raising sugarcane, the islands had attracted American planters and investors. Nominally an independent nation, Hawaii came increasingly within the American orbit. In an 1875 treaty, Hawaiian sugar gained duty-free entry to the

American market, and the islands were declared off limits to other powers. A second treaty in 1887 granted the United States naval rights at Pearl Harbor.

When Hawaii's favored access to the American market was abruptly canceled by the McKinley Tariff of 1890, sugar planters began to plot an American takeover of Hawaii. They organized a revolt in January 1893 against Queen Liliuokalani, and quickly negotiated a treaty of annexation with the Harrison administration. Before annexation could be approved by the Senate, however, Grover Cleveland returned to the presidency and withdrew the treaty. To annex Hawaii, he declared, would violate both America's "honor and morality" and its "unbroken tradition" against acquiring territory far from the nation's shores.

Meanwhile, the American presence elsewhere in the Pacific was growing. The purchase of Alaska from imperial Russia in 1867 gave the United States not only a huge territory with vast natural resources, but an unlooked-for presence stretching across the northern Pacific. Far to the south in the Samoan islands the United States secured the right in 1878 to a coaling station in Pago Pago harbor—a key link on the route to Australia—and established an informal protectorate there.

American diplomacy in these years has been characterized as a series of incidents, not the pursuit of a foreign policy. Many things happened, but intermittently and without a plan, driven by individuals and pressure groups, not by any well-founded conception of national objectives. This was possible because, as the Englishman James Bryce remarked in 1888, America still sailed "upon a summer sea." In the stormier waters that lay ahead, a different kind of diplomacy would be required.

Economic Sources of Expansionism

America's gross national product quadrupled between 1870 and 1900, and industrial output increased even faster. But were there sufficient markets to absorb the goods flowing from America's farms and factories? America itself did constitute an enormous market. Over 90 percent of American output in the late nineteenth century was consumed at home. Even so, foreign markets were important. Roughly a fifth of the nation's agricultural output was exported, and as the industrial economy expanded, so did factory exports. Between 1880 and 1900, the industrial share of total exports jumped from 15 percent to over 30 percent.

Foreign trade was important partly for reasons of international finance. As a developing economy, the United States attracted a lot of foreign capital but invested very little abroad. The result was a heavy outflow of dollars to pay interest and dividends to foreign investors. To balance this account, the United States needed to export more goods than it imported. In fact, a favorable import-export balance was achieved in 1876. But because of its dependence on foreign capital, America had to be constantly vigilant about its export trade.

Even more important, however, was the relationship that many Americans perceived between foreign markets and the nation's social stability. In hard times, farmers took up radical politics and workers became militant strikers.

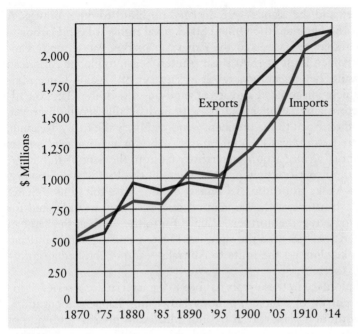

FIGURE 22.1
Balance of U.S. Imports and Exports, 1870–1914
By 1876 the United States had become a net exporting nation. The brief
reversal after 1888 aroused fears that the United States was losing its foreign markets and helped fuel the expansionist drive of the 1890s.

The problem, many thought, was that the nation's capacity to produce was
outrunning its capacity to consume. When the economy slowed, the impact
on farmers and workers was devastating, causing layoffs and farm foreclosures
across the country. The answer was to make sure that there would always be
enough buyers for America's surplus products. This meant, more than anything else, access to foreign markets.

The bulk of American exports in the late nineteenth century—over 80
percent—went to Europe and Canada. In these countries the normal instruments of diplomacy sufficed to protect the nation's economic interests. But in
Asia, Latin America, and other "backward" regions a more vigorous kind of
American intervention seemed necessary, because there the United States
found itself competing with other industrial powers.

Asia and Latin America represented only an eighth of America's export
trade in the late nineteenth century. Still, this trade was growing—it was
worth $200 million in 1900—and parts of it mattered a great deal to specific
industries, for example, the Chinese market for American textiles.

The real importance of these non-Western markets, however, was not so
much their current value as their future promise. China especially exerted a

powerful hold on the American mercantile imagination. Many felt that the China trade, although quite small, would one day be the key to American prosperity. Therefore, China and other inviting markets must not be closed to the United States.

In the mid-1880s, the pace of imperialist activity picked up. After the Berlin Conference of 1884, Africa was rapidly colonized by the European powers. In a burst of modernizing energy, Japan transformed itself into a major power. Japan easily defeated China in the Sino-Japanese War of 1894–1895, starting a scramble among the great powers, including Russia, to carve China up into spheres of influence. In Latin America, United States interests began to be challenged more aggressively by Britain, France, and Germany.

On top of all this came the Panic of 1893, setting in motion labor strikes and agrarian protests that many Americans, such as Cleveland's secretary of state, Walter Q. Gresham, took to be "symptoms of revolution." With the nation's social stability seemingly at stake, securing the markets of Latin America and Asia became an urgent necessity that inspired the expansionist diplomacy of the 1890s.

The Making of an Expansionist Foreign Policy

"Whether they will or no, Americans must now begin to look outward. The growing production of the country requires it." So wrote Captain Alfred T. Mahan, America's leading naval strategist, in his book *The Influence of Seapower upon History* (1890), which argued that first Rome and in modern times Great

Alfred T. Mahan
Mahan's theory about the influence of sea power on history came to him while he was reading Roman history in Lima, Peru, in 1885. His insight was personal as well as intellectual: embarrassed by the decrepit ships on which he served, Mahan thought the United States should have a modern fleet in which officers like himself could serve with pride (and with some hope of professional advancement).

Britain had become great empires because they had controlled the seas. From this insight Mahan developed a naval analysis that became the cornerstone of American strategic thinking.

The United States should no longer regard the oceans as barriers, Mahan argued, but as "a great highway . . . over which men pass in all directions." Traversing that highway required a robust merchant marine (America's had fallen on hard times since its heyday in the 1850s); a powerful navy to protect American commerce; and strategic overseas bases. Here technology played a role because, having converted to steam, navies required coaling stations far from home. Without such stations, Mahan warned, warships were "like land birds, unable to fly far from their own shores."

Mahan called for a canal across Central America to connect the Atlantic and the Pacific oceans. Such a canal would enable the eastern United States to "compete with Europe, on equal terms as to distance, for the markets of East Asia." The canal's approaches would need to be guarded by bases in the Caribbean Sea. And Hawaii would have to be annexed to extend American power into the Pacific.

Mahan was offering a *coherent* foreign policy, and other advocates of a powerful America flocked to him, including such coming politicians as Theodore Roosevelt and Henry Cabot Lodge. The influence of these men, few in number but strategically placed, increased during the 1890s. They pushed steadily for what Lodge called a "large policy." But mainstream politicians too accepted Mahan's underlying logic, and from the inauguration of Benjamin Harrison in 1889 onward, a surprising consistency began to emerge in the conduct of American foreign policy.

Mahan argued strongly for a battleship fleet capable of roaming the far seas and striking a decisive first blow against an enemy. In 1890 Congress appropriated funds for the first three battleships in the two-ocean fleet envisioned by Benjamin F. Tracy, Harrison's ambitious secretary of the navy. The battleship took on a special aura for those, like the young Roosevelt, who wanted to see the United States flexing its muscles. "Oh, Lord! if only the people who are ignorant about our Navy could see those great warships in all their majesty and beauty, and could realize how [well fitted they are] to uphold the honor of America!"

The incoming Cleveland administration was less spread-eagled, and by canceling Harrison's scheme for annexing Hawaii, established its antiexpansionist credentials. But after hesitating briefly, Cleveland picked up the naval program of his Republican predecessor, pressing Congress just as forcefully for more battleships (five were authorized) and making the same basic argument. The nation's commercial vitality—"free access to all markets," in the words of Cleveland's second secretary of state, Richard Olney—depended on its naval power.

While rejecting the colonialist aspects of Mahan's thinking, Cleveland absorbed the underlying strategic arguments about where America's vital interests lay. This explains the remarkable crisis that suddenly blew up in 1895 over Venezuela.

The Battleship Oregon
The battleship was the centerpiece of naval strategy in the industrial age and the key marker in the naval arms race among the Great Powers. Building a battleship fleet was America's ticket of entry to that race.

For years, a border dispute had simmered between Venezuela and British Guiana. Now the United States demanded that it be resolved. The European powers were carving up Africa and Asia. How could the United States be sure that the European nations did not have similar designs on Latin America? Indeed, prompted by President Cleveland, Secretary of State Olney made that point in a bristling note to London on July 25, 1895, insisting that Britain accept arbitration or face the consequences. Invoking the Monroe Doctrine, Olney intended to convey a clear message to Britain and the other European powers that the United States would brook no challenge to its vital interests in the Caribbean. (Note that these were America's vital interests, not those of Venezuela, which was not consulted during the entire dispute.)

Despite its suddenness, the pugnacious stand of the Cleveland administration was not an aberration, but a logical step in the new American foreign policy. Once the British realized that Cleveland meant business, they agreed to arbitration of the boundary dispute. Afterward, Olney remarked with satisfaction that as a great industrial nation, the United States needed "to accept [its] commanding position" and take its place "among the Powers of the earth." And other countries would have to accommodate the American need for access to "more markets and larger markets for the consumption and products of the industry and inventive genius of the American people."

The Ideology of Expansionism

As policymakers hammered out a new foreign policy, a sustaining body of ideology took shape. One source of expansionist dogma was the Social Darwinist theory that dominated the political thought of this era. If animals and plants evolved through the survival of the fittest, so did nations. "Nothing under the sun is stationary," warned the American social theorist Brooks Adams in *The Law of Civilization and Decay* (1895). "Not to advance is to recede." By this criterion, the United States had no choice; if it wanted to survive, it had to expand.

Linked to Social Darwinism was a spreading belief in the inherent superiority of the Anglo-Saxon "race." On both sides of the Atlantic, Anglo-Saxonism was in vogue. Thus did John Fiske, an American philosopher and historian, lecture the nation on its future responsibilities: "The work which the English race began when it colonized North America is destined to go on until every land on the earth's surface that is not already the seat of an old civilization shall become English in its language, in its religion, in its political habits, and to a predominant extent in the blood of its people."

Fiske entitled his lecture "Manifest Destiny." This term had been used half a century earlier to convey the sense of national mission—America's *Manifest Destiny*—to sweep aside the native American peoples and occupy the continent. In his widely read book *The Winning of the West* (1896), Theodore Roosevelt drew a parallel between the expansionism of his own time and the suppression of the Indians. It mattered little what happened to "backward peoples" because their conquest was "for the benefit of civilization and in the interests of mankind." More than historical parallels, however, linked the Manifest Destiny of the past and present.

In 1890 the U.S. Census reported the end of the westward movement on the American continent. The psychological impact of that news on Americans was profound, spawning, among other things, a new historical interpretation that stressed the importance of the frontier in shaping the nation's character. In his landmark essay setting out this thesis—"The Significance of the Frontier in American History" (1893)—the young historian Frederick Jackson Turner suggested a linkage between the closing of the frontier and overseas expansion. "He would be a rash prophet who should assert that the expansive character of American life has now entirely ceased," Turner wrote. "Movement has been its dominant fact, and, unless this training has no effect upon a people, the American energy will continually demand a wider field for its exercise." As Turner predicted, Manifest Destiny did turn outward.

Thus a strong current of ideas, deeply rooted in American experience and ideology, justified the new diplomacy of expansionism. The United States was eager to step onto the world stage. All it needed was the right occasion.

AN AMERICAN EMPIRE

Ever since Spain had lost its South American empire in the early nineteenth century, Cubans had yearned to join their mainland brothers and sisters in freedom. In February 1895 Cuban patriots rebelled and began a guerrilla war. A standoff developed; the Spaniards controlled the towns, the rebels much of the countryside. In early 1896 the newly appointed Spanish general, Valeriano Weyler, adopted a harsh policy of *reconcentration*, forcing entire populations into armed camps. Because no aggressive pursuit followed, reconcentration only inconvenienced the guerrilla fighters. The toll on civilians, however, was brutal. Out of a population of 1,600,000, as many as 200,000 may have died of starvation, exposure, or dysentery.

The Cuban Crisis

The rebel leaders recognized that their best hope was not military but political: they had to draw the United States into their struggle. A key group of exiles, the *junta*, set up shop in New York to make the case for *Cuba libre*. Their timing was perfect. William Randolph Hearst had just purchased the nearly bankrupt *New York Journal,* and he was in a hurry to build readership. Cuba was ideal for Hearst's purposes. Locked in a furious circulation war with Joseph Pulitzer's *New York World*, Hearst elevated Cuba's agony into flaming front-page headlines.

Across the country powerful sentiments stirred: humanitarian concern for the Cubans, sympathy with their aspirations for freedom, and a superpatriotism that became known as *jingoism.* Congress began calling for Cuban independence.

Cleveland, still in office when the rebellion broke out, took a cooler view of the situation. His concern was with America's vital interests, which, he told Congress, were "by no means of a wholly sentimental or philanthropic character." The Cuban civil war was disrupting the sizable trade between the two countries and destroying American investments, especially in Cuban sugar plantations. Cleveland was also worried that Spain's troubles might draw other European powers into the situation. A chronically unstable Cuba was incompatible with America's strategic interests, especially its plans for an interoceanic canal whose Caribbean approaches would have to be safeguarded.

If Spain could put down the rebellion, that was fine with Cleveland. But as Spain's impotence became clear, he urged the Spanish government to make reforms and resolve the crisis.

The McKinley administration, on taking office in March 1897, adopted much the same pragmatic line. Like Cleveland, McKinley was motivated by a conception of the United States as the dominant Caribbean power, with vital interests that had to be defended. McKinley, however, was inclined to be tougher on the Spaniards. For one thing, he was more appalled by their "uncivilized and inhumane conduct" in Cuba. And he had to contend with rising jingoism in the Republican party. But the notion, long held by historians, that McKinley was swept along against his better judgment by popular opinion and by a Republican war faction led by Theodore Roosevelt, Henry Cabot Lodge, and other aggressive advocates of a "large policy" was not true. McKinley was very much his own man. He was a skilled politician and a canny, if undramatic, president. He would not proceed until he sensed a broad national consensus for war. In particular, McKinley was sensitive to business interests fearful of disruption to an economy just recovering from depression.

The American pressure on Spain at first seemed to pay off. The conservative regime fell, and a liberal government, upon taking office in October 1897, moderated its Cuban policy. Spain recalled Weyler, limited reconcentration, and adopted an autonomy plan granting Cuba a degree of self-rule but not independence. Madrid's incapacity soon became clear, however. In January 1898, Spanish loyalists in Havana rioted against the offer of autonomy. The Cuban rebels, encouraged by the prospect of American intervention, demanded full independence.

On February 9, 1898, Hearst's *New York Journal* published a private letter of Dupuy de Lôme, the Spanish minister to the United States. In it de Lôme called President McKinley "weak" and "a bidder for the admiration of the crowd." Worse, his letter suggested that the Spanish government was not taking the American demands for reform seriously. De Lôme immediately resigned, but the damage had been done.

A week later the U.S. battleship *Maine*, at anchor in Havana harbor on a "courtesy" visit, blew up and sank, with the loss of 260 seamen. "Whole Country Thrills with the War Fever," proclaimed the *New York Journal*. From that moment onward, popular passions against Spain became a major factor in the march toward war.

But McKinley kept his head. He assumed that the sinking had been accidental: what motive could the Spanish have had for attacking the *Maine*? A naval board of inquiry, however, found that the sinking had been caused by a mine, not, as seems more likely, by an accidental explosion inside the ship. No evidence linked the Spanish to the sinking, but they had failed to protect the *Maine* from attack.

President McKinley had no stomach for the martial spirit engulfing the country. He was not swept along by the calls for blood to avenge the *Maine*. But he did have to attend to an aroused public opinion. Hesitant business leaders now also became impatient for the dispute with Spain to end. War was preferable to the unresolved Cuban crisis. On March 27 McKinley cabled to Madrid what was in effect an ultimatum: an immediate armistice for six months; abandonment of the practice of reconcentration; and, with the United States as mediator, peace negotiations with the rebels. A telegram the next day added that only Cuban independence would be regarded as a satisfactory outcome to the negotiations. Spain categorically rejected these humiliating demands.

On April 11 McKinley asked Congress for authority to intervene to end the fighting in Cuba. His motives were as he described them: "In the name of humanity, in the name of civilization, in behalf of endangered American interests which give us the right and the duty to speak and to act, the war in Cuba must stop." The War Hawks in Congress—a mixture of Republican jingoists and proindependence western Democrats—chafed under McKinley's cautious progress. But the president did not lose control, and he defeated the War Hawks on the crucial issue of recognizing the rebel republican government, which would have greatly reduced the administration's freedom of action in dealing with Spain.

The resolutions authorizing intervention in Cuba contained an amendment by Senator Henry M. Teller of Colorado disclaiming any intention by the United States of taking possession of Cuba. No European government should say that "when we go out to make battle for the liberty and freedom of Cuban patriots, that we are doing it for the purpose of aggrandizement." This had to be made clear with regard to Cuba, "whatever," Senator Teller added, "we may do as to some other islands."

Did McKinley have in mind "some other islands"? Was this really a war of aggression, secretly motivated by a desire to seize strategic territory from Spain? In a strict sense, almost certainly no. It was not *because* of expansionist ambitions that McKinley forced Spain into a corner. On the other hand, once war came McKinley saw it as an opportunity. As he wrote privately after hostilities began: "While we are conducting war and until its conclusion, we must keep all we get; when the war is over we must keep what we want." Precisely what would be forthcoming, of course, depended on the fortunes of battle.

The Spoils of War

Hostilities formally began when Spain declared war on April 24, 1898. Across the country, regiments began to form up. Theodore Roosevelt immediately resigned as assistant secretary of the navy, ordered a fancy uniform, and was commissioned lieutenant colonel in a volunteer cavalry regiment that would become famous as the Rough Riders. Raw recruits poured into makeshift bases around Tampa, Florida. Confusion reigned. Tropical uniforms did not arrive; the food was bad, the sanitation worse; and rifles were in short supply. No provision had been made for getting the troops to Cuba; the government hastily began to collect a miscellaneous fleet of yachts, lake steamers, and commercial boats. Fortunately, the small regular army was a disciplined, highly professional force, and its 28,000 seasoned troops provided a nucleus for the 200,000 civilians who had to be turned into soldiers inside of a few weeks.

The navy was in much better shape. Spain had nothing to match America's seven battleships and armored cruisers, and the ships it did have were undermanned and ill prepared for battle. The Spanish admiral, Pascual Cervera, gloomily expected that his fleet would "like Don Quixote go out to fight windmills and come back with a broken head."

On April 23, Commodore George Dewey's small Pacific fleet set sail from Hong Kong for the Philippines. Here, at this Spanish possession in the far Pacific, not in Cuba, the decisive engagement of the war took place. On May 1 Dewey cornered the Spanish fleet in Manila Bay and destroyed it. The victory produced euphoria in the United States. Immediately, part of the army being trained for the Cuban campaign was diverted to the Philippines. Manila, the Philippine capital, fell on August 13, 1898 (see Map 22.1).

With Dewey's victory, American strategic thinking clicked into place. "We hold the other side of the Pacific and the value to this country is almost beyond imagination," declared Senator Lodge. "We must on no account let the [Philippine] Islands go." President McKinley agreed, and so did his key advisers. An anchor in the western Pacific had long been coveted by naval strategists. At this time, too, the Great Powers were carving up China into spheres of influence. If American merchants wanted a place in that glittering market, the power of the United States would have to be projected into Asia.

Once the decision for a Philippine base had been made, other decisions followed almost automatically. The question of Hawaii was quickly resolved. After stalling the previous year, Hawaiian annexation went through Congress by joint resolution in July 1898. Hawaii had suddenly acquired a crucial strategic value: it was a halfway station to the Philippines. The navy pressed for a coaling base in the central Pacific; that meant Guam, a Spanish island in the Marianas. There was need also for a strategically located base in the Caribbean; that meant Puerto Rico. By July, before the assault on Cuba, the full scope of McKinley's war aims had taken shape.

The campaign in Cuba was something of an anticlimax. The Spanish fleet was bottled up in Santiago harbor, and the city itself became the key to the military campaign. Half trained and ill equipped, the American forces moving on Santiago might have been checked by a determined opponent. The Spaniards would fight to maintain their honor, but they had no stomach for a real war against the Americans.

The main battle, on July 1, occurred near Santiago on the heights commanded by San Juan Hill. Roosevelt's dismounted Rough Riders (there had been no room for horses on the transports) seized Kettle Hill. Then the frontal assault against the San Juan heights began. Four black regiments took the brunt of the fighting. White observers grudgingly credited much of the victory to the "superb gallantry" of the black soldiers. In fact, it was not quite a victory. The Spaniards, driven from their forward positions, retreated to a well-fortified second line. The exhausted Americans had suffered heavy casualties; whether they could have mounted a second assault was questionable. They were spared this test, however, by the Spanish. On July 3 Cervera's fleet in Santiago harbor made a suicidal daylight attempt to run the American blockade and was destroyed. A few days later, convinced that Santiago could not be saved, the Spanish forces surrendered.

The two nations then signed an armistice in which Spain agreed to give up Cuba and cede Puerto Rico and Guam to the United States. American forces would occupy Manila pending a peace treaty.

THE PHILIPPINE THEATER

CHINA

Hong Kong (Br.)

FORMOSA (Japanese)

HAINAN (China)

DEWEY

Pacific Ocean

Luzon

FRENCH INDOCHINA

Manila   PHILIPPINE ISLANDS (Spanish)

South China Sea

Sulu Sea

Mindanao

0   250   500
Miles

Bataan   Manila Bay   Manila May 1, 1898

Corregidor Is.

DEWEY'S FLEET

MAP 22.1
The Spanish-American War

The swift American victory in the Spanish-American War resulted from overwhelming naval superiority. Dewey's destruction of the Spanish fleet in Manila harbor doomed the Spaniards in the Philippines. In Cuba, American ground forces won a hard victory on San Juan Hill, for they were ill equipped and poorly supplied. With the United States in control of the seas, the Spaniards saw no choice but to give up the battle for Cuba.

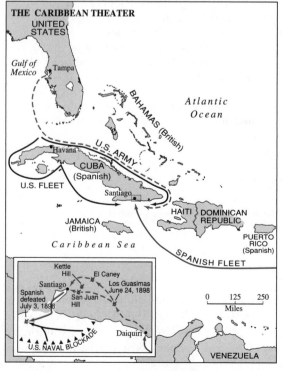

THE CARIBBEAN THEATER

UNITED STATES

Gulf of Mexico   Tampa

BAHAMAS (British)

Atlantic Ocean

Havana

U.S. ARMY

CUBA (Spanish)

U.S. FLEET

Santiago

HAITI   DOMINICAN REPUBLIC

JAMAICA (British)

PUERTO RICO (Spanish)

Caribbean Sea

SPANISH FLEET

Kettle Hill   El Caney

Santiago   Los Guasimas June 24, 1898

Spanish defeated July 3, 1898   San Juan Hill

0   125   250
Miles

Daiquiri

U.S. NAVAL BLOCKADE

VENEZUELA

Black Soldiers in a White Man's War

George W. Prioleau, the chaplain of the Ninth Cavalry regiment, expresses his bitterness against the racism experienced by black troopers in the South on their way to battle in Cuba.

Hon. H. C. Smith
Editor, *Gazette*

Dear Sir:
All the way from northwest Nebraska this regiment was greeted with cheers and hurrahs. At places where we stopped the people assembled by the thousands. While the Ninth Cavalry band would play some national air the people would raise their hats, men, women and children would wave their handkerchiefs, and the heavens would resound with their hearty cheers. . . . These demonstrations, so enthusiastically given, greeted us all the way until we reached Nashville. . . . From there until we reached Chattanooga there was not a cheer given us. . . .

    The prejudice against the Negro soldier and the Negro was great, but it was of heavenly origin to what it is in this part of Florida. . . . The southerners have made their laws and the Negroes know and obey them. They never stop to ask a white man a question. He (Negro) never thinks of disobeying. . . . Talk about fighting and freeing poor Cuba and of Spain's brutality; of Cuba's murdered thousands, and starving recon-centradoes. Is America any better than Spain? Has she not subjects in her very midst who are murdered daily without a trial of judge or jury? Has she not subjects in her own borders whose children are half-fed and half-clothed, because their father's skin is black. . . . Yet the Negro is loyal to his country's flag. . . .

    The four Negro regiments are going to help free Cuba, and they will return to their homes, some then mustered out and begin again to fight the battle of American prejudice. . . .

Yours truly,
Geo. W. Prioleau, Chaplain, Ninth Cavalry

SOURCE: *Cleveland Gazette* (May 13, 1898), reprinted in Willard B. Gatewood, *"Smoked Yankees" and the Struggle for Empire, 1898–1902* (Urbana: University of Illinois Press, 1971), 27–29.

The Imperial Experiment

The big question was the Philippines. This was an archipelago, or group, of over 7,000 islands populated—as William R. Day, McKinley's secretary of state, put it in the racist language of that era—by "eight or nine millions of absolutely ignorant and many degraded people." Not even the most avid

American expansionists advocated colonial rule over such a population: that was European-style imperialism, not the strategic bases that Mahan and his followers had in mind. Both Mahan and Lodge initially advocated keeping only Manila. It gradually became clear, however, that Manila was not defensible without the whole of Luzon, the large island on which the city is located.

McKinley and his advisers surveyed the options. One possibility was to return most of the islands to Spain, but the reputed evils of Spanish rule made that a "cowardly and dishonorable" solution. Another possibility was to partition the Philippines with one or more of the Great Powers. But as McKinley observed, to turn over valuable territory to "our commercial rivals in the Orient—that would have been bad business and discreditable."

Most plausible was the option of granting the Philippines independence. As in Cuba, Spanish rule had already stirred up a rebellion, led by the fiery patriot Emilio Aguinaldo. An arrangement might have been possible like the one being negotiated with the Cubans over Guantanamo Bay: the lease of a naval base to the Americans as the price of freedom. But after some hesitation McKinley was persuaded that "we could not leave [the Filipinos] to themselves—they were unfit for self-rule—and they would soon have anarchy and misrule over there worse than Spain's was."

As for the Spaniards, they had little choice against what they considered "the immoderate demands of a conquerer." In the Treaty of Paris they ceded the Philippines to the United States for a payment of $20 million. The treaty encountered harder going at home, and was ratified by the Senate (requiring a two-thirds majority) on February 6, 1899, with only a single vote to spare.

The narrowness of the administration's victory signaled the revival of an antiexpansionist tradition that had been briefly silenced by the patriotic passions of a nation at war. In the Senate, opponents of the treaty invoked the country's republican principles. Under the Constitution, argued the conservative Republican George F. Hoar, "no power is given to the Federal Government to acquire territory to be held and governed permanently as colonies" or "to conquer alien people and hold them in subjugation."

Leading citizens enlisted in the anti-imperialist cause, including the steelmaker Andrew Carnegie, who offered a check for $20 million to purchase the independence of the Philippines; the labor leader Samuel Gompers, who feared the competition of cheap Filipino labor; and Jane Addams, who believed that women should stand for peace. The key group, however, was a social elite of old-line Mugwump reformers such as Carl Schurz, Charles Eliot Norton, and Charles Francis Adams. In November 1898 a Boston group formed the first Anti-Imperialist League, from which blossomed a national movement over the next year.

Skillful at publicizing their cause, the anti-imperialists never managed to develop a mass following. They were an ill-assorted lot, divided in many ways, and within the Mugwump core, lacking the common touch. Nor was it easy to translate anti-imperialism into a viable political cause because the Democrats, once the treaty had been adopted, waffled over the issue. Still, if it was an accomplished fact, Philippine annexation lost the moral high ground because of the awful events that began to unfold in the Philippines.

Two days before the Senate ratified the treaty, on February 4, 1899, fighting broke out between American and Filipino patrols on the edge of Manila. Confronted by American annexation, Aguinaldo asserted his nation's independence and turned his guns on the occupying American forces.

The ensuing conflict far exceeded in ferocity the war just concluded with Spain. Fighting tenacious guerrillas, the U.S. Army resorted to the same reconcentration tactic the Spaniards had used in Cuba, moving people into towns, carrying out indiscriminate attacks outside the town limits, and burning crops and villages. In three years of warfare 4,200 Americans and many thousands of Filipinos died. The fighting ended in 1902, and Judge William Howard Taft, who had been appointed governor in 1901, set up a civilian government. He intended to make the Philippines a model of American road building and sanitary engineering.

McKinley's convincing victory over William Jennings Bryan in the 1900 election, although by no means a referendum on American expansionism, suggested popular satisfaction with America's overseas adventure. Yet a strong undercurrent of misgivings was evident. Americans had not anticipated the

Fighting the Filipinos
The United States went to war against Spain in 1898 partly out of sympathy with the Cuban struggle for independence. Yet the United States found it necessary to use the same brutal tactics to put down the Filipino struggle for independence that the Spaniards had used against the Cubans. Here the Twentieth Kansas Volunteers march through the burning village of Caloocan.

The Water Cure

In 1902, after the fighting had ceased, the U.S. Senate held hearing on the conduct of the war in the Philippines. This is the testimony of Corporal Daniel J. Evans, Twelfth Infantry, about his service on the island of Luzon.

Question: The committee would like to hear . . . whether you were the witness to any cruelties inflicted upon the natives of the Philippine Islands; and if so, under what circumstances.—*Answer:* The case I had reference to was where they gave the water cure to a native in the Ilicano Province at Ilocos Norte . . . about the month of August 1900. There were two native scouts with the American forces. They went out and brought in a couple of insurgents. . . . They tried to get from this insurgent . . . where the rest of the insurgents were at that time. . . . The first thing one of the Americans—I mean one of the scouts for the Americans—grabbed one of the men by the head and jerked his head back, and then they took a tomato can and poured water down his throat until he could hold no more. . . . Then they forced a gag into his mouth; they stood him up . . . against a post and fastened him so that he could not move. Then one man, an American soldier, who was over six feet tall, and who was very strong, too, struck this native in the pit of the stomach as hard as he could. . . . They kept that operation up for quite a time, and finally I thought the fellow was about to die, but I don't believe he was as bad as that, because finally he told them he would tell, and from that time on he was taken away, and I saw no more of him. . . .

Question: What is your observation as to the treatment of the people engaged in peaceable pursuits, as to kindness and consideration, or the reverse, from the American officers and the men?—*Answer:* They were never molested if they seemed to be peaceable natives. They would not be molested unless they showed some signs of hostility. . . . If we struck a part of the island where the natives were hostile and they would fire on our soldiers or even cut the telegraph lines, the result would be that their barrios would probably be burned.

SOURCE: Henry F. Graff, ed., *American Imperialism and the Philippine Insurrection* (Boston: Little, Brown, 1969), 80–84,

brutal methods needed to subdue the Filipino guerrillas. "We are destroying these islanders by the thousands, their villages and cities," protested the philosopher William James. "No life shall you have, we say, except as a gift from our philanthropy after your unconditional surrender to our will. . . . Could there be any more damning indictment of that whole bloated ideal termed 'modern civilization'?"

There were, moreover, disturbing constitutional issues to be resolved. Did the Constitution extend to the acquired territories? Did their inhabitants automatically become U.S. citizens? In 1901 the Supreme Court ruled negatively on both questions; these were matters for Congress to decide. A special commission appointed by McKinley recommended independence for the islands after an indefinite period of U.S. rule, during which the Filipinos would be prepared for self-government. In 1916 the Jones Act formally committed the United States to granting Philippine independence, but set no date.

The ugly business in the Philippines rubbed off some of the moralizing gloss, but left undeflected America's global aspirations. In a few years the United States had acquired the makings of a strategic overseas empire: Hawaii; Puerto Rico; Guam; the Philippines; and finally, in 1900, several of the Samoan islands that the United States had administered jointly with Germany and Britain. The United States, remarked the legal scholar John Bassett Moore in 1899, had moved "from a position of comparative freedom from entanglements into a position of what is commonly called a world power."

ONTO THE WORLD STAGE

In Europe the flexing of America's muscles against Spain caused a certain amount of consternation. At the urging of Kaiser Wilhelm II of Germany, the major powers had tried before war broke out to intercede on Spain's behalf—but tentatively, because no one was looking for trouble with the Americans. President McKinley had listened politely to the representations of their envoys on April 6, 1898, and had then, dismissively, proceeded with his war.

The decisive outcome confirmed what the Europeans already suspected. After Dewey's naval victory, the semiofficial French paper *Le Temps* observed that "what passes before our eyes is the appearance of a new power of the first order." And the London *Times* predicted, "In the future America will play a part in the general affairs of the world such as she has never played before."

A Power among Powers

The politician most ardently agreeing with the London *Times*'s vision of America's future was the man who, with the assassination of William McKinley, became president on September 14, 1901. Theodore Roosevelt was an avid student of world affairs, widely traveled and acquainted with many of the European leaders. He had no doubt about America's role in the world.

It was important, first of all, to uphold the country's honor in the community of nations. Nor should the country shrink from righteous battle. "All the great masterful races have been fighting races," Roosevelt declared. But when he spoke of war, Roosevelt had in mind actions by the "civilized" nations against "backward peoples" (such as the Filipinos whose struggle for freedom was being subdued when he entered the White House). That was why Roosevelt sympathized with European imperialism, and how he justified American dominance in the Caribbean.

As for the "civilized and orderly" policemen of the world, however, the worst thing that could happen was for them to fall to fighting among themselves. Roosevelt had an acute sense of the fragility of world peace, and he was farsighted about the chances—in this he was truly exceptional among Americans—of a catastrophic world war. He believed America was responsible for helping to maintain the balance of power.

The cornerstone of Roosevelt's thinking was Anglo-American amity. The British, increasingly isolated in world affairs, eagerly reciprocated. In the Hay-Pauncefote Agreement (1901) they gave up their treaty rights to joint participation in any Central American canal project, clearing the way for a canal under exclusive U.S. control. And two years later the last of the vexing U.S.–Canadian border disputes, this one involving British Columbia and Alaska, was settled, again to American satisfaction. No formal alliance was forthcoming, but Anglo-American friendship had been placed on such a firm basis that after 1901 the British admiralty designed its war plans on the assumption that America was "a kindred state with whom we shall never have a parricidal war."

Among nations, however, what counted was strength, not merely goodwill. Roosevelt wanted "to make all foreign powers understand that when we have adopted a line of policy we have adopted it definitely, and with the intention of backing it up with deeds as well as words." As Roosevelt famously said: "Speak softly and carry a big stick." By a "big stick" he meant above all naval power. Under Roosevelt, the battleship program went on apace. By 1904 the U.S. Navy stood fifth in the world; by 1907, it was second only to Britain's.

A canal across Panama came next on Roosevelt's agenda. With Britain's surrender of its joint rights in 1901, Roosevelt proceeded to the more troublesome task of leasing from Colombia the needed strip of land across its Panamanian province. Furious when the Colombian legislature voted down the proposed treaty, Roosevelt contemplated outright seizure of Panama, but settled on a more devious solution. Informed that an independence movement was brewing in Panama, the United States lent secret assistance that enabled the bloodless revolution against Colombia to go off on schedule. On November 7, 1903, the United States recognized Panama, and two weeks later it received a perpetually renewable lease on a canal zone. These machinations were a dirty business, but they got Roosevelt what he wanted. He never regretted the victimization of Colombia, although the United States, as a kind of conscience money, paid Colombia $25 million in 1922.

Building the canal was one of the heroic engineering feats of the century, involving a swamp-clearing project to rid the area of malaria and yellow fever,

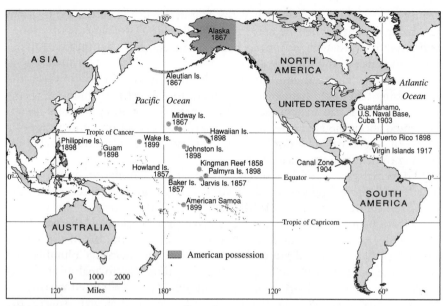

MAP 22.2
The American Empire
In 1890 Alfred T. Mahan wrote that the United States should regard the oceans as "a great highway" across which America would carry on world trade. That was precisely what resulted from the empire the United States acquired after the Spanish-American War. The Caribbean possessions, the strategically located Pacific islands, and, in 1904, the Panama Canal Zone gave the United States commercial and naval access to a wider world.

the construction of a series of great locks, and the excavation of 240 million cubic yards of earth. It took the U.S. Army Corps of Engineers eight years to finish the huge project. Opened in 1914, the Panama Canal gave the United States a commanding commercial and strategic position in the Western Hemisphere (see Map 22.2).

Next came the task of making the Caribbean basin secure. The countries there, said Secretary of State Elihu Root, had been placed "in the front yard of the United States" by the Panama Canal. Therefore, Roosevelt added, they had to "behave themselves." Believing that instability in the Caribbean invited the intervention of European powers, Roosevelt announced in 1904 that the United States would act as "policeman" of the region, stepping in, "however reluctantly, in flagrant cases . . . of wrong doing or impotence."

This policy became known as the Roosevelt Corollary to the Monroe Doctrine. It transformed what had been a broad principle of opposition against European expansionist ambitions in Latin America into an unrestricted American right to regulate Caribbean affairs. The Roosevelt Corollary was not a treaty with other states; it was a unilateral declaration sanctioned only by American power and national interest.

Under the Roosevelt Corollary the United States intervened regularly in the internal affairs of Caribbean states (see Map 22.3). In the case of Cuba, a condition of its independence had been a proviso in its constitution called the Platt amendment, which gave the United States the right to intervene if Cuba's independence or internal order was threatened. Elsewhere there was not even this semblance of legality. In 1905 American authorities took over the customs and debt management of the Dominican Republic, and similarly, Nicaragua in 1911 and Haiti in 1916. When domestic order broke down, the U.S. Marines occupied Cuba in 1906, Nicaragua in 1909, and Haiti and the Dominican Republic in later years.

The Open Door

In China, the occupying powers quickly instituted discriminatory trade regulations in their zones of control. Fearful of being frozen out of the China market, U.S. Secretary of State John Hay in 1899 sent them an "Open Door" note advancing a right of equal trade access—the Open Door—for all nations that wanted to do business in China. Even with its Philippine bases, the United States lacked real leverage and received no better than ambiguous and

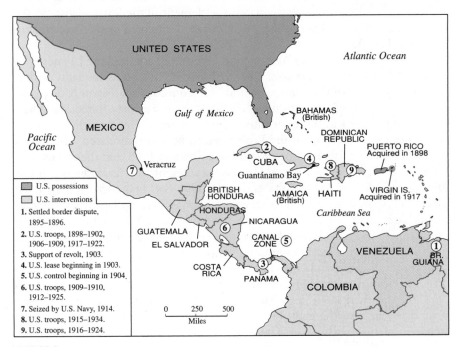

MAP 22.3
Policeman of the Caribbean
After the Spanish-American War the United States vigorously asserted its interest in the affairs of its neighbors to the south. As the record of interventions shows, the United States truly became the "policeman" of the Caribbean.

noncommital responses from the occupying powers. But Hay chose to interpret them as accepting the American Open Door position.

When a secret society of Chinese nationalists, the Boxers, rebelled against the foreigners in 1900, the United States joined the multinational campaign to raise the siege of the foreign legations in Peking (Beijing). America took this opportunity to assert a second principle of the Open Door: that China would be preserved as a "territorial and administrative entity." As long as the legal fiction of an independent China survived, so would American claims to equal access to the China market.

The European powers had acceded to American claims to preeminence in the Caribbean. But in the Far East Britain, Germany, France, and Russia were strongly entrenched, and not inclined to defer to American interests. The United States also confronted a powerful Asian nation—Japan—that had its own vital interests. Although the Open Door was important to him, Roosevelt quickly saw in the Pacific a deadlier game of power politics that called for American involvement.

In 1904 Japan, provoked by Russian demands for its military withdrawal from northern Korea, suddenly attacked the Tsar's fleet at Port Arthur, Russia's leased port in China. In a series of brilliant victories, the Japanese demolished the Russian military forces in Asia. Anxious to restore some semblance of a balance of power, Roosevelt mediated a settlement of the Russo-Japanese War at Portsmouth, New Hampshire, in 1905. Japan emerged as the predominant power in East Asia.

Contemptuous of other Asian nations, Roosevelt admired the Japanese—"a wonderful and civilized people . . . entitled to stand in absolute equality with all the other peoples of the civilized world." He conceded that Japan had "a paramount interest in what surrounds the Yellow Sea, just as the United States has a paramount interest in what surrounds the Caribbean." But American strategic and commercial interests in the Pacific had to be accommodated. The United States approved of Japan's protectorate over Korea in 1905, and then of its claim of full sovereignty six years later. However, a surge of anti-Asian feeling in California complicated Roosevelt's efforts. In 1906 San Francisco's school board placed all Asian students in a segregated school, infuriating Japan. The "gentlemen's agreement" of 1907, in which Japan agreed to restrict immigration to the United States, smoothed matters over, but the periodic resurgence of racism in California led to continuing tensions with the Japanese.

Roosevelt meanwhile moved to balance Japan's military power by increasing American naval strength in the Pacific. American battleships visited Japan in 1908 and then made a global tour in an impressive display of sea power. Late that year, near the end of his administration, Roosevelt achieved a formal accommodation with Japan. The Root-Takahira Treaty confirmed the status quo in the Pacific, as well as the principles of free oceanic commerce and equal trade opportunity in China.

However, William Howard Taft entered the White House in 1909 convinced that the United States had been shortchanged. He pressed for a larger role for American bankers and investors in the Far East, especially in the railroad construction going on in China. An exponent of Dollar Diplomacy, Taft hoped that American capital would counterbalance Japanese power and pave the way for increased commercial opportunities. When the Chinese Revolution of 1911 toppled the ruling Manchu dynasty, Taft supported the Chinese Nationalists as a counterforce to the Japanese. The United States thus entered a long-term rivalry with Japan that would end in war thirty years later.

The triumphant thrust across the Pacific lost some of its luster. The United States had become embroiled in a distant struggle that promised many future liabilities, but few of the fabulous profits that had lured Americans to Asia.

Woodrow Wilson and Mexico

When Woodrow Wilson became president in 1913, he was bent on reform in American foreign policy no less than in domestic politics. Wilson did not really differ with his predecessors on the importance of economic development overseas. He applauded the "tides of commerce" that would arise from the Panama Canal. But he opposed Dollar Diplomacy, which bullied weaker countries into inequitable financial relationships and gave undue advantage to American business. It seemed to Wilson "a very perilous thing to determine the foreign policy of a nation in terms of material interest."

The United States, Wilson insisted, should conduct its foreign policy in conformity with its democratic principles. He intended to foster the "development of constitutional liberty in the world," and above all to extend it to the nation's neighbors in Latin America. In a major policy speech in October 1913 Wilson promised those nations that the United States would "never again seek one additional foot of territory by conquest." The president committed himself to advancing "human rights, national integrity, and opportunity" in Latin America. To do otherwise would make "ourselves untrue to our own traditions."

Mexico became the primary object of Wilson's ministrations. A cycle of revolutions had begun there in 1911. The dictator Porfirio Diaz was overthrown by Francisco Madero, who spoke much as Wilson did about liberty and constitutionalism. But Madero was deposed and murdered in February 1913 by one of his generals, Victoriano Huerta. Other powers quickly recognized Huerta's provisional government, but not the United States. Wilson abhorred Huerta; he called him a murderer and pledged "to force him out."

By intervening in this way, "we act in the interest of Mexico alone. . . . We are seeking to counsel Mexico for its own good." Wilson meant that he intended to put the Mexican revolution back on the constitutional path started by Madero. Wilson was not deterred by the fact that American business interests, with enormous investments in Mexico, favored Huerta.

The emergence of armed opposition in northern Mexico under Venustiano Carranza strengthened Wilson's hand. Carranza's Constitutionalist movement, ardently nationalist, had no desire for American intervention in

Carranza
Venustiano Carranza (1859–1920) was a provincial political figure who turned revolutionary when the dictator Diaz intervened in his election for the governorship of Coahuila in 1910. Carranza proved to be only a transitional figure because, as an old-fashioned liberal, he opposed the statist direction the revolution took. Before his term as first elected president ended in 1920, he was overthrown and killed in an ambush.

Mexican affairs. Carranza angrily rebuffed Wilson's efforts to bring about elections through a compromise between the rebels and the Mexican government. He also vowed to fight any intrusion of U.S. troops in his country. All he wanted from Wilson, Carranza asserted, was recognition of the Constitutionalists' belligerent status, so they could purchase arms in the United States. In exchange for vague promises to respect property rights and "fair" foreign concessions, Carranza finally got his way in 1914. American weapons began to flow to his troops.

When it became clear that Huerta was not about to fall, the United States threw its own forces into the game. On the pretext of a minor insult to the U.S. Navy, Wilson ordered the occupation of the major port of Veracruz on April 21, 1914, an action that cost 19 American and 126 Mexican lives. At that point the Huerta regime began to crumble. Carranza nevertheless condemned the United States, and his forces came close to engaging the Americans. When he entered Mexico City in triumph in August 1914, Carranza had some cause to thank the Yankees. But if any sense of gratitude existed, it was overshadowed by the anti-Americanism inspired by Wilson's insensitivity to Mexican pride and revolutionary zeal.

This sad chapter in Mexican-American relations had a chastening effect on Wilson. It revealed to him the difficulties of acting on, or even living up to, well-meant ideals amid the confusion of war, revolution, and clashing national interests. Nor, in fact, did those ideals deter him when trouble brewed in the Caribbean. Despite his anti-imperialist pronouncements, Wilson acted just as his predecessors had by sending the U.S. Marines into Haiti in 1915 and into the Dominican Republic in 1916.

The Gathering Storm in Europe

In the meantime, Europe had begun to drift toward a great world war. There were two main sources of tension. One derived from the deadly rivalry between Germany, the new military and economic superpower of Europe, and the European states threatened by its might—above all France, which had been humiliated in the Franco-Prussian War of 1870. The second danger zone was the Balkans, where the Ottoman Empire was disintegrating and where, in the midst of explosive ethnic rivalries, Austria-Hungary and Russia were maneuvering for dominance. On the basis of these conflicts an alliance system had emerged, with Germany, Austria-Hungary, and Italy (the Triple Alliance) on one side and France and Russia (the Dual Alliance) on the other.

The tensions in Europe were partially released by European imperial adventures, especially by France in Africa and by Russia in Asia. These activities placed France and Russia in opposition to imperial Britain, effectively excluding Britain from the European alliance system. Fearful of Germany, however, Britain in 1904 composed her differences with France, and the two countries reached a friendly understanding, or *entente*. When Britain came to a similar understanding with Russia in 1907, the basis was laid for the Triple Entente. A deadly confrontation between two great European power blocs became possible.

In these European quarrels Americans had no obvious stake, nor any inclination, in the words of a cautionary Senate resolution, "to depart from the traditional American foreign policy which forbids participation . . . [in] political questions which are entirely European in scope." But on becoming president, Theodore Roosevelt had taken a lively interest in European affairs, and he was eager, as the head of a great power, to make a contribution to the cause of peace there. In 1905 he got his chance.

The Anglo-French entente of the previous year had been based partly on an agreement over North Africa: the Sudan was conceded to Britain, Morocco to France. Now Germany suddenly challenged France over Morocco— a disastrous move, contrary to Germany's interest in keeping France's attention diverted from Europe. Kaiser Wilhelm turned to Roosevelt for help. Roosevelt arranged an international conference, which was held in January 1906 at Algeciras, Spain. With U.S. diplomats playing a key role, the crisis was defused. Germany got a few token concessions, but France's dominance over Morocco was sustained.

Algeciras marked, in actuality, an ominous moment at which the power blocs that would become locked in battle in 1914 first squared off against one another. But at the time it looked like a diplomatic triumph, and Roosevelt's secretary of state, Elihu Root, boasted of America's success in "preserv[ing] world peace because of the power of our detachment." Root's words prefigured how the United States would define its role among the Great Powers: it would be the apostle of peace, distinguished by its "detachment," by its lack of selfish interest in European affairs.

But opposing this internationalist impulse was the tenacious grip of America's traditional isolationism. American had applauded the international peace movement that had been launched by the Hague Peace Conference of 1899. The Permanent Court of Arbitration created by the Hague conference offered new hope for the peaceful settlement of international disputes. Both the Roosevelt and the Taft administrations negotiated arbitration treaties with other countries, pledging to submit their disputes to the Hague Court—only to see the treaties emasculated by a Senate unwilling to permit the nation's sovereignty to be compromised in any significant way. Nor was there any sequel to Roosevelt's initiative at Algeciras. It had been coolly received in the Senate and by the nation's press.

Woodrow Wilson's secretary of state, William Jennings Bryan, was a great apostle of world peace. Bryan devoted himself to negotiating a series of "cooling-off" treaties with other countries—so called because the parties agreed to wait for one year while disputed issues were submitted to a conciliation process. These bilateral agreements were admirable, but they were irrelevant to the explosive power politics of Europe. As tensions there reached the breaking point in 1914, the United States remained effectively on the sidelines.

Yet at Algeciras Roosevelt had rightly seen what the future would demand of America. So did the French writer Andre Tardieu, who remarked in 1908:

The United States is . . . a world power. . . . Its power creates for it . . . a duty—to pronounce upon all those questions that hitherto have been arranged by agreement only among European powers. . . . The United States intervenes thus in the affairs of the universe. . . . It is seated at the table where the great game is played, and it cannot leave it.

1867	Purchase of Alaska
1871	Settlement of *Alabama* claims
1875	Treaty brings Hawaii within U.S. orbit
1876	United States achieves favorable balance of trade
1881	Secretary of State James G. Blaine inaugurates Pan-Americanism
1889	President Benjamin Harrison begins rebuilding U.S. Navy
1890	Alfred Thayer Mahan publishes *The Influence of Seapower upon History*
1893	Annexation of Hawaii fails Frederick Jackson Turner's "The Significance of the Frontier in American History" Panic of 1893 ushers in economic depression (until 1897)
1894	Sino-Japanese war begins breakup of China into spheres of influence
1895	Venezuela crisis Cuban civil war
1898	Outbreak of Spanish-American War Hawaii annexed Anti-imperialist movement launched
1899	Treaty of Paris Guerrilla war in the Philippines Open Door policy in China
1901	Theodore Roosevelt becomes president; diplomacy of the "big stick" Hay-Pauncefote Agreement
1902	U.S. withdraws from Cuba; Platt amendment gives U.S. right of intervention
1903	U.S. recognizes Panama and receives grant of Canal Zone
1904	Roosevelt Corollary
1906	U.S. mediates Franco-German crisis over Morocco at Algeciras, Spain
1907	Gentlemen's Agreement with Japan
1908	Root-Takahira Treaty
1909	William Howard Taft becomes president; Dollar Diplomacy
1913	Woodrow Wilson asserts new principles for American diplomacy
1914	Intervention in the Mexican Revolution Panama Canal opens World War I begins

THEMATIC TIMELINE

	GOVERNMENT The Rise of the State	DIPLOMACY From Isolation to World Leadership	ECONOMY Prosperity, Depression, and War	SOCIETY Migration, Consumer Culture, and Social Change
1914	Wartime agencies expand power of the federal government	U.S. enters World War I, 1917	Shift from debtor to creditor nation Agricultural glut	Blacks migrate to northern cities
1920	Republican ascendancy Prohibition, 1920–33 Business-government partnership	Treaty of Versailles rejected by U.S. Senate, 1920 Washington Conference sets naval limits, 1922	Recession, 1920–21 Booming prosperity, 1922–29 Welfare capitalism	National Origins Act Mexican immigration increases Advertising promotes consumer culture, supports radio and news magazines
1930	Franklin D. Roosevelt becomes president, 1933 The New Deal: unprecedented government intervention in economy, social welfare, arts	Good Neighbor Policy toward Latin America, 1933 Abraham Lincoln Brigade fights in Spanish Civil War U.S. neutrality proclaimed, 1939	Great Depression, 1929–1941 Rise of labor movement	Dust Bowl migration to California and the West Indian New Deal Documentary impulse Federal patronage of the arts
1940	Government mobilizes industry for war production Rationing	U.S. enters World War II, 1941 Allies defeat Axis powers; bombing of Hiroshima, 1945	War mobilization ends depression	Rural whites and blacks migrate to war jobs in cities Civil-rights movement revitalized Film industry enlisted to aid war effort

PART 5

THE MODERN STATE AND SOCIETY

1914–1945

By 1914 industrialization, economic expansion abroad, and the growth of a vibrant urban culture had laid the foundations for a distinctly *modern* American society. By 1945, after two world wars and a dozen years of economic depression, the building of the new society was largely complete.

A strong national state, an essential component of modern society, came late to America. Not until the Great Depression of the 1930s and Franklin D. Roosevelt's New Deal did the country witness a dramatic growth of federal power. An even greater expansion of the state resulted from the massive mobilization necessitated by America's entry into World War II.

America's contribution to the Allied victory in World War I demonstrated the nation's potential for world leadership. Although the United States refused to join the League of Nations, its economic strength guaranteed an active role in world affairs after the war. It led the alliance that won World War II and emerged in 1945 as the dominant world power.

In this period the American economy also took on its modern contours. With the world's most productive industrial economy, the nation's businesses—increasingly large-scale corporations—played a commanding role in the international economy. Workers, however, bore the brunt of economic downturns, which fueled the dramatic growth of the labor movement in the 1930s.

Finally, the nation was transformed by demographic change and the rise of mass consumer culture. A great wave of European immigration and the movement from farms to cities gave the nation an increasingly urban tone. Internal migration was important as well, as African-Americans moved north and Dust Bowl farmers moved west in search of a better life. Advertising and the new entertainment media—movies, radio, and magazines—promoted the quest for a rising standard of living and the values of consumerism that would shape American society for the rest of the century.

CHAPTER 23

WAR AND THE AMERICAN STATE, 1914–1920

- The Great War, 1914–1918
- War on the Home Front
- An Unsettled Peace, 1919–1920

"It would be the irony of fate if my administration had to deal chiefly with foreign affairs," Woodrow Wilson told a friend early in his first term. But the United States was no longer just a regional power—it was seated at the table of the "great game" of international politics. When war broke out in Europe in August 1914, Wilson had to play his hand. For more than two years he tried to be an honest broker between the two sides. Only when Germany's resumption of unrestricted submarine attacks threatened American lives and shipping did he reluctantly ask Congress for a declaration of war.

The American decision to enter the conflict in 1917 confirmed one of the most important shifts of power in the twentieth century. Before the outbreak of the Great War in 1914, the world had been dominated by Europe; the postwar world was increasingly dominated by the United States. The historian Akira Iriye calls this broad transformation the "globalization" of America. Increasingly the United States became "involved in security, economic, and cultural affairs in all parts of the world." This development, which is usually thought to begin with World War II and its aftermath, actually started in 1917.

Related changes that shaped the country for the rest of the twentieth century also emerged at home. New federal bureaucracies had to be created to coordinate the wartime efforts of business, labor, and agriculture—a process that hastened the emergence of a national administrative state. War meant new opportunities, albeit temporary, for women and for blacks and other ethnic minorities. It also meant new divisions among Americans and new hatreds, first of Germans and Austrians and then of "Bolshevik" Reds. When the war ended, the United States was forced to confront the deep class, racial, and ethnic divisions that had surfaced during wartime mobilization.

A potent symbol of wartime mobilization was the dramatic posters Americans encountered during the nineteen months of United States participation in "the Great War." At every turn (at the movies, in schools and libraries, in shop windows and post offices, at train stations and factories) Americans were urged to do their part: "It's Up to You—Protect the Nation's Honor—Enlist Now". . . . "Rivets Are Bayonets—Drive Them Home!". . . . "Women! Help America's Sons Win the War: Buy U.S. Government Bonds." More than colorful reminders of a bygone era, these propaganda tools were meant to unify the American people in voluntary, self-sacrificing service to the nation. They suggest not only the increased presence of the federal government in the lives of Americans, but also the fact that in modern war, victory involved more than armies. On the home front, businessmen, workers, farmers, housewives, even children had important roles to play. The story of the United States' involvement in World War I, then, is a story of battles and diplomacy abroad and mobilization at home, all of which would have a lasting impact on the nation's future.

THE GREAT WAR, 1914–1918

When war erupted in August 1914, most Americans saw no reason to involve themselves in the struggle among Europe's imperialistic powers. No vital U.S. interests were at stake; indeed, the United States had a good relationship with both sides, and its industries benefited from providing war materiel for the combatants. Many Americans placed their faith in what historians call "U.S. exceptionalism"—the belief that their superior democratic values and institutions set their country apart from the other nations of the world and made it immune from the corruption and chaos of international struggles. Horrified by the carnage and sympathetic to the suffering, Americans nevertheless expected that they would be able to follow their president's dictum, "to be neutral in fact as well as in name."

War in Europe

Almost from the moment France, Russia, and Britain formed the Triple Entente in 1907 to counter the Triple Alliance of Germany, Austria-Hungary, and Italy (see Chapter 22), European leaders began to prepare for what they saw as an inevitable conflict. The spark that ignited the war came in Europe's perennial tinderbox, the Balkans, where Austria-Hungary and Russia competed for power and influence. Austria's seizure of the provinces of Bosnia and Herzegovina in 1908 had enraged Russia and its client, the independent state

The Landscape of War
World War I devastated the countryside: this was the battleground at Ypres in 1915. The carnage of trench warfare also scarred the soldiers who served in these surreal settings, causing the "gas neurosis," "burial-alive neurosis," and "soldiers' heart"—all symptoms of shell shock.

of Serbia. Serbian terrorists responded by recruiting Bosnians to agitate against Austrian rule. On June 28, 1914, a nineteen-year-old Bosnian student, Gavrilo Princip, assassinated Franz Ferdinand, the heir to the Austro-Hungarian throne, and his wife, the Duchess of Hohenberg, in the town of Sarajevo.

   After the assassination the complex European alliance system, which had for years maintained a fragile peace, drew all the major powers into war. Austria-Hungary, blaming Serbia for the assassination, declared war on Serbia on July 28. Russia, which had a secret treaty with Serbia, mobilized its armies; Germany responded by declaring war on Russia and its ally, France, and by invading neutral Belgium. The brutality of the invasion, and Britain's commitment to Belgian neutrality, prompted Great Britain to declare war on Germany on August 4. Within a few days all the major European powers had formally entered the conflict.

   The combatants were divided into two rival blocs. The Allied Powers—Great Britain; France; Japan; Russia; and, in 1915, Italy—were pitted against the Central Powers—Germany; Austria-Hungary; Turkey; and, in 1915, Bulgaria (see Map 23.1). Because the alliance system encompassed competing imperial powers, the conflict spread to parts of the world far beyond Europe, including the Middle East, Africa, and China. Its worldwide scope gave it the name the Great War, or later, World War I.

The term "Great War" also suggested the terrible devastation the conflict produced. It was the first modern war in which extensive harm was done to civilian populations. New military technology, much of it from the United States, made armies more deadly than ever before. Soldiers carried long-range, high-velocity rifles that could hit a target at 1,000 yards—a vast improvement over the 300-yard range of the rifle-musket used in the American Civil War. Another innovation was the machine gun, whose American-born inventor, Hiram Maxim, moved to Great Britain in the 1880s to follow a friend's advice: "If you want to make your fortune, invent something which will allow those fool Europeans to kill each other more quickly."

The concentrated firepower of rifles and machine guns gave troops in defensive positions a tremendous advantage. For four bloody years, between 1914 and 1918, the Allies and the Central Powers faced each other on the

MAP 23.1
Europe at the Start of World War I
In early August 1914 a complex set of interlocking alliances drew the major European powers into war. At first the United States avoided the conflict. Not until April 1917 did America enter the war on the Allied Side.

Western Front, a narrow swath of territory in Belgium and northern France crisscrossed by 25,000 miles of heavily fortified trenches, protected by deadly barbed wire. Trench warfare produced unprecedented numbers of casualties. If one side tried to break the stalemate by venturing into the "no man's land" between the trenches, its soldiers, caught in the sea of barbed wire, were mowed down by artillery fire or poison gas, first used by the Germans at Ypres in April 1915. Between February and December 1916, the French suffered 550,000 casualties and the Germans 450,000, as Germany tried to break through the French lines at Verdun. The front did not move.

The Perils of Neutrality

As the bloody stalemate continued, the United States grappled with its role in the international conflagration. Two weeks after the outbreak of war in Europe, President Woodrow Wilson made the American position clear. In a message widely printed in the newspapers, the president called on Americans to be "neutral in fact as well as in name, impartial in thought as well as in action." Wilson wanted to keep the nation out of the war partly because he believed that if America kept aloof from the quarrel, he could arbitrate—and influence—its ultimate settlement.

The nation's divided loyalties also influenced Wilson's policy. Many Americans, including Wilson, felt deep cultural ties to the Allies, especially Britain and France. Yet most Irish-Americans resented Britain's centuries-long occupation of their home country and the cancellation of Home Rule in 1914. Pro-German sentiments were also encouraged by the presence of 10 million immigrants from Germany and Austria-Hungary. Indeed, German-Americans made up one of the largest and best-established ethnic groups in the United States, and many aspects of German culture, including classical music and the German university system, were widely admired. Wilson could not easily have rallied the nation to the Allied side in 1914.

Many Americans had no strong sympathy for either side. Some progressive leaders—both Republicans and Democrats—vehemently opposed American participation in the European conflict. Newly formed pacifist groups, among them the American Union against Militarism and the Women's Peace Party, both founded in 1915, also mobilized popular opposition. Virtually the entire political left, led principally by Eugene Debs and the Socialist party, condemned the war as imperialistic. African-American leaders such as A. Philip Randolph viewed it as a conflict of the white race only. And some prominent industrialists bankrolled antiwar activities. In December 1915 Henry Ford spent almost half a million dollars to send more than a hundred men and women to Europe on a "peace ship" in an attempt to negotiate an end to the war.

All these factors mitigated against American involvement in the war, and might have kept the nation neutral if the conflict had not spread to the high seas. There the United States initially had as many arguments with Britain as with Germany. The most troublesome issue concerned neutrality rights—freedom to trade with nations on both sides of a conflict.

By the end of August 1914 the British had imposed a naval blockade on the Central Powers, hoping to cut off military supplies and starve the German people into submission. But their actions also prevented neutral nations like the United States from trading with Germany and its allies. The United States chafed at the infringement of its neutral rights but did little besides complain, largely because the spectacular increase in trade with the Allies more than made up for the lost trade with the Central Powers. American trade with Britain and France grew from $824 million in 1914 to $3.2 billion in 1916. By 1917 U.S. banks had lent the Allies $2.5 billion. In contrast, American trade with and loans to Germany totaled only $29 million and $27 million, respectively, by 1917. This imbalance in trade translated into closer U.S. ties with the Allies, despite the nation's official posture of neutrality.

To challenge British control of the seas, the German navy launched a devastating new weapon, the U-boat. On May 7, 1915, a German U-boat submerged off the coast of Ireland torpedoed the British luxury liner *Lusitania*, killing 1,198 people, 128 of them Americans. The attack on the unarmed passenger vessel incensed Americans—newspapers branded it a "mass murder"—and prompted President Wilson to send a series of strongly worded protests to Germany. The crisis continued until September 1915, when Germany announced its submarines would no longer attack passenger ships without warning.

Throughout 1915 and 1916, Wilson tried at several points to mediate an end to the European conflict through his aide, Colonel Edward House. But House concluded that neither side was interested in serious peace negotiations. The worsening tensions with Germany caused Wilson to rethink his opposition to preparedness. In the fall of 1915 he endorsed a $1 billion buildup of the army and the navy, and by 1916 armament was well under way.

Nevertheless, public opinion still ran against entering the war, a factor that profoundly shaped the election of 1916. The Republican party passed over the belligerently prowar Theodore Roosevelt in favor of Supreme Court Justice Charles Evans Hughes, a former governor of New York. The Democrats renominated Wilson, whose campaign emphasized his progressive reform record (see Chapter 21). The Democrats also picked up some votes with their widely circulated campaign slogan, "He kept us out of war." Wilson won reelection by only 600,000 popular votes and by 23 votes in the electoral college, a slim margin that limited his options in mobilizing the nation for war.

The events of early 1917 diminished Wilson's lingering hopes of staying out of the conflict. On January 31 Germany announced the resumption of unrestricted submarine warfare, a decision dictated by the impasse in the land war. In response, Wilson broke off diplomatic relations with Germany on February 3. A few weeks later, the release of the "Zimmermann telegram" moved the country closer to war. Newspapers published an intercepted communication from Germany's foreign secretary, Arthur Zimmermann, to the German minister in Mexico City, in which Zimmermann urged Mexico to join the Central Powers in the war. In return, Germany promised to help Mexico recover "the lost territory of Texas, New Mexico, and Arizona." This threat to the territorial integrity of the United States jolted both congressional and public opinion, especially in the West, where opposition to entering the war was strong. Combined with the resumption of unrestricted submarine warfare, the Zimmermann telegram inflamed anti-German sentiment.

Although the likelihood of Mexico's reconquering the border states was small, the highly explosive situation there (see Chapter 22) continued to concern American policymakers. In the final stages of the Mexican Revolution, the United States backed the Constitutionalist movement led by Venustiano Carranza. Resentful of American support for his rival, the rebel Pancho Villa orchestrated border raids that killed sixteen U.S. citizens in January 1916. In March he razed the town of Columbus, New Mexico. In response, Wilson sent troops under General John J. Pershing into Mexico to capture the elusive Villa. Carranza, strongly supported by Mexican resentment of the apparent occupation of their country, demanded that Pershing withdraw. The two governments backed off, and U.S. troops began to leave early in 1917. Carranza's government received official recognition from Washington on March 13, 1917, less than a month before the United States entered World War I.

Meanwhile, throughout March, U-boats attacked American ships without warning, sinking three on March 18 alone. On April 2, 1917, after consulting his cabinet, Wilson appeared before a special session of Congress to ask for a declaration of war. The rights of the nation had been trampled on and its trade and citizens' lives imperiled, he charged. But while U.S. self-interest shaped the decision to go to war, years of Americans' sense of their exceptionalism, coupled with the Progressive Era's zeal to right social injustices, also played a part. Believing that the United States, in sharp contrast to other nations, was uniquely high-minded in the conduct of its international affairs, many Americans could accept Wilson's claim that "America had no selfish aims: "We desire no conquest, no dominion. We seek no indemnities for ourselves, no material compensation for the sacrifices we shall freely make. We are but one of the champions of the rights of mankind." The United States would not only help to win the war, but in doing so would earn a place at the peace table where it would spread the country's democratic ideals to the rest of the world. In a memorable phrase intended to ennoble the nation's role, Wilson proposed that U.S. participation in the war would make the world "safe for democracy."

Four days after Wilson's speech, on April 6, 1917, the United States declared war on Germany. Reflecting the divided feelings of the country as a whole, the vote was far from unanimous. Six senators and fifty members of the House voted against the action, including Representative Jeannette Rankin of Montana, the first woman elected to Congress. "I want to stand by my country," she declared, "but I cannot vote for war."

Over There

In May 1917 General John J. Pershing, recently returned from his unsuccessful pursuit of Pancho Villa in Mexico, traveled to London and Paris to determine

Call to Arms
To build popular support for the war effort, the government called on artists such as Howard Chandler Christy, Charles Dana Gibson, and James Montgomery Flagg. This 1917 recruiting poster by Flagg was adapted from a June 1916 cover of *Leslie's Illustrated Weekly Newspaper.* The model was the artist.

how the United States could best support the war effort. The answer, as Marshal Joseph Joffre of France put it, was clear: "Men, men, and more men." The problem was that the United States had never maintained a large standing army in peacetime. To field a fighting force strong enough to enter a global war, the government turned to conscription. The passage of the Selective Service Act in May 1917 demonstrated the increasing impact of the state on ordinary citizens. Though draft resistance had been common during the Civil War, no major riots occurred in 1917. The selective service system worked in part because it combined central direction from Washington with local administration and civilian control, and thus did not tread on the nation's tradition of individual freedom and local autonomy. Draft registration also demonstrated the potential bureaucratic capacity of the American state. On a single day, June 5, 1917, more than 9.5 million men between the ages of twenty-one and thirty were processed for military service in their local voting precincts. By the end of the war almost 4 million men, plus a few thousand female navy clerks and army nurses, were in uniform. Another 300,000 men, called "slackers," evaded the draft, and 4,000 were classified as conscientious objectors.

Wilson chose Pershing to head the American Expeditionary Force (AEF). But the newly raised army did not have an immediate impact on the fighting. The fresh recruits had to be trained and outfitted, then wait for transport across the submarine-infested Atlantic. Initially, the nation's main contribution was to secure the safety of the seas. Aiming for safety in numbers in the face of mounting German submarine activity, the government began sending armed convoys across the Atlantic. The plan worked: no American soldiers were killed on the way to Europe, and Allied shipping losses were cut dramatically.

Meanwhile, on the Western Front, trench warfare ground on. Allied commanders pleaded for American reinforcements, but Pershing was reluctant to put his soldiers under foreign commanders. Because the AEF was not ready to fight until May 1918, the brunt of the fighting continued to fall on the French and British. Their burden increased when the Eastern Front collapsed after the Russian Revolution in November 1917. Under the Treaty of Brest-Litovsk, signed on

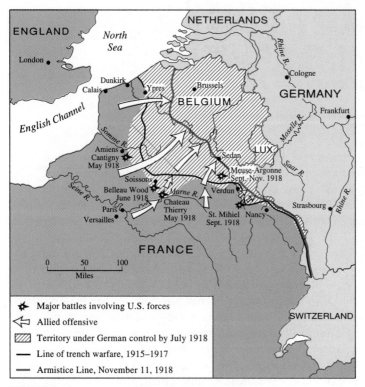

MAP 23.2
U.S. Participation on the Western Front, 1918
When American troops reached the European front in significant numbers in 1918, the Allied and Central powers had been grinding each other down in a war of attrition for almost four years. The influx of American troops and supplies broke the stalemate. Successful offensive maneuvers by the American Expeditionary Force included Belleau Wood, Château-Thierry, and the Meuse-Argonne campaign.

A Soldier Remembers

S ergeant William L. Langer, of Battery E, 1st Gas Regiment, describes the effort to work through the trenches to get to the front lines to set up devices for launching bombs at the Germans at the battle of St. Mihiel in September 1918.

There was not much activity in the trenches, certainly not enough to give reason to suppose that a large scale attack was about to start. The enemy, to be sure, kept up his Vérey lights and fired at intervals. Still, most of us were quite startled and surprised when, about 1:00 in the morning, the sky lit up behind us and the American barrage began. . . .

After depositing our loads at the position we started back for another. . . . And going back was quite a different proposition than going, for, as if by magic, the trenches had filled with men, most of them Marines . . . and troops of the 9th Infantry . . . who were to go over the top with the first wave. Those rows of cold, shivering men, equipped with grenades and with bayonets fixed, crouching in the mud of the trenches and waiting for the crucial moment, is another sight we shall never forget. . . .

We were just about to start back for the trenches [with a second load of bombs] when the Boche suddenly opened up with a concentrated bombardment of the town. Everywhere the shells were bursting. For a moment we were undecided, but then we set out on a run. . . . We reached the trenches without mishap. The first wave was just about to go over, and our machine guns had just opened a rolling barrage to precede it. For green men it was a novel experience—this stuttering breathless chatter of the machine guns behind one. The trenches were in places so congested that to get through would have been impossible had we not struck on a rather clever idea. "Heads up, men, high explosives, watch these sacks";—shouting words to that effect worked like magic and we secured an easy passage.

SOURCE: Frank Freidel, *Over There: The Story of America's First Great Overseas Crusade* (McGraw-Hill, rev. ed. 1990), 127–128.

March 3, 1918, the new Bolshevik regime under Vladimir Ilych Lenin surrendered about one-third of Russia's territories, including Russian Poland, Ukraine, the Baltic provinces, and Finland, in return for an end to hostilities.

Once hostilities with Russia had ended, the Germans launched a major offensive against the Allies on the Western Front on March 21, 1918. By May the German army had advanced to the Marne River, within 50 miles of Paris, and was attempting to subdue the city by bombardment. When Allied leaders intensified their calls for American troops, Pershing committed about 60,000 Americans to help the French repel the Germans in the battles of Château-Thierry and Belleau Wood (see Map 23.2).

American reinforcements now began to arrive in large numbers. Slowly they worked their way to the front through the clogged French transportation system. Augmented by 85,000 American troops, the Allied forces brought the German offensive to a halt in mid-July. At that point there were a million American troops in France. The counteroffensive began with a successful campaign to drive the Germans back from the Marne. In mid-September 1918, American and French troops led by General Pershing forced the Germans to retreat at Saint-Mihiel. The last major assault of the war began on September 26, when Pershing pitted over a million American soldiers against vastly outnumbered and exhausted German troops. The Meuse-Argonne campaign pushed the enemy back across the Selle River near Verdun and broke the German defenses, at a cost of over 26,000 American lives.

World War I ended on November 11, 1918, when German and Allied representatives signed an armistice in the railway car of Marshal Ferdinand Foch of France. The flood of American troops and supplies during the last six months of the war had helped secure the Allied victory. The nation's decisive contribution also signaled a shift in international power as European diplomatic and economic dominance declined and the United States emerged as a world leader.

When the war ended, about 2 million American soldiers were in France. Two-thirds of them had seen action at least briefly on the Western Front, but had escaped the horrors of sustained trench warfare that sapped the morale of Allied and German troops. During the eighteen months in which the United States fought, 48,000 American servicemen were killed in action or from wounds. Another 27,000 died from other causes, mainly the influenza epidemic that swept the world in 1918–1919. But the nation's casualties were minimal compared with the 8 million soldiers lost by the Allies and Central Powers. The French lost far more soldiers in the siege of Verdun than the United States did in the entire war.

After the armistice the war lived on in the minds of the men and women who had gone "over there." Many members of the AEF, especially those who had been spared the horror of sustained battle, experienced the war more as tourists than as soldiers. Before joining the army, most had barely traveled beyond their hometowns; for them the journey across the ocean was a monumental, once-in-a-lifetime event. Their letters described "old cathedrals, chateaux and ancient towns . . . quite wonderful . . . to eyes so accustomed to the look of the New World." In 1919 a group of former AEF officers formed the American Legion, "to preserve the memories and incidents of our association in the great war." The word *legion* captured the romantic, almost chivalric memories many veterans held of their wartime service. Only later did disillusionment over the contested legacy of World War I set in.

For African-Americans, the war experience was a bitter one. Encouraged by black leaders to enlist as a means of proving their loyalty and achieving first-class citizenship, black soldiers instead suffered continued discrimination. Placed in segregated units under white officers, they served in the most menial

A Black Veteran Returns Home
Black soldiers received segregated and unequal treatment at every stage of military service. When the war ended, black veterans faced hostility from many whites alarmed that blacks no longer "knew their place."

positions, as laborers, stevedores, and messboys. Many African-Americans emerged from the war determined to stand up for their rights, and contributed to a spirit of black militancy that characterized the early 1920s.

WAR ON THE HOME FRONT

Fighting World War I required extraordinary economic mobilization on the home front in which business, the work force, and the public all cooperated. Although the federal government did expand its power and presence during the emergency, the watchword was voluntarism. The government avoided compulsion as much as possible. Ambivalence about expanding state power, coupled with the pressures of wartime mobilization, severely damaged the impetus for progressive reforms that had characterized the prewar era. Yet even in the context of international crisis, some reformers expected that the war could serve the cause of improving American society.

Mobilization

The continuing impact of the prewar progressive reform movement was evident in the financing of the war, the cost of which would eventually mount to

$33 billion. The government paid for the war in part by using the Federal Reserve System established in 1913 (see Chapter 21) to expand the money supply, making it easier to borrow money. Two-thirds of the funds came from loans, especially the popular liberty bonds. Treasury Secretary William McAdoo encouraged the small, heavily advertised bond sales as a way of widening support for the war and demonstrating the voluntary self-sacrifice of the nation's virtuous citizenry. To augment the funds raised by bonds, McAdoo rejected a sales tax in favor of an increased federal income tax. Income taxes had been instituted by Congress after the passage of the Sixteenth Amendment to the Constitution in 1913. Now the War Revenue bills of 1917 and 1918 transformed the tax into the foremost method of federal fund raising. The Wilson administration took a progressive approach, rejecting a tax on all wages and salaries in favor of a tax on corporations and wealthy individuals. The excess-profits tax contained in the law passed in 1917 signaled a direct and unprecedented intrusion of the state into the workings of corporate capitalism. By 1918 U.S. corporations were paying over $2.5 billion in excess-profits taxes per year—more than half of all federal taxes.

The tax burden should not mask the fact that the federal government for the most part took a collaborative rather than a coercive approach to big business during the war. To the dismay of many progressives who had hoped that the war emergency would increase federal regulation of business, the government suspended antitrust laws to encourage cooperation and promote efficiency. For economic expertise the administration turned to those who knew the capacities of the economy best—the nation's business leaders. Executives flocked to Washington, where they served with federal officials on a series of boards and agencies that sought a middle ground between total state control of the economy and total freedom for business.

The central agency for mobilizing wartime industry was the War Industries Board (WIB), established in July 1917. In March 1918, after a fumbling start that showed the limits of voluntarism in a national emergency, the Wilson administration reorganized the board under the direction of Bernard Baruch, a Wall Street financier. The WIB produced an unparalleled expansion of the federal government's economic powers: it allocated scarce resources, gathered economic data and statistics, controlled the flow of raw materials, ordered the conversion from peacetime to war production, set prices, imposed efficiency and standardization procedures, and coordinated purchasing. Though the board had the authority to compel compliance, Baruch preferred to win voluntary cooperation by industry, often through personal intervention. Business generally supported this governmental oversight because it coincided so well with its own interests in improving efficiency and productivity. Despite higher taxes, corporate profits soared, aided by the suspension of antitrust laws and the institution of price guarantees for war work. War profits produced an economic boom that continued without interruption until 1920.

The reliance on voluntarism was best exemplified in the Food Administration, created in August 1917 and led by Stanford-trained engineer Herbert

Hoover, who proposed to "mobilize the spirit of self-denial and self-sacrifice in this country." Using the slogan "Food will win the war," Hoover encouraged farmers to expand production of wheat and other grains from 45 million acres in 1917 to 75 million in 1919. Although the Food Administration issued reams of rules and regulations for producers and retailers, at no time did the government contemplate domestic food rationing. Rather, Hoover sent women volunteers from door to door to secure housewives' cooperation in observing "wheatless" Mondays, "meatless" Tuesdays, and "porkless" Thursdays and Saturdays—a campaign that resulted in substantial voluntary conservation of food resources.

In some instances, new federal agencies took dramatic, decisive action. In the face of the severe winter of 1917–1918, which led to coal shortages in northeastern cities and industries, the Fuel Administration ordered all factories east of the Mississippi River to shut down for four days. An even more striking example of the temporary use of federal power came in December 1917. When a massive traffic snarl interfered with the transport of troops, the Railroad War Board, which coordinated the nation's sprawling transportation system, took over the railroads. Guaranteeing railroad owners a "standard return" equal to their average earnings between 1915 and 1917, the board promised that the carriers would be returned to private control no later than twenty-one months after the war. Although reformers hoped to continue this experiment in government control on behalf of labor and consumers, the government fulfilled that pledge after the armistice.

With the signing of the armistice in November 1918, the United States scrambled to dismantle wartime controls. Wilson, determined to "take the harness off," disbanded the WIB on January 1, 1919, resisting suggestions that the board would help stabilize the economy during demobilization. Like most Americans, Wilson could tolerate government planning power during an emergency but not as a permanent feature of the economy.

Although the nation's participation in the war lasted just eighteen months, it left an enduring legacy, the modern bureaucratic state. Entire industries had been organized as never before, linked to a maze of government agencies and executive departments. A modern system of income taxation had been established, with the potential for vastly increasing federal reserves. Finally, the collaboration between business and government had been mutually beneficial, teaching both partners a lesson they would put to use in the state building that occurred in the 1920s and afterward.

Besides mobilizing armies and business concerns to wage war, the federal government also needed to assure a reliable work force, especially in war industries. Acute labor shortages, caused by the demands of the draft and the abrupt decline in European immigration, as well as the urgency of war production, had enhanced workers' bargaining power. The National War Labor Board (NWLB), formed in April 1918, also helped to improve labor's position. Composed of representatives of labor, management, and the public, the NWLB established an eight-hour day for war workers, with time and a half

AMERICAN VOICES

A Southern Migrant

The Great Migration of southern African-Americans to the cities of the North disrupted communities and families, but the migrants kept in touch with friends and kin through letters and visits. While cities like Chicago offered new opportunities and experiences, as this letter indicates, migrants often found churches that provided important continuity with their southern past.

My dear Sister: I was agreeably surprised to hear from you and to hear from home. . . . I got here in time to attend one of the greatest revivals in the history of my life—over 500 people joined the church. . . . It was snowing some nights and if you didnt hurry you could not get standing room. Please remember me kindly to any who ask of me. The people are rushing here by the thousands and I know if you come and rent a big house you can get all the roomers you want. You write me exactly when you are coming. I am not keeping house yet I am living with my brother and his wife. . . . I can get a nice place for you to stop until you can look around and see what you want. I am quite busy. I work in Swifts packing Co. in the sausage department. My daughter and I work for the same company—We get $1.50 a day and we pack so many sausages we don't have much time to play but it is a matter of a dollar with me and I feel that god made the path and I am walking therein.

 Tell your husband work is plentiful here and he wont have to loaf if he want to work. . . . Well goodbye from your sister in Christ.

SOURCE: *Journal of Negro History,* vol. 4, no. 4, 1919, p. 457.

for overtime, and endorsed equal pay for women workers. Workers were not allowed to disrupt war production through strikes or other disturbances. In return, the NWLB supported the workers' right to organize unions, required employers to deal with shop committees, and arbitrated labor disputes.

 After years of federal hostility toward labor, the NWLB's actions brought a welcome change in labor's status and power. From 1916 to 1919 AFL membership grew by almost a million workers, reaching over 3 million at the end of the war. Few of the wartime gains lasted, however. Wartime inflation ate up most of the wage hikes, and a virulent postwar antiunion movement caused a rapid decline in union membership that lasted into the 1930s. The labor movement did not yet have enough power to bargain on an equal basis with business and government.

 While the war emergency benefited labor, it had a special effect on workers who were traditionally excluded from many industrial jobs. For the first time, northern factories actively recruited African-Americans, spawning the "Great Migration" from the South. The lure of decent jobs was potent. As one

Mississippi man described his anticipation of work in the meat-packing houses of Chicago: "You could not rest in your bed at night for thoughts of *Chicago.*" Over 400,000 African-Americans relocated to northern and midwestern cities such as St. Louis, Chicago, Cleveland, and Detroit during the war. Though they encountered discrimination there as well, they found new opportunities and an escape from the repressive southern agricultural system.

Mexican-Americans in California, Texas, New Mexico, and Arizona also found new opportunities during the war. When urban growth in the Southwest exacerbated the wartime labor shortage, many Mexican-Americans left farm labor for new industrial opportunities. Continuing political instability in Mexico following the revolution encouraged many Mexicans to relocate, temporarily or permanently, across the border, a process facilitated by newly opened railroad lines. At least 100,000 Mexicans entered the United States between 1917 and 1920, often settling in segregated neighborhoods (*barrios*) in urban areas, meeting discrimination similar to that faced by African-Americans.

Women were the largest group to take advantage of wartime opportunities. White women and, to a lesser degree, black and Mexican-American women found that factory jobs usually reserved for men had been opened to them. About 1 million women joined the labor force for the first time, while many of the 8 million women who already held jobs switched from low-paying fields like domestic service to higher-paying industrial work. Americans soon got used to the sight of female streetcar conductors, train engineers, and defense workers. But everyone—including most working women—believed that those jobs would return to men after the war.

Reform and War

Supporters of woman suffrage hoped that the war would reinvigorate the reform era. The National American Woman Suffrage Association (NAWSA) continued to lobby for the proposed woman suffrage amendment to the Constitution. It also threw the support of its 2 million members behind the Wilson administration, encouraging women to do their part to win the war. Women in communities all over the country labored exhaustively to promote food conservation, to protect children and women workers, and to distribute emergency relief through organizations like the Red Cross. Many agreed with Carrie Chapman Catt, president of NAWSA, that women's patriotic service could advance the cause of woman's suffrage.

Alice Paul and the National Woman's Party (NWP) took a more militant tack. To the dismay of NAWSA leaders, NWP militants began picketing the White House in July 1917 to protest their lack of the vote. Arrested and sentenced to seven months in jail, Paul and other women prisoners went on a hunger strike, which prison authorities met with forced feeding. Public shock at the women's treatment made them martyrs, drawing attention to the cause.

The combination of suffrage militancy and NAWSA's policy of patient persuasion finally brought results. In January 1918 Woodrow Wilson withdrew his

Wartime Opportunities
Women took on new jobs during the war, working as mail carriers, police officers, drill-press operators, and farm laborers attached to the Women's Land Army. These three women clearly enjoyed the camaraderie of working in a railroad yard in 1918. When the war ended, women usually lost such employment.

opposition to a federal woman suffrage amendment. The constitutional amendment quickly passed the House, but took eighteen months to get through the Senate. Then came another year of hard work for ratification by the states. Finally, on August 26, 1920, Tennessee gave the Nineteenth Amendment the last vote it needed. The goal that had first been declared at the Seneca Falls convention in 1848 was finally achieved seventy-two years later, in large part because of women's contributions to the war effort. The suffragists had posed a simple but effective moral challenge: How could the United States fight to make the world safe for democracy while denying half its citizens the right to vote?

Throughout the mobilization period, reformers pushed for a wide range of social reforms. In the name of army efficiency, or "keeping fit to fight," the federal government launched an ambitious anti–venereal disease campaign, forcing the shutdown of "red-light" districts in cities with military training camps. With the cooperation of the YMCA and the YWCA, the government undertook a far-reaching sex education program, designed to enlighten both men and women about the dangers of sexuality and the value of "social purity." Other reformers addressed the welfare of children. The Women's Council of National Defense, a voluntary organization with federal backing, proclaimed 1918 the year of the child, conducted a nationwide growth-monitoring program, and disseminated information about child health and nutrition. From playground directors to librarians, from educators to advocates of the Americanization of immigrants, idealistic reformers proclaimed that the war was just the start of a continuing battle for social welfare.

Especially active were temperance advocates, who viewed alcoholic beverages as the key social evil. In the early twentieth century, many Americans viewed the legal prohibition of alcohol as a progressive reform, not a denial of individual freedom. Urban reformers, concerned about good government, poverty, and public morality, supported a nationwide ban on drinking. The drive for Prohibition also had substantial backing in rural communities. Many people equated liquor with all the sins of the city: prostitution, crime, immigration, machine politics, and public disorder. In addition, the churches with the greatest strength in rural areas, including the Methodists, the Baptists, and the Mormons, strongly condemned drinking. Protestants from rural areas also dominated the membership of the Anti-Saloon League, which supplanted the Women's Christian Temperance Union as the leading proponent of Prohibition early in the century.

Support for the right to drink existed primarily in the nation's heavily urbanized areas, places where immigrants had settled. Alcoholic beverages, especially beer and whiskey, played an important role in the social life of certain ethnic cultures, especially those of German-Americans and Irish-Americans. Most saloons were in working-class neighborhoods and served as gathering places for workers. Machine politicians conducted much of their business in bars. Thus many immigrants and working-class people opposed Prohibition, rightly interpreting the attack on drinking as an imposition of middle-class cultural values on them.

Although numerous states—mostly southern and midwestern states without a significant immigrant presence—already had prohibition laws, World War I soon offered the impetus for national action. Because several major breweries (Pabst and Busch, for example) had German names, beer drinking had become unpatriotic in many people's minds. To conserve food, Congress prohibited the use of foodstuffs such as hops and barley in breweries and distilleries. Finally, in December 1917, Congress passed the proposed Eighteenth Amendment, which prohibited the "manufacture, sale, or transportation of intoxicating liquors." Ratified in 1919 and effective on January 16, 1920, the Eighteenth Amendment demonstrated the widening influence of the state in matters of personal behavior.

The Eighteenth Amendment was an example of how "progressive" reform efforts could benefit from the climate of war. But despite the stimulus the Great War gave to some types of reform, for the most part it blocked rather than furthered reforms. Though many Progressives had anticipated that the stronger federal presence in wartime would lead to stronger economic controls and corporate regulation, federal agencies were quickly disbanded once the war was over, reflecting the unease most Americans felt about a strong bureaucratic state. Moreover, the wartime collaboration between government and business gave corporate leaders more influence in shaping the economy and government policy, not less.

Promoting National Unity

For the liberal reformers who so strongly believed in the possibility that the war for democracy could promote a more just society at home, perhaps the most discouraging aspect of the war was the campaign to promote what was called "One Hundred Percent Americanism," which translated into an insistence on conformity and an intolerance of dissent. Ironically, Woodrow Wilson had predicted what came to pass: "Once lead this people into war, and they'll forget there ever was such a thing as tolerance," he had warned. But the president also recognized the need to manufacture support for the war. "It is not an army we must shape and train for war, it is a nation," he acknowledged. It was this drumming up of enthusiasm that encouraged a repressive spirit hostile to reform.

In April 1917 Wilson formed the Committee on Public Information (CPI) to promote public support for the war. This government propaganda agency, headed by the journalist George Creel, became a magnet for progressive reformers and muckraking journalists. Professing high-sounding goals such as educating citizens about democracy, promoting national unity, Americanizing immigrants, and breaking down the isolation of rural life, the committee also acted as a nationalizing force by promoting the development of a common ideology.

During the war the CPI touched the lives of practically every American. It distributed 75 million pieces of patriotic literature and sponsored speeches at local movie theaters, reaching an audience estimated at more than 300 million—three times the population of the United States at the time. In its zeal, the committee often ventured into hatemongering. In early 1918, for example, it encouraged speakers to use inflammatory stories of alleged German atrocities to build support for the war effort.

As a spirit of conformity pervaded the home front, many Americans found themselves targets of suspicion. Local businesses paid for newspaper and magazine ads that asked citizens to report to the Justice Department "the man who spreads pessimistic stories, cries for peace, or belittles our efforts to win the war." Posters encouraged Americans to be on the lookout for German spies. And quasi-vigilante groups such as the American Protective League mobilized about 250,000 self-appointed agents, furnished with badges issued by the Justice Department, to spy on neighbors and co-workers.

The CPI also urged ethnic groups to give up their Old World customs in the spirit of One Hundred Percent Americanism. German-Americans bore the brunt of this campaign. In an orgy of hostility generated by propaganda about German militarism and atrocities, everything associated with Germany became suspect. German music, especially opera, was banished from the concert halls. Publishers removed pro-German references from textbooks, and many communities banned the teaching of the German language. Sauerkraut was renamed "liberty cabbage," and hamburgers were transformed into "liberty sandwiches." Though anti-German hysteria dissipated when the war ended, hostility toward the "hyphenated" American survived into the 1920s.

In law enforcement, officials tolerated little criticism of established values and institutions, as the militant suffragists picketing the White House during wartime had discovered. The main legal tools for curbing dissent were the Espionage Act of 1917 and the Sedition Act of 1918. The Espionage Act imposed stiff penalties for antiwar activities and allowed the federal government to ban treasonous materials from the mails. The postmaster general revoked the mailing privileges of groups considered to be radical, virtually shutting down their publications.

Individuals suffered as well. Because these acts defined treason and sedition loosely, they led to the conviction of more than a thousand people. The Justice Department focused particularly on socialists who criticized the war and the draft, and on radicals like the Industrial Workers of the World (see Chapter 18), whose attacks on militarism threatened to disrupt war production in the western lumber and copper industries. Socialist party leader Eugene Debs was sentenced to ten years in jail for stating that the master classes declared war while the subject classes fought the battles. (Debs was pardoned by President Warren G. Harding in 1921.) Victor Berger, a Milwaukee socialist, who had been jailed under the Espionage Act, was twice prevented from taking the seat to which he had been elected in the U.S. House of Representatives.

The courts rarely resisted these wartime excesses. In *Schenck v. United States* (1919), the Supreme Court upheld the conviction of the general secretary of the Socialist party, Charles T. Schenck, who had been convicted of mailing pamphlets urging draftees to resist induction. In a unanimous decision, Justice Oliver Wendell Holmes ruled that an act of speech uttered under circumstances that would "create a clear and present danger to the safety of the country" could be constitutionally restricted. Because of the national war emergency, then, the Court upheld limits on freedom of speech that would not have been acceptable in peacetime. Thus in wartime, the drive for conformity reigned, dashing reformers' optimistic hopes that war could be what philosopher John Dewey had called a "plastic juncture," in which the country would be more open to reason and progressive ideas.

AN UNSETTLED PEACE, 1919–1920

In January 1917 Woodrow Wilson had proposed a "peace without victory," since only a "peace among equals" could last. His goal was "not a balance of power, but a community of power; not organized rivalries, but an organized common peace." The keystone of Wilson's postwar plans was a permanent league of nations. With victory achieved, Wilson confronted the task of constructing the new moral international order. But he would first have to win over a Senate that was Republican controlled and openly hostile to the treaty he had brought home.

The Treaty of Versailles

Wilson scored an early victory when the Allies accepted his Fourteen Points as the basis for the peace negotiations that began in January 1919. In this blueprint for the postwar world, the president called for open diplomacy, "absolute freedom of navigation upon the seas," arms reduction, the removal of trade barriers, and an international commitment to territorial integrity and national self-determination. Essential to Wilson's vision was the creation of a multinational organization "for the purpose of affording mutual guarantees of political independence and territorial integrity to great and small States alike." The League of Nations became Wilson's obsession.

The Fourteen Points were imbued with the spirit of progressivism. Widely distributed as propaganda during the final months of the war, Wilson's plan proposed to extend the ideals of America—democracy, freedom, and peaceful economic expansion—to the rest of the world. The League of Nations, acting as a kind of international Federal Trade Commission, would supervise disarmament and—according to the crucial Article X of its covenant—curb unilateralism through collective military action. More grandiosely, Wilson anticipated that the League would mediate disputes between nations, preventing future wars, and thus assuring that the Great War would be "the war to end all wars." By emphasizing these lofty goals, Wilson guaranteed disappointment: his ideals for world reformation were too far-reaching to be practical or attainable.

Twenty-seven countries sent representatives to the peace conference in Versailles, near Paris. Distrustful of the new Bolshevik regime in Russia and its call for proletarian revolution, the allies deliberately excluded its representatives. Nor was Germany invited. The Big Four—Wilson, Prime Minister David Lloyd George of Great Britain, Premier Georges Clemenceau of France, and Prime Minister Vittorio Orlando of Italy—did most of the negotiating. The three European leaders sought a peace that differed radically from Wilson's plan. They wanted to punish Germany and treat themselves to the spoils of war by demanding heavy reparations. In fact, before the war ended, Britain, France, and Italy had already made secret agreements to divide up the German colonies.

It is a tribute to Wilson that he managed to influence the peace settlement as much as he did. He was able to soften some of the harshest demands for reprisal against Germany. National self-determination, a fundamental principle of Wilson's Fourteen Points, bore fruit in the creation of the independent states of Austria, Hungary, Poland, Yugoslavia, and Czechoslovakia from the defeated empires of the Central Powers. The establishment of the new nations of Finland, Estonia, Lithuania, and Latvia not only upheld the principle of self-determination, but also served Wilson's (and the Allies') desire to isolate Soviet Russia from the rest of Europe.

Wilson had less success in achieving other goals. He won only limited concessions regarding the colonial empires of the defeated powers. The old Central and Eastern European colonial empires were dismantled, only to enlarge the overseas empire of the victorious allies. Certain topics, such as freedom of the seas and free trade, never even appeared on the agenda because of Allied resistance. Finally, Wilson had only partial success in scaling back French and British demands for reparations from Germany, which eventually were set at $33 billion.

In the face of these disappointments, Wilson consoled himself with the negotiators' commitment to his proposed League of Nations. He acknowledged that the peace treaty had defects, but expressed confidence that they could be resolved by a permanent international organization dedicated to the peaceful resolution of disputes.

On June 28, 1919, representatives gathered in the Hall of Mirrors at the Palace of Versailles to sign the peace treaty. Wilson sailed home immediately after the ceremony. He came back to a public enthusiastic about a league of nations in principle. Major newspapers and the Federal Council of Churches of Christ of America supported the treaty, and even an enemy of the proposed League, Henry Cabot Lodge, acknowledged that "[T]he people of the country are very naturally fascinated by the idea of eternal preservations of the world's peace."

But when Wilson presented the treaty to the Senate on July 10, it fell far short of the two-thirds vote necessary for ratification. The rejection was not altogether surprising, for Wilson had not paid much attention to the political realities of building support for the League of Nations and the treaty in the Senate. He had failed to include a prominent Republican in the American commission that represented the United States at Versailles. Convinced of his own rectitude and ability, he had kept the negotiations firmly in his own hands. When the Senate balked at the treaty, Wilson adamantly refused to compromise. "I shall consent to nothing," he told the French ambassador. "The Senate must take its medicine."

The Senate, however, did not oblige. And despite the president's attempt to make the 1918 congressional elections a referendum for his peace plans, Americans returned a Republican majority to Congress. Wilson and the League faced stiff opposition in the Senate. Some progressive senators, who endorsed the idea of American internationalism, felt that the peace agreement was too conservative, that it served to "validate existing empires" of the victorious Allies. The "irreconcilables," including progressive senators William E. Borah of Idaho, Hiram W. Johnson of California, and Robert M. La Follette of Wisconsin, disagreed fundamentally with the premise of permanent U.S.

participation in European affairs. More influential was a group of Republicans led by Senator Henry Cabot Lodge of Massachusetts. They proposed a list of amendments that focused on Article X, the section of the League covenant that called for collective security measures when a member nation was attacked. This provision, they argued, would restrict Congress's constitutional authority to declare war and would limit the freedom of the United States to pursue a unilateral foreign policy.

Wilson refused to budge, especially not to placate Lodge, his hated political rival. Hoping to mobilize support for the treaty, in September 1919 the president launched an extensive speaking tour during which he brought large audiences to tears with his impassioned defense of the treaty. But the tour had to be cut short when the ailing sixty-two-year-old president collapsed in Pueblo, Colorado, late in September. One week later, in Washington, Wilson suffered a severe stroke that paralyzed one side of his body. While his wife, Edith Bolling Galt Wilson; his physician; and the various cabinet heads oversaw the routine business of government, Wilson slowly recovered, but he was never the same again.

From his sickbed, Wilson remained inflexible in his refusal to compromise, ordering Democratic senators to vote against all Republican amendments. The treaty came up for a vote in November 1919, but was not ratified. When another attempt in March 1920 fell 7 votes short, the issue was dead. Wilson died in 1924, "as much a victim of the war," David Lloyd George noted, "as any soldier who died in the trenches."

The United States never ratified the Versailles treaty nor joined the League of Nations. Many wartime issues were only partially resolved, notably Germany's future, the fate of the colonial empires, and rising nationalist demands for self-determination. These unsolved problems played a major role in the coming of World War II; some, like the competing ethnic nationalisms in the Balkans, remain unresolved today.

Racial Strife and Labor Unrest

Wilson spent only ten days in the United States between December 1918 and June 1919. Totally preoccupied with the peacemaking process at Versailles, for more than six months he was practically an absentee president. Unfortunately, many urgent domestic issues demanded his attention, as the country grappled with the complex problems of demobilization, vainly hoping for a period of tranquility after war's disruptions.

The war years and the immediate postwar period witnessed a severe decline in race relations throughout the country. The volatile mix of black migration and raised black expectations as a result of service in World War I combined to exacerbate white racism. In the South the number of lynchings rose from forty-eight in 1917 to seventy-eight in 1919, and several African-American men were lynched while wearing military uniforms. In the North, race riots broke out in more than twenty-five cities, with one of the first and most deadly occurring in 1917 in East St. Louis, Illinois, where nine whites and more than forty blacks died in a conflict sparked by competition over jobs at a defense plant.

In the summer of 1919, the death toll from racial violence reached 120. One of the worst race riots in American history took place in Chicago in July, where five days of rioting left twenty-three blacks and fifteen whites dead. Tensions in Chicago mirrored those in other cities where violence erupted. In politics, black voters often determined the winners of close elections, thereby enraging white racists who resented black political influence. Blacks also competed with whites for jobs and scarce housing. Even before the July riot, blacks had suffered the bombing of their homes and other forms of harassment. Chicago blacks did not sit meekly by as whites destroyed their neighborhoods. They fought back, both in self-defense and for their rights as citizens. The war had an indirect effect on their actions, since many blacks had served in the armed forces. Wilson's rhetoric about democracy and self-determination had raised their expectations, too.

Workers harbored similar hopes for a better life after the war. The war years had brought them higher pay, shorter hours, and better working conditions. Soon after the armistice, however, many employers resumed their attacks on union activity, and many native-born Americans continued to identify unions with radicalism and foreigners. In addition, rapidly rising inflation—in 1919, the cost of living was 77 percent higher than its prewar level—threatened to wipe out workers' wage increases. Nevertheless, workers hoped to hold onto and perhaps even expand their wartime gains.

The result of workers' determination—and employers' resistance—was a dramatic wave of strikes. More than 4 million workers—one in every five—went on strike in 1919, a proportion never since equaled. The year began with a walkout by shipyard workers in Seattle, a strong union town. Their action spread into a general strike that crippled the city. Another hard-fought strike disrupted the steel industry when 350,000 steel workers demanded union recognition and an end to twelve-hour shifts and the seven-day workweek. And in the fall the Boston police force shocked many Americans by going on strike. Governor Calvin Coolidge of Massachusetts propelled himself into the political spotlight by declaring, "There is no right to strike against the public safety by anybody, anywhere, any time." Coolidge fired the entire police force, and the strike failed. The public supported this harsh reprisal, and Coolidge was rewarded with the Republican vice presidential nomination in 1920.

The Red Scare

A crucial factor in organized labor's failure to win many of its strikes in the postwar period was the pervasive fear of radicalism. This concern coincided with mainstream Americans' longstanding anxiety about unassimilated immigrants—an anxiety that the war had made worse. The Russian Revolution of 1917 so alarmed the Allies that Wilson sent several thousand troops to Russia in the summer of 1918 in hopes of weakening the Bolshevik regime. When the Bolsheviks founded the Third International (or Comintern) in 1919 to export communist doctrine throughout the world, American fears deepened. As domestic labor unrest increased, Americans began to see radicals everywhere. Hatred of the German Hun was quickly replaced by hostility toward the Bolshevik Reds.

Ironically, as public concern about domestic Bolshevism increased, radicals were rapidly losing members and political power. No more than 70,000 Americans belonged to either the fledgling U.S. Communist party or the Communist Labor party in 1919. Both the IWW and the Socialist party had been weakened by wartime repression and internal dissent. Yet the public and the press continued to blame almost every disturbance, especially labor conflicts, on alien radicals. "REDS DIRECTING SEATTLE STRIKE—TO TEST CHANCE FOR REVOLUTION," warned a typical newspaper headline.

Tensions mounted when a series of bombs exploded in the early spring. "The word 'radical' in 1919," the historian Robert Murray has observed, "automatically carried with it the implication of dynamite." In June a bomb detonated outside the Washington town house of the recently appointed attorney general, A. Mitchell Palmer. His family escaped unharmed, but the bomber was blown to bits. Angling for the presidential nomination, Palmer capitalized on the event, fanning fears of domestic radicalism.

In November 1919, on the second anniversary of the Russian Revolution, the attorney general staged the first of what became known as "Palmer raids." Federal agents stormed the headquarters of radical organizations, capturing such supposedly revolutionary booty as a set of blueprints for a phonograph (at first thought to be sketches for a bomb). The dragnet pulled in thousands of aliens who had committed no crime, but were suspect because of their anarchist or revolutionary beliefs or their immigrant backgrounds. Lacking the protection of U.S. citizenship, they faced deportation without formal trial or indictment. In December 1919 the U.S.S. *Buford*, nicknamed the "Soviet Ark," embarked for Finland and the Soviet state with a cargo of 294 deported radicals.

The peak of Palmer's power came with his New Year's raids in January 1920. In one night, with the greatest possible publicity, federal agents rounded up 6,000 radicals, invading private homes, union headquarters, and meeting halls, and arresting citizens and aliens alike. Palmer was riding high in his ambitions for the presidency, but then he overstepped himself. He predicted that on May Day 1920 an unnamed conspiracy would attempt to overthrow the U.S. government. State militia units and police went on twenty-four-hour alert to guard the nation against the threat of revolutionary violence, but not a single incident occurred. As the summer of 1920 passed without major labor strikes or renewed bombings, the hysteria of the Red Scare began to abate.

The wartime legacy of antiradicalism and anti-immigrant sentiment, however, persisted well into the next decade. In May 1920, at the height of the Red Scare, Nicola Sacco, a shoemaker, and Bartolomeo Vanzetti, a fish peddler, were arrested for the robbery and murder of a shoe company's paymaster in South Braintree, Massachusetts. The two men, self-proclaimed anarchists and alien draft evaders, were both armed at the time of their arrest.

Convicted in 1921, Sacco and Vanzetti sat on death row for six years while supporters appealed their verdicts. Although new evidence suggesting their innocence surfaced, Judge Webster Thayer denied a motion for a new trial. Scholars still debate the question of their guilt, but most agree that the two anarchists did not receive a fair trial, that both the evidence and procedures were tainted. Moreover, it is also clear the verdict stemmed as much from their status as radicals and immigrants as it did from evidence. As future Supreme Court jurist Felix Frankfurter said at the time, "The District Attorney invoked against them a riot of political passion and patriotic sentiment." Nevertheless, shortly before his execution in the electric chair on August 23, 1927, Vanzetti claimed triumph:

> If it had not been for these thing, I might have live out my life among scorning men. I might have die, unmarked, unknown, a failure.... Never in our full life can we hope to do such work for tolerance, for justice, for man's understanding of man, as now we do by an accident.

This oft-quoted elegy captures the eloquence and tolerance of a man caught in the last spasm of antiradicalism and fear that capped America's participation in the Great War.

That participation left other legacies as well. World War I did not have the catastrophic effect on the United States that it did on European countries. With relatively few casualties and no physical destruction at home, America emerged from the conflict stronger than ever before. Increased efficiency and technological advancements fostered exceptional industrial productivity, making the United States the envy of the rest of the world in the postwar decade. Consolidating developments that had begun with the Spanish-American War, the United States became a major international power, both economically and politically.

At home, Americans tended to view the war as a significant watershed. "Since the war" emerged as a persistent refrain used to described a wide range of changes in daily life and cultural values. In the 1920s, everything from rising divorce rates and changing sexual morality to African-American militancy and increased standardization and regimentation was attributed to the war. This was a simplistic assessment. The war—especially the nationalism that accompanied it—contributed to a climate that was inhospitable to liberal social reforms, a climate that would persist until the crisis of the Great Depression. And though mobilization was accompanied by an insistence on as much voluntarism as possible, the war emergency did leave a legacy of a stronger federal government and an enlarged bureaucracy. It also exacerbated a number of social tensions, including those involving the working class, ethnic and racial diversity, and the changing role of women. But World War I alone cannot account for the tremendous social transformations that swept American society in these years. Industrialization; immigration; urbanization; and changing patterns in work, politics, religion, leisure, and the family were under way well before 1914–1918. The war was not necessarily the cause of those massive social changes, but rather a magnifying lens that illuminated them.

CHAPTER 23 TIMELINE

1914	Outbreak of war in Europe
	United States declares neutrality
1915	German submarine sinks *Lusitania*
1916	Woodrow Wilson reelected
	Pershing's expedition to Mexico
1917	U.S. enters World War I
	Revenue Act passed
	Selective Service Act passed
	War Industries Board established
	Suffrage militancy
	East St. Louis race riot
	Espionage Act
	Bolshevik Revolution
	Committee on Public Information
1918	Wilson proposes Fourteen Points
	Meuse-Argonne campaign
	Sedition Act
	Eugene Debs imprisoned under Sedition Act
	Armistice ends war
	U.S. troops intervene in Soviet Union
1919	Treaty of Versailles
	Chicago race riot
	Steel strike
	Red Scare and Palmer raids; *Schenck v. United States*
	American Legion founded
	League of Nations defeated in Senate
	Eighteenth Amendment (Prohibition)
	War Industries Board disbanded
1920	Nineteenth Amendment (woman suffrage)
	"Soviet Ark" sails
1924	Woodrow Wilson dies

CHAPTER 24

MODERN TIMES: THE 1920s

- Business-Government Partnership of the 1920s
- A New National Culture
- Dissenting Values and Cultural Conflict

In 1924 the sociologists Robert Lynd and Helen Merrell Lynd arrived in Muncie, Indiana, to study the life of a small American city. They observed how the citizens of Middletown (the fictional name they gave the city) made a living, maintained a home, educated their young, practiced their religion, organized community activities, and spent their leisure time. As the Lynds' fieldwork proceeded, they were struck by how much had changed over the past thirty-five years—the actual lifetime of a middle-aged Middletown resident—and decided to contrast the Muncie of the 1890s with the Muncie of the 1920s. When *Middletown* was published in 1929, this "study in modern American culture" became an unexpected best seller. Its success spoke to Americans' desire to understand the forces that were transforming their society.

The transformation to a modern society had begun with World War I. Participation in the war had made the United States a major player in the world economy; the foundations of large-scale corporate enterprise and a modern state had been firmly established. Rather than World War I, however, the 1920s were the watershed in the development of a mass national culture. Only then did the Protestant work ethic and the old values of self-denial and frugality begin to give way to the fascination with consumption, leisure, and self-realization that is the essence of modern times. In economic organization, political outlook, and cultural values, the 1920s had more in common with the United States today than with the industrializing America of the late nineteenth century.

BUSINESS-GOVERNMENT PARTNERSHIP OF THE 1920s

The business-government partnership fostered by World War I continued on an informal basis throughout the 1920s. As the *Wall Street Journal* enthusiastically proclaimed, "Never before, here or anywhere else, has a government been so completely fused with business." From 1922 to 1929 the nation's prosperity seemed to confirm the economy's ability to regulate itself with minimal government intervention. Gone, or at least submerged, was the reform impulse of the Progressive Era. Business leaders were no longer villains but respected public figures. President Warren G. Harding captured the prevailing political mood when he offered the American public "not heroics but healing, not nostrums but normalcy."

The Republican "New Era"

Except for Woodrow Wilson's two terms, the presidency had been controlled by the Republican party since 1896. When Wilson's progressive coalition floundered by 1918, the Republicans had a chance to regain the presidency. With the ailing Wilson out of the picture, in 1920 the Democrats nominated Governor James M. Cox of Ohio. Assistant Secretary of the Navy Franklin D. Roosevelt became the vice-presidential candidate. In their platforms, the Democrats called for U.S. participation in the League of Nations and a continuation of Wilson's progressivism. The Republicans, led by Warren G. Harding and Calvin Coolidge, promised a return to "normalcy," which meant a strong probusiness stance and conservative cultural values. Harding and Coolidge won in a landslide, marking the beginning of a Republican dominance that would last until 1932.

Central to what Republicans termed the "New Era" was business-government cooperation. Although Republican administrations generally opposed expanding state power to promote progressive reforms, they did use federal policy and power to assist corporations. Thus, Harding's secretary of the treasury, financier Andrew W. Mellon, engineered a tax cut that undercut the wartime Revenue Acts, benefiting wealthy individuals and corporations. The Republican-dominated Federal Trade Commission (FTC) for the most part ignored the antitrust laws rather than using federal power to police industry. In this the Commission followed the lead of the Supreme Court, which in 1920 had dismissed the long-pending antitrust case against U.S. Steel, ruling that largeness in business was not against the law as long as some competition remained.

Perhaps the best example of government-business cooperation emerged in the Department of Commerce, headed by Herbert Hoover, a believer in what historian Ellis Hawley has called the associative state. Hoover thought that with government assistance, businessmen would work in behalf of the public interest, thereby benefiting the entire country. Under Hoover, the Commerce Department expanded dramatically, offering new services like the compilation and distribution of trade and production statistics to American business. It also assisted private trade associations in their efforts to rationalize major sectors of industry and commerce by cooperating in such areas as product standardization and wage and price controls.

Unfortunately, not all government-business cooperation was as high-minded as Hoover had anticipated. President Harding was an honest man, but some of his political associates were not. When Harding died suddenly in San Francisco in August 1923, evidence of widespread fraud and corruption in his administration had just come to light. A particularly damaging scandal concerned the secret leasing of government oil reserves in Teapot Dome, Wyoming, and in Elk Hills, California, without competitive bidding. Secretary of the Interior Albert Fall was eventually convicted of taking $300,000 in bribes; he became the first cabinet officer in American history to serve a prison sentence.

After Harding's death the taciturn vice president, Calvin Coolidge, moved into the White House. In contrast to his predecessor's political cronyism and outgoing style, Coolidge personified moral rectitude. As vice president, "Silent Cal" often sat through official functions without uttering a word. A dinner partner once challenged him by saying, "Mr. Coolidge, I've made a rather sizable bet with my friends that I can get you to speak three words this evening." Responded Coolidge icily, "You lose." Although Coolidge was quiet and unimaginative, his image of unimpeachable integrity reassured voters, and he soon announced his candidacy for the presidency in 1924.

When the Democrats gathered that July in the sweltering heat of New York City, they faced a divided party. The party drew its support mainly from the South and from northern urban political machines like Tammany Hall in New York, and the two constituencies' interests often collided. They disagreed mightily over Prohibition; immigration restriction; and, most seriously, the mounting power of the racist and anti-immigrant Ku Klux Klan. The resolutions committee remained deadlocked for days over whether the party should condemn the Klan, eventually reaching a weak compromise that affirmed its general opposition to "any effort to arouse religious or racial dissension."

With this contentious background, the convention took 103 ballots to nominate John W. Davis, a Wall Street lawyer who had served as a West Virginia congressman, for the presidency. To attract rural voters, the Democrats chose as their vice-presidential candidate Governor Charles W. Bryan of Nebraska, William Jennings Bryan's brother. But the Democrats could not mount an effective challenge to their more popular and better-financed Republican rivals, whose strength came chiefly from the native-born Protestant middle class, augmented by small business people, skilled workers, farmers, northern blacks, and wealthy industrialists. Until the Democrats could overcome their sectional and cultural divisions and build an effective national organization to rival that of the Republicans, they would remain a minority party.

The 1924 campaign also featured a third-party challenge, by Senator Robert M. La Follette of Wisconsin, who ran on the Progressive party ticket. La Follette's candidacy mobilized reformers and labor leaders as well as disgruntled farmers in an effort to reinvigorate the reform movement both major parties had abandoned. The party platform called for nationalization of railroads, public ownership of utilities, and the right of Congress to overrule Supreme Court decisions. It also favored the direct election of the president by the voters rather than by indirect election through the electoral college.

The Republicans won an impressive victory. Coolidge received 15.7 million popular votes to Davis's 8.4 million and won a decisive margin in the electoral college. La Follette got almost 5 million popular votes, but he carried only Wisconsin in the electoral college. Perhaps the most significant aspect of the election was the low voter turnout. Only 52 percent of the electorate voted in 1924, compared to more than 70 percent in presidential elections of the late nineteenth century. Newly enfranchised women voters were not to blame, however; a long-term drop in voting by men, rather than apathy among women, caused the decline.

Instead of resting after their suffrage victory, women increased their political activism in the 1920s. African-American women struggled for voting rights in the Jim Crow South and pushed unsuccessfully for a federal anti-lynching law. Many women tried to break into party politics, but Democrats and Republicans granted them only token positions on party committees. Women were more influential as lobbyists. The Women's Joint Congressional Committee, a Washington-based coalition of ten major white women's organizations, including the newly formed League of Women Voters, lobbied actively for reform legislation. Its major accomplishment was the passage in 1921 of the Sheppard-Towner Federal Maternity and Infancy Act, which appropriated $1.25 million for well-baby clinics, educational programs, and visiting-nurse projects. Such major reform legislation was rare in the 1920s, however, and its success short-lived. Once politicians realized that women did not vote as a bloc, they stopped listening to the women's lobby, and in 1929 Congress cut off the program's funding.

The roadblocks women activists faced were part of a broader public antipathy to ambitious reforms. Although some states—such as New York, where an urban liberalism was coalescing under leaders like Al Smith—did enact a flurry of legislation that promoted workmen's compensation, public health programs, and conservation measures, on the national level reforms that would strengthen federal power made little headway. After years of progressive reforms and an expanded federal presence in World War I, Americans were unenthusiastic about increased taxation or more governmental bureaucracy. The Red Scare had given ammunition to opponents of reform by making it easy to claim that legislation calling for governmental activism was the first step toward Bolshevism. The general prosperity of the 1920s further hampered the reform spirit. With a

Women Get the Vote

A lice Paul, president of the Woman's Party, was a militant whose brand of feminism and reform was not shared by all women reformers. Nonetheless, this passage from her oral history captures well the widespread excitement about the opportunities the vote could bring individual women and the power it could summon for their causes in the early 1920s.

Suddenly we were regarded as having some power in the world. I mean, people were coming to you wanting *you* to get things for them. Women were coming wanting you to have them promoted in the government because they never could get the positions they thought they ought to have, and wanting to be appointed as ambassadors and everything they imagined, we could suddenly have so much power.

Congressmen began to suddenly have women secretaries; when I first went there, there was no woman secretary in all of Congress. . . . You walked into an office—all were men. . . . Everywhere—all the employees, the people earning their living by being sent to [work for] Congress were [men], because the congressmen were trying to build up votes among their constituents, who were men. . . .

[N]ormally, if a woman came there [to a committee hearing] and asked something, she was just put aside as—nobody had to pay attention to her, whether she wanted it or not.

But this time, at our first hearing after we got the vote, everybody came and said, "I represent two million women," or whatever she said she represented. *Well*, that was two million *voters* and was a totally different situation than when she came before. . . . Most of the thing the women saw in it was to get something for themselves, to come down to see if *they* could be secretaries, and *they* could be clerks of committees.

SOURCE: Ruth Barnes Moynihan, Cynthia Russett, and Laurie Crumpacker, *Second to None: A Documentary History of American Women* (University of Nebraska Press, 1993), vol. 2, pp. 150–151.

strong economy, the Republican policy of an informal partnership between business and government seemed to work and made reforms regulating corporations and the economy seem unnecessary and even harmful.

The Economy and the Heyday of Big Business

Although prosperity and the 1920s seem almost synonymous, the decade got off to a bumpy start in the transition from a wartime to a peacetime economy. In the immediate postwar years the nation suffered rampant inflation: prices jumped by a third in 1919, accompanied by feverish business activity. Federal efforts to halt inflation—through spending cuts and a contraction of the supply of credit—produced the recession of 1920–1921, the sharpest short-term downturn the United States had ever faced. Unemployment reached 10 percent. Foreign trade dropped by almost half as European nations resumed production after the disruptions of war. Prices fell dramatically—more than 20 percent—and reversed much of the wartime inflation.

The recession was short. In 1922, stimulated by an abundance of consumer products, particularly automobiles, the economy began a recovery that continued with only brief interruptions through 1929. Between 1922 and 1929 the gross national product (GNP) grew from $74.1 billion to $103.1 billion, approximately 40 percent. Per capita income rose from $641 in 1921 to $847 in 1929. Soon the federal government was recording a budget surplus. This economic expansion provided the backdrop for the partnership between business and government that flourished in the 1920s.

An abundance of new consumer products, particularly the automobile, stimulated recovery and prosperity. Manufacturing output expanded 64 percent as industries churned out cars, appliances, chemicals, electricity, radios, aircraft, and movies. Behind the growth lay new techniques of management and mass production, which brought a 40 percent increase in workers' productivity. In most industries, the demand for goods and services kept unemployment low

The Assembly Line
The success of the automobile industry contributed significantly to the prosperity of the 1920s, and mass production made automobiles affordable for ordinary citizens, not just the well to do. This photograph suggests the aptness of the phrase "rolling off the assembly line." By 1929 there were more than 23 million cars on the road.

throughout the decade. Combined with low inflation, high employment rates enhanced the spending power of many Americans, especially skilled workers and the middle class.

The economy, however, had some weaknesses. Income distribution reflected significant disparity: 5 percent of the nation's families received one-third of all income. In addition, a number of industries were unhealthy. Agriculture never fully recovered from the 1920–1921 recession. During the inflationary period of 1914–1920, farmers had borrowed heavily to finance mortgages and equipment in response to government incentives, increased demand, and rising prices. When the war ended, European countries resumed agricultural production, glutting the world market. The price of wheat dropped 40 percent as the government withdrew wartime price supports. Corn fell 32 percent and hogs 50 percent. Farmers were not the only ones whose incomes plunged. Certain "sick industries," such as coal and textiles, had also expanded in response to wartime demand, only to face overcapacity at war's end. Their troubles foreshadowed the Great Depression of the 1930s.

But despite these signs that not all was well, for the most part the nation was in a confident mood about the economy and the corporations that shaped it. Throughout the decade, business leaders enjoyed enormous popularity and respect; their reputations often surpassed those of the era's lackluster politicians. The most revered businessman of the decade was Henry Ford, whose rise from poor farm boy to corporate giant embodied both the traditional value of individualism and the triumph of mass production. Success stories like Ford's prompted President Calvin Coolidge to declare solemnly, "The man who builds a factory builds a temple. The man who works there worships there."

In this apotheosis of big business, the 1920s saw the triumph of the managerial revolution that had been reshaping American business since the late nineteenth century (see Chapter 19), as large-scale corporate organizations with bureaucratic structures of authority replaced family-run enterprises. There were more mergers in the 1920s than at any time since the heyday of business combinations in the 1880s and 1890s, with the largest number occurring in rapidly growing industries like chemicals, electrical appliances and machinery, and automobiles. By 1930 the 200 largest corporations controlled almost half the nonbanking corporate wealth in the United States. Rarely did any single corporation monopolize an entire industry; instead, *oligopolies*, in which a few large producers controlled an industry, became the norm, as in auto manufacturing, oil, and steel. The nation's financial institutions expanded and consolidated along with its corporations. Total bank assets rose dramatically as mergers between Wall Street banks enhanced New York's role as the financial center of the world. In 1929 almost half the nation's banking resources were controlled by 1 percent, or 250, of American banks.

Most Americans benefited from corporate success in the 1920s. Although unskilled African-Americans and immigrants participated far less fully in the prosperity of the decade, many members of the working class enjoyed higher wages and a better standard of living. A shorter workweek (five full days and a half-day on Saturday) and paid vacations gave many more leisure time. But despite those benefits, labor had less power in the workplace. Scientific management techniques, first introduced in 1895 by Frederick W. Taylor, but widely implemented only in the 1920s, reduced workers' control over their labor.

The 1920s were also the heyday of "welfare capitalism," a system of labor relations that stressed management's responsibility for employees' well-being. At a time when unemployment compensation and government-sponsored pensions did not exist, large corporations offered workers stock plans, health insurance, and old-age pension plans. Employee security was not, however, the primary aim of the programs, which were established mainly to deter the formation of unions. The approach reflected the conservative values of the 1920s, which placed the responsibility for economic welfare in the private sector so as to avoid government interference on the side of labor. Coupled with an aggressive drive for what corporate leaders called the *American Plan*, or an open (nonunion) shop, and with Supreme Court decisions that limited workers' ability to strike, welfare capitalism helped to erode the unions' strength. Membership dropped from 5.1 million in 1920 to 3.6 million in 1929—about 10 percent of the nonagricultural work force—and the number of strikes also fell dramatically from the level in 1919. Technology and management had combined to undermine workers' power.

Economic Expansion and Foreign Policy

The power of American corporations, so evident in their relationship with the work force, emerged also in the international arena. During the 1920s the United States was the most productive country in the world, with an enormous capacity to compete in foreign markets that eagerly desired American consumer products such as radios, telephones, automobiles, and sewing machines. The demand for U.S. capital was just as great. American investment abroad more than doubled between 1919 and 1930: by the end of the 1920s American corporations had invested $15.2 billion in foreign countries. Soon the United States became the world's largest creditor nation, reversing its pre–World War I status as a debtor and causing a dramatic shift of power in the world's capital markets.

A wide variety of American companies aggressively sought investment opportunities abroad. General Electric built new plants in Latin America, China, Japan, and Australia; Ford had major facilities throughout the British Empire. The United Fruit Company developed plantations in Costa Rica, Honduras, and Guatemala. American capital ran sugar plantations in Cuba and rubber plantations in the Philippines, Sumatra, and Malaya. Standard Oil of New Jersey led American oil companies in acquiring oil reserves in Mexico and Venezuela.

American banks supported U.S. enterprises abroad. European countries, particularly Germany, needed American capital to finance their economic recovery from World War I. Germany had to rebuild its economy and pay reparations to the Allies; Britain and France had to repay wartime loans. As late as 1930 the Allies still owed the United States $4.3 billion. American political leaders, responding to voters' disenchantment with the cost of the war, rigidly* demanded payment. "They hired the money, didn't they?" President Coolidge scoffed.

European countries had difficulty repaying their debts because the United States was maintaining high protective tariffs against foreign-made goods. The Fordney-McCumber Tariff of 1922 and the Hawley-Smoot Tariff of 1930 advanced the longstanding Republican policy of protectionism and economic nationalism. Most American manufacturers favored high tariffs because they feared foreign competition would reduce their profits. But the difficulty of selling goods in the United States hindered European nations' efforts to pay off their debts in dollars.

In 1924, at the prodding of the United States, France, Great Britain, and Germany joined with the United States in a plan to promote European financial stability. The Dawes Plan, named for Charles G. Dawes, the Chicago banker who negotiated the agreement, offered Germany substantial loans from American banks and a reduction in the amount of reparations owed to the Allies. But the Dawes Plan did not provide a permanent solution, because the international economic system was inherently unstable. It depended on the flow of American capital to Germany, reparations payments from Germany to the Allies, and the repayment of the Allies' debts to the United States. If the outflow of capital from the United States were to slow or stop, the international financial structure could collapse.

American efforts to stabilize the international economy belie the common view of U.S. foreign affairs as isolationist in the interwar period—as representing a time when the United States, disillusioned after World War I, willfully retreated from involvement in the rest of the world. In fact, the United States played an active role in world affairs during this period. Expansion into new markets was fundamental to the prosperity of the 1920s. U.S. officials ardently sought a stable international order to facilitate American investments in Latin American, European, and Asian markets.

They continued the quest for peaceful ways to dominate the Western Hemisphere both economically and diplomatically, but retreated slightly from military intervention in Latin America. U.S. troops withdrew from the Dominican Republic in 1924, but remained in Nicaragua almost continuously from 1912 to 1933, and in Haiti from 1915 to 1934. Relations with Mexico remained tense, a legacy of U.S. intervention during the Mexican Revolution and of U.S. resentment over the Mexican government's efforts to wrest control of its oil and mineral deposits away from foreign owners, a policy that particularly alarmed American oil companies.

There was little popular or political support, however, for entangling diplomatic commitments to allies, European or otherwise. The United States never joined the League of Nations or the Court of International Justice (the World Court). International cooperation had to come through other forums, such as the 1921 Washington Naval Arms Conference. At that meeting, the leading naval powers—Britain, the United States, Japan, Italy, and France—agreed to halt construction of large battleships for ten years and to establish a permanent tonnage ratio of 5:5:3:1.75:1.75, respectively. By placing limits on naval expansion, policymakers hoped to encourage stability in areas like the Far East, and to protect the fragile postwar economy from an expensive arms race. A thinly veiled agenda was to contain Japan, whose expansionist tendencies in the Far East were alarming other nations.

Seven years later, in a similar spirit of international cooperation, the United States joined other nations in condemning militarism, through the Kellogg-Briand Peace Pact. Fifteen nations signed the pact in Paris in 1928; forty-eight more approved it later. The signatories agreed to "condemn recourse to war for the solution of international controversies, and renounce it as an instrument of national policy." U.S. peace groups such as the Women's International League for Peace and Freedom enthusiastically supported the pact, and the U.S. Senate ratified it 85 to 1. Yet critics complained that it lacked mechanisms for enforcement, calling it nothing more than an "international kiss."

In the end, fervent hopes and pious declarations were no cure for the massive economic, political, and territorial problems created by World War I. U.S. policymakers vacillated, as they would in the 1930s, between wanting to play a larger role in world events and fearing that treaties and responsibilities would limit their ability to act unilaterally. Their diplomatic efforts ultimately proved inadequate to the mounting crises of the interwar years.

A NEW NATIONAL CULTURE

The 1920s represented an important watershed in the development of a mass national culture. A new emphasis on leisure, consumption, and amusement characterized the era, although its benefits were more accessible to the white middle class than to minorities and other disadvantaged groups. Automobiles, paved roads, the parcel post service, movies, radios, telephones, mass-circulation magazines, brand names, chain stores—all linked mill towns in the southern Piedmont, rural outposts on the Oklahoma plains, and ethnic enclaves on the coasts in an expanding web of national experience. In fact, with the exportation of automobiles, radios, and movies to consumers throughout the world, the American experience began to be globalized.

Consumption and Advertising

In homes across the country in the 1920s, Americans sat down to a breakfast of Kellogg's corn flakes and toast from a General Electric toaster. Then they got into a Ford Model T to go about their business, perhaps shopping at one of the chain stores that had sprung up across the country, such as Safeway or A & P. In the evening the family gathered to listen to radio programs like "Great Moments in History" or to read the latest issue of the *Saturday Evening Post*; on weekends they might go to see the newest Charlie Chaplin film at the local theater. Millions of Americans, in other words, now shared the same daily experiences.

Yet participation in commercial mass culture was not universal, nor did it necessarily mean total conversion to mainstream values. The historian Lizabeth Cohen concluded that "Chicago's ethnic workers were not transformed into more Americanized, middle-class people by the objects they consumed. Buying an electric vacuum cleaner did not turn Josef Dobrowolski into *True Story*'s Jim Smith." What is more, the unequal distribution of income limited many consumers' ability to buy the enticing new products. At the height of the nation's prosperity in the 1920s, about 65 percent of families had incomes of less than $2,000 a year, which barely supported a decent standard of living. Many Americans stretched their incomes by buying on the newly devised installment plan: in 1927, two-thirds of the cars in the United States had been bought "on time." Once consumers saw how easily they could finance a car, they bought radios, refrigerators, and sewing machines on credit. "A dollar down and a dollar forever," one cynic remarked.

Many of the new products were household appliances made feasible by the rapid electrification of American homes. Such technological advances had a dramatic impact on women's lives, for despite enfranchisement and participation in the work force, the primary role for most women continued to be that of housewife. Electric appliances made housewives' chores less arduous. Plugging in an electric iron was far easier than heating an iron on the stove; using a vacuum cleaner was quicker and easier than wielding a broom and a rug beater. Paradoxically, however, the new products did not dramatically increase women's leisure time. Instead, more middle-class housewives began to do their own housework and laundry, replacing human servants with electric ones. The new gadgets also raised standards of cleanliness, encouraging women to spend more time doing household chores.

Few of the new consumer products could be considered necessities. But the advertising industry, which became big business in this period, spent billions of dollars annually to entice consumers into buying automobiles, cigarettes, radios, and refrigerators. Advertisers appealed to people's social aspirations by projecting images of successful and elegant sophisticates who smoked a certain brand of cigarette or drove a recognizable make of car. Ad writers also sold products by preying on people's insecurities, coming up with a variety of socially unacceptable "diseases," from "office hips" and "ashtray breath" to the dreaded "B.O." (body odor).

Yet, consumers were not merely passive victims of manipulative advertisers. The advertising industry recognized that the buying public made choices, and struggled to offer messages that appealed to the target audience. Nonetheless, advertising helped to make consumption a cultural ideal for most of the middle class. Character, religion, and social standing, once the main criteria for judging self-worth, became less important than the gratification of personal needs through the acquisition of more and better possessions.

No possession typified the new consumer culture better than the automobile. "Why on earth do you need to study what's changing this country?" a Muncie, Indiana, resident asked the sociologists Robert and Helen Lynd. "I can tell you what's happening in just four letters: A-U-T-O!" The showpiece of modern capitalism, the automobile revolutionized the way Americans spent their money and leisure time. In the wake of the automobile, the isolation of rural life broke down. Cars touched so many aspects of American life that the word *automobility* was coined to describe their impact on production methods, the landscape, and American values.

Mass production of cars stimulated the prosperity of the 1920s. Before the introduction of the moving assembly line in 1913, Ford workers took twelve and a half hours to put together an auto; on an assembly line, they took only ninety-three minutes. By 1927 Ford was producing a car every twenty-four seconds. Auto sales climbed from 1.5 million in 1921 to 5 million in 1929, a year in which Americans spent $2.58 billion on new and used cars. By the end of the decade Americans owned about 80 percent of the world's automobiles—an average of one car for every five people.

The success of the auto industry had a ripple effect on the American economy. In 1929, 3.7 million workers owed their jobs to the automobile, either directly or indirectly. Auto production stimulated the steel, petroleum, chemical, rubber, and glass industries. Highway construction became a billion-dollar-a-year enterprise, financed by federal subsidies and state gasoline taxes. Car ownership also spurred the growth of suburbs, contributed to real-estate speculation, and spawned the first shopping center, Country Club Plaza in Kansas City, in 1924. Not even the death of 25,000 people a year in traffic accidents—70 percent of them pedestrians—could dampen America's passion for the automobile.

The auto also changed the way Americans spent their leisure time. They took to the roads, becoming a nation of tourists. The American Automobile Association, founded in 1902, reported that in 1929 about 45 million people—almost a third of the population—took vacations by automobile, patronizing the "autocamps" and tourist cabins that were the forerunners of motels. And like movies and other products of the new mass culture, cars changed the dating patterns of young Americans. Contrary to many parents' views, sex was not invented in the backseat of a Ford, but a Model T offered more privacy and comfort than did the family living room or the front porch, and contributed to increased sexual experimentation among the young.

The Mass Media and New Patterns of Leisure

Equal in importance to the automobile in transforming American culture were the increasingly significant mass media. The movie industry probably did more than anything else to disseminate common values and attitudes. In contrast to Europe, where cinema developed as an avant-garde, highbrow art form, in America movies were part of popular culture almost from the start. They began around the turn of the century in nickelodeons, where for a nickel the mostly working-class audience could see a one-reel silent film like the spectacularly successful *The Great Train Robbery* (1903). Because the films, mostly comedies and melodramas, were silent, they could be understood by immigrants who did not speak English. Both democratic and highly lucrative, the new medium quickly became popular.

By 1910 the movie-making industry had concentrated in southern California, which had cheap land, plenty of sunshine, and varied scenery—mountains, deserts, cities, and the Pacific Ocean—within easy reach. Another attraction was Los Angeles's reputation as an antiunion town. By war's end the United States was producing 90 percent of the world's cinema. Foreign distribution of Hollywood films stimulated the market for the material culture so lavishly displayed on the screen.

As directors turned to feature films and began exhibiting them in large, ornate theaters, movies quickly outgrew their working-class audiences and began to appeal to the middle class. Early movie stars—the comedians Buster Keaton, Charlie Chaplin, and Harold Lloyd; Mary Pickford (though born in Canada, "America's Sweetheart"); and dashing leading men Douglas Fairbanks, Wallace Reid, and John Gilbert—became national idols who helped to set national trends in clothing and hairstyles. Then a new cultural icon, the flapper, burst on the scene to represent emancipated womanhood. Clara Bow, the "It" Girl ("It" represented "sex appeal"), was Hollywood's favorite flapper, a red-haired "jazz

The Flapper
The flapper phenomenon was not limited to Anglos. This 1921 photograph of a young Mexican-American woman shows how American fads and fashions reached into Hispanic communities across the country.

baby" who rose to stardom almost overnight. Decked out in short skirt and rolled-down silk stockings, the flapper wore makeup (once assumed to be a sign of sexual availability in lower-class women), smoked, and danced to jazz, flaunting her liberated lifestyle. Like so many cultural icons, the flapper represented only a tiny minority of women. Yet the movies, along with advertising, mass-marketed this symbol of women's emancipation, suggesting it was the norm.

Movies became even more powerful cultural influences with the advent of the "talkies." Warner Brothers' *The Jazz Singer* (1927), starring Al Jolson, was the first feature-length film to offer sound. Two years later all the major studios had made the transition to talkies. By the end of the 1920s the nation had almost 23,000 movie theaters, including elaborate picture palaces built by the studios in major cities. Movie attendance rose from 60 million in 1927 to 90 million in 1930. In two short decades, movies had become thoroughly entrenched as the most popular—and probably the most influential—form of urban-based mass media.

That the first talkie was *The Jazz Singer* was perhaps no coincidence. Jazz was such an important part of the new mass culture that the 1920s are often referred to as the "Jazz Age." An improvisational style whose notes were (and are) rarely written down, jazz originated in the dance halls and bordellos of New Orleans around the turn of the century. A synthesis of African-American music, such as ragtime and the blues, it also drew on African and European styles.

Most of the early jazz musicians were black, and their music undoubtedly expressed dissent and opposition to mainstream white values. As black musicians left the South, they took jazz to Chicago, New York, and other cities. Some of the best-known performers were the composer-pianist Ferdinand "Jelly Roll" Morton; the trumpeter Louis Armstrong; the singer Bessie Smith, the "Empress of the Blues"; and composer-bandleader Edward "Duke" Ellington. Phonograph records increased the appeal of jazz by capturing its spontaneity; jazz, in turn, boosted the infant recording industry. Soon this uniquely American art form had caught on in Europe, especially in France.

Besides movies and records, other forms of mass media helped to establish national standards of taste and behavior. In 1922, ten magazines claimed a circulation of at least 2.5 million, including the *Saturday Evening Post*, the *Ladies' Home Journal*, *Collier's Weekly*, and *Good Housekeeping*. *Reader's Digest*, *Time*, and the *New Yorker*, still found today in homes throughout the country, all started in the 1920s. Tabloid newspapers also became part of the national scene. Thanks to syndicated newspaper columns and features, people across the United States could read the same articles. They could also read the same books, preselected by a board of expert judges for the Book-of-the-Month Club, founded in 1926.

The newest instrument of mass culture, professional radio broadcasting, began in 1920. By 1929 about 40 percent of the nation's households owned a radio. More than 800 stations, most affiliated with the Columbia Broadcasting Service (CBS) or the National Broadcasting Company (NBC) were on the air. Unlike European networks, which were government monopolies, American radio stations operated for profit. Though the federal government licensed the stations, their revenue came primarily from advertisers and corporate sponsors.

Americans loved radio. They listened avidly to the World Series and other sports events and to variety shows sponsored by brand-name advertisers. One of the most popular radio shows of all time, "Amos 'n' Andy," premiered on NBC in 1928, featuring two white actors playing stereotypical black characters. Soon fractured phrases from "Amos 'n' Andy," such as "Check and double check," became part of everyday speech. So many people "tuned in" (another new phrase of the 1920s) that the country seemed to come to a halt during popular programs—a striking example of the pervasiveness of mass media.

The automobile and new forms of entertainment like movies and radio pointed to a new emphasis on leisure. As the workweek shrank and some workers won the right to paid vacations, Americans had more time and energy to spend on recreation. Like so much else in the 1920s, leisure became increasingly tied to consumption and mass culture. Public recreation flourished as cities and suburbs built baseball diamonds, tennis courts, swimming pools, and golf courses. Americans not only played sports, but had the time and money to watch professional athletes perform in increasingly commercialized enterprises. They could see a game in a comfortable stadium, as they had become accustomed to doing, or they could listen to it on the radio or catch highlights in the newsreel at the local movie theater.

Americans reveled vicariously in the accomplishments of the superb athletes of the 1920s. Baseball continued to be the national pastime, drawing as many as 10 million fans a year. Tarnished in 1919 by the "Black Sox" scandal, in which some Chicago White Sox players took bribes to throw the World Series, baseball bounced back with the rise of stars like Babe Ruth of the New York Yankees. African-Americans, however, had different heroes. Excluded from the white teams, black athletes like Satchel Paige played in Negro leagues formed in the 1920s.

Thanks to the media's attention, the popularity of sports figures rivaled that of movie stars. In football Red Grange of the University of Illinois was a major star, while Jack Dempsey and Gene Tunney attracted a loyal following in boxing and Bobby Jones helped to popularize golfing. Bill Tilden dominated men's tennis, while Helen Wills and Suzanne Lenglen reigned in the women's game. The decade's best-known swimmer was Gertrude Ederle, who crossed the English Channel in 1926 in just over fourteen hours.

The decade's most popular hero, however, was neither an athlete nor a movie star. On May 20, 1927, aviator Charles Lindbergh, flying the small, open-cockpit plane *The Spirit of St. Louis*, made the first successful nonstop solo flight between New York and Paris, a distance of 3,610 miles, in 33½ hours. Returning home to ticker-tape parades and effusive celebrations, he became *Time* magazine's first Man of the Year in 1928. Lindbergh captivated the nation by combining his mastery of the new technology (the airplane) with the pioneer virtues of individualism, self-reliance, and hard work. He symbolized Americans' desire to enjoy the benefits of modern industrialism without renouncing their traditional values.

DISSENTING VALUES AND CULTURAL CONFLICT

As movies, radio, advertising, and mass production industries helped to transform the country into a modern, cosmopolitan nation, many Americans welcomed them as exciting evidence of progress. But others were uneasy. Flappers dancing to jazz, youthful sexual experimentation in the back of Ford Model T's, hints of a decline in religious values—these harbingers of a new era worried more tradition-minded folk. In the nation's cities, the powerful presence of immigrants and African-Americans suggested the waning of white Protestant cultural dominance. Beneath the clichéd images of the "Roaring Twenties" were deeply felt tensions that surfaced in conflicts over immigration, religion, Prohibition, and race relations.

The Rise of Nativism

Tensions between the city and the country partially explain the decade's conflicts. As farmers struggled with severe economic problems, rural communities lost residents to the cities at an alarming rate. The 1920 census revealed the growing influence of cities. For the first time in the nation's history, city people outnumbered rural people. In 1920, 52 percent of the population lived in urban areas, compared with just 28 percent in 1870. Though the 1920 census exaggerated the extent of urbanization—its guidelines classified towns with only 2,500 people as cities—there was no mistaking the trend (see Map 24.1). By 1929, ninety-three cities had populations over 100,000. The mass media generally reflected the cosmopolitan values of these urban centers, and many old-stock Americans worried that the cities, and the immigrants who clustered there, would soon dominate the culture.

Yet the polarities between city and country should not be overstated. Rural people were affected by the same forces that influenced urban residents. Much of the new technology—especially automobiles—enhanced rural life. Country people, like their urban counterparts, were tempted by the materialistic new values proclaimed on the radio, in magazines, and in movies. Moreover, urban Americans were far from monolithic; and many urban residents—immigrant Catholics, for example—were just as alarmed about declining moral standards as rural Protestants were. A simplified urban-rural dichotomy flattens out the complexity of the decade's cultural conflicts.

These conflicts often centered on the question of growing racial and ethnic pluralism. When native-born white Protestants—both rural and city dwellers—looked at their communities in 1920, they saw a nation that had changed dramatically in only forty years. During that time more than 23 million immigrants had come to America, many of them Jews or Catholics, most

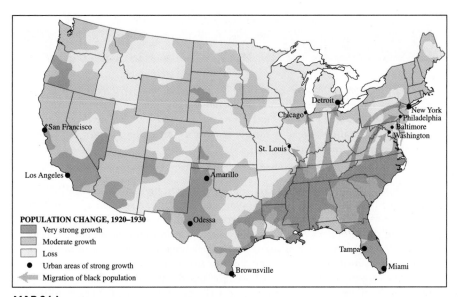

MAP 24.1
The Shift from Rural to Urban Population, 1920–1930
Despite the increasingly urban tone of modern America after 1920, regional patterns of population growth and decline were far from uniform. Cities in the South and West grew most
dramatically as southern farmers moved to more promising areas with familiar climates. An
important factor in the growth of northern cities, such as New York and Chicago, was the
migration of southern blacks set in motion by World War I.

of peasant stock. Senator William Bruce of Maryland branded them "indi-
gestible lumps" in the national stomach, implying that their large numbers and
foreign customs could not be absorbed by mainstream society. This sentiment,
termed *nativism*, was widely shared.

Nativist animosity fueled a new drive against immigration. The Chinese
had been excluded in 1882, and Theodore Roosevelt had negotiated a "gentleman's agreement" to limit Japanese immigration in 1908. Yet efforts to restrict European immigration did not meet with much success until after
World War I, which heightened suspicion of "hyphenated" Americans. During
the Red Scare, nativists had played up the supposed association of the immigrants with radicalism and labor unrest, charging that southern and Eastern
European Catholics and Jews were incapable of becoming true Americans.

In response, Congress passed an emergency bill in 1921, limiting the number
of immigrants to 3 percent of each national group as represented in the 1910
census. President Woodrow Wilson refused to sign it, but the bill was reintro-
duced and passed under Warren Harding. In 1924 a more restrictive measure,
the National Origins Act, reduced immigration until 1927 to 2 percent of each
nationality's representation in the 1890 census—which included relatively small
numbers of people from southeastern Europe and Russia. After 1927, the law set

AMERICAN VOICES

A Foreigner in America

A sian immigrants' experience of prejudice was much sharper than that of Europeans, but nonetheless Japanese immigrant Kazuo Kawai's experience echoes the problems that many young ethnic Americans in the 1920s had as they recognized that they did not belong in the old country, nor were they accepted as "One Hundred Percent Americans."

But it hurt because I couldn't say: "This is my own, my native land." What was my native land? Japan? True, I was born there. But it had seemed a queer, foreign land to me when I visited it. America? I had, until now, thought so. I had even told my father once that even in case of war between Japan and America, I would consider America as my country. In language, in thought, in ideals, in custom, in everything, I was American. But America wouldn't have me. She wouldn't recognize me in high school. She put the pictures of those of my race at the tail end of the year book. (I was a commencement speaker, so they had to put my picture near the front.) She won't let me play tennis on the courts in the city parks of Los Angeles, by city ordinance. She won't give me service when I go to a barber's shop. She won't let me own a house to live in. She won't give me a job, unless it is a menial one that no American wants. I thought I was American, but America wouldn't have me. Once I was American, but America made a foreigner out of me—Not a Japanese, but a foreigner—a foreigner to any country, for I am just as much a foreigner to Japan as to America.

SOURCE: *Stanford Survey of Race Relations* (Stanford University, 1924), Hoover Institute Archives.

a cap of 150,000 immigrants per year and continued to tie admission into the United States to a quota system that intentionally limited immigration from those regions. Japanese and Chinese immigrants were excluded entirely.

One remaining loophole in immigration law permitted unrestricted immigration from countries in the Western Hemisphere. This source became increasingly significant over the years (see Figure 24.1), as Mexicans and Central and Latin Americans crossed the border to fill jobs made available by the cutoff of immigration from Europe and Asia. Over 1 million Mexicans entered the United States between 1900 and 1930. Nativists and representatives of organized labor, who viewed Mexican immigrants as unwanted competition, lobbied Congress to close the loophole, but met with strong resistance until the 1930s and the economic devastation of the Great Depression.

Another expression of nativism in the 1920s was the revival of the Ku Klux Klan. Shortly after the premiere of *Birth of a Nation* in 1915, a group of southerners had gathered on Stone Mountain outside Atlanta to revive the racist organization. Taking as its motto "Native, white, Protestant supremacy," the modern Klan appealed to both urban and rural folk, though its largest "klaverns" were in urban areas. Spreading out from its southern base, the group found significant support in the Far West, the Southwest, and the Midwest, especially Oregon, Indiana, and Oklahoma. Unlike the Klan that was founded after the Civil War, the Klan of the 1920s did not limit its harassment to blacks; Catholics and Jews were just as likely to be its targets. Many of its tactics, however, were the same: arson, physical intimidation, and economic boycotts. The new Klan also turned to politics, succeeding in electing hundreds of Klansmen to public office. At the height of its power in 1925 the Klan had over 3 million members—including a strong contingent of women who pursued a political agenda that combined racism, nativism, and equal rights for white Protestant women.

After 1925 the Klan declined rapidly. Internal rivalries and the disclosure of rampant corruption hurt the group's image. Especially damaging was the revelation that Grand Dragon David Stephenson, the Klan's national leader,

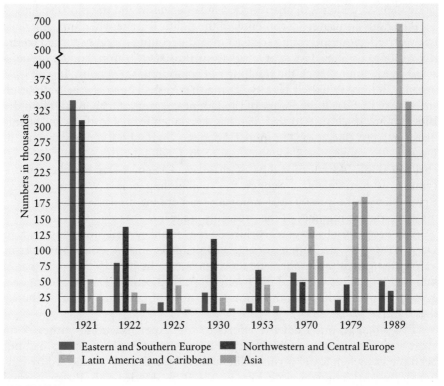

FIGURE 24.1
American Immigration after World War I
Nativism slowed the influx of immigrants after 1920, as did the dislocations brought on by depression and war in the 1930s and 1940s. Note the higher rate of non–European immigration since the 1970s.

had kidnapped and sexually assaulted his former secretary, driving her to suicide. And the passage of the National Origins Act in 1924 reduced the nativist fervor, robbing the Klan of its most potent issue.

Religious Fundamentalism and Prohibition

Other cultural tensions erupted over religion. The debate between modernist and fundamentalist Protestants, which had been simmering since the 1890s (see Chapter 20), came to a boil in the 1920s. Modernists, or liberal Protestants, tried to reconcile religion with Charles Darwin's theory of evolution and the avalanche of recent technological and scientific discoveries. Fundamentalists clung to a literal interpretation of the Bible that could not be reconciled with science. Most major Protestant denominations, especially the Baptists and the Presbyterians, experienced heated internal conflicts during the 1920s. However, the most conspicuous evangelical figures came from outside mainstream denominations. Popular preachers like Billy Sunday and Aimee Semple McPherson used revivals, storefront churches, and open-air preaching to popularize their own blends of charismatic fundamentalism and traditional values.

Religious controversy soon entered the political arena when fundamentalists, worried about increasing secularism and declining morality, turned to the law to shore up their vision of a righteous Protestant nation. Some states enacted legislation to block the teaching of evolution in the schools. In 1925, for instance, Tennessee passed a law declaring that "it shall be unlawful . . . to teach any theory that denies the story of the Divine creation of man as taught in the Bible, and to teach instead that man has descended from a lower order of animals." In a test case involving John T. Scopes, a high school biology teacher in Dayton, Tennessee, the fledgling American Civil Liberties Union (ACLU) challenged the constitutionality of that law. Clarence Darrow, the famous criminal lawyer, defended Scopes; the spellbinding orator William Jennings Bryan, three-time presidential candidate and ardent fundamentalist, was the most prominent member of the prosecution's team.

The Scopes trial was quickly dubbed the "monkey trial," referring both to Darwin's theory that human beings and primates share a common ancestor and to the circus atmosphere in the courtroom. In July 1925, more than a hundred journalists crowded the sweltering courthouse in Dayton, Tennessee, giving massive publicity to the knotty questions of faith and scientific theory that the trial addressed.

The judge rebuffed defense efforts to call expert scientific witnesses on evolution, dismissing such testimony as hearsay because the scientists had not been present when lower forms of life had evolved. Darrow countered by calling Bryan to the stand as an expert on the Bible. Under oath, Bryan asserted his belief that a "big fish" had swallowed Jonah and that God had created the world in six days. He hedged, however, about whether the "days" were literally twenty-four hours long, an inconsistency that Darrow ruthlessly exploited.

Even so, the jury took only eight minutes to delivery its verdict: guilty.

Scopes Trial
As this picture of a stall selling antievolution material in Dayton, Tennessee, suggests, the Scopes trial in 1925 became a focus of the antievolution movement. Pitting the old-time religion of rural America against modern values, the trial symbolized much of the cultural conflict of the 1920s and demonstrated the continued importance of religion to many Americans.

Though the Tennessee Supreme Court later overturned the conviction on a technicality, the reversal prevented further appeals of the case and the controversial law remained on the books more than thirty years. Historically, the trial symbolizes the conflict between the two competing value systems, cosmopolitan and traditional, that clashed in the 1920s. It suggests that despite the period's image as a frivolous and decadent time, religion continued to matter deeply to many Americans.

Like the dispute over evolution, Prohibition, the most notorious cultural debate of the 1920s, involved the power of the state to enforce social values. Americans did drink less after passage of the Eighteenth Amendment, which took effect in January of 1920 (see Chapter 23). Beer consumption declined the most, because beer was more difficult to manufacture and distribute illegally than hard liquor. But once people's willingness to flout the law became clear, this effort to legislate private morality was doomed.

More than any other issue, Prohibition gave the decade its reputation as the Roaring Twenties. In major cities, whose ethnic populations had always opposed Prohibition, noncompliance was widespread. People imitated rural moonshiners by distilling "bathtub gin." Illegal saloons called "speakeasies" sprang up everywhere—more than 30,000 of them in New York City alone. Liquor smugglers operated with ease along borders and coastlines. Organized crime, already a presence in major cities, supplied a ready-made distribution network for the bootleg liquor, using the "noble experiment," as Prohibition was called, to entrench itself more deeply in city politics. Said the decade's most notorious gangster, Al Capone, "Everybody calls me a racketeer. I call myself a businessman. When I sell liquor, it's bootlegging. When my patrons serve it on a silver tray on Lake Shore Drive, it's hospitality."

By the middle of the decade, Prohibition was clearly failing. Government appropriations for its enforcement were woefully inadequate; the few highly publicized raids hardly made a dent in the liquor trade. Forces for repeal—the "wets," as opposed to the "drys," who continued to support the Eighteenth Amendment—began the long process of gaining the necessary votes in Congress and state legislatures to amend the Constitution once more. The wets argued that Prohibition had undermined respect for the law and had seriously impinged upon individuals' liberty. The onset of the Great Depression hastened the repeal process, as politicians began to see alcohol production as a way to create jobs and prop up the faltering economy. On December 5, 1933, the Eighteenth Amendment was repealed. Ironically, drinking became more socially acceptable, though not necessarily more widespread, than it had been before the experiment began.

Intellectual Currents and Crosscurrents

The most articulate and embittered dissenters of the 1920s were writers and intellectuals disillusioned by the horrors of World War I and the crass materialism of the new consumer culture. Some artists were so repelled by what they saw as the complacent, moralistic, and anti-intellectual tone of American life that they settled in Europe—some temporarily, like the novelists Ernest Hemingway and F. Scott Fitzgerald, others permanently, like writer Gertrude Stein. Two prominent African-American artists, dancer Josephine Baker and writer Langston Hughes, sought temporary escape from racism in France. The poet T. S. Eliot, who left the United States before the war, ultimately became a British citizen. His despairing poem *The Waste Land* (1922), with its images of a fragmented civilization in ruins after the war, influenced a generation of writers. Other writers too made powerful antiwar statements, including John Dos Passos, whose first novel, *The Three Soldiers* (1921), was inspired by the war, and whose *1919* (1932), the second volume of his magnificent *USA* trilogy, railed against the obscenity of "Mr. Wilson's war." Ernest Hemingway's novels *In Our Time* (1924), *The Sun Also Rises* (1926), and *A Farewell to Arms* (1929), also powerfully described the dehumanizing consequences and the futility of war.

But the artists and writers who migrated to Europe, particularly Paris, were not simply a "lost generation" fleeing America. They were also drawn to Paris, the cultural and artistic capital of the world and a beacon of modernism. Paris, as Gertrude Stein put it, was "where the twentieth century was happening." Indeed, the *modernist* movement, which was marked by skepticism and technical experimentation in literature, art, and music, invigorated American writing both abroad and at home. Many American writers, whether they settled in Paris or remained in their home country, joined the movement, which had begun before the war as intellectuals reacted with excitement to the cultural and social changes that science, industrialization, and urbanization had brought. In the 1920s the business culture and political corruption of the Harding years caused intellectuals to cast a more critical eye on American society. One of the sharpest critics, the Baltimore journalist H. L. Mencken, directed his mordant wit against mass culture; small-town America with its guardians of public morals; and the "booboisie," his contemptuous term for the middle class. In the *American Mercury*, the journal he founded in 1922, Mencken championed writers like Sherwood Anderson, Sinclair Lewis, and Theodore Dreiser, who satirized the provincialism of American society.

The literature of the 1920s was rich and varied. Poetry enjoyed a renaissance in the works of Robert Frost, Wallace Stevens, Marianne Moore, and William Carlos Williams. Edith Wharton won a Pulitzer Prize—she was the first woman so honored—for *The Age of Innocence* (1920). Influenced by Freudian psychology, William Faulkner achieved his first critical success with *The Sound and the Fury* (1929), set in the fictional Mississippi county of Yoknapatawpha, where inhabitants clung to the values of the old agrarian South as they struggled to adjust to modern industrial capitalism. Playwright Eugene O'Neill also showed the influence of Freudian psychology in his experimental plays, including *The Hairy Ape* (1922) and *Desire under the Elms* (1924). Although both Faulkner and O'Neill went on to produce additional major works in the 1930s, the creative energy of the literary renaissance of the 1920s did not survive into the 1930s. The Great Depression, social and ideological unrest, and the rise of totalitarianism would reshape the intellectual landscape.

A different kind of cultural affirmation took place in the black community of Harlem in the 1920s. In the words of the Reverend Adam Clayton Powell, Sr., pastor of the influential Abyssinian Baptist Church, Harlem loomed as "the symbol of liberty and the Promised Land to Negroes everywhere." One aspect of this hope was the Harlem Renaissance, a movement of young writers and artists who broke with older genteel traditions of black literature to reclaim a cultural identity with African roots. Alain Locke, editor of the anthology *The New Negro* (1926), summed up the movement when he stated that, through art, "Negro life is seizing its first chances for group expression and self-determination." Authors like Claude McKay, Jean Toomer, Jessie Fauset, and Zora Neale Hurston explored the black experience and represented the "New Negro" in fiction. Countee Cullen and Langston Hughes turned to poetry, and Augusta Savage to sculpture. Their outpouring of artistic expression gave voice to the African-American struggle to find a way, as W. E. B. Du Bois put it, "to be both a Negro and an American."

The vitality of the Harlem Renaissance was short-lived. Although the NAACP's magazine *The Crisis* provided a forum for the Harlem writers, the black middle class and Harlem's intellectual elite were relatively small and could not support the group's efforts. Its major audience consisted of white intellectuals and philanthropists. The movement thus depended on white patronage for support and access to publication. During the Jazz Age, when Harlem was in vogue, publishing houses courted Harlem writers, but when the stock market crashed in 1929 their interest vanished, and the movement waned as the Depression deepened. But the legacy of the Harlem Renaissance would influence a new generation of black writers when black intellectuals rediscovered the works during the civil rights movement of the 1960s.

Although the Harlem Renaissance had little impact on the masses of African-Americans, other movements built racial pride and challenged white political and cultural hegemony. The most successful was the Universal Negro Improvement Association (UNIA), which championed black separatism under the leadership of the Jamaican-born Marcus Garvey. Based in Harlem, the UNIA was the black working class's first mass movement. At its height it

The Harlem Renaissance
The Crisis, edited by W. E. B. Du Bois, was the magazine of the National Association for the Advancement of Colored People (NAACP). This 1929 cover suggests the cultural and political awakenings associated with the Harlem Renaissance.

claimed 4 million followers, many of whom were recent migrants to northern cities. Like several nineteenth-century reformers, Marcus Garvey urged blacks to return to Africa; blacks, he reasoned, would never be treated justly in countries ruled by whites. Although he did not anticipate a massive migration, he did envision a strong black Africa which could use its power to protect blacks everywhere. Garvey's wife, Amy Jacques Garvey, appealed to black women by combining black nationalism with an emphasis on women's contributions to culture and politics.

The UNIA grew rapidly in the early 1920s. It published a newspaper called *Negro World* and undertook extensive business ventures to support black enterprise. The most ambitious project, the Black Star Line steamship company, was supposed to ferry cargo between the West Indies and the United States and take African-Americans back to Africa. Irregularities in fund raising for the project, however, led to Garvey's conviction for mail fraud in 1925, and he was sentenced to five years in prison. President Coolidge paroled him in 1927, but Garvey was deported to Jamaica. Without his charismatic leadership, the movement collapsed.

The 1928 Election

The works of the Lost Generation and the Harlem Renaissance touched only a small minority of Americans in the 1920s, but emotionally charged issues like Prohibition, fundamentalism, and nativism eventually spilled over into national politics. The Democratic party, which drew on rural Protestants in the South and the West as well as ethnic minorities in northern cities, was especially vulnerable to the cultural conflicts of the time. The 1924 Democratic national convention revealed an intensely polarized party, split between the urban machines and its rural wing.

In 1928, the urban wing held sway and succeeded in nominating New York's Governor Alfred E. Smith, a descendant of Irish immigrants and a product of Tammany Hall. Proud of his background, Smith adopted "The Sidewalks of New York" as his campaign song. His candidacy troubled many voters, however. His heavy New York accent, his brown derby, and his colorful style highlighted his urban working-class origins, and his early career in Tammany Hall suggested—incorrectly—that he was little more than a cog in the machine. Smith's stand on Prohibition—although he promised to enforce it, he wanted it repealed—alienated even more voters.

An additional handicap, however, was his religion. In 1928, most Protestants were not ready for a Catholic president. Although Smith insisted that his religion would not interfere with his duties as president, his perceived allegiance to Rome cost him the support of Democrats and Republicans alike. Protestant clergymen, who already opposed Smith because he supported the repeal of Prohibition, led the drive against him. "No Governor can kiss the papal ring and get within gunshot of the White House," declared one Methodist bishop.

Just as Smith was a new kind of presidential candidate for the Democrats, so was Herbert Hoover for the Republicans. As a professional administrator and engineer who had never before been elected to political office, Hoover embodied the new managerial and technological elite that was restructuring the nation's economic order. During his campaign, in which he gave only seven speeches, Hoover asserted that his vision of individualism and cooperative endeavor would banish poverty from the United States. That rhetoric, as well as his reputation for organizing a drive for humanitarian relief during the war, caused many voters to see him as more progressive than Smith.

Hoover won a stunning victory, receiving 58 percent of the popular vote to Smith's 41 percent, and 444 electoral votes to Smith's 87. The election reflected important underlying political changes. Despite the overwhelming loss, the Democrats' turnout increased substantially in urban areas. Smith won the industrialized states of Massachusetts and Rhode Island and carried the nation's twelve largest cities. The Democrats were on their way to fashioning a new identity as the party of the urban masses, a reorientation the New Deal completed in the 1930s.

It is unlikely that any Democratic candidate, let alone a Catholic, could have won the presidency in 1928. With a seemingly prosperous economy, national consensus on foreign policy, and strong support from the business community, the Republicans were unbeatable. Ironically, Herbert Hoover's victory would put him in the unenviable position of leading the United States when the Great Depression struck in 1929. Having claimed credit for the prosperity of the 1920s, the Republicans would not escape blame for the depression; twenty-four years would pass before a Republican won the presidency again.

But as Hoover began his presidency in early 1929, most Americans expected progress and prosperity to continue. The New Era the Republicans had touted meant more than Republican ascendancy in politics, more than business-government cooperation and a decline in the progressive reform movement. To most Americans, the New Era embodied the industrial productivity and technological advances that made consumer goods widely available, and the movies and the radio an exciting part of American life. At home and abroad the nation seemed unprecedentedly vigorous and powerful. Despite disruptive cultural conflicts and a changing workplace that was undermining workers' power, despite inequities in the racial order and in the distribution of income, the general tone was one of optimism, of faith in the modern society the country had become. That faith made the harsh realities of the Great Depression that would follow all the more shocking.

CHAPTER 24 TIMELINE

1920– 1921	Recession
1920	First commercial radio broadcast Warren G. Harding elected president Census reveals shift from farms to cities Edith Wharton, *The Age of Innocence*
1921	Sheppard-Towner Act Immigration Act passed Washington Conference on Naval Disarmament
1922	Fordney-McCumber Tariff T. S. Eliot, *The Waste Land*
1923	Calvin Coolidge succeeds Harding as president
1924	Dawes Plan reduces German reparations payments Withdrawal of American troops from Nicaragua Teapot Dome scandal U.S. troops withdrawn from Dominican Republic National Origins Act passed
1925	F. Scott Fitzgerald, *The Great Gatsby* Height of Ku Klux Klan Scopes ("monkey") trial
1926	Alain Locke, *The New Negro* anthology Book-of-the-Month Club founded
1927	*The Jazz Singer:* the first "talkie" Charles Lindbergh's solo flight
1928	Herbert Hoover elected president Kellogg-Briand Pact "Amos 'n' Andy" premieres
1929	*Middletown* Ernest Hemingway, *A Farewell to Arms* William Faulkner, *The Sound and the Fury*

THE GREAT DEPRESSION

- The Coming of the Great Depression
- Hard Times
- The Social Fabric of Depression America
- Herbert Hoover and the Great Depression

Our images of the 1920s and the decade that followed are polar opposites. Flappers and movie stars, admen and stockbrokers, caught up in what F. Scott Fitzgerald called the "world's most expensive orgy"—these are our conception of the Jazz Age. The 1930s we remember in terms of bread lines and hobos, dust bowl devastation and hapless migrants piled into dilapidated jalopies. Almost all our impressions of that decade are black and white, in part because widely distributed photographs taken by Farm Security Administration photographers etched this dark visual image of depression America on the popular consciousness.

But the contrast between the flush times of the 1920s and the hard times of the 1930s is too stark. The vaunted prosperity of the 1920s was never as widespread or as deeply rooted as many believed. Though America's mass-consumption economy was the envy of the world, many people lived on its margins. Nor was every American devastated by the depression. Those with a secure job or a fixed income survived the economic downturn in relatively good shape, and some even managed to get rich. Yet few could escape the depression's wide-ranging social, political, and cultural effects. Though not every event of the 1930s should be viewed through the lens of the depression, the great economic contraction unifies the history of the decade more than any other theme.

THE COMING OF THE GREAT DEPRESSION

Booms and busts are a permanent feature of the business cycle in capitalist economies. Since the beginning of the Industrial Revolution early in the nineteenth century, the United States had experienced recessions or panics at least once every twenty years. But none was as severe as the Great Depression of the 1930s. The downturn began slowly and almost imperceptibly. After 1927, consumer spending declined and housing construction slowed. Soon inventories piled up; in 1928 manufacturers began to cut back production and lay off workers, reducing incomes and buying power and reinforcing the slowdown. By the summer of 1929 the economy was clearly in recession.

Causes of the Depression

A crisis in the stock market signaled more serious problems. By 1929 the market had become the symbol of the nation's prosperity, an icon of American business culture. The financier John J. Raskob captured this attitude in a *Ladies' Home Journal* article, "Everyone Ought to Be Rich." Invest $15 a month in sound common stocks, Raskob advised, and in twenty years the investment would grow to $80,000. Not everyone was playing the stock market, however. Only about 4 million Americans, or roughly 10 percent of the nation's households, owned stock in 1929.

Stock prices had been rising steadily since 1921, but in 1928 and 1929 they surged forward, rising on average over 40 percent. At the time, stock market activity was essentially unregulated. Margin buying in particular proceeded at a feverish pace as customers borrowed up to 75 percent of the purchase price of stocks. But then, on "Black Thursday"—October 24, 1929, and again on "Black Tuesday"—October 29—the bubble burst. On those two bleak days, more than 28 million shares changed hands in frantic trading. Overextended investors, suddenly finding themselves heavily in debt, began to sell their stocks. Waves of panic selling ensued, during which many stocks found no buyers. Practically overnight, stock values fell from a peak of $87 billion (at least on paper) to $55 billion.

The impact of what became known as the Great Crash was felt far beyond the trading floors of Wall Street. Commercial banks had invested heavily in corporate stock. What is more, speculators who had borrowed from banks to buy their stocks could not repay their loans because they could not sell their shares. Throughout the nation, bank failures multiplied. Since bank deposits were uninsured, when a bank collapsed, depositors lost all their money. The sudden loss of their life savings was a tremendous shock to the middle class, many of whom had no other resources to cope with the crisis. Besides its immediate economic impact, the crash destroyed the optimistic view of the stock market as the crowning symbol of American prosperity, precipitating a crisis of confidence that prolonged the depression.

Although the stock market crash contributed to the Great Depression, longstanding weaknesses in the economy accounted for its length and severity. Agriculture, in particular, had never recovered from the recession of

1920–1921. Farmers faced high fixed costs for equipment and mortgages, which they had incurred during the inflationary war years. When prices fell because of overproduction, many farmers defaulted on their mortgage payments, risking foreclosure. Because farmers accounted for about a fourth of the nation's gainfully employed workers in 1929, their difficulties weakened the general economic structure.

Certain basic industries also had economic setbacks during the prosperous 1920s. Textiles, facing a steady decline after the war, abandoned New England for cheaper labor in the South, but suffered still from decreased demand and overproduction. Mining and lumbering, which had expanded in response to wartime demand, confronted the same problems. And the railroad industry, damaged by stiff competition from trucks, faced shrinking passenger revenues and stagnant freight levels, worsened by inefficient management. While these older sectors of the economy faltered, newer and more successful consumer-based industries, such as chemicals, appliances, and food processing, proved not yet strong enough to lead the way to recovery.

The unequal distribution of the nation's wealth was another underlying weakness of the economy. During the 1920s the share of national income going to families in the upper- and middle-income brackets increased. The tax policies of Secretary of the Treasury Andrew Mellon contributed to a concentration of wealth by lowering personal income tax rates, eliminating the wartime excess-profits tax, and increasing deductions that favored corporations and the very affluent. In 1929, the lowest 40 percent of the population received only 12.5 percent of aggregate family income, while the top 5 percent of the population received 30 percent. Once the depression began, this skewed income distribution prevented people from spending the amount of money that was necessary to revive the economy.

The Great Depression became self-perpetuating. The more the economy contracted, the longer people expected the depression to last. The longer they expected it to last, the more afraid they became to spend or invest their money, if they had any—and spending and investing were exactly what was needed to stimulate a recovery. The economy showed some improvement in the summer of 1931, when low prices encouraged consumption, but plunged again late that fall.

The nation's banks, already weakened by the stock market crash, contributed to the worsening contraction. When agricultural prices and income fell more steeply than usual in 1930, many farmers went bankrupt, causing rural banks to fail. By December 1930, so many rural banks had defaulted on their obligations that urban banks too began to collapse. The wave of bank failures frightened depositors, who withdrew their savings, deepening the crisis.

In 1931, a change in the nation's monetary policy compounded the banks' problems. In the first phase of the depression, the Federal Reserve System had reacted cautiously. But in October 1931 the Federal Reserve Bank of New York significantly increased the *discount rate*—the interest rate charged on loans to member banks—and reduced the amount of money placed in circulation through the purchase of government securities. This miscalculation squeezed the money supply, forcing prices down and depriving businesses of funds for investment.

In the face of that money shortage, the American people could have pulled the country out of the depression only by spending faster. But because of falling prices, rising unemployment, and a troubled banking system, Americans preferred to keep their dollars, stashing them under the mattress rather than depositing them in the bank, further limiting the amount of money in circulation. Economic stagnation solidified.

The World-Wide Depression

President Hoover later blamed the severity of the depression on the international economic situation. Although domestic factors far outweighed international causes of America's protracted decline, Hoover was correct in surmising that economic problems in the rest of the world affected the United States, and vice versa. Indeed, the international economic system had been out of kilter since World War I. It functioned only as long as American banks exported enough capital to allow European countries to repay their debts and to buy U.S. manufactured goods and foodstuffs. By the late 1920s European economies were staggering under the weight of huge debts and trade imbalances with the United States, which effectively undercut their recovery from the war. By 1931 most European economies had collapsed.

In an interdependent world, the economic downturn in America had enormous repercussions. When U.S. companies cut back production, they also cut their purchases of raw materials and supplies abroad, devastating many foreign economies. When American financiers sharply reduced their foreign investment and consumers bought fewer European goods, debt repayment became even more difficult, straining the gold standard, the foundation of multilateralism in the interwar period. As European economic conditions worsened, demand for American exports fell drastically. Finally, when the Hawley-Smoot Tariff of 1930 went into effect, raising rates to all-time highs, foreign governments retaliated by imposing their own trade restrictions, further limiting the market for American goods and intensifying the world-wide depression.

No other nation was as hard hit as the United States. From the height of its prosperity before the stock market crash in 1929 to the depths of the depression in 1932 and 1933, the U.S. gross national product (GNP) was cut almost in half, declining from $103.1 billion to $58 billion in 1932. Consumption expenditures dropped by 18 percent, construction by 78 percent; private investment plummeted 88 percent, and farm income, already low, was more than halved. In this period, 9,000 banks went bankrupt or closed their doors and 100,000 businesses failed. The consumer price index (CPI) declined by 25 percent, and corporate profits fell from $10 billion to $1 billion.

Most tellingly, unemployment rose from 3.2 percent to 24.9 percent, affecting approximately 12 million workers. Statistical measures at the time were fairly crude, so the figures were probably understated. At least one in four workers was out of a job, and even those who had jobs faced wage cuts, work for which they were overqualified, or layoffs. Their stories put a human face on the almost incomprehensible dimensions of the economic downturn.

HARD TIMES

"We didn't go hungry, but we lived lean." That statement sums up the experiences of many families during the Great Depression. The vast majority of Americans were neither very rich nor very poor. For most the depression did not mean losing thousands of dollars in the stock market, or pulling children out of boarding school; nor did it mean going on relief or living in a shantytown. In a typical family in the 1930s, the husband still had a job and the wife was still a homemaker. Though life was not easy, families usually managed to "make do."

The Invisible Scar

"You could feel the depression deepen," recalled the writer Caroline Bird, "but you could not look out the window and see it." Many people never saw a bread line or a man selling apples on the corner. The depression caused a private kind of despair that often simmered behind closed doors. "I've lived in cities for many months broke, without help, too timid to get in bread lines," the writer Meridel LeSueur remembered. "A woman will shut herself up in a room until it is taken away from her, and eat a cracker a day and be as quiet as a mouse."

The depression did not create poverty, but it did extend poverty's harsh realities to more people. Hard times weighed heavily on the nation's senior citizens, many of whom faced total destitution. Formerly solid working-class and middle-class families, who strongly believed in the Horatio Alger ethic of upward mobility through hard work, suddenly found themselves floundering in a society that no longer had a place for them. Thus, the depression challenged basic American tenets of individualism and success. Yet even in the midst of pervasive unemployment, many people blamed themselves for their misfortune. This sense of damaged pride pervaded letters written to President Franklin D. Roosevelt and his wife Eleanor, summed up succinctly in one woman's plea for assistance: "Please don't think me unworthy."

Downward mobility was especially hard for middle-class Americans. An unemployed man in Pittsburgh told the journalist Lorena Hickok, "Lady, you just can't know what it's like to have to move your family out of the nice house you had in the suburbs, part paid for, down into an apartment, down into another apartment, smaller and in a worse neighborhood, down, down, down, until finally you end up in the slums."

After exhausting their savings and credit, many families faced the humiliation of going on relief. Seeking aid from state or local government hurt their pride and disrupted the traditional custom of turning to relatives, neighbors, church, and mutual-aid society in time of need. Even if families endured the demeaning process of certification for state or local relief, the amount they

The Bread Line
Some of the most vivid images from the depression were bread lines and men selling apples on street corners. Note that all the people in this bread line are men. Women rarely appeared in bread lines, often preferring to endure private deprivation rather than violate standards of respectable behavior.

received was a pittance. In New York State, where benefits were among the highest in the nation, a family on relief received only $2.39 a week.

Such hardships left a deep wound, which Caroline Bird described as the "invisible scar." One elderly civil servant bought a plot of land outside Washington so that if the depression recurred, she would have the means to live. Virginia Durr, an Alabama civil rights activist, described another common response: "The great majority reacted by thinking money is the most important thing in the world. Get yours. And get it for your children. Nothing else matters. Not having that stark terror come at you again." For many Americans "that stark terror" of losing control over their lives was the crux of the Great Depression.

Families Face the Great Depression

Sociologists who studied family life during the 1930s found that the depression usually intensified existing behavior. If a family had been stable and cohesive before the depression, then members pulled together to overcome the new obstacles. But, if a family had shown signs of disintegration, the depression made the situation worse. On the whole, though, far more families hung together than broke apart. Men and women experienced the Great Depression differently, partly because of the gender roles that governed male and female behavior in the 1930s. From childhood men had been trained to be breadwinners; they considered themselves failures if they could no longer support their families. But while millions of men lost their jobs, few of the nation's 28 million homemakers lost their positions in the home. In contrast to men, women's sense of self-importance increased as they struggled to keep their families afloat. The sociologists Robert and Helen Lynd noticed this phenomenon in their follow-up study of Middletown (Muncie, Indiana), published in 1937:

> The men, cut adrift from their usual routine, lost much of their sense of time and dawdled helplessly and dully about the streets; while in the homes the women's world remained largely intact and the round of cooking, housecleaning, and mending became if anything more absorbing.

Even if a wife took a job when her husband lost his, she retained almost total responsibility for housework and child care. To economize, women sewed their own clothes, and canned fruits and vegetables. They bought day-old bread and heated several dishes in the oven at once to save fuel. Women who had once employed servants did their own housework. Eleanor Roosevelt described the stressful effects of the depression on these women's lives: "It means endless little economies and constant anxiety for fear of some catastrophe such as accident or illness which may completely swamp the family budget." Housewives' ability to watch every penny often made the difference in a family's survival.

Despite hard times, Americans maintained a fairly high level of consumption. As in the 1920s, households in the middle-income range—in 1935, the

A Working-Class Family Encounters the Great Depression

*Although many families endured the privations of the Great Depression with
equanimity, others, like Larry Van Dusen's family, experienced tremendous
strains. In this passage from his oral history account to journalist Studs Terkel, he
describes the pressures on male wage earners and their children.*

My father led a rough life: he drank. During the Depression, he drank more.
There was more conflict in the home. A lot of fathers—mine among them—
had a habit of taking off. They'd go to Chicago to look for work. To Topeka.
This left the family at home, waiting and hoping that the old man would find
something. And there was always the Saturday night ordeal as to whether or
not the old man would get home with his paycheck. Everything was sharpened and hurt more by the Depression.

Heaven would break out once in a while, and the old man would get a
week's work. I remember he'd come home at night, and he'd come down the
path through the trees. He always rode a bicycle. He'd stop and sometimes say
hello, or give me a hug. And that smell of fresh sawdust on those carpenter
overalls, and the fact that Dad was home, and there was a week's wages. . . .
That's the good you remember.

And then there was always the bad part. That's when you'd see your father
coming home with the toolbox on his shoulder. Or carrying it. That meant the
job was over. The tools were home now, and we were back on the treadmill
again.

I remember coming back home, many years afterwards. Things were better.
It was after the Depression, after the war. To me, it was hardly the same house.
My father turned into an angel. They weren't wealthy, but they were making
it. They didn't have the acid and the recriminations and the bitterness that I
had felt as a child.

SOURCE: Studs Terkel, *Hard Times* (New York: Pantheon Books, 1986), pp. 107–108.

50.2 percent of American families with an income of $500 to $1,500—did
much of the buying. Several trends allowed those families to maintain their
former standard of living despite pay cuts and unemployment. Between 1929
and 1935, deflation lowered the cost of living almost 20 percent. And buying
on the installment plan increased in the 1930s, permitting many families to
stretch their reduced incomes.

Americans spent their money differently in the depression. Telephone use
and clothing sales dropped sharply, but cigarettes, movies, radio, and newspapers, once considered luxuries, became necessities. The automobile proved
one of the most depression-proof items in the family budget. Though sales of

new cars dropped, gasoline sales held stable, suggesting that families bought used cars or kept their old models running longer.

Another measure of the impact of the depression on family life was the change in demographic trends in the 1930s. The marriage rate fell from 10.14 per thousand persons in 1929 to 7.87 per thousand in 1932. The divorce rate decreased as well, because couples could not afford the legal expense of dissolving failed unions. And between 1930 and 1933, the birth rate, which had fallen steadily since 1800, dropped from 21.3 live births per thousand to 18.4, a dramatic 14 percent decrease. The new level, if maintained, would have produced a decline in population. Though the birth rate rose slightly after 1934, by the end of the decade it was still only 18.8. (In contrast, at the height of the baby boom following World War II, the birth rate was 25 per thousand.)

The drop in the birth rate during the Great Depression could not have happened without increased access to effective contraception. In 1936, in *United States v. One Package of Japanese Pessaries*, a federal court struck down all federal restrictions on the dissemination of contraceptive information. The decision gave doctors wide discretion in prescribing birth control for married couples, making it legal everywhere except the heavily Catholic states of Massachusetts and Connecticut. While abortion remained illegal, the number of women who underwent the procedure increased. Because many abortionists operated under unsafe or unsanitary conditions, between 8,000 and 10,000 women died each year from the illegal operations.

Margaret Sanger played a major role in encouraging the availability and popular acceptance of birth control. Sanger began her career as a public health nurse in the 1910s in the slums of New York City. At first she joined forces with socialists trying to help working-class families to control their fertility. In the 1920s and 1930s, however, she appealed to the middle class for support, identifying those families as the key to the movement's success. Sanger also courted the medical profession, pioneering the establishment of professionally staffed birth control clinics and winning the American Medical Association's endorsement of contraception in 1937. As a result of Sanger's efforts, birth control became less a feminist issue and more a medical question. And in the context of the depression, it became an economic issue as well, as financially pressed couples sought to delay or limit their childbearing while they weathered hard times.

One way for families to make ends meet was to send an additional member of the household to work. At the turn of the century, that additional member was often a child or a young, unmarried adult; in the 1930s, it was increasingly a married woman. Instead of expelling women from the work force, the depression solidified their position in it. The 1940 census reported almost 11 million women in the work force—approximately a fourth of the nation's workers—and a small increase over 1930. The number of married women employed outside the home rose 50 percent.

Working women, especially married women, encountered sharp resentment and outright discrimination in the workplace. After calculating that the number of employed women roughly equaled total unemployment in 1939, the editor Norman Cousins suggested this tongue-in-cheek remedy: "Simply fire the women, who shouldn't be working anyway, and hire the men. Presto! No unemployment. No relief rolls. No depression." Many people agreed with the idea. In a 1936 Gallup poll, asked whether wives should work when their husbands had jobs, 82 percent of those interviewed said no. Such public disapproval encouraged restrictions on women's right to work. From 1932 to 1937 the federal government would not allow a husband and wife to hold government jobs at the same time. Many states adopted laws that prohibited married women from working.

Married or not, most women worked because they had to. A sizable minority were the sole support of their families, because their husbands had left home or lost their jobs. Single, divorced, deserted, or widowed women had no husbands to support them. Moreover, women rarely took jobs away from men. "Few of the people who oppose married women's employment," observed one feminist in 1940, "seem to realize that a coal miner or steel worker cannot very well fill the jobs of nursemaids, cleaning women, or the factory and clerical jobs now filled by women." Custom, rather than law or economics, made crossovers from one field to another rare.

The division of the work force by gender gave women a small edge during the depression. Many fields with large numbers of female employees, including clerical, sales, and service and trade occupations, suffered less from economic contraction than heavy industry, which employed men almost exclusively. As a result, unemployment rates for women, although extremely high, were somewhat lower than those for men. This small bonus came at a high price, however. The jobs women held reinforced the traditional stereotypes of female work. When the depression ended, women were even more concentrated in low-paid, dead-end jobs than when it began.

White women also benefited at the expense of minority women. To make ends meet, white women willingly took jobs usually held by blacks or other minority workers—domestic service jobs, for example—and employers were quick to act on their preference for white workers. White men also took jobs once held by minority males.

During the Great Depression there were few feminist demands for equal rights, at home or on the job. On an individual basis, women's self-esteem probably rose because of the importance of their work to family survival. Most men and women, however, continued to believe that the two sexes should have fundamentally different roles and responsibilities, and that a woman's life cycle should be shaped by marriage and her husband's career.

The depression hit other family members—the nation's 21 million young people—especially hard. Though small children often escaped the sense of bitterness and failure that gripped their elders—some youngsters thought it fun to stand in a soup line—hard times made children grow up fast. About 250,000 young people became so demoralized that they took to the road as hobos and "sisters of the road," as female tramps were called. Others chose to stay in school longer: public schools were free, and they were warm in the winter. In 1930 less than half the nation's youth attended high school, compared with three-fourths in 1940, at the end of the depression. College, however, remained the privilege of a distinct minority. About 1.2 million young people, or 7.5 percent of the population between eighteen and twenty-four, attended college in the 1930s. Forty percent of them were women. After 1935 college became slightly more affordable when the National Youth Administration (NYA) gave part-time employment to more than 2 million college and high school students. The government agency also provided work for 2.6 million out-of-school youths.

College students worked hard in the 1930s; financial sacrifice encouraged seriousness of purpose. Interest in fraternities and sororities declined as many students became involved in political movements. Fueled by disillusionment with World War I, thousands of youth took the "Oxford Pledge" never to support United States involvement in a war. In 1936 the Student Strike against War drew support from several hundred thousand students across the country.

Although youths enjoyed more education in the 1930s, the depression damaged their future prospects. Studies of social mobility confirm that young men who entered their twenties during the depression era had less successful careers than those who came before or after. After extensive interviews with these youths all over the nation, the writer Maxine Davis described them as "runners, delayed at the gun," adding, "The depression years have left us with a generation robbed of time and opportunity just as the Great War left the world its heritage of a lost generation."

Popular Culture

Americans turned to popular culture to alleviate some of the trauma of the Great Depression. As the novelist Josephine Herbst observed, it provided "an almost universal liveliness that countervailed universal suffering." Mass culture flourished in the 1930s, offering not just entertainment, but commentary on the problems that beset the nation. Movies and radio served as a forum for criticizing the system—especially politicians and bankers—as well as vehicles for reaffirming traditional ideals.

Despite the closing of one-third of the country's theaters by 1933, the movie industry and its studio system flourished. Sixty percent of Americans— some 60 to 75 million people each week—flocked to the cinema, seeking solace from the pain of the depression. In the early thirties, moviegoers might enjoy or be scandalized by Mae West, who was noted for her sexual innuendos: "I used to be Snow White, but I drifted." But in response to public outcry against immorality in the movies, especially from the Protestant and Catholic churches, the industry established a means of self-censorship, the Production Code Administration. After 1934, somewhat racy films—tame by today's standards—were supplanted by sophisticated, fast-paced, screwball comedies like *It Happened One Night*, which swept the Oscars in 1934. The musical comedies of Fred Astaire and Ginger Rogers, including *Top Hat* (1935) and *The Gay*

Divorcee (1934), in which the two dancers seemed to glide effortlessly through opulent sets, were pure entertainment.

But Hollywood, which produced 5,000 films during the decade, offered much more than mere escape, with many of its movies containing complex messages that reflected a real sense of the societal crisis that engulfed the nation. The cultural historian Lawrence W. Levine has argued that depression-era films were "deeply grounded in the realities and intricacies of the Depression" and thus offer "a rich array of insights" into the period. Even if they did not deal specifically with the economic or political crisis, many films reaffirmed traditional values like democracy, individualism, and egalitarianism. They also contained criticisms—suggestions that the system was not working, or that law and order had broken down. Thus, popular gangster movies, such as *Public Enemy* (1931), with James Cagney, or *Little Caesar* (1930), starring Edward G. Robinson, can be seen as perverse Horatio Alger tales, in which the main character struggles to succeed in a harsh environment. Often these movies suggested that incompetent or corrupt politicians, police, and businessmen were as much to blame for organized crime as the gangsters themselves.

Depression-era films repeatedly portrayed politicians as cynical and corrupt. In *Washington Merry-Go-Round* (1932), lobbyists manipulated weak congressmen to undermine democratic rule. The Marx Brothers' irreverent comedies more humorously criticized authority and most everything else. In *Duck Soup* (1933), Groucho Marx played Rufus T. Firefly, president of the mythical Freedonia, who sings gleefully:

The last man nearly ruined this place,
He didn't know what to do with it.
If you think this country's bad off now,
Just wait till I get through with it.

Few filmmakers left more of a mark on the decade than Frank Capra. An Italian immigrant who personified the possibilities for success the United States offered, Capra made films that spoke to Americans' idealism. In movies like *Mr. Deeds Goes to Town* (1936) and *Mr. Smith Goes to Washington* (1939), he pitted the virtuous small town hero against corrupt urban shysters—businessmen, politicians, lobbyists, and newspaper publishers—whose machinations subverted the nation's ideals. Though the hero usually prevailed, Capra was realistic enough to suggest that the victory was not necessarily permanent, that the problems the nation faced were serious ones.

Radio occupied an increasingly important place in popular culture during the 1930s. At the beginning of the decade about 13 million households had radios; by the end, 27.5 million owned them. Listeners tuned in to daytime serials like "Ma Perkins"; picked up useful household hints on the "The Betty Crocker Hour"; or enjoyed the Big Band "swing" of Benny Goodman, Duke Ellington, and Tommy Dorsey. Weekly variety shows featured Jack Benny; George Burns and Gracie Allen; and the ventriloquist Edgar Bergen and his impudent dummy, Charlie McCarthy. And millions of listeners followed the

Mr. Smith Goes to Washington
In director Frank Capra's classic 1939 film, *Mr. Smith Goes to Washington*, actor Jimmy Stewart plays an idealistic young senator who exposes the unscrupulous political machine that dominates his home state. In response, the machine frames Senator Smith for corruption. Although he is eventually vindicated, in this scene the despairing Smith encounters the avalanche of hostile mail generated against him by his crooked opponents.

adventures of the Lone Ranger ("Heigh-ho, Silver"), Superman, the Shadow, and Dick Tracy.

Like movies, radio offered Americans more than escape. A running gag in comedian Jack Benny's show was his stinginess; audiences could identify with an unwillingness—or inability—to spend money. Even more relevant was Benny's distrust of banks. He kept his money in an underground vault guarded by a pet polar bear named Carmichael—presumably a more reliable place than the nation's financial institutions.

"Amos 'n' Andy," a program whose main characters, two black men, were played by whites speaking an exaggerated black dialect, is remembered primarily for its racial stereotyping. But the exceptionally popular show also dealt with hard times, often referring explicitly to the depression. A central theme was the contrast between Amos's hard work and Andy's more carefree approach to life. Amos, tending to believe that the nation's economic crisis had been brought about by the extravagant spending of the 1920s, criticized his friend's fiscal irresponsibility. As the historian Arthur Frank Wertheim notes, "The way that the characters' hopes for monetary success were turned into business failures mirrored the lives of many Americans." Though "Amos 'n' Andy" reinforced racial stereotypes, it also reaffirmed the traditional values of "diligence, saving, and generosity."

Not all leisure time was filled by commercial entertainment. In a resurgence of traditionalism, attendance at religious services rose, and the home again became a center for pleasurable pastimes. An evening by the radio provided cheap family entertainment. Amateur photography and stamp collecting enjoyed tremendous vogues, as did the board game Monopoly. Reading aloud from books borrowed from the public library was another affordable diversion. But Americans bought books, too. Taking advantage of new manufacturing processes that made books cheaper, they made best sellers of Margaret Mitchell's *Gone with the Wind* (1936); James Hilton's *Lost Horizon* (1933); and Pearl Buck's *The Good Earth* (1932). Finally, "[t]alking was the Great Depression pastime," recalled the columnist Russell Baker. "Unlike the movies, talk was free."

THE SOCIAL FABRIC OF DEPRESSION AMERICA

Much writing about the 1930s has focused on white working-class or middle-class families caught suddenly in a downward spiral. For African-Americans, farmers, and Mexican-Americans, times had always been hard; during the 1930s they got much harder. As the poet Langston Hughes noted, "The depression brought everybody down a peg or two. And the Negroes had but few pegs to fall."

Blacks in the Depression

African-Americans had always known discrimination and limited opportunities, so they viewed the depression differently from most whites: "It didn't mean too much to him, the Great American Depression, as you call it," one man remarked. "There was no such thing. The best he could be is a janitor or a porter or shoeshine boy. It only became official when it hit the white man." The novelist and poet Maya Angelou, who grew up in Stamps, Arkansas, recalled, "The country had been in the throes of the Depression for two years before the Negroes in Stamps knew it. I think that everyone thought the Depression, like everything else, was for the white folks."

Despite the black migration to northern cities, which had begun before World War I, as late as 1940 more than 75 percent of African-Americans still lived in the South. Nearly all the farmers who were black lived in the South, their condition scarcely better than it had been at the end of Reconstruction. Only 20 percent of black farmers owned their own land; the rest toiled at the bottom of the South's exploitative agricultural system, as tenant farmers, farm hands, and sharecroppers. African-Americans rarely earned more than $200 a year. In one Louisiana parish, black women averaged only $41.67 a year picking cotton.

Throughout the 1920s, southern agriculture had suffered from falling prices and overproduction. The depression made an already desperate situation worse. Some black farmers tried to protect themselves by joining the Southern Tenant Farmers Union (STFU), which was founded in 1934. The STFU was one of the few southern groups that welcomed both blacks and whites. Landowners, however, had a stake in keeping sharecroppers from organizing, so they countered with repression and harassment. In the end the STFU could do little to reform an agricultural system that depended on a single crop, cotton.

All blacks faced harsh social and political discrimination throughout the South. In a celebrated case in Scottsboro, Alabama, in 1931, two white women who had been riding a freight train claimed to have been raped by nine black youths, all under twenty years old. The two women's stories contained many inconsistencies, and one woman later recanted. But in the South, when a white woman claimed to have been raped by a black, she was taken at her word. Two weeks later, juries composed entirely of white men found all nine defendants guilty of rape; eight were sentenced to death. (One defendant escaped the death penalty because he was a minor.) Though the U.S. Supreme Court overturned the sentences in 1932 and ordered new trials on grounds that the defendants had been denied adequate legal counsel, five of the men eventually were reconvicted and sentenced to long prison terms.

The youth of the defendants, their hasty trials, and the harsh sentences they received stirred public protest, prompting the International Labor Defense (ILD), a labor organization tied closely to the Communist party, to take over the defense. Though the Communist party had targeted the struggle against racism as a priority in the early 1930s, it was making little headway. "It's bad enough being black, why be red?" was a common reaction. White southerners resented radical groups' interference, noting that almost all those involved in the Scottsboro defense were northerners and Jews. Declared a local solicitor, "Alabama justice cannot be bought and sold with Jew money from New York."

The Scottsboro case received wide coverage in black communities across the country. Along with an increase in lynching in the early 1930s (twenty blacks were lynched in 1930, twenty-four in 1933), it gave black Americans a strong incentive to head for the North and the Midwest. Harlem, one of their main destinations, was already strained by the enormous influx of African-Americans in the 1920s. The depression only aggravated the housing shortage. Residential segregation kept blacks from moving elsewhere, so they paid excessive rents to live in deteriorating buildings where crowded living conditions fostered disease and premature death. As whites clamored for jobs traditionally held by blacks—waiters, domestic servants, elevator operators,

The Lynch Mob and Silent Witness
The threat of lynching remained a terrifying part of life for African-Americans in the 1930s, and not just in the South. The photograph on the top shows two young blacks who were lynched by an Indiana mob in 1930. Each day that a person was lynched, the NAACP hung a banner (bottom) outside the window of its New York office. NAACP appeals for federal antilynching legislation received little support from politicians, however.

and garbage collectors—unemployment in Harlem rose to 50 percent, twice the national rate. At the height of the depression, shelters and soup kitchens staffed by the Divine Peace Mission, under the leadership of the charismatic black religious leader Father Divine, provided 3,000 meals a day for Harlem's destitute.

In March 1935 Harlem exploded in the only major race riot of the decade. Anger about the lack of jobs, a slowdown in relief, and economic exploitation of the black community had been building for years. Although white-owned stores were entirely dependent on black trade, store owners would not employ blacks. The arrest of a black shoplifter, followed by rumors that he had been severely beaten by white police, triggered the riot. Four blacks were killed, and $2 million worth of property was damaged.

There were some signs of hope for African-Americans in the 1930s. Partly in response to the 1935 riot, but mainly in return for growing black allegiance to the Democratic party (see Chapter 26), the New Deal would channel significant amounts of relief money toward northern blacks. And the National Association for the Advancement of Colored People (NAACP) would continue to challenge the status quo of race relations. Though the call for racial justice would go largely unheeded during the depression, World War II and its aftermath would further the struggle for black equality.

Dust Bowl Migrations

A distressed agricultural sector had been one of the causes of the Great Depression. In the 1930s conditions only got worse, especially for farmers on the Great Plains. In the semiarid states of Oklahoma, Texas, New Mexico, Colorado, Arkansas, and Kansas, farmers had always risked the ravages of drought (see Chapter 17), but the years 1930–1941 witnessed the worst drought in the country's history. Low rainfall alone did not create the Dust Bowl, however. National and international market forces, like the rising demand for wheat during World War I, had caused farmers to push the farming frontier beyond its natural limits. To capture a profit, they had stripped the land of its natural vegetation, destroying the delicate ecological balance of the plains. When the rains dried up and the winds came, nothing remained to hold the soil. Huge clouds of dust rolled over the plains; streetlights blinked on as if night had fallen. Dust seeped into houses and "blackened the pillow around one's head, the dinner plates on the table, the bread dough on the back of the stove" (see Map 25.1).

The ecological disaster caused a mass exodus from the plains. Their crops ruined, their lands barren and dry, their homes foreclosed for debts they could not pay, farm families loaded their belongings into beat-up Fords. Encouraged by handbills distributed by growers that promised good jobs in California, at least 350,000 southwesterners headed west in the 1930s. Some went to metropolitan areas, but about half settled in rural areas where they worked for low wages as migratory farm laborers.

The migrants were called "Okies," whether or not they were from Oklahoma. John Steinbeck's novel *The Grapes of Wrath* (1939) immortalized them and their journey. In the novel the Joads abandon their land not only because of drought but also as a result of the transformation of American agriculture that ever since World War I had been prompting farmers to leave the land. By

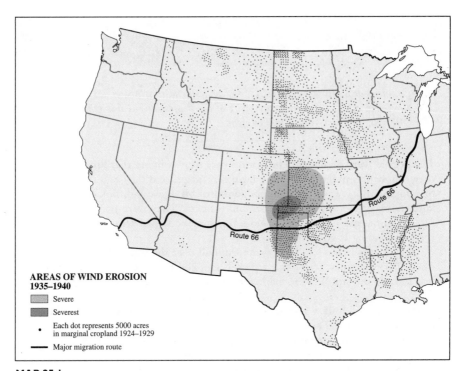

MAP 25.1
The Dust Bowl
A U.S. Weather Bureau scientist called the drought of the 1930s "the worst in the climatological history of the country." Conditions were especially severe in the southern plains, where the dramatic increases in farming on marginal land had strained production before the drought struck. Many farm families saw no choice but to follow Route 66, the highway that went west through Missouri, Oklahoma, and north Texas to California, the promised land.

the 1930s, large-scale commercialized farming had spread to the plains, where family farmers still used draft animals. In Steinbeck's novel, after the bank forecloses on the Joads' farm, a gasoline-engine tractor, the symbol of mechanized farming, plows under their crops and demolishes their home.

Though it was a powerful work, *The Grapes of Wrath* did not convey the diversity of the westward migration. Not all Okies were destitute dirt farmers; perhaps one in six was a professional, a business proprietor, or a white-collar worker. For most the drive west was fairly easy. Route 66 was a paved two-lane road: in a decent car, the journey from Oklahoma or Texas to California took only three to four days.

Before the 1930s Californians had created a different type of agriculture from that practiced in the Southwest and Midwest. Basically industrial in nature, California agriculture was large-scale, intensive, and diversified. The state's wealth came from specialty crops—citruses, grapes, potatoes—whose staggered harvests required a great deal of transient labor during short picking seasons. A

Hard Times for an Iowa Farmer

Mounting debt, plummeting prices, and widespread foreclosures led farmers to extreme measures in the early years of the depression, as this reminiscence by Harry Terrell, an Iowa farmer, makes clear.

The people were desperate. They came very near hanging that judge. Because they caught this judge foreclosing farm mortgages, and they had no other ways of stopping it. . . . They took the judge out of his court and took him to the fairgrounds and they had a rope around his neck. They were going to string him up in the old horse thief fashion. But somebody had sense enough to stop the thing before it got too far.

They had marches. . . . They came from all over the state. That was the time of the Farm Holiday. There was a picket line. The Farm Holiday movement was to hold the stuff off the market, to increase the price. It saw its violence, too.

They stopped milk wagons, dumped milk. They stopped farmers hauling their hay to market. They undertook to stop the whole agriculture process. They thought if they could block the highways and access to the packing plants, they couldn't buy these hogs at two cents a pound.

They'd say: we're gonna meet, just east of Cherokee, at the fork of the road, and so on. Now they spread it around the country that they were gonna stop everything from going through. And believe me, they stopped it. They had whatever was necessary to stop them with. Some of 'em had pitchforks. . . . You can fix the auto tire good with a pitchfork. There were blockades.

The country was getting up in arms about taking a man's property away from him. It was his livelihood. When you took a man's horses and his plow away, you denied him food, you just convicted his family to starvation. It was just that real.

SOURCE: Studs Terkel, *Hard Times* (New York: Pantheon Books, 1986), pp. 214–215.

---

steady supply of cheap migrant labor provided by Chinese, Mexicans, Okies, and (briefly) East Indians made this type of farming economically feasible.

The migrants had a lasting impact on California culture. At first they met outright hostility from old-time Californians—a demoralizing experience for white native-born Protestants, who were ashamed of the Okie stereotype. But they stayed, filling important roles in California's expanding economy. Soon some communities in the San Joaquin Valley—Bakersfield, Fresno, Merced, Modesto, and Stockton—took on a distinctly Okie cast, identifiable by southern-influenced evangelical religion and the growing popularity of country music.

Mexican-American Communities

The Mexican-American experience of the depression differed from that of the Dust Bowl refugees. In the depths of the depression, with fear of competition from foreign workers at a peak, perhaps a third of the Mexican-American population, most of them immigrants, returned to Mexico. A formal deportation policy instituted by the federal government was partly responsible for the exodus, but many more Mexicans left "voluntarily" when work ran out and local relief agencies refused to assist them. Racism, coupled with the proximity of Mexico, made Mexicans the only immigrants targeted for deportation during the depression.

In 1930 Los Angeles was home to 150,000 Mexican-Americans, giving it the largest concentration of Mexicans outside Mexico. Mexican-Americans spilled out of the downtown area, known as "Sonoratown," into neighborhoods, or *colonias*, in Belvedere and East Los Angeles. There mutual-aid societies, Spanish-language newspapers, and the Catholic Church fostered a sense of community. But Los Angeles lost approximately one-third of its Mexican population during the deportations of the 1930s, which separated families, disrupted children's education, and caused extreme financial hardship during the worst years of the depression. For those who remained in America, deportation was a constant threat, an unmistakable reminder of their fragile status in the United States.

Discrimination and exploitation were omnipresent in the Mexican community. The harsh experiences of migrant workers influenced a young Mexican-American named Cesar Chavez, who would become one of the twentieth century's most influential labor organizers. In the mid-1930s, Chavez's father became involved in several bitter labor struggles in the Imperial Valley. Thirty-seven major agricultural strikes occurred in California in 1933 alone, including one in the San Joaquin Valley that mobilized 18,000 cotton pickers. All these strikes failed, but they gave the young Chavez a background in labor organizing, which he would use to found a national farm workers' union in 1962.

Not all Mexican-Americans were migrant farm workers. Many worked as miners; others held industrial jobs, especially in steel mills, meat-packing plants, and refineries, where they established a vibrant tradition of labor activism. In California, Mexican-Americans also found employment in fruit- and vegetable-processing plants. Young single women especially preferred the higher-paid cannery work to domestic service, needlework, and farm labor. In plants owned by corporate giants like Del Monte, McNeill, and Libby, Mexican-American women earned around $2.50 a day, while their male counterparts received $3.50 to $4.50. Labor unions came to the canneries in 1939 with the formation of the United Cannery, Agricultural, Packing, and Allied Workers of America, an unusually democratic union in which women, the majority of the rank-and-file workers, played a leading role.

Mexican-American Poverty in Texas
In 1937 Antonia and Pablo Martinez lived in a one-room house in San
Antonio, Texas, with his parents and older brother. If either Pablo or Anto-
nia was employed in 1937, it was probably in San Antonio's pecan-shelling
industry, which depended heavily on the cheap labor of Mexican-
Americans.

Activism in the fields and factories demonstrated how a second generation, born in the United States, had turned increasingly to the struggle for political and economic justice in the United States, rather than retaining primary
allegiance to Mexico. According to the historian George Sánchez, they were
creating "their own version of Americanism without abandoning Mexican
culture." Joining American labor unions and becoming more involved in
American politics (see Chapter 26) were thus important steps in the creation
of a distinct Mexican-American ethnic identity.

HERBERT HOOVER AND THE GREAT DEPRESSION

In the presidential campaign of 1928, Herbert Hoover declared "the poorhouse is vanishing from among us." America was "nearer to the final triumph
over poverty than ever before in the history of any land." Once elected,
Hoover promised, he would preside over an era of Republican prosperity
and governmental restraint. When the stock market crashed in 1929, he

stubbornly insisted that the downturn was only temporary. Half a year later, Hoover greeted a business delegation, in June 1930, with these words: "Gentlemen, you have come sixty days too late. The Depression is over." When the country hit rock bottom in 1931 and 1932, the president finally acted, but by then it was too little, too late.

The Republican Response

Hoover's approach to the Great Depression was shaped by his priorities as secretary of commerce. Hoping to avoid coercive measures on the part of the federal government, he turned to the business community for leadership in overcoming the economic downturn. Hoover asked business executives to maintain wages and production levels voluntarily, and to work with the government to build people's confidence in the economic system.

Hoover did not rely solely on public pronouncements, however; he also used public funds and federal action to encourage recovery. Soon after the stock market crash he cut federal taxes, and called on state and local governments to increase their expenditures on public construction projects. He signed the 1929 Agricultural Marketing Act, which gave the federal government an unprecedented role in stabilizing agriculture. In 1930 and the first half of 1931, Hoover raised the federal budget for public works to $423 million, a dramatic increase in expenditures not traditionally considered to be the federal government's responsibility. Hoover also eased the international crisis by declaring a moratorium on the payment of Allied debts and reparations early in the summer of 1931. The depression continued, however. When the president asked Congress for a 33 percent tax increase to balance the budget, the ill-advised move choked investment and, to a lesser extent, consumption, contributing significantly to the continuation of the depression.

Hoover's most innovative program—one the New Deal would later draw on—was the Reconstruction Finance Corporation (RFC), approved by Congress in January 1932. Modeled on the War Finance Corporation of World War I, and developed in collaboration with the business and banking communities, the RFC was the first federal institution created to intervene directly in the economy during peacetime. To alleviate the credit crunch for business, the RFC would provide federal loans to railroads, financial institutions, banks, and insurance companies, in a strategy that has been called *pump priming*. In theory, money lent at the top of the economic structure would stimulate production, creating new jobs and increasing consumer spending. These benefits would eventually "trickle down" to the rest of the economy.

Unfortunately, the RFC lent its funds too cautiously to make a significant difference. Nonetheless, it represents a watershed in American political history and the rise of the state. When voluntary cooperation failed, the president turned to federal action to stimulate the economy. Yet Hoover's break with the past had clear limits. In many ways, his support of the RFC was just another attempt to encourage business confidence. Compared with previous chief executives—and in contrast to his popular image as a "do-nothing" president—Hoover responded to the national emergency on an unprecedented scale. But the nation's needs were also unprecedented, and Hoover's programs failed to meet them.

In particular, federal programs fell short of helping the growing ranks of the unemployed. Hoover remained adamant in his refusal to consider any plan for direct federal relief to the unemployed. Throughout his career he had believed that privately organized charities were sufficient to meet the nation's social welfare needs. During World War I he had headed the Commission for Relief of Belgium, a private group that distributed 5 million tons of food to Europe's suffering civilian population. And in 1927 he had coordinated a rescue and cleanup operation after a devastating flood of the Mississippi River left 16.5 million acres of land under water in seven states. The success of these and other predominantly voluntary responses to public emergencies had confirmed Hoover's belief that private charity, not federal aid, was the "American way" of solving social problems. He would not undermine the country's hallowed faith in individualism, even in the face of evidence that charities and state and local relief agencies could not meet the growing needs of the unemployed.

Rising Discontent

As the depression deepened, many citizens came to hate Herbert Hoover. Once the symbol of business prosperity, he became the scapegoat for the depression. "In Hoover we trusted, now we are busted," declared the hand-lettered signs carried by the down and out. New terms entered the vocabulary: *Hoovervilles* (shantytowns where people lived in packing crates and other makeshift shelters), *Hoover flags* (empty pockets turned inside out), *Hoover blankets* (newspapers). Hoover's declarations that nobody was starving, that hobos were better fed than ever before, seemed cruel and insensitive. His apparent willingness to bail out businesses and banks while leaving individuals to fend for themselves added to his reputation for cold-heartedness.

As the country entered the fourth year of depression, signs of rising discontent and rebellion emerged. Farmers were among the most vocal groups, banding together to harass the bank agents and government officers who enforced evictions and foreclosures and to protest the low prices they received for their crops. Midwestern farmers had watched the price of wheat fall from $3 a bushel in 1920 to barely 30 cents in 1932. Now they formed the Farm Holiday Association; barricaded local roads; and dumped milk, vegetables, and other farm produce in the dirt rather than accept prices that would not cover their costs. Nothing better captured the cruel irony of underconsumption and maldistribution than farmers dumping food at a time when thousands were going hungry.

Protest was not confined to rural America, however. Bitter labor strikes occurred in the depths of the depression, despite the threat that strikers would lose their jobs. In Harlan County, Kentucky, in 1931, miners struck over a 10 percent wage cut. Their union was crushed by mine owners and the National

Guard. In 1932, at Ford's River Rouge factory outside Detroit, a demonstration provoked violence from police and Ford security forces; three demonstrators were killed, and fifty more seriously injured. Later, some 40,000 people viewed the coffins under a banner charging that "Ford Gave Bullets for Bread."

In 1931 and 1932 violence broke out in the nation's cities. Groups of the unemployed battled local authorities over inadequate relief; citizens staged rent riots and hunger marches. Some of these actions were organized by the Communist party, still a tiny organization with only 12,000 members, as a challenge to the capitalist system. For example, the party helped to organize "unemployment councils" that agitated for jobs and food, and coordinated a hunger march on Washington, D.C., in 1931. Though the marches were well attended and often got results from local and federal authorities, they did not necessarily win converts to communism.

Not radicals but veterans staged the most publicized—and most tragic—protest. In the summer of 1932 the "Bonus Army," a ragtag group of about 15,000 unemployed World War I veterans, hitchhiked to Washington to demand immediate payment of their bonuses, originally scheduled

The Bonus Army
These children were camped out in the summer of 1932 on the Anacostia Flats of Washington, D.C., while their fathers lobbied Congress for early payment of World War I bonuses. Congress said no, and the U.S. Army violently disbanded the veterans' encampment.

for distribution in 1945. While their leaders lobbied Congress, the bonus army camped out in the capital. "We were heroes in 1917, but we're bums now," one veteran complained bitterly. When the marchers refused to leave their Anacostia Flats camp, Hoover called out riot troops to clear the area. Led by General Douglas MacArthur, assisted by Major Dwight D. Eisenhower and Major George S. Patton, the troops burned the encampment to the ground. In the fight that followed, more than a hundred marchers were injured. Newsreel footage captured the deeply disturbing spectacle of the U.S. Army moving against its own veterans, and Hoover's popularity plunged even lower.

The 1932 Election

Despite the evidence of discontent, the nation was not in a revolutionary mood as it approached the 1932 election. Having internalized Horatio Alger's ideal of the self-made man, many Americans initially blamed themselves rather than the system for their hardship. Despair and apathy, not anger, was the mood of most citizens. The Republicans, who could find no credible way to dump an incumbent president, unenthusiastically renominated Hoover. The Democrats turned to Governor Franklin Delano Roosevelt of New York, who won the nomination by capitalizing on that state's reputation for innovative relief and unemployment programs.

Roosevelt, born into a wealthy New York family in 1882, had attended Harvard College and Columbia Law School. He had served in the New York State legislature and as assistant secretary of the navy in the Wilson administration, a post that had earned him the vice-presidential nomination on the Democratic ticket in 1920. Roosevelt's rise to the presidency was interrupted in 1921 by an attack of polio that left both his legs paralyzed for life. But he fought back from this illness, emerging from the ordeal a stronger, more resilient man. "If you had spent two years in bed trying to wiggle your toe, after that anything would seem easy," he explained. His wife, Eleanor Roosevelt, strongly supported his return to public life, and helped to mastermind his successful campaign for the governorship of New York in 1928.

The 1932 campaign for the presidency foreshadowed little of the New Deal. Roosevelt hinted only vaguely at new approaches to the depression: "The country needs and, unless I mistake its temper, the country demands bold, persistent experimentation." He won easily, receiving 22.8 million votes to Hoover's 15.7 million. Despite the nation's economic collapse, Americans remained firmly committed to the two-party system. The Socialist party candidate, Norman Thomas, got fewer than a million votes, and the Communist party candidate, party leader William Z. Foster, drew only 100,000 votes.

The 1932 election marked a turning point in American politics, the emergence of a Democratic coalition that would dominate national politics for the next four decades. Roosevelt won the support of the Solid South, which returned to the Democratic fold after defecting in 1928 because of Al Smith's Catholicism and his views on Prohibition. Roosevelt drew substantial support in the West and in the cities, continuing a trend first noticed in 1928, when the Democrats appealed successfully to recent immigrants and urban ethnic groups. However, Roosevelt's election was hardly a mandate to re-shape American political and economic institutions. Many people voted as much against Hoover as for Roosevelt.

Having spoken, the voters had to wait until Roosevelt's inauguration in March 1933 to see him put his ideas into action. (The interval between the election and the inauguration was shortened by the Twentieth Amendment in 1933.) In the worst winter of the depression, Americans could do little but hope that things would get better. According to the most conservative esti-mates, unemployment stood at 20 to 25 percent nationwide. The rate was 50 percent in Cleveland, 60 percent in Akron, and 80 percent in Toledo—cities dependent on manufacturing jobs in industries that had basically shut down. The nation's banking system was so close to collapse, many state governors closed banks temporarily to avoid further panic.

By this time, the winter of 1932–1933, the depression had totally over-whelmed public welfare institutions. Private charity and public relief, both of whose expenditures had risen dramatically, still reached only a fraction of the needy. Hunger haunted cities and rural areas alike. When a teacher tried to send a coal miner's daughter home from school because she was weak from hunger, the girl replied, "It won't do any good . . . because this is sister's day to eat." In New York City, hospitals reported ninety-five deaths from starvation. This was the America that Roosevelt inherited when he took the oath of of-fice on March 4, 1933.

CHAPTER 25 TIMELINE

1929	Stock market crash Agricultural Marketing Act
1930	Midwestern drought begins Hawley-Smoot Tariff
1931	Scottsboro case Hoover declares moratorium on Allied war debts Miners strike in Harlan County, Kentucky
1932	Reconstruction Finance Corporation Bonus Army Height of deportation of Mexican migrant workers Farm Holiday Association founded Strike at Ford's River Rouge plant in Michigan Communist-led hunger marches
1933	Unemployment rises to highest level Franklin Delano Roosevelt becomes president Birth rate drops to lowest level The Marx Brothers in *Duck Soup*
1934	Southern Tenant Farmers Union founded *It Happened One Night* sweeps Oscars
1935	National Youth Administration Harlem race riot
1936	Student Strike against War Margaret Mitchell's *Gone with the Wind* Birth control legalized
1939	John Steinbeck's *The Grapes of Wrath* Frank Capra's *Mr. Smith Goes to Washington*

CHAPTER 26

THE NEW DEAL, 1933–1939

- The New Deal Begins, 1933–1935
- The Second New Deal, 1935–1938
- The New Deal's Impact on Society

I n his bold inaugural address on March 4, 1933, President Franklin Delano Roosevelt declared, "The only thing we have to fear is fear itself." That memorable phrase rallied a nation that had already endured almost four years of the worst economic contraction in its history—with no end in sight.

His demeanor grim and purposeful, Roosevelt preached his first inaugural address like a sermon. Issuing ringing declarations of his vision of governmental activism—"This Nation asks for action, and action now"—he repeatedly compared combating the Great Depression to fighting a war. The new president was willing to ask Congress for "broad Executive power to wage a war against the emergency, as great as the power that would be given to me if we were in fact invaded by a foreign foe." He promised to "assume unhesitatingly the leadership of this great army of our people dedicated to a disciplined attack upon our common problems."

To wage this war, Roosevelt proposed the *New Deal*—a term that he first used in his acceptance speech at the Democratic National Convention in 1932, and that eventually came to stand for his administration's complex set of responses to the nation's economic collapse. In a time of major crisis, the New Deal was meant to relieve suffering and conserve the nation's political and economic institutions through unprecedented activity on the part of the national government. Its legacy would be an expanded federal presence in the economy and in the lives of ordinary citizens.

THE NEW DEAL BEGINS, 1933–1935

The Great Depression destroyed Herbert Hoover's political reputation and helped to make Roosevelt's. Although some Americans hated FDR—especially wealthy conservatives—he was immensely popular and beloved by many. Ironically, the ideological differences between Hoover and Roosevelt were not that vast. Both were committed to maintaining the nation's political and economic institutions. Both believed in the basic morality of a balanced budget and extolled the values of hard work, cooperation, and sacrifice. But Roosevelt's personal charisma, his political savvy, and his willingness to experiment made all the difference. Above all, his New Deal programs put people to work, instilling hope and restoring the nation's confidence.

Roosevelt's Style of Leadership

While the New Deal represented many things to many people, one unifying factor was the personality of its master architect, Franklin Roosevelt. A superb and pragmatic politician, Roosevelt crafted his administration's program in response to shifting political and economic conditions rather than following a set ideology or plan. He experimented with an idea; then if it did not work, he tried another. Roosevelt juggled advice in the same way. Senator Huey Long of Louisiana complained, "When I talk to him, he says 'Fine! Fine! Fine!' But Joe Robinson [the Senate majority leader] goes to see him the next day and again he says 'Fine! Fine! Fine!' Maybe he says 'Fine!' to everybody."

FDR
President Franklin Delano Roosevelt was a consummate politician who loved the adulation of a crowd. He consciously adopted a cheerful mien to keep people from feeling sorry for him because of his infirmity, knowing that he could not be a successful politician if the public pitied him.

President Roosevelt established an unusually close rapport with the American people. "Mr. Roosevelt is the only man we ever had in the White House who would understand that my boss is a son of a bitch," remarked one worker. Many ordinary citizens credited Roosevelt with the positive changes in their lives, saying, "He gave me a job" or "He saved my home." Roosevelt's masterful use of the new medium of radio, typified by the sixteen "fireside chats" he broadcast during his first two terms, fostered this personal identification. In the week after the inauguration, more than 450,000 letters, many of which addressed Roosevelt as a friend or a member of the family, poured into the White House. An average of 5,000 to 8,000 arrived weekly for the rest of the decade. One person had handled public correspondence during the Hoover administration, but a staff of fifty was required under Roosevelt.

Roosevelt's personal charisma allowed him to continue the expansion of presidential power begun in the administrations of Theodore Roosevelt and Woodrow Wilson. From the beginning Roosevelt centralized decision making in the White House; in so doing, he dramatically expanded the role of the executive branch in initiating policy, and helped to create the modern presidency. For policy formulation he turned to his talented cabinet, which included Harold Ickes at the Department of the Interior, Frances Perkins at Labor, Henry A. Wallace at Agriculture, and an old friend, Henry Morgenthau, Jr., at the Treasury. During the interregnum Roosevelt relied so heavily on the advice of the Columbia University professors Raymond Moley, Rexford Tugwell, and Adolph A. Berle, Jr., that the press dubbed them the "Brain Trust."

The Hundred Days

The first problem the new president confronted was the banking crisis. Since the stock market crash, about 9 million people had lost their savings. On the eve of the inauguration, thirty-eight states had closed their banks, and the remaining ten had restricted their hours of operation. On March 5, the day after the inauguration, the president declared a national "bank holiday"—a euphemism for closing all the banks—and called Congress into special session. Four days later Congress passed Roosevelt's proposed emergency banking bill, which permitted banks to reopen beginning on March 13—but only if a Treasury Department inspection showed they had sufficient cash reserves. The House approved the plan after only thirty-eight minutes of debate.

The Emergency Banking Act, which Roosevelt developed in consultation with banking leaders, was a conservative document that could have been proposed by Herbert Hoover. The difference was the public's reaction. On the Sunday evening before the banks reopened, Roosevelt broadcast his first fireside chat to a radio audience estimated at 60 million. In simple terms, he reassured citizens that the banks were safe, and Americans believed him. When the banks reopened on Monday morning, deposits exceeded withdrawals. "Capitalism was saved in eight days," observed Raymond Moley, who had served as Roosevelt's speechwriter in the 1932 campaign. The banking bill did its job:

though more than 4,000 banks failed in 1933—the vast majority in the months before the law took effect—only 61 closed their doors in 1934.

The Banking Act was the first of fifteen pieces of major legislation enacted by Congress in the opening months of the Roosevelt administration. This legislative session, which came to be called the "Hundred Days," remains one of the most productive ever. Congress created the Home Owners Loan Corporation to refinance home mortgages threatened by foreclosure. A second banking law, the Glass-Steagall Act, curbed speculation by separating investment banking from commercial banking, and created the Federal Deposit Insurance Corporation (FDIC), which insured deposits up to $2,500. Another act established the Civilian Conservation Corps (CCC), which sent 250,000 young men to do reforestation and conservation work. The Tennessee Valley Authority (TVA) received legislative approval for its innovative plan of government-sponsored regional development and public energy. And in a move that lifted public spirits immeasurably, Roosevelt legalized beer in April. Full repeal of Prohibition came eight months later, in December 1933.

The CCC
The Civilian Conservation Corps (CCC) was one of the most popular New Deal programs. Over ten years, it enrolled 2.75 million young Americans who worked for $1 a day on projects such as soil conservation, disaster relief, reforestation, and flood control. The CCC was limited to men, although a few camps employed out-of-work young women.

To speed economic recovery, the Roosevelt administration targeted three pressing problems: agricultural overproduction, business failures, and the need for unemployment relief. Roosevelt had long felt that a healthy farming sector was crucial to the nation's economic well-being. As he put it in 1929, "if farmers starve today, we will all starve tomorrow." Thus, he viewed the Agricultural Adjustment Act (AAA) as a key step toward the nation's recovery. The AAA established an allotment system for seven major commodities (wheat, cotton, corn, hogs, rice, tobacco, and dairy products), with cash subsidies for farmers who cut production—a tradition that continues to the present day. These benefits were financed by a tax on processing (such as the milling of wheat), which was passed on to consumers. New Deal planners hoped prices would rise in response to the federally subsidized scarcity, spurring a general recovery.

Though the AAA stabilized the agricultural sector, its benefits were distributed unevenly. Subsidies for reducing production went primarily to the owners of large and medium-sized farms, who often cut production by reducing their renters' and sharecroppers' acreage rather than their own. In the South, where many sharecroppers were black and the landowners and government administrators white, that strategy had racial overtones. As many as 200,000 black tenant farmers were displaced from their land by the AAA. Thus, New Deal agricultural policies fostered the migration of marginal farmers in the South and Midwest to northern cities and California, while they consolidated the economic and political clout of larger landholders.

The New Deal's major response to the problem of economic recovery, the National Industrial Recovery Act, launched the National Recovery Administration (NRA). The NRA established a system of industrial self-government to handle the problems of overproduction, cutthroat competition, and price instability. For each industry, a code of prices and production quotas, similar to those for farm products, was hammered out. In effect, these legally enforceable agreements suspended the antitrust laws. The codes also established minimum wages and maximum hours and outlawed child labor. One of the most far-reaching provisions, Section 7(a), guaranteed workers the right to organize and bargain collectively, "through representatives of their own choosing." These union rights dramatically spurred the growth of the labor movement in the 1930s.

General Hugh Johnson, a colorful if erratic administrator, headed the NRA. Johnson supervised negotiations for more than 600 NRA codes, ranging from large industries such as coal, cotton, and steel, to small ones such as dog food, costume jewelry, and even burlesque theaters. Trade associations, controlled by large companies, tended to dominate the code-drafting process, thus solidifying the power of large businesses at the expense of smaller enterprises. Labor had little input, and consumer interests almost none.

The early New Deal also addressed the critical problem of unemployment. In the fourth year of the depression, the total exhaustion of private and local sources of charity made some form of federal relief essential. Reluctantly,

Roosevelt moved toward federal assumption of responsibility for the unemployed. The Federal Emergency Relief Administration (FERA), set up in May 1933 under the direction of Harry Hopkins, a social worker from New York, offered federal money to the states for relief programs. FERA was designed to keep people from starving until other recovery measures took hold. In his first two hours in office, Hopkins distributed $5 million. Over the program's two-year existence, FERA spent $1 billion.

Roosevelt and his advisers maintained a strong distaste for the dole. As Hopkins worried, "I don't think anybody can go year after year, month after month, accepting relief without affecting his character in some ways unfavorably. It is probably going to undermine the independence of hundreds of thousands of families." Whenever possible, then, New Deal administrators promoted work relief over cash subsidies; they also consistently favored jobs that would not compete directly with the private sector. When the Public Works Administration (PWA), under Secretary of the Interior Harold L. Ickes, received a $3.3 billion appropriation in 1933, Ickes's cautiousness in initiating public works projects limited the agency's effectiveness. But in November 1933 Roosevelt established the Civil Works Administration (CWA), and named Harry Hopkins its head. Within thirty days the CWA had put 2.6 million men and women to work; at its peak in January 1934 it employed 4 million in jobs such as repairing bridges, building highways, constructing public buildings, and setting up community projects. The CWA, regarded as a stopgap measure to get the country through the winter of 1933–1934, lapsed the next spring after spending all its funds.

Many of these early emergency measures were deliberately inflationary. That is, they were designed to trigger price increases, which were thought necessary to stimulate recovery and halt the steep deflation. Another element of this strategy was Roosevelt's executive order of April 18, 1933, to abandon the gold standard and allow gold to rise in value like any other commodity. As the price of gold rose, administrators hoped, so too would manufactured and agricultural goods' prices. Though removing the country from the gold standard did not have much impact on the domestic economy, it did allow the Federal Reserve System to manipulate the value of the dollar in response to economic conditions, an important shift in economic power from the private to the public sector.

When an exhausted Congress recessed in June 1933, much had been accomplished. Rarely had a president so dominated a legislative session. A mass of "alphabet soup agencies," as the New Deal programs came to be known, had been created. But though they gave the impression of action, despite a slight economic upturn, they did not turn the economy around.

After the Hundred Days, with no end of the depression in sight, Roosevelt and Congress continued to pass legislation to promote recovery and restore confidence. Much of it focused on reforming business practices in order to prevent future depressions. In 1934 Congress established the Securities and Exchange Commission (SEC) to regulate the stock market and prevent insider trading, fraud, and other abuses. The Banking Act of 1935 also enhanced the federal government's role in controlling the economy and business. The act authorized the president to appoint a new Board of Governors of the Federal Reserve System, placing control of interest rates and other money market policies at the federal level rather than with regional banks. By requiring all large state banks to join the Federal Reserve System by 1942 in order to take advantage of the federal deposit insurance system, the law further encouraged centralization of the nation's banking system.

The New Deal under Attack

As Congress and the president consolidated the New Deal, their work came under attack from several quarters. Although Roosevelt billed himself as the savior of capitalism, noting that "to preserve we had to reform," his actions provoked strong hostility from many Americans. To the wealthy, Roosevelt became simply "that man," a traitor to his class. Business leaders and conservative Democrats formed the Liberty League in 1934 to lobby against the New Deal and its "reckless spending" and "socialist" reforms.

The conservative majority on the Supreme Court also disagreed with the direction of the New Deal. On Black Monday, May 27, 1935, the Supreme Court struck down the NRA in *Schechter v. United States*, ruling unanimously that the National Industrial Recovery Act represented an unconstitutional delegation of legislative power to the executive. The so-called sick-chicken case concerned a Brooklyn, New York, firm convicted of violating NRA codes by selling diseased poultry. In its decision the court also ruled that the NRA regulated commerce *within* states, while the Constitution limited federal regulation to *interstate* commerce. Roosevelt protested that the Court's narrow interpretation would return the Constitution "to the horse-and-buggy definition of interstate commerce," and worried privately that the Court might invalidate the entire New Deal.

Other citizens thought the New Deal had not gone far enough. Francis Townsend, a Long Beach, California, doctor, spoke for the nation's elderly. Many Americans feared poverty in old age because few had pension plans and many had lost their life savings in bank failures. In 1933 Townsend proposed the Old Age Revolving Pension Plan, which would have given $200 a month—a considerable sum at the time—to citizens over the age of sixty. To receive payments the elderly would have had to retire from their jobs, thus opening their positions to others, and would also have had to agree to spend the money within a month. Townsend Clubs soon sprang up across the country, particularly in the Far West.

Father Charles Coughlin also challenged Roosevelt's leadership, attracting a large following, especially in the Midwest. A parish priest in the Detroit suburb of Royal Oak, Coughlin had turned to the radio in the mid-1920s to enlarge his pastorate. In 1933 about 40 million Americans listened regularly to the Radio Priest's broadcasts. At first Coughlin supported the New Deal, but

he soon broke with Roosevelt over the president's refusal to support the nationalization of the banking system and expansion of the money supply. In
1935 Coughlin organized the National Union for Social Justice to promote
his views, billing them as an alternative to those of "Franklin Double-
Crossing Roosevelt." Because he was Canadian-born and a priest, Coughlin
was not likely to make a successful run for president, but his rapidly growing
constituency threatened to complicate the 1936 election.

The most direct threat to Roosevelt came from Senator Huey Long. In a
single term as governor of Louisiana the flamboyant Long had achieved stunning popularity. He had increased the share of state taxes paid by corporations,
and had embarked on a program of public works that included construction
of new highways, bridges, hospitals, and schools. But Long's accomplishments
came at a price: to push through his reforms, he had seized almost dictatorial
control of the state government. He maintained control over Louisiana's political machine even after his election to the U.S. Senate in 1930. Though he
supported Roosevelt in 1932, he made no secret of his own presidential
ambitions.

In 1934 Senator Long broke with the New Deal, arguing that its programs
did not go far enough. Like Coughlin, he established his own national movement, the Share Our Wealth Society, which boasted over 4 million followers
by 1935. Arguing that the unequal distribution of wealth in the United States
was the fundamental cause of the depression, Long advocated taxing 100 percent of all incomes over $1 million, and all inheritances over $5 million, and
distributing the money to the rest of the population. He knew his plan was

The Kingfish
Huey Long, the Louisiana governor and senator, was one of the
most controversial figures in American political history. He took his
nickname "Kingfish" from a character in the popular radio show
"Amos 'n' Andy." Long inspired
one of the most powerful political
novels of all time, Robert Penn
Warren's *All the King's Men,* which
won a Pulitzer Prize in 1946.

unworkable, but confided privately "When they figure that out, I'll have something new for them."

Like Coughlin, Long offered easy solutions—panaceas—to the nation's economic ills. Their extreme proposals alarmed liberals. Coughlin's rhetoric, furthermore, often had anti-Semitic overtones, and both men showed little regard for the niceties of representative government. Coughlin had actually promised to dictate if necessary to preserve democracy. And the demagogic Long had dismissed complaints about his unconstitutional interference with the Louisiana legislative process by announcing, "I'm the Constitution around here." Long's and Coughlin's ideas, and their rapid rise in popularity, suggest the depth of public dissatisfaction with the Roosevelt administration. With good reason, the president's strategists feared that Long might join forces with Coughlin and Townsend to form a third party, enabling the Republicans to win the 1936 election.

THE SECOND NEW DEAL, 1935–1938

As the depression continued and attacks on the New Deal mounted, Roosevelt and his advisers embarked on a new course which historians have labeled the Second New Deal. Unlike the First New Deal, which focused on recovery, the Second New Deal emphasized reform. Pushed to the left by the popularity of movements like Long's, as well as by signs of militancy among workers, Roosevelt, his eye fixed firmly on the 1936 election, backed legislation to increase the role of the federal government in providing for the welfare of citizens.

Legislative Accomplishments

The first beneficiary of Roosevelt's change in direction was the labor movement. The rising number of strikes in 1934—about 1,800, involving a total of 1.5 million workers—reflected the dramatic growth of rank-and-file militancy. After the Supreme Court declared the NRA unconstitutional in 1935, invalidating Section 7(a), labor representatives demanded legislation that would protect the right to organize and bargain collectively.

The Wagner Act (1935), named for its sponsor, Senator Robert F. Wagner of New York, offered a degree of protection to labor. It upheld the right of industrial workers to join a union (farm workers were not covered), and outlawed many unfair labor practices used to squelch unions, such as firing or blacklisting workers for union activities. The act also established the nonpartisan National Labor Relations Board (NLRB) to protect workers from employer coercion, supervise representation elections, and guarantee the process of collective bargaining.

The Social Security Act signed by Roosevelt on August 14, 1935, was partly a response to the political mobilization of the nation's elderly through the Townsend and Long movements. But it also reflected prodding from social reformers like Grace Abbott, head of the Children's Bureau, and Secretary of Labor Frances Perkins. The Social Security Act provided pensions for most workers in the private sector, although originally agricultural workers and domestics were not covered. Pensions were to be paid out of a federal-state fund to which both employers and employees would contribute. The act also established a joint federal-state system of unemployment compensation, funded by an unemployment tax on employers.

The Social Security Act was a milestone in the creation of the modern welfare state. With its enactment, the United States joined industrialized countries like Great Britain and Germany in providing old-age pensions and unemployment compensation to citizens. (The Roosevelt administration chose not to push for national health insurance, even though most other industrialized nations offered such protection.) The act also mandated categorical assistance to the blind, deaf, and disabled and to dependent children—the so-called deserving poor, who clearly could not support themselves. Categorical assistance programs, only a small part of the New Deal, gradually expanded over the years until they became an integral part of the American welfare system.

Roosevelt was never enthusiastic about large expenditures for social welfare programs. But in the sixth year of the depression, 10 million Americans were still out of work, creating a pressing moral and political issue for FDR and the Democrats. At this point, the Works Progress Administration (WPA) became the main federal relief agency; for the rest of the depression, it addressed the needs of the unemployed. While FERA had supplied grants to state relief programs, the WPA put relief workers directly onto the federal payroll. Between 1935 and 1943 the WPA employed 8.5 million Americans, spending $10.5 billion. The agency's employees constructed 651,087 miles of roads, 125,110 public buildings, 8,192 parks, and 853 airports, and built or repaired 124,087 bridges.

Though the WPA was an extravagant operation by the standards of the 1930s (it inspired nicknames such as "We Putter Around" and "We Poke Along"), it never reached more than a third of the nation's unemployed. The average wage of $55 a month—well below the government-defined subsistence level of $100 a month—barely enabled workers to eke out a living. In 1941, the government cut the program severely. It ended in 1943, when the economy returned to full employment during World War II.

The Revenue Act of 1935 showed Roosevelt's willingness to push for reforms that were considered too controversial earlier in his presidency. Much of the business community had already turned violently against Roosevelt in reaction to the NRA, the Social Security Act, and the Wagner Act. Wealthy conservatives quickly labeled this tax reform bill, which included federal inheritance and gift taxes, higher personal income tax rates in the top brackets, and higher corporate taxes, an attempt to "soak the rich." Roosevelt, seeking to defuse the popularity of Huey Long's Share Our Wealth plan, was just as interested in the political mileage of the tax bill as its actual results, which increased federal revenue by only $250 million a year.

As the 1936 election approached, the broad range of New Deal programs brought new voters into the Democratic coalition. Many had been personally helped by federal programs; others benefited because their interests had found new support in the federal expansion. Roosevelt could count on a potent urban-based coalition of workers, organized labor, northern blacks, farmers, white ethnic groups, Catholics, Jews, liberals, intellectuals, progressive Republicans, and middle-class families concerned about unemployment and old-age dependence. The Democrats also held on, though with some difficulty, to their traditional constituency of white southerners.

The Republicans realized that they could not compete directly with Roosevelt and his New Deal coalition. To run against the president, they chose the progressive governor of Kansas, Alfred M. Landon, who accepted the general precepts of the New Deal. Landon and the Republicans concentrated on criticizing the inefficiency and expense of many New Deal programs, stridently accusing FDR of harboring dictatorial ambitions.

Roosevelt's victory in 1936 was one of the biggest landslides in American history. The assassination of Huey Long in September 1935 had deflated the threat of a serious third-party challenge; the candidate of the combined Long-Townsend-Coughlin camp, Congressman William Lemke of North Dakota, garnered fewer than 900,000 votes (1.9 percent) for the Union party ticket. Roosevelt received 60.8 percent of the popular vote and carried every state except Maine and Vermont. The New Deal was at high tide.

Stalemate

From this high point, the New Deal soon slid into retrenchment, controversy, and stalemate. The first setback came when Roosevelt attempted to make fundamental changes in the structure of the Supreme Court. Shortly after finding the NRA unconstitutional in *Schechter v. United States*, the Court had struck down the Agricultural Adjustment Act, a coal conservation act, and New York State's minimum wage law. With the Wagner Act, the TVA, and Social Security coming up on appeal, the future of New Deal reform measures seemed in doubt.

Roosevelt's response, two weeks after his second inauguration, was to propose the addition of one new justice for each sitting justice over the age of seventy—a scheme that would have increased the number of justices from nine to fifteen. Roosevelt's opponents quickly protested that he was trying to "pack" the Court with justices who favored the New Deal. The president's proposal was also regarded as an assault on the principle of the separation of powers. But the issue became a moot one when the Supreme Court upheld several key pieces of New Deal legislation, and a series of resignations created vacancies on the Court. Within four years Roosevelt managed to reshape the Supreme Court to suit his liberal philosophy through seven new appointments, including Hugo Black, Felix Frankfurter, Stanley F. Reed, and William O. Douglas. Yet his handling of the issue was a costly blunder at a time when his second-term administration was vulnerable to the lame-duck syndrome. No one yet suspected that FDR would break with tradition by seeking a third term.

Congressional conservatives had long opposed the direction of the New Deal, but the Court-packing episode galvanized them by demonstrating that Roosevelt was no longer politically invincible. Throughout Roosevelt's second term a conservative coalition, composed mainly of southern Democrats and Republicans from rural areas, blocked or impeded social legislation. Two pieces of reform legislation that did win passage were the National Housing Act of 1937, which mandated the construction of low-cost public housing, and the Fair Labor Standards Act of 1938, which made permanent the minimum wage, maximum hours, and anti–child labor provisions in the NRA codes.

The "Roosevelt recession" of 1937–1938 dealt the most devastating blow to the president's political standing in the second term. Until that point the economy had made steady progress. From 1933 to 1937 the gross national product had grown at a yearly rate of about 10 percent, and industrial output had finally returned to 1929 levels in 1937, as did real income. Unemployment had declined from 25 percent to 14 percent—which meant that almost half the people without a job in 1933 had found one by 1937. Many Americans agreed with Senator James F. Byrnes of South Carolina that "the emergency has passed."

The steady improvement of the economy cheered Roosevelt. Basically a fiscal conservative, he had never been comfortable with large federal expenditures—which had grown from $4.8 billion in 1932 to $6.5 billion in 1934, producing deficits of about $3 billion in most years. Accordingly, Roosevelt slashed the federal budget in 1937. Between January and August, Congress cut the WPA's funding in half, causing layoffs of about 1.5 million workers. The Federal Reserve, fearing inflation, tightened credit, creating a sharp drop in the stock market. Unemployment soared to 19 percent, which meant more than 10 million workers were without jobs. Roosevelt soon found himself in the same situation that had confounded Hoover. Having taken credit for the recovery between 1933 and 1937, he had to take the blame for the recession.

Shifting gears, Roosevelt spent his way out of the downturn. Large WPA appropriations and a resumption of public works projects poured enough money into the economy to lift it out of the recession by early 1938. Roosevelt and his economic advisers were groping their way toward the general theory advanced by John Maynard Keynes, a British economist who proposed that governments use deficit spending to stimulate the economy when private spending proved insufficient. But Keynes's theory would not be widely accepted until a dramatic increase in defense spending for World War II finally ended the Great Depression.

Still struggling with attacks on the New Deal, Roosevelt decided to "purge" some of his most conservative opponents from the Democratic party as the 1938 election approached. In the spring primaries he campaigned against members of his own party who had been hostile or unsympathetic to New Deal initiatives. The purge failed abysmally and widened the liberal-conservative rift in the Democratic party. In the general election of 1938, Republicans capitalized on the "Roosevelt recession" and the backlash against the Court-packing attempt to pick up 8 seats in the Senate and 81 in the House. The party also gained 13 governorships.

Even without these political reversals, the reform impetus of the New Deal probably would not have continued. Roosevelt had always set clear limits on how far he was willing to go. His instincts were basically conservative, not revolutionary; he had wanted only to save the capitalist economic system by reforming it. The new activism of the Second New Deal was a major step beyond the informal, one-sided business-government partnership of the preceding decade—a step Roosevelt took only because the emergency of the depression had pushed him in that direction.

THE NEW DEAL'S IMPACT ON SOCIETY

Despite the limits of the New Deal, it had a tremendous impact on the nation and fundamentally altered American's relationship to their government. With an optimistic faith in using government for social purposes, New Dealers sponsored programs in the arts. It created vast projects to conserve the country's natural beauty and resources and to make them more accessible to its citizens. The broker state that emerged in the New Deal also brought the voices of more citizens—women, blacks, labor, Mexican-Americans—to the public arena, helping to promote the view that Roosevelt, and his party, represented the common people.

New Deal Constituencies

The New Deal accelerated the expansion of the federal bureaucracy that had been under way since the turn of the century. In a decade, the number of civilian government employees increased 80 percent, exceeding a million by 1940. The number of federal employees who worked in Washington grew at an even faster rate, doubling between 1929 and 1940. Power was increasingly centered in the nation's capital, not in the states. In 1939 a British observer summed up the new orientation: "Just as in 1929 the whole country was 'Wall Street conscious,' now it is 'Washington conscious.'"

The growth of the federal government increased the potential impact of its decisions (and spending) on various constituencies. And the New Deal considered a broader spectrum of the population worthy of inclusion in the political process, especially if people organized themselves into pressure groups. During the 1930s the federal government operated as a *broker state*—mediating between contending groups seeking power and benefits. Democrats recognized the importance of satisfying certain blocs of voters in order to cement their allegiance to the party. Even before the depression, they had begun to

---

AMERICAN VOICES

A New Deal Activist

As an economist working for Harry Hopkins, Joe Marcus was one of thousands who formed the growing New Deal bureaucracy. Marcus's account, as told to Studs Terkel, captures some of the excitement that the New Deal generated. Marcus also suggests the way in which Roosevelt's administration expanded opportunities for Jews and other "outsiders."

I graduated college in '35. I went down to Washington and started to work in the spring of '36. The New Deal was a young man's world. Young people, if they showed any ability, got an opportunity. . . . In a few months I was made head of the department. We had a meeting with hot shots: What's to be done? I pointed out some problems: let's define what we're looking for. They immediately had me take over. . . .

The climate was exciting. You were part of a society that was on the move. You were involved in something that could make a difference. Laws could be changed. So could the conditions of people.

The idea of being involved close to the center of political life was unthinkable, just two or three years before all this happened. Unthinkable for someone like me, of lower middle-class, close to ghetto, Jewish life. Suddenly you were a significant member of society. It was not the kind of closed society you had lived in before. . . .

You were really part of something, changes could be made. Bringing *immediate* results to people who were starving. You could do something about it: that was the most important thing. . . .

We weren't thinking of remaking society. That wasn't it. I didn't buy this dream stuff. What was happening was a complete change in social attitudes at the central government level. The question was: How can you do it within this system? . . . The basic feeling—and I don't think this is just nostalgia—was one of excitement, of achievement, of happiness. Life was important, life was significant.

SOURCE: Studs Terkel, *Hard Times* (New York: Pantheon, 1986), pp. 265–266; also in the *America's History* Documents Collection, vol. 2, pp. 256–257.

---

build a coalition based on urban political machines and white ethnic voters. In the 1930s, organized labor, women, African-Americans, and other groups joined that coalition, receiving more attention from the Democrats and the federal government they controlled.

During the 1930s, labor relations became a legitimate arena for federal action and intervention, and organized labor claimed a place in national political life. Labor's dramatic growth in the 1930s represented one of the most important social and economic changes of the decade—an enormous contrast to its demoralized state at the end of the 1920s. Several factors encouraged the growth of the labor movement: the inadequacy of welfare capitalism in the face of the depression, New Deal legislation like the Wagner Act, the rise of the Congress of Industrial Organizations (CIO), and the growing militancy of rank-and-file workers. By the end of the decade the number of unionized workers had tripled to almost 9 million, or 23 percent of the nonfarm work force. Union strength grew rapidly in manufacturing, transportation, and mining. Organized labor won not only the battle for union recognition but for higher wages, seniority systems, and grievance procedures.

The CIO served as the cutting edge of the union movement by promoting industrial unionism—that is, organizing all the workers in an industry, both skilled and unskilled, into one union. John L. Lewis, leader of the United Mine Workers (UMW) and a founder of the CIO, was the foremost exponent of industrial unionism. Lewis began to detach himself from the American Federation of Labor (AFL), which favored organizing workers on a craft-by-craft basis, in 1935; by 1938 the break was complete.

The CIO achieved some of its momentum through the presence in its ranks of members of the Communist party. The rise of fascism in Europe had prompted the Soviet Union to mobilize support in democratic countries. In Europe and the United States, communist parties called for a "popular front," welcoming the cooperation of any group concerned about the threat of fascism

Organize
The Steelworkers' Organizing Committee was one of the most vital labor organizations contributing to the rise of the CIO. Note that the artist Ben Shahn chose a male figure to represent the American labor movement in this poster from the late 1930s. Such iconography reinforced the notion that the typical worker was male, despite the large number of women who joined the CIO.

to civil rights, organized labor, and world peace. Under the popular front, communists softened their revolutionary rhetoric and concentrated on becoming active leaders in many CIO unions. While few workers actually joined the Communist party, its influence in labor organizing in the thirties was far greater than its numbers, which in 1936 reached 40,000.

The CIO's success also stemmed from the recognition that to succeed, unions must be more inclusive. The CIO worked deliberately to attract new groups to the labor movement. Mexican-Americans and blacks found the CIO's commitment to racial justice a strong contrast to the AFL's long-established patterns of exclusion and segregation. And about 800,000 women workers also found a limited welcome in the CIO. Few blacks, Mexican-Americans, or women held leadership positions, however.

The CIO scored its first major victory in the automobile industry. On December 31, 1936, General Motors workers in Flint, Michigan, staged a sit-down strike, vowing to stay at their machines until management agreed to collective bargaining. The workers lived in the factories and machine shops for forty-four days before General Motors recognized their union, United Automobile Workers (UAW). Shortly after the CIO won another major victory, at the U.S. Steel Corporation. Despite a long history of bitter opposition to unionization (as demonstrated in the 1919 steel strike), Big Steel executives capitulated without a fight and recognized the Steel Workers Organizing Committee (SWOC) on March 2, 1937.

The victory in the steel industry was not complete, however. A group of companies known as "Little Steel" chose not to follow U.S. Steel's lead in making peace with the CIO. In response, steelworkers struck the Republic Steel Corporation plant in South Chicago. On Memorial Day, May 31, 1937, strikers and their families gathered for a holiday picnic and rally outside the plant's gates. Tension mounted, rocks were thrown, and the police fired on the crowd, killing ten protesters, all of them shot in the back. Workers in Little Steel did not win union recognition until 1941. The road to recognition for labor, even with New Deal protections, was still long and violent.

Labor's new vitality spilled over into political action. The AFL had always stood aloof from partisan politics, but the CIO quickly allied itself with the Democratic party, hoping to use its influence to elect candidates sympathetic to labor and social justice. Through Labor's Nonpartisan League, the CIO gave $770,000 to Democratic campaigns in 1936. Labor also provided solid support for Roosevelt's plan to reorganize the Supreme Court.

Despite the breakthroughs of the New Deal, the labor movement never developed into a dominant force in American life. Roosevelt never made the growth of the labor movement a high priority, and many workers remained indifferent or even hostile to unionization. And although the Wagner Act guaranteed unions a permanent place in American industrial relations, it did not revolutionize working conditions. The right to collective bargaining, rather than redistributing power in American industry, merely granted labor a measure of legitimacy. Management even found that unions could be used as a

Sit-down Strike

By *giving workers control of their employers' physical plant, sit-down strikes forced companies to negotiate. Bob Stinson's account of the first major sit-down strike—at General Motors in Flint, Michigan—reveals the high degree of organization and community support that characterized that forty-four-day strike.*

The Flint sit-down happened Christmas eve, 1936. . . . We had guys patrol the plant, see that nobody got involved in anything they shouldn't. If anybody got careless with company property—such as sitting on an automobile cushion without putting burlap over it—he was talked to. . . .

Governor Murphy said he hoped to God he would never have to use National Guard against people. But if there was damage to property, he would do so. This was right down our alley, because we invited him to the plant and see how well we were taking care of the place.

They'd assign roles to you. When some of the guys at headquarters wanted to tell some of the guys in the plant what was cookin', I carried the message. . . .

The merchants cooperated. There'd be apples, bushels of potatoes, crates of oranges that was beginning to spoil. Some of our members were also little farmers, they come up with a couple of baskets of junk.

The soup kitchen was outside the plant. The women handled all the cooking, outside of one chef who came from New York. He had anywhere from ten to twenty women washing dishes and peeling potatoes in the strike kitchen. Mostly stews, pretty good meals. They were put in containers and hoisted up through the window. The boys in there had their own plates and cups and saucers.

SOURCE: Studs Terkel, *Hard Times* (New York: Pantheon, 1986), p. 131.

buffer against rank-and-file militancy. New Deal social welfare programs also tended to diffuse some of the pre-1937 radical spirit by channeling economic benefits to workers whether or not they belonged to unions.

Like organized workers, white women achieved new influence in the experimental climate of the New Deal, as unprecedented numbers of them were offered positions in the Roosevelt administration. Frances Perkins, the first woman named to a cabinet post, served as secretary of labor throughout Roosevelt's presidency. Molly Dewson, a social reformer turned politician, headed the Women's Division of the Democratic National Committee, where she pushed an issue-oriented program that supported New Deal reforms. Roosevelt's appointments of women included the first female director of the mint, the head of a major WPA division, and a judge on the circuit court of appeals.

Many of those women were close friends as well as professional colleagues, and cooperated in an informal network to advance feminist and reform causes.

Eleanor Roosevelt exemplified the growing prominence of women in public life. In the 1920s she had worked closely with other reformers to increase women's power in political parties, labor unions, and education. The experience proved an invaluable apprenticeship for her White House years, when her marriage to FDR developed into one of the most successful political partnerships of all time. He was the pragmatic politician, always aware of what could be done; she was the idealist, the gadfly, always pushing him—and the New Deal—to do more. Eleanor Roosevelt served as the conscience of the New Deal.

Despite the vocal support of a female political network, grave flaws still marred the treatment of women in New Deal programs. For example, a fourth of the NRA codes set a lower minimum wage for women than for men performing the same jobs. New Deal agencies like the Civil Works Administration and the Public Works Administration gave jobs almost exclusively to men: only 7 percent of CWA workers were female. And the CCC excluded women entirely, prompting critics to ask, "where is the 'she-she-she'?"

When they did hire women, New Deal programs tended to reinforce the broader society's gender and racial attitudes. Thus program administrators resisted placing women in nontraditional jobs. Under the WPA, sewing rooms became a sort of dumping ground for unemployed women. African-American and Mexican-American women, if they had access to work relief at all, often found themselves shunted into training as domestics, whose work was not covered by the Social Security and Fair Labor Standards acts.

Eleanor Roosevelt and Civil Rights
One of Eleanor Roosevelt's greatest legacies was her commitment to civil rights. For example, she publicly resigned from the Daughters of the American Revolution (DAR) in 1939 when the group refused to let the black opera singer Marian Anderson perform at Constitution Hall. Roosevelt developed an especially close working relationship with Mary McLeod Bethune of the National Youth Administration, shown here at a conference on black youth in 1939.

Just as the New Deal did not seriously challenge gender inequities, it did little to battle racial discrimination. In the 1930s, the vast majority of the American people did not regard civil rights as a legitimate area for federal intervention. Indeed, many New Deal programs reflected prevailing racist attitudes. CCC camps segregated blacks and whites, and many NRA codes did not protect black workers. Most tellingly, Franklin Roosevelt repeatedly refused to support legislation to make lynching a federal crime, claiming it would antagonize southern members of Congress whose support he needed to pass New Deal measures.

Nevertheless, blacks did receive significant benefits from New Deal relief programs directed toward the poor, regardless of their race or ethnic background. Blacks made up about 18 percent of the WPA's recipients, although they constituted only 10 percent of the population. The Resettlement Administration, established in 1935 to help small farmers buy land, and to resettle sharecroppers and tenant farmers on more productive land, fought for the rights of black tenant farmers in the South—that is, until angry southerners in Congress drastically cut its appropriations. Still, many blacks reasoned that the tangible aid from Washington outweighed the discrimination that marred many federal programs.

African-Americans were also pleased to see blacks appointed to federal office. Mary McLeod Bethune, an educator who ran the Office of Minority Affairs of the National Youth Administration, headed the "black cabinet." This informal network worked for fairer treatment of blacks by New Deal agencies, in the same way the women's network advocated feminist causes. Both groups benefited greatly from the support of Eleanor Roosevelt. The first lady's promotion of equal treatment for blacks ranks as one of her greatest legacies.

Help from the WPA and other New Deal programs, and a belief that the White House—or at least Eleanor Roosevelt—cared about their plight, caused a dramatic change in African-Americans' voting behavior. Since the Civil War blacks had voted Republican, a loyalty based on Abraham Lincoln's freeing of the slaves. As late as 1932, black voters in northern cities overwhelmingly supported Republican candidates. But in 1936, black Americans outside the South gave Roosevelt 71 percent of their votes. In Harlem, where relief dollars increased dramatically in the wake of the 1935 riot (see Chapter 25), their support was an extraordinary 81.3 percent. Black voters have remained overwhelmingly Democratic ever since.

The election of Franklin Roosevelt also had an immediate effect on Mexican-American communities, demoralized by the depression and the deportations of the Hoover years. In cities like Los Angeles and El Paso, Mexican-Americans qualified for relief more easily under New Deal guidelines, and there was more relief to go around. Even though New Deal guidelines prohibited discrimination based on an immigrant's legal status, the new climate encouraged a marked rise in requests for naturalization papers. Mexican-Americans also benefited from New Deal labor policies; for many, joining the CIO was an important stage in becoming an American. Inspired by New Deal rhetoric about economic recovery and social progress through cooperation, Mexican-Americans increasingly identified with the United States, rather than with Mexico. This shift was especially evident among American-born children of Mexican immigrants. Increasingly, participating in the political system became part of Mexican-American life. Los Angeles activist Beatrice Griffith noted, "Franklin D. Roosevelt's name was the spark that started thousands of Spanish-speaking persons to the polls." The Democrats made it clear that they welcomed Mexican-American voters and considered them an important part of the New Deal coalition.

But what about groups that did not mobilize politically or were not recognized as key participants in the New Deal coalition? The New Deal's impact on those groups and communities often depended on whether sympathetic government administrators in Washington undertook to promote their interests. Native Americans were one of the nation's most disadvantaged and most powerless minorities. The average annual income of a native American in 1934 was only $48; the unemployment rate among native Americans was three times the national average. Concerned New Deal administrators like Secretary of the Interior Harold Ickes and Commissioner of the Bureau of Indian Affairs John Collier tried to correct some of those inequities. The Indian Section of the Civilian Conservation Corps brought needed money and projects to reservations throughout the West. Indians also received benefits from FERA and CWA work relief projects.

Of far greater significance was the Indian Reorganization Act of 1934, sometimes called the "Indian New Deal." That law reversed the Dawes Severalty Act of 1887 by promoting more extensive self-government through tribal councils and constitutions. The government also abandoned the attempt to force native Americans to assimilate into mainstream society in favor of promoting cultural pluralism. The New Deal pledged to help preserve Indian languages, arts, and traditions. The problems of native Americans were so severe, however, that these changes in federal policy did little to improve their lives or reinvigorate tribal communities.

The New Deal and the Land

Concern for the land was one of the dominant motifs of the New Deal, and the shaping of the public landscape among its most visible legacies. Roosevelt brought to the presidency a love of forestry and a conservation ethic nurtured from childhood on his Hudson River estate. The expansion of federal responsibilities in the 1930s created a climate conducive to action, as did public concern heightened by the dramatic images of drought and devastation in the Dust Bowl. The New Deal resources policy stressed scientific management of the land, conservation instead of commercial development, and the aggressive use of public authority to safeguard both private and public holdings.

The most extensive New Deal environmental undertaking was the Tennessee Valley Authority. The need for dams to control flooding and erosion in the Tennessee River Basin, a seven-state area with some of the country's heaviest rainfall, had been recognized since World War I. But not until 1933 was the Tennessee Valley Authority established to develop the region's resources under public control. The TVA was the ultimate watershed demonstration area, integrating flood control, reforestation, and agricultural and industrial development, including the production of chemical fertilizers. A hydroelectric grid provided cheap electric power for the valley's residents. Admired worldwide, the TVA became one of the most popular destinations for visitors to the United States.

The Dust Bowl helped to focus attention on land management and ecological balance. Agents from the Soil Conservation Service in the Department of Agriculture taught farmers the proper technique for tilling hillsides. Government agronomists also tried to remove marginal land from cultivation, and to prevent soil erosion through better agricultural practices. One of their most widely publicized programs was the creation of the Shelterbelts, which involved the planting of 220 million trees running roughly along the 99th meridian, from Abilene, Texas, to the Canadian border. Planted as a windbreak, the trees also prevented soil erosion.

Another priority of the Roosevelt administration was helping rural Americans to stay on the land. The Rural Electrification Administration, established in 1935, brought power to farms in an attempt to improve the quality of rural life. The New Deal also encouraged urban dwellers to return to rural areas. This "back-to-the land" motif animated many New Deal projects, especially planned cooperative communities in rural areas, such as Arthurdale in West Virginia and the "Greenbelt" residential towns outside Washington, D.C.; Cincinnati; and Milwaukee.

Today, New Deal projects to conserve environment can be seen throughout the country. CCC and WPA workers built the Blue Ridge Parkway, the consummate parkway of the 1930s, which connects the Shenandoah National Park in Virginia with the Great Smoky Mountain National Park in North Carolina. In the West, government workers built the San Francisco Zoo, Berkeley's Tilden Park, and the canals of San Antonio. The CCC helped to complete the East Coast's Appalachian Trail and the West Coast's Pacific Crest Trail through the Sierras. In state parks across the country, cabins, shelters, picnic areas, lodges, and observation towers, built in a style that has been called "government rustic," are witness to the New Deal ethos of recreation coexisting with conservation.

Although the New Deal was ahead of its time in its attention to conservation, its legacy to later environmental movements is mixed. Many of the tactics used in New Deal projects—damming rivers, blasting fire roads, altering the natural landscape through the construction of buildings and shelters—are now considered intrusive. In the 1970s, the TVA came under attack for its longstanding practice of strip mining and the pollution caused by its power plants and chemical factories. Because of environmental concerns, a project as massive as the TVA probably could not be built today—an ironic comment on what was once hailed as an enlightened use of government power.

The New Deal and the Arts

In the arts, the depression had dried up traditional sources of patronage. Like most Americans, creative artists had nowhere to turn but Washington. A WPA project known as "Federal One" put unemployed artists, actors, and writers to work, but its spirit and purpose extended far beyond relief. New Deal administrators wanted to redefine the relationship between artists and the community, so that art would no longer be the exclusive province of the elite. "Art for the millions" became a popular New Deal slogan.

The Federal Art Project (FAP) gave work to many of the twentieth century's leading painters, muralists, and sculptors at a point in their careers when the lack of private patronage might have prevented them from continuing their artistic production. Under the direction of Holger Cahill, an expert on American folk art, the FAP commissioned murals for public buildings and post offices across the country. Jackson Pollock, Alice Neel, Willem de Kooning, and Louise Nevelson all received support from the FAP.

The Federal Music Project employed 15,000 musicians under the direction of Nicholas Sokoloff, the conductor of the Cleveland Symphony Orchestra. Government-sponsored orchestras toured the country, presenting free concerts of both classical and popular music. Like many New Deal programs, the Music Project emphasized American themes. The composer Aaron Copland wrote his *Billy the Kid* (1938) and *Rodeo* (1942) ballets for the WPA, basing the compositions on western folk motifs. The distinctive "American" sound and athletic dance style of these works made them immensely appealing to audiences. The federal government also employed the musicologist Charles Seeger and his wife, the composer Ruth Crawford Seeger, to catalog hundreds of American folk songs.

The former journalist Henry Alsberg headed the Federal Writers' Project (FWP), which at its height employed about 5,000 writers. Young FWP employees who later achieved fame included Saul Bellow, Ralph Ellison, Tillie Olsen, and John Cheever. The black folklorist and novelist Zora Neale Hurston finished three novels while on the Florida FWP, among them *Their Eyes Were Watching God* (1937). And Richard Wright won the 1938 *Story* magazine prize for the best tale by a WPA writer. Wright used his spare time to complete his novel *Native Son* (1940).

Of all the New Deal arts programs, the Federal Theatre Project (FTP) was the most ambitious. American drama thrived in the 1930s, the only time at which the United States had a federally supported national theater. Under the gifted direction of Hallie Flanagan, former head of Vassar College's Experimental Theater, the Theatre Project reached an audience of 25 to 30 million people in the four years of its existence. Talented directors, actors, and playwrights, including Orson Welles, John Huston, and Arthur Miller, offered their services.

The WPA arts projects were influenced by a broad artistic trend called the *documentary impulse*. Combining social relevance with distinctively American themes, this approach—which presented actual facts and events in a way that aroused the interest and emotions of the audience—characterized the artistic expression of the 1930s. The documentary, probably the decade's most distinctive genre, influenced practically every aspect of American culture: literature, photography, art, music, film, dance, theater, and radio.

The documentary impulse is evident in John Steinbeck's fiction (see Chapter 25) and in John Dos Passos's *USA* trilogy, which used actual newspaper clippings, dispatches, and headlines in its fictional story. The *March of Time* newsreels, which movie audiences saw before feature films, presented the news of the world for the pretelevision age. The filmmaker Pare Lorentz commissioned the composer Virgil Thompson to create music that set the mood for documentary movies such as *The Plow That Broke the Plains* (1936) and *The River* (1936). The new photojournalism magazines, including *Life* and *Look*, also reflected this documentary approach. And the New Deal institutionalized the trend by sending investigators like the journalist Lorena Hickok and the writer Martha Gellhorn into the field to report on the conditions of people on relief.

Finally, the federal government played a leading role in compiling the photographic record of the 1930s. The Historical Section of the Resettlement Administration had a mandate to document and photograph the American scene for the government. Through their haunting images of sharecroppers, Dust Bowl migrants, and the urban homeless, the photographers Dorothea Lange, Walker Evans, Ben Shahn, and Margaret Bourke-White permanently shaped the image of the Great Depression. The government hired photographers solely for their professional skills, not to provide them relief, as in Federal One projects. Their photographs, collected by the Historical Section, which in 1937 became part of the newly created Farm Security Administration (FSA), rank as the best visual representation of life in the United States during the depression years.

The Legacies of the New Deal

The New Deal set in motion far-reaching changes, notably the growth of a modern state of significant size. For the first time people experienced the federal government as a concrete part of everyday life. During the 1930s more than a third of the population received direct government assistance from new federal programs, including Social Security payments, farm loans, relief work, and mortgage guarantees. Furthermore, the government had made a commitment to intervene in the economy when the private sector could not guarantee economic stability. New legislation regulated the stock market, reformed the Federal Reserve system by placing more power in the hands of Washington policymakers, and brought many practices of modern corporate life under federal regulation. Thus, the New Deal accelerated the pattern begun during the Progressive Era of using federal regulation to bring order and regularity to economic life.

The New Deal also laid the foundations of America's welfare state—that is, the federal government's acceptance of primary responsibility for the individual and collective welfare of the people. But although the New Deal offered more benefits to American citizens than they had ever received before, its safety net had many holes, especially in comparison with the far more extensive welfare systems of Western Europe. The Social Security Act did not include national health care. Another serious defect of the emerging welfare system was its failure to reach a significant minority of American workers, including domestics and farm workers, for many years. And since state governments administered the programs, benefits varied widely; southern states consistently provided the lowest amounts.

To its credit, the New Deal recognized that poverty was an economic problem, not a matter of personal failure. Reformers assumed that once the depression was over, full employment and an active economy would take care of the nation's welfare needs and poverty would wither away. It did not. When later administrations confronted the persistence of inequality and unemployment, they grafted welfare programs onto the jerry-built system left over from the New Deal. Thus the American welfare system would always be marked by its birth during the crisis atmosphere of the Great Depression.

Even if the depression-era welfare system had some serious flaws, it was brilliant politics. The Democratic party courted the allegiance of citizens who benefited from New Deal programs. Organized labor aligned itself with the administration that had made it a legitimate force in modern industrial life. Blacks voted Democratic in direct relation to the economic benefits that poured into their communities. At the grass-roots level, the Women's Division of the Democratic National Committee mobilized 80,000 women who recognized what the New Deal had done for their communities. The unemployed also looked kindly on the Roosevelt administration. According to one of the earliest Gallup polls, 84 percent of those on relief voted the Democratic ticket in 1936.

But the Democratic party did not attract only the down-and-out. Roosevelt's magnetic personality and the dispersal of New Deal benefits to families throughout the social structure brought middle-class voters, many of them first- or second-generation immigrants, into the Democratic fold. Thus the New Deal completed the transformation of the Democratic party that had begun in the 1920s toward a coalition of ethnic groups, city dwellers, organized labor, blacks, and a broad cross-section of the middle class. Those voters would form the backbone of the Democratic coalition for decades to come, and would provide support for liberal reforms that extended the promise of the New Deal.

The New Deal coalition contained potentially fatal contradictions, involving mainly the issue of race. Because Roosevelt depended on the support of southern white Democrats to pass New Deal legislation, he was unwilling to challenge the economic and political marginalization of blacks in the South. At the same time, New Deal programs were changing the face of southern agriculture by undermining the sharecropping system and encouraging the migration of southern blacks to northern and western cities. Outside the South, blacks were not prevented from voting, a disparity that guaranteed that civil rights would enter the national agenda. The resulting fissures would eventually weaken the coalition that seemed so invincible at the height of Roosevelt's power.

With all its shortcomings, the New Deal nonetheless had a profound impact on the nation, all the more remarkable in light of its short duration. After 1936, the only major pieces of reform legislation passed were the National Housing Act of 1937 and the Fair Labor Standards Act of 1938. While the Supreme Court–packing scheme, the "Roosevelt recession," and the political successes of Republicans in 1938 helped to bring an end to the New Deal, the darkening international scene also played a part. As Europe moved toward war and Japan flexed its muscles in the Far East, Roosevelt became increasingly preoccupied with international relations, and placed domestic reform further and further into the background. After the United States entered the war in 1941, Roosevelt made the end of his depression program official when he announced in 1943 that it was time for "Dr. Win the War" to take the place of "Dr. New Deal." But in reality the New Deal had long ceased to propel the nation toward social reform.

CHAPTER 26 TIMELINE	
1933	Banking crisis
	FDR's first fireside chat
	Emergency Banking Act
	Glass-Steagall Act establishes FDIC
	Agricultural Adjustment Act
	National Industrial Recovery Act
	Tennessee Valley Authority
	United States abandons gold standard
	Townsend Clubs
1934	Securities and Exchange Commission
	Indian Reorganization Act
1935	Supreme Court finds NRA unconstitutional
	National Union for Social Justice (Father Charles Coughlin)
	Resettlement Administration
	National Labor Relations (Wagner) Act
	Social Security Act
	Works Progress Administration
	CIO formed
1935–1939	Communist party at height of influence
1936	Supreme Court finds Agricultural Adjustment Act unconstitutional
	Roosevelt reelected
	The Plow That Broke the Plains and *The River*
	General Motors sit-down strike
1937	Memorial Day Massacre
	Supreme Court reorganization fails
1937–1938	"Roosevelt recession"
1938	Aaron Copland, *Billy the Kid*
	Fair Labor Standards Act
1939	Federal Theatre Project terminated

CHAPTER 27

THE WORLD AT WAR, 1939–1945

- The Road to War
- Mobilizing for Victory
- Life on the Home Front
- Fighting and Winning the War

Times Square, New York City, on August 15, 1945, was awash with people celebrating V-J (Victory over Japan) Day. World War II was over. Civilians and soldiers "jived in the streets and the crowd was so large that traffic was halted and sprinkler trucks were used to disperse pedestrians." The spontaneous street party seemed a fitting end to what had been the country's most popular war. For many Americans, World War II had been what one man described to journalist Studs Terkel as "an unreal period for us here at home. Those who lost nobody at the front had a pretty good time."

Americans had many reasons to view World War II as the "good war." Shocked by the Japanese attack on Pearl Harbor on December 7, 1941, they united in their determination to fight German and Japanese totalitarianism in defense of their way of life. When evidence of the grim reality of the Jewish Holocaust came to light, U.S. participation in the war seemed even more just. And despite their sacrifices, many people found the war a positive experience because it ended the devastating Great Depression, bringing full employment and prosperity. The unambiguous nature of the victory and the subsequent emergence of the United States as an unprecedentedly powerful nation further contributed to the sense of the war as one worth fighting.

But the good war had other sides. The period brought significant social disruption, accompanied by widespread anxiety about women's presence in the work force and a rise in juvenile delinquency. In a massive violation of civil liberties, over 100,000 people of Japanese ancestry were incarcerated in internment camps, victims of racially based hysteria. African-Americans served in a segregated military, and, with Chicanos, faced discrimination and violence at home. World War II also fostered the rise of a military industrial complex and unleashed the terrible potential of the atomic bomb. Finally, another enduring legacy developed out of the unresolved issues of the wartime alliance: the debilitating Cold War, which would dominate American foreign policy for decades.

THE ROAD TO WAR

The rise of fascism in Europe and Asia in the 1930s threatened the fragile peace that had prevailed since the end of World War I. When the League of Nations proved too weak to deal with the emerging crises, President Roosevelt foresaw the possibility of America's participation in another war. An internationalist at heart, he wanted the United States to play a prominent role in the international economic and political system to foster the long-term prosperity necessary for a lasting peace. Hampered at first by the pervasive isolationist sentiment in the country, by 1939 he was leading the nation toward war.

Depression Diplomacy

During the early years of the New Deal, America's involvement in international affairs, especially those in Europe, remained limited. One of Roosevelt's few diplomatic initiatives had been the formal recognition of the Soviet Union in November 1933. A second significant development was the Good Neighbor Policy, under which the United States voluntarily renounced the use of military force and armed intervention in the Western Hemisphere. At the core of this policy was the recognition that the friendship of Latin American countries was essential to the security of the United States. One practical outcome came in 1934, when Congress repealed the Platt Amendment, a relic of the Spanish-American War, which asserted the United States' right to intervene in Cuba's affairs. Indicating the limits to the Good Neighbor Policy, the U.S. Navy kept (and still maintains) a major base at Cuba's Guantanamo Bay and continued to meddle in Cuban politics. And in numerous Latin American countries, U.S. diplomats frequently resorted to economic pressure to solidify the influence of the United States and benefit its international corporations.

Roosevelt and his secretary of state, Cordell Hull, might have hoped to pursue more far-reaching diplomatic initiatives. But isolationism had been building in both Congress and the nation throughout the 1920s, a product in part of disillusionment with American participation in World War I. In 1934 Gerald P. Nye, a Republican senator from North Dakota, began a congressional investigation into the profits of munitions makers during World War I, and then widened the investigation to determine the influence of economic interests on America's decision to declare war. Nye's committee concluded that war profiteers, whom it called "merchants of death," had maneuvered the nation into World War I for financial gain.

Though most of the committee's charges were dubious or simplistic, they gave momentum to the isolationist movement, contributing to the passage of the Neutrality Act of 1935. Designed explicitly to prevent a recurrence of the events that had pulled the United States into World War I, the act imposed an embargo on arms trading with countries at war, and declared that American citizens traveled on the ships of belligerent nations at their own risk. In 1936, Congress expanded the Neutrality Act to ban loans to belligerents, and in 1937, it adopted a "cash-and-carry" provision: if a country at war wanted to purchase nonmilitary goods from the United States, it had to pay for them in cash and pick them up in its own ships.

The same year Congress explicitly reinforced earlier bans on sales of arms to Spain, where a bloody Civil War had erupted in 1936. There Francisco Franco, strongly supported by the fascist regimes in Germany and Italy, was leading a rebellion against the democratically elected republican government. Backed only by the Soviet Union and Mexico, the republicans, or Loyalists, relied heavily on volunteers from other countries, including the American Lincoln Brigade, which fought courageously and sustained heavy losses throughout the war. The governments of the United States, Great Britain, and France, despite their Loyalist sympathies, remained neutral, a policy that dismayed many American intellectuals and activists and virtually assured a fascist victory.

Aggression and Appeasement

The nation's neutrality was soon challenged by the aggressive actions of Germany, Italy, and Japan, all determined to expand their borders and their influence. The first crisis was precipitated by Japan, a country whose militaristic regime was intent on dominating the Pacific basin. In 1931 Japan occupied Manchuria, the northernmost province of China; then in 1937, it launched a full-scale invasion of China. In both instances, the League of Nations condemned Japan's action, but was helpless to stop the aggression. Japan simply served the required one-year notice of withdrawal from the League.

Japan's defiance of the League encouraged a fascist dictator half a world away. Italy's Benito Mussolini had long been unhappy with the Versailles treaty, which had not awarded Italy any formerly German or Turkish colonies. In 1935 Italy invaded Ethiopia, one of the few independent countries left in Africa. The Ethiopian emperor, Haile Selassie, appealed to the League of Nations, which condemned the invasion and imposed sanctions, but to little effect. By 1936 the Italian subjugation of Ethiopia was complete.

Not Italy, but Germany presented the gravest threat to the world order in the 1930s. There huge reparations payments, runaway inflation, fear of communism, labor unrest, and rising unemployment fueled the rise of Adolf Hitler and his National Socialist (Nazi) party. In 1933 Hitler became chancellor of Germany, and assumed dictatorial powers. Aiming at nothing short of world domination, as he made clear in his book *Mein Kampf* (*My Struggle*), Hitler sought to overturn the territorial settlements of the Versailles treaty, to "restore" all the Germans of Central and Eastern Europe to a single greater German fatherland, and to annex large areas of Eastern Europe. In his warped vision, "inferior races" such as Jews, gypsies, and Slavs, as well as "undesirables" such as homosexuals and the mentally impaired, would have to make way for the "master race." In 1933 Hitler established the first concentration camp at Dachau and opened a campaign of persecution against Jews.

Hitler's strategy for gaining territory provoked a series of crises that gave Britain and France no alternative but to let him have his way or risk war. British Prime Minister Neville Chamberlain was a particularly insistent proponent of what became known as "appeasement." Germany withdrew from the League of Nations in 1933; two years later Hitler announced that he planned to rearm the nation in violation of the Versailles treaty. No one stopped him. In 1936 Germany reoccupied the Rhineland, a region that had been declared a demilitarized zone under the treaty. Once again France and Britain took no action. Later that year Hitler and Mussolini joined forces in the Rome-Berlin Axis, a political and military alliance. When the Spanish Civil War broke out, Germany and Italy armed the Spanish fascists. The same year, Germany and Japan signed the Anti-Comintern Pact, a precursor to the military alliance between Japan and the Axis that was formalized in 1940.

As persecution of German Jews and other minorities escalated, Hitler's ambitions grew. In 1938 he sent troops to annex Austria, while at the same time he schemed to seize part of Czechoslovakia. Because Czechoslovakia had an alliance with France, war seemed imminent. But at the Munich Conference in September 1938, Britain and France capitulated, agreeing to let Germany annex the Sudetenland—the German-speaking border areas of Czechoslovakia—in return for Hitler's pledge to seek no more territory.

Within six months, however, Hitler's forces had overrun the rest of Czechoslovakia and were threatening to march into Poland. Britain and France realized that their policy of appeasement had been disastrous, and prepared to take a stand. Then in August 1939 Hitler shocked the world by signing the Nonaggression Pact with the Soviet Union, which allowed Germany to avoid waging war on two fronts. On September 1, 1939, German troops attacked Poland; two days later Britain and France declared war on Germany. World War II had begun.

America and the War

Because the United States had become a major world power, whatever the nation did would affect the course of the European conflict. Two days after the war started, the United States officially declared its neutrality. Roosevelt made no secret of his sympathies, however. He pointedly rephrased Woodrow Wilson's declaration of 1914: "This nation will remain a neutral nation, but I cannot ask that every American remain neutral in thought as well." The overwhelming majority of Americans supported the Allies (Britain and France) over the Nazis, but most Americans did not want to be drawn into another world war.

At first, the need for American intervention seemed remote. After the German conquest of Poland in September 1939, a false calm settled over Europe. But then on April 9, 1940, Nazi tanks overran Denmark. Norway fell to the Nazi *Blitzkrieg* ("lightning war") next, and the Netherlands, Belgium, and Luxembourg soon followed. Finally, on June 22, 1940, France fell. Britain stood alone against Hitler's plans for world domination.

In America, the debate over the nation's neutrality continued. The journalist William Allen White and his Committee to Defend America by Aiding the Allies led the interventionists. Isolationists, including the aviator Charles Lindbergh, formed the America First Committee to keep the nation out of the war. They attracted the support of the Chicago *Tribune*, the Hearst newspapers, and other conservative publications.

Despite the efforts of the America First Committee, in 1940 the United States moved closer to involvement in the war. In May Roosevelt began putting the economy and the government on a defense footing by creating the National Defense Advisory Commission and the Council of National Defense. During the summer he traded fifty World War I destroyers to Great Britain in exchange for the right to build military bases on British possessions in the Atlantic, thus circumventing the nation's neutrality law by executive order. In October Congress approved a large increase in defense spending, and instituted the first peacetime draft registration and conscription in American history.

While the war expanded in Europe, Asia, North Africa, and the Middle East, the United States was preparing for the 1940 presidential election. The conflict had convinced Roosevelt that he should seek an unprecedented third term. He submitted to a "draft" at the Democratic National Convention, and despite opposition, chose the liberal secretary of agriculture Henry A. Wallace as his running mate. The Republicans nominated Wendell Willkie of Indiana, a former Democrat who supported many New Deal policies. The two parties' platforms differed only slightly. Both pledged aid to the Allies, but stopped short of calling for American participation in the war. Though Willkie's spirited campaign resulted in a closer election than those of 1932 or 1936, Roosevelt and the Democrats won 55 percent of the popular vote and a lopsided total in the electoral college.

With the election behind him, Roosevelt concentrated on persuading the American people to increase aid to Britain, whose survival he viewed as the key to American security. In November 1939 FDR had won a bitter battle in Congress to amend the Neutrality Act of 1935 to allow the Allies to buy weapons from the United States—but only on the cash-and-carry basis established for nonmilitary goods in 1937. In March 1941, with German submarines sinking British ships faster than they could be replaced, and Britain no longer able to afford to pay cash for arms, Roosevelt convinced Congress to pass the Lend-Lease Act. The legislation authorized the president to "lease, lend, or otherwise dispose of" arms and other equipment to any country whose defense was considered vital to the security of the United States. After Germany invaded the Soviet Union in June 1941 (an abandonment of the Nazi-Soviet pact of two years earlier), the United States extended lend-lease to the Soviet Union, which became part of the Allied coalition.

In his State of the Union address to Congress in January 1941, Roosevelt had connected lend-lease to the defense of democracy at home as well as in Europe. He spoke about what he called "four essential human freedoms everywhere in the world"—freedom of speech and expression, freedom of worship, freedom from want, and freedom from fear. Although Roosevelt avoided stating explicitly that America had to enter the war to protect those freedoms, he intended to justify exactly that, for he regarded United States entry in the war as inevitable. And indeed, the implementation of lend-lease marked the unofficial entrance of the United States into the European war.

The United States became even more involved in August 1941, when Roosevelt and the British prime minister, Winston Churchill, conferred secretly to discuss goals and military strategy. Their joint press release, which became known as the Atlantic Charter, provided the ideological foundation of the western cause and of the peace to follow. Like Wilson's Fourteen Points, the Charter called for economic collaboration and guarantees of political stability after the war ended, to ensure that "all men in all the lands may live out their lives in freedom from fear and want." The Charter also supported free trade, national self-determination, and the principle of collective security.

As in World War I, when Americans started supplying the Allies, Germany attacked American and Allied ships. By September 1941 Nazi submarines and American vessels were fighting an undeclared naval war in the Atlantic, unknown to the American public. Without an actual enemy attack, however, Roosevelt hesitated to ask Congress for a declaration of war.

The final provocation came not from Germany, but from Japan. Throughout the 1930s, Japanese military advances in China had upset the balance of political and economic power in the Pacific, where the United States had long enjoyed the economic benefits of the Open Door policy. After the Japanese invasion of China in 1937, Roosevelt had denounced "the present reign of terror and international lawlessness," suggesting that aggressors such as Japan be "quarantined" by peace-loving nations. Despite such rhetoric, however, the United States avoided taking a stand. During the brutal sack of Nanking in 1937 the Japanese had sunk an American gunboat, the *Panay*, in the Yangtze River. In exchange for more than $2 million in damages, the United States allowed Japan to apologize and the incident was quickly smoothed over.

Japan soon became more expansionist in its intentions, signing the Tri-Partite Pact with Germany and Italy in 1940. In the fall of 1941 Japanese troops occupied the northern part of French Indochina. The United States retaliated by effectively cutting off trade with Japan, including vital oil shipments that accounted for almost 80 percent of Japanese consumption. But in July 1941 Japanese troops occupied the rest of Indochina. Roosevelt responded by freezing Japanese assets in the United States and instituting an embargo on trade with Japan.

In September 1941 the government of Prime Minister Hideki Tojo began secret preparations for war against the United States. By November American military intelligence knew that Japan was planning an attack, but did not know where it would come. Early on Sunday morning, December 7, 1941, Japanese bombers attacked Pearl Harbor, killing more than 2,400 Americans. Eight battleships, three cruisers, three destroyers, and almost two hundred airplanes were destroyed or heavily damaged.

Although the attack was devastating, it infused the American people with a determination to fight. Pearl Harbor Day is still etched in the memories of millions of Americans who remember precisely what they were doing when they heard about the attack. The next day Roosevelt went before Congress. Calling December 7 "a date which will live in infamy," he asked for a declaration of war against Japan. The Senate voted unanimously for war, and the House concurred by a vote of 388 to 1. The lone dissenter was Jeannette Rankin of Montana, who had also opposed American entry into World War I. Three days later Germany and Italy declared war on the United States, and the United States in turn declared war on those nations.

MOBILIZING FOR VICTORY

The task of fighting a global war accelerated the growing influence of the state on all aspects of American life. A dramatic expansion of power occurred at the presidential level when Congress passed the War Powers Act of December 18, 1941, giving Roosevelt unprecedented authority over all aspects of the conduct of the war. Coordinating the changeover from civilian to war production, raising an army, and assembling the necessary work force taxed government agencies to the limit. Mobilization on such a scale demanded cooperation between business executives and political leaders in Washington, solidifying a partnership that had been growing since World War I.

Defense Mobilization

Defense mobilization had a powerful impact on the federal government's role in the economy. During the war, the federal budget expanded by a factor of ten and the national debt grew sixfold, peaking out at $258.6 billion in 1945. Along with huge federal budgets came greater acceptance of Keynesian economics— the use of fiscal policy, especially deficit spending, to stimulate economic growth. At the same time, the national government became more closely tied to its citizens' pocketbooks. The Revenue Act of 1942 continued the income tax reform that had begun during World War I by taxing not just wealthy individuals and corporations, but average citizens as well. Tax collections rose from $2.2 billion to $35.1 billion, facilitated by payroll deductions and tax withholding, instituted in 1943. This system of mass taxation, a revolutionary change in the financing of the modern state, was sold to the taxpayers as a way to express their patriotism.

The war also brought significant changes in the federal bureaucracy. The number of civilians employed by the government increased almost fourfold, to 3.8 million—a far more dramatic growth than the New Deal period had witnessed. Leadership of federal agencies also changed as the Roosevelt administration turned to business executives to replace the reformers and social activists who had staffed New Deal relief agencies in the 1930s. Those executives became known as "dollar-a-year men," because they volunteered for government service while remaining on the corporate payroll.

Many wartime agencies extended the power of the federal government. One of the most important was the War Production Board (WPB), which awarded defense contracts, evaluated military and civilian requests for scarce resources, and oversaw the conversion of industry to military production. The WPB used the carrot more often than the stick. To encourage businesses to convert to war production, the board granted generous tax write-offs for plant construction and approved contracts with cost-plus provisions, which guaranteed a profit and promised that businesses could keep the new factories after the war. As Secretary of War Henry Stimson put it, in capitalist countries at war, "you had better let business make money out of the process or business won't work."

In the interest of efficiency and maximum production, the WPB preferred to deal with major corporations rather than with small businesses. The fifty-six largest corporations got three-fourths of the war contracts; the top ten a third. This system of allocating contracts, along with the suspension of antitrust prosecution during the war, hastened the trend toward large corporate structures. In 1940 the hundred largest companies manufactured 30 percent of the nation's industrial output; by 1945 their share was 70 percent. These very large businesses would form the core of the military-industrial complex of the postwar years, which linked the federal government, corporations, and the military in an interdependent partnership (see Chapters 28 and 29).

Although not all industries could boast of freedom from *snafus* (an acronym coined during the war from the expression "*s*ituation *n*ormal, *a*ll *f*ouled *u*p"), business and government compiled an impressive record. By

1945 the United States had turned out 86,000 tanks, 296,000 airplanes, 15 million rifles and machine guns, 64,000 landing craft, and 6,500 ships. Mobilization on this gigantic scale gave a tremendous boost to the economy, causing it to more than double, rising from a gross national product in 1940 of $99.7 billion to $211 billion by the end of the war. After years of depression, Americans' faith in the capitalist system was restored. But it was a transformed system that relied heavily on the federal government's participation in the economy.

An expanded state presence was also evident in the government's mobilization of a fighting force. By the end of World War II the armed forces of the United States numbered more than 15 million men and women. Draft boards had registered about 31 million men between the ages of eighteen and forty-four. More than half the men failed to meet the physical standards: many were rejected because of defective teeth and poor vision. The military also tried to screen out homosexuals, but its attempts were ineffectual. Once in the services, homosexuals found opportunities to participate in a gay subculture more extensive than that in civilian life.

Racial discrimination prevailed in the armed forces, directed mainly against the approximately 700,000 blacks who fought in all branches of the armed forces in segregated units. Though the National Association for the Advancement of Colored People (NAACP) and other civil rights groups chided the government with reminders such as "A Jim Crow army cannot fight for a free world," the military continued to segregate African-Americans and to assign them the most menial duties. In contrast, Mexican-Americans were never officially segregated. Unlike blacks, they were welcomed into combat units: seventeen Mexican-Americans won the Congressional Medal of Honor.

About 350,000 American women, both black and white, enlisted in the armed services and achieved a permanent status in the military, serving in agencies such as the WACS (Women's Army Corps) and the WAVES (Women Appointed for Volunteer Emergency Service). The armed forces limited the types of duty assigned to women, as it did with black men. Women were barred from combat, although nurses and medical personnel sometimes served close to the front lines, risking capture or death. Most of the jobs women did—clerical work, communications, and health care—reflected stereotypes of women's roles in civilian life.

Women, Workers, African-Americans, and the War Effort

When millions of citizens entered military service, the United States faced a critical labor shortage, which the War Manpower Commission sought to remedy. Well-organized government propaganda urged women into the work force. "Longing won't bring him back sooner . . . GET A WAR JOB!" one poster beckoned, and the artist Norman Rockwell's famous "Rosie the Riveter" appealed to women from the cover of the *Saturday Evening Post*.

AMERICAN VOICES

"A Loyal Negro Soldier"

*A*frican-Americans served in a segregated military. As shown in this letter from *"A Loyal Negro Soldier" stationed in Alexandria, Virginia, wartime experiences heightened African-American militancy. This increased militancy would be one factor that prompted the postwar civil rights movement.*

A few weeks after my arrival, at this camp, I went to a post exchange on my regimental area. I knew that each area has an exchange but I thought that I could make my purchase at any of them. Upon entering I could feel the place grow cold. All conversation ceased. It was then that I noticed that all the soldiers and the saleswomen were white. Not to be outdone I approached the counter and was told (even before asking for the article) that, "Negroes are not served here. This post-exchange is for white soldiers. You have one near your regiment. Buy what you want there." . . .

[Later, after protesting another example of discrimination, he was asked, "Don't you want to fight for the U.S.A. and its policies?"]

I am a soldier; I made no answer, but deep down inside I knew when I faced America's enemies I will fight for the protection of my loved ones at home.

Listen, Negro America, I am writing this article believing that it will act as a stimulant. You need awakening. . . . The [f]ight on the battlefield is for your existence, not for Democracy. It is upon you that each soldier depends. In my fight my thoughts will invariably return to you who can fight for Democracy. You must do this for the soldiers because Democracy will be, and Democracy must be won at home—not on battlefields but through your bringing pressure to bear on Congress.

SOURCE: Phillip McGuire, *Taps for a Jim Crow Army: Letters from Black Soldiers in World War II* (Santa Barbara, CA: ABC-Clio, 1983), pp. 85-87.

Although the government directed its propaganda at housewives, women who were already employed gladly abandoned low-paying "women's" jobs as domestic servants or file clerks for higher-paying jobs in the defense industry. Suddenly the nation's factories were full of women working as riveters, welders, blast furnace cleaners, and drill press operators. Women made up 36 percent of the labor force in 1945, compared with 24 percent at the beginning of the war. Despite their new opportunities, women war workers faced many obstacles, including discrimination on the job. In shipyards women with the most seniority and responsibility earned $6.95 a day, while the top men made as much as $22.

Wartime Workers
The photographer Dorothea Lange captured these shipyard construction workers coming off their shift at a factory in Richmond, California, in 1942. Note the large number of women workers and the presence of minority workers. Several of the workers prominently display their union buttons. (Courtesy of the Dorothea Lange Collection. The City of Oakland. The Oakland Museum, 1982)

When the men came home from war and the nation's plants returned to peacetime operations, Rosie the Riveter was out of a job. But many women refused to put on aprons and stay home. Though women's participation in the labor force dropped temporarily when the war ended, it rebounded steadily for the rest of the 1940s, especially among married women (see Chapter 29).

Wartime mobilization also opened up opportunities to advance the labor movement. By the end of the war almost 15 million workers—a third of the nonagricultural labor force, up from 9 million at the previous decade—belonged to unions. Organized labor responded to the war with an initial burst of patriotic unity. On December 23, 1941, representatives of the major unions made a "no-strike" pledge—though it was nonbinding—for the duration of the war. In January 1942 Roosevelt set up the National War Labor Board (NWLB), composed of representatives of labor, management, and the public. The NWLB established wages, hours, and working conditions, and had the authority to order government seizure of plants that did not comply. Forty plants were seized during the war.

During its tenure the NWLB handled 17,650 disputes affecting 12 million workers. It resolved the controversial issue of union membership through a compromise. Under the principle of maintenance of membership, new hires did not have to join a union, but those who already belonged had to maintain their membership over the life of a contract. Agitation for wage increases caused a more serious disagreement. Because managers wanted to keep production running smoothly and profitably, they were willing to pay higher wages. However, pay raises would conflict with the government's efforts to combat inflation, which drove prices up dramatically in the early war years. In 1942 the NWLB established the "Little Steel Formula," which granted a 15 percent wage increase to match the increase in the cost of living since January 1, 1941, and another 24 percent increase by 1945. Actually, incomes rose as much as 70 percent during the war because workers earned overtime pay, which was not covered by wage ceilings.

Although incomes were higher than anyone could have dreamed during the depression, many union members felt cheated as they watched corporate profits soar in relation to wages. The high point of their dissatisfaction came in 1943, when a nationwide railroad strike was narrowly averted. That year John L. Lewis led more than half a million United Mine Workers out on strike, demanding wages higher than the Little Steel Formula allowed. Though Lewis won concessions, he alienated Congress; and because he had defied the government, he became one of the most disliked public figures of the 1940s.

Congress countered Lewis's action by overriding Roosevelt's veto of the Smith-Connally Labor Act of 1943, which required a thirty-day cooling-off period before a strike, and prohibited entirely strikes in defense industries. Nevertheless, about 15,000 walkouts occurred during the war. Though less than one-tenth of 1 percent of working hours were lost to labor disputes, the public perceived the disruptions to be far more extensive. Thus labor's achievements during the war were mixed. Union membership increased dramatically, from 9 million to almost 15 million workers—a third of the non-agricultural work force. But these gains were accompanied by significant public and congressional hostility that would hamper the labor movement in the postwar years.

Just as labor sought to benefit from the war, African-Americans manifested a new mood of militancy. "A wind is rising throughout the world of free men everywhere," Eleanor Roosevelt wrote during the war, "and they will not be kept in bondage." Black leaders pointed out parallels between anti-Semitism in Germany and racial discrimination in America, and pledged themselves to a

"Double V" campaign: victory over Nazism abroad, and victory over racism and inequality at home.

Even before Pearl Harbor, black activism was on the rise. In 1940 only 240 of the nation's 100,000 aircraft workers were black, and most of them were janitors. Black leaders demanded that the government require defense contractors to integrate their work forces. When the government took no action, A. Philip Randolph, head of the Brotherhood of Sleeping Car Porters, a black union, announced plans for a "March on Washington" in the summer of 1941. Though Roosevelt was not a strong supporter of civil rights, he feared the embarrassment of a massive public protest. Even more, he worried about a disruption of the nation's war preparations.

In June 1941, in exchange for Randolph's cancellation of the march, Roosevelt issued Executive Order 8802, declaring "that there shall be no discrimination in the employment of workers in defense industries or government because of race, creed, color, or national origin." To oversee the policy, he established the Fair Employment Practices Commission (FEPC). Though this federal commitment to minority employment rights was unprecedented, it was limited in scope; for instance, it did not affect segregation in the armed forces. Moreover, the FEPC could not require compliance with its orders, and often found that the needs of defense production took precedence over fair employment practices. The committee resolved only about a third of the more than 8,000 complaints it received.

Encouraged by the ideological climate of the war years, civil rights organizations increased their membership: the NAACP grew ninefold to 450,000 by 1945. In 1942 James Farmer helped to found the Congress of Racial Equality (CORE). Unlike the NAACP, which favored lobbying and legal strategies, CORE used tactics such as demonstrations and sit-ins. In 1944 CORE forced several restaurants in Washington, D.C., to serve blacks after picketing them with signs that read "Are You for Hitler's Way or the American Way? Make Up Your Mind." These wartime developments—both federal intervention and resurgent African-American militancy—laid the groundwork for the civil rights revolution of the 1950s and 1960s.

Politics in Wartime

Although the federal government expanded dramatically during the war years, there was little attempt to use the state to promote social reform on the home front, as in World War I. An enlarged federal presence was justified only insofar as it assisted war aims.

During the early years of the war, Roosevelt rarely pressed for social and economic change, in part because he was preoccupied with the war. But he also faced political realities. The Republicans had picked up 10 seats in the Senate and 47 seats in the House in the 1940 elections, thus bolstering conservatives in Congress who sought to roll back New Deal measures. With little protest, Roosevelt agreed to drop several popular New Deal programs, including the Civilian

Conservation Corps and the National Youth Administration, which were less necessary once war mobilization brought full employment.

Later in the war, however, Roosevelt began to promise new social welfare measures. In his State of the Union address in 1944, he called for a second bill of rights, which would serve as "a new basis of security and prosperity." This extension of the New Deal identified jobs, adequate food and clothing, decent homes, medical care, and education as basic rights. But the president's commitment to them remained largely rhetorical; congressional support for this vast extension of the welfare state did not exist in 1944. Some of those rights did become realities for veterans, however. The Servicemen's Readjustment Act (1944), known as the GI Bill of Rights, provided education, job training, medical care, pensions, and mortgage loans for men and women who had served in the armed forces during the war.

Roosevelt's call for more social legislation was part of a plan to woo Democratic voters. In the 1942 election, Republicans gained seats in both houses of Congress and increased their share of state governorships. The Democrats realized they would have to work hard to maintain the strength of their coalition in 1944. Once again Roosevelt headed the ticket, concluding that the continuation of the war made a fourth term necessary. Democrats, concerned about Roosevelt's health and the need for a successor, dropped Vice-President Henry Wallace, whose outspoken support for labor, civil rights, and domestic reform was too extreme for many party leaders. In his place they chose Senator Harry S Truman of Missouri.

The Republicans nominated Governor Thomas E. Dewey of New York. Only forty-two years old, Dewey had won fame fighting organized crime as a U.S. attorney. He accepted the broad outlines of the welfare state, and was a member of the internationalist wing of the party. The 1944 election was the closest since 1916: Roosevelt received only 53.5 percent of the popular vote. The Democrats lost ground among farmers, but most ethnic groups remained solidly Democratic. The party's margin of victory came from the cities: in urban areas of more than 100,000 people the president drew 60 percent of the vote. A significant segment of this urban support came from organized labor. The CIO's Political Action Committee made substantial contributions to the party, canvassed door to door, and conducted voter registration campaigns—a role organized labor would continue to play after the war.

LIFE ON THE HOME FRONT

Although the United States did not suffer the physical devastation that ravaged much of Europe and the Pacific, the war affected the lives of those who stayed behind. Every time relatives of a loved one overseas saw the Western Union boy on his bicycle, they feared a telegram from the War Department reporting that their son, husband, or father would not be coming home. Other Americans tolerated small deprivations daily. "Don't you know there's a war on?" became the standard reply to any request that could not be fulfilled. People accepted the fact that their lives would be different "for the duration." They also accepted, however grudgingly, the increased role of the federal government in shaping their daily lives.

The War at Home

Just like the soldiers in uniform, people on the home front had a job to do. They worked on civilian defense committees, donated blood, collected old newspapers and scrap material, and served on local rationing and draft boards. About 20 million home "Victory gardens" produced 40 percent of the vegetables grown in the United States. All these endeavors were encouraged by various federal agencies, especially the Office of War Information (OWI), which strove to disseminate information and promote patriotism. Working closely with advertising agencies, the OWI urged them to link their clients' products to the "four freedoms," explaining that patriotic ads would not only sell goods, but would "invigorate, instruct and inspire [the citizen] as a functioning unit in his country's greatest effort."

Popular culture, especially the movies, reinforced the connections between the home front and troops serving overseas. Average weekly movie attendance soared to over 100 million during the war. Demand was so high that many theaters operated around the clock to accommodate defense workers on the swing and night shifts. Many movies, encouraged in part by the OWI, had patriotic themes; stars such as John Wayne, Anthony Quinn, and Spencer Tracy portrayed the heroism of American fighting men in films like *Back to Bataan* (1945), *Guadalcanal Diary* (1943), and *Thirty Seconds over Tokyo* (1945). Other movies, such as *Watch on the Rhine* (1943), warned of the danger of fascism at home and abroad, while the Academy Award–winning *Casablanca* (1943) demonstrated the heroism and patriotism of ordinary citizens. *Since You Went Away* (1943), starring Claudette Colbert as a wife who took a war job after her husband left for war, was one of many films that portrayed struggles on the home front. Newsreels accompanying the feature films kept the public up to date on the war, as did on-the-spot radio broadcasts by commentators such as Edward R. Murrow. Thus popular culture reflected America's new international responsibilities at the same time that it built up morale on the home front.

Perhaps the major source of Americans' high morale was wartime prosperity. Federal defense spending had solved the depression; unemployment had disappeared, and per capita income had risen from $691 in 1939 to $1,515 in 1945. Despite geographical dislocations and shortages of many items, about 70 percent of Americans admitted midway through the war that they had personally experienced "no real sacrifices." A Red Cross worker put it bluntly: "The war was fun for America. I'm not talking about the poor souls who lost sons and daughters. But for the rest of us, the war was a hell of a good time."

For many Americans, the major inconveniences of the war were the limitations placed on their consumption. In contrast to the largely voluntaristic approach used during World War I, federal agencies such as the Office of Price Administration subjected almost everything Americans ate, wore, or used during World War II to rationing or regulation. In response to depleted domestic gasoline supplies and a shortage of rubber, the government restricted the sale of tires, rationed gas, and imposed a nationwide speed limit of 35 miles per hour. By 1943 the amount of meat, butter, sugar, and other foods Americans could buy was also regulated. Most people cooperated with the restrictions and the complicated system of rationing points and coupons, but almost a fourth occasionally bought items on the black market, especially meat, gasoline, and cigarettes.

The war and the government affected not only what people ate, drank, and wore, but where they lived. When men volunteered for or were drafted into the armed services, their families often followed them to training bases or points of debarkation. The lure of high-paying defense jobs encouraged others to move. About 15 million Americans changed residence during the war years, half of them by moving to another state.

As a center of defense production, California was affected by wartime migration more than any other state. The western mecca welcomed nearly 3 million new residents during the war, a 53 percent growth in population. "The Second Gold Rush Hits the West," headlined the *San Francisco Chronicle* in 1943. During the war one-tenth of all federal dollars went to California, and the state turned out one-sixth of the total war production. People went where the defense jobs were—to Los Angeles, San Diego, and the San Francisco Bay area. Some towns grew practically overnight: just two years after the Kaiser Corporation opened a shipyard in Richmond, the population quadrupled.

Migration and relocation often caused strains. In many towns with defense industries, housing was scarce and public transportation inadequate. Conflicts over public space and recreation erupted between old-timers and newcomers. Of special concern were the young people the war had set adrift from traditional community restraints. Newspapers were filled with stories of "latchkey" children who stayed home alone while their mothers worked in defense plants. Adolescents were even more of a problem. Teenage girls who hung around army bases looking for a good time became known as "victory girls." In 1942 and 1943 juvenile delinquency seemed to be reaching epidemic proportions.

Another significant result of the growth of war industries was the migration of more than a million African-Americans to defense centers in California, Illinois, Michigan, Ohio, and Pennsylvania. The migrants' need for jobs and housing led to racial conflict in several cities. Early in 1942 black families encountered resistance and intimidation when they tried to move into the Sojourner Truth housing project, in the Polish community of Hamtramck near Detroit—the new home of a large number of southern migrants, both black and white. In June 1943 similar tensions erupted in Detroit itself, where a major race riot left thirty-four people dead, including twenty-five blacks. Racial conflicts broke out in forty-seven cities across the country during 1943.

Other Americans also experienced racial violence. In Los Angeles male Latinos who belonged to *pachuco* (youth) gangs dressed in "zoot suits"—broad-brimmed felt hats, pegged trousers, and clunky shoes—wore their long hair slicked down, and carried pocket knives on gold chains. The young women they hung out with favored long coats, huarache sandals, and pompadour hairdos. Blacks and some working-class white teenagers in Los Angeles, Detroit, New York, and Philadelphia also wore zoot suits as a symbol of alienation and self-assertion. To adults and to many Anglos, however, the zoot suit symbolized wartime juvenile delinquency.

In Los Angeles, white hostility toward Mexican-Americans had been smoldering for some time, and zoot-suiters soon became the targets. In July 1943 rumors that a *pachuco* gang had beaten a white sailor set off a four-day riot, during which white servicemen entered Mexican-American neighborhoods and attacked zoot-suiters, taking special pleasure in slashing their pegged pants. The attacks occurred in full view of white police officers, who did nothing to stop the violence.

Japanese Internment

Although racial confrontations and zoot-suit riots recalled the widespread racial tensions of World War I, the mood on the home front was generally calm in the 1940s. German culture and German-Americans did not come under suspicion, nor did Italian-Americans. Leftists and communists faced little repression, mainly because, after Pearl Harbor, the Soviet Union became an ally of the United States. The internment of Japanese-Americans on the West Coast was a glaring exception to this record of tolerance—the prejudice and hysteria directed at them was a reminder of the fragility of civil liberties in wartime.

California had a long history of antagonism toward both Japanese and Chinese immigrants (see Chapters 17 and 22). The Japanese-Americans, who clustered together in highly visible communities, were a small, politically impotent minority, numbering only about 112,100 in the three coastal states. Unlike German- and Italian-Americans, the Japanese stood out. "A Jap's a Jap," snapped General John DeWitt; "It makes no difference whether he is an American citizen or not." This sort of sentiment, coupled with fears of the West Coast's vulnerability to attack and the inflammatory rhetoric of newspapers and local politicians, fueled mounting demands that the region be rid of supposed Japanese spies.

In early 1942, in Executive Order 9022, Roosevelt approved a War Department plan to intern Japanese-Americans in relocation camps for the rest of the war. Despite the lack of any evidence of their disloyalty or sedition—no Japanese-American was ever charged with espionage—few public leaders opposed the plan. The announcement shocked Japanese-Americans, more than two-thirds of whom were native-born American citizens. (They were *Nisei*, children of the foreign-born *Issei*.) After being forced to sell their property and possessions at cut-rate prices, Japanese-Americans were rounded up in

Japanese Internment
A Japanese-American family arrives at its new "home" in Heart Mountain, Wyoming, after being relocated from the West Coast military zone. The average internee spent 900 days—more than two and a half years—confined behind the barbed wire, which is not visible in this picture.

temporary assembly centers and sent by the War Relocation Authority to internment camps in California, Arizona, Utah, Colorado, Wyoming, Idaho, and Arkansas—places "where nobody had lived before and no one has lived since," a historian commented.

Almost every Japanese-American in California, Oregon, and Washington was involuntarily detained for some period during World War II. Ironically, the Japanese-Americans who made up one-third of the population of Hawaii, and presumably posed a greater threat because of their numbers and proximity to Japan, were not affected. Less vulnerable to detention because of the islands' multiracial heritage, the Japanese also provided much of the unskilled labor on the islands. The Hawaiian economy simply could not function without them.

Cracks soon appeared in the relocation policy. A labor shortage in farming led the government to furlough seasonal agricultural workers from the camps as early as 1942. About 4,300 young people who had been in college when the relocation order came through were allowed to stay in school if they would transfer out of the West Coast military zone. Another route out of the camps was enlistment in the armed services. The 442d Infantry Combat Team, a segregated unit composed entirely of Nisei volunteers, served in Europe and became one of the most decorated units in the armed forces.

The Supreme Court upheld the constitutionality of internment as a legitimate exercise of power during wartime in *Hirabayashi v. United States* (1943) and in *Korematsu v. United States* (1944). It was not until 1988 that Congress decided to issue a public apology and to give $20,000 in cash to each of the 60,000 surviving internees—small restitution indeed. Though with each generation the memory of internment grows dimmer, this shameful episode has been burned into the national conscience.

FIGHTING AND WINNING THE WAR

World War II, noted the military historian John Keegan, was "the largest single event in human history." Fought on six continents at a cost of 50 million lives, it was far more global than World War I. At least 405,000 Americans were killed and 671,000 wounded in the global fighting—less than half of 1 percent of the U.S. population. In contrast, the Soviets lost as many as 21 million soldiers and civilians during the war, or about 8 percent of their population.

Wartime Aims and Strategies

The Allied coalition was composed mainly of Great Britain, the United States, and the Soviet Union; other nations, notably China and France, played lesser roles. President Franklin Roosevelt, Britain's Prime Minister Winston Churchill, and Premier Joseph Stalin of the Soviet Union took the lead in setting overall strategy. The Atlantic Charter, which Churchill and Roosevelt had drafted in August 1941, formed the basis of the Allies' vision of the postwar international order. But Stalin had not been part of that agreement, a fact that would later cause disagreements over its goals.

One way to wear down the Germans would have been to open a second front on the European continent, preferably in France. The Russians argued strongly for this strategy, because it would draw German troops away from Russian soil. In fact, the issue came up so many times that the Soviet foreign minister, Vyacheslav Molotov, was said to know only four English words: *yes*, *no*, and *second front*. Though Roosevelt assured Stalin informally that a second front would be opened in 1942, British opposition and the need to raise American war production to full capacity stalled the effort. At a conference in Teheran, Iran, in late November 1943, Churchill and Roosevelt agreed to open a second front within six months in return for Stalin's promise to join the fight against Japan after the war in Europe ended. Both sides kept their promises. However, the long delay in creating a second front meant that for most of the war, the Soviet Union bore the brunt of the land battle against Germany. Roosevelt and Churchill's foot-dragging angered Stalin, who was suspicious about American and British intentions. His mistrust and bitterness carried over into the Cold War that followed the Allied victory.

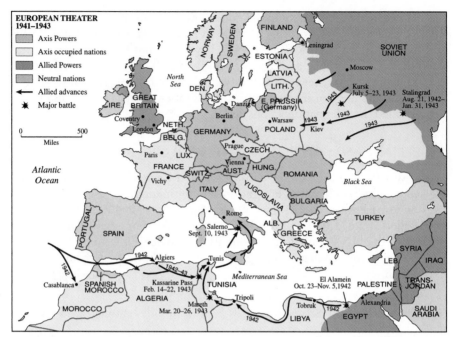

MAP 27.1
War in Europe
a. 1941–1943   Hitler's Germany reached its greatest extent in 1942, when Nazi forces stalled at Leningrad and Stalingrad. The tide of battle turned in the fall, when the Soviet army launched a massive counterattack at Stalingrad and Allied forces began to drive the Germans from North Africa. In 1943 the Allies invaded Sicily and the Italian mainland.

During the first six months of 1942 the military news was so bad it threatened to swamp the Grand Alliance. The Allies suffered severe defeats on land and sea in both Europe and Asia. German armies pushed deeper into Soviet territory, reaching the outskirts of Moscow and Leningrad. Simultaneously, they began an offensive in North Africa aimed at seizing the Suez Canal. At sea German submarines were crippling American convoys carrying vital supplies to Europe.

The major turning point of the war in Europe occurred in the winter of 1942–1943, when the Soviets halted the German advance in the Battle of Stalingrad. By 1944, Stalin's forces had driven the German army out of the Soviet Union. Meanwhile, the Allies launched a major offensive in North Africa, Churchill's substitute for a second front in France. Between November 1942 and May 1943 Allied troops under the leadership of General Dwight D. Eisenhower and General George S. Patton defeated Germany's crack Afrika Korps, led by General Erwin Rommel.

From Africa the Allied command moved to attack the Axis through what Churchill called its "soft underbelly": Sicily and the Italian peninsula. In July

b. 1944–1945   On June 6, 1944 (D-Day), the Allies finally invaded France. It would take almost a year for the Allied forces to close in on Berlin—the Soviets from the east and the Americans, British, and French from the west. Germany surrendered on May 8, 1945.

1943 Benito Mussolini's fascist regime fell, and Italy's new government joined the Allies. The Allied forces fought bitter battles against the German army during the Italian campaign, finally entering Rome in June 1944 (see Map 27.1). The last German forces in Italy did not surrender until May 1945, however.

The long-promised invasion of France came on D-Day, June 6, 1944. That morning, after an agonizing delay caused by bad weather, the largest armada ever assembled moved across the English Channel. Over the next few days, under the command of General Dwight Eisenhower, more than 1.5 million American, British, and Canadian soldiers crossed the Channel. In August Allied troops helped to liberate Paris; by September they had driven the Germans out of most of France and Belgium.

The Germans were not yet ready to give up, however. In December 1944 their forces in Belgium mounted an attack that began the Battle of the Bulge, so called because their advance made a large balloon in the Allied line on war maps. After ten days of heavy fighting in what was to be the final German offensive of the war, the Allies regained their momentum and pushed the Germans back across the Rhine River. American and British troops led the drive from the west toward Berlin, while Soviet troops advanced from the east through Poland, arriving there first. On April 30, with

Hitting the Beach at Normandy
These American reinforcements landed on the beach at Normandy two weeks after D-Day,
June 6, 1944. More than a million Allied troops came ashore during the next month. The Allies liberated Paris in August and pushed the retreating Nazi forces behind the German border
by September.

much of Berlin in rubble from intense Allied bombing, Hitler committed
suicide in his bunker. Germany surrendered on May 8, 1945, the date that
became known as V-E (Victory in Europe) Day.

When Allied troops advanced into Germany in the spring of 1945, they
came face to face with Hitler's "final solution of the Jewish question": the extermination camps where 6 million Jews had been put to death, along with
another 6 million Poles, Slavs, Gypsies, homosexuals, and other "undesirables."
Photographs of the Nazi death camps at Buchenwald, Dachau, and
Auschwitz, showing bodies stacked like cordwood and survivors so emaciated
they were barely alive, horrified the American public. But government officials could not claim that no one knew about the camps before the German
surrender. The Roosevelt administration had reliable information about the
death camps as early as November 1942.

The lack of response by the U.S. government to the systematic near annihilation of European Jewry ranks as one of the gravest failures of the Roosevelt administration. So few Jews escaped the Holocaust because the
United States and the rest of the world would not take them in. State Department policies allowed only 21,000 refugees to enter the United States
during the war. The War Refugee Board, established in 1944 with little support from the Roosevelt administration, eventually helped to save about
200,000 Jews.

An Army Nurse in Bataan

A rmy Nurse Juanita Redmond recounts her experiences as one of the last nurses to remain in Bataan in the Philippines as the Japanese advanced. She was evacuated shortly before the Americans surrendered on May 6, 1942. Her description reveals both the horror of warfare and the extraordinary service performed by military nurses.

[The bomb] landed at the hospital entrance and blew up an ammunition truck that was passing. The concussion threw me to the floor. There was a spattering of shrapnel and pebbles and earth on the tin roof. Then silence for a few minutes.

I heard the corpsmen rushing out with litters, and I pulled myself to my feet. Precious medicines were dripping to the ground from the shattered dressing carts, and I tried to salvage as much as possible.

The first casualties came in. The boys in the ammunition truck had been killed, but the two guards at the hospital gate had jumped into their foxholes. By the time they were extricated from the debris that filled up the holes they were both shell-shock cases.

There were plenty of others. . . .

Only one small section of my ward remained standing. Part of the roof had been blown into the jungle. There were mangled bodies under the ruins; a blood-stained hand stuck up through a pile of scrap; arms and legs had been ripped off and flung among the rubbish. Some of the mangled torsos were almost impossible to identify. One of the few corpsmen who had survived unhurt climbed a tree to bring down a body blown into the top branches. Blankets, mattresses, pajama tops hung in the shattered trees.

We worked wildly to get to the men who might be buried, still alive, under the mass of wreckage, tearing apart the smashed beds to reach the wounded and the dead. These men were our patients, our responsibility; I think we were all tortured by an instinctive, irrational feeling that we had failed them.

SOURCE: Judy Barrett Litoff and David C. Smith, eds., *American Women in a World at War: Contemporary Accounts from World War II* (Wilmington, Delaware: Scholarly Resource Books, 1997), pp. 85–86. Reprinted from Juanita Redmond, *I Served on Bataan* (Philadelphia: J.B. Lippincott, 1943), 106–122.

Several factors combined to inhibit U.S. action: anti-Semitism; fears of economic competition from a flood of refugees to a country just recovering from the depression; the failure of the media to grasp the magnitude of the story and to publicize it accordingly; and the failure of religious leaders, Jews and non-Jews alike, to speak out.

In justifying the American course of action, Roosevelt claimed that winning the war would be the strongest contribution America could make

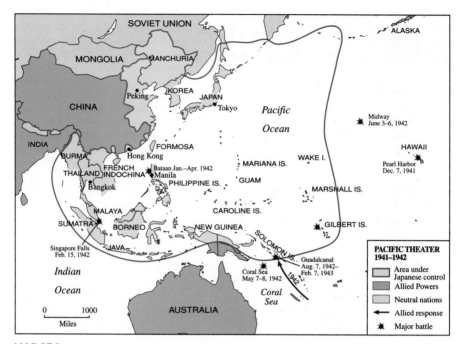

MAP 27.2
War in the Pacific
a. 1941–1942 After the attack on Pearl Harbor in December 1941 the Japanese rapidly advanced in the Pacific, as far east as the Marshall and Gilbert islands and as far south as the Solomon Islands and parts of New Guinea. Japan also controlled the Philippines, much of Southeast Asia, and parts of China, including Hong Kong. American naval victories at the Coral Sea and Midway stopped further Japanese expansion.

to liberating the camps. But one cannot escape the conclusion that the United States could have done much more to lessen the Holocaust's terrible human toll.

After the victory in Europe, the Allies still had to defeat Japan. American forces bore the brunt of the fighting in the Pacific, just as the Russians had done in the land war in Europe. In the beginning of 1942 the news from the Pacific was uniformly grim. In the wake of Pearl Harbor, Japan had scored quickly with seaborne invasions of Hong Kong, Wake Island, and Guam. Japanese forces soon conquered much of Burma, Malaya, the Philippines, and the Solomon Islands, and began to threaten Australia and India. But on May 7 and 8, 1942, in the Battle of the Coral Sea, near southern New Guinea, American naval forces halted the Japanese offensive against Australia. In June, at the island of Midway, the Americans inflicted crucial damage on the Japanese fleet. With that success, the American military command, led by General Douglas MacArthur and Admiral Chester W. Nimitz, took the offensive in the Pacific. For the next eighteen months American forces advanced arduously

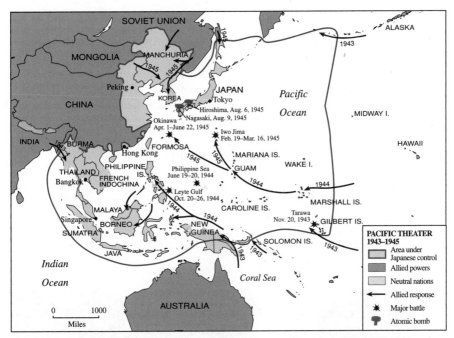

SOVIET UNION

ALASKA

1943

MONGOLIA

MANCHURIA

Peking •

JAPAN

CHINA

KOREA

Tokyo

Pacific

Hiroshima, Aug. 6, 1945

Ocean

Okinawa   Nagasaki, Aug. 9, 1945
Apr. 1–June 22, 1945

, MIDWAY I.

Iwo Jima
Feb. 19–Mar. 16, 1945

INDIA   BURMA

FORMOSA

HAWAII

Hong Kong

MARIANA IS.

WAKE I.

THAILAND

PHILIPPINE IS.

Philippine Sea
June 19–20, 1944

GUAM

Bangkok •

FRENCH
INDOCHINA

1944

1944

Leyte Gulf
Oct. 20–26, 1944

MARSHALL IS.

MALAYA

CAROLINE IS.

Tarawa
Nov. 20, 1943

Singapore

1944

BORNEO

NEW
GUINEA

GILBERT IS.

SUMATRA

SOLOMON IS.

1943

**PACIFIC THEATER
1943–1945**

JAVA

Indian

Ocean

Coral Sea

0   1000

Miles

AUSTRALIA

Area under
Japanese control

Allied powers

Neutral nations

⟵   Allied response

✴   Major battle

⚑   Atomic bomb

b. 1943–1945   Allied forces retook the islands in the Central Pacific in 1943 and 1944 and the Philippines early in 1945. The capture of Iwo Jima and Okinawa put U.S. bombers in position to attack Japan itself. The Japanese offered to surrender on August 10, after the United States dropped atomic bombs on Hiroshima and Nagasaki.

from one island to the next. In October 1944 the reconquest of the Philippines began with a victory in the Battle of Leyte Gulf, a massive naval encounter in which the Japanese lost practically their entire fleet, while the Americans suffered only minimal losses (see Map 27.2).

By early 1945, victory over Japan was in sight. The campaign in the Pacific moved slowly toward what military leaders anticipated would be a massive and costly invasion of Japan. In some of the fiercest fighting of the war, American marines won the battles for Iwo Jima and Okinawa, where they sustained more than 52,000 casualties, including 13,600 dead. The closer U.S. forces got to the Japanese home islands, the more fiercely the Japanese fought. On Iwo Jima, almost all the 21,000 Japanese died.

By mid–1945 Japan's army, navy, and air force had suffered devastating losses. American bombing of the mainland had killed about 330,000 civilians and crippled the Japanese economy. In a last-ditch effort to stem the tide, Japanese pilots began flying suicidal kamikaze missions, crashing their planes and boats into American ships. This desperate action, combined with the Japanese military leadership's refusal to surrender, suggested to military strategists that Japan would continue to fight despite overwhelming losses. American commanders grimly predicted millions of casualties in the upcoming invasion.

Planning the Postwar World

When Roosevelt, Churchill, and Stalin met in February 1945 at Yalta, a resort
on the Black Sea, victory in Europe and the Pacific was in sight, but no agreement had been reached on the peace to come. Roosevelt focused on maintaining Allied unity, the key to postwar peace and stability. The fate of British
colonies such as India, where an independence movement had already begun,
caused friction between Roosevelt and Churchill. Some of the tensions with
the Russians were resolved when, in return for additional possessions in the
Pacific, Stalin agreed to enter the war against Japan within three months of the
German surrender.

A more serious source of conflict was Stalin's desire for a band of Soviet-
controlled satellite states to protect the Soviet Union's western border. With
Soviet armies in control of much of Eastern Europe, Stalin had become increasingly inflexible on the issue of Eastern Europe, insisting that he needed
friendly (that is, Soviet-dominated) governments there to provide a buffer

The Big Three at Yalta
With victory in Europe at hand, Roosevelt journeyed to Yalta, on the Black Sea, in 1945, to
meet one last time with Churchill and Stalin. It was here that they discussed the problems of
peace settlements. The Yalta agreement mirrored a new balance of power and set the stage for
the Cold War.

zone that would guarantee the Soviet Union's national security. Roosevelt acknowledged the legitimacy of that demand but, with the Atlantic Charter's principle of self-determination in mind, hoped for democratically elected governments in Poland and the neighboring countries. Unfortunately, the two goals proved mutually exclusive.

At Yalta, Roosevelt and Churchill agreed in principle on the idea of a Soviet sphere of influence in Eastern Europe but deliberately left its dimensions vague. Stalin in return pledged to hold "free and unfettered elections" at an unspecified time. (Those elections never took place.) The compromise the three leaders reached at Yalta was open to multiple interpretations. Admiral William D. Leahy, Roosevelt's chief military aide, described the agreement as "so elastic that the Russians can stretch it all the way from Yalta to Washington without ever technically breaking it."

At Yalta the three leaders proceeded with plans to divide Germany into four zones to be controlled by the United States, Great Britain, France, and the Soviet Union. The capital city, Berlin, which lay in the middle of the Soviet zone, would also be partitioned among the four powers. The issue of German reparations remained unsettled.

The Big Three made further progress toward the establishment of an international organization in the form of the United Nations. They agreed that the Security Council of the United Nations would include the five major Allied powers—the United States, Britain, France, China, and the Soviet Union—plus six other nations elected on a rotating basis. They also decided that the permanent members of the Security Council should have veto power over decisions of the General Assembly, in which all nations would be represented. Roosevelt, Churchill, and Stalin announced that the United Nations would convene in San Francisco on April 25, 1945.

Roosevelt returned to the United States in February, visibly exhausted by his 14,000-mile trip. He neglected to inform the American public of the concessions he had made to maintain the increasingly fragile wartime alliance. When he reported to Congress on the Yalta agreements, he made an unusual acknowledgment of his physical infirmity. Referring to the heavy steel braces he wore on his legs, he asked Congress to excuse him for giving his speech while sitting down. The sixty-three-year-old president was a sick man, suffering from heart failure and high blood pressure. On April 12, 1945, during a short visit to his vacation home in Warm Springs, Georgia, Roosevelt suffered a cerebral hemorrhage and died.

When Harry Truman took over the reigns of office, he learned about the top-secret Manhattan Project, charged with developing an atomic bomb. The project, which cost $2 billion and employed 120,000 people, culminated in Los Alamos, New Mexico, where the country's top physicists assembled the first bomb. Not until the first test—at Alamogordo, New Mexico, on July 16, 1945—did scientists know that the bomb would work. A month later Truman ordered the dropping of atomic bombs on two Japanese cities, Hiroshima on August 6 and Nagasaki on August 9.

Hiroshima
This was all that remained of Hiroshima's Museum of Science and Industry on August 6, 1945. The shell of the building later became the center of a memorial to those who died in the atomic blast.

Many later questioned why the United States did not warn Japan about the attack or choose a noncivilian target; the rationale for dropping the second bomb was even less clear. Critics suggested that the fact that the Japanese were a nonwhite race facilitated the momentous decision to use the new, alarming weapon. At the time, however, the belief that Japan's military leaders would never surrender unless their country was utterly devastated convinced policy-makers that they had to deploy the atom bomb. One hundred thousand people died at Hiroshima, 60,000 at Nagasaki; tens of thousands more died slowly of radiation poisoning. Japan offered to surrender on August 10, and signed a formal treaty of surrender on September 2, 1945.

Franklin Roosevelt's death and the dropping of the atomic bomb came at a critical juncture in world affairs. Many issues had been left deliberately unre-solved, in hopes of keeping the wartime alliance intact through the transition to peace. But as the war ended, issues such as the fates of Poland and Germany demanded action. The resulting compromises, not all of which were fully re-ported to the American people, tended to promote spheres of influence as the new basis of international power, rather than the ideals of national self-determination and economic cooperation laid out in the Atlantic Charter.

Once the common enemies had been defeated, the wartime alliance be-came strained and then began to split apart in ways so fundamental that Roo-sevelt could not likely have kept it together had he lived. Perhaps the greatest legacy of World War II, then, was the Cold War that followed.

CHAPTER 27 TIMELINE

1935	Italy invades Ethiopia
1935– 1937	Neutrality Acts
1936	Rome-Berlin Axis established Japan and Germany sign Anti-Comintern Pact
1937	Japan invades China
1938	Munich agreement
1939	Nazi-Soviet Nonaggression Pact World War II breaks out in Europe
1940	Conscription reinstated
1941	Roosevelt promulgates "four freedoms" Germany invades Soviet Union Lend-Lease Act passed Fair Employment Practices Commission Atlantic Charter Japanese attack on Pearl Harbor
1942	Battles of Coral Sea and Midway Women recruited for war industries Japanese relocation
1942– 1945	Rationing
1943	Race riots in Detroit and Los Angeles Fascism falls in Italy
1944	D-Day GI Bill of Rights
1945	Germany surrenders Battles of Iwo Jima and Okinawa Yalta Conference Harry S Truman becomes president after Roosevelt's death United Nations convenes Atomic bombs dropped on Hiroshima and Nagasaki Japan surrenders

THEMATIC TIMELINE

	DIPLOMACY The Cold War Era—and After	GOVERNMENT Redefining the Role of the State	ECONOMY Rise and Fall of U.S. Economic Dominance	SOCIETY Consumerism, Social Activism, and Diversity
1945	Truman Doctrine (1947) Marshall Plan (1948) NATO founded (1949)	Truman's Fair Deal liberalism Taft-Hartley Act (1947)	Bretton Woods system established; World Bank, IMF, GATT	Urban migration Armed forces desegregated Rise of television
1950	Permanent mobilization: NSC-68 (1950) Korean War (1950–53)	Eisenhower's Modern Republicanism Warren Court activism	Rise of military-industrial complex Service sector expands	*Brown v. Board of Education* (1954) Montgomery bus boycott Growth of suburbia and the baby boom
1960	Cuban missile crisis (1962) Test ban treaty (1963) Vietnam War escalates (1965)	Great Society, War on Poverty Nixon ushers in conservative era	Kennedy-Johnson tax cut, military expenditures fuel economic growth	Shopping malls spread Student activism and youth counter culture Civil Rights Act; Voting Rights Act Revival of feminism
1970	Nixon visits China (1972)	Watergate scandal; Nixon resigns (1974) Deregulation begins under Ford and Carter	Arab oil embargo (1973–74); inflation surges Deindustrialization Income stagnation	*Roe v. Wade* (1973) New Right urges conservative agenda First Earth Day (1970) First personal computer (1977)
1980	Reagan arms buildup INF treaty (1988) Berlin Wall falls	Reagan Revolution Supreme Court conservatism	Reaganomics Budget and trade deficits soar	New Latino and Asian immigration MTV debuts AIDS epidemic
1990	War in the Persian Gulf End of Cold War U.S. peacekeeping forces in Bosnia	Democrats retrench Republican Congress shifts federal government tasks to states	Corporate downsizing NAFTA (1993) Recovery from recession	Health care crisis Information superhighway Affirmative action attacked

PART 6

AMERICA AND THE WORLD

1945 to the Present

In 1945 the United States entered an era of unprecedented international power, challenged only by the Soviet Union. The resulting conflict led to the Cold War. That bipolar struggle, which lasted until the collapse of the Soviet Union in 1991, spawned two "hot" wars, in Korea and Vietnam, fueled a debilitating nuclear arms race, and necessitated the maintenance of a large military establishment.

Government bureaucracy and power swelled in the 1950s and 1960s as Democratic presidents, especially Lyndon Johnson, dramatically expanded federal social programs. At the same time great waves of protest by African-Americans and then women, Latinos, and other groups, brought increased opportunities and progress toward legal equality for all Americans. But in the late 1970s, Republicans mounted a concerted attack on the size and role of government. In the 1980s Ronald Reagan began to whittle away at federal social programs, and in 1996 Congress terminated welfare as a federally guaranteed benefit.

In the quarter century after 1945 the growth of the military-industrial complex and the expansion of consumer culture, combined with economic dominance abroad, translated into unparalleled prosperity at home. Millions of baby-boom families flocked to new suburban developments, where they provided an expanded market for household goods and gadgets—especially television. A heady sense of unlimited progress and affluence lasted until the early 1970s, when slow growth, environmental problems, and foreign competition undermined America's economic supremacy and led to a sense of diminished expectations.

As the "old world order"—U.S. economic dominance and cold war rivalry—came to an end in the 1980s and 1990s, the outline of a "new world order" began to take shape. The United States remains the sole military superpower but shares economic leadership in a new interdependent global system. As Americans face the twenty-first century, grappling with the implications of this change will be their greatest challenge.

COLD WAR AMERICA, 1945–1960

- The Early Cold War
- Harry Truman and the Cold War at Home
- "Modern Republicanism"

When Harry Truman arrived at the White House on April 12, 1945, after Franklin Roosevelt died, he asked the president's widow, "Is there anything I can do for you?" Eleanor Roosevelt responded, "Is there anything we can do for you? For you are the one in trouble now."

Truman inherited the presidency at one of the most perilous times in modern history. Unscathed by bombs and battles on the home front, U.S. industry and agriculture had grown rapidly during World War II. The nation wielded enormous military power as the sole possessor of the atomic bomb. The most powerful country in the world, the United States became a permanent and preeminent force in the international arena. Only the Soviet Union represented an obstacle to American *hegemony*, or dominance, in global affairs. Soon the two superpowers were locked in a Cold War of economic, political, and military rivalry, but no direct engagement on the battlefield.

Soviet-American confrontations during the postwar years had important domestic repercussions. The Cold War boosted military expenditures, fueling a growing arms race. It fostered a climate of fear and suspicion of "subversives" in government, education, and the media, who might undermine American democratic institutions. But the economic benefits of internationalism also gave rise to a period of unprecedented affluence and prosperity during which the United States enjoyed the highest standard of living in the world (see Chapter 29). That prosperity helped to continue and in some cases to expand federal power, perpetuating the New Deal state in the postwar era.

THE EARLY COLD WAR

The defeat of Germany and Japan did not bring stability to the world. Six years of devastating warfare had destroyed prewar governments and geographical boundaries, creating new power relationships that helped to dissolve colonial empires. Even before the war ended, the United States and the Soviet Union were struggling for advantage in those unstable areas; after the war they engaged in a protracted global conflict. Hailed as a battle between communism and capitalism, the Cold War was in reality a more complex power struggle covering a range of economic, strategic, and ideological issues. As each side tried to protect its own national security and way of life, its actions aroused fear in the other, contributing to a cycle of distrust and animosity that would shape U.S.-Soviet relations for decades to come.

Descent into Cold War, 1945–1946

During the war Franklin Roosevelt had worked effectively with Stalin, and had determined to continue his good relations with the Soviet Union in peacetime. In particular, he hoped that the United Nations would provide a forum for resolving postwar conflicts. Avoiding the disagreements that had doomed American membership in the League of Nations after World War I, the Senate approved America's participation in the United Nations in December 1945. Coming eight months after Roosevelt's death, the vote was in part a memorial to the late president's hopes for peace.

Shortly before his death, however, Roosevelt had been disturbed by Soviet actions in Eastern Europe. As the Soviet army drove the Germans out of Russia and back through Eastern Europe, the U.S.S.R. sponsored provisional governments in the occupied countries. At the Yalta Conference in February, both America and Britain had agreed to recognize this Soviet "sphere of influence," with the proviso that "free and unfettered elections" would be held as soon as possible. But in succeeding months the Soviets made no move to hold elections and rebuffed western attempts to reorganize the Soviet-installed governments.

When Truman assumed the presidency after Roosevelt's death, he quickly took a belligerent stance toward the Soviet Union. At a meeting held shortly after he took office, the new president berated the Soviet foreign minister, V. M. Molotov, for not honoring Stalin's agreements on Poland. Truman used what he called "tough methods" that July at the Potsdam Conference, which brought together the United States, Britain, and the Soviet Union. After learning of the successful test of America's atomic bomb, Truman "told the Russians just where they got off and generally bossed the whole meeting," recalled British Prime Minister Winston Churchill. Negotiations on critical postwar issues deadlocked, revealing serious cracks in the Grand Alliance.

The one issue that was tentatively resolved at Potsdam was the fate of occupied Germany. At Yalta the defeated German state had been divided into four zones of occupation, controlled by the United States, France, Britain, and the Soviet Union. At Potsdam the Allies agreed to disarm the country, dismantle its military production facilities, and permit the occupying powers to extract reparations from the zones they controlled. Plans for future reunification stalled, however, as the United States and the Soviet Union each worried that a united Germany would fall into the other's sphere.

In both Germany and Eastern Europe, Americans and Soviets based their actions on different perspectives on the past. Since the Soviet Union had been a victim of German aggression in both world wars, Stalin was determined to prevent the rebuilding and rearming of its traditional foe; for further protection from possible invasion, he insisted on a security zone of friendly governments in Eastern Europe. Accordingly, between 1945 and 1947 the Soviets repressed democratic parties and installed puppet governments in Poland, Hungary, Rumania, and Bulgaria. Truman, recalling Britain's disastrous appeasement of Hitler in 1938, decided that the United States had to take a hard line against Soviet expansion. "There isn't any difference in totalitarian states," he said, "Nazi, Communist, or Fascist."

As tensions over Europe divided the former allies, hopes of international cooperation in the control of atomic weapons faded as well. In the Baruch Plan, submitted to the United Nations in 1946, the United States proposed a system of international control that relied on mandatory inspection and supervision but preserved the American nuclear monopoly. The Soviets rejected the plan categorically, and worked assiduously to complete their own bomb. Meanwhile, the Truman administration pursued plans to develop nuclear energy and weapons further. Thus the failure of the Baruch Plan signaled the beginning of a frenzied nuclear arms race between the two superpowers.

Containment

As tensions mounted between the superpowers, the United States increasingly perceived Soviet expansionism as a threat to its own interests, and a new American policy, called containment, began to take shape. The most articulate and influential expression of the policy came in February 1946 from George F. Kennan. In an 8,000-word cable from his post at the U.S. Embassy in Moscow to his superiors in Washington, Kennan, who was identified only as "X," warned that the U.S.S.R. was moving "inexorably along the prescribed path, like a persistent toy automobile wound up and headed in a given direction, stopping only when it meets unanswerable force." To stop Soviet expansionism, Kennan argued, the United States should pursue a policy of "firm containment . . . at every point where [the Russians] show signs of encroaching upon the interests of a peaceful and stable world."

The emerging policy of containment crystallized in 1947 over a crisis in Greece. In the spring of 1946, several thousand local communist guerrillas, whom American advisers mistakenly believed were taking orders from Moscow, launched a full-scale civil war against the government and the British occupation authorities. In February 1947 the British informed Truman that they could no longer afford to assist anticommunists in Greece. American policymakers worried that Soviet influence in Greece threatened American and European interests in the eastern Mediterranean and the Middle East, especially in strategically located Turkey and the oil-rich state of Iran.

In response, the president announced what would be known as the Truman Doctrine. In a speech to Congress on March 12, he requested large-scale military and economic assistance to Greece and Turkey. If Greece fell to communism, Truman warned, the effects would be serious not only for Turkey but for the entire Middle East. This notion of an escalating communist contagion was an early version of what Dwight Eisenhower would later call the "domino theory." Not just Greece but freedom itself was at issue, Truman declared: "If we falter in our leadership, we may endanger the peace of the world—and we shall surely endanger the welfare of our own nation." Despite the open-endedness of this military commitment, Congress quickly approved Truman's request for $300 million in aid to Greece and $100 million for Turkey. The appropriation reversed the postwar trend toward sharp cuts in foreign spending, and marked a new level of commitment to the emerging Cold War.

During this period Secretary of State George Marshall proposed a plan to provide economic as well as military aid to Europe. In June 1947, Marshall urged the nations of Europe to work out a comprehensive recovery program and then ask the United States for aid. In Truman's words, the Marshall Plan was "the other half of the walnut" (the first half being the aggressive containment of communism). By bolstering European economies devastated by war, Marshall and Truman believed, the United States could forestall severe economic dislocation, which might give rise to communism. American economic self-interest was also a contributing factor; the legislation required that foreign-aid dollars be spent on U.S. goods and services. A revitalized Europe centered on a strong West German economy would provide a better market for U.S. goods.

Within Congress, however, there was significant opposition to Truman's pledge of economic aid to European economies. Republicans castigated the Marshall Plan as a huge "international W.P.A." and a "bold Socialist blueprint." But in the midst of the congressional stalemate, on February 25, 1948, came a Communist coup in Czechoslovakia. A stark reminder of the menace of Soviet expansion in Europe, the coup served to rally congressional support for the Marshall Plan. In March 1948 Congress voted overwhelmingly to approve funds for the program. Like most other foreign policy initiatives of the 1940s and 1950s, the Marshall Plan won bipartisan support despite the opposition of an isolationist wing of the Republican party.

Over the next four years the United States contributed nearly $13 billion to a highly successful recovery effort. Western European economies revived, and industrial production increased 64 percent, opening new opportunities for international trade. The Marshall Plan did not specifically exclude Eastern Europe or the Soviet Union, but it required that all participating nations exchange economic information and work toward the elimination of tariffs and other trade barriers. Soviet leaders denounced those conditions as attempts to

The Marshall Plan in Action
Between 1948 and 1951 the European Recovery Program, popularly
known as the Marshall Plan after Secretary of State George C. Marshall,
contributed over $13 billion toward its objective of "restoring the confi-
dence of the European people in the economic future of their own countries and of Europe as a whole." Here a sign prominently announces that
Berlin is being rebuilt with help from the Marshall Plan.

draw Eastern Europe into the American orbit, and forbade the satellite states
of Czechoslovakia, Poland, and Hungary to participate.

The Marshall Plan accelerated American and European efforts to rebuild
and reunify the West German economy. In June 1948, after agreeing to fuse
their zones of occupation, the United States, France, and Britain initiated a
program of currency reform in West Berlin. The economic revitalization of
Berlin, located deep within the Soviet zone of occupation, alarmed Soviet policymakers, who feared a resurgent Germany aligned with the West. To forestall
that development, the Soviet Union imposed a blockade on all highway, rail,
and river traffic to West Berlin. Truman responded with an airlift: for nearly a
year American and British pilots, who had been dropping bombs on Berlin
only four years earlier, flew in 2.5 million tons of food and fuel—nearly a ton

for each resident. On May 12, 1949, Stalin lifted the blockade, which had made West Berlin a symbol of resistance to communism.

The coup in Czechoslovakia and the crisis in Berlin convinced U.S. policy-makers of the need for a collective security pact. In April 1949, for the first time since the American Revolution, the United States entered into a peacetime military alliance, the North Atlantic Treaty Organization (NATO). To back up America's new stance, Truman asked Congress for $1.3 billion in military assistance to NATO, and authorized the basing of four U.S. army divisions in Western Europe. Under the NATO pact, twelve nations—the United States, Canada, Britain, France, Italy, Belgium, the Netherlands, Luxembourg, Denmark, Norway, Portugal, and Iceland—agreed that "an armed attack against one or more of them in Europe or North America shall be considered an attack against them all." In May 1949 those nations also agreed to the creation of the Federal Republic of Germany (West Germany), which joined NATO in 1955 (see Map 28.1).

MAP 28.1
Cold War Europe, 1955
In 1949 the United States sponsored the creation of the North Atlantic Treaty Organization, an alliance of ten European nations, the United States, and Canada. West Germany was formally admitted to NATO in May 1955. A few days later the Soviet Union and seven other communist nations established a rival alliance, the Warsaw Pact.

In October 1949, in response to the creation of NATO, the Soviet Union tightened its grip on Eastern Europe by creating a separate government for East Germany, which became the German Democratic Republic. The Soviets also organized an economic association, the Council for Mutual Economic Assistance (COMECON) in 1949, and a military alliance for Eastern Europe, the Warsaw Pact, in 1955. The postwar division of Europe was nearly complete.

New impetus for the policy of containment came in September 1949, when American military intelligence detected a rise in radioactivity in the atmosphere—proof that the Soviet Union had set off an atomic bomb. The American atomic monopoly, which some military and political advisers had argued would last for decades, had ended in just four years, forcing a major reassessment of the nation's foreign policy.

To devise a new diplomatic and military blueprint, Truman turned to the National Security Council (NSC), an advisory body established in 1947 to set defense and military priorities. In April 1950 the NSC delivered its report, known as NSC-68, to the president. Filled with alarmist rhetoric and exaggerated assessments of Soviet capabilities, the document made several specific recommendations, including the development of a hydrogen bomb, an advanced weapon a thousand times more destructive than the atomic bombs that had destroyed Hiroshima and Nagasaki. (The United States would explode its first hydrogen bomb in November 1952; the Soviet Union its first in 1953.) NSC-68 also supported increases in U.S. conventional forces and the establishment of a strong system of alliances. Most important, it called for increased taxes to finance "a bold and massive program of rebuilding the West's defensive potential to surpass that of the Soviet world."

Though Truman was an aggressive anticommunist, he was reluctant to commit to a major defense buildup, fearing that it would overburden the budget. But the Korean War, which began just two months after NSC-68 was completed, helped to transform the report's recommendations into reality as the Cold War became a hot war.

Containment in Asia

As mutual suspicion deepened between the United States and the Soviet Union, cold war doctrines began to influence the American position in Asia as well. American policy there was based on Asia's importance to the world economy as much as on the desire to contain communism. At first, American plans for the region centered on a revitalized China, but political instability there prompted the Truman administration to focus on developing the Japanese economy instead. After dismantling Japan's military forces and weaponry, American occupation forces under General Douglas MacArthur began the job of transforming the country into a bulwark of Asian capitalism. MacArthur drafted a democratic constitution and oversaw the rebuilding of the economy, paving the way for the restoration of Japanese sovereignty in 1951.

In China the situation was more precarious. Since the 1930s a civil war had been raging, as communist forces led by Mao Zedong (Mao Tse-tung) and Zhou Enlai (Chou En-lai) contended for power with conservative Nationalist forces under Jiang Jieshi (Chiang Kai-shek). Although dissatisfied with the corrupt and inefficient Jiang regime, officials for the Truman administration did not see Mao as a good alternative, and they resigned themselves to working with the Nationalists. Between 1945 and 1949 the United States provided more than $2 billion to Jiang's forces, but to no avail. In 1947 General Albert Wedemeyer, who had tried to work with Jiang, reported to President Truman that, until the "corrupt, reactionary, and inefficient Chinese National government" undertook "drastic political and economic reforms," the United States could not accomplish its purpose. In August 1949, when those reforms did not occur, the Truman administration cut off aid to the Nationalists, sealing their fate. The People's Republic of China was formally established on October 1, 1949, and what was left of Jiang's government fled to Taiwan.

Many Americans viewed Mao's success as a defeat for the United States. A pro-Nationalist "China lobby," supported by the powerful publisher Henry R. Luce and by Republican senators Karl Mundt of South Dakota and William S. Knowland of California, protested that under Truman's newly appointed secretary of state, Dean Acheson, the State department was responsible for the "loss of China." The China lobby's influence led to the United States's refusal to recognize what it called "Red China"; instead, the nation recognized the exiled Nationalist government in Taiwan. The United States also used its influence to block China's admission to the United Nations. For almost twenty years, U.S. administrations treated mainland China, the world's most populous country, as a diplomatic nonentity.

In Korea as in China, the seeds of cold war confrontation grew out of World War II. Both the United States and the Soviet Union had troops in Korea at the end of the war. As a result, Korea was divided at the 38th parallel into competing spheres of influence. The Soviets supported a communist government, led by Kim Il Sung, in North Korea; the United States backed a longtime Korean nationalist, Syngman Rhee, in South Korea. Soon sporadic fighting broke out along the 38th parallel, and a civil war began.

On June 25, 1950, the North Koreans launched a surprise attack across the 38th parallel (see Map 28.2, following page). The initiative for Korean reunification came from Kim Il Sung, but Stalin approved of and supported the mission (although the extent of Soviet involvement was unknown at the time). Soviet and North Korean leaders may have expected Truman to ignore this armed challenge, but the president felt that the United States must take a firm stance against the spread of communism. "There's no telling what they'll do if we don't put up a fight now," he said. Truman immediately asked the United Nations Security Council to authorize a "police action" against the invaders. Because the Soviet Union was temporarily boycotting the Security Council to protest the exclusion of the People's Republic of China from the U.N., it could not veto Truman's

MAP 28.2
The Korean War, 1950–1953
From June to September 1950
North Korean troops overran most
of the territory south of the 38th
parallel. On September 15, U.N.
forces counterattacked behind
enemy lines at Inchon and pushed
north almost to the Chinese border.
Massive Chinese intervention
forced the U.N. troops to retreat to
the 38th parallel in January 1951,
and the war was at a stalemate for
the next two years.

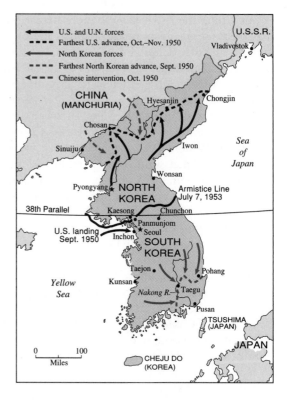

request. Three days after the Security Council voted to send a peacekeeping
force, Truman ordered U.S. troops to Korea.

Though fourteen other non-Communist nations sent troops, the rapidly
assembled United Nations army in Korea was overwhelmingly American. At
the request of the Security Council, President Truman named General Douglas MacArthur to head the U.N. forces. At first the North Koreans held an
overwhelming advantage, controlling practically the entire peninsula except
for the area around Pusan. But, on September 15, 1950, MacArthur launched
a surprise amphibious attack at Inchon, far behind the North Korean front
line, while U.N. forces staged a breakout from Pusan. Within two weeks the
U.N. forces controlled Seoul, the South Korean capital, and almost all the territory up to the 38th parallel.

Encouraged by this success, MacArthur sought the authority to lead his
forces across the 38th parallel and into North Korea. Truman's initial plan had
been to restore the 1945 border, but he managed to win U.N. support for the
broader goal of creating "a unified, independent and democratic Korea."
Though the Chinese government in Beijing warned repeatedly that such a
move would provoke retaliation, American officials did not heed the warnings.
MacArthur's troops crossed the 38th parallel on October 9, reaching the Chinese border at the Yalu River by the end of the month. Just after Thanksgiving,

a massive Chinese counterattack of almost 300,000 troops forced MacArthur to retreat to the 38th parallel. Then, on January 4, 1951, Communist troops reoccupied Seoul.

Two months later American forces and their allies counterattacked, regained Seoul, and pushed back to the 38th parallel. Then stalemate set in. Public support in the United States had dropped after Chinese intervention increased the likelihood of a long war. A poll revealed in early January 1951 that 66 percent of Americans thought the United States should withdraw; 49 percent felt intervening in the war had been a mistake. Given those domestic constraints and the stalemate in Korea, Truman and his advisers decided to work for a negotiated peace. They did not want to tie down large numbers of U.S. troops in Asia, far from what were considered more strategically important trouble spots in Europe and the Middle East.

MacArthur disagreed. Headstrong, arrogant, and brilliant, the general fervently believed that the nation's future lay in Asia, not Europe. Disregarding Truman's instructions, MacArthur traveled to Taiwan and urged the Nationalists to join in an attack on mainland China. He pleaded for permission to use the atomic bomb against China. In an inflammatory letter to the House minority leader, Republican Joseph J. Martin of Massachusetts, he denounced the Korean stalemate. "We must win"—MacArthur declared—"There is no substitute for victory."

Martin released MacArthur's letter on April 6, 1951, as part of a concerted Republican campaign to challenge Truman's conduct of the war. This strategy backfired. On April 11 Truman relieved MacArthur of his command in Korea and Japan, accusing him of insubordination—a decision the Joint Chiefs of Staff supported. Truman's decision was nonetheless highly unpopular. The allure of decisive victory under a charismatic military leader temporarily silenced the public's doubts about the war. Returning to tumultuous receptions in San Francisco, Chicago, and New York, the general delivered an impassioned address to a joint session of Congress. But when the shouting died down, Truman had the last word. After failing to get the Republican presidential nomination in 1952, MacArthur faded from public view.

The war dragged on for more than two years after MacArthur's dismissal. Truce talks began in Korea in July 1951, but a final armistice was not signed until July 1953. Approximately 45 percent of American casualties were sustained during this period. The final settlement left Korea divided very near the original border at the 38th parallel, with a demilitarized zone between the two countries. North Korea remained firmly allied with the Soviet Union; South Korea signed a mutual defense treaty with the United States in 1954.

The Korean War had a lasting impact on the conduct of American foreign policy. Truman had committed troops to Korea without congressional approval, arguing that he had the power to do so as commander in chief of the armed forces, and as executor of the treaty binding the United States to the United Nations. His act expanded executive power and set a precedent for other undeclared wars. The Korean War also widened American involvement in Asia, transforming containment into a truly global policy. During and after the war the United States stationed large numbers of troops in South Korea, and increased military aid to the Nationalist Chinese forces in Taiwan and to French forces fighting communist insurgents in Indochina (see Chapter 31). American foreign policy had become more global, more militarized, and more costly. Even in times of peace, the United States functioned in a state of permanent mobilization.

HARRY TRUMAN AND THE COLD WAR AT HOME

Harry S Truman brought a complex personality to the presidency. Alternately humble and cocky, he had none of Roosevelt's patrician ease, and was a distinctly unpopular president. Yet he handled affairs with an assurance and a crisp dispatch that have endeared him to later generations. "If you can't stand the heat, stay out of the kitchen," he liked to say of presidential responsibility. The major domestic issues he faced were reconversion to a peacetime economy and fears of communist infiltration and subversion—fears his administration played a part in perpetuating.

Truman Confronts Domestic Challenges

The public's main fear in 1945, that the depression would return once war production had ended, proved unfounded. Despite a drop in government spending after the war, consumer spending increased; workers had amassed substantial wartime savings and were eager to spend them. The Servicemen's Readjustment Act of 1944, popularly known as the GI Bill, also put money into the economy by providing educational and economic assistance to returning veterans. Despite some temporary dislocations as war production shifted back to civilian production and veterans entered the work force, unemployment did not soar.

But the transition was hardly troublefree. The main domestic problem was inflation. Consumers wanted to end wartime restrictions and price rationing, but Truman feared economic chaos if he lifted all controls immediately. In the summer of 1945 he eased industrial controls but retained the wartime Office of Price Administration (OPA). When he disbanded the OPA and lifted almost all the remaining controls in the following year, prices soared, producing an annual inflation rate of 18.2 percent. Rising prices and the persistence of food and other shortages irritated consumers.

The rapidly rising cost of living prompted demands for higher wages by the nation's workers. Under government-sanctioned agreements the labor movement had held the line on salary increases during the war. But after the war ended, union leaders expressed frustration. Corporate profits had doubled while real wages had declined as a result of inflation and the loss of overtime pay. Determined to make up for their war-induced sacrifices, workers mounted crippling strikes in the automobile, steel, and coal industries. General strikes

Helen Gahagan Douglas
Representative Helen Gahagan Douglas of California, a former Broadway
and film star, illustrated a 1947 speech supporting the reestablishment of
price controls by bringing a shopping basket of food to a press conference.
Douglas served in Congress from 1944 until 1950, when she was defeated in
a bid for the Senate by Representative Richard M. Nixon. In their bitterly
fought campaign Nixon linked her with communism by calling her pink.

effectively closed down business in more than a half dozen cities in 1946. By
the end of that year, 5 million workers had idled factories and mines for a total
of 107,476,000 workdays.

Truman responded dramatically. In the face of a devastating railway strike,
he used his executive authority to place the nation's railroad system under federal control, and asked Congress for the power to draft striking workers into
the army—a move that infuriated labor leaders, but pressured strikers to go
back to work. Three days later he seized control of the nation's coal mines to
end a strike by the United Mine Workers. Such actions won Truman support
from many Americans, but incurred the enmity of organized labor, an important partner in the Democratic coalition.

These domestic upheavals did not bode well for the Democrats at the
polls. In 1946 the Republicans gained control of both houses of Congress
and set about undoing New Deal social welfare measures, singling out labor
legislation as a special target. In 1947 Congress passed the Taft-Hartley Act,
a rollback of several provisions of the National Labor Relations Act, passed

in 1935. Unions especially disliked Section 14b of Taft-Hartley, which out-lawed the closed shop and allowed states to pass "right-to-work" laws that further limited unions' operations. The act also restricted unions' political power by prohibiting use of their dues for political activity, and allowed the president to declare an eighty-day cooling-off period in strikes that had a national impact. Truman issued a ringing veto of the Taft-Hartley bill in June 1947, calling it "bad for labor, bad for management, and bad for the country." Congress easily overrode the veto, but Truman's actions countered some of workers' hostility to his earlier antistrike activity, and kept labor in the Democratic fold.

Most observers believed that Truman faced an impossible task in the pres-idential campaign of 1948. The Republicans were united, and with Thomas E. Dewey, the politically moderate governor of New York, as their candidate once again, they had a good chance of attracting traditional Democratic voters (Chapter 27). To increase their appeal in the West, the Republicans nominated Earl Warren, governor of California, for vice-president. In their platform they promised to continue most New Deal reforms and to support a bipartisan for-eign policy.

Truman, in contrast, led a party in disarray. Both the left and the right wings of the Democratic party split off and nominated their own candidates. Henry A. Wallace, a former New Deal liberal whom Truman had fired as sec-retary of commerce in 1946 because he was perceived as too "soft" on com-munism, ran as the candidate of the new Progressive party. Wallace advocated increased government intervention in the economy, more power for labor unions, and cooperation with the Soviet Union.

The other challenge to the party came from the South. At the Democratic national convention, northern liberals such as Mayor Hubert H. Humphrey of Minneapolis had pushed through a platform calling for the repeal of the Taft-Hartley Act and increased federal commitment to civil rights. Southern Dem-ocrats, unwilling to tolerate federal interference in race relations, bolted the convention and created the States' Rights party, popularly known as the Dix-iecrats. They nominated Governor J. Strom Thurmond of South Carolina for president.

Truman responded to these challenges with one of the most effective pres-idential campaigns ever waged. He launched a strenuous cross-country speak-ing tour in which he hammered away at the Republicans' support for the antilabor Taft-Hartley Act. He also criticized Republicans for opposing legis-lation for housing, medical insurance, and civil rights. By combining these is-sues with attacks on the Soviet menace abroad, Truman began to salvage his troubled campaign. At his rallies enthusiastic listeners shouted, "Give 'em hell, Harry!"

Truman won a remarkable victory, receiving 49.6 percent of the vote to Dewey's 45.1 percent. The Democrats also regained control of both houses of Congress. Strom Thurmond carried only four southern states, and Henry Wal-lace failed to win any electoral votes. Truman retained the support of organized

Truman Triumphant
In one of the most famous photographs in American political history, Harry S Truman gloats over an inaccurate headline in the *Chicago Tribune*. Pollsters had predicted an overwhelming victory for Thomas E. Dewey. Their primitive techniques, however, did not reflect the dramatic surge in support for Truman during the last days of the campaign.

labor. Jewish and Catholic voters in the big cities, and black voters in the North, offset his losses to the Dixiecrats. Most important, Truman appealed effectively to people like himself from the farms, towns, and small cities in the nation's heartland.

Fair Deal Liberalism

Shortly after becoming president, Truman had proposed to Congress a twenty-one-point plan for expanded federal programs based on individual "rights," including the right to a "useful and remunerative" job, controls over monopolies, good housing, "adequate medical care," "protection from the economic fears of old age," and a "good education." Later, Truman added support for civil rights and called his program the Fair Deal. Although to some extent the Fair Deal represented an extension of the New Deal's liberalism—with its faith in the positive influence of government and the use of federal

power to ensure pubic welfare—it also took some new directions. Its attention to civil rights reflected the growing importance of African-Americans to
the Democratic party's coalition of urban voters. And the desire to extend a
high standard of living and other benefits of capitalism to an ever-greater
number of citizens reflected a new liberal vision of the role of the state.
Rather than rely upon extensive federal regulation of corporations and intrusive planning of the economy, as many Progressive Era and New Deal reformers had proposed, the liberals of Truman's era were more moderate. They
believed that the essential role of the federal government was to manage the
economy indirectly through fiscal policy. Drawing upon the Keynesian notion
of using government spending to spur economic growth, they expected that
welfare programs not only would provide a safety net for disadvantaged citizens but also would maintain consumer purchasing power, keeping the economy healthy.

Truman's agenda met a generally hostile Congress, despite the Democratic
majority. The same conservative coalition that had blocked Roosevelt's initiatives in his second term and dismantled or cut popular New Deal programs
during wartime continued to fight against Truman's proposals. Only parts of
the Fair Deal won adoption: the minimum wage was raised; the Social Security program was extended to cover 10 million new workers; and Social Security benefits were increased by 75 percent. The National Housing Act of 1949
called for the construction of 810,000 units of low-income housing, but only
half that number were actually built.

Interest groups successfully opposed other key items in the Fair Deal. The
American Medical Association (AMA) quashed a labor-backed movement for
national health insurance by denouncing it as the first step toward "socialized
medicine." Catholics successfully opposed aid to education because it did not
include subsidies for parochial schools. Trade associations, the National Association of Manufacturers, and other business groups also actively opposed what
they called "creeping socialism." Though most corporate leaders recognized
that some state involvement in the economy was necessary and even beneficial to business interests, the Fair Deal went too far, in their opinion. As a lob-
byist for the National Association of Real Estate Boards explained, "In our
country we prefer that government activity shall take the form of assisting and
aiding private business rather than undertake great public projects of a governmental character." Through extensive lobbying and public relations campaigns, business groups agitated not only to defeat specific pieces of Fair Deal
legislation but also to forestall increased taxes, antitrust activity, and other unwanted federal interference in corporate affairs. Their activities helped to
block the Truman administration's efforts to mobilize popular and congressional support for dramatically enlarged federal responsibilities for economic
and social welfare.

Truman's record on civil rights illustrates still other obstacles that faced the
Fair Deal. Black demands for justice, which had accelerated during World War
II (see Chapter 27), continued into the postwar years, spurred by symbolic

victories such as Jackie Robinson's breaking through the color line in major league baseball by joining the Brooklyn Dodgers in 1947. Truman offered some support for civil rights, in part because of his desire to solidify the Democrats' hold on African-American voters as they migrated from the South, where they were effectively disfranchised, to northern and western cities. Truman was also concerned about America's image abroad, especially since the Soviet Union often compared the segregation of southern blacks with the Nazis' treatment of the Jews.

Lacking a popular mandate on the civil rights issue, Truman turned to executive action. In 1946 he appointed a National Civil Rights Commission, which in its 1947 report called for an expanded federal role in civil rights that foreshadowed much of the civil rights legislation of the 1960s. He ordered the Justice department to prepare an amicus curiae ("friend of the court") brief in the Supreme Court case of *Shelley v. Kraemer* (1948), which struck down as unconstitutional restrictive covenants that enforced residential segregation by barring home buyers of a certain race or religion. In the same year Truman signed an executive order to desegregate the armed forces. The Truman administration also proposed a federal antilynching law, federal protection of voting rights (such as an end to poll taxes), and a permanent federal agency to guarantee equal employment opportunity. A filibuster by southern conservatives blocked the legislation in Congress, however.

The outbreak of the Korean War in 1950 limited the chances of the Fair Deal being passed by diverting national attention and federal funds from domestic affairs. So did the nation's growing paranoia concerning internal subversion, the most dramatic manifestation of the Cold War's effect on American life.

The Great Fear

As American relations with the Soviet Union deteriorated, fear of communism at home fueled a widespread campaign of domestic repression. Americans often call this phenomenon McCarthyism, after Senator Joseph R. McCarthy of Wisconsin, the decade's most vocal anticommunist, but more was involved than the work of just one man. The Great Fear built on the longstanding distrust of radicals and foreigners that had exploded in the Red Scare after World War I. Worsening cold war tensions intersected with those deep-seated anxieties and with partisan politics to spawn an obsessive concern with internal subversion. Ultimately, however, few Communists were found in positions of power; far more Americans became innocent victims of false accusations and innuendos.

The roots of postwar anticommunism date back to 1938, when Congressman Martin Dies of Texas and other conservatives launched the House Committee on Un-American Activities (HUAC) to investigate alleged fascist and Communist influence in labor unions and New Deal agencies. HUAC gained heightened visibility after the war, especially after revelations in 1946 of a Soviet spy ring operating in Canada and the United States accentuated fears of Soviet subversion.

Standing up to HUAC

H UAC not only asked people about their own alleged subversive activity, but compelled them to "name names," to expose friends or colleagues with links to the Communist party or other organizations the Committee deemed disloyal. Playwright Lillian Hellman was one of a small number who refused. She explains why in a letter to HUAC in May 1952.

I am most willing to answer all questions about myself. I have nothing to hide from your Committee and there is nothing in my life of which I am ashamed. I have been advised by counsel that under the Fifth Amendment I have a constitutional privilege to decline to answer any questions about my political opinions, activities and associations, on the grounds of self-incrimination. I do not wish to claim this privilege. I am ready and willing to testify before the representatives of our Government as to my own opinions and my own actions, regardless of any risks or consequences to myself. . . .

I am not willing, now or in the future, to bring bad trouble to people who, in my past association with them, were completely innocent of any talk or any action that was disloyal or subversive. I do not like subversion or disloyalty in any form and if I had ever seen any I would have considered it my duty to have reported it to the proper authorities. But to hurt innocent people whom I knew many years ago in order to save myself is, to me, inhuman and indecent and dishonorable. I cannot and will not cut my conscience to fit this year's fashions, even though I long ago came to the conclusion that I was not a political person and could have no comfortable place in any political group.

SOURCE: Lillian Hellman, *Scoundrel Time* (Boston: Little, Brown, 1976), pp. 92–94.

In 1947 HUAC helped launch the Great Fear by holding widely publicized hearings on alleged Communist infiltration in the film industry. A group of writers and directors, soon dubbed the Hollywood Ten, went to jail for contempt of Congress when they cited the First Amendment in refusing to testify about their past associations. Hundreds of other actors, directors, and writers whose names had been mentioned in the HUAC investigation, or whose associates and friends the committee had labeled as "reds," were unable to get work, victims of an unacknowledged but very real blacklist honored by industry executives. HUAC also investigated playwrights, authors, university professors, labor activists, organizations, and government officials thought to be "left wing."

Although HUAC bore much of the responsibility for spawning the witch hunt, its effects spread far beyond the congressional committee. In March 1947 President Truman issued an executive order initiating a comprehensive investigation into the loyalty of federal employees. Following

Washington's lead, many state and local governments, universities, political organizations, churches, and businesses undertook their own antisubversion campaigns, including the requirement that employees take loyalty oaths. In the labor movement, which Communists had been active in organizing in the 1930s, charges that Soviet-led Communists were taking over American unions led to a purge of Communist members. Civil rights organizations such as the NAACP and the National Urban League also purged themselves of Communists or "fellow travelers." Thus the Great Fear was particularly devastating to the political left; accusations of guilt by association affected progressives of all stripes.

The anticommunist crusade intensified in 1948 when HUAC began an investigation of Alger Hiss, a former New Dealer and a State department official who had accompanied Franklin Roosevelt to Yalta. A former Communist, Whittaker Chambers, claimed that Hiss was a member of a secret Communist cell operating within the government and had passed him classified documents in the 1930s. Hiss categorically denied the allegations, and denied even knowing Chambers. HUAC's investigation was orchestrated by Republican Congressman Richard M. Nixon of California. Because the statute of limitations on the crime Hiss was accused of had expired, Hiss was charged instead with perjury, for lying about his Communist affiliations and acquaintance with Chambers. In early 1950 Hiss was found guilty and sentenced to five years in federal prison. Even after his death in 1996, the media continued to debate the question of his guilt or innocence.

The conviction of Hiss fueled the paranoia about a Communist conspiracy in the federal government, contributing to the meteoric rise of Senator Joseph McCarthy of Wisconsin. In February 1950, McCarthy delivered a bombshell during a speech in Wheeling, West Virginia: "I have here in my hand a list of the names of 205 men that were known to the Secretary of State as being members of the Communist Party and who nevertheless are still working and shaping the policy of the State Department."

For the next four years McCarthy became the central figure in a virulent campaign of anticommunism. Like other Republicans in the late 1940s, McCarthy leveled accusations of Communist subversion in the government to embarrass President Truman and the Democratic party. Critics who disagreed with him exposed themselves to charges of being "soft" on communism. Because McCarthy charged that his critics were themselves part of "this conspiracy so immense," few political leaders challenged him. Truman called McCarthy's charges "slander, lies, character assassination," but could do nothing to curb them. When the Republican Dwight D. Eisenhower was elected president in 1952, he refrained from publicly challenging his party's most outspoken senator.

Despite McCarthy's failure to identify a single Communist in government, a series of national and international events allowed him to retain credibility. Besides the Hiss case, the sensational 1951 espionage trial of Julius and Ethel Rosenberg fueled McCarthy's allegations. Convicted of passing atomic secrets to the Soviet Union in a highly controversial trial, the Rosenbergs were executed in 1953. (As in the case of Hiss, their convictions continue to be debated; the recent release of declassified documents from a top-secret intelligence mission has provided some new evidence of Julius Rosenberg's guilt.) The Korean War, which embroiled the United States in a frustrating fight against communism in a faraway land, also made Americans susceptible to McCarthy's claims. Blaming disloyal individuals rather than complex international factors for the problems of the Cold War undoubtedly helped many Americans make sense of a disordered world of nuclear bombs, "police actions," and other world crises.

In early 1954 McCarthy overreached himself by launching an investigation into possible subversion in the U.S. Army. When the lengthy televised hearings brought McCarthy's smear tactics and leering innuendos into the nation's living rooms, support for him declined. The end of the Korean War and the death of Stalin in 1953 also undercut public interest in McCarthy's red-hunting campaign. In December 1954 the Senate voted 67 to 22 to censure McCarthy for unbecoming conduct. He died an alcoholic three years later at the age of forty-eight, his name forever attached to a period of political repression of which he was only the most flagrant manifestation.

The Army-McCarthy Hearings
These 1954 hearings contributed to the downfall of Senator Joseph McCarthy by showing his reckless accusations, bullying tactics, and sneering innuendos to a huge television audience. Some of the most heated exchanges took place between McCarthy (right) and Joseph Welch (seated, left), the lawyer representing the army. When an exasperated Welch asked, "Have you no decency left, sir?" the audience broke into applause because someone had finally had the courage to challenge McCarthy.

"MODERN REPUBLICANISM"

In 1952, in the middle of the Korean stalemate and at the height of the Great Fear, a newly elected president, Dwight D. Eisenhower, succeeded Harry Truman, ousting the Democrats from the White House. Eisenhower set the tone for what historians have called "modern Republicanism," an updated party philosophy that emphasized a slowdown, rather than a dismantling, of federal responsibilities. Compared with their predecessors in the 1920s and their successors in the 1980s and 1990s, modern Republicans were more tolerant of government intervention in social and economic affairs, though they did seek to limit the scope of federal action. More important to the average voter than Eisenhower's political philosophy, however, was his proven leadership in trying times; he seemed the right man to guide the nation through the perils of the Cold War.

"I Like Ike": Eisenhower as President

Eisenhower's status as a war hero was his greatest political asset. Born in 1890 and raised in Abilene, Kansas, he had graduated from the U.S. Military Academy at West Point in 1915. Rising quickly through the ranks, during World War II he became Supreme Commander of Allied Forces in Europe, where he had the mammoth task of coordinating the D-Day invasion of France. To hundreds of thousands of soldiers and to the millions of civilians who followed the war on newsreels, he was simply "Ike," the best known and best liked of the nation's military leaders.

As a professional military man, Eisenhower claimed to stand "above politics." While in the army he had never voted, insisting that such political activity represented an intrusion of the military into civilian affairs. Many Democrats had hoped to make him their candidate for president in 1948 and again in 1952. But Eisenhower wanted to occupy the office as a Republican. After winning several primaries, he secured the Republican nomination and asked Senator Richard M. Nixon of California to be his running mate. Nixon, young, tirelessly partisan, and with a strong anticommunist record from his crusade against Alger Hiss, brought an aggressive campaign style as well as regional balance to the Republican ticket.

The Democrats never seriously considered renominating Harry Truman, who by 1952 was a thoroughly discredited leader. Lack of popular enthusiasm for the Korean War had dealt the most severe blow to Truman's support, but a series of scandals involving federal officials in bribery, kickback, and influence-peddling schemes had caused a public outcry about the "mess in Washington." With a certain relief the Democrats turned to Governor Adlai E. Stevenson of Illinois, who enjoyed the support of respected liberals such as Eleanor Roosevelt and of organized labor. To appease southern voters who feared Stevenson's liberal agenda, the Democrats nominated Senator John A. Sparkman of Alabama for vice-president.

Throughout the 1952 campaign Stevenson advocated New Deal and Fair Deal policies with an almost literary eloquence. But Eisenhower's artfully unpretentious speeches were more effective with voters. Eager to win the support of the broadest electorate possible, Eisenhower played down specific questions of policy. Instead, he attacked the Democrats with the "K_1C_2" formula—"Korea, Communism, and Corruption." In a campaign pledge that clinched the election, he vowed to go to Korea, with the implication that he would end the stalemated war if elected.

The Republican campaign was temporarily set back by the revelation that wealthy Californians had set up a secret "slush fund" for Richard Nixon. Eisenhower contemplated dropping Nixon from the ticket, but Nixon adroitly used a televised speech to convince voters that he had not misused campaign funds. Nixon did admit to accepting one gift—a puppy his young daughters had named Checkers. That gift he would not give back, he declared earnestly. Nixon's televised speech turned an embarrassing incident into an advantage, as sympathetic viewers flooded Republican headquarters with supportive telegrams and phone calls. Outmaneuvered, Republican leaders had no choice but to keep Nixon on the ticket. The "Checkers speech" showed how the powerful new medium of television could be used to a politician's advantage.

That November, Eisenhower won 55 percent of the popular vote, carrying all the northern and western states and four southern states. Republican candidates for Congress did not fare quite as well. They regained the Senate from the Democrats, but took the House of Representatives by a slender margin of only 4 seats. In 1954 they would lose control of both houses to the Democrats. Even though the enormously popular Eisenhower would easily win re-election over Adlai Stevenson in 1956, the Republicans would remain in the minority in Congress.

The political scientist Fred Greenstein has characterized Eisenhower's style of leadership as the "hidden-hand presidency," pointing out that the president maneuvered deftly behind the scenes while seeming not to concern himself in public with partisan questions. Seeking a middle ground between liberalism and conservatism, Eisenhower did his best to set a quieter national mood, hoping to decrease the need for federal intervention in social and economic issues.

Unlike Truman, for example, Eisenhower showed little commitment to civil rights. He was disturbed by the Supreme Court decision in *Brown v. Board of Education of Topeka* (1954), which declared racial segregation in the public schools unconstitutional (see Chapter 29), asserting, "I don't believe you can change the hearts of men with laws or decisions." Nonetheless, in 1957 the president sent federal troops to enforce the integration of Central High School in Little Rock, Arkansas. Eisenhower also signed the Civil Rights Act of 1957, a Democratic bill that created the U.S. Commission on Civil Rights to study federal policies and laws concerning race. Though the act accomplished little, it was the first national civil rights legislation to be passed since Reconstruction.

Eisenhower presided over other cautious increases in federal activity. When the Soviet Union launched the first satellite, *Sputnik*, in 1957, Eisenhower supported a U.S. space program to catch up in this new cold war competition. The National Aeronautics and Space Administration (NASA) was founded the following year. The president also persuaded Congress to appropriate additional money for college scholarships and for research and development at universities and in industry. Federal outlays for veterans' benefits, unemployment compensation, housing, and Social Security were increased, and the minimum wage was raised from 75 cents an hour to $1. The creation of the new Department of Health, Education, and Welfare (HEW) in 1953 consolidated government control of social welfare programs, confirming federal commitments in that area.

Some of the most extensive federal activity during these years was in the realm of transportation. To link the Great Lakes with the Atlantic Ocean, the United States cosponsored with Canada the construction of the St. Lawrence Seaway. Congress also passed the Interstate Highway Act of 1956, which authorized $26 billion over a ten-year period for the construction of a nationally integrated highway system. The St. Lawrence Seaway and interstate highway projects were the largest public works programs to that date, surpassing anything undertaken during the New Deal.

Thus Republicans, though they resisted the unchecked expansion of the state, did not generally cut back federal power. Only in natural resource development did the Eisenhower administration move to reduce federal activity through the relinquishment of federal offshore oil contracting to the states in 1953, and the authorization of privately financed hydroelectric dams on the Snake River in 1955. In most other matters, such as social welfare programs and defense expenditures, modern Republicanism signaled an abandonment of the traditional Republican commitment to limited government. When Eisenhower retired from public life in 1961, the federal government had become an even greater presence in everyday life than it had been when he took office.

The "New Look"

Eisenhower had earned a reputation for superb judgment in military and diplomatic affairs during his years in the armed forces. One of his first acts as president was to put that skill to use in negotiating an end to the Korean War. As he had pledged in the campaign, he visited Korea in December 1952. The final settlement was signed in July 1953, after the parties reached a compromise on the tricky issue of prisoner exchange.

Once the Korean War was settled, Eisenhower turned his attention to Europe. Stalin's death in March 1953 precipitated an intraparty struggle in the Soviet Union, which lasted until 1956, when Nikita S. Khrushchev emerged as Stalin's successor. Although Khrushchev surprised westerners by calling for "peaceful coexistence" between communist and capitalist societies, he made certain that the U.S.S.R.'s Eastern European satellites did not deviate too far from the Soviet path. When nationalists revolted in Hungary in 1956 and moved to take the country out of the Warsaw Pact, Soviet tanks moved rapidly into Budapest—an action the United States could condemn, but could not realistically resist. Soviet repression of the Hungarian revolt showed that American policymakers had few, if any, options for rolling back Soviet power in Eastern Europe, short of going to war with the U.S.S.R.

Although Eisenhower strongly opposed communism, he hoped to keep the cost of containment at a manageable level. Under his "New Look" defense policy, Eisenhower and Secretary of State John Foster Dulles decided to economize by developing a massive nuclear arsenal as an alternative to more expensive conventional forces. Nuclear weapons delivered "more bang for the buck," explained Defense Secretary Charles E. Wilson. To that end, the Eisenhower administration expanded its commitment to the hydrogen bomb, approving extensive atmospheric testing in the South Pacific and in western states such as Nevada, Colorado, and Utah. To improve the nation's defenses against an air attack from the Soviet Union, the administration made a commitment to develop the long-range bombing capabilities of the Strategic Air Command, and installed the Distant Early Warning line of radar stations in Alaska and Canada in 1958.

Those measures did little to improve the nation's security, however, as the Soviets matched the United States weapon for weapon in an escalating arms race. The Soviet Union carried out atmospheric tests of its own of hydrogen bombs between 1953 and 1958, and developed a fleet of long-range bombers. By 1958, both nations had intercontinental ballistic missiles (ICBMs). When an American nuclear submarine launched an atomic-tipped Polaris missile in 1960, Soviet engineers raced to produce an equivalent weapon. While the arms race boosted the military-industrial sectors of both nations, it debilitated their social welfare programs by funneling immense resources into soon-to-be-obsolete weapons systems.

The New Look policy also extended collective security agreements between the United States and its allies. To complement the NATO alliance in Europe, for example, Secretary of State Dulles orchestrated the creation of the Southeast Asia Treaty Organization (SEATO), which linked America and its major European allies with Australia, Pakistan, Thailand, New Zealand, and the Philippines. All told, this extensive system of defense tied the United States to more than forty other countries.

In these years U.S. policymakers tended to support stable governments, no matter how repressive, as long as they were overtly anticommunist. Some of America's staunchest allies—the Philippines, Iran, Cuba, South Vietnam, and Nicaragua—were governed by dictatorships or repressive right-wing regimes that lacked broad-based popular support. In fact, Dulles often resorted to covert interventions against governments that were, in his opinion, too closely aligned with communism. For such tasks he used the newly formed Central Intelligence Agency (CIA), which had moved beyond its original mandate of intelligence gathering into active, albeit covert, involvement in the internal affairs of foreign countries. In the 1950s the CIA successfully directed the overthrow of the governments of Iran and Guatemala and helped to install new regimes viewed as more friendly to U.S. interests.

The Emerging Third World

American leaders had devised the policy of containment in response to Soviet expansion in Eastern Europe, but they soon extended it to the new nations emerging in the Third World. Before World War II, nationalism, socialism, and religion had inspired powerful anticolonial movements; in the 1940s and 1950s those forces intensified and spread, especially in the Middle East, Africa, and the Far East. Between 1947 and 1962 the British, French, Dutch, and Belgian empires all but disintegrated. Seeking to draw the new countries into an American-led world system, U.S. policymakers encouraged the development of stable market economies in those areas. They also sought to further the ideal of national self-determination that had shaped American participation in both world wars. But given the polarities of the Cold War, both the Truman and the Eisenhower administrations often failed to recognize that indigenous nationalist or socialist movements in emerging nations had their own goals, and were not necessarily under the control of either local Communists or the Soviet Union. Their failure to appreciate the complexity of local conditions limited the effectiveness of American policy.

The Middle East, an oil-rich area that was playing an increasingly central role in strategic planning, presented one of the most complicated challenges. After World War II many Jewish survivors of Nazi extermination camps had resettled in Palestine, which was still controlled by Britain under a World War I mandate. On November 29, 1947, the U.N. General Assembly voted to partition Palestine into two states, Jewish and Arab—a decision that Egypt, Jordan, and other Arab League states resisted. On May 14, 1948, the British mandate ended and Zionist leaders of the Jewish nationalist movement proclaimed the state of Israel. President Truman quickly recognized the new state, alienating the Arabs but winning crucial support from Jewish Americans in the 1948 election.

Egypt was another site of conflict with the Arab Nations, one that reflected the way in which Third World countries became embroiled in the Cold War. When Gamal Abdel Nasser came to power in Egypt in 1954, two years after his nation won independence from Britain, he pledged to lead not just Egypt but the entire Middle East out of its dependent colonial relationship with the West through a form of pan-Arab socialism. From the Soviet Union, Nasser obtained arms and promises of economic assistance, including help in building the Aswan Dam on the Nile. Secretary of State Dulles countered with an offer of American assistance, but Nasser refused to distance himself from the Soviets, declaring Egypt's neutrality in the Cold War. Unwilling to accept this stance of nonalignment, Dulles abruptly withdrew his offer in July 1956.

A week later Nasser retaliated against the withdrawal of western financial aid by nationalizing the Suez Canal, over which Britain had retained administrative authority, and through which three-quarters of Western Europe's oil passed. After several months of fruitless negotiation, Britain and France, in alliance with Israel, attacked Egypt and retook the canal. Their attack occurred at the same time as the Soviet repression of the Hungarian revolt, placing the United States in the potentially awkward position of denouncing Soviet aggression while tolerating a similar action by its own allies. President Eisenhower and the United Nations condemned the European actions in Egypt, forcing France and Britain to pull back. Egypt retook the canal and proceeded to build the Aswan Dam with Soviet support. In the end, the Suez crisis increased Soviet influence in the Third World, intensified anti-western sentiment in Arab countries, and produced dissension among leading members of the NATO alliance.

In early 1957, in the aftermath of the Suez crisis, the president persuaded Congress to approve the Eisenhower Doctrine. Addressing concerns over declining British influence in the Middle East, the joint policy stated that American forces would assist any nation in the region "requiring such aid, against overt armed aggression from any nation controlled by International Communism." Later that year Eisenhower invoked the doctrine when he sent the U.S. Sixth Fleet to the Mediterranean to aid King Hussein of Jordan. A year later he landed 8,000 troops to back a pro–United States government in Lebanon.

The attention the Eisenhower administration paid to developments in the Middle East in the 1950s demonstrated how the desire for access to steady supplies of oil increasingly affected foreign policy. Indeed, by the late 1950s the Middle East contained about 65 percent of the world's known reserves. But more broadly, attention to the Middle East confirmed the global scope of American interests. Just as the Korean War had stretched the application of the containment policy from Europe to Asia, the Eisenhower Doctrine revealed the U.S. intention to bring the Middle East into its sphere as well.

The Impact of the Cold War at Home

While the Cold War extended to the most distant corners of the globe, it also had a devastating impact on the health of American citizens at home, some of whom became unwitting guinea pigs in the nation's nuclear weapons program. In the late 1950s, a small but growing number of citizens became concerned about the effects of radioactive fallout from aboveground bomb tests. In later years federal investigators documented a host of illnesses, deaths, and birth defects among families of veterans who had worked on weapons tests and among "down-winders"—people who lived near nuclear test sites and weapons facilities. The

Testing an Atomic Bomb
Throughout the 1950s the Atomic Energy Commission conducted aboveground tests of atomic and hydrogen bombs. Thousands of soldiers were
exposed to fallout during the tests, such as this one at Yucca Flats, Nevada,
in April 1952. The AEC, ignoring or suppressing medical evidence to the
contrary, mounted an extensive public relations campaign to convince local
residents that the tests did not endanger their health.

most shocking revelations, however, came to light in 1993, when the Department
of Energy released millions of previously classified documents on human radiation experiments conducted in the late 1940s and 1950s under the auspices of
the Atomic Energy Commission (AEC) and other federal agencies. Many of the
subjects were irradiated without their consent or understanding.

Memories of a Cold War Childhood

The menacing threat of the atom bomb, the looming presence of the Soviet Union, and the fear of internal subversion were part of everyday life in the 1950s. In his autobiography, Born on the Fourth of July, *Ron Kovic conveys the anxiety Americans felt when the Soviets launched the satellite* Sputnik, *revealing that Americans were behind in the race to conquer outer space.*

We joined the cub scouts and marched in parades on Memorial Day. We made contingency plans for the cold war and built fallout shelters out of milk cartons. We wore spacesuits and space helmets. We made rocket ships out of cardboard boxes. And one Saturday afternoon in the basement Castiglia [a friend] and I went to Mars on the couch we had turned into a rocket ship. . . . And the whole block watched a thing called the space race begin. On a cold October night Dad and I watched the first satellite, called *Sputnik,* moving across the sky above our house like a tiny bright star. I still remember standing out there with Dad looking up in amazement at that thing moving in the sky above Massapequa. It was hard to believe that this thing, this *Sputnik,* was so high up and moving so fast around the world, again and again. Dad put his hand on my shoulder that night and without saying anything I quietly walked back inside and went to my room thinking that the Russians had beaten America into space and wondering why we couldn't even get a rocket off the pad. . . .

The Communists were all over the place back then. And if they weren't trying to beat us into outer space, Castiglia and I were certain they were infiltrating our schools, trying to take over our classes and control our minds. We were both certain that one of our teachers was a secret Communist agent and in our next secret club meeting we promised to report anything new he said during our next history class. We watched him very carefully that year.

SOURCE: Ron Kovic, *Born on the Fourth of July* (New York: Pocket Books, 1976), pp. 56–57.

The nuclear arms race affected all Americans by fostering a climate of fear and uncertainty. Bomb shelters, civil defense drills, and other survival measures provided a daily reminder of the threat of nuclear war. Eisenhower himself had second thoughts about a nuclear policy based on the premise of annihilating the enemy, even if one's own country was destroyed—the aptly named acronym MAD (Mutual Assured Destruction) policy. He also found spiraling arms expenditures a serious hindrance to balancing the federal budget, one of his chief fiscal goals. Consequently, Eisenhower tried to negotiate an arms limitation agreement with the Soviet Union. Progress along those lines was cut short, however, when on May 5, 1960, the Soviets shot down an American U-2 spy plane over their territory and captured and imprisoned its pilot, Francis Gary Powers. Eisenhower at first denied that the plane was engaged in espionage, but later admitted that he had authorized the mission and other secret flights over the U.S.S.R. In the midst of the dispute, a proposed summit meeting was canceled and Eisenhower's last chance to negotiate an arms agreement evaporated.

When Eisenhower left office in January 1961, he used his final address to warn against the growing power of what he termed the "military-industrial complex," which by then employed 3.5 million Americans. Its pervasive influence, he noted, was "felt in every city, every statehouse, every office of the Federal Government." Even though his administration had fostered the growth of the defense establishment, Eisenhower was gravely concerned about its implications for a democratic people. "We must guard against the acquisition of unwarranted influence, whether sought or unsought, by the military-industrial complex," he warned. "We must never let the weight of this combination endanger our liberties or democratic processes." With those words Dwight Eisenhower showed how well he understood the major transformations that the Cold War had wrought in the nation. The conflict between the Soviet Union and the United States not only had far-reaching international implications; it had powerful effects on domestic politics, the economy, and cultural values, and it permanently altered the contours of the modern state.

CHAPTER 28 TIMELINE

1945	Yalta and Potsdam conferences Harry S Truman succeeds Roosevelt as president End of World War II
1946	Kennan sends "long telegram" outlining containment policy Baruch Plan for international control of atomic weapons fails
1947	Taft-Hartley Act Truman Doctrine Marshall Plan
1948	Desegregation of armed forces State of Israel created Berlin airlift
1949	North Atlantic Treaty Organization (NATO) founded People's Republic of China established National Housing Act Soviet Union detonates atomic bomb; U.S. atomic monopoly ends
1950–1953	Korean War
1950	Alger Hiss convicted of perjury McCarthy presents his list of alleged Communists in government NSC-68 calls for permanent mobilization
1952	Dwight D. Eisenhower elected president U.S. detonates hydrogen bomb
1954	Army-McCarthy hearings *Brown v. Board of Education of Topeka*
1956	Crises in Hungary and Suez Interstate Highway Act
1957	Eisenhower Doctrine Eisenhower sends U.S. troops to Little Rock to ensure school integration
1958	NASA established
1959	St. Lawrence Seaway completed
1960	U-2 spy plane shot down over Soviet Union

CHAPTER 29

AFFLUENCE AND ITS
CONTRADICTIONS, 1945-1965

- The Postwar Capitalist Economy
- A Suburban Society
- American Society during the Baby Boom
- The Other America

Hula-Hoops and poodle skirts, sock hops and rock-'n'-roll, shiny cars and gleaming appliances—all signify the "fifties"—a period which really stretched from 1945 through the early 1960s. The postwar years are remembered as a time of affluence, consumerism, conformity, and stability, a time when Americans enjoyed an optimistic faith in progress and technology. It was an age of innocence, of a serene family-centered culture enshrined in television sitcoms such as "Father Knows Best."

This powerful myth, like many, has some truth to it. Certainly in the quarter-century after World War II, Americans enjoyed the highest standard of living in the world, and the fruits of a technologically advanced industrial sector. That affluence spawned a suburban culture in which many men and women turned inward to enjoy the private satisfactions of family, leisure, and consumerism.

But there were other sides to the story. Suburban prosperity often came at the expense of the vitality of cities; thus the roots of urban crises were to be found in this period. Heedless faith in technology sowed the seeds of serious environmental problems as well. Moreover, many "other Americans" did not lead lives of contentment in the suburbs. Although prosperity was more widespread than ever before, the poor, immigrants, and African-Americans had dramatically different experiences from the more affluent. Beneath the suburban calm, contradictions in women's lives, cultural rebellion among youth and intellectuals, and protests by African-Americans in the South, laid the foundations for significant social change in the future.

THE POSTWAR CAPITALIST ECONOMY

By the end of 1945, war-induced prosperity had made the United States the richest country in the world. Over the next two decades the gross national product expanded dramatically, rising from $213 billion in 1945 to more than $500 billion in 1960; in 1970 it approached $1 trillion. During this period, real wages rose steadily, and inflation remained low, providing a sense of security and progress to the majority of Americans. In the largest manufacturing industries, industrial workers won acceptance of their unions, and with it rising incomes, expanding benefits, and a growing rate of suburban home ownership. Affluence was so much a part of American culture in 1945 that a high standard of living characterized by an apparently endless array of consumer goods seemed inseparable from the basic freedoms guaranteed by the nation's political institutions. The "American way of life" became a crucial part of the cold war rhetoric the United States employed against the perceived communist menace.

This prosperity was, however, unevenly distributed. The rising standard of living was not accompanied by a redistribution of income; the top 10 percent of Americans still earned more than the lowest 50 percent. At the bottom of the economic ladder remained the permanently unemployed, the aged who subsisted on Social Security, female heads of households, and most nonwhites. In 1957 nearly one in four Americans lived below the official poverty line. Despite these limits, the period's economic expansion benefited a wider segment of society than anyone would have dreamed possible in the dark days of the depression. With economic growth underwritten by the federal government's outlays for defense and domestic programs, by exuberant consumer spending, and by the nation's powerful position in the international economy, Americans expected that abundance would be permanent, and that poverty would eventually be eradicated.

Sources of Affluence

The United States enjoyed overwhelming economic and political advantages at the end of World War II. Unlike the Soviet Union, Western Europe, and Japan, America emerged from the war physically unscathed, ready to build upon wartime mobilization to fashion postwar economic success. Manufacturers quickly applied the scientific and technological innovations that had been developed for military purposes to peacetime products, such as plastics and synthetic fibers. Consumers, released from wartime rationing and shortages, were eager to spend their $140 billion in accumulated savings. They provided a booming market for new housing and a rich array of consumer goods.

The nation also emerged from the war in an unprecedentedly powerful position internationally. The period from World War II through the late 1960s and the early 1970s witnessed the heyday of modern American capitalism. America's global economic supremacy stemmed in part from institutions created at a United Nations conference at Bretton Woods, New Hampshire, in 1944. The International Bank for Reconstruction and Development (known commonly as the World Bank) provided private loans for the reconstruction of war-torn Europe, as well as for the development of Third World countries. The International Monetary Fund (IMF), designed to stabilize the value of currencies, helped to guide the world economy after the war. Backed by the United States' money and influence, these international organizations tended to favor American-style internationalism over the economic nationalism traditional in most other countries. The result was stable prices, a flexible domestic market, a powerful American dollar, and reduced tariffs and trade barriers—all of which served the United States' global economic interests.

In addition to its global economic and political power, the United States was also a major military presence in the new world order. Defense spending was an important source of the nation's postwar prosperity. Between 1900 and 1930, except for the two years the United States fought in World War I, the country had spent less than 1 percent of its GNP for military purposes. By the early 1960s the figure was close to 10 percent, reflecting a dramatic shift in national priorities. Under the government-business partnership that President Eisenhower dubbed the military-industrial complex, the Defense department evolved into a massive bureaucracy that profoundly influenced the economy. Companies such as Boeing and Lockheed did so much business with the government that they became dependent on Defense department orders.

At the same time, science, corporate capitalism, and the federal government became increasingly intertwined. Federal money underwrote 90 percent of the cost of aviation and space research, and also subsidized the scientific instruments, automobile, and electronics industries. With the government footing part of the bill, corporations developed new products with unprecedented speed. After the Pentagon backed IBM's investment in integrated circuits in the 1960s, which were crucial to the computer revolution, the new devices went into commercial production in just three years.

The defense buildup brought mixed blessings. In positive terms, it created jobs: perhaps as many as one in seven Americans owed his or her job to the military-industrial complex in the 1960s. In the South and the West, where much of the new military activity was concentrated, dependence on defense spending was even greater (see Map 29.1, following page). But, even while increased spending put money in the pockets of millions of people, it limited the resources available for domestic needs. Critics of military spending calculated the trade-offs: the cost of a nuclear aircraft carrier and support ships equaled that of a subway system for Washington, D.C.; the money spent on one Huey helicopter matched the cost of sixty-six units of low-income housing.

Besides stimulating the economy, the expansion of the military-industrial complex hastened the concentration of power. Both the federal government and corporations became larger and more complex in these years. The predominant

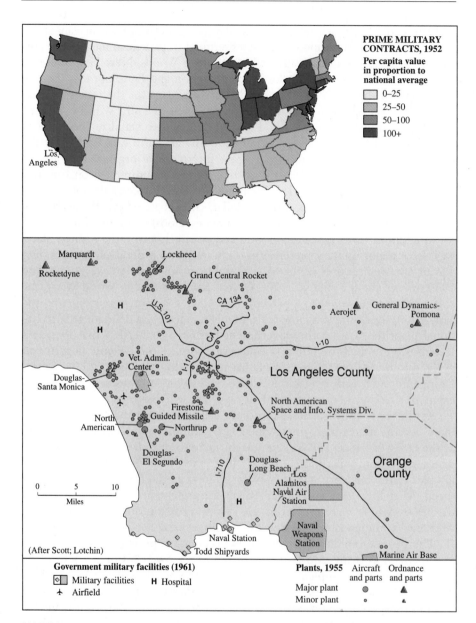

MAP 29.1

The Military-Industrial Complex in Los Angeles

The development and expansion of military facilities and defense contracting during the Cold War helped boost the populations and economies of Los Angeles and other Sun Belt cities and made the economies of some states highly dependent on defense expenditures.

trend of corporate business after 1945 continued to be the consolidation of economic and financial resources by oligopolies—a few large producers who controlled the national market, and increasingly, the world market. In 1970, for example, the top four American firms produced 91 percent of the motor vehicles sold in the domestic market.

Large firms maintained their dominance by turning to diversification. The typical corporation of the early twentieth century had produced a single line of products; its growth therefore depended on the vertical integration of related firms (see Chapter 18). After World War II, however, the most successful corporations invested heavily in research and development, produced new product lines, and moved into new markets. The Columbia Broadcasting System (CBS), for example, patented more than a hundred new devices, including a color television during the 1940s, long-playing records in the 1950s, and a video recording system in the 1960s.

Postwar managers also diversified through mergers and acquisitions, creating larger firms called *conglomerates*. International Telephone and Telegraph became a diversified conglomerate by acquiring companies in unrelated industries, including Continental Baking, Sheraton Hotels, Avis Rent-a-Car, Levitt and Sons home builders, and Hartford Fire Insurance. This pattern of corporate acquisition developed into a great wave of mergers that peaked in the 1960s.

The development of giant corporations also depended on the penetration of foreign markets. American products were considered the best in the world, and thus were widely sought after abroad. When domestic markets became saturated or recessions cut into sales, American companies adopted international strategies and turned to foreign markets. During the 1950s U.S. exports nearly doubled, producing a trade surplus of close to $5 billion in 1960, and contributing significantly to American prosperity.

The Changing World of Work

Changes in corporate structure had a powerful impact on the nature of work. Increasingly, Americans spent their workdays as part of a large bureaucracy. Since the late nineteenth century, the proportion of Americans employed in the service sector—as professionals, clerical workers, salespeople, civil servants, and other service workers—had grown steadily, while the proportion of blue-collar workers and the self-employed had declined. Industrial mobilization had temporarily halted this trend during World War II, but the growth of the service sector resumed dramatically in the postwar era to meet employers' new demands.

One of the fastest-growing groups was salaried office workers. From 1947 to 1957 the number of persons in that occupational category increased by 61 percent, while the number of factory workers decreased by 4 percent. Corporate bureaucracies also recruited increasing numbers of top executives with business-school training in information management, corporate planning, marketing, and investment. Finally, the GI Bill, which increased the public's access to college education, helped to expand the white-collar ranks.

Organization Men (and a Few Women)
The commute from home in the suburbs to corporate office in the city and back again became a weekday ritual for millions of white-collar workers in the postwar era. William H. Whyte's appropriately titled book *The Organization Man* (1956) explored the transformation of the nature of work and its impact on middle-class men who eagerly worked their way up the corporate ladder.

In the giant bureaucracies—big business, government agencies, universities, and the military—young, predominantly male college graduates used their skills to work their way up through the career ladder. To do so they had to be able to get along in a variety of situations. Corporate managers worked hard, sometimes with the assistance of the resident corporate psychologist, to become "well adjusted." Critics worried that the experience of marching off each day in gray flannel suits to work at interchangeable middle-management jobs in huge corporations was stifling men's creativity. In a best-selling book, the sociologist William Whyte painted a somber picture of "the organization man" who left home "spiritually as well as physically to take the vows of organization life."

But the popular obsession with the middle-class organization man obscured other significant changes in the postwar work force. Many of the new white-collar workers earned salaries that were lower than the total hourly wages of unionized blue-collar workers, and their jobs were as boring and repetitive as factory work. As one American Telephone and Telegraph (AT&T) operator explained in describing her routinized and carefully monitored work, "You've got a clock next to you that times every second." Millions of new service workers were blue-collar laborers who earned hourly wages toiling under factorylike conditions in laundries, restaurants, and other businesses.

Many of the new service workers were female: twice as many women worked outside the home in 1960 as in 1940. Occupational segmentation remained the norm; more than 80 percent of all working women did stereo-typical "women's work" as salespersons, health-care technicians, waitresses, domestic servants, telephone operators, and secretaries. In fact, until 1964, the classified sections of most newspapers separated employment ads into columns headed "Help Wanted Male" and "Help Wanted Female." All women had limited access to the professions. Nonwhite and working-class women were largely confined to a low-paying "pink-collar" ghetto that offered jobs in restaurants, hotels, hospitals, and beauty salons. Along with these women's jobs went women's pay, which averaged 60 percent of men's in 1963.

The changing composition of the work force and the shifting nature of work posed difficult challenges for the labor movement. The postwar era witnessed the high point of organized labor and the beginning of its decline. Unions peaked in strength around the end of World War II, when they represented over 35 percent of the nonfarm work force. They remained strong and politically influential through the 1960s, despite the limits imposed by the Taft-Hartley Act in 1947 (see Chapter 28). The strength of the labor movement in this period stemmed partly from its structural unity. In 1955 Walter P. Reuther of the United Auto Workers led the Congress of Industrial Organizations (CIO) back into a formal alliance with the American Federation of Labor (AFL). That merger created a single organization, the AFL-CIO, that represented more than 90 percent of the nation's 17.5 million union members. George Meany, a New York building-trades unionist, headed the organization for the next 24 years.

New priorities shaped labor-management relations after the war. Concerned about inflation and increased levels of consumption, unions demanded higher wages as their share of postwar prosperity. The contracts they negotiated gave many workers secure and steadily rising incomes, often with a cost-of-living adjustment, or COLA. In exchange, union leaders promised labor peace and stability, that is, fewer strikes. In return for higher wages and fringe benefits, workers for the most part put aside their traditional demand for control over the pace and duration of work and allowed technologically minded managers to exert increasing control over workers' lives on the job.

One serious challenge to workers' welfare came from new technology. Long a problem for skilled workers, mechanization in the 1950s began to affect the jobs of unskilled and semiskilled factory workers as well. The Ford Motor Company, for example, introduced automatic drilling machines at a Cleveland engine plant in 1952, in the process reducing to 41 a crew that formerly numbered 117. Thousands of workers lost their jobs in steel manufacturing, coal mining, automobile assembly, and other rapidly automating industries.

With the reduction in the number of manufacturing jobs, organized labor had to look elsewhere for new recruits. Large sectors of the work force remained unorganized in the postwar era, including the lower-skilled, lower-paying service and agricultural sectors, in which workers were often black or Latino, and the female-dominated field of office work. Although unions had only minimal success in organizing these groups, they were more effective in recruiting workers in large bureaucratic organizations such as government, health care, and education. Organizers made few gains in the small, scattered service operations where many of the lowest-paid workers toiled, and could not break the hold of antiunion forces in the South. By the mid-1950s the labor movement had stalled; union membership has declined steadily ever since.

The agricultural sector also changed markedly in the postwar years, as new technologies and an expanding corporate presence transformed farm work. In 1945 the nation's farm population accounted for 17.5 percent of the total population; by 1970 it had declined to less than 5 percent. These figures represented the culmination of a long-term trend away from family farming and toward large-scale agribusiness. New technology contributed to an astonishing increase in agricultural productivity after 1945, but it also required major capital investments. Between 1940 and 1955, the cost of fuel, fertilizer, and repairs for farm machines quadrupled, and total operating costs tripled. Family farms often lacked the capital to compete with large, technologically advanced agribusiness. Many farm families left the land in these years.

Those farmers who remained managed specialized organizations that were much like small factories. They relied on industry for fertilizer, feed, seed, and pesticides and for the fuel to run an expanding array of gasoline-powered equipment. They became increasingly dependent on national and international market conditions, scientific and technological developments, and federal farm policies such as loans and subsidies. The fuller integration of farmers into the national economy, and the diminishing number of Americans who farmed for a living greatly reduced the differences between rural and urban life.

A SUBURBAN SOCIETY

As the steady decline of the family farm indicates, Americans had been gravitating toward urban areas in large numbers throughout the twentieth century. In the postwar period, the urbanization process displayed two new patterns: a shift away from older cities in the Northeast and the Midwest, and toward newer urban centers in the South and the West; and a mass defection from the cities to the suburbs. Both processes were stimulated by the dramatic growth of a car culture and the federal government's increased promotion of economic expansion.

The Building of Suburbia

At the end of World War II many cities were surrounded by pastures and working farms. Just five or ten years later they were ringed by tract housing, factories, and shopping centers. By 1960 more Americans—particularly whites—lived in suburbs than in cities.

People flocked to the suburbs in part because they offered available housing. Very little new construction had been undertaken during the depression and the war years; as a result, returning veterans and their families faced a critical housing shortage. The difficulty was partly resolved by an innovative building contractor named Arthur Levitt, who applied mass production techniques

The Suburban Boom
Hundreds of thousands of World War II veterans took advantage of low-interest loans under the G.I. Bill to purchase new homes in suburban subdivisions like this one in Los Angeles's San Fernando Valley. (Huntington Library, San Marino, California, Whittington Collection)

to home construction. Levitt's company could build 150 homes per week, a rate of one every sixteen minutes. A basic four-room house, complete with kitchen appliances and an attic that could be converted into two additional bedrooms, was priced at less than $10,000 in 1947. Other developers soon followed suit in subdivisions all over the country, hastening the exodus from the farm and central city.

Many families financed their homes with mortgages from the Federal Housing Administration (FHA) or the Veterans Administration (VA), at rates dramatically lower than those of private lenders. In 1955 the two agencies wrote 41 percent of all nonfarm mortgages. Such lending demonstrated the quiet yet revolutionary way in which the federal government was beginning to influence citizens' daily lives.

The new suburban homes—and much of the savings and loan and Veterans Administration money—were reserved almost exclusively for whites. Many communities adopted covenants prohibiting occupation "by members of other than the Caucasian Race." Though the Supreme Court had ruled restrictive covenants illegal in *Shelley v. Kraemer* (1948), the custom continued informally until the civil rights laws of the 1960s banned private discrimination.

While observers often portrayed suburbia as a homogeneous place, strong cultural and class differences often separated suburban neighborhoods. When firefighters, machine-tool makers, and sales clerks moved to the suburbs, they were far more likely to move to a modest Levittown than to an upper-middle-class suburb such as Winnetka, Illinois, or Shaker Heights, Ohio. Though most African-Americans were shut out of white suburbs, some established their own communities, such as Lincoln Heights outside Cincinnati and Kinloch near St. Louis. For many different groups of Americans, then, the suburbs offered the ultimate postwar dream of giving every child "an opportunity to grow up with grass stains on his pants."

The Automobile Culture

Automobiles and highways were essential both to suburban growth and to the development of the "Sun Belt" states of the South and the West. Rapidly expanding cities in these regions became dependent upon motor vehicles rather than upon the mass transit systems typical of the North and the Midwest. Suburbanites throughout the country needed cars to get to work and to take their children to school and piano lessons. In 1945 Americans owned 25 million cars; by 1965 the number had tripled to 75 million. As the car culture that first emerged in the 1920s expanded dramatically in the 1950s, cars—extravagant gas guzzlers with elaborate tail fins and ostentatious chrome detail—became symbols of status and success.

More cars required more highways, which were funded largely by the federal government. In 1947 Congress authorized the construction of 37,000 miles of highways; in 1956 the National Interstate and Defense Highway Act increased that commitment by another 42,500 miles. One of the largest civil engineering projects in world history, the new interstate system would link the entire country with roads at least four lanes wide. The interstate highway promoted both urban and suburban development while altering the nation's topography. It rerouted traffic through rural areas, creating artificial communities of gas stations, fast-food outlets, and motels at its cloverleaf exchanges. In urban areas, new highways cut wide swaths through old neighborhoods. Cities were soon plagued by air pollution and traffic jams, and critics complained of "autosclerosis"—a hardening of the urban arteries.

Highway construction had far-reaching effects on everyday life. Federally funded highways siphoned funding away from mass transit, contributing to an increasing dependency on the automobile. By 1960 two-thirds of Americans drove to work each day. Instead of taking a train into the city or walking to a corner grocery store, people hopped into their cars and drove to fast-growing suburban supermarkets and shopping malls. Although the first mall had appeared in the 1920s, in 1945 there were only 8; by 1960 the number had risen to almost 4,000. A 110-store complex that opened at Roosevelt Field on suburban Long Island in 1956 was conveniently situated at an expressway exit and boasted parking space for 11,000 cars. As the suburbs, highways, and the car culture transformed the nation's commercial and physical landscape, downtown retail areas and department stores declined.

Few cities are more closely identified with shopping malls, freeways, and automobiles than Los Angeles. That city, like others in the Sun Belt, witnessed remarkable growth after the war (see Map 29.2). Corporate expansion, often underwritten by the federal government's defense spending, brought new prosperity to states such as Texas, Florida, and California, while the highway system helped to integrate them into the nation's economic system and facilitate urban development. Between 1940 and 1970, Miami's metropolitan population increased by 79 percent with the addition of more than a million new residents, many of them older or retired. Cities in Texas, especially Houston and Dallas, grew as the petrochemical industry expanded after 1945. In California, the burgeoning defense industry in the Los Angeles, San Francisco, and San Diego metropolitan areas produced dramatic growth. California added 2.6 million people in the 1940s and 3.1 million more in the 1950s, until by 1970 the state claimed about a tenth of the U.S. population.

Business boosters in California and other Sun Belt states worked tirelessly to promote regional development. Local leaders lobbied for new defense contracts and installations, and successfully wooed professional sports teams like

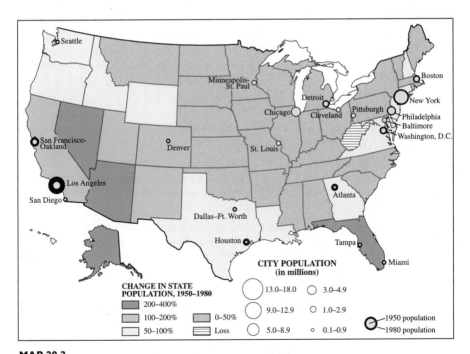

MAP 29.2
Metropolitan Growth, 1950–1980
Since the U.S. Census Bureau changed its definition of a Standard Metropolitan Statistical Area (SMSA) after 1950, it is difficult to chart urban growth precisely. This map compares the population of central cities in 1950 with population figures for the more broadly defined metropolitan areas in 1980 to illustrate the extent and geographical distribution of metropolitan growth in the postwar period.

the Brooklyn Dodgers, who relocated to Los Angeles in 1958. To attract new residents, promoters touted their region's sunny climate, attractive scenery, and relaxed lifestyles. In subsequent decades, however, the success of Sun Belt cities would create problems. Booming urban populations brought more crime and poverty, problems formerly associated with cities in the Northeast. In the West, the increasing demand for water and energy caused environmental and health problems. For example, the nuclear weapons industry, which brought jobs and income, also brought radiation contamination to residents near atomic test sites, nuclear waste facilities, and uranium mines. In the West, as elsewhere, postwar development often carried a significant social cost.

At the time, few Americans understood that trade-offs were involved in the postwar economic boom. With a strong economic position internationally and government spending to help fuel expansion at home, Americans expected an unending trajectory of progress. Their faith produced complacency—an unwillingness to look beneath the surface for the hidden implications of the forces that were transforming America.

AMERICAN SOCIETY DURING THE BABY BOOM

A term often associated with the fifties was "consensus," meaning conformity to social norms, authority, and the status quo. "Consensus" embodied the ideal that Americans could live in harmony, without social class or political conflicts. While this prevailing attitude stemmed in part from widespread affluence, it also expressed a fervent desire for stability in a period of rapid change.

In a search for tranquility—an escape from the pressures of the Cold War, the bomb, and the corporate rat race—many white middle-class Americans turned inward to the private satisfactions of home, family, and consumption. Newly married couples flocked to the suburbs, where they had more children than Americans had borne at any time since 1920. They joined the PTA, swelled church membership rosters, and raised their families in a climate of affluence, consumption, and conformity that set the tone for the period.

The Consumer Culture

In the corporate world, where work was becoming more routinized and less satisfying for both blue- and white-collar workers, consumer goods and leisure time took on growing importance as sources of meaning and pleasure. The general prosperity of the postwar period meant that even working-class families had discretionary income to spend on products such as washing machines, dryers, and the latest model car. Americans were able to stretch their rising incomes further by taking advantage of the dramatic increase in consumer credit. Between 1946 and 1958, short-term consumer credit rose from $8.4 billion to almost $45 billion. The Diners Club introduced the first credit card in 1950; by the 1970s the ubiquitous plastic credit card had revolution-ized personal and family finances.

Aggressive advertising contributed to the massive increase in consumer spending. In 1951 businesses spent more on advertising ($6.5 billion) than taxpayers did on primary and secondary education ($5 billion). The 1950s gave Americans the Marlboro man; M&M's ("They melt in your mouth, not in your hand"); the ballpoint pen that "writes under water"; and the "does she or doesn't she?" Clairol woman. Motivational researchers delved into the sub-conscious to determine what needs consumption filled and how the advertis-ing messages should be pitched. In general, the ads of the period reflected an uncritical view of American life, and suggested falsely that all Americans were white and middle class, all women were homemakers, and all families were nuclear and intact.

Consumers had more free time in which to spend their money than ever before. In 1960 the average worker put in a five-day week, with eight paid holidays a year (double the 1946 standard) plus a two-week paid vacation. Americans took to the interstate highway system by the millions, encouraging dramatic growth in motel chains, roadside restaurants, and fast-food eateries. (The first McDonald's restaurant opened in 1954 in San Bernardino, Califor-nia; the Holiday Inn motel chain started in Memphis in 1952.) Among the most popular destinations were national and state parks and Disneyland, which opened in Anaheim, California, in 1955.

Perhaps the most significant hallmark of the postwar consumer culture was television. TV quickly supplanted radio and movies as the chief diffuser of popular taste and values. By 1960, 87 percent of American families owned at least one television set. What Americans saw on television, be-sides the omnipresent commercials, was an overwhelmingly white middle-class world of nuclear families in suburban homes. "Father Knows Best," "Leave It to Beaver," "I Love Lucy," and similar sitcoms featured characters who adhered to clear-cut gender roles and plots based on small family crises that were always happily resolved by the end of the half-hour. Shows such as "The Honeymooners," starring Jackie Gleason as a Brooklyn bus driver, were rare in their treatment of working-class lives. Nonwhite char-acters appeared mainly as servants, such as Jack Benny's Rochester or the Latino gardener with the anglicized name "Frank Smith" on "Father Knows Best."

In addition to family sitcoms, Americans watched quiz shows such as "The $64,000 Question," and westerns such as "Gunsmoke"and "Bonanza" (the first TV show in color). National television coverage made professional sports into a big business with a potential far exceeding that of radio. Pro-gramming geared to children, such as "Captain Kangaroo" and Walt Disney's "Mickey Mouse Club" attracted the first generation of children to grow up glued to the tube. Although the new medium did offer some serious pro-gramming, notably live theater and documentaries, Newton Minow, head of the Federal Communications Commission, concluded in 1963 that television was "a vast wasteland." Its reassuring images of family life and postwar society, however, dovetailed with many Americans' social expectations.

The Search for Security: Religion and the Family

The dislocations of the depression and war years made Americans yearn for security and a reaffirmation of traditional values. Some of this sentiment was expressed in a renewed emphasis on religion. Church membership rose from 49 percent of the population in 1940 to 69 percent in 1960. All the major denominations shared in the growth, which was accompanied by an ecumenical movement to bring Catholics, Protestants, and Jews together. The stress on religious harmony meshed with cold war Americans' definition of themselves as a righteous people opposed to "godless communism." In 1956 Congress added "In God We Trust" to coins, and in 1954, the phrase "under God" was inserted into the Pledge of Allegiance. In the same year, President Dwight D. Eisenhower insisted that American government "makes no sense unless it is founded on a deeply felt religious faith—and I don't care what it is."

Beyond patriotism, religion also served more deep-felt needs. In his popular television program, Bishop Fulton Sheen asked, "Is life worth living?"— a question he and countless other leaders optimistically answered in the affirmative. None was more positive than Norman Vincent Peale, whose book *The Power of Positive Thinking* (1952) embodied the trend toward the therapeutic use of religion to assist men and women in coping with the stresses of modern life.

At the same time evangelical religion experienced a resurgence, most evident in the dramatic rise to popularity of the Reverend Billy Graham, who used television, radio, advertising, and print media to spread the gospel. His nondenominational Evangelistic Association, founded in 1950, was a tremendous success. Graham appealed to conservative Protestants within the major denominations. Formerly marginal churches such as the Jehovah's Witnesses and the Seventh Day Adventists also enjoyed spectacular growth in this period. Although critics suggested that middle-class interest in religion stemmed more from conformity than spirituality, the revival nonetheless spoke to Americans' search for spiritual meaning in uncertain times.

Even more dramatic testimony to the desire for stability in the postwar era was the emphasis Americans placed on the family and children. As one popular advice book put it, "The family is the center of your living. If it isn't, you've gone far astray." The families formed between 1940 and 1960 had a noteworthy demographic impact. Marriages were remarkably stable; not until the mid-1960s did the divorce rate begin to rise sharply. But the average age at marriage fell during the period, to twenty-two for men and twenty for women. In 1951 a third of all women were married by age nineteen. More important, the drop in the average age at marriage resulted in a surge of young married couples who produced a bumper crop of children. After a century and a half of declining family size, the birth rate shot up: more babies were born between 1948 and 1953 than had been born in the previous thirty years. As a result of this trend and a lengthened life expectancy due to improvements in diet, public health, and medicine, the American population rose dramatically from 140 million in 1945 to 179 million in 1960, and then to 203 million in 1970.

To rear all these baby-boom children and keep them healthy, middle-class parents increasingly relied on the advice of experts. Accepting the advice of doctors and the federal government, they had their children inoculated with the Salk polio vaccine, administered free in the nation's schools. Parents also bought millions of copies of Dr. Benjamin Spock's *Baby and Child Care*—one million in just the first year after its publication in 1946. New mothers found Spock's insistence that they abandon the rigid feeding and baby care schedules of an earlier generation liberating, though the book did not remove all their insecurities. If a mother was too protective of her children, Spock and others warned, she might hamper their adjustment to a normal adult life.

The baby boom had a broad and immediate impact on American society. It prompted a major expansion of the nation's educational system: by 1970, school expenditures were double those of the 1950 level. In addition, babies' consumer needs fueled the economy as families bought food, diapers, toys, and clothing for their expanding broods. Together with federal expenditures on national security, family spending on consumer goods fueled the unparalleled prosperity and economic growth of the 1950s and 1960s.

The parents of baby boomers experienced multiple economic and social pressures. In addition to providing for their children materially and emotionally, they were expected to adhere to rigid gender roles as a way of maintaining the family and undergirding the social order. The mass media, educators, and experts urged men to conform to a masculine ideal that emphasized their role as responsible breadwinners; women's proper place, they advised, was in the home. What Betty Friedan has called the "feminine mystique" of the 1950s—the ideal that "the highest value and the only commitment for women is the fulfillment of their own femininity"—bore a remarkable similarity to the nineteenth-century cult of true womanhood. However, the 1950s version of the cult of domesticity drew on twentieth-century science and culture, and even on Freudian psychology. Psychologists pronounced motherhood the only "normal" female sex role, and berated mothers who worked outside the home, charging that they damaged their children's development. Television, popular music, films, and advertising all reinforced that notion by depicting career women as social and sexual misfits.

Though the power of these ideas stunted the lives of many women, not all housewives were unhappy or neurotic, as Friedan would later charge in her

---

The power of the feminine mystique in the 1950s made it difficult for middle-class women who challenged the view that women's proper place was in the home. In this oral history account, "Sylvia" describes her struggle to pursue a career as an ophthalmologist.

We sat on a bench in the middle of the lobby there—I remember it looked like a train station—and he [her professor] said, "Do you plan to get pregnant or married?" I promised him I wouldn't do either. I felt like I was about ten years old. They gave me a year's trial in the research department and after that I could get a residency. Most people there, the men, had a three-year residency. I was only the second woman they'd ever accepted, and I was the only woman out of twenty men.

I had a fellowship, so when I finished with my work I'd have to go over to see how my research projects were coming along. I never, never, goofed off. These guys were watching me all the time and complaining that I wasn't doing my work. It was hard enough to be a first-year resident, where you're the bottom person who gets kicked by everybody. I had no friends. My fellow physicians were constantly telling me I should switch to obstetrics or pediatrics, I should be home having babies, that a man could earn a wonderful living for his family in my place. Finally I was at my wits' end and I called my old ophthalmology professor and told him I didn't know if I could psychologically take this for another two and a half years. He said, "You know, if you give up now I'll never be able to get another woman in there." So I went on.

SOURCE: Brett Harvey, *The Fifties: A Women's Oral History* (New York: Harper, 1993), pp. 154–155.

1963 bestseller, *The Feminine Mystique*. Many working-class women embraced their new roles as housewives; unlike their mothers and unmarried sisters, they were not compelled to take low-paid employment outside the home. But not all Americans could or did live by the norms of suburban domesticity, ideals that were out of reach of or irrelevant to many racial minorities, inner-city residents, recent immigrants, rural Americans, and homosexuals. At the height of the postwar period, more than one-third of American women held jobs outside the home. The increase in the number of working women coincided with another change of equal significance—a dramatic rise in the number of older, married middle-class women who took jobs. Once again there was a significant gap between popular culture and the reality of American lives.

How could the society of the 1950s cling so steadfastly to the domestic ideal while an increasing number of wives and mothers took jobs? Often women justified their jobs as an extension of their family responsibilities. Their paid labor allowed their families to enjoy more of the fruits of the consumer culture. Because women who took jobs outside the home still bore full responsibility for child care and household management, their families and society as a whole could avoid facing the implications of their new roles. Thus the reality of women's lives departed significantly from the cultural stereotypes glorified in advertising, sitcoms, and women's magazines. As one overburdened woman complained, she now had "two full-time jobs instead of just one—underpaid clerical worker and unpaid housekeeper."

Cultural Dissenters

Beneath the surfaces of family togetherness lay other tensions. Teenagers, especially white middle-class teenagers, had become the basis of a distinct new market that advertisers eagerly exploited. In 1956 advertisers projected an adolescent market worth $9 billion for items such as transistor radios (first introduced in 1952), clothing, and fads such as Silly Putty (1950) and Hula-Hoops (1958). Less innocuous to anxious parents were the consumer choices that teens made in books, movies, and music—choices that suggested they were rebelling against the safe and insulated suburban world their parents had worked so hard to create.

Hollywood movies played a large role in fostering and legitimizing the teenage subculture. Recognizing that young people were the largest audience for motion pictures, the studios catered to them with films such as *The Wild One* (1954), starring Marlon Brando, and *Rebel Without a Cause* (1955), starring James Dean, Natalie Wood, and Sal Mineo. "What are you rebelling against?" a waitress asked Brando in *The Wild One*. "Whattaya got?" he replied.

What really defined this generation, however, was its music. Rejecting the rigidly defined categories of traditional popular music, the teenagers of the 1950s discovered rock-'n'-roll, an amalgam of white country and western music and the black urban sound known as rhythm and blues. Young white performers such as Bill Haley, Elvis Presley, and Buddy Holly incorporated the new mixture into their own music to capitalize on the new teen market. Between 1953 and 1959, record sales increased from $213 million to $603 million, with 45-rpm rock-'n'-roll records as the driving force.

For many white youths, Elvis Presley represented the epitome of their new music. But Presley's success was based not only on his music but on his stage presence and his relationship with the audience. With his slicked-back hair, long sideburns, and tight pants, Presley cultivated a lower-class "greaser" look that proved immensely popular with teenage fans. His quivering legs, gyrating pelvis, and playful sneer drove young female fans wild; they frequently mobbed the stage, grabbing at his clothes for souvenirs.

African-Americans found Presley's success and notoriety somewhat ironic. Black musicians such as Chuck Berry had been performing similar music for

Elvis Presley
The young Elvis Presley (shown here on the cover of his first album in
1956) embodied cultural rebellion against the conservatism of adult life in
the 1950s.

years but with little commercial success among white audiences. To many, the
appropriation of black rhythm and blues by white artists was out-and-out
theft. In the long run, however, the popularity of rock-'n'-roll introduced
black performers such as Little Richard, Fats Domino, and James Brown to
white as well as black audiences.

Many white adults were appalled at the teen subculture. They saw in rock-
'n'-roll music, teen movies, and magazines such as *Mad* (introduced in 1952)
an invitation to race mixing, rebellion, and disorder. Playing on their fears, the
media featured hundreds of stories on problem teens. In 1955 a Senate sub-
committee conducted a high-profile investigation of juvenile delinquency,
blaming its origins on the popular media. Adult denunciations of the youth
culture, however, only increased its popularity among teens.

The youth rebellion was only one aspect of a broader undercurrent of
discontent with the conformist culture of the 1950s. Postwar artists, jazz musicians, and writers also expressed their alienation from mainstream society
through intensely personal, introspective art forms. In New York, Jackson
Pollock and other painters rejected the social realism of the 1930s, creating

an unconventional style that became known as abstract expressionism. Swirling and splattering paint onto giant canvases, Pollock emphasized self-expression in the act of painting, capturing the chaotic atmosphere of the nuclear age. A similar trend developed in jazz as black musicians originated a hard-driving improvisational style known as bebop. Whether the "hot" bebop of the 1940s, invented by saxophonist Charlie Parker, or the more subdued "cool" West Coast sound of the 1950s, epitomized by the trumpeter Miles Davis, postwar jazz was cerebral, intimate, and individualistic.

Black jazz musicians found eager fans not only in the African-American community, but among young white *beats* in New York and San Francisco. Beat writers and poets experimented stylistically, bringing innovation and exuberance to their works. Their messages were equally brash, as they critiqued middle-class conformity, suburban materialism, and corporate capitalism. Allen Ginsberg, in his poem *Howl* (1956), criticized the sterility of modern culture, railing against "Robot apartments! invisible suburbs! skeleton treasures! blind capitals! demonic industries!" The beats also warned against the menace of nuclear weaponry. In "Bomb" (1960), a powerful poem punctuated with lines like "Boom Boom Boom Boom," Gregory Corso called the bomb "toy of the universe."

The beats glorified spontaneity, sexual adventurism, drug use, and spirituality. In his semiautobiographical novel *On the Road* (1957), Jack Kerouac described a journey across America by his main characters—Sal Paradise and Dean Moriarity. In search of "authentic," genuine, experience, the two men often thought they found it among African-Americans or Latinos. They found black music especially exhilarating. But Kerouac's fascination with people of color could easily slip into stereotyping them as primitive. In one passage, Sal Paradise exclaimed that he walked through Denver, "wishing I were a Negro, feeling that the best the white world had offered was not enough for men, not enough life, joy, kicks, darkness, music." He wished he were a "Denver Mexican or a poor overworked Jap, anything but what I was so drearily, a white 'man' disillusioned. . . . I was only myself . . . wishing I could exchange words with the happy, true-hearted, ecstatic Negroes of America."

In his depiction of women, Kerouac also revealed the cultural biases of the society he so roundly criticized. Like other beats, he glorified sexuality, in the process often viewing women as conquests. In *On the Road*, when women became wives or mothers, they were looked upon as hindrances to the male characters' search for liberation. Almost all the well-known beat writers were male, and at least part of their rebellion focused on the circumscribed life of the organization man, on the rigid gender roles that locked men into the rat race of the breadwinner.

Important as literary innovators, the beats were also significant as outspoken social critics. Although they were apolitical—their rebellion was strictly cultural—in the 1960s they would inspire a new generation of rebels who would champion both political and cultural change.

THE OTHER AMERICA

Youth and intellectuals were not the only challengers to the status quo; many other groups lived outside the mainstream of American society. As middle-class whites flocked to the suburbs, poor and working-class migrants and immigrants, many of them nonwhite, moved into the central cities. With jobs and financial resources flowing to the suburbs, urban newcomers inherited a declining economy and a decaying environment. This "other America" remained largely invisible to affluent white suburbanites. Only in the South, where African-Americans organized to combat legal segregation, did the problem of social injustice come to the public's attention.

Postwar Immigration

Newly arrived immigrants were one of several groups that moved into the nation's cities in the postwar era. Until 1965 American immigration policy followed the restrictive quota system set up in 1924 (see Chapter 24). But during World War II and its cold war aftermath Congress slightly loosened the law for a variety of reasons. In 1948 the Displaced Persons Act admitted approximately 415,000 Europeans, but discriminated against Jews while favoring people of German origins. The Chinese Exclusion Act was repealed in 1943 in a bow to America's wartime alliance with China. And in 1952, at the height of the Cold War, the McCarran-Walter Act ended the exclusion of Japanese, Koreans, and southeast Asians from immigration and naturalization. Congress passed the measure to demonstrate to the world America's commitment to democracy. The act, however, also banned the entry of Communists and other radicals.

Foreign policy shaped immigration priorities in other ways. In 1945 Congress passed the War Brides Act, which allowed the entrance and naturalization of the wives and children of Americans who had lived abroad, mainly servicemen. Approximately 17,000 Koreans entered the United States under this law between 1950 and 1965, the vast majority of them war brides from the Korean War. Finally, in recognition of the freeing of the Philippines from American control on July 4, 1946, Filipinos received their own quota. A major increase in immigration from Asian countries, however, would not occur until after 1965 (see Chapter 30).

One of the largest groups of postwar immigrants came from Mexico. Nearly 275,000 Mexicans entered the United States in the 1950s, and almost 444,000 in the 1960s. They moved primarily to western and southwestern cities such as Los Angeles, Long Beach, El Paso, and Phoenix, where they found jobs as migrant workers or laborers in the expanding service sector. Large numbers of Mexican-Americans also settled in Chicago, Detroit, Kansas City, and Denver.

Part of the stimulus for Mexican immigration came from the reinstitution of the *bracero* program, which the Mexican and American governments had created during the labor shortages of World War II to bring temporary workers to the United States. When the Korean War produced new labor shortages, a new *bracero* program operated from 1951 to 1964. At the program's peak in 1959, 450,000 *braceros* entered the United States, and an estimated 350,000 settled permanently. But even as the federal government welcomed *braceros*, it deported those who stayed on illegally. In response to the recession of 1953–1954, which caused high unemployment throughout the nation, federal authorities deported nearly 4 million Mexicans in a program called "Operation Wetback." For a few years, the level of illegal immigration was reduced, but it rose again after the *bracero* program ended.

Another group of Spanish-speaking immigrants came from the American-controlled territory of Puerto Rico. Residents of that island had been American citizens since 1917, and thus Puerto Ricans were not subject to immigration laws. The inflow from the island increased dramatically after World War II, when mechanization of the island's sugarcane industry pushed many rural Puerto Ricans off the land. When airlines began to offer cheap direct flights between San Juan and New York City, Puerto Ricans became the first group to immigrate by air to the United States. Their massive movement, which grew from 70,000 per year in 1940 to 613,000 just twenty years later, transformed the ethnic composition of New York City. There, they faced conditions common to all recent immigrants: crowded and deteriorating housing, segregation, unemployment or restriction to menial jobs, poor schools, and the challenges of a bilingual existence.

Cuban refugees constituted the third largest group of Spanish-speaking immigrants. In the six years after Fidel Castro's seizure of power in 1959, an estimated 180,000 people fled Cuba for the United States. The Cuban refugee community grew so quickly that it turned Miami into a cosmopolitan, bilingual city almost overnight. Unlike most new immigrants, Cubans prospered, in large part because they brought with them substantial resources. Cubans differed from most other Latino immigrants in that they were predominantly middle class and politically conservative.

Migration to the City

Migration within the United States also brought people to the cities, especially African-Americans, continuing a trend that had begun during World War I (see Chapter 23). Black migration was hastened by the transformation of southern agriculture, especially its mechanization, which reduced the demand for labor. From 1930 to 1960 southern farm population fell from 16.2 million to 5.9 million.

Some of the migrants from the South settled in southern cities, where they found factory jobs. Many whites from Appalachia moved north to "hillbilly" ghettos in cities like Chicago and Cincinnati. In the most dramatic population shift, as many as 3 million black southerners headed to Chicago, New York, Washington, Detroit, Los Angeles, and other cities between 1940 and 1960.

Certain sections of Chicago seemed like the Mississippi Delta transplanted, so pervasive were the migrants. By 1960 about half the nation's black population was living outside the South, compared to only 23 percent before World War II.

In western cities, an influx of native Americans contributed to the rise in the nonwhite urban population. Congress, seeking to end federal involvement in Indian affairs, passed a resolution in 1953 authorizing a program to terminate the legal standing of native tribes and move their members off reservations and into cities. The program, which reflected the cold war preoccupation with conformity and assimilation, enjoyed strong support from mining, timber, and agricultural interests that wanted to open reservation lands for private development. But relocation proved problematic, as many Indians struggled to adjust to an urban environment and culture. Although the policy of forced termination was halted in 1958, by 1960 some 60,000 Indians had moved to the cities. Despite the program's stated goal of assimilation, most native American migrants settled together in poor urban neighborhoods alongside other nonwhite groups.

At the same time that whites were flocking to the suburbs, then, American cities saw their nonwhite populations swell. From 1950 to 1960 the nation's twelve largest cities lost 3.6 million whites and gained 4.5 million nonwhites. Tax revenues followed the more affluent whites out of the city and into the suburbs. A wealthy community such as Grosse Pointe, a suburb of Detroit, could far more easily fund first-rate schools and police than could the city of Detroit, whose tax base shrank as businesses and middle-class residents relocated to the suburbs.

By the time blacks, native Americans, and Latinos moved into the inner cities, urban America was in poor shape. Housing was a crucial problem, which city planners, politicians, and real estate developers responded to by razing blighted neighborhoods to make way for new construction. Local residents were rarely consulted about whether they wanted their neighborhoods "renewed." Urban renewal often produced grim high-rise housing projects that destroyed neighborhoods and created barren open areas vulnerable to crime. In the name of urban renewal, between 1949 and 1967, construction crews demolished almost 400,000 buildings, displacing 1.4 million people. The 575,000 units of new public housing that were built nationwide by 1964 did not begin to satisfy the need for affordable urban housing.

Increasingly, the cities became a place of last resort for the nation's poor. Unlike earlier immigrants, for whom cities had been gateways to social and economic betterment, most inner-city residents of the postwar period faced diminishing opportunities for improvement. Lured by the promise of plentiful jobs, migrants found that many employers had relocated to the suburbs. For those who needed it most, steady employment was out of reach.

Black Activism in the South

The problems of the urban poor were largely invisible to most Americans in the 1950s. But as teenagers' rebellion in musical styles and the beat generation's attack on conformity revealed currents of discontent with the cultural consensus of the period, black Americans in the South were forging a challenge to the racial status quo. Confrontations in cities like Montgomery, Alabama, and Little Rock, Arkansas, shocked white Americans, unsettling their complacency, and forcing their recognition of "other Americans" who lived outside the privileges of the affluent fifties.

Blacks who stayed in the South faced not only urban poverty but legal segregation. In most southern states in the 1950s, whites and blacks could not eat in the same rooms at restaurants and luncheonettes or use the same waiting rooms and toilets at bus and train stations. All forms of public transportation were rigidly segregated by custom or by law. Even drinking fountains were labeled "White" and "Colored."

Beginning with World War II, the National Association for the Advancement of Colored People (NAACP) redoubled its efforts to combat segregation in housing, transportation, and other areas (see Chapter 27). The first significant victory came in 1954, when the Supreme Court handed down its most far-reaching decision in *Brown v. Board of Education of Topeka*. The NAACP's chief legal counsel, Thurgood Marshall, had argued that the segregated schools mandated by the Board of Education in Topeka, Kansas, were inherently unconstitutional, because they stigmatized an entire race, denying black children the "equal protection of the laws" guaranteed by the Fourteenth Amendment. In a unanimous decision announced on May 17, 1954, the Supreme Court agreed with Marshall and overturned the longstanding "separate but equal" doctrine of *Plessy v. Ferguson* (see Chapter 19).

Over the next several years, in response to NAACP suits, the Supreme Court used the *Brown* precedent to overturn segregation in city parks, public beaches, and golf courses; in interstate and intrastate transportation; and in public housing. In the face of these Court decisions, white resistance to integration solidified. In 1956, 101 members of Congress signed the Southern Manifesto, denouncing the *Brown* decision as "a clear abuse of judicial power" and encouraging their constituents to defy it. That same year, 500,000 southerners joined White Citizens' Councils dedicated to blocking school integration and other civil rights measures. Some whites revived old tactics of violence and intimidation, swelling the ranks of the Ku Klux Klan to levels not seen since the 1920s.

In 1957, the Governor of Arkansas, Governor Orval Faubus, defied a federal court order to desegregate Little Rock's Central High School. Faubus called out the National Guard to bar nine black students who were attempting to enroll in the all-white school. After scenes of vicious mobs harassing the determined students aired on television, President Eisenhower reluctantly intervened, sending 1,000 federal troops and 10,000 nationalized members of the Arkansas National Guard to protect the students. Eisenhower thus became the first president since Reconstruction to use federal troops to enforce the rights of blacks.

Integration at Little Rock Angry crowds taunted the nine black students who tried to register in 1957 at the previously all-white Central High School in Little Rock, Arkansas, with chants such as "Two-four-six-eight, we ain't gonna integrate." The court-ordered integration proceeded only after President Eisenhower reluctantly nationalized the Arkansas National Guard.

White resistance to the *Brown* decision, as well as Eisenhower's hesitancy to act in Little Rock, showed that court victories were not enough to overturn segregation. In 1955, a new strategy, nonviolent protest, emerged from one tiny but monumental act of defiance. On December 1, Rosa Parks, a seamstress and a member of the NAACP in Montgomery, Alabama, refused to give up her seat on a city bus to a white man. "I felt it was just something I had to do," Parks stated. She was promptly arrested and charged with violating a local segregation ordinance. When the black community in Montgomery met to discuss the proper response, they turned to the Reverend Martin Luther King, Jr., who had become the pastor at a local church the year before. King endorsed a plan by a Montgomery black women's organization to boycott the city's bus system until it was integrated. For the next 381 days, members of a united black community formed carpools or walked to work. The bus company neared bankruptcy, and downtown stores saw their business decline. But not until the Supreme Court ruled in November 1956 that bus segregation was unconstitutional did the city of Montgomery finally relent, prompting one woman boycotter to proclaim, "My feets is tired, but my soul is rested."

The Montgomery bus boycott catapulted King to national prominence. In 1957, with the Reverend Ralph Abernathy and other southern black clergy, he founded the Southern Christian Leadership Conference (SCLC), based in Atlanta. The black church had long been the center of African-American social and cultural life. Through the SCLC it lent its moral and organizational strength, as well as the voices of its most inspirational preachers, to the civil-rights movement. Black churchwomen flocked to the movement, transferring the skills they had honed through years of church work to the fight for racial change. Soon the SCLC had joined the NAACP as one of the major advocates for racial justice. While the two groups achieved only limited victories in the 1950s, they laid the organizational groundwork for the dynamic civil-rights movement that would emerge in the 1960s.

AMERICAN VOICES

The Montgomery Bus Boycott

During the Montgomery, Alabama, bus boycott of 1955, many blacks walked or—as was the case with many women who worked as maids—received rides from their white employers. Others took advantage of an informal taxi system. Yancey Martin was a college freshman on Christmas vacation when he began driving for the cause.

And so all the guys who were on my street . . . and a group of other folk whose parents had cars, we would all get up in the morning as early as we could. I mean, there were some folk out there who had to leave by six o'clock in order to get to the white lady's kitchen, and many times they were just late getting there. We'd all get up in the morning and we'd drive the route. . . . And what we had to do was we had to know the names of everybody in there or else the police would stop and try to charge you with operating an illegal jitney service. . . . But the police, when they found out what we were doing, they would patrol the bus routes just as much as we would. . . .

We saw the transportation end really kinda being the backbone of the movement because folks had to work and they had to have that little money. . . . So about four or five of us said, "Well, why do we have to go back [to college]? It's important that we get a college education, but it's important that we win this thing now that we've gotten into it. . . . I could not guarantee that my daddy would find somebody who would be able to drive that car every day like I was driving it every day. So I went on and stayed.

SOURCE: Howell Raines, *My Soul Is Rested: Movement Days in the Deep South Remembered* (New York: Penguin, 1985), pp. 58–61.

"The Fifties": The Way We Were?

For many Americans the 1950s represents the norm of American society—a time when families were close-knit and intact, children happy, and the economy flourishing. Despite the fear of nuclear annihilation, Americans were confident in the 1950s that theirs was the strongest country, both economically and morally, in the world. Changes in American family, political, and social life since then are often seen as declines from this ideal.

But perhaps the fifties were not the norm but an aberration—the result of a unique combination of circumstances that could not be sustained. In a 200-year trend toward smaller families, the postwar baby boom was certainly atypical, as was the remarkable stability of marriages. Perhaps the greatest aberration—and the reason the common view of the 1950s as the norm is so misleading—was that the nation's postwar affluence was based on international economic conditions that could not continue indefinitely. Inevitably the war-devastated economies of Japan and West Germany would rebuild, taking advantage of new technology to compete with and eventually challenge American economic supremacy. If Americans regard the economic dominance the nation enjoyed in the 1950s as the norm, any decline in that dominance will appear to be a disturbing loss of American power and economic strength, rather than a return to a more balanced state of affairs.

The stereotypes of the 1950s are misleading, if not downright false, in other ways, too. In our nostalgic memories of suburban affluence, we forget those Americans who did not share equally in the postwar American dream. Many people—displaced factory workers, destitute elderly people, female heads of households, blacks, and Latinos—watched the affluent society from the outside in the fifties, wondering why they were not permitted to share in its bounty. Not until the publication of Michael Harrington's *The Other America* in 1962 did Americans begin to realize that in the richest country in the world, more than a quarter of the population was poor.

In the turbulent decade that followed, the contrast between suburban affluence and the "other America," between the lure of the city for the poor and minorities and the grim reality of its segregated existence, and between a heightened emphasis on domesticity and widening opportunities for women, would spawn protest and change. Amid the booming prosperity of the late 1940s and 1950s, however, these fundamental social and economic contradictions were barely noticed.

CHAPTER 29 TIMELINE

1944	Bretton Woods economic conference World Bank and International Monetary Fund (IMF) founded
1946	Dr. Benjamin Spock, *Baby and Child Care*
1947	Levittown, New York, built
1948	CBS and NBC begin regular television programming
1950	Reverend Billy Graham's Evangelistic Association founded
1953– **1958**	Operation Wetback and Indian termination programs
1954	Polio vaccine developed by Dr. Jonas Salk *Brown v. Board of Education of Topeka, Kansas* First McDonald's opens
1955	AFL and CIO reunited Montgomery bus boycott Disneyland opens in Anaheim, California
1956	Interstate Highway Act Elvis Presley popularizes rock-'n'-roll via television Congress adds "In God We Trust" to coins
1957	Peak of postwar baby boom Jack Kerouac, *On the Road* Eisenhower sends federal troops to protect black students during school desegregation battle in Little Rock, Arkansas Southern Christian Leadership Conference founded
1958	Brooklyn Dodgers move to Los Angeles
1963	California replaces New York as the most populous state Betty Friedan, *The Feminine Mystique*

CHAPTER 30

LIBERAL REFORM AND RADICALISM, 1960–1970

- John Kennedy and the New Frontier
- The Civil-Rights Movement
- Lyndon Johnson and the Great Society
- The Continuing Struggle for Civil Rights

I n his 1961 inaugural address President John Fitzgerald Kennedy challenged a "new generation of Americans" to take responsibility for the future. Kennedy exhorted, "Ask not what your country can do for you, ask what you can do for your country." Over the next decade many young Americans would respond to that sense of mission. As a civil-rights volunteer explained in 1964, "I want to do my part. There's a moral wave building among today's youth, and I intend to catch it."

Ironically, the roots of 1960s activism lay in the tranquil America of the 1950s. Postwar affluence produced a self-assured generation of young middle-class whites optimistic about their ability to cure the nation's social ills. It also reminded African-Americans of the economic and social gap between the races. In the 1960s the baby-boom generation swelled college enrollments, providing recruits for the civil-rights campaign and other student movements, including a revival of feminism. To them, the lofty cold war rhetoric of international freedom and democracy sounded hollow in the face of economic and racial injustice at home.

The sense of optimism and activism that characterized the 1960s also pervaded politics. The administrations of John F. Kennedy, and—to a much greater extent—Lyndon B. Johnson acted on an abiding faith in the positive influence of government. Johnson's "Great Society" marked the high tide of postwar liberalism, the deliberate use of federal power to spread the abundance of the postwar economy among greater numbers of people, through expanded federal programs in health care, education, and civil rights.

Liberal politicians also pursued an activist stance abroad. Seeking to protect American political and economic interests in the international arena, the Kennedy and Johnson administrations took aggressive action against communist influence in Europe, the Caribbean, and Vietnam (see Chapter 31), among other places. As time passed, however, the growing financial and political costs of that ambitious agenda hampered further progress on the domestic front, dividing the postwar liberal coalition.

JOHN KENNEDY AND THE NEW FRONTIER

Franklin Roosevelt's activist administration had expanded presidential power, heightening the public's expectations of presidential leadership during the Truman and Eisenhower administrations. By the 1960s, when American power and resources seemed limitless, many citizens looked to Washington for solutions to any and all problems, whether international, national, or local. Few presidents came to Washington more aware of these high expectations than John Kennedy, who promised a "New Frontier" of vigorous governmental activism at home and abroad.

The New Politics and Activism Abroad

The Republicans would have been happy to renominate Dwight D. Eisenhower for president in 1960, but they were prevented from doing so by the Twenty-second Amendment. Passed in 1951 by a Republican-controlled Congress to prevent a repetition of Franklin Roosevelt's four-term presidency, the amendment limited future presidents to two full terms. Thus in 1960, the Republicans turned to Vice-President Richard M. Nixon, who identified himself with Eisenhower's policies but was hampered by lukewarm support from Eisenhower. Asked whether Nixon had helped to make any major policy decisions in his administration, Eisenhower replied, "If you give me a week I might think of one."

The Democrats chose Senator John Fitzgerald Kennedy of Massachusetts to run for president, with Senate majority leader Lyndon Johnson of Texas as the vice-presidential nominee. Kennedy launched his "New Frontier" campaign with a platform calling for civil-rights legislation, health care for the elderly, aid to education, urban renewal, expanded military and space programs, and containment of communism abroad. With the country in the middle of a recession that had pushed unemployment to a postwar high, Kennedy vowed to "get American moving again."

At forty-three, Kennedy was poised to become the youngest man ever elected to the presidency, and the nation's first Catholic chief executive. Kennedy dealt with the issue of religion directly. In an address to a group of Protestant ministers in Houston he affirmed his belief in the separation of church and state and declared his political independence from the Vatican.

Turning his youth into a powerful campaign asset, Kennedy practiced what came to be called the "new politics"—an approach that emphasized

The Kennedy Magnetism
John Kennedy, the Democratic candidate for president in 1960, used his youth and personality
to attract voters. Here the Massachusetts senator draws an enthusiastic crowd on a campaign
stop in Elgin, Illinois.

youthful charisma, style, and personality over issues and platforms. Using the
power of the media, particularly television, to reach voters directly, practitioners of the new politics relied on professional media consultants and political
pollsters, with massive fund raising to pay for them. Kennedy's youth, attrac-
tiveness, and charm made for a superb television image.

A series of four televised debates between the two principal candidates—a
major innovation of the 1960 campaign—showed how important the new
medium of TV was becoming to political life. Nixon, far less photogenic than
Kennedy, looked sallow and unshaven under the intense studio lights.
Kennedy, in contrast, looked vigorous, cool, and self-confident on screen. Polls
showed that television did sway its viewers' political perceptions: voters who
listened to the first debate on the radio concluded that Nixon had won,
whereas those who viewed it on TV judged Kennedy the winner.

Despite the edge Kennedy enjoyed in the debates, he won only the nar-
rowest of victories, receiving 49.7 percent of the popular vote to Nixon's 49.5

percent. Kennedy had successfully appealed to the diverse elements of the Democratic coalition, attracting large numbers of Catholic and black voters and a significant sector of the middle class. The vice-presidential nominee, Lyndon Johnson, brought in southern whites. Yet only 120,000 votes separated the two candidates, and the shift of a few thousand votes in key states such as Illinois (where there were confirmed cases of voting fraud) would have reversed the outcome.

Although Kennedy's New Frontier platform had included a long list of domestic social reforms, his greatest priority as president was foreign affairs. A resolute cold warrior, Kennedy took a hard line against communist expansionism. In contrast to Eisenhower, whose cost-saving New Look program had built up the American nuclear arsenal at the expense of conventional weapons, Kennedy proposed a new policy of *flexible response*, stating that the nation must be prepared "to deter all wars, general or limited, nuclear or conventional, large or small." Congress quickly granted Kennedy's requests for increased funding, dramatically increasing the defense budget and expanding the military-industrial complex.

Flexible response measures were designed to deter direct attacks by the Soviet Union. To prepare for a new kind of warfare, evident in the wars of national liberation that had broken out in many Third World countries where inhabitants sought to overthrow colonial rulers or unpopular dictators, Kennedy adopted a new military doctrine, *counterinsurgency*. Soon U.S. Army Special Forces, called Green Berets after their distinctive headgear, were receiving intensive training in repelling the small-scale, random attacks typical of guerrilla warfare. Vietnam would soon provide a testing ground for these counterinsurgency techniques (see Chapter 31).

Another of Kennedy's projects, the Peace Corps, embodied the commitment to public service that the president had called for in his inaugural address. Thousands of young men and women, many of them recent college graduates, agreed to devote two or more years to teaching English to Filipino schoolchildren or helping African villagers obtain adequate water supplies. Embodying the idealism of the early 1960s, the Peace Corps was also a cold war weapon designed to draw Third World countries into the American orbit and away from communist influence.

For the same reason, Kennedy pushed for economic aid to developing countries. The State Department's Agency for International Development coordinated foreign aid to the Third World, including surplus agricultural products distributed to developing nations through its Food for Peace program. In Latin America, the Alliance for Progress provided funds for food, education, medicine, and other services, though it did little to enhance economic growth or improve social conditions there.

Latin America was the site of Kennedy's first major foreign policy initiative and one of his biggest failures—an effort to overthrow the new Soviet-supported regime in Cuba. The United States had long maintained a naval base at Guantánamo Bay, and had dominated the island economically and politically.

A Peace Corp Volunteer

M *any Peace Corps volunteers found their projects disillusioning, but others ide-alistically judged the Corps to be "the greatest eye-opening, mind-stretching experience any generation of Americans has ever had." Philip A. Schaefer describes the rewarding aspects of his stint of duty in Kenya at the Uaso Nyiro Settlement.*

It is my job to assist in the difficult transformation from landless worker to successful entrepreneur. At first I thought that this would be beyond my abili-ties since I am a New York City "Farm boy" whose agricultural experience was previously limited to a tour of fruit and vegetable stands on the Lower East Side of New York. But . . . I soon came to realize that "Catcher" and "Fanfare" were varieties of wheat and not terms to describe the action on the baseball diamond. . . .

Dashing around on my *piki* (motorcycle) . . . with the cooperative chairman making arrangements to harvest the wheat or to purchase cattle has been hec-tic and exciting. But ordinary life on a settlement scheme can be pretty dreary. On Uaso Nyiro we have tried to create an exciting sense of community. We have started our own scheme newspaper, an idea which is catching on with other settlement schemes. But we are most proud of recent water show which helped to raise nearly $4,000 to bring needed water to the scheme. . . .

The people have begun to work together in the spirit of *harambee* (pulling together) as preached by *Mzee* (the old one) Jomo Kenyatta, the President of Keyna. To be a small participant in positive change is probably the most exhil-arating and satisfying experience of my life. To . . . return to the wheatless streets of New York will not be entirely painless.

SOURCE: Roy Hoopes, ed., *The Peace Corps Experience* (New York: Clarkson N. Potter, Inc., 1968), p.193.

But on New Year's Day in 1959 Fidel Castro overthrew the corrupt and un-popular dictator Fulgencio Batista and called for a revolution to reshape Cuban society. When Castro began agrarian reforms and nationalized American-owned banks and industries, relations with Washington deteriorated. By early 1961 the United States had declared an embargo on all exports to Cuba, cut back on U.S. imports of Cuban sugar, and broken off diplomatic relations with the regime.

Isolated by the United States, Cuba turned increasingly toward the Soviet Union for economic and military support. Concerned about Castro's growing friendliness toward the Soviets, in early 1961 Kennedy used plans originally drawn up by the Eisenhower administration to dispatch Cuban exiles to the island to foment a counterrebellion. Though the invaders had been trained by the Central Intelligence Agency (CIA), they were ill prepared for their task and had little popular support on the island. Shortly after landing at Cuba's Bay of Pigs on April 17, the tiny force of 1,400 men was crushed by Castro's troops (see Map 30.1).

U.S.-Soviet relations, adversely affected by the Bay of Pigs invasion, deteriorated further in June 1961, when Soviet Premier Khrushchev deployed soldiers to sever East Berlin from the western sector of the German city. With congressional approval, Kennedy responded by adding 300,000 troops to the armed forces, and promptly dispatched 40,000 of them to Europe. In mid-August, to stop the rapid exodus of East Germans to the West, the Soviets ordered construction of the Berlin Wall, and East German guards began policing the border. Until it was dismantled in 1989, the Berlin Wall was the supreme symbol of the Cold War.

The climactic confrontation of the Cold War came in October 1962. After the failed Bay of Pigs invasion, the Kennedy administration increased the economic pressure on Cuba and resumed covert efforts to overthrow Castro's regime. In response, the Soviets stepped up military aid to Cuba, including the

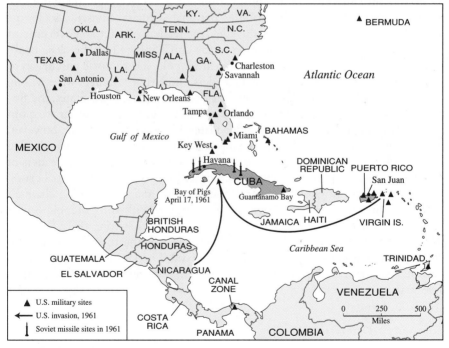

MAP 30.1

The United States and Cuba, 1961–1962

Fidel Castro's takeover in Cuba in 1959 brought cold war tensions to the Caribbean. In 1961 the United States tried unsuccessfully to overthrow Castro's regime by supporting an invasion by Cuban exiles launched from Nicaragua. In 1962 a major confrontation with the Soviet Union occurred over Soviet missile sites in Cuba. The Soviets removed the missiles after President Kennedy ordered a naval blockade of the island, which lies just 90 miles south of Florida.

installation of defensive missiles. In early October, American reconnaissance planes photographed Soviet-built bases for intermediate-range ballistic missiles (IRBMs), which could reach targets in the United States as far as 2,200 miles away. At least some of those nuclear weapons had already been installed; more were on the way.

In a somber address televised on Monday, October 22, Kennedy confronted the Soviet Union, and announced that the United States would impose a "quarantine on all offensive military equipment" intended for Cuba. As the two superpowers went on full military alert, people around the world feared that the confrontation would end in nuclear war. Americans living within range of the missiles restocked their bomb shelters or calculated the fastest route out of town. When Khrushchev denounced the quarantine, tension mounted. But as the world held its breath, ships carrying the Soviet-made missiles turned back. After a week of tense negotiations, both Kennedy and Khrushchev made concessions: Kennedy pledged not to invade Cuba, and Khrushchev promised to dismantle the missile bases.

Although the risk of nuclear war was greater during the Cuban missile crisis than at any other time in the postwar period, it led to a slight thaw in U.S.-Soviet relations. In the words of the national security adviser, McGeorge Bundy, "having come so close to the edge, the leaders of the two governments have since taken care to keep away from the cliff." Sobered by the close brush with nuclear war, Kennedy softened his earlier cold war rhetoric and began to strive for peaceful coexistence. Soviet leaders, similarly chastened, were willing to talk. In 1963 the world's three nuclear powers—the United States, the Soviet Union, and Great Britain—agreed to ban the testing of nuclear weapons in the atmosphere, in space, and under water. Underground testing, however, was allowed to continue. The new emphasis on peaceful coexistence also led to the establishment of a Washington-to-Moscow "hot line," so that leaders of the two superpowers could contact each other quickly during potential crises.

But no matter how often American leaders talked about opening channels of communication with the Soviets, the obsession with the potential Soviet military threat to American security remained a cornerstone of U.S. policy. Nor did Soviet leaders moderate their concern over the threat they believed the United States posed to their nation's survival. The Cold War—and the escalating arms race that accompanied it—would continue for another twenty-five years.

Kennedy's Domestic Policies

The expansive vision of presidential leadership that Kennedy and his advisers brought to the White House worked less well at home than it did abroad. Hampered by the lack of a popular mandate in the 1960 election, Kennedy could not mobilize public support for the domestic component of the New Frontier. A conservative coalition of southern Democrats and western and midwestern Republicans effectively stalled most of his liberal initiatives. More important, Kennedy was not nearly as impassioned about domestic reform as he was about foreign policy.

One program that did win both popular and Congressional support was increased funding for the National Aeronautics and Space Administration (NASA), whose space program had begun in 1958. On May 5, 1961, just three months after Kennedy took office, Alan Shepard became the first American to fly in space. (The Soviet cosmonaut Yuri Gagarin had become the first person ever to enter space in April 1961.) At the height of the American public's fascination with space flight, Kennedy proposed that the nation commit itself to landing a man on the moon within a decade. To support this mission (accomplished in 1969), Kennedy persuaded Congress to greatly increase NASA's budget.

Kennedy's most striking domestic achievement was his use of modern economic theory to shape government fiscal policy. New Dealers had gradually moved away from the ideal of a balanced budget, turning instead to deliberate deficit spending to stimulate economic growth. In addition to relying on federal spending to create the desired deficit, Kennedy and his advisers proposed a reduction in income taxes. A tax cut, they argued, would produce a short-term deficit, but would put more money in the hands of taxpayers, who would spend it, creating more jobs. For a time federal expenditures would exceed federal income, but after a year or two the expanding economy would raise American incomes and generate higher tax revenues.

Congress balked at this unorthodox proposal and the measure failed to pass. But Lyndon Johnson pressed for it after Kennedy's assassination, signing it into law in February 1964. Although an economic expansion began before the effects of the tax cut could be felt, Kennedy and his economic advisers got credit for it anyway. The gross national product grew at a rate of 5 percent during the 1960s—nearly twice the rate of the Eisenhower years. Much of that growth, however, was fueled by massive defense expenditures, especially spending for the escalating Vietnam War.

Kennedy's interest in stimulating economic growth did not include a commitment to spending to meet domestic social needs. He did not entirely ignore the liberal legislative agenda of Franklin Roosevelt and Harry Truman, but on some of the issues he did choose to promote—federal aid to education, wilderness preservation, investment in mass transportation, and medical insurance for the elderly—he ran into determined congressional opposition from both Republicans and dissenters in his own party.

Some of the most significant domestic reforms of the early 1960s came not from the Kennedy administration but from the Supreme Court. Much of the Court's activism in these years was linked to Earl Warren, chief justice from 1953 to 1969. Warren had influenced his Court's most important decision, *Brown v. Board of Education* (which required desegregation of public schools), in 1954 during the Eisenhower administration (see Chapter 29). In the 1960s the Court continued to make landmark decisions. It reinforced defendants' rights in cases like *Miranda v. Arizona* (1966), which required arresting officers to notify a suspect that "he has a right to remain silent, that any statement he does make may be used in evidence against him, and that he has a right to the presence of an attorney, either retained or appointed." Tackling the issue of the reapportionment of state legislatures in *Baker v. Carr* (1962) and *Reynolds v. Sims* (1964), the Court put forth the doctrine of "one person, one vote," meaning that all citizens' votes should have equal weight, no matter where they lived. The ruling substantially increased the representation of suburban and urban areas, with their concentrations of black and Spanish-speaking residents, at the expense of rural regions. Perhaps the most controversial of the Court's decisions was *Engel v. Vitale* (1962), which banned organized prayer in public schools as a violation of the First Amendment's injunction that "Congress shall make no law respecting an establishment of religion."

In allowing the Court to take the lead on such issues, Kennedy surrendered critical opportunities to exercise presidential leadership, a failure symptomatic of his first two years in office. Despite the foreign policy crises and domestic inaction that plagued his administration, however, many political observers hoped that Kennedy was maturing as a national leader. Then tragedy struck. On November 22, 1963, as he and his wife, Jacqueline, rode through Dallas in a motorcade, Kennedy was shot. He died half an hour later. Before *Air Force One* left Dallas to take the president's body back to Washington, a grim-faced Lyndon Johnson took the oath of office as president. Two days after the assassination a nightclub owner, Jack Ruby, gunned down the accused killer, Lee Harvey Oswald, in the basement of Dallas's police headquarters. Whether Oswald, a twenty-four-year-old loner who had spent three years in the Soviet Union, had been the sole gunman became a matter of considerable controversy.

In the years that followed, Kennedy's image of buoyant youth, the collective trauma of his assassination, and the American public's sense that the nation had been robbed of a promising leader contributed to a powerful mystique that enhanced his reputation far more than his record as president deserved. Though Kennedy had exercised bold presidential leadership in foreign affairs, his flexible response program and his initiatives in Cuba and Berlin had heightened the confrontations of the superpowers in the Cold War. Moreover, his enthusiasm for foreign policy had no equivalent in domestic policy. Kennedy's proposals for educational aid, medical insurance, and other liberal reforms stalled, and his tax-cut legislation languished in Congress until after his death. But perhaps Kennedy's greatest failing was his reluctance to act on civil rights.

THE CIVIL-RIGHTS MOVEMENT

Encouraged by *Brown v. Board of Education* and other favorable civil-rights decisions, black southerners had stepped up their efforts to dismantle legal segregation in the late 1950s (see Chapter 29). In the early 1960s a younger generation of activists adopted and expanded the strategy of nonviolent action developed by the Montgomery bus boycotters, Martin Luther King, Jr., and the Southern Christian Leadership Conference (SCLC) in the 1950s. Those young people, primarily black college students, used more assertive tactics to successfully challenge segregation at lunch counters and in waiting rooms, as well as at the ballot box.

New Tactics: Sit-ins, Freedom Rides, and the March on Washington

A new phase of the civil-rights movement began in Greensboro, North Carolina, on February 1, 1960, when four black college students took seats at the "whites only" lunch counter of a local Woolworth's, determined to "sit in" until they were served. Their protest demonstrated the capricious nature of southern segregation laws. At Woolworth's, blacks could buy toothpaste, underwear, and magazines alongside whites, but not a sandwich or a cup of coffee.

Although the protesters were arrested, their sit-in tactic worked, and it quickly spread to other southern cities. A few months later Ella Baker, an SCLC administrator and a lifelong activist, helped to organize the Student Non-Violent Coordinating Committee (SNCC, pronounced "snick") to facilitate student sit-ins. By the end of the year, about 50,000 people had participated in sit-ins and other demonstrations, and 3,600 of them had been jailed. White store owners quickly realized that they would lose business if the disruptions continued. Thus, black activists and a number of white supporters succeeded in desegregating lunch counters in 126 cities throughout the South.

The success of SNCC's unorthodox tactics encouraged the Congress of Racial Equality (CORE), an interracial group founded in 1942, to organize a series of *freedom rides* on interstate bus lines throughout the South. Under the direction of executive director James Farmer, CORE targeted buses, waiting rooms, and terminal restaurants to call attention to the continuing segregation of public transportation. The activists who rode the buses, mostly young and both black and white, were brutally attacked by white mobs in Anniston, Montgomery, and Birmingham, Alabama. Governor John Patterson refused to intervene, claiming, "I cannot guarantee protection for this bunch of rabble rousers."

Although the Kennedy administration generally opposed the freedom riders' activities, films of their beating and a bus burning shown on the nightly news prompted Attorney General Robert Kennedy to send federal marshals to Alabama to restore order. Faced with Justice Department intervention against those who defied the Interstate Commerce Commission's prohibition of segregation in interstate vehicles and facilities, most southern communities quietly acceded to the pressure. And civil-rights activists learned that nonviolent protest could succeed if it provoked vicious white resistance and generated nationwide publicity. Only when forced to, apparently, would federal authorities act.

This lesson was confirmed in Birmingham, Alabama, when Martin Luther King, Jr., and the Reverend Fred Shuttlesworth called for a protest against conditions in what King called "the most segregated city in the United States." In April 1963 thousands of black demonstrators marched downtown to picket Birmingham's department stores. They were met by Eugene ("Bull") Connor, the city's commissioner of public safety, who used snarling dogs, electric cattle prods, and high-pressure fire hoses to break up the crowd. Television cameras captured the scene for the evening news.

President Kennedy, realizing that he could no longer postpone decisive action, decided to step up the federal government's role in civil rights. On June 11, 1963, Kennedy went on television to promise major legislation banning discrimination in public accommodations and empowering the Justice department to enforce desegregation. Black leaders hailed the speech as the "Second Emancipation Proclamation."

To rouse the conscience of the nation and to marshal support for Kennedy's bill, civil-rights leaders adopted a tactic A. Philip Randolph had first suggested in 1941: a massive march on Washington. Martin Luther King, Jr., of the SCLC,

Racial Violence in Birmingham
When thousands of blacks marched to downtown Birmingham, Alabama, to protest racial segregation in April 1963, they were met with fire hoses and attack dogs unleashed by Police Chief "Bull" Connor. The violence, which was televised on the national evening news, shocked many Americans and helped build sympathy for the civil-rights movement among northern whites.

Roy Wilkins of the NAACP, Whitney Young of the National Urban League, and the black socialist Bayard Rustin were the principal organizers. On August 28, 1963, about 250,000 black and white demonstrators—the largest crowd at any demonstration up to that time—gathered at the Lincoln Memorial. The march culminated in a memorable speech delivered, indeed preached, by Martin Luther King, in the evangelical style of the black church. King ended with an exclamation from an old Negro spiritual: "Free at last! Free at last! Thank God almighty, we are free at last!"

King's eloquence and the sight of blacks and whites marching solemnly together did more than any other event to make the civil-rights movement acceptable to white Americans. The March on Washington seemed to justify liberals' faith that blacks and whites could work together to promote racial harmony. It marked the climax of the nonviolent phase of the civil-rights movement, confirming King's position, especially among white liberals, as the leading spokesman for the black cause. In 1964 King won the Nobel peace prize for his leadership.

Despite the impact of the march on public opinion, however, few congressional votes were changed by the event. Southern senators continued to block Kennedy's civil-rights legislation by threatening to filibuster. Even more troubling was a new outbreak of violence by white extremists determined to oppose equality for blacks at all costs. In September 1963 a Baptist church in Birmingham was bombed, and four black Sunday school students were killed. Two months later, President Kennedy was assassinated.

Landmark Legislation

On assuming the presidency, Lyndon Johnson promptly turned the passage of civil-rights legislation into a memorial to his slain predecessor—an ironic twist in light of Kennedy's lukewarm support for the cause. The Civil Rights Act, passed finally in June 1964, was a landmark in the history of American race relations. Its keystone, Title VII, outlawed discrimination in employment on the basis of race, religion, national origin, or sex. Another section barred discrimination in public accommodations. But while the act forced the desegregation of public facilities throughout the South, including many public schools, obstacles to black voting rights remained.

In 1964, with the Civil Rights Act on the brink of passage, black organizations and churches mounted a major civil-rights campaign in Mississippi. Known as Freedom Summer, the effort drew several thousand volunteers from across the country, including many idealistic white college students. Freedom Summer workers established freedom schools for black children, conducted a major voter registration drive, and organized the Mississippi Freedom Democratic party, a political alternative to the all-white Democratic organization in Mississippi. White southerners reacted swiftly and violently to their efforts. Fifteen civil-rights workers were murdered; only about 1,200 black voters were registered that summer.

A Civil-Rights Activist Remembers

A nn Moody, a CORE activist, was one of the young African-American students involved in voter registration in the South in 1963. Already discouraged by the slow progress of voter registration, she reacted to the news of the bombing of a Birmingham, Alabama, church by challenging the civil-rights movement's commitment to passive resistance.

We were all eating and listening to the radio when the music stopped abruptly in the middle of a record. "A special news bulletin just in from Birmingham," the DJ was saying. "A church was just bombed in Birmingham, Alabama. It is believed that several Sunday-school students were killed."

Why! Why! Why! Oh God, why? Why us? Why us? I found myself asking. . . . "You know, I used to go to Sunday school when I was a little girl. . . . We were taught how merciful and forgiving you are. Mama used to tell us that you would forgive us seventy-seven times a day, and I believed in you. I bet those girls in Sunday school were being taught the same as I was when I was their age. Is that teaching wrong? Are you going to forgive their killers? You not gonna answer me, God, hmm? Well, if you don't want to talk, then listen to me.

As long as I live, I'll never be beaten by a white man again. Not like in Woolworth's. Not anymore. That's out. You know something else, God? Nonviolence is out. I have a good idea Martin Luther King is talking to you, too. If he is, tell him that nonviolence has served its purpose. Tell him that for me, God, and for a lot of other Negroes who must be thinking it today.

SOURCE: Ann Moody, *Coming of Age in Mississippi* (New York: Doubleday, 1968), 317–18.

The need for federal action to support voting rights became even clearer in March 1965, when Martin Luther King and other black leaders called for a massive march from Selma, Alabama, to the state capital in Montgomery to protest the murder of a voting rights activist. As soon as the marchers left Selma, mounted state troopers attacked them with tear gas and clubs. The scene was shown on national television that night.

Calling the episode "an American tragedy," President Johnson redoubled his efforts to persuade Congress to pass the pending voting rights legislation. In a televised speech to a joint session of Congress on March 15, quoting the best-known slogan of the civil-rights movement, "We shall overcome," he proclaimed voting rights a moral imperative.

On August 6 Congress passed the Voting Rights Act of 1965, which suspended the literacy tests and other measures most southern states used to prevent blacks from registering to vote. The act authorized the attorney general to send federal examiners to register voters in any county where less than 50 percent of the voting-age population was registered. Together with the adoption in 1964 of the Twenty-fourth Amendment to the Constitution, which outlawed the federal poll tax, and successful legal challenges to state and local poll taxes, the Voting Rights Act allowed millions of blacks to register and vote for the first time. Congress reauthorized the Voting Rights Act in 1970, 1975, and 1982.

In the South, the results were stunning. In 1960 only 20 percent of eligible blacks had been registered to vote; by 1964 the figure had risen to 39 percent, and by 1971 it was 62 percent. As Hartman Turnbow, a Mississippi farmer who risked his life to register in 1964, later declared, "It won't never go back where it was."

LYNDON JOHNSON AND THE GREAT SOCIETY

Lyndon Baines Johnson brought to the presidency far more legislative experience than any other modern president. Born in the central Texas hill country in 1908, Johnson had served in government since 1932, as congressional aide, New Deal administrator, congressman, senator, Senate majority leader, and finally vice-president. In 1964, a year after Kennedy's death, Johnson won the presidency in his own right by defeating the conservative Republican senator Barry Goldwater of Arizona. With his running mate, Senator Hubert H. Humphrey of Minnesota, Johnson achieved one of the largest margins in history, 61.1 percent of the popular vote. He used his mandate and his political experience to bring to fruition the Great Society, his name for a program to end poverty and racial injustice. The Great Society, not the much less ambitious New Frontier, would fulfill and in some cases surpass the New Deal agenda of the 1930s.

Enacting the Liberal Agenda

Like most New Deal liberals, Johnson took an expansive view of presidential leadership and the role of the federal government. The 1964 election gave him not only a popular mandate, but the filibuster-proof Senate Democratic majority he needed to push his programs forward. Johnson's first major success came in education. The Elementary and Secondary Education Act, passed in 1965, authorized $1 billion in federal funds to benefit impoverished children. The same year the Higher Education Act provided the first federal scholarships for college students. The Eighty-ninth Congress also gave Johnson enough votes to enact the federal health insurance legislation first proposed by Truman. The result was two new programs: Medicare, a health plan for the elderly funded by a surcharge on Social Security payroll taxes, and Medicaid, a health plan for the poor paid for by general tax revenues.

Although the Great Society is usually associated with programs for the disadvantaged, many of the Johnson administration's initiatives benefited a wide spectrum of Americans. Federal urban renewal and home mortgage assistance helped those who could afford to live in single-family homes or modern apartments. Medicare covered every elderly person eligible for Social Security, regardless of need. And much of the federal aid to education benefited the children of the middle class. Finally, the creation of the National Endowment for the Arts and the National Endowment for the Humanities in 1965 supported artists and historians in their efforts to understand and interpret the nation's cultural and historical heritage.

Another aspect of public welfare addressed by the Great Society was the environment. President Johnson pressed for expansion of the national park system, improvement of the nation's air and water, and increased land-use planning. At the insistence of his wife, Lady Bird Johnson, he promoted the Highway Beautification Act of 1965. His approach marked a significant break with past conservation efforts, which had tended to concentrate on maintaining natural resources and national wealth. Under Secretary of the Interior Stewart Udall, Great Society programs emphasized quality of life, battling the problem "of vanishing beauty, of increasing ugliness, of shrinking open space, and of an overall environment that is diminished daily by pollution and noise and blight."

Taking advantage of the Great Society's reform climate, liberal Democrats also brought about significant changes in immigration policy. The Immigration Act of 1965 abandoned the quota system of the 1920s that had discriminated against Asians and southern and Eastern Europeans, replacing it with more equitable numerical limits on immigration from Europe, Africa, Asia, and countries in the Western Hemisphere. Since close relatives of individuals who were already legal residents of the United States could be admitted over and above the numerical limits, the legislation led to an immigrant influx far greater than anticipated, with the heaviest volume coming from Asia and Latin America.

Perhaps the most ambitious part of Johnson's liberal agenda was the War on Poverty, based on his expectation that the Great Society could put "an end to poverty in our time." During Johnson's presidency, poor people made up about a fourth of the American population; three-fourths of them were white. They included isolated farmers and miners in Appalachia, blacks and Puerto Ricans in urban ghettos, Mexican-Americans in migrant labor camps and urban barrios, native Americans on reservations, women raising families on their own, and the abandoned and destitute elderly. As Michael Harrington had pointed out in his influential book, *The Other America* (1962), the poor were everywhere.

To reduce poverty, the Johnson administration expanded long-established social insurance, welfare, and public works programs. It broadened the Social Security program to include more workers. Social welfare expenditures increased rapidly, especially for Aid to Families with Dependent Children (AFDC), public housing, rent subsidies, and Food Stamps. As during the New Deal, these social welfare programs developed in piecemeal fashion, without central coordination.

The Great Society's showcase in the War on Poverty was the Office of Economic Opportunity (OEO), established by the omnibus Economic Opportunity Act of 1964. OEO programs produced some of the most innovative measures of the Johnson administration. Head Start provided free nursery schools to prepare disadvantaged preschoolers for kindergarten. The Job Corps, Upward Bound, and Volunteers in Service to America (VISTA), modeled on the Peace Corps, provided poor youths with training and jobs. And the Community Action Program encouraged the poor to demand "maximum feasible participation" in decisions that affected them.

Cracks in the Liberal Coalition

By the end of 1965, the Johnson administration had compiled the most impressive legislative record of liberal reforms—from civil rights to health care, from environmental concerns to food stamps—since the New Deal. It had put issues of poverty, justice, and access at the center of national political life, and had expanded the federal government's role in protecting its citizens' welfare. Yet the Great Society never quite measured up to the extravagant promises made for it; by the end of the decade, many programs were troubled and under attack.

In part, the political necessity of bowing to pressure from various interest groups hampered Great Society programs. For example, the American Medical Association (AMA) used its influence to shape the Medicare and Medicaid programs, to assure that Congress did not impose a cap on medical expenses. Its intervention produced escalating federal expenditures and contributed to skyrocketing medical costs. And Democratic-controlled urban political machines criticized VISTA and Community Action Program agents who encouraged poor people to demand the public services long withheld by unresponsive local governments. In response to such political pressure, the Johnson administration gradually phased out the Community Action Program and instead channeled spending for housing, social services, and other urban poverty programs through local municipal governments.

Another inherent problem was the limited funding of Great Society programs. The annual budget for the War on Poverty was less than $2 billion. Johnson and his advisers never considered income redistribution as the solution to poverty; they counted on enhanced education and skills to raise the income level of the poor, bringing the benefits of American capitalism to more people. Despite the limited nature of the program, the statistical decline in poverty during the 1960s suggests that the Great Society was successful on some levels. From 1963 to 1968, the proportion of Americans living below the poverty line dropped from 20 percent to 13 percent. Among African-Americans, economic advancement was even more marked. In the 1960s the black poverty rate was cut in half and millions of blacks moved into the middle class, some through federal jobs in antipoverty programs. But critics charged that the reduction in the poverty rate was due to the decade's booming economy, not to the War on

Poverty. Moreover, while the nation's overall standard of living increased, distribution of wealth was still uneven. Though the poor were better off in an absolute sense, they remained far behind the middle class in a relative sense.

Other factors also hampered the success of the Great Society. Following in the steps of Roosevelt's New Deal coalition, Kennedy and Johnson had gathered an extraordinarily diverse set of groups—middle-class and poor; white and nonwhite; Protestant, Jewish, and Catholic; urban and rural—in support of an unprecedented level of federal activism. For a brief period between 1964 and 1966 the coalition held together. But inevitably the demands of certain groups—such as blacks' demands for civil rights and the urban poors' demands for increased political power—conflicted with the interests of other Democrats, such as white southerners and northern political bosses. In the end the Democratic coalition could not sustain a consensus on the purposes of governmental activism powerful enough to resist conservatives who continued to resist expanded civil-rights and social welfare legislation.

At the same time, Democrats were plagued by disillusionment over the shortcomings of their reforms. In the early 1960s the lofty rhetoric of the New Frontier and the Great Society had raised unprecedented expectations for social change. But competition for federal largesse was keen, and the shortage of funds for the War on Poverty left many promises unfulfilled, especially after 1965, when the escalation of the Vietnam War siphoned funding away from domestic programs. In 1966 the government spent $22 billion on the Vietnam War and only $1.2 billion on the War on Poverty. Ultimately, as Martin Luther King put it, the Great Society was "shot down on the battlefields of Vietnam."

THE CONTINUING STRUGGLE FOR CIVIL RIGHTS

Just as the Great Society was plagued by internal divisions and external opposition, so too was the evolving civil-rights movement. As the struggle moved outside the South and took on the more stubborn problems of entrenched poverty and racism, black frustration and anger boiled over in a new racial militance. The rhetoric and tactics of the emerging black power movement both shattered the existing civil-rights coalition and galvanized white opposition.

Rising Militance

Once the system of legal, or *de jure*, segregation had fallen, the civil-rights movement turned to the more difficult task of eliminating the *de facto* segregation, enforced by custom, that made blacks second-class citizens throughout the nation. Outside the South, racial discrimination was less flagrant, but it was pervasive, especially in education, housing, and employment. Although the *Brown* decision outlawed separate schools, it did nothing to change the educational system in areas where schools were all-black or all-white because of residential segregation. Not until 1973 did federal judges begin to extend the desegregation of schools, which had begun in the South two decades earlier, to the rest of the country.

As civil-rights leaders took on the new target of northern racism, the movement fractured along generational lines. Students who had risked assault to sit in at lunch counters or to register to vote grew impatient with the gradualism of their elders. Many repudiated the nonviolent approach pursued by Martin Luther King and urged blacks to take control of their communities through more radical, and if necessary violent, means.

Some younger activists, eager for confrontation and rapid social change, questioned the very goal of integration into white society. Black separatism, espoused by earlier black leaders such as Marcus Garvey in the 1920s (see Chapter 24), was revived in the 1960s by the Nation of Islam, which had more than 10,000 members and many more sympathizers. Popularly known as the Black Muslims, the Nation of Islam was extremely hostile to whites, whom its leader Elijah Muhammad called "blue-eyed devils." Forcefully promoting their black nationalist ideology, the group stressed black pride, unity, and self-help.

The Black Muslims' most charismatic figure was Malcolm X. Born Malcolm Little in 1925, he converted to the Nation of Islam while serving time in prison for attempted burglary. A brilliant debater and spellbinding speaker, Malcolm X preached a philosophy quite different from Martin Luther King's. He advocated militant protest and separatism, though he condoned the use of violence only for self-defense and self-assertion. Hostile to the traditional civil-rights organizations, he caustically referred to the 1963 March on Washington as the "Farce on Washington."

In 1964, after a power struggle with Elijah Muhammed, Malcolm X broke with the Nation of Islam. He then made a pilgrimage to Mecca, the holiest site of traditional Islam, and toured Africa, where he embraced the liberation struggles of all colonized peoples. On his return to the United States, Malcolm X moved away from antiwhite rhetoric toward an internationalist vision of the black future. On February 21, 1965, he was assassinated while delivering a speech at the Audubon Ballroom in Harlem. Three Black Muslims were later convicted of his murder. Malcolm X's autobiography, ghostwritten by Alex Haley and published soon after his death, became one of the decade's most influential books.

Though Malcolm X's call for black cultural and political independence appealed to young black activists in SNCC and CORE, many balked at the idea of converting to Islam, preferring a secular black nationalist movement. In 1966 the SNCC leader Stokely Carmichael christened a new era in the black struggle when he called for "Black Power." Carmichael's battle cry confirmed the militant forces already present in SNCC and other civil-rights groups. In fact, by 1966 most whites had been effectively ejected from the civil-rights movement.

In the same year Huey Newton and Bobby Seale, two college students in Oakland, California, founded the Black Panthers, a militant self-defense organization dedicated to protecting local blacks from police violence. The Panthers' organization quickly spread to other cities, where members undertook a wide range of community organizing projects, including interracial efforts. But the Panthers' affinity for Third World revolutionary movements and armed struggle became their most publicized attribute. Radical black power activists were proposing a new agenda: not nonviolence but armed self-defense; not integration but separatism; not working within the system but preparing for revolution.

Among the most significant legacies of black power was the assertion of racial pride. Many young blacks insisted on the term *Afro-American* rather than *Negro*, a term they found demeaning because of its historical association with slavery and racism. Rejecting white tastes and standards, blacks wore African clothing and hairstyles and helped to awaken interest in black history, art, and literature. By the 1970s many colleges and universities were offering programs in black studies.

The new black assertiveness alarmed many white Americans. They had been willing to go along with the moderate reforms of the 1950s and early 1960s, but became wary when blacks began demanding immediate access to higher-paying jobs, housing in white neighborhoods, education in integrated schools, and increased political power. White backlash soon became a powerful force that conservative politicans in both parties quickly seized upon (see Chapter 31).

Another major reason for the erosion of white support was a wave of riots that struck the nation's cities where African-Americans had suffered economic and political marginalization for decades. Lacking education and skills, successive generations of blacks had moved out of the rural South in search of work that paid an adequate wage. In the North, many remained unemployed. Resentful of white landlords who owned the substandard housing they were forced to live in and white shopkeepers who denied them jobs in their neighborhoods, many blacks also hated police, whose violent presence in black neighborhoods seemed that of "an occupying army." Stimulated by the successes of southern blacks who had challenged whites and gotten results, young urban blacks expressed their grievances through their own brand of "direct action."

The first "long hot summer" began in July 1964 in New York City, when police shot a young black criminal suspect in Harlem. Angry youths looted and rioted there for a week. Over the next four years, the volatile issue of police brutality set off riots in dozens of cities. In August 1965 the arrest of a young black motorist in the Watts section of Los Angeles sparked six days of rioting that left thirty-four blacks dead. Ironically, Watts erupted only five days after President Johnson signed the Voting Rights Act of 1965. For many young urban blacks the legal gains of the civil-rights movement were irrelevant to their daily experience of economic exploitation. Instead of singing "We shall overcome," Watts rioters shouted "Burn, baby, burn."

The riots of 1967 were the most serious (see Map 30.2), engulfing twenty-two cities in July and August. The most devastating outbreaks occurred in

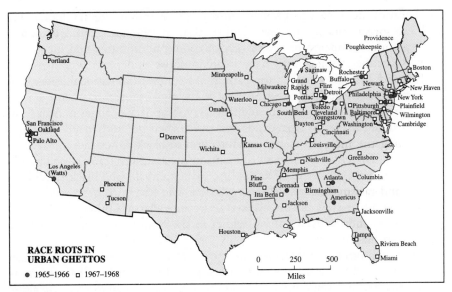

MAP 30.2
Racial Unrest in America's Cities, 1965–1968
American cities suffered through four "long hot summers" of rioting in the mid-1960s. In 1967, the worst year, riots broke out across the United States, including in the South and the West. Major riots usually did not occur in the same city two years in a row.

Newark and Detroit. Forty-three people were killed in Detroit alone, nearly all of them black, and $50 million worth of property destroyed. As in most of the riots, the arson and looting in Detroit targeted white-owned stores and property, but there was little physical violence against white people.

On July 29, 1967, President Johnson appointed a special commission to investigate the riots. The final report of the National Advisory Commission on Civil Disorders, released in March 1968, detailed the continuing inequality and racism of urban life. It also issued a warning: "Our nation is moving toward two societies, one black, one white—separate and unequal. . . . What white Americans have never fully understood—but what the Negro can never forget—is that white society is deeply implicated in the ghetto. White institutions created it, white institutions maintain it, and white society condones it."

On April 4, 1968, barely a month after the Commission on Civil Disorders released its report, Martin Luther King, Jr., was assassinated in Memphis, Tennessee, by James Earl Ray, a white ex-convict whose motive was unknown. King's death set off an explosion of urban rioting. Violence broke out in more than a hundred cities. With King's assassination the civil-rights movement lost the one leader best able to stir the conscience of white America. During the last years of his life King had moved toward a broader view of the structural problems of poverty and racism in America. In 1966 he had confronted the issue of residential segregation in a campaign for open housing in Chicago. He had also spoken out against the Vietnam War. In 1968 King was planning a poor people's campaign to raise issues of economic injustice and inequality. How successful King would have been in those endeavors will never be known. But his death marked the passing of an important national leader, and was symptomatic of the troubled course of the civil-rights movement.

The 1960s brought permanent, indeed revolutionary, changes in American race relations. Jim Crow segregation was overturned in less than a decade, and federal legislation passed to ensure protection of black Americans' most basic civil rights. The enfranchisement of blacks in the southern states ended political control by all-white state Democratic parties and allowed black candidates to enter the political arena. White candidates who had once been ardent segregationists began to court the black vote. In time Martin Luther King's greatness was recognized even among whites in the South; in 1986 his birthday became a national holiday.

Yet much remained undone. The more entrenched forms of segregation and discrimination persisted, despite the legal reforms of the 1960s. African-Americans, particularly those in the central cities, continued to make up a disproportionate number of the poor, the unemployed, and the undereducated. As the civil-rights movement gradually splintered, its agenda remained unfinished.

The Spreading Demand for Equal Rights

Despite its limitations, the black civil-rights movement provided a fresh and innovative model for social change. Although Mexican-Americans had been working actively for civil rights since the 1930s (see Chapter 25), poverty, an uncertain legal status, and language barriers made their political mobilization difficult. That situation began to change when the Mexican-American Political Association (MAPA) mobilized support for John F. Kennedy and in return Kennedy appointed several Mexican-American leaders to posts in Washington. Over the next four years, MAPA and other political organizations worked successfully to elect Mexican-American candidates to Congress: in the House, Edward Roybal of California, and Henry González and Elizo de la Garza of Texas; in the Senate, Joseph Montoya of New Mexico.

Younger Mexican-Americans quickly grew impatient with MAPA, however. The barrios of Los Angeles and other western cities produced the militant Brown Berets, modeled on the Black Panthers (who wore black berets). Rejecting the assimilationist approach of their elders, 1,500 Mexican-American students met in Denver in 1969 to hammer out a new nationalist political and cultural agenda. They proclaimed a new term, *Chicano*, to replace *Mexican-American*, and later organized a new political party, La Raza Unida ("The United Race"), to promote Chicano interests and candidates. In California and other southwestern states, students staged demonstrations and boycotts to press for bilingual education, the hiring of more Chicano teachers, and the creation of Chicano studies programs. By the 1970s dozens of such programs were offered at universities throughout the region.

Chicano strategists also pursued economic objectives. Working in the fields around Delano, California, the labor leader Cesar Chavez organized the United Farm Workers (UFW), the first union to represent migrant workers successfully. A 1965 grape pickers' strike and a nationwide boycott of table grapes brought Chavez and his union national publicity and won support from the AFL–CIO and from Senator Robert F. Kennedy of New York. Chavez soon was receiving almost as much media attention as Martin Luther King, Jr. Victory came in 1970 when California grape growers signed contracts recognizing the UFW.

North American Indians also found a model in the civil-rights movement. Native Americans, who numbered nearly 800,000 in the 1960s, were an exceedingly diverse group, divided by language, tribal history, region, and degree of integration into the mainstream of American life. But they also shared an unemployment rate ten times the national average, as well as the worst poverty, the most inadequate housing, the highest disease rates, and the least access to education of any group in the United States.

As early as World War II the National Council of American Indians had lobbied for improvement of those conditions. In the 1960s, some Indian groups became more assertive. Like the young militants in the black civil-rights movement, they challenged the accommodationist approach of their elders. Proposing a new name for themselves—native Americans—they organized protests and demonstrations to build support for their cause. In 1968 several Chipewyan from Minnesota organized the militant American Indian Movement (AIM), which drew its strength from the third of the native American population who lived in "red ghettos" in cities throughout the West.

In November 1969 AIM seized the deserted federal penitentiary on Alcatraz Island in San Francisco Bay, offering the government $24 worth of trinkets to pay for it, supposedly the sum the Dutch had paid to the native inhabitants for Manhattan Island in 1626. Their occupation of Alcatraz lasted until the summer of 1971. A year later, a thousand protesters occupied the headquarters of the Federal Bureau of Indian Affairs in Washington, D.C., to many native Americans a hated symbol of federal native American policy.

In February 1973, 200 Sioux organized by AIM leaders began an occupation of the tiny village of Wounded Knee, South Dakota, the site of an army massacre of the Sioux in 1890 (see Chapter 17). They were protesting the light sentences given to a group of white men convicted of killing a Sioux in 1972. To dramatize their cause, the protesters took eleven hostages and occupied several buildings. But when a gun battle with the FBI left one protester dead and another wounded, the seventy-one-day siege collapsed. Although the new native American activism helped to alienate many white onlookers, it did spur government action on tribal issues (see Chapter 32).

Wounded Knee Revisited
In 1973 members of the American Indian Movement staged a seventy-one-day protest at
Wounded Knee, South Dakota, the site of the 1890 massacre of 200 Sioux by U.S. soldiers.
The takeover was sparked by the murder of a local Sioux by a group of whites but quickly ex-
panded to include demands for basic reforms in federal Indian policy and tribal governance.

Civil rights, once seen as a movement exclusively for the rights of black
people, also sparked a new awareness among some predominantly white
groups. Americans of Polish, Italian, Greek, and Slavic descent, most of them
working-class and Catholic, proudly embraced their new ethnic identity.
Homosexual men and women banded together to protest legal and social oppression based on their sexual orientation. In 1969 the gay liberation movement was born in the "Stonewall riot" in New York City, when patrons of a
gay bar fought back against police harassment. The assertion of gay pride that
followed the incident drew heavily on the language and tactics of the civil-
rights movement. Activists took the new name of *gay* rather than *homosexual*;
founded advocacy groups, newspapers, and political organizations to challenge
discrimination and prejudice; and offered emotional support to those who
"came out" and publicly affirmed their homosexuality. For gays as well as
members of various ethnic and cultural groups, political activism based on
heightened group identity represented one of the most significant legacies of
the African-American struggle.

The Revival of Feminism

The black civil-rights movement also helped to reactivate feminism, a movement that had been languishing since the 1920s. Just as the abolition movement
had been the training ground for women's rights advocates in the nineteenth
century, the black struggle became an inspiration for young feminists in the

1960s. But the revival of feminism also sprang from social and demographic changes that affected women young and old. By 1970, 42.6 percent of women were working, and four out of ten working women were married. Especially significant was the growth in the number of working women with preschool children—up from 12 percent in 1950 to 30 percent in 1970. In the postwar consumer society, working mothers were becoming more accepted.

Another significant change was increased access to education for women. Immediately after World War II the percentage of college students who were women declined. The GI Bill gave men a temporary advantage in access to higher education. At the height of the baby boom, many college women dropped out of school to marry and raise families. By 1960, however, the percentage of college students who were women had risen to 35 percent; in 1970 it reached 41 percent.

The meaning of marriage was changing, too. The baby boom turned out to be only a temporary interruption of a century-long decline in the birth rate. The introduction of the birth control pill, first marketed in 1960, and the intrauterine device (IUD) helped women control their fertility. Women had fewer children, and because of an increased life expectancy (75 years in 1970—up from 54 years in 1920), they devoted proportionally fewer years to raising children. At the same time the divorce rate, which had risen slowly throughout the twentieth century, rose markedly as the states liberalized divorce laws.

As a result of these changes, traditional gender expectations were dramatically undermined. American women's lives now usually included work and marriage, often child rearing and a career, and possibly bringing up children alone after a divorce. Those changing social realities created a major constituency for the emerging women's movement of the 1960s.

During those years older, politically active professional women sought change by working through the political system. This group was galvanized in part by a report by the Presidential Commission on the Status of Women (1963), which documented the employment and educational discrimination women faced. More important than the report's rather conservative recommendations was the rudimentary nationwide network of women in public life that formed in the course of the commission's work.

Another spark that ignited the revival of feminism was Betty Friedan's best-selling book *The Feminine Mystique*, published in 1963. A pointed indictment of suburban domesticity, the book explored what Friedan called "the problem that has no name":

> As she made the beds, shopped for groceries, matched slipcover material, ate peanut butter sandwiches with her children, chauffeured Cub Scouts and Brownies, lay beside her husband at night—she was afraid to ask even of herself the silent question—"Is this all?"

Women responded enthusiastically to Friedan's book—especially white, college-educated, middle-class women. The book sold 3 million copies and was excerpted in many women's magazines. *The Feminine Mystique* gave women a vocabulary with which to express their dissatisfaction and promoted women's self-realization through employment, continuing education, and other activities outside the home.

Like so many other constituencies in postwar America, women's rights activists looked to the federal government for help. The first steps toward change had emerged in 1963, when Congress passed the Equal Pay Act, which directed that men and women be paid the same wages for doing the same job. Even more important was the Civil Rights Act of 1964, which had as great an impact on women as it did on blacks and other minorities. Title VII, which barred discrimination in employment on the basis of race, religion, national origin, or sex, eventually became a powerful tool in the fight against sex discrimination. At first, however, the Equal Employment Opportunity Commission (EEOC) avoided implementing it.

Dissatisfied with the Commission's reluctance to defend women's rights, Friedan and others founded the National Organization for Women (NOW) in 1966. Modeling itself on groups such as the NAACP, NOW aimed to be a civil-rights organization for women. "The purpose of NOW," an early statement declared, "is to take action to bring women into full participation in the mainstream of American society now, exercising all the privileges and responsibilities thereof in truly equal partnership with men." Under Friedan, who served as NOW's first president, its membership grew from 1,000 in 1967 to 15,000 in 1971. Men made up a fourth of NOW's early membership. The group is still the largest feminist organization in the United States.

Another group of new feminists, the women's liberationists, came to the women's movement through their civil-rights work. White women had made up about half the students who went south with SNCC in the Freedom Summer project of 1964. These college women developed self-confidence and organizational skills working in the South, and they found role models in older southern women like Ella Baker, Anne Braden, and Virginia Foster Durr, who were prominent in the civil-rights movement. Yet women volunteers also found they were expected to do all the cleaning and cooking at the Freedom Houses where SNCC volunteers lived. "We didn't come down here to work as a maid this summer," one complained. But the men in the movement laughed off their attempts to raise feminist issues.

After 1965 black militants made white women unwelcome in the civil-rights movement. But when these women transferred their energies to the antiwar groups that were emerging in that period (see Chapter 31), they found the New Left equally male-dominated. When the antiwar movement adopted draft resistance as a central strategy, women found themselves relegated to the role of sex objects. "Girls say yes to guys who say no" was a popular slogan. Those women who tried to raise feminist issues at conventions were shouted off the platform with jeers such as "Move on, little girl, we have more important issues to talk about here than women's liberation." Around 1967 the contradiction between the New Left's lip service to egalitarianism and women's treatment by male leaders caused women radicals to realize that they needed their own movement. In contrast to groups such as NOW, which had traditional organizational structures and dues-paying members, these women formed loose collectives whose shifting membership often lacked any formal structure. They organized independently in five or six different cities, including Chicago, San Francisco, and New York.

Members of the women's liberation movement (or "women's lib," as it was dubbed by the somewhat hostile media) went public in 1968 in a protest at the Miss America Pageant. Their demonstration featured a "freedom trash can" into which they encouraged women to throw false eyelashes, hair curlers, brassieres, and girdles—all of which they branded as symbols of female oppression. The media quickly labeled the radical feminists "bra burners." The derisive name stuck, although no brassieres were actually burned.

Feminism on the March
The visibility of the feminist movement reached a new peak in 1970 when thousands of women in New York and other cities around the country marched to celebrate the fiftieth anniversary of woman suffrage. (© Bettye Lane)

An activity with a more lasting impact was consciousness raising—group sessions in which women shared their experiences of being female. Swapping stories about being passed over for a promotion, needing a husband's signature on a credit card application, or enduring the whistles and leers of men while walking down the street helped participants to realize that their individual problems were part of a wider pattern of oppression. The slogan "The personal is political" became a rallying cry of the movement.

By 1970, a growing convergence of interests began to blur the distinction between women's rights and women's liberation. Radical women realized that key feminist goals—child care, equal pay, and abortion rights—could best be achieved in the political arena. At the same time, more traditional activists developed a broader view of the women's movement, tentatively including divisive issues such as abortion and lesbian rights. Although the movement remained largely white and middle class, feminists were beginning to think of themselves as part of a broad, growing, and increasingly influential social crusade. Their gradual convergence would lay the foundation for more vigorous activism (see Chapter 32).

By the end of the decade, the call for moderate reform that John Kennedy had sounded in his New Frontier had been superseded by far more radical demands for political and social change. Racial and ethnic minorities were challenging racial hierarchies; women were criticizing the patriarchal family; gays were speaking out against homophobia. These challenges to the status quo set up a backlash among many white, mainstream Americans, and at the same time hampered liberal reformers' efforts to maintain their fragile coalition and implement Lyndon Johnson's Great Society. But an even more ominous fault line had emerged—one that profoundly divided the nation. The quagmire of the Vietnam War would soon challenge Americans' assumptions about their nation at home and abroad.

CHAPTER 30 TIMELINE

1960	Greensboro, North Carolina, sit-ins
	John F. Kennedy elected president
1961	Freedom rides
	Peace Corps established
	Bay of Pigs invasion
	Berlin Wall erected
1962	Michael Harrington's *The Other America*
	Cuban missile crisis
1963	Betty Friedan's *The Feminine Mystique*
	Presidential Commission on the Status of Women Report
	Civil-rights protest in Birmingham, Alabama
	March on Washington
	John F. Kennedy assassinated; Lyndon B. Johnson becomes president
1964	Freedom Summer
	Civil Rights Act
	Economic Opportunity Act
	Johnson elected president
1965	Malcolm X assassinated
	Voting Rights Act
	Immigration Act
	Medicare and Medicaid
	Elementary and Secondary Education Act
	Air and Water Quality acts
1966	National Organization for Women (NOW) founded
	Stokely Carmichael proclaims black power
1967	Height of race riots in northern cities
1968	Martin Luther King, Jr., assassinated
	Women's liberation movement emerges
1969	American Indian Movement seizes Alcatraz
	Stonewall riot begins gay liberation movement

CHAPTER 31

VIETNAM AND AMERICA, 1954–1975

In February 1969, while conducting his first mass as a Catholic Priest, James Carroll seized the opportunity to criticize the U.S. war in Vietnam. Carroll's public pronouncement against the war, delivered in a U.S. Air Force base chapel before an audience of high-ranking officers, among them his father, opened a rift in his family that never healed. Carroll's stand was not unique: he joined countless other ministers and priests who used their pulpits to condemn the war. His experience provides a dramatic example of the ruptures the Vietnam War brought to families, institutions, and the American social fabric.

Vietnam spawned a vibrant antiwar protest movement, which intersected with a broader youth movement that questioned traditional American political and cultural values. The challenges posed by youth, together with the rise of the black and Chicano power movements and explosive riots in the cities, produced a profound sense of social disorder at home. Vietnam split the Democratic party and shattered the liberal consensus. The high monetary cost of the war diverted resources from domestic uses, spelling an end to the Great Society. Beyond its domestic impact, the war wreaked extraordinary damage on the country of Vietnam and undermined U.S. credibility abroad. For the first time, average Americans began to question their assumptions about the nation's cold war objectives and the beneficence of American foreign policy.

INTO THE QUAGMIRE, 1945–1968

Like many new nations that emerged from the dissolution of European empires after World War II, Vietnam was characterized by a volatile mix of nationalist sentiment, religious and cultural conflict, economic need, and political turmoil. The rise of communism there was just one phase of the nation's larger struggle, which would eventually climax in a bloody civil war. But American policymakers viewed these events through the lens of the Cold War, interpreting them as part of an internationally inspired communist movement toward global domination. Their failure to understand the complexity of Vietnam's internal conflicts led to a long and ultimately disastrous attempt to influence the course of the war.

America in Vietnam: From Truman to Kennedy

Vietnam, which had been part of the French colony of Indochina since the late nineteenth century, had been occupied by Japan during World War II. When the Japanese surrendered in 1945, Ho Chi Minh and the Vietminh, the nationalist group that had led Vietnamese resistance to the Japanese, took advantage of the resulting power vacuum. With words drawn from the American Declaration of Independence, Ho proclaimed the establishment of the independent republic of Vietnam that September. The next year, when France rejected his claim and reasserted control over the country, an eight-year struggle that the Vietminh called the Anti-French War of Resistance ensued. Appealing to American anticolonial sentiment, Ho called on President Truman to support the struggle for Vietnamese independence. But Truman ignored his pleas and instead offered covert financial support to the French, in hopes of stabilizing the politically chaotic region and rebuilding the French economy.

By the end of the decade, cold war developments had prompted the United States to step up its assistance to the French. After the Chinese revolution of 1949, the United States became concerned that China—along with the Soviet Union—might actively support anticolonial struggles in Asia, and that newly independent countries might align themselves with the communists. At the same time, Republican charges that the Democrats had "lost" China influenced Truman to take a firmer stand against perceived communist aggression both in Korea and in Vietnam. Truman also wanted to maintain good relations with France, whose support was crucial to the success of the new NATO alliance. Finally, Indochina played a strategic role in Secretary of State Dean Acheson's plans for an integrated Pacific rim economy centered on a reindustrialized Japan.

For all these reasons, when the Soviet Union and the new Chinese leaders recognized Ho's republic early in 1950, the United States—along with Great Britain—recognized the French-installed puppet government of Bao Dai. Subsequently, both the Truman and the Eisenhower administrations provided substantial military support to the French in Vietnam. President Eisenhower argued that such aid was essential to prevent the collapse of all noncommunist governments in the area, in a chain reaction he called the domino effect: "You have a row of dominoes set up, you knock over the first one, and what will happen to the last one is the certainty that it will go over very quickly."

Despite joint French-American efforts, the Vietminh forces gained strength in northern Vietnam. In the spring of 1954, they seized the isolated administrative fortress of Dienbienphu after a fifty-six-day siege. The spectacular victory gave the Vietminh negotiating leverage in the 1954 Geneva Accords, which partitioned Vietnam temporarily at the 17th parallel (see Map 31.1) and committed France to withdraw its forces north of that line. The Accords also provided that within two years, in free elections, the voters in the two sectors would choose a unified government for the entire nation. Eight of the nine national delegations in attendance signed the agreements, but the United States refused, and instead issued a separate protocol acknowledging the agreements and promising to "refrain from the threat or use of force to disturb them."

Eisenhower had no intention of allowing a communist victory in Vietnam's upcoming election. With the help of the CIA, he made sure that a pro-American government took power in South Vietnam in June 1954, just before the accords were signed. Ngo Dinh Diem, an anticommunist Catholic who had spent eight years in the United States, returned to Vietnam as the premier of the French-backed South Vietnamese government. The next year, in a rigged election, Diem became president of an independent South Vietnam. Realizing that the popular Ho Chi Minh would easily win in both north and south, Diem then called off the reunification elections that were scheduled for 1956, a move the United States supported.

In March 1956 the last French soldiers left Saigon, the capital of South Vietnam, and the United States replaced France as the dominant foreign power in the region. American policymakers quickly asserted that a noncommunist South Vietnam was vital to U.S. security interests. In reality, Vietnam was too small a country to upset the international balance of power, and its communist movement was regional and intensely nationalistic, rather than expansionist. Nevertheless, Eisenhower and subsequent U.S. presidents persisted in viewing Vietnam as part of the cold war struggle to contain the communist threat to the free world. Between 1955 and 1961 the Eisenhower administration sent Diem an average of $200 million a year in aid and stationed approximately 675 American military advisers in Saigon. Having stepped up U.S. involvement there considerably, Eisenhower left office, passing the Vietnam situation to his successor, John F. Kennedy.

President Kennedy saw Vietnam as an ideal testing ground for the counterinsurgency techniques that formed the centerpiece of his military policy (see Chapter 30). But he first had to prop up Diem's unpopular regime, which faced a growing military threat. In December 1960, the Communist party in

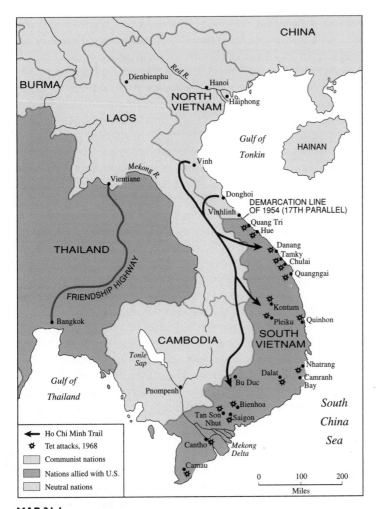

MAP 31.1
The Vietnam War, 1954–1975
The Vietnam war was a guerrilla war, fought in inconclusive skirmishes rather than decisive battles. Supporters of the National Liberation Front filtered into South Vietnam along the Ho Chi Minh Trail, which wound through Laos and Cambodia. In January 1968 Viet Cong forces launched the Tet offensive, a surprise attack on several South Vietnamese cities and provincial centers shown above. American vulnerability to these attacks fueled opposition to the war.

North Vietnam organized most of Diem's opponents in South Vietnam into a revolutionary movement known as the National Liberation Front (NLF). To counter the threat, Kennedy increased the number of American military "advisers" (an elastic term that included helicopter units and special forces), raising it to more than 16,000 by November 1963. To win the "hearts and minds" of Vietnamese peasants away from the insurgents and to increase agricultural production, he also sent economic development specialists. But Kennedy refused to send combat troops to assist the South Vietnamese.

American aid did little good in South Vietnam. Diem's political inexperience and corruption, combined with his Catholicism in a predominantly Buddhist country, prevented him from creating a stable popular government. The NLF's guerrilla forces—called the Viet Cong by their opponents—made considerable headway against Diem's regime, using the revolutionary tactics of the Chinese leader Mao Zedong to blend into South Vietnam's civilian population "like fish in the water." They found a receptive audience among peasants who had been alienated by Diem's "strategic hamlet" program, which uprooted families and whole villages and moved them into barbed-wire compounds in a vain attempt to separate them from Ho Chi Minh's sympathizers.

Anti-Diem sentiment also flourished among Buddhists, who charged the government with religious persecution. Starting in May 1963, militant Buddhists staged a dramatic series of demonstrations against Diem, including several self-immolations that were recorded by American television crews. Diem's regime retaliated with raids on temples and mass arrests of Buddhist priests in August, prompting more antigovernment demonstrations.

As opposition to Diem deepened, Kennedy decided that he would have to be removed. Ambassador Henry Cabot Lodge, Jr., let it be known in Saigon that the United States would support a military coup that had "a good chance of succeeding." On November 1, 1963, Diem was driven from office and assassinated by officers in the South Vietnamese army. America's role in the coup reinforced the links between the United States and the new regime in South Vietnam, making the prospect of withdrawal from the region less acceptable to U.S. policymakers.

Less than a month later, Kennedy himself was assassinated. Although historians continue to debate whether Kennedy would have withdrawn American forces from Vietnam had he lived, his administration's actions clearly accelerated U.S. involvement. When Lyndon Johnson became president, he retained many of Kennedy's foreign policy advisers. Asserting that "I am not going to be the President who saw Southeast Asia go the way China went," he quickly declared he would maintain U.S. support for South Vietnam.

Escalation: The Johnson Years

Diem's removal did not improve the efficiency or the popularity of the government in Saigon. Secretary of Defense Robert McNamara and other top advisers argued that only a rapid, full-scale deployment of U.S. forces could prevent the imminent defeat of the South Vietnamese. But Johnson would need at least tacit congressional support, perhaps even a declaration of war, to commit U.S. forces to an offensive strategy. During the summer of 1964, the president saw his opportunity. American naval forces were conducting surveillance missions off the North Vietnamese coast, to aid amphibious attacks on the area by the South Vietnamese. When the North Vietnamese resisted the attacks, President Johnson told the nation that on two separate occasions, North Vietnamese torpedo boats had fired on American destroyers in international waters in the Gulf of Tonkin. At Johnson's request, Congress authorized him to "take all necessary measures to repel any armed attack against the forces of the United States and to prevent further aggression." On August 7 the Gulf of Tonkin resolution passed in the Senate 88 to 2 and in the House 416 to 0. Johnson's skillful representation of the unverified attack got him what he wanted—a sweeping mandate to conduct operations in Vietnam as he saw fit. The only formal approval of American intervention in Vietnam that Congress ever granted, the Tonkin resolution represented a significant expansion of presidential power.

Once congressional support was assured, and the 1964 elections had passed (see Chapter 30), the Johnson administration moved toward the Americanization of the war. The first phase of the escalation began on March 2, 1965. Operation Rolling Thunder, a protracted bombing campaign, dropped a million tons of bombs on North Vietnam between 1965 and 1968. Each B-52 sortie cost $30,000. By early 1966 the direct costs of the air war had exceeded $1.7 billion, yet the enormous expenditure of munitions continued. From 1965 to 1973 the United States dropped three times as many bombs on North Vietnam, a country roughly the size of Texas, as had fallen on all of Europe, Asia, and Africa during World War II. The several hundred captured U.S. pilots downed in the raids then became pawns in prisoner-of-war negotiations with the North Vietnamese.

To the amazement of American advisers, the bombings did not appear to impede the North's ability to wage war. The flow of troops and supplies to the south continued unabated as the North Vietnamese quickly rebuilt roads and bridges, moved munitions plants underground, and constructed networks of tunnels and shelters. Instead of destroying enemy morale and bringing the North Vietnamese to the bargaining table, Operation Rolling Thunder intensified their nationalism and will to fight. Yet the bombing continued.

A week after the launch of Operation Rolling Thunder, the United States sent its first official ground troops into combat duty. Soon U.S. Marines were skirmishing with the enemy. Beginning in the summer of 1965, combat operations shifted from a defensive stance to a search-and-destroy offense designed to uncover and kill Viet Cong forces. Fearing congressional opposition, the Johnson administration did not reveal this major change in strategy. Over the next three years the number of American troops in Vietnam grew dramatically. Although U.S. troops were accompanied by military forces from Australia, New Zealand, and South Korea, the war increasingly became an American war, fought for American aims. By 1966 more than 380,000 American soldiers were stationed in Vietnam; by 1967, 485,000; by 1968, 536,000.

The massive commitment of troops and air power threatened to destroy Vietnam's countryside. Besides the bombardment, a defoliation campaign had seriously damaged agricultural production, undercutting the economic and

cultural base of Vietnamese society. After one devastating but not unusual engagement, a commanding officer reported, using the logic of the time, "It became necessary to destroy the town in order to save it." Graffiti on a plane that
dropped defoliants read "Only you can prevent forests." (In later years defoliants such as Agent Orange were found to have highly toxic effects on both
humans and the environment.) The destruction was not limited to North
Vietnam; South Vietnam, America's ally, absorbed more than twice the bomb
tonnage dropped on the north. In Saigon and other South Vietnamese cities,
the influx of American soldiers and dollars distorted local economies, spread
corruption and prostitution, and triggered uncontrollable inflation and black
market activity.

Why did the dramatically increased American presence in Vietnam fail to
turn the tide of the war? Some advisers argued that military intervention
would accomplish little unless it was accompanied by reform in Saigon and
increased popular support in the countryside. Other critics claimed that the
United States never fully committed itself to a total victory—although what
that term meant was never settled. Military strategy was inextricably tied to
political considerations. For domestic reasons, policymakers often searched for
an elusive "middle ground" between all-out invasion (and the possibility of
sparking a nuclear exchange between the two superpowers) and the politically
unacceptable alternative of disengagement. Hoping to win a war of attrition,
the Johnson administration assumed that American superiority in personnel
and weaponry would ultimately triumph. But that limited commitment was
never enough to ensure victory, however it was defined.

The tremendous determination of the North Vietnamese was a major factor. The Viet Cong were prepared to accept limitless casualties, and to fight on
for as many years as necessary. North Vietnamese strategists realized that the
war did not have to be won on the battlefield, and accurately predicted that
the American public would not tolerate an extended war of attrition. Time
was on the Viet Cong's side, although at enormous cost to both sides.

Soldiers' Perspectives on the War in Vietnam

Approximately 2.8 million Americans served in Vietnam. At an average age
of only nineteen, most of those servicemen and women were too young to
vote or drink (the voting age was twenty-one until passage of the Twenty-
sixth Amendment in 1971), but they were old enough to fight and die. Some
were volunteers, including 7,000 women enlistees. Many others served because they were drafted. Until the nation shifted to an all-volunteer force in
1973, the draft stood as a concrete reminder of the government's impact on
the lives of ordinary Americans. Blacks were drafted and died roughly in the
same proportion as their share of the draft-age population (about 12 to 13
percent), although black casualty rates were significantly higher than average
in the early 1960s. Even more than in other recent wars, sons of the poor and
the working class shouldered a disproportionate amount of the fighting,

forming an estimated 80 percent of the enlisted ranks. Young men from more affluent backgrounds were more likely to avoid combat through student deferments, medical exemptions, and appointments to National Guard and reserve units—alternatives that made Johnson's Vietnam policy more acceptable to the middle class.

At first, many draftees and enlistees shared common cold war assumptions about the need to fight communism and the superiority of the American military. However, their experience in Vietnam quickly challenged simple notions of patriotism and the inevitability of victory. In "Nam," long days of boring menial work were punctuated by brief flashes of intense fighting. "Most of the time, nothing happened," a soldier recalled, "but when something did, it happened instantaneously and without warning." Rarely were there large-scale battles, only skirmishes; rather than front lines and conquered territory, there were only daytime operations in areas the Viet Cong controlled at night.

Racism was a fact of everyday life. Because differentiating between friendly South Vietnamese and Viet Cong sympathizers was difficult, many soldiers lumped them together as "gooks." As a draftee noted of his indoctrination, "The only thing they told us about the Viet Cong was they were gooks. They were to be killed. Nobody sits around and gives you their historical and cultural background. They're the enemy. Kill, kill, kill."

Fighting under such conditions took its toll. One veteran explained that "The hardest thing to come to grips with was the fact that making it through Vietnam—surviving—is probably the only worthwhile part of the experience. It wasn't going over there and saving the world from communism or defending the country." Cynicism and bitterness were common. The pressure of waging war under such conditions drove many soldiers to seek escape in alcohol or drugs, which were cheap and readily available.

The American women who served in Vietnam shared many of these experiences. As WACs, nurses, and civilians serving with organizations such as the USO, women volunteers witnessed death and mutilation on a massive scale. Though they tried to maintain a professional distance, as a navy nurse recalled, "It's pretty damn hard not getting involved when you see a nineteen- or twenty-year-old blond kid from the Midwest or California or the East Coast screaming and dying. A piece of my heart would go with each."

The Cold War Consensus Unravels

President Kennedy and at first President Johnson as well enjoyed broad support for their conduct of foreign affairs. Both Democrats and Republicans approved Johnson's escalation of the war, and public opinion polls in 1965–1966 showed strong popular support for his policies. But in the late 1960s, public opinion began to turn against the war. In July 1967 a Gallup poll revealed that for the first time, a majority of Americans disapproved of Johnson's Vietnam policy, and believed the war had reached a stalemate.

Television had much to do with these attitudes. Vietnam was the first war in which television brought the films of the fighting directly into the nation's living rooms. By 1967 CBS and NBC were spending $5 million a year to cover the war from their Saigon bureaus. Reporters soon learned that combat footage—what they called "shooting bloody"—had a better chance of being aired than did pieces about social reform or political developments. Every night Americans watched U.S. soldiers advance steadily through the countryside and heard reporters detail staggering Viet Cong losses and minimal U.S. casualties.

Despite the glowing reports filed by the media and the administration on the progress of the war, by 1967 many administration officials had privately reached a more pessimistic conclusion. In November Secretary of Defense Robert McNamara sent a memo to the president arguing that continued escalation "would be dangerous, costly in lives, and unsatisfactory to the American people." Pentagon analysts confirmed McNamara's doubts, estimating that the Viet Cong could marshal 200,000 guerrillas a year, indefinitely. Despite that prognosis, however, President Johnson continued to insist that victory in Vietnam was vital to U.S. national security and prestige. Journalists, especially those who had spent time in Vietnam, soon began to warn that the Johnson

A Televised War
This harrowing scene from Saigon during the Tet offensive in 1968 depicts the head of the South Vietnamese National Police preparing to shoot a captured member of the Viet Cong. Telecast on U.S. network news, it was one of scores of disturbing images that flooded American living rooms during the Vietnam era, and helped to sway public opinion against continued participation in what commentator Walter Cronkite called a "bloody experience" that would end in "stalemate."

administration suffered from a "credibility gap." The administration, they charged, was concealing important and discouraging information about the war's progress. In February 1966 television coverage of hearings by the Senate Foreign Relations Committee (chaired by J. William Fulbright, an outspoken critic of the war) raised further questions about the administration's policy.

Economic developments put Johnson and his advisers even more on the defensive. In 1966 the federal deficit was $9.8 billion; in 1967, a year the Vietnam War cost the taxpayers $27 billion, it jumped to $23 billion. Although the war consumed just 3 percent of the gross national product, its costs became more evident as the growing federal deficit nudged the inflation rate upward. But only in the summer of 1967 did Johnson ask for a 10 percent surcharge on individual and corporate incomes, an increase that Congress did not approve until 1968. By then the inflationary spiral that would plague the U.S. economy throughout the 1970s was well under way.

Another major problem facing the Johnson administration was the growing strength and visibility of the antiwar movement. As in every American military conflict, a small group of dissenters had opposed the war from the beginning; these included pacifist organizations such as the Women's International League for Peace and Freedom, as well as religious groups such as the Quakers and the Fellowship for Reconciliation. They had been joined by a new generation of peace activists represented by groups such as SANE (the National Committee for a Sane Nuclear Policy) and Physicians for Social Responsibility. These new activists were opposed to the escalating arms race in general, and to atmospheric testing in particular. They had lobbied successfully for the 1963 nuclear test-ban treaty between the United States and the Soviet Union.

Between 1963 and 1965, peace activists in both types of organization staged periodic protests, vigils, and petition- and letter-writing campaigns against U.S. involvement in the war. After the escalation of combat in the spring of 1965, various antiwar coalitions, swelled by growing numbers of students, clergy, housewives, politicians, artists, and others opposed to the war, organized several mass demonstrations in Washington, bringing out 20,000 to 30,000 people at a time. A diverse lot, participants in these rallies shared a common skepticism about the means and aims of U.S. policy. The war was morally wrong, they argued, and antithetical to American ideals; the goal of an independent, anticommunist South Vietnam was unattainable; and American military involvement in Vietnam would not help the Vietnamese people.

Some Americans felt so strongly against the war that they adopted extreme means of protest. In November 1965 Norman Morrison, a Quaker activist, set himself on fire and burned to death near the Pentagon gates, 40 yards from Defense Secretary McNamara's office. Morrison undertook his protest after reading an account by a French priest who had despaired at seeing his Vietnamese parishioners burned by the lethal incendiary substance napalm during a bombing attack. Like the priest, Morrison was torn by his inability to stop the carnage. To his wife he wrote: "Know that I love thee but must act for the children of the priest's village."

Morrison's suicide shocked the nation. Even McNamara later admitted he was horrified by this "outcry against the killing that was destroying the lives of so many Vietnamese and American youth." Three weeks later an estimated 30,000 antiwar protesters, including a large contingent of college students, converged on the White House. Over the next few years student protesters would flock to the antiwar movement, increasing its visibility and political clout. The fervor of this new generation would drive not only the antiwar movement but a youthful rebellion that challenged authority on nearly every front.

THE CHALLENGE OF YOUTH, 1962–1970

Although some of the most potent images of the 1960s show youthful protesters rebelling against the war in Vietnam, traditional values, authority, and the "system," American youth were not monolithic. Many young people, especially those in the working class, kept their distance from the more extreme expressions of rebellion. College students, whose numbers had increased dramatically in the postwar period, formed the core of those youth who challenged authority in the 1960s.

Student Activism

In June 1962 forty students from Big Ten and Ivy League universities, disturbed by the gap they perceived between the ideals they had been taught to revere and the realities in American life, met in Port Huron, Michigan, to found Students for a Democratic Society (SDS). Tom Hayden wrote their manifesto, the Port Huron Statement, which expressed their disillusionment with the consumer culture and the gulf between the prosperous and the poor. These students rejected cold war ideology and foreign policy, including but not limited to the Vietnam conflict. They castigated the bureaucracies that dominated America's corporations, political parties, and government, and blocked citizens' access to power. They called for a reinvigorated participatory politics, designating students as the major force for social change. To distinguish themselves from the "Old Left"—communists, socialists, and other left-wing sectarians of the 1930s and 1940s—the founders of SDS referred to their movement as the "New Left." Consciously adopting the activist tactics pioneered by members of the civil-rights movement, they turned to grassroots organizing in cities and on college campuses.

　　The first student protests erupted in the fall of 1964 at the University of California at Berkeley after administrators banned political activity near the Telegraph Avenue entrance, where student groups had traditionally distributed leaflets and recruited volunteers. In protest, all the major student organizations, from SDS to the conservative Youth for Goldwater, formed a coalition called the Free Speech Movement (FSM) and organized a sit-in at the administration building. The university agreed to drop the ban.

Free Speech at Berkeley, 1964
Students at the University of California's Berkeley campus protested the administration's decision to ban political activity in the school plaza. Free speech demonstrators, many of them active in the civil-rights movement, relied on the tactics and arguments that they learned in that struggle.

The FSM owed a strong debt to the civil-rights movement. Some students had just returned from Freedom Summer in Mississippi, where they were radicalized by their experience. Mario Savio spoke for many of them:

Last summer I went to Mississippi to join the struggle there for civil rights. This fall I am engaged in another phase of the same struggle, this time in Berkeley. The two battlefields may seem quite different to some observers, but this is not the case. The same rights are at stake in both places—the right to participate as citizens in a democratic society and to struggle against the same enemy. In Mississippi an autocratic and powerful minority rules, through organized violence, to suppress the vast, virtually powerless majority. In California, the privileged minority manipulates the university bureaucracy to suppress the students' political expression.

On a deeper level Berkeley students were challenging a university that in their view had grown too big and was too far removed from the major social issues of the day. In the postwar era, the largest universities, like the largest corporations, had grown the fastest. In 1940 only two campuses in the United

States had as many as 20,000 students; by 1969 thirty-nine were that large or larger. Many students in these "multiversities" felt they were treated brusquely and impersonally. Emboldened by the Berkeley movement, students across the nation were soon protesting everything from dress codes to course requirements, from tenure decisions to academic grading.

Students also protested the universities' complicity in the problems of the ghetto. Columbia University, for example, owned substantial property in Harlem, which bordered its campus. When the university announced plans in 1968 to build a new gymnasium, which would displace local stores and housing, students tore down the fence at the construction site and took over several university buildings. Columbia officials called the police to break up the demonstration; the brutal response of New York City's Tactical Police force radicalized many more students than had originally supported the protests. As campus disturbances spread to other colleges and universities, more and more university buildings were blocked, occupied, or picketed, and classes were frequently dismissed or canceled.

Although black students participated in many protests, the student movements soon began to split along racial lines. White students focused on the antiwar movement; black students, inspired by the black power movement, demanded to study African-American history and culture. University administrators, anxious to ease campus unrest, agreed to establish Afro-American and black studies departments. By forcing the inclusion of black society and culture in the curriculum, and thus the acknowledgment of race as a key factor in American life, these students changed the way American history was taught and written. Black protesters also won university support for separate dormitories and cultural centers, to provide a sense of community for blacks residing on predominantly white campuses.

No issue provoked more impassioned and sustained protest than the Vietnam War. The highly politicized activists of the New Left, who had developed a wide-ranging critique of American society, increasingly focused on the war, and they were joined by thousands of other students in protesting American participation in the Vietnam conflict. When President Johnson escalated the war in March 1965, faculty and students at the University of Michigan organized a teach-in against the war. Abandoning their classes, they debated the political, diplomatic, and moral aspects of the nation's involvement in Vietnam. Teach-ins quickly spread to other universities as students turned from their studies to protest the war.

Many protests centered on the draft, especially after the Selective Service System abolished student deferments in January 1966. To avoid the draft, some young men enlisted in the National Guard or the reserves; others declared themselves conscientious objectors. Several thousand young men ignored their induction notices, risking prosecution for draft evasion. Others left the country, most often for Canada or Sweden. The Resistance, started at Berkeley and Stanford and widely recognized by its omega symbol, supported these draft resisters. In public demonstrations of civil disobedience, opponents of the

A Draft Resister

O*n October 16, 1967, Michael K. Ferber spoke at a Boston church in support of the organization Resistance's call for young men to turn in their draft cards. As the following passage makes clear, Ferber's motivation for resisting the draft went deeper than simple opposition to the Vietnam War; it incorporated many of the ideas of the New Left.*

We are gathered in this church today in order to do something very simple: to say No. We have come from many different places and backgrounds and we have many different ideas about ourselves and the world, but we have come here to show that we are united to do one thing: to say No. Each of our acts of returning our draft cards is our personal No; when we put them in a single container or set fire to them from a single candle we express the simple basis of our unity. . . .

But let us not be deceived. The sun will rise tomorrow as it does every day, and when we get out of bed the world will be in pretty much the same mess it is in today. American bombers will continue to drop incendiary bombs on the Vietnamese people and American soldiers will continue to "pacify" their villages. The ghettos will continue to be rotten places to live in. Black and Mexican farm workers will continue to get miserable wages. America's schools will continue to cripple the minds and hearts of its pupils. And the American Selective Service System will continue to send young men out to the slaughter.

Today is not the End. Today is the Beginning.

SOURCE: Alexander Bloom and Wini Breines, eds., *"Takin' it to the Streets": A Sixties Reader* (New York: Oxford University Press, 1995), pp. 245–248.

war burned their draft cards, closed down induction centers, and on a few occasions broke into Selective Service offices.

As antiwar and draft protests multiplied, students realized that their universities were deeply implicated in the war effort. In some cases as much as 60 percent of a university's research budget came from government contracts, especially those of the Defense department. Protesters blocked recruiters from the Dow Chemical Company, the producer of napalm and Agent Orange. Arguing that universities should not train students for war, they demanded that the Reserve Officer Training Corps (ROTC) be removed from college campuses.

In the late 1960s student protesters joined the much larger antiwar movement of peace activists, housewives, religious leaders, and a few elected officials. After 1967 nationwide student strikes, mass demonstrations, and other organized protests became commonplace. In October 1967, more than

100,000 antiwar demonstrators marched on Washington, D.C., as part of "Stop the Draft Week." The event culminated in a "siege of the Pentagon," in which protesters clashed with police and federal marshals. Hundreds of people were arrested and several demonstrators beaten. Lyndon Johnson, who had once dismissed antiwar protesters as "nervous Nellies," rebellious children, or communist dupes, had to face the reality of large-scale public opposition to his policies.

The Rise of the Counterculture

Antiwar sentiment and protest accelerated the erosion of confidence in established American institutions and values. While the New Left took to the streets in protest, a growing number of young Americans undertook their own revolution against authority and middle-class respectability. The "hippie"— attired in ragged blue jeans, tie-dyed T-shirt, beads, and army fatigues, and wearing long, unkempt hair—symbolized the new *counterculture*, a youthful movement that glorified liberation from traditional social strictures through new music and clothing styles, spiritual exploration, and experimentation with sex and drugs.

Throughout the 1960s popular music mirrored the changing political mood. The folk singer Pete Seeger set the tone for the era with idealistic songs

Flower Children
Yale law professor Charles A. Reich celebrated the new freedom of youth in his best-selling book *The Greening of America* (1970). Reich described a new consciousness that had "emerged out of the wasteland of the Corporate State, like flowers pushing up through the concrete pavement." Counterculture hippies were also called flower children.

such as the antiwar ballad "Where Have All the Flowers Gone?" Another folk singer, Joan Baez, gained national prominence singing "We Shall Overcome" and other political anthems at mid-decade protest rallies. In 1963, the year of the Birmingham demonstrations and President Kennedy's assassination, Bob Dylan's "Blowin' in the Wind" gave voice to the impatience of those whose faith in liberalism was wearing thin.

Other winds of change in popular music came from abroad. The Beatles, four working-class youths from England, burst onto the American scene early in 1964. Their music, by turns lyrical and hard driving, was phenomenally successful, spawning a commercial and cultural phenomenon called Beatlemania. American youth's eager embrace of the Beatles deepened the generational divide begun by the advent of rock-'n'-roll in the 1950s. After the Beatles came the angrier, more rebellious, music of other British groups, notably the Rolling Stones, whose raunchy 1965 hit "(I Can't Get No) Satisfaction" signaled a new openness about sexuality, while it made fun of the consumer culture ("He can't be a man 'cause he doesn't smoke the same cigarettes as me").

Drugs intertwined with music as a crucial element of the youth culture. They were hardly new to the American scene: the beats had experimented with mind-altering drugs, and many jazz musicians had used heroin and cocaine for decades. But the recreational use of drugs—especially marijuana and the hallucinogen lysergic acid diethylamide, popularly known as LSD, or "acid"—had never been so widespread, nor so celebrated in popular music. San Francisco bands, such as the Grateful Dead and the Jefferson Airplane, and musicians like the Seattle-born guitarist Jimi Hendrix developed a musical style known as "acid rock," which was characterized by long, heavily amplified guitar solos accompanied by psychedelic lighting effects. The Beatles, whose early songs had featured conventionally romantic lyrics, turned to recording tunes such as "Lucy in the Sky with Diamonds" (1967), whose "tangerine trees and marmalade skies" celebrated the new drug culture.

For a brief time, adherents of the counterculture believed a new age was dawning. In 1967 the "world's first Human Be-In" drew 20,000 people to Golden Gate Park in San Francisco. The beat poet Allen Ginsberg "purified" the site with a Buddhist ritual, and the LSD advocate Timothy Leary, a former Harvard psychology instructor, urged the gathering to "turn on to the scene, tune in to what is happening, and drop out." That summer—dubbed the "Summer of Love"—San Francisco's Haight-Ashbury, New York's East Village, and Chicago's Uptown neighborhoods swelled with young dropouts, drifters, and teenage runaways dubbed flower children by observers. Their faith in instant love and peace quickly turned sour, however, as they suffered bad drug trips, venereal disease, loneliness, and violence. In 1967 seventeen murders and more than a hundred rapes were reported in Haight-Ashbury alone.

Meanwhile, the appeal of rock music and drugs continued to grow. In August 1969 400,000 young people journeyed to Bethel, New York, to "get

AMERICAN VOICES

A Rock Musician Remembers the Counterculture

In this selection, the rock musician Joe McDonald of Country Joe and the Fish reminisces about life in the San Francisco Bay area during the 1960s. McDonald's nostalgic account of the 1960s drugs-and-music scene suggests the ways in which values of the political left often merged with those of the counterculture.

Up until that point people had just been consuming alcohol and falling down from that. But the new idea became, "Hey, take drugs and act crazy." So everybody took drugs, different kinds of drugs, whatever kinds of drugs, whatever kinds of drugs they could find. . . .

None of this stuff was happening with any sense of danger because something magical was going on that was hard to explain then, and is still hard to explain even now. An innocence, I guess.

Ultimately, though, we found out the hard way by having our innocence smashed out of us. Lots of things happened, mainly political assassinations and the war. You can't separate the era from that, from all those caskets. Ours was an era of extremes, unbelievable extremes. And inside that era we were like this little dreamland. . . . I think back fondly on that period, but I don't romanticize it. I mean, I don't think I'd want another generation to experience the negative things we experienced—mostly I mean the war.

But there were positive things, too, that sense of community, of communication. We developed family roots that were just wonderful. I love to think about that, walking down Haight Street in San Francisco and saying hello to everybody. It was a rare moment.

SOURCE: From Joe Smith, *Off the Record: An Oral History of Popular Music*, edited by Mitchell Fink (New York: Warner Books, 1988), pp. 229–231.

high" on music, drugs, and sex at the three-day Woodstock Music and Art Fair. Despite torrential rain and numerous drug overdoses, most enjoyed the festival, which was heralded as the birth of the "Woodstock nation." A few months later, however, an outdoor concert by the Rolling Stones at Altamont Speedway near San Francisco degenerated into a near riot, leaving four dead and hundreds injured.

Some young people rejected both mainstream culture and the growing anarchy of the counterculture and headed instead for rural communes. In the mountains between Santa Cruz and San Francisco and in the valleys of Vermont, communes provided economic and sexual alternatives to the traditional nuclear family. Members grew their own food, baked their own bread, and rejected materialism and commercialism in favor of old-fashioned self-sufficiency. But the communes of the 1960s did not just look backward. Their advocacy of organic farming—growing food without chemicals or pesticides—anticipated and influenced the environmental movement that would emerge in the 1970s and 1980s (see Chapter 32).

Although the counterculture and the New Left were different movements, the distinction between them sometimes blurred. Many antiwar protesters adopted hippie clothing, experimented with drugs, and embraced the more politically oriented forms of rock music. And while most flower children professed political apathy, their antiauthoritarianism threatened many adults. Furthermore, groups such as the Youth International Party, or "Yippies," led by Abbie Hoffman and Jerry Rubin, combined political and cultural rebellion in a deliberate attempt to attract media attention. During the October 1967 March on Washington, the Yippies dressed like witches and attempted to levitate the Pentagon. To many adult observers, the antiwar movement and the counterculture had become indistinguishable.

THE LONG ROAD HOME, 1968–1975

In 1968, as Lyndon Johnson planned his reelection campaign, antiwar protests and rising battlefield casualties had begun to erode public support for a war that seemed to have no end. Moreover, since Diem's assassination in 1963, South Vietnam had undergone a confusing series of military coups and countercoups. In the spring of 1966, the Johnson administration pressured the unpopular South Vietnamese government to adopt democratic reforms, including a new constitution and popular elections. In September 1967 U.S. officials helped to elect General Nguyen Van Thieu president of South Vietnam. Thieu's regime, the administration hoped, would broaden its support at home, legitimize the South Vietnamese government in the eyes of the American public, and advance the military struggle against the communists.

1968 and Its Aftermath

The administration's hopes evaporated on January 30, 1968, when the Viet Cong unleashed a massive, well-coordinated assault on major urban areas in South Vietnam. Known as the Tet offensive, the assault was timed to coincide with the lunar new year, a festive Vietnamese holiday. Viet Cong forces struck thirty-six of the forty-four provincial capitals and five of the six major cities, including Saigon, where they raided the supposedly impregnable U.S. embassy (see Map 31.1, p. 837). In strict military terms the Tet offensive was a failure for the Viet Cong since it did not provoke the intended collapse of the South Vietnamese government. But its long-term effect was quite different. The daring attack made a mockery of official pronouncements that the United States was winning the war and swung American public opinion more strongly against the war. Just before the offensive, a Gallup poll found that 56 percent of Americans considered themselves "hawks" (supporters of the war), while only 28 percent identified with the "doves" (opponents). Three months after Tet, the doves outnumbered the hawks by 42 to 41 percent. This turnaround in public opinion did not mean that a majority of Americans supported the peace movement, however. Many who called themselves doves had simply concluded that the war was unwinnable, and were therefore opposed to it on pragmatic rather than moral grounds. As a housewife told a pollster, "I want to get out, but I don't want to give up."

The growing opposition to the war spilled over into the 1968 presidential campaign. Even before Tet, Senator Eugene J. McCarthy of Minnesota had entered the Democratic primaries as an antiwar candidate. In March, President Johnson won the early New Hampshire primary, but McCarthy received a stunning 42.2 percent of the vote. His strong showing against the president reflected profound public dissatisfaction with the course of the war—even among those who were hawks.

Johnson realized that his political support was evaporating. On March 31, and at the end of an otherwise mundane televised address, he stunned the nation by announcing that he would not seek reelection. Johnson had already reversed his policy of incremental escalation of the war. Now he called a partial bombing halt and vowed to devote his remaining months in office to the search for peace. On May 10, 1968, preliminary peace talks between the United States and North Vietnam opened in Paris.

Just four days after Johnson's withdrawal from the presidential race, Martin Luther King, Jr., was assassinated in Memphis. His death provoked riots in cities across the country, leaving forty-three people dead. Soon afterward, the student confrontation at Columbia University erupted (see page 846). The next month, a massive strike by students and labor unions toppled the French government. Student unrest seemed likely to become a world-wide phenomenon.

Then came the final painful tragedy of the year. Senator Robert Kennedy, who had entered the Democratic presidential primaries in March, had quickly become a front runner. On June 5, 1968, as he celebrated his victory in the California primary, he was shot dead by a young Palestinian who was thought to oppose Kennedy's pro-Israeli stance. Robert Kennedy's assassination shattered the dreams of many who had hoped that social change could be achieved by working through the political system. His death also weakened the Democratic party. In his brief but dramatic campaign Kennedy had excited and energized the traditional members of the New Deal coalition, including blue-collar workers and black voters, in a way that the more cerebral Eugene McCarthy, who appealed mostly to the antiwar movement, never did.

The Democratic party never fully recovered from Johnson's withdrawal and Kennedy's assassination. McCarthy's campaign limped along, while Senator George S. McGovern of South Dakota entered the Democratic race in an effort to keep the Kennedy forces together. Meanwhile, Vice-

President Hubert H. Humphrey lined up pledges from traditional Democratic constituencies—unions, urban machines, and state political organizations. Democrats found themselves on the verge of nominating not an antiwar candidate, but a public figure closely associated with Johnson's war policies.

In the end, the political divisions generated by the war consumed the Democratic party. Most of the drama occurred not in the convention hall but outside, on the streets of Chicago. Led by Jerry Rubin and Abbie Hoffman, around 10,000 protesters descended on the city, calling for an end to the war, the legalization of marijuana, and the abolition of money. To mock those inside the convention hall, they nominated a pig for president. Their stunts, geared toward maximizing their media exposure, diverted attention from the more serious and far more numerous antiwar activists who had come to Chicago as convention delegates or volunteers.

Richard J. Daley, the Democratic mayor of Chicago, who had grown increasingly angry as protesters disrupted his convention, called out the police to break up the demonstrations. Several nights of skirmishes between protesters and police culminated the evening of the nominations. In what an official report later described as a "police riot," patrolmen attacked protesters with Mace, tear gas, and clubs as demonstrators chanted, "The whole world is watching!" Television networks broadcast a film of the riot as the nominating speeches were being made, cementing a popular impression of the Democrats as the party of disorder. Inside the hall, the Democrats dispiritedly nominated Hubert H. Humphrey, who chose Senator Edmund S. Muskie of Maine as his running mate. The delegates approved a middle-of-the-road platform that endorsed continued fighting in Vietnam while the administration explored diplomatic means of ending the conflict.

The disruptive Democratic convention unleashed a backlash against antiwar protesters. The general public did not differentiate between the disruptive antics of the Yippies and the more responsible behavior of those activists who were trying to work within the system. Polls showed overwhelming support for Mayor Daley and the police.

The turmoil surrounding the New Left and the antiwar movement strengthened support for proponents of "law and order," which became a conservative catch phrase for the next several years. Indeed, many Americans, though opposed to the war, were fed up with protest and dissent. Governor George C. Wallace of Alabama, a third-party candidate, skillfully exploited their growing disapproval of the antiwar movement by making student protests and urban riots his chief campaign issues. But Wallace, who in 1963 had promised to enforce "segregation now . . . segregation tomorrow . . . and segregation forever," also exploited the mounting backlash against the civil-rights movement. Articulating the resentments of many working-class whites, he combined attacks on liberal intellectuals and government elites with strident denunciations of school desegregation and forced busing.

Hard Hats
Many construction workers (and the unions they belonged to) were vocal supporters of the Vietnam War. Sometimes hard hats clashed with long-haired protesters during antiwar marches and sidewalk demonstrations.

Even more than George Wallace, Richard Nixon tapped the increasingly conservative mood of the electorate. After his unsuccessful presidential campaign in 1960 and his loss in the California gubernatorial race in 1962, Nixon engineered an amazing political comeback, and in 1968 won the Republican presidential nomination. He chose Spiro Agnew, the conservative governor of Maryland, as his running mate to attract southern voters, especially Wallace supporters, who opposed Democratic civil-rights legislation. Nixon pledged to represent the "quiet voice" of the "great majority of Americans, the forgotten Americans, the nonshouters, the nondemonstrators."

Despite the Democratic debacle in Chicago, the election was a close one. In the last weeks of the campaign, Humphrey rallied by gingerly disassociating himself from Johnson's war policies. Then, in a televised address on October 31, President Johnson announced a complete halt to the bombing of North Vietnam. Nixon countered by intimating that he had his own plan to end the war—although in reality no such plan existed. On election day Nixon received 43.4 percent of the vote to Humphrey's 42.7 percent, defeating him by a scant 510,000 votes out of the 73 million that were cast. Wallace finished with 13.5 percent of the popular vote. Though Nixon owed his election largely to the split in the Democratic coalition, the success of his southern strategy presaged the emergence of a new Republican majority. In the meantime, however, the Democrats retained a majority in both houses of Congress.

The closeness of the 1968 election suggested how polarized American society had become. Nixon appealed to a segment of society that came to be known as the *silent majority*—the hardworking, nonprotesting, generally white American. Although his victory suggested a growing consensus among voters who were "unblack, unpoor, and unyoung," heated protest and controversy would persist until the war ended.

Nixon's War

Vietnam, long Lyndon Johnson's war, now became Richard Nixon's. At first Nixon sought to end the war by expanding its scope, as a means of pressuring the North Vietnamese to negotiate. But Nixon and his national security adviser, Henry Kissinger, soon realized that the public would not support such an approach. Thus, shortly after Nixon took office, he sent a letter to the North Vietnamese leaders proposing mutual troop withdrawals. In March 1969, to convince North Vietnam that the United States meant business, Nixon ordered clandestine bombing raids on neutral Cambodia, through which the North Vietnamese had been transporting supplies and reinforcements.

When the intensified bombing failed to end the war, Nixon and Kissinger adopted a policy of *Vietnamization*. On June 8, 1969, Nixon announced that 25,000 American troops would be withdrawn by August and replaced by South Vietnamese forces. As the U.S. ambassador to Vietnam, Ellsworth Bunker, noted cynically, Vietnamization was just a matter of changing "the color of the bodies." Antiwar demonstrators denounced the new policy, which protected American lives at the expense of the Vietnamese, but would not end the war. On October 15, 1969, in cities across the country, millions of Americans joined a one-day "moratorium" against the war. A month later, more than a quarter of a million people mobilized in Washington in the largest antiwar demonstration to date.

To discredit his critics Nixon denounced student demonstrators as "bums" and stated that "North Vietnam cannot defeat or humiliate the United States. Only Americans can do that." Vice-President Spiro Agnew attacked dissenters as "ideological eunuchs" and "nattering nabobs of negativism." Nixon staunchly insisted that he would not be swayed by the mounting protests against the war. During the November 1969 march on Washington the president barricaded himself in the White House and watched football on television.

On April 30, 1970, the bombing of Cambodia, which Nixon had kept secret from both the public and from Congress, culminated in an "incursion" into Cambodia by American ground forces to destroy enemy havens there. The invasion proved only a short-term setback for the North Vietnamese, who continued to boycott the Paris peace talks. More critically, the American

action—along with the ongoing North Vietnamese intervention there—
destabilized the country, exposing it to a takeover by the ruthless Khmer
Rouge later in the 1970s.

When the *New York Times* uncovered the secret invasion of Cambodia,
antiwar leaders organized a national student strike. On May 4, at Kent State
University outside Cleveland, panicky National Guardsmen fired into a
crowd of students at an antiwar rally. Four people were killed and eleven
more wounded. Only two of those who were killed had been attending the
demonstration; the other two were just passing by on their way to class.
Soon afterward, National Guardsmen stormed a dormitory at Jackson State
College in Mississippi, killing two black students. More than 450 colleges
closed down in protest, and 80 percent of all campuses experienced some
kind of disturbance. In June 1970, immediately after the Kent State slayings,
a Gallup poll identified campus unrest as the issue that most troubled
Americans.

At the same time, however, dissatisfaction with the war continued to
spread. Congressional opposition to the war, which had been growing since
the Fulbright hearings in 1966, intensified with the invasion of Cambodia.
In June 1970 the Senate expressed its disapproval by voting to repeal the
Gulf of Tonkin resolution, and by cutting off funding for operations in
Cambodia. Even the soldiers in Vietnam were showing mounting opposition to their mission. The number of troops who refused to follow combat
orders increased steadily, and thousands of U.S. soldiers deserted. Among
the majority who fought on, many sewed peace symbols on their uniforms.
In the heat of battle, a number of overbearing junior officers were sometimes "fragged," that is, killed or wounded in grenade attacks by their own
soldiers. At home, members of a group called Vietnam Veterans against the

Kent State
The shootings by National Guardsmen of four students at Kent State
University in Ohio on May 4,
1970, set off campus demonstrations and protests across the country. The protester shown here holds
a placard memorializing the slain
students as well as the two black
students killed soon afterward at
Jackson State College in Mississippi. The president of Columbia
University called May 1970 "the
most disastrous month . . . in the
history of American higher
education."

War turned in their combat medals at demonstrations outside the U.S. Capitol.

In 1971 Americans were appalled by revelations of the sheer brutality of the war when Lieutenant William L. Calley was court-martialed for atrocities committed in the village of My Lai. In March 1968 Calley and the platoon under his command had apparently murdered 350 Vietnamese villagers in retaliation for casualties sustained in an earlier engagement. The military court sentenced Calley to life in prison for his part in the massacre. Yet George Wallace and some congressional conservatives called him a hero. President Nixon had Calley's sentence reduced; he was paroled in 1974.

After a final outbreak of protest and violence following the incident at Kent State, antiwar activism began to ebb. The antiwar movement was weakened in part by internal divisions within the New Left. In the late 1960s, SDS and other antiwar groups fell victim to police harassment, and Federal Bureau of Investigation (FBI) and Central Intelligence Agency (CIA) agents infiltrated and disrupted radical organizations. After 1968 the New Left splintered into factions, its energy spent. One radical faction broke off from SDS and formed the Weathermen, a tiny band of self-styled revolutionaries who embraced terrorist tactics that alienated more moderate activists.

Nixon's Vietnamization policy also played a role in the decline of antiwar protest by dramatically reducing the number of soldiers in combat. When Nixon took office, more than 543,000 American soldiers were serving in Vietnam; by the end of 1970 there were 334,000, and two years later there were 24,200. Nixon's promise to continue troop withdrawals, end the draft, and institute an all-volunteer army by 1973 further deprived the antiwar movement of important organizing issues, particularly on college campuses. Student commitment to social causes, however, did not disappear altogether. In the early 1970s many student activists refocused their energies on issues such as feminism and environmentalism.

Détente and the End of the War

At the same time Nixon had been prosecuting the war in Vietnam, ostensibly to halt the spread of communism, he had been formulating a new policy toward the Soviet Union and China. Known as *détente* (the French word for a relaxation of tensions), Nixon's policy was to seek peaceful coexistence with the two communist powers, and to link his overtures of friendship with a plan to end the Vietnam War. In his talks with Chinese and Soviet leaders, Nixon urged them to reduce their military aid to the North Vietnamese as a means of pressuring them to the negotiating table.

A lifelong anticommunist crusader, Nixon was better able to reach out to the two communist superpowers than a Democratic president would have been. Since the Chinese revolution of 1949 the United States had refused to recognize the government of the People's Republic of China. Instead, the

State Department had recognized the Nationalist Chinese government in Taiwan. Nixon moved away from that policy, reasoning that the United States could exploit the growing rift between the People's Republic of China and the Soviet Union. In February 1972 Nixon journeyed to China in a symbolic visit that set the stage for the establishment of formal diplomatic relations, which took place in 1979.

In a similar spirit Nixon journeyed to Moscow in May 1972 to sign the first Strategic Arms Limitations Treaty (SALT I) between the United States and the Soviet Union. Although SALT I fell far short of ending the arms race, it did limit the production and deployment of intercontinental ballistic missiles (ICBMs) and antiballistic missile systems (ABMs). The treaty also signified that the United States could no longer afford the massive military spending that would have been necessary to regain the nuclear and military superiority it had enjoyed immediately following World War II. By the early 1970s, inflation, domestic dissent, and the decline in American hegemony had limited and reshaped American aims and options in international relations. Most of all, Nixon hoped that a rapprochement with the Soviets would help to resolve the prolonged crisis in Vietnam.

The Paris peace talks had been in stalemate since 1968. Though the war had been "Vietnamized," and American casualties had decreased, the South Vietnamese military proved unable to hold its own. In late 1971, as American troops withdrew from the region, communist forces stepped up their attacks on Laos, Cambodia, and South Vietnam. The next spring North Vietnamese forces launched a major new offensive against South Vietnam. In April, as the fighting intensified, Nixon ordered B-52 bombing raids against North Vietnam, and a month later he approved the mining of North Vietnamese ports.

That spring the increased combat activity and growing political pressure at home helped revive the Paris peace negotiations. Nixon hoped to undercut antiwar critics by making concessions to the North Vietnamese in the peace talks. In October Henry Kissinger and the North Vietnamese negotiator Le Duc Tho reached a cease-fire agreement calling for the withdrawal of the remaining U.S. troops; the return of all American prisoners of war; and the continued presence of North Vietnamese troops in South Vietnam. Nixon and Kissinger also promised the North Vietnamese substantial aid for postwar reconstruction. On the eve of the 1972 presidential election Kissinger announced "peace is at hand," and Nixon returned to the White House with a resounding electoral victory (see Chapter 32).

The peace initiative, however, soon stalled when the South Vietnamese rejected the provision concerning North Vietnamese troop positions, and the North declined to compromise further. With negotiations deadlocked, Nixon stepped up military action once more. From December 17 to December 30, 1972, American planes subjected civilian and military targets in Hanoi and Haiphong to the most devastating bombing of the war, referred to in the press as the Christmas bombings. Finally, on January 27, 1973, representatives of the

United States, North and South Vietnam, and the Viet Cong signed a cease-fire in Paris. But the Paris Peace Accords, which differed little from the proposal that had been rejected in October, did not fulfill Nixon's promise of "peace with honor." Basically, they mandated the unilateral withdrawal of American troops in exchange for the return of American prisoners of war from North Vietnam. For most Americans, that was enough.

Nor did the 1973 accords resolve Vietnam's civil war. Without massive U.S. military and economic aid, and with North Vietnamese guerrillas operating freely throughout the countryside, the South Vietnamese government of General Nguyen Van Thieu soon fell to the more disciplined and popular communist forces. In March 1975 North Vietnamese forces launched a final offensive. Horrified American television viewers watched as South Vietnamese officials and soldiers struggled with American embassy personnel to board the last helicopters that would fly out of Saigon before North Vietnamese troops entered the city. On April 29, 1975, Vietnam was reunited, and Saigon was renamed Ho Chi Minh City in honor of the communist leader, who had died in 1969.

The Legacy of Vietnam

Spanning nearly thirty years, the Vietnam War occupied American administrations from Truman to Nixon's successor Gerald Ford. U.S. troops fought in Vietnam for more than eleven years, from 1961 to 1973. In human terms, the nation's longest war exacted an enormous cost. Some 58,000 U.S. troops died, and another 300,000 were wounded. Even those who returned unharmed encountered a sometimes hostile or indifferent reception. Arriving home alone, with no counseling, most Vietnam veterans found the transition to civilian life abrupt and disorienting. The psychological tensions of serving in Vietnam and the difficulty of reentry sowed the seeds of what is now recognized as post-traumatic stress disorder—recurring physical and psychological problems that often lead to divorce, unemployment, and suicide. Only in the 1980s did America begin to make its peace with those who had served in the nation's most unpopular war.

In Southeast Asia, the damage was far greater. The war claimed an estimated 1.5 million Vietnamese lives and devastated the country's physical and economic infrastructure. Neighboring Laos and Cambodia also suffered, particularly Cambodia, where between 1975 and 1979 the Khmer Rouge killed an estimated 2 million Cambodians—a quarter of the population—in a brutal relocation campaign. All told, the war produced nearly 10 million refugees, many of whom immigrated to the United States. Among them were thousands of Amerasians, the offspring of American soldiers and Vietnamese women. Spurned by their fathers and by most Vietnamese, more than 30,000 Amerasians immigrated to the United States in the 1990s.

The defeat in Vietnam prompted Americans to think differently about foreign affairs, and to acknowledge the limits of U.S. power abroad. The United

States became less willing to plunge into overseas military commitments, a controversial change that conservatives dubbed the "Vietnam syndrome." In 1973 Congress declared its hostility to undeclared wars like those in Vietnam and Korea by passing the War Powers Act, which required the president to report any use of military force within forty-eight hours, and directed that hostilities must cease within sixty days without a declaration of war by Congress. On those occasions when Congress did agree to foreign intervention, as in the Persian Gulf War of 1990–1991, American leaders would insist on obtainable military objectives and careful handling of the news media—elements that had often been lacking in Vietnam. Perhaps most important, in the future, any foreign entanglement would be evaluated in terms of its potential to become "another Vietnam."

The Vietnam War also distorted American economic and social affairs. At a total price of over $150 billion, the war siphoned resources from domestic needs, added to the deficit, and fueled inflation (see Chapter 32). Lyndon Johnson's Great Society programs had been pared down, and domestic reform efforts slowed thereafter. Moreover, the war shattered the liberal consensus that had supported the Democratic coalition. Even more seriously, the conduct of the war—the lies about American successes on the battlefield, the questionable representation of events in the Gulf of Tonkin, the secret war in Cambodia—spawned a deep distrust of government among American citizens. The discrediting of liberalism, the increased cynicism toward government, and the growing social turmoil that accompanied the war would continue into the next decade, paving the way for a resurgence of the Republican party and a new mood of conservatism.

CHAPTER 31 TIMELINE

1946	War begins between French and Vietminh
1950	China and Soviet Union recognize Ho Chi Minh's government United States begins sending military aid to Vietnam
1954	French defeat at Dienbienphu Ngo Dinh Diem takes power in South Vietnam Geneva Accords
1960	Founding of National Liberation Front (NLF) in South Vietnam
1962	Students for a Democratic Society (SDS) founded
1963	Ngo Dinh Diem ousted in coup
1964	Gulf of Tonkin Resolution Free Speech Movement at Berkeley
1965	Operation Rolling Thunder First U.S. combat troops arrive in Vietnam
1967	Hippie counterculture's Summer of Love
1968	Tet offensive Martin Luther King, Jr., assassinated Peace talks open in Paris Robert F. Kennedy assassinated Riot at Democratic National Convention in Chicago
1969	Woodstock festival Vietnam moratorium
1970	Nixon orders invasion of Cambodia; renewed antiwar protests Kent State and Jackson State killings Gulf of Tonkin resolution repealed
1972	Nixon visits People's Republic of China SALT I with Soviet Union signed Christmas bombings of North Vietnam
1973	Paris Peace Accords War Powers Act
1975	Fall of Saigon

CHAPTER 32

THE LEAN YEARS: 1969–1980

- The Nixon Years
- Diminished Expectations and New Challenges
- Social Gridlock: Reform and Reaction in the 1970s
- Post-Watergate Politics: Failed Leadership

As the Vietnam War ended, Americans turned inward, just as they had done in the years after World Wars I and II. But the 1970s, unlike the 1920s and the 1950s, were not a time of prosperity and optimism. To many Americans, the nation's withdrawal from Vietnam represented an ignominious defeat that underscored its diminished power. In the early 1970s, growing economic problems—rising oil prices, runaway inflation, declining productivity, and stagnating incomes—compounded that sense of disillusionment, signaling the end of the nation's overwhelming economic superiority. Americans also grew disenchanted with their political leadership in the 1970s, as one public official after another, including President Richard Nixon, resigned for misconduct. In the wake of Nixon's resignation, the lackluster administrations of Presidents Gerald Ford and Jimmy Carter failed to provide the leadership necessary to cope with the nation's economic and international insecurities—a failure that fed Americans' growing skepticism about government and its capacity to improve people's lives.

Paradoxically, in the midst of this growing disaffection and skepticism, a commitment to social change persisted. Some of the social movements born in the 1960s, such as feminism and environmentalism, had their greatest impact in the 1970s. As former student radicals moved into the political mainstream, they took their struggles with them, from streets and campuses into courts, schools, workplaces, and local communities. But, like the civil-rights

862

and antiwar movements of the 1960s, the social activism of the 1970s stirred fears and uncertainties among many Americans. Furthermore, the darkening economic climate of the new decade undercut the sense of social generosity that had characterized the 1960s, fueling a new conservatism that would become a potent political force by the decade's end.

THE NIXON YEARS

Richard Nixon set the stage for the conservative political resurgence that would influence the nation for the next several decades. His "new federalism" heralded a long-term Republican effort to trim back the Great Society and shift some federal responsibilities back to the states. At the same time, Nixon actively embraced the use of federal power—within limits—to uphold governmental responsibility for social welfare, environmental protection, and economic stability.

The Republican Domestic Agenda

In a 1968 campaign pledge to "the average American," Nixon had vowed to "reverse the flow of power and resources from the states and communities to Washington and start power and resources flowing back . . . to the people." One hallmark of this *new federalism* was the 1972 *revenue sharing* program, which distributed a portion of federal tax revenues to the states as block grants, to be spent as state officials saw fit. In later years revenue sharing would become a key Republican strategy for reducing federal social programs and federal bureaucracy.

Nixon also worked to scale down certain federal government programs that had grown dramatically during the two preceding administrations. He reduced funding for many War on Poverty programs, and dismantled the Office of Economic Opportunity altogether in 1971. Urban renewal, pollution control, and other environmental initiatives suffered when Nixon *impounded* (refused to spend) billions of dollars appropriated for them by Congress. Nixon's lack of interest in extending the gains of the civil-rights movement, as well as his effort, albeit unsuccessful, to reform the social welfare system, further exemplified the Republicans' desire to roll back the consolidation of federal power that had characterized American political life since the New Deal.

Still, with Democratic majorities in both houses of Congress, Nixon needed to be flexible in legislative matters. He agreed to the growth of major entitlement programs, such as Medicare, Medicaid, and Social Security. In 1970 he signed a bill establishing the Environmental Protection Agency (EPA), and in 1972 he approved legislation creating the Occupational Safety and Health Administration (OSHA) and the Consumer Products Safety Commission. Thus, his administration witnessed the expansion of federal power in numerous areas.

Nixon demonstrated his conservative social values most clearly in his appointments to the Supreme Court. In 1969, he nominated the conservative

Warren Burger to replace retired Chief Justice Earl Warren. After some difficulties in getting other nominees confirmed by the Senate—the nomination
of G. Harold Carswell failed in part because Carswell had participated in a
white segregationists' scheme to buy a public golf course in Florida to prevent
its integration—Nixon eventually named three other conservative justices:
Harry Blackmun, Lewis F. Powell, Jr., and William Rehnquist.

Nixon's appointees did not always hand down decisions the president approved, however. Despite attempts by the Justice department to halt further
desegregation in the face of determined white opposition, the Court ordered
busing to achieve racial balance. In 1972, it issued restrictions on the implementation of capital punishment, though it did not rule the death penalty unconstitutional. And in the controversial 1973 case *Roe v. Wade*, Justice Harry
Blackmun wrote the decision that struck down laws prohibiting abortion in
Texas and Georgia.

The 1972 Election

Nixon's reelection in 1972 was never much in doubt. In May, the threat of a
conservative third-party challenge from Alabama governor George Wallace
ended abruptly when an assailant shot Wallace, paralyzing him from the waist
down. With Wallace out of the picture, Nixon's strategy of wooing southern
white voters away from the Democrats got a boost (see Chapter 31). Nixon
also benefited from the disarray of the Democratic party. Divided over Vietnam and civil rights, the Democrats were plagued by tensions between their
newer, more liberal constituencies—women, minorities, and young adults—
and the old-line officeholders and labor union leaders who had always dominated the party. Recent changes in the party's system of selecting delegates
and candidates benefited the newer groups, and they helped to nominate Senator George McGovern of South Dakota, a noted liberal and an outspoken
opponent of the Vietnam War.

McGovern's campaign quickly ran into trouble. On learning that his running mate, Senator Thomas F. Eagleton of Missouri, had undergone elec-
troshock therapy for depression some years earlier, McGovern first supported
him and then abruptly insisted that he quit the ticket. Sargent Shriver, the former head of the Peace Corps and the Office of Economic Opportunity, replaced Eagleton. But McGovern's waffling on the matter made him appear
weak and indecisive. Moreover, he was far too liberal for many traditional
Democrats, who rejected his ill-defined proposals for welfare reform and his
call for unilateral withdrawal from Vietnam.

Nixon's campaign took full advantage of McGovern's weaknesses. Although the president had failed to end the war, his Vietnamization policy had
virtually eliminated American combat deaths by 1972. Henry Kissinger's premature declaration that "peace is at hand" raised voters' hopes for a negotiated
settlement (see Chapter 31). Not only did those initiatives rob the Democrats
of their greatest appeal—their antiwar stance—but an improving economy

further favored the Republicans. Nixon won handily, receiving nearly 61 percent of the popular vote and carrying every state except Massachusetts and the District of Columbia. Yet the president failed to kindle strong loyalty in the electorate. Only 55.7 percent of eligible voters bothered to go to the polls, and the Democrats maintained control of both houses of Congress.

Watergate

Though the Watergate scandal, one of the great constitutional crises of the twentieth century, broke in 1972, its roots lay in the early years of Nixon's first administration. Obsessed with the antiwar movement, the White House had repeatedly authorized illegal surveillance—opening mail, tapping phones, arranging break-ins—of citizens such as Daniel Ellsberg, a former Defense department analyst who had become disillusioned with the war. In 1971 Ellsberg had leaked the so-called Pentagon Papers to the *New York Times*. This secret study, commissioned by Secretary of Defense McNamara in 1967, detailed so many American blunders that, after reading it, McNamara had commented, "You know, they could hang people for what is in there." The administration had tried to get a court order to block publication of the papers. To discredit Ellsberg, White House underlings broke into his psychiatrist's office to search for damaging personal information, but the burglars failed to turn up anything embarrassing. When their break-in was revealed, the court dismissed the case against Ellsberg.

In another abuse of presidential power committed prior to the 1972 campaign, the White House had established a clandestine intelligence group, known as the "plumbers," because they were supposed to plug leaks of government information. They relied on tactics such as using the Internal Revenue Service and other government agencies to harass the administration's opponents who were named on an "enemies list" drawn up by presidential counsel John Dean. One of the plumbers' major targets was the Democratic party, whose front-running primary candidate, Senator Edmund Muskie of Maine, became the object of several of their "dirty tricks," including the distribution of phony campaign posters reading "Help Muskie in Busing More Children Now."

These secret and highly questionable activities were financed by massive illegal fund-raising efforts by Nixon's Committee to Re-Elect the President (known as CREEP). To obtain contributions from major corporations, Nixon's fund-raisers had used high-pressure tactics that included implied threats of federal tax audits and other punitive measures if companies failed to cooperate. CREEP raised over $20 million, a portion of which was used to finance the plumbers' dirty tricks, including a break-in that led to the Watergate scandal.

Early in the morning of June 17, 1972, police arrested five men carrying cameras, wiretapping equipment, and a large amount of cash, and charged them with breaking into the Democratic National Committee's headquarters

Watergate Diary

Journalist Elizabeth Drew kept a diary during the Watergate crisis. This passage, written on August 5, 1974, shortly after President Nixon was forced to release some exceptionally damaging tape transcripts, explores the implications of the revelations for Americans' faith in the presidency.

For those who believed that the President was aware of, and even directed, the cover-up, it must still be a shock to *read his conversation* about it. . . .

There is an inexplicable difference between the experiences of suspecting a lie and being whacked in the face with the evidence of one. Many Americans had become accustomed to thinking of the President as a liar, and had alternately suspended belief in, scoffed at, or become enraged at his statements. But I wonder whether the enormity of his lying has sunk in yet—whether we have, or can, come to terms with the thought that so much of what he said to us was just noise, words, and that we can no longer begin by accepting any of it as the truth. This is a total reversal of the way we were brought up to think about Presidents, a departure from deeply ingrained habits. One's mind resists the thought of our President as a faithless man, capable of looking at us in utter sincerity from the other side of the television camera and telling us multiple, explicit, barefaced lies. One is torn between the idea that people must be able to have some confidence in their leaders and the idea that in this day of image manipulation a certain skepticism may serve them well. I do not think there is much comfort to be taken from the fact that eventually Nixon's lies— like Johnson's—caught up with him. It took a long time, and a great deal of damage was done meanwhile.

SOURCE: Elizabeth Drew, *Washington Journal: The Events of 1973–1974* (New York: Random House, 1974), pp. 391–392.

at the Watergate apartment complex in Washington, D.C. Two accomplices were apprehended soon afterward. Three of the men had worked in the White House or for CREEP, and four had CIA connections. Nixon later claimed that White House counsel John Dean had conducted a full investigation of the incident (no such investigation ever took place), and that "no one on the White House staff, no one in this administration, presently employed, was involved in this very bizarre incident."

Subsequent investigations revealed that shortly after the break-in, the president had ordered his chief of staff, H. R. Haldeman, to instruct the CIA to tell the FBI not to probe too deeply into connections between the White House and the burglars. When the burglars were convicted in January 1973, John Dean, with Nixon's approval, tried to buy their continued silence with $400,000 in hush money and hints of presidential pardons.

The coverup of the White House's involvement began to unravel when one of the convicted burglars began to talk. Two tenacious investigative reporters at the Washington *Post*, Carl Bernstein and Bob Woodward, exposed the attempt to hide the truth and traced it back to the White House. Reports of CREEP's "dirty tricks" and illegal fund-raising soon compounded the public's suspicions about the president. In February the Senate voted 77 to 0 to establish a select committee to investigate the widening scandal. Two months later Nixon accepted the resignations of Haldeman, Assistant Secretary of Commerce Jeb Stuart Magruder, and chief domestic adviser John Ehrlichman, all of whom had been implicated in the cover-up. He fired Dean, who had agreed to testify in the case in exchange for immunity from prosecution.

In May the Senate Watergate committee, chaired by Senator Sam Ervin of North Carolina, began holding nationally televised hearings. On June 14 Magruder testified before the committee, confessing his guilt and implicating former Attorney General John Mitchell, Dean, and others. Dean, in turn, implicated Nixon in the plot. Even more startling testimony from a Nixon aide revealed that Nixon had installed a secret taping system in the Oval Office.

The president steadfastly "stonewalled" the committee's demand that he surrender the tapes, citing executive privilege and national security. But Archibald Cox, a special prosecutor whom Nixon had appointed to investigate the case, successfully petitioned a federal court to order the president to hand the tapes over. Still Nixon refused to comply. When he ordered Attorney General Elliott Richardson to fire Cox, Richardson resigned in protest, as did the assistant attorney general. Nixon finally got the solicitor general, Robert Bork, to carry out his order, but this action backfired. The "Saturday Night Massacre" sparked public outrage and renewed demands for release of the tapes.

After receiving additional federal subpoenas the following spring, Nixon finally released a heavily edited transcript of the tapes, peppered with the words "expletive deleted." Senate Republican leader Hugh Scott called the transcripts "deplorable, disgusting, shabby, immoral." Most suspicious was an eighteen-minute gap in the tape covering a crucial meeting between Nixon, Haldeman, and Ehrlichman on June 20, 1972—three days after the break-in.

The Watergate affair moved into its final phase when on June 30 the House of Representatives voted three articles of impeachment against Richard Nixon: obstruction of justice, abuse of power, and acting to subvert the Constitution. Two days later the Supreme Court ruled unanimously that Nixon could not claim executive privilege as a justification for refusing to turn over additional tapes. Under duress, on August 5 Nixon released the unexpurgated tapes, which contained evidence that he had ordered the cover-up as early as six days after the break-in. Facing certain conviction in a Senate trial, on August 9, 1974, Nixon became the first U.S. president to resign.

The next day Vice-President Gerald Ford was sworn in as president. Ford, a former Michigan congressman and house minority leader, had replaced Vice-President Spiro Agnew in 1973 after Agnew resigned under indictment

Nixon Resigns
On August 9, 1974, Richard M. Nixon became the first American president to resign. He is shown here minutes after turning over the presidency to Gerald R. Ford. Nixon retired to his home in San Clemente, California, refusing to admit guilt for what had happened.

for accepting kickbacks on construction contracts. The transfer of power proceeded smoothly. A month later, however, Ford stunned the nation by granting Nixon a "full, free, and absolute" pardon "for all offenses he had committed or might have committed during his presidency." Ford took that action, he said, to spare the country the agony of rehashing Watergate. While Nixon retired to his estate in San Clemente, California, twenty-five members of his administration went to prison. Named only as an "unindicted coconspirator" in their trials, Nixon refused to admit guilt for what had happened, conceding only that he had made an error in judgment.

In response to the abuses of the Nixon administration and to contain the power of what the historian Arthur M. Schlesinger, Jr., called "the imperial presidency," Congress adopted several reforms. In 1974 a strengthened Freedom of Information Act gave citizens greater access to files federal agencies had amassed on them. The Fair Campaign Practices Act of 1974 limited campaign contributions and provided for stricter accountability and public financing of presidential campaigns. Ironically, because the act allowed an unlimited number of political action committees (PACs) to donate up to $5,000 per candidate, corporations and lobbying groups found they could actually increase their influence by making multiple donations. By the end of the decade close to 3,000 PACs were playing an increasingly pivotal—and some would argue unethical—role in national elections.

Perhaps the most significant legacy of Watergate, however, was the wave of cynicism that swept the country in its wake. Beginning with Lyndon Johnson's "credibility gap" during the Vietnam War, public distrust of government had risen steadily with the disclosure of the secret bombing of Cambodia and the illegal surveillance and harassment of antiwar protesters and other political opponents. The saga of Watergate confirmed what many Americans had long suspected: that politicians were hopelessly corrupt, and that the federal government was out of control.

DIMINISHED EXPECTATIONS AND NEW CHALLENGES

Economic difficulties compounded Americans' political disillusionment. Growing international demand for natural resources, particularly oil, coupled with unstable access to foreign oil supplies, wreaked havoc with the American economy. At the same time, foreign competitors successfully expanded their share of the world market, edging out American-made products. The resulting sharp downturn in the domestic economy marked the end of America's twenty-five-year dominance of the world economy.

The Hydrocarbon Age

Until well into the twentieth century, the United States was the world's leading producer and consumer of oil. During World War II the nation had produced two-thirds of the world's oil, but by 1972 its share had fallen to only 22 percent, even though domestic production had continued to rise. By the late 1960s the United States was buying more and more of its oil on the world market to keep up with shrinking domestic reserves and growing demand.

The imported oil came primarily from the Middle East, where production had increased a stupendous 1,500 percent in the twenty-five years following World War II. The rise of nationalism and the corresponding decline of colonialism in the postwar era had encouraged the Persian Gulf nations to wrest control from the European and American oil companies that once dominated petroleum exploration and production in that region. In 1960, joining with other Third World oil-producing countries, they had formed the Organization of Petroleum Exporting Countries (OPEC). Just five of the founding countries—the Middle Eastern states of Saudi Arabia, Kuwait, Iran, and Iraq, plus Venezuela—were the source of more than 80 percent of the world's crude oil exports. During the early 1970s, when world demand climbed and oil reserves fell, they took advantage of market forces to maximize their profits. Between 1973 and 1975 OPEC deliberately raised the price of a barrel of oil from $3 to $12. By the end of the decade the price had peaked at $34 a barrel, setting off a round of furious inflation in the oil-dependent United States.

OPEC members also found that oil could be used as a weapon in global politics. In 1973 OPEC instituted an oil embargo against the United States, Western Europe, and Japan, in retaliation for their aid to Israel during the Yom Kippur War, which had begun when Egypt and Syria invaded Israel. The embargo, which lasted until 1974, forced Americans to curtail their driving or spend long hours in line at the pumps; in a matter of months, gas prices climbed 40 percent. Since the U.S. automobile industry had little to offer except "gas-guzzlers" built to run on cheap fuel, Americans turned to cheaper, more fuel-efficient foreign cars manufactured in Japan and West Germany. Soon the auto industry was in a slump, weakening the American economy.

The energy crisis was an enormous shock to the American psyche. Suddenly Americans felt like hostages to economic forces that were beyond their control. As OPEC's leaders pushed prices higher and higher, they seemed to be able to determine whether western economies would grow or stagnate. Despite an extensive public conservation campaign and a second gas shortage in 1979, caused by the Iranian revolution, Americans could not wean themselves from foreign oil. In fact, they used even more foreign oil after the energy crisis

No Gas
During the energy crisis of 1973–1974 American motorists faced widespread gasoline shortages for the first time since World War II. Although gas was not rationed, gas stations were closed on Sundays, air travel was cut by 10 percent, and a national speed limit of 55 miles per hour was imposed.

than they had before—a testimony to the enormous thirst of modern industrial and consumer societies for petroleum.

Economic Woes

While the energy crisis dealt a swift blow to the U.S. economy, other developments had equally damaging results. The high cost of the Vietnam War and the Great Society had contributed to a steadily growing federal deficit and spiraling inflation. A business downturn in 1970 had led to rising unemployment (6 percent) and declining productivity. In the industrial sector the reviving economies of West Germany and Japan over time had reduced demand for American goods worldwide. In 1955 American-made goods had accounted for 32 percent of all imports by major capitalist countries; by 1970 the proportion was only 18 percent, and it continued to decline in the 1970s. As a result, in 1971 the dollar fell to its lowest level on the world market since 1949, and the United States posted its first trade deficit in almost a century.

That year Nixon took several bold steps to turn the economy around. To stem the decline in currency and trade, he suspended the Bretton Woods system that had been set up at the United Nations monetary conference in 1944 (see Chapter 29). Once again, the dollar would fluctuate in relation to the price of an ounce of gold. The change, which effectively devalued the dollar in hopes of encouraging foreign trade, represented a frank acknowledgment that America's currency was no longer the world's strongest. Nixon also instituted wage and price controls to curb inflation, and to boost the sluggish economy he offered a "full employment" budget for 1972, including $11 billion in deficit spending.

Though these measures brought a temporary improvement in the economy, the general decline persisted. Overall economic growth, as measured by the gross national product (GNP), had averaged 4.1 percent per year in the 1960s; in the 1970s it dropped to only 2.9 percent, contributing to a noticeable decline in most Americans' standard of living. Between 1973 and the early 1980s, discretionary income per worker decreased 18 percent. At the same time, galloping inflation forced consumer prices upward, peaking at 10 percent in 1974 and over 13 percent in 1980. Housing prices, in particular, rose rapidly: the average cost of a single-family home more than doubled in the 1970s, making home ownership inaccessible to a growing segment of the working and middle classes.

Young adults faced a constricted job market in the late 1970s, as a record number of baby boomers competed for a limited number of jobs. Unemployment peaked at around 9 percent in 1975, declined briefly, then edged upward again to around 6 to 7 percent in the late 1970s. A devastating combination of inflation and unemployment—dubbed *stagflation*—bedeviled presidential administrations from Nixon to Reagan, whose remedies (such as deficit spending and tax reduction) failed to eradicate the double scourge.

American economic woes were most acute in the industrial sector, which entered a prolonged period of decline, or *deindustrialization*. Investors who had formerly bought stock in basic U.S. industries began to speculate on the stock market or put their money into mergers or foreign companies. Many U.S. firms relocated overseas, partly to take advantage of cheaper labor and production costs. By the end of the 1970s the hundred largest multinational corporations and banks were earning more than a third of their overall profits abroad.

The most dramatic consequences of deindustrialization occurred in the older industrial regions of the northeast and midwest, which came to be known as the Rust Belt. There the dominant images of American industry in the mid-twentieth century—huge factories such as Ford's River Rouge outside Detroit and the General Electric plant in Lynn, Massachusetts— were fast becoming relics. When a community's major employer closed down and left town, the devastating effect rippled through communities in America's heartland. Many workers moved to the cities of the Sun Belt, which continued the dramatic growth that began after World War II (see Chapter 29).

Deindustrialization and the changing economic conditions that provoked it posed a critical problem for the labor movement. In the heyday of labor during the 1940s and 1950s, American managers had often cooperated with unions; with profits high, there was room for accommodation. But as foreign competition cut into corporate profits in the 1970s, industry became less willing to bargain, and the labor movement's power declined. In the 1970s union membership dropped from 28 to 23 percent of the American work force. Facing strikes or labor problems, some employers simply moved their operations abroad, where they found a cheaper, more compliant work force. In a competitive global environment, labor's prospects seemed dim.

SOCIAL GRIDLOCK: REFORM AND REACTION IN THE 1970s

The nation's economic problems and growing cynicism about government led to deep public anxiety and resentment. Many Americans turned inward to private satisfactions. The journalist Tom Wolfe labeled the 1970s the "Me Decade" because of the widespread obsession with lifestyles and personal well-being, while the historian Christopher Lasch referred derisively to what he called a "culture of narcissism." Yet those labels hardly do justice to a decade in which environmentalism, feminism, lesbian and gay rights, and other social movements blossomed. Furthermore, such characterizations neglect the growing social conservatism that was in part a response to such movements. In fact, the confluence of these trends produced a pattern of shifting crosscurrents that made the 1970s a complex transitional decade.

The New Activism: Environmental and Consumer Movements

After 1970 many baby boomers left the counterculture behind and settled down to pursue careers and material goods. But these young adults sought personal fulfillment as well. In a quest for physical and spiritual well-being, millions of Americans began jogging, riding bicycles, and working out at the gym. The fitness craze coincided with a heightened environmental awareness that spurred the demand for pesticide-free foods and vegetarian cookbooks. For spiritual support, some young people embraced the self-help techniques of the human potential, or New Age, movement; others turned to religious cults such as the Hare Krishna, the Church of Scientology, and the Unification Church of Reverend Sun Myung Moon.

A few baby boomers continued to pursue the unfinished social and political agendas of the 1960s. Moving into law, education, social work, medicine, and other fields, these former radicals continued their activism on a grass-roots level. Some joined the left wing of the Democratic party; others helped to establish community-based organizations, including health clinics, food co-ops, and day-care centers. On the local level, at least, the progressive spirit of the 1960s lived on.

One of the most dynamic sources of activism in the 1970s was the environmental movement. In contrast to the older generation of environmental activists, which advocated resource management and worked within the political system through organizations such as the Sierra Club (see Chapter 17), many of the new environmentalists had been 1960s-style activists. They brought their radical political sensibilities to the environmental movement, infusing it with new life. For example, they construed the search for alternative technologies (especially solar power) as a political statement against a corporate structure that was increasingly inhospitable to human-scale technology—and to humans, as well. The new activists used sit-ins and other protest tactics developed in the civil-rights and antiwar movements to mobilize mass support for specific issues or legislation.

The birth of the modern environmental movement is often dated to the publication in 1962 of Rachel Carson's *Silent Spring*, a powerful analysis of the impact of pesticides on the food chain. Other issues that galvanized public opinion included the environmental impact of industrial projects such as the Alaska pipeline and the harmful effects of chlorofluorocarbons and increased carbon dioxide levels on the earth's atmosphere. In January 1969 a huge oil spill off the coast of Santa Barbara, California, provoked an outcry, as did the discovery in 1978 that a housing development outside Niagara Falls, New York, had been built on a toxic waste site. The abnormally high rates of illness and birth defects recorded in this Love Canal neighborhood deepened public awareness of the culpability of business in generating environmental hazards. Concerned Americans also worried about the federal government's lax control of nuclear weapons plants, such as the uranium-processing plant at Fernald, Ohio, where liquid wastes were dumped into open-air storage pits.

Nuclear energy became the subject of citizen action in the 1970s, when rising prices and oil shortages pitted environmental concerns against the need for alternative energy sources. To reduce the nation's dependence on foreign oil, some politicians and utility companies began to promote the expansion of nuclear power. By January 1974, forty-two nuclear power plants were in operation,

Environmental Activist

*S*am Lovejoy participated in the Clamshell Alliance, a group that used peaceful civil disobedience in its protest against a nuclear power plant in Seabrook, New Hampshire. His account, as given to journalist Studs Terkel, reveals the persistence of 1960s-style political activism in the environmental movement that emerged in the 1970s.

Terkel: We are told that some issues are too complex for ordinary people, that experts . . .
Lovejoy: Bullshit. It's the best argument to delude the people. It's the same thing we heard about the Vietnam War. If we're gonna have democracy in this country, by God, we're gonna have to start telling people the facts. Einstein said it thirty years ago: We must take the facts of nuclear power to the village square, and from the village square must come America's voice. . . .
[At Seabrook] We made a commitment to nonviolent civil disobedience to stop the plant. . . .
On April 30, we brought over two thousand people to the site. The governor distrusted his state police and mobilized the National Guard. Over fourteen hundred people were arrested and locked up in the five armories for two weeks. It created more publicity than the Clamshell Alliance had ever anticipated. The arrestees conducted workshops. The National Guard guys were standing around, listening and participating. They're just funky people from local towns, just like you and me. They got called off local jobs and didn't see what the hell they were doing here, guarding a bunch of very nice people. . . .
The media is selling us on the notion of apathy and paralysis in the country. Bullshit. The movement did not die. It did the most intelligent thing it could do: it went to find a home. It went into the community. It's working, unnoticed, in the neighborhood. They're starting to blossom and make alliances, connections. I've been all over the country, and I have not been into one community where I did not meet people exactly like me.

SOURCE: Studs Terkel, *American Dreams: Lost and Found* (New York: Pantheon, 1980), pp. 459–460.

and over a hundred more were planned. Suddenly, the construction of nuclear power plants and reactors, which had gone largely unchallenged in the 1950s and 1960s, became controversial. Community activists protested plans for new reactors, citing inadequate evacuation plans and the unresolved problem of the disposal of radioactive waste. In Seabrook, New Hampshire, and Shoreham, New York, the mass protests of the Clamshell Alliance and other antinuclear groups, reminiscent of the antiwar demonstrations of the 1960s, helped to delay or prevent the start-up of nuclear reactors.

Public fears about nuclear safety seemed to be confirmed in March 1979 when a nuclear plant at Three Mile Island near Harrisburg, Pennsylvania, came critically close to a meltdown of its central core reactor. A prompt shutdown of the plant brought the problem under control before radioactive material seeped into the environment, but as a member of the panel that investigated the accident admitted, "We were damn lucky." Ultimately, Three Mile Island caused Americans to rethink the question of whether nuclear power could be a viable solution to the nation's energy needs. Grass-roots activism, combined with public fear of the potential dangers of nuclear energy, convinced many utility companies to abandon nuclear power, despite its short-term economic advantages.

Americans' concerns about nuclear power, chemical contamination, pesticides, and other environmental issues helped to turn environmentalism into a mass movement. On the first Earth Day, April 22, 1970, 20 million citizens gathered in communities across the country to show their support for the endangered planet. Although environmentalists failed to garner support for a "Green" political party, modeled on those in European countries, they did create bipartisan support for a spate of new federal legislation. In 1969 Congress passed the National Environmental Policy Act, which required the developers of public projects to file an environmental impact statement. The next year Nixon established the Environmental Protection Agency (EPA) and signed the Clean Air Act, which toughened standards for auto emissions in order to reduce smog and air pollution. Two years later Congress banned the use of the pesticide DDT. And in 1973 the Endangered Species Act expanded the protection provided by the Endangered Animals Act of 1964, granting species such as snail darters and spotted owls protected status. Thus environmental protection joined social welfare, defense, and national security as targets of federal intervention.

The environmental movement did not go uncontested. The EPA-mandated fuel economy standards for cars, for example, provoked criticism for threatening the health of the auto industry as it struggled to keep up with foreign competitors. Corporations resented environmental regulations, but so did many of their workers, who believed that tightened standards threatened their jobs and privileged nature over human beings. "IF YOU'RE HUNGRY AND OUT OF WORK, EAT AN ENVIRONMENTALIST" read one labor union's bumper sticker. Thus, in a time of rising unemployment and deindustrialization, activists clashed head-on with proponents of economic development, full employment, and global competitiveness.

The rise of environmentalism was paralleled by a growing movement to eliminate harmful consumer products and curb dangerous practices by American corporations. The consumer protection movement had originated in the Progressive Era, with the founding of government agencies such as the Food and Drug Administration (FDA) (see Chapter 21). In the 1960s, after decades of inertia, the movement reemerged under the leadership of Ralph Nader, a young lawyer whose book *Unsafe at Any Speed* (1965) attacked General Motors for putting style ahead of safety and fuel economy in its engineering. In 1969 Nader launched a Washington-based organization that gave rise to the Public Interest Research Group, a national network of consumer groups that focused on issues ranging from product safety to consumer fraud and environmental pollution. His organization pioneered legal tactics, such as the class-action suit, which allowed people with common grievances to sue as a group. It became the model for dozens of other groups that emerged in the 1970s and afterward to combat the health hazards of smoking, unethical insurance and credit practices, and other consumer problems. With the establishment of the federal Consumer Products Safety Commission in 1972 Congress acknowledged the growing need for consumer protection.

Challenges to Tradition: The Women's Movement and Gay Rights Activism

Feminism proved the most enduring movement to emerge from the 1960s. In the next decade the women's movement grew more sophisticated, generating an array of services and organizations, from rape crisis centers and battered women's shelters to feminist health collectives and women's bookstores. In 1972 Gloria Steinem and other journalists founded *Ms.* magazine, the first consumer magazine aimed at a feminist audience. Formerly all-male bastions, such as Yale, Princeton, and the U.S. Military Academy, admitted women undergraduates for the first time, while the proportion of women attending graduate and professional schools rose markedly. Several new national women's organizations emerged, and established groups such as The National Organization for Women (NOW) continued to grow. In 1977, 20,000 women went to Houston for the first National Women's Conference. Their "National Plan of Action" represented a hard-won consensus on topics ranging from violence against women to homemakers' rights; the needs of older women; and, most controversially, abortion and other reproductive issues.

Women were also increasingly visible in politics and public life. The National Women's Political Caucus, founded in 1971, actively promoted the election of women to public office. Their success stories included Shirley Chisholm, Patricia Schroeder, and Geraldine Ferraro, all of whom served in Congress, and Ella Grasso, who won election as Connecticut's governor in 1974.

Women's political mobilization produced significant legislative and administrative gains. With the passage of Title IX of the Educational Amendments Act of 1972, which broadened the 1964 Civil Rights Act to include educational institutions, Congress prohibited colleges and universities that received federal funds from discriminating on the basis of sex, a change that particularly benefited women athletes. In 1972 Congress authorized child-care deductions for working parents; in 1974 it passed the Equal Credit Opportunity Act, which significantly improved women's access to credit.

The Expanding Women's Movement
By the late 1970s the feminist movement had broadened its base, attracting women of all ages and backgrounds, such as this delegate to the 1977 National Women's Conference in Houston, Texas. As the slogan on her hat implies, though, the women's movement was already on the defensive against right-wing claims that the feminist movement was undermining traditional values. (© Bettye Lane)

The Supreme Court also significantly advanced women's rights. In several rulings the Court read a right of privacy into the Ninth and Fourteenth amendments' concept of personal liberty, to give women more control over their reproductive lives. In 1965 *Griswold v. Connecticut* had overturned state laws against the sale of contraceptive devices to married adults, a protection that was later extended to single persons. In 1973, in *Roe v. Wade*, the Court struck down Texas and Georgia statutes that allowed an abortion only if the mother's life was in danger. According to this 7–2 decision, states could no longer outlaw abortions performed during the first trimester of pregnancy.

Roe v. Wade nationalized the liberalization of state abortion laws, which had begun in New York in 1970, but also fueled the development of a powerful antiabortion movement. Charging that the rights of a fetus took precedence over a woman's right to decide whether or not to terminate a pregnancy, abortion opponents worked to circumvent or overturn *Roe v. Wade*. In 1976 they convinced Congress to deny Medicaid funds for abortions for poor women, one of the opening rounds in a protracted legislative and judicial campaign to chip away at the *Roe* decision.

Another battlefront for the women's movement was the proposed Equal Rights Amendment (ERA) to the Constitution. The ERA, first introduced in Congress in 1923 by the National Woman's party, stated in its entirety, "Equality of rights under the law shall not be denied or abridged by the United States or any State on the basis of sex." In 1970 feminists revived the amendment, which passed the House but died in the Senate. In the next session it passed both houses and was submitted to the states for ratification. But though thirty-four states quickly passed the ERA between 1972 and 1974, growing opposition by conservative groups slowed its momentum (see Map 32.1). By 1982 the amendment was dead.

The fate of the ERA and the battle over abortion rights showed that by the mid-1970s, the women's movement was beginning to weaken. Increasingly its members were divided over issues of race, class, age, and sexual orientation. For many nonwhite and working-class women, the feminist movement seemed to stand for the interests of self-seeking white career women. At the same time, the women's movement faced growing social conservatism among Americans in general. Although 63 percent of women polled in 1975 said they favored "efforts to strengthen and change women's status in society," a growing minority of both sexes expressed concern over what seemed to be revolutionary changes in women's traditional roles.

Lawyer Phyllis Schlafly, long active in conservative causes, led the antifeminist backlash. Despite the active career she had pursued while raising five

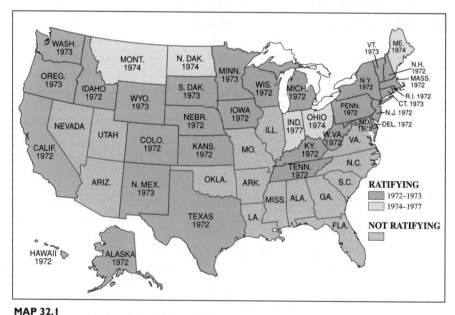

MAP 32.1
States Ratifying the Equal Rights Amendment
The Equal Rights Amendment quickly won support in 1972 and 1973 but then stalled. ERAmerica, a coalition of women's groups formed in 1976, lobbied extensively, particularly in Florida, North Carolina, and Illinois, but failed to sway the conservative legislatures in those states. Efforts to revive the ERA in the 1980s were unsuccessful.

children, Schlafly advocated traditional roles for women. Schlafly's STOP ERA organization claimed that the amendment would create a "unisex society" in which women could be drafted, homosexuals could be married, and separate toilets for men and women would be prohibited. (Feminists argued that those charges were groundless.) Alarmed, conservative women in grassroots networks mobilized, showing up at statehouses with home-baked bread and apple pies, symbols of their traditional domestic role. Their message, that women would lose more than they would gain if the ERA passed, resonated with many men and women, especially those who were troubled by the rapid pace of social change.

Although the feminist movement was on the defensive by the mid-1970s, women's lives showed no signs of returning to the patterns of the 1950s. Because of increasing economic pressures, the proportion of women in the paid work force continued to rise, from 44 percent in 1970 to 51 percent in 1980. Easier access to birth control permitted married and unmarried women to enjoy greater sexual freedom (although they also became more vulnerable to male sexual pressure). With a growing number of career options available to them, many women, particularly educated white women, stayed single or delayed marriage and child rearing. The birth rate continued its postwar decline, reaching an all-time low in the mid-1970s. At the same time, the divorce rate rose 82 percent in the 1970s, as more men and women elected to leave unhappy marriages.

Although such changes brought increased autonomy for many women, they also caused new hardships, particularly in poor and working-class families. Divorce left many women with low-paying jobs and inadequate child care. Meanwhile, more tolerant attitudes toward premarital sex, along with other social and economic factors, had contributed to rising teenage pregnancy rates. The rise in divorce and adolescent pregnancy produced a sharp increase in the number of female-headed families, contributing to the "feminization" of poverty. By 1980 women accounted for 66 percent of adults who lived below the poverty line, a development that fueled a growing wave of social reaction.

Another major focus of social activism, the gay liberation movement, achieved heightened visibility in the 1970s. Thousands of gay men and lesbians "came out," publicly proclaiming their sexual orientation. In New York's Greenwich Village, San Francisco's Castro, and other urban enclaves, growing gay communities gave rise to hundreds of new gay and lesbian clubs, churches, businesses, and political organizations. In 1973 the National Gay Task Force launched a campaign to include gay men and lesbians as a protected group under laws covering employment and housing rights. Such efforts were most successful on the local level; during the 1970s Detroit, Boston, Los Angeles, Miami, San Francisco, and other cities passed laws barring discrimination on the basis of sexual preference.

Like abortion and the ERA, gay rights came under attack from conservatives, who believed that protecting gay people's rights would encourage immoral behavior. When the Miami city council passed a measure banning discrimination against gay men and lesbians in 1977, the singer Anita Bryant led a campaign to repeal the law by popular referendum. Later that year voters overturned the measure by a 2–1 majority, prompting similar antigay campaigns around the country.

Racial Minorities

Although the civil-rights movement was in disarray by the late 1960s, in the next decade, minority group protests brought social and economic gains. Native Americans realized some of the most significant changes. In 1971 the Alaska Native Land Claims Act restored 40 million acres to Eskimos, Aleuts, and other native peoples, along with $960 million in compensation. Most important, the federal government abandoned the tribal termination program of the 1950s (see Chapter 29). Under the Indian Self-Determination Act of 1974, Congress restored the tribes' right to govern themselves and gave them authority over federal programs on their reservations (see Map 32.2).

The busing of children to achieve school desegregation proved the most disruptive social issue of the 1970s. Progress in achieving the desegregation mandated by *Brown v. Board of Education of Topeka* (see Chapter 29) had been slow. In the 1970s both the courts and the Justice department pushed for more action, not just in the South but in other parts of the country. In *Milliken v. Bradley* (1974), for example, the Supreme Court ordered cities with deeply ingrained patterns of residential segregation to use busing to integrate their classrooms. The decision sparked intense and sometimes violent opposition. In Boston in 1974–1975, the strongly Irish-Catholic working-class neighborhood of South Boston responded to the arrival of black students from Roxbury with mob action reminiscent of that in Little Rock in 1957. Threatened by court-ordered busing, many white parents transferred their children to private schools or moved to the suburbs. The resulting "white flight" exacerbated the racial imbalance busing was supposed to redress. Some black parents also opposed busing, calling instead for better schools in predominantly black neighborhoods. By the late 1970s federal courts had begun to back away from their insistence on busing to achieve racial balance.

Almost as divisive as busing was the implementation of *affirmative action* procedures—hiring and enrollment goals and recruitment and training programs designed to redress a history of discrimination against nonwhites and women in employment and education. First introduced by Lyndon Johnson's administration in 1965, affirmative action programs had expanded opportunities for blacks and Latinos. The number of black students enrolled in colleges and universities doubled between 1970 and 1977 to 1.1 million, or 9.3 percent of the total student enrollment. A small but growing number of blacks moved into white-collar professions in corporations and universities. Others found new opportunities in civil service occupations such as law enforcement or entered apprenticeships in the skilled construction trades. Latinos experienced similar gains in education and "token" advances in the job market. On the whole, however, both groups enjoyed only marginal economic improvement, since poor and working-class nonwhites bore the brunt of job loss and unemployment in the 1970s.

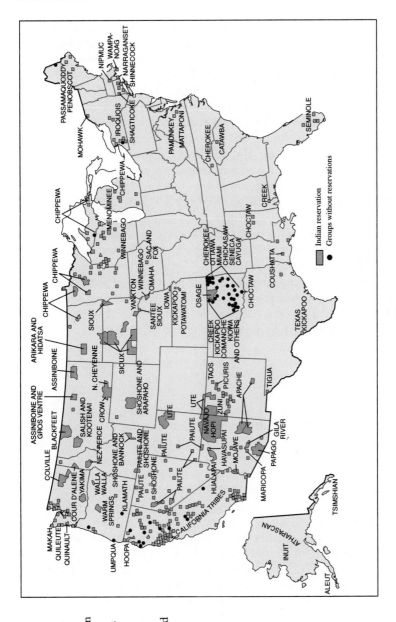

MAP 32.2
American Indian
Reservations
Although native Americans have been able to preserve small enclaves in the northeastern states, most Indian reservations are in the West. Beginning in the 1970s, various tribes filed land claims against federal and state governments.

Nevertheless, many whites, especially men, who were feeling the economic pinch of stagflation, came to resent affirmative action programs as an infringement of their rights. In 1978 Allan Bakke, a white man, sued the University of California Medical School at Davis for rejecting him in favor of less qualified minority candidates. The Supreme Court ruling in *Bakke v. University of California* was inconclusive. Though it branded the medical school's strict quota system illegal and ordered Bakke admitted, it stated that racial factors could be considered in hiring and admission decisions, thus upholding the principle of affirmative action. But the Bakke decision was clearly a setback for proponents of affirmative action, and it prepared the way for subsequent efforts to eliminate those programs.

The activists who supported racial minorities, women, gays, consumers, and the environment had distinct agendas. However, they also had much in common. They were part of "a rights revolution"—a wide-ranging movement in the 1960s and 1970s to bring issues of social justice and welfare to the forefront of public policy. Growing out of the Great Society's liberalism, they invariably turned to the federal government for protection of individual rights and—in the case of environmentalists—the world's natural resources. The activists of this period made substantial progress in widening the notion of the federal government's responsibilities, but by the end of the 1970s their movements faced growing opposition.

The Politics of Resentment

Together with the rapidly growing antiabortion movement, the often vociferous public opposition to busing, affirmative action, gay rights ordinances, and the Equal Rights Amendment constituted a broad backlash against the social changes of the previous decade. Many Americans believed that their interests had been slighted by the rights revolution and resented a federal government that protected women who sought abortions or minorities who benefited from affirmative action. The economic changes of the 1970s, which left many working-class and middle-class Americans with lower disposable incomes, rising prices, and higher taxes, further fueled what the conservative writer Alan Crawford has termed the "politics of resentment"—a grass-roots revolt against "special-interest groups" (women, minorities, gays, and so on) and growing expenditures on social welfare. Special groups and programs, conservatives believed, robbed other Americans of educational and employment opportunities, and saddled the working and middle classes with an extra financial burden.

Although the politics of resentment most often centered on socioeconomic issues, it also took the form of local taxpayers' revolts. In 1978 California voters passed Proposition 13, a measure that reduced property taxes and eventually undercut local governments' ability to maintain schools and other essential services. Promising tax relief to middle-class homeowners and reduced funding for busing and other programs to benefit the poor—who were

An Antibusing Confrontation in Boston
Tensions over court-ordered busing ran high in Boston in 1976. When a black lawyer tried to cross the city hall plaza during an antibusing demonstration, he became another victim of Boston's climate of racial hatred and violence. This photograph by Stanley Forman for the *Boston Herald American*, showing protesters trying to impale the man with a flagstaff, won a Pulitzer Prize.

invariably viewed as nonwhite—Proposition 13 became the model for similar tax measures around the country in the late 1970s and 1980s.

The rising popularity of evangelical religion also fueled the conservative resurgence of the 1970s. Fundamentalist groups that fostered a "born-again" experience had been growing steadily since World War II, under the leadership of charismatic preachers such as Billy Graham. According to a Gallup poll conducted in 1976, some 50 million Americans—about a quarter of the population—were affiliated with evangelical movements. These groups set up their own school systems and newspapers. Through broadcasting networks, like the Christian Broadcasting Network founded by the Virginia preacher Pat Robertson, a new breed of *televangelists* such as Jerry Falwell built vast and influential electronic ministries.

As evangelicals spoke out on a broad range of issues, denouncing abortion, busing, sex education, pornography, feminism, and gay rights, they sought ways to bring their religious values to a wider public. In 1979 Jerry Falwell founded the Moral Majority, a political pressure group that promoted Christian "family values"—traditional gender roles, heterosexuality, family cohesion—and staunch anticommunism. Soon the extensive media and fund-raising networks of the Christian right became the organizational base for a larger conservative movement known as the New Right. Using computerized mass-mailing campaigns that targeted evangelical constituencies, New Right political groups mobilized thousands of followers and millions of dollars to support conservative candidates and causes.

POST-WATERGATE POLITICS: FAILED LEADERSHIP

It is not surprising that in the wake of Watergate, when many Americans became disillusioned with politics as usual, the New Right could energize voters around a new set of issues. Many citizens had become cynical about the federal government and about politicians in general. "Don't vote. It only encourages them" read one bumper sticker during the 1976 campaign. Indeed, political leaders were proving unable to deal with the rising inflation, stagnant growth, and declining productivity that plagued the U.S. economy in the 1970s. The fall of Saigon in 1975 reminded Americans of the failure of the nation's Vietnam policy. The world was changing; Americans grappled with the unsettling idea that perhaps the United States would not continue to be the all-powerful nation it had been for much of the postwar era.

Ford's Caretaker Presidency

During the two years Gerald Ford held the nation's highest office, he failed to establish his legitimacy as president. Ford's pardon of Nixon hurt his credibility as a political leader, but an even bigger problem was his handling of the economy, which was reeling from the inflation set in motion by the Vietnam War, rising oil prices, and the growing trade deficit. In 1974 the inflation rate soared to almost 12 percent, and in the following year the economy entered its deepest downturn since the Great Depression. Though many of the nation's economic problems were beyond the president's control, Ford's failure to take more vigorous action made him appear timid and powerless.

In foreign policy Ford was equally lacking in leadership. He maintained Nixon's détente initiatives by asking Henry Kissinger to stay on as secretary of state. Though Ford met with Soviet leaders hoping to hammer out the details of a SALT II (Strategic Arms Limitation Treaty) agreement, he made little progress. Ford and Kissinger also continued Nixon's policy of increasing support for the shah of Iran, ignoring the bitter opposition and antiwestern sentiment that the shah's policy of rapid modernization was provoking among the growing Muslim fundamentalist population in Iran.

Jimmy Carter: The Outsider as President

The 1976 presidential campaign was one of the blandest in years. President Ford chose as his running mate the conservative Senator Robert J. Dole of

Kansas. The Democratic choice, Jimmy Carter, Governor of Georgia, shared the ticket with Senator Walter F. Mondale of Minnesota, who had ties to the traditional Democratic constituencies of labor, liberals, blacks, and big-city machines. Avoiding issues and controversy, Carter played up his role as a Washington outsider, pledging to restore morality to government. "I will never lie to you," he earnestly told voters. Carter won the election with 50 percent of the popular vote to Ford's 48 percent.

Despite his efforts to overcome the post-Watergate climate of skepticism and apathy, Carter never became an effective leader. His outsider strategy distanced him from traditional sources of power, and he did little to heal the breach. Shying away from established Democratic leaders, Carter turned to advisers and friends who had worked with him in Georgia, none of whom had national experience. When his budget director, Bert Lance, was questioned about financial irregularities at the Atlanta bank he had headed, Carter's campaign pledge to restore integrity and morality to the government rang hollow.

Inflation was Carter's major domestic challenge. When he took office, the nation was still recovering from the severe recession of 1975–1976. Carter embarked on a fiscal policy that eroded both business and consumer confidence. Unemployment hovered between 6 and 7 percent, while inflation rose from 6.5 percent in 1977 to 13.4 percent in 1980. To counter inflation, the Federal Reserve Board raised interest rates repeatedly; in 1980 they topped 20 percent, a historic high. A deep recession finally broke the inflationary spiral in 1982, a year after Carter left office.

The Carter administration expanded the federal bureaucracy in some cases and limited its reach in others. Carter enlarged the cabinet by creating the departments of energy and education and approved new environmental protection measures, such as the $1.6 billion "Superfund" to clean up chemical pollution sites, as well as new park and forest lands in Alaska. But he continued President Nixon's efforts to reduce the scope of federal activities by reforming the civil service and deregulating the airline, trucking, and railroad industries. With deregulation, prices often dropped, but the resulting cutthroat competition drove many firms out of business and encouraged corporate consolidation. Carter also failed in his effort to decontrol oil and natural gas prices as a spur to domestic production and conservation.

Carter's attempt to provide leadership during the energy crisis also failed. He called energy conservation efforts "the moral equivalent of war," but the media reduced the phrase to "MEOW." In early 1979 a revolution in Iran raised oil prices higher, and gas lines again reminded Americans of their dependence on foreign oil. That summer Carter's approval rating dropped to 26 percent—lower than Richard Nixon's during the worst part of the Watergate scandal.

In foreign affairs, President Carter made human rights the centerpiece of his policy. He criticized the suppression of dissent in the Soviet Union—especially as it affected the right of Jewish citizens to emigrate—and withdrew economic and military aid from Argentina, Uruguay, Ethiopia, and other countries that violated human rights. Carter also established the Office of Human Rights in the State Department. Unable to change the internal policies of long-time U.S. allies who were serious violators of human rights, such as the Philippines, South Korea, and South Africa, he did manage to raise public awareness of the human rights issue, making it one future administrations would have to address.

In Latin America, Carter's most important contribution was the resolution of the lingering dispute over control of the Panama Canal. In a treaty signed on September 7, 1977, the United States agreed to turn over control of the canal to Panama on December 31, 1999. In return, the United States retained the right to send its ships through the canal in case of war, even though the canal itself would be declared neutral territory. Despite a conservative outcry that the United States was giving away more than it got, the Senate narrowly approved the treaty.

Though Carter had campaigned to free the United States from its "inordinate fear of Communism," relations with the Soviet Union soon became tense, largely because of problems surrounding arms limitation talks. Eventually the Soviet leader Leonid Brezhnev signed SALT II (1979), but hopes for Senate ratification of the treaty collapsed when the Soviet Union invaded Afghanistan that December. In retaliation for this aggression, which Carter viewed as a threat to Middle Eastern oil supplies, the United States curtailed grain sales to the U.S.S.R. and boycotted the 1980 summer Olympics in Moscow. (The Soviets returned the gesture by boycotting the 1984 summer games in Los Angeles.) When Carter left office in 1981, relations with the Soviet Union were worse than they had been when he took over.

President Carter achieved both his most stunning success and his greatest failure in the Middle East. Relations between Egypt and Israel had remained tense since the 1973 Yom Kippur War. In 1978 Carter helped to break the diplomatic stalemate by inviting Israel's prime minister Menachem Begin and Egyptian president Anwar Sadat to Camp David, the presidential retreat in Maryland. Two weeks of discussions and Carter's promise of additional foreign aid to Egypt persuaded Sadat and Begin to adopt a "framework for peace." The framework included Egypt's recognition of Israel's right to exist and Israel's return of the Sinai peninsula, which it had occupied since 1967. Transfer of the territory to Egypt took place from 1979 to 1982.

Dramatically less successful was U.S. foreign policy toward Iran. Ever since the CIA had helped to install Muhammad Reza Pahlavi on the throne in 1953, the United States had counted Iran as a faithful ally in the troubled Middle East. Overlooking the repressive tactics of Iran's CIA-trained secret police, SAVAK, Carter followed in the footsteps of previous cold war policymakers for whom access to Iranian oil reserves and the shah's consistently anticommunist stance outweighed all other considerations.

Early in 1979, however, the shah's government was overthrown and driven into exile by a revolution led by fundamentalist Muslim leader Ayatollah Ruhollah Khomeini. In late October 1979 the Carter administration admitted the deposed shah, who was suffering from incurable cancer, to the United

States for medical treatment. Though Iran's new leaders had warned that such an action would provoke retaliation, Henry Kissinger and other foreign policy leaders had argued that the United States should assist the shah, both for humanitarian reasons and in return for his years of support for American policy. In response, on November 4, 1979, fundamentalist Muslim students under Khomeini's direction seized the U.S. embassy in Teheran, taking Americans there hostage in a flagrant violation of the principle of diplomatic immunity. The hostage takers demanded that the shah be returned to Iran for trial and punishment, but the United States refused. Instead, President Carter suspended arms sales to Iran, froze Iranian assets in American banks, and threatened to deport Iranian students in the United States.

For the next fourteen months the Iranian hostage crisis paralyzed Jimmy Carter's presidency. Night after night, humiliating pictures of blindfolded hostages appeared on television newscasts. The extensive media coverage, and Carter's insistence that the safe return of the 52 hostages was his top priority, enhanced the value of the hostages to their captors. An attempt to mount a military rescue of the hostages failed miserably in April 1980, six months into the crisis, because of helicopter equipment failures in the desert. The abortive rescue mission reinforced the public's view of Carter as a bumbling and ineffective executive.

American Hostages in Iran
Images of blindfolded, handcuffed American hostages seized by Iranian militants at the American embassy in Teheran in November 1979 shocked the nation and created a foreign policy crisis that eventually cost Jimmy Carter the presidency.

The Reagan Revolution

With Carter embroiled in the hostage crisis, the Republicans gained momentum by nominating former California governor Ronald Reagan. A movie actor in the late 1930s, the 1940s, and the early 1950s, Reagan had served as president of the Screen Actors Guild and had been deeply affected by the postwar anticommunist crusade in Hollywood. He had endorsed Barry Goldwater in 1964 and had begun his own political career shortly after, serving as governor of California from 1967 to 1975. After losing a bid for the Republican nomination in 1976, Reagan secured it easily in 1980, and chose former CIA director George Bush as his running mate.

In the final months of the campaign, Carter took on an embattled and defensive tone, while Reagan remained upbeat and decisive. The Republicans benefited from superior financial resources, which allowed them to make sophisticated use of television and direct mail appeals. Reagan also had a powerful issue to exploit: the hostage stalemate. Calling the Iranians "barbarians" and "common criminals," he hinted that he would take strong action to win the hostages' return. More important, Reagan effectively appealed to the politics of resentment that flourished during the lean years of the 1970s. In a televised debate between the candidates, Reagan emphasized the economic plight of working- and middle-class Americans when he posed the rhetorical question, "Are you better off today than you were four years ago?" Battered by inflation, unemployment, and income stagnation, and resentful of the rights revolution they felt slighted them, many viewers answered no.

In November Reagan won easily, with 51 percent of the popular vote to Carter's 41 percent. The landslide also gave the Republicans control of the Senate for the first time since 1954, though the Democrats maintained their hold on the House. Voter turnout, however, was at the lowest since the 1920s: only 53 percent of those eligible to vote went to the polls. Many poor and working-class voters stayed home. Nevertheless, the election confirmed the growth in the power of the Republican party since Richard Nixon's victory in 1968.

The core of the Republican party that elected Ronald Reagan remained the upper-middle-class white Protestant voters who supported balanced budgets, disliked government activism, feared crime and communism, and believed in a strong national defense. But new groups had gravitated toward the Republican vision: southern whites disaffected by big government and black civil-rights gains; blue-collar workers, especially Catholics; young voters who identified themselves as conservatives; and residents in the West, especially those in the rapidly growing suburbs. By wooing these "Reagan Democrats," the Republican party made deep inroads into Democratic territory, eroding that party's traditional coalition of southerners, blacks, laborers, and urban ethnics.

But perhaps the most significant constituency in the Republican party was the New Right, whose emphasis on traditional values and fundamentalist Christian morality dovetailed well with conservative Republican ideology. In 1980 New Right concerns formed the basis for the party's platform, which called for a constitutional ban on abortion, voluntary prayer in public schools, and a mandatory death penalty for certain crimes. The Republicans also demanded an end to court-mandated busing, and for the first time in forty years opposed the Equal Rights Amendment. A key factor in the 1980 election, the New Right contributed to the rebirth of the Republican party under Ronald Reagan.

On January 20, 1981, at the moment Carter turned over the presidency to Ronald Reagan, the Iranian government released the American hostages. After 444 days of captivity, the hostages returned home to an ecstatic welcome, a reflection of the public's frustration over their long ordeal. While most Americans continued to maintain "We're Number One," the hostage crisis in Iran came to symbolize the loss of America's power to control world affairs. Its psychological impact was enhanced by its occurrence at the end of a decade that had witnessed Watergate, the American defeat in Vietnam, and the OPEC embargo. To a great extent, the decline in American influence had been magnified by the unusual predominance the United States had enjoyed after World War II—an advantage that could not have been expected to last forever. The return of Japan and Western Europe to economic and political power, the control of vital oil resources by Middle Eastern countries, and the industrialization of some Third World nations had widened the cast of characters on the international stage. Still, many Americans were unable to let go of the presumption of economic and political supremacy born in the postwar years. Ronald Reagan rode their frustrations to victory in 1980.

CHAPTER 32 TIMELINE

1968	Richard Nixon elected president
1970	First Earth Day Environmental Protection Agency established
1971	Pentagon Papers published
1972	Revenue sharing begins Watergate break-in Congress passes Equal Rights Amendment Consumer Products Safety Commission established Nixon reelected
1973	Spiro Agnew resigns; Gerald Ford appointed vice-president *Roe v. Wade* legalizes abortion OPEC oil embargo begins; gas shortages
1974	*Milliken v. Bradley* mandates busing within cities Nixon resigns; Ford becomes president and pardons Nixon Freedom of Information Act strengthened Fair Campaign Practices Act passed
1974– 1975	Busing controversy in Boston Economic recession
1976	Jimmy Carter elected president
1977	National Women's Conference in Houston Miami voters overturn a gay rights measure
1978	Carter brokers Camp David accords *Bakke v. University of California* limits affirmative action Exposure of the toxic waste site at Love Canal
1979	Three Mile Island nuclear accident Second oil crisis Hostages seized at American embassy in Teheran, Iran U.S.S.R. invades Afghanistan
1980	Superfund created to clean up chemical pollution Ronald Reagan elected president

A NEW DOMESTIC AND WORLD ORDER, 1981 TO THE PRESENT

- The Reagan-Bush Years, 1981–1993
- Foreign Relations under Reagan and Bush
- An Age of Anxiety
- The Clinton Presidency: Public Life since 1993

On April 19, 1995, a truck bomb ripped apart the Federal Building in Oklahoma City, killing 168 people. Though suspicion initially focused on Middle Eastern terrorists, two years later Timothy McVeigh, an American with links to a right-wing citizens' militia group, was convicted of the crime. Resentful of big government and often sympathetic to white supremacy, men like McVeigh had been swelling the ranks of paramilitary organizations throughout the country, especially in the western states. They were extreme examples of widespread disenchantment with government, politics, and American society in general at the end of the twentieth century. Indeed, a sense of social disorder rippled through the nation and the world as the century and the millennium came to an end. With the breakup of the Soviet Union in 1991, the Cold War had ended, but new sources of conflict soon threatened world peace. In the new world order, the United States was increasingly linked to a global economy that directly affected American interest rates, consumption patterns, and job opportunities. At home, Americans grappled with racial, ethnic, and cultural conflict; crime and economic inequities; the shrinking role of the federal government; and the failure of their political leaders to solve many of the nation's pressing social problems.

THE REAGAN-BUSH YEARS, 1981–1993

George Bush's one term as president often seems indistinguishable from the two terms of his predecessor Ronald Reagan, in part because Bush followed the basic policies of the previous administration. But Bush was also over-shadowed because Reagan, while he was not a particularly capable president, possessed extraordinary charisma. First elected at sixty-nine, he was the oldest man ever to serve as president, yet he conveyed a sense of physical vigor. By capitalizing on his skills as an actor and a public speaker, and by winning the support of the emerging New Right within the Republican party, Reagan became one of the most popular presidents of the twentieth century. Distrust-ful of the federal government, both Bush and Reagan turned away from the state as a source of solutions for America's social problems, calling into ques-tion almost half a century of governmental activism. "Government is not the solution to our problem," Reagan declared, "Government is the problem."

Reaganomics

The economic and tax policies that emerged under Reagan, quickly dubbed *Reaganomics*, were based on *supply-side* economics theory. According to the

The Great Communicator
Ronald Reagan felt totally at home in front of the camera, trading stories and one-liners with audiences and the press. Commen-tator Gary Wills observed, "Reagan runs continuously in everyone's home movies of the mind. . . . He is, in the strictest sense, what Hol-lywood promoters used to call 'fabulous.'"

theory, high taxes siphoned off capital that would otherwise be invested, stimulating growth. Tax cuts would therefore promote investment, causing an economic expansion that would increase tax revenues. Together with cuts in government spending, especially on entitlement programs, tax cuts would also shrink the federal budget deficit. That, at least, was the theory. Critics charged that conservative Republicans deliberately cut taxes to force reductions in federal funding for the social programs that they abhorred.

The Economic Recovery Tax Act passed in 1981 reduced income tax rates by 25 percent over three years. The reductions were supposed to be linked to drastic cutbacks in federal expenditures. But while cuts were made in food stamps, unemployment compensation, and welfare programs such as Aid to Families with Dependent Children (AFDC), congressional resistance kept the Social Security and Medicare programs intact. The net impact of Reaganomics was to further the redistribution of income from the poor to the wealthy.

Another tenet of Reaganomics was that many federal regulations impeded economic growth and productivity. Insisting that a safety net existed for the truly needy, the administration moved to abolish or reduce federal regulation of the workplace, health care, consumer protection, and the environment. The responsibility and cost of such regulations were transferred to the states. One of the results of their policy was the deinstitutionalization of many of the mentally ill, forcing them onto the streets.

The money saved by these means—and more—was plowed into a five-year, $1.2 trillion defense buildup. This huge increase fulfilled Reagan's campaign pledge to "make America number one again." The B-1 bomber, which President Carter had canceled, was resurrected, and development of a new missile system, the MX, was begun. Reagan's most ambitious and controversial weapons plan, proposed in 1983, was the Strategic Defense Initiative (SDI), popularly known as "Star Wars." A computerized satellite and laser shield to detect and intercept incoming missiles, SDI would supposedly render nuclear war obsolete.

Reagan's programs benefited from the Federal Reserve Board's tight money policies, as well as a serendipitous drop in world oil prices, which reduced the disastrous inflation rates that had bedeviled the nation in the 1970s. Between 1980 and 1982 the inflation rate dropped from 12.4 percent to just 4 percent. Unfortunately, the Fed's tightening of the money supply also brought on the "Reagan Recession" of 1981–1982, which threw some 10 million Americans out of work. But as the recession bottomed out in early 1983, the economy began to grow, and for the rest of the decade inflation remained low. Despite rather unexceptional growth in the gross national product, the Reagan administration presided over the longest peacetime economic expansion in American history.

Reagan's Second Term

This economic growth played a role in the 1984 elections. Reagan campaigned on the theme "It's Morning in America," suggesting that a new day of prosperity and pride was dawning. The Democrats nominated former vice-president

Walter Mondale of Minnesota to run against Reagan. With strong ties to labor unions, minority groups, and party leaders, Mondale epitomized the New Deal coalition that had dominated the Democratic party since Roosevelt. To appeal to women voters, Mondale selected Representative Geraldine Ferraro of New York as his running mate—the first woman to run on a major party ticket. Nevertheless, Reagan won a landslide victory, carrying the entire nation except for Minnesota and the District of Columbia. Democrats, however, held onto the House, and in 1986 would regain control of the Senate.

A major scandal marred Reagan's second term when in 1986 news leaked out that the administration had negotiated an arms-for-hostages deal with the revolutionary government of Iran—the same government Reagan had denounced during the 1980 hostage crisis. In an attempt to gain Iran's help in freeing some American hostages held by pro-Iranian forces in Lebanon, the U.S. had covertly sold arms to Iran. Some of the profits generated by the arms sales were diverted to the Contras, counterrevolutionaries in Nicaragua, whom the administration supported over the leftist regime of the Sandinistas. The covert diversion of funds, which was both illegal and unconstitutional, seemed to have been the brainstorm of Marine Lieutenant Colonel Oliver North, a National Security Council aide at the time. One key memo linked the White House to his plan. But when Congress investigated the mounting scandal in 1986 and 1987, White House officials testified that the president knew nothing about the diversion. Ronald Reagan's defense remained simple and consistent: "I don't remember."

The scandal bore many similarities to Watergate, including the possibility that the president had acted illegally. Early in Reagan's administration, one of his critics had coined the phrase "Teflon presidency" to describe Reagan's resiliency—bad news didn't stick; it just rolled off. No matter that the president was often confused or ill informed, or that he relied heavily on close advisers, especially his wife. Even the news that Nancy Reagan was in the habit of consulting an astrologer before planning major White House events failed to shake public confidence in the president. Reagan weathered "Iran-Contragate," but the scandal did weaken his presidency.

The president proposed no bold domestic policy initiatives in his last two years in office. He had promised to place drastic limits on the federal government and to give free-market forces freer reign. Despite reordering the federal government's priorities, he failed to reduce its size or scope. And although spending for most poverty programs had been cut, Social Security and other entitlement programs remained untouched. Despite Reagan's failure to achieve his goals, his spending cuts and antigovernment rhetoric shaped the terms of political debate for the rest of the century.

One of Reagan's most significant legacies was his conservative judicial appointments. In 1981 he had nominated Sandra Day O'Connor, the first woman ever to serve on the Supreme Court. In his second term he appointed two more justices, Antonin Scalia (1986) and Anthony Kennedy (1988), both of whom were far more conservative than the moderate O'Connor. Justice William Rehnquist, a noted conservative, was elevated to chief justice in

1986. Under his leadership the Court, often by a 5–4 margin, chipped away at the Warren Court's legacy in decisions on individual liberties, affirmative action, and the rights of criminal defendants.

Ironically, though Reagan had promised to balance the budget by 1984, his most enduring legacy was the national debt, which tripled during his two terms. The huge deficit reflected the combined effects of increased military spending, tax reductions for high-income taxpayers, and Congress's refusal to approve deep cuts in domestic programs. By 1989 the national debt had climbed to $2.8 trillion—more than $11,000 for every American citizen.

The nation was also running an annual deficit in its trade with other nations. Exports had been falling since the 1970s, when American products began to encounter increasing competition in world markets. In the early 1980s a high exchange rate for dollars made U.S. goods more expensive for foreign buyers and imports more affordable for Americans. The budget and trade deficits contributed to a major shift in 1985: for the first time since 1915 the United States became a debtor rather a creditor nation. Since then, with phenomenal speed, the United States has accumulated the world's largest foreign debt.

The Bush Presidency

George Herbert Walker Bush won the Republican nomination in 1988, despite challenges from Senate minority leader Robert Dole, television evangelist Pat Robertson, and congressional representative Jack Kemp. Bush's choice for vice-president, a young conservative Indiana senator, Dan Quayle, who had used family connections to avoid service in Vietnam, added little to the ticket. In the Democratic primaries, the contest was between Governor Michael Dukakis of Massachusetts and the charismatic civil-rights leader Jesse Jackson, whose populist Rainbow Coalition had embraced the diversity of Democratic constituencies. Dukakis received the party's nomination and chose Senator Lloyd Bentsen of Texas as his running mate.

The 1988 campaign had a harsh tone: brief televised attack ads replaced meaningful discussion of the issues. The sound bite "Read My Lips: No New Taxes," drawn from George Bush's acceptance speech at the Republican convention, became the party's campaign mantra. In a television ad featuring Willie Horton, a black man convicted of murder who had killed again while on furlough from a Massachusetts prison, Republicans, pandering to voters' racist fears, charged Dukakis with being soft on crime. Dukakis, forced on the defensive, failed to mount an effective counterattack. Bush carried thirty-eight states, winning the popular vote by 53.4 percent to 45.6 percent. Only 50 percent of eligible voters went to the polls.

Though Bush did not share many of Reagan's conservative views, he failed to develop a distinctive domestic agenda. The impact of Reagan's Supreme Court nominees shaped one of the most significant domestic trends during the Bush administration—the Supreme Court's continued move away from liberal activism and toward a more conservative stance, especially on the issue of abortion. The 1989 *Webster v. Reproductive Health Services* decision permitted states to restrict abortion. The next year the Court upheld a federal regulation barring personnel at federally funded health clinics from discussing abortion with their clients. In 1992 the Court upheld a Pennsylvania law mandating informed consent and a twenty-four-hour waiting period before an abortion could be performed. But the justices also reaffirmed the "essential holding" in *Roe v. Wade*: women had a constitutional right to abortion.

In 1990 David Souter, a little known federal judge from New Hampshire, easily won confirmation to the Supreme Court. But the next year a major controversy erupted over President Bush's nomination of Clarence Thomas, a black conservative with little judicial experience. Just as Thomas's confirmation hearings were drawing to a close, a former colleague, Anita Hill, testified publicly that Thomas had sexually harassed her in the early 1980s. After widely watched and widely debated televised testimony by both Thomas and Hill before the all-male Senate Judiciary Committee, the Senate confirmed Thomas by a narrow margin. In the wake of the hearings, national polls confirmed the pervasiveness of sexual harassment on the job: four out of ten women said that they had been the object of unwanted sexual advances from men at work.

Besides developments in the Supreme Court, a key issue during Bush's four years as president was the economy. His campaign promise of a "kinder, gentler administration" was doomed by his predecessor's failed economic policies, especially the budget deficit. The Gramm-Rudman Act, passed in 1985, had mandated automatic cuts if budget targets were not met in 1991. Facing the prospect of a halt in nonessential government services and the layoff of thousands of government employees, Congress resorted to new spending cuts and one of the largest tax increases in history. Bush's failure to keep his "No New Taxes" promise earned him the enmity of Republican conservatives, which would dramatically hurt his chances for reelection in 1992.

Reagan's decision to shift the cost of many federal programs, including housing, education, public works, and social services, to state and local governments caused problems for Bush. In 1990 a recession began to erode state and local tax revenues. As incomes declined and industrial and white-collar layoffs increased, poverty and homelessness increased sharply. In 1991 unemployment approached 7 percent nationwide. To save money, state and local governments laid off workers even as demand for social services and unemployment compensation climbed.

FOREIGN RELATIONS UNDER REAGAN AND BUSH

The collapse of détente during the Carter administration, after the Soviet invasion of Afghanistan, underlay Reagan's confrontational approach to what he called the "evil empire." Backed by Republican hard-liners, and determined to reduce Communist influence in developing nations, Reagan articulated some of the harshest anti-Soviet rhetoric since the 1950s. The collapse of the Soviet Union in 1991 removed that nation as a credible threat, but new post–cold war challenges quickly appeared.

Interventions in the Third World and the End of the Cold War

Despite Reagan's rhetoric, not all his international problems involved U.S.-Soviet confrontations. In 1983, after Israel invaded Lebanon, the U.S. Embassy in Beirut was bombed by anti-Israeli Muslim fundamentalists. A second bombing killed 239 Marine peacekeepers barracked in the city. Around the world, terrorist assassins struck down Indira Gandhi in India and Anwar Sadat in Egypt. But it was the airplane hijackings and countless terrorist incidents in the Middle East that led Reagan to order air strikes against one highly visible source of terrorism, Muammar Khadafy of Libya.

The administration reserved its most concerted attention for Central America. Halting what was seen as the spread of communism in that region became an obsession. In 1983 Reagan ordered the marines to invade the tiny Caribbean island of Grenada, claiming that its Cuban-supported Communist regime posed a threat to other states in the region. Reagan's top priority, however, was to topple the leftist Sandinista government in Nicaragua. In 1981 the United States suspended aid to Nicaragua, charging that the Sandinistas were supplying arms to rebels against a repressive right-wing regime in El Salvador. At the same time, the CIA began to provide extensive covert support to the Nicaraguan opposition, the "Contras," whom Reagan called "freedom fighters." Congress, wary of the assumption of unconstitutional powers by the executive branch, responded in 1984 by passing the Boland Amendment, which banned the CIA and other intelligence agencies from providing military support to the Contras—a provision violated in the Iran-Contra affair.

Surprisingly, given Reagan's rhetoric, his second term brought a reduction in tensions with the Soviet Union. In 1985, Reagan met with the new Soviet premier, Mikhail Gorbachev, at the first superpower summit meeting since 1979. Two years later, the two leaders agreed to eliminate all intermediate-range missiles based in Europe. Although a summit in Moscow in 1988 produced no further cuts in nuclear arms, the sight of the two first families attending the Bolshoi Ballet together and strolling amiably in Red Square exemplified the thaw in the Cold War.

Under Bush's administration, even more dramatic changes abroad brought about an end to the Cold War. In 1989 the grip of communism on Eastern Europe loosened and then let go completely in a series of mostly nonviolent revolutions that climaxed in the destruction of the Berlin Wall in November. Soon the Soviet Union itself began to succumb to the forces of change. The background for these dramatic upheavals lay in the changes set in motion by Soviet president Mikhail Gorbachev after 1985. Through his policies of *glasnost* (openness) and *perestroika* (economic restructuring), Gorbachev had signaled a willingness to tolerate significant changes. But Gorbachev, who was always more popular outside his country than at home, found that to call for the dismantling of an old system was easier than to build a new system.

On August 19, 1991, alarmed Soviet military leaders seized Gorbachev and attempted unsuccessfully to oust him. The failure of the coup broke the Communist party's dominance over the Soviet Union. Lithuania had declared its independence in March 1990 and now the Baltic Republics of Latvia and Estonia followed suit. In December the Union of Soviet Socialist Republics formally dissolved itself to make way for an eleven-member Commonwealth of Independent States (CIS). Gorbachev resigned, and Boris Yeltsin, president of the new state of Russia, the largest and most populous republic, became the preeminent leader in the region.

The suddenness of the collapse of the Soviet Union and the end of the Cold War stunned America and the world. In the future, in the absence of superpower confrontations, international conflicts would arise from regional, religious, and ethnic differences. Suddenly, the United States faced unfamiliar military and diplomatic challenges.

War in the Persian Gulf, 1990–1991

The first new challenge arose in the Middle East. On August 2, 1990, Iraq, led by Saddam Hussein, invaded Kuwait, its small but oil-rich neighbor. In response, President Bush sponsored a series of resolutions in the U.N. Security Council, condemning Iraq, calling for its withdrawal, and imposing an embargo and trade sanctions. When Hussein showed no signs of yielding, Bush prodded the international organization to create a legal framework for a military offensive against the man he called "the butcher of Baghdad." In November the Security Council voted to use force if Iraq did not withdraw by January 15. In a close 52–48 vote on January 12, the U.S. Senate authorized military action. Four days later President Bush announced to the nation that "the liberation of Kuwait has begun."

The forty-two-day war was a resounding success for the United Nations' coalition forces, which were predominantly American. Under the leadership of General Colin Powell, chairman of the Joint Chiefs of Staff, and the com-

Women at War
Women played key and visible roles in the Persian Gulf War, comprising approximately 10 percent of the American troops. Increasing numbers of women are choosing to make a career out of the military, despite widespread reports of sexual harassment and other forms of discrimination.

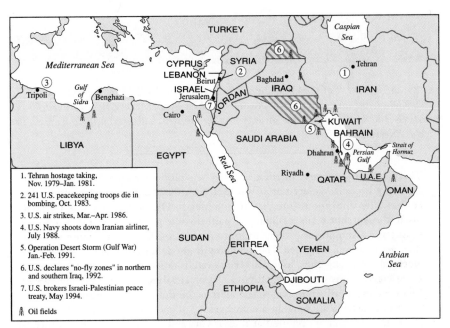

MAP 33.1
U.S. Involvement in the Middle East, 1980–1994
The United States has long played an active role in the Middle East, pursuing the twin goals of protecting Israel's security and assuring a reliable supply of low-cost oil from the Persian Gulf states. By far the largest intervention came in 1991, when, under United Nations auspices, President Bush sent 540,000 American troops to liberate Kuwait from Iraq. The United States also played a major role in the 1994 agreement allowing for Palestinian self-rule in the Gaza Strip and parts of the West Bank.

manding general, H. Norman Schwarzkopf, Operation Desert Storm opened with a month of air strikes to crush communications, destroy armaments, and pummel Iraqi ground troops. A land offensive followed. Within days thousands of Iraqi troops had fled or surrendered, and the fighting quickly ended, although Hussein remained in power (see Map 33.1).

Operation Desert Storm's success, and the amazingly low U.S. casualties (only 145 Americans were killed in action), produced a euphoric reaction at home. For many, the American victory over a vastly inferior fighting force seemed to banish the ghost of Vietnam. "By God, we've kicked the Vietnam Syndrome once and for all," Bush gloated. The president's approval rating shot up precipitously, but declined almost as quickly when a new recession showed that the easy victory had masked the country's serious economic problems.

AN AGE OF ANXIETY

Opinion polls taken in the early 1990s showed that Americans were deeply concerned about the future. They worried about crime in the streets,

The Age of Anxiety

In the aftermath of the Oklahoma City bombing in April 1995, journalist Joe Klein wrote an essay for Newsweek *in which he drew connections between the shock Americans felt over the disaster and the broader challenges facing the nation in the "Nervous Nineties."*

These are the Nervous Nineties. Life—by any rational standard—is good. The economy is good. We are not at war. But we are not quite at peace, either. We are beset by amorphous threats. The bombing in Oklahoma City was a unique, discrete event, but it fits a subliminal pattern—the growing sense that our most basic assumptions of security, of rationality, of decency are more tenuous than we had ever imagined. The economy is good, but a majority (60 percent) worry about losing their jobs. The crime rate is down, but everyone knows someone who has been mugged (and 89 percent think crime is getting worse). Medicine can perform miracles, but there is the threat of new viruses . . . and some old bacteria are making a comeback. . . . Finally, the cold war is over: Russian missiles aren't pointed at Kansas City, but a terrorist bomb can turn Oklahoma City into Beruit. . . .

Not just innocence, but economic hegemony has been lost. . . . Most important, there is competition from the rest of the world. This month's *International Business* magazine predicts a "global oversupply" of *skilled* workers that will, no doubt, further depress American wages. . . . Two salaries [in the household] yield more, but also less—less time (and supervision) for children, for civic activities, for relaxation. "The dual-earner household is creating a lot more stress than people ever imagined," says the pollster Daniel Yankelovich. "And John Kennedy was wrong: a rising tide doesn't necessarily lift all boats. Right now, it seems to be lifting only yachts. The disparity in incomes is growing. That's cause for a lot of anxiety."

SOURCE: Joe Klein, "Nervous '90s," *Newsweek*, May 1, 1995, pp. 59–60.

increases in poverty and homelessness, the decline of the inner cities, illegal immigration, the environment, the failure of public schools, the unresolved abortion issue, and AIDS. But above all they worried about their own economic security, whether they would be able to keep their jobs in an era of global competition.

The Economy

One of the most salient economic trends of the past two decades has been the growing inequality in income distribution. In the 1980s, as economist Lester

Thurow noted, "all of the gains in male earnings went to the top 20 percent of the workforce and an amazing 64 percent accrued to the top 1 percent." At the same time, the pay of leading corporate executives went from "35 to 157 times that of the average production worker." America was becoming a nation of haves and have-nots. Even relatively well-advantaged Americans felt a sense of diminished expectations. Earlier generations had aspired to doing better than their parents financially; now many young adults wondered whether they could achieve even a modest middle-class lifestyle.

These diminished expectations stemmed in part from changes in the job market. By the end of the twentieth century, the average employee could typically expect to make several job shifts over the course of a lifetime. Following an established pattern, the number of minimum-wage service jobs continued to grow, while the number of union-protected manufacturing jobs was shrinking. For many—one-fifth of the labor force in 1994—part-time or temporary work was the only work that was available. Moreover, in the 1980s and 1990s the downsizing trend, in which companies deliberately shed permanent workers to cut wage costs, spread to middle management. From 1980 to 1995 IBM shrank its mostly white-collar work force from 400,000 to 220,000—a 45 percent decrease. Although most laid-off middle managers eventually found new jobs, many took a large pay cut.

These economic trends put even more pressure on women to seek paid employment. In 1994, 58.8 percent of women were in the labor force, up from 38 percent in 1962, compared with 75.1 percent of men. The traditional nuclear family of employed father, homemaker wife, and children characterized less than 15 percent of U.S. households. Although women continued to make inroads in traditionally male-dominated fields—medicine, law, law enforcement, the military, and skilled trades—one out of five held a clerical or secretarial job, the same proportion as in 1950. Women's pay lagged behind men's; among black and Latino women the gender gap was even wider than among white women.

Another major cause of diminished economic expectations was the widespread fear that American corporations were no longer competitive in the global marketplace. Americans viewed with alarm the economic success of Germany and Japan, the growing U.S. trade deficit, and the infusion of foreign workers and investment money into the United States. In order to compete, American corporations adopted new technologies, including microelectronics, biotechnology, computers, and robots, and by the late 1990s saw their competitiveness return. Bethlehem Steel, which invested $6 billion to modernize its operations, doubled its productivity between 1989 and 1997. Other firms retooled their corporate vision. In 1980–1981 the Ford Motor Company had lost $2.5 billion despite laying off 150,000 workers. In the face of this desperate situation, Ford shifted its focus from maximizing output to improving quality and consumer satisfaction, making assembly-line workers more involved in the company and its products by giving them more responsibility. The popular Ford Taurus, introduced in 1986, typified the new focus on quality.

While management struggled to improve productivity, the labor movement, hurt by downsizing, foreign competition, fear of layoffs, government hostility, and a failure to organize unskilled workers, continued to decline. By 1993, 16.6 million Americans were union members, just 15.8 percent of the work force. The Reagan administration took a tough antiunion stance from the start, breaking a nationwide strike by the Professional Air Traffic Controllers (PATCO) in 1981 and ultimately destroying the union. Reagan's action signaled to the business community that an antiunion posture was acceptable, encouraging sharp labor confrontations at Eastern Airlines, Caterpillar, and other corporations. In the mid-1990s new union leadership, a wave of union mergers, and vigorous efforts to recruit new members raised hopes that organized labor would reverse its long decline. In August 1997 the success of a dramatic strike against United Parcel Service (UPS) seemed to confirm this promise. The Teamster-backed strike won crucial concessions—union control of pensions and the conversion of part-time jobs to full-time positions with company benefits—that most observers viewed as a major victory for organized labor.

These gains for labor took place in the context of a brightening national economic picture. By the late 1990s, the United States led the world in information technology and its industries' efforts to improve manufacturing efficiency resulted in expanded productivity. In 1997, U.S. economic growth, measured at 4 percent, was among the healthiest in the world, while one of its most serious competitors in the 1980s, Japan, limped along with only a 1.1 percent growth rate. Working Americans benefited from these developments: new jobs were added to the economy at the rate of 213,000 per month in 1997. A booming stock market, which daily seemed to reach new highs, fueled the wealth and potential retirement savings of middle- and upper-class Americans. But there were downsides to the picture as well. Many stock market analysts worried that a steep drop in the stock market might create a recession. Moreover, prosperity was not equally distributed. As former Secretary of Labor Robert Reich put it, "There are still millions of people desperately trying to stay afloat. One in five children lives in poverty. Forty-four million Americans have no health insurance. The average 50-year-old without a college education hasn't seen a wage or benefit increase in 20 years. But Americans are segregated by income as never before, so it is far easier to pretend the worse off don't exist. They're out of sight."

An Increasingly Pluralistic Society

In 1996 the United States had a population of 265.5 million people, one-fourth of whom claimed African, Asian, Latino, or American Indian ancestry. Ethnic and racial diversity, always a source of conflict in American culture, became a defining theme of the 1990s, as Americans coped with racial violence, dramatically increased immigration, and widespread ethnic antagonism, especially on the part of native-born whites.

New Immigrants
In the 1980s many Korean immigrants got their start by opening small grocery stores in urban neighborhoods. Their success sometimes led to conflict with other racial groups, such as blacks and Hispanics, who were often their customers as well as competitors.

In the 1980s over 7 million immigrants entered the country, accounting for more than a third of the population growth in that decade. The greatest number of the newcomers were Latinos. Although Mexico continued to provide the largest group of Spanish-speaking immigrants, large numbers also arrived from El Salvador and the Dominican Republic. The 1986 Immigration Reform and Control Act (Simpson-Mazzoli Act), which granted amnesty to some immigrants, primarily benefited Mexicans and other Latinos who had entered the United States illegally before 1982. The second largest minority group in the United States after African-Americans and the second fastest-growing after Asians, the Latino population reached 24.3 million in 1992. Once concentrated in California, Texas, and New Mexico, Latinos now lived in urban areas throughout the country, and made up about 13 percent of the population of Florida and New York (see Map 33.2).

Asia was the other major source of new immigrants. This migration, which increased almost 108 percent from 1980 to 1990, consisted mainly of people from China, the Philippines, Vietnam, Laos, Cambodia, Korea, India, and Pakistan. More than 700,000 Indochinese refugees came to escape upheavals in Southeast Asia in the decade following the Vietnam War. The first arrivals, many of them well educated, adapted successfully to their new homeland. Later refugees lacked professional or vocational skills and took low-paying jobs where they could find them.

The new immigrants' impact on the country's social, economic, and cultural landscape has been tremendous. In many places they have created thriving ethnic communities, such as Koreatown in Los Angeles. In the 1980s tens of thousands of Jews fleeing religious and political persecution in the Soviet Union created Little Odessa in Brooklyn, New York. Ethnic restaurants and shops have sprung up across the country, while some 300 specialized periodicals serve immigrant readers.

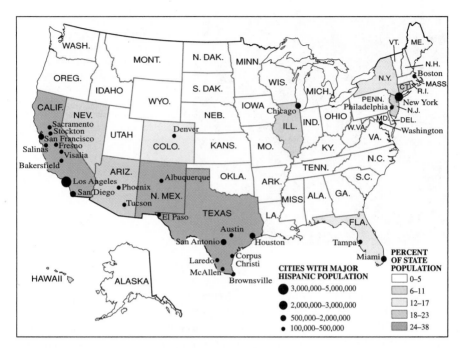

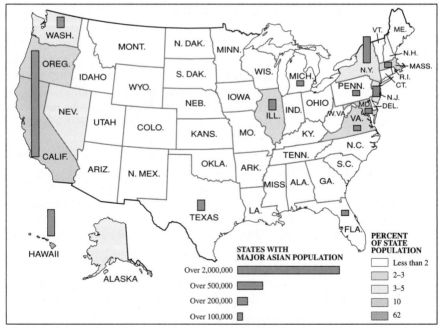

MAP 33.2

Hispanic Population and Asian-American Population, 1990

In 1990 Latinos made up almost 10 percent of the U.S. population, and Asian-Americans just under 3 percent. Demographers predict that Latinos will overtake African-Americans as the largest minority group early in the twenty-first century and that by the year 2050 only about half the U.S. population will be composed of non-Latino whites.

The Undocumented Worker

In this oral history, Cuauhtémoc Mendez, an immigrant construction worker, re-flects on the controversial issue of undocumented Mexican workers—an issue that helped fuel anti-immigration sentiment in the 1980s and 1990s.

In the United States, to get rid of all the illegals, you don't need a border or the Immigration. Simply, if there is no work, what would the illegals do there?. . . For the United States it is a great advantage, because Mexican labor is very cheap. The illegal produces his product much cheaper, and they can sell it cheaper to the American people. In this sense the illegal helps the United States.

He also helps Mexico. All of the *mojados* bring money back. We don't take money out of Mexico. Those of us who work in the United States help our country more than the rich who send their Mexican money out. We support our country.

Normally the Mexican who goes to the United States goes to work in jobs that many Americans don't want. In the first place, it's hard work. I'm not going to say that they can't do the work, but they don't want to work for the same price as the Mexican. It's clear there is this contradiction, this antipathy toward the Mexican who is there illegally. They look at the *mojados* as scabs. The Chicanos and Mexican-Americans look at us from this perspective because they think we are the reason they don't have jobs. But it's not true. We are there at the convenience of the owners and bosses who want cheap labor, cheaper than they can get there. It isn't our fault. We have the necessity to work. I don't think it's a sin to subsist in another country that offers the opportunity to live a little better than is possible for us in Mexico.

SOURCE: Marilyn P. Davis, *Mexican Voices, American Dreams: An Oral History of Mexican Immigration to the United States* (New York: Henry Holt and Co., 1990), p. 110.

In 1990 the immigration quota was expanded to 700,000 per year (modified in 1995 to 675,000), with priority given to skilled workers and relatives of current residents. But by then the new immigrants had become scapegoats for all that was wrong with the United States. Though a 1997 study by the National Academy of Science reported that immigration has benefited the nation, adding some $10 billion a year to the economy, many American-born workers felt threatened by immigrants. The unfounded assumption that immigrants were lured to the United States by generous public services influenced provisions of a 1996 welfare reform act (see page 497), which severely curtailed legal immigrants' access to welfare benefits, especially food stamps. Also in 1996 Congress enacted legislation that increased the financial requirements for sponsors of new immigrants.

The most dramatic challenges to immigrants have emerged on the state level. In the 1980s California absorbed far more immigrants than any other state: more than a third of its population growth in that decade came from foreign immigration. In 1994 California voters overwhelmingly approved Proposition 187, a ballot initiative provocatively named "Save Our State," which barred undocumented aliens from public schools, nonemergency care at public health clinics, and all other state social services. The initiative also required law enforcement officers, school administrators, and social workers to report suspected illegal immigrants to the Immigration and Naturalization Service. Though opponents challenged the constitutionality of Proposition 187, anti-immigrant feeling soon spread to other parts of the country, becoming a hotly debated issue in the 1996 election.

Though the National Academy of Sciences report did find that "some black workers have lost their jobs to immigrants," for the most part African-Americans were not adversely affected by the new immigration. But urban African-Americans and new immigrants were forced by economic necessity and entrenched segregation patterns to fight for space in decaying, crime-ridden, ghettos, where unemployment rates sometimes hit 60 percent. Overcrowded and underfunded, inner city schools had fallen into disrepair and were unable to provide a proper education.

In April 1992 the frustration and anger of impoverished urban Americans erupted in five days of race riots in Los Angeles. The worst civil disorder since the 1960s, the violence took sixty lives and caused $850 million in damage. The riot was set off by the acquittal on all but one charge of four white Los Angeles police officers accused of using excessive force in arresting a black motorist, Rodney King, the year before. A graphic eighty-one-second amateur video showing the policemen kicking, clubbing, and beating King had not swayed the predominantly white jury. Three of the officers were later convicted on federal civil-rights charges.

The Los Angeles riot exposed the cleavages in urban neighborhoods. Trapped in the nation's inner cities, many blacks resented recent immigrants who were struggling to get ahead, and often succeeding. As a result, some blacks had targeted Korean-owned stores during the arson and looting. Latinos were also frustrated by high unemployment and crowded housing conditions. According to the Los Angeles Police Department, Latinos accounted for more than half of those arrested and a third of those killed during the rioting. Thus the riots were not simply a case of black rage at white injustice; they contained a strong element of class-based protest against the failure of the American system to address the needs of all poor people.

One of the ways federal and state governments had tried to help poor blacks and Latinos was through the establishment of affirmative action programs in government hiring, contracts, and university admissions. From the inception of affirmative action programs in 1965 and their extension in 1967 to include women, many white men had viewed them as unfair and discriminatory. But affirmative action remained official government policy until the 1990s, when white resentment deepened against the "rights revolution" (see Chapter 32) and fueled renewed debate on the issue.

The impact of affirmative action was most evident in college admissions. In 1994, the student population at the University of California, Berkeley campus was 39 percent Asian, 32 percent white, 14 percent Latino, 6 percent black, and 1 percent native American (8 percent of students did not identify their race). In 1995, under pressure from the Republican governor, Pete Wilson, the Regents of the University of California voted to scrap the university's twenty-year-old policy of affirmative action, despite protests from the faculty and from university presidents. In the November 1996 elections, the struggle over affirmative action was intensified by California's passage of Proposition 209, which banned all preference based on race or gender. As appeals worked their way through the federal courts, and black and Latino enrollments declined, the University of California actively sought new admissions criteria that would circumvent the restrictions imposed by Proposition 209.

One reason affirmative action became a political issue in the 1990s was that many, including prominent conservatives like George F. Will, William Bennett, and Patrick Buchanan, saw it as a threat to core American values. Simplistically lumping affirmative action together with multiculturalism—the attempt to represent the diversity of American society and its peoples—critics feared that all this counting by race, gender, sexual preference, and age would lead to a "balkanization," or fragmentation, of American society. Attempts to revise American history textbooks along multicultural lines aroused much anger, as did efforts by universities such as Stanford to revise college curricula to include the study of non-European cultures. Conservatives also took aim at the antiracist and antisexist regulations and speech codes that had been adopted by many colleges. Under the guise of protecting First Amendment rights, conservatives derided the attempt to regulate hate speech as politically correct (PC).

Other Culture Wars: Women and Gays

Conservative critics also targeted the women's movement. In the widely read *Backlash: The Undeclared War on American Women* (1991), the journalist Susan Faludi described a powerful reaction against the gains American women had won in the 1960s and 1970s. Spearheaded by New Right leaders and aided by the media, conservatives held the women's movement responsible for every ill afflicting modern women, from infertility to rising divorce rates; yet polls showed strong support for many feminist demands, including equal pay, reproductive rights, and a more equitable distribution of household and child-care responsibilities.

The deep national divide over abortion, one of the main issues associated with feminism, continued to polarize the country. In the 1980s and 1990s harassment and violence toward those who sought or provided abortions became common. In 1994 four workers were murdered at Boston abortion clinics. Although only a fraction of antiabortion activists supported such extreme acts, disruptive confrontational tactics had made receiving what was still a woman's legal right more dangerous.

Gay rights was another field of battle. As gays and lesbians gained legal protection against housing and job discrimination across the country, Pat Robertson, North Carolina senator Jesse Helms, and others denounced these civil-rights gains as undeserved "special rights." To conservatives, gay rights threatened America's traditional family values. In 1992 Coloradans passed a referendum (overturned by the Supreme Court in 1996) that barred local jurisdictions from passing ordinances protecting gays and lesbians. Across the nation, "gay bashing" and other forms of violence against homosexuals continued. But in 1997, when the comedian Ellen DeGeneres "came out" on national TV in both her real life and sitcom persona, "Ellen," it marked a victory for homosexuals and a blow to conservative watchdogs.

A grim backdrop to gay men's struggle against discrimination was the AIDS epidemic. Acquired immune deficiency syndrome (AIDS) was first recognized by physicians in 1981, and its cause identified as the human immunodeficiency virus (HIV). At first little government funding was directed toward AIDS research or treatment; critics charged that the lack of attention to the syndrome reflected society's antipathy toward gay men, the earliest victims of the disease. Only when heterosexuals, such as hemophiliacs who had received the virus through blood transfusions, began to be affected did AIDS begin to gain significant public attention. The death of the film star Rock

ACT UP
This poster *Untitled* (1989) by artist Keith Haring for the group ACT UP (AIDS Coalition to Unleash Power) was used to mobilize public action against the deadly disease, which would later claim Haring's life.

Hudson from AIDS in 1985 finally broke the barrier of public apathy. Another galvanizing moment came in 1991, when the basketball great Earvin "Magic" Johnson announced that he was HIV-positive.

As early as the mid-1980s, AIDS cases had begun to increase among heterosexuals, especially intravenous drug addicts and their sexual partners, as well as bisexuals. Women now constitute the group with the fastest-growing incidence of HIV infection. To date, more Americans have died of AIDS than were killed in the Korean and Vietnam wars combined. Between 1996 and 1997, however, deaths from AIDs in the United States dropped 19 percent. This decline—the result of new treatment strategies using a combination of drugs, or a "cocktail"—has led to cautious optimism about controlling the disease, though scientists warn that the drugs have not been effective for between 30 and 50 percent of patients.

Popular Culture and Popular Technology

Image was everything in the 1980s and 1990s—or so commentators said, pointing to rock stars Michael Jackson and Madonna, and even to President Reagan. One strong influence on popular culture was MTV, which premiered in 1981. With its creative choreography, flashy colors, and rapid cuts, it seemed perfect for a generation raised on "Sesame Street." The MTV style soon showed up in mainstream media and even political campaigns, which adapted the 30-second sound bites common on television news shows to their own purposes. The national newspaper *USA Today*, which debuted in 1982, adapted the style, featuring eye-catching graphics, color photographs, and short, easy-to-read articles. Soon more staid newspapers followed suit. At the same time, new technology, especially satellite transmission and live "minicam" broadcasting, reshaped the television industry. Also new was the increased availability of cable and satellite dishes. By the mid-1990s viewers could choose from well over a hundred channels, including upstarts such as Ted Turner's Cable News Network (CNN) and the Entertainment Sports Network (ESPN), an all-sports channel. Media, communications, and entertainment were big business, increasingly drawn into global financial networks, markets, and mergers.

Technology also reshaped the home in the late twentieth century. The 1980s saw the introduction of videocassette recorders (VCRs), compact disc (CD) players, cellular phones, and inexpensive fax machines. By 1993 more than three-quarters of American households had VCRs. Video was everywhere—stores, airplanes, tennis courts, operating rooms. With the introduction of camcorders, the family photo album could be supplemented by a video of a high school graduation, a marriage, or a birth.

But it was the personal computer that revolutionized both the home and office. The big breakthrough came in 1977 when the upstart Apple Computer Company offered the Apple II personal computer for $1,195—a price middle-class Americans could afford. When the Apple II became a runaway success, other companies scrambled to get into the market. IBM offered its first personal computer in the summer of 1981. Software companies such as Microsoft, whose founder, Bill Gates, is now the richest person in America, grew rapidly by providing operating systems and other software for the expanding personal computer market. In 1995, 37 percent of American households had at least one personal computer.

More than any other technological advance, the computer created the modern electronic office. Even the smallest business could keep all its records, and do all its correspondence, billing, and other business on a single desktop machine. The very concept of the office was changing as a new class of telecommuters worked at home via computer, fax machine, and electronic mail.

Today, new technologies utilizing fiberoptics, microwave relays, and satellites can transmit massive quantities of information to and from almost any place on earth, and even in outer space, via the *information superhighway*. By 1996, 40 million people in the United States alone used the Internet, and experts predict that by the year 2000 more than 250 million people in over 170 countries will have access to cyberspace. At first scientists and other professionals, who communicated with their peers through electronic mail (*E-mail*) were the primary users of the Internet. But the debut of the World Wide Web in 1991 enhanced the commercial possibilities of the Internet. The Web allowed companies, organizations, political campaigns, and even the White House to create their own "home pages," incorporating both visual and textual information. Although theoretically available to all, the glories of cyberspace are still available mostly to those who can afford them: in 1997 65 percent of Americans who used the Internet had incomes of $50,000 or more. The trend toward wiring public schools and libraries, however, should significantly increase access to the new technology.

The Environmental Movement at Twenty-five

Americans'—and increasingly the world's—love affair with technology continued to be tempered by the recognition that industrial development and economic growth had environmental consequences. On April 26, 1995, when Americans came together for the twenty-fifth anniversary of Earth Day, they had much to celebrate. The nation's rivers and waterways were cleaner; air pollution had been reduced by a third; and lead emissions from fuel, a cause of retardation in children, had been cut by an astounding 98 percent. The bald eagle and the California condor had come back from the brink of extinction. More than 6,000 communities across the country had established recycling programs.

There still was much to be done. Despite efforts to reduce urban smog, two out of five Americans lived in areas with unhealthy air. Many rivers and lakes were still unsafe for fishing and swimming. And one out of four Americans lived within 4 miles of toxic waste dumps, a trend with disproportionate effect on lower-income communities, which constituted what activists termed *environmental racism*.

In addition to addressing problems in their own communities, Americans were also becoming increasingly aware that the environment required action not just from the United States but from the global community as a whole. Three pressing environmental problems demanded international attention: the depletion of the ozone layer, acid rain, and global warming. An important precedent for international action on environmental issues was set by the Montreal Protocol (1987), in which thirty-four nations agreed to phase out ozone-damaging chlorofluorocarbons (CFCs) by 1999. In June 1992 delegates to the Earth Summit in Rio de Janeiro adopted a treaty on global warming, and in 1994 the United States joined sixty-three other countries in signing the Basel Convention, which banned the export of hazardous wastes from industrialized to developing countries. In the future, U.S. environmental policy would operate more and more within an international framework.

THE CLINTON PRESIDENCY: PUBLIC LIFE SINCE 1993

If Americans hoped to make progress on the environment, the faltering economy, and the deep social cleavages surrounding race, gender, and sexual orientation, they would need strong leadership. Yet, low voter turnout in the 1992 presidential election signaled deep dissatisfaction with the American political system. The strong showing of the independent candidate Ross Perot that year, and the early support for the conservative Republican Pat Buchanan four years later, reflected Americans' disenchantment with the two major parties. In the administration of Bill Clinton, their disaffection helped to continue the rollback of federal power begun by Reagan and Bush.

The Clinton Years

As the 1992 election campaign got under way, the economy was the overriding issue, for the recession that had begun in 1990 showed no sign of abating. Bush easily won renomination as the Republican candidate. To solidify the support of the New Right, his running mate, Dan Quayle, spoke out strongly for "family values" and other conservative social agendas. Bill Clinton, the long-time governor of Arkansas, survived charges of marital infidelity and draft dodging, as well as questions about a dubious Arkansas real estate deal called Whitewater, to win the Democratic nomination. For his running mate he chose Al Gore, a second-term senator from Tennessee. At age forty-four, Gore was a year and a half younger than Clinton, making the two men the first of the baby-boom generation to occupy the national ticket.

In the middle of the primary season, the Texas billionaire H. Ross Perot, capitalizing on voters' desire for a change from politics as usual, announced he would run as an independent candidate. Although Perot dropped out of the race on the last day of the Democratic convention, he reentered it less than five weeks before the election, adding a well-financed wild card to an unusual election year.

The Democrats mounted an effective, aggressive campaign that highlighted Clinton's plans to solve domestic problems, especially education, health care, and the economy. Gore added expertise on defense and environmental issues. Bush was hurt by the weak economy, and especially by his reneging on the "No New Taxes" pledge. On election day Clinton received 43 percent of the popular vote to Bush's 38 percent and Perot's 19 percent. Although Perot did not win a single state, his popular vote was the highest for an independent candidate since Theodore Roosevelt's in 1912. The Democrats retained control of both houses of Congress, ending twelve years of divided government. But the narrowness of Clinton's victory, and the public's perception that he did not really stand for anything, did not augur well for his ability to lead the country.

The liberals who supported Clinton hoped that a Democratic presidency could erase the Reagan-Bush legacy and oversee the creation of a new democratic social agenda. Initially, Clinton seemed to fulfill that promise. In 1993 he nominated the liberal Ruth Bader Ginsberg for a seat on the Supreme Court; she was confirmed. The president also appointed Janet Reno as attorney general—the first woman to hold that post. Other trailblazing cabinet appointments included Secretary of Health and Human Services Donna E. Shalala, and, in Clinton's second term, Secretary of State Madeline Albright. Clinton chose an African-American, Ron Brown, as secretary of commerce, and two Latinos, Henry Cisneros and Frederico Peña, to head the Department of Housing and Urban Development (HUD) and the Department of Transportation, respectively.

Clinton's early legislative and administrative record was mixed. In early 1993 he signed into law the Family and Medical Leave Act, twice vetoed by Bush, which provided workers with up to twelve weeks of unpaid leave to tend to a newborn or an adopted child or to respond to a family medical emergency. But when Clinton tried to implement a campaign promise to lift the ban on gays serving in the armed forces, he ran into such ferocious opposition that he backed off, offering a weak compromise policy—"Don't ask, don't tell, don't pursue"—instead. The solution was an ineffective palliative at best, one that called into question Clinton's willingness to stand firm on issues of principle.

By the time Clinton took office, the economy had pulled out of the 1990 recession, enabling him to focus on other economic issues, especially the opening of foreign markets to U.S. goods. In 1992 President Bush had signed the North American Free Trade Agreement (NAFTA), in which the United States, Canada, and Mexico agreed to create a free-trade zone covering all of North America. Strongly supported by the business community, NAFTA was bitterly opposed by labor unions worried about the loss of jobs to lower-paid Mexican workers, and by environmentalists concerned about the weak enforcement of antipollution laws south of the border. Nonetheless, with Clinton's support, Congress narrowly passed NAFTA in November 1993. Another major development in international trade was the revision in 1994 of the General Agreement on Tariffs and Trade (GATT), which had been created at the end of World War II. The new provisions cut tariffs on many manufactured products and for the first time established regulations protecting intellectual property such as patents; copyrights; and trademarks on software, entertainment, and pharmaceuticals.

With the recession over, crime replaced the economy as a major concern among voters. In 1993 Congress passed the Brady Handgun Violence Prevention Act, over the opposition of the National Rifle Association. A much more wide-ranging piece of legislation was the Omnibus Violent Crime Control and Prevention Act (1994), which authorized $30.2 billion for stepped-up law enforcement, crime prevention, and prison construction and administration. The act also extended the death penalty to more than fifty federal crimes, and banned the sale and possession of certain kinds of assault weapons.

Responding to the deep anxieties Americans had about their economic security, Clinton had staked his political fortunes on his campaign promise of universal health care. Though the United States spent more on health care than any other country in the world, it remained the only major industrialized country not to provide national health insurance to all. Furthermore, spiraling medical costs and rising insurance premiums had brought the health-care system to a crisis.

The president chose his wife, Hillary Rodham Clinton, to head the task force that would draft the legislation—a controversial move since no first lady had ever played a formal role in policy making. The resulting proposal was based on the idea of managed competition: market forces, not the government, would control health-care costs and expand citizen's access to health care. But even this mild form of social engineering ran into intense opposition from the well-financed pharmaceutical and insurance industries. By September 1994 congressional leaders were admitting that health reform was dead. In 1995 an estimated 40.3 million Americans—over 17 percent of the population under sixty-five—had no health insurance, and experts predicted that these statistics would climb.

Clinton seems never to have had the time to devote his full attention to pushing health reform through Congress. Three days before assuming office he had to commit his support to a missile attack President Bush had ordered on Iraq. In February foreign terrorists bombed the World Trade Center in New York City, and in April, FBI agents made a misguided assault on the Branch Davidian compound in Waco, Texas. At the White House in September, Israeli Prime Minister Yitzhak Rabin and Yasir Arafat, chairman of the Palestine Liberation Organization, signed an agreement allowing limited Palestinian self-rule in the Gaza Strip and Jericho. In October 1993, just after Clinton announced his health plan, twelve American soldiers were killed on a United Nations peacekeeping mission in Somalia. Constantly shifting from crisis to crisis, Clinton appeared to the American public to be vacillating, indecisive, and lacking in vision, especially in his handling of foreign affairs.

In the former Soviet Union, the increasing unpopularity of the Russian president Boris Yeltsin, who was trying to bring about fundamental market reforms, made American leaders less optimistic about the chances for democracy in that country. Yeltsin's harsh repression of dissent in the breakaway region of Chechnya strained Russia's already difficult relationship with the United States.

Nothing seemed more intractable than the problems that engulfed the former state of Yugoslavia, which had broken into five independent states in 1991. The province of Bosnia and Herzegovina, made up largely of Muslims and committed to a multiethnic state—Serb, Croat, and Muslim—had declared its independence in 1992. But Bosnian Serbs, supported financially and militarily by what remained of Yugoslavia, formed their own breakaway state, and began a siege of the Bosnian capital, Sarajevo. In the countryside the Serbs launched a ruthless campaign of "ethnic cleansing," driving Bosnian Muslims and Croats from their homes and into concentration camps, or shooting them to death in mass executions. More than 250,000 people were killed or reported missing after the outbreak of war in April 1992. After three years of unsuccessful efforts by the European powers to stop the carnage, President Clinton and Secretary of State Warren Christopher facilitated a peace accord in November 1995. A NATO-led peacekeeping force, backed by U.S. troops, would end the fighting, at least temporarily.

At the same time, the end of cold war superpower rivalry presented unexpected opportunities to resolve other longstanding conflicts. In Haiti, the threat of a U.S. invasion in October 1993 led to the restoration of the exiled president, Jean-Bertrand Aristide, who had been ousted by a military coup in 1991. In South Africa, the end of a fifty-year policy of racial separation was capped by the election of the rebel leader Nelson Mandela, who had spent twenty-seven years in prison for challenging apartheid, as the country's first black president in May 1994. And in a move that was seen as the symbolic end to the American experience in Vietnam, the United States established diplomatic relations with Hanoi in July 1995, two decades after the fall of Saigon.

"The Era of Big Government Is Over"

In the 1994 midterm elections, Republicans gained 52 seats in the House of Representatives, which gave them a majority in the House as well as the Senate. In the House, the centerpiece of the new Republican majority was the "Contract with America," a list of proposals that Newt Gingrich of Georgia, the new Speaker of the House, vowed would be voted on in the first 100 days of the new session. The contract included constitutional amendments to balance the budget and set term limits for congressional office; $245 billion in tax cuts for individuals, and tax incentives for small businesses; cuts in welfare and other entitlement programs; anticrime initiatives, and cutbacks in federal regulations. President Clinton, bowing to political reality, acknowledged in his State of the Union message in January 1996 that "the era of big government is over."

But the Republicans were frustrated in their commitment to cut taxes and balance the budget by the year 2002, because both practical and political considerations made many items in the budget immune to serious reductions. Interest on the national debt had to be paid. Defense spending had declined only slightly in the post–cold war world. That left Medicare and Medicaid, Social Security, and all other government programs. Since Social Security was considered untouchable, Congress looked to health care and discretionary spending for savings.

In the fall of 1995 Congress passed a budget that cut $270 billion from projected spending on Medicare, and $170 billion from spending on Medicaid over the next seven years. Other savings came from cuts in discretionary programs, including education and the environment. Clinton accepted Congress's resolve to balance the budget in seven years but, vowing to protect the nation from an "extremist" Congress, vetoed the budget itself. In the standoff that followed, nonessential departments of the government were forced to shut down twice for lack of funding, but polls showed that a majority of Americans held Congress, not the president, responsible. The budget that Clinton finally signed in April 1996 left Medicare and Social Security intact, though it did meet the Republicans' goal of cutting $23 billion from discretionary spending.

As part of the Contract with America, House Republicans were especially determined to cut welfare, a joint federal-state program that represented a fairly small part of the budget. To Republicans, the program had become a prime example of misguided government priorities. The benefits of the main welfare program, Aid for Dependent Children (AFDC), were far from generous: the average annual welfare payment to families (including Food Stamps) was $7,740, well below the established poverty line. Still, in the 1990s both Democratic and Republican statehouses sought ways to change the behavior of welfare recipients by imposing work requirements or denying benefits for additional children born to women on AFDC. In August 1996, after vetoing two Republican-authored bills, President Clinton, who had campaigned on a promise of welfare reform, signed into law the Personal Responsibility and Work Opportunity Act, a historic overhaul of federal entitlements. The 1996 law ended the federal guarantee of cash assistance to poor children by abolishing AFDC; required most adult recipients to find work within two years; set a five-year limit on payments to any one family; and gave states wide discretion in running their welfare programs.

The Republican takeover of Congress had one unintended consequence: it united the usually fractious Democrats behind the president. Unopposed in the 1996 primaries, Clinton was able to burnish his image as a moderate "New Democrat." His political fortunes were aided by the unpopularity of the Republican Congress following the government shutdowns. He also benefited from the continuing strength of the economy. Economic indicators released shortly before election day painted a promising picture. The "misery index"—a combination of the unemployment rate and inflation—was the lowest it had been in twenty-seven years.

The Republicans settled on Senate Majority Leader Bob Dole of Kansas as their presidential candidate. Acceptable to both the conservative and the moderate wings of the party, Dole had a detached campaign style that failed to generate much enthusiasm. He made a 15 percent across-the-board tax cut the centerpiece of his campaign, and selected former representative Jack Kemp, a leading proponent of supply-side economics, as his running mate.

Americans seemed to have made up their minds early about the candidates, which made for a rather desultory campaign. Clinton emphasized his success in reducing the budget deficit, raising the minimum wage to $5.15 an hour, and reforming welfare, and he took credit for the 10 million new jobs created during his first term. In November, Clinton became the first Democratic president since Franklin Roosevelt to win reelection. Voter turnout was the lowest since Calvin Coolidge won the presidency in 1924. Republicans retained control in a majority of the nation's statehouses and in the House of Representatives, and increased their majority in the Senate. Thus a key factor in Bill Clinton's second term would be the necessity, as a Democratic president working with a Republican-dominated Congress, of pursuing bipartisan policies or facing complete stalemate.

In his 1998 state of the union address, Bill Clinton outlined an impressive program of federal spending for schools, tax credits for child care, a hike in the minimum wage, and protection for the beleaguered social security system. His ability to pursue this domestic agenda was seriously compromised, however, by two crises. One revolved around an issue that had plagued him since 1992: allegations of sexual misconduct. In January 1998, attorneys representing Paula Jones, who claimed that the then governor Clinton had propositioned her when she was an Arkansas state employee, revealed that they planned to depose a former White House intern, Monica Lewinsky, about an alleged affair with President Clinton. Kenneth Starr, the independent counsel initially charged with investigating the Whitewater scandal, widened his investigation to explore whether Clinton or his aides had encouraged Lewinsky to lie in her statement. Predictably, a media frenzy—and even speculation about impeachment—ensued. Ironically, Clinton's approval rating remained exceptionally high, perhaps because Americans doubted the political motives of his attackers, and almost certainly because a strong economy kept most citizens content with the President's performance. Whatever the outcome of the investigation, the scandal detracted attention from more pressing domestic issues.

A second crisis was far more serious. The 1991 defeat of Iraq in Operation Desert Storm and the United Nation's imposition of economic sanctions left Saddam Hussein in power. In late 1997 Hussein challenged the authority of the U.N. to inspect Iraqi sites in search of hidden weapons "of mass destruction," which included nuclear, biological, and chemical warfare materials.

Domestic Terrorism
On April 19, 1995, a powerful car bomb exploded outside the Alfred P. Murrah Federal Building in Oklahoma City, killing 168 people, including nineteen children in the building's day-
care center. Antigovernment hostility was suspected as a possible motive of the two accused
bombers, Timothy McVeigh and Terry Nichols.

When Hussein ejected American members of the U.N. inspection team in
October, the United States, with limited international support, began a military buildup in the Gulf. The threatened air strike against Iraq was averted
when U.N. Secretary-General Kofi Annan went to Baghdad and brokered an
agreement that allowed Hussein to save face. The U.N. inspection teams
would have unrestricted access to all suspected weapon sites, but would be accompanied by diplomatic representatives. Although the threat of force accomplished the short term goal of permitting U.N. weapons inspectors to
continue their task, it neither assured the world that Hussein's "weapons of
mass destruction" could be discovered and destroyed nor undercut Hussein's
regime. The crisis served as a potent reminder that despite its position as the
most powerful nation in the world, the United States was limited in its ability
to achieve its foreign policy aims.

Making Sense of the Late Twentieth Century

In 1995 the *New York Times* asked readers to choose a name for the time
they were living in. Perhaps not surprisingly, the responses were fairly pes-

simistic, often including words such as *uncertainty, fragmentation*, and *disillusionment*. Reflecting the importance of new technology, one reader suggested the Silicon Age; another submitted *Kokusaika* (Japanese for "internationalization"), arguing that a non-English word would best capture the internationalization of economics, politics, culture, and society in the late twentieth century.

Indeed, the period since 1980 has brought enormous changes: the end of the four-decade Cold War; a dramatic rethinking of the role of the state in modern American life; the growing globalization of political and economic life; and a growing diversity in American culture and public affairs. The last fifteen years of the twentieth century will probably turn out to have been as important a period of realignment as the 1930s and 1940s, when the New Deal state was formed and the United States took on global responsibilities. These times are certainly as dramatic as the 1890s, when the nation completed the process of industrialization, absorbed a huge wave of immigrants, and secured an overseas empire.

Several themes from twentieth-century American history will certainly endure into the twenty-first. By the late 1990s the United States had dramatically improved its position in the world economy, but nonetheless decisions made beyond the United States continued to affect the daily lives of American workers, managers, and consumers. A startling 554-point drop in the stock market in November 1997—in part a reaction to severe economic crises in several Asian countries—served as a potent reminder of just how interconnected the global economy had become. With trade barriers falling and the Internet opening the entire world to instant communication, national boundaries and economies will become increasingly less important.

In the international political arena, the world appears to be returning to a situation in which power, both economic and military, is dispersed among a number of key players, of which the United States is the most preponderant. However, as the showdown in Iraq suggests, the nation's dominance in the new world order is offset by the limits to its power. Permanent peace in the Persian Gulf or in other hot spots will undoubtedly prove elusive.

Finally, in politics, a significant shift has occurred in the ways that Americans and their leaders seem to be thinking about government and the political system. Decisions made in the mid 1990s will probably ensure that the federal deficit will be tamed, at least temporarily, and the size of government reduced. But given all the challenges the nation will face at home and abroad, it is far too soon to declare an end to the activist American state. All that can be predicted with any assurance in that the dramatic late twentieth-century changes in domestic and world realities will shape the future of the United States and the globe in the twenty-first century and beyond.

CHAPTER 33 TIMELINE

1981	Economic Recovery Tax Act Sandra Day O'Connor nominated to Supreme Court MTV premieres Beginning of AIDS epidemic
1981–1982	Recession
1983	Star Wars proposed
1984	Geraldine Ferraro runs for vice-president
1985	Gramm-Rudman Act
1986	Iran-Contra scandal Immigration Reform and Control Act
1987	Montreal protocol Stock market collapse
1988	George Bush elected president
1989	*Webster v. Reproductive Health Services*
1990–1991	Persian Gulf War
1990–1992	Recession
1991	Dissolution of Soviet Union ends Cold War Clarence Thomas–Anita Hill hearings
1992	Los Angeles riots Bill Clinton elected president
1993	North American Free Trade Agreement (NAFTA) ratified
1994	Health-care reform fails Republicans gain control of Congress
1995	Congress passes parts of the Contract with America University of California Regents vote to end affirmative action Twenty-fifth anniversary of Earth Day U.S. troops enforce peace in Bosnia
1996	Personal Responsibility and Work Opportunity Act Bill Clinton reelected president

ABOUT THE AUTHORS

James A. Henretta is Priscilla Alden Burke Professor of American History at the University of Maryland, College Park. He received his undergraduate education at Swarthmore College and his Ph.D. from Harvard University. He has taught at the University of Sussex, England; Princeton University; UCLA; Boston University; as a Fulbright lecturer in Australia at the University of New England; and at Oxford University as the Harmsworth Professor of American History. His publications include *The Evolution of American Society, 1700–1815: An Interdisciplinary Analysis; "Salutary Neglect": Colonial Administration under the Duke of Newcastle; Evolution and Revolution: American Society, 1600–1820; The Origins of American Capitalism*; and important articles in early American and social history. He recently completed a fellowship at the Woodrow Wilson Center working on a study of *The Transformation of the Liberal State in America, 1800–1970.*

David Brody is Professor Emeritus of History at the University of California, Davis. He received his B.A., M.A., and Ph.D. from Harvard University. He has taught at the University of Warwick in England, at Moscow State University in the former Soviet Union, and at Sydney University in Australia. He is the author of *Steelworkers in America; Workers in Industrial America: Essays on the 20th Century Struggle*; and *In Labor's Cause: Main Themes on the History of the American Worker.* He has been awarded fellowships from the Social Science Research Council, the Guggenheim Foundation, and the National Endowment for the Humanities. He is past president (1991–92) of the Pacific Coast Branch of the American Historical Association. His current research is on industrial labor during the Great Depression.

Lynn Dumenil is Professor of History at Occidental College in Los Angeles. She is a graduate of the University of Southern California and received her Ph.D. from the University of California, Berkeley. She has written *The Modern Temper: American Culture and Society in the 1920s* and *Freemasonry and American Culture: 1880–1930.* Her articles and reviews have appeared in *Journal of American History; Journal of American Ethnic History; Reviews in American History*; and *American Historical Review.* She has been a historical consultant to several documentary film projects and has served on committees of the Organization of American Historians, the American Studies Association, and the Immigration History Society. Her current work is on World War I, citizenship, and the state.

DOCUMENTS

THE DECLARATION OF INDEPENDENCE

The Unanimous Declaration of the Thirteen United States of America

When in the Course of human events, it becomes necessary for one people to dissolve the political bands which have connected them with another, and to assume among the Powers of the earth, the separate and equal station to which the Laws of Nature and of Nature's God entitle them, a decent respect to the opinions of mankind requires that they should declare the causes which impel them to the separation.

We hold these truths to be self-evident, that all men are created equal, that they are endowed by their Creator with certain unalienable rights, that among these are Life, Liberty, and the pursuit of Happiness. That to secure these rights, Governments are instituted among Men, deriving their just powers from the consent of the governed. That whenever any Form of Government becomes destructive of these ends, it is the Right of the People to alter or to abolish it, and to institute new Government, laying its foundation on such principles and organizing its powers in such form, as to them shall seem most likely to effect their Safety and Happiness. Prudence, indeed, will dictate that Governments long established should not be changed for light and transient causes; and accordingly all experience hath shown, that mankind are more disposed to suffer, while evils are sufferable, than to right themselves by abolishing the forms to which they are accustomed. But when a long train of abuses and usurpations, pursuing invariably the same Object evinces a design to reduce them under absolute Despotism, it is their right, it is their duty, to throw off such Government, and to provide new Guards for their future security.—Such has been the patient sufferance of these Colonies; and such is now the necessity which constrains them to alter their former Systems of Government. The history of the present King of Great Britain is a history of repeated injuries and usurpations, all having in direct object the establishment of an absolute Tyranny over these States. To prove this, let Facts be submitted to a candid world.

He has refused his Assent to Laws, the most wholesome and necessary for the public good.

He has forbidden his Governors to pass Laws of immediate and pressing importance, unless suspended in their operation till his Assent should be obtained; and, when so suspended, he has utterly neglected to attend to them.

He has refused to pass other Laws for the accommodation of large districts of people, unless those people would relinquish the right of Representation in the Legislature, a right inestimable to them and formidable to tyrants only.

He has called together legislative bodies at places unusual, uncomfortable, and distant from the depository of their public Records, for the sole purpose of fatiguing them into compliance with his measures.

He has dissolved Representative Houses repeatedly, for opposing with manly firmness his invasions on the rights of the people.

He has refused for a long time, after such dissolutions, to cause others to be elected; whereby the Legislative powers, incapable of Annihilation, have returned to the People at large for their exercise; the State remaining in the mean time exposed to all the dangers of invasion from without and convulsions within.

He has endeavoured to prevent the population of these States; for that purpose obstructing the Laws of Naturalization of Foreigners; refusing to pass others to encourage their migrations hither, and raising the conditions of new Appropriations of Lands.

He has obstructed the Administration of Justice, by refusing his Assent to Laws for establishing Judiciary powers.

He has made Judges dependent on his Will alone, for the tenure of their offices, and the amount and payment of their salaries.

He has erected a multitude of New Offices, and sent hither swarms of Officers to harass our People, and eat out their substance.

He has kept among us, in times of peace, Standing Armies without the Consent of our legislature.

He has combined with others to subject us to a jurisdiction foreign to our constitution, and unacknowledged by our laws; giving his Assent to their Acts of pretended Legislation:

For quartering large bodies of armed troops among us:

For protecting them, by a mock Trial, from Punishment for any Murders which they should commit on the Inhabitants of these States:

For cutting off our Trade with all parts of the world:

For imposing taxes on us without our Consent:

For depriving us of many cases, of the benefits of Trial by jury:

For transporting us beyond Seas to be tried for pretended offences:

For abolishing the free System of English Laws in a neighbouring Province, establishing therein an Arbitrary government, and enlarging its Boundaries so as to render it at once an example and fit instrument for introducing the same absolute rule into these Colonies:

For taking away our Charters, abolishing our most valuable Laws, and altering fundamentally the Forms of our Governments:

For suspending our own Legislatures, and declaring themselves invested with Power to legislate for us in all cases whatsoever.

He has abdicated Government here, by declaring us out of his Protection and waging War against us.

He has plundered our seas, ravaged our Coasts, burnt our towns, and destroyed the lives of our people.

He is at this time transporting large armies of foreign mercenaries to compleat the works of death, desolation, and tyranny, already begun with circumstances of Cruelty & perfidy scarcely paralleled in the most barbarous ages, and totally unworthy the Head of a civilized nation.

He has constrained our fellow Citizens taken Captive on the high Seas to bear Arms against their Country, to become the executioners of their friends and Brethren, or to fall themselves by their Hands.

He has excited domestic insurrections amongst us, and has endeavoured to bring on the inhabitants of our frontiers, the merciless Indian Savages, whose known rule of warfare, is an undistinguished destruction of all ages, sexes, and conditions.

In every stage of these Oppressions We have Petitioned for Redress in the most humble terms: Our repeated Petitions have been answered only by repeated injury. A Prince, whose character is thus marked by every act which may define a Tyrant, is unfit to be the ruler of a free people.

Nor have We been wanting in attention to our British brethren. We have warned them from time to time of attempts by their legislature to extend an unwarrantable jurisdiction over us. We have reminded them of the circumstances of our emigration and settlement here. We have appealed to their native justice and magnanimity, and we have conjured them by the ties of our common kindred to disavow these usurpations, which, would inevitably interrupt our connections and correspondence. They too have been deaf to the voice of justice and of consanguinity. We must, therefore, acquiesce in the necessity, which denounces our Separation, and hold them, as we hold the rest of mankind, Enemies in War, in Peace Friends.

We, therefore, the Representatives of the United States of America, in General Congress, Assembled, appealing to the Supreme Judge of the world for the rectitude of our intentions, do, in the Name, and by Authority of the good People of these Colonies, solemnly publish and declare, That these United Colonies are, and of Right ought to be FREE AND INDEPENDENT STATES; that they are Absolved from all Allegiance to the British Crown, and that all political connection between them and the State of Great Britain, is and ought to be totally dissolved; and that as Free and Independent States, they have full Power to levy War, conclude Peace, contract Alliances, establish Commerce, and to do all other Acts and Things which Independent States may of right do. And for the support of this Declaration, with a firm reliance on the Protection of Divine Providence, we mutually pledge to each other our Lives, our Fortunes, and our sacred Honor.

John Hancock

Button Gwinnett	George Wythe	James Wilson	Josiah Bartlett
Lyman Hall	Richard Henry Lee	Geo. Ross	Wm. Whipple
Geo. Walton	Th. Jefferson	Caesar Rodney	Saml. Adams
Wm. Hooper	Benja. Harrison	Geo. Read	John Adams
Joseph Hewes	Thos. Nelson, Jr.	Thos. M'Kean	Robt. Treat Paine
John Penn	Francis Lightfoot Lee	Wm. Floyd	Elbridge Gerry
Edward Rutledge	Carter Braxton	Phil. Livingston	Step. Hopkins
Thos. Heyward, Junr.	Robt. Morris	Frans. Lewis	William Ellery
Thomas Lynch, Junr.	Benjamin Rush	Lewis Morris	Roger Sherman
Arthur Middleton	Benja. Franklin	Richd. Stockton	Sam'el Hunington
Samuel Chase	John Morton	Jno. Witherspoon	Wm. Williams
Wm. Paca	Geo. Clymer	Fras. Hopkinson	Oliver Wolcott
Thos. Stone	Jas. Smith	John Hart	Matthew Thornton
Charles Carroll	Geo. Taylor	Abra. Clark	
of Carrollton			

THE ARTICLES OF CONFEDERATION AND PERPETUAL UNION

Between the states of New Hampshire, Massachusetts Bay, Rhode Island and Providence Plantations, Connecticut, New York, New Jersey, Pennsylvania, Delaware, Maryland, Virginia, North Carolina, South Carolina, Georgia.*

Article 1.

The stile of this confederacy shall be "The United States of America."

Article 2.

Each State retains its sovereignty, freedom and independence, and every power, jurisdiction, and right, which is not by this confederation expressly delegated to the United States, in Congress assembled.

Article 3.

The said states hereby severally enter into a firm league of friendship with each other for their common defence, the security of their liberties and their mutual and general welfare; binding themselves to assist each other against all force offered to, or attacks made upon them, or any of them, on account of religion, sovereignty, trade, or any other pretence whatever.

Article 4.

The better to secure and perpetuate mutual friendship and intercourse among the people of the different states in this union, the free inhabitants of each of these states, paupers, vagabonds, and fugitives from justice excepted, shall be entitled to all privileges and immunities of free citizens in the several states; and the people of each State shall have free ingress and regress to and from any other State, and shall enjoy therein all the privileges of trade and commerce, subject to the same duties, impositions, and restrictions, as the inhabitants thereof respectively; provided, that such restrictions shall

---

*This copy of the final draft of the Articles of Confederation is taken from the *Journals*, 9:907–925, November 15, 1777.

not extend so far as to prevent the removal of property, imported into any State, to any other State of which the owner is an inhabitant; provided also, that no imposition, duties, or restriction, shall be laid by any State on the property of the United States, or either of them.

If any person guilty of, or charged with treason, felony, or other high misdemeanor in any State, shall flee from justice and be found in any of the United States, he shall, upon demand of the governor or executive power of the State from which he fled, be delivered up and removed to the State having jurisdiction of his offence.

Full faith and credit shall be given in each of these states to the records, acts, and judicial proceedings of the courts and magistrates of every other State.

Article 5.

For the more convenient management of the general interests of the United States, delegates shall be annually appointed, in such manner as the legislature of each State shall direct, to meet in Congress, on the 1st Monday in November in every year, with a power reserved to each State to recal its delegates, or any of them, at any time within the year, and to send others in their stead for the remainder of the year.

No State shall be represented in Congress by less than two, nor by more than seven members; and no person shall be capable of being a delegate for more than three years in any term of six years; nor shall any person, being a delegate, be capable of holding any office under the United States, for which he, or any other for his benefit, receives any salary, fees, or emolument of any kind.

Each State shall maintain its own delegates in a meeting of the states, and while they act as members of the committee of the states.

In determining questions in the United States, in Congress assembled, each State shall have one vote.

Freedom of speech and debate in Congress shall not be impeached or questioned in any court or place out of Congress: and the members of Congress shall be protected in their persons from arrests and imprisonments, during the time of their going to and from, and attendance on Congress, *except for treason*, felony, or breach of the peace.

Article 6.

No State, without the consent of the United States, in Congress assembled, shall send any embassy to, or receive any embassy from, or enter into any conference, agreement, alliance, or treaty with any king, prince, or state; nor shall any person, holding any office of profit or trust under the United States, or any of them, accept of any present, emolument, office or title, of any kind whatever, from any king, prince, or foreign state; nor shall the United States, in Congress assembled, or any of them, grant any title of nobility.

No two or more states shall enter into any treaty, confederation, or alliance, whatever, between them, without the consent of the United States, in Congress assembled, specifying accurately the purposes for which the same is to be entered into, and how long it shall continue.

No state shall lay any imposts or duties which may interfere with any stipulations in treaties entered into by the United States, in Congress assembled, with any king, prince, or state, in pursuance of any treaties already proposed by Congress to the courts of France and Spain.

No vessels of war shall be kept up in time of peace by any State, except such number only as shall be deemed necessary by the United States, in Congress assembled, for the defence of such State or its trade; nor shall any body of forces be kept up by any State, in time of peace, except such number only as, in the judgment of the United States, in Congress assembled, shall be deemed requisite to garrison the forts necessary for the defence of such State; but every State shall always keep up a well regulated and disciplined militia, sufficiently armed and accoutred, and shall provide, and constantly have ready for use, in public stores, a due number of field pieces and tents, and a proper quantity of arms, ammunition and camp equipage.

No State shall engage in any war without the consent of the United States, in Congress assembled, unless such State be actually invaded by enemies, or shall have received certain advice of a resolution being formed by some nation of Indians to invade such State, and the danger is so imminent as not to admit of a delay till the United States, in Congress assembled, can be consulted; nor shall any State grant commissions to any ships or vessels of war, nor letters of marque or reprisal, except it be after a declaration of war by the United States, in Congress assembled, and then only against the kingdom or state, and the subjects thereof, against which war has been so declared, and under such regulations as shall be established by the United States, in Congress assembled, unless such State be infested by pirates, in which case vessels of war may be fitted out for that occasion, and kept so long as the danger shall continue, or until the United States, in Congress assembled, shall determine otherwise.

Article 7.

When land forces are raised by any State for the common defence, all officers of or under the rank of colonel, shall be appointed by the legislature of each State respectively, by whom such forces shall be raised, or in such manner as such State shall direct; and all vacancies shall be filled up by the State which first made the appointment.

Article 8.

All charges of war and all other expences, that shall be incurred for the common defence or general welfare, and allowed by the United States, in Congress assembled, shall be defrayed out of a common treasury, which shall be supplied by the several states, in proportion to the value of all land within each State, granted to or surveyed for any person, as such land and the buildings and improvements thereon shall be estimated according to such mode as the United States, in Congress assembled, shall, from time to time, direct and appoint.

The taxes for paying that proportion shall be laid and levied by the authority and direction of the legislatures of the several states, within the time agreed upon by the United States, in Congress assembled.

Article 9.

The United States, in Congress assembled, shall have the sole and exclusive right and power of determining on peace and war, except in the cases mentioned in the 6th article; of sending and receiving ambassadors; entering into treaties and alliances, provided that no treaty of commerce shall be made, whereby the legislative power of the respective states shall be restrained from imposing such imposts and duties on foreigners as their own people are subjected to, or from prohibiting the exportation or importation of any species of goods or commodities whatsoever; of establishing rules for deciding, in all cases, what captures on land or water shall be legal, and in what manner prizes, taken by land or naval forces in the service of the United States, shall be divided or appropriated; of granting letters of marque and reprisal in times of peace; appointing courts for the trial of piracies and felonies committed on the high seas, and establishing courts for receiving and determining, finally, appeals in all cases of captures; provided, that no member of Congress shall be appointed a judge of any of the said courts.

The United States, in Congress assembled, shall also be the last resort on appeal in all disputes and differences now subsisting, or that hereafter may arise between two or more states concerning boundary, jurisdiction or any other cause whatever; which authority shall always be exercised in the manner following: whenever the legislative or executive authority, or lawful agent of any State, in controversy with another, shall present a petition to Congress, stating the matter in question, and praying for a hearing, notice thereof shall be given, by order of Congress, to the legislative or executive authority of the other State in controversy, and a day assigned for the appearance of the parties by their lawful agents, who shall then be directed to appoint, by joint consent, commissioners or judges to constitute a court for hearing and determining the matter in question; but, if they cannot agree, Congress shall name three persons out of each of the United States, and from the list of such persons each party shall alternately strike out one, the petitioners beginning, until the number shall be reduced to thirteen; and from that number not less than seven, nor more than nine names, as Congress shall direct, shall, in the presence of Congress, be drawn out by lot; and the persons whose names shall be so drawn, or any five of them, shall be commissioners or judges to hear and finally determine the controversy, so always as a major part of the judges who shall hear the cause shall agree in the determination; and if either party shall neglect to attend at the day appointed, without shewing reasons which Congress shall judge sufficient, or, being present, shall refuse to strike, the Congress shall proceed to nominate three persons out of each State, and the secretary of Congress shall strike in behalf of such party absent or refusing; and the judgment and sentence of the court to be appointed, in the manner before prescribed, shall be final and conclusive; and if any of the parties shall refuse to submit to the authority of such court, or to appear or defend their claim or cause, the court shall nevertheless proceed to pronounce sentence or judgment, which shall, in like manner, be final and decisive, the judgment or sentence and other proceedings begin, in either case, transmitted to Congress, and lodged among the acts of Congress for the security of the parties concerned: provided, that every commissioner, before he sits in judgment, shall take an oath, to be administered by one of the judges of the supreme or superior court of the State where the cause shall be tried, "well and truly to hear and determine the matter in question, according to the best of his judgment, without favour, affection, or hope of reward:" provided, also, that no State shall be deprived of territory for the benefit of the United States.

All controversies concerning the private right of soil, claimed under different grants of two or more states, whose jurisdictions, as they may respect such lands and the states which passed such grants, are adjusted, the said grants, or either of them, being at the same time claimed to have originated antecedent to such settlement of jurisdiction, shall, on the petition of either party to the Congress of the United States, be finally determined, as near as may be, in the same manner as is before prescribed for deciding disputes respecting territorial jurisdiction between different states.

The United States, in Congress assembled, shall also have the sole and exclusive right and power of regulating the alloy and value of coin struck by their own authority, or by that of the respective states; fixing the standard of weights and measures throughout the United States; regulating the trade and managing all affairs with the Indians not members of any of the states; provided that the legislative right of any State within its own limits be not infringed or violated; establishing and regulating post offices from one State to another throughout all the United States, and exacting such postage on the papers passing through the same as may be requisite to defray the expences of the said office; appointing all officers of the land forces in the service of the United States, excepting regimental officers; appointing all the officers of the naval forces, and commissioning all officers whatever in the service of the United States; making rules for the government and regulation of the said land and naval forces, and directing their operations.

The United States, in Congress assembled, shall have authority to appoint a committee to sit in the recess of Congress, to be denominated "a Committee of the States," and to consist of one delegate from each State, and to appoint such other committees and civil officers as may be necessary for managing the general affairs of the United States, under their direction; to appoint one of their number to preside; provided that no person be allowed to serve in the office of president more than one year in any term of three years; to ascertain the necessary sums of money to be raised for the service of the United States, and to appropriate and apply the same for defraying the public expences; to borrow money or emit bills on the credit of the United States, transmitting, every half year, to the respective states, an account of the sums of money so borrowed or emitted; to build and equip a navy; to agree upon the number of land forces, and to make requisitions from each State for its quota, in proportion to the number of white inhabitants in such State; which requisitions shall be binding; and thereupon, the legislature of each State shall appoint the regimental officers, raise the men, and cloathe, arm, and equip them in a soldier-like manner, at the expence of the United States; and the officers and men so cloathed, armed, and equipped, shall march to the place appointed and within the time agreed on by the United States, in Congress assembled; but if the United States, in Congress assembled, shall, on consideration of circumstances, judge proper that any State should not raise men, or should raise a smaller number than its quota, and that any other State should raise a greater number of men than the quota thereof, such extra number shall be raised, officered, cloathed, armed, and equipped in the same manner as the quota of such State, unless the legislature of such State shall judge that such extra number cannot be safely spared out of the same, in which case they shall raise, officer, cloathe, arm, and equip as many of such extra number as they judge can be safely spared. And the officers and men so cloathed, armed, and equipped, shall march to the place appointed and within the time agreed on by the United States, in Congress assembled.

The United States, in Congress assembled, shall never engage in a war, nor grant letters of marque and reprisal in time of peace, nor enter into any treaties or alliances, nor coin money, nor regulate the value thereof, nor ascertain the sums and expences necessary for the defence and welfare of the United States, or any of them: nor emit bills, nor borrow money on the credit of the United States, nor appropriate money, nor agree upon the number of vessels of war to be built or purchased, or the number of land or sea forces to be raised, nor appoint a commander in chief of the army or navy, unless nine states assent to the same; nor shall a question on any other point, except for adjourning from day to day, be determined, unless by the votes of a majority of the United States, in Congress assembled.

The Congress of the United States shall have power to adjourn to any time within the year, and to any place within the United States, so that no period of adjournment be for a longer duration than the space of six months, and shall publish the journal of their proceedings monthly, except such parts thereof, relating to treaties, alliances or military operations, as, in their judgment, require secrecy; and the yeas and nays of the delegates of each State on any question shall be entered on the journal, when it is desired by any delegate; and the delegates of a State, or any of them, at his, or their request, shall be furnished with a transcript of the said journal, except such parts as are above excepted, to lay before the legislatures of the several states.

Article 10.

The committee of the states, or any nine of them, shall be authorized to execute, in the recess of Congress, such of the powers of Congress as the United States, in Congress assembled, by the consent of nine states, shall, from time to time, think expedient to vest them with; provided, that no power be delegated to the said committee, for the exercise of which, by the articles of confederation, the voice of nine states, in the Congress of the United States assembled, is requisite.

Article 11.

Canada acceding to this confederation, and joining in the measures of the United States, shall be admitted into and entitled to all the advantages of this union; but no other colony shall be admitted into the same, unless such admission be agreed to by nine states.

Article 12.

All bills of credit emitted, monies borrowed and debts contracted by, or under the authority of Congress before the assembling of the United States, in pursuance of the present confederation, shall be deemed and considered as a charge against the United States, for payment and satisfaction whereof the said United States and the public faith are hereby solemnly pledged.

Article 13.

Every State shall abide by the determinations of the United States, in Congress assembled, on all questions which, by this confederation, are submitted to them. And the articles of this confederation shall be inviolably observed by every State, and the union shall be perpetual; nor shall any alteration at any time hereafter be made in any of them, unless such alteration be agreed to in a Congress of the United States, and be afterwards confirmed by the legislatures of every State.

These articles shall be proposed to the legislatures of all the United States, to be considered, and if approved of by them, they are advised to authorize their delegates to ratify the same in the Congress of the United States; which being done, the same shall become conclusive.

THE CONSTITUTION OF THE UNITED STATES

We the People of the United States, in Order to form a more perfect Union, establish Justice, insure domestic Tranquility, provide for the common defence, promote the general Welfare, and secure the Blessings of Liberty to ourselves and our Posterity, do ordain and establish this Constitution for the United States of America.

Article I

Section 1
All legislative Powers herein granted shall be vested in a Congress of the United States, which shall consist of a Senate and a House of Representatives.

Section 2
The House of Representatives shall be composed of Members chosen every second Year by the People of the several States, and the Electors in each State shall have the Qualifications requisite for Electors of the most numerous Branch of the State Legislature.

No Person shall be a Representative who shall not have attained to the Age of twenty-five Years, and been seven Years a Citizen of the United States, and who shall not, when elected, be an Inhabitant of that State in which he shall be chosen.

Representatives and direct Taxes shall be apportioned among the several States which may be included within this Union, according to their respective Numbers, *which shall be determined by adding to the whole Number of free Persons, including those bound to Service for a Term of Years, and excluding Indians not taxed, three fifths of all other Persons.** The actual Enumeration shall be made within three Years after the first Meeting of the Congress of the United States, and within every subsequent Term of ten Years, in such Manner as they shall by Law direct. The Number of Representatives shall not exceed one for every thirty Thousand, but each State shall have at Least one Representative; and *until such enumeration shall be made, the State of New Hampshire shall be entitled to chuse three, Massachusetts eight, Rhode Island and Providence Plantations one, Connecticut five, New-York six, New Jersey four, Pennsylvania eight, Delaware one, Maryland six, Virginia ten, North Carolina five, South Carolina five, and Georgia three.*

Note: The Constitution became effective March 4, 1789. Provisions in italics have been changed by constitutional amendment.

*Changed by Section 2 of the Fourteenth Amendment.

When vacancies happen in the Representation from any State, the Executive Authority thereof shall issue Writs of Election to fill such Vacancies.

The House of Representatives shall chuse their Speaker and other Officers; and shall have the sole Power of Impeachment.

Section 3

The Senate of the United States shall be composed of two Senators from each State, *chosen by the Legislature thereof,*[†] for six Years; and each Senator shall have one Vote.

Immediately after they shall be assembled in Consequence of the first Election, they shall be divided as equally as may be into three Classes. The Seats of the Senators of the first Class shall be vacated at the Expiration of the second Year, of the second Class at the Expiration of the fourth Year, and of the third Class at the Expiration of the sixth Year, so that one-third may be chosen every second Year; *and if Vacancies happen by Resignation, or otherwise, during the Recess of the Legislature of any State, the Executive thereof may make temporary Appointments until the next Meeting of the Legislature, which shall then fill such Vacancies.*[‡]

No person shall be a Senator who shall not have attained to the Age of thirty Years, and been nine Years a Citizen of the United States, and who shall not, when elected, be an Inhabitant of that State for which he shall be chosen.

The Vice President of the United States shall be President of the Senate, but shall have no Vote, unless they be equally divided.

The Senate shall chuse their other Officers, and also a President pro tempore, in the absence of the Vice President, or when he shall exercise the Office of President of the United States.

The Senate shall have the sole Power to try all Impeachments. When sitting for that Purpose, they shall be on Oath or Affirmation. When the President of the United States is tried, the Chief Justice shall preside: And no Person shall be convicted without the Concurrence of two thirds of the Members present.

Judgment in Cases of Impeachment shall not extend further than to removal from Office, and disqualification to hold and enjoy any Office of honor, Trust or Profit under the United States: but the Party convicted shall nevertheless be liable and subject to Indictment, Trial, Judgment and Punishment, according to Law.

Section 4

The Times, Places and Manner of holding Elections for Senators and Representatives, shall be prescribed in each State by the Legislature thereof; but the Congress may at any time by Law make or alter such Regulations, except as to the Places of Chusing Senators.

The Congress shall assemble at least once in every Year, and such Meeting *shall be on the first Monday in December, unless they shall by Law appoint a different Day.*[*]

Section 5

Each House shall be the Judge of the Elections, Returns and Qualifications of its own Members, and a Majority of each shall constitute a Quorum to do Business; but a smaller number may adjourn from day to day, and may be authorized to compel the Attendance of absent Members, in such Manner, and under such Penalties, as each House may provide.

[†]Changed by Section 1 of the Seventeenth Amendment.
[‡]Changed by Clause 2 of the Seventeenth Amendment.
[*]Changed by Section 2 of the Twentieth Amendment.

Each House may determine the Rules of its Proceedings, punish its Members for disorderly Behavior, and, with the Concurrence of two thirds, expel a Member.

Each House shall keep a Journal of its Proceedings, and from time to time publish the same, excepting such Parts as may in their Judgment require Secrecy; and the Yeas and Nays of the Members of either House on any question shall, at the Desire of one-fifth of those Present, be entered on the Journal.

Neither House, during the Session of Congress, shall, without the Consent of the other, adjourn for more than three days, nor to any other Place than that in which the two Houses shall be sitting.

Section 6

The Senators and Representatives shall receive a Compensation for their Services, to be ascertained by Law, and paid out of the Treasury of the United States. They shall in all Cases, except Treason, Felony and Breach of the Peace, be privileged from Arrest during their Attendance at the Session of their respective Houses, and in going to and returning from the same; and for any Speech or Debate in either House, they shall not be questioned in any other Place.

No Senator or Representative shall, during the Time for which he was elected, be appointed to any civil Office under the Authority of the United States, which shall have been created, or the Emoluments whereof shall have been increased, during such time; and no Person holding any Office under the United States, shall be a Member of either House during his Continuance in Office.

Section 7

All Bills for raising Revenue shall originate in the House of Representatives; but the Senate may propose or concur with Amendments as on other Bills.

Every Bill which shall have passed the House of Representatives and the Senate, shall, before it becomes a Law, be presented to the President of the United States; If he approve he shall sign it, but if not he shall return it, with his Objections to that House in which it shall have originated, who shall enter the Objections at large on their Journal, and proceed to reconsider it. If after such Reconsideration two thirds of that House shall agree to pass the Bill, it shall be sent, together with the Objections, to the other House, by which it shall likewise be reconsidered, and if approved by two thirds of that House, it shall become a Law. But in all such Cases the Votes of both Houses shall be determined by Yeas and Nays, and the Names of the Persons voting for and against the Bill shall be entered on the Journal of each House respectively. If any Bill shall not be returned by the President within ten Days (Sundays excepted) after it shall have been presented to him, the Same shall be a Law, in like Manner as if he had signed it, unless the Congress by their Adjournment prevent its Return, in which Case it shall not be a Law.

Every Order, Resolution, or Vote to which the Concurrence of the Senate and the House of Representatives may be necessary (except on a question of Adjournment) shall be presented to the President of the United States; and before the Same shall take Effect, shall be approved by him, or being disapproved by him, shall be repassed by two thirds of the Senate and House of Representatives, according to the Rules and Limitations prescribed in the Case of a Bill.

Section 8

The Congress shall have Power To lay and collect Taxes, Duties, Imposts and Excises, to pay the Debts and provide for the common Defence and general Welfare of the United States; but all Duties, Imposts and Excises shall be uniform throughout the United States;

To borrow money on the credit of the United States;

To regulate Commerce with foreign Nations, and among the several States, and with the Indian Tribes;

To establish an uniform Rule of Naturalization, and uniform Laws on the subject of Bankruptcies throughout the United States;

To coin Money, regulate the Value thereof, and of foreign Coin, and fix the Standard of Weights and Measures;

To provide for the Punishment of counterfeiting the Securities and current Coin of the United States;

To establish Post Offices and post Roads;

To promote the Progress of Science and useful Arts, by securing for limited Times to Authors and Inventors the exclusive Right to their respective Writings and Discoveries;

To constitute Tribunals inferior to the supreme Court;

To define and punish Piracies and Felonies committed on the high Seas, and Offenses against the Law of Nations;

To declare War, grant Letters of Marque and Reprisal, and make Rules concerning Captures on Land and Water;

To raise and support Armies, but no Appropriation of Money to that Use shall be for a longer Term than two Years;

To provide and maintain a Navy;

To make Rules for the Government and Regulation of the land and naval Forces;

To provide for calling forth the Militia to execute the Laws of the Union, suppress Insurrections and repel Invasions;

To provide for organizing, arming, and disciplining the Militia, and for governing such Part of them as may be employed in the Service of the United States, reserving to the States respectively, the Appointment of the Officers, and the Authority of training the Militia according to the discipline prescribed by Congress;

To exercise exclusive Legislation in all Cases whatsoever, over such District (not exceeding ten Miles square) as may, by Cession of particular States, and the acceptance of Congress, become the Seat of Government of the United States, and to exercise like Authority over all Places purchased by the Consent of the Legislature of the State in which the Same shall be, for the Erection of Forts, Magazines, Arsenals, dock-Yards, and other needful Buildings;—And

To make all Laws which shall be necessary and proper for carrying into Execution the foregoing Powers, and all other Powers vested by this Constitution in the Government of the United States, or in any Department or Officer thereof.

Section 9
The Migration or Importation of such Persons as any of the States now existing shall think proper to admit, shall not be prohibited by the Congress prior to the Year one thousand eight hundred and eight but a tax or duty may be imposed on such Importation, not exceeding ten dollars for each Person.

The privilege of the Writ of Habeas Corpus shall not be suspended, unless when in Cases of Rebellion or Invasion the public Safety may require it.

No Bill of Attainder or ex post facto Law shall be passed.

No capitation, or other direct, Tax shall be laid, unless in Proportion to the Census or Enumeration herein before directed to be taken.*

No Tax or Duty shall be laid on Articles exported from any State.

---

*Changed by the Sixteenth Amendment.

No Preference shall be given by any Regulation of Commerce or Revenue to the Ports of one State over those of another: nor shall Vessels bound to, or from, one State, be obliged to enter, clear, or pay Duties in another.

No Money shall be drawn from the Treasury, but in Consequence of Appropriations made by law; and a regular Statement and Account of the Receipts and Expenditures of all public Money shall be published from time to time.

No Title of Nobility shall be granted by the United States: And no Person holding any Office of Profit or Trust under them, shall, without the Consent of the Congress, accept of any present, Emolument, Office, or Title, of any kind whatever, from any King, Prince, or foreign State.

Section 10
No State shall enter into any Treaty, Alliance, or Confederation; grant Letters of Marque and Reprisal; coin Money; emit Bills of Credit; make any Thing but gold and silver Coin a Tender in Payment of Debts; pass any Bill of Attainder, ex post facto Law, or Law impairing the Obligation of Contracts, or grant any Title of Nobility.

No State shall, without the Consent of the Congress, lay any Imposts or Duties on Imports or Exports, except what may be absolutely necessary for executing its inspection Laws: and the net Produce of all Duties and Imposts, laid by any State on Imports or Exports, shall be for the Use of the Treasury of the United States; and all such Laws shall be subject to the Revision and Control of the Congress.

No State shall, without the Consent of the Congress, lay any duty of Tonnage, keep Troops, or Ships of War in time of Peace, enter into any Agreement or Compact with another State, or with a foreign Power, or engage in War, unless actually invaded, or in such imminent Danger as will not admit of delay.

Article II

Section 1
The executive Power shall be vested in a President of the United States of America. He shall hold his Office during the Term of four Years, and, together with the Vice President, chosen for the same Term, be elected, as follows:

Each State shall appoint, in such Manner as the Legislature thereof may direct, a Number of Electors, equal to the whole Number of Senators and Representatives to which the State may be entitled in the Congress; but no Senator or Representative, or Person holding an Office of Trust or Profit under the United States, shall be appointed an Elector.

The Electors shall meet in their respective States, and vote by Ballot for two Persons, of whom one at least shall not be an Inhabitant of the same State with themselves. And they shall make a List of all the Persons voted for, and of the Number of Votes for each; which List they shall sign and certify, and transmit sealed to the Seat of the Government of the United States, directed to the President of the Senate. The President of the Senate shall, in the Presence of the Senate and House of Representatives, open all the Certificates, and the Votes shall then be counted. The Person having the greatest Number of Votes shall be the President, if such Number be a Majority of the whole Number of Electors appointed; and if there be more than one who have such Majority, and have an equal Number of Votes, then the House of Representatives shall immediately chuse by Ballot one of them for President; and if no Person have a Majority, then from the five highest on the List the said House shall in like Manner chuse the President.

But in chusing the President, the Votes shall be taken by States, the Representation from each State having one Vote; a quorum for this Purpose shall consist of a Member or Members from two thirds of the States, and a Majority of all the States shall be necessary to a Choice. In every Case, after the Choice of the President, the Person having the greatest Number of Votes of the Electors shall be the Vice President. But if there should remain two or more who have equal Votes, the Senate shall chuse from them by Ballot the Vice President.*

The Congress may determine the Time of chusing the Electors, and the Day on which they shall give their Votes; which Day shall be the same throughout the United States.

No Person except a natural born Citizen, or a Citizen of the United States, at the time of the Adoption of this Constitution, shall be eligible to the Office of President; neither shall any Person be eligible to that Office who shall not have attained to the Age of thirty five Years, and been fourteen Years a Resident within the United States.

In Case of the Removal of the President from Office, or of his Death, Resignation, or Inability to discharge the Powers and Duties of the said Office, the same shall devolve on the Vice President, *and the Congress may by Law provide for the Case of Removal, Death, Resignation, or Inability, both of the President and Vice President, declaring what Officer shall then act as President, and such Officer shall act accordingly, until the Disability be removed, or a President shall be elected.*†

The President shall, at stated Times, receive for his Services a Compensation, which shall neither be increased nor diminished during the Period for which he shall have been elected, and he shall not receive within that Period any other Emolument from the United States, or any of them.

Before he enter on the Execution of his Office, he shall take the following Oath or Affirmation:—"I do solemnly swear (or affirm) that I will faithfully execute the Office of President of the United States, and will to the best of my Ability, preserve, protect and defend the Constitution of the United States."

Section 2

The President shall be Commander in Chief of the Army and Navy of the United States, and of the Militia of the several States, when called into the actual Service of the United States; he may require the Opinion, in writing, of the principal Officer in each of the executive Departments, upon any Subject relating to the Duties of their respective Offices, and he shall have Power to Grant Reprieves and Pardons for Offences against the United States, except in Cases of Impeachment.

He shall have Power, by and with the Advice and Consent of the Senate, to make Treaties, provided two thirds of the Senators present concur; and he shall nominate, and by and with the Advice and Consent of the Senate, shall appoint Ambassadors, other public Ministers and Consuls, Judges of the supreme Court, and all other Officers of the United States, whose Appointments are not herein otherwise provided for, and which shall be established by Law: but the Congress may by Law vest the Appointment of such inferior Officers, as they think proper, in the President alone, in the Courts of Law, or in the Heads of Departments.

The President shall have Power to fill up all Vacancies that may happen during the Recess of the Senate, by granting Commissions which shall expire at the End of their next Session.

---

*Superseded by the Twelfth Amendment.

†Modified by the Twenty-Fifth Amendment.

Section 3

He shall from time to time give to the Congress Information of the State of the Union, and recommend to their Consideration such Measures as he shall judge necessary and expedient; he may, on extraordinary Occasions, convene both Houses, or either of them, and in Case of Disagreement between them, with Respect to the Time of Adjournment, he may adjourn them to such Time as he shall think proper; he shall receive Ambassadors and other public Ministers; he shall take Care that the Laws be faithfully executed, and shall Commission all the Officers of the United States.

Section 4

The President, Vice President and all civil Officers of the United States, shall be removed from Office on Impeachment for, and Conviction of, Treason, Bribery, or other high Crimes and Misdemeanors.

Article III

Section 1

The judicial Power of the United States, shall be vested in one supreme Court, and in such inferior Courts as the Congress may from time to time ordain and establish. The Judges, both of the supreme and inferior Courts, shall hold their Offices during good Behaviour, and shall, at stated Times, receive for their Services a Compensation, which shall not be diminished during their Continuance in Office.

Section 2

The judicial Power shall extend to all Cases, in Law and Equity, arising under this Constitution, the Laws of the United States, and Treaties made, or which shall be made, under their Authority;—to all Cases affecting Ambassadors, other public Ministers and Consuls;—to all Cases of admiralty and maritime Jurisdiction;—to Controversies to which the United States shall be a Party;—to Controversies between two or more States;—between a State and Citizens of another State;*—between Citizens of different States;—between Citizens of the same State claiming Lands under Grants of different States, and between a State, or the Citizens thereof, and foreign States, Citizens or Subjects.

In all Cases affecting Ambassadors, other public Ministers and Consuls, and those in which a State shall be Party, the supreme Court shall have original Jurisdiction. In all the other Cases before mentioned, the supreme Court shall have appellate Jurisdiction, both as to Law and Fact, with such Exceptions, and under such Regulations as the Congress shall make.

The trial of all Crimes, except in Cases of Impeachment, shall be by Jury; and such Trial shall be held in the State where said Crimes shall have been committed; but when not committed within any State, the Trial shall be at such Place or Places as the Congress may by Law have directed.

Section 3

Treason against the United States, shall consist only in levying War against them, or in adhering to their Enemies, giving them Aid and Comfort. No Person shall be convicted of Treason unless on the Testimony of two Witnesses to the same overt Act, or on Confession in open Court.

---

*Restricted by the Eleventh Amendment.

The Congress shall have Power to declare the Punishment of Treason, but no Attainder of Treason shall work Corruption of Blood, or Forefeiture except during the Life of the Person attainted.

Article IV

Section 1
Full Faith and Credit shall be given in each State to the public Acts, Records, and judicial Proceedings of every other State. And the Congress may by general Laws prescribe the Manner in which such Acts, Records, and Proceedings shall be proved, and the Effect thereof.

Section 2
The Citizens of each State shall be entitled to all Privileges and Immunities of Citizens in the several States.

A Person charged in any State with Treason, Felony, or other Crime, who shall flee from Justice, and be found in another State, shall on demand of the executive Authority of the State from which he fled, be delivered up, to be removed to the State having Jurisdiction of the Crime.

No Person held to Service or Labour in one State, under the Laws thereof, escaping into another, shall, in Consequence of any Law or Regulation therein, be discharged from such Service or Labour, but shall be delivered up on Claim of the Party to whom such Service or Labour may be due.*

Section 3
New States may be admitted by the Congress into this Union; but no new State shall be formed or erected within the Jurisdiction of any other State; nor any State be formed by the Junction of two or more States, or parts of States, without the Consent of the Legislatures of the States concerned as well as of the Congress.

The Congress shall have Power to dispose of and make all needful Rules and Regulations respecting the Territory or other Property belonging to the United States; and nothing in this Constitution shall be so construed as to Prejudice any Claims of the United States, or of any particular State.

Section 4
The United States shall guarantee to every State in this Union a Republican Form of Government, and shall protect each of them against Invasion; and on Application of the Legislature, or of the Executive (when the Legislature cannot be convened) against domestic Violence.

Article V

The Congress, whenever two thirds of both Houses shall deem it necessary, shall propose Amendments to this Constitution, or, on the Application of the Legislatures of two thirds of the several States, shall call a Convention for proposing Amendments, which, in either Case, shall be valid to all Intents and Purposes, as Part of this Constitution, when ratified by the Legislatures of three fourths of the several States, or by Conventions in three fourths thereof, as the one or the other Mode of Ratification

---

*Superseded by the Twelfth Amendment.

may be proposed by the Congress; Provided that no Amendment which may be made prior to the Year One thousand eight hundred and eight shall in any Manner affect the first and fourth Clauses in the Ninth Section of the first Article; and that no State, without its Consent, shall be deprived of its equal Suffrage in the Senate.

Article VI

All Debts contracted and Engagements entered into, before the Adoption of this Constitution, shall be as valid against the United States under this Constitution, as under the Confederation.

This Constitution, and the Laws of the United States which shall be made in Pursuance thereof; and all Treaties made, or which shall be made, under the Authority of the United States, shall be the supreme Law of the Land; and the Judges in every State shall be bound thereby, any Thing in the Constitution or Laws of any State to the Contrary notwithstanding.

The Senators and Representatives before mentioned, and the Members of the several State Legislatures, and all executive and judicial Officers, both of the United States and of the several States, shall be bound by Oath or Affirmation, to support this Constitution; but no religious Test shall ever be required as a Qualification to any Office or public Trust under the United States.

Article VII

The Ratification of the Conventions of nine States shall be sufficient for the Establishment of this Constitution between the States so ratifying the Same.

Done in Convention by the Unanimous Consent of the States present the Seventeenth Day of September in the Year of our Lord one thousand seven hundred and Eighty seven and of the Independence of the United States of America the Twelfth. In Witness whereof We have hereunto subscribed our Names.

Go.Washington
President and deputy from Virginia

New Hampshire	*New Jersey*	*Delaware*	*North Carolina*
John Langdon	Wil. Livingston	Geo. Read	Wm. Blount
Nicholas Gilman	David Brearley	Gunning Bedford jun	Richd. Dobbs Spaight
Massachusetts	Wm. Paterson	John Dickenson	Hu Williamson
Nathaniel Gorham	Jona. Dayton	Richard Bassett	*South Carolina*
Rufus King	*Pennsylvania*	Jaco. Broom	J. Rutledge
Connecticut	B. Franklin	*Maryland*	Charles Cotesworth Pickney
Wm. Saml. Johnson	Thomas Mifflin	James McHenry	Pierce Butler
Roger Sherman	Robt. Morris	Dan. of St. Thos. Jenifer	*Georgia*
New York	Geo. Clymer	Danl. Carroll	William Few
Alexander Hamilton	Thos. FitzSimons	*Virginia*	Abr. Baldwin
	Jared Ingersoll	John Blair	
	James Wilson	James Madison, Jr.	
	Gouv. Morris		

AMENDMENTS TO THE CONSTITUTION

Amendment I [1791]*

Congress shall make no law respecting an establishment of religion, or prohibiting the free exercise thereof; or abridging the freedom of speech, or of the press; or the right of the people peaceably to assemble, and to petition the Government for a redress of grievances.

Amendment II [1791]

A well regulated Militia, being necessary to the security of a free State, the right of the people to keep and bear Arms shall not be infringed.

Amendment III [1791]

No Soldier shall, in time of peace, be quartered in any house, without the consent of the Owner, nor in time of war, but in a manner to be prescribed by law.

Amendment IV [1791]

The right of the people to be secure in their persons, houses, papers, and effects, against unreasonable searches and seizures, shall not be violated, and no Warrants shall issue, but upon probable cause, supported by Oath or affirmation, and particularly describing the place to be searched, and the persons or things to be seized.

Amendment V [1791]

No person shall be held to answer for a capital or otherwise infamous crime, unless on a presentment or indictment of a Grand Jury, except in cases arising in the land or naval forces, or in the Militia, when in actual service in time of War or public danger; nor shall any person be subject for the same offence to be twice put in jeopardy of life or limb; nor shall be compelled in any criminal case to be a witness against himself, nor be deprived of life, liberty, or property, without due process of law; nor shall private property be taken for public use, without just compensation.

Amendment VI [1791]

In all criminal prosecutions, the accused shall enjoy the right to a speedy and public trial, by an impartial jury of the State and district wherein the crime shall have been committed, which district shall have been previously ascertained by law, and to be informed of the nature and cause of the accusation; to be confronted with the witnesses against him; to have compulsory process for obtaining witnesses in his favor, and to have the Assistance of Counsel for his defence.

---

*The dates in brackets indicate when the amendments were ratified.

Amendment VII [1791]

In suits at common law, where the value in controversy shall exceed twenty dollars, the right of trail by jury shall be preserved, and no fact tried by a jury, shall be otherwise reexamined in any Court of the United States, than according to the Rules of the common law.

Amendment VIII [1791]

Excessive bail shall not be required, nor excessive fines imposed, nor cruel and unusual punishments inflicted.

Amendment IX [1791]

The enumeration in the Constitution, of certain rights, shall not be construed to deny or disparage others retained by the people.

Amendment X [1791]

The powers not delegated to the United States by the Constitution, nor prohibited by it to the States, are reserved to the States respectively, or to the people.

Amendment XI [1798]

The Judicial power of the United States shall not be construed to extend to any suit in law or equity, commenced or prosecuted against one of the United States by Citizens of another State, or by Citizens or subjects of any foreign state.

Amendment XII [1804]

The Electors shall meet in their respective States and vote by ballot for President and Vice-President, one of whom, at least, shall not be an inhabitant of the same State with themselves; they shall name in their ballots the person voted for as President, and in distinct ballots the person voted for as Vice-President, and they shall make distinct lists of all persons voted for as President, and of all persons voted for as Vice-President, and of the number of votes for each, which lists they shall sign and certify, and transmit sealed to the seat of the government of the United States, directed to the President of the Senate;—the President of the Senate shall, in the presence of the Senate and House of Representatives, open all the certificates and the votes shall then be counted;—The person having the greatest number of votes for President, shall be the President, if such number be a majority of the whole number of Electors appointed; and if no person have such majority, then from the persons having the highest numbers not exceeding three on the list of those voted for as President, the House of Representatives shall choose immediately, by ballot, the President. But in choosing the President, the votes shall be taken by States, the representation from each State having one vote; a quorum for this purpose shall consist of a member or members from two-thirds of the States, and a majority of all the States shall be necessary to a choice. And if the House of Representatives shall not choose a President whenever the right of choice shall devolve upon them, before *the fourth day of March* next following, then the Vice-President shall act as President, as in the case of the death or other constitutional disability of the President.*—The person having the greatest number of votes as Vice-President, shall be the Vice-President, if such number be a majority of the whole number of Electors appointed, and if no person have a majority, then from the two highest numbers on the list, the Senate shall choose the Vice-President; a quorum for the purpose shall consist of two-thirds of the whole number of Senators, and a majority of the whole number shall be necessary to a choice. But no person constitutionally ineligible to the office of President shall be eligible to that of Vice-President of the United States.

Amendment XIII [1865]

Section 1
Neither slavery nor involuntary servitude, except as a punishment for crime whereof the party shall have been duly convicted, shall exist within the United States, or any place subject to their jurisdiction.

Section 2
Congress shall have power to enforce this article by appropriate legislation.

Amendment XIV [1868]

Section 1
All persons born or naturalized in the United States, and subject to the jurisdiction thereof, are citizens of the United States and of the State wherein they reside. No State shall make or enforce any law which shall abridge the privileges or immunities of citizens of the United States; nor shall any State deprive any person of life, liberty, or property, without due process of law; nor deny to any person within its jurisdiction the equal protection of the laws.

Section 2
Representatives shall be apportioned among the several States according to their respective numbers, counting the whole number of persons in each State, excluding Indians not taxed. But when the right to vote at any election for the choice of electors for President and Vice-President of the United States, Representatives in Congress, the Executive and Judicial officers of a State, or the members of the Legislature thereof, is denied to any of the male inhabitants of such State, being twenty-one years of age, and citizens of the United States, or in any way abridged, except for participation in rebellion, or other crime, the basis of representation therein shall be reduced in the proportion which the number of such male citizens shall bear to the whole number of male citizens twenty-one years of age in such State.

Section 3
No person shall be a Senator or Representative in Congress, or elector of President and Vice-President, or hold any office, civil or military, under the United States, or

---

*Superseded by Section 3 of the Twentieth Amendment.

under any State, who, having previously taken an oath, as a member of Congress, or as an officer of the United States, or as a member of any State legislature, or as an executive or judicial officer of any State, to support the Constitution of the United States, shall have engaged in insurrection or rebellion against the same, or given aid or comfort to the enemies thereof. Congress may by a vote of two-thirds of each house, remove such disability.

Section 4
The validity of the public debt of the United States, authorized by law, including debts incurred for payment of pensions and bounties for services in suppressing insurrection or rebellion, shall not be questioned. But neither the United States nor any State shall assume or pay any debt or obligation incurred in aid of insurrection or rebellion against the United States, or any claim for the loss or emancipation of any slave; but all such debts, obligations and claims shall be held illegal and void.

Section 5
The Congress shall have power to enforce, by appropriate legislation, the provisions of this article.

Amendment XV [1870]

Section 1
The right of citizens of the United States to vote shall not be denied or abridged by the United States or by any State on account of race, color, or previous condition of servitude—

Section 2
The Congress shall have power to enforce this article by appropriate legislation.

Amendment XVI [1913]

The Congress shall have power to lay and collect taxes on incomes, from whatever source derived, without apportionment among the several States, and without regard to any census or enumeration.

Amendment XVII [1913]

The Senate of the United States shall be composed of two Senators from each State, elected by the people thereof, for six years; and each Senator shall have one vote. The electors in each State shall have the qualifications requisite for electors of the most numerous branch of the State legislatures.

When vacancies happen in the representation of any State in the Senate, the executive authority of such State shall issue writs of election to fill such vacancies: *Provided,* That the legislature of any State may empower the executive thereof to make temporary appointments until the people fill the vacancies by election as the legislature may direct.

This amendment shall not be so construed as to affect the election or term of any Senator chosen before it becomes valid as part of the Constitution.

Amendment XVIII [1919]

Section 1
After one year from the ratification of this article the manufacture, sale, or transportation of intoxicating liquors within, the importation thereof into, or the exportation thereof from the United States and all territory subject to the jurisdiction hereof for beverage purposes hereby prohibited.

Section 2
The Congress and the several States shall have concurrent power to enforce this article by appropriate legislation.

Section 3
This article shall be inoperative unless it shall have been ratified as an amendment to the Constitution by the legislatures of the several States, as provided by the Constitution, within seven years from the date of submission hereof to the States by the Congress.*

Amendment XIX [1920]

The right of citizens of the United States to vote shall not be denied or abridged by the United States or by any State on account of sex.

Congress shall have power to enforce this article by appropriate legislation.

Amendment XX [1933]

Section 1
The terms of the President and Vice-President shall end at noon on the 20th day of January, and the terms of Senators and Representatives at noon on the 3d day of January, of the years in which such terms would have ended if this article had not been ratified; and the terms of their successors shall then begin.

Section 2
The Congress shall assemble at least once in every year, and such meeting shall begin at noon on the 3d day of January, unless they shall by law appoint a different day.

Section 3
If, at the time fixed for the beginning of the term of the President, the President elect shall have died, the Vice-President elect shall become President. If a President shall not have been chosen before the time fixed for the beginning of his term, or if the President elect shall have failed to qualify, then the Vice-President elect shall act as President until a President shall have qualified; and the Congress may by law provide for the case wherein neither a President elect nor a Vice-President elect shall have qualified, declaring who shall then act as President, or the manner in which one who is to act shall be selected, and such person shall act accordingly until a President or Vice-President shall have qualified.

---

*Repealed by Section 1 of the Twenty-First Amendment.

Section 4

The Congress may by law provide for the case of the death of any of the persons from whom the House of Representatives may choose a President whenever the right of choice shall have devolved upon them, and for the case of the death of any of the persons from whom the Senate may choose a Vice-President whenever the right of choice shall have devolved upon them.

Section 5

Sections 1 and 2 shall take effect on the 15th day of October following the ratification of this article.

Section 6

This article shall be inoperative unless it shall have been ratified as an amendment to the Constitution by the legislatures of three-fourths of the several States within seven years from the date of its submission.

Amendment XXI [1933]

Section 1

The eighteenth article of amendment to the Constitution of the United States is hereby repealed.

Section 2

The transportation or importation into any State, Territory, or possession of the United States for delivery or use therein of intoxicating liquors, in violation of the laws thereof, is hereby prohibited.

Section 3

This article shall be inoperative unless it shall have been ratified as an amendment to the Constitution by conventions in the several States, as provided in the Constitution, within seven years from the date of submission hereof to the States by the Congress.

Amendment XXII [1951]

Section 1

No person shall be elected to the office of President more than twice, and no person who has held the office of President, or acted as President, for more than two years of a term to which some other person was elected President shall be elected to the office of the President more than once. But this Article shall not apply to any person holding the office of President when this Article was proposed by the Congress, and shall not prevent any person who may be holding the office of President, or acting as President, during the term within which this Article becomes operative from holding the office of the President or acting as President during the remainder of such term.

Section 2

This article shall be inoperative unless it shall have been ratified as an amendment to the Constitution by the legislatures of three-fourths of the several States within seven years from the date of its submission to the States by the Congress.

Amendment XXIII [1961]

Section 1
The District constituting the seat of Government of the United States shall appoint in such manner as the Congress may direct:

A number of electors of President and Vice-President equal to the whole number of Senators and Representatives in Congress to which the District would be entitled if it were a State, but in no event more than the least populous State; they shall be in addition to those appointed by the States, but they shall be considered, for the purposes of the election of President and Vice-President, to be electors appointed by a State; and they shall meet in the District and perform such duties as provided by the twelfth article of amendment.

Section 2
The Congress shall have power to enforce this article by appropriate legislation.

Amendment XXIV [1964]

Section 1
The right of citizens of the United States to vote in any primary or other election for President or Vice-President, for electors for President or Vice-President, or for Senator or Representative in Congress, shall not be denied or abridged by the United States or any State by reason of failure to pay any poll tax or other tax.

Section 2
The Congress shall have power to enforce this article by appropriate legislation.

Amendment XXV [1967]

Section 1
In case of the removal of the President from office or of his death or resignation, the Vice-President shall become President.

Section 2
Whenever there is a vacancy in the office of the Vice-President, the President shall nominate a Vice-President who shall take office upon confirmation by a majority vote of both houses of Congress.

Section 3
Whenever the President transmits to the President pro tempore of the Senate and the Speaker of the House of Representatives his written declaration that he is unable to discharge the powers and duties of his office, and until he transmits to them a written declaration to the contrary, such powers and duties shall be discharged by the Vice-President as Acting President.

Section 4
Whenever the Vice-President and a majority of either the principal officers of the executive departments or of such other body as Congress may by law provide, transmit

to the President pro tempore of the Senate and the Speaker of the House of Representatives their written declaration that the President is unable to discharge the powers and duties of his office, the Vice-President shall immediately assume the powers and duties of the office as Acting President.

Thereafter, when the President transmits to the President pro tempore of the Senate and the Speaker of the House of Representatives his written declaration that no inability exists, he shall resume the powers and duties of his office unless the Vice-President and a majority of either the principal officers of the executive department or of such other body as Congress may by law provide, transmit within four days to the President pro tempore of the Senate and the Speaker of the House of Representatives their written declaration that the President is unable to discharge the powers and duties of his office. Thereupon Congress shall decide the issue, assembling within forty-eight hours for that purpose if not in session. If the Congress, within twenty-one days after receipt of the latter written declaration, or, if Congress is not in session, within twenty-one days after Congress is required to assemble, determines by two-thirds vote of both Houses that the President is unable to discharge the powers and duties of his office, the Vice-President shall continue to discharge the same as Acting President; otherwise, the President shall resume the powers and duties of his office.

Amendment XXVI [1971]

Section 1
The right of citizens of the United States, who are eighteen years of age or older, to vote shall not be denied or abridged by the United States or by any state on account of age.

Section 2
The Congress shall have power to enforce this article by appropriate legislation.

Amendment XXVII [1992]

No law varying the compensation for services of the Senators and Representatives, shall take effect, until an election of Representatives shall have intervened.

APPENDIX

Territory	Date Acquired	Square Miles	How Acquired
Original states and territories	1783	888,685	Treaty of Paris
Louisiana Purchase	1803	827,192	Purchased from France
Florida	1819	72,003	Adams-Onís Treaty
Texas	1845	390,143	Annexation of independent country
Oregon	1846	285,580	Oregon Boundary Treaty
Mexican cession	1848	529,017	Treaty of Guadalupe Hidalgo
Gadsden Purchase	1853	29,640	Purchased from Mexico
Midway Islands	1867	2	Annexation of uninhabited islands
Alaska	1867	589,757	Purchased from Russia
Hawaii	1898	6,450	Annexation of independent country
Wake Island	1898	3	Annexation of uninhabited island
Puerto Rico	1899	3,435	Treaty of Paris
Guam	1899	212	Treaty of Paris
The Philippines	1899–1946	115,600	Treaty of Paris; granted independence
American Samoa	1900	76	Treaty with Germany and Great Britain
Panama Canal Zone	1904–1978	553	Hay–Bunau-Varilla Treaty
U.S. Virgin Islands	1917	133	Purchased from Denmark
Trust Territory of the Pacific Islands★	1947	717	United Nations Trusteeship

★A number of these islands have recently been granted independence: Federated States of Micronesia, 1990; Marshall Islands, 1991; Palau, 1994.

A–1

THE LABOR FORCE

(thousands of workers)

Year	Agricul-ture	Mining	Manufac-turing	Construc-tion	Trade	Other	Total
1810	1,950	11	75	—	—	294	2,330
1840	3,570	32	500	290	350	918	5,660
1850	4,520	102	1,200	410	530	1,488	8,250
1860	5,880	176	1,530	520	890	2,114	11,110
1870	6,790	180	2,470	780	1,310	1,400	12,930
1880	8,920	280	3,290	900	1,930	2,070	17,390
1890	9,960	440	4,390	1,510	2,960	4,060	23,320
1900	11,680	637	5,895	1,665	3,970	5,223	29,070
1910	11,770	1,068	8,332	1,949	5,320	9,041	37,480
1920	10,790	1,180	11,190	1,233	5,845‾	11,372	41,610
1930	10,560	1,009	9,884	1,988	8,122	17,267	48,830
1940	9,575	925	11,309	1,876	9,328	23,277	56,290
1950	7,870	901	15,648	3,029	12,152	25,870	65,470
1960	5,970	709	17,145	3,640	14,051	32,545	74,060
1970	3,463	516	20,746	4,818	15,008	34,127	78,678
1980	3,364	979	21,942	6,215	20,191	46,612	99,303
1990	3,186	730	21,184	7,696	24,269	60,849	117,914
1994	3,409	669	20,157	7,493	25,699	65,633	123,060

SOURCE: *Historical Statistics of the United States, Colonial Times to 1970* (1975), 139; *Statistical Abstract of the United States*, 1995, Table 653.

Changing Labor Patterns

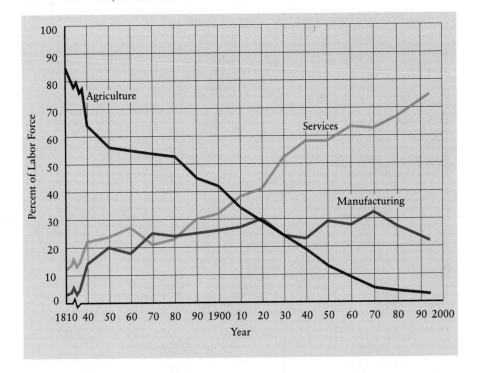

AMERICAN POPULATION

Year	Population	Percent Increase	Year	Population	Percent Increase
1610	350	—	1810	7,239,881	36.4
1620	2,300	557.1	1820	9,638,453	33.1
1630	4,600	100.0	1830	12,866,020	33.5
1640	26,600	478.3	1840	17,069,453	32.7
1650	50,400	90.8	1850	23,191,876	35.9
1660	75,100	49.0	1860	31,443,321	35.6
1670	111,900	49.0	1870	39,818,449	26.6
1680	151,500	35.4	1880	50,155,783	26.0
1690	210,400	38.9	1890	62,947,714	25.5
1700	250,900	19.2	1900	75,994,575	20.7
1710	331,700	32.2	1910	91,972,266	21.0
1720	466,200	40.5	1920	105,710,620	14.9
1730	629,400	35.0	1930	122,775,046	16.1
1740	905,600	43.9	1940	131,669,275	7.2
1750	1,170,800	29.3	1950	150,697,361	14.5
1760	1,593,600	36.1	1960	179,323,175	19.0
1770	2,148,100	34.8	1970	203,235,298	13.3
1780	2,780,400	29.4	1980	226,545,805	11.5
1790	3,929,214	41.3	1990	248,709,873	9.8
1800	5,308,483	35.1	1993	259,383,000	4.3

Note: These figures largely ignore the native American population. Census takers never made any effort to count the native American population that lived outside their political jurisdictions and compiled only casual and incomplete enumerations of those living within their jurisdictions until 1890. In that year the federal government attempted a full count of the Indian population: the Census found 125,719 Indians in 1890, compared with only 12,543 in 1870 and 33,985 in 1880.

SOURCE: *Historical Statistics of the United States, Colonial Times to 1970* (1975); *Statistical Abstract of the United States,* 1995.

SUGGESTED READINGS

CHAPTER 1

One of the few works that cover the history of the various European and native American peoples is Eric Wolf, *Europe and the People without History*. See also Alfred W. Crosby, Jr., *Ecological Imperialism: The Biological Expansion of Europe, 900–1900* (1986); Robert R. Reynolds, *Europe Emerges: Transition toward an Industrial World-Wide Society, 600–1750* (1961); and G. V. Scammell, *The World Encompassed: The First European Maritime Empires* (1981).

Native American Worlds

Brian M. Fagan, *The Great Journey: The People of Ancient America* (1987), synthesizes recent scholarship on the prehistoric Indians of the United States, while his *Kingdoms of Gold, Kingdoms of Jade: The Americas before Columbus* (1991) does the same for the Mesoamerican peoples. See also Stuart J. Fiedel, *Prehistory of the Americas* (1992); Inga Clendinnen, *Aztecs: An Interpretation* (1991); John S. Henderson, *The World of the Maya* (1981); David Carrasco, *Quetzalcoatl and the Irony of Empire* (1982); R. C. Padden, *The Hummingbird and the Hawk* (1962); and R. Tom Zuidema, *Inca Civilization in Cuzco* (1992). Two fine supplements are Michael Coe et al., *Atlas of Ancient America* (1986), and Manuel Lucena Salmoral, *America in 1492* (1991), a photographic survey of dress, artifacts, and architecture.

Alfred W. Crosby, Jr., *The Columbian Exchange: Biological and Cultural Consequences of 1492* (1972), traces the impact of European diseases. See also Russell Thornton, *American Indian Holocaust and Survival: A Population History since 1492* (1987); Henry F. Dobyns, *Their Numbers Became Thinned: Native American Population Dynamics in Eastern North America* (1983); and William M. Denevan, *The Native Population of the Americas in 1492* (1992).

On North America, consult Alvin M. Josephy, Jr., ed., *America in 1492* (1993); Linda S. Cordell, *Ancient Pueblo Peoples* (1994); Bruce D. Smith, ed., *The Mississippian Emergence* (1990); Carl Waldman and Molly Braun, *Atlas of the North American Indian* (1985); and Robert Silverberg, *Mound Builders of Ancient America: The Archaeology of a Myth* (1968). Roger Kennedy, *Hidden Cities* (1994), surveys the early Indian civilizations of the Mississippi Valley.

Traditional European Society in 1450

Barbara W. Tuchman, *A Distant Mirror: The Calamitous Fourteenth Century* (1978), and Johan Huizinga, *The Waning of the Middle Ages* (1947), present vivid portraits of the late medieval world. Two wide-ranging studies of subsequent developments are

George Huppert, *After the Black Death: A Social History of Modern Europe* (1986), and Henry Kamen, *European Society, 1500–1700* (1984). Illuminating specialized studies include Peter Burke, *Popular Culture in Early Modern Europe* (1978); Pierre Goubert, *The French Peasantry in the Seventeenth Century* (1986); Philippe Ariès, *Centuries of Childhood* (1962); B. H. Slicher Van Bath, *The Agrarian History of Western Europe, A.D. 500–1850* (1963); and Emanuel Le Roy Ladurie, *The Peasants of Languedoc* (1974). See also Joel Mokyr, *The Lever of Riches: Technological Creativity and Economic Progress* (1990), and E. P. Thompson, *Customs in Common: Studies in Traditional Popular Culture* (1991).

Europe and the World, 1450–1550

The preconditions for European expansion are treated in James D. Tracy, ed., *Rise of Merchant Empires: Long Distance Trade in the Early Modern World, 1350–1750* (1990). For the southern European background, read selectively in Fernand Braudel's massive and stimulating *The Mediterranean and the Mediterranean World in the Age of Philip II* (1949).

Paul H. Chapman, *The Norse Discovery of America* (1981), and Boies Penrose, *Travel and Discovery in the Renaissance, 1420–1620* (1952), illuminate the growth of geographical knowledge. For the expansion of the Iberian peoples, see Bailey W. Diffie and George Winius, *Foundations of the Portuguese Empire, 1415–1580* (1977), and Henry Kamen, *Crisis and Change in Early Modern Spain* (1993). A good short biography of Columbus and his times is Felipe Fernández-Armesto, *Columbus* (1991).

For the Spanish and Portuguese colonial empires, see Charles R. Boxer, *The Portuguese Seaborne Empire* (1969), and James Lockhard and Stuart B. Schwartz, *Early Latin America: Colonial Spanish America and Brazil* (1984). Fine accounts of the Spanish conquest include the memorable firsthand report by Bernal Diaz del Castillo, *The Discovery and Conquest of Mexico* (ed. by I. A. Leonard, 1956); Leon Portilla, *Broken Spears: The Aztec Account of the Conquest of Mexico* (1962); and Hugh Thomas, *Conquest: Montezuma, Cortés and the Fall of Old Mexico* (1994). The impact on native society in New Spain is portrayed in Daniel T. Reff, *Disease, Depopulation, and Culture Change in Northwestern New Spain, 1518–1764* (1991); for the story north of the Rio Grande, see David J. Weber, *The Spanish Frontier in North America* (1992), and Ramón Gutiérrez, *When Jesus Came, the Corn Mothers Went Away: Marriage, Sexuality, and Power in New Mexico, 1500–1846* (1991).

The Protestant Reformation and the Rise of England, 1500–1630

On the European Reformation, consult William J. Bouwsma, *John Calvin* (1987), and De Lamar Jensen, *Reformation Europe: Age of Reform and Revolution* (1981). For England, see Patrick Collinson, *The Religion of the Protestants: The Church in English Society, 1559–1625* (1982), and Susan Doran and Christopher Durston, *Princes, Pastors, and People: The Church and Religion in England, 1529–1689* (1991).

On the decline of Spain, consult Henry Kamen, *Spain: A Society in Conflict, 1479–1714* (2d ed., 1991), and John Lynch, *The Hispanic World in Crisis and Change, 1598–1700* (1992), which also traces the growing economic independence of New Spain. For a general analysis of economic change in Europe, see T. S. Ashton, ed., *The Brenner Debate* (1987).

A brilliant and forceful portrait of English preindustrial society is offered by Peter Laslett, *The World We Have Lost* (3d ed., 1984). Other important works are

Keith Wrightson, *English Society, 1580–1680* (1982), and two books by Lawrence Stone, *The Crisis of the Aristocracy* (1965) and *Family, Sex, and Marriage in England, 1500–1800* (1977). On the movement of people, see Ida Altman and James Horn, eds., *"To Make America": European Emigration in the Early Modern Period* (1991).

CHAPTER 2

David Weber, *The Spanish Frontier in North America* (1992), and Richard White, *The Middle Ground: Indians, Empires, and Republics in the Great Lakes Region, 1650–1815* (1991), are magisterial studies, while Bernard Bailyn, *The Peopling of British North America* (1986), offers a useful overview of the early English colonies.

Imperial Conflicts and Rival Colonial Models

For Spain's northern empire, see, in addition to Weber, Ramón Gutiérrez, *When Jesus Came, the Corn Mothers Went Away: Marriage, Sexuality, and Power in New Mexico, 1500–1846* (1991). The French threat to its domain is traced by Robert S. Weddle, *The French Thorn: Rival Explorers in the Spanish Sea, 1682–1762* (1991), and Daniel H. Usner, Jr., *Indians, Settlers, and Slaves in a Frontier Exchange Economy: The Lower Mississippi Valley before 1783* (1991).

The best general studies of French Canada are by W. J. Eccles, *The Canadian Frontier, 1534–1760* (1983) and *France in America* (rev. ed, 1990). French interaction with native Americans is covered by Bruce G. Trigger, *The Children of Aataentsic: A History of the Huron People to 1660* (1976); Daniel K. Richter, *The Ordeal of the Long House: The Peoples of the Iroquois League in the Era of European Colonization* (1992); and Patricia O. Dickason, *Canada's First Nations: A History of the Founding Peoples from Earliest Times* (1992).

For English expansion, see Kenneth Andrews, *Trade, Plunder, and Settlement: Maritime Enterprise and the Genesis of the British Empire, 1480–1630* (1984); Nicholas Canny, *Kingdom and Colony: Ireland in the Atlantic World, 1560–1800* (1988); A. L. Rowse, *Sir Walter Raleigh* (1962); David B. Quinn, *England and the Discovery of America, 1481–1620* (1974); and Karen O. Kupperman, *Roanoke* (1984). The interaction of the English and Dutch with native Americans can be followed in Gary B. Nash, *Red, White, and Black: The Peoples of Early America* (1982); Francis Jennings, *The Invasion of America* (1975); and two works by James Axtell, *The European and the Indian* (1981) and *The Invasion Within: The Contest of Cultures in Colonial North America* (1985).

The Chesapeake Experience

Alden Vaughan, *American Genesis: Captain John Smith and the Founding of Virginia* (1975), covers the earliest years, while Edmund S. Morgan, *American Slavery, American Freedom: The Ordeal of Colonial Virginia* (1975), provides a brilliant analysis of the rest of the colonial period. Important essays appear in Thad W. Tate and David L. Ammerman, eds., *The Chesapeake in the Seventeenth Century* (1979), and Lois Green Carr, Philip D. Morgan, and Jean B. Russo, *Colonial Chesapeake Society* (1989). Significant community studies include Carville Earle, *The Evolution of a Tidewater Settlement Pattern: All Hallows Parish, Maryland, 1650–1783* (1975), and Lois Green Carr, et al., *Robert Cole's World: Agriculture and Society in Early Maryland* (1991).

For a discussion of political institutions, see W. F. Craven, *The Southern Colonies in the Seventeenth Century, 1607–1689* (1949), and David W. Jordan, *Foundations of Representative Government in Maryland, 1632–1715* (1988). Contrasting accounts of Bacon's Rebellion can be found in T. J. Wertenbaker, *Torchbearer of the Revolution* (1940), and Wilcomb B. Washburn, *The Governor and the Rebel* (1958).

Puritan New England

For the Puritan migration, see Edmund Morgan, *The Puritan Dilemma: The Story of John Winthrop* (1955); Sumner Chilton Powell, *Puritan Village: The Formation of a New England Town* (1963); David Grayson Allen, *In English Ways: The Movement of Societies and the Transferral of English Local Law and Custom to Massachusetts Bay in the Seventeenth Century* (1981); and David Cressy, *Coming Over: Migration and Communication between England and New England in the Seventeenth Century* (1987).

Puritanism as an intellectual movement is best explored in the works of Perry Miller; see especially *The New England Mind: The Seventeenth Century* (1939). Charles Hambrick-Stowe, *The Practice of Piety: Puritan Devotional Disciplines* (1982), discusses the emotional dimension of Puritanism, while David D. Hall, *World of Wonder, Days of Judgment: Popular Religious Belief in Early New England* (1989), explores its nonrational aspects. See also Andrew Delbanco, *The Puritan Ordeal* (1989).

For a discussion of dissent in early New England, consult Philip Gura, *A Glimpse of Sion's Glory: Puritan Radicalism in New England, 1620–1660* (1984); Edwin S. Gaustad, *Liberty of Conscience: Roger Williams in America* (1991); Amy Schrager Lang, *Prophetic Woman: Anne Hutchinson and the Problem of Dissent in the Literature of New England* (1987); Paul Boyer and Steven Nissenbaum, *Salem Possessed: The Social Origins of Witchcraft* (1974); Carol F. Karlsen, *The Devil in the Shape of a Woman: Witchcraft in New England* (1987); and David D. Hall, ed., *Witch Hunting in Seventeenth-Century New England: A Documentary History, 1632–1691* (1991).

Community studies that reveal the lives of ordinary New England men and women include John Demos, *The Little Commonwealth: Family Life in Plymouth Colony* (1971), and Kenneth A. Lockridge, *A New England Town . . . Dedham, Massachusetts, 1636–1736* (1970). See also John Demos, *The Unredeemed Captive: A Family Story from Early America* (1994).

The Indians' New World

James H. Merrell, *The Indians' New World: Catawbas and Their Neighbors from European Contact through the Era of Removal* (1989), is a pathbreaking study. Douglas Leach, *Flinthawk and Tomahawk: New England in King Philip's War* (1958), is the standard treatment of the conflict. See also Karen Ordahl Kupperman, *Settling with the Indians: The Meeting of English and Indian Cultures in America, 1580–1640* (1981); Bernard Sheehan, *Savagism and Civility: Indians and Englishmen in Colonial Virginia* (1980); and Daniel K. Richter and James H. Merrell, *Beyond the Covenant Chain: The Iroquois and Their Neighbors in Indian North America* (1987). Two illuminating ecological studies are Calvin Martin, *Keepers of the Game: Indian-Animal Relations and the Fur Trade* (1978), and William Cronon, *Changes in the Land: Indians, Colonists, and the Ecology of New England* (1983).

CHAPTER 3

The best short overview of England's empire is Michael Kammen, *Empire and Interest: The American Colonies and the Politics of Mercantilism* (1970), but see also Alison Olson, *Making the Empire Work: London and American Interest Groups, 1690–1790.* On Africa, see Paul Bohannan and Philip Curtin, *Africa and the Africans* (3d ed., 1988). For the mingling of cultures in Virginia, read Mechel Sobel, *The World They Made Together* (1987).

The Politics of Empire, 1660–1713

Robert Bliss, *Revolution and Empire: English Politics and the American Colonies in the Seventeenth Century* (1990), explores the impact of the Puritan Revolution, while Jack M. Sosin, *English America and the Restoration Monarchy of Charles II: Transatlantic Politics, Commerce, and Kinship* (1980), does the same for the restored king. See also Stephen S. Webb, *1676: The End of American Independence* (1984). For the events of 1688–1689, consult David S. Lovejoy, *The Glorious Revolution in America* (1972). A good case study is Lois Green Carr and David W. Jordan, *Maryland's Revolution of Government, 1689–1692* (1974). Ethnic tension in New York can be traced in Robert C. Ritchie, *The Duke's Province: Politics and Society in New York, 1660–1691* (1977); Thomas J. Archdeacon, *New York City, 1664–1710: Conquest and Change* (1976); Donna Merwick, *Possessing Albany, 1630–1710: The Dutch and English Experiences* (1990); and Joyce Goodfriend, *Before the Melting Pot: Society and Culture in Colonial New York City, 1664–1730* (1992). Jack M. Sosin, *English America and Imperial Inconstancy: The Rise of Provincial Autonomy, 1696–1715* (1985), outlines the new imperial system.

The Imperial Slave Economy

For the African background, see John Thornton, *Africa and Africans in the Making of the Atlantic World, 1400–1680* (1992), and Richard Olaniyan, *African History and Culture* (1982). Specialized studies of forced African migration include Philip Curtin, *The Atlantic Slave Trade: A Census* (1969); Paul Lovejoy, ed., *Africans in Bondage: Studies in Slavery and the Slave Trade* (1986); James A. Rawley, *The Transatlantic Slave Trade* (1981); Joseph E. Inikori and Stanley L. Engerman, eds., *The Atlantic Slave Trade* (1992); and Barbara L. Solow, ed., *Slavery and the Rise of the Atlantic System* (1991).

Richard S. Dunn, *Sugar and Slaves: The Rise of the Planter Class in the English West Indies, 1624–1713* (1972), provides a graphic portrait of the brutal slave-based economy, while Sidney W. Mintz, *Sweetness and Power: The Place of Sugar in Modern History* (1985), explores the impact of its major crop. Winthrop D. Jordan, *White over Black, 1550–1812* (1968), remains the best account of Virginia's decision for slavery, but see also Thomas D. Morris, *Southern Slavery and the Law, 1619–1860* (1996). T. H. Breen and Stephen Innes, *"Myne Owne Ground": Race and Freedom on Virginia's Eastern Shore, 1640–1676* (1980), closely examines the lives of the first Africans on Virginia's Eastern Shore. For the creation of African-American society, see Allan Kulikoff, *Tobacco and Slaves: Southern Cultures in the Chesapeake, 1680–1800* (1986); Daniel C. Littlefield, *Rice and Slaves: Ethnicity and the Slave Trade in Colonial South Carolina* (1981); Peter H. Wood, *Black Majority: Negroes in Colonial South Carolina through the Stono Rebellion* (1974); and Marvin L. Michael Kay and Lorin Lee Cary, *Slavery in North Carolina, 1748–1775* (1995). See also Richard Price, ed., *Maroon Societies: Rebel Slave*

Communities in the Americas (1973), and Ira Berlin and Philip D. Morgan, eds., *Cultivation and Culture: Labor and the Shaping of Slave Life in the Americas* (1992).

On white society in the South, read Daniel Blake Smith, *Inside the Great House: Planter Family Life in Eighteenth-Century Chesapeake Society* (1980); Rhys Isaac, *The Transformation of Virginia, 1740–1790* (1982); Timothy H. Breen, *Tobacco Culture* (1985); and a fine older study of political practices, Charles Sydnor, *American Revolutionaries in the Making* (1952). Urban society and trade are explored in Gary B. Nash, *The Urban Crucible* (1979); Gary M. Walton and James F. Shephard, *The Economic Rise of Early America* (1979); and Christine L. Heyrman, *Commerce and Culture: The Maritime Communities of Colonial Massachusetts, 1690–1750* (1984). See also Marcus Rediker, *Between the Devil and the Deep Blue Sea: Merchant Seamen, Pirates, and the Anglo-American Maritime World, 1700–1750* (1987).

The New Politics of Empire, 1713–1750

The appearance of a distinctive American polity is traced in Bernard Bailyn, *The Origins of American Politics* (1968). Studies of various colonies include Jack P. Greene, *The Quest for Power: The Lower Houses of Assembly in the Southern Royal Colonies, 1689–1776* (1963); Patricia U. Bonomi, *A Factious People: Politics and Society in Colonial New York* (1971); A. Roger Ekirch, *"Poor Carolina": Politics and Society in Colonial North Carolina, 1729–1776* (1981); and Richard Bushman, *King and People in Provincial Massachusetts* (1985). John Schutz, *William Shirley* (1961), shows how a competent colonial governor wielded power, while Thomas C. Barrow, *Trade and Empire: The British Customs Service in Colonial America, 1660–1775* (1967), and Alison G. Olson, *Anglo-American Politics, 1660–1775* (1973), explore various aspects of British mercantilism.

Douglas E. Leach, *Roots of Conflict: British Armed Forces and Colonial Americans, 1677–1763* (1986), and Howard H. Peckham, *The Colonial Wars, 1689–1762* (1964), cover the diplomatic and military conflicts of the period, but these Anglo-American perspectives should be balanced by David J. Weber, *The Spanish Frontier in North America* (1992).

CHAPTER 4

A fine collection of important articles can be found in Stanley Katz, John Murrin, and Douglas Greenberg, eds., *Colonial America: Essays in Politics and Social Development* (4th ed., 1993). John J. McCusker and Russell R. Menard, *The Economy of British America, 1607–1783* (1985), survey economic change, while Jon Butler, *Awash in a Sea of Faith: Christianizing the American People* (1990), covers religious developments. Jack P. Greene, *Pursuits of Happiness* (1988), offers a provocative comparative analysis of regional social evolution.

Freehold Society in New England

A good local study is Daniel Vickers, *Farmers & Fishermen: Two Centuries of Work in Essex County Massachusetts, 1630–1830* (1994), while Bruce C. Daniels, *The Fragmentation of New England: Comparative Perspectives on Economic, Political, and Social Divisions in the Eighteenth Century* (1988), and Allan Kulikoff, *The Agrarian Origins of American Capitalism* (1992), offer a wider view. See also Robert Gross, *The Minutemen and Their*

World (1976), and Richard Bushman, *From Puritan to Yankee: Character and the Social Order in Connecticut, 1690–1765* (1967). On women's lives, see Laurel Thatcher Ulrich, *Good Wives: Image and Reality in the Lives of Women of Northern New England, 1650–1750* (1982), and Marylynn Salmon, *Women and the Law of Property in Early America* (1986). For studies of material culture that reveal the character of society, see Robert B. St. George, ed., *Material Life in America, 1600–1860* (1988), and Cary Carson, et al., eds., *Of Consuming Interest* (1994).

The Mid-Atlantic: Toward a New Society, 1720–1765

On Pennsylvania, consult Michael Zuckerman, ed., *Friends and Neighbors: Group Life in America's First Plural Society* (1982), and Barry J. Levy, *Quakers and the American Family* (1988). James T. Lemon, *The Best Poor Man's Country* (1972), pays some attention to ethnicity, as does Marilyn J. Westerkamp, *Triumph of the Laity: Scots-Irish Piety and the Great Awakening, 1625–1760* (1988). On white indentured servants and ethnic migration, see the classic study by Abbot E. Smith, *Colonists in Bondage* (1947); A. G. Roeber, *Palatines, Liberty, and Property: German Lutherans in Colonial British America* (1993); R. J. Dickson, *Ulster Immigration to Colonial America, 1718–1775* (1966); Jon Butler, *The Huguenots in America* (1983); Ned Landsman, *Scotland and Its First American Colony, 1683–1775* (1985); and A. Roger Ekirch, *Bound for America: The Transportation of British Convicts to the Colonies, 1718–1775* (1987). Important studies on mid-Atlantic politics include Patricia U. Bonomi, *A Factious People: Politics and Society in Colonial New York* (1971); Thomas L. Purvis, *Proprietors, Patronage, and Money: New Jersey, 1703–1776* (1986); Alan Tully, *Forming American Politics* (1994); and Benjamin H. Newcomb, *Political Partisanship in the American Middle Colonies, 1700–1776* (1995).

The Enlightenment and the Great Awakening, 1740–1765

Henry F. May, *The Enlightenment in America* (1976), is still the standard treatment, but see also Paul Merrill Spurlin, *The French Enlightenment in America* (1984), and Herbert Leventhal, *In the Shadow of the Enlightenment: Occultism and Renaissance Science in Eighteenth-Century America* (1976). For medical knowledge, consult Richard Shryock, *Medicine and Society in America, 1660–1860* (1960). Brooke Hindle, *The Pursuit of Science in Revolutionary America, 1735–1789* (1956), and John C. Greene, *American Science in the Age of Jefferson* (1984), are also relevant.

Good studies of the Great Awakening include David S. Lovejoy, *Religious Enthusiasm in the New World: Heresy to Revolution* (1985); Patricia U. Bonomi, *Under the Cope of Heaven: Religion, Society, and Politics in Colonial America* (1986); and Harry S. Stout, *The New England Soul: Preaching and Religious Culture in Colonial New England* (1986). Three good biographies of New England revivalists are Patricia Tracy, *Jonathan Edwards, Pastor* (1979); W. G. McLoughlin, *Isaac Backus and American Pietistic Tradition* (1957); and Christopher Jedrey, *The World of John Cleaveland* (1979). Harry Stout, *The Divine Dramatist* (1991), is a biography of George Whitefield. Richard Bushman, ed., *The Great Awakening* (1970), and Rhys Isaac, *The Transformation of Virginia, 1740–1790* (1982), capture the emotions of ordinary participants. William L. Joyce et al., eds., *Printing and Society in Early America* (1983), assesses the impact of books, pamphlets, and newspapers on the American mind.

The Midcentury Challenge: War, Trade, and Land, 1750–1765

Douglas E. Leach, *Roots of Conflict: British Armed Forces and Colonial Americans, 1677–1763* (1986), sets the Great War for Empire in a larger context. See also Edward P. Hamilton, *The French and Indian Wars* (1962); Guy Fregault, *Canada: The War of the Conquest* (1969); George F. G. Stanley, *New France: The Last Phase, 1744–1760* (1968); and Fred Anderson, *A People's Army: Massachusetts Soldiers and Society in the Seven Years' War* (1984). Richard White, *The Middle Ground* (1991), and Francis Jennings, *Empire of Fortune: Crown, Colonies, and Tribes in the Seven Years' War* (1988), describe the crucial role played by Indians in the conflict. See also Richard Aquila, *The Iroquois Restoration: Iroquois Diplomacy on the Colonial Frontier, 1701–1754* (1983), and David H. Corkran, *The Cherokee Frontier: Conflict and Survival, 1740–1762* (1966).

Gary M. Walton and James F. Shepherd, *The Economic Rise of Early America* (1979), trace the growing importance of commerce. See also Paul G. E. Clemens, *The Atlantic Economy and Colonial Maryland's Eastern Shore: From Tobacco to Grain* (1980).

Backcountry political agitation forms the focus of Richard D. Brown, *The South Carolina Regulators* (1963), and some of the essays in Alfred Young, ed., *The American Revolution: Essays in the History of American Radicalism* (1976). See also W. Stitt Robinson, *The Southern Colonial Frontier, 1607–1763* (1979); Richard Beeman, *The Evolution of the Southern Backcountry* (1984); and Rachel N. Klein, *Unification of a Slave State: The Rise of the Planter Class in the South Carolina Backcountry, 1660–1808* (1994).

CHAPTER 5

Jack P. Greene and J. R. Pole, eds., *The Blackwell Encyclopedia of the American Revolution* (1991), illuminates both obscure and well-known aspects of the Revolutionary Era. A good interpretive synthesis is Edward Countryman, *The American Revolution* (1985).

The Reform Movement, 1763–1765

For the state of the empire in 1763, see Alison Gilbert Olson, *Making the Empire Work: London and the American Interest Groups, 1690–1790* (1992), and Jack P. Greene, *Peripheries and Center: Constitutional Development . . .1607–1788* (1986). The impact of the Seven Years' War is traced in the classic study by Lawrence H. Gipson, *The Coming of the Revolution, 1763–1775* (1954), and in the following works: Richard Middleton, *The Bells of Victory: The Pitt-Newcastle Ministry and the Conduct of the Seven Years' War, 1757–1762* (1985); Alan Rogers, *Empire and Liberty: American Resistance to British Authority, 1755–1763* (1974); Howard H. Peckham, *Pontiac and the Indian Uprising* (1947); and Joseph A. Ernst, *Money and Politics in America, 1755–1775* (1973). Marc Egnal, *A Mighty Empire: The Origins of the Revolution* (1988), provides an interpretive synthesis.

British politics and imperial reform can be traced in John Brewer, *Party Ideology and Popular Politics at the Accession of George III* (1976); P. D. G. Thomas, *British Politics and the Stamp Act Crisis . . . 1763–1767* (1975); Thomas C. Barrow, *Trade and Empire: The British Customs Service in Colonial America, 1660–1775* (1967); John L. Bullion, *A Great and Necessary Measure: George Grenville and the Genesis of the Stamp Act, 1763–1765* (1982); Carl Ubbelohde, *The Vice-Admiralty Courts and the American Revolution* (1960); and Philip Lawson, *George Grenville* (1984).

The Dynamics of Rebellion, 1765–1766

For the American response to the British reform laws, see Edmund S. Morgan and Helen M. Morgan, *The Stamp Act Crisis* (1963); Pauline Maier, *From Resistance to Revolution . . . 1765–1776* (1972); and Gary B. Nash, *The Urban Crucible: Social Change, Political Consciousness, and the Origins of the American Revolution* (1979). Merrill Jensen, *The Founding of a Nation . . . 1763–1776* (1968), and Robert Middlekauff, *The Glorious Cause: The American Revolution, 1763–1789* (1982), provide detailed narratives of the struggle.

Studies of individual colonies capture the spirit of the resistance movement. See Paul A. Gilje, *The Road to Mobocracy: Popular Disorder in New York City, 1763–1834* (1986); David Lovejoy, *Rhode Island Politics and the American Revolution* (1958); and Ronald Hoffman, *A Spirit of Dissension: Economics, Politics, and the Revolution in Maryland* (1973). The motives of Patriots are best addressed through biographies. See Francis Jennings, *Benjamin Franklin, Politician* (1996); Pauline Maier, *The Old Revolutionaries: Political Lives in the Age of Samuel Adams* (1980); Milton E. Flower, *John Dickinson, Conservative Revolutionary* (1983); Richard R. Beeman, *Patrick Henry: A Biography* (1974); John R. Alden, *George Washington: A Biography* (1984); Helen Hill Miller, *George Mason: Gentleman Revolutionary* (1975); and Page Smith, *John Adams* (1962).

The most important single study of Patriot ideology is Bernard Bailyn, *The Ideological Origins of the American Revolution* (1967), but see also Robert M. Calhoon, *Dominion and Liberty: Ideology in Anglo-American Political Thought, 1660–1801* (1994). Other works include Caroline Robbins, *The Eighteenth-Century Commonwealthman* (1959); Morton White, *The Philosophy of the American Revolution* (1978); Garry Wills, *Inventing America: Jefferson's Declaration of Independence* (1978); and H. T. Dickinson, *Liberty and Property: Political Ideology in Eighteenth-Century Britain* (1978). For a discussion of the legal tradition, see Charles H. McIlwain, *The American Revolution: A Constitutional Interpretation* (1923), and the various volumes of John Phillip Reid's *Constitutional History of the American Revolution* (1986–1996).

The Growing Confrontation, 1767–1770

Peter D. G. Thomas, *The Townshend Duties Crisis . . . 1767–1773* (1987), is the most comprehensive treatment, but see also Colin Bonwick, *English Radicals and the American Revolution* (1977), and Ian R. Christie and Benjamin W. Labaree, *Empire or Independence, 1760–1776* (1976). On American resistance, consult Richard Alan Ryerson, *The Revolution Is Now Begun: The Radical Committees of Philadelphia, 1765–1776* (1978); Peter Shaw, *American Patriots and the Rituals of Revolution* (1981); and Stanley Godbold, Jr., and Robert W. Woody, *Christopher Gadsden* (1982). The confrontation between Patriots and British authority is covered in John Shy, *Toward Lexington: The Role of the British Army in the Coming of the American Revolution* (1965), and Hiller B. Zobel, *The Boston Massacre* (1970).

The Road to War, 1771–1775

Benjamin Labaree, *The Boston Tea Party* (1964), is comprehensive and stimulating and can be supplemented by Peter D. G. Thomas, *Tea Party to Independence* (1991); Bernard Donoughue, *British Politics and the American Revolution: The Path to War, 1773–75*

(1972); and David Ammerman, *In the Common Cause: American Response to the Coercive Acts of 1774* (1968). A fine study of the resistance movement is Edward F. Country-man, *A People in Revolution: The American Revolution and Political Society in New York* (1983). On prewar Loyalism, see Bernard Bailyn, *The Ordeal of Thomas Hutchinson* (1974), and Janice Potter, *The Liberty We Seek: Loyalist Ideology in Colonial New York and Massachusetts* (1983). For the rising of the countryside, see David Hackett Fischer, *Paul Revere's Ride* (1994); Gregory H. Nobles, *Divisions throughout the Whole: Politics and Society in Hampshire County, Massachusetts, 1740–1775* (1983); Jere R. Daniell, *Experiment in Republicanism: New Hampshire Politics and the Revolution, 1741–1790* (1970); and Richard Bushman, *King and People in Provincial Massachusetts* (1985). The transfer of authority is described in Jerrilyn Greene Marston, *King and Congress: The Transfer of Political Legitimacy, 1774–1776* (1987).

CHAPTER 6

Gordon Wood, *The Radicalism of the American Revolution* (1992), offers a fine overview. For a contrasting interpretation, see the essays in Alfred F. Young, ed., *Beyond the American Revolution: Explorations in the History of American Radicalism* (1993).

Toward Independence, 1775–1776

Jerrilyn Green Marston, *King and Congress: The Transfer of Political Legitimacy, 1774–1776* (1987), and Jack N. Rakove, *The Beginnings of National Politics* (1979), discuss the movement toward independence. See also Eric Foner, *Tom Paine and Revolutionary America* (1976); Jack Fruchtman, Jr., *Thomas Paine: Apostle of Freedom* (1994); and Pauline Maier, *American Scripture: Making the Declaration of Independence* (1997). On Loyalism, read William N. Nelson, *The American Tory* (1961); Robert M. Calhoon et al., *The Loyalist Perception* (1989); and the essays collected in Robert M. Calhoon, Timothy M. Barnes, and George A. Rawlyk, eds., *Loyalists and Community in North America* (1994).

The Perils of War and Finance, 1776–1778

The military history of the war is covered in James L. Stokesbury, *A Short History of the American Revolution* (1991), and Piers Mackesy, *The War for America, 1775–1783* (1964). Don Higginbotham, *George Washington and the American Military Tradition* (1985), and Ronald Hoffman and Peter Albert, eds., *Arms and Independence: The Military Character of the American Revolution* (1984), offer a more analytic perspective. The war in the North can be followed in Ira D. Gruber, *The Howe Brothers and the American Revolution* (1972), and Richard J. Hargrove, Jr., *General John Burgoyne* (1983).

Studies of ordinary soldiers include Rodney Attwood, *The Hessians* (1980); Sylvia R. Frey, *The British Soldier in America* (1981); Robert K. Wright, Jr., *The Continental Army* (1983); Charles P. Neimeyer, *America Goes to War: A Social History of the Continental Army* (1996); and John C. Dann, ed., *The Revolution Remembered: Eyewitness Accounts of the War for Independence* (1980). For the military bureaucracy, see R. Arthur Bowler, *Logistics and the Failure of the British Army in America, 1775–1783* (1975), and E. Wayne Carp, *To Starve the Army at Pleasure: Continental Army Administration and American Political Culture, 1775–1783* (1984).

Local studies include Jean Butenhoff Lee, *The Price of Nationhood: The American Revolution in Charles County* (1994); David Hackett Fischer, *Paul Revere's Ride* (1994); Robert Gross, *The Minutemen and Their World* (1976); Richard Buel, Jr., *Dear Liberty: Connecticut's Mobilization for the Revolutionary War* (1980); and Donald Wallace White, *A Village at War: Chatham, New Jersey, and the American Revolution* (1979).

African–American participation in the war is discussed by Gary A. Puckrein, *The Black Regiment in the American Revolution* (1978); Sidney Kaplan, *The Black Presence in the Era of the American Revolution* (rev. ed., 1989); and Gary B. Nash, *Race and Revolution* (1990).

The native American response is described in Barbara Graymont, *The Iroquois in the American Revolution* (1972); Isabel T. Kelsey, *Joseph Brant, 1743–1807* (1984); and James H. O'Donnell III, *Southern Indians in the American Revolution* (1973).

Two classic discussions of the fiscal problems created by the war are E. James Ferguson, *The Power of the Purse: A History of American Public Finance: 1776–1790* (1961), and Clarence L. Ver Steeg, *Robert Morris, Revolutionary Financier* (1954). A more recent study is William G. Anderson, *The Price of Liberty: The Public Debt of the American Revolution* (1983).

The Path to Victory, 1778–1783

Bradford Perkins, *The Creation of a Republican Empire, 1776–1865* (1993), and Jonathan R. Dull, *A Diplomatic History of the American Revolution* (1985), provide good overviews. More specialized studies include James H. Hutson, *John Adams and the Diplomacy of the American Revolution* (1980); Richard B. Morris, *The Peacemakers: The Great Powers and American Independence* (1965); and Ronald Hoffman and Peter Albert, eds., *Peace and the Peacemakers: The Treaty of 1783* (1986).

For the southern campaign, consult W. Robert Higgins, ed., *The Revolutionary War in the South* (1979); Ronald Hoffman, Thad W. Tate, and Peter J. Albert, eds., *An Uncivil War: The Southern Backcountry during the American Revolution* (1985); and Jeffrey J. Crow and Larry E. Tise, eds., *The Southern Experience in the American Revolution* (1978). Studies of military action include Hugh F. Rankin, *Francis Marion: The Swamp Fox* (1973), and John S. Pancake, *The Destructive War, 1780–1782* (1985).

Republicanism Defined and Challenged

Milton M. Klein et al., *The Republican Synthesis Revisited* (1992), explores the debate over the importance of republican thought. See also Charles Royster, *A Revolutionary People at War: The Continental Army and American Character, 1775–1783* (1979). On women's lives, see Ronald Hoffman and Peter J. Albert, eds., *Women in the Age of the American Revolution* (1989); Mary Beth Norton, *Liberty's Daughters: The Revolutionary Experience of American Women, 1750–1800* (1980); Lynn Withey, *Dearest Friend: A Life of Abigail Adams* (1980); and Joy Day Buel and Richard Buel, Jr., *The Way of Duty: A Woman and Her Family in Revolutionary America* (1984).

On the black experience, consult Sylvia R. Frey, *Water from the Rock: Black Resistance in a Revolutionary Age* (1991); Ira Berlin and Ronald Hoffman, eds., *Slavery and Freedom in the Age of the American Revolution* (1983); Gary B. Nash, *Forging Freedom: The Formation of Philadelphia's Black Community, 1720–1840* (1988); and David Brion Davis, *The Problem of Slavery in the Age of Revolution, 1770–1823* (1975). See also James W. St. G. Walker, *The Black Loyalists: The Search for a Promised Land in Nova Scotia and*

Sierra Leone, 1783–1870 (1976), and Shane White, *Somewhat More Independent: The End of Slavery in New York City, 1770–1810* (1991).
    On changes in American religion, see Ronald Hoffman and Peter J. Albert, eds., *Religion in a Revolutionary Age* (1994); Rhys Isaac, *The Transformation of Virginia, 1740–1790* (1982); Fred Hood, *Reformed America 1783–1837* (1980); and Nathan O. Hatch, *The Democratization of American Christianity* (1989). The spiritual roots of a new secular religion are traced by Catharine Albanese, *Sons of the Fathers: The Civil Religion of the American Revolution* (1976), and Ruth Bloch, *Visionary Republic: Millennial Themes in American Thought* (1985).

CHAPTER 7

Jack N. Rakove, *Original Meaning: Politics and Ideas in the Making of the Constitution* (1996), and Richard B. Bernstein and Kym S. Rice, *Are We to Be a Nation? The Making of the Constitution* (1987), are the best recent overviews, while Stanley Elkins and Eric McKitrick, *The Age of Federalism: The Early Republic, 1788–1800* (1993), offers a comprehensive assessment of the 1790s.

Creating New Institutions, 1776–1789

Elisha P. Douglass, *Rebels and Democrats* (1965), documents the struggle for equal political rights. See also Jackson T. Main, *The Sovereign States, 1775–1783* (1973), and Ronald L. Hoffman and Peter Albert, eds., *Sovereign States in an Age of Uncertainty* (1981). Important studies of state constitutions include Willi Paul Adams, *The First American Constitutions* (1980); Edward Countryman, *A People in Revolution: The American Revolution and Political Society in New York, 1760–1790* (1981); Donald Lutz, *Popular Consent and Popular Control: Whig Political Theory in the Early State Constitutions* (1980); and J. R. Pole, *Political Representation in England and the Origins of the American Republic* (1966).
    On women and republicanism, see Linda K. Kerber, *Women of the Republic* (1980), and Ronald Hoffman and Peter Albert, eds., *Women in the Age of the American Revolution* (1989). Fine in-depth studies include Rosemarie Zagarri, *A Woman's Dilemma: Mercy Otis Warren and the American Revolution* (1995); Judith Sargent Murray, *The Gleaner*, ed. by Nina Baym (1992); and Lynn Withey, *Dearest Friend: A Life of Abigail Adams* (1982).
    Gordon Wood, *The Creation of the American Republic, 1776–1790* (1965), links state and national constitutional development. Other important works on the 1780s include Peter S. Onuf, *The Origins of the Federal Republic: Jurisdictional Controversies in the United States, 1775–1787* (1983); Roger H. Brown, *Redeeming the Republic: Federalists, Taxation, and the Origins of the Constitution* (1993); Richard B. Morris, *The Forging of the Union, 1781–1789* (1987); and Robert A. Gross, ed., *In Debt to Shays* (1993).

The Constitution of 1787

In 1913 two studies initiated the modern analysis of the Constitution: Charles A. Beard, *An Economic Interpretation of the Constitution of the United States*, and Max Farrand, *The Framing of the Constitution*. For critiques of Beard's work, see Leonard Levy, ed., *Essays on the Making of the Constitution* (rev. ed., 1987); for an update of Farrand, read Christopher Collier and James L. Collier, *Decision in Philadelphia* (1987).

Other significant works include Forrest McDonald, *Novus Ordo Seculorum: The Intellectual Origins of the Constitution* (1985); Edmund S. Morgan, *Inventing the People: The Rise of Popular Sovereignty in England and America* (1988); and Michael Kammen, *A Machine That Would Go by Itself: The Constitution in American Culture* (1986). Three fine collections of essays are Richard R. Beeman et al., eds., *Beyond Confederation: Origins of the Constitution* . . . (1987); Ellen Frankel Paul and Howard Dickman, eds., *Liberty, Property and the Foundations of the American Constitution* (1989); and Herman Belz et al., eds., *To Form a More Perfect Union: The Critical Ideas of the Constitution* (1992).

On the Antifederalists and ratification, see Patrick T. Conley and John P. Kaminiski, eds., *The Constitution and the States* (1988); Stephen L. Schechter, *The Reluctant Pillar: New York and the Adoption of the Federal Constitution* (1985); and Herbert Storing, *The Antifederalists* (1985). Two recent studies of the Federalist papers are David F. Epstein, *The Political Theory of "The Federalist"* (1984), and Charles R. Kesler, ed., *Saving the Revolution* (1987).

R. A. Rutland, *The Birth of the Bill of Rights, 1776–1791* (rev. ed., 1983), offers the basic narrative; more analytic treatments include Michael J. Lacey and Knud Haakonssen, *A Culture of Rights* (1991); David J. Bodenhemer and James W. Ely, Jr., *The Bill of Rights in Modern America* (1993); and Joyce Lee Malcolm, *To Keep and Bear Arms: The Origins of an Anglo-American Right* (1993).

The Political Crisis of the 1790s

A good synthesis is James Rogers Sharp, *American Politics in the Early Republic: The New Nation in Crisis* (1993). Studies of important statesmen include Forrest McDonald, *Alexander Hamilton: A Biography* (1979), and James T. Flexner, *George Washington and the New Nation, 1783–1793* (1970) and *George Washington: Anguish and Farewell, 1793–1799* (1972). For Jeffersonian ideology, see Joyce Appleby, *Capitalism and a New Social Order: The Republican Vision of the 1790s* (1984); Drew McCoy, *The Elusive Republic: Political Economy in Jeffersonian America* (1982); Lance Banning, *The Jeffersonian Persuasion: The Evolution of a Party Ideology* (1978); and John R. Nelson, Jr., *Liberty and Property: Political Economy and Policymaking in the New Nation, 1789–1812* (1987).

Richard Hofstadter, *The Idea of a Party System: The Rise of Legitimate Opposition in the United States, 1790–1840* (1969), offers an overview of the subject; see also John F. Hoadley, *Origins of American Political Parties, 1789–1803* (1986). More detailed studies are Thomas P. Slaughter, *The Whiskey Rebellion* (1986), and Richard J. Twomey, *Jacobins and Jeffersonians* (1989). On diplomatic and military history, consult Henry Ammon, *The Genêt Mission* (1973); Jerald A. Combs, *The Jay Treaty* (1970); Richard H. Kohn, *Eagle and Sword* (1975); and Lawrence D. Cress, *Citizens in Arms: The Army and the Military to the War of 1812* (1982).

On Adams's administration, see Ralph Brown Adams, *The Presidency of John Adams* (1975). More specialized studies are William Sinchcombe, *The XYZ Affair* (1980); Leonard Levy, *The Emergence of a Free Press* (1985); and James M. Smith, *Freedom's Fetters: The Alien and Sedition Laws and American Civil Liberties* (rev. ed., 1966).

Good state histories include Patricia Watlington, *The Partisan Spirit: Kentucky Politics, 1779–1792* (1972); Richard R. Beeman, *The Old Dominion and the New Nation, 1788–1801* (1972); and Mary K. Bonsteel Tachau, *Federal Courts in the Early Republic: Kentucky, 1789–1816* (1978).

CHAPTER 8

Gregory Evans Dowd, *A Spirited Resistance: The North American Indian Struggle for Unity, 1745–1815* (1992), presents a fine survey of the Indian peoples, while Donald R. Wright, *African-Americans in the Early Republic, 1789–1831* (1993), provides a good overview of the black population. Donald R. Hickey, *The War of 1812: A Forgotten Conflict* (1989), puts the war in an economic and diplomatic context.

Westward Expansion

For studies of white policy toward native Americans, see Bernard Sheehan, *Seeds of Extinction: Jeffersonian Philanthropy and the American Indian* (1973); Reginald Horsman, *Expansion and American Indian Policy, 1783–1812* (1967); Dorothy Jones, *License for Empire: Colonialism by Treaty in Early America* (1982); and Richard Slotkin, *Regeneration through Violence: The Mythology of the American Frontier* (1973). Works dealing with the impact of Christian missions include Henry Warner Bowden, *American Indians and Christian Missions: Studies in Cultural Conflict* (1981); William W. Fitzhugh, ed., *Cultures in Contact* (1985); William G. McLoughlin, *Cherokees and Missionaries, 1789–1839* (1984); and Earl P. Olmstead, *Blackcoats among the Delaware* (1991). Other analyses of cultural interaction are William G. McLoughlin, *Cherokee Renascence in the New Republic* (1986); J. Leitch Wright, Jr., *Creeks and Seminoles: The Destruction and Regeneration of the Muscogulge People* (1986); Katherine E. H. Braund, *Deerskins and Duffels* (1993); and John Mack Faragher, *Daniel Boone* (1992).

Two fine accounts of settlers and speculators are Alan Taylor, *Liberty Men and Great Proprietors . . . on the Maine Frontier, 1760–1820* (1990) and *William Cooper's Town* (1995). For developments west of the mountains, see Malcolm J. Rohrbough, *The Transappalachian Frontier: Peoples, Societies, and Institutions, 1775–1850* (1978), and John Mack Faragher, *Sugar Creek: Life on the Illinois Prairie* (1986).

Republican Policy and Diplomacy

Two good general accounts are Marshall Smelser, *The Democratic Republic, 1801–1815* (1968), and Ralph Ketcham, *Presidents above Party: The First American Presidency, 1789–1829* (1984). Detailed studies of Jefferson's presidency include Daniel Sisson, *The Revolution of 1800* (1974); Dumas Malone, *Jefferson the President* (2 vols., 1970 and 1974); and Richard E. Ellis, *The Jeffersonian Crisis: Courts and Politics in the New Republic* (1971). For the Louisiana Purchase, see Stephen E. Ambrose, *Undaunted Courage: Meriwether Lewis, Thomas Jefferson, and the Opening of the American West* (1996); Donald Jackson, *The Letters of the Lewis and Clark Expedition* (1963); and James P. Ronda, *Lewis and Clark among the Indians* (1984).

The activities of Aaron Burr are covered in Milton Lomask, *Aaron Burr* (1979), while the Federalists are discussed in David Hackett Fischer, *The Revolution of American Conservatism: The Federalist Party in the Age of Jeffersonian Democracy* (1965); Linda K. Kerber, *Federalists in Dissent: Imagery and Ideology in Jeffersonian America* (1970); and James Banner, *To the Hartford Convention: The Federalists and the Origins of Party Politics in the Early Republic, 1789–1815* (1970).

American attempts to avoid involvement in the Napoleonic Wars are traced in Lawrence Kaplan, *"Entangling Alliances with None": American Foreign Policy in the Age of Jefferson* (1987), and Bradford Perkins, *The First Rapprochement: England and the United*

States, 1795–1805 (1967) and *Prologue to War: England and the United States, 1805–1812* (1963). See also Clifford L. Egan, *Neither Peace nor War: Franco-American Relations, 1803–1812* (1983), and Doron S. Ben-Atar, *The Origins of Jeffersonian Commercial Policy and Diplomacy* (1993). On Madison, see Robert A. Rutland, *The Presidency of James Madison* (1990); J. C. A. Stagg, *Mr. Madison's War: Politics, Diplomacy, and Warfare in the Early Republic, 1783–1830* (1983); and Drew McCoy, *The Last of the Fathers: James Madison and the Republican Legacy* (1989). Native American involvement in the war is discussed by R. David Edmunds, *The Shawnee Prophet* (1983) and *Tecumseh and the Quest for Indian Leadership* (1984), as well as by H. S. Halbert and T. H. Ball, *The Creek War of 1813 and 1814* (1970).

Regional Diversity and National Identity

For life in the northern seaboard states, see Benjamin W. Labaree, *The Merchants of Newburyport, 1764–1815* (1962), and Sean Wilentz, *Chants Democratic: New York City and the Rise of the American Working Class, 1788–1850* (1984). The essays in R. A. Burchell, ed., *The End of Anglo-America* (1991), document various shifts in cultural identity.

A sophisticated analysis of the Old Northwest is Andrew R. L. Cayton and Peter S. Onuf, *The Midwest and the Nation* (1990). More detailed studies include Richard C. Wade, *The Urban Frontier: The Rise of Western Cities, 1790–1840* (1973), and Andrew Cayton, *The Frontier Republic: Ideology and Politics in the Ohio Country, 1789–1812* (1986).

Peter Kolchin, *American Slavery, 1619–1877* (1993), provides a fine overview. On the expansion of slavery, see Ira Berlin and Ronald Hoffman, eds., *Slavery and Freedom in the Age of the American Revolution* (1983); Donald L. Robinson, *Slavery in the Structure of American Politics, 1765–1820* (1971); and Albert Raboteau, *Slave Religion* (1968). Also see Ira Berlin and Philip D. Morgan, eds., *Cultivation and Culture: Labor and the Shaping of Slave Life* (1993), and Dena J. Epstein, *Sinful Tunes and Spirituals: Black Folk Music to the Civil War* (1977). Two good studies of the Carolina region are Joyce E. Chaplin, *Agricultural Innovation and Modernity in the Lower South, 1730–1815* (1993), and Peter A. Coclanis, *The Shadow of a Dream: Economic Life and Death in the South Carolina Low Country, 1670–1920* (1988).

For blacks in the northern states, see Gary B. Nash, *Forging Freedom: Philadelphia's Black Community, 1720–1840* (1988). Glover Moore, *The Missouri Compromise* (1953), provides a detailed analysis of that crisis. See also Merton L. Dillon, *Slavery Attacked: Southern Slaves and Their Allies, 1619–1865* (1990).

Spain's quest for empire is covered in David Weber, *The Spanish Frontier in North America* (1992), while American initiatives are the subject of Walter LaFeber, ed., *John Quincy Adams and American Continental Empire* (1965); Ernest May, *The Making of the Monroe Doctrine* (1976); and Henry Ammon, *James Monroe: The Quest for National Identity* (1971).

CHAPTER 9

Three fine local studies—Alan Taylor, *William Cooper's Town: Power and Persuasion on the Frontier of the Early American Republic* (1995); Christopher Clark, *The Roots of Rural Capitalism* (1990); and Laurel Thatcher Ulrich, *A Midwife's Tale: The Life of Martha Ballard*

(1990)—capture the texture of life in the early republic. Nathan O. Hatch, *The Democratization of American Christianity* (1987), offers an interpretation of religious change.

Political Economy: The Capitalist Commonwealth

Thomas Doerflinger, *A Vigorous Spirit of Enterprise: Merchants and Economic Development in Revolutionary Philadelphia* (1986); John Denis Haeger, *John Jacob Astor* (1991); and Stuart Bruchey, *Robert Oliver: Merchant of Baltimore* (1956), are fine studies of merchant enterprise. The standard history is Curtis R. Nettels, *The Emergence of a National Economy, 1775–1815* (1965). See also Ronald Hoffman, John J. McCusker, and Peter Albert, eds., *The Economy of Revolutionary America* (1987), and Daniel P. Jones, *The Economic and Social Transformation of Rhode Island, 1780–1850* (1992).

On banking, consult the classic study by Bray Hammond, *Banks and Politics in America* (1957), and Richard H. Timberlake, *Monetary Policy in the United States* (1992). Studies of manufacturing include Thomas C. Cochran, *Frontiers of Change: Early Industrialism in America* (1981); David Jeremy, *Transatlantic Industrial Revolution: The Diffusion of Textile Technology* . . . (1981); and Judith A. McGaw, *Early American Technology* (1994).

The classic studies of state mercantilism are Oscar and Mary Handlin, *Commonwealth: A Study of the Role of Government in the American Economy: Massachusetts, 1774–1861* (1947), and Louis Hartz, *Economic Policy and Democratic Thought: Pennsylvania, 1776–1860* (1948). State support for transportation can be traced in Carter Goodrich, *Government Promotion of American Canals and Railroads* (1960); Erik F. Hiates et al., *Western River Transportation: The Era of Early Internal Development, 1810–1860* (1975); and Harry N. Scheiber, *Ohio Canal Era: A Case Study of Government and the Economy* (1969).

The legal implications of commonwealth ideology are analyzed in Leonard Levy, *The Law of the Commonwealth and Chief Justice Shaw* (1955), and Morton Horwitz, *The Transformation of American Law, 1790–1860* (1976). R. Kent Newmyer, *The Supreme Court under Marshall and Taney* (1968), offers a concise treatment. See also Robert K. Faulkner, *The Jurisprudence of John Marshall* (1968); Francis N. Stites, *John Marshall: Defender of the Constitution* (1981); and Thomas C. Shevory, ed., *John Marshall's Achievement* (1989). A fine case study is C. Peter McGrath, *Yazoo: Law and Politics in the New Republic* (1966). William R. Casto, *The Supreme Court in the Early Republic: The Chief Justiceships of John Jay and Oliver Ellsworth* (1995), looks at the pre-Marshall court.

Visions of a Republican Social Order

Warren S. Tryon, *A Mirror for Americans: Life and Manners in the United States, 1790–1870, as Recorded by European Travelers* (3 vols., 1952), suggests the distinctive features of republican society. Clement Eaton, *Henry Clay and the Art of American Politics* (1957), perceptively describes the coming of political democracy. More detailed studies are Ronald Formisano, *The Transformation of Political Culture: Massachusetts Parties, 1790s–1840s* (1983), and Chilton Williamson, *American Suffrage from Property to Democracy* (1960).

Michael Grossberg, *Governing the Hearth* (1985), discusses changing marriage rules. Catherine M. Scholten, *Childrearing in American Society, 1650–1850* (1985), should be supplemented by Philip Greven's pathbreaking analysis, *The Protestant Temperament: Patterns of Childrearing, Religious Experience, and the Self in Early America*

(1977). On sentimentalism, see Shirley Samuels, *The Culture of Sentiment: Race, Gender and Sentimentality in Nineteenth Century America* (1992). Other important works include Daniel Blake Smith, *Inside the Great House: Planter Family Life in Eighteenth-Century Chesapeake Society* (1980); Bernard Wishy, *The Child and the Republic* (1970); and Jan Lewis, *The Pursuit of Happiness: Family and Values in Jefferson's Virginia* (1983).

Protestant Christianity and Women's Lives

Perry Miller, *The Life of the Mind in America* (1966), offers a good overview of the Second Great Awakening. For revivalism, see Stephen A. Marini, *Radical Sects of Revolutionary New England* (1982); Bernard A. Weisberger, *They Gathered at the River* (1958); Jon Butler, *Awash in a Sea of Faith* (1989); P. Jeffrey Potash, *Vermont's Burned Over District* (1991); and Ian H. Murray, *Revival and Revivalism: The Making and Marring of American Evangelicalism, 1750–1858* (1994). The course of religious thought in New England is traced in Daniel Walker Howe, *The Unitarian Conscience* (1970).

Some of the many recent studies touching on evangelical religion include Christine L. Heyrman, *Southern Cross: The Beginnings of the Bible Belt* (1997); Diana Hockstedt Butler, *Standing against the Whirlwind: Evangelical Episcopalians in Nineteenth-Century America* (1995); Randy J. Sparks, *On Jordan's Stormy Banks: Evangelicalism in Mississippi, 1773–1876* (1994); and John G. West, Jr., *The Politics of Revelation and Reason: Religion and Civic Life in the New Nation* (1996).

For women's lives, see Susan Juster, *Disorderly Women: Sexual Politics and Evangelicalism in Revolutionary New England* (1994); Harriet B. Applewhite and Darline G. Levy, eds., *Women and Politics in the Age of Democratic Revolution* (1990); and Linda Kerber, *Women of the Republic: Intellect and Ideology in Revolutionary America* (1980). Specialized studies include Joan M. Jensen, *Loosening the Bonds: Mid-Atlantic Farm Women, 1750–1850* (1986); Nancy F. Cott, *The Bonds of Womanhood: "Women's Sphere" in New England, 1780–1835* (1977); and Jeanne Boydston, *Home and Work* (1990).

Women's religious initiatives are discussed in Mary P. Ryan, *Cradle of the Middle Class* (1981); Barbara Epstein, *The Politics of Domesticity: Women, Evangelism, and Temperance* (1978); and Keith Melder, *Beginnings of Sisterhood: The American Women's Rights Movement, 1800–1850* (1977), which also traces the growth of female academies.

CHAPTER 10

Two important studies of American economic transformation are Stuart Bruchey, *Enterprise: The Dynamic Economy of a Free People* (1990), and Charles G. Sellers, Jr., *The Market Revolution: Jacksonian America, 1815–1840* (1991).

The Coming of Industry: Northeastern Manufacturing

Surveys of the broad economic setting and impact of the Industrial Revolution include W. Elliot Brownlee, *Dynamics of Ascent: A History of the American Economy* (1979); Thomas C. Cochran, *Frontiers of Change: Early Industrialism in America* (1981); and Douglass C. North, *The Economic Growth of the United States, 1790–1860* (1961). Another useful survey is the pioneering work in economic geography, Donald W. Meinig, *The Shaping of America: A Geographical Perspective*, Volume 2: *Continental America, 1800–1867* (1993).

Books on the role of technological change include Gary Cross and Rick Szostak, *Technology and American Society: A History* (1995); H. J. Habakkuk, *American and British Technology in the Nineteenth Century: The Search for Labour-Saving Inventions* (1962); David Freeman Hawke, *Nuts and Bolts of the Past: A History of American Technology, 1776–1860* (1988); Brooke Hindle and Steven Lubar, *Engines of Change: The American Industrial Revolution, 1790–1860* (1986); Donald K. Hoke, *Ingenious Yankees: The Rise of the American System of Manufactures in the Private Sector* (1990); David A. Hounshell, *From the American System to Mass Production, 1800–1932: The Development of Manufacturing Technology in the United States* (1984); Harold C. Livesay, *American Made: Men Who Shaped the American Economy* (1979); Judith A. McGaw, ed., *Early American Technology: Making and Doing Things from the Colonial Era to 1850* (1994); Nathan Rosenberg, *Perspectives on Technology* (1976); and Barbara M. Tucker, *Samuel Slater and the Origins of the American Textile Industry* (1984).

Stanley Lebergott, *Manpower in Economic Growth: The United States Record since 1800* (1964), provides a useful survey of the contribution of labor to the Industrial Revolution. Two in-depth studies of an important group of women workers are by Thomas Dublin, *Women at Work: The Transformation of Work and Community in Lowell, Massachusetts, 1826–1860* (1979) and *Transforming Women's Work: New England Lives in the Industrial Revolution* (1994). Regional studies of the early Industrial Revolution include Peter J. Coleman, *The Transformation of Rhode Island* (1963); Dianne Lindstrom, *Economic Development in the Philadelphia Region, 1810–1850* (1978); and Anthony F. C. Wallace, *Rockdale: The Growth of an American Village in the Early Industrial Revolution* (1978).

The Expansion of Markets

Urban development in this period is best explored in R. G. Albion, *The Rise of New York Port, 1815–1860* (1939); Eric E. Lampard, "The Evolving System of Cities in the United States: Urbanization and Economic Development," in *Issues in Urban Economics* (Harvey S. Perloff and Lowdon Wingo, Jr., eds., 1968); Richard C. Wade, *The Urban Frontier: Pioneer Life in Early Pittsburgh, Cincinnati, Lexington, Louisville, and St. Louis* (1964); and Alan R. Pred, *Urban Growth and the Circulation of Information: The United States System of Cities, 1790–1840* (1973). The best introductions to agricultural expansion in this period are Paul W. Gates, *The Farmer's Age: Agriculture, 1815–1860* (1960), and Lewis C. Gray, *History of Agriculture in the Southern United States to 1860* (1933). The classic history of the role of transportation is George R. Taylor, *The Transportation Revolution, 1815–1860* (1951). On the role of canals, consult Carter Goodrich et al., *Canals and American Economic Development* (1961); Ronald E. Shaw, *Canals for a Nation: The Canal Era in the United States, 1790–1860* (1990); Carol Sherrif, *The Artificial River: The Erie Canal and the Paradox of Progress, 1817–1862* (1996); and Peter Way, *Common Labour: Workers and the Digging of North American Canals* (1993). On the contribution of the law to the economic revolution, see Oscar Handlin and Mary Flug Handlin, *Commonwealth: A Study in the Role of Government in the American Economy, Massachusetts, 1774–1861* (1947); Morton J. Horwitz, *The Transformation of American Law, 1780–1860* (1977); James Willard Hurst, *Law and the Conditions of Freedom in the Nineteenth-Century United States* (1964); and Christopher L. Tomlins, *Law, Labor and Ideology in the Early American Republic* (1993).

A Changing Social Structure

The following works provide a good introduction to the study of the distribution of wealth and income in the early nineteenth century: Frederic C. Jaher, *The Urban Establishment: Upper Strata in Boston, New York, Charleston, Chicago, and Los Angeles* (1982); Edward Pessen, *Riches, Class, and Power before the Civil War* (1973); and Jeffrey G. Williamson and Peter H. Lindert, *American Inequality: A Macroeconomic History* (1980). These studies should be supplemented with analyses of social mobility such as Robert Doherty, *Society and Power: Five New England Towns, 1800–1860* (1977); Don H. Doyle, *The Social Order of a Frontier Community: Jacksonville, Illinois, 1825–1870* (1978); Peter R. Knights, *The Plain People of Boston, 1830–1860* (1976); and Stanley Lebergott, *The American Economy: Income, Wealth, and Want* (1976). Some of the disruptive effects of economic change are addressed in Karen Haltunen, *Confidence Men and Painted Women: A Study of Middle-Class Culture in America, 1830–1870* (1982); Alan Dawley, *Class and Community: The Industrial Revolution in Lynn* (1976); Bruce Laurie, *Working People of Philadelphia* (1980); Jonathan Prude, *The Coming of Industrial Order: Town and Factory Life in Rural Massachusetts* (1983); W. J. Rorabaugh, *The Alcoholic Republic: An American Tradition* (1979); Christine Stansell, *City of Women: Sex and Class in New York, 1789–1860* (1986); and Sam Bass Warner, Jr., *The Private City* (1968). For a stimulating discussion of the effects of markets and manufacturing on the countryside, see Christopher Clark, *The Roots of Rural Capitalism: Western Massachusetts, 1789–1860* (1990).

The concept of the business class is developed in Michael Katz et al., *The Social Organization of Early Industrial Capitalism* (1982). Surveys of reform movements closely linked to the Second Great Awakening include Alice F. Tyler, *Freedom's Ferment: Phases of Social History from the Colonial Period to the Outbreak of the Civil War* (1944), and Ronald G. Walters, *American Reformers, 1815–1860* (1978). Studies of the relationship between religious evangelism and reform are particularly abundant for communities in New York State. See Paul E. Johnson, *A Shopkeeper's Millennium: Society and Revivals in Rochester, New York, 1815–1837* (1978), and Mary Ryan, *Cradle of the Middle Class: The Family in Oneida County, New York, 1790–1865* (1981). On the relationship between religion and labor protest, see Jama Lazerow, *Religion and the Working Class in Antebellum America* (1996). For more general studies of religious ferment in the early republic, see John Butler, *Awash in a Sea of Faith: Christianizing the American People* (1990); Nathan O. Hatch, *The Democratization of American Christianity* (1989); and R. Lawrence Moore, *Selling God: American Religion in the Marketplace of Culture* (1994).

CHAPTER 11

Two fine surveys of the Jacksonian era are Charles Sellers, *The Market Revolution: Jacksonian America, 1814–1846* (1992), and Harry L. Watson, *Liberty and Power: The Politics of Jacksonian America* (1990). See also Daniel Feller, *The Jacksonian Promise: America, 1815–1840* (1995).

Democratizing Politics and the Jacksonian Presidency

Arthur M. Schlesinger, Jr., *The Age of Jackson* (1945), initiated the modern reexamination of Andrew Jackson and his significance. Among the most provocative subsequent studies are: Lee Benson, *The Concept of Jacksonian Democracy: New York as a Test Case* (1961); Marvin Meyers, *The Jacksonian Persuasion: Politics and Belief* (1957); and John William Ward, *Andrew Jackson; Symbol for an Age* (1962). For studies of Jackson and political institutions, see Donald Cole, *The Presidency of Andrew Jackson* (1992), and Leonard D. White, *The Jacksonians: A Study in Administrative History, 1828–1861* (1954). On the politics of the Bank war, see Robert V. Remini, *Andrew Jackson and the Bank War* (1967). On the nullification crisis, see William W. Freehling, *Prelude to Civil War* (1966), and Richard E. Ellis, *The Union at Risk* (1987). Works treating Jackson's Indian policy include Ralph S. Cotterill, *The Southern Indians* (1954); Grant Forman, *Indian Removal* (1953); Michael D. Green, *The Politics of Indian Removal* (1982); William G. McLoughlin, *Cherokee Renascence in the New Republic* (1986); Gary E. Moulton, *John Ross: Cherokee Chief* (1978); Francis P. Prucha, *American Indian Policy in the Formative Years* (1962) and *American Indian Treaties: The History of a Political Anomaly* (1994); and Ronald N. Satz, *American Indian Policy in the Jacksonian Era* (1975). For a comprehensive view of Jackson's life, see Robert V. Remini, *Andrew Jackson and the Course of American Freedom, 1822–1833* (1977), *Andrew Jackson and the Course of American Democracy, 1833–1845* (1984), and *The Life of Andrew Jackson* (1988). For important biographies of other leading politicians, consult Samuel Flagg Bemis, *John Quincy Adams and the Union* (1956); Leonard L. Richards, *The Life and Times of Congressman John Quincy Adams* (1986); John Niven, *Martin Van Buren: The Romantic Age of American Politics* (1983); Robert V. Remini, *Martin Van Buren and the Making of the Democratic Party* (1959); and James C. Curtis, *The Fox at Bay* (1970). For studies of the leading Whigs, see Richard N. Current, *John C. Calhoun* (3 vols., 1944–1951); Irving H. Bartlett, *Daniel Webster* (1978); and Robert V. Remini, *Henry Clay: Statesman for the Union* (1991).

Class, Culture, and the Second Party System

A rich literature describes the emergence of the Whigs in the context of a changing political culture and the creation of the Second Party System. Books that deal broadly with these topics include John Ashworth, *"Agrarians" & "Aristocrats": Party Political Ideology in the United States, 1837–1846* (1983); Richard Hofstadter, *The Idea of a Party System* (1972); Daniel W. Howe, *The Political Culture of the American Whigs* (1979); Robert Kelley, *The Cultural Pattern in American Politics: The First Century* (1979); Lawrence F. Kohl, *The Politics of Individualism: Parties and the American Character in the Jacksonian Era* (1989); Richard P. McCormick, *The Second American Party System: Party Formation in the Jacksonian Era* (1966); and Joel H. Silbey, *The Partisan Imperative: The Dynamics of American Politics before the Civil War* (1985). More specialized studies include Thomas Brown, *Politics and Statesmanship: Essays on the American Whig Party* (1985); Ronald P. Formisano, *The Birth of Mass Political Parties: Michigan, 1827–1861* (1972) and *The Transformation of Political Culture: Massachusetts Parties, 1790's–1840's* (1983); William G. Shade, *Banks or No Banks: The Money Issue in Western Politics, 1832–1865* (1972); Harry L. Watson, *Jacksonian Politics and Community Conflict: The Emergence of the Second Party System in Cumberland County, North Carolina* (1981); and Chilton Williamson, *American Suffrage from Property to Democracy, 1760–1860* (1960). For the presidency of John Tyler, see Robert J. Morgan, *A Whig Embattled* (1954).

An earlier generation of historians of labor emphasized the organization of unions during early industrialization. See Norman Ware, *The Industrial Worker, 1840–1860* (1924), and John R. Commons, *History of Labor in the United States*, Vol. 1 (1918). More recently, historians have explored the political and social context of the labor movement. See Mary H. Blewett, *Men, Women, and Work: Class, Gender, and Protest in the New England Shoe Industry, 1780–1910* (1988); Jeanne Boydston, *Home and Work: Housework, Wages, and the Ideology of Labor in the Early Republic* (1990); Alan Dawley, *Class and Community: The Industrial Revolution in Lynn, 1780–1860* (1976); Paul G. Faler, *Mechanics and Manufacturers in the Early Industrial Revolution* (1981); Paul A. Gilje and Howard B. Rock, eds., *Keepers of the Revolution: New Yorkers at Work in the Early Republic* (1992); Susan E. Hirsch, *Roots of the American Working Class: The Industrialization of Crafts in Newark, 1800–1860* (1978); Bruce Laurie, *Working People of Philadelphia, 1800–1860* (1980); Jonathan Prude, *The Coming of the Industrial Order: Town and Factory Life in Rural Massachusetts, 1810–1860* (1983); Ronald Schultz, *The Republic of Labor: Philadelphia Artisans and the Politics of Class* (1993); and Sean Wilentz, *Chants Democratic, New York City and the Rise of the American Working Class, 1788–1850* (1984). See also Christopher L. Tomlins, *Law, Labor and Ideology in the Early American Republic* (1993).

CHAPTER 12

General surveys of antebellum reform movements include Robert H. Abzug, *Cosmos Crumbling: American Reform and the Religious Imagination* (1994); C. S. Griffen, *The Ferment of Reform, 1830–1860* (1967); Alice F. Tyler, *Freedom's Ferment* (1944); and Ronald G. Walters, *American Reformers, 1815–1860* (1978).

Individualism

The leading study that connects transcendentalism with reform movements is Ann C. Rose, *Transcendentalism as a Social Movement, 1830–1850* (1981). See also Catherine L. Albanese, *Corresponding Motion: Transcendental Religion and the New America* (1977). Studies that link literary developments to reform themes and cultural history include Harold Kaplan, *Democratic Humanism and American Literature* (1972); David S. Reynolds, *Beneath the American Renaissance: The Subversive Imagination in the Age of Emerson and Melville* (1988) and *Walt Whitman's America: A Cultural Biography* (1995); R. Jackson Wilson, *Figures of Speech: American Writers and the Literary Marketplace, from Benjamin Franklin to Emily Dickinson* (1989); and Larzer Ziff, *Literary Democracy: The Declaration of Cultural Independence in America* (1981). On Margaret Fuller, see Paula Blanchard, *Margaret Fuller: From Transcendentalism to Revolution* (1978); Charles Capper, *Margaret Fuller: An American Romantic Life* (1992); and Joan von Mehren, *Minerva and the Muse: A Life of Margaret Fuller* (1995).

Communalism

On communitarian experiments, see Arthur Bestor, Jr., *Backwoods Utopias: The Sectarian and Owenite Phases of Communitarian Life in America* (1970); Lawrence Foster, *Religion and Sexuality: Three American Communal Experiments of the Nineteenth Century* (1981); Jean McMahon Humez, ed., *Gifts of Power: The Writings of Rebecca Jackson, Black Visionary, Shaker Eldress* (1981); Louis J. Kern, *An Ordered Love: Sex Roles and Sexuality in Victorian Utopias—The Shakers, the Mormons, and the Oneida Community* (1981); Spencer Klaw, *Without Sin: The Life and Death of the Oneida Community* (1995); Charles Nordhoff, *The Communistic Societies of the United States* (1875, reprinted 1960); and

Stephen J. Stein, *The Shaker Experience in America* (1992). On the Mormon experience, see James B. Allen and Glen M. Leonard, *The Story of the Latter-Day Saints* (1992); Leonard J. Arrington, *The Mormon Experience: A History of the Latter-Day Saints* (1992); John L. Brooke, *The Refiner's Fire: The Making of Mormon Cosmology, 1644–1844* (1994); Grant Underwood, *The Millennarian World of Early Mormonism* (1993); and Kenneth H. Winn, *Exiles in a Land of Liberty: Mormons in America, 1830–1846* (1989). On the linkages between religion and the utopians, see Paul E. Johnson and Sean Wilentz, *The Kingdom of Matthias: A Story of Sex and Salvation in 19th-Century America* (1995), and Timothy L. Smith, *Revivalism and Social Reform: American Protestantism on the Eve of the Civil War* (1980).

The Women's Movement

The most comprehensive history of women in the United States is Nancy Woloch, *Women and the American Experience* (1992). On the social history of women, see W. Elliot Brownlee and Mary M. Brownlee, *Women in the American Economy: A Documentary History, 1675–1929* (1976); Nancy F. Cott, *The Bonds of Womanhood: "Women's Sphere" in New England, 1780–1835* (1977); Carl N. Degler, *At Odds: Women and the Family in America from the Revolution to the Present* (1980); and Mary P. Ryan, *Cradle of the Middle Class: The Family in Oneida County, New York, 1790–1865* (1981). The most thorough description of the participation of women in benevolence and reform is Keith Melder, *Beginnings of Sisterhood: The American Women's Rights Movement, 1800–1850* (1977). For studies of more specific aspects of women's involvement in reform, see Barbara J. Berg, *The Remembered Gate: Origins of American Feminism: The Woman and the City, 1800–1860* (1978); Estelle B. Freedman, *Their Sisters' Keepers: Women's Prison Reform in America, 1830–1860* (1981); Lori D. Ginzberg, *Women and the Work of Benevolence: Morality, Politics, and Class in the Nineteenth-Century United States* (1990); Nancy A. Hewitt, *Women's Activism and Social Change: Rochester, New York, 1822–1872* (1984); and Jean F. Yellin, *Women and Sisters: The Antislavery Feminists in American Culture* (1989). On Dorothea Dix, see David Gollaher, *Voice for the Mad: The Life of Dorothea Dix* (1995), and Charles M. Snyder, *The Lady and the President: The Letters of Dorothea Dix and Millard Fillmore* (1975). The leading histories of feminists and the early women's rights movement include Kathleen Barry, *Susan B. Anthony—A Biography: A Singular Feminist* (1988); Ellen Du Bois, *Feminism and Suffrage: The Emergence of an Independent Women's Movement, 1848–1869* (1978); and Eleanor Flexner, *Century of Struggle: The Woman's Rights Movement in the United States* (1959).

Abolitionism

Surveys of antislavery reform include Robert H. Abzug, *Passionate Liberator: Theodore Dwight Weld and the Dilemma of Reform* (1980); David Brion Davis, *The Problems of Slavery in the Age of Revolution, 1770–1823* (1975); Louis Filler, *The Crusade against Slavery, 1830–1860* (1960); Stanley Harrold, *The Abolitionists and the South, 1831–1861* (1995); Leon F. Litwack, *North of Slavery: The Negro in the Free States, 1790–1860* (1961); Stephen B. Oates, *To Purge This Land with Blood: A Biography of John Brown* (1970); Lewis Perry, *Childhood, Marriage, and Reform: Henry Clarke Wright, 1797–1870* (1980); Benjamin Quarles, *Black Abolitionists* (1969); James B. Stewart, *Holy Warriors: The Abolitionists and American Slavery* (1976); John L. Thomas, *The Liberator: William*

Lloyd Garrison (1963); and Bertram Wyatt-Brown, *Lewis Tappan and the Evangelical War against Slavery* (1959). For the role of women in the antislavery movement, consult Edmund Fuller, *Prudence Crandall: An Incident of Racism in Nineteenth-Century America* (1971); Blanche Hersh, *The Slavery of Sex: Female Abolitionists in Nineteenth-Century America* (1978); Gerda Lerner, *The Grimké Sisters from South Carolina: Pioneers for Women's Rights and Abolition* (1967); and Alma Lutz, *Crusade for Freedom: Women of the Antislavery Movement* (1968). On northern hostility to abolition, see Leonard L. Richards, *"Gentlemen of Property and Standing": Anti-Abolition Mobs in Jacksonian America* (1970).

CHAPTER 13

Useful books on the social history of sections and sectionalism in the 1840s and 1850s include Stuart M. Blumin, *The Emergence of the Middle Class: Social Experience in the American City, 1760–1900* (1989); David Alan Johnson, *Founding the Far West: California, Oregon, and Nevada, 1840–1890* (1992); James Oakes, *The Ruling Race: A History of American Slaveholders* (1982); and William R. Taylor, *Cavalier and Yankee: The Old South and American National Character* (1961).

The Slave South: A Distinctive Society

The culture of the planter class and non-slaveholding whites can be explored in O. Vernon Burton, *In My Father's House Are Many Mansions: Family and Community in Edgefield, South Carolina* (1985); Drew Gilpin Faust, *Southern Stories: Slaveholders in Peace and War* (1992); Robert W. Fogel, *Without Consent or Contract* (1989); and Eugene Genovese, *The Slaveholder's Dilemma: Freedom and Progress in Southern Conservative Thought, 1820–1860* (1992). The best studies of women in southern slave society are Catherine Clinton, *The Plantation Mistress* (1983), and Elizabeth Fox-Genovese, *Within the Plantation Household: Black and White Women of the Old South* (1988). Catherine Clinton, ed., *Half Sisters of History: Southern Women and the American Past* (1994) is a collection of important articles. Efforts to connect southern culture with southern politics include George M. Frederickson, *White Supremacy: A Comparative Study in American and South African History* (1981), and J. Mills Thornton III, *Politics and Power in a Slave Society: Alabama, 1800–1860* (1978). On the nature of violence in southern society, see John Hope Franklin, *The Militant South 1800–1861* (1956), and Bertram Wyatt-Brown, *Southern Honor: Ethics and Behavior in the Old South* (1982).

On the role of family life and religion in helping African-Americans cope with the oppression of slavery, the pioneering studies were John W. Blassingame, *The Slave Community: Plantation Life in the Antebellum South* (1979); Albert J. Raboteau, *Slave Religion* (1978); Eugene D. Genovese, *Roll, Jordan, Roll* (1974); Herbert G. Gutman, *The Black Family in Slavery and Freedom, 1750–1925* (1976); and Lawrence W. Levine, *Black Culture and Black Consciousness* (1977). More recent studies include Jacqueline Jones, *Labor of Love, Labor of Sorrow: Black Women, Work, and the Family from Slavery to the Present* (1986), and Deborah G. White, *Ar'n't I a Woman? Female Slaves in the Plantation South* (1985).

On slave revolts, see Stephen B. Oates, *The Fires of Jubilee: Nat Turner's Fierce Rebellion* (1975), and Eugene D. Genovese, *From Rebellion to Revolution: Afro-American Slave*

Revolts in the Making of the Modern World (1979). On the ambiguous position of free blacks in a slave society, consult Ira Berlin, *Slaves without Masters: The Free Negro in the Antebellum South* (1974).

The Northeast: Industry and Culture

The economic changes in the North during the 1840s and 1850s can be studied in many of the economic history sources listed in Chapter 10. In addition, see Albert Fishlow, *American Railroads and the Transformation of the Ante-Bellum Economy* (1965).

On European immigration, consult Maldwyn Allen Jones, *American Immigration* (1960), and Philip Taylor, *The Distant Magnet: European Immigration to the U.S.A.* (1971). The most useful introduction to the nature of immigrant communities in the 1840s and 1850s is Oscar Handlin, *Boston's Immigrants: A Study in Acculturation* (1979). See also Kathleen Neils Conzen, *Immigrant Milwaukee, 1836–1860* (1976), and Bruce Laurie, *Working People in Philadelphia, 1800–1850* (1980).

Studies of women and popular literature include Ann Douglas, *The Feminization of American Culture* (1977), and Mary Kelley, *Private Woman, Public Stage: Literary Domesticity in Nineteenth-Century America* (1984). On birth control, see Linda Gordon, *Woman's Body, Woman's Rights: A Social History of Birth Control in America* (1976), and James Reed, *From Private Vice to Public Virtue: The Birth Control Movement and American Society since 1830* (1978). On educational reform, see Lawrence A. Cremin, *American Education: The National Experience, 1783–1876* (1980), and Carl F. Kaestle, *Pillars of the Republic: Common Schools and American Society, 1780–1860* (1983). See also Kathryn Kish Sklar, *Catharine Beecher: A Study in American Domesticity* (1973), a definitive biography.

The West: Manifest Destiny

Historians have recently begun to examine the development of the Midwest as a region. See Stephen Aron, *How the West Was Lost: The Transformation of Kentucky from Daniel Boone to Henry Clay* (1996); Andrew R. L. Cayton and Peter S. Onuf, *The Midwest and the Nation* (1990); and Nicole Etcheson, *The Emerging Midwest: Upland Southerners and the Political Culture of the Old Northwest, 1787–1861* (1996). See also William Cronon, *Nature's Metropolis* (1992).

Manifest Destiny is treated in Norman Graebner, *Empire on the Pacific: A Study of American Continental Expansion* (1955); Reginald Horsman, *Race and Manifest Destiny: The Origins of American Racial Anglo-Saxonism* (1981); and Frederick Merk, *Manifest Destiny and Mission in American History* (1963).

In recent years a number of books have opened up exciting new approaches to the history of western America. Leading examples include Patricia Nelson Limerick, *The Legacy of Conquest: The Unbroken Past of the Unbroken West* (1987); Clyde A. Milner II, *The Oxford History of the American West* (1994); David J. Weber, *The Mexican Frontier, 1821–1846* (1982); and Richard White, *"It's Your Misfortune and None of My Own": A History of the American West* (1991). This newer scholarship presents a more complete view of women in the West. See, for example, Susan Armitage and Elizabeth Jameson, eds., *The Women's West* (1987); John Mack Faragher, *Women and Men on the Overland Trail* (1979); Julie R. Jeffrey, *Frontier Women: The Trans-Mississippi West, 1840–1860* (1979); and Joanna L. Stratton, *Pioneer Women: Voices from the Kansas Frontier* (1981).

On the politics of expansion to the Pacific, see William J. Cooper, *The South and the Politics of Slavery, 1828–1856* (1978), and Charles G. Sellers, *James K. Polk: Continentalist, 1843–1846* (1966).

CHAPTER 14

Histories that discuss the disruption of the Union between the Mexican War and the onset of the Civil War in a comprehensive fashion are rare. The best is David M. Potter, *The Impending Crisis, 1848–1861* (1976).

War, Expansion, and Slavery, 1846–1850

Study of expansionism in the 1840s should begin with Frederick Merk, *The Monroe Doctrine and American Expansion, 1843–1849* (1972). On the coming of the Mexican War, consult Paul H. Bergeron, *The Presidency of James K. Polk* (1987); David Pletcher, *The Diplomacy of Annexation: Texas, Oregon, and the Mexican War* (1973); and Charles G. Sellers, *James K. Polk: Continentalist, 1843–1846* (1966). On the fighting of the war, see K. Jack Bauer, *The Mexican War, 1846–1848* (1974), and Otis A. Singletary, *The Mexican War* (1960). For an analysis of the relationship between the war experience and American culture, see Robert W. Johannsen, *To the Halls of the Montezumas: The Mexican War in the American Imagination* (1985), and John H. Schroeder, *Mr. Polk's War: American Opposition and Dissent* (1973). For the Mexican viewpoint, see Gene M. Brack, *Mexico Views Manifest Destiny, 1821–1846: An Essay on the Origins of the Mexican War* (1975). On congressional politics during the 1840s, see Chaplain Morrison, *Democratic Politics and Sectionalism: The Wilmot Proviso Controversy* (1967); Merrill Peterson, *The Great Triumvirate: Webster, Clay, and Calhoun* (1987); and Joel H. Silbey, *The Shrine of Party: Congressional Voting Behavior, 1841–1852* (1967). On the Compromise of 1850, see Holman Hamilton, *Prologue to Conflict: The Crisis and Compromise of 1850* (1964). For an interpretation stressing the contingency of the South's commitment to the Union, consult William W. Freehling, *The Road to Disunion: Secessionists at Bay, 1776–1854* (1991).

The End of the Second Party System, 1850–1858

General studies of sectional conflict in the 1850s include Avery O. Craven, *The Growth of Southern Nationalism* (1953). On the Fugitive Slave Act, consult Stanley W. Campbell, *The Slave Catchers* (1970). The best study of the politics of southern expansionism is Robert E. May, *The Southern Dream of a Caribbean Empire, 1854–1861* (1973). The leading studies of Frederick Douglass include Nathan I. Huggins, *Slave and Citizen: The Life of Frederick Douglass* (1980), and William S. McFeely, *Frederick Douglass* (1991). Essential sources on Douglass include *The Narrative of the Life of Frederick Douglass, An American Slave* (1845) and *Life and Times of Frederick Douglass, Written by Himself* (1881).

On the development of the Republican party, see Eric Foner, *Free Soil, Free Labor, Free Men: The Ideology of the Republican Party before the Civil War* (1970), and William E. Gienapp, *The Origins of the Republican Party, 1852–1856* (1987). The crisis over Kansas is discussed in James A. Rawley, *Race and Politics: Bleeding Kansas and the Coming of the Civil War* (1969), and Gerald W. Wolff, *The Kansas-Nebraska Bill: Party, Section, and the*

Coming of the Civil War (1977). On the Buchanan administration, see Kenneth M. Stampp, *America in 1857: A Nation on the Brink* (1990). On Dred Scott, see Don E. Fehrenbacher, *The Dred Scott Case: Its Significance in American Law and Politics* (1978). For a biography of Stephen A. Douglas, see Robert W. Johannsen, *Stephen A. Douglas* (1973). The best biography of John Brown is Stephen Oates, *To Purge this Land with Blood: A Biography of John Brown* (1970).

Abraham Lincoln and the End of Union, 1858–1860

The fate of the Democratic party is discussed in Roy F. Nichols, *The Disruption of American Democracy* (1948), and Michael Holt, *The Political Crisis of the 1850s* (1978). Abraham Lincoln has inspired a host of biographies. Classic studies include James G. Randall, *Mr. Lincoln* (1957); Carl Sandburg, *Abraham Lincoln: The Prairie Years* (1929); and Benjamin Thomas, *Abraham Lincoln: A Biography* (1952). The most recent major biography of Lincoln is David Herbert Donald, *Lincoln* (1995). For a stimulating set of essays, see Richard N. Current, *The Lincoln Nobody Knows* (1958). The most valuable book on Lincoln's formative political years is Don E. Fehrenbacher, *Prelude to Greatness: Lincoln in the 1850s* (1962). For other interpretations, see George B. Forgie, *Patricide and the House Divided* (1979); Stephen Oates, *With Malice toward None: A Life of Abraham Lincoln* (1977); and Garry Wills, *Lincoln at Gettysburg* (1992).

CHAPTER 15

The best up-to-date, comprehensive one-volume surveys of the Civil War are James M. McPherson's *Battle Cry of Freedom: The Civil War Era* (1988) and *Ordeal by Fire: The Civil War and Reconstruction* (1993). An excellent brief survey is Charles P. Roland, *An American Iliad: The Story of the Civil War* (1991). For a compelling older survey, see Shelby Foote, *The Civil War: A Narrative*, 3 vols. (1958–1974).

Secession and Military Stalemate, 1861–1863

Classic studies of the secession crisis include Richard N. Current, *Lincoln and the First Shot* (1963); David M. Potter, *Lincoln and His Party in the Secession Crisis, 1860–61* (1950); and Kenneth M. Stampp, *And the War Came: The North and the Secession Crisis, 1860–61* (1950). Histories of the secession of the Deep South include William L. Barney, *The Secessionist Impulse: Alabama and Mississippi in 1860* (1974), and Michael P. Johnson, *Toward a Patriarchal Republic: The Secession of Georgia* (1977). On the Upper South, see Daniel Crofts, *Reluctant Confederates: Upper South Unionists in the Secession Crisis* (1989).

Toward Total War

To study northern society and politics during the war, consult Iver Bernstein, *The New York City Draft Riots* (1990); Gabor S. Boritt, ed., *Lincoln the War President: The Gettysburg Lectures* (1992); George M. Fredrickson, *The Inner Civil War: Northern Intellectuals and the Crisis of Union* (2d ed., 1993); J. Matthew Gallman, *The North Fights the Civil War: The Home Front* (1994); Mary E. Massey, *Bonnet Brigades: American Women and the Civil War* (1966); Mark E. Neely, Jr., *The Fate of Liberty: Abraham Lincoln and Civil Liberties* (1991);

Phillip S. Paludan, *The Presidency of Abraham Lincoln* (1994); Susan M. Reverby, *Ordered to Care: The Dilemma of American Nursing, 1850–1945* (1987); Joel Silbey, *A Respectable Minority: The Democratic Party in the Civil War Era* (1977); Hans Trefousse, *The Radical Republicans* (1969); and Garry Wills, *Lincoln at Gettysburg* (1992). Important biographies of Union leaders include Michael Fellman, *Citizen Sherman: A Life of William Tecumseh Sherman* (1995); William McFeely, *Grant: A Biography* (1981); Stephen B. Oates, *With Malice towards None: The Life of Abraham Lincoln* (1977); Stephen W. Sears, *George B. McClellan: The Young Napoleon* (1988); and the Abraham Lincoln studies cited in Chapter 14.

Among the best histories of the Confederacy are George C. Rable, *The Confederate Republic: A Revolution against Politics* (1994), and Emory M. Thomas, *The Confederate Nation: 1861–1865* (1979). Important biographies of leading Confederates include William C. Davis, *Jefferson Davis, the Man and His Hour: A Biography* (1991), and Thomas E. Schott, *Alexander H. Stephens of Georgia: A Biography* (1988).

Studies of the Confederacy include Paul Escott, *After Secession: Jefferson Davis and the Failure of Southern Nationalism* (1978); Drew Gilpin Faust, *The Creation of Confederate Nationalism: Ideology and Identity in the Civil War* (1988); and Philip S. Paludan, *Victims: A True History of the Civil War* (1981).

The Turning Point: 1863

Studies of wartime emancipation include Herman Belz, *A New Birth of Freedom: The Republican Party and Freedmen's Rights, 1861–1866* (1976); John Hope Franklin, *The Emancipation Proclamation* (1963); Louis S. Gerteis, *From Contraband to Freedom: Federal Policy toward Southern Blacks, 1861–1865* (1973); and James M. McPherson, *The Struggle for Equality: Abolitionists and the Negro in the Civil War and Reconstruction* (1964). The best scholarship on the lives of slaves during the war is found in Ira Berlin et al., eds., *Freedom: A Documentary History of Emancipation, 1861–1867*, Series I, Volume I: *The Destruction of Slavery* (1985), and Series I, Volume III: *The Wartime Genesis of Free Labor: The Lower South* (1990).

The Union Victorious, 1864–1865

The most useful introduction to the military aspects of the war is T. Harry Williams, *The History of American Wars* (1981). On the experiences of Civil War soldiers, see Albert Castel, *Decision in the West: The Atlanta Campaign* (1992); Gerald F. Linderman, *Embattled Courage: The Experience of Combat in the American Civil War* (1987); James M. McPherson, *What They Fought For, 1861–1865* (1994); and Reid Mitchell, *Civil War Soldiers* (1988) and *The Vacant Chair: The Northern Soldier Leaves Home* (1993). On the participation of African-Americans in the war, see Ira Berlin et al., eds., *Freedom: A Documentary History of Emancipation, 1861–1867*, Series II: *The Black Military Experience* (1982), and Joseph T. Glatthaar, *Forged in Battle: The Civil War Alliance of Black Soldiers and White Officers* (1990). On Confederate military tactics, see Grady McWhiney and Perry D. Jamieson, *Attack and Die: Civil War Military Tactics and the Southern Heritage* (1982), and Steven E. Woodworth, *Jefferson Davis and His Generals: The Failure of Confederate Command in the West* (1990). An innovative exploration of the dynamics of violence is found in Charles Royster, *The Destructive War: William Tecumseh Sherman, Stonewall Jackson, and the Americans* (1991). The most graphic account of a single battle is Stephen W. Sears, *Landscape Turned Red: The Battle of Antietam* (1983). On the Civil

War in the Far West, consult Alvin M. Josephy, Jr., *The Civil War in the American West* (1991). For insightful analyses of the war's outcome, see Richard E. Beringer et al., *Why the South Lost the Civil War* (1986); Herman Hattaway and Archer Jones, *How the North Won: A Military History of the Civil War* (1983); and Archer Jones, *Civil War Command and Strategy: The Process of Victory and Defeat* (1992).

CHAPTER 16

The starting point for the study of Reconstruction is Eric Foner's major synthesis, *Reconstruction: America's Unfinished Revolution, 1863–1877* (1988), which is also available in a shorter version. Two older surveys that provide useful introductions are John Hope Franklin, *Reconstruction: After the Civil War* (1961), and Kenneth M. Stampp, *The Era of Reconstruction* (1965). *Black Reconstruction in America* (1935), by the black activist and scholar W. E. B. Du Bois, deserves attention as the first book to challenge traditional racist interpretations of Reconstruction as carpetbagger rule unjustly imposed on the defeated South by Radical Republicans.

Presidential Reconstruction

For important studies of presidential efforts to rebuild the Union, see the books on Abraham Lincoln listed in Chapter 15 and the following works on Andrew Johnson: Albert Castel, *The Presidency of Andrew Johnson* (1979); Eric L. McKitrick, *Andrew Johnson and Reconstruction* (1960); and James Sefton, *Andrew Johnson and the Uses of Constitutional Power* (1979). On the Radical resistance to presidential Reconstruction, see James M. McPherson, *The Struggle for Equality: Abolitionists and the Negro in the Civil War and Reconstruction* (1965). Books that focus on Congress include LaWanda Cox and John H. Cox, *Politics, Principle, and Prejudice, 1865–1867* (1963); David Donald, *The Politics of Reconstruction, 1863–1867* (1965); and William B. Brock, *An American Crisis: Congress and Reconstruction, 1865–1867* (1963). For insight into developments in the South, see Dan T. Carter, *When the War Was Over: The Failure of Self-Reconstruction in the South, 1865–1867* (1985). Michael Perman, *Reunion without Compromise: The South and Reconstruction, 1865–1868* (1973), stresses the South's handling of Johnson. On the freedmen, Willie Lee Rose, *Rehearsal for Reconstruction: The Port Royal Experiment* (1964); Peter Kolchin, *First Freedom: The Responses of Alabama's Blacks to Emancipation and Reconstruction* (1972); Leon F. Litwack, *Been in the Storm So Long: The Aftermath of Slavery* (1979); Ira Berlin et al., eds., *Freedom: A Documentary History of Emancipation, 1861–1867: The Wartime Genesis of Free Labor* (1990); Berlin et al., eds., *Slaves No More: Three Essays on Emancipation and the Civil War* (1992); Julie Saville, *The Work of Reconstruction: From Slave to Wage Laborer in South Carolina, 1860–1870* (1994). Jacqueline Jones, *Labor of Love, Labor of Sorrow: Black Women, Work, and the Family from Slavery to the Present* (1985), is a pioneering work on the impact of emancipation on black women.

Radical Reconstruction

For Congress's role in radical Reconstruction, see Michael Les Benedict, *A Compromise of Principle: Congressional Republicans and Reconstruction* (1974), and Hans L. Trefousse, *Impeachment of a President: Andrew Johnson, the Blacks, and Reconstruction* (1975). William

S. McFeely, *Grant: A Biography* (1981), deftly explains the politics of Reconstruction. Also helpful is Brooks D. Simpson, *Let Us Have Peace: Ulysses S. Grant and the Politics of War and Reconstruction, 1861–1868* (1991). State studies of Reconstruction include Richard Lowe, *Republicans and Reconstruction in Virginia, 1856–1870* (1991), and Otto Olsen, ed., *Reconstruction and Redemption in the South* (1980). The best account of carpetbaggers is Richard N. Current, *Those Terrible Carpetbaggers: A Reinterpretation* (1988). On blacks during radical Reconstruction, see Joel Williamson, *After Slavery: The Negro in South Carolina during Reconstruction, 1861–1877* (1965); Robert Cruden, *The Negro in Reconstruction* (1969); Thomas Holt, *Black over White: Negro Political Leadership in South Carolina during Reconstruction* (1977); and Barry A. Crouch, *The Freedmen's Bureau and Black Texans* (1992). Other studies covering southern race relations over a longer time span include John Blassingame, *Black New Orleans, 1860–1880* (1973); Howard N. Rabinowitz, *Race Relations in the Urban South, 1865–1890* (1977); Barbara Fields, *Slavery and Freedom on the Middle Ground: Maryland during the Nineteenth Century* (1985); and Jonathan M. Bryant, *How Curious a Land: Conflict and Change in Greene County, Georgia, 1850–1885* (1996).

Redemption

The most thorough study of the Ku Klux Klan is Allen W. Trelease, *White Terror: The Ku Klux Klan Conspiracy and Southern Reconstruction* (1972). To survey Reconstruction politics in the South, consult Michael Perman, *The Road to Redemption: Southern Politics, 1869–1879* (1984). On politics in the North, see Eugene H. Berwanger, *The West and Reconstruction* (1981); James Mohr, ed., *The Radical Republicans in the North: State Politics during Reconstruction* (1976); and William Gillette, *Retreat from Reconstruction, 1863–1879* (1979). The emergence of the sharecropping system is explored in Roger L. Ransom and Richard Sutch, *One Kind of Freedom: The Economic Consequences of Emancipation* (1977); Jay Mandle, *The Roots of Black Poverty: The Southern Plantation Economy after the Civil War* (1978); Gavin Wright, *Old South, New South: Revolutions in the Southern Economy since the Civil War* (1986); Edward Royce, *The Origins of Southern Sharecropping* (1993); Harold Woodman, *New South, New Law: The Legal Foundations of Credit and Labor Relations in the Postbellum Agricultural South* (1995). On yeomen farmers, consult Steven Hahn, *The Roots of Southern Populism: Yeoman Farmers and the Transformation of the Georgia Upcountry, 1850–1890* (1983). For the impact of Reconstruction on the national state, see Morton Keller, *Affairs of State: Public Life in Late Nineteenth-Century America* (1977), and Richard F. Bensel, *Yankee Leviathan: The Origins of Central State Authority in America, 1859–1877* (1990). On political corruption, see Mark W. Summers, *The Era of Good Stealings* (1993). On the Compromise of 1877, see C. Vann Woodward's classic *Reunion and Reaction* (1956), and K. I. Polakoff, *The Politics of Inertia: The Election of 1876 and the End of Reconstruction* (1973).

CHAPTER 17

Western history has become a bitterly contested ground in recent years. The fountainhead of the voluminous traditional scholarship is Frederick Jackson Turner's famous essay "The Significance of the Frontier in American History" (1893), reprinted in Ray A. Billington, ed., *Frontier and Section: Selected Essays of Frederick Jackson Turner* (1961). The "new" western history is critical of Turnerian scholarship for being "Eurocentric"—for seeing western history only through the eyes of frontiersmen and settlers—and for masking the rapacious and environmentally destructive underside of western settlement. Patricia N. Limerick's skillfully argued *The Legacy of Conquest: The Unbroken Past of the American West* (1987) opened the debate. Richard White, *"It's Your Misfortune and None of My Own": A New History of the American West* (1991), provides the fullest synthesis of the new scholarship. For an authoritative, balanced treatment of the main themes of western history, see the essays in Clyde A. Milner II et al., *The Oxford History of the American West* (1994). On women's experience—another primary concern of the new western history—the starting point is Susan Armitage and Elizabeth Jameson, eds., *The Women's West* (1987). There are incisive environmental essays in Donald Worster, *Under Western Skies: Nature and History in the American West* (1992).

The Great Plains

The classic book, stressing the settlers' adaptation to climate and environment, is Walter P. Webb, *The Great Plains* (1931). Robert M. Utley, *The Indian Frontier of the American West, 1846–1890* (1984), is a good introduction; Robert H. Lowie, *Indians of the Great Plains* (1954), is a classic anthropological study. On the religious life of the Plains Indians, see Howard L. Harrod, *Renewing the World: Plains Indians Religion and Morality* (1987). The assault on Indian culture is told in Fredrick E. Hoxie, *A Final Promise: The Campaign to Assimilate the Indians, 1880–1920* (1984). On phases of plains settlement see Oscar Winther, *The Transportation Frontier: The Trans-Mississippi West, 1865–1890* (1964); Lewis Atherton, *The Cattle Kings* (1964); Gilbert Fite, *The Farmer's Frontier, 1865–1900* (1966); and Mary W. M. Hargreaves, *Dry-Farming in the Northern Great Plains* (1954). Ecological impact is subtly probed in Frieda Knobloch, *The Culture of Wilderness: Agriculture as Colonization in the American West* (1996). The peopling of the plains can be explored in Craig Miner, *West of Wichita: Settling the High Plains of Kansas, 1865–1890* (1986); Frederick C. Luebke, ed., *Ethnicity and the Great Plains* (1980); Nell Irvin Painter, *Exodusters: Black Migration to Kansas after Reconstruction* (1976); Julie Roy Jeffrey, *Frontier Women: The Trans-Mississippi West, 1840–1880*; Deborah Fink, *Agrarian Women: Wives and Mothers in Rural Nebraska, 1880–1940* (1992); and Elaine Lindgren, *Land in Her Own Name: Women as Homesteaders in North Dakota* (1991). On the integration of the plains economy with the wider world, an especially rich book is William Cronon, *Nature's Metropolis: Chicago and the Great West* (1991). Richard Slotkin, *The Fatal Environment: The Myth of the Frontier in the Age of Industrialization, 1800–1890* (1985), deals with the process by which Americans translated the hard realities of conquering the West into a national mythology.

The Far West

The best book on western mining is Rodman Paul, *Mining Frontiers of the Far West: 1848–1880s* (1963). An important case study of women in a mining town is Paula Petrik, *Women and Family on the Rocky Mountain Frontier: Helena, Monotana, 1865–1900* (1987). On western miners the standard book is Mark Wyman, *Hard Rock Epic: Western Miners and the Industrial Revolution, 1860–1910* (1979); and on the western labor movement, an important new interpretation is David Brundage, *The Making of Western Working-Class Radicalism: Denver's Organized Workers, 1878–1905* (1994). Two valuable regional histories are Carlos A. Schwantes, *The Pacific Northwest: An Interpretive History* (1989), and David Alan Johnson, *Founding the Far West: California, Oregon, and*

Nevada (1992). A very imaginative recent treatment of the New Mexico peasantry is Sarah Deutsch, *No Separate Refuge* (1987). On Hispanic Texas an important book is David Montejano, *Anglos and Mexicans in the Making of Texas* (1987). Important local studies of laboring Hispanics and their communities are Mario T. Garcia, *Desert Immigrants: The Mexicans of El Paso, 1880–1920* (1981), and Richard Griswold del Castillo, *The Los Angeles Barrio, 1850–1890* (1979). On the Asian migration to America, the best introduction is Ronald Takaki, *Strangers from a Different Shore: A History of Asian Americans* (1989), which can be supplemented with Gunther Barth, *Bitter Strength: A History of the Chinese in the United States, 1850–1870* (1964), and Sucheng Chan, *This Bittersweet Soil: The Chinese in California Agriculture, 1860–1910* (1986). Labor's opposition to the Chinese is skillfully treated in Alexander Saxton, *The Indispensable Enemy: Labor and the Anti-Chinese Movement in California* (1971). Kevin Starr, *California and the American Dream, 1850–1915* (1973), provides a comprehensive account of the emergence of a distinctive California culture.

CHAPTER 18

The most useful introduction to the economic history of this period is Edward C. Kirkland, *Industry Comes of Age, 1860–1897* (1961). A more sophisticated analysis can be found in W. Elliot Brownlee, *Dynamics of Ascent* (rev. ed., 1979). For essays on many of the topics covered in this chapter, consult Glenn Porter, ed., *Encyclopedia of American Economic History* (3 vols., 1980).

Industrial Capitalism Triumphant

On railroads a convenient introduction is John F. Stover, *American Railroads* (1970). The growth of the railroads as an integrated system has been treated in George R. Taylor and Irene D. Neu, *The American Railway Network, 1861–1890* (1956). Julius Grodinsky, *Jay Gould: His Business Career, 1867–1892* (1957), is a complex study demonstrating the contributions this railroad buccaneer made to the transportation system. Books such as Grodinsky's have gone a long way to resurrect Gilded Age businessmen from the debunking tradition first set forth with great power in Matthew Josephson, *Robber Barons: Great American Fortunes* (1934). Peter Temin, *Iron and Steel in the Nineteenth Century* (1964), is the best treatment of that industry. Joseph F. Wall, *Andrew Carnegie* (1970), is the definitive biography of the great steelmaker. Equally definitive on the oil king is Allan Nevins, *A Study in Power: John D. Rockefeller* (2 vols., 1953). On the development of mass production the key book is David A. Hounsell, *From the American System to Mass Production, 1800–1932* (1984). Alfred D. Chandler, *The Visible Hand: The Managerial Revolution in American Business* (1977), is not an easy book but will amply repay the labors of interested students.

On the New South the standard work has long been C. Vann Woodward, *Origins of the New South, 1877–1913* (1951). Equally essential as a modern reconsideration is Edward L. Ayers, *The Promise of the New South: Life after Reconstruction* (1992). A brilliant reinterpretation of the causes of the South's economic retardation is Gavin Wright, *Old South, New South: Revolutions in the Southern Economy since the Civil War* (1986). Jacqueline Jones, *The Dispossessed: America's Underclasses from the Civil War to the Present* (1992), contains an excellent treatment of southern labor.

The World of Work

To understand the impact of industrialism on American workers, three collections of essays make the best starting points: Herbert G. Gutman, *Work, Culture and Society in Industrializing America* (1976); Michael S. Frisch and Daniel J. Walkowitz, eds., *Working-Class America: Essays on Labor, Community and American Society* (1983); and Leon Fink, *In Search of the Working Class* (1994). On the introduction of Taylorism, the most useful book is Daniel Nelson, *Managers and Workers: Origins of the New Factory System* (2d ed., 1995). The impact of Taylorism on American workers is treated with insight in David Montgomery, *The Fall of the House of Labor: The Workplace, the State, and American Labor Activism, 1865–1925* (1987).

Two valuable collections of essays on immigrant workers are Richard Ehrlich, ed., *Immigrants in Industrial America* (1977), and Dirk Hoerder, ed., *American Labor and Immigration History, 1877–1920: Recent European Research* (1983). John Bodnar, *Immigration and Industrialization: Ethnicity in an American Mill Town* (1977), is an important case study of a single community. On women workers the best introduction is Alice Kessler-Harris, *Out to Work* (1982). Ava Baron, ed., *Work Engendered: Toward a New History of American Labor* (1991), is a rich collection of essays that apply gender analysis to the history of working people. On black workers useful introductions are William H. Harris, *The Harder We Run: Black Workers Since the Civil War* (1982), and Philip S. Foner, *Organized Labor and the Black Worker* (1974). Walter Licht, *Getting Work: Philadelphia, 1840–1950* (1992), is a pioneering history of a labor market in operation.

The Labor Movement

The standard book on the struggle between labor reform and trade unionism is Gerald N. Grob, *Workers and Utopia, 1865–1900* (1961). For the Knights of Labor, it should be supplemented by Leon Fink, *Workingmen's Democracy: The Knights of Labor and American Politics* (1983), which captures the cultural dimensions of labor reform not seen by earlier historians. The place of labor in the political environment is the subject of David Montgomery, *Citizen Worker* (1993). Paul Krause, *The Battle for Homestead, 1880–1892* (1992), puts the great strike in a larger social context. The most recent survey, incorporating much of the latest scholarship, is Bruce Laurie, *Artisans into Workers: Labor in Nineteenth Century America* (1989).

The founder of the AFL is the subject of a lively brief biography by Harold Livesay, *Samuel Gompers and Organized Labor in America* (1978). Among the many books on individual unions, Robert Christie, *Empire in Wood* (1956), best reveals the way pure-and-simple unionism worked out in practice. On industrial conflict, the most vivid book is Robert V. Bruce, *1877: Year of Violence* (1959). The best book on the IWW is Melvyn Dubofsky, *We Shall Be All* (1969). On socialism, David Shannon, *The Socialist Party of America* (1955), remains the standard account. There is, however, a fine biography of that party's leader that supersedes previous studies: Nick Salvatore, *Eugene V. Debs: Citizen and Socialist* (1982). A dimension of American radicalism long neglected has received sensitive attention in Mari Jo Buhle, *Women and American Socialism, 1870–1920* (1982).

CHAPTER 19

The best introductions to American politics in the late nineteenth century are John A. Garraty, *The New Commonwealth, 1877–1890* (1968), and R. Hal Williams, *Years of*

Decision: American Politics in the 1890s (1978). More detailed and comprehensive is Morton Keller, *Affairs of State: Public Life in Late Nineteenth-Century America* (1977). Joel L. Silbey, *The American Political Nation, 1838–1893* (1991), focuses on the party system and political behavior.

The Politics of the Status Quo, 1877–1893

Various aspects of national politics are discussed in Robert D. Marcus, *Grand Old Party: Political Structure in the Gilded Age* (1971); J. Rogers Hollingsworth, *The Whirligig of Politics: The Democracy of Cleveland and Bryan* (1963); H. Wayne Morgan, *From Hayes to McKinley: National Party Politics, 1877–1896* (1969); and David J. Rothman, *Politics and Power: The Senate, 1869–1901* (1966). On the development of public administration, see Leonard D. White, *The Republican Era, 1869–1901* (1958), and Stephen Skowronek, *Building a New American State: The Expansion of National Administrative Capacities* (1982).

The ideological basis for conservative national politics is fully treated in Sidney Fine, *Laissez Faire and the General Welfare State, 1865–1901* (1956); Robert G. Mc-Closkey, *American Conservatism in the Age of Enterprise* (1951); and the opening section of Morton J. Horwitz, *The Transformation of American Law, 1870–1960* (1992). On the popular sources of political participation, see especially Michael E. McGerr, *The Decline of Popular Politics: The American North, 1865–1928* (1986), and Paul Kleppner, *The Third Electoral Party System, 1853–1892: Parties, Voters, and Political Cultures* (1979). On the Mugwump reformers, see John G. Sproat, *The "Best Men": Liberal Reformers in the Gilded Age* (1965); and Ari Hoogenboom, *Outlawing the Spoils: The Civil Service Reform Movement, 1865–1883* (1961). The existence of a women's political culture in the late nineteenth century can be traced in Carl N. Degler, *At Odds: Women and the Family from the Revolution to the Present* (1979). A valuable book setting the stage is Ellen Carol Du Bois, *Feminism and Suffrage: The Emergence of an Independent Women's Movement in America, 1848–1869* (1978).

The Crisis of American Politics: The 1890s

The most recent synthesis on Populism is Robert C. McMath, *American Populism* (1993). Richard D. Hofstadter, *The Age of Reform* (1955), stresses the darker side of Populism, in which intolerance and paranoia figure heavily. Hofstadter's thesis, which once dominated debate among historians, has given way to a much more positive assessment. The key book here is Lawrence Goodwyn, *Democratic Promise: The Populist Moment in America* (1976), which argues that Populism was a broadly based radical response to industrial capitalism. Peter H. Argesinger, *The Limits of Agrarian Radicalism: Western Politics and American Politics* (1995), stresses the capacity of the political status quo to frustrate western Populism. Two stimulating books that follow the history of Populism into the twentieth century are Grant McConnell, *The Decline of Agrarian Democracy* (1953), which focuses on farm organizations, and Michael Kazin, *The Populist Persuasion* (1995), which describes how the language of Populism entered the discourse of mainstream American politics.

The money question is elucidated in Walter Nugent, *Money and American Society, 1865–1880* (1968), and Allan Weinstein, *Prelude to Populism: Origins of the Silver Issue* (1970). On the politics of the 1890s, see especially Robert F. Durden, *Climax of Populism: The Election of 1896* (1965), and Paul W. Glad, *McKinley, Bryan, and the People* (1964).

Race and Politics in the South

On southern politics the seminal book for the post-Reconstruction period is C. Vann Woodward, *Origins of the New South, 1877–1913* (1951), which still defines the terms of discussion among historians. The most far-reaching revision is Edward L. Ayers, *The Promise of the New South* (1992). Complementary books on the social basis of southern politics are Dwight B. Billings, *Planters and the Making of "New South": North Carolina, 1865–1900* (1979), and Paul Escott, *Many Excellent People: Power and Privilege in North Carolina, 1850–1900* (1985).

The classic book on segregation is C. Vann Woodward, *The Strange Career of Jim Crow* (2d ed., 1968), but it should be supplemented by Howard N. Rabinowitz, *Race Relations in the Urban South, 1865–1890* (1978). A powerful analysis of southern racism, stressing its psychosocial roots, is Joel Williamson, *A Rage for Order: Black/ White Relations in the American South since Emancipation* (1986). Disfranchisement is treated with great analytic sophistication in J. Morgan Kousser, *The Shaping of Southern Politics: Suffrage Restriction and the Establishment of the One-Party South, 1880–1910* (1974), and as an aspect of progressivism in Jack Temple Kirby, *Darkness at the Dawning: Race and Reform in the Progressive South* (1972). August Meier, *Negro Thought in America, 1880–1915* (1963), is a key analysis of black accommodation and protest. The preeminent exponent of accommodation is the subject of a superb two-volume biography by Louis B. Harlan, *Booker T. Washington: The Making of a Black Leader* (1973) and *Wizard of Tuskegee* (1983); and equally fine on Washington's main critic is David Levering Lewis, *W. E. B. Du Bois: Biography of a Race 1868–1919* (1993).

CHAPTER 20

Useful introductions to urban history are Charles N. Glaab and A. Theodore Brown, *A History of Urban America* (1967), and Arthur M. Schlesinger, *The Rise of the City* (1936), a pioneering study; and Blake McKelvey, *The Urbanization of America, 1860–1915* (1963). A sampling of the innovative scholarship that opened new historical paths can be found in Stephan Thernstrom and Richard Sennett, eds., *Nineteenth-Century Cities: Essays in the New Urban History* (1969).

Urbanization

Allan Pred, *Spatial Dynamics of U.S. Urban Growth, 1800–1914* (1971), traces the patterns in which cities grew. On the revolution in urban transit, see the pioneering book by Sam B. Warner, *Streetcar Suburbs: The Process of Growth in Boston, 1870–1900* (1962). In a subsequent work, *The Private City: Philadelphia in Three Periods* (1968), Warner broadened his analysis to show how private decision making shaped the character of the American city. Innovations in urban construction are treated in Carl Condit, *American Building Art: Nineteenth Century* (1969) and *Chicago School of Architecture* (1964); Robert C. Twombly, *Louis Sullivan* (1986); Alan Trachtenberg, *The Brooklyn Bridge* (1965); and Harold L. Platt, *The Electric City: Energy and the Growth of the Chicago Area, 1880–1930* (1991). The problems of meeting basic human needs are treated in Jon C. Teaford, *The Unheralded Triumph: City Government in America, 1870–1900* (1984); Eric H. Monkkonen, *Police in Urban America, 1860–1920* (1981); and David B. Tyack, *The One Best System: A History of American Urban Education* (1974). The struggle to reshape the chaotic nineteenth-century city can be explored in John D. Fairchild, *The*

Mysteries of the Great City: The Politics of Urban Design, 1877–1937 (1993); William H. Wilson, *The City Beautiful Movement in Kansas City* (1964); and David Schuyler, *The New Urban Landscape: The Redefinition of City Form in Nineteenth-Century America* (1986).

City People

Among the leading books on immigrants and the city are Moses Rischin, *The Promised City: New York's Jews, 1870–1914* (1962); Joseph Barton, *Peasants and Strangers: Italians, Rumanians, and Slovaks in an American City, 1890–1950* (1975); and Humbert S. Nelli, *The Italians in Chicago, 1860–1920* (1970). On blacks in the city, see Gilbert Osofsky, *Harlem: The Making of a Ghetto, 1890–1930* (1966); Allan H. Spear, *Black Chicago, 1860–1920* (1966); and Kenneth L. Kusmer, *A Ghetto Takes Shape: Black Cleveland, 1870–1930* (1976). David C. Hammack, *Power and Society: Greater New York at the Turn of the Century* (1982), is a sophisticated treatment that places the party machine in the larger context of municipal power politics. The encounter of Protestantism with the city is treated in Henry F. May, *Protestant Churches and Urban America* (1949); Aaron I. Abell, *The Urban Impact on American Protestantism* (1943); and William G. McLoughlin, *Modern Revivalism* (1959). On the Catholic Church, see Robert D. Cross, *The Emergence of Liberal Catholicism in America* (1958). Aspects of an emerging city culture are studied in Gunther Barth, *City People: The Rise of Modern City Culture in Nineteenth-Century America* (1982); Susan Porter Benson, *Counter Cultures: Saleswomen, Managers, and Customers in American Department Stores, 1890–1940* (1986); John F. Kasson, *Amusing the Million: Coney Island at the Turn of the Century* (1978); Timothy J. Gilfoyle, *City of Eros: New York City, Prostitution and the Commercialization of Sex, 1790–1920* (1991); Kathy Peiss, *Cheap Amusements: Working Women and Leisure in Turn-of-the-Century New York* (1986); and David Nasaw, *Going Out: The Rise and Fall of Public Amusements* (1993). George Chauncey, *Gay New York: Gender, Urban Culture, and the Making of the Gay New York World, 1890–1940* (1994), reveals a terrain hitherto invisible to the historian.

Upper Class/Middle Class

Urban social mobility is the focus of Stephan Thernstrom, *The Other Bostonians: Poverty and Progress in an American City, 1880–1970* (1973), which also contains a useful summary of mobility research on other cities. On the social elite see Frederic C. Jaher, *The Urban Establishment: Upper Strata in Boston, New York, Charleston, Chicago, and Los Angeles* (1982). Two recent books greatly advance our understanding of the urban middle class: Stuart S. Blumin, *The Emergence of the Middle Class: Social Experience in the American City, 1760–1900* (1989), and Olivier Zunz, *Making Corporate America, 1870–1920* (1990). Aspects of middle-class life are revealed in Margaret Marsh, *Suburban Lives* (1990); Gwendolyn Wright, *Moralism and the Model Home: Domestic Architecture and Cultural Conflict in Chicago, 1873–1913* (1980); Susan Strasser, *Never Done: A History of American Housework* (1983); John F. Kasson, *Rudeness and Civility: Manners in Nineteenth-Century America* (1990); and, on the entry of immigrants into the middle class, Andrew R. Heinze, *Adapting to Abundance: Jewish Immigrants, Mass Consumption, and the Search for American Identity* (1990). Contemporary notions of sexuality are skillfully captured in John S. Haller and Robin M. Haller, *The Physician and Sexuality in Victorian America* (1980). Whether those views actually applied to the private world of the middle class is strongly questioned in Karen Lystra, *The Searching Heart: Women, Men, and Romantic*

Love in Nineteenth-Century America (1989). Control over reproduction is fully explored in Janet Farrell Brodie, *Contraception and Abortion in Nineteenth-Century America* (1994). On the fostering of high culture in the American city, see Daniel M. Fox, *Engines of Culture: Philanthropy and Art Museums* (1963). The best introduction to intellectual currents in the emerging urban society is Alan Trachtenberg, *The Incorporation of America: Culture and Society, 1865–1893* (1983).

CHAPTER 21

The most recent survey of the Progressive Era is John Milton Cooper, *Pivotal Decades: The United States, 1900–1920* (1990). Two older but still serviceable narrative accounts are George E. Mowry, *The Era of Theodore Roosevelt, 1900–1912* (1958), and Arthur S. Link, *Woodrow Wilson and the Progressive Era, 1910–1917* (1954). A highly influential interpretation of progressive reform that is worth reading despite its disputed central arguments is Richard Hofstadter, *Age of Reform* (1955). Robert H. Wiebe, *The Search for Order, 1877–1920* (1967), places progressive reform in a broader context of organizational development. On the debate over progressivism as a movement, see Daniel Rodgers, "In Search of Progressivism," *Reviews in American History* 10 (1982).

The Course of Reform

The progressive mind has been studied from many different angles. The religious underpinnings are stressed in Robert M. Crunden, *Ministers of Reform: The Progressives' Achievement in American Civilization, 1889–1920* (1982). In *The New Radicalism in America, 1889–1963* (1965), Christopher Lasch sees progressivism as a form of cultural revolt. Most useful on political thinkers is Charles Forcey, *The Crossroads of Liberalism: Croly, Weyl, Lippmann, and the Progressive Era* (1961). A provocative study set in an international context is James T. Kloppenberg, *Uncertain Victory: Social Democracy and Progressivism in European and American Thought, 1870–1920* (1986). On the journalists, see David M. Chalmers, *The Social and Political Ideas of the Muckrakers* (1964), and Harold S. Wilson, *McClure's Magazine and the Muckrakers* (1970).

Political reform has been the subject of a voluminous literature. Wisconsin progressivism can be studied in David P. Thelen, *The New Citizenship: Origins of Progressivism in Wisconsin, 1885–1900* (1972). Important progressives are discussed in Spencer C. Olin, *California's Prodigal Son: Hiram Johnson and the Progressive Movement* (1968), and Richard Lowitt, *George W. Norris: The Making of a Progressive* (1963). On city reform, see Bradley R. Rice, *Progressive Cities: The Commission Government Movement* (1972); Jack Tager, *The Intellectual as Urban Reformer: Brand Whitlock and the Progressive Movement* (1968); and Melvin G. Holli, *Reform in Detroit: Hazen S. Pingree and Urban Politics* (1969).

The best treatment of the settlement-house movement is Allen F. Davis, *Spearheads of Reform* (1967). Allen F. Davis, *American Heroine: Jane Addams* (1973); George Martin, *Madame Secretary: Frances Perkins* (1976); and Kathryn Kish Sklar, *Florence Kelley and the Nation's Work: The Rise of Women's Political Culture* (1995), deal with leading woman progressives. The connection to working women is effectively treated in Nancy S. Dye, *As Equals and Sisters: Feminism, the Labor Movement, and the Women's Trade Union League of New York* (1980). Women garment workers, the key labor constituency for women progressives, are studied with great skill and insight in Susan A. Glenn, *Daughters of the Shtetl: Life and Labor in the Immigrant Generation* (1990). Two path-breaking books on the origins of American feminism are Rosalind Rosenberg, *Beyond Separate Spheres: The Intellectual Origins of Modern Feminism* (1982), and Nancy F. Cott, *The Grounding of Modern Feminism* (1987). The leading social reformer to spring from feminism is treated in Ellen Chesler, *Woman of Valor: Margaret Sanger and the Birth Control Movement* (1992).

On urban liberalism, the standard book is John D. Buenker, *Urban Liberalism and Progressive Reform* (1973). The relationship to organized labor can be followed in Irwin Yellowitz, *Labor and the Progressive Movement in New York State* (1965). Two important recent books by historical sociologists treat the halting progress toward the welfare state: Theda Skocpol, *Protecting Soldiers and Mothers* (1992), and, in a comparison of the United States with Canada and Britain, Ann Shola Orloff, *The Politics of Pensions* (1993). The most comprehensive survey is Morton Keller, *Regulating a New Society: Public Policy and Social Change In America, 1900–1933* (1994). On the South, see Dewey Grantham, *Southern Progressivism* (1983); on southern black women as social reformers, see Glenda Elizabeth Gilmore, *Gender amd Jim Crow: Women and the Politics of White Supremacy in North Carolina, 1869–1920* (1996); and on the racial conservatism of social progressives, see Elizabeth Lasch-Quinn, *Black Neighbors: Race and the Limits of Reform in the American Settlement-House Movement* (1993). The revival of black protest is vigorously described in Stephen R. Fox, *The Guardian of Boston: William Monroe Trotter* (1971), and in David Levering Lewis, *W. E. B. Du Bois: Biography of a Race, 1868–1919* (1993).

Progressivism and National Politics

National progressivism is best approached through its leading figures. John Milton Cooper, *The Warrior and the Priest* (1983), is a provocative joint biography of Roosevelt and Wilson that emphasizes their shared world view. Lewis S. Gould, *The Presidency of Theodore Roosevelt* (1991), provides a useful synthesis. Aspects of national progressive politics can be followed in James Penick, *Progressive Politics and Conservation: The Ballinger-Pinchot Affair* (1968); James Holt, *Congressional Insurgents and the Party System* (1969); and David Sarasohn, *The Party of Reform: The Democrats in the Progressive Era* (1989). Naomi Lamoreaux, *The Great Merger Movement in American Business, 1895–1904* (1985), offers a sophisticated modern analysis of trust activity, and Thomas K. McCraw, ed., *Regulation in Perspective* (1981), contains valuable interpretive essays on the problems of trust regulation. A comprehensive rethinking of the progressive struggle to fashion a regulatory policy for big business is offered in Martin J. Sklar, *The Corporate Reconstruction of American Capitalism, 1890–1916: The Market, the Law, and Politics* (1988).

CHAPTER 22

Two useful surveys of late nineteenth-century diplomatic history are Foster R. Dulles, *Prelude to World Power, 1865–1900* (1965), and Charles S. Campbell, *The Transformation of American Foreign Relations, 1865–1900* (1976). Invaluable as a historiographical guide is Robert L. Beisner, *From the Old Diplomacy to the New, 1865–1900* (2d ed., 1986).

The Roots of Expansionism

Standard works on the preexpansionist era are David M. Pletcher, *The Awkward Years: American Foreign Relations under Garfield and Arthur* (1963), and Milton Plesur, *America's Outward Thrust: Approaches to American Foreign Affairs, 1865–1890* (1971). Walter LaFeber's highly influential *The New Empire, 1860–1898* (1963) places economic interest—especially the need for overseas markets—at the center of scholarly debate over the sources of American expansionism. On American business overseas the definitive work is Myra Wilkins, *The Emergence of the Multinational Enterprise: American Business Abroad from the Colonial Era to 1914* (1970). Other important books dealing with aspects of American expansionism are David Healy, *U.S. Expansionism: The Imperialist Urge in the 1890s* (1970); Robert Seager, *Alfred Thayer Mahan* (1977); Michael Hunt, *Ideology and U.S. Foreign Policy* (1987); Mark R. Shulman, *Navalism and the Emergence of American Sea Power, 1882–1893* (1995); and Kenneth J. Hagan, *This People's Navy: The Making of American Seapower* (1991).

An American Empire

On the war with Spain, see John Offner, *An Unwanted War: The Diplomacy of the United States and Spain over Cuba, 1895–1898* (1988); David S. Trask, *The War with Spain in 1898* (1981); Frank Freidel, *A Splendid Little War* (1958); and Lewis Gould, *The Spanish-American War and President McKinley* (1982), which emphasizes McKinley's strong leadership. Ernest R. May, *Imperial Democracy: The Emergence of America as a Great Power* (1961), exemplifies the earlier view that McKinley was a weak figure driven to war by jingoistic pressures. On the Philippines, see Richard E. Welch, *Response to Imperialism: The United States and the Philippine-American War, 1898–1903* (1979), and, for the subsequent history, Peter Stanley, *A Nation in the Making: The Philippines and the United States, 1899–1921* (1974). Robert L. Beisner, *Twelve against Empire: The Anti-Imperialists, 1898–1900* (1968), remains the best book on that subject.

Onto the World Stage

On the European context a useful introduction can be found in the early chapters of Felix Gilbert, *The End of the European Era, 1890 to the Present* (4th ed., 1991). For a stimulating interpretation, see L. C. B. Seaman, *From Vienna to Versailles* (1955). On American relations with Britain the standard work is Bradford Perkins, *The Great Rapprochement: England and the United States, 1895–1914* (1968). On Roosevelt's diplomacy the starting point remains Howard K. Beale, *Theodore Roosevelt and the Rise of America to World Power* (1956). There are keen insights into the diplomatic views of both Roosevelt and Wilson in John Milton Cooper, *The Warrior and the Priest* (1983). On the thrust into the Caribbean, see Walter LaFeber, *The Panama Canal* (1979); Richard Lael, *Arrogant Diplomacy: U.S. Policy toward Colombia, 1903–1922* (1987); David Healy, *Drive to Hegemony: The United States in the Caribbean, 1898–1917* (1988); and Thomas D. Schoonover, *The United States in Central America, 1860–1911* (1991). America's Asian involvements are treated in Thomas J. McCormick, *China Market: America's Quest for Informal Empire, 1893–1901* (1967); Michael H. Hunt, *The Making of a Special Relationship: The United States and China to 1914* (1983); and Akira Iriye, *Pacific Estrangement: Japanese and American Expansion, 1897–1911* (1972). On the Mexican involvement, see John S. D. Eisenhower, *Intervention! The United States and the Mexican Revolution* (1993). There is a lively and critical analysis of Wilson's misguided policies in Robert E. Quirk, *An Affair of Honor: Woodrow Wilson and the Occupation of Veracruz* (1962). The revolution as experienced by the Mexicans is brilliantly depicted in John Womack, *Zapata and the Mexican Revolution* (1968).

CHAPTER 23

Ronald Schaffer, *America in the Great War* (1991), and David M. Kennedy, *Over Here* (1980), provide comprehensive overviews of the period. A less scholarly, but highly readable account is Meirion and Susie Harries, *The Last Days of Innocence* (1997). On the links between the Progressive Era and the war, see Neil A. Wynn, *From Progressivism to Prosperity* (1986); John A. Thompson, *Reformers and War* (1987); John F. McClymer, *War and Welfare* (1980); and Robert M. Crunden, *Ministers of Reform* (1982). Ellis W. Hawley, *The Great War and the Search for a Modern Order, 1917–1933* (1979), stresses the continuities between the war years and the 1920s.

The Great War, 1914–1918

On America's entry into World War I, see John Coogan, *The End to Neutrality* (1981); Ross Gregory, *The Origins of American Intervention in the First World War* (1971); and Thomas A. Bailey and Paul Ryan, *The Lusitania Disaster* (1975). There is a large body of material on the policies and personality of Woodrow Wilson, beginning with Arthur Link's five-volume biography (1947–1965) and his *Woodrow Wilson: Revolution, War and Peace* (1979). Other studies of Wilson include August Hecksher, *Woodrow Wilson* (1991); Kendrick Clements, *The Presidency of Woodrow Wilson* (1992); Robert Ferrell, *Woodrow Wilson and World War I* (1985); Arthur S. Link, ed., *Woodrow Wilson and a Revolutionary World* (1982); and John Milton Cooper, Jr., *The Warrior and the Priest: Woodrow Wilson and Theodore Roosevelt* (1983).

On American participation in the war, Russell Weigley, *The American Way of War* (1973), and Edward M. Coffman, *The War to End All Wars* (1968) provide useful introductions. They can be supplemented by Laurence Stallings, *The Doughboys* (1963), and A. E. Barbeau and Florette Henri, *The Unknown Soldiers: Black Troops in World War I* (1974). John Whiteclay Chambers II, *To Raise an Army* (1987), covers the draft. Allan Brandt, *No Magic Bullet* (1985), discusses anti–venereal disease campaigns. Mary E. Odem, *Delinquent Daughters* (1995), provides a discussion of the attempt to control sexuality during the war years. On Prohibition, see Joseph R. Gusfield, *Symbolic Crusade* (1963); James H. Timberlake, *Prohibition and the Progressive Movement* (1963); and K. Austin Ker, *Organized for Prohibition* (1985).

War on the Home Front

Robert D. Cuff, *The War Industries Board* (1973), provides an excellent case study of mobilization for war. Lawrence E. Gelfand, ed., *Herbert Hoover* (1979), includes several essays on Hoover's role in food conservation. See also Stephen Skowronek, *Building a New American State* (1982); Charles Gilbert, *American Financing of World War I* (1970); and David F. Noble, *America by Design* (1977). Valerie Jean Conner, *The National War Labor Board* (1983), covers federal policies toward labor, and Melvyn Dubofsky, *The State and Labor in Modern America* (1994), offers a valuable discussion of the "positive state" and labor during the war.

Maurine Greenwald, *Women, War, and Work* (1980), and Barbara Steinson, *American Women's Activism in World War I* (1982), provide good overviews of women's wartime experiences. Ellen Carol Du Bois, *Harriet Stanton Blatch and the Winning of Woman's Suffrage* (1997); Eleanor Flexner, *Century of Struggle* (1959); and Christine A. Lunardini, *From Equal Suffrage to Equal Rights: Alice Paul and the National Woman's Party, 1910–1928* (1986), cover the final stages of the woman suffrage campaign. On the peace movement, see C. Roland Marchand, *The American Peace Movement and Social Reform, 1898–1918* (1973); Charles Chatfield, *For Peace and Justice* (1971); and Charles DeBenedetti, *Origins of the Modern Peace Movement* (1978).

Efforts to promote national unity are covered in Stephen Vaughan, *Holding Fast the Inner Lines: Democracy, Nationalism, and the CPI* (1980); William J. Breen, *Uncle Sam at Home* (1984); Paul L. Murphy, *World War I and the Origins of Civil Liberties* (1979); William Preston, Jr., *Aliens and Dissenters* (1963); and Frederick Luebke, *Bonds of Loyalty: German-Americans and World War I* (1974). On free speech, see Richard Polenberg, *Fighting Faiths: The Abrams Case, the Supreme Court, and Free Speech* (1987), as well as Zechariah Chaffee, Jr.'s, classic *Free Speech in the United States* (1941). For the experiences of Mexican-Americans, see Rodolfo Acuña, *Occupied America* (1980), George Sánchez, *Becoming Mexican American* (1993); Ricardo Romo, *History of a Barrio: East Los Angeles* (1977); and Wayne Cornelius, *Building the Cactus Curtain* (1980).

An Unsettled Peace, 1919–1920

On Wilson's diplomacy, see Thomas Knock, *To End All Wars* (1992); Lloyd Ambrosius, *Woodrow Wilson and the American Diplomatic Tradition* (1987); Arthur Walworth, *Wilson and the Peacemakers* (1986); and N. Gordon Levin, Jr., *Woodrow Wilson and World Politics* (1968). For more on Versailles and the League of Nations, see Ralph A. Stone, *The Irreconcilables* (1970), and Arno J. Mayer, *Politics and Diplomacy of Peacemaking* (1967). See also William Widenor, *Henry Cabot Lodge and the Search for an American Foreign Policy* (1980). On American intervention in Russia, see George F. Kennan, *The Decision to Intervene* (1958); John L. Gaddis, *Russia, The Soviet Union, and the United States* (1978); and Peter Filene, *Americans and the Soviet Experiment, 1917–1933* (1967).

Robert K. Murray, *The Red Scare* (1955), summarizes the antiradicalism of the postwar period. See also James Weinstein, *The Decline of Socialism in America, 1912–1923* (1967); and John Higham, *Strangers in the Land* (1955). David Brody, *Labor in Crisis* (1965), describes the steel strike of 1919; for a more general overview, see David Montgomery, *The Fall of the House of Labor* (1987). On race relations, see Joe William Trotter, Jr., ed., *The Great Migration in Historical Perspective* (1991); James R. Grossman, *Land of Hope: Chicago, Black Southerners, and the Great Migration* (1989); William M. Tuttle, Jr., *Race Riot* (1970); Jacqueline Jones, *Labor of Love, Labor of Sorrow* (1985); Robert V. Haynes, *A Night of Violence: The Houston Riot of 1917* (1976); and Elliot M. Rudwick, *Race Riot at East St. Louis, July 2, 1917* (1964). An invaluable primary source is Chicago Commission on Race Relations, *The Negro in Chicago* (1922). For an introduction to the Sacco and Vanzetti case, see Louis Joughin and Edmund Morgan, *The Legacy of Sacco and Vanzetti* (1948), and Roberta Strauss Feuerlicht, *Justice Crucified* (1977).

CHAPTER 24

General overviews of the 1920s are provided by Lynn Dumenil, *The Modern Temper* (1994); Ellis Hawley, *The Great War and the Search for a Modern Order, 1917–1933* (1979); William Leuchtenburg, *The Perils of Prosperity*, 2d ed. (1995); and Frederick

Lewis Allen, *Only Yesterday* (1931). Ann Douglas, *Terrible Honesty: Mongrel Manhattan in the 1920s* (1995), uses New York City to look broadly at culture in the 1920s. Robert S. Lynd and Helen Merrell Lynd, *Middletown* (1929), remains a superb study of American life and values in the 1920s.

Business-Government Partnership of the 1920s

Discussion of corporate developments can be found in Alfred Chandler, *The Visible Hand* (1977), and James Gilbert, *Designing the Industrial State* (1972). Irving Bernstein, *The Lean Years* (1960); David Brody, *Workers in Industrial America* (1980); Dana Frank, *Purchasing Power: Consumer Organizing, Gender, and the Seattle Labor Movement, 1919–1929* (1994); and David Montgomery, *The Fall of the House of Labor* (1987), cover labor developments.

The domestic and international aspects of the economy are treated in Jim Potter, *The American Economy between the Wars* (1974); Mira Wilkins, *The Maturing of Multinational Enterprise* (1974); and Emily Rosenberg, *Spreading the American Dream* (1982). Interpretations of foreign policy include Akira Iriye, *The Globalizing of America, 1913–1945* (1993); Warren Cohen, *Empire without Tears* (1987); William Appleman Williams, *The Tragedy of American Diplomacy* (1962); and Walter LaFeber, *Inevitable Revolutions* (1983).

General introductions to politics in the 1920s can be found in John D. Hicks, *Republican Ascendancy* (1960); David Burner, *The Politics of Provincialism* (1967); and Robert Murray, *The Politics of Normalcy* (1973). Alan Dawley, *Struggles for Justice* (1991), analyzes the fate of reform. Biographies of the decade's major political figures include Donald McCoy, *Calvin Coolidge* (1967); David Burner, *Herbert Hoover* (1979); Joan Hoff Wilson, *Herbert Hoover* (1975); and Paula Elder, *Governor Alfred E. Smith* (1983). On women in politics, see J. Stanley Lemons, *The Woman Citizen* (1973); Clarke A. Chambers, *Seedtime of Reform* (1963); Nancy Cott, *The Grounding of Modern Feminism* (1987); and Elisabeth Israels Perry, *Belle Moskowitz* (1987).

A New National Culture

Daniel Boorstin, *The Americans: The Democratic Experience* (1973); David Nasaw, *Going Out: The Rise and Fall of Public Amusements* (1993); and essays in Catherine L. Covert and John D. Stevens, eds., *Mass Media between the Wars* (1984), provide excellent introductions to the emerging mass culture. On movies, see Robert Sklar, *Movie-Made America* (1975); Lary May, *Screening Out the Past* (1980); Lewis A. Erenberg, *Steppin' Out* (1981); David Stenn, *Clara Bow, Runnin' Wild* (1988); and Sumiko Higashi, *Virgins, Vamps and Flappers* (1978). Erik Barnouw, *A Tower in Babel* (1966); Susan Douglas, *Inventing American Broadcasting* (1987); and Philip Rosen, *The Modern Stentors* (1980), discuss radio. See also Melvin Patrick Ely, *The Adventures of Amos 'n' Andy* (1991), and Claude E. Fischer, *America Calling: A Social History of the Telephone to 1940* (1992). Stewart Ewen, *Captains of Consciousness* (1976); Daniel Pope, *The Making of Modern Advertising* (1983); Roland Marchand, *Advertising the American Dream* (1985); Vincent Vinikas, *Soft Soap, Hard Sell* (1992); and T. J. Jackson Lears, *Fables of Abundance* (1994), cover advertising. Paula Fass, *The Damned and the Beautiful* (1977), and Beth L. Bailey, *From Front Porch to Back Seat* (1988), cover youth, while Susan Strasser, *Never Done* (1982), and Ruth Schwartz Cowan, *More Work for Mother* (1983), discuss white middle-class women. Lizabeth Cohen, *Making a New Deal* (1990), suggests how working-class communities adapted mass culture for their purposes. Joan Shelley Rubin describes the middle class in *The Making of Middlebrow Culture* (1992).

The impact of the automobile on modern American life is documented by James Flink, *The Car Culture* (1975) and *The Automobile Age* (1988), and by Clay McShane, *Down the Asphalt Path: The Automobile and the American City* (1994), and Virginia Scharff, *Taking the Wheel* (1991). For sports, see Allen Guttmann, *A Whole New Ball Game* (1988); Harvey Green, *Fit for America* (1986); and Susan Cahn, *Coming on Strong: Gender and Sexuality in 20th Century Women's Sport* (1994). The Negro Leagues are covered in Robert W. Peterson, *Only the Ball Was White* (1970), and Donn Rogosin, *Invisible Men* (1985).

Dissenting Values and Cultural Conflict

Paul Carter, *Another Part of the Twenties* (1977), outlines the decade's deeply felt cultural controversies. Background on rural and urban life is provided by Don Kirschner, *City and Country* (1970); Zane Miller, *The Urbanization of America* (1973); and Jon Teaford, *The Twentieth-Century American City* (1986). John Higham, *Strangers in the Land* (1955), describes immigration restriction and nativism. Richard K. Tucker, *The Dragon and the Cross* (1991), and Leonard Moore, *Citizen Klansmen* (1991), cover the Klan's rise and fall, while Kathleen M. Blee, *Women of the Klan* (1991), and Nancy MacLean, *Behind the Mask of Chivalry* (1994), offer provocative discussions of racism and gender in the 1920s. See also Kenneth Jackson, *The Ku Klux Klan in the City, 1915–1930* (1965). George M. Marsden, *Fundamentalism and American Culture* (1980), and William G. McLoughlin, *Fundamentalism in American Culture* (1983), cover religion. Lawrence W. Levine, *Defender of the Faith* (1965), traces the last years of William Jennings Bryan's career. Robert Crunden, *From Self to Society, 1919–1941* (1972); Roderick Nash, *The Nervous Generation* (1969); Frederick J. Hoffman, *The 20s* (1962); and Daniel Singal, ed., *Modernist Culture in America* (1991), cover key intellectual developments. On the Harlem Renaissance see Jervis Anderson, *This Was Harlem, 1900–1950* (1982); Nathan Huggins, *Harlem Renaissance* (1971); and Gloria T. Hull, *Color, Sex, and Poetry: Three Women Writers of the Harlem Renaissance* (1987); see also Burton Peretti, *The Creation of Jazz* (1992). Judith Stein, *The World of Marcus Garvey* (1985), and Theodore Vincent, *Black Power and the Garvey Movement* (1970), describe Marcus Garvey. On prohibition, see Andrew Sinclair, *Prohibition* (1962); Joseph R. Gusfield, *Symbolic Crusade* (1963); and Norman Clark, *Deliver Us from Evil* (1976). The 1928 election is covered in David Burner, *The Politics of Provincialism* (1967); Oscar Handlin, *Al Smith and His America* (1958); Kristi Andersen, *The Creation of a Democratic Majority, 1928–1936* (1979); and Allan J. Lichtman's quantitative study, *Prejudice and the Old Politics* (1979).

CHAPTER 25

Useful overviews of the Great Depression are T. H. Watkins, *The Great Depression: America in the 1930s* (1993); John A. Garraty, *The Great Depression* (1987); and Robert S. McElvaine, *The Great Depression, 1929–1941* (1984).

The Coming of the Great Depression

Historians and economists continue to debate the causes of the Great Depression. See John Kenneth Galbraith, *The Great Crash* (1954); Milton Friedman and Anna Schwartz, *The Great Contraction, 1929–1933* (1965); Charles Kindelberger, *The World in Depression* (1974); Peter Temin, *Did Monetary Forces Cause the Great Depression?* (1976); and Michael Bernstein, *The Great Depression* (1988).

Hard Times

A wealth of material brings the voices of the 1930s to life. The Federal Writers' Project, *These Are Our Lives* (1939); Tom Terrill and Jerrold Hirsch, eds., *Such as Us: Southern Voices of the Thirties* (1978); and Ann Banks, ed., *First-Person America* (1980), all draw on oral histories collected by the Works Progress Administration during the 1930s. See also Richard Lowitt and Maurine Beasley, eds., *One-Third of a Nation: Lorena Hickock Reports the Great Depression* (1981), and Robert S. McElvaine, ed., *Down and Out in the Great Depression* (1983), for firsthand accounts. Evocative secondary sources include Studs Terkel, *Hard Times: An Oral History of the Great Depression* (1970); Irving Bernstein, *The Lean Years* (1960); and Caroline Bird, *The Invisible Scar* (1966).

Descriptions of family life in the 1930s include Robert and Helen Lynd, *Middletown in Transition* (1937); Mirra Komarovsky, *The Unemployed Man and His Family* (1940); and Roger Angell, *The Family Encounters the Depression* (1936). Russell Baker's autobiography, *Growing Up* (1982), provides an often humorous description of family life in the 1930s. Glen H. Elder, Jr., *Children of the Great Depression* (1974), and John A. Clausen, *American Lives: Looking Back at the Children of the Great Depression* (1993), look at the long-term effects. For more on youth, see Maxine Davis, *The Lost Generation* (1936); Eileen Eagan, *Class, Culture, and the Classroom* (1981); Beth L. Bailey, *From Front Porch to Back Seat* (1988); and John Modell, *Into One's Own: From Youth to Adulthood, 1920–1975* (1989).

Frederick Lewis Allen, *Since Yesterday* (1939), provides an impressionistic overview of popular culture in the 1930s. See also the essays in Lawrence W. Levine, *The Unpredictable Past* (1993). Specific studies of movies and Hollywood include Robert Sklar, *Movie-Made America* (2d ed., 1987); Andrew Bergman, *We're in the Money* (1971); Molly Haskell, *From Reverence to Rape: The Treatment of Women in the Movies* (2d ed., 1987); and Thomas Schatz, *The Genius of the System: Hollywood Film Making in the Studio Era* (1988). On radio, see Arthur Frank Wertheim, *Radio Comedy* (1979).

Material on women in the 1930s can be found in Susan Ware, *Holding Their Own* (1982); Winifred Wandersee, *Women's Work and Family Values, 1920–1940* (1981); and Lois Scharf, *To Work and to Wed* (1981). For the special dimensions of white rural women's lives, see Margaret Hagood, *Mothers of the South* (1939). Jeane Westin, *Making Do: How Women Survived the '30s* (1976), is a lively account drawn from interviews. The birth control movement is surveyed in Linda Gordon, *Woman's Body, Woman's Right* (2d ed., 1990); James Reed, *From Private Vice to Public Virtue* (1978); Estelle Freedman and John D'Emilio, *Intimate Matters: A History of Sexuality in America* (1988); and Ellen Chesler, *Woman of Valor: Margaret Sanger and the Birth Control Movement in America* (1992).

The Social Fabric of Depression America

Developments in the black community during the 1930s are covered in Cheryl Lyn Greenberg, *"Or Does It Explode?": Harlem in the Great Depression* (1991); Gilbert Osofsky, *Harlem: The Making of a Ghetto* (1966); Gunnar Myrdal, *An American Dilemma* (1944); David Lewis, *When Harlem Was in Vogue* (1981); Jervis Anderson, *This Was Harlem, 1900–1950* (1982); and Robert Weisbrot, *Father Divine and the Struggle for Racial Equality* (1983). James Goodman, *Stories of Scottsboro* (1994), and Dan T. Carter, *Scottsboro* (1969), cover that case. Donald Grubbs, *Cry from Cotton* (1971), tells the story of the Southern Tenant Farmers Union. Robin D. G. Kelley, *Hammer and Hoe* (1990), is an excellent account of Alabama communists during the Great Depression. Donald Worster, *Dust Bowl* (1979), evokes the plains during the "Dirty Thirties," as does Ann Marie Low's memoir, *Dust Bowl Diary* (1984). James N. Gregory, *American Exodus: The Dust Bowl Migration and Okie Culture in California* (1989), treats the experiences of migrants in and their impact on California culture and the economy.

On the experiences of Mexican-Americans during the 1930s see Mario T. Garcia, *Mexican Americans: Leadership, Ideology, and Identity, 1930–1960* (1989); Devra Weber, *Dark Sweat, White Gold: California Farm Workers, Cotton, and the New Deal* (1994); and Mario T. Garcia, *Memories of Chicano History: The Life and Narrative of Bert Corona* (1994). George J. Sánchez, *Becoming Mexican American* (1993), examines Chicano Los Angeles from 1900 to 1945. See also Carey McWilliams, *North from Mexico* (1948), and Richard A. Garcia, *The Rise of the Mexican-American Middle Class* (1990). For Mexican-American women's lives, see Vicki Ruiz, *Cannery Women, Cannery Lives: Mexican Women, Unionization, and the California Food Processing Industry, 1930–1950* (1987), and Patricia Zavella, *Women's Work and Chicano Families* (1987).

Herbert Hoover and the Great Depression

Hoover's response to the depression is chronicled in Alfred Romasco, *The Poverty of Abundance* (1965), and Jordan Schwartz, *The Interregnum of Despair* (1970). See also David Burner, *Herbert Hoover* (1978); Joan Hoff Wilson, *Herbert Hoover: Forgotten Progressive* (1975); and William Barber, *Herbert Hoover, the Economists, and American Economic Policy, 1921–1933* (1986). Eliot Rosen, *Hoover, Roosevelt, and the Brain Trust* (1977), treats the transition between the two administrations, as does Frank Freidel, *Launching the New Deal* (1973). On the 1932 election and the beginnings of the New Deal coalition, see David Burner, *The Politics of Provincialism* (1967); Samuel Lubell, *The Future of American Politics* (1952); and John Allswang, *The New Deal in American Politics* (1978).

CHAPTER 26

Comprehensive introductions to the New Deal include Robert S. McElvaine, *The Great Depression* (1984); Anthony J. Badger, *The New Deal* (1989); William E. Leuchtenburg, *Franklin D. Roosevelt and the New Deal* (1963); Barry Karl, *The Uneasy State* (1983); John A. Garraty, *The Great Depression* (1987); Roger Biles, *A New Deal for the American People* (1991); and Harvard Sitkoff, ed., *Fifty Years Later: The New Deal Evaluated* (1985).

The New Deal Begins, 1933–1935

The New Deal has inspired a voluminous bibliography. Frank Freidel, *Launching the New Deal* (1973), covers the first hundred days in detail. Monographs include Bernard Bellush, *The Failure of the NRA* (1975); Thomas K. McCraw, *TVA and the Power Fight* (1970); John Salmond, *The Civilian Conservation Corps* (1967); Roy Lubove, *The Struggle for Social Security* (1968); Susan Kennedy, *The Banking Crisis of 1933* (1973); Michael Parrish, *Securities Regulation and the New Deal* (1970); Mark Leff, *The Limits of Symbolic Reform: The New Deal and Taxation, 1933–1939* (1984); James Olson, *Saving Capitalism: The Reconstruction Finance Corporation and the New Deal, 1933–1940* (1988); and Bonnie Fox Schwartz, *The Civilian Works Administration, 1933–1934* (1984). Ellis Hawley, *The New Deal and the Problem of Monopoly* (1966), provides a stimulating account of economic policy. Agricultural developments are covered in Theodore Saloutos, *The American Farmer and the New Deal* (1982); Paul Mertz, *The New Deal and Southern Rural Poverty* (1978); and Sidney Baldwin, *Poverty and Politics: The Rise and*

Decline of the Farm Security Administration (1968). Greg Mitchell, *The Campaign of the Century* (1992), describes Upton Sinclair's campaign for the California governorship, and Alan Brinkley, *Voices of Protest* (1982), covers the Coughlin and Long movements. See also Leo Ribuffo, *The Old Christian Right* (1983).

The Second New Deal, 1935–1938

Roosevelt's second term has drawn far less attention than has the 1933–1936 period. James MacGregor Burns, *Roosevelt* (1956), provides an overview, as does Barry Karl, *The Uneasy State* (1983). Alan Brinkley, *The End of Reform* (1995), discusses the New Deal and liberalism between 1937 and 1945. The growing opposition to the New Deal is treated in James T. Patterson, *Congressional Conservatism and the New Deal* (1967); Richard Polenberg, *Reorganizing Roosevelt's Government* (1966); and Barry Karl, *Executive Reorganization and Reform in the New Deal* (1963).

The New Deal's Impact on Society

Katie Louchheim, ed., *The Making of the New Deal: The Insiders Speak* (1983), provides an engaging introduction to some of the men and women who shaped the New Deal. See also Peter Irons, *New Deal Lawyers* (1982), and Jordan A. Schwartz, *The New Dealers* (1993). On women in the New Deal, see Susan Ware, *Beyond Suffrage* (1981). Blanche Cook, *Eleanor Roosevelt* (1991), takes the story to 1933; see also Lois Scharf, *Eleanor Roosevelt* (1987). George Martin, *Madam Secretary* (1976), covers the career of Frances Perkins.

On minorities and the New Deal, see Harvard Sitkoff, *A New Deal for Blacks* (1978); John B. Kirby, *Black Americans in the Roosevelt Era* (1980); Robert Zangrando, *The NAACP Crusade against Lynching, 1909–1950* (1980); and Nancy J. Weiss, *Farewell to the Party of Lincoln* (1983). George J. Sánchez, *Becoming Mexican American: Ethnicity, Culture and Identity in Chicano Los Angeles, 1900–1945* (1993), describes the politicization of Mexican-Americans in the 1930s.

Irving Bernstein, *The Turbulent Years* (1970), and *A Caring Society: The New Deal, the Worker, and the Great Depression* (1985), chronicle the story of the labor movement through 1941. Additional studies include Peter Friedlander, *The Emergence of a UAW Local* (1975); Melvin Dubofsky and Warren Van Tine, *John L. Lewis* (1977); Sidney Fine, *Sit-Down: The General Motors Strike of 1936–1937* (1969); David Brody, *Workers in Industrializing America* (1980); Ronald Schatz, *The Electrical Workers* (1983); Bruce Nelson, *Workers on the Waterfront* (1988); and Lizabeth Cohen, *Making a New Deal* (1990). Steven Fraser, *Labor Will Rule* (1991), is a fine biography of Sidney Hillman.

On Indian policy see Donald Parman, *Navajoes and the New Deal* (1976); Laurence Hauptman, *The Iroquois and the New Deal* (1981); and Laurence C. Kelly, *The Assault on Assimilation: John Collier and the Origins of Indian Policy Reform* (1983). For material on rural electrification, see D. Clayton Brown, *Electricity for Rural America* (1980), and Marquis Childs, *The Farmer Takes a Hand* (1952).

The creation of the New Deal's welfare system is treated in James T. Patterson, *America's Struggle against Poverty* (1981), which carries the story through 1980. Linda Gordon, *Pitied but Not Entitled* (1994), looks at single mothers and the history of welfare. See also Michael Katz, *In the Shadow of the Poorhouse* (1986); John Garraty, *Unemployment in History* (1978); and Otis Graham, *Towards a Planned Society* (1976). For the enduring impact of Franklin Roosevelt on the political system, see William Leuchtenburg, *In the Shadow of FDR* (1983).

The various New Deal programs have found historians in Jerry Mangione, *The*

Dream and the Deal: The Federal Writers' Project, 1935–1943 (1972); Monty Penkower, *The Federal Writers' Project* (1977); Richard McKinzie, *The New Deal for Artists* (1973); and Jane DeHart Mathews, *The Federal Theater, 1935–1939* (1967). Marlene Park and Gerald Markowitz, *Democratic Vistas* (1984), surveys New Deal murals and art. General studies of cultural expression include William Stott, *Documentary Expression and Thirties America* (1973), and Richard Pells, *Radical Visions and American Dreams* (1973). See also Karen Becker Ohrn, *Dorothea Lange and the Documentary Tradition* (1980), and F. Jack Hurley, *Portrait of a Decade: Roy Stryker and the Development of Documentary Photography in the Thirties* (1972).

Daniel Aaron, *Writers on the Left* (1961), provides an overview of literary currents in the decade. Material on the relationship between intellectuals and the Communist party can be found in Harvey Klehr, *The Heyday of American Communism* (1984), and Irving Howe and Lewis Coser, *The American Communist Party* (1957). Warren Susman provides a provocative analysis of culture and commitment in the 1930s in *Culture as History* (1984).

CHAPTER 27

John Morton Blum, *V Was for Victory* (1976); William O'Neill, *A Democracy at War* (1993); Michael C. C. Adams, *The Best War Ever* (1994); Richard Polenberg, *War and Society* (1972); and Geoffrey Perret, *Days of Sadness, Years of Triumph* (1973), offer good introductions to American politics and culture during the war years. A valuable collection of articles is Lewis A. Erenberg and Susan E. Hirsch, eds., *The War In American Culture* (1996). A powerful and provocative oral history of the war is Studs Terkel, *The Good War: An Oral History of World War Two* (1984). John Keegan, *The Second World War* (1990), offers the best one-volume account of the battlefront aspects.

The Road to War

Depression and wartime diplomacy are covered in Robert Dallek, *Franklin D. Roosevelt and American Foreign Policy, 1932–1945* (1979); Akira Iriye, *The Globalizing of America, 1913–1945* (1993); Robert Divine, *The Reluctant Belligerent* (2d ed., 1979); Arnold Offner, *American Appeasement* (1976); and David Schmitz, *The United States and Fascist Italy, 1922–1940* (1988). On American isolationism, see Wayne Cole, *Roosevelt and the Isolationists, 1932–1945* (1983). Warren T. Kimball, *The Juggler* (1991), provides an overview of Roosevelt's wartime leadership. Roberta Wohlstetter, *Pearl Harbor* (1962), and Gordon W. Prange, *At Dawn We Slept* (1981), describe the events that led to American entry.

Mobilizing for Victory

Gerald T. White, *Billions for Defense* (1980), and Harold G. Vatter, *The U.S. Economy in World War II* (1985), discuss America's economic mobilization. Alan Winkler, *The Politics of Propaganda* (1978), covers the Office of War Information. On labor's role during war, see George Lipsitz, *Rainbow at Midnight* (1994), and Nelson Lichtenstein, *Labor's War at Home* (1982). Michael S. Sherry, *In the Shadow of War* (1995), provides an account of the World War II origins of the militarization of the United States. For more on politics in wartime, see James McGregor Burns, *Roosevelt: The Soldier of Freedom* (1970), and Alan Brinkley, *The End of Reform* (1995).

Women's roles in wartime are covered by Susan Hartmann, *The Home Front and Beyond* (1982); Leila J. Rupp, *Mobilizing Women for War* (1978); D'Ann Campbell, *Women at War with America* (1984); Ruth Milkman, *Gender at Work* (1987); and Sherna B. Gluck, *Rosie the Riveter Revisited* (1987). Judy Barrett Litoff and David C. Smith, *We're in This War, Too* (1994), includes letters from American women in uniform.

Life on the Home Front

William M. Tuttle, Jr., *"Daddy's Gone to War"* (1993), describes World War II from the perspective of the nation's children. Alan Clive, *State of War* (1979), provides a case study of Michigan during the war; Marilynn S. Johnson, *The Second Gold Rush* (1993), describes Oakland and the East Bay. See also Gerald D. Nash, *The American West Transformed* (1985), and Marc Scott Miller, *The Irony of Victory: World War II and Lowell, Massachusetts* (1988). Clayton R. Koppes and Gregory D. Black, *Hollywood Goes to War* (1987), covers the film industry. The experience of black Americans is treated in Albert Russell Buchanan, *Black Americans in World War II* (1977), and Neil Wynn, *The Afro-American and the Second World War* (1975). On racial tensions, see Dominic Capeci, Jr., *Race Relations in Wartime Detroit* (1984), and Mauricio Mazan, *The Zoot Suit Riots* (1984). August Meier and Elliott Rudwick, *CORE* (1973), describes the founding of an important civil-rights organization. Richard Dalfiume, *Desegregation of the U.S. Armed Forces* (1969), covers black soldiers in the military, and Phillip McGuire, comp., *Taps for a Jim Crow Army* (1993), offers a collection of letters from black soldiers. Alan Berube, *Coming Out under Fire* (1990), is an oral history of gay men and lesbians in the military. Two accounts of Japanese relocation are Audre Girdner and Anne Loftus, *The Great Betrayal* (1969), and Roger Daniels, *Prisoners without Trial* (1993). See also John Tateishi, ed., *And Justice for All: An Oral History of the Japanese-American Detention Camps* (1984), and Peter Irons, *Justice at War: The Story of the Japanese-American Internment Cases* (1983). Valerie Matsumoto, *Farming the Home Place* (1993), describes a Japanese-American community in California from 1919 to 1982.

Fighting and Winning the War

Extensive material chronicles the American military experience during World War II. Albert Russell Buchanan, *The United States and World War II* (1962), and Russell F. Weigley, *The American Way of War* (1973), provide overviews. Cornelius Ryan, *The Last Battle* (1966); John Toland, *The Last Hundred Days* (1966); and Stephen Ambrose, *D-Day, June 6, 1944* (1994), describe the end of the fighting in Europe. David S. Wyman, *The Abandonment of the Jews* (1984), describes the lack of American response to the Holocaust from 1941 to 1945. On the Far East, see John W. Dower, *War without Mercy* (1986); Ronald H. Spector, *Eagle against the Sun* (1984); and John Toland, *Rising Sun* (1970). See Geoffrey Perret, *Old Soldiers Never Die* (1996), on General Douglas MacArthur.

American diplomacy and the strategy of the Grand Alliance are surveyed in Lloyd Gardner, *Spheres of Influence* (1993). The relationship between the wartime conferences and the onset of the Cold War are treated in Walter LaFeber, *America, Russia, and the Cold War* (7th ed., 1993); Stephen Ambrose, *Rise to Globalism* (7th ed., 1993); John L. Gaddis, *The United States and the Origins of the Cold War* (1972); and Herbert Feis, *Between War and Peace* (1960). Richard Rhodes, *The Making of the Atomic Bomb* (1987); McGeorge Bundy, *Danger and Survival* (1988); and Martin Sherwin, *A World Destroyed* (1975), provide compelling accounts of the development of the bomb. See also Gar Alperowitz, *The Decision to Use the Atomic Bomb* (1995); Ronald Takaki, *Hiroshima* (1995); Gregg Herken, *The Winning Weapon* (1980); John Hersey, *Hiroshima* (2d ed., 1985); and Robert Jay Lifton and Greg Mitchell, *Hiroshima in America: Fifty Years of Denial* (1995).

CHAPTER 28

General works on the politics and diplomacy of the cold war era include William Chafe, *The Unfinished Journey* (3d ed., 1995); Paul Boyer, *Promises to Keep* (1995); and James T. Patterson, *Grand Expectations: The United States, 1945–1974* (1996).

The Early Cold War

The best overviews of the Cold War are Walter LaFeber, *America, Russia, and the Cold War, 1945–1990* (7th ed., 1992); Stephen Ambrose, *Rise to Globalism* (7th ed., 1993); and Thomas G. Paterson, *On Every Front* (rev. ed., 1992). Melvyn P. Leffler presents a masterful and exhaustive synthesis of Truman's foreign policy in *A Preponderance of Power* (1992). For critical views of American aims, see H. W. Brands, *The Devil We Knew* (1993); and Richard Ned Lebow and Janice Gross Stein, *We All Lost the Cold War* (1994). John Lewis Gaddis, *Strategies of Containment* (1982), blames the Cold War on both the United States and the Soviet Union, although his more recent works, *The Long Peace* (1987) and *The United States and the End of the Cold War* (1992), are more sympathetic to American policy making. For international perspectives on the Cold War, see Melvyn P. Leffler and David S. Painter, eds., *Origins of the Cold War* (1994); Thomas J. McCormick, *America's Half-Century* (1989); and Warren I. Cohen, *America in the Age of Soviet Power* (1993).

For collective accounts of key policymakers, see Walter Isaacson and Evan Thomas, *The Wise Men* (1986), and Donald R. Mcloy, *The Making of the American Establishment* (1992).

McGeorge Bundy, *Danger and Survival* (1989); Martin J. Sherwin, *A World Destroyed* (1975); and Gar Alperovitz, *Atomic Diplomacy* (2d ed., 1994), cover the impact of atomic weapons on American policy. For general discussions of America and nuclear weapons, see Paul Boyer, *By the Bomb's Early Light* (1985); Richard G. Hewlett and Jack Hall, *Atoms for Peace and War, 1953–1961* (1989); Howard Ball, *Justice Downwind* (1986); and Lawrence S. Wittner, *One World or None* (1993).

For developments in Asia, Akira Iriye, *The Cold War in Asia* (1974), is a good starting point. See also William Borden, *The Pacific Alliance* (1984), and Warren I. Cohen, *America's Response to China* (2d ed., 1980). There is an abundance of scholarship on the Korean War, including Callum McDonald, *Korea* (1987); Burton Kaufman, *The Korean War* (1986); and Bruce Cumings, *Liberation and the Emergence of Separate Regions, 1945–1947* (1981) and *The Roaring of the Cataract, 1945–1950* (1990). Sergei N. Goncharov et al., *Uncertain Partners* (1994), uses newly released Soviet and Chinese documents to analyze the role of those countries in the war.

Harry Truman and the Cold War at Home

Harry Truman, in his *Memoirs* (1952–1962), tells his own story. See also two recent biographies, Alonzo Hamby, *Man of the People* (1995), and Robert Ferrell, *Harry S. Truman* (1994). General accounts of the Truman presidency can be found in Robert J. Donovan, *Tumultuous Years* (1982); Alonzo Hamby, *Beyond the New Deal* (1973); and William Pemberton, *Harry S. Truman* (1989). Critical perspectives are presented in Barton J. Bernstein, ed., *Politics and Policies of the Truman Administration* (1970), and Michael J. Lacey, ed., *The Truman Presidency* (1989).

The literature on McCarthyism is voluminous. Two recent overviews are Richard Fried, *Nightmare in Red* (1990), and Stephen J. Whitfield, *The Culture of the Cold War* (1991). David Caute, *The Great Fear* (1978), provides another introduction, which can be supplemented by Victor Navasky, *Naming Names* (1980). Two biographies of McCarthy are Thomas C. Reeves, *The Life and Times of Joe McCarthy* (1982), and David Oshinsky, *A Conspiracy So Immense* (1983). Robert Griffith, *The Politics of Fear* (1970), and Richard Fried, *Men against McCarthy* (1976), look at the politics involved.

Allen Weinstein, *Perjury* (1978), covers the still-debated Hiss case. Walter and Miriam Schneir, *Invitation to an Inquest* (1965), and Ronald Radosh and Joyce Milton, *The Rosenberg File* (1983), cover the Rosenberg case. Griffin Fariello, ed., *Red Scare* (1995), provides a compelling oral history of McCarthyism, and Eric Bentley, ed., *Thirty Years of Treason* (1971), collects excerpts from testimony before the House Committee on Un-American Activities.

"Modern Republicanism"

Two standard overviews of the Eisenhower administration, Herbert S. Parmet, *Eisenhower and the American Crusades* (1972), and Charles C. Alexander, *Holding the Line* (1975), can be supplemented by Fred I. Greenstein, *The Hidden-Hand Presidency* (1982), and Stephen Ambrose, *Eisenhower the President* (1984). Blanche Wiesen Cook, *The Declassified Eisenhower* (1981), contrasts the covert activities of the administration with its public image. On specific aspects of the Eisenhower administration, see Jeff Broadwater, *Seeing Red: Eisenhower and the Anti-Communist Crusade* (1992), and Robert F. Burk, *The Eisenhower Administration and Black Civil Rights* (1984).

For the complex foreign policy of the 1950s, consult Walter LaFeber, *America, Russia, and the Cold War* (1996), and Thomas J. McCormick, *America's Half-Century*. Other overviews are provided in Robert Divine, *Eisenhower and the Cold War* (1981), and Ronald Steel, *Pax Americana* (1967). An excellent book on the CIA is Victor Marchetti and John D. Marks, *The CIA and the Cult of Intelligence* (1974). For the links among economics, corporations, and the defense industry, see Mira Wilkins, *The Maturing of Multinational Enterprise* (1974); Richard Barnet and Ronald Muller, *Global Reach* (1974); and Paul Hammond, *Organizing for Defense* (1971). Gabriel Kolko, *Confronting the Third World, 1945–1980* (1988), offers a highly critical view of U.S. policy. On American involvement in the Middle East, see Bruce Kuniholm, *The Origins of the Cold War in the Near East* (1980), and Michael Stoff, *Oil, War, and American Security* (1980). On Latin America, see Peter H. Smith, *Talons of the Eagle: Dynamics of U.S.–Latin American Relations* (1996), and Stephen Rabe, *Eisenhower and Latin America* (1988).

On specific policy situations in the 1950s, see Robert Divine, *Blowing in the Wind: The Nuclear Test Ban Debate, 1954–1960* (1978); Robert Stookey, *America and the Arab States* (1975); and John Snetsinger, *Truman, the Jewish Role, and the Creation of Israel* (1974). Steven Z. Freiberger, *Dawn over Suez* (1992), and Diane B. Kunz, *The Economic Diplomacy of the Suez Crisis* (1991), examine the Suez crisis of 1956.

CHAPTER 29

General introductions to postwar society include Paul Boyer, *Promises to Keep* (1995); William Chafe, *The Unfinished Journey* (3d ed., 1995); James T. Patterson, *Grand Expectations: The United States, 1945–1974* (1996); and David Halberstam, *The Fifties* (1993).

The Postwar Capitalist Economy

For overviews on the economic changes of the postwar period, see W. Elliot Brownlee, *Dynamics of Ascent* (1979), and David P. Calleo, *The Imperious Economy* (1982). Robert Kuttner, *The End of Laissez-Faire* (1991), provides ample background on the Bretton Woods system. Herman P. Miller, *Rich Man, Poor Man* (1971), and Gabriel Kolko, *Wealth and Power in America* (1962), discuss inequality in income distribution. Michael Harrington, *The Other America* (1962), documents the persistence of poverty in the postwar era, as does Harry M. Caudill, *Night Comes to the Cumberlands* (1963). Michael B. Katz, *In the Shadow of the Poorhouse* (1986), and James Patterson, *America's Struggle against Poverty, 1900–1980* (1981), offer longer-term perspectives. John Kenneth Galbraith, *The Affluent Society* (1958) and *The New Industrial State* (1967), shaped much of the public discussion of the economy in the period.

John L. Shover, *First Majority–Last Minority* (1976), analyzes the transformation of rural life in America. David Brody, *Workers in Industrial America* (1980); James R. Green, *The World of the Worker* (1980); and Robert Zeiger, *American Workers, American Unions, 1920–1985* (1994), provide overviews of labor in the twentieth century. On the impact of technology and automation, see Elting E. Morison, *From Know-how to Nowhere* (1974), and David F. Noble, *Forces of Production* (1984). Harry Braverman, *Labor and Monopoly Capital* (1974), looks at the degradation of work from a Marxist perspective.

The most influential study of the new middle class remains David Reisman et al., *The Lonely Crowd* (1950). See also William H. Whyte, *The Organization Man* (1956), and the work of C. Wright Mills, especially *White Collar* (1951) and *The Power Elite* (1956).

Alfred D. Chandler, *The Visible Hand* (1977), is the definitive history of American corporate structure and strategy. Myra Wilkin, *The Maturing of Multinational Enterprise* (1974), and Richard J. Barnet and Ronald E. Muller, *Global Reach* (1974), describe American business abroad. See also Robert Sobel, *The Age of Giant Corporations* (1972), and Barry Bluestein and Bennett Harrison, *The Deindustrialization of America* (1982).

A Suburban Society

The best overviews of urbanization in the South and the West are Carl Abbott, *The New Urban America* (1981), and Richard Bernard and Bradley Rice, eds., *Sunbelt Cities* (1983). Mark H. Rose, *Interstate* (1979), describes the politics of building the highway system. On the development of suburbs, see Kenneth Jackson, *Crabgrass Frontier* (1985); Jon C. Teaford, *City and Suburb* (1979); Robert Fishman, *Bourgeois Utopias* (1987); and Zane Miller, *Suburb* (1981).

American Society during the Baby Boom

Books that highlight the social and cultural history of the 1950s include Elaine Tyler May, *Homeward Bound* (1988); Larry May, ed., *Recasting America* (1989); Douglas T. Miller and Marion Nowak, *The Fifties* (1977); and Stephen Whitfield, *The Culture of the Cold War* (1991).

For popular culture, George Lipsitz, *Time Passages* (1991) and *Rainbow at Midnight* (2d ed., 1994), look at working-class culture and rock-'n'-roll. Eric Barnouw, *Tube of Plenty* (2d. ed., 1982), chronicles the impact of television and Karal Ann Marling, *As Seen on TV* (1994), challenges many assumptions about television and culture. Other treatments of the mass media include James L. Baughman, *The Republic of Mass Culture* (1992), and Nora Sayre, *Running Time* (1982). Vance Packard's influential unmasking of the advertising industry, *The Hidden Persuaders* (1957), can be supplemented by Stephen Fox, *The Mirror Makers* (1984). Daniel Horowitz's biography, *Vance Packard* (1994), provides valuable insights into intellectuals and the consumer culture.

Richard Easterlin, *American Baby Boom in Historical Perspective* (1962) and *Birth and Future* (1980), analyze the demographic changes, as does Landon Y. Jones, *Great Expectations* (1980). Jane S. Smith, *Patenting the Sun* (1990), looks at Salk's development of the polio vaccine. Diane Ravitch describes education from 1945 to 1980 in *The Troubled Crusade* (1983).

Elaine May's *Homeward Bound* (1990) is the classic introduction to postwar family life, providing a historical corollary to Betty Friedan's *Feminine Mystique* (1963), but see also Joanne Meyerowitz, ed., *Not June Cleaver* (1994), and Wini Breines, *Young, White, and Miserable* (1992). Alice Kessler-Harris, *Out to Work* (1982), surveys women's role in the work force.

Youth culture is the subject of William Graeber's *Coming of Age in Buffalo* (1990). James Gilbert, *A Cycle of Outrage* (1986), looks at juvenile delinquency in the 1950s. Peter Guralnick, *Last Train to Memphis* (1994), is the definitive biography of Elvis Presley's early years. Discussions of cultural dissent in the 1950s can be found in Bruce Cook, *The Beat Generation* (1971), and Dan Wakefield, *New York in the Fifties* (1992).

The Other America

Reed Ueda, *Postwar Immigrant America* (1994), and David Reimers, *Still the Open Door* (1985), examine new trends in immigration since 1945. Nicholas Lemann examines postwar black migration in *The Promised Land* (1991), while Jacqueline Jones compares black and white urban migrants in *The Dispossessed* (1992). Donald Fixico, *Termination and Relocation* (1986), looks at federal native American policy from 1945 to 1970.

Jon C. Teaford, *Rough Road to Renaissance* (1990); John Mollenkopf, *The Contested City* (1983); and Kenneth Fox, *Metropolitan America* (1985), offer the most complete accounts of postwar urban development. Herbert Gans, *The Urban Villagers* (1962), tells the story of a Boston Italian community displaced by urban renewal.

Richard Kluger, *Simple Justice* (1975), and Mark Tushnet, *The NAACP's Legal Strategy against Segregated Education* (1987), analyze the *Brown* decision, while Anthony Lewis, *Portrait of a Decade* (1964), covers southern reaction to the decision. J. Harvey Wilkinson III continues the story of the Supreme Court and integration through the 1970s in *From Brown to Bakke* (1979). Taylor Branch, *Parting the Waters: America in the King Years, 1954–1963* (1988), provides a good account of Martin Luther King's early years and of the importance of black churches to the civil-rights movement. Henry Hampton and Steve Fayer provide an oral history of the movement in *Voices of Freedom* (1990).

CHAPTER 30

Among the best surveys of the 1960s are David Steigerwald, *The Sixties and the End of Modern America* (1995); David Chalmers, *And Crooked Places Made Straight* (1991); David Farber, *The Age of Great Dreams* (1994); Todd Gitlin, *The Sixties* (1987); and Allen J. Matusow, *The Unraveling of America* (1984). Overviews of American foreign policy in the 1960s include Stephen Ambrose, *Rise to Globalism* (7th ed., 1993); Walter LaFeber, *America, Russia, and the Cold War* (7th ed., 1992); and Diane Kunz, ed., *The Diplomacy of the Crucial Decade* (1994).

John Kennedy and the New Frontier

Among the best general accounts of the Kennedy years are Richard Reeves, *President Kennedy* (1993); James Giglio, *The Presidency of JFK* (1991); and David Burner, *JFK and a New Generation* (1988). Critical views appear in David Halberstam, *The Best and the Brightest* (1972); Henry Fairlie, *The Kennedy Promise* (1973); and Garry Wills, *The Kennedy Imprisonment* (1980).

On foreign policy, see Michael Beschloss, *The Crisis Years: Kennedy and Khrushchev, 1960–1963* (1990); Thomas Paterson, *Kennedy's Quest for Victory* (1989); and Richard Walton, *Cold War and Counterrevolution* (1972). James Nathan, *The Cuban Missile Crisis Revisited* (1992); Raymond Garthoff, *Reflections on the Cuban Missile Crisis* (1989); and Thomas Paterson, *Contesting Castro* (1994), assess the Cuban missile crisis. On U.S. relations with the Third World, see John L. S. Girling, *America and the Third World* (1980), and Samuel Baily, *The United States and the Development of South America, 1945–1975* (1977). Gerald T. Rice, *The Bold Experiment* (1985), and Karen Schwarz, *What You Can Do for Your Country* (1991), cover the Peace Corps.

Kennedy's domestic policies are treated in the general works on his presidency noted above. On the Warren Court, see Bernard Schwartz, *Super Chief* (1983). Earl Warren was the chief author of the Warren Report (1964), investigating the Kennedy assassination. More recently, Gerald Posner, *Case Closed* (1993), provides the most definitive treatment of that event.

The Civil-Rights Movement

Robert Weisbrot, *Freedom Bound* (1990), and Harvard Sitkoff, *The Struggle for Black Equality* (2d ed., 1993), offer comprehensive overviews. Two fine oral histories of the civil-rights movement are Howell Raines, *My Soul Is Rested* (1977), and Henry Hampton and Steve Fayer, *Voices of Freedom* (1990). Local accounts of grass-roots organizing include William H. Chafe's superb study of Greensboro, North Carolina, *Civilities and Civil Rights* (1980), and two recent studies of Mississippi: John Dittmer, *Local People* (1994), and Charles M. Payne, *I've Got the Light of Freedom* (1995). The role of women in the civil-rights movement is examined in Vicki L. Crawford et al., *Women in the Civil Rights Movement* (1990). On federal policy making, see Hugh Davis Graham, *Civil Rights and the Presidency* (1992), and Mark Stern, *Calculating Visions* (1992). Martin Luther King, Jr., told his own story in *Why We Can't Wait* (1964). His biographers include David Garrow, *Bearing the Cross* (1986), and Taylor Branch, *Parting the Waters* (1988).

Lyndon Johnson and the Great Society

Lyndon Johnson's account of his presidency can be found in *The Vantage Point* (1971). Doris Kearns, *Lyndon Johnson and the American Dream* (1976), and Merle Miller, *Lyndon* (1980), are based on extensive conversations with LBJ. Other accounts of Johnson's career include Robert A. Caro, *The Path to Power* (1982) and *Means of Ascent* (1989); Robert Dallek in *Lone Star Rising* (1991); and Joseph A. Califano, Jr., *The Triumph and Tragedy of Lyndon Johnson* (1991).

A major synthesis of the Great Society is Irwin Unger, *The Best of Intentions* (1996). Michael Harrington called attention to poverty in *The Other America* (1962), and later critiqued the War on Poverty in *The New American Poverty* (1984). Charles Murray's conservative viewpoint in *Losing Ground: American Social Policy, 1950–1980* (1983) can be balanced by Michael Katz's liberal perspective in *The Undeserving Poor* (1989).

The Continuing Struggle for Civil Rights

Major texts of the black power movement include Stokely Carmichael and Charles Hamilton, *Black Power* (1967); James Baldwin, *The Fire Next Time* (1963); and Eldridge Cleaver, *Soul on Ice* (1968). *The Autobiography of Malcolm X* (cowritten with Alex Haley, 1965) has become a literary classic. William L. Van Deburg, *New Day in Babylon* (1992), provides a general historical account of the black power movement. Hugh Pearson in *The Shadow of the Panther* (1994) looks at Huey Newton and the Black Panthers, as does the former Black Panther Elaine Brown in *A Taste of Power* (1992).

Report of the National Advisory Commission on Civil Disorders (1968) analyzes the decade's major race riots. Sidney Fine's book on the Detroit riot, *Violence in the Model City* (1989), provides the most thorough historical treatment of race rioting in this period.

Carlos Muñoz, Jr., *Youth, Identity and Power* (1989), and Juan Gomez-Quiñones, *Chicano Politics* (1990), examine the rise of the Chicano movement in the 1960s. Peter Matthiessen, *In the Spirit of Crazy Horse* (1983), and Vine DeLoria, Jr., *Behind the Trail of Broken Treaties* (1974) and *Custer Died for Your Sins* (1969), convey the new Indian assertiveness. John D'Emilio, *Sexual Politics, Sexual Communities* (1983), describes the emergence of gay identity between 1940 and 1970, while Martin Duberman, *Stonewall* (1993), looks at the birth of the gay movement in the late 1960s.

Jo Freeman, *The Politics of Women's Liberation* (1975); Barbara Deckard, *The Women's Movement* (1975); and Judith Hole and Ellen Levine, *The Rebirth of Feminism* (1971), chronicle the revival of feminism in the 1960s and 1970s. Sara Evans, *Personal Politics* (1979), traces the roots of feminism in the civil-rights movement and the New Left, while Alice Echols, *Daring to Be Bad* (1989), examines radical feminism. General histories of women's activism in the 1960s include Cynthia Harrison, *On Account of Sex* (1988); Leila J. Rupp and Verta Taylor, *Survival in the Doldrums* (1987); and Susan M. Hartmann, *From Margin to Mainstream* (1989).

Important feminist works of the period include Robin Morgan, ed., *Sisterhood Is Powerful* (1970); Kate Millett, *Sexual Politics* (1970); Germaine Greer, *The Female Eunuch* (1972); and Susan Brownmiller, *Against Our Will: Men, Women, and Rape* (1975).

CHAPTER 31

Among the best general accounts of the Vietnam War are George Herring, *America's Longest War* (2d ed., 1986); Stanley Karnow, *Vietnam* (rev. ed., 1991); Gary R. Hess,

Vietnam and the United States (1990); and Marilyn Young, *The Vietnam Wars, 1945–1990* (1991). Guenter Lewy offers a controversial defense of American involvement in *America in Vietnam* (1978).

Into the Quagmire, 1945–1968

The origins of American involvement in Vietnam are covered in Loren Baritz, *Backfire* (1985); Larry Berman, *Planning a Tragedy* (1982) and *Lyndon Johnson's War* (1989); Lloyd Gardner, *Approaching Vietnam* (1988); Conrad Gibbons, *The U.S. Government and the Vietnam War* (1986–1989); David Halberstam, *The Best and the Brightest* (1972) and *The Making of a Quagmire* (rev. ed., 1987); and Brian VanDeMark, *Into the Quagmire* (1991). A fascinating insight into Vietnam policy making in the 1960s can be found in Neil Sheehan, *The Pentagon Papers* (1971). Secretary of Defense Robert McNamara offers an insider's view and a belated apologia in *In Retrospect* (1995). James C. Thompson, *Rolling Thunder* (1980), and John Galloway, *The Gulf of Tonkin Resolution* (1970), cover specific topics. Eric Bergerud, *Dynamics of Defeat* (1991), examines the military aspects of the war, and Daniel Hallin, *The Uncensored War* (1986), and Clarence R. Wyatt, *Paper Soldiers* (1993), look at the role of the media. Frances FitzGerald, *Fire in the Lake* (1972), discusses the war in the context of South Vietnamese society.

For a sense of what the war felt like to the soldiers who fought it, see Mark Baker, *Nam* (1982); Philip Caputo, *Rumor of War* (1977); Gloria Emerson, *Winners and Losers* (1976); Michael Herr, *Dispatches* (1977); Tim O'Brien, *If I Die in a Combat Zone* (1973); Bernard Edelman, ed., *Dear America: Letters Home from Vietnam*; and Ron Kovic, *Born on the Fourth of July* (1976). Wallace Terry, *Bloods* (1984), surveys the experiences of black veterans, and Keith Walker, *A Piece of My Heart* (1985), introduces the often forgotten stories of the women who served in Vietnam. Lawrence Baskir and William A. Strauss, *Chance and Circumstance* (1978), explains who was drafted and why. Christian G. Appy offers a class analysis of the Vietnam experience in *Working-Class War* (1993). Neil Sheehan surveys the entire Vietnam experience through the life of the career soldier John Paul Vann in *A Bright and Shining Lie* (1988).

The Challenge of Youth, 1962–1970

On the student activism of the 1960s, see Kenneth Keniston, *The Uncommitted* (1965) and *Young Radicals* (1969); Daniel Bell and Irving Kristol, *Confrontation* (1969); and Nathan Glazer, *Remembering the Answers* (1970). On student revolt, see, W. J. Rorabaugh, *Berkeley at War* (1989); Seymour Lipset and Sheldon Wolin, eds., *The Berkeley Student Revolt* (1965); Jerry Avorn, *Up against the Ivy Wall* (1968); Kirkpatrick Sale, *SDS* (1973); Wini Breines, *Community and Organization in the New Left, 1962–1968* (1982); and James Miller, *Democracy Is in the Streets* (1987). Terry Anderson, *The Movement and the Sixties* (1994), and Irwin Unger, *The Movement: A History of the American New Left* (1974), provide general accounts of 1960s activism. Todd Gitlin, *The Whole World Is Watching* (1980), discusses the impact of the mass media on the New Left.

The definitive book on the antiwar movement is Charles DeBenedetti, with Charles Chatfield, *An American Ordeal* (1990). Nancy Zaroulis and Gerald Sullivan, *Who Spoke Up* (1984), examine the role of the New Left in the antiwar movement, while Melvin Small and William D. Hoover, eds., *Give Peace a Chance* (1992), is an anthology of recent work. An eloquent account of one man's embrace of the movement is James Carroll, *An American Requiem* (1996).

Morris Dickstein, *Gates of Eden* (1977), is an excellent account of cultural developments in the 1960s. Todd Gitlin, *The Sixties* (1987), also treats the counterculture extensively. Other sources include Theodore Roszak, *The Making of a Counter-Culture* (1969), and Charles Reich, *The Greening of America* (1970). Gerald Howard, ed., *The Sixties* (1982), is a good anthology of the decade's art, politics, and culture, and *Takin' It to the Streets*, edited by Alexander Bloom and Wini Breines (1995), is an excellent collection of documents. Philip Norman, *Shout! The Beatles in Their Generation* (1981), and Jon Weiner, *Come Together: John Lennon in His Times* (1984), cover developments in popular music. Tom Wolfe, *Electric Kool-Aid Acid Test* (1965), describes the antics of Ken Kesey and his Merry Pranksters, key players in the counterculture. Joan Didion, *Slouching toward Bethlehem* (1968) and *The White Album* (1979), explore some of the darker side of the hippie phenomenon. David Farber, *The Age of Great Dreams* (1994), and David Farber, ed., *The Sixties* (1994), an anthology of articles, provide excellent insights into the Vietnam era.

The Long Road Home

The Tet offensive is the subject of Don Oberdoffer, *Tet!* (1971), whereas the domestic events of 1968 are covered in David Caute, *The Year of the Barricades* (1968); David Farber, *Chicago '68* (1988); and Lewis Chester, Godfrey Hodgson, and Bruce Page, *An American Melodrama* (1970). Norman Mailer provides a contemporary view of the conventions in *Miami and the Siege of Chicago* (1968). Dan Carter, *The Politics of Rage* (1996), examines the political career of George Wallace, while Kevin Phillips, *The Emerging Republican Majority* (1969), and Richard Scammon and Ben J. Wattenberg, *The Real Majority* (1970), describe the voters Richard Nixon tried to reach. Theodore H. White, *The Making of the President—1968* (1969), covers the divisive election of 1968.

Robert S. Litwak, *Détente and the Nixon Doctrine* (1984); Seymour Hersh, *The Price of Power* (1983); and Tad Szulc, *The Illusion of Peace* (1978), are overviews of Nixon's foreign policy. On his Vietnam policy see the general works on Vietnam listed above, as well as the highly critical study by William Shawcross, *Sideshow: Kissinger, Nixon, and the Destruction of Cambodia* (1979). An account of the My Lai massacre can be found in Seymour Hersh, *Cover-Up* (1972). Frank Snepp, *Decent Interval* (1977), examines the Paris peace process. Robert Jay Lifton, *Home from the War* (1973); Paul Starr, *The Discarded Army* (1973); and Lawrence Baskir and William A. Strauss, *Chance and Circumstance* (1978), discuss the problems of returning Vietnam veterans.

CHAPTER 32

A definitive scholarly history of the 1970s has yet to be written. Peter N. Carroll's popular history, *It Seemed Like Nothing Happened* (1982), provides a general overview of the period, as do the chapters on the 1970s in Paul Boyer, *Promises to Keep* (1995), and William H. Chafe, *The Unfinished Journey* (1995).

The Nixon Years

Jonathan Schell, *The Time of Illusion* (1976), offers an insightful discussion of the Nixon administration. Herbert Parmet, *Richard Nixon and His America* (1990), and Stephen Ambrose's three-volume *Nixon* (1987, 1991) are two of many biographies.

Kim McQuaid, *The Anxious Years* (1989), is an overview of the Nixon era. See also William Safire, *Before the Fall* (1975); Leonard Silk, *Nixonomics* (1972); and Garry Wills, *Nixon Agonistes* (rev. ed., 1990).

Stanley Kutler, *The Wars of Watergate* (1990); Anthony Lukas, *Nightmare* (1976); and Theodore H. White, *Breach of Faith* (1975), are comprehensive accounts of the Watergate scandal. See also Carl Bernstein and Bob Woodward, *All the President's Men* (1974) and *The Final Days* (1976). John Dean, *Blind Ambition* (1976), is the best account by a participant; see also H. R. Haldeman, *The Ends of Power* (1978), and Richard M. Nixon, *RN: The Memoirs of Richard Nixon* (1978). Arthur M. Schlesinger, Jr., *The Imperial Presidency* (1973), analyzes the changes in the presidency that provided a backdrop for the Watergate affair.

Lowered Expectations and New Challenges

Barry Commoner, *The Closing Circle* (1971) and *The Poverty of Power* (1976), and Robert Heilbroner, *An Inquiry into the Human Prospect* (1974), cogently assess the origins of the energy crisis and the prospects for the future. See also Lester C. Thurow, *The Zero-Sum Society* (1980), and Robert Stobaugh and Daniel Yergin, *Energy Future* (1980). Daniel Yergin, *The Prize* (1991); John M. Blair, *The Control of Oil* (1976); and J. C. Hurewitz, ed., *Oil, the Arab-Israeli Dispute, and the Industrial World* (1976), treat OPEC developments.

General introductions to the economic developments of the decade are Barry Bluestone and Bennett Harrison, *The Deindustrialization of America* (1982); Richard J. Barnet and Ronald E. Muller, *Global Reach* (1974); Richard J. Barnet, *The Lean Years* (1980); John P. Hoerr, *And the Wolf Finally Came: The Decline of the Steel Industry* (1988); Robert Calleo, *The Imperious Economy* (1982); and Gardner Means et al., *The Roots of Inflation* (1975).

Social Gridlock: Reform and Reaction in the 1970s

Tom Wolfe gave the decade its name in "The Me Decade and the Third Great Awakening," *New York Magazine* (August 23, 1976). Influential books include Christopher Lasch, *The Culture of Narcissism* (1978), and Gail Sheehy, *Passages* (1976).

For a general overview of the environmental movement, see Samuel P. Hays, *Beauty, Health, and Permanence* (1987). Roderick Nash provides a history of environmental ethics in *The Rights of Nature* (1989). Books that were influential in shaping public awareness of ecological issues include Rachel Carson, *Silent Spring* (1962); Paul R. Ehrlich, *The Population Bomb* (1968); Frances Moore Lappé, *Diet for a Small Planet* (1971); and Philip Slater, *Earthwalk* (1974). Charles McCarry chronicles Ralph Nader's crusade for consumer protection in *Citizen Nader* (1972).

On women and feminism in the 1970s, see Alice Echols, *Daring to Be Bad* (1989); Susan M. Hartmann, *From Margin to Mainstream* (1989); and Winifred D. Wandersee, *On the Move* (1988). Donald G. Mathews and Jane S. De Hart analyze the struggle over the ERA in *Sex, Gender, and the Politics of ERA* (1990), while Carol Felsenthal examines the life of the ERA opponent Phyllis Schlafly in *The Sweetheart of the Silent Majority* (1981). David Garrow, *Liberty and Sexuality* (1994), is an in-depth examination of the 1973 abortion decision. On the abortion debate, see Faye Ginsberg, *Contested Lives* (1989), and Kristen Luker, *Abortion and the Politics of Motherhood* (1984).

Leigh W. Rutledge surveys the gay and lesbian movement in *The Gay Decades*

(1992). Thomas Byrne Edsall with Mary D. Edsall, *Chain Reaction: The Impact of Race, Rights and Taxes on American Politics* (1991), examines some of the divisive social issues of the 1970s. Stanley Aronowitz, *False Promises* (1973); Richard Krickus, *Pursuing the American Dream* (1976); and Michael Novak, *The Rise of the Unmeltable Ethnics* (1977), describe the concerns of the white ethnic middle class. J. Anthony Lukas, *Common Ground* (1985), tells the story of the Boston busing crisis. Nathan Glazer, *Affirmative Discrimination* (1975); Thomas Sowell, *Race and Economics* (1975); and Allan P. Sindler, *Bakke, Defunis, and Minority Admissions* (1978), treat affirmative action.

Alan Crawford, *Thunder on the Right* (1980), and Peter Steinfels, *The Neo-Conservatives* (1979), survey the new conservatism. John Woodridge, *The Evangelicals* (1975), and Quentin J. Schultze, *Televangelism and American Culture* (1991), analyze the rise of evangelical religion. On the political role of the Christian right, see Michael Liensch, *Redeeming America* (1993).

Post-Watergate Politics: Failed Leadership

Much of the material on post-Watergate politics has been provided by journalists rather than historians. James Cannon, *Time and Chance: Gerald Ford's Appointment with History* (1993), and John Osborne, *White House Watch: The Ford Years* (1977), cover the Ford presidency. See also A. James Reichley, *Conservatives in an Age of Change: The Nixon and Ford Administrations* (1981). Jules Witcover, *Marathon* (1977), describes the pursuit of the presidency in 1976.

Generally unfavorable portraits of the Carter presidency are found in Burton Kaufman, *The Presidency of James Earl Carter, Jr.* (1993); Robert Shogan, *Promises to Keep* (1977); Haynes Johnson, *In the Absence of Power* (1980); and Clark Mollenhoff, *The President Who Failed* (1980). See also Erwin Hargrove, *Jimmy Carter as President* (1989), and Charles Jones, *The Trusteeship Presidency* (1988). James Wooten, *Dasher* (1978), and Betty Glad, *Jimmy Carter* (1980), are competent biographies. See also Jimmy Carter's presidential memoirs, *Keeping Faith* (rev. ed., 1995). James Fallows, *National Defense* (1981), provides an incisive overview of defense developments. See also A. Glenn Mower, Jr., *Human Rights and American Foreign Policy: The Carter and Reagan Experiences* (1987). Gary Sick, *All Fall Down* (1986), provides an account of the Iranian hostage crisis, and Jack Germond, *Blue Smoke and Mirrors* (1981), examines the presidential election of 1980.

CHAPTER 33

Few historians have turned their attention to the period after 1980, leaving the field to journalists, economists, and political scientists. The Bureau of the Census offers a fine introduction to the period in its *Statistical Abstract of the United States* (114th ed., 1994). Essays on important issues are available in the *Congressional Quarterly Researcher*. Indexes to newspapers and periodicals identify stories on major events.

The Reagan-Bush Years, 1981–1993

Haynes Johnson, *Sleepwalking through History* (1991), provides an excellent overview of America in the Reagan years. See also Robert Dallek, *Ronald Reagan* (1982); Michael Rogin, *Ronald Reagan* (1987); and Lou Cannon, *President Reagan* (1991). On electoral politics, see Jack W. Germond and Jules Witcover, *Wake Us When It's Over* (1985), and Frances Fox Piven and Richard Cloward, *Why Americans Don't Vote* (1988).

On Reaganomics, George Gilder's *Wealth and Poverty* (1981) represents the views held by many in the Reagan administration, but David Stockman's memoir, *The Triumph of Politics* (1986), is more revealing. See also Benjamin Friedman, *Day of Reckoning* (1988).

On the Bush administration, see James A. Baker, *The Politics of Diplomacy* (1995); Barbara Bush, *Barbara Bush: A Memoir* (1994); and Stephen R. Graubard, *Mr. Bush's War* (1992). For an insider's critical account of the Bush White House, see Charles Kolb, *White House Daze* (1994). On politics, see E. J. Dionne, *Why Americans Hate Politics* (1992); William Greider, *Who Will Tell the People?* (1992); and Kevin Phillips, *The Politics of Rich and Poor* (1990).

Foreign Relations under Reagan and Bush

For foreign policy, Stephen Ambrose, *Rise to Globalism* (7th ed., 1993), provides a comprehensive overview of the Reagan and Bush years. The Iran-Contra scandal is covered in Jane Hunter et al., *The Iran-Contra Connection* (1987). Good introductions to the United States and Central and South America include Walter LaFeber, *Inevitable Revolutions* (1984); Abraham F. Lowenthal, *Partners in Conflict: The United States and Latin America* (1987); and Kenneth Coleman and George C. Herring, eds., *The Central America Crisis* (1985).

The emergence of a new world order has provoked commentary from economists, journalists, and historians, including Paul Kennedy, *The Rise and Fall of the Great Powers* (1987); Joseph Nye, *Bound to Lead: The Changing Nature of American Power* (1990); Robert Kuttner, *The End of Laissez Faire: National Purpose and the Global Economy after the Cold War* (1991); and Henry R. Nau, *The Myth of America's Decline* (1990). Bernard Gwertzman and Michael T. Kaufman, eds., *The Collapse of Communism* (1990), reviews the events of 1989 through articles published in the *New York Times*. See also Michael Beschloss and Strobe Talbott, *At the Highest Levels: The Inside Story of the End of the Cold War* (1994). H. Norman Schwartzkopf's autobiography, *It Doesn't Take a Hero* (1992), recounts the Gulf War, as does former chairman of the Joint Chiefs of Staff Colin Powell in *My American Journey* (1995).

An Age of Anxiety

Paul Krugman, *Peddling Prosperity* (1994), and Jeffrey Madrick, *The End of Affluence* (1995), provide overviews of economic trends since the 1970s. Lester C. Thurow offers an insightful analysis of the world economic changes accompanying the collapse of communism in *The Future of Capitalism* (1996). For overviews of U.S. competitiveness in the global marketplace, see Hedrick Smith, *Rethinking America* (1995); Lester Thurow, *Head to Head: The Coming Economic Battle among Japan, Europe, and America* (1992); and Robert B. Reich, *The Work of Nations* (1991). Books that address the growing inequality in American life include William J. Wilson, *The Truly Disadvantaged* (1987); Michael Katz, *The Undeserving Poor* (1989); Nicholas Lemann, *The Promised Land* (1989); and Linda Gordon, *Pitied but Not Entitled: Single Mothers and the History of Welfare* (1994). A lively work that provides statistics on America's world standing on a variety of social and economic measures is Andrew L. Shapiro, *We're Number One* (1992).

On the problems of women, work, and families, see Hilda Scott, *Working Your Way to the Bottom* (1985); Arlie Hochschild, *The Second* (1989); and Juliet Schor, *The Over-*

worked American (1991). For feminism and its critics, see Susan Faludi, *Backlash* (1991). Toni Morrison, ed., *Race-ing Justice, En-gendering Power* (1992), covers the Clarence Thomas–Anita Hill hearings.

David Reimers, *Still the Golden Door* (2d ed., 1992), covers immigration policy in the postwar period. Linda Chavez, *Out of the Barrio* (1991), discusses Hispanic assimilation, while Ronald Takaki, *Strangers from a Different Shore* (1989), covers Asian-Americans, and Julian Simon, *The Economic Consequences of Immigration* (1989), assesses the economic implication of immigration. Various analyses of the 1992 racial uprising in Los Angeles are provided in Haki R. Madhubuti, ed., *Why L.A. Happened* (1993).

Randy Shilts, *And the Band Played On* (1987), is a controversial critique of inaction in the early years of the AIDS epidemic. See also Elinor Burkett, *The Gravest Show on Earth* (1995). Allan Bloom, *The Closing of the American Mind* (1987), and E. D. Hirsch, Jr., *Cultural Literacy* (1988), deal with issues of curriculum, learning, and literacy. Lawrence W. Levine, *The Opening of the American Mind* (1996), challenges many of their assumptions. For differing views on affirmative action, see Stephen L. Carter, *Reflections of an Affirmative Action Baby* (1991), and Gertrude Ezorsky, *Racism and Justice* (1991). For the story of Bill Gates and Microsoft, see Steven Manes, *Gates* (1993); James Wallace, *Hard Drive* (1992); and Gates's own *The Road Ahead* (1995).

Gregg Easterbrook provides a general overview of the environment in *A Moment on the Earth* (1995). Al Gore, *Earth in the Balance* (1992), reports on how well or poorly the world is doing on environmental awareness. Daniel Yergin, *The Prize* (1991), chronicles how oil dominates modern life, with both economic and environmental consequences.

The Clinton Presidency: Public Life since 1993

For an excellent overview of Clinton's first year, see Elizabeth Drew, *Finding His Voice* (1994). Other sources include Bob Woodward, *The Agenda* (1994); Roger Morris, *Promises of Change* (1996); and Richard Cohen, *Changing the Guard* (1993). James B. Stewart, *Blood Sport* (1996), analyzes the Whitewater scandal. On the Republican agenda, see Newt Gingrich, *To Renew America* (1995).

CREDITS

Illustrations

Chapter 1   **p. 4** Robert Knight/Leo de Wys; **p. 7** Amerind Foundation, Dragoon, AZ. Photo by Robin Stancliff; **p. 9** Bailey/Howe Library, University of Vermont; **p. 12** Mathias Grünwald, *Isenheim Altar Piece* (central panel), early 16th c., Musée Unterlinden, Colmar/ Giraudon/Art Resource; **p. 24** *Elizabeth I*, Armada Portrait by Anonymous. Private Collection/Bridgeman Art Library, London.

Chapter 2   **p. 32** Nettie Lee Benson Latin American Collection, University of Texas at Austin, General Libraries; **p. 39** Colonial Williamsburg Foundation; **p. 48** Courtesy, Peabody Essex Museum, Salem, MA; **p. 50** Courtesy, American Antiquarian Society; **p. 53** Shelburne Museum, Shelburne, VT. Photograph by Ken Burris.

Chapter 3   **p. 61** *James II*, by Godfrey Kneller, late 17th c. Courtesy of the National Portrait Gallery, London; **p. 69** Benin Bronze Plaque: Mounted King and Attendants, c. 1550–1680. The Metropolitan Museum of Art, NY The Michael C. Rockefeller Memorial Collection; **p. 74** Courtesy, Georgia Department of Archives and History, Atlanta; **p. 75** Abby Aldrich Rockefeller Folk Art Center, Williamsburg, VA; **p. 80** The Connecticut Historical Society.

Chapter 4   **p. 88** The Connecticut Historical Society, Hartford; **p. 95** Courtesy, Museum of Fine Arts, Boston. Bequest of Maxim Karolik; **p. 99** John Steper and Henry Dawkins, *A Southeast Prospect of the Pennsylvania Hospital*, c. 1761. The Library Company of Philadelphia; **p. 109** Stock Montage, Inc.; **p. 112** *View from Bushango Tavern, 5 miles from York Town on the Baltimore Road, July 1788*, Columbian Magazine. Collection of the New-York Historical Society.

Chapter 5   **p. 120** Print Collection. Miriam and Ira D. Wallach Division of Art, Prints and Photographs. The New York Public Library. Astor, Lenox and Tilden Foundations; **p. 123** Courtesy of the John Carter Brown Library at Brown University, Providence, RI; **p. 128** Courtesy, Peabody Essex Museum, Salem, MA; **p. 133** Anon, *Patrick Henry*, n.d. Shelburne Museum, Shelburne, VT. Photograph by Ken Burris; **p. 137** Courtesy of the John Carter Brown Library at Brown University, Providence, RI.

Chapter 6   **p. 148** Library of Congress; **p. 155** Library of Congress; **p. 160** Virginia Historical Society, Richmond; **p. 162** Anne S. K. Brown Military Collection, Brown University Library, Providence; **p. 166** Woodcut from *A Now Touch on the Times . . . By a Daughter of Liberty, Living in Marblehead*, 1779. Collection of the New-York Historical Society.

Chapter 7   **p. 177** John Singleton Copley, *Judith Sargent (Murray) at age 19*. Private Collection. Photo, courtesy Frick Art Reference Library; **p. 190** Ralph Earl, *Oliver Ellsworth and Abigail Wolcott Ellsworth*, c. 1792, Wadsworth Atheneum, Hartford, CT. Gift of the Ellsworth Heirs; **p. 195** Rembrandt Peale, *Thomas Jefferson*, c. 1800. White House Historical Collection.

Photograph by the National Geographic Society; **p. 195** John Trumbull, *Alexander Hamilton*, n.d., Yale University Art Gallery, New Haven.

Chapter 8   **p. 202** Thomas Birch, *Conestoga Wagon on the Pennsylvania Turnpike*, 1816. Shelburne Museum, Shelburne, VT. Photograph by Ken Burris; **p. 206** Courtesy of the Wethersfield Historical Society, CT; **p. 212** Library Company of Philadelphia; **p. 224** Mount Bethel A.M.E. Church, Philadelphia.

Chapter 9   **p. 233** Print Collection, Miriam and Ira D. Wallach Division of Art, Prints and Photographs. The New York Public Library, Astor, Lenox and Tilden Foundations; **p. 235** Shelburne Museum, Shelburne, VT. Photograph by Ken Burris; **p. 239** Chester Harding, *John Marshall*, c. 1830, Boston Atheneum; **p. 245** Ambrose Andrews, *Schuyler Family*, c. 1824, Collection of The New-York Historical Society; **p. 253** John L. D. Mathies, *Jemima Wilkinson*, c. 1816, Collection of the Yates County Historical Society. Reproduced Courtesy the Village Board, Penn Yan, NY.

Chapter 10   **p. 260** Collection of the New-York Historical Society; **p. 264** Smithsonian Institution; **p. 279** Oberlin College Archives.

Chapter 11   **p. 288** Philip Haas, *John Quincy Adams* (daguerreotype), c. 1843, The Metropolitan Museum of Art, Gift of I. N. Phelps Stokes, Edward S. Hawes, Alice Mary Hawes, Marion Augusta Hawes, 1937; **p. 293** The Gibbes Museum of Art, Carolina Art Association, Charleston, SC; **p. 297** George Catlin, *muk a tah mish o kah kaik, the Black Hawk*, mid 19th c., water color on paper. Courtesy of the Thomas Gilcrease Institute of American History and Art, Tulsa, OK; **p. 301** Collection of the New-York Historical Society; **p. 305** Collection of the New-York Historical Society; **p. 308** Collection of the New-York Historical Society.

Chapter 12   **p. 314** Culver Pictures; **p. 321** Culver Pictures; **p. 325** Library of Congress; **p. 325** Library of Congress; **p. 328** Harriet Beecher Stowe Center, Hartford, CT; **p. 332** Unknown, *William Lloyd Garrison* (daguerreotype), 19th c., The Metropolitan Museum of Art, Gift of I. N. Stokes, Edward S. Hawes, Alice Mary Hawes, Marion Augusta Hawes, 1937.

Chapter 13   **p. 340** Franz Holzlhuber, *Sugarcane Harvest in Louisiana & Texas*, c. 1856–1860, Collection of Glenbow Museum, Calgary, Alberta, Canada.; **p. 346** Sophia Smith Collection, Smith College, Northampton, MA; **p. 349** Culver Pictures; **p. 354** Library of Congress.

Chapter 14   **p. 372** Courtesy of the California History Room, California State Library, Sacramento, CA; **p. 377** Chicago Historical Society; **p. 382** The Kansas State Historical Society, Topeka; **p. 387** The Lincoln Museum, Fort Wayne, IN, a part of the Lincoln National Corporation.

Chapter 15   **p. 400** Culver Pictures; **p. 403** Massachusetts Commandery Military Order of the Loyal Legion and the US Army Military History Institute; **p. 412** Library of Congress; **p. 415** Library of Congress.

Chapter 16   **p. 421** Library of Congress; **p. 426** Collection of the New-York Historical Society; **p. 433** Library of Congress; **p. 434** From *Harper's Weekly*, June 23, 1866, Courtesy of the Newberry Library, Chicago; **p. 439** Rutherford B. Hayes Presidential Center, Speigel Grove, Fremont, OH; **p. 441** Brown Brothers.

Chapter 17   **p. 453** Culver Pictures; **p. 456** The Kansas State Historical Society, Topeka; **p. 462** Smithsonian Institution, Photo no. 3200-b-8 (National Anthropological Archives); **p. 469** Bancroft Library, University of California, Berkeley; **p. 472** Yosemite National Park Research Library, Yosemite National Park, CA.

Chapter 18   **p. 484** International Museum of Photography at George Eastman House, Rochester, NY; **p. 487** Corbis-Bettmann; **p. 495** The George Meany Memorial Archives Negative # 91; **p. 499** The Newberry Library.

Chapter 19   **p. 503** Culver Pictures; **p. 506** Brown Brothers; **p. 511** From the Collection of the Newport Historical Society, Newport, RI (P292); **p. 515** The Kansas State Historical Society, Topeka; **p. 527** Library of Congress.

Chapter 20   **p. 532** Corbis-Bettmann; **p. 533** Museum of the City of New York, Gift of Louis Stearns, 1889-1914; **p. 541** Archives of Industrial Society, University Library System, University of Pittsburgh; **p. 545** Brown Brothers; **p. 551** Museum of the City of New York, Byron Collection.

Chapter 21   **p. 559** State Historical Society of Wisconsin, Madison, WI; **p. 561** Chicago Historical Society; **p. 563** Corbis-Bettmann; **p. 572** Edward Steichen, *J. Pierpont Morgan*, 1903, Plate V from the boxed edition deluxe of the Steichen supplement to *Camera Work*, April 1906. Published simultaneously with XIV April 1906. Gravure, 8⅛ in. × 6¼ in. Collection, The Museum of Modern Art, New York. Gift of A. Conger Goodyear; **p. 574** Library of Congress.

Chapter 22   **p. 587** Culver Pictures; **p. 589** U.S. Naval Historical Center, Washington, DC; **p. 598** GW Peters in *Harper's Weekly*, April 22, 1899, Courtesy of The Newberry Library, Chicago; **p. 606** Aultman Collection, El Paso Public Library.

Chapter 23   **p. 614** Imperial War Museum, London; **p. 620** Library of Congress; **p. 623** UPI/Corbis-Bettmann; **p. 628** National Archives, photo by M. Rudolph Vetter.

Chapter 24   **p. 644** Brown Brothers; **p. 651** *Portrait of Luisa Ronstadt Espinel,* c. 1921. Courtesy of the Arizona Historical Society/Tucson Gift of Edward Ronstadt, Mexican Heritage Project; **p. 659** Corbis-Bettmann; **p. 662** Henry Lee Moon Library and Civil Rights Archive of the NAACP.

Chapter 25   **p. 671** Franklin D. Roosevelt Library, Hyde Park, NY; **p. 678** MOMA-Film Stills Archive; **p. 681** (top) UPI/Corbis-Bettmann; (bottom) Schomburg Center for Research in Black Culture, The New York Public Library. Astor, Lenox, and Tilden Foundations; **p. 686** University of Texas, The Institute of Texan Cultures, The *San Antonio Light* Collection; **p. 689** Corbis-Bettmann.

Chapter 26   **p. 694** AP/Wide World Photos; **p. 696** Library of Congress; **p. 700** UPI/Corbis-Bettmann; **p. 707** Ben Shahn, *Steel Workers Organizing Committee* Poster, 1930s, Library of Congress; **p. 710** AP/Wide World Photos.

Chapter 27   **p. 729** Courtesy of the Dorothea Lange Collection, The City of Oakland, The Oakland Museum 1982; **p. 736** Myron Davos, *Life Magazine* © Time Warner, Inc; **p. 740**

UPI/Corbis-Bettmann; **p. 744** Franklin D. Roosevelt Library, Hyde Park, NY (Photographed by US Army Signal Corps); **p. 746** UPI/Corbis-Bettmann.

Chapter 28   **p. 754** UPI/Corbis-Bettmann; **p. 761** Carl Albert Center Congressional Archives, University of Oklahoma; **p. 763** UPI/Corbis-Bettmann; **p. 768** Robert Phillips/Black Star; **p. 775** FPG International.

Chapter 29   **p. 784** Photo by Dan Weiner, Courtesy Sandra Weiner; **p. 787** The Huntington Library, San Marino, California (Whittington Collection); **p. 796** © 1956 BMG Music; **p. 802** AP/Wide World Photos.

Chapter 30   **p. 808** AP/Wide World Photos; **p. 816** Charles Moore/Black Star; **p. 828** UPI/Corbis-Bettmann; **p. 831** Bettye Lane.

Chapter 31   **p. 842** AP/Wide World Photos; **p. 845** Bancroft Library, University of California, Berkeley; **p. 848** Paul Fusco/Magnum; **p. 854** Burt Glinn/Magnum; **p. 856** Michael Abramson/Black Star.

Chapter 32   **p. 868** Dennis Brack/Black Star; **p. 870** Tony Korody/Sygma; **p. 877** Bettye Lane; **p. 880** Stanley Forman; **p. 887** Mingam/Gamma Liaison.

Chapter 33   **p. 892** Rick Rickman/Matrix; **p. 898** Luc Delahaye/SIPA Press; **p. 903** Kay Chernush/The Image Bank; **p. 908** Estate of Keith Haring; **p. 917** Sygma.

Text

Chapter 1   **p. 17** From Bartolomé de Las Casas, *The Journal of Christopher Columbus.* Translated by Cecil Jane, revised and annotated by L. A. Vigneras (London: Hakluyt Society, 1960). Reprinted by permission. **p. 19** Bernardino de Sahagún, *The Florentine Codex: A General History of the Things of New Spain.* Translated by Arthur J. O. Anderson and Charles E. Dibble (Salt Lake City and Sante Fe: The University of Utah Press and The School of American Research, 1975), Bk 12, pp. 17–20, 26, 83. Reprinted courtesy of the University of Utah Press.

Chapter 2   **p. 54** From *The Unredeemed Captive: A Family Story from Early America* by John Demos. Copyright © 1994 by John Demos. Reprinted by permission of Alfred A. Knopf, Inc.

Chapter 3   **p. 76** Reprinted from Hunter Dickinson Farish, ed., *Journal and Letters of Philip Vickers Fithian, 1773–1774: A Plantation Tutor of the Old Dominion*, published by the Colonial Williamsburg Foundation, 1965, pp. 38–39.

Chapter 4   **p. 94** From *Voyagers to the West* by Bernard Bailyn. Copyright © 1986 by Bernard Bailyn. Reprinted by permission of Alfred A. Knopf, Inc.

Chapter 6   **p. 156** Henry Steele Commanger and Richard B. Morris, eds., *The Spirit of Seventy-Six* (New York: Harper & Row, 1967). Reprinted by permission.

Chapter 7   **p. 183** Reprinted by permission of The Putnam Publishing Group from *American Populism* by George McKenna. Copyright © 1974 by George McKenna. **p. 176** J. P.

INDEX

white supremacy, in the South, 422, 425,
    523–526
Whitlock, Brand, 509, 558
Whitman, Walt, 314–315, 316, 371
Whitney, Eli, 219, 265
Whyte, William H., 784, 784*i*
Wickersham, George W., 576
Wilderness, Battle of the (1864), 413
Wild One, The (film), 795
Wilhelm II, Kaiser, 600, 607
Wilkes, Charles, 360
Wilkes, John, 118, 132
Wilkins, Roy, 817
Wilkinson, Eliza, 176
Wilkinson, James, 210
Wilkinson, Jemima, 253, 253*i*
Will, George F., 907
Willamette Valley, Oregon, 360, 361, 463, 465
Willard, Emma, 254
Willard, Frances, 513
William III, King of England (William of Orange),
    61, 62
Williams, Eunice, 54
Williams, Roger, 47, 49
Williams, William Carlos, 661
Williams v. Mississippi (1898), 524
Willkie, Wendell, 723
Wills, Helen, 653
Wilmington, Delaware, 273
Wilmot, David, 369
Wilmot Proviso, 369, 370, 371, 388, 406
Wilson, Augusta Evans, 351
Wilson, Charles E., 773
Wilson, Pete, 907
Wilson, Woodrow, 568, 577–580, 655, 723
    1916 election and, 618
    death of, 634
    economic policy, 578–580
    foreign policy, 605, 608
    League of Nations and, 632, 633–634
    as New Jersey governor, 577
    social policy, 580
    Treaty of Versailles and (1919), 633–634
    World War I and, 617, 618, 625, 630
    postwar plans and goals, 631–633
Wilson-Gorman Tariff (1894), 519
Winning of the West, The (T. Roosevelt), 590
Winthrop, John, 45, 46, 49
Wisconsin, 6, 33, 180, 268, 352, 374, 376–377
Wise, John, 99
Wissler, Clark, 451
witchcraft, Puritans and, 51
Wobblies, 500
Wolfe, James, 107, 108, 117
Wolfe, Tom, 872
Wollstonecraft, Mary, 248
Wolsey, Cardinal Thomas, 21
Woman in the Nineteenth Century (Fuller), 314
Woman's Christian Temperance Union (WCTU),
    513, 629

women. *See also* abortion; families; feminism; mar-
    riage; mothers
    1840 election and, 307–308
    in 1920s, 642–643, 649
        flapper, 651–652
    1940s–1960s, 793
    in 1970s, 879
    abolitionism and, 323, 325–327, 333, 335
    American Revolution and, 143, 165, 166*i*
    antiwar movement and, 830–831
    in the armed forces
        Persian Gulf War, 898*i*
        Vietnam War, 841
        World War II, 727
    beat writers and poets and, 797
    Benevolent Empire and, 278
    black, 569, 642
        Reconstruction and, 435
        slaves, 223, 342
    charitable organizations and, 252–254, 278
    Civil War and, 402, 403*i*
    in colonial period, 39, 79
        Chesapeake Bay colonies, 71, 72
        indentured servants, 40
        New England, 87–89
        nonimportation movement and homespun
            textiles, 131
        Puritans, 49
        Quakers, 95*i*
    domestic role of, 248
    domestic servants, 551
    education of, 178, 248, 254, 829
    in Europe, 15th century, 10, 11
    farm, 205, 206*i*
    Fourierist view of, 319
    Great Depression and, 672
    household appliances and, 649
    Mexican-American, 685
    middle-class
        1820s–1840s, 324, 350–352
        in 1920s, 649
        families and, 551–553
        Progressive Era, 559–560
    native American, 32, 34
        agriculture and, 8, 9*i*, 225
    New Deal and, 709–710
    pioneer (homesteading), 456
    planters' wives, 342
    in politics, 1870s–1880s, 512–513
    Populism and, 517
    prostitution, 324, 544
    protective laws for, 560
    reform movements and, 324
    religion and, 1790s–1820s, 253–255
        Protestant Christianity (1790–1820), 249
    in Revolutionary Era (1776–1790), 176–178
    "separate sphere" for, 248, 324, 351
    Shakers and, 318
    suffrage (voting rights), 243, 329, 427, 563*i*
        1870s–1880s, 512, 513

Wovoka, 461–462
Wright, Richard, 714
writers, artists, and intellectuals, in 1920s, 660–663
Wyandot Indians, 203
Wyllys, George, 80*i*

XYZ affair, 198

Yalta conference and agreements (1945), 744*i*,
  744–745, 751
Yamasee Indians, 58
Yancey, William Lowndes, 342, 389
Yazoo Land Company, 241
Yellow Bird, 462, 462*i*
yellow-dog contracts, 496
yellow journalism, 546
Yeltsin, Boris, 898, 913–914
yeomen, 26, 27, 42, 139
  in the South, 342–343
Yippies (Youth International Party), 851
Yom Kippur War (1973), 870, 886

Yorktown, Battle of (1781), 161, 162*i*
Yosemite Valley, 471–472, 472*i*
Young, Brigham, 321, 322
Young, Whitney, 817
young people. *See also* children; youth culture
  1962–1970, 844–851
    student activism, 844–848
  city amusements and, 544
  Great Depression and, 675–676
  during World War II, 734
youth culture, 554. *See also* counterculture
  of 1950s, 795–796
Ypres, Battle of (1915), 614
Yucatan Peninsula, 3–4
Yugoslavia, 633, 914

Zhou Enlai (Chou En-lai), 757
Zimmermann telegram (1917), 618
zoot-suiters, 735
Zuni Indians, 7